THE Java™ Class Libraries

The Java™ Series

Lisa Friendly, Series Editor
Bill Joy, Technical Advisor

The Java™ Programming Language
Ken Arnold and James Gosling
ISBN 0-201-63455-4

The Java™ Language Specification
James Gosling, Bill Joy, and Guy Steele
ISBN 0-201-63451-1

The Java™ Virtual Machine Specification
Tim Lindholm and Frank Yellin
ISBN 0-201-63452-X

The Java™ Application Programming Interface, Volume 1: Core Packages
James Gosling, Frank Yellin, and the Java Team
ISBN 0-201-63453-8

The Java™ Application Programming Interface, Volume 2: Window Toolkit and Applets
James Gosling, Frank Yellin, and the Java Team
ISBN 0-201-63459-7

The Java™ Tutorial: Object-Oriented Programming for the Internet
Mary Campione and Kathy Walrath
ISBN 0-201-63454-6

The Java™ Class Libraries: An Annotated Reference
Patrick Chan and Rosanna Lee
ISBN 0-201-63458-9

Concurrent Programming in Java™ : Design Principles and Patterns
Doug Lea
ISBN 0-201-69581-2

The Java™ FAQ: Frequently Asked Questions
Jonni Kanerva
ISBN 0-201-63456-2

THE Java™ Class Libraries:

An Annotated Reference

Patrick Chan
and
Rosanna Lee

ADDISON-WESLEY

An imprint of Addison Wesley Longman, Inc.

Reading, Massachusetts • Harlow, England • Menlo Park, California
Berkeley, California • Don Mills, Ontario • Sydney
Bonn • Amsterdam • Tokyo • Mexico City

The publisher offers discounts on this book when ordered in quantity for special sales.

For more information, please contact:

Corporate & Professional Publishing Group
Addison-Wesley Publishing Company
One Jacob Way
Reading, Massachusetts 01867

Library of Congress Cataloging-in-Publication Data

Chan, Patrick, 1961-
The Java class libraries: an annotated reference / Patrick Chan, Rosanna Lee
p. cm. -- (The Java series)
Includes bibliographical references and index.
ISBN 0-201-63458-9 (hc)
1. Java (Computer program language) I. Lee, Rosanna. 1960- II. Title. III. Series.
QA76.73.J38C47 1996
005.13'3--dc20 96-34046
CIP

ISBN 0-201-63458-9

Text printed on recycled and acid-free paper
1 2 3 4 5 6 7 8 9-MA-99989796

First Printing, September 1996

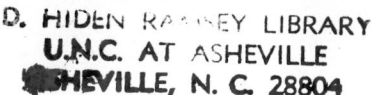

To our parents

Agatha and Fai Chan
Patricia and Warren Lee

Contents

Contents

List of Figures

Java Package Overviews

Java Class Libraries

List of Tables

Preface

How to Use This Book

This book is intended as a reference rather than a tutorial. Its structure is designed to optimize the time it takes for you to look up a class or class member. This book does not explain any part of the Java language. There are several books that you can use to learn the language. *The Java™ Programming Language*, by Ken Arnold and James Gosling, and *The Java™ Language Specification*, by James Gosling, Bill Joy, and Guy Steele are good sources of material for learning the language.

Part I: Java Package Overviews

These chapters briefly describe each package and all the classes that appear in them. Also included are diagrams that show the inheritance hierarchy of the classes that appear in a package.

Part II: Alphabetical Reference to the Java Class Libraries

These chapters cover the alphabetical listing of the classes. Probably the most notable aspect about the structure of this book is the order in which the classes appear. Most other Java books that contain an API alphabetically order the classes within a package and then alphabetically order the packages. The problem with this format is that it always takes two or more steps to locate a class. If you do not know the package, you basically need to go through each of the eight packages looking for the class. If you do know the package, you first need to find the package and then find the class. Even if an index were available for all the classes, you first need to locate the index and then locate the class.

The classes in this book are ordered alphabetically without regard to package name. This makes looking up a class as straightforward as looking up a word in a dictionary.

Each class is described in its own chapter. Each chapter contains a class description, a picture of the class hierarchy, a class example, a member summary, and descriptions for every member in the class.

Class Descriptions

In the class descriptions, we describe all the properties of the class. For example, the properties of the `Graphics` class includes the current color, font, paint mode, origin, and clipping rectangle. Describing in one place all of a class's available properties and how the properties behave rather than scattering the property descriptions throughout the member descriptions makes learning all the capabilities of a class much easier.

Any terminology used in the member descriptions is introduced and described in the class descriptions. If you find that the description for a member is lacking in detail, go to the class description for more information.

Class Hierarchy Diagrams

A class diagram appears for each class in the Java API. The class diagram shows all the ancestors of the class, its siblings, its immediate descendents, and any interfaces that the class implements. In these diagrams, if a package name precedes a class or interface name, the class or interface is not in the same package as the current class.

In the diagrams, we visually distinguish only three kinds of Java entities:

1. The class
2. The abstract class
3. The interface

The mneumonic we use to represent the entities is based on how much of the entity is implemented. For example, in a class all the methods are implemented, so a class appears "full." In an abstract class, one or more methods have not been implemented, so an abstract class appears "partially full." Finally, an interface does not have any methods implemented (only method signatures), so the interface appears "empty."

Examples

Ideally we would have liked to include a unique example for every single member in the Java API. We simply did not have enough time. So we tried to make sure that every member appeared in at least one example.

We worked to make the examples as useful as possible so that they demonstrate the member as it would typically be used. For example, in the example for a button we not only show how a button is created; we also show how button events are handled. In some cases, we also try to demonstrate some other class in the Java API. For example, in the `Graphics.drawOval()` example, we not only demonstrate how to draw an oval. We also demonstrate how to use the `DataInputStream` class to read integers from standard input that are used to locate the ovals. As long as the introduction does not confuse the example, we feel that gently introducing other classes in the Java API is a good way to help you become aware of all available classes in the Java API.

The names and structures of most of the examples are the same mainly to make approaching an example easier. As you read more examples, you will become used to the structure and it will become one less thing on which you have to put your attention.

Member Summary

The Member Summary section for each class is to help you when you approach an unfamiliar class. It groups the members of the class into catagories that are specific to that class. For example, in the `List` class the Selection Methods catagory lists all methods having to do with selections. It is meant to be a quick summary of the class's members, so it does not contain any syntax information other than the name of the method.

Member Descriptions

The member descriptions appear in alphabetical order within a class chapter regardless of what kind of method or field they are. Again, this was done to make locating a member proceed as fast as possible.

Overloaded methods are placed together in one member description because they have very similar functionality. The different overloaded forms are typically provided as a convenience for the programmer when specifying parameters. For instance, some overloads eliminate parameters by providing common defaults. To describe overloads with missing parameters, we use a phrase of the form "if the parameter `p` is not specified, it defaults to the value 3.14." Other overloads take different representations of a value. For example, one overload could take a particular parameter as an integer, while another could take the same parameter as a string containing an integer.

Each member description contains some or all of the following fields:

PURPOSE	A brief description of the purpose of this member
SYNTAX	The syntactic declaration of this member
DESCRIPTION	A full description of this member
PARAMETERS	The parameters accepted by this member, if any, listed in alphabetical order
RETURNS	The value returned by this member, if any
EXCEPTIONS	The exceptions and errors thrown by this member, if any, listed in alphabetical order
SEE ALSO	Other related classes or members, if any, listed in alphabetical order
OVERRIDES	The method that this member overrides, if any
EXAMPLE	A code example that illustrates how this member is used. This is sometimes a reference to an example that illustrates the use of this method in another member example or class example.

How to Get the Examples

All the code examples in this book have been compiled and run on the FCS version of Java release 1.0.2, either on Solaris or Windows95 or both. Most of the complete examples are available online. You can access them and other information about this book using the URL

```
http://aw.com/cp/chan-lee.html
```

Conventions Used in This Book

`Lucida San Typewriter` is used for examples, syntax declarations, class names, method names, and field names.

Italics is used when defining a new term and for emphasis.

Acknowledgments

We want to thank the many people who made this book possible.

Mike Hendrickson, the Acquisition Editor for this book, coordinated the project and, more important, sustained our spirits as the months progressed.

Lisa Friendly, as Series Editor, got this project started and believed in us every step of the way.

Katie Duffy, Simone Payment, Avanda Peters, Laura Michaels, and Marty Rabinowitz assisted in the production of this book, from coordination with the reviewers, to creating figures and class hierarchy diagrams, to polishing the book's format.

Despite the daunting size of this book, Tom Wrensch and Maurice Fitzgerald II gave thorough reviews. Other reviewers who gave useful feedback include Kevin Kluge, Doug Kramer, Bhavesh Mehta, James Robins, and Roland Schemers.

Jayashree Vasudevan was tremendously helpful in assisting us with formatting early drafts of this book.

Most important, thanks to all of Patrick's fellow Java team members for the wonderful friendships and the incredible journey.

And finally, we can't forget our 3 and 5 year olds, Melissa and Kevin, who patiently endured our "Not now's" and stayed home with us, weekend after weekend while we typed and typed and typed for 6 months. What are we all going to do now that we've published our book? Why, we're going to Disneyland, of course!

Patrick Chan
Rosanna Lee
June, 1996

java.applet

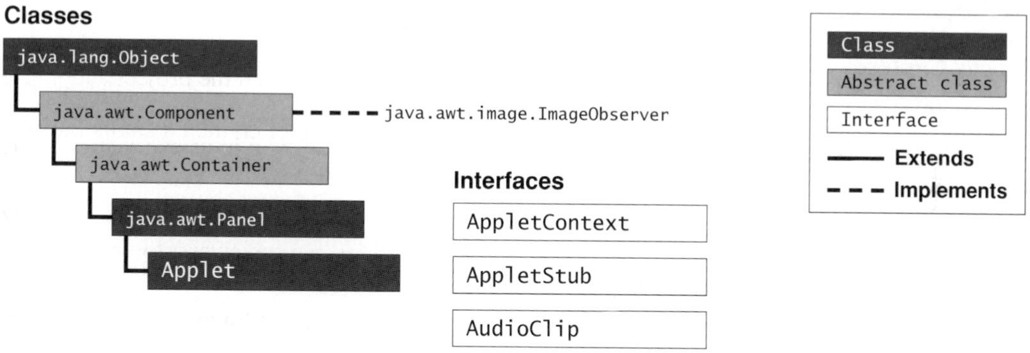

The applet framework involves two entities: the *applet context* and the *applet*. The applet context is an application that is responsible for loading and running applets. For example, the applet context could be a Web browser or an applet development environment, as shown in Figure 1.

An applet is an embeddable window (see `Panel` class) with a few extra methods that the applet context can use to initialize, start, and stop the applet.

This package contains the classes necessary to create an applet and the classes an applet uses to communicate with its applet context.

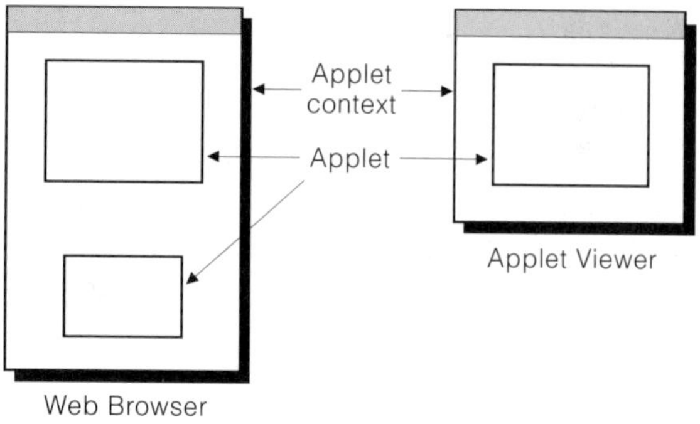

FIGURE 1 Relationship Between Applet Contexts and Applets

Applet

A class becomes an applet by subclassing this class. It contains methods that the applet can override and methods for retrieving media via a URL.

`Applet`	Used for building an applet. All applets must be a subclass of this class.

Audio

This class contains methods for fetching and playing sound clips at a URL. A sound clip can be played once or in a continuous loop.

`AudioClip`	Used to play and stop sound clips.

Applet Context

These interfaces specify the methods that all applet contexts must provide to applets. For example, there are methods to display a status message in the applet context's status bar and methods for discovering other applets that the applet context may contain.

`AppletContext`	Used by an applet for communicating with the applet context.
`AppletStub`	Used in the implementation of the `AppletContext`. Not directly used.

java.awt

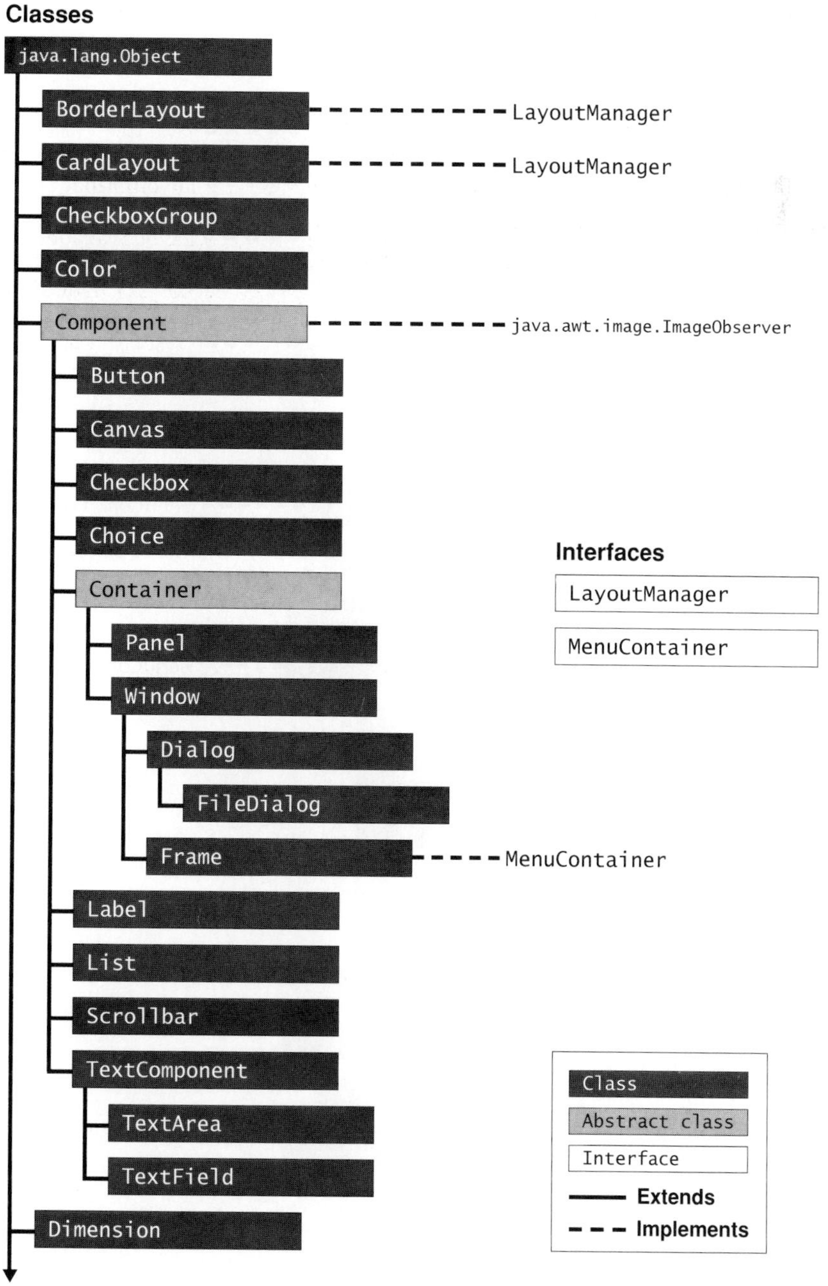
Classes
java.lang.Object
BorderLayout
LayoutManager
CardLayout
LayoutManager
CheckboxGroup
Color
Component
java.awt.image.ImageObserver
Button
Canvas
Checkbox
Choice
Container
Panel
Window
Dialog
FileDialog
Frame
MenuContainer
Label
List
Scrollbar
TextComponent
TextArea
TextField
Dimension
Interfaces
LayoutManager
MenuContainer
Class
Abstract class
Interface
Extends
Implements

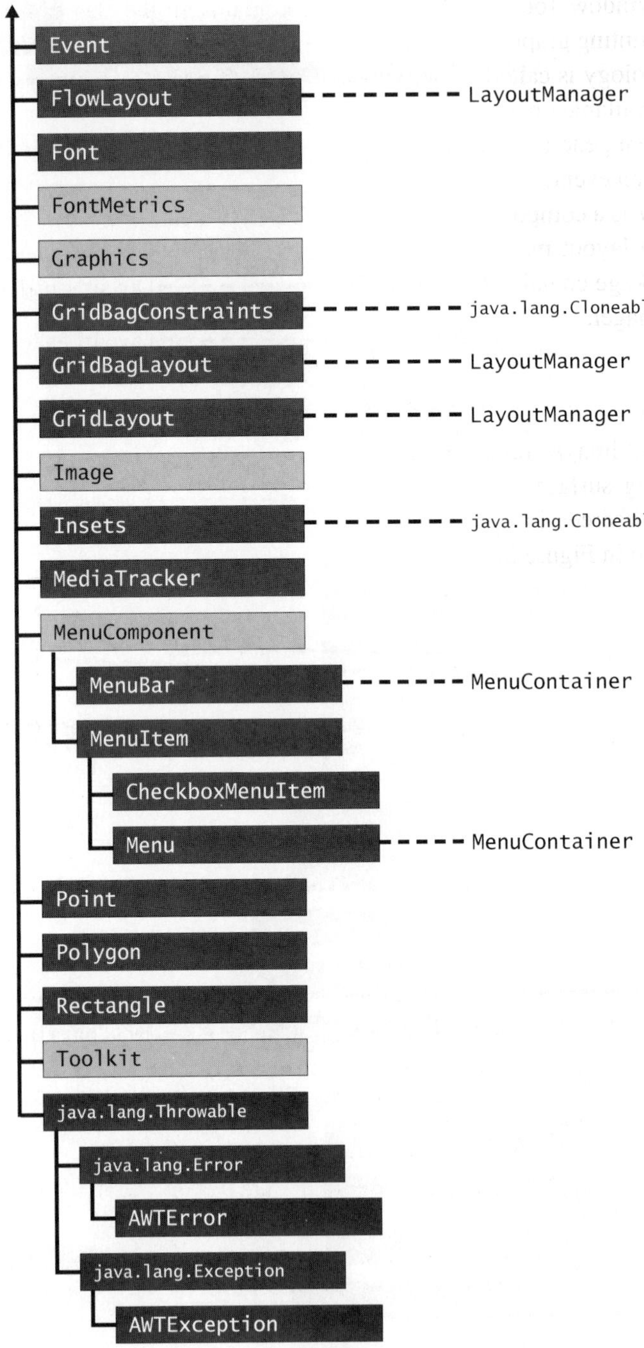
Event
FlowLayout
LayoutManager
Font
FontMetrics
Graphics
GridBagConstraints
java.lang.Cloneable
GridBagLayout
LayoutManager
GridLayout
LayoutManager
Image
Insets
java.lang.Cloneable
MediaTracker
MenuComponent
MenuBar
MenuContainer
MenuItem
CheckboxMenuItem
Menu
MenuContainer
Point
Polygon
Rectangle
Toolkit
java.lang.Throwable
java.lang.Error
AWTError
java.lang.Exception
AWTException

The Abstract Window Toolkit (AWT) package contains all the classes for creating user interfaces and for painting graphics and images. A user interface object such as a button or scrollbar in AWT terminology is called a *component*. The AWT provides a number of standard components that are available on all platforms.

A component generates events when a user interacts with it. The `Event` class encapsulates all the states in an event.

A *container* is a component that can contain components and other containers. A container can also have a layout manager that controls the visual placement of components in a container. This package contains several layout manager classes and an interface for building your own layout manager.

Graphics

This set of classes is used to draw shapes, text, and images on a drawing surface. Drawing surfaces can include the screen, an offscreen-image, and the printer, as shown in Figure 2.

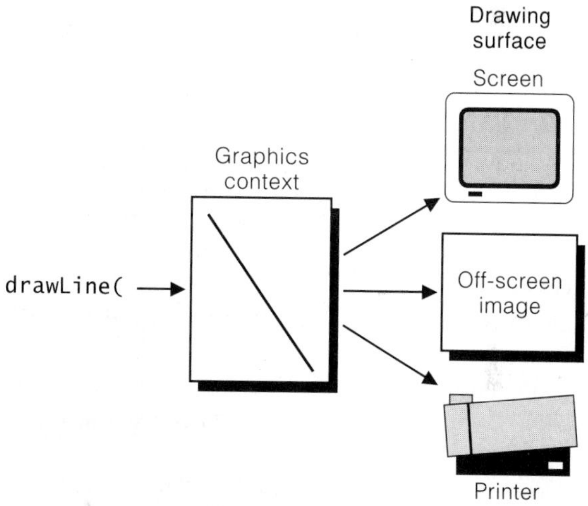

FIGURE 2 Graphics Contexts and Drawing Surfaces

`Graphics`	Used for painting basic shapes like lines and rectangles and for painting images.
`Color`	Represents a color with methods for converting between RGB and HSB values.
`Font`	Represents a font.
`FontMetrics`	Used for determining information about a font, such as height and character widths.
`Image`	Represents an image with methods for retrieving its dimensions.
`MediaTracker`	Used for preloading images.

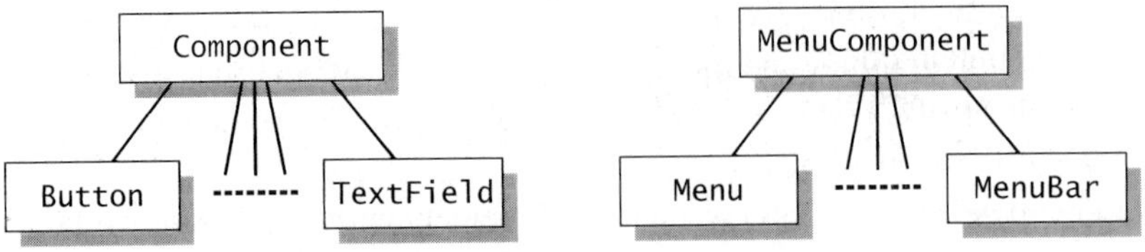

FIGURE 3 **Component and MenuComponent**

Components

These classes represent the components that the AWT provides for building user interfaces. Each component generates a different set of events, so you must check with the documentation to determine the type of events a component generates.

All the classes in this group and in the following containers group, are either subclasses of `Component` or of `MenuComponent`, as shown in Figure 3. See these classes to learn about the set of properties common to all components.

`Button`	A component that generates an event when clicked.
`Canvas`	A component typically used to render graphics.
`Checkbox`	A component that maintains a boolean state.
`CheckboxGroup`	Used for implementing a set of radio buttons.
`CheckboxMenuItem`	A menu item that maintains a boolean state.
`Choice`	A component that implements a drop-down list.
`Component`	The superclass of components.
`Label`	A component that displays a text string.
`List`	A component that displays a list of items.
`Menu`	A menu that contains menu items.
`MenuBar`	A menu bar that contains menus.
`MenuComponent`	The superclass of menu components.
`MenuContainer`	The superclass of menu containers.
`MenuItem`	A menu item that can be inserted in a menu.
`Scrollbar`	A component that implements a scrollbar.
`TextArea`	A component that provides editing for a multiline text string.
`TextComponent`	The superclass of text components.
`TextField`	A component that provides editing for a one-line text string.

Containers

A container can contain components and other containers. A container can also have a layout manager that controls the visual placement of components in a container. Some containers are top-level windows that cannot be embedded in another container.

`Container`	The superclass of containers.
`Dialog`	The superclass of dialog boxes.
`FileDialog`	A dialog box for selecting an existing file or naming a new file.
`Frame`	A top-level window with a title, menu bar, and borders.
`Panel`	A container that can be embedded in other containers.
`Window`	A top-level window without a title, menu bar, or borders.

Layout

The AWT provides a number of useful layout managers. The most versatile but difficult to use is the `GridBagLayout` layout manager. If none of these are appropriate, you can build your own using the `LayoutManager` interface.

`BorderLayout`	A layout manager that places components along each edge and in the center.
`CardLayout`	A layout manager that displays one component at a time.
`FlowLayout`	A layout manager that places components left-to-right, top-to-bottom.
`GridBagConstraints`	Used to specify constraints in a `GridBagLayout` object.
`GridBagLayout`	A layout manager that places components in a grid with flexible-sized cells.
`GridLayout`	A layout manager that places components in a rigid grid with fixed-sized cells.
`LayoutManager`	The interface that a layout manager must implement.

Geometry

These classes are used to hold collections of values. For example, a `Rectangle` object holds four values that represent the locations of the edges of a rectangle.

`Dimension`	Used for specifying the size of a rectangle (width and height).
`Insets`	Used for specifying the insets of a rectangle (top, left, bottom, and right).
`Point`	Used for specifying a point using *x*, *y* coordinates.
`Polygon`	Used for holding an array of points.
`Rectangle`	Used for specifying the location and size of a rectangle (*x*, *y*; width; and height).

Event

An *event* is an object that is generated by a component when the user interacts with it. There are many kinds of mouse and keyboard events that a component can generate. The event automatically flows up the component hierarchy and is handled by one or more *event handlers*. Figure 4 shows a component hierarchy and an event flowing through that hierarchy. Figure 4 shows a user event first being delivered to a button component and then passing through all of its ancestors. As the event flows up the hierarchy, any component receiving the event can handle the event and therefore stop the event from continuing upward.

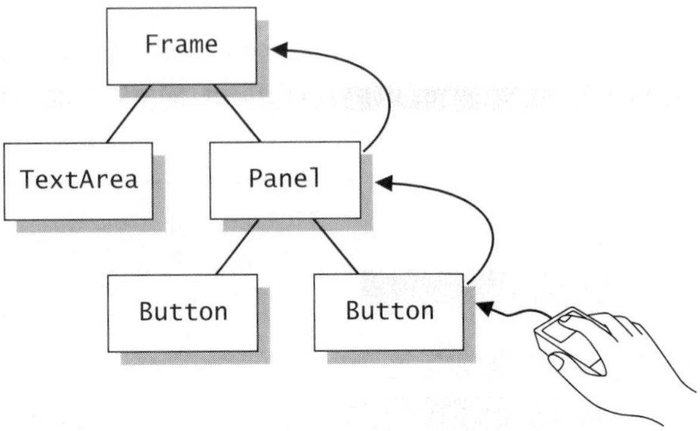

FIGURE 4 Events and the Component Hierarchy

See `Component.handleEvent()` for a description of event handlers. The `Event` class encapsulates all the details of an AWT event.

`Event`	Encapsulates all the information of an event.

Toolkit

This class contains methods that return information about the platform's screen, such as its dimension and resolution. This class also contains methods that create native versions of Java components called *peers*. For example, when you create a `Button` component, the `Button` class uses the `Toolkit` class to create a button peer. These peer creation methods are not normally used directly, since each component class automatically calls the `Toolkit` methods to create and destroy its associated peers.

`Toolkit`	Used for retrieving information about the screen.

Errors and Exceptions

These are the errors and exceptions declared in the AWT package.

`AWTError`	Thrown if an unrecoverable condition arises. This error should not be caught.
`AWTException`	Thrown if an error occurs in an AWT operation. This exception must be caught or declared in a `throws` clause.

java.awt.image

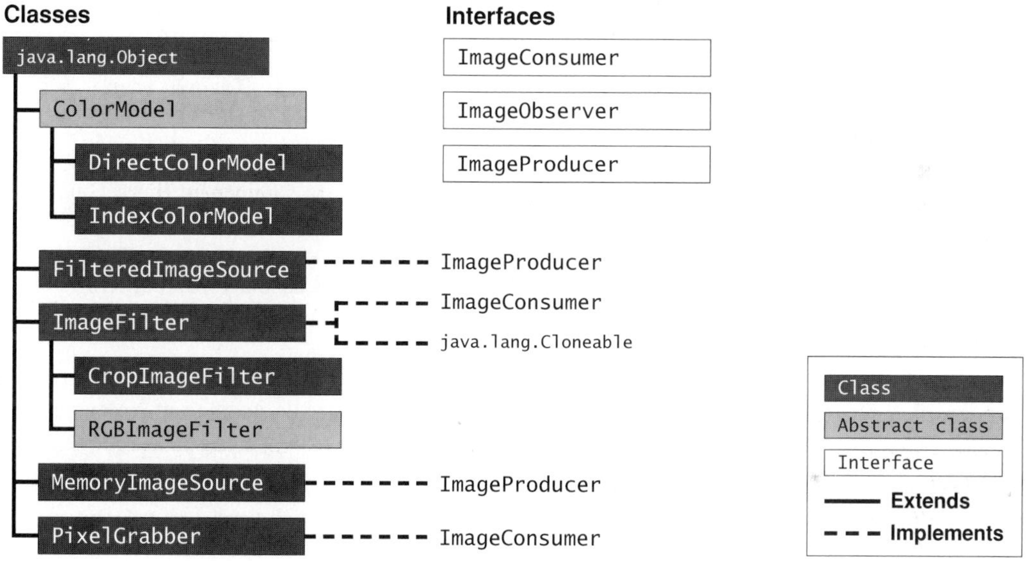

This package contains classes for creating and modifying images. Images are processed using a streaming framework that involves an image producer and an image consumer. This framework makes it possible to progressively render an image while it is being fetched or generated. Moreover, the framework allows an application to discard the storage used by an image and to regenerate it at any time.

In between the image producer and the consumer, you can insert one or more image filters that can modify the image data as it passes through it. Figure 5 shows an image stream.

This package provides a number of image producers, consumers, and filters that you can configure for your image processing needs. If none of the provided classes suits your needs, you can construct your own image producers, consumers, and filters using the supplied classes, which serve as excellent examples.

Another participant in the image streaming framework is the image observer, which can receive notifications on the progress of an image as it is being loaded. A class can become an image observer by implementing the `ImageObserver` interface.

Also included in this package are classes that deal with an image's color model, which specifies how to translate the image's pixel value into colors.

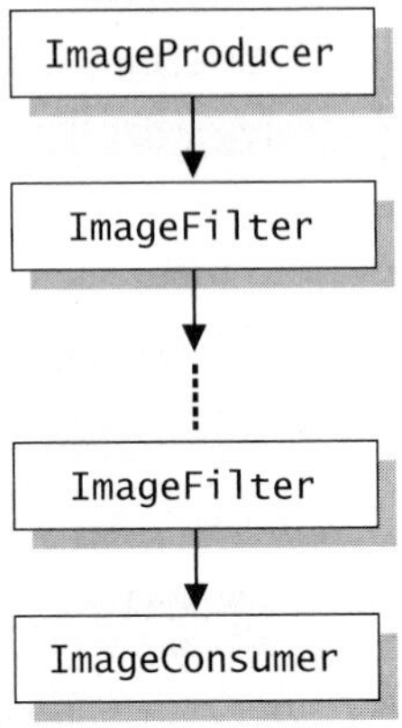

FIGURE 5 Image Producer, Consumers, and Filters

Image Observer

A class must implement this interface if it wants to receive the progress status of an image as the image is being loaded.

`ImageObserver`	Used for obtaining progress status of the loading of an image.

Image Producers

The `ImageProducer` class is used to build image producers. One image producer is provided for producing an image from an array of pixels.

`ImageProducer`	The superclass of all image producers.
`MemoryImageSource`	Used for producing an image from an array of pixels.

Image Consumers

The `ImageConsumer` class is used to build image consumers. One image consumer, `PixelGrabber`, is provided for extracting pixel values from an image.

`ImageConsumer`	The superclass of all image consumers.
`PixelGrabber`	Used for extracting the pixel values from an image.

Image Filters

The `ImageFilter` class is used to build image consumers. Three image filter classes are available for various kinds of image filtering.

`ImageFilter`	The superclass of all image filters.
`CropImageFilter`	An image filter for creating a subimage from an image.

`FilteredImageSource`	Used for inserting an image filter into an image stream.
`RGBImageFilter`	Used for creating an image filter.

Color Models

A color model is associated with an image and specifies how to translate the image's pixel values into colors.

`ColorModel`	The superclass of all color models.
`DirectColorModel`	A color model whereby the colors are encoded in the pixel values.
`IndexColorModel`	A color model whereby pixel values are indices into a color table.

java.awt.peer

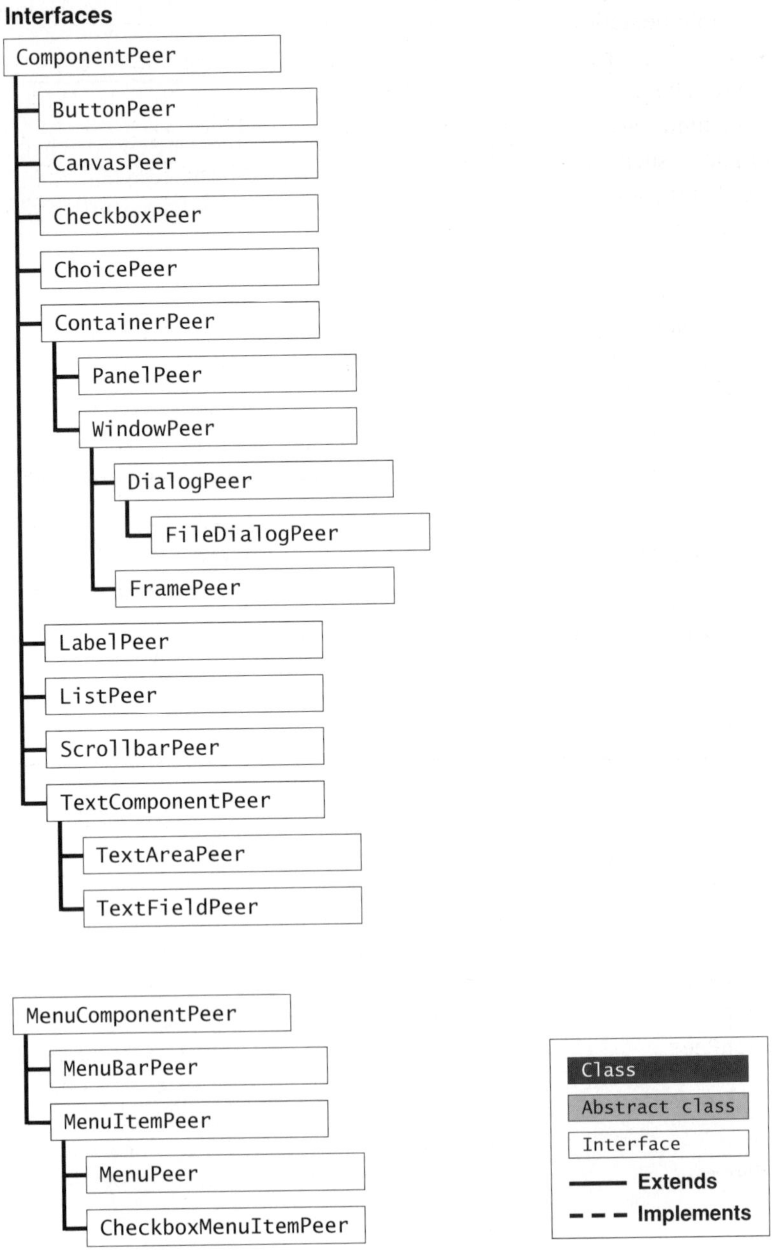

Interfaces
ComponentPeer
ButtonPeer
CanvasPeer
CheckboxPeer
ChoicePeer
ContainerPeer
PanelPeer
WindowPeer
DialogPeer
FileDialogPeer
FramePeer
LabelPeer
ListPeer
ScrollbarPeer
TextComponentPeer
TextAreaPeer
TextFieldPeer
MenuComponentPeer
MenuBarPeer
MenuItemPeer
MenuPeer
CheckboxMenuItemPeer
Class
Abstract class
Interface
Extends
Implements

An AWT component such as a button uses the platform's native implementation of a button. For example, on Solaris the AWT button uses the Motif button widget, while on Windows 95 the AWT button uses the button control. To make the AWT button component behave the same on all platforms, the button is assigned a *peer* that takes care of translating the behavior of the platform's native button to the behavior of the AWT button.

For the AWT subsystem to be able to use a set of peers with a platform and a vendor-dependent implementation, the peers must implement a set of common interfaces called the *peer interfaces*. These peer interfaces are all contained in this package as part of the Java package hierarchy. The *peer classes* that implement these interfaces, however, are *not* part of the Java package hierarchy. Rather, they are located in a package that has a platform- and vendor-dependent name, such as `sun.awt.win32`. The name of the package is contained in a system property so that the AWT subsystem can find it. Figure 6 shows a component hierarchy and its corresponding peer hierarchy.

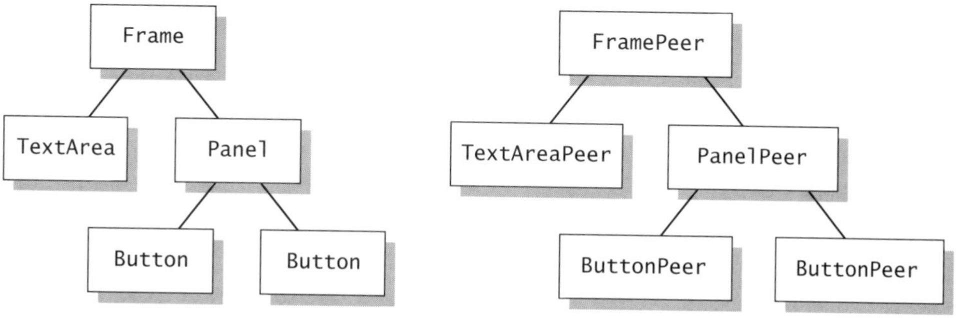

FIGURE 6 The Component Hierarchy and Its Corresponding Peer Class Hierarchy

Peer Classes

`ButtonPeer`	The peer interface for the `Button` component.
`CanvasPeer`	The peer interface for the `Canvas` component.
`CheckboxMenuItemPeer`	The peer interface for the `CheckboxMenuItem` component.
`CheckboxPeer`	The peer interface for the `Checkbox` component.
`ChoicePeer`	The peer interface for the `Choice` component.
`ComponentPeer`	The peer interface for the `Component` component.
`ContainerPeer`	The peer interface for the `Container` component.
`DialogPeer`	The peer interface for the `Dialog` component.
`FileDialogPeer`	The peer interface for the `FileDialog` component.
`FramePeer`	The peer interface for the `Frame` component.
`LabelPeer`	The peer interface for the `Label` component.
`ListPeer`	The peer interface for the `List` component.
`MenuBarPeer`	The peer interface for the `MenuBar` component.

MenuComponentPeer	The peer interface for the MenuComponent component.
MenuItemPeer	The peer interface for the MenuItem component.
MenuPeer	The peer interface for the Menu component.
PanelPeer	The peer interface for the Panel component.
ScrollbarPeer	The peer interface for the Scrollbar component.
TextAreaPeer	The peer interface for the TextArea component.
TextComponentPeer	The peer interface for the TextComponent component.
TextFieldPeer	The peer interface for the TextField component.
WindowPeer	The peer interface for the Window component.

java.io

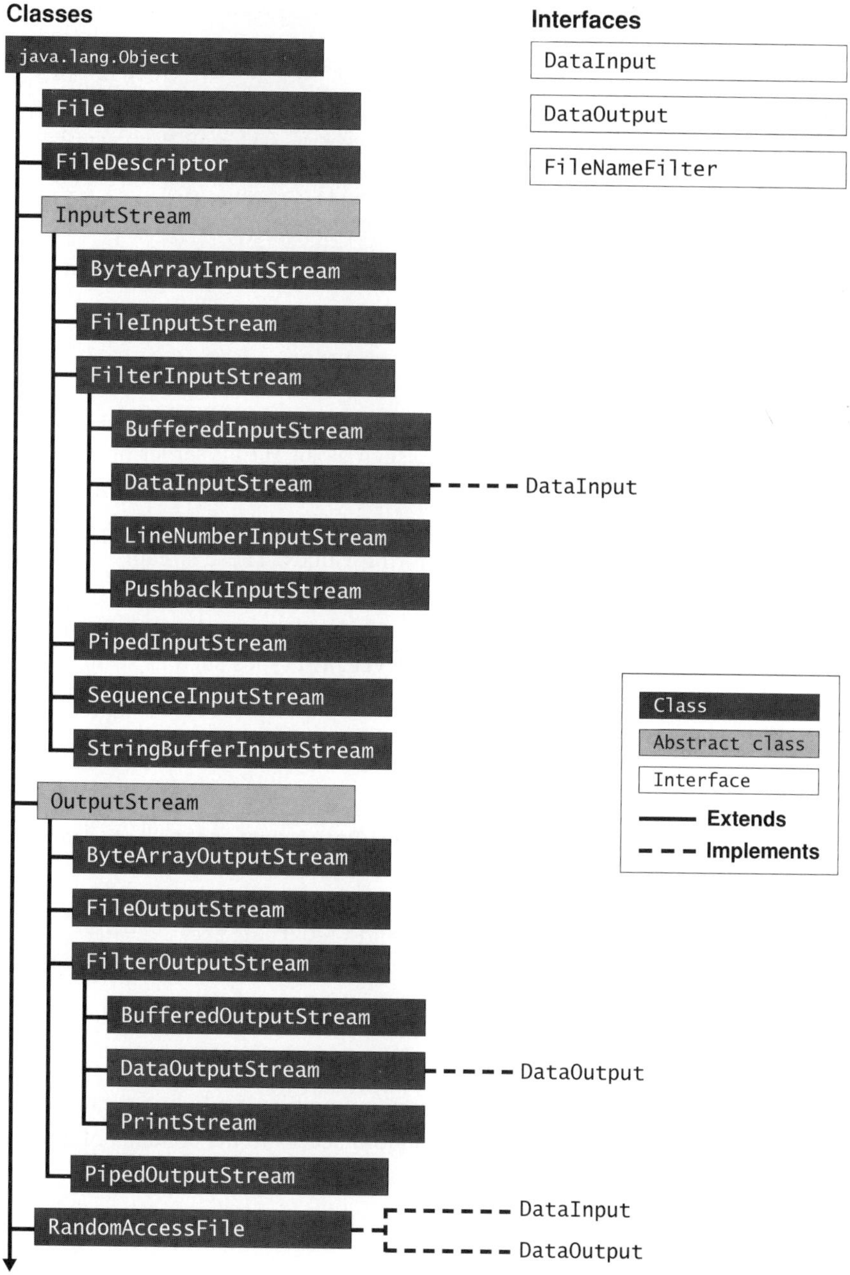
Classes
java.lang.Object
File
FileDescriptor
InputStream
ByteArrayInputStream
FileInputStream
FilterInputStream
BufferedInputStream
DataInputStream
DataInput
LineNumberInputStream
PushbackInputStream
PipedInputStream
SequenceInputStream
StringBufferInputStream
OutputStream
ByteArrayOutputStream
FileOutputStream
FilterOutputStream
BufferedOutputStream
DataOutputStream
DataOutput
PrintStream
PipedOutputStream
RandomAccessFile
DataInput
DataOutput
Interfaces
DataInput
DataOutput
FileNameFilter
Class
Abstract class
Interface
Extends
Implements

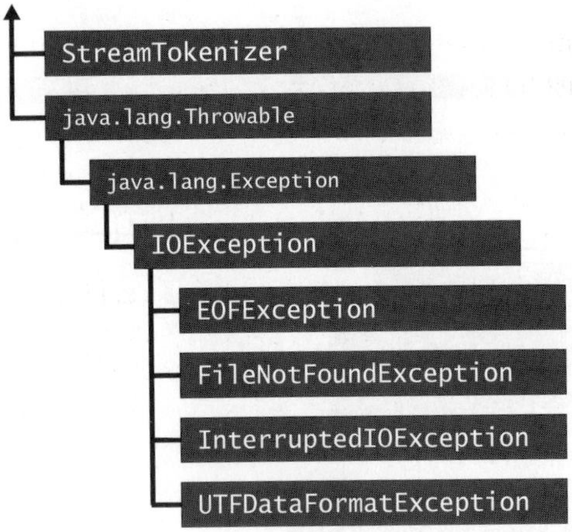

This package contains classes for building *data streams*. A data stream is either an *input* stream for reading values from a data source, such as an HTTP server or a Java string, or an *output* stream for writing values to a data repository such as a file or an array of bytes.

A data container such as a file typically provides a method that returns an input stream for reading its contents or an output stream for storing values. These streams can be composed to form a chain of streams through which data flows and can be transformed by each stream. For example, after obtaining an input stream from a file a data input stream could be added that would transform a stream of bytes into higher-level Java types such as strings and integers, as shown in Figure 7.

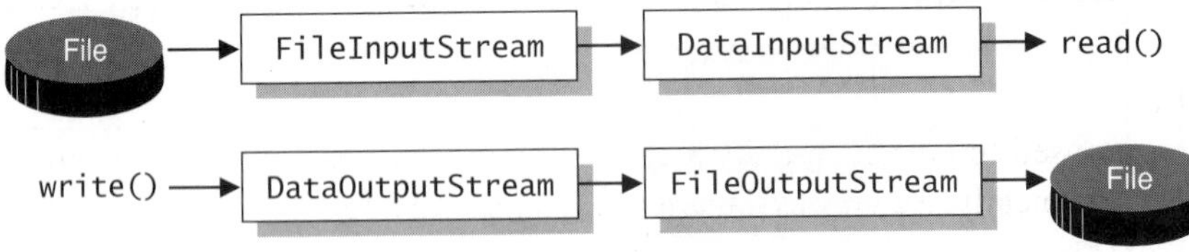

FIGURE 7 Composing IO Streams

This package also contains classes for operating on files, including creating and removing files. The `RandomAccessFile` class allows random access to the contents of a file.

Stream Superclasses

These classes define a minimum set of operations that a stream must implement. All input, output, and filter streams must be a subclass of one of these classes.

`FilterInputStream`	The superclass of all input filter streams.
`FilterOutputStream`	The superclass of all output filter streams.
`InputStream`	The superclass of all input streams. Provides basic input methods for reading data from an input stream.
`OutputStream`	The superclass of all output streams. Provides basic output methods for writing data to an output stream.

Buffered Streams

These filter streams buffer the data flows through them to improve the performance of small read and write operations.

`BufferedInputStream`	A filter input stream that maintains a buffer of bytes read from the original input stream.
`BufferedOutputStream`	A filter output stream that maintains a buffer of bytes to be written to its destination output stream.

Byte Array and String Streams

The `StringBufferInputStream` allows you to create an input stream from a string. The other two classes create input and output streams from byte arrays.

`ByteArrayInputStream`	An input stream that reads data from a byte array.
`ByteArrayOutputStream`	An output stream that writes its data to a byte array.
`StringBufferInputStream`	An input stream that reads data from a string.

Data Streams

These classes are used to encode and decode Java primitive types in a compact binary form. These classes are typically used to save and retrieve values in a file.

`DataInput`	An interface for reading Java primitive data types.
`DataInputStream`	A filter input stream for retrieving Java primitive data types from a binary form.

`DataOutput`	An interface for writing Java primitive data types.
`DataOutputStream`	A filter output stream for encoding Java primitive data types to a binary form.

File Classes and Streams

These classes provide all file-related operations available in Java.

`File`	Represents a file with methods for operating on a file.
`FileDescriptor`	Represents a handle to an open file.
`FileInputStream`	A filter input stream for reading data from a file.
`FileOutputStream`	A filter output stream for writing data to a file.
`FilenameFilter`	An interface for defining selection criteria for a list of filenames.
`RandomAccessFile`	Used for accessing the contents of a file nonsequentially.

Pipes

This pair of classes can be used to create a stream of data between two threads. Such a stream of data is called a *pipe*. One thread can write into one end of the pipe, while the other thread can read from the other end of the pipe.

`PipedInputStream`	An input stream for reading input from a pipe.
`PipedOutputStream`	An output stream for writing output to a pipe.

Input Stream Sequence

This class is used to combine a sequence of input streams into a single input stream. When one input stream is exhausted, the class seamlessly starts reading from the next input stream.

`SequenceInputStream`	Creates a single input stream from two or more input streams.

Miscellaneous Filter Streams

These classes implement various useful streams.

`LineNumberInputStream`	A filter input stream for counting the number of lines.

`PrintStream`	A filter output stream for converting Java primitive types to a printable form.
`PushbackInputStream`	A filter input stream that allows 1 byte to be unread from the stream.
`StreamTokenizer`	A filter input stream for parsing the stream into a sequence of tokens.

Exceptions

These are the exceptions declared in this package. They are not subclasses of `RuntimeException`, so they must be either caught or declared in the `throws` clause.

`EOFException`	Thrown if the End-Of-File has been reached when reading from a data input stream.
`FileNotFoundException`	Thrown if attempting to access a nonexistent file.
`IOException`	The superclass of the other IO exceptions in this package.
`InterruptedIOException`	Thrown if a stream operation has been interrupted.
`UTFDataFormatException`	Thrown if a Unicode string in a malformed Unicode Transfer Format has been encountered.

java.lang

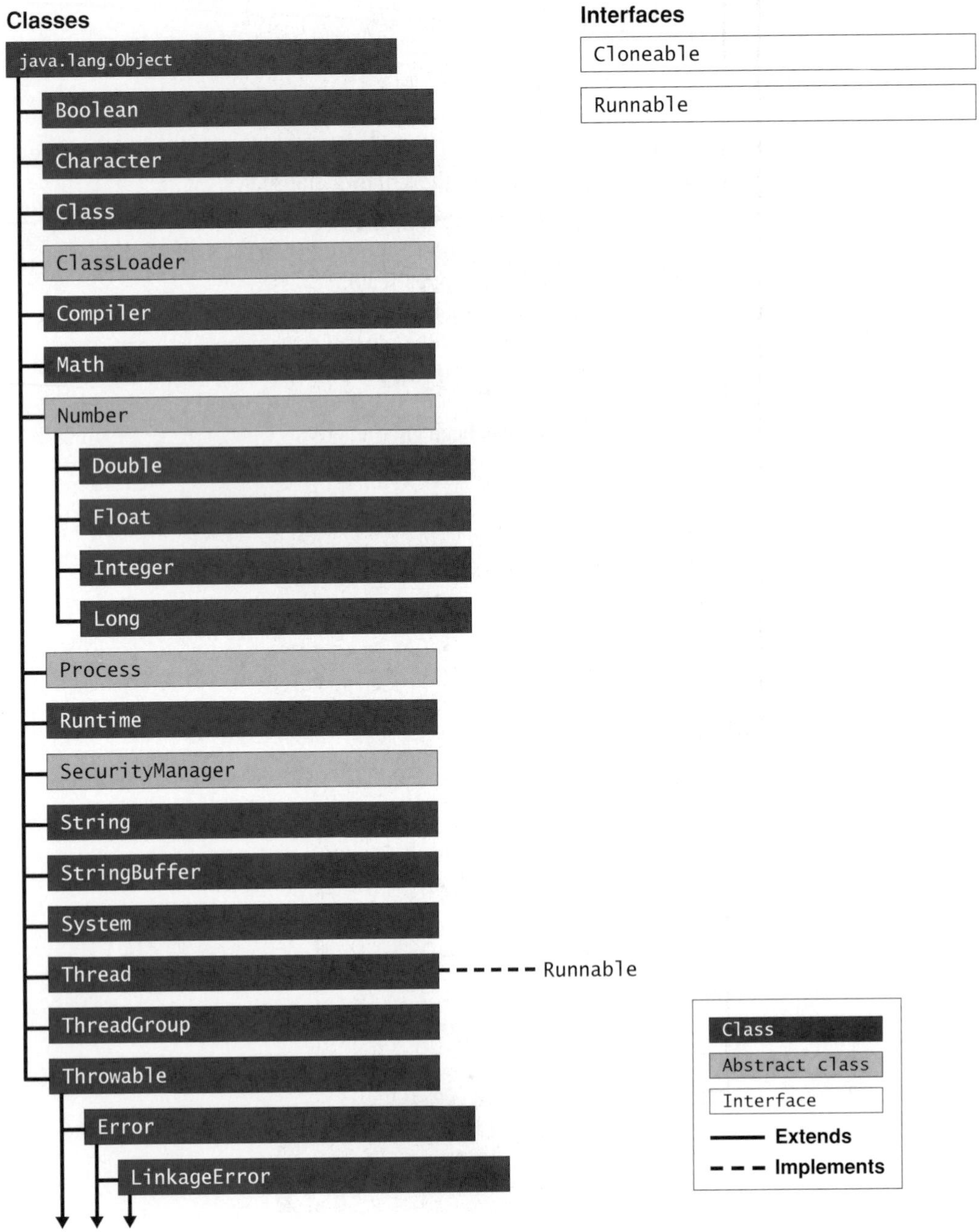

Classes
java.lang.Object
Boolean
Character
Class
ClassLoader
Compiler
Math
Number
Double
Float
Integer
Long
Process
Runtime
SecurityManager
String
StringBuffer
System
Thread
Runnable
ThreadGroup
Throwable
Error
LinkageError
Interfaces
Cloneable
Runnable
Class
Abstract class
Interface
Extends
Implements

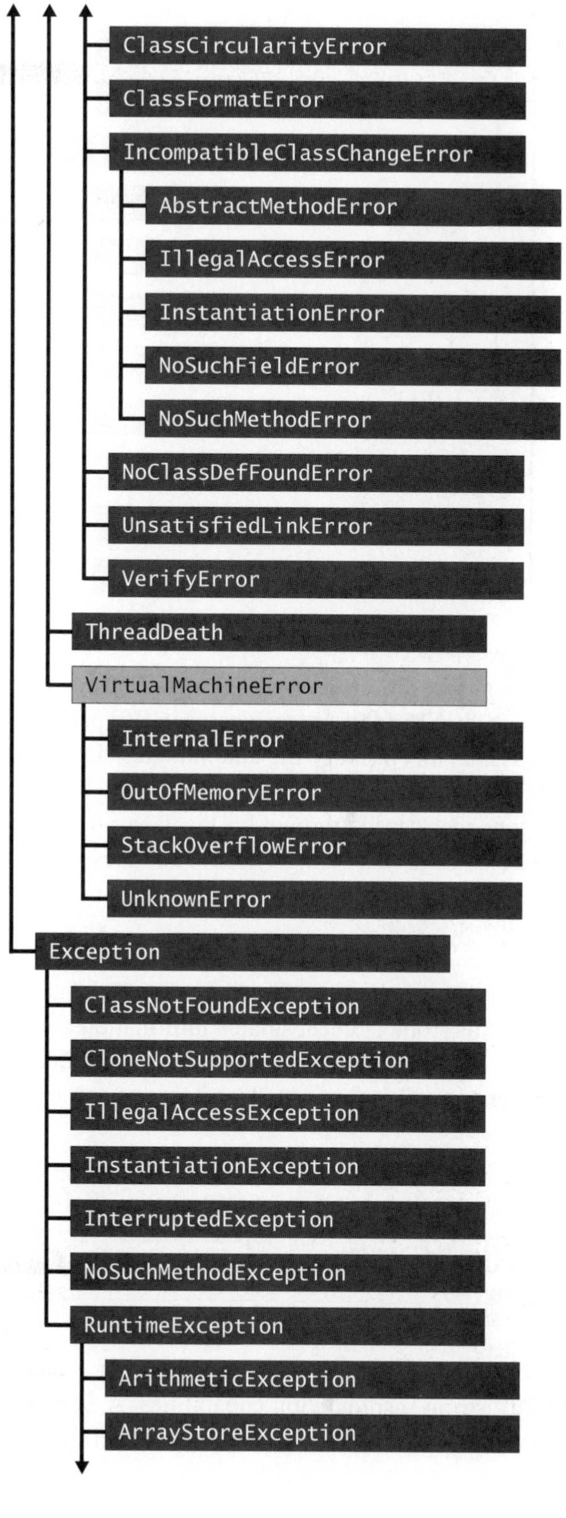
ClassCircularityError
ClassFormatError
IncompatibleClassChangeError
AbstractMethodError
IllegalAccessError
InstantiationError
NoSuchFieldError
NoSuchMethodError
NoClassDefFoundError
UnsatisfiedLinkError
VerifyError
ThreadDeath
VirtualMachineError
InternalError
OutOfMemoryError
StackOverflowError
UnknownError
Exception
ClassNotFoundException
CloneNotSupportedException
IllegalAccessException
InstantiationException
InterruptedException
NoSuchMethodException
RuntimeException
ArithmeticException
ArrayStoreException

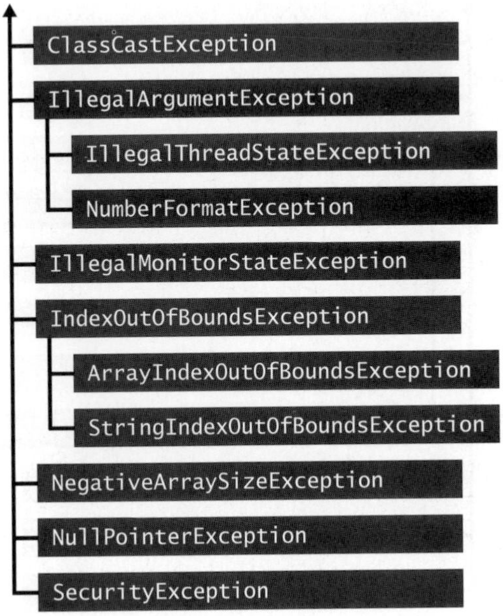

This package contains classes that are an integral part of the Java language. These include `Object`, `Throwable`, `String`, and `Thread`. If any classes in this package are missing, the runtime will not start. The classes in this package are automatically imported into every Java program, so there is no need to explicitly import them.

All errors and exceptions that can be thrown by the Java virtual machine appear in this package. Also included are classes for accessing system resources, primitive type object wrappers, a math class, and a security class.

Root Classes

The `Object` class is the superclass of all classes, so the methods defined in this class are inherited by all other classes. A `Class` object encapsulates information about a Java class that has been loaded into the system; there is one `Class` object for each loaded class. The `Throwable` class is the root of all Java errors and exceptions. To be an error or an exception, a class must inherit from `Throwable`.

`Class`	Used for obtaining information about a Java class.
`Object`	The superclass of all Java objects.
`Throwable`	The superclass of all Java errors and exceptions.

Strings

These classes provide Java's string manipulation capabilities. A `String` object is immutable. This means that any operation on it always results in a new `String` object, while the original object is left intact. A `StringBuffer` object maintains an expandable sequence of characters and should be used in applications where you expect to modify a string quite a bit. In most applications, `String` objects are typically used and result in fewer programming errors. Consider using a `StringBuffer` object only if efficiency becomes an issue.

`String`	An immutable sequence of characters with lots of string-related operations.
`StringBuffer`	A mutable, expandable sequence of characters with lots of string-related operations.

Math

`Math`	A collection of mathematical operations for doing trigonometry, for rounding, and for finding logs and square roots.

System

These classes are used to access system-related services such as the current time, processes, garbage collector, and memory management.

`ClassLoader`	Used for loading Java classes and defining loading policies.
`Process`	Used for obtaining information about and communicating with processes spawned off to execute system programs.
`Runtime`	Used for performing environment-related and system-related operations, such as loading libraries, executing system programs, and performing garbage collection.
`System`	Used for examining and manipulating system-related information such as the current time and system properties in a platform-independent manner. Contains fields for standard input, output, and error.

Threads

Threads allow a program to have multiple threads of execution occurring concurrently. The following classes provide the support for defining, creating, and manipulating Java threads.

`Runnable`	An interface that a class can implement to be runnable by a thread.
`Thread`	Used for defining, creating, and manipulating a thread.
`ThreadGroup`	Used for creating and manipulating a set of threads.

Cloneable

This interface is used by classes that want to support the `clone()` method. Unless a class implements this interface, an attempt to clone an object will result in the `CloneNotSupportedException` being thrown.

`Cloneable`	An interface that a class must implement in order to support the `clone()` method.

Primitive Type Wrappers

These classes are used to work around the fact that primitive types such as `int` and `float` are not Java objects and that Java does not support templates. For example, classes that implement a data structure such as a tree or a hash table are typically implemented to handle objects for maximal reusability. This means that a primitive type like `int` cannot be used with the class. By wrapping an `Integer` object around an `int` value, the `int` value can then be used by the class. Of course, this introduces some overhead, so if efficiency is absolutely critical you'll need to implement a version of the data structure specifically for the desired primitive type.

`Boolean`	An object wrapper for `boolean` values.
`Character`	An object wrapper for `char` values.
`Double`	An object wrapper for `double` values.
`Float`	An object wrapper for `float` values.
`Integer`	An object wrapper for `int` values.
`Long`	An object wrapper for `long` values.
`Number`	The abstract superclass for the number objects (`Double`, `Float`, `Integer`, and `Long`).

Security

This class is used to define the security policies of a Java program. It controls what a Java program can and cannot do. It is typically used by an application that executes Java programs, such as a Web browser. It can be set once and cannot be removed.

`SecurityManager`	Used for defining the security policy for a Java program.

Compiler

This class is used to control a compiler that compiles Java byte codes directly into machine code for a particular platform. Such a compiler is not included in the Java development kit from Sun Microsystems and must be obtained from a third-party source.

`Compiler`	Used for compiling Java byte codes into machine code.

Errors

A Java *error* is a type of exception thrown by the Java virtual machine to indicate that an unrecoverable erroneous condition has occurred. For example, an error would be thrown if there were an attempt to load a corrupted class.

`AbstractMethodError`	Thrown if attempting to invoke an abstract method.
`ClassCircularityError`	Thrown if attempting to load classes that have cyclic class inheritance.
`ClassFormatError`	Thrown if attempting to load a class that is not in an acceptable format.
`Error`	The superclass of all error classes.
`IllegalAccessError`	Thrown if attempting to access a member of a class to which it does not have access (such as a `protected` method).
`IncompatibleClassChangeError`	The superclass of errors that are thrown if attempting to access a member of a class in a way that violates Java language semantics.
`InstantiationError`	Thrown if attempting to instantiate an abstract class or an interface.

`InternalError`	Thrown if the Java virtual machine encounters an unrecoverable error that involves the virtual machine's internal logic.
`LinkageError`	The superclass of errors that result when attempting to load a class that has changed in an incompatible manner and consequently cannot be loaded.
`NoClassDefFoundError`	Thrown if the system's default class loader cannot find the class to load.
`NoSuchFieldError`	Thrown if attempting to access a nonexistent field of a class.
`NoSuchMethodError`	Thrown if attempting to access a nonexistent method of a class.
`OutOfMemoryError`	Thrown if the Java runtime runs out of memory and consequently cannot continue execution.
`StackOverflowError`	Thrown if the Java execution stack limit has been exceeded during the execution of a thread.
`ThreadDeath`	Thrown by the runtime to indicate that the current thread is about to be terminated.
`UnknownError`	Thrown if a condition that cannot be described by any other error has occurred.
`UnsatisfiedLinkError`	Thrown if a library cannot be loaded and linked successfully.
`VerifyError`	Thrown if a class cannot be loaded because it violates the Java byte code specification.
`VirtualMachineError`	The superclass of errors that are thrown if the Java virtual machine encounters an unrecoverable error, such as lack of memory or lack of stack size.

Runtime Exceptions

These exceptions inherit from `RuntimeException`, so it is not necessary to catch them or declare them in a `throws` clause. However, exceptions of this type are considered programming bugs and should be corrected. Therefore these exceptions should not be caught.

`ArithmeticException`	Thrown if attempting to perform an illegal arithmetic operation (such as division by zero).
`ArrayIndexOutOfBoundsException`	Thrown if attempting to access an array element with an index outside the array bounds.
`ArrayStoreException`	Thrown if attempting to store an object of the wrong type in an array.
`ClassCastException`	Thrown if attempting to cast an object to an incompatible class.

`IllegalArgumentException`	Thrown if an illegal argument has been passed to a method.
`IllegalMonitorStateException`	Thrown if calling an object's synchronized method but does not own the object's lock.
`IllegalThreadStateException`	Thrown if attempting to perform an operation on a thread while the thread is in a state not suitable for that operation.
`IndexOutOfBoundsException`	The superclass of exceptions that are thrown when accessing an element with an index that is out of bounds.
`NegativeArraySizeException`	Thrown if attempting to create an array with a negative size.
`NullPointerException`	Thrown if attempting to de-reference a `null` reference.
`NumberFormatException`	Thrown if a string is not in a format that can be parsed into a number of the desired type.
`RuntimeException`	The superclass of all runtime exceptions that indicate a programming error.
`StringIndexOutOfBoundsException`	Thrown if attempting to access an element of a string using an index that is outside the bounds of the string.

Exceptions

These exceptions directly inherit from `Exception`, so they must be either caught or declared in the `throws` clause. Exceptions of this type typically indicate some error condition that can sometimes arise in an operation. For example, when loading a class the operation normally returns a reference to the class. However, if the class cannot be found, the `ClassNotFoundException` is raised. A program should catch this error, notify the user of the error, and then continue running.

`ClassNotFoundException`	Thrown if a class loader cannot find the class to load on explicit instructions from the program (rather than implicitly by the runtime, which loads classes as they are referenced).
`CloneNotSupportedException`	Thrown if attempting to clone an object that belongs to a class that does not implement the `Cloneable` interface.
`Exception`	The superclass used for representing exceptional conditions that must be caught.
`IllegalAccessException`	Thrown if not permitted to access a member of a class.

`InstantiationException`	Thrown if attempting to instantiate an abstract class or an interface.
`InterruptedException`	Thrown when a thread receives an interrupt invoked by another thread.
`NoSuchMethodException`	Thrown if attempting to access a nonexistent method from a user-defined class loader.

java.net

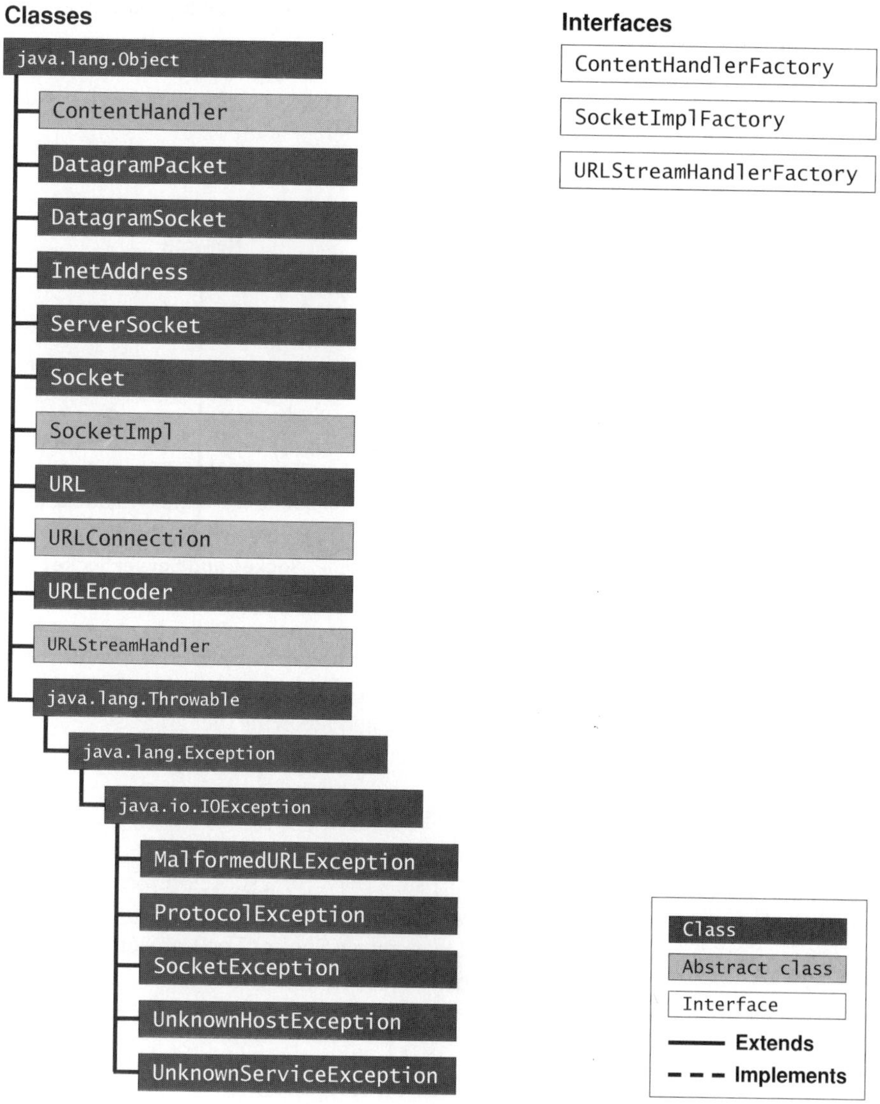
Classes
java.lang.Object
ContentHandler
DatagramPacket
DatagramSocket
InetAddress
ServerSocket
Socket
SocketImpl
URL
URLConnection
URLEncoder
URLStreamHandler
java.lang.Throwable
java.lang.Exception
java.io.IOException
MalformedURLException
ProtocolException
SocketException
UnknownHostException
UnknownServiceException
Interfaces
ContentHandlerFactory
SocketImplFactory
URLStreamHandlerFactory
Class
Abstract class
Interface
Extends
Implements

This package contains classes for implementing networking applications. Using the socket classes, you can communicate with any server on the Internet or implement your own Internet server.[1] A number of classes are provided to make it convenient to use *Universal Resource Locators* (URLs) to retrieve data on the Internet.

Host Name Resolution

This class is used to resolve a host name to an Internet address.

`InetAddress`	Represents an Internet address with methods for resolving a host name to an Internet address.

Sockets

These classes provide the necessary functionality for communicating with servers on the Internet. These classes can also be used to implement an Internet server. See Figure 8.

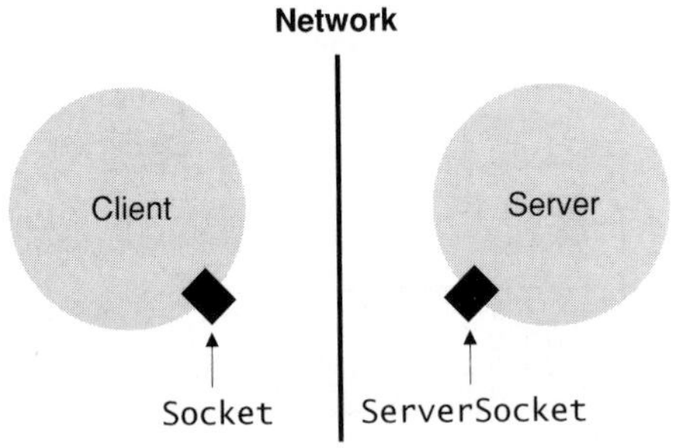

FIGURE 8 Socket and ServerSocket

`DatagramPacket`	A datagram used in a connectionless protocol such as UDP.
`DatagramSocket`	Used for sending and receiving datagrams.
`ServerSocket`	Used by a server in a connection-oriented protocol such as TCP.
`Socket`	Used by a client or server in connectionless or connection-oriented protocols.
`SocketImpl`	The abstract superclass for a socket implementation. Not directly used.
`SocketImplFactory`	A factory that creates `SocketImpl` objects. Not directly used.

1. Restrictions may be placed by the security manager as to which servers you can communicate with. For example, some Web browsers allow only applets to communicate with the server from which the applet was loaded.

URL

These classes make it convenient to use URLs to retrieve data on the Internet. The data can be retrieved as a complete object or as a stream. Figure 9 shows the use of the `URL` and `URLConnection` classes in accessing Web services.

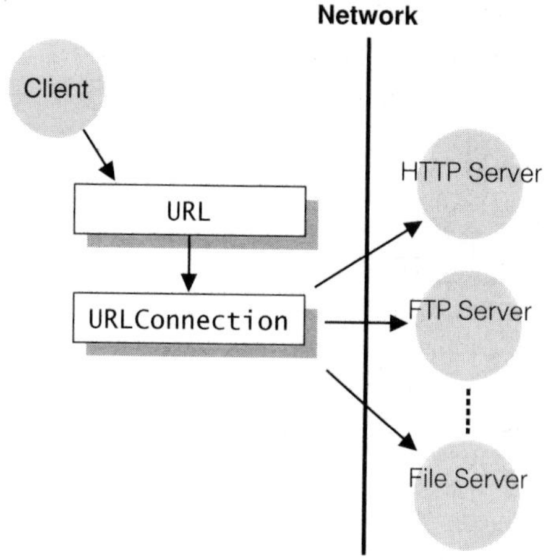

FIGURE 9 Use of `URL` and `URLConnection`, to access Web Services

`ContentHandler`	The abstract superclass of content handlers for producing an object based on a MIME. Not directly used.
`ContentHandlerFactory`	A factory that returns a new `ContentHandler` object based on a MIME type. Not directly used.
`URL`	Represents a URL with methods for parsing the URL and creating a connection to the URL's host.
`URLConnection`	Used for creating a connection to a URL's host and retrieving the data.
`URLEncoder`	Used for encoding a string in `x-www-form-urlencoded` format.
`URLStreamHandler`	The abstract superclass for URL protocol handlers (e.g., "http," "ftp," "telnet," etc.). Not directly used.
`URLStreamHandlerFactory`	A factory that creates instances of `URLStreamHandler` for different URL protocols. Not directly used.

Exceptions

These are exceptions declared in this package. They are not subclasses of `RuntimeException`, so they must be either caught or declared in the `throws` clause.

`MalformedURLException`	Thrown if arguments to the `URL` constructor are invalid.
`ProtocolException`	Thrown if attempting to connect to a socket of the wrong type.

`SocketException`	Thrown if attempting to create a socket to an unsupported service or if attempting to install a socket implementation factory when one has already been installed.
`UnknownHostException`	Thrown if cannot resolve a host name to an Internet address.
`UnknownServiceException`	Thrown if attempting to use a service that is not supported by a URL connection.

java.util

This package contains a number of utility classes that are useful in typical Java programs. Included in this package are classes that implement a few data structures, a class to manipulate dates, a simple string tokenizer, and a random-number generator.

Data Structures

These classes implement a few data structures that are often used by a typical Java application. The `Enumeration` class provides a convenient way to visit all the elements in a data structure.

This is particularly useful for data structures whose elements cannot be retrieved with an index, such as a hash table.

`BitSet`	A space-efficient bit vector that automatically expands.
`Dictionary`	The abstract superclass for data structures that maintain a set of key/value pairs.
`Enumeration`	An interface consisting of methods for enumerating a list of objects.
`Hashtable`	A hash table for efficiently associating an object with another object.
`Stack`	A last-in, first-out stack of objects.
`Vector`	An array of objects that automatically expands.

Date Class

This class encapsulates date and time functionality. Methods are provided for obtaining the current time and date and converting them to and from a string.

`Date`	Represents a time and date with methods to operate on the time and date.

Observer Classes

An *observable object* is an object that holds some data that is constantly modified. An observer is an object that when registered with an observable object, gets notifications whenever the data held by the observable object changes.

`Observable`	The superclass of observable objects.
`Observer`	The interface that an observer must implement.

Properties

A *property* is a key/value pair where both the key and value are strings. This class is used to implement system properties; this is how a user customizes a Java program. This class contains methods for saving and retrieving all the data in the property table.

`Properties`	A set of properties that has methods for saving and retrieving those properties.

Random Numbers

This class is used to generate pseudo-random numbers of all the Java primitive number types - `int`, `long`, `float`, and `double`.

`Random`	Used to generate pseudo-random numbers.

Parser

This class is used to separate a string into smaller strings based on a set of characters that define the separators. The separators are typically whitespace characters like the space and tab.

`StringTokenizer`	Used to parse a string to a sequence of tokens.

Exceptions

These are the exceptions declared in this package. They are subclasses of `RuntimeException` and so should not be caught.

`EmptyStackException`	Thrown if attempting to access an element on an empty stack.
`NoSuchElementException`	Thrown if attempting to access an element in an enumeration after the enumeration is exhausted.

java.lang

AbstractMethodError

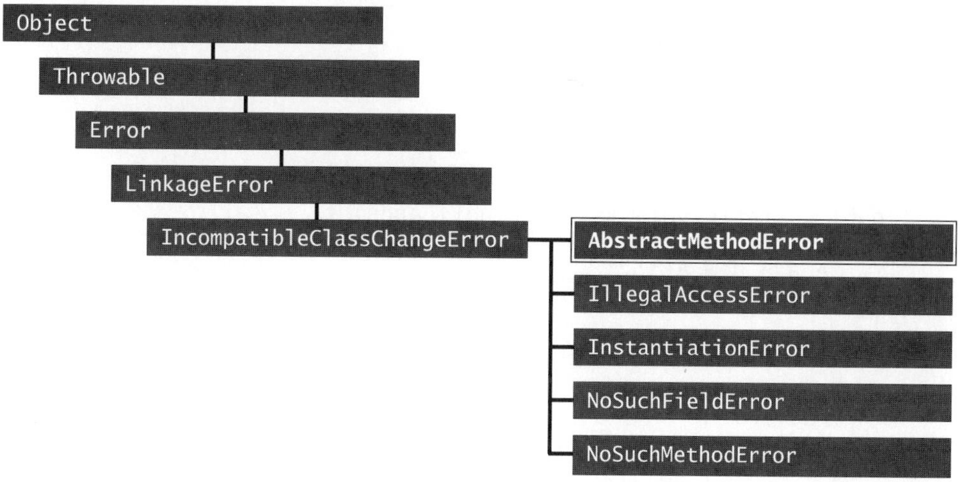

Syntax

```
public class AbstractMethodError extends IncompatibleClassChangeError
```

Description

`AbstractMethodError` is a runtime linkage error that is raised when the Java virtual machine detects that the program is trying to invoke an abstract method. Normally, when you compile a program that attempts to invoke an abstract method, you would get a compilation error pinpointing the problem so that a linkage error at runtime would not occur. However, the problem could be introduced when classes used by the program become inconsistent; for example, by making an incompatible change and then recompiling only some of its classes.

`AbstractMethodError` should not be caught or declared in the `throws` clause of a method.

MEMBER SUMMARY	
Constructor	
`AbstractMethodError()`	Constructs an `AbstractMethodError` instance.

See Also

`Error`, `IncompatibleClassChangeError`.

A
B
C
D
E
F
G
H
I
J
K
L
M
N
O
P
Q
R
S
T
U
V
W
X
Y
Z

Example

In this example, method1() in class B used to be nonabstract. The following main program compiled fine with it.

In Main.java:

```
class A extends B {
    public void method2(int i) {
        System.out.println(i);
    }
}
class Main {
    public static void main(String[] args) {
        System.out.println("AbstractMethodError example");
        A a = new A();
        a.method1(0);
    }
}
```

In B.java:

```
abstract class B {
    public void method1(int i) {
        System.out.println("method1:" + i);
    }
    abstract public void method2(int i);
}
```

However, if method1() is subsequently made abstract (by adding the abstract keyword and removing its body), running main() would raise AbstractMethodError.

In the modified B.java:

```
abstract class B {
    abstract public void method1(int i);
    abstract public void method2(int i);
}
```

AbstractMethodError()

PURPOSE Constructs an AbstractMethodError instance.

SYNTAX
```
public AbstractMethodError()
public AbstractMethodError(String msg)
```

DESCRIPTION These constructors create a new instance of AbstractMethodError. An optional string msg can be supplied that describes this particular instance of the error.

PARAMETERS

msg A string that gives details about this error.

java.applet
Applet

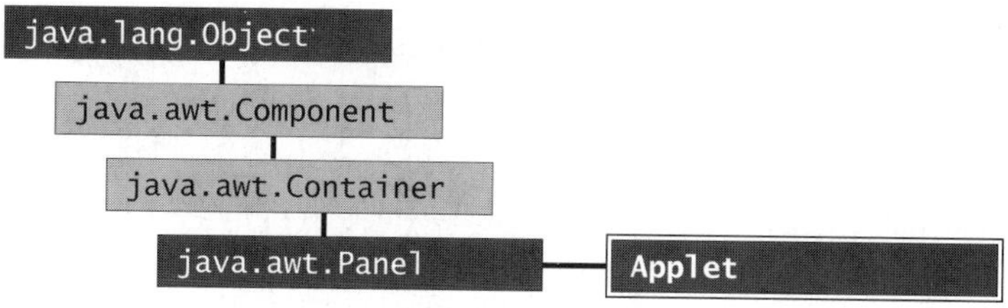

Syntax

```
public class Applet extends Panel
```

Description

Applets and Applet Contexts

An *applet* is basically a specialized panel (see `Panel`) that is embedded in a specialized component container called an *applet context*. An applet context can be a Web browser or other type of application that can display applets. It can contain more than one applet. An applet implements a number of methods that the applet context calls when it wants to initialize, start, stop, or destroy the applet. An applet also has access to a number of methods for retrieving resources such as images and audio clips based on URLs. Although they do not provide any more functionality that is available by other Java classes, they have been specially designed to be convenient to use by an applet. An applet can also access applet context information, such as the URL of the document containing the applet and, in some cases, control the applet context, such as to display a status message.

Handling Events and Painting

Since an applet is a subclass of `Panel`, you handle events in an applet just as you do events in a component. See the `Component` and `Event` classes for more information on event handling. Similarly, an applet paints itself in exactly the same way that a component paints itself. That is, it overrides the `paint()` and `update()` methods. See the `Component` class for more information.

Since an applet is a subclass of `Panel`, it is possible to embed components in the applet. The default layout manager of an applet is a flow layout (see `FlowLayout`).

States

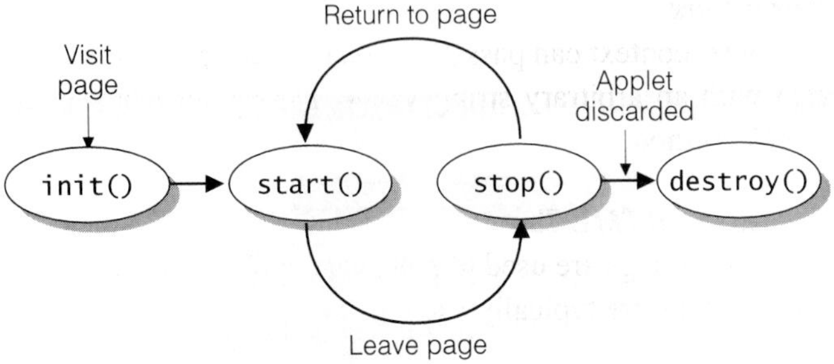

FIGURE 10 Applet Transitions

An applet can be in an *active* or *inactive* state. When the applet is first loaded, it is inactive states. When the applet is first displayed on the screen, it becomes active. The applet then moves between active and inactive states until it is destroyed by the applet context. Exactly what causes the applet to become active or inactive is up to the applet context. For example, the applet context might decide to make the applet inactive if the applet is scrolled out of view. Or it might make the applet inactive if the user views another document and leaves the document with the applet. Or it might make the applet inactive if the user clicks a special button. Figure 10 shows the transitions that an applet can go through.

Creating an Applet

An applet is created by declaring a class that extends from the `Applet` class. The applet then overrides one or more methods to implement the behavior. There are only six methods that can be overridden, any of which are optional: `destroy()`, `init()`, `start()`, `stop()`, `getAppletInfo()`, and `getParameterInfo()`. The `init()` method is called just after the applet is loaded. The `start()` method is called just after the applet becomes active. The `stop()` method is called just after the applet becomes inactive. The `destroy()` method is called just before the applet context destroys the applet. The `getAppletInfo()` and `getParameterInfo()` methods return some textual information about the applet and is typically called by the applet context when the user wants to display the information.

Code and Document Bases

An applet can fetch resources by way of a URL object. If it is desirable to fetch the applet using a relative URL, then there are two prefixes available to the applet. The code base is the URL prefix that contains the applet code. For example, suppose an applet were located at `http://www.sun.com/applets/Main.class`. The code base would be `http://www.sun.com/applets/`. The code base is typically used to fetch resources specific to the applet, such as icons and configuration information.

The document base is the URL prefix that contains the document that contains the applet. For example, suppose the document containing the applet were located at `http://www.sun.com/products/sparcstation/index.html`. The document base would be `http://www.sun.com/products/sparcstation/`. The document base is typically used to fetch resources specific to the document. For example, if some animation were to be designed for a particular HTML document, the animation images would typically be located somewhere relative to that document.

Parameters

An applet context can pass parameters to an applet. Parameters are simply string names associated with an arbitrary string value. The applet retrieves a parameter using the `getParameter()` method.

The Applet HTML Tag

Two HTML tags are used to embed an applet in an HTML document: `<applet>` and `<param>`. The two tags are typically used as follows:

```
<applet name=Main codebase=http://www.sun.com code=Main width=300
height=200>
<param name=name1 value="value1">
<param name=name2 value="value2">
<param name=name3 value="value3">

If you don't have a Java enabled browser ... get one.

<a href="http://www.sun.com"><IMG SRC="javacup.gif" height=60 width=60
alt="get Java"></a>
</applet>
```

A Java enabled browser recognizes the `<applet>` tag and interprets everything up to the `</applet>` tags. Between the `<applet>` and `</applet>` tags, it recognizes only `<param>` tags; it ignores everything else. A non-Java enabled browser on the other hand ignores the `<applet>`, `</applet>`, and `<param>` tags and interprets everything else. In this way, you can set up an HTML document that serves up the Java applet in a Java-enabled browser and displays something else for a non-Java enabled browser. Tables 1 and 2 give the attributes of the `<applet>` and `<param>` tags.

TABLE 1 Attributes of the `<applet>` Tag

`name`	Specifies the name of the applet. An applet can name itself, thereby allowing other applets to retrieve a reference to it. This attribute is equivalent to specifying a parameter with the name `"name"`. Therefore an applet can retrieve its name by calling `getParameter("name")`. This attribute is optional and defaults to `null`.
`codebase`	Specifies the applet's code base. This can be any absolute URL or a URL relative to the document containing the applet. This attribute is optional and defaults to `"."`.
`code`	Specifies the class name of the applet. The code tag specifies only the name of the class file and cannot contain any part of the path to the class file. This tag is mandatory.

TABLE 2 Attributes of the <param> Tag

`name`	Specifies the name of the parameter. The name must be different from the names of other parameters in the same pair of `<applet>` and `</applet>` tags. This attribute is mandatory. A special parameter called `"name"` is the name of the applet. There are two ways to name an applet: through the name attribute of the applet tag or by specifying a parameter called `"name"`.
`value`	Specifies a string that is associated with the parameter name. This attribute is mandatory.

MEMBER SUMMARY

Methods to Override	
`destroy()`	Called by the applet context to destroy the applet.
`init()`	Called by the applet context just after the applet is loaded.
`start()`	Called by the applet context just after the applet is made active.
`stop()`	Called by the applet context just after the applet is made inactive.
`getParameterInfo()`	Retrieves information about parameters that the applet recognizes.
`getAppletInfo()`	Retrieves a string containing information about the applet.
State Method	
`isActive()`	Retrieves the active state of the applet.
Audio and Image Methods	
`getAudioClip()`	Retrieves an audio clip from a URL.
`getImage()`	Retrieves an image at a URL.
`play()`	Fetches and plays an audio clip.
Parameter Methods	
`getCodeBase()`	Retrieves the applet's code base URL.
`getDocumentBase()`	Retrieves the applet's document base URL.
`getParameter()`	Retrieves the value of a parameter.
Applet Context Methods	
`getAppletContext()`	Retrieves the applet context.
`showStatus()`	Displays a message in the applet context.
Size Method	
`resize()`	Resizes the bounds of the applet.
Stub Method	
`setStub()`	Sets the applet's stub.

Example

This example implements a game. The goal is to catch duke while he's jumping around. If you catch him, he plays a sound. You also can drag him around. If the applet is active, the game plays some background music using the `loop()` method so that it plays continuously until stopped. All the images and sounds are fetched relative to the document base.

A button is created and embedded in the applet. If you click the button, `getAppletContext().showDocument()` is called to display the source code. Since the source code is typically located with the compiled applet code, `getCodeBase()` is used to locate the source code.

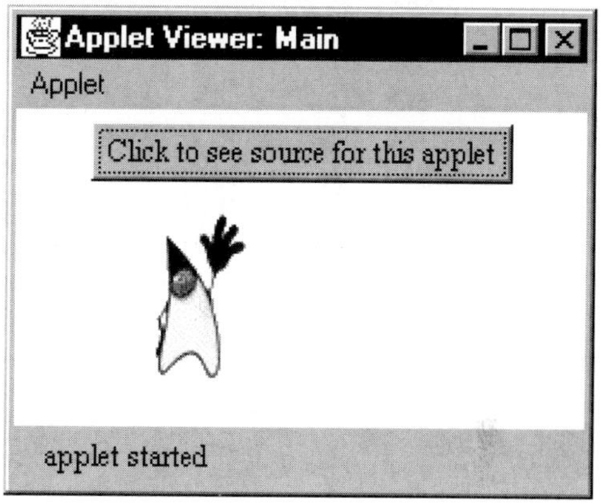

FIGURE 11 Applet

To eliminate flashing, the applet first paints the duke image into a second buffer and then displays the second buffer on the screen. To keep things simple, the applet paints the entire buffer every time Duke moves. It is much more efficient to paint only the parts of the image that have changed.

```
import java.applet.*;
import java.awt.*;
import java.net.*;
public class Main extends Applet implements Runnable {
    Image backBuffer;       // image for double-buffering.
    Graphics backBufferG;   // graphics context for double-buffer.

    AudioClip bgAudio;
    Image image;
    int imageX, imageY;     // current position of image.

    // Applet State Methods
    public void init() {
        backBuffer = createImage(400, 200);
        backBufferG = backBuffer.getGraphics();

        // load resources
        image = getImage(getDocumentBase(), getParameter("image"));
        bgAudio = getAudioClip(getDocumentBase(),
            getParameter("bg-audio"));

        add(new Button("Click to see source for this applet"));
        resize(400, 200);
    }
```

Example

```
    public void start() {
        startTickThread(true);
        bgAudio.loop();
    }

    public void stop() {
        startTickThread(false);
        bgAudio.stop();
    }

    public void destroy() {
        backBufferG.dispose();
        backBuffer.flush();
        image.flush();
    }

    // Paint Methods
    public void paint(Graphics g) {
        update(g);
    }

    public void update(Graphics g) {
        int w = size().width;
        int h = size().height;

        if (backBuffer == null
                || backBuffer.getWidth(this) < w
                || backBuffer.getHeight(this) < h) {
            backBuffer = createImage(w, h);
        }
        backBufferG.clearRect(0, 0, w, h);
        backBufferG.drawImage(image, imageX, imageY, this);
        g.drawImage(backBuffer, 0, 0, this);
    }

    // Event Methods
    public boolean mouseDown(Event evt, int x, int y) {
        if (x > imageX && x < imageX + image.getWidth(this)
            && y > imageY && y < imageY + image.getHeight(this)) {
            startTickThread(false);
            imageX = x-image.getWidth(this)/2;
            imageY = y-image.getHeight(this)/2;
            getAppletContext().showStatus("OWWW! Ya got me! Let go!");
            play(getDocumentBase(), getParameter("audio"));
            repaint();
        }
    return true;
    }

    public boolean mouseDrag(Event evt, int x, int y) {
        if (tickThread == null) {
            imageX = x-image.getWidth(this)/2;
            imageY = y-image.getHeight(this)/2;
            repaint();
```

```
        }
        return true;
    }

    public boolean mouseUp(Event evt, int x, int y) {
        if (tickThread == null) {
            startTickThread(true);
            getAppletContext().showStatus("Nah, Nah!");
        }
    return true;
    }

    public boolean action(Event evt, Object arg) {
        if (evt.target instanceof Button) {
            try {
                getAppletContext().showDocument(
                    new URL(getCodeBase(), getParameter("source")));
            } catch (MalformedURLException e) {
                e.printStackTrace();
            }
        return true;
        }
        return false;
    }

    // Tick Thread Methods
    Thread tickThread;
    void startTickThread(boolean start) {
        if (start) {
            tickThread = new Thread(this);
            tickThread.start();
        } else {
            tickThread = null;
        }
    }

    public void run() {
        int delay = Integer.parseInt(getParameter("delay"));
        while (Thread.currentThread() == tickThread) {
            try {
                imageX = (int)Math.floor(Math.random()*size().width);
                imageX = Math.min(imageX,
                                  size().width-image.getWidth(this));
                imageY = (int)Math.floor(Math.random()*size().height);
                imageY = Math.min(imageY,
                                  size().height-image.getHeight(this));
                repaint();
                Thread.sleep(delay);
            } catch (InterruptedException e) {
            }
        }
    }

    public String getAppletInfo() {
```

```
            return "Patrick Chan and Rosanna Lee (c) 1996";
        }

        String[][] parameterInfo = {
            {"image", "document-based url", "image to move around"},
            {"audio", "document-based url",
                         "sound to play when image is hit"},
            {"bg-audio", "document-based url", "background music"},
            {"audio", "code-based url",
                          "sound to play when image is hit"},
            {"delay", "integer", "delay between moves in milliseconds"},
        };
        public String[][] getParameterInfo() {
            return parameterInfo;
        }
    }
```

destroy()

PURPOSE Called by the applet context to destroy the applet.

SYNTAX `public void destroy()`

DESCRIPTION This method is called by the applet context when it decides to destroy the applet. This may occur if the applet context is low on space or when it exits. A subclass should override this method if it needs to dispose of any resources created by the applet. For example, if the applet creates a thread to do some background work, this method should be overridden so as to destroy the thread.

If an applet is active, the applet context will always call the `stop()` method before calling the `destroy()` method.

SEE ALSO `stop()`.

EXAMPLE See the class example.

getAppletContext()

PURPOSE Retrieves the applet context.

SYNTAX `public AppletContext getAppletContext()`

DESCRIPTION See the class description for more information about the applet context.

RETURNS The non-`null` reference to the applet context.

SEE ALSO `AppletContext`.

EXAMPLE See the class example.

A B C D E F G H I J K L M N O P Q R S T U V W X Y Z

getAppletInfo()

PURPOSE Retrieves a string containing information about the applet.

SYNTAX `public String getAppletInfo()`

DESCRIPTION This method can be overridden by an applet to return information about itself. This returned string typically includes information about the author, version, and copyright.

RETURNS A possibly `null` string containing information about the applet.

EXAMPLE See the class example.

getAudioClip()

PURPOSE Retrieves an audio clip from a URL.

SYNTAX
```
public AudioClip getAudioClip(URL url)
public AudioClip getAudioClip(URL url, String name)
```

DESCRIPTION This method retrieves an audio clip at the URL `url`. If `name` is specified, the audio clip is fetched from a new url created by appending `name` to `url`.

PARAMETERS

`name` The non-`null` name to append to `url`.

`url` The non-`null` url at which to fetch the audio clip.

RETURNS The audio clip at `url`. Returns `null` if the audio clip cannot be found.

SEE ALSO `AudioClip`, `java.net.URL`.

EXAMPLE See the class example.

getCodeBase()

PURPOSE Retrieves the applet's code base URL.

SYNTAX `public URL getCodeBase()`

DESCRIPTION The code base is the URL prefix that contains the applet code. For example, suppose an applet were located at `http://www.sun.com/applets/Main.class`. The code base would be `http://www.sun.com/applets/`. The code base is typically used to fetch resources specific to the applet, such as icons and configuration information.

RETURNS	The non-`null` applet's code base URL.
SEE ALSO	`getDocumentBase()`, `URL`.
EXAMPLE	See the class example.

getDocumentBase()

PURPOSE Retrieves the applet's document base URL.

SYNTAX
```
public URL getDocumentBase()
```

DESCRIPTION The document base is the URL prefix of the document that contains the applet. For example, suppose the document containing the applet were located at `http://www.sun.com/products/sparcstation/index.html`. The document base would be `http://www.sun.com/products/sparcstation/`. The document base is typically used to fetch resources specific to the document. For example, if some animation were to be designed for a particular HTML document, the animation images would typically be located somewhere relative to that document.

SEE ALSO `getCodeBase()`, `URL`.

EXAMPLE See the class example.

getImage()

PURPOSE Retrieves an image at a URL.

SYNTAX
```
public Image getImage(URL url)
public Image getImage(URL url, String name)
```

DESCRIPTION This method retrieves an image at the URL `url`. If `name` is specified, the image is fetched from a new URL created by appending `name` to `url`. This method returns immediately and does not actually fetch the pixels of the image. The pixels are fetched at the time they are needed (see `Image`).

As long as the image is found, the return image reference will not be `null`. However, an error may occur while loading the image. To check for errors, use the `Component.checkImage()` method call.

PARAMETERS

`name`	The non-`null` name to append to `url`.
`url`	The non-`null` URL at which to fetch the image.

RETURNS The image at `url`. Returns `null` if the image cannot be found.

SEE ALSO `Image`, `Component.checkImage()`, `URL`.

EXAMPLE See the class example.

getParameter()

PURPOSE Retrieves the value of a parameter.

SYNTAX `public String getParameter(String name)`

DESCRIPTION See the class description about applet parameters and the `param` HTML tag.

PARAMETERS

`name` The non-`null` name of the parameter value to retrieve.

RETURNS Returns the value of the parameter; otherwise returns `null` if the parameter does not exist.

EXAMPLE See the class example.

getParameterInfo()

PURPOSE Retrieves information about parameters that the applet recognizes.

SYNTAX `public String[][] getParameterInfo()`

DESCRIPTION This method is called by the applet context when it needs to display information about the applet parameters. This method returns an array of string arrays containing the desired information. Each parameter is described using three strings: the name of the parameter, the type of the parameter value (which is an arbitrary string), and a short description of the parameter.

RETURNS A possibly `null` array of string arrays containing information about the applet parameters.

EXAMPLE The `getParameterInfo()` method in this example describes an applet that displays an image and a message underneath the image.

```
String[][] parameterInfo = {
    {"location", "x y",
        "the location to display the image"},
    {"image", "url",
        "the location of the image"},
```

```
        {"message",  "string",
           "the message to display under the image"},
    };
    public String[][] getParameterInfo() {
            return parameterInfo;
    }
```

init()

PURPOSE Called by the applet context just after the applet is loaded.

SYNTAX `public void init()`

DESCRIPTION A subclass should override this method if it needs to implement behavior that occurs before the applet becomes active for the first time. For example, if the applet needs a background thread to do some work regardless of the applet's state, then this method should be overridden to create the thread.

SEE ALSO `destroy()`.

EXAMPLE See the class example.

isActive()

PURPOSE Retrieves the active state of the applet.

SYNTAX `public boolean isActive()`

DESCRIPTION An applet becomes active just before the `start()` method is called and becomes inactive just before the `stop()` method is called.

RETURNS `true` if the applet is active; `false` otherwise.

SEE ALSO `start()`.

EXAMPLE This example implements an applet that simply fetches a list of images. See Figure 12. A fetcher thread is created when the applet is loaded. When the fetcher thread finishes fetching an image, it calls `repaint()` to update the display, but only if the applet is active. Otherwise, it avoids calling `repaint()` and continues fetching images.

The list of images to fetch are supplied through the parameters. The applet looks for parameter names of the form `imageN`, where `N` starts at 0. Once a parameter name doesn't exist, the applet stops looking and assumes that all the images have been specified.

FIGURE 12 `Applet.isActive()`

```
import java.applet.*;
import java.awt.*;
public class Main extends Applet implements
    Runnable
{
    String[] imagesToFetch;
    Image[] fetchedImages;
    int fetched;    // number fetched
    Thread fetcherThread;

    // Applet State Methods
    public void init() {
        int i = 0;

        while (getParameter("image"+i) !=
            null) { i++;
        }
        imagesToFetch = new String[i];
        fetchedImages = new Image[i];

        if (i > 0) {
            fetcherThread = new Thread(this);
            fetcherThread.start();
        }
        for (i=0; i<imagesToFetch.length; i++) {
            imagesToFetch[i] = getParameter("image"+i);
        }
        resize(200, imagesToFetch.length * 70);
    }

    public void destroy() {
        fetcherThread = null;
    }

    // Paint Methods
    public void paint(Graphics g) {
        int w = size().width;
        int h = size().height;
        FontMetrics fm = g.getFontMetrics();
        int y = 0;
```

```
            for (int i=0; i<imagesToFetch.length; i++) {
                if (i < fetched) {
                    g.drawImage(fetchedImages[i], 0, y, 50, 50, this);
                }
                g.drawString(imagesToFetch[i], 60, y + fm.getAscent());
                y += 70;
            }
        }

        public void run() {
            while (Thread.currentThread() == fetcherThread
                    && fetched < imagesToFetch.length) {
                try {
                    fetchedImages[fetched]= getImage(
                        getDocumentBase(), imagesToFetch[fetched]);
                    while (!prepareImage(fetchedImages[fetched], this)) {
                        Thread.sleep(2000);
                    }
                    fetched++;
                    if (isActive()) {
                        repaint();
                    }
                } catch (InterruptedException e) {
                }
            }
        }
    }
```

play()

PURPOSE Fetches and plays an audio clip.

SYNTAX
```
public void play(URL url)
public void play(URL url, String name)
```

DESCRIPTION This method fetches the audio clip from the URL `url` and immediately plays the audio clip. If `name` is specified, the image is fetched from a new URL created by appending `name` to `url`. This method is ignored if the audio clip could not be fetched from `url`.

PARAMETERS

`name` The non-`null` name to append to `url`.

`url` The non-`null` URL at which to fetch the audio clip.

EXAMPLE See the class example.

resize()

PURPOSE Resizes the bounds of the applet.

SYNTAX
```
public void resize(Dimension d)
public void resize(int width, int height)
```

DESCRIPTION The bounds of the applet is the area in which it can paint. The `resize()` method makes a request to the applet context to resize the bounds of the applet. This request can be ignored by the applet context. The new bounds can be specified either as a width and height or as a dimension.

PARAMETERS

`d` The non-`null` dimension containing the new size in pixels.

`height` The height of the new bounds in pixels.

`width` The width of the new bounds in pixels.

SEE ALSO `Dimension`.

EXAMPLE See the class example.

setStub()

PURPOSE Sets the applet's stub.

SYNTAX
```
public final void setStub(AppletStub stub)
```

DESCRIPTION The stub is used internally by the `Applet` class. It is called by the applet context just after the applet is loaded. The stub is part of the implementation of the applet context and is not used by the applet programmer.

PARAMETERS

`stub` The non-`null` stub.

showStatus()

PURPOSE Displays a message in the applet context.

SYNTAX
```
public void showStatus(String msg)
```

DESCRIPTION This method can be ignored by the applet context. But typically the applet context displays `msg` in a status bar, which is often located at the bottom of its window.

PARAMETERS

`msg`	The message to display. If `null`, the previous message is cleared.

EXAMPLE See the class example.

start()

PURPOSE Called by the applet context just after the applet is made active.

SYNTAX `public void start()`

DESCRIPTION A subclass should override this method if it needs to implement behavior that occurs when the applet becomes active. For example, if the applet plays background music only when it is active, this method should be overridden to start the background music.

SEE ALSO `stop()`.

EXAMPLE See the class example.

stop()

PURPOSE Called by the applet context just after the applet is made inactive.

SYNTAX `public void stop()`

DESCRIPTION A subclass should override this method if it needs to implement behavior that occurs when the applet becomes inactive. For example, if the applet plays background music only when it is active, this method should be overridden to stop the background music.

If an applet is active, the applet context will always call this method before calling `destroy()`.

SEE ALSO `destroy()`, `start()`.

EXAMPLE See the class example.

java.applet

AppletContext

```
AppletContext
```

Syntax

`public interface AppletContext`

Description

This interface corresponds to an applet's environment. It can be used by an applet to obtain information from the applet's environment, which is usually the browser or the applet viewer.

MEMBER SUMMARY

Audio and Image Methods	
`getAudioClip()`	Retrieves an audio clip at a URL.
`getImage()`	Retrieves an image at a URL.
Applet Methods	
`getApplet()`	Retrieves a reference to an applet.
`getApplets()`	Enumerates the accessible applets in this applet context.
Display Methods	
`showDocument()`	Causes the applet context to display another HTML document.
`showStatus()`	Displays a message in the applet context.

See Also

`Applet`.

Example

This example implements two kinds of applets that communicate with each other through the applet context: The master applet keeps track of a color. The bullet applet simply paints an oval in the color maintained by the master. See Figures 13 and 14. The master applet has a choice component containing several color names. Changing the selected color in the master causes all the bullet applets to redisplay their bullets in the selected color. The master applet notifies all the bullet applets by calling their `repaint()` method.

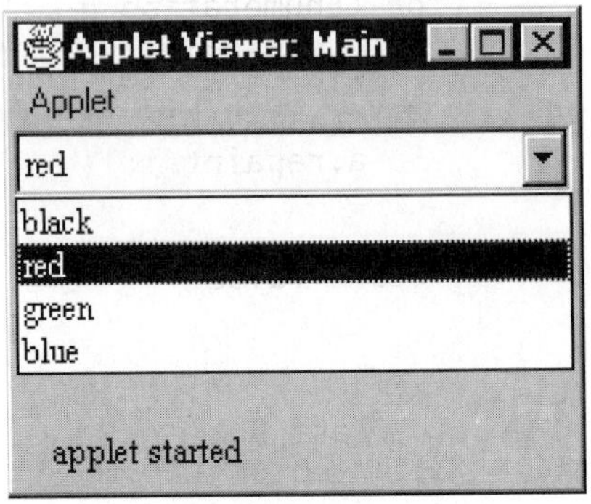

FIGURE 13 Master Applet

FIGURE 14 Bullet Applet

```
import java.applet.*;
import java.awt.*;
import java.util.*;
public class Main extends Applet {
    Color color;

    public void init() {
        Choice c = new Choice();

        setLayout(new BorderLayout());
        c.addItem("black");
        c.addItem("red");
        c.addItem("green");
        c.addItem("blue");
        add("Center", c);
    }

    public Color getColor() {
        return color;
    }

    public boolean action(Event evt, Object arg) {
        if (evt.target instanceof Choice) {
            if ("black".equals(arg)) {
                color = Color.black;
            } else if ("red".equals(arg)) {
                color = Color.red;
            } else if ("green".equals(arg)) {
                color = Color.green;
            } else if ("blue".equals(arg)) {
                color = Color.blue;
            }
        }
```

```
        for (Enumeration e=getAppletContext().getApplets();
                e.hasMoreElements(); ) {
            Applet a = (Applet)e.nextElement();
            if (a != null && a != this) {
                a.repaint();
            }
        }
        return false;
    }
}

public class Bullet extends Applet {
    Color color = Color.black;

    public void paint(Graphics g) {
        Main applet = (Main)getAppletContext().getApplet("Master");
        g.setColor(applet.getColor());
        g.fillOval(0, 0, size().width-1, size().height-1);
    }
}
```

getApplet()

PURPOSE Retrieves a reference to an applet.

SYNTAX `Applet getApplet(String appletName)`

DESCRIPTION This method retrieves the applet with the name `appletName`. If there is more than one applet with the name `appletName`, one of them will be returned. You cannot predict which one will be returned.

PARAMETERS

`appletName` The name of the applet. See the `Applet` class for a description of how to name an applet.

RETURNS A reference to the applet; otherwise returns `null` if the applet does not exist.

SEE ALSO `Applet`.

EXAMPLE See the class example.

getApplets()

PURPOSE Enumerates the accessible applets in this applet context.

SYNTAX `Enumeration getApplets()`

DESCRIPTION This method returns an enumeration of the accessible applets in this applet context. The enumeration always includes the current applet.

Some applet references in the enumeration could be `null`. This can happen if applets are being added or destroyed in the applet context during the enumeration.

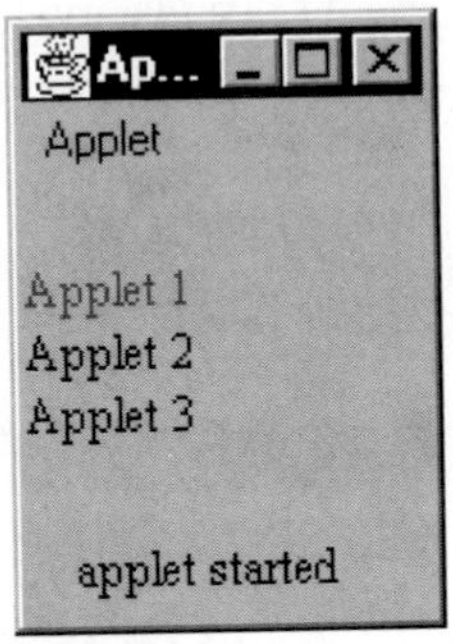

FIGURE 15
`AppletContext.getApplets()`

RETURNS A non-`null` enumeration of applet references. An applet reference in the enumeration can be `null`.

EXAMPLE This example creates three identical applets, each with a different name. The applets call `getApplets()` to get a list of all accessible applets. The applets then display the names of all the applets, highlighting their names in red.

```
import java.applet.*;
import java.awt.*;
import java.util.*;
public class Main extends Applet {
    public void paint(Graphics g) {
        FontMetrics fm = g.getFontMetrics();
        int y = fm.getAscent() + 20;

        for (Enumeration e=getAppletContext().getApplets();
                e.hasMoreElements(); ) {
            Applet a = (Applet)e.nextElement();
            if (a == null) {
                continue;
            } else if (a == this) {
                g.setColor(Color.red);
            } else {
                g.setColor(Color.black);
            }
            if (a.getParameter("name") != null) {
                g.drawString(a.getParameter("name"), 0, y);
            } else {
                g.drawString("no name", 0, y);
            }
            y += fm.getHeight();
        }
    }
}
```

getAudioClip()

PURPOSE Retrieves an audio clip at a URL.

SYNTAX `AudioClip getAudioClip(URL url)`

DESCRIPTION This method retrieves an audio clip at the URL `url`.

PARAMETERS

`url` The non-`null` URL at which to fetch the audio clip.

RETURNS The audio clip at `url`. Returns `null` if the audio clip cannot be found.

SEE ALSO `AudioClip`, `URL`.

EXAMPLE See the `Applet` class example.

getImage()

PURPOSE Retrieves an image at a URL.

SYNTAX `Image getImage(URL url)`

DESCRIPTION This method retrieves an image at the URL `url`. It returns immediately and does not actually fetch the pixels of the image. The pixels are fetched at the time they are needed (see `Image`).

PARAMETERS

`url` The non-`null` URL at which to fetch the image.

RETURNS The image at `url`. Returns `null` if the image cannot be found.

SEE ALSO `Image`, `URL`.

EXAMPLE See the `Applet` class example.

showDocument()

PURPOSE Causes the applet context to display another HTML document.

SYNTAX

```
public void showDocument(URL url)
public void showDocument(URL url, String target)
```

DESCRIPTION This method shows a new document in a target window or frame. The frame is an HTML frame, not an AWT frame. If `target` is not specified, it defaults to `"_self"`. This method may be ignored by the applet context.

Table 3 shows the list of valid target strings.

TABLE 3 `AppletContext.showDocument()` **Targets**

`_self`	Show in current frame.
`_parent`	Show in parent frame.
`_top`	Show in topmost frame.
`_blank`	Show in new unnamed top-level window.
`<other>`	Show in new top-level window named `<other>`.

PARAMETERS

`url` The non-`null` URL containing the document to display.

`target` The name of the frame in which to display the document.

EXAMPLE See the `Applet` class example.

showStatus()

PURPOSE Displays a message in the applet context.

SYNTAX `public void showStatus(String msg)`

DESCRIPTION This method can be ignored by the applet context. But typically the applet context displays `msg` in a status bar, which is often located at the bottom of its window.

PARAMETERS

`msg` The message to display. If `null`, the previous message is cleared.

EXAMPLE See the `Applet` class example.

java.applet
AppletStub

`AppletStub`

Syntax

`public interface AppletStub`

Description

This interface is essentially an internal interface used by the applet context. It is not normally used by applet programmers. This interface differs from the `AppletContext` interface mainly in that it supports methods that set and retrieve information specific for one particular applet. The applet context, on the other hand, maintains information for all the applets that it contains.

MEMBER SUMMARY

Stub Methods	
`appletResize()`	Resizes the bounds of the applet.
`getAppletContext()`	Retrieves the applet context.
`getCodeBase()`	Retrieves the applet's code base URL.
`getDocumentBase()`	Retrieves the applet's document base URL.
`getParameter()`	Retrieves the value of a parameter.
`isActive()`	Retrieves the active state of the applet.

See Also

`AppletContext`.

Example

See the `Applet` class.

appletResize()

PURPOSE Resizes the bounds of the applet.

SYNTAX `void appletResize(int w, int h)`

DESCRIPTION The bounds of the applet is the area in which it can paint. This request may be ignored. If the request is satisfied, the new bounds will have the width `w` and the height `h`.

PARAMETERS

`h` The height of the new bounds in pixels.

`w` The width of the new bounds in pixels.

EXAMPLE See `Applet.resize()`.

getAppletContext()

PURPOSE Retrieves the applet context.

SYNTAX `public AppletContext getAppletContext()`

DESCRIPTION See the `Applet` class for more information about applet contexts.

RETURNS The non-`null` reference to the applet context.

SEE ALSO `AppletContext`.

EXAMPLE See `Applet.getAppletContext()`.

getCodeBase()

PURPOSE Retrieves the applet's code base URL.

SYNTAX `URL getCodeBase()`

DESCRIPTION The code base is the URL prefix that contains the applet code. For example, suppose an applet were located at `http://www.sun.com/applets/Main.class`. The code base would be `http://www.sun.com/applets/`. The code base is typically used to fetch resources specific to the applet, such as icons and configuration information.

RETURNS The non-`null` applet's code base URL.

SEE ALSO `getDocumentBase()`, `URL`.

EXAMPLE See `Applet.getCodeBase()`.

A B C D E F G H I J K L M N O P Q R S T U V W X Y Z

getDocumentBase()

PURPOSE Retrieves the applet's document base URL.

SYNTAX `URL getDocumentBase()`

DESCRIPTION The document base is the URL prefix that contains the document that contains the applet. For example, suppose the document containing the applet were located at `http://www.sun.com/products/sparcstation/index.html`. The document base would be `http://www.sun.com/products/sparcstation/`. The document base is typically used to fetch resources specific to the document. For example, if some animation were to be designed for a particular HTML document, the animation images would typically be located somewhere relative to that document.

SEE ALSO `getCodeBase()`, `URL`.

EXAMPLE See `Applet.getDocumentBase()`.

getParameter()

PURPOSE Retrieves the value of a parameter.

SYNTAX `String getParameter(String name)`

DESCRIPTION This method returns the value of the parameter identified by the name `name`.

PARAMETERS

`name` The non-`null` name of the parameter value to retrieve.

RETURNS Returns the value of the parameter; otherwise returns `null` if the parameter does not exist.

EXAMPLE See `Applet.getParameter()`.

isActive()

PURPOSE Retrieves the active state of the applet.

SYNTAX `boolean isActive()`

A B C D E F G H I J K L M N O P Q R S T U V W X Y Z

DESCRIPTION An applet becomes active just before the `start()` method is called and becomes inactive just before the `stop()` method is called. See the `Applet` class for more information about applet states.

RETURNS `true` if the applet is active; `false` otherwise.

SEE ALSO `Applet.start()`.

EXAMPLE See `Applet.isActive()`.

ArithmeticException

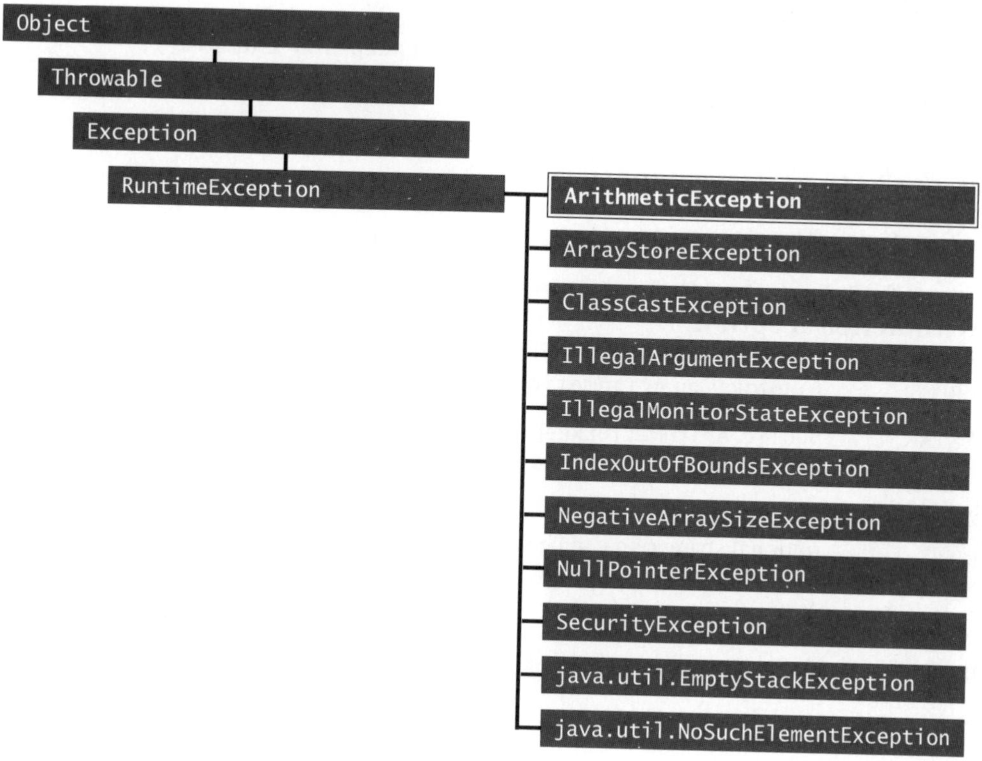

Syntax

```
public class ArithmeticException extends RuntimeException
```

Description

`ArithmeticException` is a runtime exception that is thrown when the program attempts to perform an illegal arithmetic operation. It should not be caught or declared in the `throws` clause of a method.

MEMBER SUMMARY	
Constructor	
`ArithmeticException()`	Constructs an `ArithmeticException` instance.

A B C D E F G H I J K L M N O P Q R S T U V W X Y Z

A B C D E F G H I J K L M N O P Q R S T U V W X Y Z

Example

The following code is attempting to divide by 0. It generates an `ArithmeticException`.

```
class Main {
    public static void main(String[] args) {
        System.out.println("ArithmeticException Example");

        int a = 100;
        a /= 0;
    }
}
```

ArithmeticException()

PURPOSE Constructs an `ArithmeticException` instance.

SYNTAX
```
public ArithmeticException()
public ArithmeticException(String msg)
```

DESCRIPTION This constructor creates a new instance of `ArithmeticException`. An optional string `msg` can be supplied that describes this particular instance of the exception.

PARAMETERS

`msg` A string that gives details about this exception.

ArrayIndexOutOfBoundsException

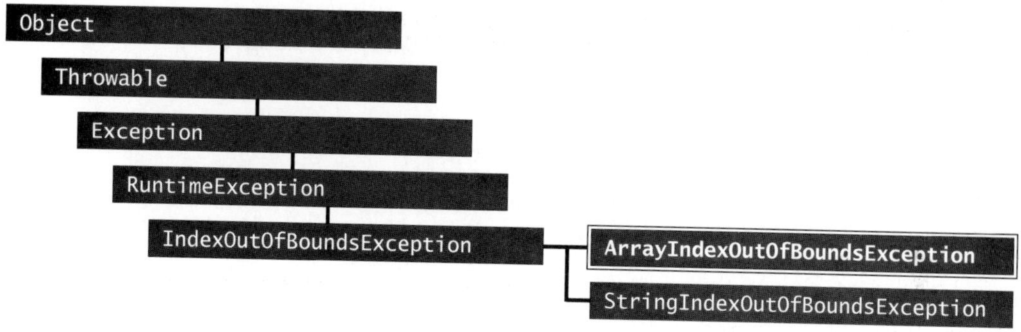

Syntax

```
public class ArrayIndexOutOfBoundsException extends IndexOutOfBoundsException
```

Description

`ArrayIndexOutOfBoundsException` is a runtime exception that is thrown when the program attempts to access an element within an array by using an index that is not within the bounds of the array. Because array indices use a zero-based numbering scheme, the index is usually either negative or a number greater than or equal to the array's length.

`ArrayIndexOutOfBoundsException` is a runtime exception that should not be caught or declared in the `throws` clause of a method.

MEMBER SUMMARY	
Constructor	
`ArrayIndexOutOfBoundsException()`	Constructs an `ArrayIndexOutOfBoundsException` instance.

See Also

`IndexOutOfBoundsException`, `RuntimeException`.

A B C D E F G H I J K L M N O P Q R S T U V W X Y Z

B C D E F G H I J K L M N O P Q R S T U V W X Y Z

Example

The following example generates an `ArrayIndexOutOfBoundsException`:

```
class Main {
    public static void main(String[] args) {
        System.out.println("ArrayIndexOutOfBoundsException example");

        char[] buf = {'a', 'b', 'c'};
        int i;

        for (i = 0; i < buf.length; i++)
            System.out.println(buf[i]);

        System.out.println(buf[i]); // index out of bounds
    }
}
```

ArrayIndexOutOfBoundsException()

PURPOSE Constructs an `ArrayIndexOutOfBoundsException` instance.

SYNTAX
```
public ArrayIndexOutOfBoundsException()
public ArrayIndexOutOfBoundsException(String idx)
public ArrayIndexOutOfBoundsException(String msg)
```

DESCRIPTION These constructors create a new instance of `ArrayIndexOutOfBoundsException`. An optional string `msg` can be supplied that describes this particular instance of the exception. Alternatively, the index `idx` that caused the exception can be supplied to the constructor, which will use `idx` to construct a message for describing this exception.

PARAMETERS

`idx` The index that caused the exception.

`msg` A string that gives details about this exception.

ArrayStoreException

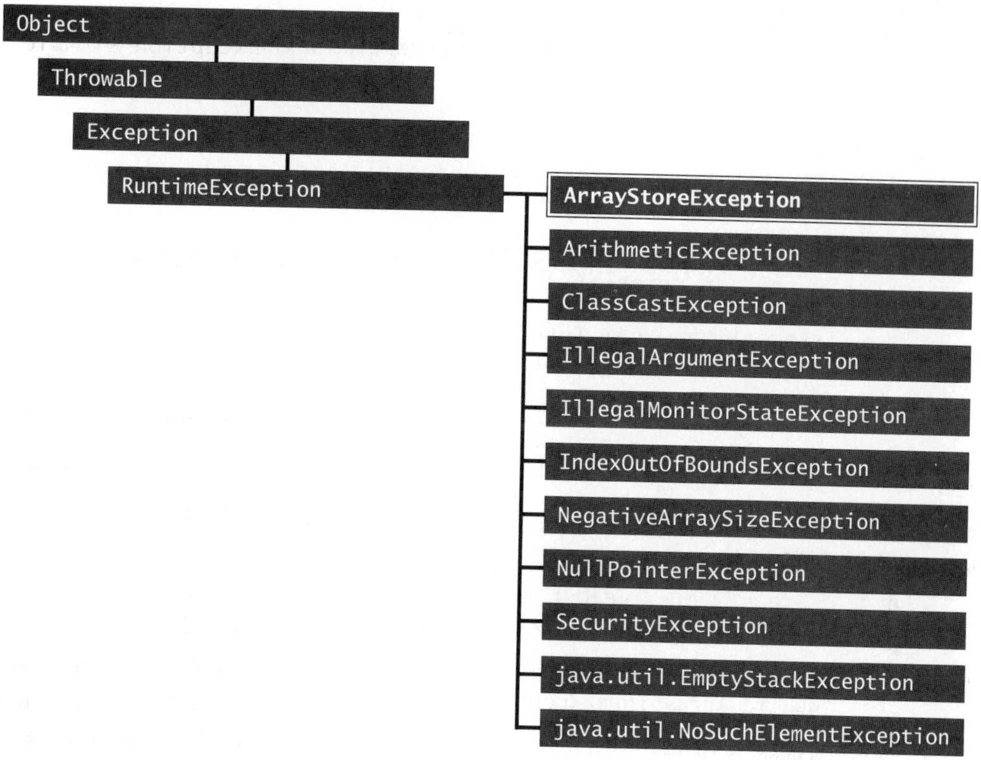

Syntax

```
public class ArrayStoreException extends RuntimeException
```

Description

`ArrayStoreException` is a runtime exception that is thrown when the program attempts to store an object of the wrong type into an array. It should not be caught or declared in the `throws` clause of a method.

MEMBER SUMMARY	
Constructor	
`ArrayStoreException()`	Constructs an `ArrayStoreException` instance.

A B C D E F G H I J K L M N O P Q R S T U V W X Y Z

See Also

RuntimeException.

Example

The following example generates an ArrayStoreException when it tries to store a String instance in an Integer array:

```
class Main {
    private static void storeItem(Object[]a, int i, Object item) {
        a[i] = item;
    }
    public static void main(String[] args) {
        System.out.println("ArrayStoreException Example");

        Integer[] a = new Integer[3];
        storeItem(a, 2, new String("abc"));
    }
}
```

ArrayStoreException()

PURPOSE Constructs an ArrayStoreException instance.

SYNTAX
```
public ArrayStoreException()
public ArrayStoreException(String msg)
```

DESCRIPTION These constructors create a new instance of ArrayStoreException. An optional string msg can be supplied that describes this particular instance of the exception.

PARAMETERS

msg A string that gives details about this exception.

java.applet

AudioClip

```
AudioClip
```

Syntax

`public interface AudioClip`

Description

An *audio clip* is a sample of audio data. This class has minimal support for playing audio clips. You can start and stop playing an audio clip, and you can play an audio clip in a repeat loop.

MEMBER SUMMARY	
Play and Stop Methods	
`loop()`	Starts playing the audio clip in a loop.
`play()`	Starts playing the audio clip.
`stop()`	Stops playing the audio clip.

Example

See the `Applet` class example.

loop()

PURPOSE Starts playing the audio clip in a loop.

SYNTAX `void loop()`

DESCRIPTION When this method is called, the audio clip is restarted at the beginning, regardless of whether the audio clip was already playing.

EXAMPLE See the `Applet` class example.

play()

PURPOSE Starts playing the audio clip.

SYNTAX `void play()`

DESCRIPTION The audio clip is played from the beginning, regardless of whether the audio clip was already playing. The audio clip is played once and does not repeat. In particular, if the audio clip was being played in a loop (see `loop()`), the `play()` method will terminate the loop and play the audio clip from the start one more time.

EXAMPLE See the `Applet` class example.

stop()

PURPOSE Stops playing the audio clip.

SYNTAX `void stop()`

DESCRIPTION If the audio clip is playing, either in a loop or not, it is immediately stopped.

EXAMPLE See the `Applet` class example.

java.awt

AWTError

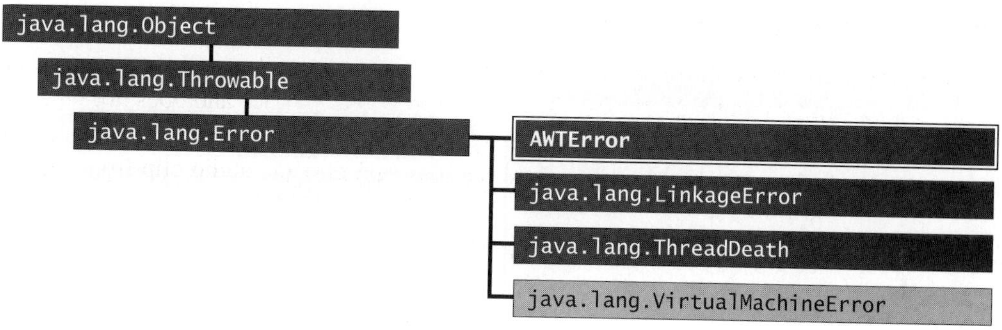

Syntax

`public class AWTError extends Error`

Description

This error is raised if the AWT encounters a fatal problem that renders the AWT usable. Currently, it is raised only by `Toolkit.getDefaultToolkit()`.

MEMBER SUMMARY	
Constructor	
`AWTError()`	Constructs an `AWTError` instance.

AWTError()

PURPOSE Constructs an `AWTError` instance.

SYNTAX `public AWTError(String msg)`

DESCRIPTION This constructor creates a new instance of `AWTError` with a string `msg` that describes the details of this particular instance of the error.

PARAMETERS

`msg` A string that gives details about this error.

java.awt

AWTException

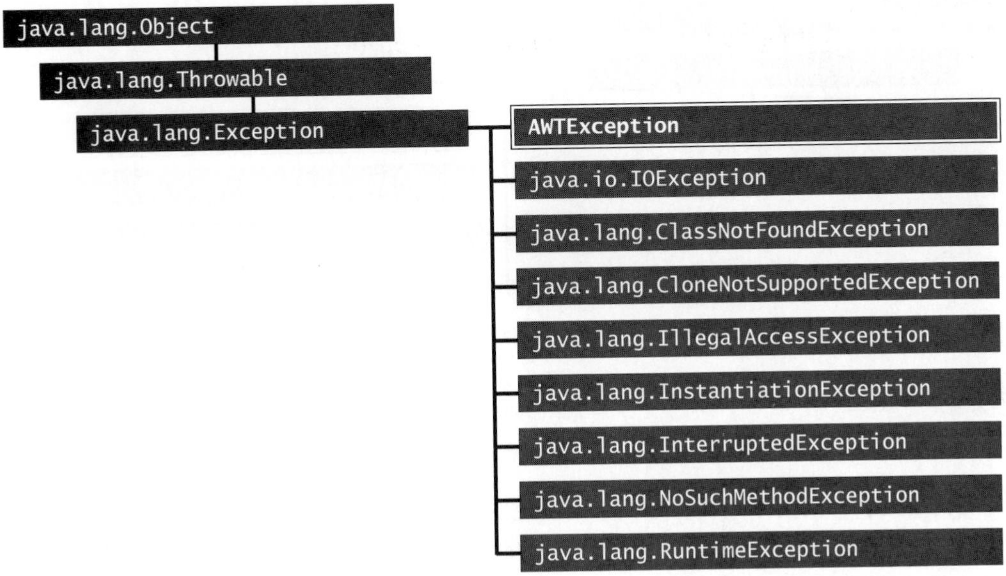

Syntax

```
public class AWTException extends Exception
```

Description

`AWTException` is an exception that is thrown when the program encounters an exception in the AWT. It currently is not thrown by any method in the Java runtime or its libraries.

MEMBER SUMMARY	
Constructor	
`AWTException()`	Constructs an `AWTException` instance.

AWTException()

PURPOSE Constructs an `AWTException` instance.

SYNTAX `public AWTException(String msg)`

DESCRIPTION This constructor creates a new instance of `AWTException`. The string `msg` describes this particular instance of the exception.

PARAMETERS

`msg` A string that gives details about this exception.

java.util
BitSet

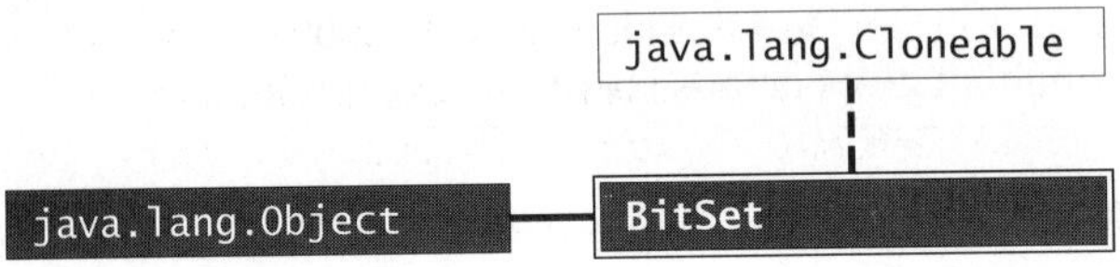

Syntax

```
public final class BitSet implements Cloneable
```

Description

The `BitSet` class is used to represent a bit array.[1] Each element in the bit array is a bit that is either set (1) or cleared (0). You create a bit array with an initial size. The bit array will grow automatically as bits beyond its initial size are set/cleared. You can access and update the bits in the bit array individually by their indices, and you can perform bitwise logical operations on the entire bit array.

You can use a bit array as a compact way of representing a set of `boolean` flags. You can also use a bit array to record `boolean` information about an array of objects, for example, on/off switch settings on a bank of lights.

MEMBER SUMMARY

Constructor	
`BitSet()`	Constructs a new bit array with all bits initialized to 0.
Bit Manipulation Methods	
`and()`	Applies the logical AND of this bit array with another bit array.
`clear()`	Clears a bit in this bit array.
`get()`	Retrieves a bit from this bit array.
`or()`	Applies logical OR of this bit array with another bit array.
`set()`	Sets a bit in this bit array.
`size()`	Determines the number of bits in this bit array.
`xor()`	Applies logical XOR of this bit array with another bit array.

1. `BitSet` is a misnomer because "sets" are unordered. `BitArray` would be a more correct class name.

MEMBER SUMMARY

Object Override Methods	
`clone()`	Makes a copy of this bit array.
`equals()`	Compares this bit array with another object for equality.
`hashCode()`	Computes the hash code for this bit array.
`toString()`	Generates the string representation of this bit array.

See Also

`Vector`.

Example

This example shows the use of two `BitSet` instances, `english` and `french`, to represent whether a person in a group speaks English and/or French, respectively. These two instances are then used to determine which persons are bilingual, and which are unilingual. The example uses the bitwise logical methods as well as `set()`/`get()` methods on the bit arrays.

```
import java.util.BitSet;

class Main {
    private static void initBitSets(BitSet e, BitSet f) {
        for(int i = 0; i < 10; i++)
            e.set(i);
        for (int i = 5; i <15; i++)
            f.set(i);
        System.out.println("english: " + e);
        System.out.println("french: " + f);
    }
    public static void main(String[] args) {
        BitSet english = new BitSet(100);  // tracks English speakers
        BitSet french = new BitSet(100);   // tracks French speakers

        // initialize bit arrays with data
        initBitSets(english, french);

        BitSet bilingual = (BitSet)english.clone();
        bilingual.and(french);

        if (bilingual.equals(english))
            // this means entire English class is bilingual
            System.out.println("Completely bilingual class");
        else
            System.out.println("Bilingual: " + bilingual.toString());

        BitSet either = (BitSet)english.clone();
        either.or(french);
        int eitherCount = 0;
```

B C D E F G H I J K L M N O P Q R S T U V W X Y Z

```
            // count how many speak either English or French or both
            for (int i=0; i < either.size(); i++) {
                if (either.get(i))
                    ++eitherCount;
            }
            System.out.println("Either(" + eitherCount + "):" + either);

            // find those who speak either French or English but not both
            BitSet one = (BitSet)english.clone();
            one.xor(french);
            System.out.println("One: " + one);

            // Another way to do this is to take 'either' and
            // eliminate those who are bilingual

            // fast way
            one = (BitSet)either.clone();
            one.xor(bilingual);
            System.out.println("One:" + one);

            // slow way
            one = (BitSet)either.clone();
            for (int i = 0; i < one.size(); i++)
                if (bilingual.get(i))
                    one.clear(i);
            System.out.println("One:" + one);
        }
    }
```

and()

PURPOSE Applies logical AND of this bit array with another bit array.

SYNTAX `public void and(BitSet bs)`

DESCRIPTION This method applies logical AND of this bit array with the bit array `bs`. For all indices of this bit array, if the *i*th bit in this bit array and the *i*th bit in `bs` are both set, the *i*th bit of this array will remain set. Otherwise the *i*th bit will be cleared. If `bs` has fewer bits than this bit array, the rest of the bits in this bit array that are not AND'ed are set to 0. If `bs` has more bits than this bit array does, the extra bits are not used.

PARAMETERS

`bs` The bit array with which to logically AND.

EXAMPLE See the class example.

BitSet()

PURPOSE Constructs a new bit array with bits initialized to 0.

SYNTAX

```
public BitSet()
public BitSet(int nbits)
```

DESCRIPTION There are two forms of the constructor for the `BitSet` class. The first form creates a new bit array with a default initial size of 64 bits. The second form creates a new bit array with the initial size of `nbits` bits, which is always rounded up to the next 64 increment. For example, if `nbits` is 8, the size of the new bit array is 64. For both forms of the constructor, the bit array will automatically grow if bits in positions higher than this initial size are set (by `clear()` or `set()`).

Also for both forms of the constructor, all bits in the new bit array are initialized to 0.

PARAMETERS

`nbits` The initial size of the bit array.

SEE ALSO `clear()`, `set()`.

EXAMPLE See the class example and `hashCode()`.

clear()

PURPOSE Clears a bit in this bit array.

SYNTAX

```
public void clear(int pos)
```

DESCRIPTION This method sets the bit at index `pos` in this bit array to 0. If `pos` is beyond the size of this bit array, the bit array is grown automatically so that `pos` identifies a bit in the new larger bit array. Any new bits added are initialized to 0.

PARAMETERS

`pos` The 0-based index of the bit to clear.

SEE ALSO `set()`.

EXAMPLE See the class example.

clone()

PURPOSE Makes a copy of this bit array.

B

C

SYNTAX `public Object clone()`

DESCRIPTION This method makes a copy of all the bits in this bit array.

RETURNS A new bit array that has the same bits as this bit array.

OVERRIDES `Object.clone()`.

EXAMPLE See the class example.

equals()

PURPOSE Compares this bit array with another bit array for equality.

SYNTAX `public boolean equals(Object obj)`

DESCRIPTION This method compares the bits in this bit array with the bits in `obj` for equality. If `obj` is `null` or if `obj` is not a `BitSet`, `equals()` returns `false`. If all the bits in this bit array are identical to those in `obj`, this method returns `true`. If one bit array is longer than the other, the extra bits in the longer bit array are logically AND'ed with zero bits. If not all the bits are identical, `equals()` returns `false`.

PARAMETERS
`obj` The object with which to compare.

RETURNS `true` if `obj` is a bit array and has the same bits as this bit array; `false` otherwise.

OVERRIDES `Object.equals()`.

EXAMPLE See the class example.

get()

PURPOSE Retrieves a bit from this bit array.

SYNTAX `public boolean get(int pos)`

DESCRIPTION This method retrieves the bit at index `pos` of this bit array. It returns `true` if the bit has been set (to 1) and `false` if the bit has been cleared (zeroed). If `pos` is beyond the size of this bit array, `false` is returned.

PARAMETERS
`pos` The index of the bit to retrieve. `pos` must be greater than or equal to 0.

RETURNS The `boolean` value of the specified bit in this bit array.

SEE ALSO `clear()`, `set()`.

EXAMPLE See the class example.

hashCode()

PURPOSE Computes the hash code for this bit array.

SYNTAX `public int hashCode()`

DESCRIPTION This method computes and returns the hash code for this bit array. The hash code is calculated using an algorithm involving all the bits in this bit array.

RETURNS The hash code of this bit array.

OVERRIDES `Object.hashCode()`.

SEE ALSO `Hashtable`.

EXAMPLE

```
BitSet bs = new BitSet(128);
...
int[] hits = new int[13];
int hashval = bs.hashCode();                // generate hash code
++hits[Math.abs(hashval%hits.length)];      // count hits
```

or()

PURPOSE Applies logical OR of this bit array with another bit array.

SYNTAX `public void or(BitSet bs)`

DESCRIPTION This method applies logical OR of this bit array with the bit array `bs`. For all indices of this bit array, if the *i*th bit in `bs` is set, the *i*th bit of this array will be set. Otherwise the *i*th bit in this bit array remains unchanged (if it was 0 before, it will remain 0; if it was set before, it will remain set). If `bs` has fewer bits than this bit array, the extra bits in this bit array are left unchanged. If `bs` has more bits than this bit array, the extra bits are not used.

PARAMETERS

`bs` The bit array with which to logically OR.

EXAMPLE See the class example.

A
B
C
D
E
F
G
H
I
J
K
L
M
N
O
P
Q
R
S
T
U
V
W
X
Y
Z

set()

PURPOSE Sets a bit in this bit array.

SYNTAX `public void set(int pos)`

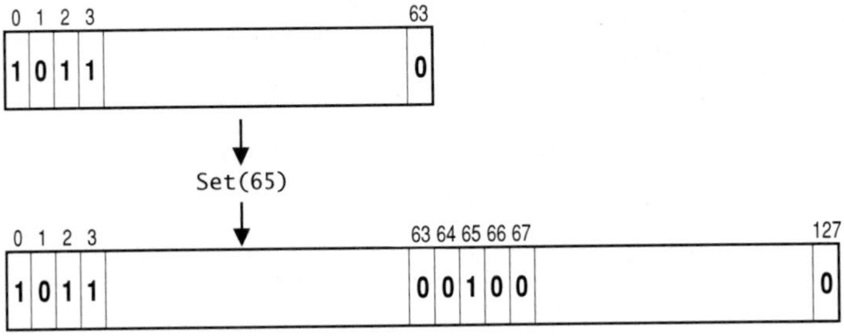

FIGURE 16 **`BitSet.set()`**

DESCRIPTION This method sets the bit at index `pos` in this bit array to 1. If `pos` is beyond the size of this bit array, the bit array is grown automatically so that `pos` identifies a bit in the new larger bit array. Except for the bit at `pos`, any new bits added are initialized to 0, as shown in Figure 16.

PARAMETERS

`pos` The index of the bit to set `pos` must be greater than or equal to 0.

SEE ALSO `clear()`.

EXAMPLE See class example.

size()

PURPOSE Determines the number of bits in this bit array.

SYNTAX `public int size()`

DESCRIPTION The number of bits in a bit array is always rounded up to its closest 64-bit increment. For example, creating a bit array with an initial size of 8 bits actually creates one that is 64 bits in size. Creating a bit array with an initial size of 65 bits actually creates one that is 128 bits in size. This method returns the number of bits in this bit array.

RETURNS The number of bits in this bit array.

SEE ALSO `BitSet()`, `clear()`, `set()`.

EXAMPLE See class example.

toString()

PURPOSE Generates the string representation for this bit array.

SYNTAX `public String toString()`

DESCRIPTION The string representation of a bit array consists of a comma-separated list of the indices of the bits in the bit array that have been set (to 1). The indices of the bits that are clear are not included in the string. This method returns this string representation.

RETURNS The string representation of this bit array.

OVERRIDES `Object.toString()`.

EXAMPLE See class example.

xor()

PURPOSE Applies logical XOR of this bit array with another bit array.

SYNTAX `public void xor(BitSet bs)`

DESCRIPTION This method applies logical XOR of this bit array with the bit array `bs`. For all indices in this array, if the *i*th bit in this bit array and the *i*th bit in `bs` are the same, the *i*th bit in this bit array is cleared. If the two *i*th bits are different (one is set and the other is not), the *i*th bit is set. If `bs` has fewer bits than this bit array, the extra bits in this bit array are left unchanged. If `bs` has more bits than this bit array, the extra bits are not used.

PARAMETERS

`bs` The bit array with which to logically XOR.

EXAMPLE See class example.

java.lang

Boolean

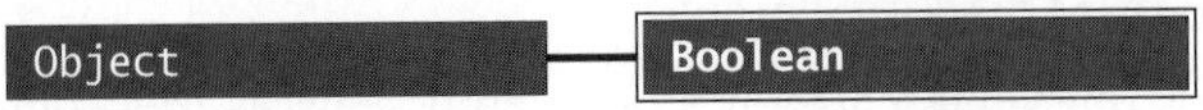

Syntax

```
public final class Boolean extends Object
```

Description

The `Boolean` class provides an object wrapper for `boolean` data values. This allows `bool-eans` to be passed to methods in Java class libraries that accept Java objects as parameters.

MEMBER SUMMARY

Constuctor

`Boolean`	Constructs a `Boolean` object using its string representation or `boolean` value.

Constant Fields

`TRUE`	A `Boolean` object that has the `boolean` value `true`.
`FALSE`	A `Boolean` object that has the `boolean` value `false`.

Value and Parsing Methods

`booleanValue()`	Retrieves the `boolean` value of this `Boolean` object.
`getBoolean()`	Retrieves the `boolean` value of a system property.
`valueOf()`	Creates a `Boolean` object using its string representation.

Object Override Mehtods

`equals()`	Compares this object with another object for equality.
`hashCode()`	Computes the hash code for this object.
`toString()`	Generates the string representation of this object.

Example

```
class Main {
    public static void main(String args[]) {
        Boolean tb = new Boolean(true);
        Boolean fb = new Boolean(false);

        if (tb.booleanValue() && fb.booleanValue())
            System.err.println("logic error");
```

```
        if (tb.equals(Boolean.TRUE) && fb.equals(Boolean.FALSE))
            System.err.println("expected behavior");

        System.out.println("tb :" + tb.toString());
        System.out.println("fb :" + fb.toString());
    }
}
```

Boolean( )

PURPOSE Constructs a `Boolean` object using its string representation or `boolean` value.

SYNTAX
```
public Boolean(boolean boolVal)
public Boolean(String strVal)
```

DESCRIPTION These constructors create a `Boolean` object using a `boolean` value `boolVal` or a string representation of the `boolean` value `strVal`.

PARAMETERS

`boolVal` The `boolean` value that the new object will have.

`strVal` The string representation of the `boolean` value that the new object will have. If `strVal` is the case-insensitive equivalent of "`true`", the `boolean` value of the new object will be `true`; otherwise the `boolean` value will be `false`.

SEE ALSO `valueOf()`.

EXAMPLE

```
Boolean status = new Boolean(true);        // true
Boolean b1 = new Boolean("True");          // true
Boolean b2 = new Boolean("false");         // false
Boolean b3 = new Boolean("neither");       // false
```

booleanValue( )

PURPOSE Retrieves the `boolean` value of this `Boolean` object.

SYNTAX `public boolean booleanValue()`

RETURNS The `boolean` value of this object.

EXAMPLE

```
Boolean status = new Boolean(false);
boolean bval = status.booleanValue();
if (bval)
    return (-1);
```

C

equals()

D

PURPOSE Compares this object with another object for equality.

E

SYNTAX `public boolean equals(Object obj)`

F

DESCRIPTION This method compares the `boolean` value of this object with the `boolean` value of `obj`. It returns `true` if the two values are equal. It returns `false` if the two values are not equal or if `obj` is `null` or not a `Boolean` object.

G

PARAMETERS

H

`obj` The object against which this object will be compared.

I

RETURNS `true` if `obj` has the same `boolean` value as this object; `false` otherwise.

OVERRIDES `Object.equals()`.

J

EXAMPLE

K

```
Object obj1 = new Boolean(true);
Object obj2 = new Boolean(false);
if (obj1.equals(obj2))
    return (-1);
```

L

M

N

FALSE

O

PURPOSE A `Boolean` object that has the `boolean` value `false`.

P

SYNTAX `public static final Boolean FALSE`

SEE ALSO `TRUE`.

Q

EXAMPLE

R

```
Boolean status = new Boolean(true);
...
// Returns -1 if status is false
if(status.equals(Boolean.FALSE))
    return (-1);
```

S

T

U

getBoolean

V

W

PURPOSE Retrieves the `boolean` value of a system property.

X

SYNTAX `public static boolean getBoolean(String property)`

DESCRIPTION This method retrieves the system property identified by `property` and parses its value to determine whether it has the case-insensitive string value "`true`".

Y

Z

It returns `true` if the string value is "`true`". If the string value is not "`true`" or if the property is not found, this method returns `false`.

PARAMETERS

`property` The string name of the property of interest.

RETURNS A `boolean` value indicating whether the specified property has the string value "`true`".

SEE ALSO `Properties`, `System.getProperty()`.

EXAMPLE

```
if (Boolean.getBoolean("os.password.required")) {
    password = Login.getPassword("Password:");
}
```

hashCode()

PURPOSE Computes the hash code for this object.

SYNTAX `public int hashCode()`

DESCRIPTION This method returns the hash code for this object. The hash code of a `Boolean` object is calculated using its `boolean` value. `Boolean` objects with the same `boolean` value have the same hash value.

RETURNS An `int` representing the hash code of this object.

OVERRIDES `Object.hashCode()`.

SEE ALSO `Hashtable`.

EXAMPLE

```
Boolean b1 = new Boolean("true");         // true
Boolean b2 = new Boolean(false);
Boolean b3 = new Boolean(true);

if (b1.hashCode() == b3.hashCode())       // equal
    System.out.println("hash equal");
else
    System.out.println("hash different");

if (b1.hashCode() == b2.hashCode())       // different
    System.out.println("hash equal");
else
    System.out.println("hash different");
```

toString()

PURPOSE Generates the string representation of this object.

SYNTAX `public String toString()`

DESCRIPTION This method generates and returns the string representation of this `Boolean` object. The string representation of a `Boolean` object is either "`true`" or "`false`", depending on the object's `boolean` value.

This method is the inverse of `valueOf()`.

RETURNS The string representation of this `Boolean` object's `boolean` value.

OVERRIDES `Object.toString()`.

SEE ALSO `valueOf()`.

EXAMPLE

```
Boolean status = new Boolean(true);
String strval = status.toString();
System.out.println("Value of status is: " + strval); // "true"
```

TRUE

PURPOSE A `Boolean` object that has the `boolean` value `true`.

SYNTAX `public static final Boolean TRUE`

SEE ALSO `FALSE`.

EXAMPLE

```
Boolean status = new Boolean(true);
...
if(status.equals(Boolean.TRUE))
    return (-1);
```

valueOf()

PURPOSE Creates a `Boolean` object using its string representation.

SYNTAX `public static Boolean valueOf(String str)`

DESCRIPTION

This method creates a Boolean object by parsing the string str. If str contains the string "true" (case is not significant), the resulting object has the boolean value true; otherwise its value is false.

This method is the inverse of toString().

PARAMETERS

str — The string representation of a boolean value (i.e., "true" or "false").

RETURNS

A new Boolean object with the boolean value represented by str.

SEE ALSO

toString().

EXAMPLE

```
Boolean b1 = Boolean.valueOf("True");
if (b1.booleanValue())
    System.out.println("correct");
```

java.awt

BorderLayout

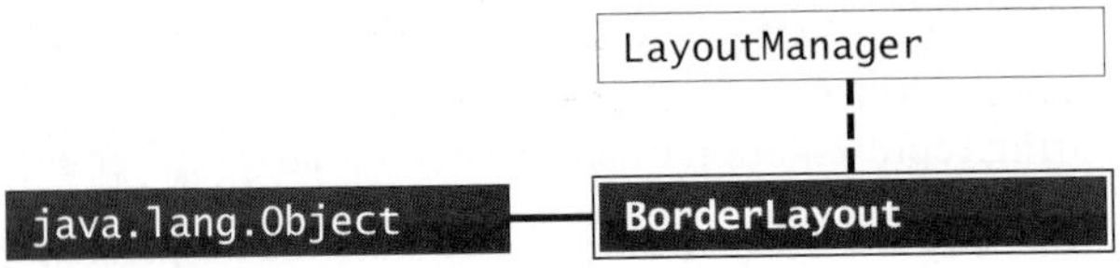

Syntax

```
public class BorderLayout implements LayoutManager
```

Description

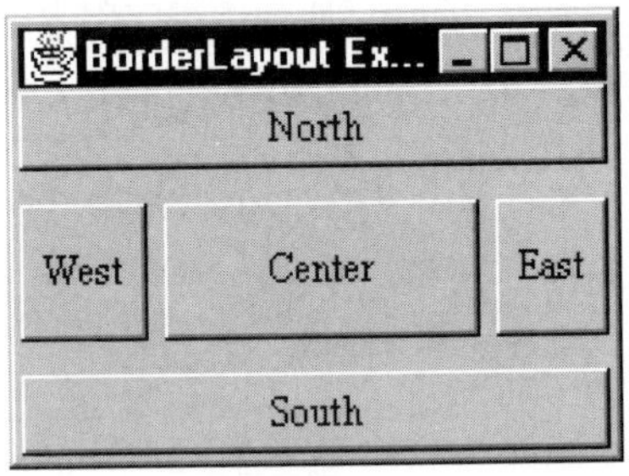

FIGURE 17 The Five Border Layout Locations

The border layout manager has exactly five locations at which it places its components. Figure 17 shows a container with a border layout manager and five buttons occupying all five locations. The locations are named North, South, East, West, and Center. When a component is added to a container with a border layout manager, one of these five names must be used. The names are case-sensitive.

Not all five locations must be filled. If a location is not used, the space is distributed to the other locations. Figure 18 shows a North and West component, with the Center component claiming all remaining space. An invisible component in a location is ignored during the layout, so the location is treated as if it were not occupied. Also notice that the border layout manager does not always fill up all available space.

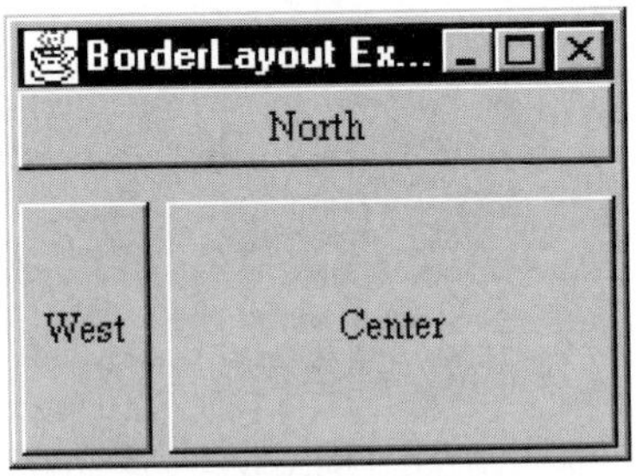

FIGURE 18 Buttons at Three Locations

For example, in Figure 19, although there is space between the North and South components, the border layout manager does not attempt to stretch the two components to fill up this space. Finally, the border layout manager places the components in a particular order. First, the North and South components are placed. Next, the West and East components are placed. Finally, the Center component takes up all remaining space. Note that opposite-facing components are placed simultaneously. In other words, it is not the case that one component is placed first and the other takes up the remaining space. Figure 20 shows a container that is shorter than the combined widths of the West and East components. Notice that they overlap. You cannot control which one will appear on top.

You must always name any components added to a container by using a border layout manager. You also should be careful to use the correct name. The border layout manager does not warn you if you misspell the name or use a name more than once. If this happens, the components simply won't be laid out correctly.

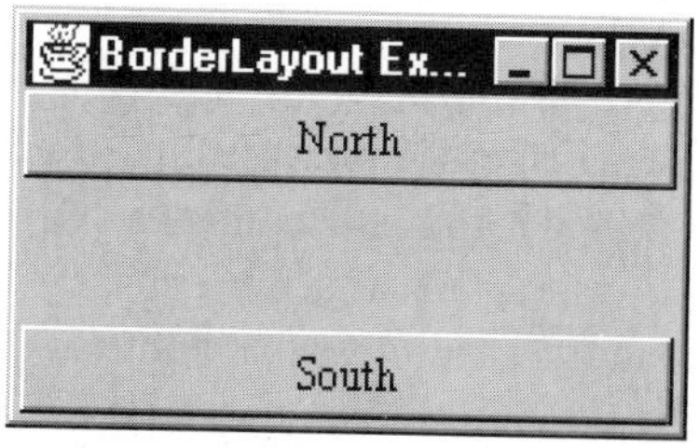

FIGURE 19 Buttons at Two Locations

Gaps

The border layout manager allows you to separate the locations by gaps. The vertical gap specifies the space between the bottom of the North component, the top of the South component, and the components in between. The horizontal gap specifies the space between the West, Center, and East components. Note that if there are no components between the North and South components, the gap between them is two times the vertical gap. This is also true of the West and East components. This means that if you have a container with only two opposite-facing components and you pack the container to its minimum size, the gap may be larger than you want. If your gap size is even, you can simply set a gap that's half the size. If your gap size is odd, you'll have to subclass the border layout manager and implement your own gap rules.

FIGURE 20 Overlapping Locations

MEMBER SUMMARY

Constructor	
`BorderLayout()`	Constructs a `BorderLayout` instance.
Layout Manager Interface Methods	
`addLayoutComponent()`	Places a component at a location.
`layoutContainer()`	Lays out the container's components according to the settings of the layout manager.
`minimumLayoutSize()`	Calculates the minimum dimensions needed to lay out the components.
`preferredLayoutSize()`	Calculates the preferred dimensions needed to lay out the components.
`removeLayoutComponent()`	Removes a component from a location.
Debugging Method	
`toString()`	Generates a string representation of the layout manager's state.

A B C D E F G H I J K L M N O P Q R S T U V W X Y Z

Example

This example demonstrates the typical way a border layout manager is used (see Fig. 21). The Center location is assigned a component that can stretch with the frame (in this case, just a blank canvas). The East location is assigned a scrollbar that controls the Center component. The South position contains a window that displays status information. The North location contains buttons.

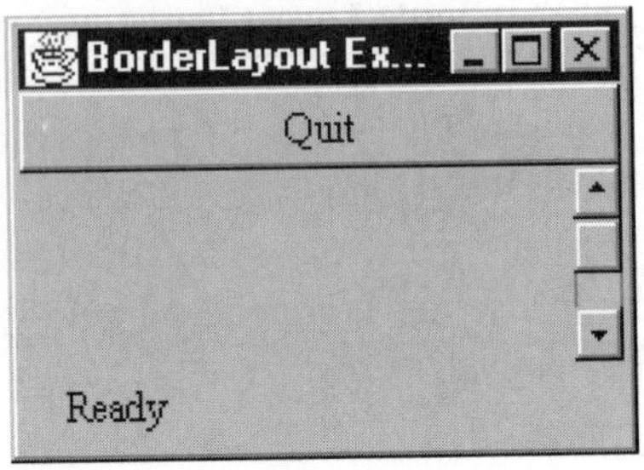

FIGURE 21 `BorderLayout`

```
import java.awt.*;

class Main {
    public static void main(String[] args) {
        Frame f = new Frame("BorderLayout Example");

        f.setLayout(new BorderLayout());
        f.add("North", new Button("Quit"));
        f.add("Center", new Canvas());
        f.add("East", new Scrollbar());
        f.add("South", new Label("Ready"));
        f.resize(200, 200);
        f.pack();
        f.show();
    }
}
```

addLayoutComponent()

PURPOSE Places a component in a location.

SYNTAX `public void addLayoutComponent(String name, Component comp)`

DESCRIPTION This method places `comp` at the location `name`, which can be one of five strings: `"North"`, `"South"`, `"West"`, `"East"`, and `"Center"`. The use of any other name results in incorrectly laid out components.

PARAMETERS

`comp` The non-`null` named component that has just been added to the container. Table 4 details the resizing rules for each location in the border layout.

`name` The string specifying the location.

EXAMPLE See the `LayoutManager`.

TABLE 4 BorderLayout Locations

`North, South`	As wide as the container and as tall as the component's preferred height.
`West, East`	As wide as the component's preferred width and as tall as the space between the bottom of the North and South components (if any) minus twice the vertical gap.
`Center`	As wide as the space between the West and East components (if any) minus twice the horizontal gap. As high as the space between the North and South components (if any) minus twice the vertical gap.

BorderLayout()

PURPOSE Constructs a new `BorderLayout` instance.

SYNTAX

```
public BorderLayout()
public BorderLayout(int hgap, int vgap)
```

DESCRIPTION This constructor creates a new `BorderLayout` manager instance with the gaps `hgap` and `vgap`. If the gaps are not specified, they both default to 0.

The association between a location and a component is maintained in the border layout manager, so each container requires its own `BorderLayout` instance. That is, you cannot use the same `BorderLayout` instance in more than one container. Also, a container can be set to use a border layout only when the container has no components.

PARAMETERS

`hgap` A non-negative integer specifying the horizontal gap in pixels.

`vgap` A non-negative integer specifying the vertical gap in pixels.

EXAMPLE See the class example.

layoutContainer()

PURPOSE Lays out the container's components according to the settings of the layout manager.

SYNTAX

```
public void layoutContainer(Container container)
```

DESCRIPTION This method is called by `container` when the layout is invalidated and needs to be redone. It uses a component's preferred size when determining the dimensions of its location. The locations are also dependent on the current size of the container.

PARAMETERS

`container` The non-`null` container using this layout instance.

EXAMPLE See `LayoutManager`.

minimumLayoutSize()

PURPOSE Calculates the minimum dimensions needed to lay out the components.

SYNTAX `public Dimension minimumLayoutSize(Container container)`

DESCRIPTION The minimum dimension is calculated by determining each visible component's minimum size and laying them out using just enough space so that they do not overlap. The minimum size also adds enough space for the gaps.

PARAMETERS

`container` The non-`null` container using this layout instance.

RETURNS A new non-`null` `Dimension` instance containing the minimum size of the border layout.

SEE ALSO `Component.minimumSize()`.

EXAMPLE See `LayoutManager`.

preferredLayoutSize()

PURPOSE Calculates the preferred dimensions needed to lay out the components.

SYNTAX `public Dimension preferredLayoutSize(Container container)`

DESCRIPTION The preferred dimension is calculated by determining each visible component's preferred size and laying them out using just enough space so that they don't overlap. The preferred size also adds enough space for the gaps.

PARAMETERS

`container` The non-`null` container using this layout instance.

RETURNS A new non-`null` `Dimension` object containing the preferred size of the border layout.

SEE ALSO `Component.preferredSize()`.

EXAMPLE See `LayoutManager`.

removeLayoutComponent()

PURPOSE Removes a component from a location.

SYNTAX `public void removeLayoutComponent(Component comp)`

DESCRIPTION This method removes the component `comp` from the border layout manager's list of components. The border layout manager will no longer place `comp`. If `comp` does not have a name, the method call is ignored. This method is normally called by the container in response to the removal of any component from the container.

PARAMETERS

`comp` The non-`null` component about to be removed from the container.

EXAMPLE See `LayoutManager`.

toString()

PURPOSE Generates a string representation of the layout manager's state.

SYNTAX `public String toString()`

DESCRIPTION The string representation of a layout manager contains the layout manager's class name, the size of the two gaps, and which locations are occupied. This method returns this string representation.

This method is typically used for debugging.

RETURNS A non-`null` string representing the layout manager's state.

OVERRIDES `Object.toString()`.

EXAMPLE See `Object.toString()`.

java.io
BufferedInputStream

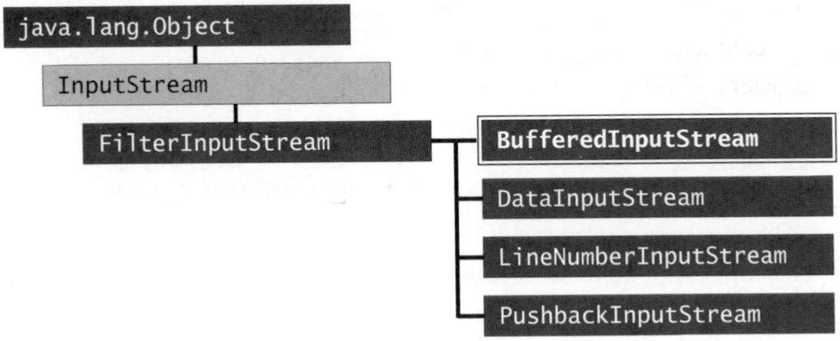

Syntax

```
public class BufferedInputStream extends FilterInputStream
```

Description

`BufferedInputStream` implements a buffered input stream. A buffered input stream is a filter input stream. You can compose it with an existing input stream to allow buffering of input when reading from that stream. The buffered input stream maintains a buffer of bytes read from the original input stream. Requests to read from the buffered input stream retrieve bytes from this buffer, rather than performing read operations on the original input stream. When all bytes from the buffer have been read, the buffer is refilled with input from the original input stream. If read operations on the original input stream have a high per-read overhead, buffering the stream can improve the performance significantly because it can reduce the number of read operations on the original input stream. The buffered input stream incurs extra memory overhead because it must maintain the buffer. It also incurs an extra level of copying because bytes must first be copied into the buffer.

Marks/Resets

You can mark a buffered input stream using a stream *mark,* which marks a position in the input stream so that you can subsequently return to it. Stream marks are intended to be used in situations in which you need to read ahead a little to see what is in the stream. Parsers often make use of this feature instead of remembering the read data itself. When you set the mark, you supply a *mark limit,* which indicates the number of bytes in the input stream from the marked position that are to be saved. If you subsequently read beyond this mark limit, the mark becomes *invalidated* and you cannot return the stream to its mark.

The `BufferedInputStream` provides implementations for the `mark()` and `reset()` methods (declared in the `InputStream` class). In Figure 22, the buffered input stream initially contains the characters "`abcdefg`". `mark()` is called after three characters were read. After four more characters ("`defg`") have been read, `reset()` is called. This method resets the read pointer back four positions, after which "`defg`" can then be re-read.

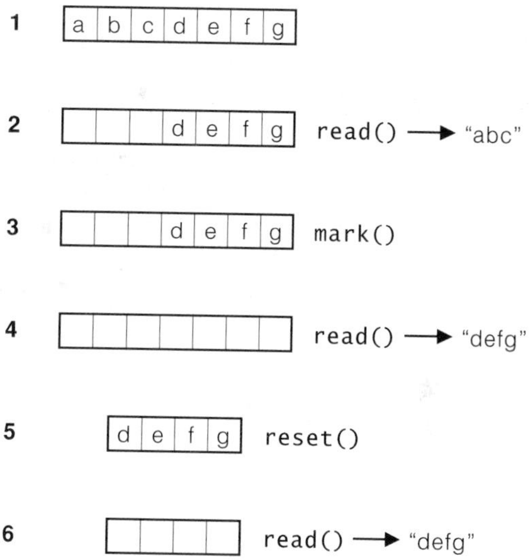

FIGURE 22 **`BufferedInputStream`**

MEMBER SUMMARY

Constructor	
`BufferedInputStream()`	Constructs a new buffered stream from an input stream.
Input Methods	
`available()`	Determines the number of bytes that can be read without blocking.
`read()`	Reads bytes from this buffered input stream.
`skip()`	Skips the specified number of bytes in this buffered input stream.
Mark/Reset Methods	
`mark()`	Marks the current position in the buffered input stream.
`markSupported()`	Determines whether this stream supports re-reading of its data.
`reset()`	Repositions the buffered input stream to the last marked position.
Protected Fields	
`buf`	The buffer that stores the input stream data.
`count`	The number of bytes in the buffer.
`marklimit`	The maximum read-ahead allowed before the mark is invalidated.
`markpos`	The position in the buffer of the current mark.
`pos`	The current read position in the buffer.

See Also

`BufferedOutputStream`, `FilterInputStream`, `InputStream`.

Example

This example shows the use of a buffered input stream to read in a file and print it out twice to standard output. It uses the mark/reset of the buffered input stream to avoid reading the file twice.

```
import java.io.BufferedInputStream;
import java.io.FileInputStream;
import java.io.IOException;

// reads in a file and sends it to standard output 2 times
class Main {
    public static void main(String[] args) {
        if (args.length != 1) {
            System.err.println("Usage: java Main <file>");
            System.exit(-1);
        }
        try {
            FileInputStream in = new FileInputStream(args[0]);
            // create buffered input stream for 'in'
            BufferedInputStream bufin = new BufferedInputStream(in);
            if (bufin.markSupported()) {
                int limit;
                // create mark for size of file
                bufin.mark(limit=bufin.available());

                // first copy; read just before EOF
                for (int i = 0; i < limit; i++)
                    System.out.print((char)(bufin.read()));
                // reset to beginning of file
                bufin.reset();
            }
            int c;
            while ((c=bufin.read()) >= 0)   // second copy
                System.out.print((char)c);
            bufin.close();
        } catch (IOException e) {
            e.printStackTrace();
        }
    }
}
```

available()

PURPOSE Determines the number of bytes that can be read without blocking.

SYNTAX `public synchronized int available() throws IOException`

DESCRIPTION This method returns the number of bytes that can be read without blocking. This is the sum of the number of unread bytes in the buffer and the number of bytes available from the input stream.

RETURNS The number of bytes that can be read without blocking.

EXCEPTIONS

`IOException` If an IO error occurred while attempting to determine the number of bytes available.

OVERRIDES `FilterInputStream.available()`.

SEE ALSO `InputStream.available()`.

EXAMPLE See the class example.

buf

PURPOSE The buffer that stores the input stream data.

SYNTAX `protected byte[] buf`

DESCRIPTION This field stores the input stream data. It is allocated when the buffer input stream is first created. `buf` may expand as required to support marking with a mark limit larger than its current buffer size. The bytes in `buf` are filled from the input stream for which this buffer input stream was created. Bytes that are read from this buffer input stream are retrieved from `buf`.

SEE ALSO `count`, `pos`.

EXAMPLE This example is taken from the source of `BufferedInputStream`. It shows how the `read()` method uses the protected fields `buf`, `count`, and `pos`.

```
public synchronized int read() throws IOException {
    if (pos >= count) {
        fill();
        if (count == 0)
            return -1;
    }
    return buf[pos++] & 0xff;
}
```

BufferedInputStream()

PURPOSE Constructs a new buffered stream from an input stream.

SYNTAX
```
public BufferedInputStream(InputStream in)
public BufferedInputStream(InputStream in, int size)
```

DESCRIPTION There are two forms of the constructor for `BufferedInputStream`. The first form constructs a new buffered input stream for the input stream `in`, with the default buffer size of 2 kilobytes. The second form constructs a new buffered input stream for `in` with the buffer size `size`. The buffer size may increase after the stream has been created if the stream is asked to support a mark limit larger than its current buffer size.

A buffer of the specified size is created to cache the bytes read. The larger the buffer, the more bytes can be retrieved from each read operation from the actual input stream `in`, thus requiring fewer reads from `in`. A bigger buffer might result in significant performance improvements if read operations on `in` are slow. However, it also means more memory is required to store the bytes. Thus you should select a size that balances performance requirements and memory demand.

PARAMETERS

`in`	The input stream.
`size`	The buffer size.

SEE ALSO `BufferedOutputStream`.

EXAMPLE See the class example and `skip()`.

count

PURPOSE The number of bytes in the buffer.

SYNTAX `protected int count`

DESCRIPTION This field records the total number of bytes, read and unread, in the buffer `buf`.

SEE ALSO `pos`, `markpos`.

EXAMPLE See `buf`.

mark()

PURPOSE Marks the current position in the buffered input stream.

SYNTAX `public synchronized void mark(int readlimit)`

DESCRIPTION Buffered input streams support marks and resets. This method marks the current position in the input stream and records that `readlimit` of bytes can be read or skipped from this position before this marked position becomes invalidated (i.e., can no longer reset to this mark). A subsequent call to `reset()` will reposition the stream at the last marked position so that subsequent reads will re-read the same bytes.

PARAMETERS

`readlimit` The number of bytes that can be read or skipped from this marked position before the mark becomes invalidated.

OVERRIDES `FilterInputStream.mark()`.

SEE ALSO `marklimit`, `markpos`, `reset()`.

EXAMPLE See the class example.

marklimit

PURPOSE The maximum read-ahead allowed before the current mark is invalidated.

SYNTAX `protected int marklimit`

DESCRIPTION When you set a mark on the input stream by calling `mark()`, you specify the number of bytes that can be read or skipped before the mark is invalidated. This number is recorded in the field `marklimit`. If you subsequently read or skip beyond `marklimit` number bytes, a subsequent call to `reset()` will not reset the read position to that previously marked.

SEE ALSO `mark()`, `markpos`, `read()`, `skip()`, `reset()`.

EXAMPLE This example is taken from the source of `BufferedInputStream`. It shows how `mark()` sets the fields `marklimit` and `markpos`.

```
public synchronized void mark(int readlimit) {
    marklimit = readlimit;
    markpos = pos;
}
```

markpos

PURPOSE The position in the buffer of the current mark.

SYNTAX `protected int markpos`

DESCRIPTION When you set a mark on the input stream by calling `mark()`, the current read position is recorded in the field `markpos`. When `reset()` is invoked, the current read position is reset to `markpos`. If no mark has been set, the value of `markpos` is `-1`.

SEE ALSO `mark()`, `pos`, `reset()`.

EXAMPLE See `marklimit`.

markSupported()

PURPOSE Determines whether this stream supports re-reading of its data.

SYNTAX `public boolean markSupported()`

DESCRIPTION This method returns whether this stream supports re-reading of its data (i.e., mark/reset). Buffered input streams support this feature, and hence, this method always returns `true`.

RETURNS `true`.

OVERRIDES `FilterInputStream.markSupported()`.

SEE ALSO `mark()`, `reset()`.

EXAMPLE See the class example.

pos

PURPOSE The current read position in the buffer.

SYNTAX `protected int pos`

DESCRIPTION This field records the current read position in the buffer. `read()` and `skip()` methods start from this position when reading or skipping bytes from this stream.

SEE ALSO `read()`, `skip()`.

EXAMPLE See `buf`.

read()

PURPOSE Reads bytes from the buffered input stream.

SYNTAX
```
public synchronized int read() throws IOException
public synchronized int read(byte[] buffer, int offset, int
    count) throws IOException
```

DESCRIPTION The `read()` method reads bytes from this buffered input stream, starting at the current read position. If all the bytes buffered earlier have been read, the buffer is refilled with data from this buffered input stream's original input stream. The current read position is usually that of the next byte after the last byte read during the previous `read()` or `skip()` invocation. However, the current read position can be changed using `reset()`.

The first form of `read()` returns the byte in the current read position in this buffered input stream. If the end of the stream has been reached, this method returns `-1`.

The second form of `read()` reads `count` bytes from this buffered input stream starting at the current read position and stores the bytes read into the byte array `buffer` starting at index `offset`. The actual number of bytes read, which could be different from `count` (when the number of bytes available is less than that requested) is returned. If no bytes can be read because the end of the stream has been reached, this method returns `-1`.

PARAMETERS

`buffer` The buffer into which the data is read.
`count` The number of bytes to read.
`offset` The index in `buffer` in which to start storing the bytes read.

RETURNS The first form returns the byte read; the second returns the actual number of bytes read. Both forms return `-1` when the end of the stream is reached.

EXCEPTIONS

`IOException` If an IO error occurred while attempting to read the requested bytes.

OVERRIDES `FilterInputStream.read()`.

SEE ALSO `mark()`, `reset()`, `skip()`.

EXAMPLE See the class example and `skip()`.

reset()

PURPOSE Repositions the stream to the last marked position.

SYNTAX
```
public synchronized void reset() throws IOException
```

DESCRIPTION This method repositions the stream to the last marked position. If the stream has not been marked or if the mark has been invalidated by reading or skipping beyond the mark, an `IOException` is thrown.

EXCEPTIONS

`IOException` If the stream has not been marked or if the mark has been invalidated.

OVERRIDES `FilterInputStream.reset()`.

SEE ALSO `mark()`.

EXAMPLE See the class example.

skip()

PURPOSE Skips the specified number of bytes in this buffered input stream.

SYNTAX `public synchronized long skip(long count) throws IOException`

DESCRIPTION This method skips `count` number of bytes of this buffered input stream, starting at the current read position. It returns the actual number of bytes skipped, which differs from `count` if there are fewer bytes available in the stream. The current read position is updated to reflect the number of bytes skipped. The next `read()` will not return those skipped bytes.

It returns `0` if it cannot skip any bytes.

PARAMETERS

`count` The number of bytes to be skipped.

RETURNS The actual number of bytes skipped.

EXCEPTIONS

`IOException` If an IO error occurred while attempting to skip.

OVERRIDES `FilterInputStream.skip()`.

EXAMPLE This example reads in a file and skips the first half before echoing the second half to standard output.

```
import java.io.BufferedInputStream;
import java.io.FileInputStream;
import java.io.IOException;

//  read a file and skips first half, and echos rest
class Main {
```

```
    public static void main(String[] args) {
        if (args.length != 1) {
            System.err.println("Usage: java Main <file>");
            System.exit(-1);
        }
        try {
            FileInputStream in = new FileInputStream(args[0]);
            // create buffered input stream with initial buffer
            BufferedInputStream bufin = new BufferedInputStream(in,
              1024);
            int count, half = bufin.available()/2;

            bufin.skip(half);        // skip first half of file

            // echo the rest
            byte[] buf = new byte[1024];
            while ((count=bufin.read(buf, 0, buf.length)) > 0)
                for (int i = 0; i<count; i++)
                    System.out.print((char)buf[i]);

            System.out.flush();
            bufin.close();
        } catch (IOException e) {
            e.printStackTrace();
        }
    }
}
```

java.io

BufferedOutputStream

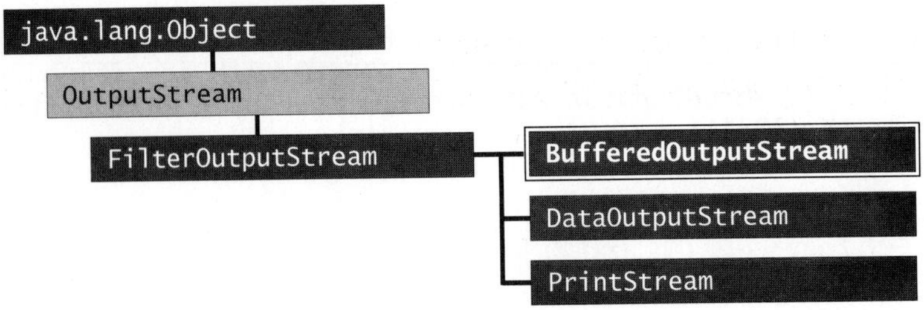

Syntax

```
public class BufferedOutputStream extends FilterOutputStream
```

Description

`BufferedOutputStream` implements a buffered output stream. A buffered output stream is a filter output stream. You can compose it with an existing output stream to allow buffering of output when writing to that stream. The buffered output stream maintains a buffer of bytes to be written to the original output stream. Requests to write to the buffered output stream store bytes in a buffer, rather than performing write operations on the original output stream. When the buffer becomes full or when the stream is flushed, the bytes in it are written out to the original output stream. If write operations to the original output stream have a high per-operation overhead, buffering the stream can improve the performance significantly because it can reduce the number of write operations on the original output stream. The buffered output stream incurs extra memory overhead because it must maintain the buffer. It also incurs an extra level of copying because the bytes must first be copied to the buffer.

MEMBER SUMMARY	
Constructor	
`BufferedOutputStream()`	Constructs a new buffered output stream from an output stream.
Output Methods	
`flush()`	Flushes the buffered bytes into the output stream.
`write()`	Writes bytes to the buffered output stream.
Protected Fields	
`buf`	The buffer in which data is stored.
`count`	The number of bytes stored in the buffer.

See Also

BufferedInputStream, FilterOutputStream, OutputStream.

Example

This example shows how a buffered output stream can be used with a socket. Operations on sockets are relatively expensive, so putting a buffer in front of the socket helps cut down the cost of using the socket.

```
import java.io.OutputStream;
import java.io.BufferedOutputStream;
import java.io.IOException;
import java.net.Socket;

class Main {
    public static void main(String[] args) {
        try {
            //  9 == 'discard' port, false == not a stream socket
            Socket sock = new Socket("localhost", 9, false);

            OutputStream so = sock.getOutputStream();
            BufferedOutputStream out = new BufferedOutputStream(so,
                8192);

            String msg = "this is a test";
            byte[] ob = new byte[msg.length()];
            msg.getBytes(0, ob.length, ob, 0);

            for (int i = 0; i < 5000; i++)
                out.write(ob, 0, ob.length);

            out.flush();
            out.close();
            sock.close();
        } catch (IOException e) {
            e.printStackTrace();
        }
    }
}
```

buf

PURPOSE The buffer in which data is stored.

SYNTAX `protected byte[] buf`

DESCRIPTION This field is used to store the bytes written to the buffered output stream before they get written to the output stream of this buffered output stream.

SEE ALSO count.

EXAMPLE This example is taken from the source of `BufferedOutputStream`. It shows how the `write()` method uses the fields `buf` and `count`.

```
public synchronized void write(int b) throws IOException {
    if (count == buf.length) {
        flush();
    }
    buf[count++] = (byte)b;
}
```

BufferedOutputStream()

PURPOSE Constructs a new buffered output stream from an output stream.

SYNTAX
```
public BufferedOutputStream(OutputStream out)
public BufferedOutputStream(OutputStream out, int size)
```

DESCRIPTION There are two forms of the constructor for `BufferedOutputStream`. The first form constructs a new buffered output stream for the output stream `out` with the default buffer size of 512 bytes. The second form constructs a new buffered output stream for `out` with the buffer size `size`.

A buffer of the specified size is created to cache the bytes to be written. The larger the buffer, the more bytes that can be cached before being written out to `out`. A bigger buffer might result in significant performance improvements if write operations on `out` are slow. However, it also means more memory is required to store the bytes. Thus you should select a size that is balanced between performance requirements and memory usage.

The buffered output is written out to `out` either when the buffer becomes full or when `flush()` is invoked.

PARAMETERS

`out` The output stream.

`size` The buffer size.

SEE ALSO `FilterOutputStream`.

EXAMPLE See the class example.

count

PURPOSE The number of bytes stored in the buffer.

SYNTAX `protected int count`

DESCRIPTION This field records the number of bytes that are stored in this buffer and that have yet to be written to the output stream of this buffered output stream.

SEE ALSO `buf`, `flush()`.

EXAMPLE See `buf`.

flush()

PURPOSE Flushes the buffered bytes into the output stream.

SYNTAX `public synchronized void flush() throws IOException`

DESCRIPTION This method writes any buffered bytes to the output stream (`out`) of this buffered output stream and clears the buffer. `out` is also flushed, in case it is another buffered output stream.

EXCEPTIONS

`IOException` If an IO error occurred while attempting to flush the stream.

OVERRIDES `FilterOutputStream.flush()`.

SEE ALSO `buf`, `count`, `write()`.

EXAMPLE See the class example.

write()

PURPOSE Writes bytes to the buffered output stream.

SYNTAX

```
public synchronized void write(int oneByte)
public synchronized void write(byte[] buffer, int offset, int
    count) throws IOException
```

DESCRIPTION The `write()` method writes the specified byte or bytes to this buffered output stream. The first form of `write()` writes a single byte `oneByte` to the buffered output stream. The second form writes `count` bytes from the buffer `buffer` starting at index `offset` to the buffered output stream.

If there is room in the buffer of this stream to hold the bytes, they are buffered. Otherwise any buffered bytes and these new bytes are written out to the output stream of this buffered output stream. This clears the buffer and allows bytes in subsequent `write()` calls to be buffered.

write()

PARAMETERS

`buffer`	The buffer containing data to be written.
`count`	The number of bytes from `buffer` to be written.
`offset`	The index in `buffer` of the bytes to be written.
`oneByte`	The byte to be written.

EXCEPTIONS

`IOException`	If an IO error occurred while attempting to write the bytes.

OVERRIDES	`FilterOutputStream.write()`.
SEE ALSO	`flush()`.
EXAMPLE	See the class example.

java.awt
Button

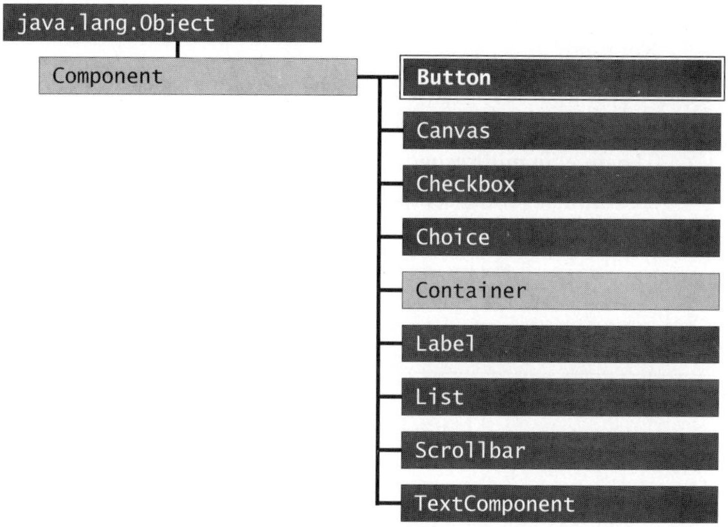

Syntax

```
public class Button extends Component
```

Description

A button is a component that has a label and generates an event when pressed. A button is typically used when a command needs to be invoked. For example, a stopwatch application is shown in Figure 23 with three buttons to operate the stopwatch.

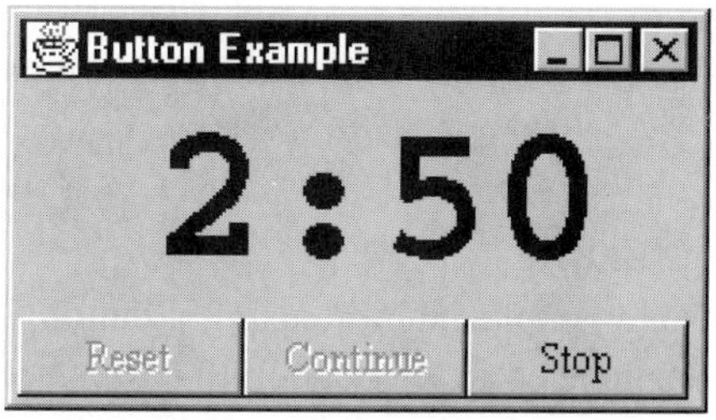

FIGURE 23 A Simple Stopwatch with Three Buttons

Event

A button generates an action event whenever it is pressed. See the `Event` class for details on how to filter or handle events. Table 5 describes how a button fills the fields in the event.

TABLE 5 Action Event from a `Button`

`arg`	The button's label.
`clickCount`	Not used.
`id`	`Event.ACTION`.
`key`	Not used.
`modifiers`	The state of the modifier keys when the component was clicked.
`target`	Reference to the component that generated this event.
`when`	The time, in milliseconds, that the event was generated.
`x`	*x*-coordinate of the component in pixels.
`y`	*y*-coordinate of the component in pixels.

MEMBER SUMMARY

Constructor	
`Button()`	Constructs a new `Button` instance.
Label Methods	
`getLabel()`	Retrieves the button's label.
`setLabel()`	Sets the button's label.
Peer Method	
`addNotify()`	Creates the button's peer.
Debugging Method	
`paramString()`	Generates a string representing the button's state.

Example

For a simple example using a button, see the `Button()` constructor. This is a more elaborate example of an application that uses buttons. The application is a (not very accurate) stopwatch with three buttons: "Reset," "Start," and "Stop." Figure 23 shows a screen shot of the example. Depending on the mode of the stopwatch, certain buttons will be enabled or disabled to indicate which operations are or are not currently appropriate. For example, if the stopwatch is stopped, the "Stop" button will be disabled.

A thread is created whenever the stopwatch is ticking and killed when no longer needed.

```
import java.awt.*;
public class Main extends Frame implements Runnable {
    Label timeDisp = new Label("  0:0  ", Label.CENTER);
    Thread timerThread;
    int time = 0;    // The time in seconds.
```

```
Button btReset = new Button("Reset");
Button btStart = new Button("Start");
Button btStop = new Button("Stop");

Main() {
    super("Button Example");
    Panel p = new Panel();

    // Use a grid layout manager for the 3 buttons.
    p.setLayout(new GridLayout(1, 0));
    btReset.disable();
    btStop.disable();
    p.add(btReset);
    p.add(btStart);
    p.add(btStop);
    add("South", p);

    // Make the time display very large.
    timeDisp.setFont(new Font("Courier", Font.BOLD, 60));
    add("Center", timeDisp);
    pack();
    show();
}

// Returns only when the timerThread has terminated.
void stop() {
    Thread t = timerThread;
    if (t != null) {
        timerThread = null;
        try { t.join(); } catch (Exception e) {}
    }
}

public boolean action(Event evt, Object what) {
    if (evt.target == btReset) {
        stop();
        timeDisp.setText("0:0");
        time = 0;
        btReset.disable();
        btStart.enable();
        btStop.disable();
        btStart.setLabel("Start");
        return true;
    } else if (evt.target == btStop) {
        stop();
        btReset.enable();
        btStart.enable();
        btStop.disable();
        btStart.setLabel("Continue");
        return true;
    } else if (evt.target == btStart) {
        // Create and start the timer thread.
        timerThread = new Thread(this);
        timerThread.start();
```

```
                btReset.disable();
                btStart.disable();
                btStop.enable();
                btStart.setLabel("Continue");
                return true;
            }
            return false;
        }

        public void run() {
            while (timerThread == Thread.currentThread()) {
                timeDisp.setText("" + time/10 + ":" + time%10 + "0");
                time++;
                try { Thread.sleep(100); } catch (Exception e) {};
            }
        }

        static public void main(String[] args) {
            new Main();
        }
    }
```

addNotify()

PURPOSE Creates the button's peer.

SYNTAX `public synchronized void addNotify()`

DESCRIPTION This method creates the peer if it does not yet exist. The peer is created by a call to the `Toolkit.createButton()` method. The `addNotify()` method should never be called directly. It is normally called by the parent.

OVERRIDES `Component.addNotify()`.

SEE ALSO `Component`, `Toolkit`.

Button()

PURPOSE Constructs a new `Button` instance.

SYNTAX `public Button()`
`public Button(String label)`

DESCRIPTION These constructors create a new `Button` instance with the label `label`. If `label` is not specified, it defaults to "".

PARAMETERS

`label` The non-`null` string specifying the button's label.

EXAMPLE This is the simplest example of a complete program that uses a button. A button labeled "Button" is created and added to a frame. The frame's event handler prints "Button pressed" whenever the button is pressed. See also Figure 24.

FIGURE 24 `Button()`

```
import java.awt.*;
public class Main extends Frame {
    Button b = new Button("Button");

    Main() {
        super("Button Example");
        add("Center", b);
        pack();
        show();
    }

    public boolean action(Event evt, Object what) {
        if (evt.target == b) {
            System.out.println("Button pressed");
            return true;
        }
        return false;
    }

    static public void main(String[] args) {
        new Main();
    }
}
```

getLabel()

PURPOSE Retrieves the button's label.

SYNTAX `public String getLabel()`

RETURNS A non-`null` string containing the button's label.

SEE ALSO `setLabel()`.

EXAMPLE See `setLabel()`.

paramString()

PURPOSE Generates a string representing the button's state.

SYNTAX `protected String paramString()`

DESCRIPTION The returned string includes the button's label. A subclass of this class should override this method and return a concatenation of its state with the results of `super.paramString()`. This method is called by the `toString()` method and is typically used for debugging.

RETURNS A non-`null` string representing the button's state.

OVERRIDES `Component.paramString()`.

SEE ALSO `Object.toString()`.

EXAMPLE See `Component.paramString()`.

setLabel()

PURPOSE Sets the button's label.

SYNTAX `public void setLabel(String label)`

DESCRIPTION This method sets the button's label to be `label`. As a result of the label's being set, the minimum and preferred sizes of the button may change, so resizing the button may be necessary. The example shows how to cause the button's parent to resize the button.

PARAMETERS

`label` The non-`null` string specifying the button's new label.

SEE ALSO `getLabel()`.

EXAMPLE This example creates a button and a text field. Pressing Return in the text field causes the button label to be set to the contents of the text field. Changing the label does not automatically resize the button in the layout. This needs to be done explicitly. To do this, the button's container must first be invalidated and then immediately validated. See Figure 25.

FIGURE 25 `Button.setLabel()`

To force the button to be as small as possible, a blank canvas is inserted in the Center location of the border layout.

```
import java.awt.*;
class Main extends Frame {
    Button bt = new Button("Button");
    TextField tf = new TextField(40);
```

```
    Main() {
        super("setLabel Example");
        add("Center", new Canvas());
        add("West", bt);
        add("South", tf);
        tf.setText(bt.getLabel());     // init with current label
        pack();
        show();
    }

    public boolean action(Event evt, Object what) {
        if (evt.target == tf) {
            bt.setLabel(tf.getText());

            // the size has changed so get parent to validate itself.
            bt.getParent().invalidate();
            bt.getParent().validate();
            return true;
        }
        return false;
    }
    static public void main(String[] args) {
        new Main();
    }
}
```

java.awt.peer

ButtonPeer

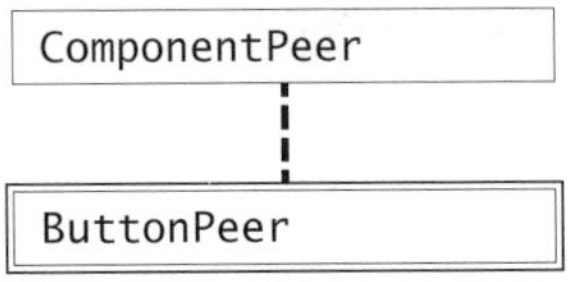

Syntax

```
public interface ButtonPeer extends ComponentPeer
```

Description

The button component (see the `Button` class) in the Abstract Windowing Toolkit (AWT) uses the platform's native implementation of a button. To make the AWT button component behave the same on all platforms, the button is assigned a peer whose task is to translate the behavior of the platform's native button to the behavior of the AWT button.

AWT programmers normally do not directly use peer classes and interfaces. Instead they deal with AWT components in the `java.awt` package. These in turn automatically manage their peers. Only someone who is porting the AWT to another platform should be concerned with the peer classes and interfaces. Consequently, most peer documentation refers to `java.awt` counterparts.

See `Component` and `Toolkit` for additional information about component peers.

MEMBER SUMMARY	
Peer Method	
`setLabel()`	Sets the button's label.

See Also

`Button`, `Component`, `Toolkit`.

setLabel()

PURPOSE Sets the button's label.

SYNTAX `void setLabel(String label)`

PARAMETERS

`label` The non-`null` string specifying the button peer's new label.

SEE ALSO `Button.setLabel()`.

java.io

ByteArrayInputStream

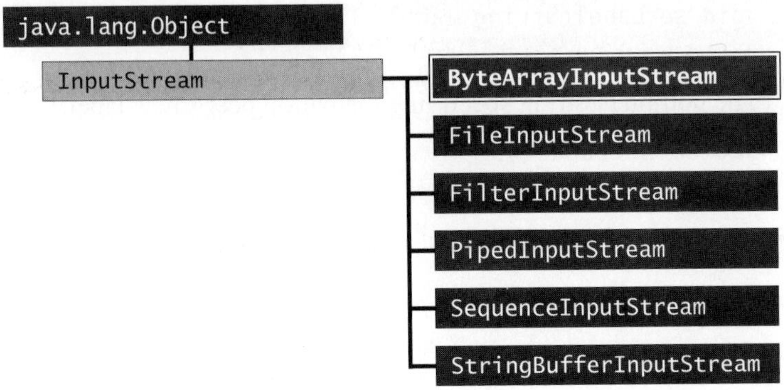

Syntax

`public class ByteArrayInputStream extends InputStream`

Description

`ByteArrayInputStream` implements a byte array input stream. You can use a byte array input stream to turn a byte array into an input stream on which you can perform read operations. Requests to read from the byte array input stream retrieve bytes from the original byte array (see Figure 26).

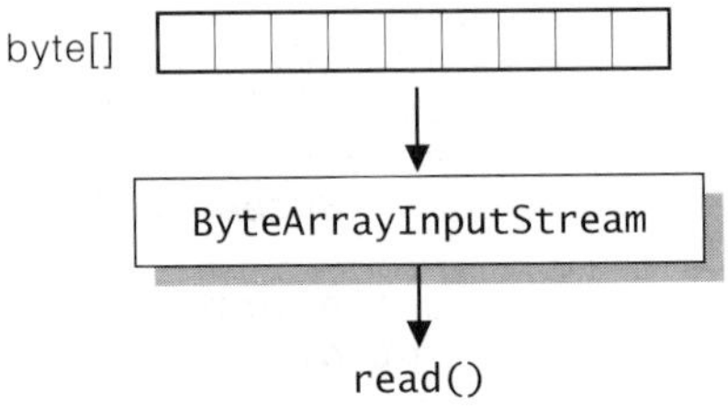

FIGURE 26 `ByteArrayInputStream`

MEMBER SUMMARY	
Constructor	
`ByteArrayInputStream()`	Constructs a byte array input stream using a byte array.
Input Methods	
`available()`	Determines the number of unread bytes in this stream.
`read()`	Reads bytes from this byte array input stream.
`skip()`	Skips a specified number of bytes in the input stream.
Reset Method	
`reset()`	Resets to the beginning of the byte array.

MEMBER SUMMARY

Protected Fields

`buf`	The byte array containing the bytes to be read.
`count`	The ending index of the byte array to be read.
`pos`	The current read position in the byte array.

See Also

`ByteArrayOutputStream`, `FilterOutputStream`, `OutputStream`.

Example

This example exercises all the methods in the `ByteArrayInputStream` class. It reads all the bytes from the stream, resets the stream, skips 3 bytes, and then reads the rest of the bytes from the stream.

```
import java.io.ByteArrayInputStream;

class Main {
    public static void main(String[] args) {
        byte[] inputbytes = { 'a', 'b', 'c', 'd', 'e'};
        ByteArrayInputStream in = new
            ByteArrayInputStream(inputbytes);

        System.out.println("Available: " + in.available());
        int b;

        while ((b=in.read()) >= 0)        // reads "abcde"
            System.out.print((char)b);
        in.reset();
        System.out.println();

        in.skip(3);                       // skips "abc"

        while ((b=in.read()) >= 0)        // reads "de"
            System.out.print((char)b);
        System.out.println();
    }
}
```

available()

PURPOSE Determines the number of unread bytes in this byte array input stream.

A B C D E F G H I J K L M N O P Q R S T U V W X Y Z

SYNTAX `public synchronized int available()`

DESCRIPTION This method returns the number of bytes that have yet to be read from this byte array input stream.

RETURNS The number of bytes yet to be read from this stream.

OVERRIDES `InputStream.available()`.

EXAMPLE See the class example.

buf

PURPOSE The byte array contains the bytes to be read.

SYNTAX `protected byte[] buf`

DESCRIPTION `buf` is a reference to the byte array used to create this byte array input stream. Because this is a reference, any changes to the original byte array are reflected in this byte array input stream.

SEE ALSO `count`, `pos`.

EXAMPLE This example is taken from the source of `ByteArrayInputStream`. It shows the usage of all the three protected fields of `ByteArrayInputStream`.

```
public synchronized int read() {
    return (pos < count) ? (buf[pos++] & 0xff) : -1;
}
```

ByteArrayInputStream()

PURPOSE Constructs a byte array input stream using a byte array.

SYNTAX
```
public ByteArrayInputStream(byte[] buffer)
public ByteArrayInputStream(byte[] buffer, int offset, int count)
```

DESCRIPTION These constructors are used to create a byte array input stream using an existing byte array `buffer`. `buffer` is used directly and not copied, so any changes to `buffer` subsequent to the creation of this stream also affect this input stream. The bytes to be read from `buffer` are the `count` number of bytes starting at index `offset`. If `offset` and `count` are not specified, all the bytes in the entire buffer will be read.

PARAMETERS

`buffer`	The buffer containing the bytes to be read (not copied).
`count`	The number of bytes that can be read from `buffer`. If `count + offset` exceeds `buffer.length`, `count` is automatically lowered to the limit imposed by `buffer`.
`offset`	The index in `buffer` from where to start reading.

EXAMPLE See the class example.

count

PURPOSE The ending index of the byte array to be read.

SYNTAX `protected int count`

DESCRIPTION This field records the exclusive ending index of the byte array to be read. It is calculated initially when the byte array input stream is first created, and it remains unchanged.

SEE ALSO `pos`, `ByteArrayInputStream()`.

EXAMPLE See `buf`.

pos

PURPOSE The current read position in the byte array.

SYNTAX `protected int pos`

DESCRIPTION This field records the current read position in the byte array of this byte array input stream. The next `read()` or `skip()` operation will start reading from this position. This field is set initially when the byte array input stream is first created and is updated during `read()` and `skip()` operations to record which byte to read next. `reset()` sets `pos` to 0 so that subsequent reading and skipping will start at the beginning of the byte array (regardless of the value of `offset` supplied in the `ByteArrayInputStream()` constructor).

SEE ALSO `count`.

EXAMPLE See `buf`.

A B C D E F G H I J K L M N O P Q R S T U V W X Y Z

read()

PURPOSE Reads bytes from this byte array input stream.

SYNTAX
```
public synchronized int read()
public synchronized int read(byte[] buffer, int offset, int count)
```

DESCRIPTION The `read()` method reads bytes from this byte array input stream, starting at the current read position. The current read position is usually that of the next byte after the last byte read during the previous `read()` or `skip()` invocation. However, the current read position can be changed using `reset()`.

The first form of `read()` returns the byte at the current read position in this byte array input stream. If the end of the stream has been reached, this method returns `-1`.

The second form of `read()` reads `count` bytes from this byte array input stream starting at the current read position and stores the bytes read into the byte array `buffer` starting at index `offset`. The actual number of bytes read is returned. This number could differ from `count` when the number of bytes available is less than that requested. If no bytes can be read because the end of the stream has been reached, this method returns `-1`.

PARAMETERS

`buffer` The buffer into which the data is read.

`count` The number of bytes to read.

`offset` The index in `buffer` in which to start storing the bytes read.

RETURNS The first form returns the byte read. The second returns the actual number of bytes read. Both forms return `-1` when the end of the stream is reached.

EXCEPTIONS

`IOException` If an IO error occurred while attempting to read the requested bytes.

OVERRIDES `InputStream.read()`.

SEE ALSO `reset()`, `skip()`.

EXAMPLE See the class example.

reset()

PURPOSE Resets the buffer to the beginning of the byte array.

SYNTAX `public synchronized void reset()`

DESCRIPTION This method resets the current read position of this stream to be the beginning of the byte array (`0`). Note that this is the actual beginning of the byte array with which this input stream was created, rather than the `offset` parameter to the `ByteArrayInputStream()` constructor. For example, regardless of whether `offset` was `10` or `0`, `reset()` always sets the current read position to `0`. The ending index of the byte array to read (that calculated originally using `offset` and `count` arguments to the constructor) remains unchanged.

OVERRIDES `InputStream.reset()`.

SEE ALSO `count`, `pos`, `read()`, `skip()`.

EXAMPLE See the class example.

skip()

PURPOSE Skips the specified number of bytes in this byte array input stream.

SYNTAX `public synchronized long skip(long count)`

DESCRIPTION This method skips `count` number of bytes of this byte array input stream starting at the current read position. It returns the actual number of bytes skipped, which may differ from `count` if there are fewer bytes available in the stream. The current read position is updated to reflect the number of bytes skipped. The next `read()` will not return those bytes skipped.

It returns `0` if it cannot skip any bytes.

OVERRIDES `InputStream.skip()`.

PARAMETERS

`count` The number of bytes to be skipped.

RETURNS The actual number of bytes skipped.

SEE ALSO `read()`.

EXAMPLE See the class example.

A B C D E F G H I J K L M N O P Q R S T U V W X Y Z

java.io

ByteArrayOutputStream

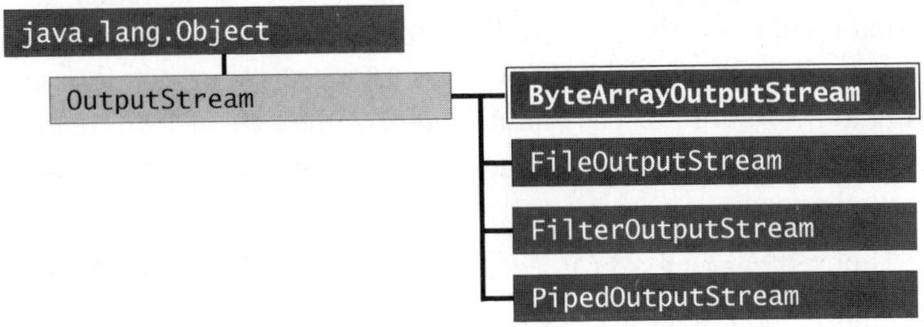

Syntax

```
public class ByteArrayOutputStream extends OutputStream
```

Description

`ByteArrayOutputStream` implements a byte array output stream. You can use a byte array output stream to treat a byte array as an output stream on which you can perform write operations. Requests to write bytes to the stream store the bytes into an automatically expandable byte array whose contents can later be retrieved as a byte array or as a string. This is helpful when you want to capture output from methods that operate on output streams in the form of a byte array (for which you can subsequently obtain a string representation). See Figure 27.

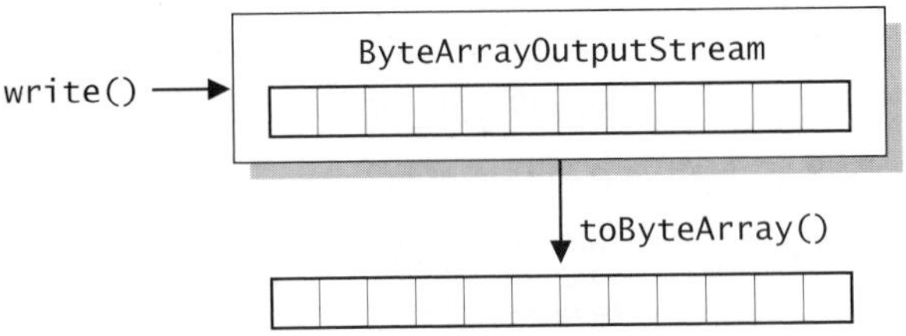

FIGURE 27 **ByteArrayOutputStream**

MEMBER SUMMARY

Constructor	
`ByteArrayOutputStream()`	Constructs a new byte array output stream.
Output Methods	
`size()`	Retrieves the number of bytes in this stream.
`write()`	Writes bytes to this stream.
Reset Method	
`reset()`	Resets this stream so that it can be reused.

MEMBER SUMMARY	
Externalizing Methods	
`toByteArray()`	Retrieves the contents of this stream as a byte array.
`toString()`	Generates the string representation of this stream.
`writeTo()`	Writes the contents of this stream to another stream.
Protected Fields	
`buf`	The buffer in which data of this stream is stored.
`count`	The number of bytes in this stream.

See Also

`ByteArrayInputStream`, `OutputStream`.

Example

This example shows the use of a byte array output stream to add a backslash character to escape meta characters that appear in a string.

```
import java.io.ByteArrayOutputStream;

class Main {
    // for any meta character that appears in the string 's',
    // escape it with the backslash.
    public static String encode(String s, char[] metachars) {
        // start off with length of string; stream will grow
        // automatically
        ByteArrayOutputStream out = new
            ByteArrayOutputStream(s.length());

        for (int i = 0; i < s.length(); i++) {
            int c = (int)s.charAt(i);
            for (int j = 0; j < metachars.length; j++) {
                if (c == metachars[j]) {
                    out.write('\\');
                    break;
                }
            }
            out.write(c);
        }
        return out.toString();
    }
    public static void main(String[] args) {
        char[] meta = {'\\', '\''};
        String raw = "'abc'\\b2+3";
        String answer = encode(raw, meta);

        System.out.println("Raw: " + raw);
        System.out.println("Encoded: " + answer);
    }
}
```

buf

PURPOSE The buffer in which data of this stream is stored.

SYNTAX `protected byte[] buf`

DESCRIPTION This field is used to store the bytes written to the byte array output stream. `buf`'s initial size is determined by the arguments to the `ByteArrayOutputStream()` constructor but is expanded as needed as more bytes are written to the stream.

SEE ALSO `count`, `size()`.

EXAMPLE This example is taken from the source of `ByteArrayOutputStream`. It shows the use of the protected fields `buf` and `count` in the `write()` method.

```
public synchronized void write(int b) {
    int newcount = count + 1;
    if (newcount > buf.length) {
        byte newbuf[] = new byte[Math.max(buf.length << 1, newcount)];
        System.arraycopy(buf, 0, newbuf, 0, count);
        buf = newbuf;
    }
    buf[count] = (byte)b;
    count = newcount;
}
```

ByteArrayOutputStream()

PURPOSE Constructs a new byte array output stream.

SYNTAX
```
public ByteArrayOutputStream()
public ByteArrayOutputStream(int size)
```

DESCRIPTION There are two forms of the constructor for `ByteArrayOutputStream`. The first form constructs a new byte array output stream with the default buffer size of 32 bytes. The second form constructs a new byte array output stream buffer size `size`.

A buffer of the specified size is created to store the bytes written to this stream. As the number of bytes written to this stream exceeds the buffer size, the buffer will be grown automatically to accommodate the additional bytes.

PARAMETERS

`size` The initial buffer size.

SEE ALSO `size()`.

EXAMPLE See the class example, `reset()`, and `toByteArray()`.

count

PURPOSE The number of bytes in this stream.

SYNTAX `protected int count`

DESCRIPTION This field records the number of bytes that have been written to this stream since its most recent reset or since it was created if it has never reset. This number is incremented as more bytes are written to this stream and is set to `0` when `reset()` is invoked.

RETURNS The number of bytes in this stream.

SEE ALSO `reset()`, `size()`.

EXAMPLE See `buf`.

reset()

PURPOSE Resets this stream so that it can be reused.

SYNTAX `public synchronized void reset()`

DESCRIPTION This method resets the current write position of this stream to be the beginning of the byte array. The size of this stream becomes 0, and all bytes written earlier to the current stream are lost. Subsequent write operations to this stream start at the beginning of the byte array.

OVERRIDES `OutputStream.reset()`.

SEE ALSO `write()`, `writeTo()`.

EXAMPLE This example shows the use of `reset()` and `writeTo()` to write a list of HTML anchors when their descriptions and references are provided. It uses the byte array output stream to construct each anchor and then writes the result to the output stream. Before processing the next anchor, it resets the byte array output stream.

```
import java.io.ByteArrayOutputStream;
import java.io.OutputStream;
import java.io.IOException;

class Anchor {
    // writes out an HTML anchor:    <A HREF="ref"> desc </A>
    public static void anchor(String[] desc, String[] ref,
        OutputStream out)
```

```
        throws IOException{
            ByteArrayOutputStream buf = new ByteArrayOutputStream();
            byte[] prefix = {‘<‘, ‘A’, ‘ ‘, ‘H’, ‘R’, ‘E’, ‘F’, ‘=’, ‘”’};
            byte[] suffix = {‘ ‘, ‘<‘, ‘/’, ‘A’, ‘>’};

            for (int a = 0; a < desc.length; a++) {
                    buf.write(prefix, 0, prefix.length);
                    for (int i = 0; i < ref[a].length(); i++)
                            buf.write((int)ref[a].charAt(i));

                    buf.write(‘”’);
                    buf.write(‘>’);
                    buf.write(‘ ‘);
                    for (int i = 0; i < desc[a].length(); i++)
                            buf.write((int)desc[a].charAt(i));

                    buf.write(suffix, 0, suffix.length);
                    buf.write(‘\n’);
                    buf.writeTo(out);
                    buf.reset();        // reset stream to start of buffer
            }
        }
        public static void main(String[] args) {
            String[] desc = {“Preface”, “Table of Contents”,
                             “Index”, “Glossary”};
            String[] ref = {“preface.htm”, “toc.htm”,
                            “index.htm”, “glossary.htm”};
            try {
                anchor(desc, ref, System.out);
            } catch (IOException e) {
                e.printStackTrace();
            }
        }
    }
```

size()

PURPOSE Retrieves the number of bytes in this stream.

SYNTAX `public int size()`

DESCRIPTION This method returns the number of bytes that have been written to this stream since its most recent reset or since it was created if it has never been reset. This number is incremented as more bytes are written to this stream and is set to `0` when `reset()` is invoked.

RETURNS The number of bytes in this stream.

SEE ALSO `count`, `reset()`.

EXAMPLE This example shows the use of a byte array output stream to concatenate the string representations of a vector of objects and returns the result as a `byte` array.

```
import java.util.Vector;
import java.io.ByteArrayOutputStream;

class Concat {
    public static byte[] concat(Vector objs, boolean printSize) {
        ByteArrayOutputStream out = new ByteArrayOutputStream();

        for (int i = 0; i < objs.size(); i++) {
            String str = objs.elementAt(i).toString();
            for (int j = 0; j < str.length(); j++)
                out.write((int)str.charAt(j));
        }
        if (printSize)
            System.out.println("Size: " + out.size());
        return (out.toByteArray());
    }
    public static void main(String[] args) {
        Vector objs = new Vector(args.length);

        for (int i = 0; i < args.length; i++)
            objs.addElement(args[i]);

        byte[] all = concat(objs, true); // print size of total string

        for (int i = 0; i < all.length; i++)
            System.out.print((char)all[i]);
        System.out.println();
    }
}
```

toByteArray()

PURPOSE Retrieves the contents of this stream as a byte array.

SYNTAX `public synchronized byte[] toByteArray()`

DESCRIPTION This method is used to retrieve the contents of this stream as a byte array. The contents of this stream are copied to a newly created byte array, and this new byte array is returned. Subsequent changes to this stream do not affect the byte array that is being returned.

RETURNS A new byte array containing the contents of this stream.

EXAMPLE See `size()`.

C

toString()

D

PURPOSE Generates the string representation of this stream.

E

SYNTAX
```
public String toString()
public String toString(int hibyte)
```

F

DESCRIPTION This method creates a string using the contents of this byte array output stream. If `hibyte` is supplied, the high-order byte of each 16-bit Unicode character of the string is set to `hibyte`. If `hibyte` is not supplied, the high-order byte of each character is filled with 0. The string that is returned is a snapshot of the current contents of this stream. It is not affected by any subsequent changes to this stream.

G H I J

PARAMETERS
`hibyte` The byte used to fill the high-order byte of each character in the resulting string.

K

RETURNS The string representation of this stream.

L

OVERRIDES `Object.toString()`.

SEE ALSO `toByteArray()`.

M

EXAMPLE See the class example.

N O

write()

P

PURPOSE Writes bytes to this byte array output stream.

Q

SYNTAX
```
public synchronized void write(int oneByte)
public synchronized void write(byte[] buffer, int offset, int
    count)
```

R S

DESCRIPTION The `write()` method writes the specified byte or bytes to this byte array output stream. The first form of `write()` writes a single byte `oneByte` to this stream. The second form writes `count` bytes from the byte array `buffer` starting at index `offset` to this stream.

T U

The bytes written are copied to the stream starting at the current write position. The current write position is usually the next index after the point at which the last byte from the previous `write()` occurred, unless set to 0 via `reset()`. The current write position is incremented to reflect the new bytes written. The internal byte array used to hold the contents of the stream expands dynamically as required to hold all the new data.

V W X Y Z

PARAMETERS

`buffer`	The byte array containing data to be written.
`count`	The number of bytes from `buffer` to be written.
`offset`	The index in `buffer` of the bytes to be written.
`oneByte`	The byte to be written.

OVERRIDES `OutputStream.write()`.

SEE ALSO `reset()`.

EXAMPLE See the class example, `buf`, `reset()`, and `size()`.

writeTo()

PURPOSE Writes the contents of this stream to another stream.

SYNTAX

```
public synchronized void writeTo(OutputStream out) throws
    IOException
```

DESCRIPTION This method writes the entire contents of this stream to the output stream `out`. The output consists of all the bytes from the beginning of this stream to the current write position of this stream. This method does not change the current write position.

PARAMETERS

`out` The stream to which to write.

EXCEPTIONS

`IOException` If an IO error occurred while attempting to write to `out`.

SEE ALSO `OutputStream`.

EXAMPLE See `size()`.

java.awt
Canvas

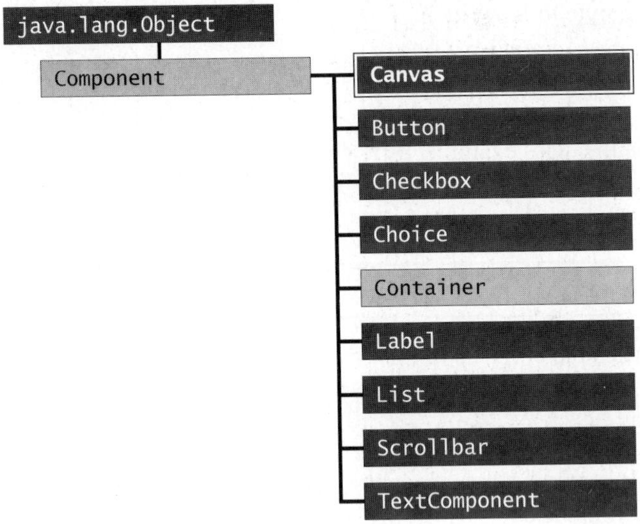

Syntax

```
public class Canvas extends Component
```

Description

A canvas component is a primitive component meant to be either subclassed into custom components or used for painting graphics. A canvas has no border or other bars. A canvas generates all the mouse, keyboard, and focus events defined in the `Event` class.

MEMBER SUMMARY	
Peer Method	
`addNotify()`	Creates the canvas's peer.
Paint Override	
`paint()`	Paints the canvas.

Example

This example demonstrates how to build a custom button. The button displays a blinking colored circle rather than a text string. A thread is created to blink the button. The custom button also overrides the enabled and disabled methods in order to paint different images depending on the state of this property. The custom button also generates an action event when clicked.

This example creates three colored buttons to control the color of the main canvas. See Figure 28. After a color is chosen, the corresponding button becomes disabled.

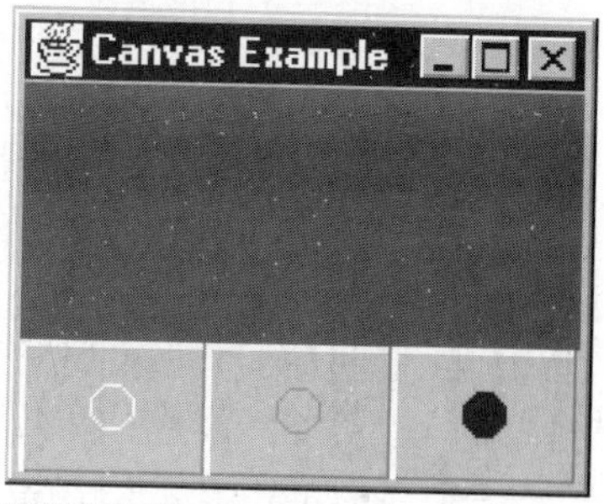

FIGURE 28 Canvas

```
import java.awt.*;
class Main extends Frame {
    String[] colorNames = {"red", "green", "blue"};
    Color[] colorValues = {Color.red, Color.green, Color.blue};
    MainButton[] buttons = new MainButton[colorNames.length];
    Canvas cv = new Canvas();

    Main() {
        super("Canvas Example");
        Panel p = new Panel();

        p.setLayout(new GridLayout(1, 0));
        for (int i=0; i<colorNames.length; i++) {
            p.add(buttons[i] = new MainButton(colorNames[i],
                colorValues[i]));
        }
        add("South", p);
        cv.resize(150, 150);
        add("Center", cv);
        pack();
        show();
    }

    public boolean action(Event evt, Object arg) {
        if (evt.target instanceof MainButton) {
            for (int i=0; i<colorNames.length; i++) {
                if (colorNames[i].equals(arg)) {
                    buttons[i].disable();
                    cv.setBackground(colorValues[i]);
                    cv.repaint();
                } else {
                    buttons[i].enable();
                }
            }
            return true;
        }
        return false;
    }
```

Example

```
    static public void main(String[] args) {
        new Main();
    }
}

class MainButton extends Canvas implements Runnable {
    boolean on;
    boolean engaged;
    String label;
    Thread timerThread;

    MainButton(String label, Color color) {
        this.label = label;
        (timerThread = new Thread(this)).start();
        resize(40, 40);
        setForeground(color);
    }

    public void enable() {
        super.enable();
        if (timerThread == null) {
            (timerThread = new Thread(this)).start();
        }
        repaint();
    }

    public void disable() {
        super.disable();
        timerThread = null;
        on = false;
        repaint();
    }

    public void paint(Graphics g) {
        update(g);
    }

    public void update(Graphics g) {
        FontMetrics fm = g.getFontMetrics();
        int w = size().width;
        int h = size().height;
        int ovalSize = Math.min(w/3, h/3);

        g.clearRect(0, 0, w, h);
        if (isEnabled()) {
            if (engaged || on) {
                g.fillOval((w-ovalSize)/2, (h-ovalSize)/2,
                    ovalSize, ovalSize);
            } else {
                g.drawOval((w-ovalSize)/2, (h-ovalSize)/2,
                    ovalSize, ovalSize);
            }
        } else {
```

```
            g.setColor(Color.white);
            g.drawOval((w-ovalSize)/2, (h-ovalSize)/2, ovalSize,
              ovalSize);
        }
        g.setColor(getBackground());
        g.draw3DRect(0, 0, w-1, h-1, !engaged);
        g.draw3DRect(1, 1, w-2, h-2, !engaged);
    }

    public boolean mouseDown(Event evt, int x, int y) {
        engaged = true;
        repaint();
        return true;
    }

    public boolean mouseUp(Event evt, int x, int y) {
        engaged = false;
        repaint();
        postEvent(new Event(this, Event.ACTION_EVENT, label));
        return true;
    }

    public void run() {
        while (timerThread == Thread.currentThread()) {
            on = !on;
            repaint();
            try { Thread.sleep(1000); } catch (Exception e) {};
        }
    }
}
```

addNotify()

PURPOSE Creates the canvas's peer.

SYNTAX `public synchronized void addNotify()`

DESCRIPTION This method creates the peer if it does not yet exist. The peer is created by calling the `Toolkit.createCanvas()` method. This method should never be called directly. It is normally called by the parent.

OVERRIDES `Component.addNotify()`.

SEE ALSO `Component`, `Toolkit`.

paint()

PURPOSE Paints the canvas.

SYNTAX `public void paint(Graphics graphics)`

DESCRIPTION This method is called when part of the canvas that was previously occluded by some other window is now exposed. You can determine the bounds of the exposed area by using the `getClipRect()` method on the graphics context. This method by default simply clears the exposed area with the canvas's background color. Override this method to implement your drawing routines. Note that the system does not automatically clear the exposed area, so you need to explicitly do this if necessary.

PARAMETERS

`graphics` The non-`null` graphics context used to paint on the component.

OVERRIDES `Component.paint()`.

EXAMPLE This is the simplest example of a program that uses a canvas to draw a graphic. A subclass of canvas is defined and its `paint()` method overridden. The `paint()` method simply draws an oval. See Figure 29.

FIGURE 29 `Canvas.paint()`

```
import java.awt.*;
class Main {
    static public void main(String[] args) {
        Frame f = new Frame("paint Example");
        f.add("Center", new MainCanvas());
        f.resize(200, 100);
        f.show();
    }
}
class MainCanvas extends Canvas {
    public void paint(Graphics g) {
        g.drawOval(0, 0, size().width, size().height);
    }
}
```

CanvasPeer

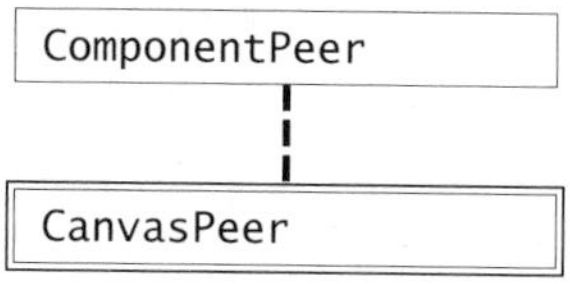

Syntax

```
public interface CanvasPeer extends ComponentPeer
```

Description

The canvas component (see the `Canvas` class) in the Abstract Windowing Toolkit (AWT) uses the platform's native implementation of a canvas. So that the AWT canvas component behaves the same on all platforms, the canvas is assigned a peer, whose task is to translate the behavior of the platform's native canvas to the behavior of the AWT canvas.

AWT programmers normally do not directly use peer classes and interfaces. Instead they deal with AWT components in the `java.awt` package. These in turn automatically manage their peers. Only someone who is porting the AWT to another platform should be concerned with the peer classes and interfaces. Consequently, most peer documentation refers to `java.awt` counterparts.

See `Component` and `Toolkit` for additional information about component peers.

See Also

`Canvas`, `Component`, `Toolkit`.

java.awt

CardLayout

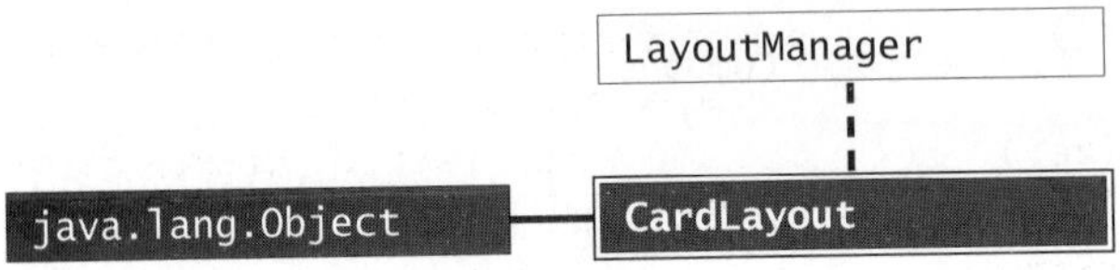

Syntax

```
public class CardLayout implements LayoutManager
```

Description

The card layout manager shows only one component in the container at a time; all other components in the container are hidden. The visible component, called the current component, is resized to take up the entire visible area of the container (that is, the container's bounds less space taken up by the container insets and card layout manager gaps).

Several methods allow you to change the current component. One of them is the `show()` method, which allows you to make any component current via its name. Unless you need to use the `show()` method, it is not necessary to name the components.

The card layout manager uses the visibility state of the components to keep track of the current component, so you should not directly change the visibility state of the components while they are under the control of a card layout manager.

Gaps

The card layout's gaps are really insets. The vertical gap specifies the space between the top and bottom edges of the container and the current component. The horizontal gap specifies the space between the left and right edges of the container and the current component.

MEMBER SUMMARY	
Constructor	
`CardLayout()`	Constructs a new `CardLayout` instance.
Show Methods	
`first()`	Makes the container's first component current.
`last()`	Makes the container's last component current.
`next()`	Makes the next component current.
`previous()`	Makes the previous component current.
`show()`	Makes a named component current.

MEMBER SUMMARY

LayoutManager Methods	
`addLayoutComponent()`	Associates a name with a component.
`layoutContainer()`	Lays out the container's components according to the settings of the layout manager.
`minimumLayoutSize()`	Calculates the minimum dimensions needed to lay out the components.
`preferredLayoutSize()`	Calculates the preferred dimensions needed to lay out the components.
`removeLayoutComponent()`	Removes a component from the layout.
Debugging Method	
`toString()`	Generates the string representation of this `CardLayout's` values.

Example

This example creates a panel with a card layout manager (see Figure 30). A number of buttons are added to the panel, each labeled with its position in the container. A row of buttons at the bottom controls the current component in the card layout.

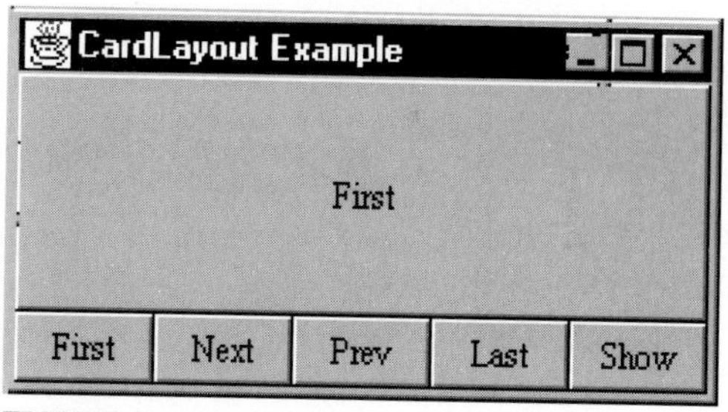

FIGURE 30 `CardLayout`

```
import java.awt.*;
class Main extends Frame {
    CardLayout cardLayout = new CardLayout();
    Panel cardCont = new Panel();
    Main() {
        super("CardLayout Example");

        cardCont.setLayout(cardLayout);
        cardCont.add("First", new Button("First"));
        cardCont.add("Second", new Button("Second"));
        cardCont.add("Third", new Button("Third"));
        cardCont.add("Show", new Button("Show"));
        cardCont.add("Last", new Button("Last"));
        add("Center", cardCont);

        Panel p = new Panel();
        p.setLayout(new GridLayout(1, 0));
        p.add(new Button("First"));
        p.add(new Button("Next"));
        p.add(new Button("Prev"));
        p.add(new Button("Last"));
```

```
            p.add(new Button("Show"));
            add("South", p);
            pack();
            show();
        }

        public boolean action(Event evt, Object arg) {
            if ("First".equals(arg)) {
                cardLayout.first(cardCont);
                return true;
            } else if ("Prev".equals(arg)) {
                cardLayout.previous(cardCont);
                return true;
            } else if ("Next".equals(arg)) {
                cardLayout.next(cardCont);
                return true;
            } else if ("Last".equals(arg)) {
                cardLayout.last(cardCont);
                return true;
            } else if ("Show".equals(arg)) {
                cardLayout.show(cardCont, (String)arg);
                return true;
            }
            return false;
        }

        public static void main(String args[]) {
            new Main();
        }
    }
```

addLayoutComponent()

PURPOSE Associates a name with a component.

SYNTAX `public void addLayoutComponent(String name, Component comp)`

DESCRIPTION This method associates the name `name` with the component `comp`. If another component in the same layout already has the same name, `name` becomes associated with `comp` and the old association is lost. The component that was previously associated with `name` can no longer be addressed by a name, but it can still be displayed using `first()`, `last()`, `next()`, and `previous()` methods.

PARAMETERS

`comp` The non-`null` named component that has just been added to the container.

`name` The non-`null` string specifying the name of the component.

EXAMPLE See `LayoutManager`.

CardLayout()

PURPOSE Constructs a new `CardLayout` instance.

SYNTAX
```
public CardLayout()
public CardLayout(int hgap, int vgap)
```

DESCRIPTION These constructors create a new card layout manager instance with the gaps `hgap` and `vgap`. If the gaps are not specified, they both default to 0.

The first component added to the container becomes the default current component. The component names are maintained in the card layout manager, so each container requires its own `CardLayout` instance. A container can be set to use a card layout only when the container has no components.

PARAMETERS

`hgap` A non-negative integer specifying the horizontal gap in pixels.

`vgap` A non-negative integer specifying the vertical gap in pixels.

EXAMPLE See the class example.

first()

PURPOSE Makes the container's first component current.

SYNTAX
```
public void first(Container cont)
```

DESCRIPTION The current component in the container `cont` is hidden and `cont`'s first component is made current. The component need not have a name.

PARAMETERS

`cont` The non-`null` container using this layout instance.

SEE ALSO `last()`, `next()`, `previous()`, `show()`.

EXAMPLE See the class example.

last()

PURPOSE Makes the container's last component current.

SYNTAX
```
public void last(Container cont)
```

DESCRIPTION The current component in the container `cont` is hidden and `cont`'s last component is made current. The component need not have a name.

PARAMETERS

`cont` The non-`null` container using this layout instance.

SEE ALSO `first()`, `next()`, `previous()`, `show()`.

EXAMPLE See the class example.

layoutContainer()

PURPOSE Lays out the container's components according to the settings of the layout manager.

SYNTAX `public void layoutContainer(Container cont)`

DESCRIPTION This method is called by the container when the layout is invalidated and needs to be redone. The current component in the container `cont` is resized to `cont`'s current dimensions, less the space used by the gaps and the container's insets.

PARAMETERS

`cont` The non-`null` container using this layout instance.

EXAMPLE See `LayoutManager`.

minimumLayoutSize()

PURPOSE Calculates the minimum dimensions needed to lay out the components.

SYNTAX `public Dimension minimumLayoutSize(Container cont)`

DESCRIPTION The minimum dimension is calculated by determining the minimum size of each component in the container `cont`. The minimum dimension of the layout is the maximum of these minimum dimensions plus the added space for the gaps and `cont`'s insets.

PARAMETERS

`cont` The non-`null` container using this layout instance.

RETURNS A non-`null` `Dimension` object containing the minimum size of the card layout.

SEE ALSO `Component.minimumSize()`.

EXAMPLE See `LayoutManager`.

next()

PURPOSE Makes the next component current.

SYNTAX `public void next(Container cont)`

DESCRIPTION The current component in the container `cont` is hidden and the component after the current component is made current. If the current component is already the last component, the method call is ignored. The component need not have a name.

PARAMETERS

`cont` The non-`null` container using this layout instance.

SEE ALSO `first()`, `last()`, `previous()`, `show()`.

EXAMPLE See the class example.

preferredLayoutSize()

PURPOSE Calculates the preferred dimensions needed to lay out the components.

SYNTAX `public Dimension preferredLayoutSize(Container cont)`

DESCRIPTION The preferred dimension is calculated by determining the preferred size of each component in the container `cont`. The preferred dimension of the layout is the maximum of these preferred dimensions plus the added space for the gaps and `cont`'s insets.

PARAMETERS

`cont` The non-`null` container using this layout instance.

RETURNS A non-`null` `Dimension` object containing the preferred size of the card layout.

SEE ALSO `Component.preferredSize()`.

EXAMPLE See `LayoutManager`.

previous()

PURPOSE Makes the previous component current.

SYNTAX `public void previous(Container cont)`

DESCRIPTION The current component in the container `cont` is hidden and the component before the current component is made current. If the current component is already the first component, the method call is ignored. The component need not have a name.

PARAMETERS

`cont` The non-`null` container using this layout instance.

SEE ALSO `first()`, `last()`, `next()`, `show()`.

EXAMPLE See the class example.

removeLayoutComponent()

PURPOSE Removes a component from the layout.

SYNTAX `public void removeLayoutComponent(Component comp)`

DESCRIPTION This method removes the component `comp` from the layout.

PARAMETERS

`comp` The non-`null` component about to be removed from the container.

EXAMPLE See `LayoutManager`.

show()

PURPOSE Makes a named component current.

SYNTAX `public void show(Container cont, String name)`

DESCRIPTION This method makes the component named by `name` the current component in the container `cont`. `name` is the component's name as declared via the `addLayout()` method call. This call is ignored if `name` does not name a component in `cont`.

PARAMETERS

`cont` The non-`null` container containing the component.
`name` The non-`null` string specifying the component's name.

EXAMPLE See the class example.

A B C D E F G H I J K L M N O P Q R S T U V W X Y Z

A B C D E F G H I J K L M N O P Q R S T U V W X Y Z

toString()

PURPOSE Generates a string representation of the layout manager's state.

SYNTAX `public String toString()`

DESCRIPTION The string representation contains the layout manager's class name and the size of the two gaps. This method returns this string representation.

This method is typically used for debugging.

RETURNS A non-`null` string representing the layout manager's state.

OVERRIDES `Object.toString()`.

EXAMPLE See `Object.toString()`.

java.lang

Character

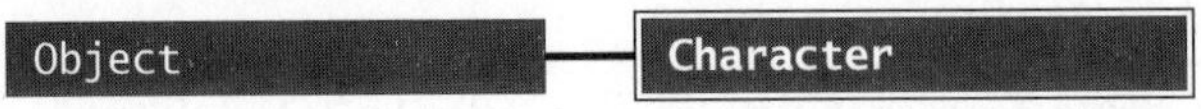

Syntax

```
public final class Character extends Object
```

Description

The `Character` class provides an object wrapper for Java `char` data values, which are Unicode characters. This wrapper allows characters to be passed to methods in Java class libraries that accept Java objects as parameters. In addition, the `Character` class provides methods that operate on characters, such as determining whether a character is uppercase or lowercase and converting a character to its numeric value.

```
Character charobj = new Character('A');
char[] str = new char[3];
  ...
str[2] = charobj.charValue();
  ...
if (charobj.equals(anotherObject))
    return 0;
```

Digit Characters

A *digit character* is a character that represents a digit in a number system. The *base*, or *radix*, of the number system determines the numeric value of a digit. For example, in radix 16, the numeric value of the digit character 'A' (or 'a') is 10.

The `Character` class provides methods that convert a digit character to and from its numeric value, as well as a method to determine whether a character is a digit character.

Character Case

Many Roman character sets support the notion of *uppercase* and *lowercase* characters. For example, 'A' and 'a' are uppercase and lowercase characters, respectively, in the ISO-LATIN-1 character set. In addition, Java supports the notion of *titlecase*, which some characters have for displaying the character as the first character in a title. There are only four characters in the Unicode character set with a true titlecase form; the uppercase forms are used as the titlecase for characters that have only uppercase and no titlecase forms.

The `Character` class provides methods for converting a character to and from the cases and for determining the case of a character.

A B C D E F G H I J K L M N O P Q R S T U V W X Y Z

Whitespace Characters

Whitespace characters are defined in Java to be blanks, tabs, line feed characters, form feed characters, and newline characters. The `Character` class contains a method to determine whether a character is a whitespace character by this definition.

MEMBER SUMMARY

Constructor	
`Character()`	Constructs a `Character` object using a `char` value.
Digit Character Fields and Methods	
`digit()`	Retrieves the numeric value of a digit character in the specified radix.
`forDigit()`	Retrieves the `char` value (digit character) of a number in the specified radix.
`isDigit()`	Determines whether a character is a digit character.
`MAX_RADIX`	The maximum radix available for converting a digit character to/from a number.
`MIN_RADIX`	The minimum radix available for converting a digit character to/from a number.
Case Methods	
`isLowerCase()`	Determines whether a character is lowercase.
`isTitleCase()`	Determines whether a character is a titlecase character.
`isUpperCase()`	Determines whether a character is uppercase.
`toLowerCase()`	Retrieves the lowercase form of a character.
`toTitleCase()`	Retrieves the titlecase form of a character.
`toUpperCase()`	Retrieves the uppercase form of a character.
Whitespace Method	
`isSpace()`	Determines whether a character is a whitespace character.
Character Value Fields and Methods	
`charValue()`	Retrieves the value of this object as a `char`.
`MAX_VALUE`	The maximum value that a `char` can have.
`MIN_VALUE`	The minimum value that a `char` can have.
Comparison Methods	
`equals()`	Compares this object with another object for equality.
`isDefined()`	Determines whether a character is defined in Unicode.
`isJavaLetter()`	Determines whether a character is a valid first character in a Java identifier.
`isJavaLetterOrDigit()`	Determines whether a character is a valid first character in a Java identifier or a digit character.

Continued

MEMBER SUMMARY	
`isLetter()`	Determines whether a character is a letter.
`isLetterOrDigit()`	Determines whether a character is a letter or a digit.
General Methods	
`hashCode()`	Computes the hash code for this object.
`toString()`	Generates the string representation of this object.

Character()

PURPOSE Constructs a `Character` object using a `char` value.

SYNTAX `public Character(char ch)`

DESCRIPTION This constructor creates a `Character` object using the `char` value `ch`.

PARAMETERS

`ch` The value that the `Character` object will have.

EXAMPLE

```
Character newch = new Character('A');
```

charValue()

PURPOSE Retrieves the value of this object as a `char`.

SYNTAX `public char charValue()`

RETURNS The `char` value of this object.

EXAMPLE

```
Character charobj = new Character('A');
char ch = charobj.charValue(); // returns ('A');
```

digit()

PURPOSE Retrieves the numeric value of a digit character in the specified radix.

SYNTAX `public static int digit(char ch, int radix)`

DESCRIPTION This method returns the numeric value of the given digit character `ch` using the specified radix `radix`. If `radix` is not a valid radix or if `ch` is not a valid digit character in radix `radix`, this method returns `-1`. This method is the inverse of `forDigit()`.

PARAMETERS

`ch` The digit character for which to get the numeric value.

`radix` The radix of the number system to use.

RETURNS The numeric value of `ch` in radix `radix`. This method returns `-1` if `ch` is not a valid digit character in radix `radix`.

SEE ALSO `forDigit()`, `isDigit()`, `MAX_RADIX`, `MIN_RADIX`.

EXAMPLE

```
// Given a char array and radix, return its numeric value
// Assume array contains only valid digits
static int charsToNumber(char[] str, int radix) {
    int number = 0;
    for (int magnitude = 1, i = str.length - 1;
         i >= 0;
         magnitude *= radix, i--)
        number += (Character.digit(str[i], radix)) * magnitude;
    return number;
}
```

equals()

PURPOSE Compares this object with another object for equality.

SYNTAX `public boolean equals(Object obj)`

DESCRIPTION This method compares the `char` value of this object against that of the object `obj`. It returns `true` if the two values are equal. It returns `false` if the two values are not equal or if `obj` either is `null` or is not a `Character` object.

PARAMETERS

`object` The object against which this object will be compared.

RETURNS `true` if `obj` has the same `char` value as this object; `false` otherwise.

OVERRIDES `Object.equals()`.

EXAMPLE

```
Character c1 = new Character('\u23f3');
Character c2 = new Character('A');
if (c1.equals(c2))
        ...
```

A B C D E F G H I J K L M N O P Q R S T U V W X Y Z

A B C D E F G H I J K L M N O P Q R S T U V W X Y Z

forDigit()

PURPOSE Retrieves the char value (digit character) of a number in the specified radix.

SYNTAX `public static char forDigit(int digit, int radix)`

DESCRIPTION This method returns the digit character of the given number `digit` in the specified radix, `radix`. If `digit` is not a valid digit in radix `radix`, the null character ('\0') is returned. This method is the inverse of `digit()`.

PARAMETERS

`digit` The number for which to generate the digit character.

`radix` The radix of the number system to use.

RETURNS The `char` value of the digit character. If `digit` or `radix` are invalid, the `null` character ('\0') is returned.

SEE ALSO `digit()`, `isDigit()`, `MAX_RADIX`, `MIN_RADIX`.

EXAMPLE

```
char ch = Character.forDigit(10, 16); // returns 'A'
```

hashCode()

PURPOSE Computes the hash code for this object.

SYNTAX `public int hashCode()`

DESCRIPTION This method returns the hash code for a `Character` object. The hash code of a `Character` object is calculated using its `char` value. Two `Character` objects with the same `char` values have the same hash code.

RETURNS An `int` representing this object's hash code.

OVERRIDES `Object.hashCode()`.

SEE ALSO `Hashtable`.

EXAMPLE

```
int[] hits = new hits[1023];
Character cobj = new Character('A');
int hashval = cobj.hashCode();          // generate hash code
++hits[Math.abs(hashval%hits.length)];  // count hits
```

isDefined()

PURPOSE Determines whether a character is defined in Unicode.

SYNTAX `public static boolean isDefined(char ch)`

DESCRIPTION This method returns `true` if `ch` is defined in Unicode. Some characters in the range `MIN_VALUE` and `MAX_VALUE` do not have a meaning in Unicode.

PARAMETERS

`ch` The character to check.

RETURNS `true` if `ch` is defined in Unicode; `false` otherwise.

SEE ALSO `isDigit()`, `isLetter()`, `isLetterOrDigit()`, `isUpperCase()`, `isLowerCase()`, `isTitleCase()`, `MAX_VALUE`, `MIN_VALUE`.

EXAMPLE See `isLetter()`.

isDigit()

PURPOSE Determines whether a character is a digit character.

SYNTAX `public static boolean isDigit(char ch)`

DESCRIPTION This method determines whether the character `ch` is a digit character. A digit character is one of the ISO-LATIN-1 characters 0 to 9 or one of the Unicode characters representing digits in other languages (such as Arabic-Indic digits).

PARAMETERS

`ch` The character being checked.

RETURNS `true` if `ch` is a digit character; `false` otherwise.

SEE ALSO `isJavaLetterOrDigit()`.

EXAMPLE

```
if (Character.isDigit(ch))
    number += Character.digit(ch, 10);
```

isJavaLetter()

PURPOSE Determines whether a character is valid as the first character in a Java identifier.

SYNTAX `public static boolean isJavaLetter(char ch)`

DESCRIPTION This method determines whether the character `ch` is valid as the first character in a Java identifier. A valid first character in a Java identifier is one of `isLetter(ch)` or '$' or '_'.

PARAMETERS

`ch` The character being checked.

RETURNS `true` if `ch` is valid as the first character in a Java identifier; `false` otherwise.

SEE ALSO `isJavaLetterOrDigit()`, `isLetter()`.

EXAMPLE This example defines a function that checks whether a string is a valid Java identifier.

```
class JChar {
    public static boolean validJavaIdentifier(String str) {
        char[] buf = new char[str.length()];
        str.getChars(0, buf.length, buf, 0);

        if (!Character.isJavaLetter(buf[0]))
            return false;

        for (int i = 1; i < buf.length; i++) {
            if (!Character.isJavaLetterOrDigit(buf[i]))
                return false;
        }
        return true;
    }

    public static void main(String[] args) {
        for (int i = 0; i < args.length; i++)
            System.out.println(args[i] + ":" +
                (validJavaIdentifier(args[i]) ? "OK" : "Invalid"));
    }
}
```

isJavaLetterOrDigit()

PURPOSE Determines whether a character is valid as the first character in a Java identifier or a digit character.

SYNTAX `public static boolean isJavaLetter(char ch)`

DESCRIPTION This method determines whether the character `ch` is valid as the first character in a Java identifier. Such a character is one of `isLetterOrDigit(ch)` or '$' or '_'.

PARAMETERS

ch The character being checked.

RETURNS true if ch is valid as the first character in a Java identifier or is a digit character; false otherwise.

SEE ALSO isDigit(), isJavaLetter(), isLetter(), isLetterOrDigit().

EXAMPLE See isJavaLetter().

isLetter()

PURPOSE Determines whether a character is a letter.

SYNTAX `public static boolean isLetter(char ch)`

DESCRIPTION This method determines whether the character ch is a letter. A letter is defined as one of the ISO-LATIN-1 characters 'a' to 'z', 'A' to 'Z', or one of the Unicode characters representing letters in other languages (such as extended Latin sets and Basic Arabic). Although letters derived from Roman character sets have the notion of uppercase and lowercase, some letters, such as Asian or Arabic characters, do not.

PARAMETERS

ch The character being checked.

RETURNS true if ch is a letter; false otherwise.

SEE ALSO isDigit(), isJavaLetter(), isJavaLetterOrDigit(), isLetterOrDigit(), isLowerCase(), isTitleCase(), isUpperCase().

EXAMPLE This example defines a function that prints out information about a particular character. It demonstrates the use of isDefined(), isLowerCase(), isUpperCase(), isTitleCase(), isLetter(), isDigit(), and isSpace().

```
class WhatCase {
    public static void charInfo(char ch) {
        System.out.print("'" + ch + "': ");
        if (!Character.isDefined(ch)) {
            System.out.println("**");
            return;
        }
        // case
        if (Character.isLowerCase(ch))
            System.out.print('l');
        else if (Character.isUpperCase(ch))
            System.out.print('u');
        else if (Character.isTitleCase(ch))
            System.out.print('t');
```

A B C D E F G H I J K L M N O P Q R S T U V W X Y Z

```
            else
                System.out.print('-');

            // letter or digit or space
            if (Character.isLetter(ch))
                System.out.println('l');
            else if (Character.isDigit(ch))
                System.out.println('d');
            else if (Character.isSpace(ch))
                System.out.println('s');
            else System.out.print('-');
            System.out.println();
        }

        public static void main(String[] args) {
            char[] buf = {'a', 'b', 'T', '5', '\t'};
            for (int i = 0; i < buf.length; i++)
                charInfo(buf[i]);
        }
    }
```

isLetterOrDigit()

PURPOSE Determines whether a character is a letter or a digit.

SYNTAX `public static boolean isLetterOrDigit(char ch)`

DESCRIPTION This method determines whether the character `ch` is a letter or a digit character. It returns `true` if `ch` is a letter or a digit character; `false` otherwise.

PARAMETERS

`ch` The character being checked.

RETURNS `true` if `ch` is a letter or a digit; false otherwise.

SEE ALSO `isDigit()`, `isJavaLetter()`, `isJavaLetterOrDigit()`, `isLetter()`.

EXAMPLE See similar usage of `isLetter()` in `isLetter()` example.

isLowerCase()

PURPOSE Determines whether a character is lowercase.

SYNTAX `public static boolean isLowerCase(char ch)`

DESCRIPTION This method determines whether the character `ch` is lowercase. A lowercase character is one of 'a' to 'z' or one of the characters with Unicode value in the inclusive range \u00df to \u00ff. This method returns `true` if `ch` is lowercase and `false` otherwise.

PARAMETERS

`ch` The character being tested.

RETURNS `true` if `ch` is a lowercase character; `false` otherwise.

SEE ALSO `isTitleCase()`, `isUpperCase()`, `toLowerCase()`.

EXAMPLE See also `isLetter()` example.

```
if (Character.isLowerCase(ch))
    return (Character.toUpperCase(ch));
```

isSpace()

PURPOSE Determines whether a character is a whitespace character.

SYNTAX `public static boolean isSpace(char ch)`

DESCRIPTION A whitespace character is either a blank (' '), tab character ('\t'), form feed character ('\f'), return character ('\r'), or newline character ('\n'). This method returns whether the character `ch` is one of these whitespace characters.

PARAMETERS

`ch` The character being tested.

RETURNS `true` if `ch` is a whitespace character; `false` otherwise.

EXAMPLE

```
// Returns the number of white space characters in char array
static int countWhiteSpaces(char[] str) {
    int count = 0;
    for (int i = 0; i < str.length; i++)
        if (Character.isSpace(str[i]))
              ++count;
    return (count);
}
```

isTitleCase()

PURPOSE Determines whether a character is a titlecase character.

SYNTAX `public static boolean isTitleCase(char ch)`

DESCRIPTION This method determines whether the character `ch` is a titlecase character. In Unicode, there are only 4 characters that are titlecase characters: `\u01c5 \u01c8 \u01cb \u01f2`

This method returns `true` if `ch` is one of these and `false` otherwise.

PARAMETERS

`ch` The character being checked.

RETURNS `true` if `ch` is a titlecase character; `false` otherwise.

SEE ALSO `isLowerCase()`, `isUpperCase()`, `toTitleCase()`, `toUpperCase()`.

EXAMPLE See `isLetter()`.

isUpperCase()

PURPOSE Determines whether a character is uppercase.

SYNTAX `public static boolean isUpperCase(char ch)`

DESCRIPTION This method determines whether the character `ch` is an uppercase character. An uppercase character is one of 'A' to 'Z' and/or one of the characters with Unicode value in the inclusive range `\u00c0` and `\u00de`. This method returns `true` if `ch` is uppercase and `false` otherwise.

PARAMETERS

`ch` The character being checked.

RETURNS `true` if `ch` is an uppercase character; `false` otherwise.

SEE ALSO `isLowerCase()`, `isTitleCase()`, `toUpperCase()`.

EXAMPLE

```
if (Character.isUpperCase(ch))
    return (Character.toLowerCase(ch));
```

MAX_RADIX

PURPOSE The maximum radix available for converting a digit character to/from a number.

SYNTAX `public static final int MAX_RADIX`

DESCRIPTION This constant is the maximum radix available for conversion of a digit character or a string consisting of digit characters to and from its numeric value. The value of this field is 36.

SEE ALSO `digit()`, `forDigit()`, `Integer.toString()`, `MIN_RADIX`.

EXAMPLE

```
if (radix >= Character.MIN_RADIX &&
    radix <= Character.MAX_RADIX)
    number = Character.digit(ch, radix);
```

MAX_VALUE

PURPOSE The maximum value that a `char` can have.

SYNTAX `public static final char MAX_VALUE`

DESCRIPTION A `char` value in Java represents a Unicode character. `MAX_VALUE` represents the maximum value that a `char` can have, which is `\uffff`.

SEE ALSO `MIN_VALUE`.

EXAMPLE

```
char ch = 'a';
        ...
if (ch <= Character.MAX_VALUE && ch >= Character.MIN_VALUE)
        ...
```

MIN_RADIX

PURPOSE The minimum radix available for converting a digit character to/from a number.

SYNTAX `public static final int MIN_RADIX`

DESCRIPTION This constant is the minimum radix available for conversion of a digit character, or a string consisting of digit characters to and from its numeric value. The value of this field is 2.

SEE ALSO `digit()`, `forDigit()`, `Integer.toString()`, `MAX_RADIX`.

EXAMPLE See `MAX_RADIX`.

MIN_VALUE

PURPOSE The minimum value that a char can have.

SYNTAX `public static final char MIN_VALUE`

DESCRIPTION A char value in Java represents a Unicode character. MIN_VALUE represents the minimum value that a char can have, which is \u0000.

SEE ALSO MAX_VALUE.

EXAMPLE See MAX_VALUE.

toLowerCase()

PURPOSE Retrieves the lowercase form of a character.

SYNTAX `public static char toLowerCase(char ch)`

DESCRIPTION This method returns the lowercase form of ch. If ch does not have a lowercase form, ch is returned unmodified.

PARAMETERS

ch The character for which to get the lowercase form.

RETURNS The lowercase form of ch if it has one; ch otherwise.

SEE ALSO isLowerCase(), toTitleCase(), toUpperCase().

EXAMPLE See also the toTitleCase() example.

```
// Make all characters in the char array 'name' lowercase
for (int i = 0; i < name.length; i++)
    name[i] = Character.toLowerCase(name[i]);
```

toString()

PURPOSE Generates the string representation of this object.

SYNTAX `public String toString()`

DESCRIPTION This method returns the string representation of a Character object. The string representation of a Character object is its char value.

OVERRIDES Object.toString().

EXAMPLE

```
Character ch = new Character('A');
String chstr = ch.toString();
System.out.println("Value of ch is " + chstr);
```

toTitleCase()

PURPOSE Retrieves the titlecase form of a character.

SYNTAX `public static char toTitleCase(char ch)`

DESCRIPTION This method returns the titlecase form of `ch`. If `ch` does not have a true title-case form, its uppercase form is returned. If `ch` has no uppercase form, `ch` is returned unmodified.

PARAMETERS

`ch` The character for which to get the titlecase form.

RETURNS The titlecase form of `ch` if it has one; `ch` otherwise.

SEE ALSO `isTitleCase()`, `toLowerCase()`, `toUpperCase()`.

EXAMPLE The following example shows the use of `toTitleCase()` in returning the title case form of a string. It capitalizes the first character of each word.

EXAMPLE

```
class CMain {
    public static String makeTitle(String name) {
        char[] buf = new char[name.length()];
        boolean title = true;
        name.getChars(0, name.length(), buf, 0);

        // Capitalize first letter of each word

        for (int i = 0; i < buf.length; i++) {
            if (title)
                buf[i] = Character.toTitleCase(buf[i]);
            else
                buf[i] = Character.toLowerCase(buf[i]);
            title = Character.isSpace(buf[i]);
        }
        return (new String(buf));
    }
```

```
        public static void main(String[] args) {
            if (args.length == 1)
                System.out.println(makeTitle(args[0]));
            else
                System.out.println(makeTitle("this is a tEst"));
        }
    }
```

toUpperCase()

PURPOSE Retrieves the uppercase form of a character.

SYNTAX `public static char toUpperCase(char ch)`

DESCRIPTION This method returns the uppercase form of `ch`. If `ch` does not have an uppercase form, `ch` is returned unmodified.

PARAMETERS

`ch` The character for which to get the uppercase form.

RETURNS The uppercase form of `ch` if it has one; `ch` otherwise.

SEE ALSO `isUpperCase()`, `toLowerCase()`, `toTitleCase()`.

EXAMPLE

```
    // Make all characters in the char array 'name' uppercase
    for (int i = 0; i < name.length; i++)
        name[i] = Character.toUpperCase(name[i]);
```

java.awt

Checkbox

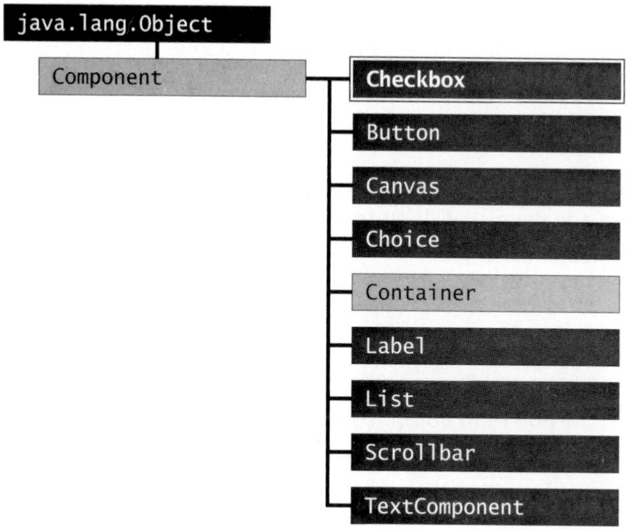

Syntax

```
public class Checkbox extends Component
```

Description

The checkbox is a component that maintains and displays a check state that can be either on or off. The check state can be changed by either the user or the program. A checkbox is typically used to indicate a two-value choice in an application. For example, in a mail application you may or may not want an audible signal of new mail. A checkbox with the label "Play sound for new mail" would be a typical way to display the current preference and to allow the user to change it.

FIGURE 31 **Checkbox**

Figure 31 shows a checkbox component with the label "Checkbox"; the checkbox is set to *on*.

B C D E F G H I J K L M N O P Q R S T U V W X Y Z

Checkbox Groups

Two or more checkbox boxes can be grouped together so that at most one of the checkboxes in the group is set to *on*. That checkbox which is called the current checkbox. Figure 32 shows a checkbox group containing four checkboxes. See the `CheckboxGroup` class for more information about checkbox groups.

FIGURE 32 `CheckboxGroup`

Events

A checkbox generates an action event whenever it is clicked.

See the `Event` class for details on how to filter or handle events. Table 6 describes how a checkbox fills the fields in the event.

TABLE 6 `Checkbox` Action Event

`arg`	The `Boolean` object containing the checkbox's new check state.
`clickCount`	Not used.
`id`	`Event.ACTION`.
`key`	Not used.
`modifiers`	The state of the modifier keys when the component was clicked.
`target`	A reference to the component that generated this event.
`when`	The time, in milliseconds, that the event was generated.
`x`	*x*-coordinate of the component in pixels.
`y`	*y*-coordinate of the component in pixels.

A grouped checkbox generates an action event whenever it is clicked. The event is generated only by the new current checkbox. The previous current checkbox does not generate an event indicating that it has been turned off. If the current checkbox is clicked, an event is generated because the modifiers may have changed.

See the `Event` class for details on how to filter or handle events. Table 7 describes how a grouped checkbox fills the fields in the event.

TABLE 7 Grouped Checkbox Action Event

`arg`	The `Boolean` object containing the value `true`.
`clickCount`	Not used.
`id`	`Event.ACTION`.
`key`	Not used.
`modifiers`	The state of the modifier keys when the component was clicked.
`target`	A reference to the component that generated this event.
`when`	The time, in milliseconds, that the event was generated.
`x`	*x*-coordinate of the component in pixels.
`y`	*y*-coordinate of the component in pixels.

MEMBER SUMMARY

Constructor

`Checkbox()`	Constructs a new `Checkbox` instance.

Checkbox Group Methods

`getCheckboxGroup()`	Retrieves the checkbox's checkbox group.
`setCheckboxGroup()`	Sets the checkbox's checkbox group to the specified group.

Property Methods

`getLabel()`	Retrieves the checkbox's label.
`getState()`	Retrieves the check state of the checkbox.
`setLabel()`	Sets the checkbox's label.
`setState()`	Sets the checkbox's check state.

Peer Method

`addNotify()`	Creates the checkbox's peer.

Debugging Method

`paramString()`	Generates a string representation of the checkbox's state.

Example

For a simple example using a checkbox, see the `Checkbox()` constructor. This is a more elaborate example of a program that displays a set of options that can be applied to the purchase of a car. As more options are enabled, the price of the car increases. See Figure 33.

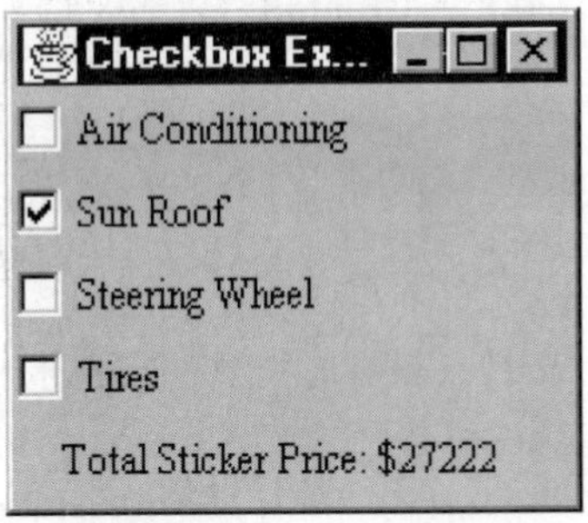

FIGURE 33 Use of Checkbox for Multiple Options

```
import java.awt.*;
class Main extends Frame {
    Checkbox cbAC = new Checkbox("Air Conditioning");
    Checkbox cbSR = new Checkbox("Sun Roof");
    Checkbox cbSW = new Checkbox("Steering Wheel");
    Checkbox cbTR = new Checkbox("Tires");
    Label status = new Label();

    Main() {
        super("Checkbox Example");
        Panel gridPanel = new Panel();

        gridPanel.setLayout(new GridLayout(0, 1));
        gridPanel.add(cbAC);
        gridPanel.add(cbSR);
        gridPanel.add(cbSW);
        gridPanel.add(cbTR);
        add("Center", gridPanel);

        computeTotal();
        add("South", status);
        pack();
        show();
    }

    public boolean action(Event evt, Object what) {
        computeTotal();
        return true;
    }

    void computeTotal() {
        int total = 25000;
        if (cbAC.getState()) total += 510;
        if (cbSR.getState()) total += 2222;
        if (cbSW.getState()) total += 150;
        if (cbTR.getState()) total += 320;
        status.setText("Total Sticker Price: $" + total);
    }
```

```
        static public void main(String[] args) {
            new Main();
        }
    }
```

addNotify()

PURPOSE Creates the checkbox's peer.

SYNTAX `public synchronized void addNotify()`

DESCRIPTION This method creates the peer if it does not yet exist. The peer is created by calling the `Toolkit.createCheckbox()` method.

This method should never be called directly. It is normally called by the parent.

OVERRIDES `Component.addNotify()`.

SEE ALSO `Component`, `Toolkit`.

EXAMPLE See `Component.show()`.

Checkbox()

PURPOSE Constructs a new `Checkbox` instance.

SYNTAX

```
public Checkbox()
public Checkbox(String label)
public Checkbox(String label, CheckboxGroup group, boolean state)
```

DESCRIPTION These three forms of the constructor create a new visible checkbox component with the label `label`, checkbox group `group`, and initial check state `state`. A `null` label is the same as `"  "`. If the label is not specified, it defaults to `null`. If `state` is not specified, it defaults to `false`. If `group` is `null`, the checkbox will not be included in any checkbox group. If `group` is not specified, it defaults to `null`.

PARAMETERS

`group` The checkbox group in which to include the new checkbox. May be `null`.

`label` A string specifying the label on the checkbox. May be `null`.

`state` A `boolean` specifying the checkbox's initial check state.

EXAMPLE This simple example creates a checkbox with the label "Checkbox" and prints the current state of the checkbox each time it is clicked. See Figure 34.

FIGURE 34 `Checkbox()`

```
import java.awt.*;
class Main extends Frame {
    Checkbox cb = new Checkbox("Checkbox");

    Main() {
        super("Checkbox Example");
        add("North", cb);
        pack();
        show();
    }

    public boolean action(Event evt, Object arg) {
        if (evt.target == cb) {
            System.out.println("checkbox: "+((Boolean)arg).
                booleanValue());
        }
        return true;
    }

    static public void main(String[] args) {
        new Main();
    }
}
```

getCheckboxGroup()

PURPOSE Retrieves the checkbox's checkbox group.

SYNTAX `public CheckboxGroup getCheckboxGroup()`

DESCRIPTION If the return value is `null`, the checkbox is not a group checkbox.

RETURNS The checkbox's checkbox group. The return value may be `null`, which means the checkbox is not in a checkbox group.

SEE ALSO `setCheckboxGroup()`.

EXAMPLE See `setCheckboxGroup()`.

getLabel()

PURPOSE Retrieves the checkbox's label.

SYNTAX `public String getLabel()`

RETURNS A string containing the checkbox's label. The result value may be `null`.

SEE ALSO `setLabel()`.

EXAMPLE See `setLabel()`.

getState()

PURPOSE Retrieves the check state of the checkbox.

SYNTAX `public boolean getState()`

RETURNS `true` if the check state is set to *on*; `false` otherwise.

SEE ALSO `setState()`.

EXAMPLE This example creates a checkbox and a text area. If the checkbox is set to *off*, the text area behaves normally. If the checkbox is set to *on*, all characters typed in the text area are converted to uppercase. See Figure 35.

FIGURE 35 **`Checkbox.getState()`**

```
import java.awt.*;
class Main extends Frame {
    Checkbox cb = new Checkbox("Upper Case");
    TextArea ta = new TextArea(10, 40);

    Main() {
        super("getState Example");
        add("North", cb);
        add("Center", ta);
        pack();
        show();
    }

    public boolean keyDown(Event evt, int key) {
        char ch = (char)key;

        if (evt.target == ta && cb.getState()
                && Character.isLowerCase(ch)) {
            ch = Character.toUpperCase(ch);
            ta.insertText(String.valueOf(ch), ta.getSelectionEnd());
            return true;
```

A B C D E F G H I J K L M N O P Q R S T U V W X Y Z

```
            }
            return false;
        }

        static public void main(String[] args) {
            new Main();
        }
    }
```

paramString()

PURPOSE Generates a string representation of the checkbox's state.

SYNTAX `protected String paramString()`

DESCRIPTION The returned string includes the checkbox's label and check state. A subclass of this class should override this method and return a concatenation of its state with the results of `super.paramString()`. This method is called by the `toString()` method and is typically used for debugging.

RETURNS A non-`null` string representing the checkbox's state.

OVERRIDES `Component.paramString()`.

SEE ALSO `toString()`.

EXAMPLE See `Component.paramString()`.

setCheckboxGroup()

PURPOSE Sets the checkbox's checkbox group.

SYNTAX `public void setCheckboxGroup(CheckboxGroup group)`

DESCRIPTION This method is used to change a checkbox's checkbox group. It is not used very often, as checkboxes do not typically change groups after they are created. The checkbox group of a checkbox is typically known at the time the checkbox is created, so it is supplied to the checkbox constructor method.

PARAMETERS

`group` The checkbox's new checkbox group. A value of `null` removes the checkbox from its current group.

SEE ALSO `getCheckboxGroup()`.

A B C D E F G H I J K L M N O P Q R S T U V W X Y Z

EXAMPLE This example creates two checkbox groups called "Left" and "Right." By using the choice component at the bottom, the user can make the checkbox at the top part of either group or of no group. See Figure 36.

FIGURE 36 `Checkbox.setCheckboxGroup()`

```
import java.awt.*;
class Main extends Frame {
    CheckboxGroup cgLeft = new CheckboxGroup();
    CheckboxGroup cgRight = new CheckboxGroup();
    Choice choice = new Choice();
    Checkbox cb = new Checkbox("Left", cgLeft, true);

    Main() {
        super("setCheckboxGroup Example");
        Panel p = new Panel();

        add("North", cb);

        p.setLayout(new GridLayout(0, 1));
        p.add(new Checkbox("Left", cgLeft, false));
        p.add(new Checkbox("Left", cgLeft, false));
        add("West", p);

        p = new Panel();
        p.setLayout(new GridLayout(0, 1));
        p.add(new Checkbox("Right", cgRight, false));
        p.add(new Checkbox("Right", cgRight, false));
        add("East", p);

        choice.addItem("None");
        choice.addItem("Left");
        choice.addItem("Right");
        choice.select("Left");
        add("South", choice);

        pack();
        show();
    }

    public boolean action(Event evt, Object what) {
        if (evt.target instanceof Choice) {
            cb.setLabel((String)what);
            if ("None".equals(what)) {
                cb.setCheckboxGroup(null);
            } else if ("Left".equals(what)) {
                cb.setCheckboxGroup(cgLeft);
```

```
                } else if ("Right".equals(what)) {
                    cb.setCheckboxGroup(cgRight);
                }
                return true;
            }
            return false;
        }

        static public void main(String[] args) {
            new Main();
        }
    }
```

setLabel()

PURPOSE Sets the menu item's label.

SYNTAX `public void setLabel(String label)`

DESCRIPTION Note that the minimum and preferred sizes of the checkbox may change, so it may be necessary to resize the checkbox. The example shows how to cause the checkbox's parent to resize the checkbox.

PARAMETERS

`label` The non-`null` string specifying the checkbox's new label.

SEE ALSO `getLabel()`.

EXAMPLE This example creates a checkbox and a text field. Pressing `Return` in the text field causes the checkbox label to be set to the contents of the text field. When the label changes, so does its minimum size. This example also shows how to cause the checkbox's parent to properly resize the checkbox.

FIGURE 37 `Checkbox.setLabel()`

The canvas to the right of the checkbox is there to force the checkbox to be as narrow as possible. See Figure 37.

```
import java.awt.*;
class Main extends Frame {
    Checkbox cb = new Checkbox("Checkbox");
    TextField tf = new TextField(40);

    Main() {
        super("setLabel Example");
        add("Center", new Canvas());
```

```
        add(“West”, cb);
        add(“South”, tf);
        tf.setText(cb.getLabel());        //init with current label
        pack();
        show();
    }

    public boolean action(Event evt, Object what) {
        if (evt.target == tf) {
            cb.setLabel(tf.getText());

      //the size has changed so the parent must be invalidated
      //and re-laid out.
            cb.getParent().invalidate();
            cb.getParent().validate();
            return true;
        }
        return false;
    }

    static public void main(String[] args) {
        new Main();
    }
}
```

setState()

PURPOSE Sets the checkbox's check state.

SYNTAX `public void setState(boolean state)`

DESCRIPTION The method call is ignored when this is both a group checkbox and the current checkbox.

PARAMETERS

`state` If `true`, the checkbox's check state is set to on; otherwise it is set to off.

SEE ALSO `getState()`.

EXAMPLE This example creates a checkbox and a checkbox menu item and synchronizes their check states: if the checkbox is set to *on*, so is the checkbox menu item. See Figure 38.

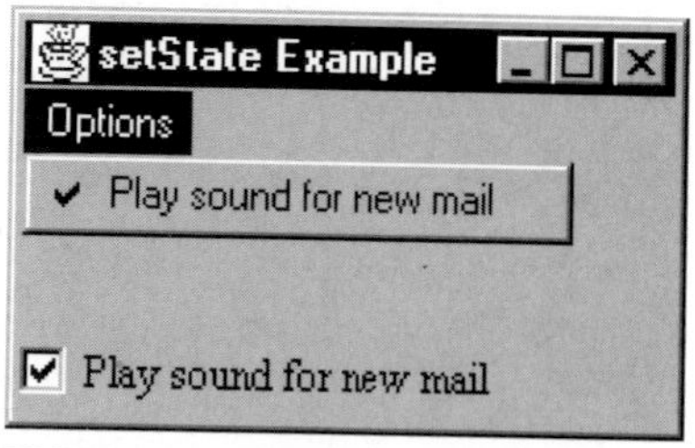

FIGURE 38 `Checkbox.setState()`

```
import java.awt.*;
class Main extends Frame {
    CheckboxMenuItem mi =
            new CheckboxMenuItem("Play sound for new mail");
    Checkbox cb = new Checkbox("Play sound for new mail");

    Main() {
        super("setState Example");
        MenuBar mb = new MenuBar();
        Menu m = new Menu("Options");

        m.add(mi);
        mb.add(m);
        setMenuBar(mb);
        add("South", cb);
        pack();
        show();
    }

    public boolean action(Event evt, Object what) {
        if (evt.target == mi) {
            cb.setState(mi.getState());
        } else {
            mi.setState(cb.getState());
        }
        // playSoundForNewMail();
        return true;
    }

    static public void main(String[] args) {
        new Main();
    }
}
```

CheckboxGroup

java.lang.Object — CheckboxGroup

Syntax

```
public class CheckboxGroup
```

Description

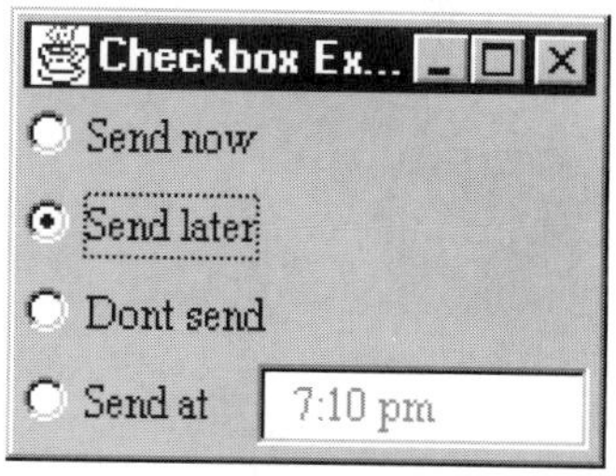

FIGURE 39 CheckboxGroup

The checkbox group is used to group checkbox components; it is not an AWT component. In a checkbox group, at most one checkbox is in the *on* state. This checkbox is called the *current* checkbox. Selecting any of the other checkboxes in the group causes that checkbox to become current and all other checkboxes in the group to be automatically set to *off*. Figure 39 shows a checkbox group that contains four checkboxes; the "Send later" checkbox is set to on. See the `Checkbox` class for more information about checkboxes.

It is possible that none of the checkboxes in the group are set to on. This can happen in one of two ways:

1. If none of the checkboxes that are added to the group are set to on.
2. If the current checkbox in the group is removed from the group.

Checkbox Group versus Choice Component

The choice component is similar to the checkbox group in that it lets the user choose from a fixed set of items (see the `Choice` class). Following are two design guidelines to consider when deciding between the checkbox group and the choice component. As with all user interface "principles," these guidelines are intended to summarize the issues and not mandate your design.

1. The larger the number of items, the more appropriate the choice component becomes. You should probably use a choice component if you have five or more items.
2. If a group of one or more components is related to one particular item and is therefore enabled only if that item is selected, a checkbox group might be appropriate.

MEMBER SUMMARY

Constructor

`CheckboxGroup()`	Constructs a new `CheckboxGroup` instance.

The Current Checkbox Methods

`getCurrent()`	Retrieves the current checkbox.
`setCurrent()`	Sets the current checkbox.

Debugging Method

`toString()`	Generates a string representation of the checkbox group's state.

Example

This example creates a checkbox group and a collection of colored canvases. Clicking a checkbox causes its associated color canvas to be selected. Also, clicking a colored canvas causes its associated checkbox to be current. See Figure 40.

FIGURE 40 **Use of CheckboxGroup for Exclusive Options**

```
import java.awt.*;
class Main extends Frame {
    Color[] cbColor = {Color.red, Color.green, Color.blue};
    String[] cbName = {"Red", "Green", "Blue"};
    MainCanvas[] cbCanvas = new MainCanvas[3];
    CheckboxGroup cgroup = new CheckboxGroup();

    Main() {
        super("CheckboxGroup Example");
        Panel p = new Panel(), colorPanel = new Panel();

        p.setLayout(new GridLayout(0, 1));
        colorPanel.setLayout(new GridLayout(1, 0));
        for (int i=0; i<cbColor.length; i++) {
            Checkbox cb = new Checkbox(cbName[i], cgroup, i == 0);
            p.add(cb);
            colorPanel.add(cbCanvas[i] = new MainCanvas(cbColor[i],
                cb));
            cbCanvas[i].resize(70, 70);
        }
        add("West", p);
```

```
        add("Center", colorPanel);
        pack();
        show();
    }

    public boolean action(Event evt, Object what) {
        if (evt.target instanceof Checkbox) {
            for (int i=0; i<cbCanvas.length; i++) {
                cbCanvas[i].repaint();
            }
            return true;
        }
        return false;
    }

    static public void main(String[] args) {
        new Main();
    }
}

class MainCanvas extends Canvas {
    Checkbox cb;

    MainCanvas(Color color, Checkbox cb) {
        setBackground(color);
        this.cb = cb;
    }

    public boolean mouseDown(Event evt, int x, int y) {
        cb.getCheckboxGroup().setCurrent(cb);
        // repaint all sibling canvases.
        for (int i=0; i<getParent().countComponents(); i++) {
            getParent().getComponent(i).repaint();
        }
        return true;
    }

    public void paint(Graphics g) {
        if (cb.getCheckboxGroup().getCurrent() == cb) {
            Dimension d = size();
            g.setColor(Color.black);
            g.fillOval(d.width/3, d.height/3, d.width/3, d.height/3);
        }
    }
}
```

CheckboxGroup()

PURPOSE Constructs a new CheckboxGroup instance.

SYNTAX `public CheckboxGroup()`

EXAMPLE This example creates a checkbox group that has three buttons. When a checkbox is clicked, it prints out the new state of the checkbox. See Figure 41.

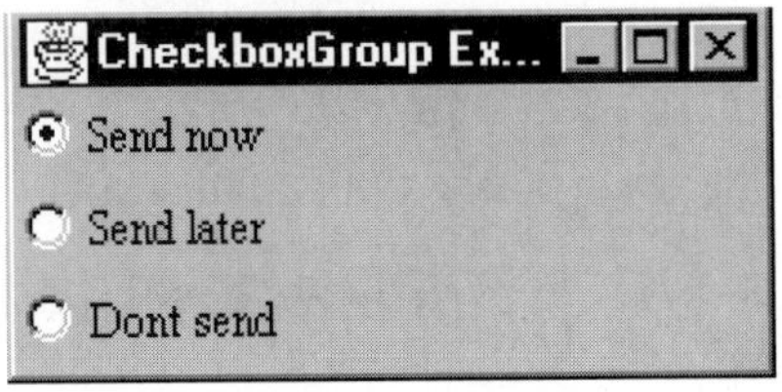

FIGURE 41 CheckboxGroup()

```
import java.awt.*;
class Main extends Frame {
    CheckboxGroup cg = new CheckboxGroup();

    Main() {
        super("Checkbox Example");
        Panel p = new Panel();

        p.setLayout(new GridLayout(0, 1));
        p.add(new Checkbox("Send now", cg, true));
        p.add(new Checkbox("Send later", cg, false));
        p.add(new Checkbox("Dont send", cg, false));
        add("Center", p);
        pack();
        show();
    }

    public boolean action(Event evt, Object what) {
        if (evt.target instanceof Checkbox) {
            System.out.println(what);
            return true;
        }
        return false;
    }

    static public void main(String[] args) {
        new Main();
    }
}
```

getCurrent()

PURPOSE Retrieves the current checkbox.

SYNTAX `public Checkbox getCurrent()`

A B C D E F G H I J K L M N O P Q R S T U V W X Y Z

DESCRIPTION This method retrieves the current checkbox. The check state of the current checkbox will always be set to on. If the return value is `null`, then either there are no checkboxes in the group or none of the checkboxes are set to on.

RETURNS The current checkbox in the group. The return value may be `null`.

SEE ALSO `setCurrent()`.

EXAMPLE See the class example.

setCurrent()

PURPOSE Sets the current checkbox.

SYNTAX `public synchronized void setCurrent(Checkbox checkbox)`

DESCRIPTION This method sets the current checkbox to be `checkbox`. If `checkbox` is `null`, none of the checkboxes in the group will be made current. The method is ignored if `checkbox` belongs to a different group.

PARAMETERS

`checkbox` The new current checkbox. May be `null`.

SEE ALSO `getCurrent()`.

EXAMPLE See the class example.

toString()

PURPOSE Generates a string representation of the checkbox group's state.

SYNTAX `public String toString()`

DESCRIPTION This method returns the string representation of this checkbox group's state. It is typically used for debugging.

RETURNS A non-`null` string representing the checkbox group's state.

OVERRIDES `Object.toString()`.

EXAMPLE

```
CheckboxGroup gb = new CheckboxGroup();
Checkbox cb = new Checkbox("Read-only", gb, true);
System.out.println(gb);
```

java.awt
CheckboxMenuItem

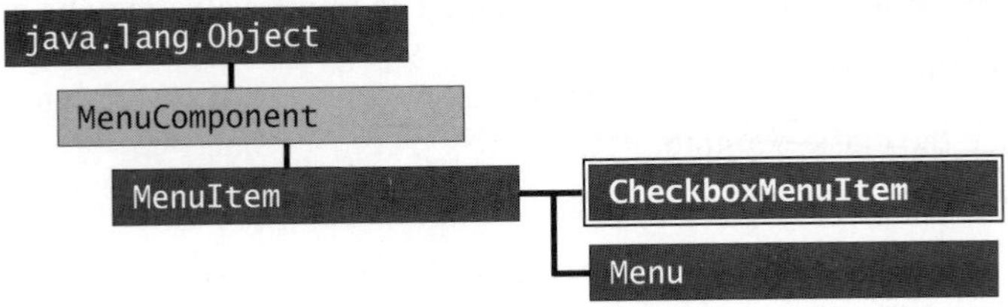

Syntax

```
public class CheckboxMenuItem extends MenuItem
```

Description

A checkbox menu item adds an additional property to a `MenuItem` object: the *check state*. The checkbox menu item's check state is always in one of two states: *on* or *off*. It can be changed at any time by either the user or a program. A checkbox menu item is typically used to indicate a two-value choice in an application. For example, in a mail application you may or may not want an audible signal of new mail. A checkbox menu item with the label "Play sound for new mail" would be a typical way to display the current preference and to allow the user to change it.

Figure 42 shows a menu displaying two checkbox menu items. The one labeled "Play sound for new mail" is set to *on*, while the one labeled "Pop dialog for new mail" is set to off.

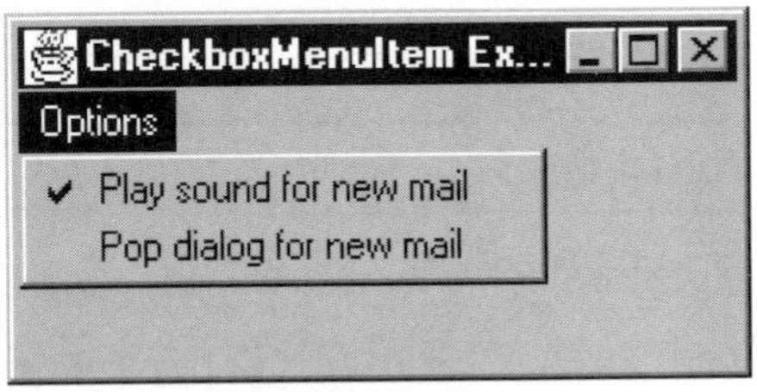

FIGURE 42 `CheckboxMenuItem`

Events

The checkbox menu item generates the same event as the menu item. The checked state of the checkbox menu item is automatically set before the event is generated. For example, if the checked state is currently `true` and the user selects the checkbox menu item, the checked state is set to `false` and then the event is generated.

See the `MenuItem` class for more details about the generated event.

MEMBER SUMMARY	
Constructor	
`CheckboxMenuItem()`	Constructs a new `CheckboxMenuItem` instance.
State Methods	
`getState()`	Retrieves the checked state of the checkbox menu item.
`setState()`	Sets the checkbox menu item's check state.
Peer Method	
`addNotify()`	Creates the checkbox menu item's peer.
Debugging Method	
`paramString()`	Generates a string representation of the checkbox menu's state.

Example

This example creates a menu with two menu items. The one labeled "Play sound for new mail" is enabled and the one labeled "Pop dialog for new mail" is disabled. See Figure 42 for a screen shot of the example. The menu is installed in a menu bar, which in turn is installed in a frame. This example also shows you how to handle events generated by a menu item.

```
import java.awt.*;
class Main extends Frame {
    Main() {
        super("CheckboxMenuItem Example");
        MenuBar mb = new MenuBar();
        Menu m = new Menu("Options");

        m.add(new CheckboxMenuItem("Play sound for new mail"));
        m.add(new CheckboxMenuItem("Pop dialog for new mail"));
        mb.add(m);

        // Set the menu bar on the frame.
        setMenuBar(mb);
        resize(100, 50);
        show();
    }

    public boolean action(Event evt, Object what) {
        if ("Play sound for new mail".equals(what)) {
            // playSound();
            return true;
        } else if ("Pop dialog for new mail".equals(what)) {
            // popDialog();
            return true;
        }
        return false;
```

```
        }

        static public void main(String[] args) {
            new Main();
        }
    }
```

addNotify()

PURPOSE	Creates the checkbox menu item's peer.
SYNTAX	`public synchronized void addNotify()`
DESCRIPTION	This method creates the checkbox menu item's peer if it does not yet exist. The peer is created by calling the `Toolkit.createCheckboxMenuItem()` method. This method should never be called directly. It is normally called by the checkbox menu item's parent.
OVERRIDES	`Component.addNotify()`.
SEE ALSO	`Component`, `Toolkit`.
EXAMPLE	See `Component.show()`.

CheckboxMenuItem()

PURPOSE	Constructs a new `CheckBoxMenuItem` instance.
SYNTAX	`public CheckboxMenuItem(String label)`
DESCRIPTION	This constructor creates a new `CheckBoxMenuItem` instance with the label `label`. The checked state is `false` by default. If `label` is "-", a separator is created.
PARAMETERS	
`label`	The non-`null` string specifying the checkbox menu item's label.
SEE ALSO	`MenuItem`.
EXAMPLE	See the class example.

getState()

PURPOSE Retrieves the checked state of the checkbox menu item.

SYNTAX `public boolean getState()`

RETURNS `true` if the checkbox menu item is checked; `false` otherwise.

EXAMPLE This method prints the checked state of all checkbox menu items in the menu bar.

```
void printMenuLabels(MenuBar menubar) {
    for (int i=0; i<menubar.countMenus(); i++) {
        Menu menu = menubar.getMenu(i);
        for (int j=0; j<menu.countItems(); j++) {
            if (menu.getItem(j) instanceof CheckboxMenuItem) {
                CheckboxMenuItem mi = (CheckboxMenuItem)menu.getItem(j);
                System.out.println(mi.getLabel() + ": "
                    + mi.getState());
            }
        }
    }
}
```

paramString()

PURPOSE Generates a string representation of the checkbox menu item's state.

SYNTAX `public String paramString()`

DESCRIPTION The string includes the label, enabled, and checked states of the checkbox menu item component. This method is called by the `toString()` method and is typically used for debugging.

RETURNS A non-`null` string representing the checkbox menu item's state.

OVERRIDES `Component.paramString()`.

SEE ALSO `Object.toString()`.

setState()

PURPOSE Sets the checkbox menu item's check state.

SYNTAX `public void setState(boolean state)`

setState()

DESCRIPTION The method call is ignored if the check state does not change.

PARAMETERS

`state` If `true`, the checkbox's check state is set to on; otherwise it is set to off.

SEE ALSO `getState()`.

EXAMPLE This example creates a checkbox and a checkbox menu item and synchronizes their check states. If the checkbox is on so is the checkbox menu item. See Figure 43.

FIGURE 43 `CheckboxMenuItem.setState()`

```
import java.awt.*;
class Main extends Frame {
    CheckboxMenuItem mi =
        new CheckboxMenuItem("Save All Files On Exit");
    Checkbox cb = new Checkbox("Save All Files On Exit");

    Main() {
        super("setState Example");
        MenuBar mb = new MenuBar();
        Menu m = new Menu("File");

        m.add(mi);
        m.add("Exit");
        mb.add(m);
        setMenuBar(mb);

        // Add the checkbox
        add("South", cb);
        pack();
        show();
    }

    public boolean action(Event evt, Object what) {
        if (evt.target == mi) {
            cb.setState(mi.getState());
        } else {
            mi.setState(cb.getState());
        }
        // saveAllFiles();
        return true;
    }

    static public void main(String[] args) {
        new Main();
    }
}
```

java.awt.peer

CheckboxMenuItemPeer

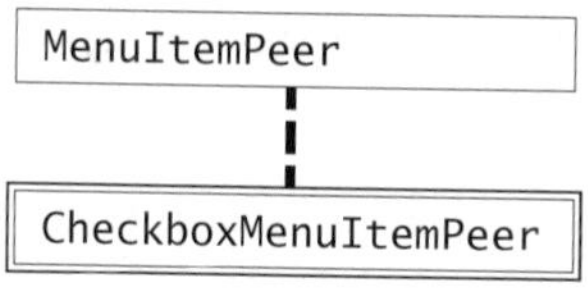

Syntax

```
public interface CheckboxMenuItemPeer extends MenuItemPeer
```

Description

The checkbox menu item component (see `CheckboxMenuItem` class) in the Abstract Windowing Toolkit (AWT), uses the platform's native implementation of a checkbox menu item. So that the AWT checkbox menu item component behaves the same on all platforms, the checkbox menu item is assigned a peer, whose task is to translate the behavior of the platform's native checkbox menu item to the behavior of the AWT checkbox menu item.

AWT programmers normally do not directly use peer classes and interfaces. Instead they deal with AWT components in the `java.awt` package. These in turn automatically manage their peers. Only someone who is porting the AWT to another platform should be concerned with the peer classes and interfaces. Consequently, most peer documentation refers to `java.awt` counterparts.

See `Component` and `Toolkit` for additional information about component peers.

MEMBER SUMMARY	
Peer Method	
`setState()`	Sets the checkbox menu item's check state.

See Also

`CheckboxMenuItem`, `Component`, `Toolkit`.

setState()

PURPOSE Sets the checkbox menu item's check state.

SYNTAX `void setState(boolean state)`

PARAMETERS

`state` If `true`, the checkbox's check state is set to on; otherwise it is set to off.

SEE ALSO `CheckboxMenuItem.setState()`.

java.awt.peer
CheckboxPeer

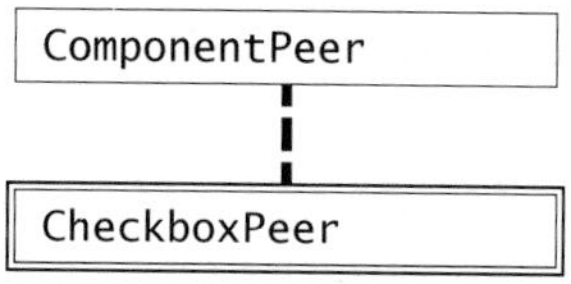

Syntax

```
public interface CheckboxPeer extends ComponentPeer
```

Description

The checkbox component (see the `Checkbox` class) in the Abstract Windowing Toolkit (AWT), uses the platform's native implementation of a checkbox. So that the AWT checkbox component behaves the same on all platforms, the checkbox is assigned a peer, whose task is to translate the behavior of the platform's native checkbox to the behavior of the AWT checkbox.

AWT programmers normally do not directly use peer classes and interfaces. Instead they deal with AWT components in the `java.awt`. These in turn automatically manage their peers. Only someone who is porting the AWT to another platform should be concerned with the peer classes and interfaces. Consequently, most peer documentation refers to `java.awt` counterparts.

See `Component` and `Toolkit` for additional information about component peers.

MEMBER SUMMARY	
Peer Methods	
`setCheckboxGroup()`	Sets the checkbox peer's checkbox group.
`setLabel()`	Sets the checkbox peer's label.
`setState()`	Sets the checkbox peer's check state.

See Also

`Checkbox`, `Component`, `Toolkit`.

setCheckboxGroup()

PURPOSE Sets the checkbox peer's checkbox group.

SYNTAX `void setCheckboxGroup(CheckboxGroup g)`

PARAMETERS

`g` The checkbox peer's new checkbox group. A value of `null` removes the checkbox peer from its current group.

SEE ALSO `Checkbox.setCheckboxGroup()`.

setLabel()

PURPOSE Sets the checkbox peer's label.

SYNTAX `void setLabel(String label)`

PARAMETERS

`label` The non-`null` string specifying the checkbox peer's new label.

SEE ALSO `Checkbox.setLabel()`.

setState()

PURPOSE Sets the checkbox peer's check state.

SYNTAX `void setState(boolean state)`

PARAMETERS

`state` If `true`, the checkbox peer's check state is set to on; otherwise it is set to off.

SEE ALSO `Checkbox.setState()`.

java.awt
Choice

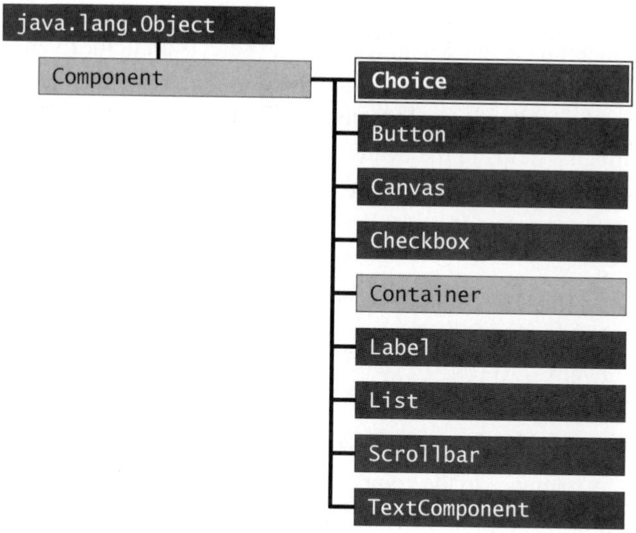

Syntax

```
public class Choice extends Component
```

Description

A Choice is a component that lets the user choose from a fixed set of string items. It is similar to a list except that it occupies much less screen space in its normal state. In its normal state, the choice displays the currently selected item. In its activated state, it displays the entire list of choices. Once a selection has been made, it shrinks back to a single line and displays the newly selected item.

The checkbox group is a component that is similar to a choice component in that it lets the user choose from a fixed set of items (see the `Checkbox` class). Following are two design guidelines to consider when deciding between the choice component and the checkbox group. As with all user interface "principles," these guidelines are intended to summarize the issues and not mandate your design.

1. The larger the number of items, the more appropriate the choice component becomes. You should probably use a choice component if you have five or more items.
2. If a group of one or more components is related to one particular item and is therefore enabled only if that item is selected, a checkbox group might be more appropriate.

Description

B C D E F G H I J K L M N O P Q R S T U V W X Y Z

The Selected Item

If there are any items in the choice, one is always selected, called the *selected item*. The selected item can be changed by either the program or the user.

Events

A choice generates an action event whenever the user selects an item. Even if the selected item is reselected, an action event is generated, since the modifier keys may have changed.

See the `Event` class for details on how to filter or handle events. Table 8 describes how a choice component fills the fields in the event.

TABLE 8 `Choice` Action Event

`arg`	The newly selected item.
`clickCount`	Not used.
`id`	`Event.ACTION`.
`key`	Not used.
`modifiers`	The state of the modifier keys when the component was clicked.
`target`	A reference to the component that generated this event.
`when`	The time, in milliseconds, that the event was generated.
`x`	*x*-coordinate of the component in pixels.
`y`	*y*-coordinate of the component in pixels.

MEMBER SUMMARY

Constructor	
`Choice()`	Constructs a new `Choice` instance.
Item Methods	
`addItem()`	Adds an item to the choice.
`countItems()`	Retrieves the number of items in the choice.
`getItem()`	Retrieves an item in the choice.
Selection Methods	
`getSelectedIndex()`	Retrieves the index of the choice's selected item.
`getSelectedItem()`	Retrieves the choice's selected item.
`select()`	Selects an item in the choice.
Peer Method	
`addNotify()`	Creates the choice's peer.
Debugging Method	
`paramString()`	Generates a string representing the choice's state.

A B C D E F G H I J K L M N O P Q R S T U V W X Y Z

Example

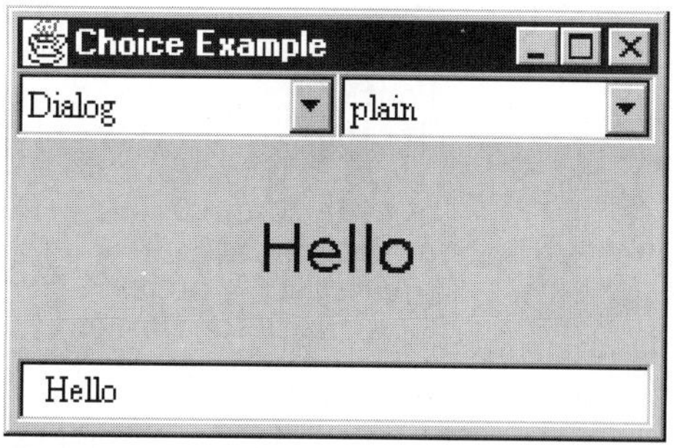

FIGURE 44 `Choice`

For a simple example using the choice component, see the example for the `Choice()` constructor. This more elaborate example creates two choice components for controlling the appearance of a message that is displayed in the center (see Figure 44). One choice controls the font name, and the other controls the font style. You can use the text field at the bottom to change the text of the message. The message is painted in the middle of the frame container. Since frame containers have insets, the `paint()` method needs to subtract the insets from the frame's bounds. For containers without insets (such as the `Panel`), this calculation is not necessary.

```
import java.awt.*;
class Main extends Frame {
    String[] styleNames = {"plain", "italic", "bold", "bold-italic"};
    int[] styleValues = {Font.PLAIN, Font.ITALIC, Font.BOLD,
                         Font.ITALIC|Font.BOLD};
    Choice chFont = new Choice();
    Choice chStyle = new Choice();
    TextField tf = new TextField("Hello");

    Main() {
        super("Choice Example");
        Panel p = new Panel();

        // Retrieve all the font names.
        for (int i=0; i<getToolkit().getFontList().length; i++) {
            chFont.addItem(getToolkit().getFontList()[i]);
        }
        // Initialize the font style choice.
        for (int i=0; i<styleNames.length; i++) {
            chStyle.addItem(styleNames[i]);
        }
        p.setLayout(new GridLayout(1, 0));
        p.add(chFont);
        p.add(chStyle);
        add("North", p);
        add("South", tf);
        resize(300, 150);
        show();
    }

    public void paint(Graphics g) {
        Insets insets = insets();
        int w = size().width-insets.left-insets.right-2;
        int h = size().height-insets.top-insets.bottom-2;
```

```
            Font f = new Font(chFont.getSelectedItem(),
                styleValues[chStyle.getSelectedIndex()], 24);
            FontMetrics fm = g.getFontMetrics(f);
            String str = tf.getText();

            g.clearRect(0, 0, w, h);
            g.setFont(f);
            g.drawString(str, (w-fm.stringWidth(str))/2,
                (h-fm.getHeight())/2+fm.getAscent());
        }

        public boolean action(Event evt, Object arg) {
            repaint();
            return true;
        }

        static public void main(String[] args) {
            new Main();
        }
    }
```

addItem()

PURPOSE Adds an item to the choice.

SYNTAX `public synchronized void addItem(String item)`

DESCRIPTION This method adds the item `item` to the end of the choice. If the item is the first one in the list, then the item is selected; otherwise the selected item does not change.

PARAMETERS

`item` The non-`null` item.

EXAMPLE See the class example.

addNotify()

PURPOSE Creates the choice's peer.

SYNTAX `public synchronized void addNotify()`

DESCRIPTION This method creates the peer if it does not yet exist. The peer is created by calling the `Toolkit.createChoice()` method. This method should never be called directly. It is normally called by the parent.

OVERRIDES `Component.addNotify()`.

SEE ALSO Component, Toolkit.

EXAMPLE See Component.show().

Choice()

PURPOSE Constructs a new Choice instance.

SYNTAX `public Choice()`

DESCRIPTION This constructor constructs a new visible choice component.

EXAMPLE This example creates a choice component with two items. The program simply prints out the current item whenever the current item in the choice changes. See Figure 45.

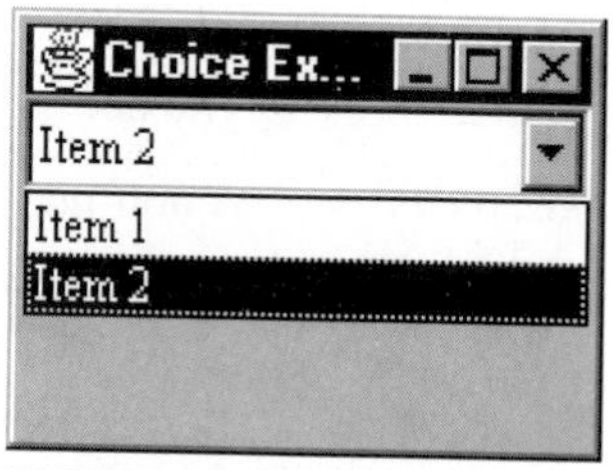

FIGURE 45 Choice()

```
import java.awt.*;
class Main extends Frame {
    Main() {
        super("Choice Example");
        Choice choice = new Choice();

        choice.addItem("Item 1");
        choice.addItem("Item 2");
        add("Center", choice);
        resize(200, 200);
        show();
    }

    public boolean action(Event evt, Object arg) {
        if (evt.target instanceof Choice) {
            System.out.println(arg);
            return true;
        }
        return false;
    }

    static public void main(String[] args) {
        new Main();
    }
}
```

countItems()

PURPOSE Retrieves the number of items in the choice.

SYNTAX `public int countItems()`

RETURNS	The number of items in the choice.
EXAMPLE	See `select()`.

getItem()

PURPOSE	Retrieves an item in the choice.
SYNTAX	`public String getItem(int index)`
DESCRIPTION	This method retrieves the item at index `index`.
PARAMETERS	
`index`	The non-negative 0-based index of the item.
RETURNS	A non-`null` string containing the item's name.
SEE ALSO	`addItem()`.
EXAMPLE	See `select()`.

getSelectedIndex()

PURPOSE	Retrieves the index of the choice's selected item.
SYNTAX	`public int getSelectedIndex()`
RETURNS	The 0-based index of the selected item; `-1` if the choice does not have any items.
SEE ALSO	`getSelectedItem()`.
EXAMPLE	See the class example.

getSelectedItem()

PURPOSE	Retrieves the choice's selected item.
SYNTAX	`public String getSelectedItem()`
RETURNS	The selected item; `null` if the choice does not have any items.
SEE ALSO	`getSelectedIndex()`.
EXAMPLE	See the class example.

paramString()

PURPOSE
Generates a string representing the choice's state.

SYNTAX
```
protected String paramString()
```

DESCRIPTION
This method returns the string representation of this choice's state; the returned string includes the selected item. A subclass of this class should override this method and return a concatenation of its state with the results of `super.paramString()`. This method is called by the `toString()` method and is typically used for debugging.

RETURNS
A non-`null` string representing the choice's state.

OVERRIDES
`Component.paramString()`.

SEE ALSO
`Object.toString()`.

EXAMPLE
See `Component.paramString()`.

select()

PURPOSE
Selects an item in the choice.

SYNTAX
```
public synchronized void select(int index)
public void select(String string)
```

DESCRIPTION
This method selects an item either by its name or by its index. If `index` is specified, the item at index `index` is selected. If `string` is specified the item's name is `string`. If several matches exist, the item with the smallest index is selected. If `string` does not match any items, then the method call is ignored. See Figure 46.

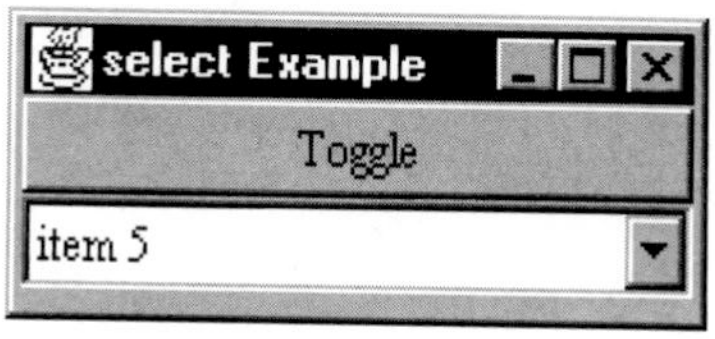

FIGURE 46 Toggle to Choice

PARAMETERS

`index`	The non-negative 0-based index of the item.
`string`	The non-`null` item to select.

SEE ALSO
`getSelectedIndex()`, `getSelectedItem()`.

EXAMPLE This example creates a frame with a button and initially with a choice component (Figure 46). Clicking the button causes the choice component to be replaced by a list component (Figure 47). Clicking the button again causes the list to revert to a choice component (Figure 45). The program uses select() to maintain the selected item between transformations.

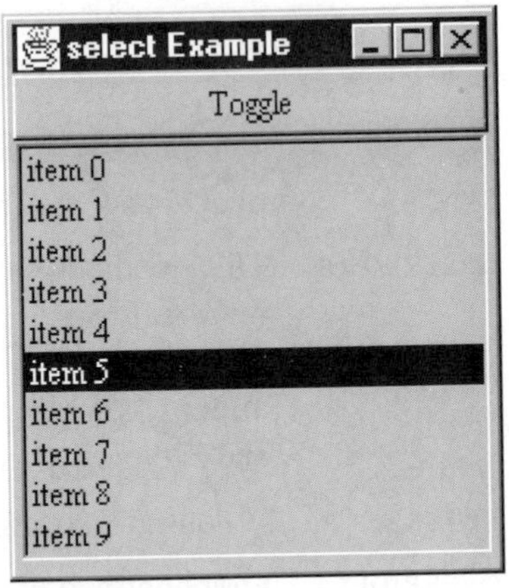

FIGURE 47 Toggle to List

```
import java.awt.*;
class Main extends Frame {
    List list;
    Choice choice = new Choice();

    Main() {
        super("select Example");

        for (int i=0; i<10; i++) {
            choice.addItem("item "+i);
        }
        add("South", choice);
        add("North", new Button("Toggle"));
        pack();
        show();
    }
    public boolean action(Event evt, Object arg) {
        if ("Toggle".equals(arg)) {
            if (choice != null) {
                // create a list and transfer items to the list.
                list = new List(choice.countItems(), false);
                for (int i=0; i<choice.countItems(); i++) {
                    list.addItem(choice.getItem(i));
                    if (i == choice.getSelectedIndex()) {
                        list.select(i);
                    }
                }
                add("Center", list);
                remove(choice);
                choice = null;
            } else {
                // create a choice and transfer items to the list.
                choice = new Choice();
                for (int i=0; i<list.countItems(); i++) {
                    choice.addItem(list.getItem(i));
                    if (i == list.getSelectedIndex()) {
                        choice.select(i);
                    }
```

```
                }
                add("South", choice);
                remove(list);
                list = null;
            }
            pack();
            return true;
        }
        return false;
    }
    static public void main(String[] args) {
        new Main();
    }
}
```

java.awt.peer
ChoicePeer

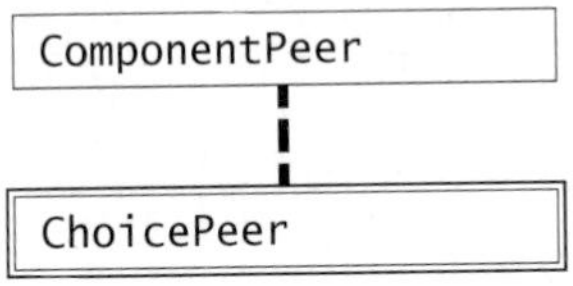

Syntax

`public interface ChoicePeer extends ComponentPeer`

Description

The choice component (see `Choice` class) in the Abstract Windowing Toolkit (AWT), uses the platform's native implementation of a choice component. So that the AWT choice component behaves the same on all platforms, the choice component is assigned a peer, whose task is to translate the behavior of the platform's native choice component to the behavior of the AWT choice component.

AWT programmers normally do not directly use peer classes and interfaces. Instead they deal with AWT components in the `java.awt` package. These in turn automatically manage their peers. Only someone who is porting the AWT to another platform should be concerned with the peer classes and interfaces. Consequently, most peer documentation refers to its `java.awt` counterparts.

See `Component` and `Toolkit` for additional information about component peers.

MEMBER SUMMARY	
Peer Methods	
`addItem()`	Adds an item to the choice.
`select()`	Selects an item in the choice.

See Also

`Choice`, `Component`, `Toolkit`.

addItem()

PURPOSE Adds an item to the choice.

SYNTAX `void addItem(String item, int index)`

DESCRIPTION This method adds the item `item` to the choice list at the index specified by `index`.

PARAMETERS

`index` The position in the choice list to place `item`.

`item` The non-`null` item to be added.

SEE ALSO `Choice.addItem()`.

select()

PURPOSE Selects an item in the choice.

SYNTAX `void select(int index)`

DESCRIPTION This method selects the item at the index indicated by `index`.

PARAMETERS

`index` The non-negative 0-based index of the item.

SEE ALSO `Choice.select()`.

A B C D E F G H I J K L M N O P Q R S T U V W X Y Z

java.lang
Class

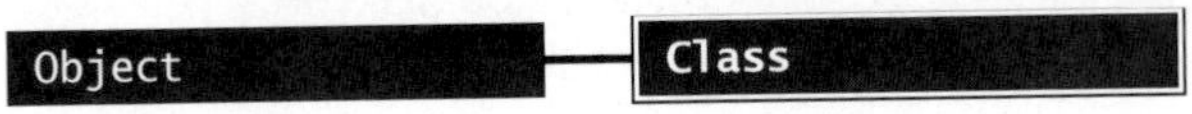

Syntax

```
public final class Class extends Object
```

Description

Every object in Java is an instance of a class. For each class, Java maintains an immutable `Class` object that contains information about the class. This information includes the class's string name, the superclass that it extends, the interfaces that it implements, and the class loader used to load this class. Although an interface is different from a class, the `Class` object is also used to represent information about interfaces. The `Class` class provides methods that return this information about a class or an interface, as well as a method to generate new instances of the class.

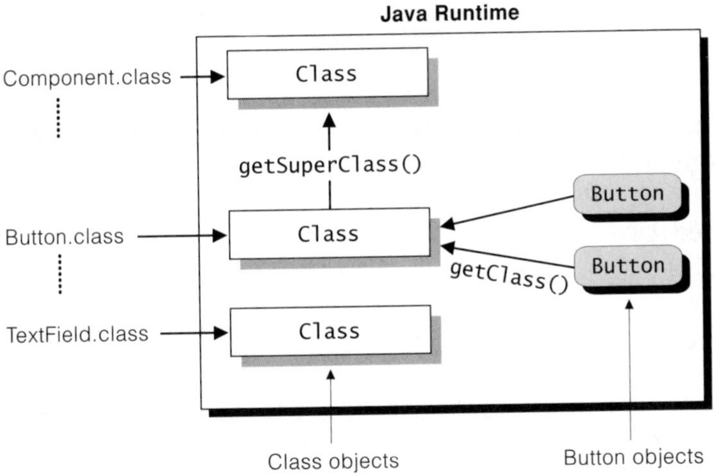

FIGURE 48 Examples of Classes

In Figure 48, each class file (`Component.class`, `Button.class`, etc.) that has been loaded has a corresponding `Class` object. When you invoke `getSuperClass()` on the `Button` class's `Class` object, you get back the `Class` object for `Component`. When you invoke `getClass()` on an instance of a `Button` object, you get back the `Class` object for `Button`.

MEMBER SUMMARY

Informational Methods	
`getClassLoader()`	Retrieves the class loader for this class.
`getInterfaces()`	Retrieves the interfaces that this class implements.
`getName()`	Retrieves the name of this class.
`getSuperclass()`	Retrieves the superclass that this class extends.
`isInterface()`	Determines whether this class definition is an interface.
Class Methods	
`forName()`	Finds the `Class` object using its class name.
`newInstance()`	Creates a new instance of this class.
Description Method	
`toString()`	Generates the string representation of this object.

See Also

`ClassLoader`, `Object.getClass()`.

Example

```
// Prints details of class with given name and
// returns a new instance of it
static Object printClassDetails(String className) {
    try {
        Class c = Class.forName(className);
        Class ifs[] = c.getInterfaces();

        System.out.println("Name of" +
            (c.isInterface() ? "interface: " : "class: ") +
            c.getName());
        System.out.println("Superclass is: " + c.getSuperclass());
        System.out.println("Class Loader is : " + c.getClassLoader());
        System.out.println("Description is : " + c.toString());
        for (int i = 0; i < ifs.length; i++)
            System.out.println("Interface[" + i + "] is " + ifs[i]);

        Object obj = null;
        try {
            obj = c.newInstance();
        } catch (InstantiationException e) {
            System.err.println(e);
        } catch (IllegalAccessException e) {
            System.err.println(e);
        }
        return (obj);
    } catch (ClassNotFoundException e) {
```

```
            System.err.println("Could not find class: " + e);
        }
        return (null);
    }
```

forName()

PURPOSE Finds the `Class` object using its class name.

SYNTAX `public static native Class forName(String className) throws ClassNotFoundException`

DESCRIPTION This method returns a `Class` object for the given class name `className`. The class name is the package-qualified name of the class (e.g., `java.lang.Class`).

PARAMETERS

`className` The non-`null` package-qualified name of the class for which to return a `Class` object.

RETURNS The `Class` object for `className`.

EXCEPTIONS

`ClassNotFoundException`
If `className` does not name a class.

SEE ALSO `getName()`.

EXAMPLE

```
    try {
        Class c = Class.forName("java.lang.String");
    } catch (ClassNotFoundException e) {
        System.err.println("Couldn't find class" + e );
    }
```

getClassLoader()

PURPOSE Retrieves the class loader for this class.

SYNTAX `public native ClassLoader getClassLoader()`

DESCRIPTION Each class is loaded into the runtime system using a *class loader*. A class loader can be used to enforce policies related to loading classes (e.g., determining where to find class files if the classes are contained in files, getting classes from network sockets, and getting classes from secure network sockets). A class loader is represented in the system by using a `ClassLoader` object. This method returns the ClassLoader object used to load this Class object. A value of null indicates that the default system class loader was used to load this class.

RETURNS A ClassLoader object for this Class object; null if the default system class loader was used.

SEE ALSO ClassLoader.

EXAMPLE

```
Class c = obj.getClass();
ClassLoader loader = c.getClassLoader();
if (loader == null)
    System.out.println("Default system class loader");
else
    System.out.println(loader);
```

getInterfaces()

PURPOSE Retrieves the interfaces being implemented by this class.

SYNTAX `public native Class[] getInterfaces()`

DESCRIPTION A class can inherit from a single superclass and zero or more interfaces. This method returns a Class array containing the Class objects of interfaces being implemented by this class.

RETURNS A non-null array of Class objects of interfaces implemented by this class. An array of length 0 is returned if this class does not implement any interfaces.

SEE ALSO getSuperclass().

EXAMPLE

```
// print out interfaces implemented by class
Class c = obj.getClass();
Class[] ifs = c.getInterfaces();
for (int i = 0; i < ifs.length; i++)
    System.out.println("Interface[" + i + "] is " + ifs[i]);
```

getName()

PURPOSE Retrieves the name of this class.

SYNTAX `public native String getName()`

DESCRIPTION This method returns the package-qualified name of this `Class` object (e.g., `java.lang.Boolean`).

RETURNS A string containing the name of this class.

SEE ALSO `forName()`, `toString()`.

EXAMPLE

```
Class c = obj.getClass();
System.out.println("name of class: " + c.getName());
```

getSuperclass()

PURPOSE Retrieves the superclass that this class extends.

SYNTAX `public native Class getSuperClass()`

DESCRIPTION This method returns the superclass that this class extends. Except for `Object`, all classes have a superclass. The superclass of an interface is `Object`.

RETURNS The `Class` object for the superclass of this `Class` object; `null` if this `Class` does not have a superclass.

SEE ALSO `Object.getClass()`.

EXAMPLE

```
Class c = obj.getClass();
Class super_c = c.getSuperclass();
```

isInterface()

PURPOSE Determines whether this class definition is for an interface.

SYNTAX `public native boolean isInterface();`

DESCRIPTION A `Class` object is used to described either a Java class or a Java interface. This method returns whether this `Class` object is for an interface or for a class.

RETURNS `true` if this `Class` object is describing an interface; `false` otherwise.

SEE ALSO `toString()`.

EXAMPLE

```
try {
    Class c = Class.forName(className);
```

```
    if (c.isInterface())
        System.out.print("Interface");
    else
        System.out.print("Class");
} catch (ClassNotFoundException e) {
    System.err.println(e);
}
```

newInstance()

PURPOSE Creates a new instance of this class.

SYNTAX
```
public native Object newInstance() throws
    InstantiationException, IllegalAccessException
```

RETURNS A new object that is an instance of this class.

EXCEPTIONS

`InstantiationException`
If the object could not be instantiated because the class is an abstract class, if the class is an interface, or because of some other reason.

`IllegalAccessException`
If the class or initializer for the instance is not accessible. For example, when trying to create a new instance of a class in another package, this exception will occur if either the class or its `null` constructor is not declared `public`.

EXAMPLE

```
try {
    Class c = Class.forName("java.lang.String");
    try {
        // create and cast new instance to 'String' class
        String str = (String)c.newInstance();
    } catch (InstantiationException e) {
        System.err.println("Problem instantiating object" + e);
    } catch (IllegalAccessException e) {
        System.err.println("Could not access class" + e);
    }
} catch (ClassNotFoundException e) {
    System.err.println("String class not found");
}
```

toString()

PURPOSE Generates the string representation of this object.

SYNTAX `public String toString()`

DESCRIPTION This method returns the string representation of this `Class` object. The string representation of a `Class` object contains either the string "`class`" or the string "`interface`" (depending on the type of the `Class` object) and the name of the class.

OVERRIDES `Object.toString()`.

SEE ALSO `getName()`, `isInterface()`.

EXAMPLE

```
Class c = obj.getClass();
String classDesc = c.toString();
```

ClassCastException

Syntax

```
public class ClassCastException extends RuntimeException
```

Description

`ClassCastException` is a runtime exception that is thrown when the program attempts to cast an instance of a class to another class and that cast is not allowed.

`ClassCastException` should not be caught or declared in the `throws` clause of a method.

MEMBER SUMMARY	
Constructor	
`ClassCastException()`	Constructs a `ClassCastException` instance.

See Also

`RuntimeException`.

Example

The following example generates a `ClassCastException` when it attempts to cast a `String` instance to an `Integer` instance:

```
class Main {
    private static void storeItem(Integer[]a, int i, Object item) {
        a[i] = (Integer) item;
    }
    public static void main(String[] args) {
        System.out.println("ClassCastException Example");

        Integer[] a = new Integer[3];
        storeItem(a, 2, new String("abc"));
    }
}
```

ClassCastException()

PURPOSE Constructs a `ClassCastException` instance.

SYNTAX

```
public ClassCastException()
public ClassCastException(String msg)
```

DESCRIPTION These two forms of the constructor create a new instance of `ClassCastException`. An optional string `msg` can be supplied that describes this particular instance of the exception.

PARAMETERS

`msg` A string that gives details about this exception.

java.lang

ClassCircularityError

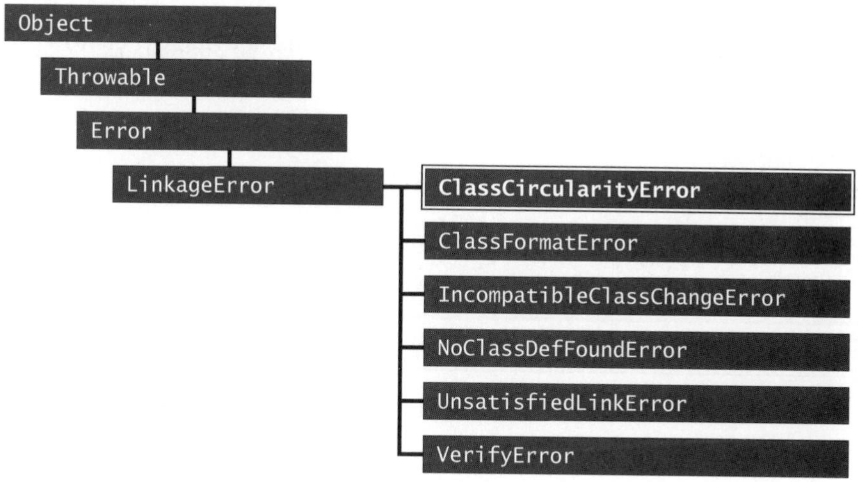

Syntax

`public class ClassCircularityError extends LinkageError`

Description

`ClassCircularityError` is a runtime linkage error that is thrown when the class loader attempts to load in classes that have cyclic class inheritance. Normally, when you compile classes that have cyclic class inheritance, you get a compilation error pinpointing the problem so that a linkage error at runtime does not occur. However, the circularity could be introduced when classes of a program become inconsistent, for example, by making an incompatible change and then recompiling only some of the classes.

`ClassCircularityError` should not be caught or declared in the `throws` clause of a method.

MEMBER SUMMARY	
Constructor	
`ClassCircularityError()`	Constructs a `ClassCircularityError` instance.

See Also

`Error`, `LinkageError`.

Example

The following code is an example of two classes that would raise a `ClassCircularityError`.

```
class A extends B {
}

class B extends A {
}
```

ClassCircularityError()

PURPOSE Constructs a `ClassCircularityError` instance.

SYNTAX
```
public ClassCircularityError()
public ClassCircularityError(String msg)
```

DESCRIPTION These two forms of the constructor create a new instance of `ClassCircularityError`. An optional string `msg` can be supplied that describes this particular instance of the error.

PARAMETERS

`msg` A string that gives details about this error.

java.lang

ClassFormatError

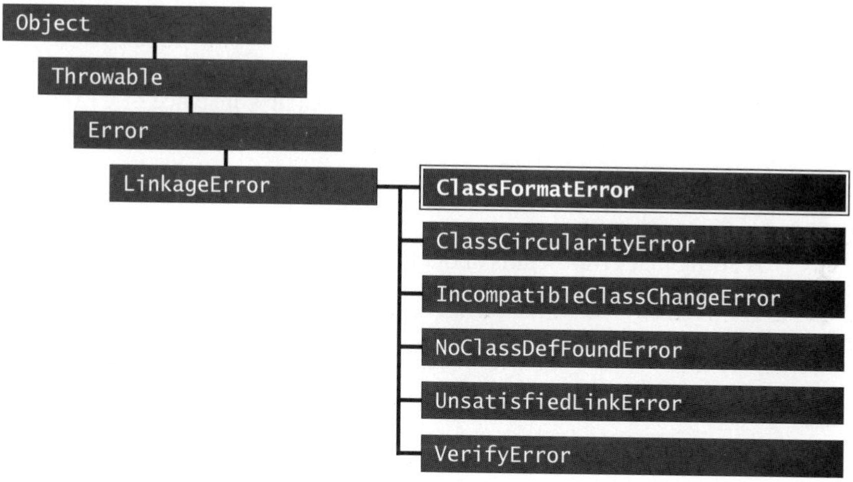

Syntax

`public class ClassFormatError extends LinkageError`

Description

`ClassFormatError` is a runtime linkage error that is thrown when the class loader attempts to load in a class that is not in a format that it accepts. This can happen, for example, if the class file in which the class is stored becomes corrupted or, if the class is being loaded across a network, the server sending the class is not sending it in an acceptable format.

`ClassFormatError` should not be caught or declared in the `throws` clause of a method.

MEMBER SUMMARY	
Constructor	
`ClassFormatError()`	Constructs a `ClassFormatError` instance.

See Also

`Error`, `LinkageError`.

ClassFormatError()

PURPOSE Constructs a `ClassFormatError` instance.

SYNTAX
```
public ClassFormatError()
public ClassFormatError(String msg)
```

PURPOSE These two forms of the constructor create a new instance of `ClassFormatError`. An optional string `msg` can be supplied that describes this particular instance of the error.

PARAMETERS

`msg` A string that gives details about this error.

java.lang
ClassLoader

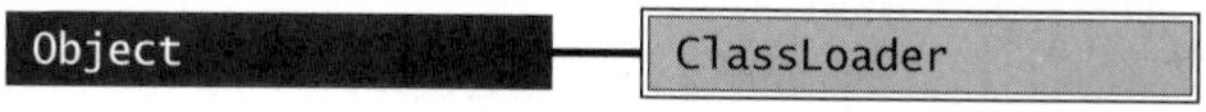

Syntax

```
public abstract class ClassLoader
```

Description

`ClassLoader` is an abstract class that can be used to define policies for loading Java classes into the runtime environment. Such policies include the format that the classes are stored in (e.g., byte code, zip, compressed), the source for the classes (e.g., file system, network), how to locate the classes within the source (e.g., the directories to search, the zip files to use, the machines to contact), and security conditions to apply when loading the classes. Figure 49 shows examples of two different implementations of `ClassLoader`. One loads classes from the network, while the other loads classes from the file system.

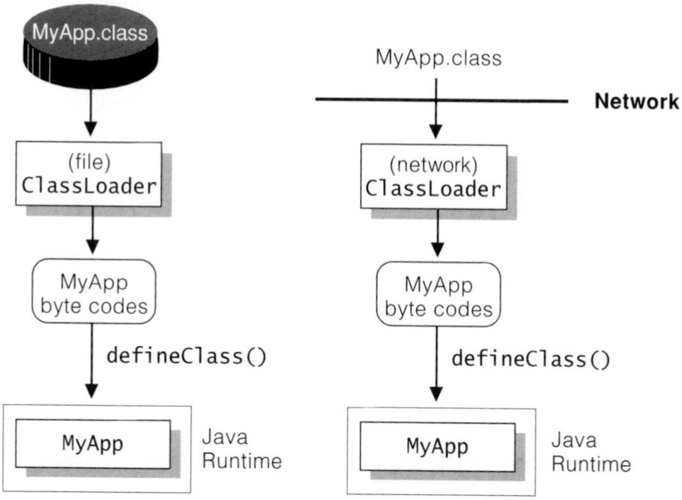

FIGURE 49 A File System-based `ClassLoader` and a Network-based `ClassLoader`

Default System Class Loader

The default system class loader loads classes from files in directories or zip files specified by the `java.class.path` system property, which in turn is determined by the CLASSPATH environment variable. `java.class.path` contains an ordered list of directory names or zip files in which to search for a given class. The default setting is the `classes` subdirectory of where

Java has been installed and the zip file containing the Java classes. The following are the default settings for Solaris and Windows 95/NT.

```
Solaris        $JAVAHOME/classes:$JAVAHOME/lib/classes.zip
Windows95, NT  C:\java\classes;C:\java\classes.zip
```

You can collect your own classes into a zip file and add that zip file to this path. The zip file can be created using any zip tool that supports long filenames. The only restriction is that the class files within the zip file are not compressed.

Defining New Class Loaders

New class loaders can be created by defining subclasses of `ClassLoader` and providing implementations for the abstract method `loadClass()`. Some examples of different class loading policies are loading classes from a network socket, from a secure network socket, from files in a particular directory, and from a stream generated by a program.

Any subclass of `ClassLoader` must provide an implementation of the `loadClass()` method. `loadClass()` defines the policy regarding where the definition of classes are found and how to load them.

The `ClassLoader` class defines methods that can be used by subclasses of `ClassLoader` in the implementation of their own `loadClass()` method. These include methods to obtain a `Class` object given the definition of the class in byte code form, to resolve classes referenced by a given class, and to load a class using the default system class loader.

MEMBER SUMMARY	
Constructor	
`ClassLoader()`	Constructs a new class loader.
Abstract Method	
`loadClass()`	Loads a class using the policy defined by this `ClassLoader`.
Final Methods	
`defineClass()`	Generates a new `Class` object using an array of byte codes.
`findSystemClass()`	Loads a class using the default system class loader.
`resolveClass()`	Resolves the classes referenced by a class using this class loader.

See Also

`Class`, `Object`, `System.getProperties()`.

Example

The following code implements a class loader that checks a special directory for class files before using the default class loader. Note the use of the hash table as a cache for previously loaded classes.

```
class DirClassLoader extends ClassLoader {
    private Hashtable cache = new Hashtable();
    private File classdir;
    DirClassLoader(String dir) {
        super();
        classdir = new File(dir);
    }
    // load the class data from the class file in specified dir
    private byte[] loadClassData(String name)
        throws ClassNotFoundException {
        File target = new File(classdir, name + ".class");
        byte[] data = null;
        try {
            long bytecount = target.length();
            if (bytecount > 0) {
                data = new byte[(int)bytecount];
                FileInputStream in = new FileInputStream(target);
                in.read(data);
                in.close();
            }
        } catch (IOException e) {
            throw new ClassNotFoundException(name);
        }
        return (data);
    }
    public synchronized Class loadClass(String name, boolean resolve)
        throws ClassNotFoundException {
        Class c = (Class) cache.get(name);
        if (c == null) {
            byte[] data = loadClassData(name);
            if (data != null) {
               cache.put(name, c = defineClass(data, 0, data.length));
                if (resolve && c != null)
                    resolveClass(c);
            } else {
                // Try default System loader
                c = findSystemClass(name);
            }
        }
        if (c == null)
            throw new ClassNotFoundException(name);
        return c;
    }
}
```

ClassLoader()

PURPOSE Constructs a new `ClassLoader` object.

SYNTAX `protected ClassLoader()`

EXAMPLE The following example defines a class loader for debugging. It is identical to the default system class loader except it prints out the classes being loaded.

```
class DebugClassLoader extends ClassLoader {
    public synchronized Class loadClass(String name, boolean resolve)
        throws ClassNotFoundException {
            System.out.println("Loading " + name);
            return (findSystemClass(name));
        }
}
DebugClassLoader loader = new DebugClassLoader();
Class c = loader.loadClass(className, true);
```

defineClass()

PURPOSE Generates a new `Class` object using an array of byte codes.

SYNTAX
```
protected final Class defineClass(byte[] bytecode, int offset,
   int length)
```

DESCRIPTION The Java compiler compiles Java programs into a machine-independent representation called *byte codes* to be used by the Java interpreter and runtime system. A class is introduced into the runtime system by generating a `Class` object using information encoded in a sequence of byte codes. This is the task performed by the `defineClass()` method. When defining a new `ClassLoader`, the implementation of `loadClass()` needs to call `defineClass()` by using the byte codes that it retrieved in order to introduce the class into the runtime system.

PARAMETERS

`bytecode` An array of bytes containing the byte codes for the class.
`offset` The start position in `bytecode` of the class's byte codes.
`length` The number of bytes occupied by the class's byte codes.

RETURNS A `Class` object generated by using given byte codes.

SEE ALSO `loadClass()`, `Class`.

EXAMPLE See `loadClass()`.

findSystemClass()

PURPOSE Loads a class by using the default system class loader.

SYNTAX
```
protected final Class findSystemClass(String className) throws
    ClassNotFoundException
```

DESCRIPTION The default system class loader loads classes from files in directories and zip files specified by the `java.class.path` system property. `findSystemClass()` uses this default loader to load the definition of the class named by `className`.

PARAMETERS

`className` The package-qualified name of the class to load.

RETURNS A new `Class` object with name `className`.

EXCEPTIONS

`ClassNotFoundException`
If a class with name `className` was not found in the directories and zip files specified by the `java.class.path` system property.

SEE ALSO `loadClass()`, `Class`.

EXAMPLE See `ClassLoader`.

loadClass()

PURPOSE Loads a class using the policy defined by this `ClassLoader`.

SYNTAX
```
protected abstract Class loadClass(String className, boolean
    resolve) throws ClassNotFoundException
```

DESCRIPTION This method loads the specified class `className` by using the policy defined by this class loader. This is an abstract method that must be defined by the subclass of `ClassLoader`. The general flow of `loadClass()` is to first obtain the byte codes for the specified class and then call `defineClass()` to turn the byte codes into a `Class` object. If `resolve` is `true`, `loadClass()` should then call `resolveClass()` to load classes referenced by the class being loaded. To load the referenced classes, the Java runtime uses the class loader originally used to load the class.

PARAMETERS

`className` The name of the class to be loaded.

`resolve` `true` if the classes referenced by this class need to be resolved; `false` otherwise.

RETURNS A new `Class` object with name `className`.

EXCEPTIONS

`ClassNotFoundException`
If a class with name `className` could not be found according to the policy of this class loader.

SEE ALSO `findSystemClass()`, `defineClass()`, `Hashtable`, `resolveClass()`.

REMARKS The implementation of `loadClass()` can use a hash table for caching classes in order to avoid reloading a class, provided this action is consistent with the policy of this `ClassLoader`.

EXAMPLE The following example illustrates the necessary calls made by a typical `loadClass()` definition. After obtaining the byte code `data`, it must call `defineClass()` to introduce the class `c` represented by `data` to the system. It must then resolve any classes referenced by `c` by calling `resolveClass()` on it.

```
class TestClassLoader extends ClassLoader {
    private byte[] loadClassData(String className) {
     ...
    }
    public synchronized Class loadClass(String className, boolean
        resolve) throws ClassNotFoundException {
            byte[] data = loadClassData(className);
            if (data != null) {
                Class c = defineClass(data, 0, data.length);
                if (resolve && c != null)
                    resolveClass(c);
                return (c);
            } else
                throw new ClassNotFoundException(className);
        }
}
TestClassLoader loader = new TestClassLoader();
try {
    Class c = loader.loadClass(className, true);
} catch (ClassNotFoundException e) {
  ...
}
```

resolveClass()

PURPOSE Resolves the classes referenced by a class by using this class loader.

SYNTAX `protected final void resolveClass(Class c)`

DESCRIPTION This method resolves the classes referenced by the class `c` by loading these classes using the `loadClass()` method of this class loader. This must be done before the class `c` is used.

PARAMETERS

`c` The class whose references are being resolved.

SEE ALSO `defineClass()`, `loadClass()`.

EXAMPLE See `loadClass()`.

java.lang

ClassNotFoundException

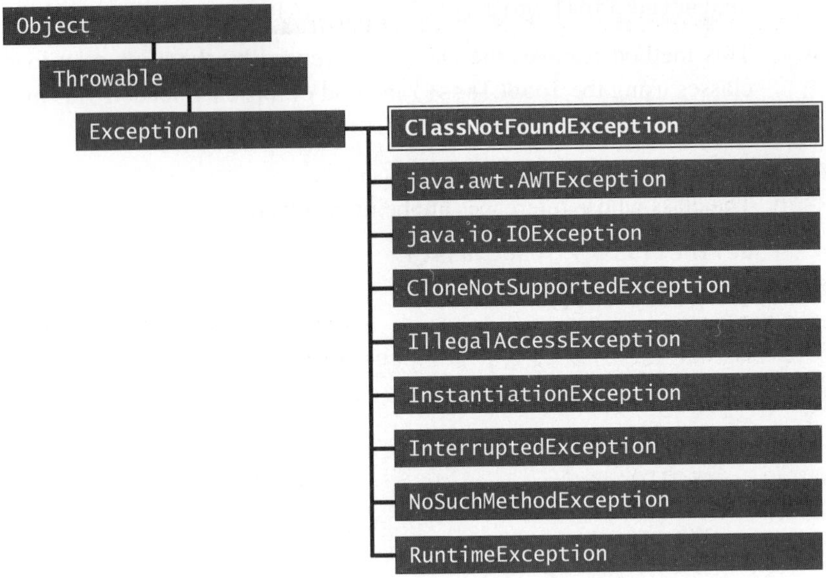

Syntax

```
public class ClassNotFoundException extends Exception
```

Description

`ClassNotFoundException` is an exception that is thrown when a class loader cannot find the class to load. This can happen if you define a class loader and it fails to find the class defined.

`ClassNotFoundException` and `NoClassDefFoundError` both report the same error, that is, the requested class cannot be found. The difference is that `ClassNotFoundException` is an exception thrown by a program-defined class loader or the user's invocation of a method to find a class (such as the use of `Class.forName()` and `ClassLoader.findSystemClass()`). On the other hand, `NoClassDefFoundError` is a runtime linkage error thrown by the Java virtual machine when it is attempting to load and resolve class references.

A method that throws `ClassNotFoundException` must declare it or any of its superclasses in its `throws` clause.

MEMBER SUMMARY	
Constructor	
`ClassNotFoundException()`	Constructs a `ClassNotFoundException` instance.

See Also

`Class`, `Class.forName()`, `ClassLoader.loadClass()`, `ClassLoader.findSystemClass()`, `NoClassDefFoundError`.

Example

This program defines a class `DebugClassLoader` that just echoes the class being loaded. You can make this program throw `ClassNotFoundException` by giving it a bogus class name. A valid class name is qualified by its package name (e.g., `java.io.String`).

```
class DebugClassLoader extends ClassLoader {
    public synchronized Class loadClass(String name, boolean resolve)
        throws ClassNotFoundException {
            System.out.println("Loading " + name);
            return (findSystemClass(name));
        }
}
class Main {
    public static void main(String[] args) {
        System.out.println("ClassNotFound Example");
        if (args.length != 1) {
            System.err.println("usage: java Main <classname>");
            System.exit(1);
        }
        DebugClassLoader loader = new DebugClassLoader();
        try {
            loader.loadClass(args[0], true);
        } catch (ClassNotFoundException e) {
            e.printStackTrace();
        }
    }
}
```

A
B
C
D
E
F
G
H
I
J
K
L
M
N
O
P
Q
R
S
T
U
V
W
X
Y
Z

ClassNotFoundException()

PURPOSE Constructs a `ClassNotFoundException` instance.

SYNTAX
```
public ClassNotFoundException()
public ClassNotFoundException(String msg)
```

DESCRIPTION These constructors create a new instance of `ClassNotFoundException`. An optional string `msg` can be supplied that describes this particular instance of the exception.

PARAMETERS

`msg` A string that gives details about this exception.

java.lang
Cloneable

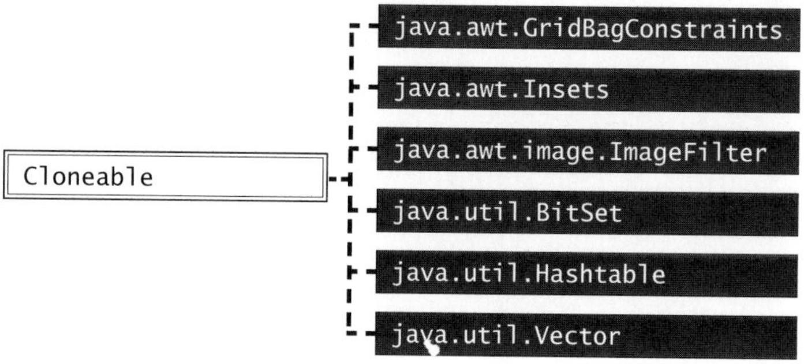

Syntax

`public interface Cloneable`

Description

If you want a class to support the `clone()` method (defined in `Object`), it is not sufficient to just override that method. You must provide the definition of the overridden `clone()` method, as well as declare the class to implement the `Cloneable` interface. Invoking `clone()` on an instance of a class that does not implement `Cloneable` will raise the exception `CloneNotSupportedException`.

See Also

`CloneNotSupportedException`, `Object`.

Example

This example comes from the `Hashtable` class, which overrides the `clone()` method. This `clone()` makes a duplicate of the table as well as duplicates of all the entries (buckets) in the table.

```
public class Hashtable extends Dictionary implements Cloneable {
    ...
    public synchronized Object clone() {
        try {
            Hashtable t = (Hashtable)super.clone();
            t.table = new HashtableEntry[table.length];
            for (int i = table.length ; i-- > 0 ; ) {
                t.table[i] = (table[i] != null) ?
                    (HashtableEntry)table[i].clone() : null;
            }
```

A B C D E F G H I J K L M N O P Q R S T U V W X Y Z

Example

```
                return t;
            } catch (CloneNotSupportedException e) {
                // this shouldn't happen, since we are Cloneable
                throw new InternalError();
            }
        }
    }
```

CloneNotSupportedException

Syntax

```
public class CloneNotSupportedException extends Exception
```

Description

`CloneNotSupportedException` is an exception that is thrown when the program attempts to clone an object that does not explicitly support the `clone()` method or whose class does not implement the `Cloneable` interface.

A method that throws `CloneNotSupportedException` must declare it or any of its superclasses in its `throws` clause.

MEMBER SUMMARY	
Constructor	
`CloneNotSupportedException()`	Constructs a `CloneNotSupportedException` instance.

A B C D E F G H I J K L M N O P Q R S T U V W X Y Z

See Also

Cloneable, Exception, Object.clone().

Example

The following example throws a CloneNotSupportedException because A was not declared to support the Cloneable interface:

```
class A {
    private static int a;
    public A(int i) {
        a = i;
    }
    public Object clone() {
        try {
            Object newa = super.clone();
            ((A)(newa)).a = a;
            return (newa);
        } catch (CloneNotSupportedException e) {
            e.printStackTrace();
        }
        return (null);
    }
}
class Main {
    public static void main(String[] args) {
        System.out.println("CloneNotSupportedException example");
        A i = new A(10);

        A j = (A)i.clone();
    }
}
```

CloneNotSupportedException()

PURPOSE Constructs a CloneNotSupportedException instance.

SYNTAX
```
public CloneNotSupportedException()
public CloneNotSupportedException(String msg)
```

DESCRIPTION These constructors create a new instance of CloneNotSupportedException. An optional string msg can be supplied that describes this particular instance of the exception.

PARAMETERS

msg A string that gives details about this exception.

A B C D E F G H I J K L M N O P Q R S T U V W X Y Z

java.awt
Color

java.lang.Object — Color

Syntax

```
public final class Color
```

Description

A `Color` instance specifies a color that is used in graphics operations. Colors are also used when setting the background and foreground colors of components. The actual color displayed by the system may not exactly match the desired color because of limitations in the rendering device. In this case, the closest matching color is used.

A color can be specified using either the *RGB* (*red, green, blue*) or *HSB* (*hue, saturation, brightness*) color coding system. In the RGB system, the three color components are values in the range `0`–`255`; the higher the value, the brighter the component. An RGB value of (`0`, `0`, `0`) is black and an RGB value of (`255`, `255`, `255`) is white. In the HSB system, the three color components are values between `0.0` and `1.0`. An HSB value of (`0.0`, `0.0`, `0.0`) is black and an HSB value of (`0.0`, `0.0`, `1.0`) is white.

MEMBER SUMMARY

Constructor

`Color()`	Constructs a new `Color` instance.

Pre-defined Colors

`black`	This constant field holds the color black (`0`, `0`, `0`).
`blue`	This constant field holds the color blue (`0`, `0`, `255`).
`cyan`	This constant field holds the color cyan (`0`, `255`, `255`).
`darkGray`	This constant field holds the color dark gray (`64`, `64`, `64`).
`gray`	This constant field holds the color gray (`128`, `128`, `128`).
`green`	This constant field holds the color green (`0`, `255`, `0`)
`lightGray`	This constant field holds the color light gray (`192`, `192`, `192`).
`magenta`	This constant field holds the color magenta (`255`, `0`, `255`).
`orange`	This constant field holds the color orange (`255`, `200`, `0`).
`pink`	This constant field holds the color pink (`255`, `175`, `175`).
`red`	This constant field holds the color red (`255`, `0`, `0`).
`white`	This constant field holds the color white (`255`, `255`, `255`).
`yellow`	This constant field holds the color yellow (`255`, `255`, `0`).

Continued

A B C D E F G H I J K L M N O P Q R S T U V W X Y Z

MEMBER SUMMARY

Color Converter	
`brighter()`	Calculates a brighter version of the color.
`darker()`	Calculates a darker version of the color.
Color Component Methods	
`getBlue()`	Retrieves the blue component of the color.
`getGreen()`	Retrieves the green component of the color.
`getRed()`	Retrieves the red component of the color.
`getRGB()`	Retrieves the 24-bit RGB representation of the color.
HSB Methods	
`getHSBColor()`	Creates a new `Color` instance from an HSB specification.
`HSBtoRGB()`	Converts an HSB color specification to a 24-bit RGB color specification.
`RGBtoHSB()`	Converts an RGB color specification to an HSB color specification.
Property Method	
`getColor()`	Retrieves a color from a system property.
Debugging Method	
`toString()`	Generates a string representation of the color.
General Methods	
`equals()`	Determines if an object is equal to the color.
`hashCode()`	Calculates the hash code for the color.

Example

This example creates two sets of scrollbars that are used to pick a color (Figure 50). One set is based on RGB values, while the other is based on HSB values. Changing a scrollbar in one set modifies the scrollbars in the other. An uneditable text field is located at the bottom of the frame and shows the current color in both the RGB and HSB color coding systems.

Since the HSB values are in the range `0–1.0` and scrollbars only handle integer values, you must multiply the HSB values by `1000` to get an integer value. Hence a scrollbar representing an HSB component uses the range `0–1000`.

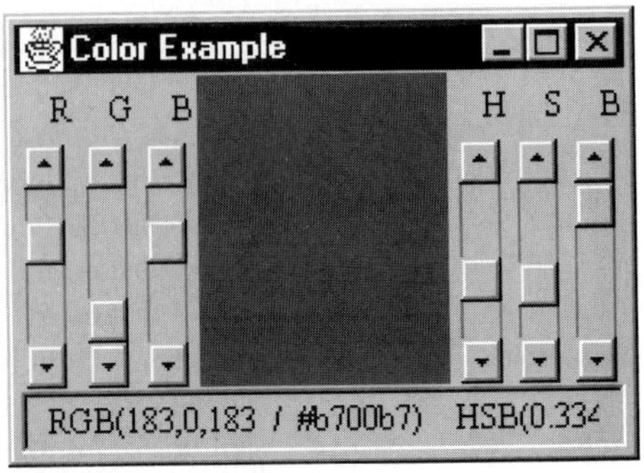

FIGURE 50 `Color`

The scrollbar sets the value `0` at the top of the scrollbar. However, since it is more intuitive to have the value `0` appear at the bottom of the scrollbar, the direction of the scrollbar is "reversed." To reverse the direction of the scrollbar, the value of the scrollbar is subtracted from the maximum value.

A gridbag layout (see `GridBagLayout`) is used to lay out a set of scrollbars. The first row is a row of labels, while the second is a row of scrollbars. The weight is given to the second row so that if the window is enlarged, the scrollbars, rather than the labels, stretch.

```
import java.awt.*;

class Main extends Frame {
    Scrollbar sbRed = new Scrollbar(Scrollbar.VERTICAL);
    Scrollbar sbGreen = new Scrollbar(Scrollbar.VERTICAL);
    Scrollbar sbBlue = new Scrollbar(Scrollbar.VERTICAL);
    Scrollbar sbH = new Scrollbar(Scrollbar.VERTICAL);
    Scrollbar sbS = new Scrollbar(Scrollbar.VERTICAL);
    Scrollbar sbB = new Scrollbar(Scrollbar.VERTICAL);
    TextField status = new TextField();
    int r = 256;
    int g = 256;
    int b = 256;
    float[] hsb;

    Main() {
        super("Color Example");
        add("West", makeScrollbars("R", sbRed, "G", sbGreen,
            "B", sbBlue));
        add("East", makeScrollbars("H", sbH, "S", sbS, "B", sbB));
        status.setEditable(false);
        add("South", status);
        resize(300, 300);
        show();
        setBackground(adjustHSBScrollbars());
        adjustRGBScrollbars();
    }

    Panel makeScrollbars(String l1, Scrollbar sb1,
            String l2, Scrollbar sb2, String l3, Scrollbar sb3) {
        double[] rowWeights = {0.0, 1.0};
        Panel p = new Panel();
        GridBagLayout gbl = new GridBagLayout();

        gbl.rowWeights = rowWeights;
        p.setLayout(gbl);
        add(p, gbl, new Label(l1, Label.CENTER),
            0, 0, GridBagConstraints.NONE);
        add(p, gbl, sb1, 0, 1, GridBagConstraints.VERTICAL);
        add(p, gbl, new Label(l2, Label.CENTER),
            1, 0, GridBagConstraints.NONE);
        add(p, gbl, sb2, 1, 1, GridBagConstraints.VERTICAL);
        add(p, gbl, new Label(l3, Label.CENTER),
            2, 0, GridBagConstraints.NONE);
```

Example

```
        add(p, gbl, sb3, 2, 1, GridBagConstraints.VERTICAL);
        return p;
    }

    void add(Panel p, GridBagLayout gbl, Component comp, int x,
        int y, int fill) {
        GridBagConstraints gbc = new GridBagConstraints();
        gbc.gridx = x;
        gbc.gridy = y;
        gbc.fill = fill;
        gbl.setConstraints(comp, gbc);
        p.add(comp);
    }

    public boolean handleEvent(Event evt) {
        Color c = getBackground();

        if (evt.target == sbRed) {
            r = 255-sbRed.getValue();
            c = adjustHSBScrollbars();
        } else if (evt.target == sbGreen) {
            g = 255-sbGreen.getValue();
            c = adjustHSBScrollbars();
        } else if (evt.target == sbBlue) {
            b = 255-sbBlue.getValue();
            c = adjustHSBScrollbars();
        } else if (evt.target == sbH) {
            hsb[0] = (1000-sbH.getValue()) / 1000.0f;
            c = adjustRGBScrollbars();
        } else if (evt.target == sbS) {
            hsb[1] = (1000-sbS.getValue()) / 1000.0f;
            c = adjustRGBScrollbars();
        } else if (evt.target == sbB) {
            hsb[2] = (1000-sbB.getValue()) / 1000.0f;
            c = adjustRGBScrollbars();
        }
        setBackground(c);
        repaint();
        status.setText("RGB("+r+","+g+","+b+"   /   "+
            "#"+Integer.toString(c.getRGB()&0xffffff, 16)+")"+
            "     HSB("+hsb[0]+","+hsb[1]+","+hsb[2]+")");
        return super.handleEvent(evt);
    }

    Color adjustHSBScrollbars() {
        hsb = Color.RGBtoHSB(r, g, b, null);
        sbH.setValues(1000-(int)(hsb[0] * 1000), 1, 0, 1000);
        sbS.setValues(1000-(int)(hsb[1] * 1000), 1, 0, 1000);
        sbB.setValues(1000-(int)(hsb[2] * 1000), 1, 0, 1000);
        return new Color(r, g, b);
    }

    Color adjustRGBScrollbars() {
        Color c = Color.getHSBColor(hsb[0], hsb[1], hsb[2]);
```

```
        // An alternate way of converting the HSB values to RGB:
        // Color c = new Color(Color.HSBtoRGB(hsb[0], hsb[1], hsb[2]));

        sbRed.setValues(255-(r = c.getRed()), 1, 0, 255);
        sbGreen.setValues(255-(g = c.getGreen()), 1, 0, 255);
        sbBlue.setValues(255-(b = c.getBlue()), 1, 0, 255);
        return c;
    }

    public static void main(String[] args) {
        new Main();
    }
}
```

black

PURPOSE This constant field holds the color black (0, 0, 0).

SYNTAX `public final static Color black`

EXAMPLE This example paints dots at random positions on the screen using random colors taken from the predefined palette of colors. This example also demonstrates the use of a thread to continually paint a dot every 16 milliseconds. See Figure 51.

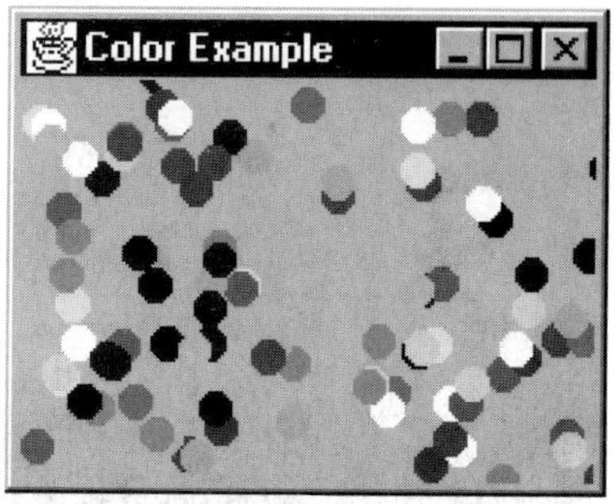

FIGURE 51 Pre-defined Colors

```
import java.awt.*;
class Main extends Frame implements Runnable {
    Color[] colors = {Color.black, Color.blue, Color.cyan,
        Color.darkGray,
        Color.gray, Color.green, Color.lightGray, Color.magenta,
        Color.orange,
        Color.pink, Color.red, Color.white, Color.yellow}

    Main() {
        resize(200, 200);
        show();
        (new Thread(this)).start();
    }

    int random(int r) {
        return (int)Math.floor(Math.random() * r);
    }
```

```
    public void update(Graphics g) {
        g.setColor(colors[random(colors.length)]);
        g.fillOval(random(size().width), random(size().height),
        10, 10);
    }

    public void run() {
        while (true) {
            repaint();
            try {
                Thread.sleep(16);
            } catch (Exception e) {
            }
        }
    }

    public static void main(String[] args) {
        new Main();
    }
}
```

blue

PURPOSE This constant field holds the color blue (0, 0, 255).

SYNTAX `public final static Color blue`

EXAMPLE See `black`.

brighter()

PURPOSE Calculates a brighter version of the color.

SYNTAX `public Color brighter()`

RETURNS A new non-`null` color instance containing a brighter version of the color.

EXAMPLE See `getColor()`.

Color()

PURPOSE Constructs a new `Color` instance.

SYNTAX `public Color(int red, int green, int blue)`

```
public Color(float redF, float greenF, float blueF)
public Color(int rgb)
```

DESCRIPTION This constructor creates a new `Color` with the specified RGB values. The RGB values can be specified in three ways. The first is with three integers in the range `0`–`255`. If an integer is larger than `255`, only the lower 8 bits are used.

The second way is with three floats in the range `0.0`–`1.0`. These floating-point numbers are converted into integers in the range `0`–`255`.

The third way is with a 24-bit integer. See `getRGB()` for information about how the values are encoded. If the integer is larger than 24 bits, only the lower 24 bits are used.

PARAMETERS

`blue` The blue component of the color. This value must be in the range `0`–`255`.

`blueF` The blue component of the color. This value must be in the range `0`–`1`.

`green` The green component of the color. This value must be in the range `0`–`255`.

`greenF` The green component of the color. This value must be in the range `0`–`1`.

`red` The red component of the color. This value must be in the range `0`–`255`.

`redF` The red component of the color. This value must be in the range `0`–`1`.

`rgb` The RGB value encoded as 24 bits. See `getRGB()` for details about the encoding.

FIGURE 52 Example `Color()`

EXAMPLE This simple example creates a frame and draws a yellow oval in the middle of the frame.

```
import java.awt.*;
class Main extends Frame {
    Main() {
        super("Color Example");
        resize(100, 100);
        show();
    }

    public void paint(Graphics g) {
        int w = size().width - insets().left - insets().right;
        int h = size().height - insets().top - insets().bottom;

        g.setColor(new Color(255, 255, 0));
        g.fillOval(w/4, h/4, w/2, h/2);
    }
```

A B C D E F G H I J K L M N O P Q R S T U V W X Y Z

```
        public static void main(String[] args) {
            new Main();
        }
    }
```

cyan

PURPOSE This constant field holds the color cyan (0, 255, 255).

SYNTAX `public final static Color cyan`

EXAMPLE See `black`.

darker()

PURPOSE Calculates a darker version of the color.

SYNTAX `public Color darker()`

RETURNS A new non-`null` `Color` instance containing a darker version of the color.

EXAMPLE See `getColor()`.

darkGray

PURPOSE This constant field holds the color dark gray (64, 64, 64).

SYNTAX `public final static Color darkGray`

EXAMPLE See `black`.

equals()

PURPOSE Determines if an object is equal to the color.

SYNTAX `public boolean equals(Object obj)`

DESCRIPTION An object `obj` is equal to this color if `obj` is a `Color` instance and their red, green, and blue component values are identical to those of this color.

PARAMETERS

`obj` The object to compare with. `obj` may be `null`.

RETURNS `true` if object is equal to this color; `false` otherwise.

OVERRIDES `Object.equals()`.

EXAMPLE See `getColor()`.

getBlue()

PURPOSE Retrieves the blue component of the color.

SYNTAX `public int getBlue()`

RETURNS The blue component of the color that is a value in the range `0–255`.

SEE ALSO `Color()`.

EXAMPLE See the class example.

getColor()

PURPOSE Retrieves a color from a system property.

SYNTAX

```
public static Color getColor(String propertyName)
public static Color getColor(String propertyName, int defaultInt)
public static Color getColor(String propertyName, Color
   defaultColor)
```

DESCRIPTION These methods retrieve the color associated with the system property `propertyName`. If `propertyName` is not defined or the value is not an integer, then one of three things can be returned. First, if `defaultInt` is defined, then a new color instance containing the 24-bit RGB `defaultInt` value is returned. Second, if `defaultColor` is specified, it is returned. Third, if neither `defaultInt` nor `defaultColor` are specified, then `null` is returned.

PARAMETERS

`defaultColor`	The color instance to use if the system property is not defined or the value is malformed.
`defaultInt`	The 24-bit color value to use if the system property is not defined or the value is malformed.
`propertyName`	The non-`null` name of the system property.

RETURNS A new non-`null` color instance containing the color as defined by the system property `propertyName`.

SEE ALSO `getRGB()`.

EXAMPLE This example reads in some properties from a file that defines some text, the color of the text, and its background color. Figure 53 shows the contents of the properties file. Figure 54 shows the frame displaying the text.

To see how the two methods `brighter()` and `darker()` work, click the window; the text brightens and the background color darkens.

```
# text
text.value=Java

# blue text
text.fg=#000088

# yellow background
text.bg=#eeee00
```

FIGURE 53 `properties.txt`

FIGURE 54 `Color.getColor()`.

```
import java.awt.*;
import java.io.*;
import java.util.*;

class Main extends Frame {
    Color fg, originalFg;
    Color bg, originalBg;
    String str;

    Main() {
        super("getColor Example");
        try {
            System.getProperties().load(
                new FileInputStream("properties.txt"));
            System.getProperties().list(System.out);
            fg = originalFg = Color.getColor("text.fg", 0x000000);
            bg = originalBg = Color.getColor("text.bg", Color.white);
            str = System.getProperties().getProperty("text.value");
        } catch (Exception e) {
            e.printStackTrace();
        }
        resize(200, 100);
        show();
    }
```

```
    public void paint(Graphics g) {
        Insets insets = insets();
        int w = size().width-insets.left-insets.right;
        int h = size().height-insets.top-insets.bottom;
        Font f = new Font("Helvetica", Font.BOLD, 40);
        FontMetrics fm = g.getFontMetrics(f);

        g.setFont(f);
        g.setColor(bg);
        g.fillRect(0, 0, w, h);
        g.setColor(fg);
        g.drawString(str, (w-fm.stringWidth(str))/2,
                          (h-fm.getHeight())/2+fm.getAscent());
    }

    public boolean mouseDown(Event evt, int x, int y) {
        // If darkening or brightening either color has no
        // effect, simply swap the colors.
        if (originalFg.brighter().equals(originalFg)
            || originalBg.brighter().equals(originalBg)) {
            fg = originalBg;
            bg = originalFg;
        } else {
            fg = originalFg.brighter();
            bg = originalBg.darker();
        }
        repaint();
        return true;
    }

    public boolean mouseUp(Event evt, int x, int y) {
        fg = originalFg;
        bg = originalBg;
        repaint();
        return true;
    }

    public static void main(String[] args) {
        new Main();
    }
}
```

getGreen()

PURPOSE Retrieves the green component of the color.

SYNTAX `public int getGreen()`

RETURNS The green component of the color. It is a value in the range `0–255`.

A B C D E F G H I J K L M N O P Q R S T U V W X Y Z

SEE ALSO `Color()`.

EXAMPLE See the class example.

getHSBColor()

PURPOSE Creates a new `Color` instance from an HSB specification.

SYNTAX
```
public static Color getHSBColor(float hue, float saturation,
   float brightness)
```

DESCRIPTION This method is equivalent to
```
new Color(HSBtoRGB(hue, saturation, brightness));
```

PARAMETERS

`brightness`	The brightness component of the color. This value must be in the range `0–1.0`.
`hue`	The hue component of the color. This value must be in the range `0–1.0`.
`saturation`	The saturation component of the color. This value must be in the range `0–1.0`.

RETURNS A new non-`null` `Color` instance based on the specified HSB values.

EXAMPLE See the class example.

getRed()

PURPOSE Retrieves the red component of the color.

SYNTAX `public int getRed()`

RETURNS The red component of the color. It is a value in the range `0–255`.

SEE ALSO `Color()`.

EXAMPLE See the class example.

getRGB()

PURPOSE Retrieves the 24-bit RGB representation of the color.

SYNTAX `public int getRGB()`

DESCRIPTION This method returns the RGB representation of the color. It always has the following format. Bits 24–31 always have the value `0xff`. Bits 16–23 contain the value of the red component. Bits 8–15 contain the value of the green component. Bits 0–7 contain the value of the blue component.

RETURNS The 24-bit RGB representation of the color.

SEE ALSO `Color()`.

EXAMPLE See the class example.

gray

PURPOSE This constant field holds the color gray (`128`, `128`, `128`).

SYNTAX `public final static Color gray`

EXAMPLE See `black`.

green

PURPOSE This constant field holds the color green (`0`, `255`, `0`).

SYNTAX `public final static Color green`

EXAMPLE See `black`.

hashCode()

PURPOSE Calculates the hash code for the color.

SYNTAX `public int hashCode()`

DESCRIPTION This method calculates this color's hash code from its RGB value. If `equals(c1, c2)` is `true`, then `c1` and `c2` will have the same hash codes; otherwise `c1` and `c2` will likely have different hash codes.

A B C D E F G H I J K L M N O P Q R S T U V W X Y Z

RETURNS The color's hash code.

OVERRIDES `Object.hashCode()`.

SEE ALSO `equals()`.

EXAMPLE See `Object.hashCode()`.

HSBtoRGB()

PURPOSE Converts an HSB color specification to a 24-bit RGB color specification.

SYNTAX
```
public static int HSBtoRGB(float hue, float saturation, float
    brightness)
```

DESCRIPTION The RGB color as a 24-bit integer. See `getRGB()` for details about the encoding.

PARAMETERS

`brightness` The brightness component of the color. This value must be in the range `0`– `1.0`.

`hue` The hue component of the color. This value must be in the range `0`–`1.0`.

`saturation` The saturation component of the color. This value must be in the range `0`– `1.0`.

SEE ALSO `ColorModel.getRGBdefault()`, `getRGB()`.

EXAMPLE See the class example.

lightGray

PURPOSE This constant field holds the color light gray (`192`, `192`, `192`).

SYNTAX
```
public final static Color lightGray
```

EXAMPLE See `black`.

magenta

PURPOSE This constant field holds the color magenta (`255`, `0`, `255`).

SYNTAX
```
public final static Color magenta
```

EXAMPLE See `black`.

orange

PURPOSE This constant field holds the color orange (255, 200, 0).

SYNTAX `public final static Color orange`

EXAMPLE See `black`.

pink

PURPOSE This constant field holds the color pink (255, 175, 175).

SYNTAX `public final static Color pink`

EXAMPLE See `black`.

red

PURPOSE This constant field holds the color red (255, 0, 0).

SYNTAX `public final static Color red`

EXAMPLE See `black`.

RGBtoHSB()

PURPOSE Converts an RGB color specification to an HSB color specification.

SYNTAX

```
public static float[] RGBtoHSB(int red, int green, int blue,
    float[] hsbReturnValues)
```

DESCRIPTION If `hsbReturnValues` is not `null`, the HSB values are placed in the `hsbReturnValues` and `hsbReturnValues` itself is returned. If `hsbReturnValues` is `null`, a new array containing the HSB values is returned.

PARAMETERS

`blue` The blue component of the color. This value must be in the range 0–255.

`green` The green component of the color. This value must be in the range 0–255.

`hsbReturnValues`	The array to be used to return the three HSB values—hue, saturation, and brightness—or `null`. If non-`null`, the array must have length of at least 3.
`red`	The red component of the color. This value must be in the range `0`–`255`.

RETURNS A non-`null` array containing three values in the range `0`–`1.0`. The first element contains the hue, the second contains the saturation, and the third contains the brightness.

SEE ALSO `ColorModel.getRGBdefault()`, `getRGB()`, `Image`.

EXAMPLE See the class example.

toString()

PURPOSE Generates a string representation of the color.

SYNTAX `public String toString()`

DESCRIPTION This method returns the string representation of this color, which consists of its RGB values.

This method is typically used for debugging.

RETURNS A non-`null` string representing the color.

OVERRIDES `Object.toString()`.

EXAMPLE See `Object.toString()`.

white

PURPOSE This constant field holds the color white (`255`, `255`, `255`).

SYNTAX `public final static Color white`

EXAMPLE See `black`.

yellow

PURPOSE This constant field holds the color yellow (`255`, `255`, `0`).

SYNTAX `public final static Color yellow`

EXAMPLE See `black`.

java.awt.image
ColorModel

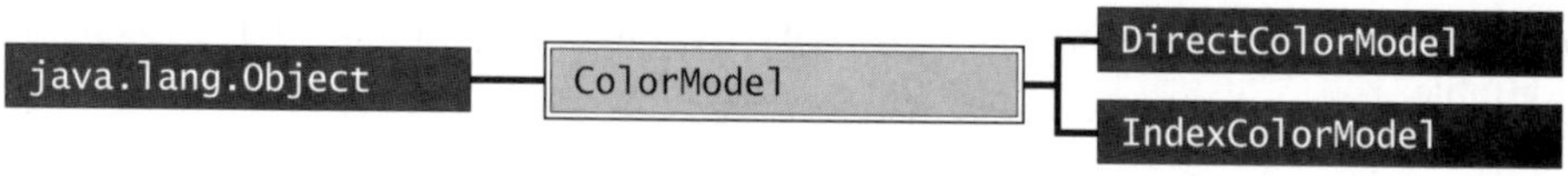

Syntax

```
public abstract class ColorModel
```

Description

An image is a collection of pixels. Each pixel has a location in the image and a value. The purpose of the `ColorModel` class is to convert these pixel values into colors. There are many ways to encode a color as a pixel value; the two main ones are described in the following sections. However, the important fact to remember is that a set of pixel values is meaningless unless it is associated with an instance of `ColorModel` to interpret those pixel values.

The Index Color Model

In the *index color model*, pixel values do not themselves contain any information from which you could extract a color. Rather, pixel values are used to index into a color table (see Figure 55 a). The actual set of colors in the table are encapsulated in a `ColorModel` instance and can vary from instance to instance.

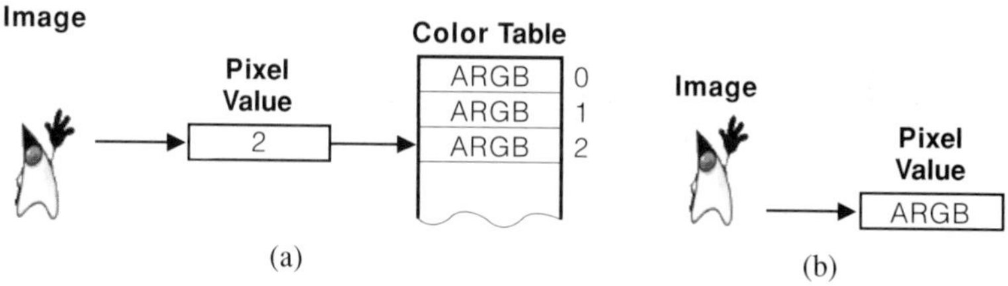

FIGURE 55 The Two Types of Color Models

You can tell if a color model instance is using the index color model by determining if it is an instance of `IndexColorModel`. Using the `IndexColorModel` class, you can create an instance with your own set of colors. See the `IndexColorModel` class for additional methods.

The Direct Color Model

In the *direct color model*, the pixel values actually contain the color information. In this case, the color mode is to extract the color information from the pixel value (see Figure 55 b). The typical encoding used in a direct color model is to divide the bits in a pixel value among the components of a color. For example, in one encoding you could allow 2 bits for red and green, 10 bits for blue, and 4 bits for alpha.

You can tell if a color model instance is using the direct color model by determining if it is an instance of `DirectColorModel`. The `DirectColorModel` class allows you to specify an encoding that divides the bits of a pixel value among the four color components. See the `DirectColorModel` class for additional methods.

The main advantage of the index color model over the direct color model is that an image using an index color model can be represented in much less space (three to four times smaller). The disadvantage is that the available colors that the image can use are limited to the ones in the color table.

The Default Color Model

The AWT package specifies what is called the *default color model,* which is used as a "standard" when converting between different color models. If a method is described to return pixel values in the default color model, it doesn't need to return an instance of any other color model. To interpret such pixels, you only need to retrieve the default color model using the `getRGBdefault()` method in this class.

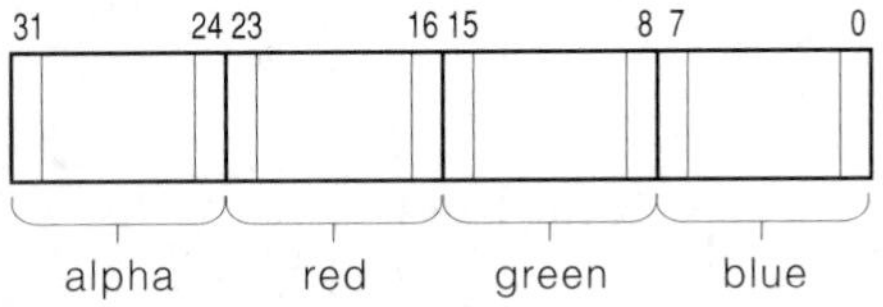

FIGURE 56 Pixel Value Format for the Default Color Model

The format for pixel values in the default color model is an integer with 8 bits each of alpha, red, green, and blue color components ordered correspondingly from the most significant byte to the least significant byte. This is shown in Figure 56.

MEMBER SUMMARY	
Constructor Method	
`ColorModel()`	Constructs a new `ColorModel` instance.
Color Component Methods	
`getAlpha()`	Retrieves the alpha component of a pixel value.
`getBlue()`	Retrieves the blue component of a pixel value.
`getGreen()`	Retrieves the green component of a pixel value.
`getRed()`	Retrieves the red component of a pixel value.
`getRGB()`	Converts a pixel value to a pixel value in the default color model.
Pixel Size Members	
`getPixelSize()`	Retrieves the bit size of pixel values in the color model.
`pixel_bits`	This field holds the bit size of pixel values using this color model.
Default Color Model Method	
`getRGBdefault()`	Retrieves the default color mode.

Example

This example retrieves the color model used by an AWT component (which is platform-dependent). If an index color model is used, all the colors in the color model's color table are displayed in a grid (see Figure 57). If a direct color model is used, 256 random colors are generated and displayed.

When the cursor is moved over a displayed color, the program displays the color components of the color in a label located at the top of the window.

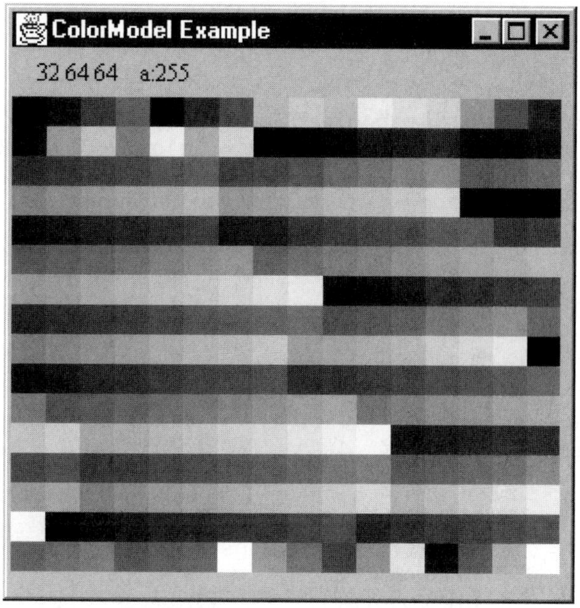

FIGURE 57 `ColorModel`

```
import java.awt.*;
import java.awt.image.*;
import java.util.Random;

class Main extends Frame {
    ColorGrid cgrid;
    Label label = new Label();

    Main() {
        super("ColorModel Example");
        ColorModel colorModel =
            Toolkit.getDefaultToolkit().getColorModel();
        int bitsize = colorModel.getPixelSize();

        if (colorModel instanceof IndexColorModel) {
            // index color model
            cgrid = new ColorGrid(1 << bitsize);
            for (int i=0; i<1<<bitsize; i++) {
                cgrid.setColor(i, colorModel.getRGB(i));
            }
        } else {
            // direct color model
            Random r = new Random();
            cgrid = new ColorGrid(256);
            for (int i=0; i<256; i++) {
                cgrid.setColor(i, r.nextInt());
            }
        }
        add("Center", cgrid);
        add("North", label);
```

Example

```
            resize(300, 300);
            show();
        }

        public boolean mouseMove(Event evt, int x, int y) {
            ColorModel cm = ColorModel.getRGBdefault();
            int rgb = cgrid.getRGB(x - cgrid.bounds().x,
                y - cgrid.bounds().y);

            label.setText(cm.getRed(rgb) + " " + cm.getGreen(rgb)
                + " " + cm.getBlue(rgb) + "    a:" + cm.getAlpha(rgb));
            return true;
        }

        public static void main(String[] args) {
            new Main();
        }
    }

    // This class displays a grid that is used for displaying colors.
    class ColorGrid extends Canvas {
        int rows, cols;
        int colors[];
        ColorGrid(int numColors) {
            colors = new int[numColors];
            cols = Math.min(16, numColors);
            rows = (numColors - 1) / cols + 1;
        }

        // Sets the color at the cell located at position 'i'.
        // 'rgb' is a color in the default RGB color model.
        void setColor(int i, int rgb) {
            colors[i] = rgb;
        }

        // Returns the pixel value at (x, y).  The pixel value is encoded
        // using the default color model.
        int getRGB(int x, int y) {
            int cellW = size().width / cols;
            int cellH = size().height / rows;

            x /= cellW;
            y /= cellH;

            // Return the last color if out of bounds.
            return colors[Math.min(colors.length-1, y * cols + x)];
        }

        public void paint(Graphics g) {
            int cellW = size().width / cols;
            int cellH = size().height / rows;
```

```
            for (int i=0; i<colors.length; i++) {
                int r = i / cols;
                int c = i % cols;

                g.setColor(new Color(colors[i]));
                g.fillRect(c * cellW, r * cellH, cellW, cellH);
            }
        }
    }
```

ColorModel()

PURPOSE Constructs a new `ColorModel` instance.

SYNTAX `public ColorModel(int b)`

DESCRIPTION This constructor is used by subclasses of this class to specify that the bit size of pixel values of this color model instance is `b` bits wide. This class cannot be directly instantiated.

PARAMETERS

`b` A non-negative number specifying the bit size of pixel values using this color model.

EXAMPLE This class cannot be directly instantiated. See the `ColorModel` subclasses `IndexColorModel` and `DirectColorModel` for examples for constructing `ColorModel` instances.

getAlpha()

PURPOSE Retrieves the alpha component of a pixel value.

SYNTAX `public abstract int getAlpha(int pixelValue)`

DESCRIPTION Subclasses must implement this method to return the alpha component of a color specified by the pixel value `pixelValue`. The return value must be in the range `0`–`255`, where the value `0` means completely transparent and `255` means completely opaque.

PARAMETERS

`pixelValue` The pixel value specifying a color in the color model.

RETURNS The alpha transparency component in the range `0`–`255`.

EXAMPLE See the class example.

getBlue()

PURPOSE Retrieves the blue component of a pixel value.

SYNTAX `public abstract int getBlue(int pixelValue)`

DESCRIPTION Subclasses must implement this method to return the blue component of the color specified by the pixel value `pixelValue`. The return value must be in the range `0`–`255`, where the value `0` means no blue and `255` means maximum blue.

PARAMETERS

`pixelValue` The pixel value specifying a color in the color model.

RETURNS The blue color component in the range from `0`–`255`.

EXAMPLE See the class example.

getGreen()

PURPOSE Retrieves the green component of a pixel value.

SYNTAX `public abstract int getGreen(int pixelValue)`

DESCRIPTION Subclasses must implement this method to return the green component of the color specified by the pixel value `pixelValue`. The return value must be in the range `0`–`255`, where the value `0` means no green and `255` means maximum green.

PARAMETERS

`pixelValue` The pixel value specifying a color in the color model.

RETURNS The green color component in the range `0`–`255`.

EXAMPLE See the class example.

getPixelSize()

PURPOSE Retrieves the bit size of pixel values in the color model.

SYNTAX `public int getPixelSize()`

DESCRIPTION The returned value is the same as the one supplied to the constructor.

RETURNS The bit size of pixel values in the color model.

EXAMPLE See the class example.

getRed()

PURPOSE Retrieves the red component of a pixel value.

SYNTAX `public abstract int getRed(int pixelValue)`

DESCRIPTION Subclasses must implement this method to return the red component of the color specified by the pixel value `pixelValue`. The return value must be in the range `0–255`, where the value `0` means no red and `255` means maximum red.

PARAMETERS

`pixelValue` The pixel value specifying a color in the color model.

RETURNS The red color component in the range from `0–255`.

EXAMPLE See the class example.

getRGB()

PURPOSE Converts a pixel value to a pixel value in the default color model.

SYNTAX `public int getRGB(int pixelValue)`

DESCRIPTION The pixel value `pixelValue` is converted to an equivalent pixel value that must be interpreted using the default color model. The color of the new pixel value may not necessarily be identical to the color of `pixelValue`. There may be some loss of color information.

PARAMETERS

`pixelValue` The pixel value specifying a color in the color model.

RETURNS A pixel value that specifies a color in the default color model.

SEE ALSO `ColorModel.getRGBdefault()`.

EXAMPLE See the class example.

A B C D E F G H I J K L M N O P Q R S T U V W X Y Z

getRGBdefault()

PURPOSE Retrieves the default color model.

SYNTAX `public static ColorModel getRGBdefault()`

DESCRIPTION The color model instance returned by this method is used to translate pixel values encoded with the default color model into colors.

RETURNS A non-`null` instance of the default color model.

EXAMPLE See the class example.

pixel_bits

PURPOSE This field holds the bit size of pixel values using this color model.

SYNTAX `protected int pixel_bits`

DESCRIPTION This holds the value that was specified by the `ColorModel` constructor.

SEE ALSO See `ColorModel()`.

Compiler

Object — Compiler

Syntax

```
public final class Compiler
```

Description

The `Compiler` class is used to control a compiler that compiles Java byte codes directly into machine code for a particular platform. Such a compiler is not included in the Java development kit from Sun Microsystems and must be obtained from a third-party source.

If the system property `java.compiler` exists, it defines the name of the library that contains the compiler. The value of the `java.compiler` property is passed into `System.loadLibary()` to load the library. When a class is compiled into machine code, the machine code is not returned. Rather, the Java runtime maintains the compiled machine code and runs it automatically whenever a method in the class is called.

MEMBER SUMMARY

Compiler Methods	
`command()`	Sends a command to the compiler.
`compileClass()`	Compiles a class into machine code.
`compileClasses()`	Compiles classes by name into machine code.
`disable()`	Disables the compiler.
`enable()`	Enables the compiler.

command()

PURPOSE Sends a command to the compiler.

SYNTAX `public static native Object command(Object arg)`

DESCRIPTION This method allows an application to communicate with the compiler. Since different compilers will have different commands that they respond to, you need to read the documentation supplied by the compiler vendor to determine the commands that are available.

A B C D E F G H I J K L M N O P Q R S T U V W X Y Z

PARAMETERS

`arg` A compiler-specific argument.

RETURNS A compiler-specific return value. `null` is returned if the compiler is not loaded or is disabled.

SEE ALSO `disable()`, `enable()`.

compileClass()

PURPOSE Compiles a class into machine code.

SYNTAX `public static native boolean compileClass(Class oneClass)`

DESCRIPTION This method compiles the class `oneClass` into machine code.

PARAMETERS

`oneClass` The non-`null` class to compile.

RETURNS `true` if the compilation succeeds; `false` otherwise. `false` is also returned if the compiler is not loaded or is disabled.

SEE ALSO `disable()`, `enable()`.

compileClasses()

PURPOSE Compiles classes by name into machine code.

SYNTAX `public static native boolean compileClasses(String classNames)`

DESCRIPTION The string `classNames` specifies the names of the classes to compile. In the simple case, `classNames` names a single class. To name more than one class, check with the compiler documentation to determine how multiple class names are specified.

PARAMETERS

`classNames` The non-`null` string containing the name of the classes to compile.

RETURNS `true` if the compilation of all the classes succeed; `false` otherwise. `false` is also returned if the compiler is not loaded or is disabled.

SEE ALSO `disable()`, `enable()`.

disable()

PURPOSE Disables the compiler.

SYNTAX `public static native void disable()`

DESCRIPTION This method disables the compiler. When the compiler has been disabled, `command()` returns `null`, while `compileClass()` and `compileClasses()` return `false`.

SEE ALSO `command()`, `compileClass()`, `compileClasses()`.

enable()

PURPOSE Enables the compiler.

SYNTAX `public static native void enable()`

DESCRIPTION This method enables the compiler so that classes can be compiled.

SEE ALSO `command()`, `compileClass()`, `compileClasses()`.

java.awt
Component

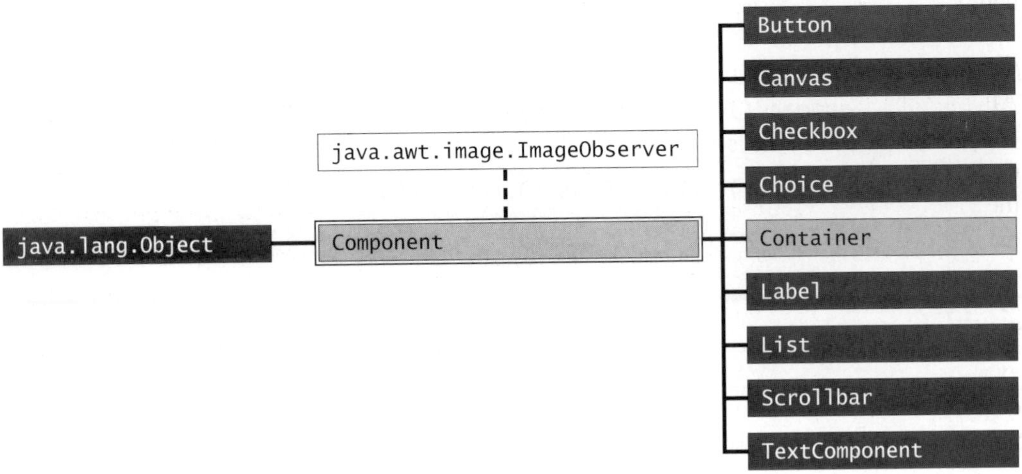

Syntax

```
public abstract class Component implements ImageObserver
```

Description

A *component* is a user interface object that can be displayed on the screen and interact with the user. Such user interface objects include buttons, scrollbars, and text fields. The `Component` class is the superclass of all nonmenu-related components (the `MenuComponent` class is the superclass of all menu-related components).

The Component Hierarchy

Some components are containers that have all the properties of a component and the additional ability to contain other components (called *children*). A user interface is made of many components and containers. All components (and containers) must exist inside another container (called the *parent*); only the top-most container lacks a parent. This arrangement produces a hierarchy of components that affects how components are laid out and how events travel from one component to another. Figure 58 shows an example of a component hierarchy. More information about layout and events are described below.

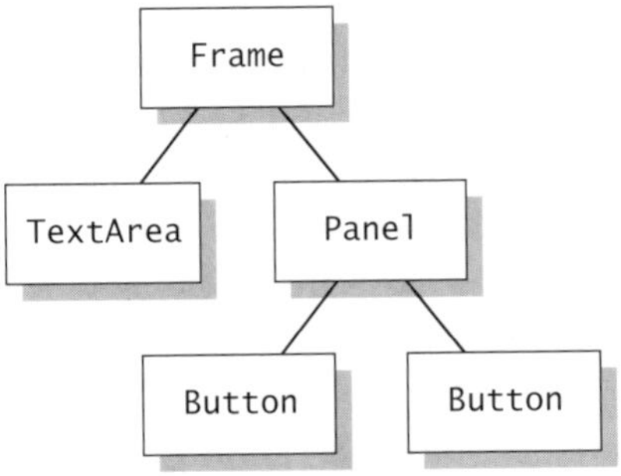

FIGURE 58 Component Hierarchy

Bounds

The *bounds* of a component specify the absolute size of the component and its location within its parent. The width and height of the bounds specify the dimensions of the component without regard to any insets (see `Container`). The *x*- and *y*-coordinates of the bounds specify the coordinates of the component relative to the bounds of its parent.

Coordinates

All coordinates used by the classes in the AWT package, such as in mouse events or graphics painting, are either relative to a component's bounds or inset area. The inset area applies to components that are containers. See the `Container` class for details on the inset area. Only if the component's inset area differs from its bounds is it necessary to determine whether a method using coordinates interprets them relative to the bounds or inset area.

Minimum and Preferred Sizes

Every component has a *minimum* size and a *preferred* size. The minimum size of a button, for example, is such that the button's label can be properly displayed in its current font. For non-container components like buttons and scrollbars, the preferred and minimum sizes are usually the same.

It's important to note that the results of calling the `preferredSize()` or `minimumSize()` differ depending on whether or not the component's peer exists. In general, the peers of the component hierarchy should be created before the minimum or preferred size of the component hierarchy is calculated.

Layout and the Valid State

Layout normally applies to components that are containers. A container has associated with it a layout manager that controls the placement of children within the container. See the `Container` class for more information about layout managers. However, all components maintain a valid state that is used by the layout manager. In particular, if a component is invalid, the component's `layout()` method will be called the next time the layout manager is invoked.

The Enabled Property

A component can be either enabled or disabled. When enabled, the user can interact with the component to cause it to generate events. When disabled, the component will not respond to user gestures and so will not generate events. Enabled and disabled components look different so that they can be visually distinguished.

The Visible Property

A component can be made visible or invisible. Components are typically created visible by default. Only top-level components like frames and windows are created invisible by default.

Events

Components interact with a program that uses them through the use of *events*. For example, clicking a component with the mouse generates a mouse down event. For a complete discussion on available events, event handlers, and event flow through a component hierarchy, see the `Event` class.

Peers

A component such as a button uses the platform's native implementation of a button. For example, on Solaris, the AWT button uses the Motif button widget, while on Windows 95, the AWT button uses the button control. So that the AWT button component behaves the same on all platforms, the button is assigned a peer that takes care of translating the behavior of the platform's native button to the behavior of the AWT button.

When constructing a user interface with components and containers, the component hierarchy is created without any peers. Even without the peers, it is possible to initialize all the properties on the components. When the user interface is ready to be displayed on the screen, the peers for each component are finally created and properly initialized with the current state of the component. Once the peer exists, any modifications to the component's properties are forwarded directly to the peer. (With the peers in existence, the component may or may not maintain the state changes. However, when the peer is destroyed, any state that the peer maintained for the component must be transferred back to the component.)

The peers of a component hierarchy are created by calling the `addNotify()` method of the top-level container. Although all components have an `addNotify()` method, the method can not be called directly. Only the `addNotify()` method of a subclass of `Window` can be called. When this happens, it sets off a chain reaction that results in a call to the `addNotify()` method of every component in the hierarchy. The opposite sequence occurs when the `removeNotify()` method is called on the top-level container.

Figure 59 shows a component hierarchy and its corrsponding peer hierarchy.

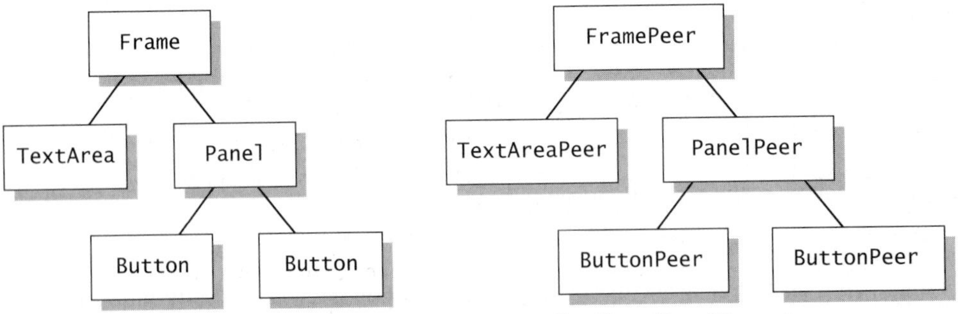

FIGURE 59 A Component Hierarchy and Its Corresponding Peer Class Hierarchy

MEMBER SUMMARY

Enable Methods	
`disable()`	Disables a component.
`enable()`	Enables a component.
`isEnabled()`	Determines if the component is enabled.
Visibility Methods	
`hide()`	Makes the component invisible.
`isShowing()`	Determines if the component is visible and has a peer.
`isVisible()`	Retrieves the component's visible state.
`show()`	Makes the component visible.
Color Methods	
`getBackground()`	Retrieves the component's background color.
`getColorModel()`	Retrieves the component's color model.
`getForeground()`	Retrieves the component's foreground color.
`setBackground()`	Sets the component's background color.
`setForeground()`	Sets the component's foreground color.
Font Methods	
`getFont()`	Retrieves the component's font.
`getFontMetrics()`	Retrieves the font metrics for a font.
`setFont()`	Sets the component's font.
Graphics Method	
`getGraphics()`	Creates a graphics context for the component.
Layout Methods	
`bounds()`	Retrieves the component's bounds.
`inside()`	Determines if a point is inside the component.
`invalidate()`	Invalidates the component.
`isValid()`	Retrieves the component's valid state.
`layout()`	Invokes the layout manager on the component.
`locate()`	Locates a subcomponent at a point in the component.
`location()`	Retrieves the location of the component.
`minimumSize()`	Calculates the component's minimum size dimensions.
`preferredSize()`	Calculates the component's preferred size dimensions.
`move()`	Moves the component.
`nextFocus()`	Sets the focus to the next component.
`requestFocus()`	Requests that the focus be given to the component.
`reshape()`	Moves and resizes a component.
`resize()`	Resizes a component.
`size()`	Retrieves the size of the component.
`validate()`	Validates the component.

Continued

MEMBER SUMMARY

Event Methods	
`action()`	Called when an action event occurs.
`deliverEvent()`	Delivers an event to the component.
`gotFocus()`	Called to notify the component that it has received the focus.
`handleEvent()`	Called when the component receives an event.
`keyDown()`	Called when a key is pressed.
`keyUp()`	Called when a key is released.
`lostFocus()`	Called to notify the component that it has lost the focus.
`mouseDown()`	Called when the user presses a mouse button.
`mouseDrag()`	Called when the user drags the mouse while some mouse button is down.
`mouseEnter()`	Called when the user moves the cursor into the component's bounds.
`mouseExit()`	Called when the user moves the cursor outside the component's bounds.
`mouseMove()`	Called whenever the user moves the cursor.
`mouseUp()`	Called when the user releases a mouse button.
`postEvent()`	Delivers an event to the component.
Image Methods	
`checkImage()`	Retrieves the construction status of an image.
`createImage()`	Creates an off-screen image or an image from an image producer.
`imageUpdate()`	Called to deliver status information about the loading of an image.
`prepareImage()`	Triggers the loading of image data for an image.
Paint Methods	
`paint()`	Called to repaint the component.
`paintAll()`	Called to repaint the component and any descendents.
`repaint()`	Requests that the component be repainted.
`update()`	Called in response to a `repaint()` method call.
Print Methods	
`print()`	Prints the component on a graphics context.
`printAll()`	Prints all the components on a graphics context.
`Parent Method`	
`getParent()`	Retrieves the component's parent.
Peer Methods	
`addNotify()`	Creates the component's peer.
`getPeer()`	Retrieves the component's peer.
`getToolkit()`	Retrieves the component's toolkit.
`removeNotify()`	Destroys the component's peer.

MEMBER SUMMARY	
Debugging Methods	
`list()`	Prints out information about the component.
`paramString()`	Generates a string representation of the component's state.
`toString()`	Generates a string representation of the component's state.

Example

This example demonstrates most of the methods in this class by implementing a simple text field component using a canvas component (see Figure 60). When the text field has the focus, a block cursor appears, indicating where the next character will go. If the text field is not full, the block cursor blinks.

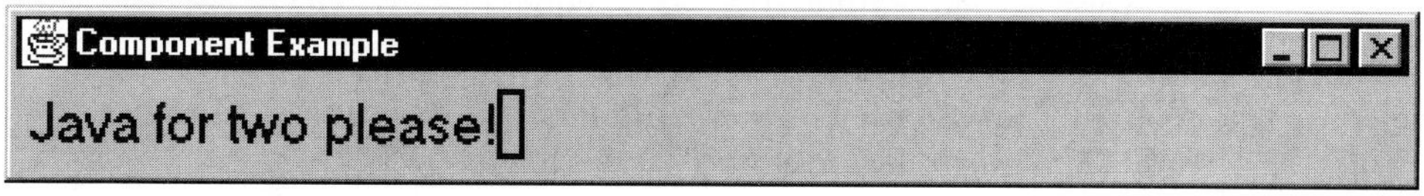

FIGURE 60 `Component`

When the cursor is in the text field, the cursor is changed to a `Frame.TEXT_CURSOR`. To change the cursor, a reference to the top-level frame is necessary. This is done by moving up the component hierarchy using `getParent()` until a frame is found.

Hitting `Return` in the text field causes it to generate an action event using the `postEvent()` method. The `arg` field of the action event is filled with the current contents of the text field.

```
import java.awt.*;
class Main extends Frame {
    Main() {
        super("Component Example");
        add("Center", new InputCanvas(30, 5));
        pack();
        show();
    }

    public boolean action(Event evt, Object arg) {
        System.out.println(evt);
        return true;
    }

    static public void main(String[] args) {
        new Main();
    }
}
```

Example

```
class InputCanvas extends Canvas implements Runnable {
    int border;
    int length;
    Font font;
    FontMetrics fontM;
    char[] buffer;
    int bufferIx;

    boolean hasFocus;
    boolean cursorVisible;
    boolean cursorOn;
    int saveCursor;

    InputCanvas(int len, int bor) {
        border = bor;
        length = len;
        buffer = new char[len];
        font = getFont();
        if (font == null) {
            font = new Font("Dialog", Font.PLAIN, 20);
        }
        fontM = getFontMetrics(font);

        (new Thread(this)).start();
    }

    public void paint(Graphics g) {
        int y = (size().height-fontM.getHeight())/2;

        g.setFont(font);
        g.drawChars(buffer, 0, bufferIx, border, y
            + fontM.getAscent());

        // Draw blinking cursor.
        int x = fontM.charsWidth(buffer, 0, bufferIx) + border;
        int w = fontM.charWidth('c');
        if (hasFocus) {
            g.setColor(getForeground());
            g.fillRect(x, y, w, fontM.getHeight());
            if (cursorOn) {
                if (bufferIx < buffer.length) {
                    g.setColor(getBackground());
                    g.fillRect(x+2, y+2, w-4, fontM.getHeight()-4);
                }
            }
        }
    }

    public Dimension minimumSize() {
        int w = fontM.charWidth('m') * length;
        return new Dimension(w + 2*border,
            fontM.getHeight() + 2*border);
    }
```

```
public Dimension preferredSize() {
    return minimumSize();
}

public boolean mouseEnter(Event evt, int x, int y) {
    Component p = getParent();
    while (p != null && !(p instanceof Frame)) {
        p = getParent();
    }
    if (p != null) {
        saveCursor = ((Frame)p).getCursorType();
        ((Frame)p).setCursor(Frame.TEXT_CURSOR);
    }
    return false; // Allow subclass to receive event.
}

public boolean mouseExit(Event evt, int x, int y) {
    Component p = getParent();
    while (p != null && !(p instanceof Frame)) {
        p = getParent();
    }
    if (p != null) {
        ((Frame)p).setCursor(saveCursor);
    }
    return false; // Allow subclass to receive event.
}

public boolean mouseDown(Event evt, int x, int y) {
    requestFocus();
    return true;
}

public boolean gotFocus(Event evt, Object what) {
    hasFocus = true;
    repaint();
    return true;
}

public boolean lostFocus(Event evt, Object what) {
    hasFocus = false;
    repaint();
    return true;
}

public boolean keyDown(Event evt, int key) {
    if (key == 127 || key == 8) {
        if (bufferIx > 0) {
            bufferIx--;
            repaint();
        }
    } else if (key == 9) {    // tab
        nextFocus();
    } else if (key == 10) {   // return
        evt.id = Event.ACTION_EVENT;
```

```
                evt.arg = String.valueOf(buffer, 0, bufferIx);
                postEvent(evt);
            } else if (bufferIx < buffer.length) {
                buffer[bufferIx++] = (char)key;
                repaint();
            }
            return true;
        }

        public void run() {
            while (true) {
                try {
                    Thread.sleep(1000);
                    cursorOn = !cursorOn;
                    repaint();
                } catch (Exception e) {
                    e.printStackTrace();
                }
            }
        }
    }
```

action()

PURPOSE Called when an action event occurs.

SYNTAX `public boolean action(Event evt, Object arg)`

DESCRIPTION The component should override this method to handle events generated when the user holds down a key. This method is called by the `handleEvent()` method in response to an `Event.ACTION_EVENT` type event. `arg` is the same as the `evt.arg` field and can be any object. Each component fills the `arg` field differently, you need to check the component's documentation to determine what the component places in the event's `arg` field. For example, a button fills the `arg` field with the name of its label, while a checkbox fills the `arg` field with the new state.

PARAMETERS

`arg` An object that depends on the component that generated the event.
`evt` The non-`null` event.

RETURNS `false` if the event should be passed up to the component's parent; `true` otherwise.

SEE ALSO `Event.ACTION_EVENT`, `handleEvent()`.

EXAMPLE See the class example.

addNotify()

PURPOSE Creates the component's peer.

SYNTAX `public void addNotify()`

DESCRIPTION This method must be overridden by a component subclass to create the peer. This method can be called directly only if the component is a top-level window such as a frame or dialog (See `Window.addNotify()`).

SEE ALSO `getPeer()`, `removeNotify()`.

EXAMPLE See `show()`.

bounds()

PURPOSE Retrieves the component's bounds.

SYNTAX `public Rectangle bounds()`

DESCRIPTION The bounds of a component specify the size of the component and its location within its parent. The width and height of the bounds specify the dimensions of the component without regard to any insets. The *x*- and *y*-coordinates of the bounds specify the location of the component relative to its parent.

RETURNS A new non-`null` rectangle containing the bounds of the component.

SEE ALSO `location()`, `reshape()`.

EXAMPLE See `createImage()`.

checkImage()

PURPOSE Retrieves the construction status of an image.

SYNTAX

```
public int checkImage(Image image, ImageObserver obs)
public int checkImage(Image image, int width, int height,
    ImageObserver obs)
```

DESCRIPTION This method retrieves the status of an image that is being constructed. As far as this method is concerned, an image that has been scaled is treated as a completely different image. Therefore, when checking the status of an image, you must also indicate which scaled version of the image to check by setting the `width` and `height` parameters to the dimension of the scaled image.

The image may not be in the process of being constructed; this method does not start the process. To start the image construction process, use `prepareImage()`.

Any status changes are delivered to the image observer `obs` if not `null`.

PARAMETERS

`height`	If >= 0, specifies the height of the scaled version of the image to check.
`image`	The non-`null` image to check.
`obs`	If non-`null`, specifies the image observer to be notified whenever the status changes.
`width`	If >= 0, specifies the width of the scaled version of the image to check.

RETURNS The combination of status bits as defined by the `ImageObserver` interface.

SEE ALSO `ImageObserver`, `prepareImage()`.

EXAMPLE While an image is being loaded and displayed, a background thread is created to create a scaled version of the image. The thread uses the `checkImage()` to wait until the scaled image is complete. When the scaled image is complete, it is displayed on the screen. See Figure 61 for a screen shot of this example.

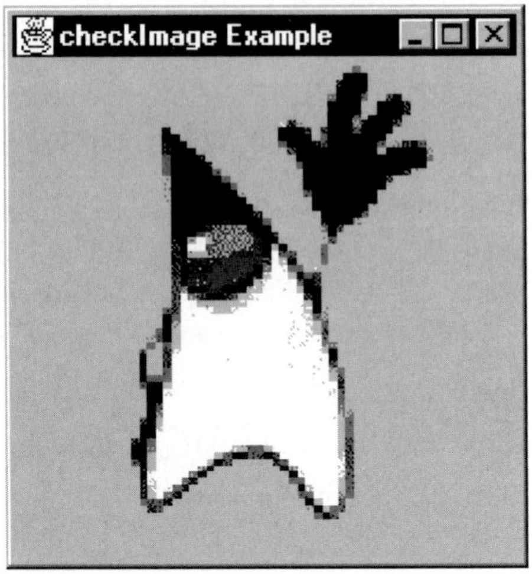

FIGURE 61 `Component.checkImage()`

```
import java.awt.*;
import java.awt.image.*;
import java.net.*;
class Main extends Frame {
    Main(String filename) {
        super("checkImage Example");
        add("Center",
            new ImageCanvas(getToolkit(). getImage(filename)));
        resize(300, 300);
        show();
    }

    static public void main(String[] args) {
        if (args.length == 1) {
            new Main(args[0]);
        } else {
            System.err.println("usage: java Main <image file>");
        }
    }
}
```

```
class ImageCanvas extends Canvas implements Runnable {
    int newWidth = 200, newHeight = 200;
    boolean drawScaled;
    Image image;

    ImageCanvas(Image image) {
        this.image = image;
        (new Thread(this)).start();
    }

    public void paint(Graphics g) {
        update(g);
    }
    public void update(Graphics g) {
        if (drawScaled) {
            g.clearRect(0, 0, size().width, size().height);
            g.drawImage(image, 0, 0, newWidth, newHeight, this);
        } else {
            g.drawImage(image, 0, 0, this);
        }
    }

    public void run() {
        prepareImage(image, newWidth, newHeight, null);
        while (true) {
            int status = checkImage(image, newWidth, newHeight, null);
            if ((status&ImageObserver.ERROR) != 0) {
                System.out.println(
                    "Error encountered while scaling image");
                System.exit(1);
            }
            if ((status&ImageObserver.ALLBITS) != 0) {
                drawScaled = true;
                repaint();
                break;
            }
            try {
                Thread.sleep(100);
            } catch (InterruptedException e) {
            }
        }
    }
}
```

createImage()

PURPOSE Creates an off-screen image or an image from an image producer.

SYNTAX

```
public Image createImage(int width, int height)
public Image createImage(ImageProducer prod)
```

A B C D E F G H I J K L M N O P Q R S T U V W X Y Z

DESCRIPTION There are two forms of `createImage()`. The first form uses a `width` and `height` to create an off-screen image on which you can paint. The off-screen image is often used to achieve smooth animation. The image is first constructed in the off-screen image and then painted on the screen in its entirety. This technique is called *double-buffering*. The following example demonstrates the use of `createImage()` for double-buffering.

The second form of `createImage()` takes an image producer `prod` and creates an image based on the data supplied by the image producer. See the `RGBImageFilter` class for an example that uses this form of `createImage()`.

PARAMETERS

`height`	The height of the off-screen image in pixels.
`prod`	The non-`null` image producer `prod`.
`width`	The width of the off-screen image in pixels.

RETURNS The image or `null`.

EXAMPLE This example implements a simple animation of the word "Java" slowly rising in the center of a "brown bubbling liquid," as shown in Figure 62. To eliminate flickering, the program calls `createImage()` to create an off-screen image and uses it to implement the double-buffering technique. Each frame of the animation is first generated on the off-screen image and then painted whole on the screen.

FIGURE 62 `Component.createImage()`

```
import java.awt.*;
class Main {
    static public void main(String[] args) {
        Frame f = new Frame("createImage Example");
        f.add("Center", new MainCanvas());
        f.resize(200, 100);
        f.show();
    }
}

class MainCanvas extends Canvas implements Runnable {
    Image backBuffer;
    Graphics backG;
```

```
String str = "Java";
int pointSize = 15;
Point[] points = new Point[10];
int[] pointRates = new int[points.length];
Point stringPt = new Point(0, 0);

MainCanvas() {
    for (int i=0; i<points.length; i++) {
        points[i] = new Point(0, 0);
        initPoint(i);
    }
    (new Thread(this)).start();
}

void initPoint(int i) {
    points[i].x = (int)(Math.floor(Math.random()*size().width));
    points[i].y = size().height;
    pointRates[i] = (int)(Math.floor(Math.random()*30)) + 5;
}

public void paint(Graphics g) {
    update(g);
}

public void update(Graphics g) {
    int w = bounds().width;
    int h = bounds().height;

    if (backBuffer == null
            || backBuffer.getWidth(null) != w
            || backBuffer.getHeight(null) != h) {
        backBuffer = createImage(w, h);
        if (backBuffer != null) {
            if (backG != null) {
                backG.dispose();
            }
            backG = backBuffer.getGraphics();
            backG.setFont(new Font("Helvetica", Font.BOLD, 48));
            FontMetrics fm = backG.getFontMetrics();
            stringPt.x = (w-fm.stringWidth(str))/2;
        }
    }

    if (backBuffer != null) {
        backG.setColor(new Color(130, 80, 80));  // brown
        backG.fillRect(0, 0, w, h);

        // Bubbles behind the string.
        backG.setColor(Color.white);
        for (int i=0; i<points.length/3; i++) {
            backG.fillOval(points[i].x, points[i].y, pointSize,
                pointSize);
        }
```

B C D E F G H I J K L M N O P Q R S T U V W X Y Z

```
                // Paint the string
                backG.setColor(Color.black);
                backG.drawString(str, stringPt.x, stringPt.y % h + h);
                backG.drawString(str, stringPt.x, stringPt.y % h + 2*h);

                // Bubbles in front of the string.
                backG.setColor(Color.white);
                for (int i=points.length/3; i<points.length; i++) {
                    backG.fillOval(points[i].x, points[i].y, pointSize,
                        pointSize);
                }
                g.drawImage(backBuffer, 0, 0, null);
            }
        }

        public void run() {
            while (true) {
                for (int i=0; i<points.length; i++) {
                    points[i].y -= pointRates[i];
                    if (points[i].y < -pointSize) {
                        initPoint(i);
                    }
                }
                stringPt.y--;
                repaint();
                try { Thread.sleep(80); } catch (Exception e) {};
            }
        }
    }
```

deliverEvent()

PURPOSE Delivers an event to the component.

SYNTAX `public void deliverEvent(Event e)`

DESCRIPTION This method simply makes a call to `postEvent()` with `e`. See `postEvent()` for details.

PARAMETERS

`e` The non-`null` event.

SEE ALSO `Event`, `handleEvent()`, `postEvent()`.

EXAMPLE See `postEvent()`.

A B C D E F G H I J K L M N O P Q R S T U V W X Y Z

disable()

PURPOSE Disables a component.

SYNTAX `public synchronized void disable()`

DESCRIPTION When this is disabled, a component will not respond to user input and so cannot generate events.

SEE ALSO `enable()`, `isEnabled()`.

EXAMPLE See the `Button` class example.

enable()

PURPOSE Enables a component.

SYNTAX

```
public void enable()
public void enable(boolean cond)
```

DESCRIPTION If `cond` is `true`, this method enables the component; otherwise it disables the component. When enabled, a component is able to respond to user input. If `cond` is not specified, it defaults to `true`.

PARAMETERS

`cond` If `true`, the component is enabled; otherwise the component is disabled.

SEE ALSO `disable()`, `enable()`.

EXAMPLE See the `Button` class example.

getBackground()

PURPOSE Retrieves the component's background color.

SYNTAX `public Color getBackground()`

DESCRIPTION Some part of a component's visual appearance is painted using the background color. For example, a button is painted in the background color, while the label is painted in the foreground color.

If the component does not have a background color set (for example, by calling `setBackground()` with a `null` color), the component inherits its background color from the closest ancestor whose background color has been set.

RETURNS	The component's background color. If the background color has not been set in the component or in any of its ancestors, `null` is returned.
SEE ALSO	`getForeground()`, `setBackground()`.
EXAMPLE	See the class example.

getColorModel()

PURPOSE	Retrieves the component's color model.
SYNTAX	`public synchronized ColorModel getColorModel()`
DESCRIPTION	If the component's peer exists, this returns the peer's color model. Otherwise it returns the default toolkit's color model (see `Toolkit.getDefaultToolkit()`).
RETURNS	A non-`null` color model instance.
SEE ALSO	`ColorModel`, `Toolkit.getDefaultToolkit()`.
EXAMPLE	See the `ColorModel` class example.

getFont()

PURPOSE	Retrieves the component's font.
SYNTAX	`public Font getFont()`
DESCRIPTION	This method returns the font supplied in the most recent call to `setFont()` on this component. If `setFont()` has never been called on this component, this method returns the font of the component's parent. If this font also has never been set, the search continues up the parent chain until an ancestor component whose font has been set is encountered. If the search finds no such component, `null` is returned.
RETURNS	The component's font or the font of the closest ancestor whose font has been set. `null` is returned if no ancestor has a font set.
SEE ALSO	`setFont()`.
EXAMPLE	See the class `example`.

getFontMetrics()

PURPOSE Retrieves the font metrics for a font.

SYNTAX `public FontMetrics getFontMetrics(Font fnt)`

DESCRIPTION If the component's peer exists, this method asks the peer for the font metrics of the font `fnt`. Otherwise, this method returns the result of calling `Toolkit.getFontMetrics(fnt)`. The results are typically the same.

PARAMETERS

`fnt` The non-`null` font.

RETURNS The non-`null` font metrics for `fnt`.

SEE ALSO `getFont()`.

EXAMPLE See the class example.

getForeground()

PURPOSE Retrieves the component's foreground color.

SYNTAX `public Color getForeground()`

DESCRIPTION Some part of a component's visual appearance is painted using the foreground color. For example, a button is painted in the background color, while the label is painted in the foreground color.

If the component does not have a foreground color set (for example, by calling `setForeground()` with a `null` color), the component inherits its foreground color from the closest ancestor whose foreground color has been set.

RETURNS The component's foreground color. If the foreground color has not been set in the component or in any of its ancestors, `null` is returned.

SEE ALSO `getBackground()`, `setForeground()`.

EXAMPLE See the class example.

getGraphics()

PURPOSE Creates a graphics context for the component.

SYNTAX `public Graphics getGraphics()`

A B C D E F G H I J K L M N O P Q R S T U V W X Y Z

DESCRIPTION	The graphics context inherits the component's background color, foreground color, and font. The origin of the new graphics context is based on the component's peer inset area origin.
RETURNS	A graphics context on the component. The resulting value will be `null` if the component's peer does not exist.
SEE ALSO	`Graphics`, `paint()`.

getParent()

PURPOSE	Retrieves the component's parent.
SYNTAX	`public Container getParent()`
DESCRIPTION	This method retrieves the component's parent. It returns `null` if the component does not have a parent. If the component hierarchy is part of a standalone application rather than an applet, the top-level window can be determined by following the parent chain until a component without a parent is found.
RETURNS	The parent of the component; `null` if the component does not have a parent.
EXAMPLE	See the class example.

getPeer()

PURPOSE	Retrieves the component's peer.
SYNTAX	`public ComponentPeer getPeer()`
RETURNS	The component's peer; `null` if the component does not have a peer.
SEE ALSO	`addNotify()`.
EXAMPLE	See `show()`.

getToolkit()

PURPOSE	Retrieves the component's toolkit.
SYNTAX	`public Toolkit getToolkit()`

DESCRIPTION This method retrieves the component's toolkit, which in turn can be used to retrieve information about the screen on which the components are painted. If the component's peer exists, the peer returns the component's toolkit. Otherwise, this method searches up the component hierarchy looking for a component whose peer exists and returns a non-`null` toolkit. If none is found, this method returns `Toolkit.getDefaultToolkit()`. Note that if a component is moved from one frame to another, the returned toolkit may be different.

RETURNS A non-`null` reference to the component's toolkit.

SEE ALSO `Toolkit`.

EXAMPLE See `Toolkit.getImage()`.

gotFocus()

PURPOSE Called to notify the component that it has received the focus.

SYNTAX `public boolean gotFocus(Event evt, Object arg)`

DESCRIPTION The component should override this method to handle events generated when the component receives the focus. This method is called by the `handleEvent()` method in response to an `Event.GOT_FOCUS` type event. `arg` is the same as the `evt.arg` field and can be any object. Each component fills the `arg` field differently, you need to check the component's documentation to determine what the component places in the event's `arg` field.

PARAMETERS

`arg` An object that depends on the component that generated the event.

`evt` The non-`null` event.

RETURNS `false` if the event should be passed up to the component's parent; `true` otherwise.

SEE ALSO `Event.GOT_FOCUS`, `lostFocus()`, `requestFocus()`.

EXAMPLE See the class example.

handleEvent()

PURPOSE Called when the component receives an event.

SYNTAX `public boolean handleEvent(Event evt)`

DESCRIPTION This method is called to deliver the event `evt` to the component. Depending on the type of event in the `evt.id`, this method calls another method in this class. For example, if `evt` is an action event, the component's `action()` method is called with `evt`. Table 9 gives the list of event types and their corresponding methods. To handle event types that do not appear in this table, you must override the `handleEvent()` method.

TABLE 9 Event Methods

Event Type	Event Method
Event.ACTION_EVENT	action()
Event.GOT_FOCUS	gotFocus()
Event.KEY_DOWN	keyDown()
Event.KEY_UP	keyUp()
Event.LOST_FOCUS	lostFocus()
Event.MOUSE_DOWN	mouseDown()
Event.MOUSE_DRAG	mouseDrag()
Event.MOUSE_ENTER	mouseEnter()
Event.MOUSE_EXIT	mouseExit()
Event.MOUSE_MOVE	mouseMove()
Event.MOUSE_UP	mouseUp()

If the `handleEvent()` method is overridden and not all events are handled, the result of calling `super.handleEvent()` must be returned so that the event can be dispatched to the appropriate event handler method.

PARAMETERS

`evt` The non-`null` event.

RETURNS `false` if the event should be passed up to the component's parent; `true` otherwise.

SEE ALSO `mouseEnter()`, `mouseExit()`, `mouseMove()`, `mouseDown()`, `mouseDrag()`, `mouseUp()`, `keyDown()`, `action()`.

EXAMPLE See the `Event` class.

hide()

PURPOSE Makes the component invisible.

SYNTAX `public synchronized void hide()`

DESCRIPTION This method makes the component invisible if it is not already invisible.

SEE ALSO `isShowing()`, `isVisible()`, `show()`.

EXAMPLE See `show()`.

imageUpdate()

PURPOSE Called to deliver status information about the loading of an image.

SYNTAX `public boolean imageUpdate(Image img, int infoflags, int x, int y, int w, int h)`

DESCRIPTION This method is called if the component had requested some information about the image `img` and the information was not yet available. For example, if the component called `Image.getWidth()` and the width information was not yet available (that is, the method returned `-1`), the `imageUpdate()` method will be called as soon as the width becomes available.

See `ImageObserver.imageUpdate()` for more details.

PARAMETERS

`height`	This value depends on the status bits enabled in `infoflags`.
`img`	The non-`null` image being updated.
`infoflags`	A set of status bits.
`width`	This value depends on the status bits enabled in `infoflags`.
`x`	This value depends on the status bits enabled in `infoflags`.
`y`	This value depends on the status bits enabled in `infoflags`.

RETURNS `true` if no further calls to `imageUpdate()` are needed.

EXAMPLE See the `ImageObserver` example.

inside()

PURPOSE Determines if a point is inside the component.

SYNTAX `public synchronized boolean inside(int x, int y)`

DESCRIPTION This method determines if `x` and `y` are within the component's bounds. In particular, `x` and `y` are inside the component if `x >= 0 && x < width && y >= 0 && y < height`.

PARAMETERS	
`x`	The *x*-coordinate relative to the component.
`y`	The *y*-coordinate relative to the component.
RETURNS	`true` if `x` and `y` are within the component's bounds.
SEE ALSO	`locate()`.

invalidate()

PURPOSE	Invalidates the component.
SYNTAX	`public void invalidate()`
DESCRIPTION	This method invalidates the component and all of its ancestors. See the class description and the `validate()` method for more details about the valid state.
SEE ALSO	`isValid()`, `validate()`.
EXAMPLE	See `validate()`.

isEnabled()

PURPOSE	Determines if the component is enabled.
SYNTAX	`public boolean isEnabled()`
DESCRIPTION	See the class description for more information about a component's enabled state.
RETURNS	`true` if the component is enabled; `false` otherwise.
SEE ALSO	`disable()`, `enable()`.
EXAMPLE	See the `Canvas` class example.

isShowing()

PURPOSE	Determines if the component is visible and has a peer.
SYNTAX	`public boolean isShowing()`
DESCRIPTION	A component can be "visible" even though it doesn't appear on the screen. However, if the component's visible state is `true` and the component has a

peer, the component will appear on the screen. This method is used to determine if the component is visible on the screen.

RETURNS `true` if the component is visible and has a peer.

SEE ALSO `hide()`, `show()`.

EXAMPLE See `show()`.

isValid()

PURPOSE Retrieves the component's valid state.

SYNTAX `public boolean isValid()`

DESCRIPTION See the class description and the `validate()` method for more details about the valid state.

RETURNS `true` if the component is valid; `false` otherwise.

SEE ALSO `invalidate()`, `validate()`.

EXAMPLE See `validate()`.

isVisible()

PURPOSE Retrieves the component's visible state.

SYNTAX `public boolean isVisible()`

DESCRIPTION Most components are by default components created visible. Top-level windows such as frames are created invisible.

RETURNS `true` if the component is visible; `false` otherwise.

SEE ALSO `hide()`, `show()`.

EXAMPLE See `show()`.

keyDown()

PURPOSE Called when a key is pressed.

SYNTAX `public boolean keyDown(Event evt, int key)`

DESCRIPTION The component should override this method to handle events generated when the user presses down on a key. This method is called by the `handleEvent()` method in response to an `Event.KEY_DOWN` event. `key` is the same value as the `evt.key` field and is either the ASCII key that was pressed or a special function key. See `Event` for more details.

PARAMETERS

`evt` The non-`null` event.

`key` The key that was pressed.

RETURNS `false` if the event should be passed up to the component's parent; `true` otherwise.

SEE ALSO `handleEvent()`.

EXAMPLE See `Event.key`.

keyUp()

PURPOSE Called when a key is released.

SYNTAX `public boolean keyUp(Event evt, int key)`

DESCRIPTION The component should override this method to handle events generated when the user releases a key. This method is called by the `handleEvent()` method in response to an `Event.KEY_UP` event. `key` is either the ASCII key that was pressed or a special function key. See `Event` for more details.

PARAMETERS

`evt` The non-`null` event.

`key` The key that was released.

RETURNS `false` if the event should be passed up to the component's parent; `true` otherwise.

SEE ALSO `handleEvent()`.

EXAMPLE See `Event.key`.

layout()

PURPOSE Invokes the layout manager on the component.

SYNTAX `public void layout()`

DESCRIPTION If the component is a container, the container's layout manager is invoked (see `Container.layout()` for more details). Otherwise, this method does not do anything by default.

SEE ALSO `Container.layout()`.

EXAMPLE See `Container.layout()`.

list()

PURPOSE Prints out information about the component.

SYNTAX
```
public void list()
public void list(PrintStream out)
public void list(PrintStream out, int indent)
```

DESCRIPTION This method prints the results of calling `toString()` to the output stream `out`.

If the component is a container, this method recursively prints the results of calling `toString()` on each of the container's descendents. The component hierarchy is traversed in depth-first order. Children that are further down the hierarchy are printed with more indents. The first line of output is printed with indent spaces.

If `out` is not specified, it defaults to `System.out`. If `indent` is not specified, it defaults to `0`.

PARAMETERS

`indent` The indentation of the first line of output.

`out` The non-`null` output stream in which to print.

SEE ALSO `toString()`.

EXAMPLE See `Container.list()`.

locate()

PURPOSE Locates a subcomponent at a point in the component.

SYNTAX
```
public Component locate(int x, int y)
```

DESCRIPTION This method is used to determine what, if any, component is at the pixel coordinate `x, y`. The coordinates must be relative to the component's bounds. If the component is not a container, then this method returns `inside(x, y)`. If the component is a container, see `Container.locate()` for details on the effects.

PARAMETERS

`x`	The *x*-coordinate relative to the component's bounds.
`y`	The *y*-coordinate relative to the component's bounds.

RETURNS The sub-component at `x`, `y` or the component itself if no component is at `x`, `y` but `x`, `y` is in the component. Returns `null` if `x`, `y` is not in the component.

SEE ALSO `inside()`.

EXAMPLE See `Container.locate()`.

location()

PURPOSE Retrieves the location of the component.

SYNTAX `public Point location()`

DESCRIPTION The location of the component is the top-left corner of the component's bounds. The location of the component is relative to the component's parent.

RETURNS A new non-`null` point containing the component's location relative to the component's parent.

SEE ALSO `move()`.

EXAMPLE See `Container` class example.

lostFocus()

PURPOSE Called to notify the component that it has lost the focus.

SYNTAX `public boolean lostFocus(Event evt, Object arg)`

DESCRIPTION The component should override this method to handle events generated when the component loses the focus. This method is called by the `handleEvent()` method in response to an `Event.LOST_FOCUS` type event. `arg` is the same as the `evt.arg` field and can be any object. Each component fills the `arg` field differently; you need to check the component's documentation to determine what it places in the event's `arg` field.

PARAMETERS

`arg`	An object that depends on the component that generated the event.
`evt`	The non-`null` event.

A B C D E F G H I J K L M N O P Q R S T U V W X Y Z

RETURNS `false` if the event should be passed up to the component's parent; `true` otherwise.

SEE ALSO `Event.LOST_FOCUS`, `gotFocus()`.

EXAMPLE See the class example.

minimumSize()

PURPOSE Calculates the component's minimum size dimensions.

SYNTAX `public synchronized Dimension minimumSize()`

DESCRIPTION The result of this method for some components depends on whether the component's peer exists. In general, the component's peer should be created before size information is calculated. If the component is a container, see `Container.minimumSize()` for more information on how the preferred size is calculated.

RETURNS A new non-`null` dimension object containing the component's minimum size.

SEE ALSO `preferredSize()`.

EXAMPLE See the `LayoutManager` class example.

mouseDown()

PURPOSE Called when the user presses a mouse button.

SYNTAX `public boolean mouseDown(Event evt, int x, int y)`

DESCRIPTION The component should override this method to handle events generated when the user presses down on a mouse button. This method is called by the `handleEvent()` method in response to an `Event.MOUSE_DOWN` event. `x` and `y` are the same values as `evt.x` and `evt.y` and refer to the coordinates of the cursor relative to the component's bounds. That is, if `x` and `y` are 0, the cursor is located at the top-left corner of the component. See `Event.MOUSE_DOWN` for more details.

PARAMETERS

`evt` The non-`null` event.

`x` The *x*-coordinate of the cursor relative to the component's bounds at the time of the mouse event.

`y` The *y*-coordinate of the cursor relative to the component's bounds at the time of the mouse event.

RETURNS `false` if the event should be passed up to the component's parent; `true` otherwise.

SEE ALSO `Event.MOUSE_DOWN`, `handleEvent()`.

EXAMPLE See the class example.

mouseDrag()

PURPOSE Called when the user drags the mouse while some mouse button is down.

SYNTAX `public boolean mouseDrag(Event evt, int x, int y)`

DESCRIPTION The component should override this method to handle events generated when the user moves the mouse while a mouse button is pressed. This method is called by the `handleEvent()` method in response to an `Event.MOUSE_DRAG` event. `x` and `y` are the same values as `evt.x` and `evt.y` and refer to the coordinates of the cursor relative to the component's bounds. That is, if `x` and `y` are 0, the cursor is located at the top-left corner of the component. See `Event.MOUSE_DRAG` for more details.

PARAMETERS

`evt` The non-`null` event.

`x` The *x*-coordinate of the cursor relative to the component's bounds at the time of the mouse event.

`y` The *y*-coordinate of the cursor relative to the component's bounds at the time of the mouse event.

RETURNS `false` if the event should be passed up to the component's parent; `true` otherwise.

SEE ALSO `Event.MOUSE_DRAG`, `handleEvent()`.

mouseEnter()

PURPOSE Called when the user moves the cursor into the component's bounds.

SYNTAX `public boolean mouseEnter(Event evt, int x, int y)`

DESCRIPTION The component should override this method to handle events generated when the user moves the cursor into the component's bounds. This event is generated regardless of whether a mouse button is down. This method is called by the `handleEvent()` method in response to an `Event.MOUSE_ENTER` event. `x` and y are the same values as `evt.x` and `evt.y` and refer to the coordinates of the cursor relative to the component's bounds. That is, if x and y are 0, the cursor is located at the top-left corner of the component. See `Event.MOUSE_ENTER` for more details.

PARAMETERS

`evt`	The non-`null` event.
`x`	The *x*-coordinate of the cursor relative to the component's bounds at the time of the mouse event.
`y`	The *y*-coordinate of the cursor relative to the component's bounds at the time of the mouse event.

RETURNS `false` if the event should be passed up to the component's parent; `true` otherwise.

SEE ALSO `Event.MOUSE_ENTER`, `handleEvent()`.

EXAMPLE See the class example.

mouseExit()

PURPOSE Called when the user moves the cursor outside the component's bounds.

SYNTAX `public boolean mouseExit(Event evt, int x, int y)`

DESCRIPTION The component should override this method to handle events generated when the user moves the cursor outside the component's bounds. This event is generated regardless of whether a mouse button is down. This method is called by the `handleEvent()` method in response to an `Event.MOUSE_EXIT` event. x and y are the same values as `evt.x` and `evt.y` and refer to the coordinates of the cursor relative to the component's bounds. That is, if x and y are 0, the cursor is located at the top-left corner of the component. See `Event.MOUSE_EXIT` for more details.

PARAMETERS

`evt`	The non-`null` event.
`x`	The *x*-coordinate of the cursor relative to the component's bounds at the time of the mouse event.
`y`	The *y*-coordinate of the cursor relative to the component's bounds at the time of the mouse event.

RETURNS `false` if the event should be passed up to the component's parent; `true` otherwise.

SEE ALSO `Event.MOUSE_EXIT`, `handleEvent()`.

EXAMPLE See the class example.

mouseMove()

PURPOSE Called whenever the user moves the cursor.

SYNTAX `public boolean mouseMove(Event evt, int x, int y)`

DESCRIPTION The component should override this method to handle events generated whenever the user moves the cursor while no mouse buttons are pressed. This method is called by the `handleEvent()` method in response to an `Event.MOUSE_MOVE` event. `x` and `y` are the same values as `evt.x` and `evt.y` and refer to the coordinates of the cursor relative to the component's bounds. That is, if `x` and `y` are 0, the cursor is located at the top-left corner of the component. See `Event.MOUSE_MOVE` for more details.

PARAMETERS

`evt` The non-`null` event.

`x` The *x*-coordinate of the cursor relative to the component's bounds at the time of the mouse event.

`y` The *y*-coordinate of the cursor relative to the component's bounds at the time of the mouse event.

RETURNS `false` if the event should be passed up to the component's parent; `true` otherwise.

SEE ALSO `Event.MOUSE_MOVE`, `handleEvent()`.

EXAMPLE This example creates a frame with four custom canvases, as shown in Figure 63. The canvas merely displays the cursor position of a mouse move event and pretends not to handle it. The mouse move event is then forwarded to the frame and displayed in the label at the bottom. This example demonstrates two points. First, when a mouse event is passed up the component hierarchy, the mouse coordinates are translated relative to the component that is handling the event. Second, the mouse coordinates are independent of a container's insets. To see this, move the cursor to the northwest corner of the frame's paintable area. Notice that the mouse coordinates are relative to the northwest corner of the frame rather than at (0, 0).

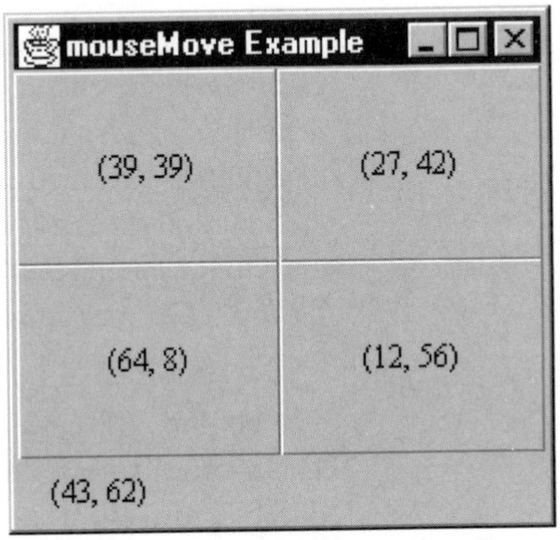

FIGURE 63 `Component.mouseMove()`

```
import java.awt.*;
public class Main extends Frame {
    Label l = new Label();

    Main() {
        super("mouseMove Example");
        Panel p = new Panel();
        p.setLayout(new GridLayout(2, 2));
        for (int i=0; i<4; i++) {
            p.add(new MainCanvas());
        }
        add("Center", p);
        add("South", l);
        resize(200, 200);
        show();
    }

    public boolean mouseMove(Event evt, int x, int y) {
        l.setText("("+x+", "+y+")");
        return true;
    }

    static public void main(String[] args) {
        new Main();
    }
}

class MainCanvas extends Canvas {
    String label = "";

    public void paint(Graphics g) {
        int w = size().width;
        int h = size().height;
        FontMetrics fm = g.getFontMetrics();

        g.drawString(label, (w-fm.stringWidth(label))/2,
            (h-fm.getHeight())/2+fm.getAscent());
        g.setColor(getBackground());
        g.draw3DRect(0, 0, w-1, h-1, true);
    }

    public boolean mouseMove(Event evt, int x, int y) {
        label = "("+x+", "+y+")";
        repaint();
        return false;
    }
}
```

mouseUp()

PURPOSE
: Called when the user releases a mouse button.

SYNTAX
: `public boolean mouseUp(Event evt, int x, int y)`

DESCRIPTION
: The component should override this method to handle events generated when the user releases a mouse button. This method is called by the `handleEvent()` method in response to an `Event.MOUSE_UP` event. `x` and `y` are the same values as `evt.x` and `evt.y` and refer to the coordinates of the cursor relative to the component's bounds. That is, if `x` and `y` are 0 the cursor is located at the top-left corner of the component. See `Event.MOUSE_UP` for more details.

PARAMETERS

`evt`
: The non-`null` event.

`x`
: The *x*-coordinate of the cursor relative to the component's bounds at the time of the mouse event.

`y`
: The *y*-coordinate of the cursor relative to the component's bounds at the time of the mouse event.

RETURNS
: `false` if the event should be passed up to the component's parent; `true` otherwise.

SEE ALSO
: `Event.MOUSE_UP`, `handleEvent()`.

EXAMPLE
: See the `Container` class example.

move()

PURPOSE
: Moves the component.

SYNTAX
: `public void move(int x, int y)`

DESCRIPTION
: Moves the component such that its top-left corner coincides with `x, y` in the bounds of the component's parent. Note that unlike graphics and events whose coordinates are relative to a component's inset area, move coordinates are relative to a component's bounds.

PARAMETERS

`x`
: The new *x*-coordinate.

`y`
: The new *y*-coordinate.

SEE ALSO
: `bounds()`, `reshape()`, `resize()`.

EXAMPLE
: See the `Container` class example.

nextFocus()

PURPOSE Sets the focus to the next component.

SYNTAX `public void nextFocus()`

DESCRIPTION The focus is given to the next component in the container. If the component is the last component in the container, the focus is given to the first component in the container.

SEE ALSO `requestFocus()`.

EXAMPLE See the class example.

paint()

PURPOSE Called to repaint the component.

SYNTAX `public void paint(Graphics gc)`

DESCRIPTION This method is called whenever the component is exposed because some window that was occluding it was removed. The graphics context `gc` should be used to repaint the damaged area. The system automatically clears the damaged area with the component background color.

The damaged area is not necessarily the whole area of the component. To discover the damaged area, call `gc.getClipRect()`. Note that when the component is made larger, the clipping rectangle may actually encompass only the new area. If by enlarging the component some other part of the component changes and needs to be redrawn, a call to `repaint()` must be made so that the area can be redrawn.

PARAMETERS

`gc` The non-`null` graphics context in which to paint the component.

SEE ALSO `getBackground()`, `repaint()`, `update()`.

EXAMPLE See `createImage()`.

paintAll()

PURPOSE Called to repaint the component and any descendents.

SYNTAX `public void paintAll(Graphics gc)`

DESCRIPTION This method is called by the AWT system in response to a request to paint an AWT component hierarchy. The component should paint itself on the graphics context `gc` and then, if the component is a container, invoke the `paintAll()` method on all its children.

PARAMETERS

`gc` The non-`null` graphics context in which to paint the component.

SEE ALSO `paint()`.

paramString()

PURPOSE Generates a string representation of the component's state.

SYNTAX `protected String paramString()`

DESCRIPTION A subclass of this class should override this method and return a concatenation of its state with the results of `super.paramString()`. This method is called by the `toString()` method and is typically used for debugging.

RETURNS A non-`null` string representing the component's state.

SEE ALSO `toString()`.

EXAMPLE This example shows how a subclass should override the `paramString()` method. The override appends three extra pieces of state to the superclass's state.

```
boolean myBool = false;
int myInt = 59;
String myStr = "Testing";
protected String paramString() {
     String str = super.paramString();
     str += ",myBool=" + myBool;
     str += ",myInt=" + myInt;
     if (myStr != null) {
        str += ",myStr=" + myStr;
     }
     return str;
   }
```

postEvent()

PURPOSE Delivers an event to the component.

SYNTAX `public boolean postEvent(Event evt)`

DESCRIPTION The event `evt` is delivered to the component by calling its `handleEvent()` method. If `handleEvent()` returns `false`, the event is delivered to its parent by calling its `handleEvent()` method. This continues up the component hierarchy until one of the component's `handleEvent()` methods returns `true`. If none returns `true`, the event is discarded. This method actually makes the call to all the `handleEvent()` methods; it does not, for example, queue the event.

PARAMETERS

`evt` The non-`null` event.

RETURNS `false` if the event should be passed up to the component's parent; `true` otherwise.

SEE ALSO `Event`, `handleEvent()`.

EXAMPLE See the class example.

preferredSize()

PURPOSE Calculates the component's preferred size dimensions.

SYNTAX `public Dimension preferredSize()`

DESCRIPTION The result of this method for some components depends on whether the component's peer exists. In general, the component's peer should be created before size information is calculated. If the component is a container, see `Container.preferredSize()` for more information on how the preferred size is calculated.

RETURNS A non-`null` dimension object containing the component's preferred size.

SEE ALSO `minimumSize()`.

EXAMPLE See the `LayoutManager` class example.

prepareImage()

PURPOSE Triggers the loading of image data for an image.

SYNTAX

```
public boolean prepareImage(Image img, ImageObserver obs)
public boolean prepareImage(Image img, int w, int h, ImageObserver
    obs)
```

DESCRIPTION This method starts the loading or production of image data associated with image `img` or a scaled version of `img`. If `w` and `h` are `-1`, no scaling of `img` is done. If `w` and `h` are non-negative, they specify that `img` should not only be loaded but also scaled so that its width is `w` and its height is `h`. The image observer `obs` will receive image update notifications as the image is being loaded or produced.

This method is typically used to pre-load image data for an image or a scaled version of an image so that `Graphics.drawImage()` can operate as quickly as possible.

If `w` and `h` are not specified, they default to `-1`, which specifies that the image should not be scaled.

PARAMETERS

`h`	`-1` or the scaled height of the returned image in pixels.
`img`	The non-`null` image to load.
`obs`	The non-`null` image observer.
`w`	-1 or the scaled width of the returned image in pixels.

RETURNS `true` if all the image data for `img` is available; `false` otherwise.

SEE ALSO `ImageObserver`.

EXAMPLE See `checkImage()`.

print()

PURPOSE Prints the component on a graphics context.

SYNTAX `public void print(Graphics gc)`

DESCRIPTION By default, this method calls `paint(gc)`. If the component does not look the same when it is displayed on the screen and when it is printed, this method should be overridden to render the printed appearance of the component.

PARAMETERS

`gc`	The non-`null` graphics context on which to print.

SEE ALSO `paint()`.

printAll()

PURPOSE Prints all the components on a graphics context.

SYNTAX `public void printAll(Graphics gc)`

DESCRIPTION	This method prints all the components on the graphics context `gc`. If a component is a container, the component is first validated and then the component and all its descendents are also printed on `gc`.
PARAMETERS	
`gc`	The non-`null` graphics context on which to print.
SEE ALSO	`print()`, `validate()`.

removeNotify()

PURPOSE	Destroys the component's peer.
SYNTAX	`public synchronized void removeNotify()`
DESCRIPTION	This method must be overridden by a component subclass to destroy the peer. This method can be called directly only if the component is a top-level window such as a frame or dialog (see `Window.addNotify()`).
SEE ALSO	`addNotify()`, `getPeer()`.
EXAMPLE	See `show()`.

repaint()

PURPOSE Makes a request to repaint the component.

SYNTAX

```
public void repaint()
public void repaint(long ms)
public void repaint(int x, int y, int width, int height)
public void repaint(long ms, int x, int y, int width, int height)
```

DESCRIPTION This method makes a request to repaint the rectangular area of the component specified by `x`, `y`, `width`, and `height`. If `x`, `y`, `width`, and `height` are not specified, they default to the bounds of the component. The scheduled repaint will occur no later than `ms` milliseconds later. If `ms` is not specified, it defaults to `0`.

The AWT system will repaint the component by calling the `update()` method.

PARAMETERS

`height`	The height of the rectangular area to repaint.
`ms`	Maximum delay in milliseconds before the `update()` method is called.
`width`	The width of the rectangular area to repaint.
`x`	The *x*-coordinate of the rectangular area to repaint.
`y`	The *y*-coordinate of the rectangular area to repaint.

SEE ALSO `update()`.

EXAMPLE This example paints various four-leaved roses and cardoids. As a figure is painted, a path of the figure is left behind. A thread is used to update the location of the dot and then to invoke the repaint method to paint the dot every 50 milliseconds. See Figure 64.

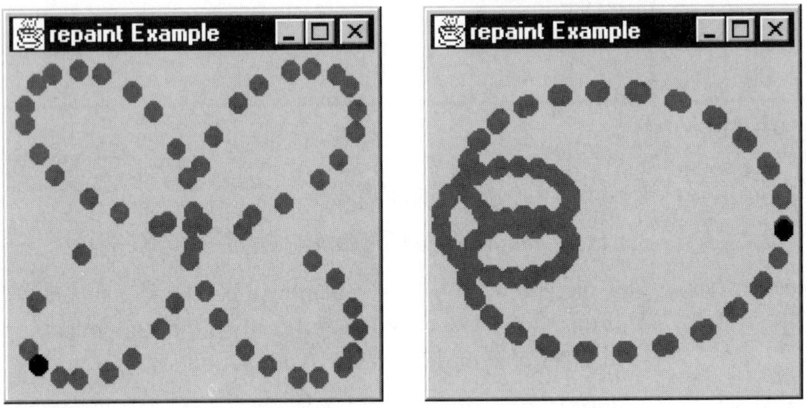

FIGURE 64 `Component.repaint()`

```
import java.awt.*;
class Main extends Frame implements Runnable {
    int curX = -100, curY = -100;
    double newX, newY;
    double angle = 0.0;
    double maxX, maxY, minX, minY;
    int figure;
    boolean clearBg = true;

    Main() {
        super("repaint Example");
        resize(200, 200);
        show();
        (new Thread(this)).start();
    }

    public void update(Graphics g) {
        int dotSize = 10;
        Insets insets = insets();
        int w = size().width-insets.left-insets.right-dotSize;
        int h = size().height-insets.top-insets.bottom-dotSize;

        if (clearBg) {
            g.clearRect(0, 0, size().width, size().height);
            curX = curY = -100;
            clearBg = false;
        } else {
            g.setColor(Color.red);
```

```
            g.fillOval(curX, curY, dotSize, dotSize);
            g.setColor(Color.black);
            g.fillOval(curX = (int)(newX*w), curY = (int)(newY*h),
                dotSize, dotSize);
        }
    }

    public boolean mouseDown(Event evt, int x, int y) {
        figure++;
        angle = 0;
        clearBg = true;
        return true;
    }

    double plot(double theta) {
        switch (figure % 5) {
        case 0:
            maxX = .8; maxY = .8; minX = -.8; minY = -.8;
            return Math.sin(2 * theta);
        case 1:
            maxX = 1; maxY = 1; minX = -1; minY = -1;
            return Math.cos(2 * theta);
        case 2:
            maxX = 2; maxY = 2; minX = -1.3; minY = -2;
            return Math.cos(theta/2) + 1;
        case 3:
            maxX = 3; maxY = 3; minX = -1.5; minY = -3;
            return 2 * Math.cos(theta/2) + 1;
        case 4:
            maxX = 4; maxY = 4; minX = -2; minY = -4;
            return 3 * Math.cos(theta/2) + 1;
        }
        return 0;
    }

    public void run() {
        while (true) {
            double r = plot(angle);
            newX = (r * Math.cos(angle)-minX)/(maxX-minX);
            newY = (r * Math.sin(angle)-minY)/(maxY-minY);
            repaint();
            try { Thread.sleep(50); } catch (Exception e) {};
            angle += .2;
        }
    }

    static public void main(String[] args) {
        new Main();
    }
}
```

requestFocus()

PURPOSE Requests that the focus be given to the component.

SYNTAX `public void requestFocus()`

DESCRIPTION This method makes a request that the focus be given to the component. If the request is granted, an `Event.GOT_FOCUS` event will be posted to the component. The conditions under which a component is granted or denied the focus is platform-dependent.

SYNTAX `gotFocus()`.

EXAMPLE See the class example.

reshape()

PURPOSE Moves and resizes a component.

SYNTAX `public synchronized void reshape(int x, int y, int w, int h)`

DESCRIPTION Moves the component to position `x`, `y` and resizes it to have width `w` and height `h`. `x` and `y` are relative to the component's parent bounds.

PARAMETERS

`h`	The new height of the component in pixels.
`w`	The new width of the component in pixels.
`x`	The new *x*-coordinate of the component in pixels.
`y`	The new *y*-coordinate of the component in pixels.

SEE ALSO `bounds()`, `move()`, `resize()`.

EXAMPLE See the `Container` class example.

resize()

PURPOSE Resizes a component.

SYNTAX
```
public void resize(int w, int h)
public void resize(Dimension d)
```

DESCRIPTION This method resizes the component so that it has width `w` and height `h`. If dimension `d` is specified instead, the component will have width `d.width` and height `d.height`. The current location is not altered.

PARAMETERS

`d` The non-`null` component dimension.

`h` The new height of the component in pixels.

`w` The new width of the component in pixels.

SEE ALSO `bounds()`, `reshape()`, `size()`.

EXAMPLE See the `Container` class example.

setBackground()

PURPOSE Sets the component's background color.

SYNTAX `public synchronized void setBackground(Color c)`

DESCRIPTION This method sets the component's background color to `c`. The background color affects each component differently. For example, a button is painted in the background color, while its label is painted in the foreground color. See Figure 65.

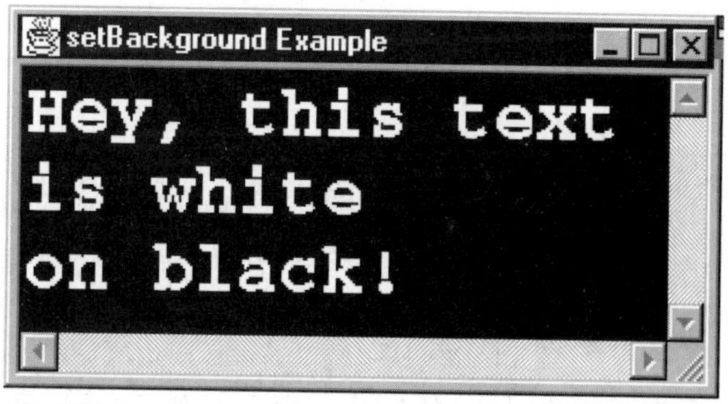

FIGURE 65 **`Component.setBackground()`**

If `c` is `null`, the component will inherit its background color from the closest ancestor whose background color has been set.

If the component is already displayed, the `repaint()` method must be called to force the component to redraw itself using the new background color.

PARAMETERS

`c` The new background color, which can be `null`.

SEE ALSO `getBackground()`, `setForeground()`.

EXAMPLE This method creates a text area with a black background and white foreground. The white foreground causes the text to be painted in white. Also, the text area is set with a very large font.

```
import java.awt.*;
class Main extends Frame {
    Main() {
        super("setBackground Example");
        TextArea ta = new TextArea();
```

```
            ta.setBackground(Color.black);
            ta.setForeground(Color.white);
            ta.setFont(new Font("Courier", Font.BOLD, 30));
            add("Center", ta);
            resize(200, 200);
            show();
        }

        static public void main(String[] args) {
            new Main();
        }
    }
```

setFont()

PURPOSE Sets the component's font.

SYNTAX `public synchronized void setFont(Font f)`

DESCRIPTION If `f` is not `null`, this method sets the component's font so that if the component paints any strings, it will paint them in the font `f`. Moreover, any graphics context that is created on the component will be initialized to `f`.

If `f` is `null`, the component's font is cleared. This means that the component's font will be inherited from the closest ancestor whose font has been set.

PARAMETERS

`f` The font. This parameter can be `null`.

SEE ALSO `getFont()`.

EXAMPLE See the class example.

setForeground()

PURPOSE Sets the component's foreground color.

SYNTAX `public synchronized void setForeground(Color c)`

DESCRIPTION This method sets the component's foreground color to `c`. The foreground color affects each component differently. For example, a button is painted in the background color, while its label is painted in the foreground color.

If `c` is `null`, the component will inherit its foreground color from the closest ancestor whose foreground color has been set.

If the component is already displayed, `repaint()` must be called to force the component to redraw itself using the new foreground color.

PARAMETERS

`c` The new foreground color, which can be `null`.

SEE ALSO `getForeground()`, `setBackground()`.

EXAMPLE See `setBackground()`.

show()

PURPOSE Makes the component visible.

SYNTAX

```
public synchronized void show()
public void show(boolean vis)
```

DESCRIPTION If `vis` is `true`, the component is made visible if not already visible. Otherwise the component is made invisible if not already invisible. If `vis` is not specified, the method defaults to `true`. Some layout managers completely ignore invisible components, so when the component is made visible, it appears at the wrong location and size. To update the component's bounds, the component's container should be invalidated and validated immediately after the component is made visible.

PARAMETERS

`vis` If `true`, the component is made visible; otherwise the component is hidden.

SEE ALSO `hide()`, `isShowing()`, `isVisible()`.

EXAMPLE This example creates two buttons. One has a blinking label, and the other shows or hides the blinking button. See Figure 66.

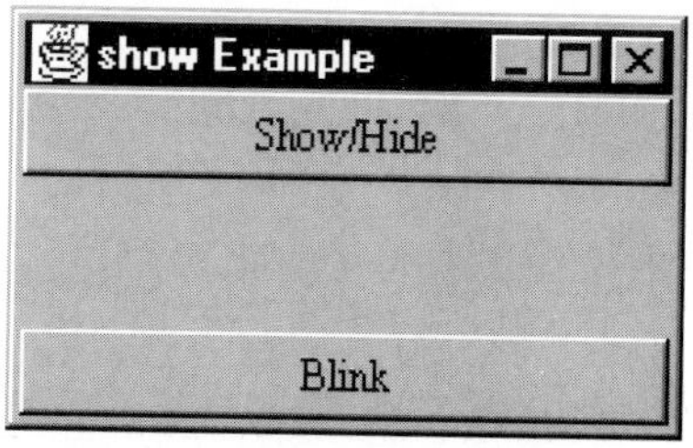

FIGURE 66 **`Component.show()`**

The blinking button overrides the `addNotify()` method to start the blinking thread which periodically sets and clears the button's label. The blinking button also overrides the `removeNotify()` method to add the `synchronized` keyword to the method signature. The blinking thread does not modify the label if the label is not visible. The thread terminates if the peer has been removed. To avoid a race condition, the blinking thread acquires the button's lock. Inside the lock, it checks whether the peer exists. If it doesn't, the thread terminates. Since the removeNotify() method is synchronized, the peer cannot be removed while the blinking thread holds the lock.

```
import java.awt.*;
class Main extends Frame {
    BlinkButton b = new BlinkButton("Blink");
    Main() {
        super("show Example");
        add("North", new Button("Show/Hide"));
        add("South", b);
        pack();
        show();
    }

    public boolean action(Event evt, Object arg) {
        if ("Show/Hide".equals(arg)) {
            if (b.isVisible()) {
                b.hide();
            } else {
                b.show();
                invalidate();
                validate();
            }
            // OR b.show(!b.isVisible());
            return true;
        }
        return false;
    }

    static public void main(String[] args) {
        new Main();
    }
}

class BlinkButton extends Button implements Runnable {
    String label;

    BlinkButton(String label) {
        super(label);
        this.label = label;
    }

    public void addNotify() {
        super.addNotify();
        (new Thread(this)).start();
    }

    public synchronized void removeNotify() {
        super.removeNotify();
    }

    public void run() {
        boolean on = false;
```

```
            while (true) {
                synchronized (this) {
                    if (getPeer() == null) {
                        break;
                    }

                    // Actually, isVisible() could have been used
                    // instead of isShowing() since the previous
                    // statement guarantees that the button's peer exists.
                    if (isShowing()) {
                        if (on) {
                            setLabel(label);
                        } else {
                            setLabel("");
                        }
                        on = !on;
                    }
                }
                try {
                    Thread.sleep(1000);
                } catch (Exception e) {
                }
            }
        }
    }
```

size()

PURPOSE Retrieves the size of the component.

SYNTAX `public Dimension size()`

DESCRIPTION The size of the component is derived from the component's bounds. In particular, `size().width == bounds().width` and `size().height == bounds().height`.

RETURNS A non-`null` `Dimension` object containing the size of the component.

SEE ALSO `resize()`.

EXAMPLE See the class example.

toString()

PURPOSE Generates a string representation of the component's state.

SYNTAX `public String toString()`

DESCRIPTION
The result string contains the component's class name and the results of calling `paramString()`. The Java compiler automatically generates code to call this method when it needs to translate the component instance to a string. This method is typically used for debugging.

RETURNS
A non-`null` string representing the component's state.

OVERRIDES
`Object.toString()`.

SEE ALSO
`paramString()`.

EXAMPLE
See `Object.toString()`.

update()

PURPOSE
Called in response to a `repaint()` method call.

SYNTAX
`public void update(Graphics gc)`

DESCRIPTION
The `update()` method is called in response to a call to `repaint()`. By default, this method clears the background of the component and calls `paint()`. Here is the default implementation:

```
public void update(Graphics g) {
    g.setColor(getBackground());
    g.fillRect(0, 0, width, height);
    g.setColor(getForeground());
    paint(g);
}
```

This method is typically overridden to avoid the background repaint. This is critical to smooth animation. Use the graphics context `gc` to update the area. `gc` is initialized with a clipping rectangle as large as the update area, so you cannot paint outside this area. You can determine the bounds of the update area by calling `gc.getClipRect()`. Note that it is possible for two or more `repaint()` method calls to be batched into a single call to the `update()` method. When this happens, the resulting update area is enlarged to include all the smaller update areas.

See the `Graphics` class for a description of the initial state of the graphics context `gc` (for example, font, color).

PARAMETERS

`gc`
The non-`null` graphics context on which to paint the component.

SEE ALSO
`paint()`, `repaint()`.

EXAMPLE
See `repaint()`.

validate()

PURPOSE Validates the component.

SYNTAX `public void validate()`

DESCRIPTION This method validates the component if it is invalid. If the component is invalid, its `layout()` method is called. If the component is a container, the `validate()` method goes further and finds all invalid children and invokes their `validate()` methods. However, note that for efficiency, the `validate()` method is not invoked on valid children. So if the valid child contains an invalid child, the invalid child will not be validated. This situation rarely arises because, by default, calling `invalidate()` on a component also invalidates all of its ancestors. This method is normally used on components that are containers.

See the `Container` class for more information about layout.

SEE ALSO `invalidate()`, `layout()`.

EXAMPLE This example demonstrates that layouts are not automatically validated. In the program, when a button is clicked its font is increased by one point and the button is invalidated. The button label becomes too big and needs to be validated. Clicking the button labeled "Validate" invokes the `validate()` method on the frame, thereby validating the entire component hierarchy.

Figure 67(a) shows a button whose label has increased in size and is therefore invalid. Figure 67(b) shows the same button after the component hierarchy has been validated.

```
import java.awt.*;
class Main extends Frame {
    Main() {
        super("validate Example");

        add("North", new Button("Validate"));
        add("Center", makePanel("East",
            makePanel("South",
            makePanel("West",
            makePanel(null, null)))));
        resize(300, 300);
        show();
    }

    Panel makePanel(String name, Component c) {
        Panel p = new Panel();

        p.setLayout(new BorderLayout());
        p.add("North", new Button("North"));
        p.add("South", new Button("South"));
```

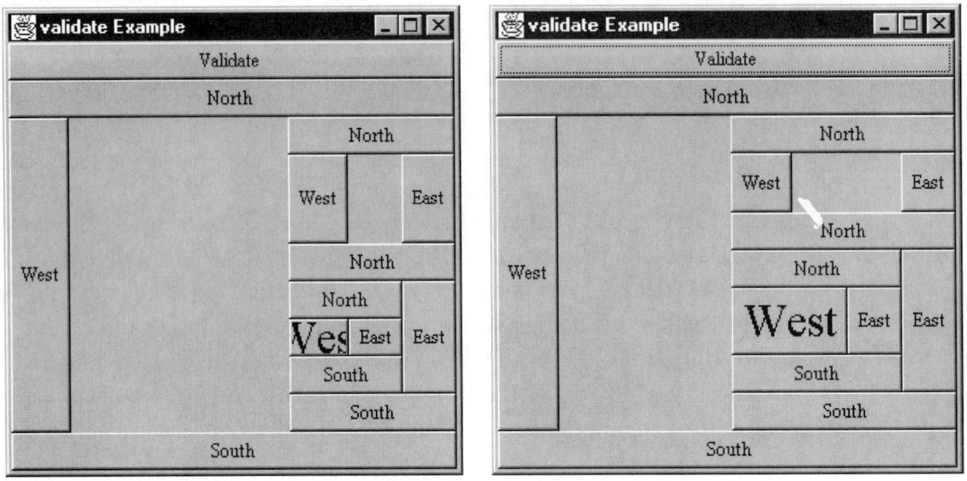

(a) (b)

FIGURE 67 **`Component.validate()`**

```
            p.add("West", new Button("West"));
            p.add("East", new Button("East"));
            if (name != null) {
                p.add(name, c);
            }
            return p;
        }

        public boolean action(Event evt, Object arg) {
            if ("Validate".equals(arg)) {
                validate();
            } else {
                Font f = ((Component)evt.target).getFont();

                f = new Font(f.getFamily(), f.getStyle(), f.getSize()+1);
                ((Component)evt.target).setFont(f);
                ((Component)evt.target).invalidate();
            }
            return true;
        }

        static public void main(String[] args) {
            new Main();
        }
    }
```

A B C D E F G H I J K L M N O P Q R S T U V W X Y Z

java.awt.peer

ComponentPeer

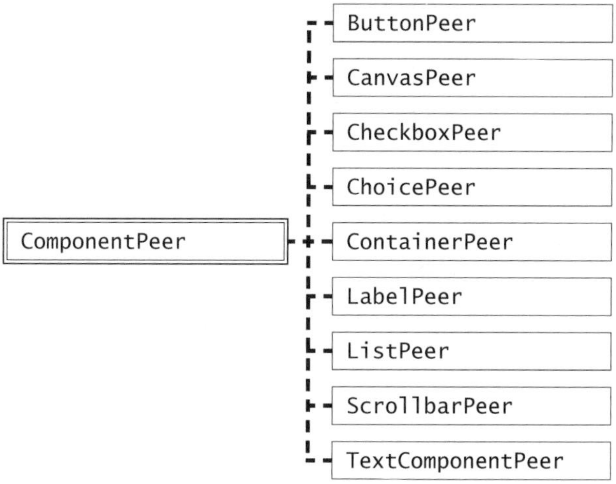

Syntax

```
public interface ComponentPeer
```

Description

A component such as a button uses the platform's native implementation of a button. For example, on Solaris, the Abstract Windowing Toolkit (AWT) button uses the Motif button widget, while on Windows 95, the AWT button uses the button control. So that the AWT button component behaves the same on all platforms, the button is assigned a peer that takes care of translating the behavior of the platform's native button to the behavior of the AWT button.

Every component in the AWT has a peer associated with it. Just as the `Component` class is the superclass of all AWT components, the `ComponentPeer` class is the superclass of all peer classes.

AWT programmers normally do not directly use peer classes and interfaces. Instead they deal with AWT components in the `java.awt` package. These in turn automatically manage their peers. Only someone who is porting the AWT to another platform should be concerned with the peer classes and interfaces. Consequently, most peer documentation refers to `java.awt` counterparts.

See `Component` and `Toolkit` for additional information about component peers.

MEMBER SUMMARY

Peer Methods

`checkImage()`	Retrieves the construction status of an image.
`createImage()`	Creates an off-screen image or an image from an image producer.
`disable()`	Disables a component.
`dispose()`	Destroys a component.
`enable()`	Enables a component.
`getColorModel()`	Retrieves the component's color model.
`getFontMetrics()`	Retrieves the font metrics for a font.
`getGraphics()`	Creates a graphics context for the component.
`getToolkit()`	Retrieves the component's toolkit.
`handleEvent()`	Called when the component receives an event.
`hide()`	Makes the component invisible.
`minimumSize()`	Calculates the component's minimum size dimensions.
`nextFocus()`	Sets the focus to the next component.
`paint()`	Called to repaint the component.
`preferredSize()`	Calculates the component's preferred size dimensions.
`prepareImage()`	Triggers the loading of image data for an image.
`print()`	Prints the component on a graphics context.
`repaint()`	Makes a request to repaint a component.
`requestFocus()`	Requests that the focus be given to the component.
`reshape()`	Moves and resizes a component.
`setBackground()`	Sets the component's background color.
`setFont()`	Sets the component's font.
`setForeground()`	Sets the component's foreground color.
`show()`	Makes the component visible.

See Also

`Component`, `Toolkit`.

checkImage()

PURPOSE Retrieves the construction status of an image.

SYNTAX
```
int checkImage(Image image, int width, int height,
   ImageObserver obs)
```

PARAMETERS

`height`	If >= 0, specifies the height of the scaled version of the image to check.
`image`	The non-`null` image to check.

`obs`	If non-`null`, specifies the image observer to be notified whenever the status changes.
`width`	If >= 0, specifies the width of the scaled version of the image to check.

RETURNS The combination of status bits as defined by the `ImageObserver` interface.

SEE ALSO `Component.checkImage()`.

createImage()

PURPOSE Creates an off-screen image or an image from an image producer.

SYNTAX
```
Image createImage(int width, int height)
Image createImage(ImageProducer prod)
```

PARAMETERS

`height`	The height of the off-screen image in pixels.
`prod`	The non-`null` image producer.
`width`	The width of the off-screen image in pixels.

RETURNS A new off-screen image.

SEE ALSO `Component.createImage()`.

disable()

PURPOSE Disables a component.

SYNTAX
```
void disable()
```

SEE ALSO `Component.disable()`.

dispose()

PURPOSE Destroys this component.

SYNTAX
```
void dispose()
```

DESCRIPTION This method releases any resources associated with this component.

A B C D E F G H I J K L M N O P Q R S T U V W X Y Z

enable()

PURPOSE Enables a component.

SYNTAX `void enable()`

SEE ALSO `Component.enable()`.

getColorModel()

PURPOSE Retrieves the component's color model.

SYNTAX `ColorModel getColorModel()`

RETURNS A non-`null` color model instance.

SEE ALSO `Component.getColorModel()`.

getFontMetrics()

PURPOSE Retrieves the font metrics for a font.

SYNTAX `FontMetrics getFontMetrics(Font font)`

PARAMETERS

`font` The non-`null` font.

RETURNS The non-`null` font metrics for `font`.

SEE ALSO `Component.getFontMetrics()`.

getGraphics()

PURPOSE Creates a graphics context for the component.

SYNTAX `Graphics getGraphics()`

RETURNS A graphics context on the component.

SEE ALSO `Component.getGraphics()`.

A B C D E F G H I J K L M N O P Q R S T U V W X Y Z

getToolkit()

PURPOSE Retrieves the component's toolkit.

SYNTAX `Toolkit getToolkit()`

RETURNS A non-`null` reference to the component's toolkit.

SEE ALSO `Component.getToolkit()`, `Toolkit`.

handleEvent()

PURPOSE Called when the component receives an event.

SYNTAX `boolean handleEvent(Event evt)`

PARAMETERS

`evt` The non-`null` event.

RETURNS `false` if the event should be passed up to the component's parent; `true` otherwise.

SEE ALSO `Component.handleEvent()`.

hide()

PURPOSE Makes the component invisible.

SYNTAX `void hide()`

SEE ALSO `Component.hide()`.

minimumSize()

PURPOSE Calculates the component's minimum size dimensions.

SYNTAX `Dimension minimumSize()`

RETURNS A non-`null` dimension object containing the component's minimum size.

SEE ALSO `Component.minimumSize()`.

nextFocus()

PURPOSE Sets the focus to the next component.

SYNTAX `void nextFocus()`

SEE ALSO `Component.nextFocus()`.

paint()

PURPOSE Called to repaint the component.

SYNTAX `void paint(Graphics gc)`

PARAMETERS

`gc` The non-`null` graphics context in which to paint the component.

SEE ALSO `Component.paint()`.

preferredSize()

PURPOSE Calculates the component's preferred size dimensions.

SYNTAX `Dimension preferredSize()`

RETURNS A non-`null` dimension object containing the component's preferred size.

SEE ALSO `Component.preferredSize()`.

prepareImage()

PURPOSE Triggers the loading of image data for an image.

SYNTAX `boolean prepareImage(Image img, int w, int h, ImageObserver obs)`

PARAMETERS

`h` `-1` or the scaled height of the returned image.
`img` The non-`null` image to load.
`obs` The non-`null` image observer
`w` `-1` or the scaled width of the returned image.

RETURNS `true` if all the image data for `img` is available; `false` otherwise.

SEE ALSO `Component.prepareImage()`.

print()

PURPOSE Prints the component on a graphics context.

SYNTAX `void print(Graphics gc)`

PARAMETERS

`gc` The non-`null` graphics context on which to print.

SEE ALSO `Component.print()`.

repaint()

PURPOSE Makes a request to repaint a component.

SYNTAX `void repaint(long ms, int x, int y, int w, int h)`

PARAMETERS

`h` The height of the rectangular area to repaint.
`ms` Maximum delay in milliseconds before the `update()` method is called.
`w` The width of the rectangular area to repaint.
`x` The *x*-coordinate of the rectangular area to repaint.
`y` The *y*-coordinate of the rectangular area to repaint.

SEE ALSO `Component.repaint()`.

requestFocus()

PURPOSE Requests that the focus be given to the component.

SYNTAX `void requestFocus()`

SEE ALSO `Component.requestFocus()`.

reshape()

PURPOSE Moves and resizes a component.

SYNTAX `void reshape(int x, int y, int w, int h)`

PARAMETERS

`h` The new height of the component in pixels.

`w`	The new width of the component in pixels.
`x`	The new *x*-coordinate of the component in pixels.
`y`	The new *y*-coordinate of the component in pixels.
SEE ALSO	`Component.reshape()`.

setBackground()

PURPOSE Sets the component's background color.

SYNTAX `void setBackground(Color c)`

PARAMETERS

`c` The new background color, which can be `null`.

SEE ALSO `Component.setBackground()`.

setFont()

PURPOSE Sets the component's font.

SYNTAX `void setFont(Font f)`

PARAMETERS

`f` The font. This parameter can be `null`.

SEE ALSO `Component.setFont()`.

setForeground()

PURPOSE Sets the component's foreground color.

SYNTAX `void setForeground(Color c)`

PARAMETERS

`c` The new foreground color, which can be `null`.

SEE ALSO `Component.setForeground()`.

show()

PURPOSE Makes the component visible.

SYNTAX `void show()`

SEE ALSO `Component.show()`.

java.awt

Container

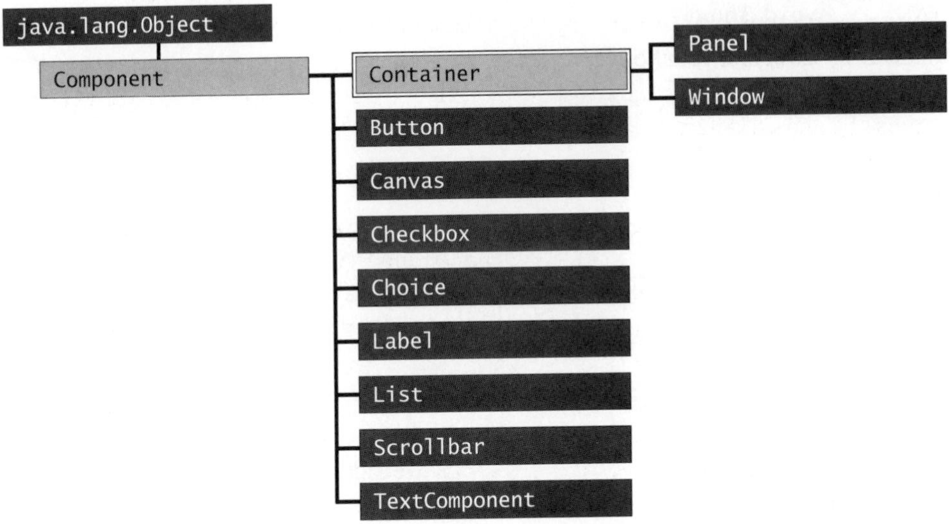

Syntax

```
public abstract class Container extends Component
```

Description

A container is a component that can contain other components. A container has a list of child components and a layout manager to lay out the children.

Layout Management

A container can have a layout manager associated with it to determine the size and placement of its components. A container maintains a *valid* state, which indicates whether the children of the container are properly laid out. Actions such as removing or adding a component to a container cause the container to become invalid. Only when the user causes the resizing of the container (by resizing the top-level window) is the layout manager automatically invoked by the system. Otherwise the layout manager needs to be invoked explicitly (for example, when you are adding a new button).

When the layout manager is invoked on a container, it first checks whether the container is valid. If so, it does not lay out the container. If not, it lays out all the children and then proceeds to invoke the layout manager of any invalid children. The layout process continues recursively until all reachable components are valid. Note that if a component is invalid but is embedded in a valid container, the layout process will not be applied to the invalid component.

Although the layout manager recursively traverses the component hierarchy, it does not recurse below valid components. Note that with this behavior an invalid component will *not* be validated if it is in a valid container. To remedy this, you need to either invoke the layout manager directly on the invalid component or invalidate the component's container.

Certain operations on the container automatically invalidate the container. However, in many cases the container needs to be explicitly invalidated. For example, if a component's size is changed (such as by changing its label), its container is not automatically marked invalid. See `layout()` and `validate()` for more details.

Insets

An *inset* is a distance from a rectangle's edge (see `Insets`). A container maintains four insets—left, top, right, bottom—that correspond to the edges of the container. The insets are applied to a container's bounds to yield another, typically smaller, area called the *inset area*, in which the container's components are constrained. Insets are most often used by containers that have borders such as the frame (see `Frame`).

When dealing with insets, you need to understand the distinction between the container's insets and the container's peer insets. By default, the container's insets are identical to the peer's insets. However, if the container's insets are overridden to produce a different inset, the override should always take into account the peer's insets. For example, if you want to reduce a container's inset area by 2 pixels on all sides, have the override retrieve the peer's insets, add 2 pixels on all sides, and then use the result.

A container's insets are primarily used by the layout manager. However, other objects are also affected by the container's insets. One is a mouse event, which is based on the peer's inset area rather than on the container's bounds. More precisely, the mouse coordinate (0, 0) is located at the top-left corner of the peer's inset area. So overriding a container's insets does not affect the mouse coordinates.

Another object affected by the container's peer insets is the graphics context. When a graphics context is created on a container, it is created in the container's inset area. As with the mouse event, the origin of a graphics context is coincident with the top-left corner of the peer's inset area. And as with the mouse event, overriding the container's insets does not affect the graphics context origin.

Figure 68(a) shows the two coordinate systems of a container. Figure 68(b) shows how the location of components are relative to the container's bounds. Figure 68(c) shows how mouse coordinates are relative to the container's inset area.

Disabled Containers

Disabling a container intercepts the delivery of all mouse and keyboard events made by the user to the container's child components. Disabling the container is not the same as disabling all components in the container. For example, most components look different when disabled. In a disabled container, the components will appear as though they were enabled.

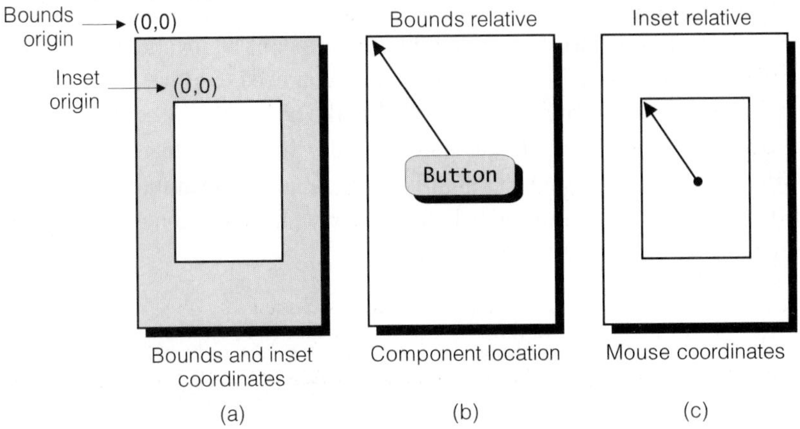

FIGURE 68 Bounds and Inset Coordinates in a Container

Z Ordering

Presently, the AWT does not define the back-to-front ordering of the components. Therefore when a component is appended to the container's component list, it is not possible to predict whether the new component will appear in front or behind all the other components.

MEMBER SUMMARY	
Component Methods	
`add()`	Adds the specified component.
`countComponents()`	Retrieves the number of components in the container.
`getComponent()`	Retrieves a component in the container.
`getComponents()`	Retrieves all the components in the container.
`locate()`	Locates the component at a point in the container.
`paintComponents()`	Paints the container's components on a graphics context.
`printComponents()`	Prints the container's components on a graphics context.
`remove()`	Removes a component from the container.
`removeAll()`	Removes all the components from the container.
Layout Methods	
`insets()`	Retrieves the container's insets.
`getLayout()`	Retrieves the container's layout manager.
`layout()`	Invokes the layout manager on the container.
`minimumSize()`	Calculates the container's minimum size dimensions.
`preferredSize()`	Calculates the container's preferred size dimensions.
`setLayout()`	Sets the layout manager for the container.
`validate()`	Validates the container by re-laying out its components.

MEMBER SUMMARY	
Event Method	
`deliverEvent()`	Delivers an event to a component in the container.
Peer Methods	
`addNotify()`	Creates the peers for the container and all its children.
`removeNotify()`	Destroys the peer hierarchy of the container and all its children.
Debugging Methods	
`list()`	Prints out the container's component hierarchy.
`paramString()`	Generates a string representing the container's state.

Example

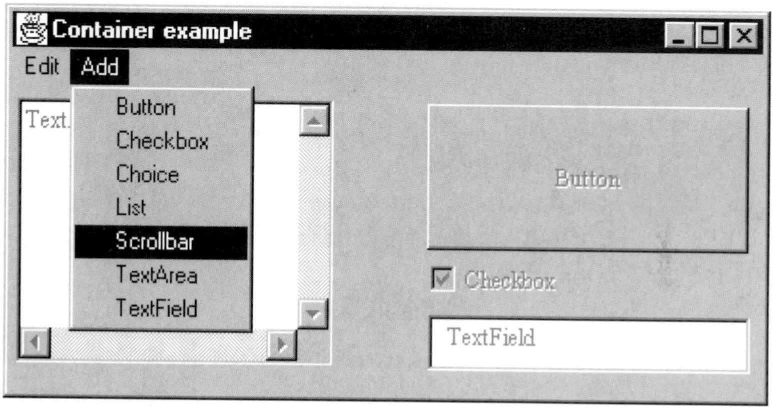

FIGURE 69 `Container`

This example program implements a rudimentary user interface builder. Using it, the user can create AWT components on the canvas and then move them about. The Add menu contains the names of various components that, when selected, create the component on the canvas. See Figure 69. The components are created disabled so that they can respond to mouse events. Any mouse event directed at a disabled component is delivered to its parent. In this case, the program catches the mouse event and determines if it occurred over a component. If so, one of several actions can occur. If the left mouse button was pressed, the component can be dragged around. If the right mouse button was pressed, the component is resized. If both the Shift and Control modifier keys were held down during the mouse click, the component is removed.

Example

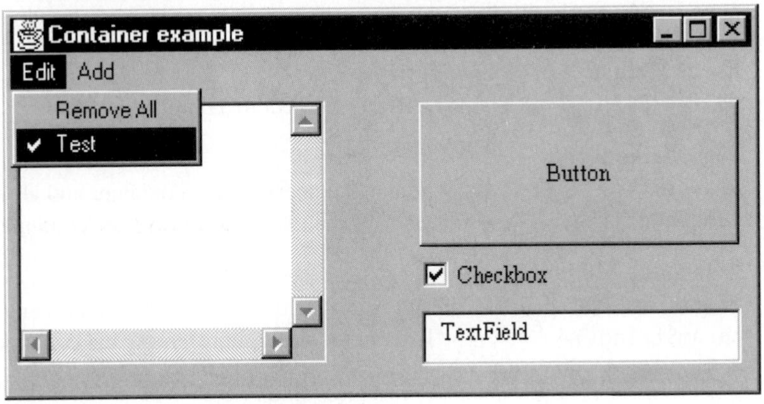

FIGURE 70 `Container`: **Edit Menu**

The Edit menu contains two commands: Remove All and Test. See Figure 70. Remove All removes all the components on the canvas. Test changes the enabled state of all the components on the canvas. In test mode, the components are enabled and so behave normally; the components cannot be moved or resized. When not in test mode, the components are disabled and can be moved and resized.

```
import java.awt.*;
class Main extends Frame {
    Main() {
        super("Container example");
        MenuBar mb = new MenuBar();

        // Edit Menu
        Menu m = new Menu("Edit");
        m.add("Remove All");
        m.add(new CheckboxMenuItem("Test"));
        mb.add(m);

        // Add Menu
        m = new Menu("Add");
        m.add("Button");
        m.add("Checkbox");
        m.add("Choice");
        m.add("List");
        m.add("Scrollbar");
        m.add("TextArea");
        m.add("TextField");
        mb.add(m);

        setMenuBar(mb);

        // Remove the default layout manager.
        setLayout(null);

        resize(400, 200);
        show();
    }
```

```
Component dragging;
Component stretching;
Point offset;
public boolean mouseDown(Event evt, int x, int y) {
    x += insets().left;
    y += insets().top;
    Component c = locate(x, y);
    if (c != null && c != this) {
        if (evt.shiftDown() && evt.controlDown()) {
            remove(c);
        } else if (evt.metaDown()) {
            stretching = c;
        } else {
            offset = new Point(x-c.location().x, y-c.location().y);
            dragging = c;
        }
    }
    return true;
}

public boolean mouseDrag(Event evt, int x, int y) {
    x += insets().left;
    y += insets().top;
    if (dragging != null) {
        dragging.move(x-offset.x, y-offset.y);
    } else if (stretching != null) {
        stretching.resize(x-stretching.bounds().x,
                          y-stretching.bounds().y);
    }
    return true;
}

public boolean mouseUp(Event evt, int x, int y) {
    stretching = dragging = null;
    return true;
}

int newX, newY;
public boolean action(Event evt, Object arg) {
    newX = Math.max(insets().left, newX);
    newY = Math.max(insets().top, newY);
    Component c = null;

    if (evt.target instanceof MenuItem) {
        if ("Button".equals(arg)) {
            add(c = new Button("Button"));
        } else if ("Checkbox".equals(arg)) {
            add(c = new Checkbox("Checkbox"));
        } else if ("Choice".equals(arg)) {
            add(c = new Choice());
        } else if ("List".equals(arg)) {
            add(c = new List());
        } else if ("Scrollbar".equals(arg)) {
            add(c = new Scrollbar());
```

B C D E F G H I J K L M N O P Q R S T U V W X Y Z

```
                } else if ("TextArea".equals(arg)) {
                    add(c = new TextArea("TextArea", 3, 20));
                } else if ("TextField".equals(arg)) {
                    add(c = new TextField("TextField"));
                } else if ("Remove All".equals(arg)) {
                    removeAll();
                } else if ("Test".equals(arg)) {
                    Component[] all = getComponents();

                    for (int i=0; i<all.length; i++) {
                        all[i].enable(((CheckboxMenuItem)evt.target).
                            getState());
                    }
                }
            }
            if (c != null) {
                Dimension d = c.preferredSize();

                c.reshape(newX, newY, d.width, d.height);
                c.disable();
                newX += 20;
                newY += 20;
                if (newX > size().width*3/4) {
                    newX = 0;
                }
                if (newY > size().height*3/4) {
                    newY = 0;
                }
                return true;
            }
            return false;
        }

        static public void main(String[] args) {
            new Main();
        }
    }
```

add()

PURPOSE Adds a component to the container.

SYNTAX
```
public Component add(Component comp)
public synchronized Component add(Component comp, int pos)
public synchronized Component add(String name, Component comp)
```

DESCRIPTION This method adds the component `comp` to the container at position `pos`. If `pos` is `0`, the new component will be the first component in the container. If `pos` is `-1`, the new component will be the last component in the container. If `pos` is not specified, it defaults to `-1`.

The component's name, if specified, is not used by the container in any way; it is used by the container's layout manager. In particular, if `name` is specified or is `null`, the component is added to the container. The container's layout manager is notified of the addition via a call to the `LayoutManager.addLayoutComponent()` method. If `name` is not specified, the container's layout manager will not be notified of the component's insertion.

PARAMETERS

`comp`	The non-`null` component to be added to the container.
`name`	The component name, which may be `null`.
`pos`	The position at which to insert the component. `0` means the first position and `-1` means the last position.

SEE ALSO `LayoutManager`.

EXAMPLE See the class example.

addNotify()

PURPOSE Creates the peers for the container and all its children.

SYNTAX `public synchronized void addNotify()`

DESCRIPTION This method creates the container's peer if it does not yet exist. Since `Container` is an abstract class, the actual peer created is based on a subclass of `Container`. This method also calls `addNotify()` on all the container's children.

OVERRIDES `Component.addNotify()`.

SEE ALSO `Component`, `Toolkit`.

countComponents()

PURPOSE Retrieves the number of components in the container.

SYNTAX `public int countComponents()`

RETURNS The number of components in the container.

EXAMPLE See `deliverEvent()`.

deliverEvent()

PURPOSE
Delivers an event to a component in the container.

SYNTAX
`public void deliverEvent(Event e)`

DESCRIPTION
This method delivers the event `e` to the component in the container at location `(e.x, e.y)`. If no component is located at `(e.x, e.y)`, the event is delivered to the container itself.

PARAMETERS

`e` The non-`null` event to be delivered.

OVERRIDES
`Component.deliverEvent()`.

SEE ALSO
`Component.handleEvent()`.

EXAMPLE
This example creates a frame with two buttons. See Figure 71(a). Clicking the buttons changes the fonts of all the components in the frame. In particular, clicking the SmallFont button causes the components to assume a small font, while clicking the LargeFont button causes all the components to assume a large font. See Figure 71(b).

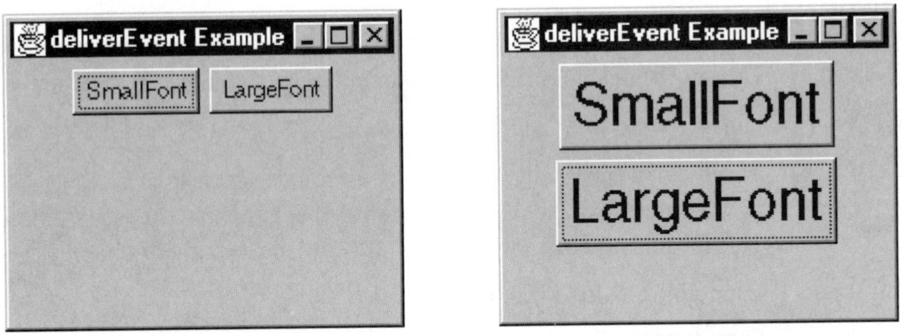

FIGURE 71 **`Container.deliverEvent()`: (a)Initial State and (b) After Changing Font Sizes**

Changing the font of the container's components could have been achieved by simply calling their `setFont()` methods. However, for the purposes of this example, the action is achieved by delivering a special action event to the components. To distinguish the action event from normal events, the `arg` field of the event is set to an instance of a `Font` object.

```
import java.awt.*;
class Main extends Frame {
    Main() {
        super("deliverEvent Example");

        setLayout(new FlowLayout());
```

```
        add(new MainButton("SmallFont"));
        add(new MainButton("LargeFont"));
        resize(200, 200);
        show();
    }

    public boolean action(Event evt, Object arg) {
        Font f = null;

        if ("SmallFont".equals(arg)) {
            f = new Font("Helvetica", Font.PLAIN, 12);
        } else if ("LargeFont".equals(arg)) {
            f = new Font("Helvetica", Font.PLAIN, 30);
        }
        if (f != null) {
            for (int i=0; i<countComponents(); i++) {
                Component c = getComponent(i);
                deliverEvent(new Event(this, 0, Event.ACTION_EVENT,
                    c.bounds().x, c.bounds().y, 0, 0, f));
            }
            layout();
            /* instead of layout(), the following would also work:
              invalidate();
              validate();
            */
            return true;
        }
        return false;
    }

    public static void main(String[] args) {
        new Main();
    }
}

class MainButton extends Button {
    MainButton(String label) {
        super(label);
    }

    public boolean action(Event evt, Object arg) {
        if (arg instanceof Font) {
            setFont((Font)arg);
            return true;
        }
        return false;
    }
}
```

getComponent()

PURPOSE Retrieves a component in the container.

SYNTAX `public synchronized Component getComponent(int n)`

DESCRIPTION This method retrieves a reference to the component at index `n` in the container. The index is zero-based, so the index of first component is 0.

PARAMETERS

`n` The zero-based index of the component in the container.

RETURNS The non-`null` component at index `n`.

EXCEPTIONS

`ArrayIndexOutOfBoundsException`

If `n` does not refer to a component.

EXAMPLE See `deliverEvent()`.

getComponents()

PURPOSE Retrieves all the components in the container.

SYNTAX `public synchronized Component[] getComponents()`

DESCRIPTION The length of the returned array indicates the number of children in the container.

RETURNS A non-`null` array of all the components in the container.

EXAMPLE See the class example.

getLayout()

PURPOSE Retrieves the container's layout manager.

SYNTAX `public LayoutManager getLayout()`

RETURNS The container's layout manager. The return value may be `null`.

SEE ALSO `layout()`, `setLayout()`.

EXAMPLE See `setLayout()`.

insets()

PURPOSE
Retrieves the container's insets.

SYNTAX

```
public Insets insets()
```

DESCRIPTION
If the container's peer has not been created, the returned insets will be (0, 0, 0, 0).

A container can override this method to modify the container's default insets. The override should take into account the peer's insets (i.e., the override should call `super.insets()`). Therefore if the override increases the default insets, it should first retrieve the peer's insets and then add the extra insets.

A container's insets are primarily used by the layout manager. Other objects such as mouse events and graphics context are based on the container peer's insets and ignore the results of an overridden `insets()` method. In particular, the mouse coordinate (0, 0) is situated at

```
(bounds().x+peer.insets().left,
    bounds().y+peer.insets().top).
```

Also, when a graphics context is created on the container, (0, 0) of the graphics context is at the same location.

RETURNS
A new non-`null` instance of the container's insets.

SEE ALSO
`Insets`.

EXAMPLE
This example creates a frame that contains a panel with a grid layout manager. See Figure 72. The frame overrides the `insets()` method and increases the insets on all sides. This causes the grid layout panel to be positioned and resized within the new insets.

FIGURE 72 `Container.insets()`

The frame also paints a 3-D border around the grid layout panel. This demonstrates that although the container's insets are increased, the origin of the graphics context supplied by `paint()` ignores the frame's `insets()` override and is still relative to the peer's insets.

The panel also prints out the mouse coordinates as the cursor moves around the panel. This is to demonstrate that as with the graphics context, the origin of mouse coordinates do not depend on the frame's `insets()` override and are still relative to the peer's insets.

```
import java.awt.*;
import java.awt.peer.ContainerPeer;
class Main extends Frame {
    Main() {
        super(“insets Example”);
        Panel p = new MainPanel(new GridLayout(0, 1), 8);
        Canvas cv;

        p.add(cv = new Canvas());
        cv.setBackground(Color.black);
        p.add(cv = new Canvas());
        cv.setBackground(Color.white);
        add(“Center”, p);
        resize(150, 200);
        show();
    }

    static public void main(String[] args) {
        new Main();
    }
}

class MainPanel extends Panel {
    int borderSize;

    MainPanel(LayoutManager layout, int size) {
        setLayout(layout);
        borderSize = size;
    }

    public Insets insets() {
        Insets insets = super.insets();
        insets.top += borderSize;
        insets.left += borderSize;
        insets.bottom += borderSize;
        insets.right += borderSize;
        return insets;
    }

    // Use the peer’s insets to determine the size of the paintable
    // area.
    public void paint(Graphics g) {
        Insets insets = ((ContainerPeer)getPeer()).insets();
        int w = size().width-insets.left-insets.right;
        int h = size().height-insets.top-insets.bottom;

        g.setColor(new Color(200, 100, 100));
        for (int i=0; i<borderSize; i++) {
            g.draw3DRect(i, i, w-2*i-1, h-2*i-1, i<borderSize/2);
        }
    }
```

```
    public boolean mouseMove(Event evt, int x, int y) {
        System.out.println(x + "," + y);
        return true;
    }
}
```

layout()

PURPOSE Invokes the layout manager on the container.

SYNTAX `public synchronized void layout()`

DESCRIPTION This method invokes the layout manager to resize and position the container's components. Unlike `validate()`, this method ignores the valid state of the container. Moreover, `validate()` attempts to validate all the descendents of the container, while `layout()` does not.

OVERRIDES `Component.layout()`.

SEE ALSO `getLayout()`, `setLayout()`.

EXAMPLE See `deliverEvent()`. This example causes the components in the frame to change font size. Since changing the size of the button label's font does not invalidate the button's container, the button's size will not change. Calling `layout()` corrects the position and size of the button. An alternative to calling `layout()` is calling `validate()`. However, since the container is not automatically invalidated, the `invalidate()` method needs to be called first.

list()

PURPOSE Prints out the container's component hierarchy.

SYNTAX `public void list(PrintStream out, int indent)`

DESCRIPTION This method recursively prints the results of calling `toString()` on each of the container's descendents. The component hierarchy is traversed in depth-first order. Children that are deeper down the hierarchy are printed with more indents. The first line of output is printed with `indent` spaces.

PARAMETERS

`indent` The indentation of the first line of output.

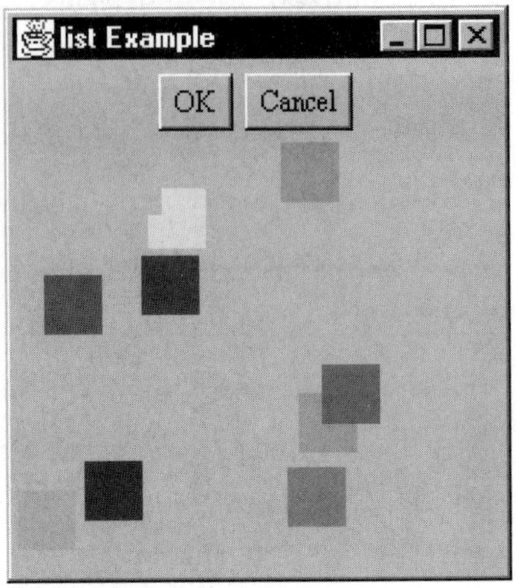

FIGURE 73 `Container.list()`

out — The non-`null` output stream in which to print.

OVERRIDES — `Component.list()`.

SEE ALSO — `Object.toString()`.

EXAMPLE — This example creates a frame with many nested containers. See Figure 73. Pressing F1 prints the frame's entire component hierarchy.

```
import java.awt.*;
class Main extends Frame {
    Main() {
        super("list Example");
        Panel p = new Panel();

        setLayout(new BorderLayout());

        Panel card = new Panel();
        card.setLayout(new CardLayout());
        add("North", card);

        p = new Panel();
        p.setLayout(new FlowLayout());
        p.add(new Button("OK"));
        p.add(new Button("Cancel"));
        card.add("1", p);

        p = new Panel();
        p.setLayout(new GridLayout(1, 0));
        p.add(new Box());
        card.add("2", p);

        p = new Panel();
        p.setLayout(null);
        for (int i=0; i<10; i++) {
            p.add(new Box());
        }
        p.add(new Button("Button"));
        add("Center", p);

        resize(350, 350);
        show();
    }

    public boolean keyDown(Event evt, int key) {
        if (key == Event.F1) {
            list(System.out);
            return true;
        }
        return false;
```

```
    }

    static public void main(String[] args) {
        new Main();
    }
}

class Box extends Canvas {
    Color c = new Color(random(256), random(256), random(256));

    Box() {
        reshape(random(150), random(150), 25, 25);
    }

    int random(int r) {
        return (int)(Math.floor(Math.random()*r));
    }

    public void paint(Graphics g) {
        g.setColor(c);
        g.fillRect(0, 0, size().width, size().height);
        g.setColor(Color.black);
    }

    protected String paramString() {
        String str = super.paramString();

        return str + ",color=" + c;
    }
}
```

OUTPUT

```
Main[0,0,218x241,layout=java.awt.BorderLayout,resizable,title=list
Example]
  java.awt.Panel[4,23,210x34,layout=java.awt.CardLayout]
    java.awt.Panel[4,23,210x34,layout=java.awt.FlowLayout]
      java.awt.Button[63,5,32x24,label=OK]
      java.awt.Button[100,5,46x24,label=Cancel]
    java.awt.Panel[0,0,0x0,hidden,layout=java.awt.GridLayout]
      Box[4,23,0x0,color=java.awt.Color[r=245,g=49,b=99]]
  java.awt.Panel[4,57,210x180]
    Box[115,0,25x25,color=java.awt.Color[r=147,g=183,b=170]]
    Box[55,47,25x25,color=java.awt.Color[r=68,g=42,b=86]]
    Box[39,5,25x25,color=java.awt.Color[r=174,g=169,b=240]]
    Box[132,93,25x25,color=java.awt.Color[r=70,g=101,b=217]]
    Box[58,19,25x25,color=java.awt.Color[r=182,g=236,b=107]]
    Box[122,105,25x25,color=java.awt.Color[r=255,g=140,b=121]]
    Box[13,55,25x25,color=java.awt.Color[r=97,g=88,b=233]]
    Box[30,133,25x25,color=java.awt.Color[r=152,g=18,b=87]]
    Box[1,145,25x25,color=java.awt.Color[r=187,g=176,b=42]]
    Box[117,136,25x25,color=java.awt.Color[r=147,g=134,b=177]]
    java.awt.Button[0,0,0x0,label=Button]
```

locate()

PURPOSE Locates the component at a point in the container.

SYNTAX `public Component locate(int x, int y)`

DESCRIPTION This method is used to determine what, if any, component is at the pixel coordinate `x`, `y`. The coordinates must be relative to the container's bounds and not its insets.

The returned component is a direct descendent of the container; that is, it does not recurse down the component hierarchy to find the actual component at `x`, `y`. So, for example, if the container contains another container of buttons, then `locate()` can return only a reference to the subcontainer and not to any of its buttons.

PARAMETERS

`x` The *x*-coordinate relative to the container's bounds.

`y` The *y*-coordinate relative to the container's bounds.

RETURNS The component at `x`, `y` or the container itself if no component is at `x`, `y` but `x`, `y` is in the container. Returns `null` if `x`, `y` is not in the container.

OVERRIDES `Component.locate()`.

EXAMPLE See the class example.

minimumSize()

PURPOSE Calculates the container's minimum size dimensions.

SYNTAX `public synchronized Dimension minimumSize()`

DESCRIPTION By default, this method uses the container's layout manager to determine the container's minimum size. In particular, if the layout manager is not `null`, the result of calling the layout manager's `minimumLayoutSize()` method is returned.

Note that if this method is overridden, the minimum size must include the container's insets. For example, if the container must display a 10-×-10 pixel image and has an inset border of 3 pixels on all edges, then the minimum size is 16-×-16.

RETURNS A non-`null` dimension object containing the container's minimum size.

OVERRIDES `Component.minimumSize()`.

EXAMPLE See the `LayoutManager` class example.

A B C D E F G H I J K L M N O P Q R S T U V W X Y Z

paintComponents()

PURPOSE Paints the container's components on a graphics context.

SYNTAX `public void paintComponents(Graphics gc)`

DESCRIPTION This method is called by the AWT system in response to a request to paint an AWT component hierarchy. The container should paint all its components on the graphics context `gc`. It can either paint directly on `gc` or call each of the component's `paint()` methods.

PARAMETERS

`gc` The non-`null` graphics context in which to paint the container's components.

SEE ALSO `Component.paint()`, `Component.paintAll()`.

paramString()

PURPOSE Generates a string representing the container's state.

SYNTAX `protected String paramString()`

DESCRIPTION The returned string includes the container's layout manager. A subclass of this class should override this method and return a concatenation of its state with the results of `super.paramString()`. This method is called by the `toString()` method and is typically used for debugging.

RETURNS A non-`null` string representing the container's state.

OVERRIDES `Component.paramString()`.

SEE ALSO `Object.toString()`.

EXAMPLE See `Component.paramString()`.

preferredSize()

PURPOSE Calculates the container's preferred size dimensions.

SYNTAX `public synchronized Dimension preferredSize()`

DESCRIPTION By default, this method uses the container's layout manager to determine the container's preferred size. In particular, if the layout manager is not `null`, the result of calling the layout manager's `preferredLayoutSize()` method is returned.

Note that if this method is overridden, the preferred size must include the container's insets. For example, if the container must display a 10-×-10 pixel image and has an inset border of 3 pixels on all edges, then the preferred size is 16-×-16.

RETURNS A non-`null` dimension object containing the container's preferred size.

OVERRIDES `Component.preferredSize()`.

EXAMPLE See the `LayoutManager` class example.

printComponents()

PURPOSE Prints the container's components on a graphics context.

SYNTAX `public void printComponents(Graphics gc)`

DESCRIPTION This method is called by the AWT system in response to a request to print an AWT component hierarchy. The container should print all its components on the graphics context `gc`. It can either print directly on `gc` or call each of the component's `print()` methods.

PARAMETERS

`gc` The non-`null` graphics context in which to print the container's components.

SEE ALSO `Component.print()`, `Component.printAll()`.

remove()

PURPOSE Removes a component from the container.

SYNTAX `public synchronized void remove(Component comp)`

DESCRIPTION When a component is removed, its peer is first destroyed and then removed from the container's list of components. The layout manager also is notified of the removal by way of the `LayoutManager.removeLayoutComponent()` method. The container and all of its ancestors are also invalidated.

PARAMETERS

`comp` The non-`null` component to be removed.

SEE ALSO `add()`, `LayoutManager.removeLayoutComponent()`, `removeAll()`.

EXAMPLE See the class example.

A B C D E F G H I J K L M N O P Q R S T U V W X Y Z

removeAll()

PURPOSE Removes all the components in the container.

SYNTAX `public synchronized void removeAll()`

DESCRIPTION This method removes all the components in the container. It is equivalent to calling `remove()` on each component. The layout manager is notified of the removal of each by way of the `LayoutManager.removeLayoutComponent()` method. The container and all of its ancestors are also invalidated.

SEE ALSO `add()`, `LayoutManager.removeLayoutComponent()`, `remove()`.

EXAMPLE See the class example.

removeNotify()

PURPOSE Destroys the peer hierarchy of the container and all its children.

SYNTAX `public synchronized void removeNotify()`

DESCRIPTION This method destroys the peer hierarchy of the container and all its children, if they exist. This method should never be called directly. It is normally called by the component's container.

OVERRIDES `Component.removeNotify()`.

SEE ALSO `Component`, `Toolkit`.

setLayout()

PURPOSE Sets the layout manager for the container.

SYNTAX `public void setLayout(LayoutManager mgr)`

DESCRIPTION This method sets `mgr` to be the container's layout manager. `mgr` can be `null`, which means that the components in the container will not be moved or resized.

PARAMETERS

mgr — The layout manager to set for the container.

SEE ALSO — `getLayout()`, `layout()`.

EXAMPLE — This example creates a row of buttons and a panel with a card layout manager. See Figure 74. Clicking a button causes the card layout panel to display the component identified by the button. For example, clicking the TextArea button displays a `TextArea` component.

FIGURE 74 `Container.setLayout()`

```
import java.awt.*;
class Main extends Frame {
    Panel flow = new Panel();
    Panel card = new Panel();
    Main() {
        super("setLayout Example");
        card.setLayout(new CardLayout());
        flow.setLayout(new FlowLayout());

        addComp("Button", new Button());
        addComp("TextArea", new TextArea());
        addComp("List", new List());

        add("North", flow);
        add("Center", card);

        resize(200, 200);
        show();
    }

    void addComp(String label, Component c) {
        card.add(label, c);
        flow.add(new Button(label));
    }

    public boolean action(Event evt, Object arg) {
        if (arg instanceof String) {
            CardLayout l = (CardLayout)card.getLayout();
            l.show(card, (String)arg);
            return true;
        }
```

```
            return false;
        }

        static public void main(String[] args) {
            new Main();
        }
    }
```

validate()

PURPOSE Validates the container by re-laying out its components.

SYNTAX `public synchronized void validate()`

DESCRIPTION If the container is invalid, this method validates it by calling the `layout()` method; otherwise the method call is ignored. After the container is validated, this method calls `validate()` on each of the container's components.

OVERRIDES `Component.invalidate()`.

SEE ALSO `LayoutManager`.

EXAMPLE See `deliverEvent()`. This example causes the components in the frame to change font size. Since changing the size of the button's label does not invalidate its container, the button's size will not change. For the container to lay out the components again, the container must first be invalidated and then validated.

java.awt.peer

ContainerPeer

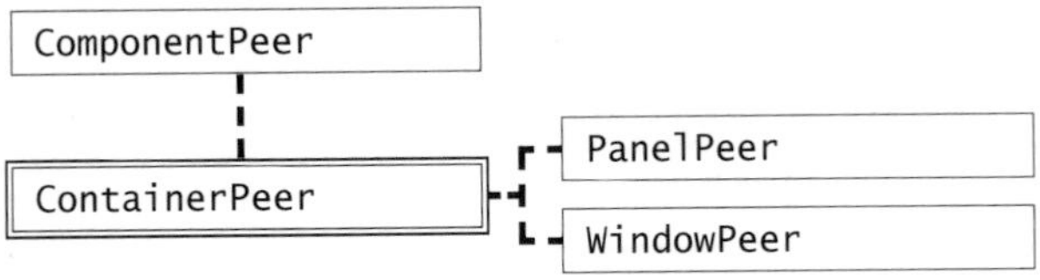

Syntax

`public interface ContainerPeer extends ComponentPeer`

Description

The container component (see the `Container` class) in the Abstract Windowing Toolkit (AWT), uses the platform's native implementation of a container. So that the AWT container behaves the same on all platforms, the container is assigned a peer, whose task is to translate the behavior of the platform's native container to the behavior of the AWT container.

AWT programmers normally do not directly use peer classes and interfaces. Instead they deal with AWT components in the `java.awt` package. These in turn automatically manage their peers. Only someone who is porting the AWT to another platform should be concerned with the peer classes and interfaces. Consequently, most peer documentation refers to `java.awt` counterparts.

See `Component` and `Toolkit` for additional information about component peers.

MEMBER SUMMARY	
Peer Method	
`insets()`	Retrieves the container's insets.

See Also

`Component`, `Container`, `Toolkit`.

insets()

PURPOSE Retrieves the container's insets.

SYNTAX `Insets insets()`

RETURNS A new non-`null` instance of the container's insets.

SEE ALSO `Container.insets()`, `Insets`.

java.net
ContentHandler

java.lang.Object — ContentHandler

Syntax

```
abstract public class ContentHandler
```

Description

Each document returned by an HTTP server has a document header. This header describes various properties about the document's contents. One such property is the MIME type of the document. For example, an HTML file has a type of "text" and a subtype of "html" ("text/html"), while a movie might have a type of "video" and a subtype of "mpeg" ("video/mpeg"). `ContentHandler` is an abstract class that is the basis for implementing handlers for documents of different MIME types. Different instances of `ContentHandler` are created by the `ContentHandlerFactory` object used by the program (usually a Web browser). The factory decides which subclass of `ContentHandler` to create an instance of. It does this by examining the MIME type of the document to be read from the HTTP server. Once a content handler has been created, you use the `getContent()` method implemented by the handler to retrieve a Java object that represents the contents of the document read from the HTTP server. If you use `URL.getContent()` or `URLConnection.getContent()`, this process of examining document headers, creating content handlers, and getting an object that represents the contents is done automatically for you.

MEMBER SUMMARY	
Communication Method	
`getContent()`	Generates an object by reading its representation from a URL connection.

See Also

`ContentHandlerFactory`, `URL`, `URLConnection`.

A B C D E F G H I J K L M N O P Q R S T U V W X Y Z

Example

This example shows an implementation of a content handler that reads the contents from the connection and returns the contents read in the form of a string.

See related examples in `ContentHandlerFactory` and `URLConnection.setContentHandlerFactory()`.

```
import java.net.ContentHandler;
import java.net.URLConnection;
import java.io.InputStream;
import java.io.IOException;

// Content handler that expects content to be Text String
class SimpleStringHandler extends ContentHandler {
    public Object getContent(URLConnection conn) throws IOException {
        InputStream input = conn.getInputStream();
        StringBuffer buf = new StringBuffer();
        int c;
        while ((c = input.read()) >= 0) {
            buf.append((char) c);
        }
        input.close();
        return (buf.toString());
    }
}
```

getContent()

PURPOSE Generates an object by reading its representation from a URL connection.

SYNTAX `abstract public Object getContent(URLConnection urlconn) throws IOException`

DESCRIPTION This method reads from the URL connection `urlconn` the representation of an object whose type is expected by this particular `ContentHandler` class. If the representation is not in the correct format expected for this particular `ContentHandler` class, `IOException` is thrown.

PARAMETERS

`urlconn` The URL connection from which to read the object.

EXCEPTIONS

`IOException` If the object is not in the format expected by this content handler or if an IO error occurred while reading the object.

SEE ALSO `ContentHandlerFactory`, `URL`, `URL.getContent()`, `URLConnection.getContent()`.

EXAMPLE See the class example.

A B C D E F G H I J K L M N O P Q R S T U V W X Y Z

java.net

ContentHandlerFactory

ContentHandlerFactory

Syntax

`public interface ContentHandlerFactory`

Description

Each document that is returned by an HTTP server has a document header. This header describes various properties about the document contents. One such property is the MIME type of the document. For example, an HTML file has a type of "text" and a subtype of "html" ("text/html"), while a movie might have a type of "video" and a subtype of "mpeg" ("video/mpeg"). `ContentHandler` is an abstract class that is the basis for implementing handlers for documents of different MIME types. Different instances of `ContentHandler` are created by the `ContentHandlerFactory` object used by the program (usually a Web browser). The factory decides which subclass of `ContentHandler` to create an instance of. It does this by examining the MIME type of the document being read from the HTTP server. Once a content handler has been created, you use the `getContent()` method implemented by the handler to retrieve a Java object that represents the contents of the document read from the HTTP server.

There can be only one content handler factory installed in a program at any one time. Once installed, the content handler factory cannot be replaced.

MEMBER SUMMARY	
Handler Creation Method	
`createContentHandler()`	Creates a content handler for documents of a MIME type.

See Also

`ContentHandler`, `URL`, `URLConnection.setContentHandlerFactory()`, `URLStream-Handler`.

Example

The following is an example of a ContentHandlerFactory implementation. See related examples in ContentHandler and URLConnection.setContentHandlerFactory().

```
// Sample factory that uses same policy as default Java policy.
class SampleFactory implements ContentHandlerFactory {
    Hashtable handlers = new Hashtable();
    static private ContentHandler defaultHandler =
        new SimpleStringHandler();
    private static String content_class_prefix =
        "sun.net.www.content.";

    // Construct fully-qualified class name for content handler
    // for mimeType; expects default Sun configuration
    private String mapMIMETypeToClassName(String mimeType) {
        int i = content_class_prefix.length();
        int j = mimeType.length();
        char nm[] = new char[i + j];
        content_class_prefix.getChars(0, i, nm, 0);
        mimeType.getChars(0, j, nm, i);
        while (--j >= 0) {
            char c = nm[i];
            // clean up characters in class name
            if (c == '/')
                nm[i] = '.';
            else if (!('A' <= c && c <= 'Z' ||
                       'a' <= c && c <= 'z' ||
                       '0' <= c && c <= '9'))
                nm[i] = '_';
            i++;
        }
        return (new String(nm));
    }
    public ContentHandler createContentHandler(String mimeType) {
        ContentHandler handler = null;
        if (mimeType == null)
            return defaultHandler;          // no type specified

        // Check cache first
        handler = (ContentHandler)handlers.get(mimeType);
        if (handler != null)
            return handler;

        // Get class name from MIME Type and create handler
        String className = mapMIMETypeToClassName(mimeType);
        if (className != null) {
            try {
                handler = (ContentHandler)
                    Class.forName(className).newInstance();
```

```
                } catch(Exception e) {
                    // cannot get handler, just use default
                    handler = defaultHandler;
                }
            } else
                handler = defaultHandler;

            // Add newly found handler to cache
            handlers.put(mimeType, handler);
            return handler;
        }
    }
```

createContentHandler()

PURPOSE Creates a content handler for documents of a MIME type.

SYNTAX `ContentHandler createContentHandler(String mimeType)`

DESCRIPTION This method creates a new content handler for processing documents with MIME type `mimeType`.

PARAMETERS

`mimeType` The MIME type for which to create the content handler.

RETURNS A new content handler for `mimeType`.

SEE ALSO `ContentHandler`, `URL`, `URL.getContent()`, `URLConnection.getContent()`.

EXAMPLE See the class example.

CropImageFilter

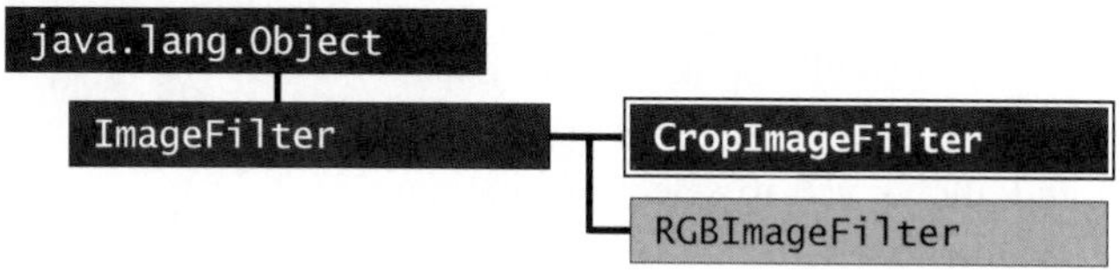

Syntax

```
public class CropImageFilter extends ImageFilter
```

Description

This class extends the basic `ImageFilter` class to extract a given rectangular region of an existing `Image` and to provide a source for a new image containing just the extracted region. It is meant to be used in conjunction with a `FilteredImageSource` object to produce cropped versions of existing images.

Here is how the crop image filter is typically used:

```
Image copySubImage(Image image, Rectangle r) {
    CropImageFilter filter =
        new CropImageFilter(r.x, r.y, r.width, r.height);
    return getToolkit().createImage(
        new FilteredImageSource(image.getSource(), filter));
}
```

MEMBER SUMMARY

Constructor Method

`CropImageFilter()`	Constructs a new `CropImageFilter` instance.

Image Consumer Methods

`setDimensions()`	Called by the image producer to deliver the dimensions of the source image.
`setPixels()`	Called by the image producer to deliver pixels to the image consumer.
`setProperties()`	Called by the image producer to deliver the properties for the source image.

A B C D E F G H I J K L M N O P Q R S T U V W X Y Z

See Also

`FilteredImageSource`, `ImageFilter`, `Toolkit.createImage()`.

Example

FIGURE 75 CropImageFilter

This example implements a small application for copying areas in an image (see Figure 75). The application reads in an image and allows you to select rectangular areas in the image. To make a selection, you click and hold the left mouse button and drag downward and to the right. The pixels in the selected area are painted in XOR mode (see `Graphics.setXORMode()`).

To make a copy of the selected area, press the 'c' key. The copy is created using the `CropImageFilter` image filter. Now you can move the copy around the image just by moving the cursor around. To paint the copy on the image, click the mouse. To delete either the selected area or the copy, press any key.

When moving the copy around the image, you will notice a lot of flickering. You can eliminate the flickering by using the double-buffering techniques demonstrated in the `Component.createImage()` example.

```
import java.awt.*;
import java.awt.image.*;
class Main extends Frame {
    Main(String filename) {
        super("CropImage Example");
        try {
            Image fileImage = getToolkit().getImage(filename);

            // Use a media tracker object to wait until all the pixels
            // have been retrieved.
            MediaTracker tracker = new MediaTracker(this);
            tracker.addImage(fileImage, 0);
            tracker.waitForID(0);

            // Now copy the retrieved image to an offscreen image.
            addNotify();    // otherwise the following code will fail.
            Image image = createImage(fileImage.getWidth(this),
                                      fileImage.getHeight(this));
            Graphics g = image.getGraphics();
            g.drawImage(fileImage, 0, 0, this);
            g.dispose();

            add("Center", new ImageCanvas(image));
        } catch (Exception e) {
            e.printStackTrace();
```

```
        }
        resize(300, 300);
        show();
    }

    static public void main(String[] args) {
        if (args.length == 1) {
            new Main(args[0]);
        } else {
            System.err.println("usage: java Main <image file>");
        }
    }
}

class ImageCanvas extends Canvas {
    Image image;
    Rectangle selected = new Rectangle();
    Image cropImage;
    Rectangle cropImageRect = new Rectangle();

    ImageCanvas(Image image) {
        this.image = image;
    }

    public void update(Graphics g) {
        paint(g);
    }
    public void paint(Graphics g) {
        g.drawImage(image, 0, 0, this);
        if (cropImage != null) {
            g.drawImage(cropImage, cropImageRect.x, cropImageRect.y,
                this);
        } else if (!selected.isEmpty()) {
            g.setXORMode(getBackground());
            g.fillRect(selected.x, selected.y,
                       selected.width, selected.height);
            g.setPaintMode();
        }
    }

    // Convenience method.
    void repaintRect(Rectangle r) {
        repaint(r.x, r.y, r.width, r.height);
    }

    public boolean mouseDown(Event evt, int x, int y) {
        if (cropImage != null) {
            // Add cropImage to main image.
            Graphics g = image.getGraphics();
            g.drawImage(cropImage, cropImageRect.x, cropImageRect.y,
                this);
```

Example

```
                g.dispose();
                cropImage = null;
            }
            repaintRect(selected);
            selected.move(x, y);
            repaintRect(selected);
            return true;
        }
        public boolean mouseDrag(Event evt, int x, int y) {
            repaintRect(selected);
            selected.width = Math.max(0, x - selected.x);
            selected.height = Math.max(0, y - selected.y);
            repaintRect(selected);
            return true;
        }
        public boolean mouseUp(Event evt, int x, int y) {
            mouseDrag(evt, x, y);
            return true;
        }
        public boolean mouseMove(Event evt, int x, int y) {
            if (cropImage != null) {
                // Move the cropped image around.
                repaintRect(cropImageRect);
                cropImageRect.move(x, y);
                repaintRect(cropImageRect);
                return true;
            }
            return false;
        }
        public boolean keyDown(Event evt, int key) {
            if (key == 'c') {
                if (!selected.isEmpty()) {
                    // Create crop image using a CropImageFilter.
                    CropImageFilter imgf = new CropImageFilter(
                        selected.x, selected.y, selected.width,
                            selected.height);
                    ImageProducer ip = image.getSource();
                    ip = new FilteredImageSource(ip, imgf);
                    cropImage = getToolkit().createImage(ip);
                    cropImageRect = new Rectangle(selected.x, selected.y,
                        selected.width, selected.height);
                }
            } else if (cropImage != null) {
                repaintRect(cropImageRect);
                cropImage = null;
            }
            // Delete the selection.
            repaintRect(selected);
            selected.width = selected.height = 0;
            return true;
        }
    }
```

A B C D E F G H I J K L M N O P Q R S T U V W X Y Z

CropImageFilter()

PURPOSE Constructs a new `CropImageFilter` instance.

SYNTAX
```
public CropImageFilter(int x, int y, int width, int height)
```

DESCRIPTION The new crop image filter will extract the pixels in the rectangular region specified by `x`, `y`, `width`, and `height` of the source image. The crop image filter will translate the locations of the extracted pixels to the image consumer such that the top-left pixel will have the coordinate (0, 0).

PARAMETERS

`height`	The height of the rectangle in pixels.
`width`	The width of the rectangle in pixels.
`x`	The *x*-coordinate of the left edge of the rectangle in pixels.
`y`	The *y*-coordinate of the top of the rectangle in pixels.

EXAMPLE See the class example.

setDimensions()

PURPOSE Called by the image producer to deliver the dimensions of the source image.

SYNTAX
```
public void setDimensions(int width, int height)
```

DESCRIPTION The `CropImageFilter` class implements this method as part of the `ImageConsumer` interface. It should not be used.

PARAMETERS

`height`	The height of the image in pixels.
`width`	The width of the image in pixels.

OVERRIDES `ImageFilter.setDimensions()`.

SEE ALSO `ImageConsumer.setDimensions()`.

setPixels()

PURPOSE Called by the image producer to deliver pixels to the image consumer.

SYNTAX
```
public void setPixels(int x, int y, int w, int h, ColorModel
   model, byte[] pixels, int offset, int scansize)
public void setPixels(int x, int y, int w, int h, ColorModel
   model, int[] pixels, int offset, int scansize)
```

DESCRIPTION The `CropImage` class implements this method as part of the `ImageConsumer` interface. It should not be used.

PARAMETERS

`h`	The height of the rectangle in which the pixels are destined.
`model`	The non-`null` color model used to translate the pixel values.
`offset`	The index of the first pixel in the pixel array.
`pixels`	The non-`null` array of pixel values.
`scansize`	The width to use when extracting pixels from `pixels`.
`w`	The width of the rectangle in which the pixels are destined.
`x`	The *x*-coordinate of the rectangle in which the pixels are destined.
`y`	The *y*-coordinate of the rectangle in which the pixels are destined.

OVERRIDES `ImageFilter.setPixels()`.

SEE ALSO `ImageConsumer.setPixels()`.

setProperties()

PURPOSE Called by the image producer to deliver the properties for the source image.

SYNTAX `public void setProperties(Hashtable props)`

DESCRIPTION The `CropImage` class implements this method as part of the `ImageConsumer` interface. It should not be used.

PARAMETERS

`props` A non-`null` hashtable of properties.

OVERRIDES `ImageFilter.setProperties()`.

SEE ALSO `ImageConsumer.setProperties()`.

java.net

DatagramPacket

`java.lang.Object` — `DatagramPacket`

Syntax

```
public final class DatagramPacket
```

Description

All protocols can be classified as *connection-oriented* or *connectionless*. In connection-oriented protocols, a *connection* is established between the communicating parties such that data sent from one party to the other is received in the same order in which the data is sent. Furthermore, the data sent from one party to the other behaves like a *stream*. That is, if any piece of data (or *packet*) is lost in transmission from one party to the other, the sending party will retransmit that packet to ensure that the receiver gets it. The sending and receiving parties keep track of what packets have been sent and received, thus maintaining a logical stream of the data.

In a connectionless protocol, no state is kept about each packet that is sent. The receiver cannot tell whether a packet is missing or whether a packet has been received twice. Each packet, referred to as a *datagram*, is a separate, self-contained unit with no relationship to other packets being sent and received. Data sent between the communicating parties is limited by the size of the packet.

The `DatagramPacket` class represents datagrams in a connectionless protocol. A datagram that is sent contains the address of the destination of the datagram and its contents. A datagram that is received contains the address of the source of the datagram and its contents.

MEMBER SUMMARY	
Constructor	
`DatagramPacket()`	Constructs a `DatagramPacket` instance for sending/receiving datagrams.
Field Access Methods	
`getAddress()`	Retrieves the destination address or source address of this packet.
`getData()`	Retrieves the contents of this packet.
`getLength()`	Retrieves the length of this packet.
`getPort()`	Retrieves the destination port of this packet.

A B C D E F G H I J K L M N O P Q R S T U V W X Y Z

See Also

`DatagramSocket`.

Example

The following is a standalone program that makes a datagram exchange using `DatagramPacket`. By default, it uses port 13 (the `daytime` port) on the local machine. You can supply a port number of any datagram service (either your own or standard ones like `echo` (7)) that sends a request and then expects a reply (in string format).

```
import java.net.*;
import java.io.*;

class Main {
    public static String dgExchange(String msg, InetAddress dst, int
        port) {
        byte[] outbuf = new byte[msg.length()];
        msg.getBytes(0, outbuf.length, outbuf, 0);
        byte[] inbuf = new byte[256];  // default size

        try {
            DatagramPacket request =
                new DatagramPacket(outbuf, outbuf.length, dst, port);
            DatagramPacket reply =
                new DatagramPacket(inbuf, inbuf.length);

            DatagramSocket sock = new DatagramSocket();
            sock.send(request);
            sock.receive(reply);
            System.out.println(
                "Received packet from:" + reply.getAddress() +
                " port: " + reply.getPort() +
                " length: " + reply.getLength());

            sock.close();
            return (new String(reply.getData(), 0));
        } catch (SocketException e) {
            e.printStackTrace();
        } catch (IOException e) {
            e.printStackTrace();
        }
        return (null);
    }

    public static void main(String[] args) {
        try {
            String msg = "\n";
            int port = 13;
            InetAddress dst = InetAddress.getLocalHost();

            if (args.length > 0) {
                port = Integer.parseInt(args[0]);
```

```
                if (args.length >= 2)
                    msg = args[1];
                if (args.length == 3)
                    dst = InetAddress.getByName(args[2]);
            }

            System.out.println(dgExchange(msg, dst, port));

        } catch (UnknownHostException e) {
            e.printStackTrace();
        }
    }
}
```

DatagramPacket()

PURPOSE
Constructs a `DatagramPacket` object for sending/receiving datagrams.

SYNTAX

```
public DatagramPacket(byte[] inBuffer, int max)
public DatagramPacket(byte[] outBuffer, int count, InetAddress
   dst, int port)
```

DESCRIPTION
This class has two constructor forms. The first form constructs a `DatagramPacket` instance for receiving a datagram. You specify an existing buffer `inBuffer` in which to put the incoming packet, and you specify the maximum number of bytes, `max`, you expect to receive into `inBuffer`.

The second form constructs a `DatagramPacket` instance for sending a datagram. You specify the buffer `outBuffer` that contains the bytes to be sent, the number of bytes to send (`count`), and the destination of the packet (`dst` and `port`). Any direct updates to `outBuffer` after this `DatagramPacket` has been created affects the contents of this packet as well.

PARAMETERS

`count`	The number of bytes in `outBuffer` to send.
`dst`	The destination address to which to send the packet.
`inBuffer`	The buffer in which to receive the data.
`max`	The maximum number of bytes to receive into `inBuffer`.
`outBuffer`	The buffer containing the data to send.
`port`	The port to which to send the packet.

SEE ALSO
`DatagramSocket.receive()`, `DatagramSocket.send()`, `InetAddress`.

EXAMPLE
See the class example.

getAddress()

PURPOSE Retrieves the destination or source address of this datagram packet.

SYNTAX `public InetAddress getAddress()`

DESCRIPTION If this is an outgoing packet, `getAddress()` returns the destination address of the packet. If this is an incoming packet, `getAddress()` returns the source address of the packet (i.e., who sent the packet). The address of a datagram packet is its Internet address.

RETURNS The destination or source address of this packet.

SEE ALSO `getPort()`, `InetAddress`.

EXAMPLE See the class example.

getData()

PURPOSE Retrieves the contents of this datagram packet.

SYNTAX `public byte[] getData()`

RETURNS A byte array containing the data to be sent or the data received. Any changes to this byte array also affect the `DatagramPacket` from which it came.

SEE ALSO `getLength()`.

EXAMPLE Seet the class example.

getLength()

PURPOSE Retrieves the packet length.

SYNTAX `public int getLength()`

DESCRIPTION If this is an outgoing packet, `getLength()` returns the number of bytes in this packet. If this is an incoming packet, `getLength()` returns the number of bytes received into this packet.

RETURNS The number of bytes in this packet.

SEE ALSO `getData()`.

EXAMPLE See the class example.

getPort()

PURPOSE Retrieves the destination port of this packet.

SYNTAX `public int getPort()`

RETURNS Each machine has an IP address containing network addressing information that allows packets to be routed to the machine. On a single machine, there can be many logical entities (called *servers*) that perform different functions. For example, there can be a time server, a file server, and a calendar server all on the same machine. A client application is typically interested in communicating with a particular server on a machine. Hence it must identify the server within the machine. A *port number* is a logical address within a machine. Each server uses a port number so that it can be further identified within the machine. Once a packet reaches a machine, the port number is used to route the packet to the appropriate server. `getPort()` returns the port number on the destination machine to which to send this packet.

SEE ALSO `getAddress()`, `DatagramSocket.getLocalPort()`.

EXAMPLE See the class example.

A
B
C
D
E
F
G
H
I
J
K
L
M
N
O
P
Q
R
S
T
U
V
W
X
Y
Z

java.net
DatagramSocket

`java.lang.Object` — **`DatagramSocket`**

Syntax

```
public class DatagramSocket
```

Description

A *socket* is a communications endpoint. A *datagram socket* is an endpoint for sending and receiving *datagram packets* between applications.

In a client/server application that uses datagram sockets to communicate, the server creates a datagram socket for a "well-known" port. Clients learn about these ports either by convention or through a naming service that maps service names to port numbers. The server then waits for clients to send datagrams to this port (on its machine). When it receives a datagram, it processes the datagram and, if appropriate, sends a reply to the client.

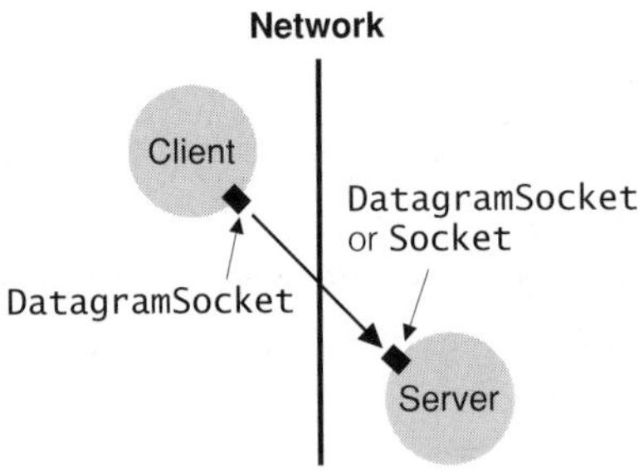

FIGURE 76 `DatagramSocket`

The client interacts with the server by creating a datagram packet with the server's address (machine address plus port number) in it and then filling it with the contents of the request to be sent to the server. It then creates a datagram socket and sends this packet through the socket to the server (see Figure 76). The server can receive the packet using either a `Socket` or a `DatagramSocket`. If the client is expecting a reply, it waits until the server sends a reply.

MEMBER SUMMARY

Constructor	
`DatagramSocket()`	Creates a datagram socket.
Communication Methods	
`close()`	Closes this datagram socket.
`receive()`	Receives a datagram from this socket.
`send()`	Sends a datagram to its destination using this socket.

MEMBER SUMMARY

Field Access Method	
`getLocalPort()`	Retrieves the local port to which this socket is bound.
Object Override Method	
`finalize()`	Closes this datagram socket when this datagram socket is garbage-collected.

See Also

`DatagramPacket`, `InetAddress`, `ServerSocket`, `Socket`.

Example

This example shows the use of `DatagramSocket` by both the server and the client. The server implements `EchoServer`, which creates a `DatagramSocket` and waits for requests. When it receives a request, it sends back to the client a copy of the datagram that it received. The client implements the `echo()` method, which creates a `DatagramSocket` to communicate with the server.

```
class EchoServer extends Thread {
    private DatagramSocket sock = null;
    EchoServer(int port) {
        super();
        try {
            sock = new DatagramSocket(port);
        } catch (SocketException e) {
            e.printStackTrace();
        }
    }

    public void run() {
        if (sock == null)
            return;

        byte[] inbuf = new byte[1024];
        DatagramPacket request = new DatagramPacket(inbuf,
            inbuf.length);
        try {
            while (true) {
                sock.receive(request);
                sock.send(request); // just return what was sent
            }
        } catch (IOException e) {
            e.printStackTrace();
```

```
            }
        }
        protected void finalize() {
            if (sock != null) {
                sock.close();
                sock = null;
            }
        }
    }

    public static void echo(String msg, InetAddress dst, int port) {
        byte[] inbuf = new byte[1024];  // default size
        byte[] outbuf = new byte[msg.length()];
        msg.getBytes(0, outbuf.length, outbuf, 0);

        try {
            DatagramSocket client = new DatagramSocket(); // any port
            DatagramPacket request = new DatagramPacket(outbuf,
                outbuf.length,
                dst, port);
           DatagramPacket reply = new DatagramPacket(inbuf, inbuf.length);
            client.send(request);
            client.receive(reply);
            client.close();
            System.out.println(new String(reply.getData(), 0));
        } catch (SocketException e) {
            e.printStackTrace();
        } catch (IOException e) {
            e.printStackTrace();
        }
    }
```

close()

PURPOSE	Closes this datagram socket.
SYNTAX	`public synchronized void close()`
DESCRIPTION	This method closes this datagram socket. It should be used when the socket is no longer needed. Closing a socket frees the port that it was bound to and frees any resources (like file descriptors) associated with the socket. After the socket has been closed, it can no longer be used.
SEE ALSO	`DatagramSocket()`, `finalize()`.
EXAMPLE	See the class example.

DatagramSocket()

PURPOSE Creates a new datagram socket.

SYNTAX
```
public DatagramSocket() throws SocketException
public DatagramSocket(int port) throws SocketException
```

DESCRIPTION These constructors create a datagram socket and bind it to the specified local port `port`. If `port` is not supplied or if `port` is `0`, the new socket is bound to any locally available port. Use of certain ports is restricted (for example, those well-known ports for Internet protocols like FTP, Telnet, SMTP, etc.) and use of *any* port is permitted only if allowed by the security manager.

PARAMETERS

`port` The port to which to bind this socket.

EXCEPTIONS

`SecurityException`
If cannot use `port` due to security reasons.

`SocketException`
If cannot create a datagram socket using `port`.

SEE ALSO `Security.checkListen()`.

EXAMPLE See the class example.

finalize()

PURPOSE Closes this datagram socket when this datagram socket is garbage-collected.

SYNTAX
```
protected synchronized void finalize()
```

DESCRIPTION The `finalize()` method of an object is called when the object is garbage-collected. Sockets are a limited resource. This method ensures that this socket is closed and freed when it is finalized.

OVERRIDES `Object.finalize()`.

SEE ALSO `close()`, `System.gc()`, `System.runFinalization()`.

getLocalPort()

PURPOSE Retrieves the local port to which this socket is bound.

SYNTAX
```
public int getLocalPort()
```

DESCRIPTION A socket has two endpoints: the sending end and the receiving end. Each end is identified by the Internet address of the machine that it is connected to and the port on the machine being used. `getLocalPort()` returns the port number that is being used by this socket on the local machine to send and receive data.

RETURNS The port number being used for the socket on the local machine.

SEE ALSO `DatagramPacket.getPort()`.

EXAMPLE

```
try {
    DatagramSocket client = new DatagramSocket();
    System.out.println("Using port number " + client.getLocalPort());
    ...
    client.close();
} catch (SocketException e) {
    e.printStackTrace();
}
```

receive()

PURPOSE Receives a datagram from this socket.

SYNTAX `public synchronized void receive(DatagramPacket dgram) throws IOException`

DESCRIPTION This method reads from this socket a datagram `dgram`. It blocks until `dgram` is read. `dgram` must contain a preallocated buffer in which to receive the incoming data. Upon return, `dgram` will contain the incoming data, as well as the address of the sender of the datagram.

Because the socket is a datagram socket, there is no guarantee the same packet `dgram` will arrive just once. There also is no guarantee that successive calls to `receive()` will retrieve the datagrams in the same order in which they were sent or that a datagram will arrive at all.

This method can be executed only if the security manager permits communication with the sender of the datagram.

PARAMETERS

`dgram` The datagram into which to receive. Upon return, `dgram` will contain the data of the packet and the address of the sender. The buffer in `dgram` for holding the data must have been preallocated.

EXCEPTIONS

`IOException` If an I/O error occurred while receiving the datagram.

`SecurityException`
If not allowed to communicate with the sender specified in `dgram` due to security reasons.

SEE ALSO `SecurityManager.checkConnect()`, `send()`.

EXAMPLE See the class example.

send()

PURPOSE Sends a datagram to its destination using this socket.

SYNTAX `public void send(DatagramPacket dgram) throws IOException`

DESCRIPTION Using the destination address found inside the datagram packet `dgram`, `send()` sends the datagram's contents to its destination by using this socket.

Because this is a datagram socket, delivery of `dgram` to its destination is not guaranteed because datagram protocols have unreliable delivery.

This method can be executed only if the security manager permits communication with the destination (host address and port number) specified in `dgram`.

PARAMETERS

`dgram` The datagram being sent through this socket. `dgram` contains the address of the destination as well as the packet contents to send.

EXCEPTIONS

`IOException` If an I/O error occurred during the transmission of the datagram.

`SecurityException`
If not allowed to communicate with the destination specified in `dgram` due to security reasons.

SEE ALSO `receive()`, `SecurityManager.checkConnect()`.

EXAMPLE See the class example.

java.io

DataInput

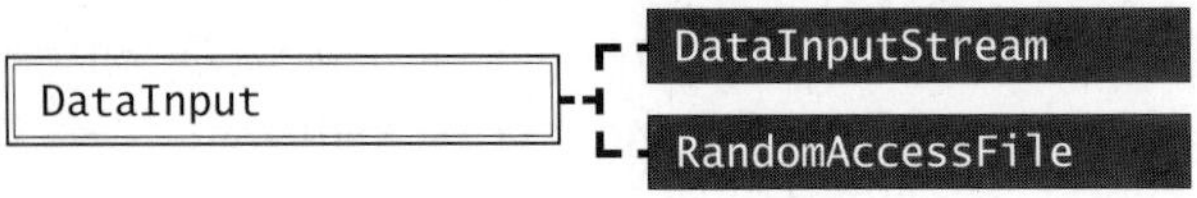

Syntax

```
public interface DataInput
```

Description

`DataInput` is an interface that declares methods for reading in data values and returning them as Java primitive data types. The format of the data values read is determined by the class that implements the `DataInput` interface. The types supported include `byte`, 16-bit Unicode `char`, 16-bit `short`, 32-bit `int`, 32-bit `float`, 64-bit `long`, 64-bit `double`, byte strings, and Unicode strings.

MEMBER SUMMARY

Methods for Reading a Boolean, a Byte, a Character, or a Number	
`readBoolean()`	Reads a `boolean`.
`readByte()`	Reads an 8-bit `byte`.
`readChar()`	Reads a 16-bit `char`.
`readDouble()`	Reads a 64-bit `double`.
`readFloat()`	Reads a 32-bit `float`.
`readInt()`	Reads a 32-bit `int`.
`readLong()`	Reads a 64-bit `long`.
`readShort()`	Reads a 16-bit `short`.
`readUnsignedByte()`	Reads an unsigned 8-bit `byte`.
`readUnsignedShort()`	Reads an unsigned 16-bit `short`.
Methods for Reading or Skipping Bytes	
`readFully()`	Reads the requested number of bytes.
`skipBytes()`	Skips the requested number of bytes.
Methods for Reading a String	
`readLine()`	Reads in a sequence of bytes terminated by a line terminator.
`readUTF()`	Reads a Unicode string.

See Also

`DataInputStream`, `DataOutput`, `EOFException`, `RandomAccessFile`.

Example

See the class examples of `DataInputStream` and `RandomAccessFile`.

readBoolean()

PURPOSE Reads a `boolean`.

SYNTAX `boolean readBoolean() throws IOException`

RETURNS The `boolean` read.

EXCEPTIONS

`EOFException` If end-of-file was reached.

`IOException` If an IO error occurred.

readByte()

PURPOSE Reads an 8-bit byte.

SYNTAX `byte readByte() throws IOException`

RETURNS The `byte` read.

EXCEPTIONS

`EOFException` If end-of-file was reached.

`IOException` If an IO error occurred.

SEE ALSO `readUnsignedByte()`.

readChar()

PURPOSE Reads a 16-bit `char`.

SYNTAX `char readChar() throws IOException`

RETURNS The `char` read.

EXCEPTIONS

`EOFException` If end-of-file was reached.

`IOException` If an IO error occurred.

readDouble()

PURPOSE Reads a 64-bit `double`.

SYNTAX `double readDouble() throws IOException`

RETURNS The 64-bit `double` read.

EXCEPTIONS

`EOFException` If end-of-file was reached.

`IOException` If an IO error occurred.

SEE ALSO `readFloat()`.

readFloat()

PURPOSE Reads a 32-bit float.

SYNTAX `float readFloat() throws IOException`

RETURNS The 32-bit `float` read.

EXCEPTIONS

`EOFException` If end-of-file was reached.

`IOException` If an IO error occurred.

SEE ALSO `readDouble()`.

readFully()

PURPOSE Reads the requested number of bytes.

SYNTAX

```
void readFully(byte[] buffer) throws IOException
void readFully(byte[] buffer, int offset, int count) throws
   IOException
```

A B C D E F G H I J K L M N O P Q R S T U V W X Y Z

DESCRIPTION This method reads bytes to store into the byte array `buffer`, blocking until the requested number of bytes have been read. The first form of the method reads `buffer.length` number of bytes and stores them starting at index 0. The second form of the method reads `count` number of bytes and stores them starting at index `offset`.

PARAMETERS

`buffer`	The buffer into which the data is read.
`count`	The number of bytes to read.
`offset`	The index in `buffer` to start storing the data read.

EXCEPTIONS

`EOFException`	If end-of-file was reached.
`IOException`	If an IO error occurred.

SEE ALSO `skipBytes()`.

readInt()

PURPOSE Reads a 32-bit `int`.

SYNTAX `int readInt() throws IOException`

RETURNS The `int` read.

EXCEPTIONS

`EOFException`	If end-of-file was reached.
`IOException`	If an IO error occurred.

SEE ALSO `readLong()`, `readShort()`, `readUnsignedShort()`.

readLine()

PURPOSE Reads in a sequence of bytes terminated by a line terminator.

SYNTAX `String readLine() throws IOException`

DESCRIPTION A line is a sequence of bytes terminated by a newline character or carriage return character or a combination thereof.

RETURNS A string containing the bytes of the line read (not including the line terminating character).

EXCEPTIONS
`EOFException` If end-of-file was reached.
`IOException` If an IO error occurred.

SEE ALSO `readUTF()`.

readLong()

PURPOSE Reads a 64-bit `long`.

SYNTAX `long readLong() throws IOException`

RETURNS The 64-bit `long` read.

EXCEPTIONS
`EOFException` If end-of-file was reached.
`IOException` If an IO error occurred.

SEE ALSO `readInt()`.

readShort()

PURPOSE Reads a 16-bit `short`.

SYNTAX `short readShort() throws IOException`

RETURNS The `short` value read.

EXCEPTIONS
`EOFException` If end-of-file was reached.
`IOException` If an IO error occurred.

SEE ALSO `readUnsignedShort()`.

readUnsignedByte()

PURPOSE Reads an unsigned 8-bit `byte`.

SYNTAX `int readUnsignedByte() throws IOException`

DESCRIPTION This method reads an 8-bit byte and returns it as an unsigned number. The only difference between this method and `readByte()` is that `readByte()` returns the value read as a `byte`, while this method returns the value as an `int`. The higher-order 3 bytes of an `int` are unused and zeroed when an `int` is used to store an 8-bit byte; consequently, the `int` is always unsigned.

RETURNS An `int` containing the 8 bits read.

EXCEPTIONS

`EOFException` If end-of-file was reached.

`IOException` If an IO error occurred.

SEE ALSO `readByte()`, `readInt()`, `readUnsignedShort()`.

readUnsignedShort()

PURPOSE Reads an unsigned 16-bit `short`.

SYNTAX `int readUnsignedShort() throws IOException`

DESCRIPTION This method reads 16 bits and returns them as an unsigned number. The only difference between this method and `readShort()` is that `readShort()` returns the value read as a `short`, while this method returns the value as an `int`. The higher-order 2 bytes of an `int` are unused and zeroed when an `int` is used to store a 16-bit `short`; consequently, the `int` is always unsigned.

RETURNS An `int` containing the 16 bits read.

EXCEPTIONS

`EOFException` If end-of-file was reached.

`IOException` If an IO error occurred.

SEE ALSO `readInt()`, `readShort()`.

readUTF()

PURPOSE Reads a Unicode string.

SYNTAX `String readUTF() throws IOException`

DESCRIPTION This method reads a UTF-encoded sequence of characters and returns it as a string. UTF stands for Unicode Transfer Format, a character encoding scheme for Unicode characters.

RETURNS A string containing the characters read.

SEE ALSO `readLine()`.

EXCEPTIONS

`EOFException` If end-of-file was reached.

`IOException` If an IO error occurred.

skipBytes()

PURPOSE Skips the requested number of bytes.

SYNTAX `int skipBytes(int count) throws IOException`

DESCRIPTION This method skips `count` number of bytes. It blocks until `count` number of bytes have been skipped.

PARAMETERS

`count` The number of bytes to skip.

RETURNS The actual number of bytes skipped.

EXCEPTIONS

`EOFException` If end-of-file was reached.

`IOException` If an IO error occurred.

java.io

DataInputStream

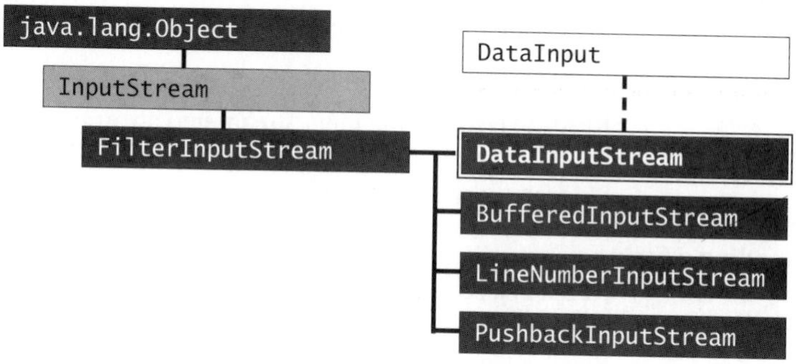

Syntax

```
public class DataInputStream extends FilterInputStream implements DataInput
```

Description

The `DataInputStream` class is a filter input stream that implements the `DataInput` interface. It can be composed with another stream to allow data from that stream to be read and interpreted (through this data input stream) as representations of Java primitive data types. The types supported include `byte`, 16-bit Unicode `char`, 16-bit `short`, 32-bit `int`, 32-bit `float`, 64-bit `long`, 64-bit `double`, byte strings, and Unicode strings.

Typically, you use a `DataInputStream` to read data created by using a `DataOutputStream`.

MEMBER SUMMARY

Constructor	
`DataInputStream()`	Constructs a new data input stream from an existing input stream.
Methods for Reading a Boolean, a Byte, a Character, or a Number	
`readBoolean()`	Reads a `boolean` from the input stream.
`readByte()`	Reads a `byte` from the input stream.
`readChar()`	Reads a 16-bit Unicode `char` from the input stream.
`readDouble()`	Reads a 64-bit `double` from the input stream.
`readFloat()`	Reads a 32-bit `float` from the input stream.
`readInt()`	Reads a 32-bit `int` from the input stream.
`readLong()`	Reads a 64-bit `long` from the input stream.

Continued

MEMBER SUMMARY	
readShort()	Reads 16-bit short from the input stream.
readUnsignedByte()	Reads an unsigned 8-bit byte from the input stream.
readUnsignedShort()	Reads an unsigned 16-bit short from the input stream.
Methods for Reading or Skipping Bytes	
read()	Reads bytes from the input stream into an array of bytes.
readFully()	Reads the requested number of bytes from the input stream.
skipBytes()	Skips the requested number of bytes from the input stream.
Methods for Reading a String	
readLine()	Reads in a sequence of bytes terminated by a line terminator from the input stream.
readUTF()	Reads a Unicode string from the input stream.

See Also

DataInput, DataOutputStream, InputStream, RandomAccessFile.

Example

This example shows the use of the methods in DataInputStream. It reads in a file generated by the class example of DataOutputStream and prints out what was read.

```
import java.io.*;

class Main {
    public static void main(String[] args) {
        if (args.length != 1) {
            System.err.println(
                "Usage: java Main <output from DataOutput example>");
            System.exit(-1);
        }
        FileInputStream file_in;
        DataInputStream data_in;

        try {
            file_in = new FileInputStream(args[0]);
            data_in = new DataInputStream(file_in);

            System.out.println("Available: " + data_in.available());

            byte b;
            byte[] b2 = new byte[1];
            b = data_in.readByte();
            System.out.println("Byte: " + b);
```

A B C D E F G H I J K L M N O P Q R S T U V W X Y Z

```
            data_in.read(b2);
            System.out.println("Byte[0]: " + (char)b2[0]);
            data_in.read(b2, 0, b2.length);
            System.out.println("Byte[0]: " + (char)b2[0]);
            int ub = data_in.readUnsignedByte();
            System.out.println("Unsigned Byte: " + b);
            System.out.println("Boolean: " + data_in.readBoolean());
            char a = data_in.readChar();
            System.out.println("Char: " + a);

            byte[] b3 = new byte[3];
            data_in.readFully(b3);
            System.out.println("readFully: " + (char)b3[0]
                               + (char)b3[1] + (char)b3[2]);
            data_in.skipBytes(6); // skip string 'abc'
            double d1 = data_in.readDouble();
            float f1 = data_in.readFloat();
            int i = data_in.readInt();
            long l = data_in.readLong();
            short s = data_in.readShort();
            String str = data_in.readUTF();
            ub = data_in.readUnsignedByte();
            int us = data_in.readUnsignedShort();
            System.out.println("UTF String" + str);
        } catch (IOException e) {
            System.out.println(e);
        }
    }
}
```

DataInputStream()

PURPOSE: Constructs a new data input stream from an existing stream.

SYNTAX: `public DataInputStream(InputStream in)`

DESCRIPTION: This constructor creates a new data input stream for an existing input stream `in`. The input for this new data input stream comes from the input stream `in`. When a read operation is performed on this data input stream, the stream reads bytes from `in` and returns the answer in the data type requested.

PARAMETERS

`in` The input stream from which the data values will be read.

SEE ALSO: `FilterInputStream`.

EXAMPLE: See the class example.

read()

PURPOSE Reads bytes from the input stream into an array of bytes.

SYNTAX
```
public final int read(byte[] buffer) throws IOException
public final int read(byte[] buffer, int offset, int count) throws
   IOException
```

DESCRIPTION These methods read bytes from the data input stream and copy them into the byte array `buffer`. If `offset` and `count` are specified, `count` bytes are read and placed into `buffer` starting at index `offset`. If they are not specified, `buffer.length` bytes are read and placed into `buffer` starting at index 0. These methods might block if no bytes are available to be read. The requested number of bytes to be read (either `count` or `buffer.length`) might not all be read if there are not that many bytes available. If you want to block waiting for all the number of bytes requested, use `readFully()`.

PARAMETERS

`buffer` The byte array into which the data is read.

`count` The maximum number of bytes to read.

`offset` The index in `buffer` to start putting the bytes read.

RETURNS The actual number of bytes read. `-1` is returned when no bytes are read because the end of the stream has been reached.

EXCEPTIONS

`IOException` If an IO error occurred while attempting to read from this stream.

OVERRIDES `FilterInputStream.read()`.

SEE ALSO `DataOutputStream.write()`, `DataOutputStream.writeByte()`, `readByte()`, `readLine()`, `readFully()`, `readUnsignedByte()`.

EXAMPLE See the class example.

readBoolean()

PURPOSE Reads a `boolean` from the input stream.

SYNTAX
```
public final boolean readBoolean() throws IOException
```

DESCRIPTION This method reads a `boolean` value from the input stream. A `boolean` is represented as a single byte. If the byte is nonzero, the `boolean` value is `true`. If the byte is 0, the `boolean` value is `false`.

RETURNS The `boolean` value read (`true` or `false`).

EXCEPTIONS
`EOFException` If end-of-file was reached while attempting to read from this stream.
`IOException` If an IO error occurred while attempting to read from this stream.

SEE ALSO `DataOutputStream.writeBoolean()`.

EXAMPLE See the class example.

readByte()

PURPOSE Reads a `byte` from the input stream.

SYNTAX `public final byte readByte() throws IOException`

RETURNS The 8-bit `byte` read.

EXCEPTIONS
`EOFException` If end-of-file was reached while attempting to read from this stream.
`IOException` If an IO error occurred while attempting to read from this stream.

SEE ALSO `DataOutputStream.writeByte()`, `DataOutputStream.writeBytes()`, `readUnsignedByte()`.

EXAMPLE See the class example.

readChar()

PURPOSE Reads a 16-bit Unicode `char` from the input stream.

SYNTAX `public final char readChar() throws IOException`

DESCRIPTION A Unicode `char` is represented by a 16-bit unsigned integer. This method reads a `char` by reading two consecutive bytes from the input stream, and interpreting those as a 16-bit unsigned integer (first byte read is the high-order byte) to be used as the value of the `char`.

RETURNS The `char` read.

EXCEPTIONS
`EOFException` If end-of-file was reached while attempting to read from this stream.
`IOException` If an IO error occurred while attempting to read from this stream.

SEE ALSO `DataOutputStream.writeChar()`, `DataOutputStream.writeChars()`.

EXAMPLE See the class example.

A B C D E F G H I J K L M N O P Q R S T U V W X Y Z

readDouble()

PURPOSE Reads a 64-bit `double` from the input stream.

SYNTAX
```
public final double readDouble() throws IOException
```

DESCRIPTION This method reads 8 bytes from the input stream and returns the `double` value represented by the bits of those 8 bytes.

RETURNS The `double` value read.

EXCEPTIONS

`EOFException` If end-of-file was reached while attempting to read from this stream.

`IOException` If an IO error occurred while attempting to read from this stream.

SEE ALSO `DataOutputStream.writeDouble()`, `Double.longBitsToDouble()`.

EXAMPLE See the class example.

readFloat()

PURPOSE Reads a 32-bit `float` from the input stream.

SYNTAX
```
public final float readFloat() throws IOException
```

DESCRIPTION This method reads 4 bytes from the input stream and returns the `float` value represented by the bits of those 4 bytes.

RETURNS The `float` value read.

EXCEPTIONS

`EOFException` If end-of-file was reached while attempting to read from this stream.

`IOException` If an IO error occurred while attempting to read from this stream.

SEE ALSO `DataOutputStream.writeFloat()`, `Float.intBitsToFloat()`.

EXAMPLE See the class example.

readFully()

PURPOSE Reads the requested number of bytes from the input stream.

SYNTAX
```
public final void readFully(byte[] buffer) throws IOException
public final void readFully(byte[] buffer, int offset, int count)
    throws IOException
```

DESCRIPTION These methods read bytes from the data input stream and copy them into the byte array `buffer`. If `offset` and `count` are specified, `count` bytes are read and placed into `buffer` starting at index `offset`. If they are not specified, `buffer.length` bytes are read and placed into `buffer` starting at index 0. These methods will block waiting for all the requested number of bytes to be read (either `count` or `buffer.length`).

PARAMETERS

`buffer`	The byte array into which the data is read.
`count`	The maximum number of bytes to read.
`offset`	The index in `buffer` in which to place the bytes read.

EXCEPTIONS

`EOFException`	If end-of-file was reached while attempting to read from this stream.
`IOException`	If an IO error occurred while attempting to read from this stream.

EXAMPLE See the class example.

readInt()

PURPOSE Reads a 32-bit `int` from the input stream.

SYNTAX `public final int readInt() throws IOException`

DESCRIPTION This method reads 4 bytes from the input stream and returns the `int` value represented by the bits of those 4 bytes. The higher-order bytes are read in order from the input stream.

RETURNS The `int` value read.

EXCEPTIONS

`EOFException`	If end-of-file was reached while attempting to read from this stream.
`IOException`	If an IO error occurred while attempting to read from this stream.

SEE ALSO `DataOutputStream.writeInt()`.

EXAMPLE See the class example.

readLine()

PURPOSE Reads in a sequence of bytes terminated by a line terminator from the input stream.

SYNTAX `public final String readLine() throws IOException`

DESCRIPTION This method reads a line of characters from the input stream and returns it as a string. A line is defined as a sequence of bytes terminated by a newline (`\n`), return(`\r`), newline-return(`\r\n`), or end-of-file. The high-order byte of each character in the string is set to 0. The string does not include the line terminator character.

RETURNS A string copy of a line from the input stream; `null` if no byte is read before end-of-file is reached.

EXCEPTIONS
`IOException` If an IO error occurred while attempting to read from this stream.

SEE ALSO `DataOutputStream.writeBytes()`.

EXAMPLE See the class example.

readLong()

PURPOSE Reads a 64-bit `long` from the input stream.

SYNTAX `public final long readLong() throws IOException`

DESCRIPTION This method reads 8 bytes from the input stream and returns the `long` value represented by the bits of those 8 bytes. The higher-order bytes are read in order from the input stream.

RETURNS The `long` value read.

EXCEPTIONS
`EOFException` If end-of-file was reached while attempting to read from this stream.
`IOException` If an IO error occurred while attempting to read from this stream.

SEE ALSO `DataOutputStream.writeLong()`.

EXAMPLE See the class example.

readShort()

PURPOSE Reads a 16-bit `short` from the input stream.

SYNTAX `public final short readShort() throws IOException`

DESCRIPTION This method reads 2 bytes from the input stream and returns the `short` value represented by the bits of those 2 bytes. The higher-order byte is read first from the input stream.

RETURNS The `short` value read.

EXCEPTIONS

`EOFException` If end-of-file was reached while attempting to read from this stream.
`IOException` If an IO error occurred while attempting to read from this stream.

SEE ALSO `DataOutputStream.writeShort()`, `readUnsignedShort()`.

EXAMPLE See the class example.

readUnsignedByte()

PURPOSE Reads an unsigned 8-bit byte from the input stream.

SYNTAX `public final int readUnsignedByte() throws IOException`

DESCRIPTION This method reads a byte from the input stream and returns it as the lowest byte in an `int`. The only difference between this method and `readByte()` is that this method returns the byte in an `int`, while `readByte()` returns the byte in a `byte`. Because `byte` is a signed type, the highest-order bit will determine the sign of the value. When a byte is returned in an `int`, the higher-order 3 bytes are unused (0). Consequently, the `int` value returned is always unsigned.

RETURNS An `int` containing the byte read.

EXCEPTIONS

`EOFException` If end-of-file was reached while attempting to read from this stream.
`IOException` If an IO error occurred while attempting to read from this stream.

SEE ALSO `DataOutputStream.writeByte()`, `readByte()`.

EXAMPLE See the class example.

readUnsignedShort()

PURPOSE Reads an unsigned 16-bit `short` from the input stream.

SYNTAX `public final int readUnsignedShort() throws IOException`

DESCRIPTION This method reads 2 bytes from the input stream and returns the unsigned integer value represented by the bits of those 2 bytes. The higher-order byte is read first from the input stream. The only difference between this method and `readShort()` is that this method returns the result as an `int`, while `readShort()` returns the result as a `short`.

Because `short` is a signed type, the highest-order bit will determine the sign of the value. When a `short` is returned in an `int`, it occupies the lower-order 2 bytes of the `int`; the higher-order 2 bytes are unused (0). Consequently, the `int` value returned is always unsigned.

RETURNS An `int` containing the 16-bit short value read.

EXCEPTIONS

`EOFException` If end-of-file was reached while attempting to read from this stream.

`IOException` If an IO error occurred while attempting to read from this stream.

SEE ALSO `DataOutputStream.writeShort()`, `readShort()`.

EXAMPLE See the class example.

readUTF()

PURPOSE Reads a Unicode string from this data input stream.

SYNTAX

```
public final String readUTF() throws IOException
public final static String readUTF(DataInput in) throws
   IOException
```

DESCRIPTION This method reads a Unicode string and returns it as a `String`. The first form of this method reads the string from this data input stream. The second form reads the string from the data input stream `in`.

UTF stands for Unicode Transfer Format. It is an encoding scheme for Unicode characters. The size of the string is specified in the encoded form. When writing a string to a data stream, use `DataOutputStream.writeUTF()` and read it back using `readUTF()`.

PARAMETERS

`in` The stream from which to read the string.

RETURNS The Unicode string read as a `String`.

EXCEPTIONS

`EOFException` If end-of-file was reached while attempting to read the string.

`IOException` If an IO error occurred while attempting to read the string.

`UTFDataFormatException`
If the string being read is a malformed UTF string.

SEE ALSO `DataOutputStream.writeUTF()`.

EXAMPLE See the class example.

skipBytes()

PURPOSE Skips the requested number of bytes from this input stream.

SYNTAX `public final int skipBytes(int count) throws IOException`

DESCRIPTION This method skips `count` number of bytes from the input stream. It blocks until all `count` number of bytes are skipped.

PARAMETERS

`count` The number of bytes to be skipped.

RETURNS The actual number of bytes skipped.

EXCEPTIONS

`EOFException` If end-of-file was reached while attempting to skip the requested number of bytes.

`IOException` If an IO error occurred while attempting to skip the requested number of bytes.

EXAMPLE See the class example.

java.io
DataOutput

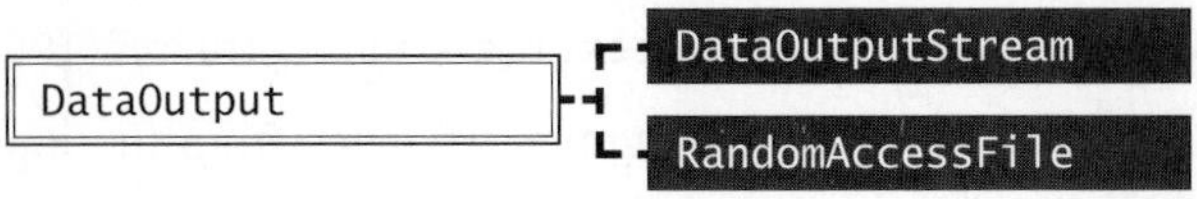

Syntax

```
public interface DataOutput
```

Description

`DataOutput` is an interface that declares methods for writing Java primitive data values. The format of the data values written is determined by the class that implements the `DataOutput` interface. The types supported include `byte`, 16-bit Unicode `char`, 16-bit `short`, 32-bit `int`, 32-bit `float`, 64-bit `long`, 64-bit `double`, byte strings, and Unicode strings.

MEMBER SUMMARY

Methods for Writing a Byte, a Boolean, a Character, or a Number

`writeBoolean()`	Writes a `boolean`.
`writeByte()`	Writes an 8-bit `byte`.
`writeChar()`	Writes a 16-bit `char`.
`writeDouble()`	Writes a 64-bit `double`.
`writeFloat()`	Writes a 32-bit `float`.
`writeInt()`	Writes a 32-bit `int`.
`writeLong()`	Writes a 64-bit `long`.
`writeShort()`	Writes a 16-bit `short`.

Method for Writing Bytes

`write()`	Writes a single byte or an array of bytes.

Methods for Writing a String

`writeBytes()`	Writes a string as a sequence of bytes.
`writeChars()`	Writes a string as a sequence of `char`s.
`writeUTF()`	Writes a string in UTF.

See Also

`DataInput`, `DataOutputStream`, `RandomAccessFile`.

Example

See the class examples of `DataOutputStream` and `RandomAccessFile`.

write()

PURPOSE Writes a single byte or an array of bytes.

SYNTAX

```
void write(int oneByte) throws IOException
void write(byte[] buffer) throws IOException
void write(byte[] buffer, int offset, int count) throws
   IOException
```

DESCRIPTION This method writes bytes. The first form writes the lowest 8 bits of `oneByte`. The second form writes all the bytes from the byte array `buffer`. The third form writes `count` number of bytes starting at the index `offset` from the byte array `buffer`.

PARAMETERS

`buffer`	The bytes to be written.
`count`	The number of bytes to be written.
`offset`	The index in `buffer` from which to get the bytes to be written.
`oneByte`	The byte to be written.

EXCEPTIONS

`IOException`	If an IO error occurred.

SEE ALSO `writeByte()`, `writeBytes()`.

writeBoolean()

PURPOSE Writes a `boolean` value.

SYNTAX

```
void writeBoolean(boolean val) throws IOException
```

DESCRIPTION This method writes the `boolean` value `val`. The output consists of a single byte whose value is `1` if `val` is `true` and `0` if `val` is `false`.

PARAMETERS

`val`	The `boolean` to be written.

EXCEPTIONS

`IOException`	If an IO error occurred while attempting to write.

SEE ALSO `DataInput.readBoolean()`.

writeByte()

PURPOSE Writes an 8-bit byte.

SYNTAX `void writeByte(int val) throws IOException`

DESCRIPTION This method writes an 8-bit byte. The output consists of a single byte whose value is the lowest-order byte of `val`.

PARAMETERS

`val` The byte value to be written.

EXCEPTIONS

`IOException` If an IO error occurred while attempting to write.

SEE ALSO `write()`, `writeBytes()`.

writeBytes()

PURPOSE Writes a string as a sequence of bytes.

SYNTAX `void writeBytes(String str) throws IOException`

DESCRIPTION This method writes the string `str` as a sequence of 8-bit bytes. Because a string consists of 16-bit Unicode `char`s, only the lower-order 8 bits of each `char` are written.

PARAMETERS

`str` The string of bytes to be written.

EXCEPTIONS

`IOException` If an IO error occurred.

SEE ALSO `writeChars()`, `writeUTF()`.

writeChar()

PURPOSE Writes a 16-bit `char`.

SYNTAX `void writeChar(int val) throws IOException`

DESCRIPTION This method writes `val` as a 16-bit `char`. Because an `int` is a 32-bit entity, only the lower-order 16 bits of `val` are written.

PARAMETERS

`val` The `char` value to be written.

EXCEPTIONS

`IOException` If an IO error occurred.

SEE ALSO `writeByte()`, `writeChars()`.

writeChars()

PURPOSE Writes a string as a sequence of `char`s.

SYNTAX `void writeChars(String str) throws IOException`

DESCRIPTION This method writes the string `str` as a sequence of 16-bit `char` values.

PARAMETERS

`str` The string to be written.

EXCEPTIONS

`IOException` If an IO error occurred.

SEE ALSO `writeBytes()`, `writeChar()`, `writeUTF()`.

writeDouble()

PURPOSE Writes a 64-bit `double`.

SYNTAX `void writeDouble(double val) throws IOException`

DESCRIPTION This method writes the `double` value `val`.

PARAMETERS

`val` The `double` value to be written.

EXCEPTIONS

`IOException` If an IO error occurred.

SEE ALSO `writeFloat()`.

writeFloat()

PURPOSE Writes a 32-bit `float`.

SYNTAX `void writeFloat(float val) throws IOException`

DESCRIPTION This method writes the `float` value `val`.

PARAMETERS
`val` The `float` value to be written.

EXCEPTIONS
`IOException` If an IO error occurred.

SEE ALSO `writeDouble()`.

writeInt()

PURPOSE Writes a 32-bit `int`.

SYNTAX `void writeInt(int val) throws IOException`

DESCRIPTION This method writes the `int` value `val`.

PARAMETERS
`val` The `int` value to be written.

EXCEPTIONS
`IOException` If an IO error occurred.

SEE ALSO `writeShort()`, `writeLong()`.

writeLong()

PURPOSE Writes a 64-bit `long`.

SYNTAX `void writeLong(long val) throws IOException`

DESCRIPTION This method writes the `long` value `val`.

PARAMETERS
`val` The `long` value to be written.

EXCEPTIONS
`IOException` If an IO error occurred.

SEE ALSO `writeInt()`, `writeShort()`.

writeShort()

PURPOSE Writes a 16-bit short.

SYNTAX `void writeShort(int val) throws IOException`

DESCRIPTION This method writes the `short` value `val`. Because a `short` is only 16 bits, only the lower-order 2 bytes of `val` are written.

PARAMETERS

`val` The `short` value to be written.

EXCEPTIONS

`IOException` If an IO error occurred.

SEE ALSO `writeInt()`, `writeLong()`.

writeUTF()

PURPOSE Writes a string in UTF.

SYNTAX `void writeUTF(String str) throws IOException`

DESCRIPTION This method writes the string `str` out in UTF. UTF stands for Unicode Transfer Format, an encoding scheme for Unicode characters.

PARAMETERS

`str` The string to be written.

EXCEPTIONS

`IOException` If an IO error occurred.

SEE ALSO `writeChars()`.

java.io
DataOutputStream

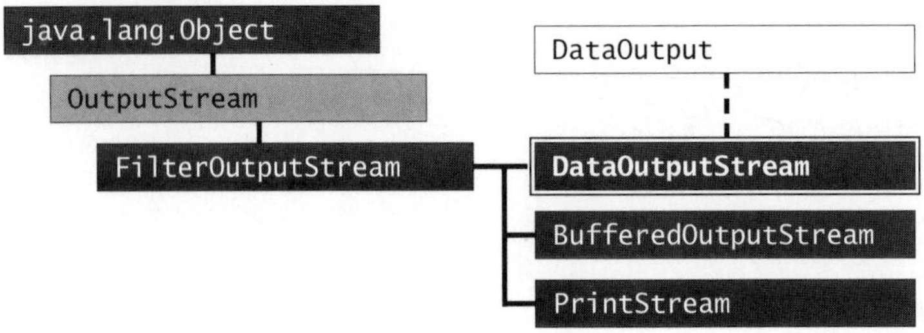

Syntax

```
public class DataOutputStream extends FilterOutputStream implements DataOutput
```

Description

The `DataOutputStream` class is a filter that implements the `DataOutput` interface. It can be composed with another stream so that you can use this data output stream to write typed data to that stream. The types supported include `byte`, 16-bit Unicode `char`, 16-bit `short`, 32-bit `int`, 32-bit `float`, 64-bit `long`, 64-bit `double`, byte strings, and Unicode strings.

Typically, you use `DataOutputStream` to generate the output that will be read subsequently using a `DataInputStream` (see Figure 77).

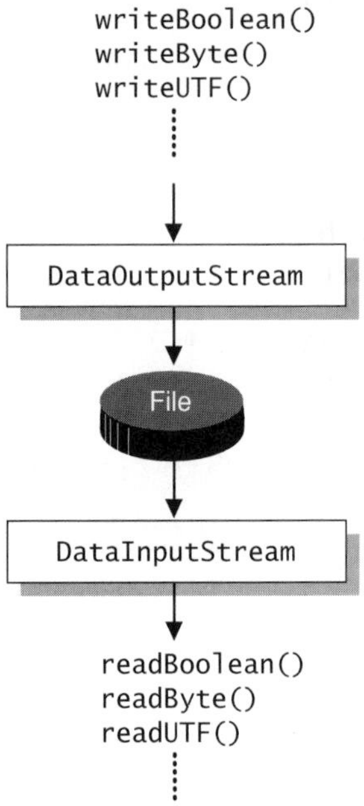

FIGURE 77 `DataOutputStream` and `DataInputStream`

MEMBER SUMMARY	
Constructor	
`DataOutputStream()`	Constructs a new data output stream for an existing output stream.
Methods for Writing a Byte, a Boolean, a Character, or a Number	
`writeBoolean()`	Writes a `boolean` to the output stream.
`writeByte()`	Writes an 8-bit `byte` to the output stream.
`writeChar()`	Writes a 16-bit `char` to the output stream.
`writeDouble()`	Writes a 64-bit `double` to the output stream.
`writeFloat()`	Writes a 32-bit `float` to the output stream.
`writeInt()`	Writes a 32-bit `int` to the output stream.
`writeLong()`	Writes a 64-bit `long` to the output stream.
`writeShort()`	Writes a 16-bit `short` to the output stream.
Method for Writing Bytes	
`write()`	Writes bytes to the output stream.
Methods for Writing a String	
`writeBytes()`	Writes a string as a sequence of bytes to the output stream.
`writeChars()`	Writes a string as a sequence of `char`s to the output stream.
`writeUTF()`	Writes a string in UTF to the output stream.
Size and Flush Methods	
`flush()`	Writes any buffered output to the output stream.
`size()`	Determines the number of bytes written to this stream so far.
Protected Field	
`written`	The number of bytes written to this stream so far.

See Also

`DataInputStream`, `DataOutput`, `OutputStream`.

Example

This example shows the use of the methods in `DataOutputStream`. It generates a file that can be read back in using the class example of `DataInputStream`.

```
import java.io.*;

class Main {
    public static void main(String[] args) {
```

```
            if (args.length != 1) {
                System.err.println(“Usage: java Main <output file>”);
                System.exit(-1);
            }
            FileOutputStream file_out;
            DataOutputStream data_out;

            try {
                file_out = new FileOutputStream(args[0]);
                data_out = new DataOutputStream(file_out);

                char a = ‘a’;
                byte b = 2;
                String c = “abc”;
                short d = 4;
                byte[] b2 = {‘a’, ‘b’, ‘c’};

                data_out.write(b);
                data_out.write(b2, 0, b2.length);
                data_out.writeBoolean(true);
                data_out.writeChar(a);
                data_out.writeBytes(c);
                data_out.writeChars(c);
                data_out.writeDouble(123.456);
                data_out.writeFloat(123.456f);
                data_out.writeInt(678);
                data_out.writeLong(678l);
                data_out.writeShort(d);
                data_out.writeUTF(c);
                data_out.writeUTF(“abc\n”);
                data_out.write(b);
                data_out.writeShort(d);
                data_out.flush();
                System.out.println(“Size of file written: “
                                   + data_out.size());
                data_out.close();
            } catch (IOException e) {
                System.out.println(e);
            }
        }
    }
```

DataOutputStream()

PURPOSE Constructs a data output stream for an existing output stream.

SYNTAX `public DataOutputStream(OutputStream out)`

A B C D E F G H I J K L M N O P Q R S T U V W X Y Z

DESCRIPTION This constructor creates a new data output stream (filter) for the existing output stream `out`. You can use the methods of this newly created data output stream to write typed output to `out`.

PARAMETERS

`out` The output stream to which data will be written.

SEE ALSO `FilterOutputStream`.

EXAMPLE See the class example.

flush()

PURPOSE Writes any buffered output to the output stream.

SYNTAX `public void flush() throws IOException`

DESCRIPTION `DataOutputStream` is simply a filter stream that passes data written onto its output stream. It does no buffering. `flush()` on this data output stream invokes `flush()` on the output stream associated with this data output stream. If the output stream (or any of its filters) does any buffering, any unwritten output will be written out.

EXCEPTIONS

`IOException` If an IO error occurred while attempting to flush the output stream.

OVERRIDES `FilterOutputStream.flush()`.

EXAMPLE See the class example.

size()

PURPOSE Determines the number of bytes written to this stream so far.

SYNTAX `public final int size()`

DESCRIPTION The data output stream keeps track of how many bytes have been written to the output stream so far. This number is updated after each write operation. `size()` returns this number.

RETURNS The number of bytes written to this stream so far.

SEE ALSO `written`.

EXAMPLE See the class example.

write()

PURPOSE Writes bytes to the output stream.

SYNTAX
```
public synchronized void write(int oneByte) throws IOException
public synchronized void write(byte[] buffer, int offset, int
    count) throws IOException
```

DESCRIPTION The `write()` method writes the specified byte or bytes to this data output stream. The first form of `write()` writes a single byte `oneByte` to this stream. The second form writes `count` bytes from the byte array `buffer` starting at index `offset` to this stream.

PARAMETERS

`buffer`	The byte array containing data to be written.
`count`	The number of bytes from `buffer` to be written.
`offset`	The index in `buffer` of the bytes to be written.
`oneByte`	The byte to be written.

EXCEPTIONS

`IOException` If an IO error occurred while attempting to write.

OVERRIDES `FilterOutputStream.write()`.

SEE ALSO `DataInputStream.readByte()`, `DataInputStream.readLine()`, `DataInputStream.readFully()`, `DataInputStream.readUnsignedByte()`, `writeByte()`, `writeBytes()`.

EXAMPLE See the class example.

writeBoolean()

PURPOSE Writes a `boolean` to the output stream.

SYNTAX
```
public final void writeBoolean(boolean val) throws IOException
```

DESCRIPTION This method writes the `boolean` value `val` to the output stream. The output consists of a single byte whose value is `1` if `val` is `true` and `0` if `val` is `false`.

PARAMETERS

`val` The `boolean` value to be written.

EXCEPTIONS

`IOException` If an IO error occurred while attempting to write.

SEE ALSO `DataInputStream.readBoolean()`.

EXAMPLE See the class example.

writeByte()

PURPOSE Writes an 8-bit byte to the output stream.

SYNTAX `public final void writeByte(int val) throws IOException`

DESCRIPTION This method writes the 8-bit byte (in the lowest-order byte of `val`) to the output stream. The output consists of a single byte whose value is the lowest-order byte of `val`.

PARAMETERS

`val` The byte value to be written.

EXCEPTIONS

`IOException` If an IO error occurred while attempting to write.

SEE ALSO `DataInputStream.read()`, `DataInputStream.readByte()`, `DataInputStream.readFully()`, `DataInputStream.readLine()`, `DataInputStream.readUnsignedByte()`, `write()`.

EXAMPLE See the class example.

writeBytes()

PURPOSE Writes a string as a sequence of bytes to the output stream.

SYNTAX `public final void writeBytes(String str) throws IOException`

DESCRIPTION This method writes the string `str` to the output stream as a sequence of bytes (8 bits). Because a string consists of 16-bit Unicode `char` values, only the lower-order 8 bits of each `char` is written; the higher-order 8 bits are lost (and not written). Use `writeChar()` and `writeChars()` to write all 16 bits of a Unicode `char` or `char` string.

PARAMETERS

`str` The string to be written.

EXCEPTIONS

`IOException` If an IO error occurred while attempting to write.

SEE ALSO `DataInputStream.read()`, `DataInputStream.readByte()`, `DataInputStream.readFully()`, `DataInputStream.readLine()`, `DataInputStream.readUnsignedByte()`, `write()`, `writeChar()`, `writeChars()`.

EXAMPLE See the class example.

writeChar()

PURPOSE Writes a 16-bit `char` to the output stream.

SYNTAX `public final void writeChar(int val) throws IOException`

DESCRIPTION This method writes a 16-bit Unicode `char val` to the output stream. Only the lower-order 2 bytes of `val` are written; the higher-order 2 bytes are ignored. The output consists of 2 bytes (higher-order written first), which represent the Unicode value of `val`.

PARAMETERS

`val` The `char` value to be written.

EXCEPTIONS

`IOException` If an IO error occurred while attempting to write.

SEE ALSO `DataInputStream.readChar()`, `writeByte()`, `writeChars()`.

EXAMPLE See the class example.

writeChars()

PURPOSE Writes a string to the output stream as a sequence of `char`s.

SYNTAX `public final void writeChars(String str) throws IOException`

DESCRIPTION This method writes the string `str` to the output stream as a sequence of chars (16 bits). Each `char` written consists of 2 bytes (higher-order written first), which represent its Unicode value.

PARAMETERS

`str` The string to be written.

EXCEPTIONS

`IOException` If an IO error occurred while attempting to write.

SEE ALSO `DataInputStream.readChar()`, `writeChar()`, `writeBytes()`.

EXAMPLE See the class example.

writeDouble()

PURPOSE Writes a 64-bit `double` to the output stream.

SYNTAX `public final void writeDouble(double val) throws IOException`

DESCRIPTION This method writes the `double` value `val` to the output stream. The output generated consists of 8 bytes, which make up the bit representation of `val`.

PARAMETERS

`val` The `double` value to be written.

EXCEPTIONS

`IOException` If an IO error occurred while attempting to write.

SEE ALSO `DataInputStream.readDouble()`, `Double.doubleToLongBits()`.

EXAMPLE See the class example.

writeFloat()

PURPOSE Writes a 32-bit `float` to the output stream.

SYNTAX `public final void writeFloat(float val) throws IOException`

DESCRIPTION This method writes the `float` value `val` to the output stream. The output generated consists of 4 bytes, which make up the bit representation of `val`.

PARAMETERS

`val` The `float` value to be written.

EXCEPTIONS

`IOException` If an IO error occurred while attempting to write.

SEE ALSO `DataInputStream.readFloat()`, `Float.floatToIntBits()`.

EXAMPLE See the class example.

writeInt()

PURPOSE Writes a 32-bit `int` to the output stream.

SYNTAX `public final void writeInt(int val) throws IOException`

DESCRIPTION This method writes the `int` value `val` to the output stream. The output generated consists of 4 bytes, highest-to-lowest byte order, that represent the value of `val`.

PARAMETERS

`val` The `int` value to be written.

EXCEPTIONS

`IOException` If an IO error occurred while attempting to write.

SEE ALSO `DataInputStream.readInt()`.

EXAMPLE See the class example.

writeLong()

PURPOSE Writes a 64-bit `long` to the output stream.

SYNTAX `public final void writeLong(long val) throws IOException`

DESCRIPTION This method writes the `int` value `val` to the output stream. The output generated consists of 8 bytes, highest-to-lowest byte order, that represent the value of `val`.

PARAMETERS

`val` The `long` value to be written.

EXCEPTIONS

`IOException` If an IO error occurred while attempting to write.

SEE ALSO `DataInputStream.readLong()`.

EXAMPLE See the class example.

writeShort()

PURPOSE Writes a 16-bit `short` to the output stream.

SYNTAX `public final void writeShort(int val) throws IOException`

DESCRIPTION This method writes the `short` value `val` to the output stream (the lower-order 2 bytes of `val` are used). The output generated consists of 2 bytes, with the higher-order byte written first.

PARAMETERS

`val` The value to be written. The 2 lower-order bytes of `val` are used as the value of the `short` to be written.

EXCEPTIONS

`IOException` If an IO error occurred while attempting to write.

SEE ALSO `DataInputStream.readShort()`, `DataInputStream.readUnsignedShort()`.

EXAMPLE See the class example.

writeUTF()

PURPOSE Writes a string in UTF to the output stream.

SYNTAX `public final void writeUTF(String str) throws IOException`

DESCRIPTION This method writes a string `str` to the output stream in UTF. UTF stands for Unicode Transfer Format, an encoding scheme for Unicode characters. When writing a string to a data stream, use the `writeUTF()` method and read it back using `DataInputStream.readUTF()`.

PARAMETERS

`str` The string to be written.

EXCEPTIONS

`IOException` If an IO error occurred while attempting to write.

SEE ALSO `DataInputStream.readUTF()`, `writeBytes()`, `writeChars()`.

EXAMPLE See the class example.

written

PURPOSE The number of bytes written so far.

SYNTAX `protected int written`

DESCRIPTION This field records the number of bytes written to this stream so far. It is updated after each write operation.

SEE ALSO `size()`.

EXAMPLE See the class example.

A B C D E F G H I J K L M N O P Q R S T U V W X Y Z

java.util
Date

`java.lang.Object` — `Date`

Syntax

```
public class Date
```

Description

The `Date` class is used to represent a date (a time of day). `Date` provides methods to create, modify, and display date values.

UTC and GMT

Coordinated Universal Time (UTC) is a standard for keeping time using atomic clocks. GMT, (Greenwich Mean Time) is another standard for keeping time. Each uses slightly different algorithms for keeping time. They also have slightly different formats for displaying the time in a string form. Different locales may also have different ways of displaying time. Here are some examples of different string representations of dates:

```
Sat Apr 20 09:32:58 EST 1996
August 1, 1981 15:32:44 PST
18 Feb 1978 00:06:23 GMT 0430
```

Number of Milliseconds Since Epoch

A date can be compactly represented in a single `long` value. The value counts the number of elapsed milliseconds since January 1, 1970 00:00:00 UTC. This is also referred to as the number of milliseconds since *epoch*. The methods `Date()`, `getTime()`, `parse()`, `setTime()`, and `UTC()` use this representation.

Specifying Time

The `Date` class provides many ways of specifying the time that a `Date` object should have. You can get the current time of day or supply a specific time that you want the `Date` object to reflect. For the latter, you can specify the time in terms of units such as year/month/day/hour/minutes/seconds, the number of milliseconds since epoch, or the string representation of the date in commonly used standards (e.g., "`12 Aug 1995 09:00:00 GMT`"). The time zone of the date is assumed to be the local time zone (in which the Java program is running, not from where it was loaded) unless otherwise specified.

The methods that can be used in specifying time include the `Date()` constructor, `parse()`, and `UTF()`.

Modifying Time

After creating a Date object, you can modify the time it represents by setting any or all of a date's component (year, month, day, hour, minutes, seconds). Any of these modifications will cause the date's value to be recalculated; the Date object will then refer to a new date. For example, changing the month of a Date object will result in a different day of the week and in a different number of milliseconds since the epoch value for that Date.

Modifications to Date object update only the Date objects themselves and do not affect the system's clock (date).

MEMBER SUMMARY

Constructor	
`Date()`	Constructs a new `Date` object.
Date Field Access Methods	
`getDate()`	Retrieves the day of the month (`1`–`31`) of this date.
`getDay()`	Retrieves the day of the week (`0`–`6`, with Sunday=`0`) of this date.
`getHours()`	Retrieves the hour of the day (`0`–`23`, with midnight=`0`) of this date.
`getMinutes()`	Retrieves the minute of the hour (`0`–`59`) of this date.
`getMonth()`	Retrieves the month of the year (`0`–`11`, with January=`0`) of this date.
`getSeconds()`	Retrieves the second of the minute (`0`–`59`) of this date.
`getTime()`	Retrieves the value of this date in milliseconds since epoch.
`getTimezoneOffset()`	Retrieves the time zone offset of this date.
`getYear()`	Retrieves the year of this date.
Update Methods	
`setDate()`	Sets the day of the month of this date.
`setHours()`	Sets the hour of the day of this date.
`setMinutes()`	Sets the minute of the hour of this date.
`setMonth()`	Sets the month of the year of this date.
`setSeconds()`	Sets the second of the minute of this date.
`setTime()`	Sets the value of this date using milliseconds since epoch.
`setYear()`	Sets the year of this date.
Comparison Methods	
`after()`	Determines whether this date comes after another date.
`before()`	Determines whether this date comes before another date.
`equals()`	Compares this date with another object for equality.

Continued

MEMBER SUMMARY	
Date Format Methods	
`parse()`	Computes the date value from the string representation of a date.
`toGMTString()`	Generates the string representation of this date using GMT conventions.
`toLocaleString()`	Generates the string representation of this date using local conventions.
`toString()`	Generates the string representation of this date object.
`UTC()`	Calculates a UTC value from year/month/date/hour/minute/second values.
Hash Code Method	
`hashCode()`	Computes the hash code for this date object.

See Also

`System.currentTimeMillis()`.

Example

```
Date today = new Date();
System.out.println(today.getDay()); // print day of the week
```

after()

PURPOSE Determines whether this date comes after another date.

SYNTAX `public boolean after(Date when)`

DESCRIPTION This method determines whether this date comes after the date `when`. If this date comes after `when`, this method returns `true`; otherwise, it returns `false`.

PARAMETERS

`when` The date against which to compare.

RETURNS `true` if this date comes after `when`; `false` otherwise.

SEE ALSO `before()`.

EXAMPLE See `parse()`.

before()

PURPOSE
Checks whether this date comes before another date.

SYNTAX
```
public boolean before(Date when)
```

DESCRIPTION
This method determines whether this date comes before the date `when`. If this date comes before `when`, this method returns `true`; otherwise, it returns `false`.

PARAMETERS

`when` The date to compare against.

RETURNS
`true` if this date comes before `when`; `false` otherwise.

SEE ALSO
`after()`.

EXAMPLE
See `parse()`.

Date()

PURPOSE
Constructs a new instance of `Date`.

SYNTAX
```
public Date()
public Date(long msSinceEpoch)
public Date(int year, int month, int day)
public Date(int year, int month, int day, int hours, int minutes)
public Date(int year, int month, int day, int hours, int minutes,
    int seconds)
public Date (String dateStr)
```

DESCRIPTION
This constructor creates a `Date` object. The first form of the constructor creates a `Date` object for the current time.

The second form creates a `Date` object for the date represented by the number of milliseconds since epoch, `msSinceEpoch`.

The third, fourth, and fifth forms create a `Date` object for the time specified using year/month/day and, optionally, hours/minutes/seconds. If hours/minutes/seconds are not specified, their default values are `0`.

The last form creates a `Date` object for the time as specified using a string `dateStr`. `dateStr` must be a string that can be parsed by `parse()`.

PARAMETERS

`day` The day of the month. `day` must be in the range `1`–`31` inclusive.

`dateStr` The string representation of the date.

`hours` The hour of the day. `hours` must be in the range `0`–`23` inclusive.

A B C D E F G H I J K L M N O P Q R S T U V W X Y Z

`minutes`	The minute of the hour. `minutes` must be in the range `0`–`59` inclusive.
`month`	The month of the year. `month` must be in the range `0`–`11` inclusive; January=`0`.
`msSinceEpoch`	The date as specified by the number of milliseconds since epoch.
`seconds`	The second within the minute. `seconds` must be in the range `0`–`59` inclusive.
`dateStr`	A string representing the date in a syntax accepted by `parse()`.
`year`	The year. `year` must be a positive number. It is added to 1900 to get the complete year number (e.g., 97 means 1997).

SEE ALSO `parse()`, `System.currentTimeMillis()`.

EXAMPLE

```
Date today = new Date();                       // today
Date ymd = new Date(89, 9, 17);                // Oct 17, 1989
Date ymdhm = new Date(89, 9, 17, 17, 4);       // Oct 17, 1989, 5:04pm
Date ymdhms = new Date(89, 9, 17, 17, 4, 15);  // Oct 17, 1989,
                                                  5:04:15pm
Date s1 = new Date("17 Oct 1989 17:04:15");
Date s2 = new Date("17 Oct 1989");
Date s3 = new Date("Thu, 2 Nov 1995");
Date s4 = new Date("Sat, 12 Aug 1995 13:30:00 GMT+0430");

// self-correcting date; "Mon" will get changed to "Sat"
Date s5 = new Date("Mon, 12 Aug 1995 13:30:00 GMT+0430");

if (s2.hashCode() == ymd.hashCode())
    System.out.println("dates maybe equal");   // expected case
else
    System.out.println("dates not equal");
```

equals()

PURPOSE Compares this date object with another object for equality.

SYNTAX `public boolean equals(Object obj)`

DESCRIPTION This method compares this date with the object `obj` for equality. If `obj` is a `Date` object and if it has the same date value as this date, the objects are equal and this method returns `true`. If the date values are not equal or if `obj` is `null` or not a `Date` object, this method returns `false`.

PARAMETERS

`obj` The object with which to compare. `obj` can be `null`.

RETURNS `true` if the objects are the same; `false` otherwise.

OVERRIDES `Object.equals()`.

EXAMPLE See `parse()`.

getDate()

PURPOSE Retrieves the day of the month of this date.

SYNTAX `public int getDate()`

RETURNS The day of the month of this date. It is a number in the range 1–31 inclusive.

SEE ALSO `setDate()`.

EXAMPLE This example shows how to write a date printing routine that makes use of the various access methods to display the date in a user-friendly format.

```
import java.util.Date;

class Main {
    private final static String[] WeekDays =
        {"Sun", "Mon", "Tue", "Wed", "Thu", "Fri", "Sat"};
    private final static String[] Months =
        {"Jan", "Feb", "Mar", "Apr", "May", "Jun",
         "Jul", "Aug", "Sep", "Oct", "Nov", "Dec"};
    private static String fixWidth(int num) {
        if (num == 0)
            return "00";
        if (num < 10)
            return ("0" + num);
        return (Integer.toString(num, 10));
    }
    // prints out date in the form
    // Tue Oct 17 1995 hh:mm:ss GMT+HHMM
    private static String dateToString(Date d) {
        String buf = WeekDays[d.getDay()] + " " +
            Months[d.getMonth()] + " " +
            d.getDate() + " " +
            (d.getYear() + 1900) + " " +
            d.getHours() + ":" +
            d.getMinutes() + ":" +
            d.getSeconds() + " GMT" +
            ((d.getTimezoneOffset() >= 0) ? "+" : "-") +
            fixWidth((d.getTimezoneOffset()/60)) +
            fixWidth((d.getTimezoneOffset()%60));
        return (buf);
    }
    public static void main(String[] args) {
        Date d = new Date();
        System.out.println("today: " + dateToString(d));
    }
}
```

getDay()

PURPOSE Retrieves the day of the week of this date.

SYNTAX `public int getDay()`

RETURNS The day of the week of this date. It is a number in the range `0`–`6` inclusive, with Sunday=`0`.

EXAMPLE See `getDate()`.

getHours()

PURPOSE Retrieves the hour of the day of this date.

SYNTAX `public int getHours()`

RETURNS The hour of the day of this date. It is a number in the range `0`–`23` inclusive, with midnight=0.

SEE ALSO `setHours()`.

EXAMPLE See `getDate()`.

getMinutes()

PURPOSE Retrieves the minute of the hour of this date.

SYNTAX `public int getMinutes()`

RETURNS The minute of the hour of this date. It is a number in the range `0`–`59` inclusive.

SEE ALSO `setMinutes()`.

EXAMPLE See `getDate()`.

getMonth()

PURPOSE Retrieves the month of the year of this date.

SYNTAX `public int getMonth()`

RETURNS The month of the year of this date. It is a number in the range `0`–`11` inclusive, with January=`0`.

SEE ALSO `setMonth()`.

EXAMPLE See `getDate()`.

getSeconds()

PURPOSE Retrieves the second within the minute of this date.

SYNTAX `public int getSeconds()`

RETURNS The second within the minute of this date. It is a number in the range `0`–`59` inclusive.

SEE ALSO `setSeconds()`.

EXAMPLE See `getDate()`.

getTime()

PURPOSE Retrieves the date value of this date in milliseconds since epoch.

SYNTAX `public long getTime()`

RETURNS The number of milliseconds since epoch of this date.

SEE ALSO `UTC()`.

EXAMPLE

```
import java.util.Date;
import java.io.DataInputStream;
import java.io.IOException;

class Test {
    public static void tests() {
        try {
            Thread.sleep(5);
        } catch (InterruptedException e) {
        }
    }
}
class Main {
    public static void main(String[] args) {
        Date startTime = new Date();
        Test.tests();
```

```
            Date endTime = new Date();
            System.out.println("Tests took: " +
                               (endTime.getTime() - startTime.getTime()) +
                               " ms");
        }
    }
```

getTimezoneOffset()

PURPOSE Retrieves the time zone offset of this date.

SYNTAX `public int getTimezoneOffset()`

DESCRIPTION This method returns the time zone offset in minutes for the current locale for this date. For a particular locale, this value is constant except for locales that use daylight savings. For example, in a locale that supports Daylight Savings Time, a date in February might have a time zone offset of 480 minutes, while a date in October might have a time zone offset of 420 minutes.

RETURNS The time zone offset in number of minutes.

EXAMPLE See `getDate()`.

getYear()

PURPOSE Retrieves the year of this date.

SYNTAX `public int getYear()`

RETURNS The year of this date. It is added to 1900 to get the complete year number (e.g., 97 means 1997).

SEE ALSO `setYear()`.

EXAMPLE See `getDate()`.

hashCode()

PURPOSE Computes the hash code for this date.

SYNTAX `public int hashCode()`

DESCRIPTION The hash code of a `Date` object is computed using its time value (`getTime()`). Two `Date` objects with the same time value have the same hash code. However, two `Date` objects with the same hash code may not necessarily have the same time value.

RETURNS The hash code of this date.

OVERRIDES `Object.hashCode()`.

EXAMPLE See `Date()`.

parse()

PURPOSE Computes the date value from the string representation of a date.

SYNTAX `public static long parse(String str)`

DESCRIPTION This method parses the string `str` and computes its corresponding date value in the number of milliseconds since epoch. The syntaxes supported by `parse()` include these:

- The Internet GMT convention (e.g., "`12 Aug 1995 09:00:00 GMT (class)`")
- The UNIX `ctime` syntax (e.g., "`Sat Aug 12 02:00:00 PDT 1995`")

Month names and weekday names can appear either abbreviated or in their full form (e.g., both "Monday" and "Mon" refer to the same weekday). If the weekday is inconsistent with the rest of the date as specified, it is corrected to reflect the right day of the week on which the date falls.

The year can either be abbreviated or appear in its full form (that is, "`95`" and "`1995`" are equivalent). For constant field width support, the day of the month, hour, minutes, and seconds can have an optional 0 (i.e., "`01`" and "`1`" are equivalent).

Time zones are specified using U.S. time zone abbreviations (e.g., "`pdt`", "`est`"). If no time zone is specified, the local time zone is assumed. Time zone offsets are specified using the syntax "`gmt+hhmm`" (e.g., "`gmt+0430`" means 4 hours and 30 minutes west of GMT).

PARAMETERS

`str` The string to be parsed.

RETURNS The date value of `str` in number of seconds since epoch.

EXCEPTIONS

`IllegalArgumentException`
If `str` does not contain a date representation that can be parsed.

SEE ALSO `getTime()`, `toGMTString()`, `toLocaleString()`, `toString()`.

EXAMPLE

```
long utcTime = Date.UTC(95,10,2,10,30,4);
long parsedTime = Date.parse("11 November 1996");

Date utcDate = new Date(utcTime);
Date parsedDate = new Date("11 Nov 1996");
int tracker;

if (utcDate.before(parsedDate)) {
    tracker = -1;
    utcDate.setTime(parsedTime); // reset
} else if (utcDate.after(parsedDate)) {
    tracker = 1;
    utcDate.setTime(parsedTime); // reset
} else if (utcDate.equals(parsedDate))
    tracker = 0;
// Print the date in the three formats
System.out.println("GMT: " + utcDate.toGMTString());
System.out.println("Locale: " + utcDate.toLocaleString());
System.out.println("ctime: " + utcDate.toString());
```

setDate()

PURPOSE Sets the day of the month of this date.

SYNTAX `public void setDate(int day)`

DESCRIPTION This method sets the day of the month of this date to be `day`. This causes the value of this date to be recalculated.

PARAMETERS

`day` The day of the month to which to set this date. `day` must be a number in the range 1–31 inclusive.

SEE ALSO `getDate()`, `getTime()`.

EXAMPLE This example is a simplified fortune-teller program that loops, querying for a birthdate and returning a fortune for that birthdate. It uses a single `Date` instance and updates its year/month/day fields based on the user's input. The program could also be written instead to use a new `Date` instance for each query using the `Date(hh,mm,ss)` constructor.

```
import java.util.Date;
import java.util.Vector;
import java.io.IOException;
import java.io.DataInputStream;

class Main {
    private final static Vector monthVec = new Vector(12);
    static {
        String[] months = {
            "Jan", "Feb", "Mar", "Apr", "May", "Jun",
            "Jul", "Aug", "Sep", "Oct", "Nov", "Dec"};
        for (int i = 0; i < months.length; i++)
            monthVec.addElement(months[i]);
    }
    public static int readFromUser(String query, Vector map) {
        System.out.print("Enter " + query + ": ");
        System.out.flush();
        try {
            DataInputStream in = new DataInputStream(System.in);
            String numStr = in.readLine();
            return (map.indexOf(numStr));
        } catch (IOException e) {
        }
        return (0);
    }
    public static int readFromUser(String query) {
        System.out.print("Enter " + query + ": ");
        System.out.flush();
        try {
            DataInputStream in = new DataInputStream(System.in);
            String numStr = in.readLine();
            return (Integer.parseInt(numStr));
        } catch (IOException e) {
            return (0);
        } catch (NumberFormatException e) {
            return (0);
        }
    }
    private final static String[] fortunes = {
        "There is good prospect in store for you",
        "Don't travel aboard",
        "A mysterious stranger is in your future"
    };
    public static String getFortune(Date d) {
        // use birth date to determine fortune
        int days = (int)(d.getTime()/(24*60*60*1000));
        return (fortunes[days%fortunes.length]);
    }
    // Gets birth date from user and tells him his fortune
    public static void FortuneTeller(Date bday) {
        int year = readFromUser("Year");
        if (year > 1900)
            year -= 1900;
```

```
            int month = readFromUser("Month", monthVec);
            if (month < 0)
                month = 0;  // ignore
            int day = readFromUser("Day");

            // Set birth date
            bday.setYear(year);
            bday.setMonth(month);
            bday.setDate(day);
            System.out.println("Your fortune is: " + getFortune(bday)
                + ".");
        }
        public static void main(String[] args) {
            Date d = new Date();
            while (true)
                FortuneTeller(d);
        }
    }
```

setHours()

DESCRIPTION Sets the hour of the day of this date.

SYNTAX `public void setHours(int hour)`

DESCRIPTION This method sets the hour of the day of this date to be `hour`. This causes the value of this date to be recalculated.

PARAMETERS

`hour` The hour to which to set this date. `hour` must be in the range `0`–`23` inclusive, with midnight=`0`.

SEE ALSO `getHours()`, `getTime()`.

EXAMPLE This example uses the set hours/minutes/seconds method to update a `Date` instance that represents a clock (on a device such as a clock radio or VCR).

```
    import java.util.Date;

    class Clock {
        private Date clockTime = new Date(96, 0, 1, 0, 0, 0);

        private static String fixWidth(int num) {
            if (num == 0)
                return "00";
            if (num < 10)
                return ("0" + num);
            return (Integer.toString(num, 10));
        }
```

```
    private void updateLCD(boolean blink) {
        // could be replaced by more fancy GUI
        System.out.println(fixWidth(clockTime.getHours()) + ":" +
                           fixWidth(clockTime.getMinutes()) + ":" +
                           fixWidth(clockTime.getSeconds()));
        if (blink)
            updateLCD(false);       // recurse once
    }
    public void set(int hh, int mm, int ss) {
        clockTime.setHours(hh);
        clockTime.setMinutes(mm);
        clockTime.setSeconds(ss);

        updateLCD(false);       // do not blink after setting
    }
    public void display(boolean blink) {
        updateLCD(blink);
    }
}

class Main {
    public static void main(String[] args) {
        if (args.length != 3) {
            System.err.println("Usage: java Main <hh> <mm> <ss>");
            System.exit(-1);
        }
        int hours = Integer.parseInt(args[0]);
        int mins = Integer.parseInt(args[1]);
        int secs = Integer.parseInt(args[2]);

        Clock c = new Clock();
        c.display(true);  // blink

        c.set(hours, mins, secs);

        // ...
    }
}
```

setMinutes()

PURPOSE Sets the minute of the hour of this date.

SYNTAX `public void setMinutes(int minute)`

DESCRIPTION This method sets the minute of the hour of this date to be `minute`. This causes the value of this date to be recalculated.

PARAMETERS

`minute` The minute of the hour to which to set this date. `minute` must be in the range `0`–`59` inclusive.

SEE ALSO `getMinutes()`, `getTime()`.

EXAMPLE See `setHours()`.

setMonth()

PURPOSE Sets the month of the year of this date.

SYNTAX `public void setMonth(int month)`

DESCRIPTION This method sets the month of the year of this date to be `month`. This causes the value of this date to be recalculated.

PARAMETERS

`month` The month of the year to which to set this date. `month` must be in the range `0`–`11` inclusive, with January=0.

SEE ALSO `getMonth()`, `getTime()`.

EXAMPLE See `setDate()`.

setSeconds()

PURPOSE Sets the second of the minute of this date.

SYNTAX `public void setSeconds(int second)`

DESCRIPTION This method sets the second of the minute of this date to be `second`. This causes the value of this date to be recalculated.

PARAMETERS

`second` The second of the minute to which to set this date. `second` must be in the range `0`–`59` inclusive.

SEE ALSO `getSecond()`, `getTime()`.

EXAMPLE See `setHours()`.

setTime()

PURPOSE Sets the value of this date using milliseconds since epoch.

SYNTAX `public void setTime(long msSinceEpoch)`

DESCRIPTION This method sets the time value of this date to be `msSinceEpoch` in milliseconds since epoch. If `msSinceEpoch` is `0`, this corresponds to January 1, 1970 00:00:00 UTC. This method causes the value of this date to be recalculated.

PARAMETERS

`msSinceEpoch` The new time value in milliseconds since the epoch.

SEE ALSO `getTime()`.

EXAMPLE See `parse()`.

setYear()

PURPOSE Sets the year of this date.

SYNTAX `public void setYear(int year)`

DESCRIPTION This method sets the year of this date to be `year`. This causes the value of this date to be recalculated.

PARAMETERS

`year` The year to which to set this date. `year` must be a positive number. It is added to 1900 to get the complete year number (e.g., 95 means 1995).

SEE ALSO `getYear()`, `getTime()`.

EXAMPLE See `setDate()`.

toGMTString()

PURPOSE Generates the string representation of this date using GMT conventions.

SYNTAX `public native String toGMTString()`

DESCRIPTION The Internet GMT string representation of a date has the following format:

Day Month Year HH:*MM*:*SS GMT*

where the following holds:

- *Day* is the day of the month (`01`–`31`).
- *Month* is the abbreviated string name of the month (e.g., "`Jan`")
- *Year* is the year (e.g., "`1995`").
- *HH* is the hour (`00`–`23`).

A B C D E F G H I J K L M N O P Q R S T U V W X Y Z

A B C D E F G H I J K L M N O P Q R S T U V W X Y Z

- *MM* is the minutes (`00`–`59`).
- *SS* is the seconds (`00`–`59`).

All fields are constant width.

The following is an example of a GMT string representation of a date:

```
12 Aug 1995 09:00:00 GMT
```

RETURNS The string representation of this date using GMT convention.

SEE ALSO `toLocaleString()`, `toString()`.

EXAMPLE See `parse()`.

toLocaleString()

PURPOSE Generates the string representation of this date using the local convention.

SYNTAX `public native String toLocaleString()`

DESCRIPTION This method returns the string representation of this date using the convention specific to the current locale.

RETURNS The string representation of this date using local conventions.

SEE ALSO `toGMTString()`, `toString()`.

EXAMPLE See `parse()`.

toString()

PURPOSE Generates the string representation of this date using UNIX `ctime` convention.

SYNTAX `public native String toString()`

DESCRIPTION This method returns the string representation of this date using the UNIX `ctime` convention. This format is

Wday Month Mday HH:MM:SS TZone Year

where the following holds:

- *Wday* is the weekday abbreviated string (e.g., "`Wed`").
- *Month* is the abbreviated string of the month (e.g., "`Jan`").
- *Mday* is the day of the month (`01`–`31`).
- *HH* is the hour (`00`–`23`).

- *MM* is the minutes (`00`–`59`).
- *SS* is the seconds (`00`–`59`).
- *TZone* is the time zone (e.g., "`PDT`").
- *Year* is the year (e.g., "`1995`").

All fields have constant width.

The following is an example of a `ctime` string:

```
Sat Aug 12 02:00:00 PDT 1995
```

RETURNS The string representation of this date using UNIX `ctime` convention.

OVERRIDES `Object.toString()`.

SEE ALSO `toGMTString()`, `toLocaleString()`.

EXAMPLE See `parse()`.

UTC()

PURPOSE Calculates a UTC value from year/month/date/hour/minute/second values.

SYNTAX

```
public static long UTC(int year, int month, int day, int hours,
   int minutes, int seconds)
```

DESCRIPTION This method calculates a UTC value using the `year`, `month`, `day`, `hours`, `minute` and `second` parameters. These values are interpreted in the UTC and not the local time zone.

PARAMETERS

`day` The day of the month. `day` must be in the range `1`–`31` inclusive.
`hours` The hour of the day. `hours` must be in the range `0`–`23` inclusive.
`minutes` The minute of the hour. `minutes` must be in the range `0`–`59` inclusive.
`month` The month of the year. `month` must be in the range `0`–`11` inclusive; January=`0` .
`seconds` The second within the minute. `seconds` must be in the range `0`–`59` inclusive.
`year` The year. `year` must be a positive number. It is added to 1900 to get the complete year number (e.g., 95 means 1995).

RETURNS The time in milliseconds since epoch.

SEE ALSO `Date()`, `getTime()`, `parse()`.

EXAMPLE See `parse()`.

java.awt

Dialog

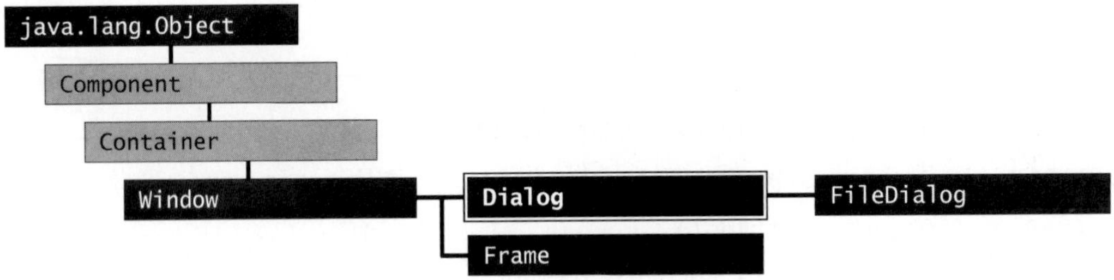

Syntax

```
public class Dialog extends Window
```

Description

A `Dialog` is a top-level window with a title bar and a border. A dialog can be modal. It resembles a frame but has fewer properties. It does not have, for example, an icon image, a cursor, etc.

The Modal Property

When a *modal* dialog is visible, it prevents the user from interacting with any other AWT window. A *modeless* dialog does not have this affect, as it behaves more like a frame. The modal property cannot be changed after the dialog is created.

The Title Property

The title bar is a strip across the top of the dialog that displays a short description of the dialog. The title can be changed at any time.

The Resizable Property

A resizable dialog allows the user to change the size of the dialog. The resizable property can be changed at any time. The precise manner in which the user resizes the dialog is platform-dependent.

Events

The dialog generates the same events as a window does. See the `Window` class for more details.

MEMBER SUMMARY

Constructor	
`Dialog()`	Constructs a new `Dialog` instance.
Property Methods	
`getTitle()`	Retrieves the dialog's title.
`isModal()`	Retrieves the dialog's modal state.
`isResizable()`	Retrieves the dialog's resizable state.
`setResizable()`	Sets the resizable property.
`setTitle()`	Sets the dialog's title.
Peer Method	
`addNotify()`	Creates the dialog's peer hierarchy.
Debugging Method	
`paramString()`	Generates a string representation of the dialog's state.

Example

This example creates a frame with two buttons. One creates a modal dialog; the other creates a modeless dialog. Figure 78 shows the dialog creator as well as the newly created modal and modeless dialogs.

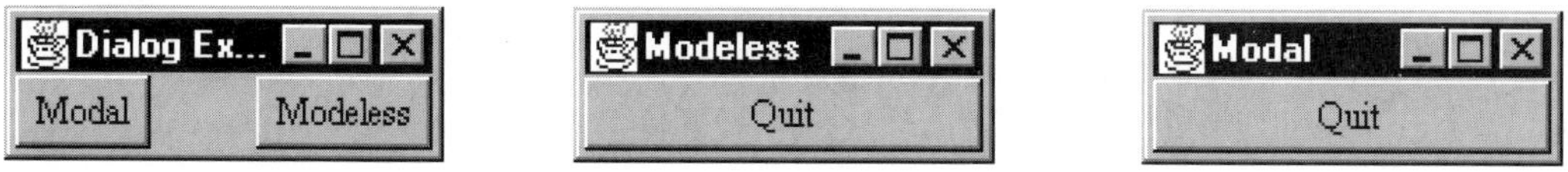

FIGURE 78 `Dialog` Creator, Modeless, and Modal Dialogs

This example also shows how to create the dialog at a particular position on the screen. This is done by calling the `move()` method before calling the `show()` method on the dialog.

```
simport java.awt.*;
class Main extends Frame {
    Main() {
        super("Dialog Example");
        add("West", new Button("Modal"));
        add("East", new Button("Modeless"));
        pack();
        show();
    }
```

A B C D E F G H I J K L M N O P Q R S T U V W X Y Z

B
C
D
E
F
G
H
I
J
K
L
M
N
O
P
Q
R
S
T
U
V
W
X
Y
Z

```
        public boolean action(Event evt, Object what) {
            if ("Modal".equals(what)) {
                new MainDialog(this, true);
                return true;
            } else if ("Modeless".equals(what)) {
                new MainDialog(this, false);
                return true;
            }
            return false;
        }

        static public void main(String[] args) {
            new Main();
        }
    }
    class MainDialog extends Dialog {
        // These two integers hold the location of the last window.
        // New windows are created at an offset to the previous one.
        static int offsetX, offsetY;

        MainDialog(Frame frame, boolean modal) {
            super(frame, modal);
            add("Center", new Button("Quit"));
            offsetX += 20;
            offsetY += 20;
            move(offsetX, offsetY);
            pack();
            show();
        }

        public boolean action(Event evt, Object what) {
            if ("Quit".equals(what)) {
                dispose();
                return true;
            }
            return false;
        }
    }
```

addNotify()

PURPOSE Creates the dialog's peer hierarchy.

SYNTAX `public synchronized void addNotify()`

DESCRIPTION This method creates the dialog's peer hierarchy if necessary. The hierarchy is created by calling the `Toolkit.createDialog()` method. This method should be called before calculating the dialog's minimum or preferred size. The methods `Window.pack()` and `Window.show()` automatically call `addNotify()`.

OVERRIDES `Component.addNotify()`.

SEE ALSO `Component`, `Component.minimumSize()`, `Component.preferredSize()`, `Toolkit`, `Window.pack()`, `Window.show()`.

EXAMPLE See `Component.show()`.

Dialog()

PURPOSE Constructs a new `Dialog` instance.

SYNTAX

```
public Dialog(Frame parent, boolean modal)
public Dialog(Frame parent, String title, boolean modal)
```

DESCRIPTION These constructors create a new invisible `Dialog` instance. If `parent` is not `null`, events not handled by the dialog will flow to the parent. If `title` is `null`, the dialog's title is blank. If `title` is not specified, it defaults to `null`. If `modal` is `true`, the dialog is modal; otherwise the dialog is modeless. The default layout manager for the dialog is `BorderLayout`.

PARAMETERS

`modal` If `true`, dialog is modal; otherwise the dialog is modeless.
`parent` The parent of the dialog. Can be `null`.
`title` The string specifying the dialog's title. Can be `null`.

EXAMPLE See the class example.

getTitle()

PURPOSE Retrieves the dialog's title.

SYNTAX `public String getTitle()`

RETURNS A string containing the dialog's title. The result value may be `null`.

EXAMPLE See `setTitle()`.

isModal()

PURPOSE Retrieves the dialog's modal state.

SYNTAX `public boolean isModal()`

A B C D E F G H I J K L M N O P Q R S T U V W X Y Z

DESCRIPTION When a modal dialog is visible, it prevents the user from interacting with any other AWT window. A modeless dialog does not have this affect, as it behaves more like a frame. The modal property cannot be changed after the dialog is created.

RETURNS `true` if the dialog is modal; `false` if the dialog is modeless.

EXAMPLE See the class example.

isResizable()

PURPOSE Retrieves the dialog's resizable state.

SYNTAX `public boolean isResizable()`

RETURNS `true` if the dialog is currently resizable; `false` otherwise.

EXAMPLE See `setResizable()`.

paramString()

PURPOSE Generates a string representation of the dialog's state.

SYNTAX `protected String paramString()`

DESCRIPTION If you subclass `dialog`, you can override this method to add your additional state to the dialog's state. This method is called by the `toString()` method and is typically used for debugging.

RETURNS A non-`null` string representing the dialog's state.

OVERRIDES `Container.paramString()`.

SEE ALSO `toString()`.

EXAMPLE This example shows how to override the `paramString()` method. The override appends an extra piece of state (`myData`) to the returned string. Figure 79 shows the output of the example.

```
Main[0,0,0x0,invalid,hidden,layout=java.awt.BorderLay-
out,modeless,title=paramString Example,myData=Testing]
```

FIGURE 79 `Dialog.paramString()` Output

```
import java.awt.*;
class Main extends Dialog {
    String myData = "Testing";

    Main() {
        super(null, "paramString Example", false);
    }

    protected String paramString() {
        String str = super.paramString();
        if (myData != null) {
            str += ",myData=" + myData;
        }
        return str;
    }

    static public void main(String[] args) {
        Main m = new Main();
        System.out.println(m);
    }
}
```

setResizable()

PURPOSE Sets the resizable property.

SYNTAX `public void setResizable(boolean resizable)`

DESCRIPTION This method sets this dialog box to be resizable or non-resizable. If `resizable` is `true`, resizing is enabled; otherwise it is disabled.

PARAMETERS

`resizable` If `true`, the dialog becomes resizable; otherwise the dialog becomes non-resizable.

EXAMPLE This example creates a dialog with a checkbox indicating whether the dialog can be resized. Clicking the checkbox changes the resizable property of the dialog. See Figure 80.

FIGURE 80 `Dialog.setResizable()`

```
import java.awt.*;
class Main extends Dialog {
    Checkbox cb;
    Main() {
        super(null, "setResizable Example", false);
        cb = new Checkbox("Resizable", null, isResizable());
```

```
            add("North", cb);
            pack();
            show();
        }

        public boolean action(Event evt, Object what) {
            if (evt.target == cb) {
                setResizable(cb.getState());
                return true;
            }
            return false;
        }

        static public void main(String[] args) {
            new Main();
        }
    }
```

setTitle()

PURPOSE Sets the dialog's title.

SYNTAX `public void setTitle(String title)`

DESCRIPTION This method sets the dialog's title to be the string `title`.

PARAMETERS

`title` The string specifying the dialog's new title. A value of `null` clears the title.

SEE ALSO `getTitle()`.

EXAMPLE This example creates a text field in a dialog. The text field is initialized with the current title of the frame. If you press Return in the text field, the frame's title is set to the text in the text field. See Figure 81.

FIGURE 81 **`Dialog.setTitle()`**

```
    import java.awt.*;
    class Main extends Dialog {
        TextField t;

        Main() {
            super(null, "setTitle Example", false);
            // Initialize the text field with the current title.
            t = new TextField(getTitle(), 50);
            add("North", t);
```

Example

This example implements a binary tree using the `Dictionary` class. There are three classes in this example, as shown in Figure 82. `Tree` is a binary tree implemented using the `Dictionary` class. Each node in the tree is represented by `TreeNode` and the key in each node must be a string. The class `TreeEnumerator` is used when enumerating the nodes in a tree.

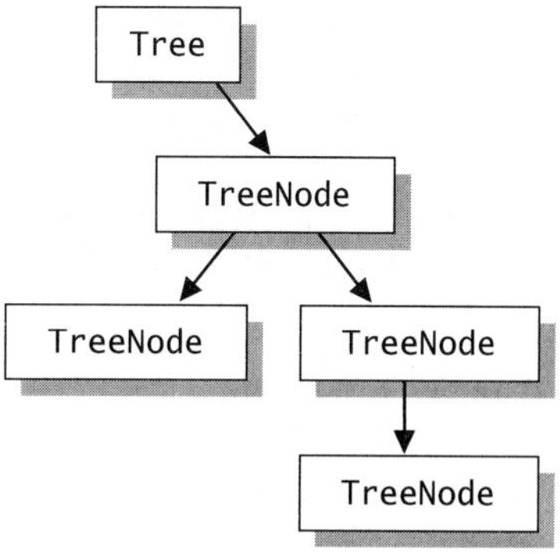

FIGURE 82 `Dictionary`

```
import java.util.*;

class Main {
    static public void main(String[] args) {
        Tree t = new Tree();

        // Add 20 random numbers.
        for (int i=0; i<20; i++) {
            double r = Math.random();
            t.put(““+Math.floor(r * 10), new Double(r));
        }
        // Display the elements in the tree.
        String key;
        for (Enumeration e = t.keys(); e.hasMoreElements(); ) {
            key = e.nextElement();
            System.out.print(key + “: “);
            System.out.println(t.get(key));
        }
    }
}

// This class implements a node in the binary tree.
// The node contains a reference to the key and element.
// The node also contains a reference to left and right branch
// of the tree.
class TreeNode {
    // 0 -> left, 1 -> right
    TreeNode[] branch = new TreeNode[2];
    String key;
    Object value;
    TreeNode(String k, Object v) {
        key = k;
        value = v;
    }
}
```

Example

```
class Tree extends Dictionary {
    TreeNode root;
    int count;

    public int size() {
        return count;
    }

    public boolean isEmpty() {
        return root == null;
    }

    public Enumeration keys() {
        return new TreeEnumerator(this, true);
    }

    public Enumeration elements() {
        return new TreeEnumerator(this, false);
    }


    // Recurse the tree, looking for 'key'.
    public Object get2(TreeNode n, String key) {
        if (n == null) return null;
        int cmp = key.compareTo(n.key);

        if (cmp == 0) return n.value;
        return get2(n.branch[cmp = Math.min(1, Math.max(0, cmp))],
            key);
    }
    public Object get(Object key) {
        return get2(root, (String)key);
    }

    // n is never null.  Smaller elements are added to the left branch.
    public Object put2(TreeNode n, String key, Object value) {
        int cmp = key.compareTo(n.key);
        if (cmp == 0) {
            Object old = n.value;
            n.value = value;
            return old;
        }
        cmp = Math.min(1, Math.max(0, cmp));
        if (n.branch[cmp] != null) {
            return put2(n.branch[cmp], key, value);
        } else {
            n.branch[cmp] = new TreeNode(key, value);
            count++;
            return null;
        }
    }
    public Object put(Object key, Object value) {
```

```
        if (root == null) {
            root = new TreeNode((String)key, value);
            count++;
            return null;
        } else {
            return put2(root, (String)key, value);
        }
    }

    public Object remove(Object key) {
        // not implemented
        return null;
    }
}

// The enumerator create a list of tree nodes, large enough
// to hold all the tree nodes in the tree.  The enumerator
// then recurses the tree and places all tree nodes in the list.
class TreeEnumerator implements Enumeration {
    boolean keys;
    int index;
    TreeNode[] list;

    void traverse(TreeNode n) {
        if (n == null) return;
        traverse(n.branch[0]);
        list[index++] = n;
        traverse(n.branch[1]);
    }
    TreeEnumerator(Tree tree, boolean keys) {
        this.keys = keys;
        list = new TreeNode[tree.count];
        traverse(tree.root);
        index = 0;
    }
    public boolean hasMoreElements() {
        return index < list.length;
    }
    public Object nextElement() {
        if (keys) {
            return list[index++].key;
        } else {
            return list[index++].value;
        }
    }
}
```

elements()

PURPOSE Retrieves an enumeration of all the elements in this dictionary.

SYNTAX `abstract public Enumeration elements()`

DESCRIPTION This method retrieves a list of all the elements in this dictionary. This list can be enumerated using methods in the `Enumeration` class. There is no guaranteed relationship between the order in which elements are added to this dictionary and the order of elements in this list. Neither is there any guaranteed relationship between the order of this list and the order of the list generated using `keys()`. Any such relationships depend on the implementation of the subclass of `Dictionary`. The effects of modifying the dictionary while the dictionary is being enumerated also depends on the subclass.

RETURNS A list of all the elements in this dictionary.

SEE ALSO `keys()`, `size()`, `Enumeration`.

EXAMPLE See the `Dictionary` and `Hashtable` class examples.

get()

PURPOSE Retrieves the element associated with a key in this dictionary.

SYNTAX `abstract public Object get(Object key)`

DESCRIPTION This method retrieves the element associated with the key `key` in this dictionary. It returns `null` if `key` is not in this dictionary.

PARAMETERS

`key` The key for which to search.

RETURNS The element associated with `key` or `null` if `key` is not found in this dictionary.

SEE ALSO `put()`.

EXAMPLE See the class example and `Hashtable.get()`.

isEmpty()

PURPOSE Determines whether this dictionary has any elements.

SYNTAX `abstract public boolean isEmpty()`

RETURNS `true` if there are no elements in this dictionary; `false` if there are elements.

SEE ALSO `size()`.

EXAMPLE See the `Dictionary` and `Hashtable` class examples.

keys()

PURPOSE Retrieves a list of all the keys in this dictionary.

SYNTAX `abstract public Enumeration keys()`

DESCRIPTION This method retrieves a list of all the keys in this dictionary. This list can be enumerated using methods in the `Enumeration` class. There is no guaranteed relationship between the order in which keys are added to this dictionary and the order of keys in this list. Neither is there any guaranteed relationship between the order of this list and the order of the list generated using `elements()`. Any such relationships depend on the implementation of the subclass of `Dictionary`. The effects of modifying the dictionary while the dictionary is being enumerated also depends on the subclass.

RETURNS A list of all the keys in this dictionary.

SEE ALSO `elements()`, `size()`, `Enumeration`.

EXAMPLE See the `Dictionary` and `Hashtable` class examples.

put()

PURPOSE Adds a key/element pair to this dictionary.

SYNTAX `abstract public Object put(Object key, Object elem)`

DESCRIPTION This method adds the pair of key `key` and element `elem` to this dictionary. `put()` returns the element previously associated with `key`, if any; it returns `null` if `key` was not in the dictionary. Any existing entry with the key `key` is removed. After this call to `put()`, `elem` can be retrieved from this dictionary using the call

```
elem = dictionary.get(key);
```

or returned as part of the enumeration returned by `elements()`. `key` can be obtained as part of the enumeration returned by `keys()`.

PARAMETERS

`elem` The non-`null` element to add.

`key` The non-`null` key to add.

RETURNS The element previously associated with `key`; `null` if `key` was not in this dictionary.

SEE ALSO `elements()`, `get()`, `keys()`.

EXAMPLE See the `Dictionary` and `Hashtable` class examples.

A B C D E F G H I J K L M N O P Q R S T U V W X Y Z

remove()

PURPOSE Removes a key/element pair from this dictionary.

SYNTAX `abstract public Object remove(Object key)`

DESCRIPTION This method removes the element with the key `key` from this dictionary and returns the element. If `key` is not in this dictionary, this method returns `null`.

PARAMETERS

`key` The key associated with the element to be removed.

RETURNS The element associated with `key`; `null` if key was not in the dictionary.

SEE ALSO `get()`, `put()`.

EXAMPLE See the class example and `Hashtable.get()`.

size()

PURPOSE Retrieves the number of elements in this dictionary.

SYNTAX `abstract public int size()`

RETURNS The number of elements in this dictionary.

SEE ALSO `elements()`, `keys()`.

EXAMPLE See the `Dictionary` and `Hashtable` class examples.

Dimension

java.lang.Object — **Dimension**

Syntax

```
public class Dimension
```

Description

A dimension is used to represent a size. It holds two values: a width and height. In general, when returning a dimension instance in a method call, you should either have a copy returned, if you need to retain the instance, or have the instance discarded after it is returned. If you have a dimension instance passed in a method call and wish to continue using the instance, note whether the method will retain the instance or copy the values.

MEMBER SUMMARY

Constructor	
`Dimension()`	Constructs a new `Dimension` instance.
Fields	
`height`	This field holds the dimension's height.
`width`	This field holds the dimension's width.
Debugging Method	
`toString()`	Generates a string representation of the dimension's values.

Example

This example implements a circle class, which is an object that has an origin and radius. This circle class implements the `size()` method, which returns the dimension of the circle. The example creates a circle object and paints it in a frame. See Figure 83.

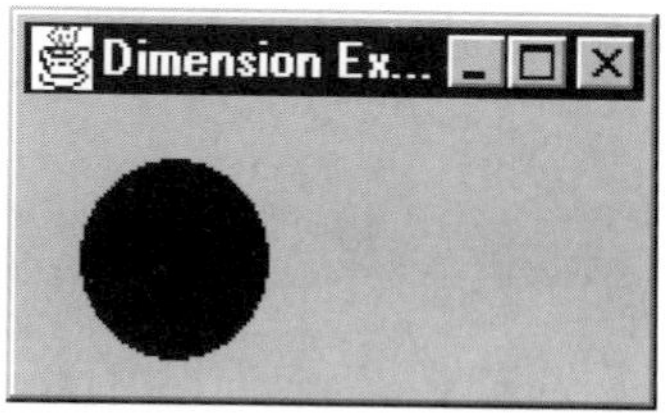

FIGURE 83 `Dimension`

A B C D E F G H I J K L M N O P Q R S T U V W X Y Z

```
import java.awt.*;
class Main extends Frame {
    Circle c = new Circle(new Point(40, 40), 25);

    Main() {
        super("Dimension Example");
        resize(100, 100);
        show();
    }

    public void paint(Graphics g) {
        c.draw(g);
    }

    public static void main(String[] args) {
        new Main();
    }
}

class Circle {
    Point origin;
    int radius;

    Circle(Point origin, int radius) {
        this.origin = origin;
        this.radius = radius;
    }

    public Dimension size() {
        return new Dimension(2 * radius, 2 * radius);
    }

    public void draw(Graphics g) {
        g.fillOval(origin.x-radius, origin.y-radius, size().width,
            size().height);
    }
}
```

Dimension()

PURPOSE Constructs a new `Dimension` instance.

SYNTAX
```
public Dimension()
public Dimension(Dimension dimension)
public Dimension(int width, int height)
```

DESCRIPTION These constructors create a new `Dimension` instance that has the specified initial values. If `dimension` is specified, the initial values for the new dimension are taken from `dimension`. If neither `dimension` nor `width` and `height` are specified, they default to `0`.

PARAMETERS

`dimension`	The non-`null` dimension containing the initial values.
`height`	The dimension's height.
`width`	The dimension's width.

EXAMPLE See the class example.

height

PURPOSE This field holds the dimension's height.

SYNTAX `public int height`

EXAMPLE See the class example.

toString()

PURPOSE Generates a string representation of the dimension.

SYNTAX `public String toString()`

DESCRIPTION This method generates the string representation of this dimension, which consists of its width and height.

This method is typically used for debugging.

RETURNS A non-`null` string representing the dimension's state.

OVERRIDES `Object.toString()`.

EXAMPLE See `Object.toString()`.

width

PURPOSE This field holds the dimension's width.

SYNTAX `public int width`

EXAMPLE See the class example.

java.awt.image
DirectColorModel

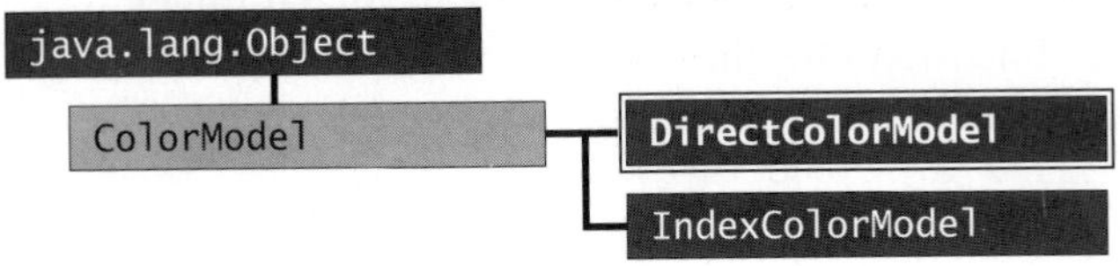

Syntax

```
public class DirectColorModel extends ColorModel
```

Description

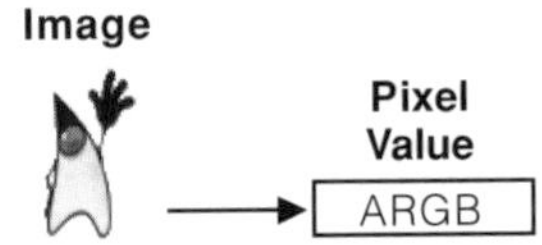

FIGURE 84 Direct Color Model Pixel Values

A pixel value in an image can be encoded in either a *direct color model* or an *indexed color model*. In the direct color model encoding, pixel values actually contain the color information, and the color model is used to extract the color information from the pixel value (see Figure 84). The typical encoding used in a direct color model is to divide the bits in a pixel value among the components of a color. For example, in one encoding you could allow 2 bits for red and green and 10 bits for blue and 4 bits for alpha.

See the `ColorModel` class for more information about color models. See `IndexColorModel` for more information about indexed color models.

MEMBER SUMMARY	
Constructor	
`DirectColorModel()`	Constructs a `DirectColorModel` from the given masks.
Color Component Retrieval Methods	
`getAlpha()`	Retrieves the alpha component of a pixel value.
`getBlue()`	Retrieves the blue component of a pixel value.
`getGreen()`	Retrieves the green component of a pixel value.
`getRed()`	Retrieves the red component of a pixel value.
`getRGB()`	Converts a pixel value to a pixel value in the default color model.
Color Component Mask Retrieval Methods	
`getAlphaMask()`	Retrieves the bit mask for the alpha transparency component.
`getBlueMask()`	Retrieves the bit mask for the blue color component.
`getGreenMask()`	Retrieves the bit mask for the green color component.
`getRedMask()`	Retrieves the bit mask for the red color component.

Example

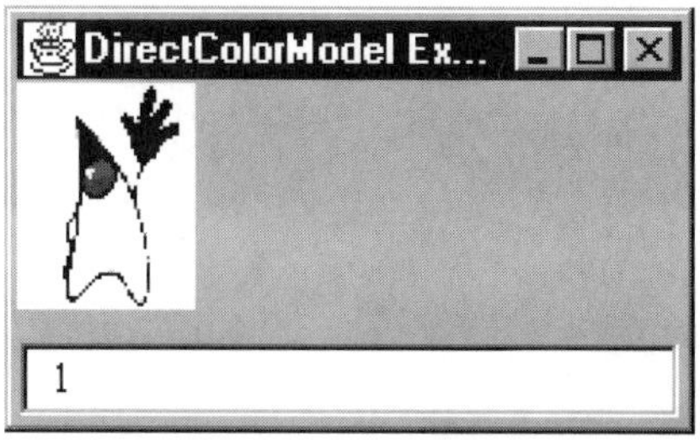

FIGURE 85 `DirectColorModel`

This example creates a low-resolution color filter that reduces the number of bits of a color. See Figure 85. A frame is created that displays an image plus a text field for entering the number of bits per color component. When you change the value in the text field, the image is passed through the filter and then redisplayed. For example, if you enter the value `1` in the text field, each of the four color components—red, green, blue, and alpha—of every pixel value in the image will be reduced to 1 bit.

The filter is derived from `RGBImageFilter`. This makes it convenient for modifying image colors by flowing all pixel values through a single method called `filterRGB()` (see `RGBImageFilter` for details). Whenever the bit size for the color components is changed, a new direct color model is created to represent the new encoding. As pixels flow through the filter, the colors of the pixel values are reduced and the filter's direct color model is substituted for the image producer's color model.

```
import java.awt.*;
import java.awt.image.*;
import java.net.*;
import java.util.*;
class Main extends Frame {
    TextField textField = new TextField();
    ImageCanvas icv;

    Main(String filename) {
        super(“DirectColorModel Example”);
        try {
            // Retrieve the image.
            Image image = getToolkit().getImage(filename);

            add(“Center”, icv = new ImageCanvas(image));
                add(“South”, textField);
        } catch (Exception e) {
            e.printStackTrace();
        }
        resize(50, 100);
        show();
    }

    public boolean action(Event evt, Object arg) {
        if (evt.target == textField) {
            icv.setColorBits(Integer.parseInt(textField.getText()));
            return true;
        }
        return false;
    }
```

```
    static public void main(String[] args) {
        if (args.length == 1) {
            new Main(args[0]);
        } else {
            System.err.println("usage: java Main <image file>");
        }
    }
}

class ImageCanvas extends Canvas {
    Image newImage;
    Image image;
    LowResFilter imgf = new LowResFilter();

    ImageCanvas(Image image) {
        this.image = image;
        processImage();
    }

    void setColorBits(int bits) {
        imgf.setColorBits(bits);
        processImage();
    }

    public void paint(Graphics g) {
        update(g);
    }

    public void update(Graphics g) {
        g.drawImage(newImage, 0, 0, this);
    }

    void processImage() {
        ImageProducer ip = image.getSource();

        ip = new FilteredImageSource(ip, imgf);
        newImage = getToolkit().createImage(ip);
        repaint();
    }
}

class LowResFilter extends RGBImageFilter {
    int bits;    // bits for each color.
    DirectColorModel lowResColorModel =
        (DirectColorModel)ColorModel.getRGBdefault();

    void setColorBits(int bits) {
        int mask = 0;
        this.bits = bits;

        for (int i=0; i<bits; i++) {
            mask |= (mask<<1) + 1;
        }
```

```
        lowResColorModel = new DirectColorModel(bits * 3,
            mask<<(2 * bits), mask<<bits, mask);
        System.out.println(
            Integer.toString(lowResColorModel.getAlphaMask(), 16));
        System.out.println(
            Integer.toString(lowResColorModel.getRedMask(), 16));
        System.out.println(
            Integer.toString(lowResColorModel.getGreenMask(), 16));
        System.out.println(
            Integer.toString(lowResColorModel.getBlueMask(), 16));
    }

    public void setColorModel(ColorModel model) {
        consumer.setColorModel(lowResColorModel);
    }

    public int filterRGB(int x, int y, int rgb) {
        int res = 1 << bits;
        int a = ColorModel.getRGBdefault().getAlpha(rgb);
        int r = ColorModel.getRGBdefault().getRed(rgb);
        int g = ColorModel.getRGBdefault().getGreen(rgb);
        int b = ColorModel.getRGBdefault().getBlue(rgb);

        return ((a * res / 256) << 3*bits)
            | ((r * res / 256) << 2*bits)
            | ((g * res / 256) << bits)
            | ((b * res / 256));
    }

    public void filterRGBPixels(int x, int y, int w, int h,
             int pixels[], int off, int scansize) {
        int index = off;
        for (int cy = 0; cy < h; cy++) {
            for (int cx = 0; cx < w; cx++) {
       pixels[index] =
              filterRGB(x + cx, y + cy, pixels[index]);
              index++;
        }
        index += scansize - w;
   }
        consumer.setPixels(x, y, w, h, lowResColorModel, pixels, off,
        scansize);
    }
    }
```

DirectColorModel()

PURPOSE Constructs a `DirectColorModel` instance.

A B C D E F G H I J K L M N O P Q R S T U V W X Y Z

SYNTAX
```
public DirectColorModel(int bits, int rmask, int gmask, int
    bmask)
public DirectColorModel(int bits, int rmask, int gmask, int bmask,
    int amask)
```

DESCRIPTION These constructors construct a new `DirectColorModel` object based on the specified masks. A mask for a color component specifies which bit positions in the pixel values are occupied by the color component. For example, the value 3 specifies the bit positions 0 and 1 (small endian). The bit positions in a mask must be contiguous and the masks must not overlap. The sum of all the masks must be no more than the number of bits specified by `bits`.

PARAMETERS

`amask`	The mask for the alpha color component.
`bits`	The total number of bits used by the pixel values.
`bmask`	The mask for the blue color component.
`gmask`	The mask for the green color component.
`rmask`	The mask for the red color component.

EXAMPLE See the class example.

getAlpha()

PURPOSE Retrieves the alpha component of a pixel value.

SYNTAX
```
final public int getAlpha(int pixelValue)
```

DESCRIPTION This method retrieves the alpha component of the pixel value `pixelValue`. The return value must be in the range `0`–`255`, where the value `0` means completely transparent and `255` means completely opaque.

PARAMETERS

`pixelValue`	The pixel value specifying a color in the color model.

RETURNS The alpha transparency component in the range `0`–`255`.

EXAMPLE See the class example.

getAlphaMask()

PURPOSE Retrieves the bit mask for the alpha transparency component.

SYNTAX
```
final public int getAlphaMask()
```

DESCRIPTION The return value is identical to the one supplied to the constructor.

RETURNS The mask for the alpha component.

EXAMPLE See the class example.

getBlue()

PURPOSE Retrieves the blue component of a pixel value.

SYNTAX `final public int getBlue(int pixelValue)`

DESCRIPTION This method retrieves the blue component of the pixel value `pixelValue`. The return value must be in the range `0`–`255`, where the value `0` means no blue and `255` means maximum blue.

PARAMETERS

`pixelValue` The pixel value specifying a color in the color model.

RETURNS The blue color component in the range `0`–`255`.

EXAMPLE See the class example.

getBlueMask()

PURPOSE Retrieves the bit mask for the blue color component.

SYNTAX `final public int getBlueMask()`

DESCRIPTION The return value is identical to the one supplied to the constructor.

RETURNS The mask for the blue component.

EXAMPLE See the class example.

getGreen()

PURPOSE Retrieves the green component of a pixel value.

SYNTAX `final public int getGreen(int pixelValue)`

DESCRIPTION This method retrieves the green component of the pixel value `pixelValue`. The return value must be in the range `0`–`255`, where the value `0` means no green and `255` means maximum green.

PARAMETERS

`pixelValue` The pixel value specifying a color in the color model.

RETURNS The green color component in the range `0`–`255`.

EXAMPLE See the class example.

getGreenMask()

PURPOSE Retrieves the bit mask for the green color component.

SYNTAX `final public int getGreenMask()`

DESCRIPTION The return value is identical to the one supplied to the constructor.

RETURNS The mask for the green component.

EXAMPLE See the class example.

getRed()

PURPOSE Retrieves the red component of a pixel value.

SYNTAX `final public int getRed(int pixelValue)`

DESCRIPTION This method retrieves the red component of the pixel value `pixelValue`. The return value must be in the range `0`–`255`, where the value `0` means no red and `255` means maximum red.

PARAMETERS

`pixelValue` The pixel value specifying a color in the color model.

RETURNS The red color component in the range from `0`–`255`.

EXAMPLE See the class example.

getRedMask()

PURPOSE Retrieves the mask that specifies which bits in the pixel value contain the red color component.

SYNTAX `final public int getRedMask()`

DESCRIPTION The return value is identical to the one supplied to the constructor.

RETURNS The mask for the red component.

EXAMPLE See the class example.

getRGB()

PURPOSE Converts a pixel value to a pixel value in the default color model.

SYNTAX `final public int getRGB(int pixelValue)`

DESCRIPTION The pixel value `pixelValue` is converted to an equivalent pixel value that must be interpreted using the default color model. The color of the new pixel value might not be identical to the color of `pixelValue`, so there may be some loss of color information.

PARAMETERS

`pixelValue` The pixel value specifying a color in the direct color model.

RETURNS A pixel value that specifies a color in the default color model.

OVERRIDES `ColorModel.getRGB()`.

SEE ALSO `ColorModel.getRGBdefault()`.

EXAMPLE See the `ColorModel` class example.

java.lang

Double

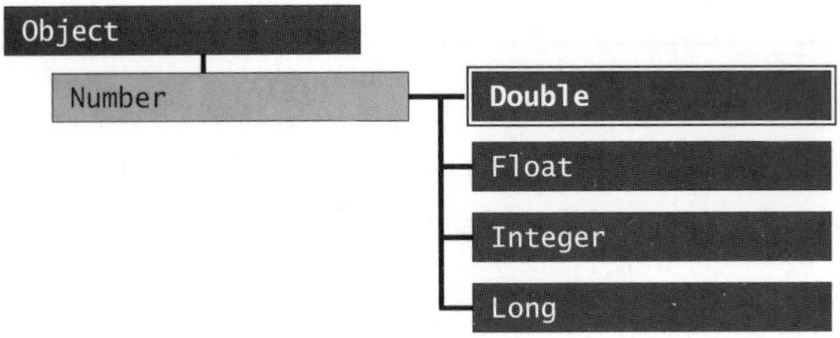

Syntax

```
public final class Double extends Number
```

Description

A `double` in Java is a 64-bit floating-point number. The `Double` class provides an object wrapper for `double` data values. This wrapper allows doubles to be passed to methods in Java class libraries that accept Java objects as parameters. In addition, the `Double` class provides methods that convert to and from doubles and perform other operations on doubles.

A `Double` instance cannot be used in an arithmetic expression in place of `double`. For example, the following are not allowed:

```
Double d1 = new Double(243.34);
Double d2 = new Double(5);
Double d3 = d1 * d2;                                        // Illegal
```

To perform an arithmetic operation using a `Double` instance, you first must use access methods defined in the `Double` class to obtain its numeric value as follows:

```
double d3 = d1.doubleValue() * d2.doubleValue();
long lnum = d1.longValue() + d2.intValue();
```

MEMBER SUMMARY

Constructor	
`Double()`	Constructs a `Double` object using a `double` value or a string.
Constant Fields	
`MAX_VALUE`	The maximum value a `double` can have.
`MIN_VALUE`	The smallest positive value a `double` can have.
`NaN`	The special Not-a-Number value.

MEMBER SUMMARY

`NEGATIVE_INFINITY`	Negative infinity for a `double`.
`POSITIVE_INFINITY`	Positive infinity for a `double`.
Number Methods	
`doubleValue()`	Retrieves the value of this object as a `double`.
`floatValue()`	Retrieves the value of this object as a `float`.
`intValue()`	Retrieves the value of this object as an `int`.
`longValue()`	Retrieves the value of this object as a `long`.
Methods for Converting to/from Other Representations	
`doubleToLongBits()`	Retrieves the bit representation of a `double`.
`longBitsToDouble()`	Retrieves the `double` corresponding to a given bit representation.
`toString()`	Generates the string representation of a `double` or a `Double` object.
`valueOf()`	Creates a new `Double` object using its string representation.
Comparison Methods	
`equals()`	Compares this object with another object for equality.
`isInfinite()`	Determines whether a `double` is infinitely large in magnitude.
`isNaN()`	Determines whether a `double` is the special `NaN` value.
Hash Code Method	
`hashCode()`	Computes the hash code for this object.

See Also

`Float`, `Integer`, `Number`, `Long`.

Double()

PURPOSE Constructs a `Double` object using a `double` value or a string.

SYNTAX
```
public Double(double dVal)
public Double(String strVal) throws NumberFormatException
```

DESCRIPTION The first form of the constructor creates a new instance of `Double` using a `double dVal`. The second form creates a new instance of `Double` using its string representation `strVal`.

PARAMETERS

`dVal` The `double` value that the new object will have.

A B C D E F G H I J K L M N O P Q R S T U V W X Y Z

`strVal` The string representation of the `double` value that the new object will have.

EXCEPTIONS

`NumberFormatException`
If `strVal` contains an invalid string representation of a `double` value.

SEE ALSO `valueOf()`.

EXAMPLE

```
// Create new Double object called 'pi'
Double pi = new Double(3.14159);
try {
    // Create new Double object using a string
    Double dobj = new Double("29.5");
    if (dobj.equals(pi))
        ...
} catch (NumberFormatException e) {
  ...
}
```

doubleToLongBits()

PURPOSE Retrieves the bit representation of a `double` value.

SYNTAX `public static native long doubleToLongBits(double value)`

DESCRIPTION A `double` is a 64-bit floating-point number. This method returns in a `long` (64-bit integer) the bit representation of the `double` value `value`. The bit representation is the IEEE standard format for 64-bit floating-point numbers. This method is the inverse of the method `longBitsToDouble()`.

PARAMETERS

`value` The `double` value for which to get the bit representation.

RETURNS A `long` value containing the bit representation.

SEE ALSO `longBitsToDouble()`.

EXAMPLE

```
double dnum = 22.45915;
long bitrepr = Double.doubleToLongBits(dnum);       // get bit repr
double reconst = Double.longBitsToDouble(bitrepr); // reconstruct dnum

if (reconst == dnum) // should be true
    System.out.println("correct");
```

doubleValue()

PURPOSE Retrieves the value of this object as a `double`.

SYNTAX `public double doubleValue()`

RETURNS The value of this object as a `double`.

EXAMPLE

```
Double dobj = new Double(0.47712);

double dval = dobj.doubleValue(); // get double value
float fval = dobj.floatValue();   // get float value
int ival = dobj.intValue();       // round to 0
long lval = dobj.longValue();     // round to 0
```

equals()

PURPOSE Compares this object with another object for equality.

SYNTAX `public boolean equals(Object obj)`

DESCRIPTION This method compares the `double` value of this `Double` object against that of the object `obj`. It returns `true` if the two values are equal. It returns `false` if the two values are not equal or if `obj` is `null` or is not a `Double` object. This method considers two `NaN` `double` values to be equal in order to be useful in hash tables. This is contrary to the IEEE specification.

PARAMETERS

`obj` The object with which this object will be compared.

RETURNS `true` if `obj` has the same `double` value as this object; `false` otherwise.

OVERRIDES `Object.equals()`.

EXAMPLE

```
Double d1 = new Double(4.8123);
Double d2 = new Double(4.8123);

// Check whether the value of two Doubles are equal
if (d1.equals(d2))
    System.out.println("equal");
```

floatValue()

PURPOSE Retrieves the value of this object as a `float`.

SYNTAX `public float floatValue()`

DESCRIPTION This method returns the value of this object as a `float` by casting its `double` value to a `float` value. This might result in a loss of precision because `double` is a 64-bit floating-point value, while `float` is a 32-bit floating-point value.

RETURNS The value of this object as a `float`.

EXAMPLE See `doubleValue()`.

hashCode()

PURPOSE Computes the hash code for this object.

SYNTAX `public int hashCode()`

DESCRIPTION This method returns the hash code for this `Double` object. The hash code for a `Double` object is calculated using the object's `double` value. Two `Doubles` with the same `double` value have the same hash code. However, two `Doubles` with the same hash code may not necessarily have the same `double` value.

RETURNS An `int` representing the hash code.

OVERRIDES `Object.hashCode()`.

SEE ALSO `Hashtable`.

EXAMPLE

```
// Keep track of hits on hash code
int[] hits = new int[1023];
Double dnum = new Double(1.61803);
int hashval = dnum.hashCode();
++hits[Math.abs(hashval%hits.length)];  // count hits
```

intValue()

PURPOSE Retrieves the value of this object as an `int`.

SYNTAX `public int intValue()`

DESCRIPTION This method returns the value of this object as an `int` by casting its `double` value to an `int`. The `double` value is rounded to a whole number. If the whole number does not fit in a 32-bit `int`, `-1` is returned.

RETURNS The value of this object as an `int`.

EXAMPLE See `doubleValue()`.

isInfinite()

PURPOSE Determines whether a `double` is infinitely large in magnitude.

SYNTAX
```
public boolean isInfinite()
public static boolean isInfinite(double value)
```

DESCRIPTION The first form of this method returns `true` if the `double` value of this `Double` object is infinitely large in magnitude. It returns `false` otherwise. The second form returns `true` if the `double` value `value` is infinitely large in magnitude. It returns `false` otherwise.

PARAMETERS

`value` The `double` value to check for infinity.

RETURNS `true` if the `double` value is infinitely large in magnitude; `false` otherwise.

EXAMPLE

```
Double dnum = new Double(1.6878);
  ...
if (dnum.isInfinite())          // instance version
    throw new ArithmeticException();
if (Double.isInfinite(85.1))    // class version
    break;
```

isNaN()

PURPOSE Determines whether a `double` value is the special Not-a-Number (`NaN`) value.

SYNTAX
```
public boolean isNaN()
public static boolean isNaN(double value)
```

DESCRIPTION The first form of this method returns `true` if the `double` value of this `Double` object is the special `NaN` value. It returns `false` otherwise. The second form returns `true` if the double value `value` is the special `NaN` value. It returns `false` otherwise.

PARAMETERS

`value` The `double` value to check whether it is `NaN`.

RETURNS `true` if the `double` is `NaN`; `false` otherwise.

EXAMPLE

```
Double dnum = new Double(1.523E24);
if (dnum.isNaN())                      // instance version
    throw new ArithmeticException();
if (Double.isNaN(dnum.doubleValue())) // class version
 ...
```

longBitsToDouble()

PURPOSE Retrieves the `double` value corresponding to a given bit representation.

SYNTAX `public static native double longBitsToDouble(long bits)`

DESCRIPTION This method returns the `double` value corresponding to the bit representation `bits`. This method is the inverse of `doubleToLongBits()`.

PARAMETERS

`bits` The bits to use to generate the `double` value.

RETURNS The `double` value represented by `bits`.

SEE ALSO `doubleToLongBits()`.

EXAMPLE See `doubleToLongBits()`.

longValue()

PURPOSE Retrieves the value of this object as a `long`.

SYNTAX `public long longValue()`

DESCRIPTION This method returns the value of this object as a `long` by casting its `double` value to a `long`.

RETURNS The value of this object as a `long`.

EXAMPLE See `doubleValue()`.

MAX_VALUE

PURPOSE The maximum value a `double` can have.

SYNTAX `public static final double MAX_VALUE`

DESCRIPTION This constant represents the maximum value a `double` can have, which is 1.79769313486231570e+308d.

SEE ALSO `MIN_VALUE`.

EXAMPLE

```
// test if number is less than MAX_VALUE
double dnum = 3.1415927;
if (dnum < Double.MAX_VALUE)
    dnum *= 100;
```

MIN_VALUE

PURPOSE The smallest positive value a `double` can have.

SYNTAX `public static final double MIN_VALUE`

DESCRIPTION This constant represents the smallest positive value a `double` can have, which is 2.2250738585072014e-308d.

SEE ALSO `MAX_VALUE`.

EXAMPLE

```
// test if number is greater than MIN_VALUE
double dnum = 2.71828;
if (dnum > Double.MIN_VALUE)
    dnum = 1/dnum;
```

NaN

PURPOSE The special Not-a-Number value.

SYNTAX `public static final double NaN`

DESCRIPTION This constant represents the special Not-a-Number (`NaN`) value. The value of `NaN` is not equal to anything, including `NaN` itself. However, to be useful in hash tables, the `Double.equals()` method considers two `NaN`s equal. This is contrary to the IEEE specification. The equals operator ('=='), however, is consistent with the IEEE, that is, two `NaN`s are not equal when the equals operator is used.

EXAMPLE

```
double dnum = Double.NaN;
// test if number is Not-A-Number
if (Double.isNaN(dnum))                  // succeeds
    System.out.println("correct");
if (Double.isNaN(Double.NaN))            // succeeds
    System.out.println("correct");

// A NaN is not equal to itself except when using equals()
if (dnum == Double.NaN)                  // fails
    System.out.println("incorrect");
Double d1 = new Double(Double.NaN);
Double d2 = new Double(Double.NaN);
if (d1.equals(d2))                       // succeeds
    System.out.println("correct");
```

NEGATIVE_INFINITY

PURPOSE Negative infinity for a `double`.

SYNTAX `public static final double NEGATIVE_INFINITY`

EXAMPLE

```
double dnum;
 ...
// reset to 0 if number reached neg infinity
if (dnum == Double.NEGATIVE_INFINITY)
    dnum = 0;
```

POSITIVE_INFINITY

PURPOSE Positive infinity for a `double`.

SYNTAX `public static final double POSITIVE_INFINITY`

EXAMPLE

```
double dnum;
 ...
// reset to 0 if number reached pos infinity
if (dnum == Double.POSITIVE_INFINITY)
    dnum = 0;
```

toString()

PURPOSE Generates the string representation of a `double` or a `Double` object.

SYNTAX
```
public String toString()
public static native String toString(double dval)
```

DESCRIPTION The two forms of this method return the string representation of a `double`. The first form returns the string representation of this `Double` object (basically the string form of its `double` value). This method is the inverse of `valueOf()`.

The second form returns the string representation of `dval`.

PARAMETERS

`dval` The `double` value for which to return the string representation.

RETURNS The string representation of a `double`.

OVERRIDES `Object.toString()`.

SEE ALSO `valueOf()`.

EXAMPLE

```
Double dnum = new Double(0.843);
String str = dnum.toString();          // get string form of Double obj
String str2 = Double.toString(0.432); // string form of double
String pstr = "The values are " + str + ", " + str2;
```

valueOf()

PURPOSE Creates a new `Double` object using its string representation.

SYNTAX
```
public static native Double valueOf(String str) throws
   NumberFormatException
```

DESCRIPTION This method creates a new `Double` object by parsing `str` into a `double`. This method is the inverse of `toString()`.

PARAMETERS

`str` The string to be parsed.

RETURNS A new `Double` object with the `double` value of the number parsed from `str`.

SEE ALSO `toString()`.

EXCEPTIONS

`NumberFormatException`

If `str` cannot be parsed into a `double` value.

valueOf()

EXAMPLE

```
String str = "1.0871E3";
try {
    Double r = Double.valueOf(str);
     ...
} catch (NumberFormatException e) {
    System.err.println("Could not convert string to number " + str);
}
```

java.util

EmptyStackException

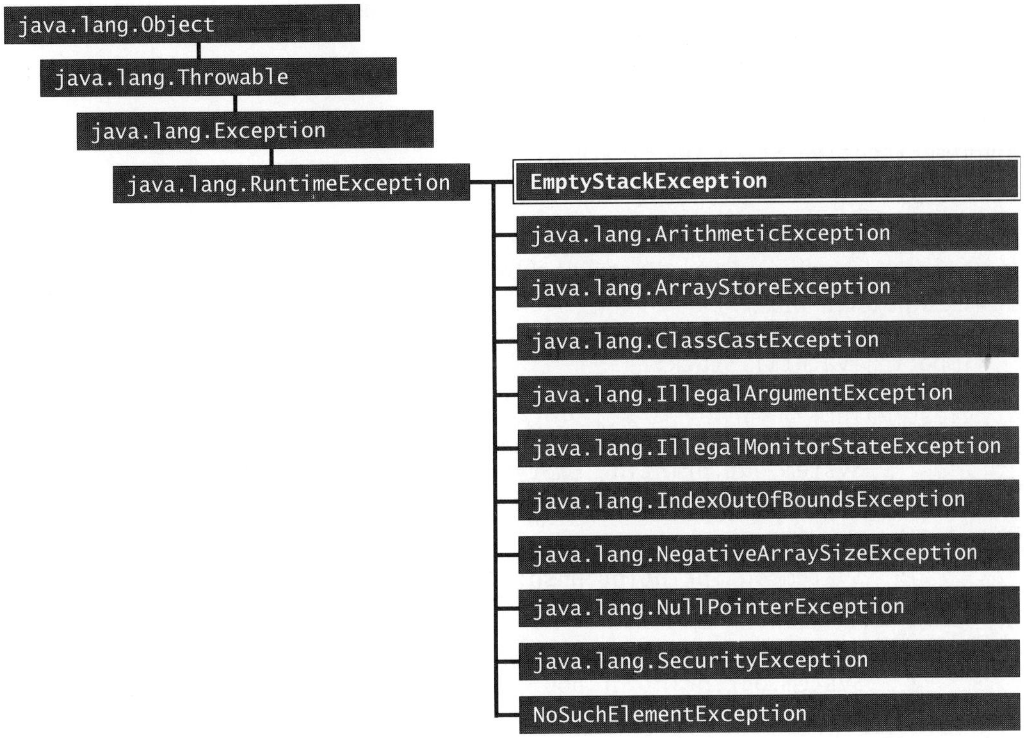

Syntax

```
public class EmptyStackException extends RuntimeException
```

Description

`EmptyStackException` is a runtime exception that is thrown when the program attempts to access an item on a stack when the stack is empty (see the `Stack` class).

`EmptyStackException` should not be caught or declared in the `throws` clause of a method.

A B C D E F G H I J K L M N O P Q R S T U V W X Y Z

MEMBER SUMMARY	
Constructor	
`EmptyStackException()`	Constructs a new `EmptyStackException` instance.

See Also

`RuntimeException`, `Stack.pop()`, `Stack.peek()`.

Example

In this example, `main()` throws `EmptyStackException` when it attempts to pop an item off the stack the fourth time:

```
import java.util.Stack;

class Main {
    public static void main(String[] args) {
        System.out.println("EmptyStackException example");
        Stack s = new Stack();

        System.out.println("push: " + s.push(new Integer(1)));
        System.out.println("push: " + s.push(new Integer(2)));
        System.out.println("push: " + s.push(new Integer(3)));

        System.out.println("pop: " + s.pop());
        System.out.println("pop: " + s.pop());
        System.out.println("pop: " + s.pop());

        System.out.println("pop: " + s.pop()); // empty stack
    }
}
```

EmptyStackException()

PURPOSE Constructs a new `EmptyStackException` instance.

SYNTAX `public EmptyStackException()`

java.util
Enumeration

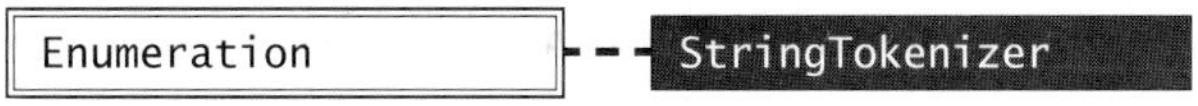

Syntax

```
public interface Enumeration
```

Description

The `Enumeration` interface provides methods for enumerating a list of objects. An individual object on this list to be enumerated is called an *element*. The order in which elements are enumerated depends on the subclass that implements `Enumeration`.

You typically use this interface in a `for` loop. Each step retrieves a single element from the enumeration via `nextElement()`. `hasMoreElements()` serves as the terminating condition for the loop. For example, the following code to print all elements of a vector `vec` typifies how the methods in the `Enumeration` interface are used:

```
for (Enumeration e = vec.elements() ; e.hasMoreElements() ;) {
    System.out.println(e.nextElement());
}
```

Typically, `hasMoreElements()` should be invoked once each time before `nextElement()` is invoked. Some implementations (such as the `Enumeration` implemented by `Hashtable`) have side effects and depend on this behavior. For example, if you call `hasMoreElements()` twice in a row before calling `nextElement()`, you might miss one of the elements. Also, it is up to the class implementing `Enumeration` whether modifications to the object being enumerated (such as a dictionary) invalidates or has any effect on the enumeration in progress.

MEMBER SUMMARY

Enumeration Methods

`hasMoreElements()`	Determines whether there are any more elements in the enumeration.
`nextElement()`	Retrieves the next element in the enumeration.

See Also

`Hashtable`, `Properties`, `SequenceInputStream`, `StringTokenizer`, `Vector`.

A B C D E F G H I J K L M N O P Q R S T U V W X Y Z

Example

In addition to the previous sample usage, see TreeEnumerator in the class example of Dictionary and see the class example of Hashtable for example implementations of Enumeration.

hasMoreElements()

PURPOSE Determines whether there are any more elements in the enumeration.

SYNTAX `boolean hasMoreElements()`

RETURNS `true` if there are more elements in this enumeration; `false` otherwise.

SEE ALSO `nextElement()`.

EXAMPLE See the example in the class description.

nextElement()

PURPOSE Retrieves the next element in the enumeration.

SYNTAX `Object nextElement()`

DESCRIPTION This method returns the next element in this enumeration. You can retrieve all the elements in this enumeration by successively calling `nextElement()` until `hasMoreElements()` returns `false`. If there are no more elements in the enumeration, a `NoSuchElementException` is thrown.

RETURNS The next element in this enumeration.

EXCEPTIONS

`NoSuchElementException`
If there are no more elements in this enumeration.

SEE ALSO `hasMoreElements()`.

EXAMPLE See the example in the class description.

java.io
EOFException

Syntax

```
public class EOFException extends IOException
```

Description

`EOFException` is an IO exception that is thrown when a program reading from a `DataInput` stream reaches the end of the stream (either through the use of `DataInputStream` or `RandomAccessFile`). Other input streams in the Java IO library typically use a value of `-1` to indicate that the end of the stream has been reached. However, because read methods on streams that implement the `DataInput` interface can return negative values, including `-1`, these methods use the `EOFException` to denote that the end of the stream has been reached.

A method that throws `EOFException` must declare it or any of its superclasses in its `throws` clause.

MEMBER SUMMARY	
Constructor	
`EOFException()`	Constructs an `EOFException` instance.

See Also

`DataInput`, `DataInputStream`, `IOException`, `RandomAccessFile`.

Example

This example writes out a string to a random access file and then reads it back and echoes its contents to standard output. When reading from the file, it catches the `EOFException` to terminate the reading.

```
import java.io.RandomAccessFile;
import java.io.EOFException;
import java.io.IOException;

class Main {
    public static void main(String[] args) {
        if (args.length != 1) {
            System.err.println("java Main <outputfile>");
            System.exit(-1);
        }
        try {
            RandomAccessFile raf = new RandomAccessFile(args[0],
                                                        "rw");
            String str = "This is a test";
            raf.writeChars(str);
            raf.close();

            // read the stuff back
            raf = new RandomAccessFile(args[0], "r");
            try {
                while (true)
                    System.out.print(raf.readChar());
            } catch (EOFException e) {
                // end of file reached
                System.out.println();
            }
            raf.close();
        } catch (IOException e) {
            e.printStackTrace();
        }
    }
}
```

EOFException( )

PURPOSE Constructs an `EOFException` instance.

SYNTAX

```
public EOFException()
public EOFException(String msg)
```

DESCRIPTION These constructors create a new instance of `EOFException`. An optional string `msg` can be supplied that describes this particular instance of the exception.

PARAMETERS

`msg` A string that gives details about this exception.

java.lang
Error

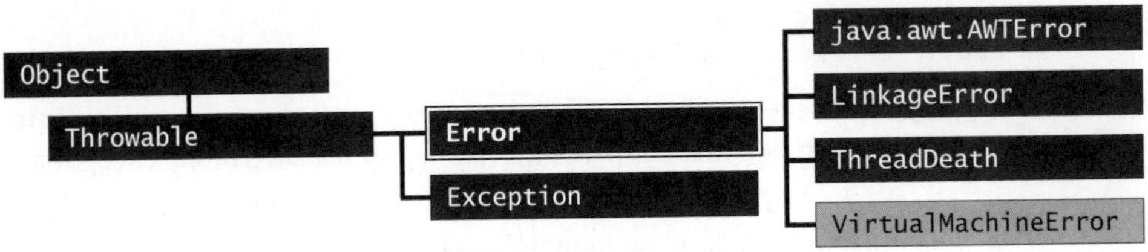

Syntax

```
public class Error extends Throwable
```

Description

The `Error` class is the superclass of classes used to represent erroneous, abnormal events. Errors are thrown only by the Java virtual machine. `Error` and its subclasses should not be thrown or subclassed by user programs. Nor should they be caught by user programs. Furthermore, `Error` and its subclasses need not be specified in the `throws` clause of a method, even if that method throws the `Error`.

MEMBER SUMMARY	
Constructor	
`Error()`	Constructs an `Error` object.

See Also

`Exception`, `RuntimeException`, `Throwable`.

Example

See examples for subclasses of `Error`.

Error()

PURPOSE Constructs an `Error` object.

SYNTAX
```
public Error()
public Error(String msg)
```

DESCRIPTION This class has two constructors. The first form creates an `Error` object with no additional description other than the class name of the `Error` object. The second form creates an `Error` object using the string `msg`, which provides information about the error in addition to the class name of the `Error` object.

PARAMETERS

`msg` A string containing information about the error.

A B C D E F G H I J K L M N O P Q R S T U V W X Y Z

java.awt
Event

java.lang.Object — **Event**

Syntax

```
public class Event
```

Description

Events that flow between the AWT components are represented by objects of the `Event` class. When an event such as a mouse click or a keyboard press occurs, a new platform-independent `Event` object is created to contain various information about the event. All events use the `Event` class and so have the same fields, but not all fields are used for all events. The event type determines which fields are to be used.

Generating Events

Events can be generated by a component as the user interacts with it. At present, not all components generate events such as mouse and keyboard events. Instead, the component may hide all mouse and keyboard events and generate only a single action event. In a future release of the AWT, all components will be able to generate mouse and keyboard events. To determine what events a component generates, check with the component's documentation.

Events can also be generated other than in response to user interaction. For example, you may want a component to become enabled when some asynchronous activity completes. The thread doing the asynchronous activity could either disable the component directly or send it a special event to perform that task itself. The latter method would be more appropriate if disabling the component also involved other activities known only to the component.

Special events can be created either by subclassing `Event` or by creating an action event and filling in the `arg` and `target` fields. The event handler can then identify the special event by testing the `arg` and/or `target` fields using the `instanceof` operator.

Event Flow

Events flow up the component hierarchy. For example, a button that generates an action event can either handle the event itself or not. If it doesn't, the AWT framework automatically forwards the event onto the button's parent. The parent can either handle the event or not. If it doesn't, the AWT framework again forwards the event, this time to the next parent. If no one handles the event, the event is simply discarded.

Event Handlers

Events are handled by overriding a component's `handleEvent()` method. See `Component.handleEvent()` for details.

A B C D E F G H I J K L M N O P Q R S T U V W X Y Z

Mouse Events

For portability purposes, the AWT assumes that the mouse has only one button. This means that on a mouse with more than one button, pressing any of the buttons generates the same event type. A specific bit set in the event's modifiers field indicates which button was pressed. In particular, if the `ALT_MASK` bit is set, the middle mouse button was pressed; if the `META_MASK` bit is set, the right mouse button was pressed. On platforms with mice that have fewer than three buttons, the extra buttons can be simulated by holding down the appropriate modifier key (Shift, Control, or Alt) while pressing the mouse button.

This design does not allow you to determine, for example, on a platform with a three-button mouse, whether the right button was pressed or whether the left button was pressed while holding down the `META_MASK`.

Cursor Coordinates

With some event types, such as the mouse-related events, the coordinates of the cursor are captured in the `x` and `y` fields. As an event travels up the component hierarchy, the cursor coordinates are automatically translated to be relative to the bounds of the component currently holding the event. What this means is that the cursor coordinates are always relative to the bounds of the component that handles the event, not the bounds of the component that generates the event. For example, if an event was generated by a button in a panel and the event was handled by the panel, the cursor coordinates in `x` and `y` would be relative to the bounds of the panel, not the bounds of the button.

Another important fact about cursor coordinates in an event is that if the component handling the event is a container with non-zero insets, the cursor coordinates are relative to the container's inset area rather than the container's bounds; see the `Container` class for more details.

MEMBER SUMMARY

Constructor	
`Event()`	Constructs an `Event` instance.
Event Types	
`ACTION_EVENT`	Event type that triggers a command in the application.
`GOT_FOCUS`	Event type indicating that a component received the keyboard focus.
`KEY_ACTION`	Event type indicating that some non-ASCII key was pressed.
`KEY_ACTION_RELEASE`	Event type indicating that some non-ASCII key was released.
`KEY_PRESS`	Event type indicating that some ASCII key was pressed.
`KEY_RELEASE`	Event type indicating that some ASCII key was released.
`LIST_DESELECT`	Event type indicating that an item in a component has been deselected.

Continued

MEMBER SUMMARY	
`LIST_SELECT`	Event type indicating that an item in a component has been selected.
`LOAD_FILE`	Event type indicating that a file is being loaded.
`LOST_FOCUS`	Event type indicating that a component lost the focus.
`MOUSE_DOWN`	Event type indicating that a mouse button was pressed.
`MOUSE_DRAG`	Event type indicating that the cursor moved while some button was being pressed.
`MOUSE_ENTER`	Event type indicating that the cursor has reentered the component's bounds.
`MOUSE_EXIT`	Event type indicating that the cursor has left the component's bounds.
`MOUSE_MOVE`	Event type indicating that the cursor moved while no buttons were being pressed.
`MOUSE_UP`	Event type indicating that a mouse button was released.
`SAVE_FILE`	Event type specifying that a file is being saved.
`SCROLL_ABSOLUTE`	Event type indicating that the scrollbar's scroll box was dragged.
`SCROLL_LINE_DOWN`	Event type indicating that the scrollbar's line down button was clicked.
`SCROLL_LINE_UP`	Event type indicating that the scrollbar's line up button was clicked.
`SCROLL_PAGE_DOWN`	Event type indicating that the scrollbar's page down button was clicked.
`SCROLL_PAGE_UP`	Event type indicating that the scrollbar's page up button was clicked.
`WINDOW_DEICONIFY`	Event type indicating that a top-level window has been deiconified.
`WINDOW_DESTROY`	Event type indicating that the Close button on a top-level window has been pressed.
`WINDOW_EXPOSE`	Event type indicating that a top-level window has been exposed.
`WINDOW_ICONIFY`	Event type indicating that a top-level window has been iconified.
`WINDOW_MOVED`	Event type indicating that a top-level window has been moved.
Event Fields	
`arg`	Contains an arbitrary object associated with the event.
`clickCount`	Contains the number of consecutive `MOUSE_DOWN` events.
`evt`	Refers to another event object.
`id`	Contains the event type.
`key`	Contains the key that was pressed in a keyboard event.
`modifiers`	Contains the state of the modifier keys.
`target`	Contains a reference to the object that generated the event.
`when`	Contains the event's time stamp.

MEMBER SUMMARY

`x`	Contains the *x*-coordinate of the cursor at the time of the event.
`y`	Contains the *y*-coordinate of the cursor at the time of the event.
Keyboard Modifier Masks	
`ALT_MASK`	Modifier mask used to determine the state of the Alt key.
`CTRL_MASK`	Modifier mask used to determine the state of the Control key.
`META_MASK`	Modifier mask used to determine the state of the Meta key.
`SHIFT_MASK`	Modifier mask used to determine the state of the Shift key.
Keyboard Modifier Methods	
`controlDown()`	Retrieves the state of the Control modifier key.
`metaDown()`	Retrieves the state of the Meta modifier key.
`shiftDown()`	Retrieves the state of the Shift modifier key.
Non-ASCII Key Constants	
`DOWN`	Key constant representing the down arrow key.
`END`	Key constant representing the End key.
`F1`	Key constant representing the F1 function key.
`F10`	Key constant representing the F10 function key.
`F11`	Key constant representing the F11 function key.
`F12`	Key constant representing the F12 function key.
`F2`	Key constant representing the F2 function key.
`F3`	Key constant representing the F3 function key.
`F4`	Key constant representing the F4 function key.
`F5`	Key constant representing the F5 function key.
`F6`	Key constant representing the F6 function key.
`F7`	Key constant representing the F7 function key.
`F8`	Key constant representing the F8 function key.
`F9`	Key constant representing the F9 function key.
`HOME`	Key constant representing the Home key.
`LEFT`	Key constant representing the left arrow key.
`PGDN`	Key constant representing the page down key.
`PGUP`	Key constant representing the page up key.
`RIGHT`	Key constant representing the right arrow key.
`UP`	Key constant representing the up arrow key.
Translate Method	
`translate()`	Translates the event's *x*- and *y*-coordinates.
Debugging Method	
`paramString()`	Generates a string representing the event's state.
`toString()`	Produces a string representation of the event's state.

Example

As mentioned previously in this section, the events that are generated by the AWT components are currently not consistent. To cope with this, you can use the following example to experiment with each component to determine exactly what events it generates and in what situations. The program handles every event that is generated by any of the components and prints the details of the event to standard output. See Figure 86 for a screenshot of this example.

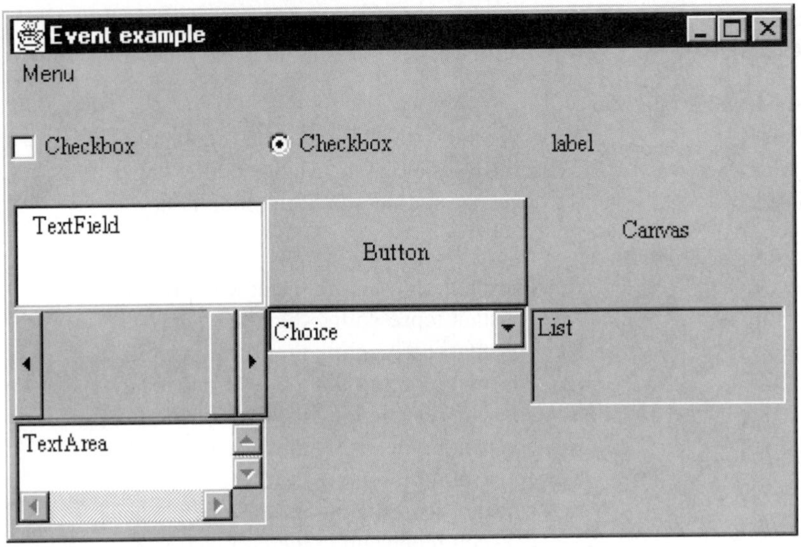

FIGURE 86 A Container of All AWT Components

```
import java.awt.*;
class Main extends Frame {
    Main() {
        super("Event example");

        // Menu bar with a menu and menu item
        MenuBar mb = new MenuBar();
        Menu m = new Menu("Menu");
        m.add("MenuItem");
        m.add(new CheckboxMenuItem("CheckboxMenuItem"));
        mb.add(m);
        setMenuBar(mb);

        setLayout(new GridLayout(0, 3));

        // checkbox, grouped checkbox, label, text field, scrollbar,
        //     button
        add(new Checkbox("Checkbox"));
        add(new Checkbox("Checkbox", new CheckboxGroup(), true));
        add(new Label("label"));
        add(new TextField("TextField"));
```

```
        add(new Button("Button"));
        add(new MyCanvas());

        // scrollbar
        Scrollbar sb = new Scrollbar(Scrollbar.HORIZONTAL);
        sb.setValues(50, 50, 0, 100);
        add(sb);

        // choice
        Choice choice = new Choice();
        choice.addItem("Choice");
        choice.addItem("a choice item");
        add(choice);

        // list
        List list = new List();
        list.addItem("List");
        list.addItem("a list item");
        add(list);

        // text area
        TextArea textArea = new TextArea("TextArea");
        textArea.resize(100, 50);
        add(textArea);

        pack();
        show();
    }

    public boolean handleEvent(Event evt) {
        if (evt.target instanceof Button) {
            System.out.print("Button");
        } else if (evt.target instanceof Choice) {
            System.out.print("Choice");
        } else if (evt.target instanceof Checkbox) {
            System.out.print("Checkbox");
        } else if (evt.target instanceof CheckboxGroup) {
            System.out.print("CheckboxGroup");
        } else if (evt.target instanceof Label) {
            System.out.print("Label");
        } else if (evt.target instanceof TextField) {
            System.out.print("TextField");
        } else if (evt.target instanceof Scrollbar) {
            System.out.print("Scrollbar");
        } else if (evt.target instanceof Canvas) {
            System.out.print("Canvas");
        } else if (evt.target instanceof List) {
            System.out.print("List");
        } else if (evt.target instanceof TextField) {
            System.out.print("TextField");
        } else if (evt.target instanceof TextArea) {
            System.out.print("TextArea");
        } else if (evt.target instanceof MenuItem) {
            System.out.print("MenuItem");
```

```
} else if (evt.target instanceof Container) {
   System.out.print("Container");
}
System.out.print(" ");

switch (evt.id) {
    case Event.ACTION_EVENT:
        System.out.print("ACTION_EVENT"); break;
    case Event.GOT_FOCUS:
        System.out.print("GOT_FOCUS"); break;
    case Event.KEY_ACTION:
        System.out.print("KEY_ACTION"); break;
    case Event.KEY_ACTION_RELEASE:
        System.out.print("KEY_ACTION_RELEASE"); break;
    case Event.KEY_PRESS:
        System.out.print("KEY_PRESS"); break;
    case Event.KEY_RELEASE:
        System.out.print("KEY_RELEASE"); break;
    case Event.LIST_DESELECT:
        System.out.print("LIST_DESELECT"); break;
    case Event.LIST_SELECT:
        System.out.print("LIST_SELECT"); break;
    case Event.LOAD_FILE:
        System.out.print("LOAD_FILE"); break;
    case Event.LOST_FOCUS:
        System.out.print("LOST_FOCUS"); break;
    case Event.MOUSE_DOWN:
        System.out.print("MOUSE_DOWN"); break;
    case Event.MOUSE_DRAG:
        System.out.print("MOUSE_DRAG"); break;
    case Event.MOUSE_ENTER:
        System.out.print("MOUSE_ENTER"); break;
    case Event.MOUSE_EXIT:
        System.out.print("MOUSE_EXIT"); break;
    case Event.MOUSE_MOVE:
        System.out.print("MOUSE_MOVE"); break;
    case Event.MOUSE_UP:
        System.out.print("MOUSE_UP"); break;
    case Event.SAVE_FILE:
        System.out.print("SAVE_FILE"); break;
    case Event.SCROLL_ABSOLUTE:
        System.out.print("SCROLL_ABSOLUTE"); break;
    case Event.SCROLL_LINE_DOWN:
        System.out.print("SCROLL_LINE_DOWN"); break;
    case Event.SCROLL_LINE_UP:
        System.out.print("SCROLL_LINE_UP"); break;
    case Event.SCROLL_PAGE_DOWN:
        System.out.print("SCROLL_PAGE_DOWN"); break;
    case Event.SCROLL_PAGE_UP:
        System.out.print("SCROLL_PAGE_UP"); break;
    case Event.WINDOW_DEICONIFY:
        System.out.print("WINDOW_DEICONIFY"); break;
    case Event.WINDOW_DESTROY:
        System.out.print("WINDOW_DESTROY"); break;
```

```
            case Event.WINDOW_EXPOSE:
                System.out.print("WINDOW_EXPOSE"); break;
            case Event.WINDOW_ICONIFY:
                System.out.print("WINDOW_ICONIFY"); break;
            case Event.WINDOW_MOVED:
                System.out.print("WINDOW_MOVED"); break;
        }
        System.out.print(" ("+evt.x+" "+evt.y+") w("+evt.when+")");
        System.out.print(" k("+(char)evt.key+
            ")m("+evt.modifiers+")");
        System.out.print(" c("+evt.clickCount+") a("+evt.arg+")");
        System.out.println();
        return false;
    }

    static public void main(String[] args) {
        new Main();
    }
}

class MyCanvas extends Canvas {
    public void paint(Graphics g) {
        FontMetrics fm = g.getFontMetrics();
        g.drawString("Canvas",
            (size().width-fm.stringWidth("Canvas"))/2,
            (size().height-fm.getAscent())/2);
    }
}
```

Output

```
Canvas KEY_RELEASE (540 183) w(827558080120) k(_) m(0) c(0) a(null)
Canvas LOST_FOCUS (540 183) w(0) k(_) m(0) c(0) a(null)
Canvas MOUSE_ENTER (347 454) w(827558089680) k(_) m(0) c(0) a(null)
Canvas MOUSE_MOVE (347 454) w(827558089680) k(_) m(0) c(0) a(null)
Canvas GOT_FOCUS (302 452) w(0) k(_) m(0) c(0) a(null)
Canvas MOUSE_MOVE (343 465) w(827558090010) k(_) m(0) c(0) a(null)
Canvas MOUSE_DOWN (343 464) w(827558090010) k(_) m(0) c(1) a(null)
Canvas MOUSE_DRAG (331 480) w(827558092040) k(_) m(0) c(0) a(null)
Canvas MOUSE_UP (331 480) w(827558092040) k(_) m(0) c(0) a(null)
Canvas MOUSE_MOVE (331 480) w(827558092040) k(_) m(0) c(0) a(null)
Canvas MOUSE_MOVE (309 477) w(827558092150) k(_) m(0) c(0) a(null)
Canvas MOUSE_EXIT (251 467) w(827558092260) k(_) m(0) c(0) a(null)
Canvas LOST_FOCUS (302 452) w(0) k(_) m(0) c(0) a(null)
Button ACTION_EVENT (153 93) w(0) k(_) m(0) c(0) a(Button)
TextField KEY_PRESS (4 93) w(827558094240) k(k) m(0) c(0) a(null)
TextField KEY_RELEASE (4 93) w(827558094340) k(k) m(0) c(0) a(null)
TextField KEY_PRESS (4 93) w(827558094450) k(l) m(0) c(0) a(null)
Checkbox ACTION_EVENT (4 42) w(0) k(_) m(0) c(0) a(true)
Checkbox ACTION_EVENT (4 42) w(0) k(_) m(0) c(0) a(false)
Scrollbar SCROLL_PAGE_UP (4 144) w(0) k(_) m(0) c(0) a(40)
Scrollbar SCROLL_ABSOLUTE (4 144) w(0) k(_) m(0) c(0) a(20)
Scrollbar SCROLL_LINE_UP (4 144) w(0) k(_) m(0) c(0) a(17)
Scrollbar SCROLL_ABSOLUTE (4 144) w(0) k(_) m(0) c(0) a(22)
```

```
Scrollbar SCROLL_LINE_DOWN (4 144) w(0) k(_) m(0) c(0) a(23)
List LIST_SELECT (302 144) w(0) k(_) m(0) c(0) a(0)
List ACTION_EVENT (302 144) w(0) k(_) m(0) c(0) a(List)
TextArea KEY_PRESS (4 195) w(827558105110) k(k) m(0) c(0) a(null)
TextArea KEY_RELEASE (4 195) w(827558105490) k(j) m(0) c(0) a(null)
Container MOUSE_MOVE (799 10) w(827558114500) k(_) m(0) c(0) a(null)
Container MOUSE_MOVE (799 2) w(827558114670) k(_) m(0) c(0) a(null)
Container WINDOW_DESTROY (0 0) w(0) k(_) m(0) c(0) a(null)
```

ACTION_EVENT

PURPOSE Event type that triggers a command in the application.

SYNTAX `public static final int ACTION_EVENT`

DESCRIPTION This event is typically generated by a component to trigger some high-level activity in the application. For example, double-clicking a filename in a list component might cause the application to open the file. The component generating an action event must fill the event's `arg` field with some detail about the event. For example, a button fills the `arg` field with the name of its label. Because each component fills the `arg` field differently, you need to check the component's documentation to determine what it places in the event's `arg` field.

EXAMPLE See the class example.

ALT_MASK

PURPOSE Modifier mask used to determine the state of the Alt key.

SYNTAX `public static final int ALT_MASK`

DESCRIPTION This mask should be bitwise and'ed with the `modifiers` field to determine the state of the Alt key. If the result is `0`, the Alt key is not pressed; otherwise the key is pressed.

SEE ALSO `CONTROL_MASK`, `META_MASK`, `modifiers`, `SHIFT_MASK`.

EXAMPLE This example shows how to test if the Alt key is pressed. The method returns `true` if the key is pressed and `false` otherwise.

```
public boolean altDown() {
   return (modifiers & ALT_MASK) != 0;
}
```

arg

PURPOSE Contains an arbitrary object associated with the event.

SYNTAX `public Object arg`

DESCRIPTION This field is filled in by certain event types and contains an object whose type is determined by the event. For example, the `arg` field for buttons generating an `ACTION_EVENT` event contains the label of the button. The `arg` field for scrollbars generating a `SCROLL_ABSOLUTE` event contains the new value of the scrollbar in an `Integer` object. To determine whether an event type uses the `arg` field, check with the documentation for that event type.

EXAMPLE See the class example.

clickCount

PURPOSE Contains the number of consecutive `MOUSE_DOWN` events.

SYNTAX `public int clickCount`

DESCRIPTION This field is used only by the `MOUSE_DOWN` event and then typically to detect double- and triple-click gestures. The value in the field is at least `1` and indicates the *n*th click in a multiple-click sequence. For example, a value of `1` indicates a single-click and a value of `2` indicates a double-click.

SEE ALSO `MOUSE_DOWN`.

EXAMPLE See the class example.

controlDown()

PURPOSE Retrieves the state of the Control modifier key.

SYNTAX `public boolean controlDown()`

DESCRIPTION This method uses `CTRL_MASK` on the `modifiers` field to determine if the Control key was pressed.

RETURNS `true` if the Control key is down; `false` otherwise.

SEE ALSO `metaDown()`, `modifiers`, `SHIFT_MASK`, `shiftDown()`.

EXAMPLE See the `key` example.

A B C D E F G H I J K L M N O P Q R S T U V W X Y Z

CTRL_MASK

PURPOSE Modifier mask used to determine the state of the Control key.

SYNTAX `public static final int CTRL_MASK`

DESCRIPTION This mask should be bitwise and'ed with the `modifiers` field to determine the state of the Control key. If the result is `0`, the Control key is not pressed; otherwise the key is pressed.

SEE ALSO `ALT_MASK`, `META_MASK`, `modifiers`, `SHIFT_MASK`.

EXAMPLE This example shows how the `controlDown()` method uses `CTRL_MASK` to determine the state of the Control key. The method returns `true` if the Control key is pressed and `false` otherwise.

```
public boolean controlDown() {
    return (modifiers & CTRL_MASK) != 0;
}
```

DOWN

PURPOSE Key constant representing the down arrow key.

SYNTAX `public static final int DOWN`

DESCRIPTION This key constant is delivered via the `KEY_ACTION` and `KEY_ACTION_RELEASE` events.

SEE ALSO `KEY_ACTION`, `KEY_ACTION_RELEASE`.

EXAMPLE See the `key` example.

END

PURPOSE Key constant representing the End key.

SYNTAX `public static final int END`

DESCRIPTION This key constant is delivered via the `KEY_ACTION` and `KEY_ACTION_RELEASE` events.

SEE ALSO `KEY_ACTION`, `KEY_ACTION_RELEASE`.

EXAMPLE See the `key` example.

A B C D E F G H I J K L M N O P Q R S T U V W X Y Z

Event()

PURPOSE Constructs an `Event` instance.

SYNTAX
```
public Event(Object target, long when, int id, int x, int y, int
   key, int modifiers, Object arg)
public Event(Object target, long when, int id, int x, int y, int
   key, int modifiers)
public Event(Object target, int id, Object arg)
```

DESCRIPTION These constructors construct an `Event` object whose fields are initialized with the specified parameters. For details on what a field contains, see the documentation for that field in this class. If `arg` is not specified, this method defaults to `null`. For any field that is not initialized by a parameter, it defaults to `0`.

PARAMETERS

`arg`	The object to be associated with this event.
`id`	The event type.
`key`	The key that generated the event; used by keyboard-related event types.
`modifiers`	The state of the modifier keys at the time of the event.
`target`	The non-`null` component that generated the event.
`when`	The event's time stamp at the time of the event.
`x`	The *x*-coordinate of the cursor at the time of the event.
`y`	The *y*-coordinate of the cursor at the time of the event.

EXAMPLE See the class example.

evt

PURPOSE Refers to another `Event` object.

SYNTAX `public Event evt`

DESCRIPTION This field is used when the event needs to be inserted into a linked list.

EXAMPLE This example defines a method that simply inserts an event to the head of a linked list.

```
Event list;
void queueEvent(Event event) {
    event.evt = list;
    list = event;
}
```

F1

PURPOSE Key constant representing the F1 function key.

SYNTAX `public static final int F1`

DESCRIPTION This key constant is delivered via the `KEY_ACTION` and `KEY_ACTION_RELEASE` events.

SEE ALSO `KEY_ACTION`, `KEY_ACTION_RELEASE`.

EXAMPLE See the `key` example.

F10

PURPOSE Key constant representing the F10 function key.

SYNTAX `public static final int F10`

DESCRIPTION This key constant is delivered via the `KEY_ACTION` and `KEY_ACTION_RELEASE` events.

SEE ALSO `KEY_ACTION`, `KEY_ACTION_RELEASE`.

EXAMPLE See the `key` example.

F11

PURPOSE Key constant representing the F11 function key.

SYNTAX `public static final int F11`

DESCRIPTION This key constant is delivered via the `KEY_ACTION` and `KEY_ACTION_RELEASE` events.

SEE ALSO `KEY_ACTION`, `KEY_ACTION_RELEASE`.

EXAMPLE See the `key` example.

F12

PURPOSE Key constant representing the F12 function key.

SYNTAX `public static final int F12`

DESCRIPTION This key constant is delivered via the KEY_ACTION and KEY_ACTION_RELEASE events.

SEE ALSO KEY_ACTION, KEY_ACTION_RELEASE.

EXAMPLE See the key example.

F2

PURPOSE Key constant representing the F2 function key.

SYNTAX `public static final int F2`

DESCRIPTION This key constant is delivered via the KEY_ACTION and KEY_ACTION_RELEASE events.

SEE ALSO KEY_ACTION, KEY_ACTION_RELEASE.

EXAMPLE See the key example

F3

PURPOSE Key constant representing the F3 function key.

SYNTAX `public static final int F3`

DESCRIPTION This key constant is delivered via the KEY_ACTION and KEY_ACTION_RELEASE events.

SEE ALSO KEY_ACTION, KEY_ACTION_RELEASE.

EXAMPLE See the key example.

F4

PURPOSE Key constant representing the F4 function key.

SYNTAX `public static final int F4`

DESCRIPTION This key constant is delivered via the KEY_ACTION and KEY_ACTION_RELEASE events.

SEE ALSO KEY_ACTION, KEY_ACTION_RELEASE.

EXAMPLE See the key example.

F5

PURPOSE Key constant representing the F5 function key.

SYNTAX `public static final int F5`

DESCRIPTION This key constant is delivered via the `KEY_ACTION` and `KEY_ACTION_RELEASE` events.

SEE ALSO `KEY_ACTION`, `KEY_ACTION_RELEASE`.

EXAMPLE See the `key` example.

F6

PURPOSE Key constant representing the F6 function key.

SYNTAX `public static final int F6`

DESCRIPTION This key constant is delivered via the `KEY_ACTION` and `KEY_ACTION_RELEASE` events.

SEE ALSO `KEY_ACTION`, `KEY_ACTION_RELEASE`.

EXAMPLE See the `key` example.

F7

PURPOSE Key constant representing the F7 function key.

SYNTAX `public static final int F7`

DESCRIPTION This key constant is delivered via the `KEY_ACTION` and `KEY_ACTION_RELEASE` events.

SEE ALSO `KEY_ACTION`, `KEY_ACTION_RELEASE`.

EXAMPLE See the `key` example.

F8

PURPOSE Key constant representing the F8 function key.

SYNTAX `public static final int F8`

DESCRIPTION This key constant is delivered via the KEY_ACTION and KEY_ACTION_RELEASE events.

SEE ALSO KEY_ACTION, KEY_ACTION_RELEASE.

EXAMPLE See the key example.

F9

PURPOSE Key constant representing the F9 function key.

SYNTAX `public static final int F9`

DESCRIPTION This key constant is delivered via the KEY_ACTION and KEY_ACTION_RELEASE events.

SEE ALSO KEY_ACTION, KEY_ACTION_RELEASE.

EXAMPLE See the key example.

GOT_FOCUS

PURPOSE Event type indicating a component received the keyboard focus.

SYNTAX `public static final int GOT_FOCUS`

DESCRIPTION The event's target field contains a reference to the component that received the keyboard focus.

SEE ALSO LOST_FOCUS.

EXAMPLE See the class example.

HOME

PURPOSE Key constant representing the Home key.

SYNTAX `public static final int HOME`

DESCRIPTION This key constant is delivered via the KEY_ACTION and KEY_ACTION_RELEASE events.

SEE ALSO KEY_ACTION, KEY_ACTION_RELEASE.

EXAMPLE See the key example.

id

PURPOSE Contains the event type.

SYNTAX `public int id`

DESCRIPTION This field contains one of the event types as summarized in the "Member Summary" section.

EXAMPLE See the class example.

key

PURPOSE Contains the key that was pressed in a keyboard event.

SYNTAX `public int key`

DESCRIPTION This field is set only by one of the four keyboard event types: `KEY_ACTION`, `KEY_ACTION_RELEASE`, `KEY_PRESS`, or `KEY_RELEASE`. In a `KEY_PRESS` event and a `KEY_RELEASE` event, the `key` field contains the ASCII representation of the key that was pressed. For example, pressing the 'A' key generates 'a' and pressing Shift-A generates 'A.' In a `KEY_ACTION` event and a `KEY_ACTION_RELEASE` event, the `key` field contains one of the `key` constants, such as `HOME` or `DOWN`, defined in this class.

SEE ALSO `KEY_ACTION`, `KEY_ACTION_RELEASE`, `KEY_PRESS`, `KEY_RELEASE`.

EXAMPLE This example creates two frames. One displays an image in its natural size and a rectangle called the *lens* on the image. The other frame magnifies the original image by taking the pixels inside the lens and scaling them to fill its entire paintable area. See Figure 87. The size and position of the lens is controlled by

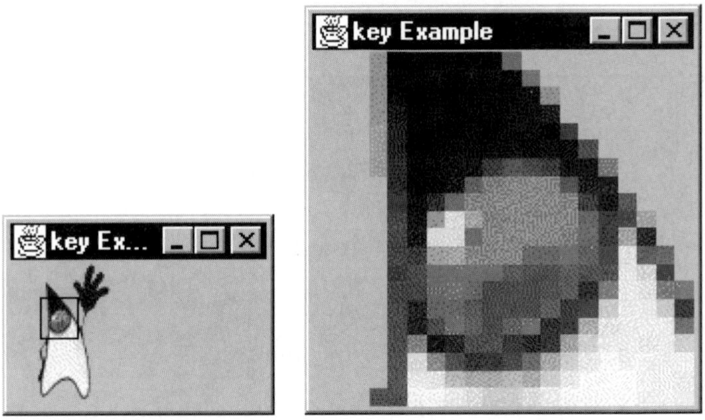

FIGURE 87 **`Event.key`: Original and Magnified Images**

keystrokes. The direction keys—UP, DOWN, LEFT, and RIGHT—move the lens. Typing a direction key with the Shift modifier key enabled adjusts the size of the lens. Finally, typing F1 causes the pixels inside the lens to be magnified in the other frame.

A crop image filter (see `CropImageFilter`) is used to create a scaled image from the pixels in the lens. A `MediaTracker` object is used to preload the image before it is displayed. This is done because the width and height of the image are needed right away.

```
import java.awt.*;
import java.awt.image.*;
class Main extends Frame {
    Main(String filename) {
        super("key Example");
        Image image = getToolkit().getImage(filename);

        MediaTracker tracker = new MediaTracker(this);
        tracker.addImage(image, 0);
        try {
            tracker.waitForAll();
        } catch (Exception e) {
            e.printStackTrace();
        }

        ImageCanvas c = new ImageCanvas(image, new ScaledFrame());
        add("Center", c);
        resize(50, 100);
        show();
    }

    static public void main(String[] args) {
        if (args.length == 1) {
            new Main(args[0]);
        } else {
            System.err.println("usage: java Main <image file>");
        }
    }
}

class ImageCanvas extends Canvas {
    int imageW, imageH;
    Image image;
    Rectangle lens = new Rectangle(0, 0, 20, 20);
    ScaledFrame frame;

    ImageCanvas(Image i, ScaledFrame f) {
        image = i;
        frame = f;
        imageW = image.getWidth(null);
        imageH = image.getHeight(null);
    }
```

```
    public void paint(Graphics g) {
        g.drawImage(image, 0, 0, this);
        g.setColor(Color.black);
        g.drawRect(lens.x, lens.y, lens.width-1, lens.height);
    }

    public boolean keyDown(Event evt, int key) {
        Rectangle oldRect = lens.union(lens);
        int delta = evt.controlDown() ? 5 : 1;

        switch (key) {
        case Event.UP:
            if (evt.shiftDown()) {
                lens.resize(lens.width, lens.height-delta);
            } else {
                lens.translate(0, -delta);
            }
            break;
        case Event.DOWN:
            if (evt.shiftDown()) {
                lens.resize(lens.width, lens.height+delta);
            } else {
                lens.translate(0, delta);
            }
            break;
        case Event.LEFT:
            if (evt.shiftDown()) {
                lens.resize(lens.width-delta, lens.height);
            } else {
                lens.translate(-delta, 0);
            }
            break;
        case Event.RIGHT:
            if (evt.shiftDown()) {
                lens.resize(lens.width+delta, lens.height);
            } else {
                lens.translate(delta, 0);
            }
            break;
        case Event.PGUP:
            lens.translate(0, -lens.height);
            break;
        case Event.PGDN:
            lens.translate(0, lens.height);
            break;
        case Event.HOME:
            lens.move(0, 0);
            break;
        case Event.END:
            lens.move(imageW-lens.width, imageH-lens.height);
            break;
        case Event.F1:
            frame.rescale(image, lens);
            break;
```

```
        }
        if (!oldRect.equals(lens)) {
            lens.width = Math.max(1, lens.width);
            lens.height = Math.max(1, lens.height);
            lens.move(Math.min(imageW-lens.width, lens.x),
                Math.min(imageH-lens.height, lens.y));
            lens.move(Math.max(0, lens.x), Math.max(0, lens.y));
            repaint();
        }
        return true;
    }
}

class ScaledFrame extends Frame {
    Image image;

    ScaledFrame() {
        super("key Example");
        resize(200, 200);
        show();
    }

    void rescale(Image image, Rectangle r) {
        CropImageFilter imgf = new CropImageFilter(
            r.x, r.y, r.width, r.height);
        this.image = getToolkit().createImage(
            new FilteredImageSource(image.getSource(), imgf));
        repaint();
    }

    public void paint(Graphics g) {
        int w = size().width - insets().right - insets().left;
        int h = size().height - insets().bottom - insets().top;

        if (image != null) {
            g.drawImage(image, 0, 0, w, h, this);
        }
    }
}
```

KEY_ACTION

PURPOSE Event type indicating that some non-ASCII key was pressed.

SYNTAX `public static final int KEY_ACTION`

DESCRIPTION The `key` field contains one of the key constants, such as `HOME` or `DOWN`, defined in this class. The `modifiers` field contains the state of the modifiers when the key was pressed.

Note that transitions of the modifier keys are not generated. Also, a modifier key that was pressed in a `KEY_ACTION` event possibly may not be pressed in a `KEY_ACTION_RELEASE` event.

SEE ALSO `modifiers`.

EXAMPLE See the class example.

KEY_ACTION_RELEASE

PURPOSE Event type indicating that some non-ASCII key was released.

SYNTAX `public static final int KEY_ACTION_RELEASE`

DESCRIPTION The `key` field contains one of the key constants, such as `HOME` or `DOWN`, defined in this class. The `modifiers` field contains the state of the modifiers when the key was released.

Note that transitions of the modifier keys are not generated. Also, a modifier key that was pressed in a `KEY_ACTION` event possibly may not be pressed in a `KEY_ACTION_RELEASE` event.

SEE ALSO `modifiers`.

EXAMPLE See the class example.

KEY_PRESS

PURPOSE Event type indicating that some ASCII key was pressed.

SYNTAX `public static final int KEY_PRESS`

DESCRIPTION The `key` field contains the ASCII encoding of the key that was pressed. For example, pressing the 'A' key generates 'a' and pressing Shift-A generates 'A.' The `modifiers` field contains the state of the modifiers when the key was pressed.

Note that transitions of the modifier keys are not generated. Also, a modifier key that was pressed in a `KEY_PRESS` event possibly may not be pressed in a `KEY_RELEASE` event.

SEE ALSO `modifiers`.

EXAMPLE See the class example.

KEY_RELEASE

PURPOSE Event type indicating that some ASCII key was released.

SYNTAX `public static final int KEY_RELEASE`

DESCRIPTION The `key` field contains the ASCII encoding of the key that was released. For example, releasing 'A' generates 'a' and releasing Shift-A generates 'A.' The `modifiers` field contains the state of the modifiers when the key was released.

Note that transitions of the modifier keys are not generated. Also, a modifier key that was pressed in a `KEY_PRESS` event possibly may not be pressed in a `KEY_RELEASE` event.

SEE ALSO `modifiers`.

EXAMPLE See the class example.

LEFT

PURPOSE Key constant representing the left arrow key.

SYNTAX `public static final int LEFT`

DESCRIPTION This key constant is delivered via the `KEY_ACTION` and `KEY_ACTION_RELEASE` events.

SEE ALSO `KEY_ACTION`, `KEY_ACTION_RELEASE`.

EXAMPLE See the `key` example.

LIST_DESELECT

PURPOSE Event type indicating that an item in a component has been deselected.

SYNTAX `public static final int LIST_DESELECT`

DESCRIPTION This event is generated by the list component. The `arg` field contains the index of the deselected item wrapped in an `Integer` object.

SEE ALSO `Integer`, `List`.

EXAMPLE See the class example.

LIST_SELECT

PURPOSE Event type indicating that an item in a component has been selected.

SYNTAX `public static final int LIST_SELECT`

DESCRIPTION This event is generated by the list component. The `arg` field contains the index of the selected item wrapped in an `Integer` object.

SEE ALSO `Integer`, `List`.

EXAMPLE See the class example.

LOAD_FILE

PURPOSE Event type indicating that a file is being loaded.

SYNTAX `public static final int LOAD_FILE`

DESCRIPTION This event type is generated by a file selection dialog after the user chooses a filename. This constant field is not currently being used.

SEE ALSO `SAVE_FILE`.

LOST_FOCUS

PURPOSE Event type indicating that a component lost the focus.

SYNTAX `public static final int LOST_FOCUS`

DESCRIPTION The event's `target` field contains a reference to the component that lost the keyboard focus.

SEE ALSO `GOT_FOCUS`.

EXAMPLE See the class example.

META_MASK

PURPOSE Modifier mask used to determine the state of the meta key.

SYNTAX `public static final int META_MASK`

DESCRIPTION This mask should be bitwise and'ed with the modifiers field to determine the state of the meta key. If the result is 0, the key is not pressed; otherwise the key is pressed.

SEE ALSO ALT_MASK, CONTROL_MASK, modifiers, SHIFT_MASK.

EXAMPLE This example shows how the metaDown() method uses META_MASK to determine the state of the meta key. The method returns true if the meta key is pressed and false otherwise.

```
public boolean metaDown() {
   return (modifiers & META_MASK) != 0;
}
```

metaDown()

PURPOSE Retrieves the state of the meta modifier key.

SYNTAX `public boolean metaDown()`

DESCRIPTION This method uses META_MASK on the modifiers field to determine if the meta key was pressed.

RETURNS true if the meta key is down; false otherwise.

SEE ALSO controlDown(), META_MASK, modifiers, shift().

EXAMPLE See the key example.

modifiers

PURPOSE Contains the state of the modifier keys.

SYNTAX `public int modifiers`

DESCRIPTION This field contains the state of the modifier keys when a keyboard event or mouse event is generated. The state of each modifier is represented by a bit in the modifiers field. Use the modifier masks to determine the state of a particular modifier key.

In the case of mouse events, the state of the modifiers also identifies which mouse button was pressed. In particular, if the ALT_MASK bit is set, the middle button was pressed; if the META_MASK bit is set, the right button was pressed. For platforms with mice that have fewer than three buttons, the extra buttons can be simulated by holding down the appropriate modifier key while pressing the mouse button.

SEE ALSO `ALT_MASK`, `CTRL_MASK`, `META_MASK`, `SHIFT_MASK`.

MOUSE_DOWN

PURPOSE Event type indicating that a mouse button was pressed.

SYNTAX `public static final int MOUSE_DOWN`

DESCRIPTION The `x` and `y` fields contain the location of the cursor relative to the component's bounds at the time the button was pressed; see the class description for more details. The `modifiers` field contains the identity of which mouse button was pressed and the state of the modifiers at the time the event was generated. The `clickcount` field contains the number of consecutive `MOUSE_DOWN` events.

For every `MOUSE_DOWN` event that is generated, there will be a corresponding `MOUSE_UP` event generated. That is, the `MOUSE_UP` event will be generated even if the mouse is not released in the component that generated the `MOUSE_DOWN` event.

SEE ALSO `clickcount`, `modifiers`, `MOUSE_UP`, `x`, `y`.

EXAMPLE See the class example.

MOUSE_DRAG

PURPOSE Event type indicating that the cursor moved while some button was being pressed.

SYNTAX `public static final int MOUSE_DRAG`

DESCRIPTION The `x` and `y` fields contain the location of the cursor relative to the container's bounds. That is, if `x` and `y` are 0, the cursor is located at the top-left corner of the container.

The `modifiers` field contains the identity of which mouse button was pressed and the state of the modifiers at the time the event was generated.

SEE ALSO `modifiers`, `x`, `y`.

EXAMPLE See the class example.

MOUSE_ENTER

PURPOSE Event type indicating that the cursor has reentered the component's bounds.

SYNTAX `public static final int MOUSE_ENTER`

DESCRIPTION The `x` and `y` fields contain the location of the cursor relative to the component's bounds when it reentered the component's bounds; see class description for more details. The `modifiers` field contains the identity of which mouse button was pressed and the state of the modifiers at the time the event was generated. This event is generated regardless of whether a mouse button is down.

SEE ALSO `modifiers`, `x`, `y`.

EXAMPLE See the class example.

MOUSE_EXIT

PURPOSE Event type indicating that the cursor has left the component's bounds.

SYNTAX `public static final int MOUSE_EXIT`

DESCRIPTION The `x` and `y` fields contain the location of the cursor relative to the component's bounds when it left the component's bounds; see class description for more details. The `modifiers` field contains the identity of which mouse button was pressed and the state of the modifiers at the time the event was generated. This event is generated regardless of whether a mouse button is down.

SEE ALSO `modifiers`, `x`, `y`.

EXAMPLE See the class example.

MOUSE_MOVE

PURPOSE Event type indicating that the cursor moved while no button was being pressed.

SYNTAX `public static final int MOUSE_MOVE`

DESCRIPTION The `x` and `y` fields contain the current location of the cursor relative to the component's bounds; see class description for more details. The `modifiers` field contains the identity of which mouse button was pressed and the state of the modifiers at the time the event was generated.

MOUSE_UP

SEE ALSO `modifiers`, x, y.

EXAMPLE See the class example.

MOUSE_UP

PURPOSE Event type indicating that a mouse button was released.

SYNTAX `public static final int MOUSE_UP`

DESCRIPTION The `x` and `y` fields contain the location of the cursor relative to the component's bounds at the time the button was released; see class description for more details. The `modifiers` field contains the identity of which mouse button was pressed and the state of the modifiers at the time the event was generated. For every `MOUSE_DOWN` event generated, there will be a corresponding `MOUSE_UP` event generated. That is, the `MOUSE_UP` event will be generated even if the mouse button is not released in the component that generated the `MOUSE_DOWN` event.

SEE ALSO `modifiers`, x, y.

EXAMPLE See the class example.

paramString()

PURPOSE Generates a string representing the event's state.

SYNTAX `protected String paramString()`

DESCRIPTION The returned string includes the selected item. A subclass of this class should override this method and return a concatenation of its state with the results of `super.paramString()`. This method is called by the `toString()` method and is typically used for debugging.

RETURNS A non-`null` string representing the event's state.

SEE ALSO `toString()`.

EXAMPLE See `Component.paramString()`.

PGDN

PURPOSE Key constant representing the page down key.

SYNTAX `public static final int PGDN`

DESCRIPTION This key constant is delivered via the KEY_ACTION and KEY_ACTION_RELEASE events.

SEE ALSO KEY_ACTION, KEY_ACTION_RELEASE.

EXAMPLE See the key example.

PGUP

PURPOSE Key constant representing the page up key.

SYNTAX `public static final int PGUP`

DESCRIPTION This key constant is delivered via the KEY_ACTION and KEY_ACTION_RELEASE events.

SEE ALSO KEY_ACTION, KEY_ACTION_RELEASE.

EXAMPLE See the key example.

RIGHT

PURPOSE Key constant representing the right arrow key.

SYNTAX `public static final int RIGHT`

DESCRIPTION This key constant is delivered via the KEY_ACTION and KEY_ACTION_RELEASE events.

SEE ALSO KEY_ACTION, KEY_ACTION_RELEASE.

EXAMPLE See the key example.

SAVE_FILE

PURPOSE Event type specifying that a file is being saved.

SYNTAX `public static final int SAVE_FILE`

DESCRIPTION This event type is generated by a file selection dialog after the user chooses a filename. This constant field is not currently being used.

SEE ALSO LOAD_FILE.

SCROLL_ABSOLUTE

PURPOSE Event type indicating that the scrollbar's scroll box was dragged.

SYNTAX `public static final int SCROLL_ABSOLUTE`

DESCRIPTION This event is generated only by the scrollbar component. The `arg` field contains an `Integer` object, which in turn holds the new value of the scrollbar. See the `Scrollbar` class for more details.

SEE ALSO `Scrollbar`.

EXAMPLE See the class example.

SCROLL_LINE_DOWN

PURPOSE Event type indicating that the scrollbar's line down button was clicked.

SYNTAX `public static final int SCROLL_LINE_DOWN`

DESCRIPTION This event is generated only by the scrollbar component. The `arg` field contains an `Integer` object, which in turn holds the new value of the scrollbar. See the `Scrollbar` class for more details.

SEE ALSO `Scrollbar`.

EXAMPLE See the class example.

SCROLL_LINE_UP

PURPOSE Event type indicating that the scrollbar's line up button was clicked.

SYNTAX `public static final int SCROLL_LINE_UP`

DESCRIPTION This event is generated only by the scrollbar component. The `arg` field contains an `Integer` object, which in turn holds the new value of the scrollbar. See the `Scrollbar` class for more details.

SEE ALSO `Scrollbar`.

EXAMPLE See the class example.

SCROLL_PAGE_DOWN

PURPOSE Event type indicating that the scrollbar's page down button was clicked.

SYNTAX `public static final int SCROLL_PAGE_DOWN`

DESCRIPTION This event is generated only by the scrollbar component. The `arg` field contains an `Integer` object, which in turn holds the new value of the scrollbar. See the `Scrollbar` class for more details.

SEE ALSO `Scrollbar`.

EXAMPLE See the class example.

SCROLL_PAGE_UP

PURPOSE Event type indicating that the scrollbar's page up button was clicked.

SYNTAX `public static final int SCROLL_PAGE_UP`

DESCRIPTION This event is generated only by the scrollbar component. The `arg` field contains an `Integer` object, which in turn holds the new value of the scrollbar. See the `Scrollbar` class for more details.

SEE ALSO `Scrollbar`.

EXAMPLE See the class example.

SHIFT_MASK

PURPOSE Modifier mask used to determine the state of the Shift key.

SYNTAX `public static final int SHIFT_MASK`

DESCRIPTION This mask should be bitwise and'ed with the `modifiers` field to determine the state of the Shift key. If the result is `0`, the Shift key is not pressed; otherwise the key is pressed.

SEE ALSO `CTRL_MASK`, `META_MASK`, `modifiers`.

EXAMPLE This example shows how the `shiftDown()` method uses `SHIFT_MASK` to determine the state of the Shift key. The method returns `true` if the Shift key is pressed and `false` otherwise.

```
public boolean shiftDown() {
    return (modifiers & SHIFT_MASK) != 0;
}
```

shiftDown()

PURPOSE Determines the state of the Shift modifier key.

SYNTAX `public boolean shiftDown()`

DESCRIPTION This method uses `SHIFT_MASK` on the `modifiers` field to determine if the Shift key was pressed.

RETURNS `true` if the Shift key is down; `false` otherwise.

SEE ALSO `controlDown()`, `metaDown()`, `modifiers`, `SHIFT_MASK`.

EXAMPLE See the `key` example.

target

PURPOSE Contains a reference to the object that generated the event.

SYNTAX `public Object target`

EXAMPLE See the class example.

toString()

PURPOSE Produces a string representation of the event's state.

SYNTAX `public String toString()`

DESCRIPTION The string contains the event's class name and the values in its public fields. The Java compiler automatically generates code to call this method when it needs to translate the `Event` instance to a string. This method is typically used for debugging.

RETURNS A non-null string representing the event's state.

OVERRIDES `Object.toString()`.

EXAMPLE See `Object.toString()`.

translate()

PURPOSE Translates the event's *x*- and *y*-coordinates.

SYNTAX `public void translate(int x, int y)`

DESCRIPTION This method simply adds x to the event's x field and y to the event's y field. It is typically used by the AWT event framework as it passes an event up the component hierarchy. In particular, the framework adjusts the event's coordinates so that they are relative to the component that is receiving the event.

PARAMETERS

x The value to add to the event's *x*-coordinate.

y The value to add to the event's *y*-coordinate.

EXAMPLE This example implements a variant of `Component.postEvent()`. The `postToTopLevel()` method finds the component's top-most container and posts the event to that container. As each parent of the component is retrieved, the event is translated to be relative to that parent's coordinates.

```
void postEventToTopLevel(Event e) {
    Component prev = this;
    Component p = prev.getParent();
    while (p != null) {
        e.translate(prev.bounds().x, prev.bounds().y);
        prev = p;
        p = p.getParent();
    }
    prev.postEvent(e);
}
```

UP

PURPOSE Key constant representing the up arrow key.

SYNTAX `public static final int UP`

DESCRIPTION This key constant is delivered via the `KEY_ACTION` and `KEY_ACTION_RELEASE` events.

SEE ALSO KEY_ACTION, KEY_ACTION_RELEASE.

EXAMPLE See the key example.

when

PURPOSE Contains the event's time stamp.

SYNTAX `public long when`

DESCRIPTION The time stamp is a time value in milliseconds. The time stamp is used to distinguish and order the events if necessary. The time stamp value is not based on the current time and so cannot be converted to the current time.

EXAMPLE See the class example.

WINDOW_DEICONIFY

PURPOSE Event type indicating that a top-level window has been deiconified.

SYNTAX `public static final int WINDOW_DEICONIFY`

DESCRIPTION The `target` field contains a reference to the window that was deiconified.

EXAMPLE See the class example.

WINDOW_DESTROY

PURPOSE Event type indicating that the Close button on a top-level window has been clicked.

SYNTAX `public static final int WINDOW_DESTROY`

DESCRIPTION This event is generated when the user clicks the window's Close button. The program should destroy the window if necessary, since the AWT does not automatically destroy the window. The `target` field contains a reference to the window requesting to be destroyed.

EXAMPLE See the class example.

WINDOW_EXPOSE

PURPOSE Event type indicating that a top-level window has been exposed.

SYNTAX `public static final int WINDOW_EXPOSE`

DESCRIPTION A top-level window is exposed if some part of the window had been occluded by another window and is now visible. The `target` field contains a reference to the window that has been exposed.

EXAMPLE See the class example.

WINDOW_ICONIFY

PURPOSE Event type indicating that a top-level window has been iconified.

SYNTAX `public static final int WINDOW_ICONIFY`

DESCRIPTION The `target` field contains a reference to the window that was iconified.

EXAMPLE See the class example.

WINDOW_MOVED

PURPOSE Event type indicating that a top-level window has been moved.

SYNTAX `public static final int WINDOW_MOVED`

DESCRIPTION The `target` field contains a reference to the window that was iconified. The `x` and `y` fields contain the new coordinates of the window.

EXAMPLE See the class example.

x

PURPOSE Contains the *x*-coordinate of the cursor at the time of the event.

SYNTAX `public int x`

DESCRIPTION As an event travels up the component hierarchy, the `x-` and `y-` coordinates are automatically translated to be relative to the bounds of the component currently holding the event. In other words, when a component is delivered an event, the cursor coordinates in the event will be relative to the bounds of that component, rather than to the bounds of the component that created the event (the target). For example, if an event was generated by a button in a panel and the event was handled by the panel, the cursor coordinates in `x` and `y` would be relative to the bounds of the panel, not the bounds of the button.

If the component handling this event is a container with non-zero insets, the cursor coordinates are relative to the container's inset area rather than the container's bounds; see the `Container` class for more details.

EXAMPLE See the class example.

y

PURPOSE Contains the *y*-coordinate of the cursor at the time of the event.

SYNTAX `public int y`

DESCRIPTION As an event travels up the component hierarchy, the `x-` and `y`-coordinates are automatically translated to be relative to the bounds of the component currently holding the event. In other words, when a component is delivered an event, the cursor coordinates in the event will be relative to the bounds of that component, rather than to the bounds of the component that created the event (the target). For example, if an event was generated by a button in a panel and the event was handled by the panel, the cursor coordinates in `x` and `y` would be relative to the bounds of the panel, not the bounds of the button.

If the component handling this event is a container with non-zero insets, the cursor coordinates are relative to the container's inset area rather than the container's bounds; see the `Container` class for more details.

EXAMPLE See the class example.

java.lang
Exception

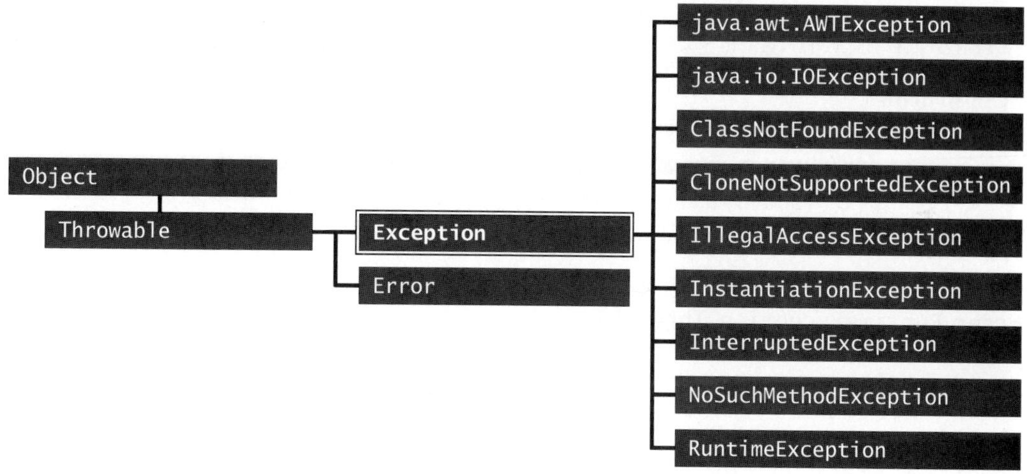

Syntax

```
public class Exception extends Throwable
```

Description

The `Exception` class is the superclass of classes used to represent exceptional conditions. There are two types of exceptional conditions: (1) runtime exceptions thrown by the Java runtime system that are considered unrecoverable and should not be caught and (2) all others. The former is represented by `RuntimeException` and its subclasses and the latter by all other subclasses of `Exception`. This latter category includes exceptions thrown by the Java runtime system that are considered to be nonfatal. Even though they are thrown by the runtime system, these exceptions are not subclasses of `RuntimeException`. This is because they are recoverable by user programs and therefore must be declared in the `throws` clause of a method and caught by using `try/catch` statements.

Any method that throws any instance of `Exception` that is not a `RuntimeException` must declare the exception(s) in its `throws` clause as part of the method's declaration. This is a Java language requirement. Any method that calls this method must either catch the exception(s) by using `try/catch` statements or declare the exception(s) in its own `throws` clause. The Java compiler will generate a compilation error for any code that does not follow these rules.

`RuntimeException` and its subclasses should not be declared in a method's `throws` clause. Nor should they be caught by using `try/catch` statements. These exceptions should be allowed to percolate to the top level of the user's program, where they will be dealt with by the Java runtime system. The system displays to the user executing the faulty program a stack trace of where the `RuntimeException` occurred. User programs should not subclass `RuntimeException` (or its subclasses); these are reserved for the Java runtime system.

MEMBER SUMMARY	
Constructor	
`Exception()`	Constructs an `Exception` object.

See Also

`Error`, `RuntimeException`, `Throwable`.

Example

The following example defines a stack and two exceptions: `StackOverflow` and `Stack-Underflow`. `StackOverflow` is thrown when you attempt to push an item onto a full stack. `StackUnderflow` is thrown when you attempt to pop an item off an empty stack.

```
// attempting to add to stack when it is full
class StackOverflow extends Exception {
};

// attempting to access stack when it is empty
class StackUnderflow extends Exception {
};

// A stack that has a 3 item limit
class ThreeDeep {
    static final int STACK_SIZE = 3;
    private int[] stack_store = new int[STACK_SIZE];
    private int stack_ptr = 0;

    // push item onto stack
    public void push(int item) throws StackOverflow {
        if (stack_ptr >= STACK_SIZE)
            throw new StackOverflow();
        else
            stack_store[stack_ptr++] = item;
    }

    // pop item off top of stack
    public int pop() throws StackUnderflow {
        if (stack_ptr == 0)
            throw new StackUnderflow();
        else
            return (stack_store[--stack_ptr]);
```

```
        }
    }

    ThreeDeep s = new ThreeDeep();
    try {
        s.push(i);
    } catch (StackOverflow e) {
        System.err.println("overflow " + i);
    }
      ...
    try {
        System.out.println("pop " + s.pop());
    } catch (StackUnderflow e) {
        System.err.println("underflow " + e);
    }
```

Exception()

PURPOSE Constructs an `Exception` object.

SYNTAX
```
public Exception()
public Exception(String msg)
```

DESCRIPTION This class has two constructors. The first returns an `Exception` object containing only the class name of the `Exception` object. The second returns an `Exception` object by using the string `msg`, which provides information about the exception in addition to the `Exception` object's class name.

Subclasses of `Exception` not only provide support for these constructors. They also can define their own constructors. In addition, subclasses can define new methods and instance variables that can be used to store state information about the exception, as appropriate.

PARAMETERS

`msg` A string containing information about the exception.

EXAMPLE This example illustrates how an exception `PrinterOutOfPaperException` can be defined to include additional information about the exception. In this case, the exception records the time at which the exception occurred and the number of pages printed so far in a print job, if known.

```
import java.util.Date;

class PrinterOutOfPaperException extends Exception {
    public Date when;
    public int pagecount = 0;
    public PrinterOutOfPaperException() {
        super();
```

```
            when = new Date();
        }
        public PrinterOutOfPaperException(String msg) {
            super(msg);
            when = new Date();
        }
        public PrinterOutOfPaperException(int count) {
            super();
            when = new Date();
            pagecount = count;
        }
    }


    try {
      ...
        throw new PrinterOutOfPaperException();
    } catch (PrinterOutOfPaperException e) {
        System.err.println(e + " since " + e.when);
      ... <wait for paper and continue>
    }

    try {
      ...
        throw new PrinterOutOfPaperException("ATTENTION");
    } catch (PrinterOutOfPaperException e) {
        System.err.println(e + " since " + e.when);
      ... <wait for paper and continue>
    }

    try {
        int i = 0;
      ...
        throw new PrinterOutOfPaperException(i);
    } catch (PrinterOutOfPaperException e) {
        System.err.println(e + " since " + e.when);
        System.err.println(e.pagecount + " pages printed so far");
      ... <wait for paper and continue printing from 'i'>
    }
```

java.io

File

java.lang.Object — File

Syntax

```
public class File
```

Description

The `File` class represents a filename. The filename can be absolute, in which case it is resolved relative to the root directory of the file system. Or it can be relative, in which case it is resolved relative to the current directory in which the Java program is running. The filename is specified in the filename convention of the file system on which the Java program is running.

This class not only manipulates the filename itself. It also provides methods for performing file-related operations that actually interact with the underlying file system. Such operations include creating directories, obtaining the status of the file/directory, renaming the file, and checking permission on the file.

MEMBER SUMMARY

Constructor	
`File()`	Constructs a new instance of `File`.
File Status Methods	
`canRead()`	Determines whether allowed to read this file.
`canWrite()`	Determines whether allowed to write to this file.
`exists()`	Determines whether this file exists.
`getAbsolutePath()`	Generates the absolute (complete) pathname of this file.
`getName()`	Retrieves the filename (no directory) of this file.
`getParent()`	Retrieves the pathname of the parent directory of this file.
`getPath()`	Retrieves the pathname of this file.
`isAbsolute()`	Determines whether the pathname of this file is absolute.
`isDirectory()`	Determines whether this file names a directory.
`isFile()`	Determines whether this file names a regular file (nondirectory).
`lastModified()`	Retrieves the last modification time of this file.
`length()`	Retrieves the size of this file in bytes.

Continued

MEMBER SUMMARY	
File Namespace Methods	
`delete()`	Deletes this file.
`list()`	Lists the files in the directory named by this file using a filter.
`mkdir()`	Creates a directory with the pathname of this file.
`mkdirs()`	Creates all directories in the pathname of this file.
`renameTo()`	Renames this file.
File System Property Fields (Static)	
`pathSeparator`	The operating system's path variable separator string.
`pathSeparatorChar`	The operating system's path variable separator character.
`separator`	The file system's file directory separator string.
`separatorChar`	The file system's file directory separator character.
Object Override Methods	
`equals()`	Compares this object with another object for equality.
`hashCode()`	Computes the hash code for the file.
`toString()`	Generates the string representation for this object.

See Also

`FileInputStream`, `FileOutputStream`.

Example

This example shows the use of methods in the `File` class to print a detailed listing of files in a directory.

```
import java.io.File;
import java.util.Date;

class Ls {
    public static void printOne(File f) {
      if (f.exists()) {
          System.out.print(f.canRead() ? "r" : "-");
          System.out.print(f.canWrite() ? "w" : "-");
          System.out.print(f.isDirectory() ? "d" : "-");
          System.out.print('\t');

          System.out.print(f.length());
          System.out.print('\t');

          System.out.print(new Date(f.lastModified()));
          System.out.print('\t');
```

A B C D E F G H I J K L M N O P Q R S T U V W X Y Z

```
        } else {
            System.out.print("\t\t\t\t\t");
        }
        System.out.println(f.getName());
    }
    public static void main(String[] args) {
        if (args.length != 1) {
            System.err.println("Usage: java Ls <filepath>");
            System.exit(-1);
        }
        File f1 = new File(args[0]);
        String[] ls;
        int i;
        for (ls = f1.list(), i = 0;
             ls != null && i < ls.length;
             printOne(new File(f1, ls[i])), i++);
    }
}
```

canRead()

PURPOSE Determines whether the current execution context is allowed to read this file.

SYNTAX `public boolean canRead()`

DESCRIPTION This method determines whether the current execution context is allowed, by the security manager and the underlying file system, to read this file. It returns `true` if allowed; `false` otherwise.

RETURNS `true` if allowed to read this file; `false` otherwise.

EXCEPTIONS

`SecurityException`

If this file cannot be read for security reasons.

SEE ALSO `SecurityManager.checkRead()`.

EXAMPLE See the class example.

canWrite()

PURPOSE Determines whether the current execution context is allowed to write to this file.

SYNTAX `public boolean canWrite()`

A B C D E F G H I J K L M N O P Q R S T U V W X Y Z

DESCRIPTION	This method determines whether the current execution context is allowed, by the security manager and the underlying file system, to write to this file. It returns `true` if allowed; `false` otherwise.
RETURNS	`true` if allowed to write to this file; `false` otherwise.

EXCEPTIONS

`SecurityException`
If this file cannot be written to for security reasons.

SEE ALSO	`SecurityManager.checkWrite()`.
EXAMPLE	See the class example.

delete()

PURPOSE	Deletes this file.
SYNTAX	`public boolean delete()`
DESCRIPTION	This method deletes this file. It can delete this file only if the current execution context is allowed by the security manager and the underlying file system. Only files can be deleted by this method; directories cannot.
RETURNS	`true` if this file has been successfully deleted; `false` otherwise.

EXCEPTIONS

`SecurityException`
If this file cannot be deleted for security reasons.

SEE ALSO	`SecurityManager.checkDelete()`.
EXAMPLE	This example shows the use of `delete()`, `mkdir()`, and `mkdirs()`. The program creates the specified directory (and any parent directories required) and a subdirectory beneath it. The `delete()` calls at the end of the program always fail because you cannot delete a directory using `delete()`.

```
import java.io.File;

class Mods {
    public static void main(String[] args) {
        if (args.length != 1) {
            System.err.println("Usage: java Mods <newDirPath>");
            System.exit(-1);
        }

        File dir = new File(args[0]);
```

```
        if (dir.exists()) {
                System.out.println((dir.delete() ? "Deleted " :
                                    "Could not delete ") +
                                        dir.getPath());
        }
        if (dir.mkdirs()) {
            System.out.println("Created directory " +
                dir.getAbsolutePath());
            File subdir = new File(dir, "newSub");

            if (subdir.mkdir()) {
                System.out.println("Created subdirectory " +
                                   subdir.getAbsolutePath());
                System.out.println((subdir.delete() ? "Deleted " :
                                    "Could not delete ") +
                                        subdir.getPath());
            }
            else
                System.out.println("Could not create subdirectory " +
                                   subdir.getAbsolutePath());
                System.out.println((dir.delete() ? "Deleted " :
                                "Could not delete ") + dir.getPath());
        } else {
            System.out.println("Could not create directory " +
                               dir.getAbsolutePath());
        }
    }
}
```

equals()

PURPOSE Compares this object with another object for equality.

SYNTAX `public boolean equals(Object obj)`

DESCRIPTION This method determines whether this `File` object has the same path as that of `obj`. It returns `true` if the two paths are equal. It returns `false` if the two are not equal or if `obj` is `null` or is not a `File` object. The path comparison uses string comparison. Consequently, for file systems that support case-insensitive file pathnames, two paths that have characters that are the same but of different cases would not be equal.

PARAMETERS

`obj` The object against which this object will be compared.

RETURNS `true` if `obj` has the same path as this object; `false` otherwise.

OVERRIDES `Object.equals()`.

EXAMPLE See `renameTo()`.

exists()

PURPOSE Determines whether this file exists.

SYNTAX `public boolean exists()`

DESCRIPTION This method determines whether this file exists. The check can be made only if this current execution context is allowed, by the security manager and the underlying file system, to examine this file. It returns `true` if this file exists; `false` otherwise.

RETURNS `true` if this file exists; `false` otherwise.

EXCEPTIONS
`SecurityException`
If this file cannot be examined for security reasons.

SEE ALSO `SecurityManager.checkRead()`.

EXAMPLE See the class example, `delete()`, `getAbsolutePath()`.

File()

PURPOSE Constructs a new `File` object.

SYNTAX
```
public File(String path)
public File(String dirPath, String name)
public File(File dir, String name)
```

DESCRIPTION There are three forms of the constructor for the `File` class. The first creates a new instance of `File` for the file pathname `path`. `path` can be absolute or relative (or even a single-component filename). If it is not an absolute pathname, it is taken to be relative to the current working directory of the program. The second form creates a new instance of `File` using a file directory pathname `dirPath` and a pathname `name` to be taken relative to `dirPath`. `dirPath` and `name` are composed together (using the file directory separator in between) to obtain the path for this new `File` instance. `dirPath` can be an absolute pathname or a relative pathname. The third form is similar to the second, except it takes a `File` object as the directory to which `name` is relative.

PARAMETERS

`dir`	The `File` instance of the directory to which `name` is relative.
`dirPath`	The pathname of the directory to which `name` is relative.
`name`	The file pathname relative to the directory specified (`dirPath` or `dir`).
`path`	The file pathname.

EXAMPLE See the class example, `delete()`, `getAbsolutePath()`, and `renameTo()`.

getAbsolutePath()

PURPOSE Generates the absolute (complete) pathname of this file.

SYNTAX `public String getAbsolutePath()`

DESCRIPTION An *absolute* pathname is a pathname that names a file starting at the root of the file system. Its precise definition is file system-dependent. This method generates the absolute pathname of this file. If this `File` instance was created with an absolute pathname, that pathname is returned. Otherwise, the current working directory of this program is composed with the pathname of this file (using the file directory separator) to generate the absolute pathname.

RETURNS The absolute file pathname of this file.

SEE ALSO `getPath()`, `isAbsolute()`.

EXAMPLE This example shows the `File` methods related to obtaining information about a `File` instance's name. This example prints out the file's absolute path, directory name, and filename and the name components of the file's absolute path.

```
import java.io.File;
import java.util.StringTokenizer;
import java.util.NoSuchElementException;

class Stat {
    public static void stat(File f) {
        if (!f.isAbsolute())
            System.out.println("Absolute Pathname:" +
                               f.getAbsolutePath());

        String parent = f.getParent();
        if (parent == null)
            parent = File.separator;
        System.out.println("Directory name:" + parent);
```

```
            System.out.println("File name:" + f.getName());

            System.out.println("Type: " +
                (f.isDirectory() ? "directory" :
                 (f.isFile() ? "file" : "unknown")));
        }
        public static void components(File f) {
            StringTokenizer parser =
                new StringTokenizer(f.getAbsolutePath(), File.separator);
            System.out.println("There are " + parser.countTokens() +
                                " components in the pathname");
            try {
                while(parser.hasMoreTokens()) {
                    System.out.println(parser.nextToken());
                }
            } catch (NoSuchElementException e) {
                System.err.println(e);
            }
        }
        public static void main(String[] args) {
            if (args.length != 1) {
                System.err.println("Usage: java Stat <filepath>");
                System.exit(-1);
            }
            File f1 = new File(args[0]);

            if(f1.exists()) {
                stat(f1);
                components(f1);
            } else
                System.err.println(f1.getPath() + " does not exists");
        }
    }
```

getName()

PURPOSE Retrieves the filename (no directory) of this file.

SYNTAX `public String getName()`

DESCRIPTION This method returns the last (lowest-level) component of the pathname of this file. This is the name of the file (with no path/directory information).

RETURNS The filename of this file.

SEE ALSO `getParent()`, `getPath()`.

EXAMPLE See `getAbsolutePath()`.

getParent()

PURPOSE Retrieves the pathname of the parent directory of this file.

SYNTAX `public String getParent()`

DESCRIPTION This method retrieves the pathname of the parent directory of this file. This is the pathname of the file, excluding the last (lowest-level) component.

RETURNS The pathname of the parent directory; `null` if none is found.

SEE ALSO `getName()`, `getPath()`.

EXAMPLE See `getAbsolutePath()`.

getPath()

PURPOSE Retrieves the pathname of this file.

SYNTAX `public String getPath()`

DESCRIPTION The pathname of this file is the path with which this instance of `File` was created.

RETURNS The pathname of this file.

SEE ALSO `File()`, `getAbsolutePath()`, `getName()`.

EXAMPLE See `delete()`, `getAbsolutePath()`, and `renameTo()`.

hashCode()

PURPOSE Computes the hash code for this file.

SYNTAX `public int hashCode()`

DESCRIPTION The hash code for a `File` object is calculated using the character values of its path. Two `Files` with the same path have the same hash code. However, two `Files` with the same hash code may not necessarily have the same path. This method returns the hash code for this `File` object.

RETURNS The hash code of this file.

OVERRIDES `Object.hashCode()`.

A B C D E F G H I J K L M N O P Q R S T U V W X Y Z

SEE ALSO `Hashtable`.

EXAMPLE See `renameTo()`.

isAbsolute()

PURPOSE Determines whether the pathname of this file is absolute.

SYNTAX `public native boolean isAbsolute()`

DESCRIPTION An *absolute* pathname is a pathname that names a file starting at the root of the file system. Its precise definition is file system-dependent. This method determines whether the pathname of this file is an absolute pathname.

RETURNS `true` if the pathname of this file is absolute; `false` otherwise.

SEE ALSO `getAbsolute()`, `getPath()`.

EXAMPLE See `getAbsolutePath()`.

isDirectory()

PURPOSE Determines whether this file names a directory.

SYNTAX `public boolean isDirectory()`

DESCRIPTION This method determines whether this file names a directory. This check can be made only if the current execution context is allowed, by the security manager and the underlying file system, to read this file.

RETURNS `true` if this file names a directory; `false` otherwise.

EXCEPTIONS

`SecurityException`
If this file cannot be examined due to security reasons.

SEE ALSO `isFile()`, `SecurityManager.checkRead()`.

EXAMPLE See the class example `getAbsolutePath()`.

isFile()

PURPOSE Determines whether this file names a regular file (nondirectory).

SYNTAX `public boolean isFile()`

DESCRIPTION This method determines whether this file names a regular file (i.e., not a directory). This check can be made only if the current execution context is allowed, by the security manager and the underlying file system, to read this file.

RETURNS `true` if this file names a regular file; `false` otherwise.

EXCEPTIONS
`SecurityException`
If this file cannot be examined due to security reasons.

SEE ALSO `isDirectory()`, `SecurityManager.checkRead()`.

EXAMPLE See `getAbsolutePath()`.

lastModified()

PURPOSE Retrieves the last modification time of this file.

SYNTAX `public long lastModified()`

DESCRIPTION This method retrieves the last modification time of this file. This method can be invoked only if the current execution context is allowed, by the security manager and the underlying file system, to read this file.

RETURNS The last modification time (in number of milliseconds since epoch).

EXCEPTIONS
`SecurityException`
If this file cannot be examined due to security reasons.

SEE ALSO `Date`, `SecurityManager.checkRead()`.

EXAMPLE See the class example.

length()

PURPOSE Retrieves the size of this file in bytes.

SYNTAX `public long length()`

DESCRIPTION This method retrieves the size of this file in bytes. It can be invoked only if the current execution context is allowed, by the security manager and the underlying file system, to read this file.

RETURNS The number of bytes in this file.

EXCEPTIONS

`SecurityException`
If this file cannot be examined due to security reasons.

SEE ALSO `SecurityManager.checkRead()`.

EXAMPLE See the class example.

list()

PURPOSE Lists the files in the directory named by this file by using a filter.

SYNTAX
```
public String[] list()
public String[] list(FilenameFilter filter)
```

DESCRIPTION This method lists the files in the directory named by this file. If a filename filter `filter` is supplied, the names returned are the subset of files found in the directory that satisfy `filter`. If no filter is supplied, the names of all the files found in this directory are returned.

This method can be invoked only if the current execution context is allowed, by the security manager and the underlying file system, to read this file.

PARAMETERS

`filter` The filter used to select filenames.

RETURNS The filter-selected files in the directory named by this file.

EXCEPTIONS

`SecurityException`
If this file cannot be examined due to security reasons.

SEE ALSO `FilenameFilter`, `SecurityManager.checkRead()`.

EXAMPLE See the class example of `File` and of `FilenameFilter`.

mkdir()

PURPOSE Creates a directory with the pathname of this file.

SYNTAX
```
public boolean mkdir()
```

DESCRIPTION This method creates a directory with the pathname of this file. This method can be executed only if this current execution context is allowed, by the security manager and the underlying file system, to write to (create) this directory. This method returns `true` if the directory was created successfully. It returns `false` otherwise or if the directory already exists.

RETURNS `true` if the directory was created successfully; `false` otherwise.

EXCEPTIONS

`SecurityException`
If this directory could not be created due to security reasons.

SEE ALSO `mkdirs()`, `SecurityManager.checkWrite()`.

EXAMPLE See `delete()`.

mkdirs()

PURPOSE Creates all directories in the pathname of this file.

SYNTAX `public boolean mkdirs()`

DESCRIPTION This method creates all directories in the pathname of this file, including this file itself. It returns `true` if all the directories were successfully created. If any of the intermediate directories already exist, `mkdirs()` will skip it and attempt the next directory below. If the terminal directory itself exists, this method returns `false`.

This method can be executed only if this current execution context is allowed, by the security manager and the underlying file system, to write to (create) this directory.

RETURNS `true` if all directories in this path have been successfully created (or already exist); `false` otherwise.

SEE ALSO `mkdir()`, `SecurityManager.checkWrite()`.

EXAMPLE See `delete()`.

pathSeparator

PURPOSE The operating system's path variable separator string.

SYNTAX `public static final String pathSeparator`

DESCRIPTION *Path variables* are used by operating systems and programs to specify an ordered search path. For example, Java defines a CLASSPATH variable that specifies the search order for Java classes for the default Java class loader. Each item in the search path is separated by a *path variable separator* character. This character varies depending on the operating system. On UNIX, the separator is the colon character (':'). On Windows95, it is the semicolon character (';').

The `pathSeparator` field represents the operating system's path variable separator character as a string.

SEE ALSO `pathSeparatorChar`.

EXAMPLE This method parses a path variable string into its component.

```
import java.io.File;
import java.util.StringTokenizer;
import java.util.NoSuchElementException;

class ParsePath {
    public static void main(String[] args) {
        if (args.length != 1) {
            System.err.println("Usage: java ParsePath
                                   <path_variable>");
            System.exit(-1);
        }
        StringTokenizer parser =
            new StringTokenizer(args[0], File.pathSeparator);
        System.out.println("\nInput: " + args[0]);
        System.out.println("There are " + parser.countTokens() +
                               " entries in the path");
        try {
            while(parser.hasMoreTokens()) {
                System.out.println(parser.nextToken());
            }
        } catch (NoSuchElementException e) {
            System.err.println(e);
        }
    }
}
```

pathSeparatorChar

PURPOSE The operating system's path variable separator character.

SYNTAX `public static final char pathSeparatorChar`

SEE ALSO `pathSeparator`.

EXAMPLE Usage of this field is similar to that of `pathSeparator`.

renameTo()

PURPOSE
Renames this file.

SYNTAX
`public boolean renameTo(File dest)`

DESCRIPTION
This method renames this file to the new filename `dest`. Successful renaming of this file does not affect the filename of this instance of `File`. For example, `getPath()` would still return the same string that it did before `renameTo()` was called.

This method can be executed only if this current execution context is allowed, by the security manager and the underlying file system, to rename this file to `dest`.

PARAMETERS

`dest` The new filename.

RETURNS
`true` if this file has been successfully renamed to `dest`; `false` otherwise.

EXCEPTIONS

`SecurityException`
If this file cannot be renamed to `dest` for security reasons.

SEE ALSO
`SecurityManager.checkWrite()`.

EXAMPLE
This example renames a file.

```
import java.io.File;

class Mv {
    public static void main(String[] args) {
        if (args.length != 2) {
            System.err.println("Usage: java Mv <file1> <file2>");
            System.exit(-1);
        }
        File f1 = new File(args[0]);
        File f2 = new File(args[1]);

        if (f1.equals(f2)) {
            System.err.println("Cannot rename a file to itself");
            System.exit(-1);
        }
        System.out.println(f1.getPath() +
           (f1.renameTo(f2) ? " renamed to " :
               " could not be renamed to ") +
                           f2.getPath());
```

```
            // check f1 and f2: their path and hash codes remain unchanged
            System.out.println("f1: " + f1.toString() + " " +
                f1.hashCode());
            System.out.println("f2: " + f2.toString() + " " +
                f2.hashCode());
        }
    }
```

separator

PURPOSE The file system's file directory separator string.

SYNTAX `public static final String separator`

DESCRIPTION Each directory name in a file pathname is separated by a *directory separator* character. This character is file system-dependent. On UNIX, the character is the forward slash character ('/'). On Windows95, it is the backward slash character ('\').

The `separator` field contains the directory separator character in a string.

SEE ALSO `separatorChar`.

EXAMPLE See `getAbsolutePath()`.

separatorChar

PURPOSE The file system's file directory separator character.

SYNTAX `public static final char separatorChar`

SEE ALSO `separator`.

EXAMPLE This usage of this field is similar to that of `separator`; see `getAbsolutePath()` for an example of `separator`.

toString()

PURPOSE Generates the string representation for this file.

SYNTAX `public String toString()`

DESCRIPTION	The string representation of a `File` object is the file pathname with which it was created. `toString()` returns this string representation.
RETURNS	The string representation of this file.
OVERRIDES	`Object.toString()`.
SEE ALSO	`File()`, `getPath()`.
EXAMPLE	See `renameTo()`.

java.io
FileDescriptor

java.lang.Object — FileDescriptor

Syntax

```
public final class FileDescriptor
```

Description

A *file descriptor* is a compact representation of information required to access and manipulate an open file or device (such as a socket). When you open a file, you get back a file descriptor for it. Thereafter, you use this file descriptor for reading from or writing to the file. The operations allowed on the file descriptor are determined by the mode with which you have opened the file. For example, if you opened a file for reading, then the file descriptor you get back will allow read operations on the file.

The `FileDescriptor` class is used to represent a file descriptor.

In the Java class libraries, you typically need not manipulate file descriptors directly. Java defines input/output stream classes for files and sockets that use file descriptors internally. Therefore, instead of using file descriptors directly, you typically use file/socket stream references to perform IO operations. However, for those special cases in which you want to use file descriptors directly, these IO classes provide constructors that accept a file descriptor as an argument.

Standard Input/Output

There are three open file descriptors associated with the three standard open files: input, output, and error output. Standard input is used by the program to read data input by the user who is running the program. Standard output is used by the program to print text output for display to the user. Standard error output is used by the program to print error messages to the user. The `FileDescriptor` class defines three fields that correspond to each of these standard descriptors: `in`, `out`, and `err`. You can use these fields directly when doing standard IO. However, you are advised to use the corresponding IO streams in `System` (`System.in`, `System.out`, and `System.err`), which provide a much easier-to-use abstraction for doing standard IO.

MEMBER SUMMARY	
Standard IO Fields	
`err`	File descriptor for standard error output.
`in`	File descriptor for standard input.
`out`	File descriptor for standard output.
File Descriptor Method	
`valid()`	Determines whether this file descriptor is valid.

See Also

`FileInputStream`, `FileOutputStream`, `RandomAccessFile`, `SocketImpl`, `System.err`, `System.in`, `System.out`.

Example

This example shows how standard `in`, `out`, and `err` can be accessed using file descriptors instead of `System.in`, `System.out`, and `System.err`.

```
import java.io.*;

class Main {
    public static void main(String[] args) {
        FileOutputStream stderr =
            new FileOutputStream(FileDescriptor.err);
        FileOutputStream stdout =
            new FileOutputStream(FileDescriptor.out);
        FileInputStream stdin =
            new FileInputStream(FileDescriptor.in);
        try {
            StringBuffer sb = new StringBuffer();
            int c;
            while ((c=stdin.read()) > -1) {
                if (c == '\n' || c == '\r')
                    break;
                sb.append((char)c);
            }
            // print to standard out
            byte[] buf = new byte[sb.length()];
            sb.toString().getBytes(0, buf.length, buf, 0);
            stdout.write(buf);
            stdout.write('\n');
            stdout.flush();
        } catch (IOException e) {
            e.printStackTrace();
        }
    }
}
```

A B C D E F G H I J K L M N O P Q R S T U V W X Y Z

in

PURPOSE File descriptor for standard input.

SYNTAX `public static final FileDescriptor in`

SEE ALSO `System.in`.

EXAMPLE See the class example.

out

PURPOSE File descriptor for standard output.

SYNTAX `public static final FileDescriptor out`

SEE ALSO `System.out`.

EXAMPLE See the class example.

err

PURPOSE File descriptor for standard error output.

SYNTAX `public static final FileDescriptor err`

SEE ALSO `System.err`.

EXAMPLE See the class example.

valid()

PURPOSE Determines whether this file descriptor is valid.

SYNTAX `public native boolean valid()`

DESCRIPTION A file descriptor is associated with an open file. A file descriptor is valid if it has not been closed. This method determines whether this file descriptor is valid.

RETURNS `true` if the file descriptor is valid; `false` otherwise.

EXAMPLE

```
import java.io.FileInputStream;
import java.io.IOException;
import java.io.FileDescriptor;

class Main {
    public static void main(String[] args) {
        if (args.length != 1) {
            System.err.println("Usage: java Main <input_file>");
            System.exit(-1);
        }
        try {
            FileInputStream in = new FileInputStream(args[0]);
            if (in.getFD().valid())
                System.out.println("got valid file descriptor");
            // ...

            in.close();
        } catch (IOException e) {
            e.printStackTrace();
        }
    }
}
```

A B C D E F G H I J K L M N O P Q R S T U V W X Y Z

FileDialog

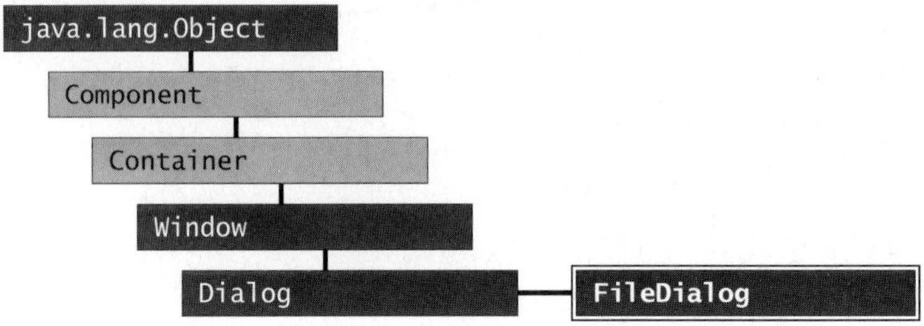

Syntax

```
public class FileDialog extends Dialog
```

Description

The `FileDialog` component displays a dialog for selecting a file in the file system. The file dialog can be used to either load or save a file. It is a modal dialog and blocks the calling thread until the user has chosen a file.

The Mode Property

There are two file dialog modes: *load* and *save*. A load file dialog is used to select an existing file in the file system. A save file dialog is used either to select an existing file or to select an existing directory and then to allow the user to name a new file. The mode is set at the time a file dialog instance is created and cannot be changed later.

The Directory and File Property

The *directory property* of a file dialog indicates the directory the file dialog is current displaying. The *file property* indicates either the file that is currently selected in the file dialog or the text in the filename entry text field.

These properties can be set before the file dialog is displayed and queried after the dialog is closed.

The Filter Property

The *filter property* controls which files are displayed in the file dialog. The filter is a class that implements the `FilenameFilter` interface that defines the `accept()` method. The `accept()` method is passed a directory and filename. It returns `true` if the file should be displayed and `false` otherwise.

A B C D E F G H I J K L M N O P Q R S T U V W X Y Z

MEMBER SUMMARY	
Constructor	
`FileDialog()`	Constructs a new `FileDialog` instance.
File Dialog Types	
`LOAD`	The file dialog mode that specifies a load file dialog.
`SAVE`	The file dialog mode that specifies a save file dialog.
Property Methods	
`getDirectory()`	Retrieves the file dialog's directory property.
`getFile()`	Retrieves the file dialog's file property.
`getFilenameFilter()`	Retrieves the filename filter object.
`getMode()`	Retrieves the file dialog's mode.
`setDirectory()`	Sets the file dialog's directory property.
`setFile()`	Sets the file dialog's file property.
`setFilenameFilter()`	Sets the file dialog's filename filter.
Peer Method	
`addNotify()`	Creates the file dialog's peer hierarchy.
Debugging Method	
`paramString()`	Generates a string representing the file dialog's state.

See Also

`FilenameFilter`.

Example

This example creates a frame with two buttons (Figure 88). One button creates a load file dialog (Figure 89), while the other creates a save file dialog (Figure 90). In addition, the frame contains three text fields—directory, file, and filter—for showing and changing the current values of the file dialog's properties. Just before the file is displayed, the directory and file properties are initialized to the values in the respective text fields. After a file has been selected and the file dialog is closed, the two text fields are updated with the values in the dialog.

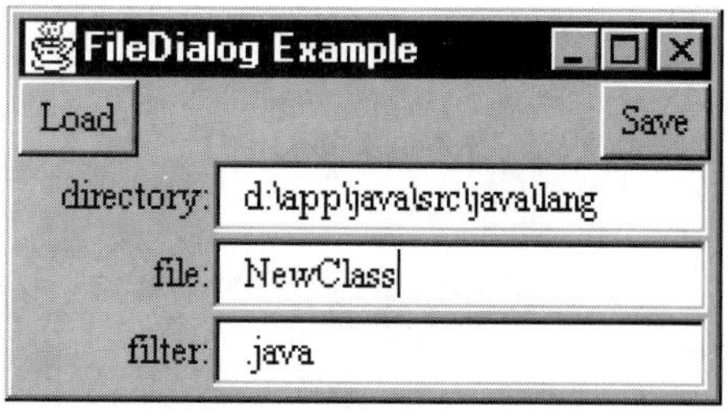

FIGURE 88 `FileDialog`: Control Panel

The file filter is implemented by the `accept()` method. It returns `true` if the file dialog mode is `LOAD` and the filename suffix matches the contents of the filter text field. If the file dialog mode is `SAVE`, `accept()` always returns `true`.

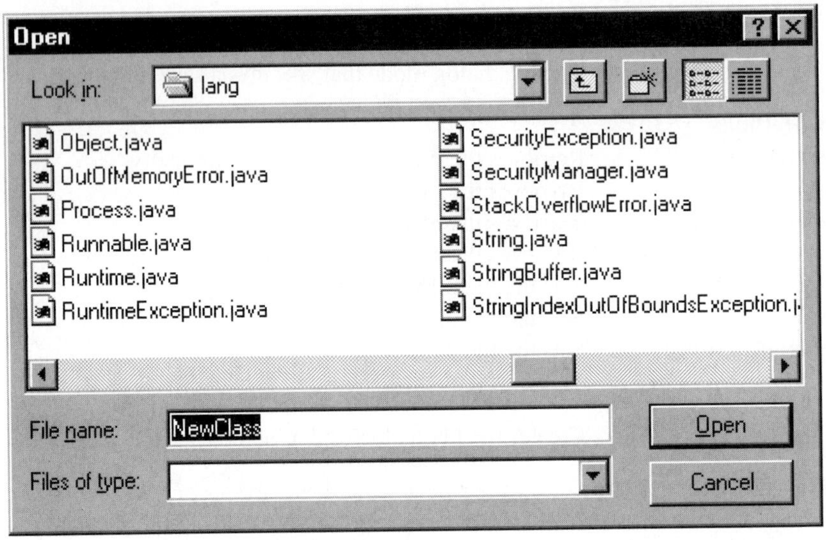

FIGURE 89 A Load File Dialog

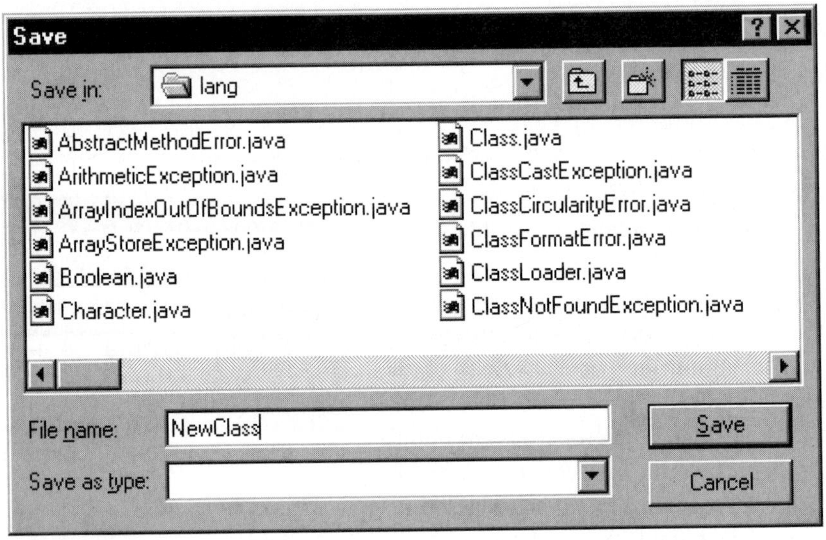

FIGURE 90 A Save File Dialog

```
import java.awt.*;
import java.io.*;
class Main extends Frame implements FilenameFilter {
    FileDialog fd;
    TextField tfDirectory = new TextField();
    TextField tfFile = new TextField();
    TextField tfFilter = new TextField();

    Main() {
        super("FileDialog Example");
        add("West", new Button("Load"));
        add("East", new Button("Save"));

        Panel p = new Panel();
        p.setLayout(new GridBagLayout());
        addRow(p, new Label("directory:", Label.RIGHT), tfDirectory);
        addRow(p, new Label("file:", Label.RIGHT), tfFile);
        addRow(p, new Label("filter:", Label.RIGHT), tfFilter);

        add("South", p);
        pack();
        show();
    }

    // Adds a row in a gridbag layout where the c2 is stretchy
    // and c1 is not.
    void addRow(Container cont, Component c1, Component c2) {
        GridBagLayout gbl = (GridBagLayout)cont.getLayout();
        GridBagConstraints c = new GridBagConstraints();
        Component comp;

        c.fill = GridBagConstraints.BOTH;
        cont.add(c1);
        gbl.setConstraints(c1, c);

        c.gridwidth = GridBagConstraints.REMAINDER;
        c.weightx = 1.0;
        cont.add(c2);
        gbl.setConstraints(c2, c);
    }

    public boolean accept(File dir, String name) {
        if (fd.getMode() == FileDialog.LOAD) {
            return name.lastIndexOf(tfFilter.getText()) > 0;
        }
        return true;
    }

    public boolean action(Event evt, Object what) {
        boolean load = "Load".equals(what);

        if (load || "Save".equals(what)) {
            FileDialog fd = new FileDialog(this, null,
                load ? FileDialog.LOAD : FileDialog.SAVE);
```

A B C D E F G H I J K L M N O P Q R S T U V W X Y Z

```
                fd.setDirectory(tfDirectory.getText());
                fd.setFile(tfFile.getText());
                fd.setFilenameFilter(this);
                fd.show();
                tfDirectory.setText(fd.getDirectory());
                tfFile.setText(fd.getFile());

                // Filter must be the same
                if (fd.getFilenameFilter() != this) {
                    throw new RuntimeException("Internal error");
                }
                return true;
            }
            return false;
        }

        static public void main(String[] args) {
            new Main();
        }

    }
```

addNotify()

PURPOSE Creates the file dialog's peer hierarchy.

SYNTAX `public synchronized void addNotify()`

DESCRIPTION This method creates the file dialog's peer hierarchy, if necessary. The file dialog's peer is created by calling the `Toolkit.createFileDialog()` method.

OVERRIDES `Dialog.addNotify()`.

SEE ALSO `Component`, `Toolkit`.

FileDialog()

PURPOSE Constructs a new `FileDialog` instance.

SYNTAX `public FileDialog(Frame parent, String title)`
`public FileDialog(Frame parent, String title, int mode)`

DESCRIPTION These two forms of the constructor create a new invisible `FileDialog` instance with the parent `parent`, title `title`, and file dialog mode `mode`. If `mode` is not specified, it defaults to `LOAD`. The title can be `null`, in which case it defaults to "`Open`" for a load file dialog and "`Save`" for a save file dialog.

By default, all the properties of the file dialog—directory, file, and filter—are set to `null`.

PARAMETERS

`mode`	An integer specifying the file dialog mode.
`parent`	The file dialog's parent. It can be `null`.
`title`	The string specifying the title of the file dialog. If `null`, it defaults to either "`Open`" or "`Save`", depending on the mode.

SEE ALSO `LOAD`, `SAVE`.

EXAMPLE See the class example.

getDirectory()

PURPOSE Retrieves the file dialog's directory property.

SYNTAX `public String getDirectory()`

DESCRIPTION This method should not be called while the dialog is visible.

RETURNS The non-`null` directory of the file dialog.

SEE ALSO `setDirectory()`.

EXAMPLE See the class example.

getFile()

PURPOSE Retrieves the file dialog's file property.

SYNTAX `public String getFile()`

DESCRIPTION This method should not be called while the dialog is visible.

RETURNS The file property. A return value of `null` indicates that no file was selected.

SEE ALSO `setFile()`.

EXAMPLE See the class example.

getFilenameFilter()

PURPOSE Retrieves the filename filter object.

SYNTAX `public FilenameFilter getFilenameFilter()`

RETURNS The object that is implementing the filename filter. May be `null`.

SEE ALSO `FilenameFilter`, `setFilenameFilter()`.

EXAMPLE See the class example.

getMode()

PURPOSE Retrieves the file dialog's mode.

SYNTAX `public int getMode()`

RETURNS An integer indicating the file dialog's mode, which can be either `LOAD` or `SAVE`.

SEE ALSO `LOAD`, `SAVE`.

EXAMPLE See the class example.

LOAD

PURPOSE The file dialog mode that specifies a load file dialog.

SYNTAX `public static final int LOAD`

DESCRIPTION This integer constant is used to specify a load file dialog when a file dialog is created.

EXAMPLE See the class example.

paramString()

PURPOSE Generates a string representing the file dialog's state.

SYNTAX `protected String paramString()`

DESCRIPTION This method returns a string representing the file dialog, including the selected item. A subclass of this class should override this method and return a concatenation of its state with the results of `super.paramString()`. This method is called by the `Object.toString()` method and is typically used for debugging.

RETURNS A non-`null` string representing the file dialog's state.

OVERRIDES `Dialog.paramString()`.

SEE ALSO `Object.toString()`.

EXAMPLE See `Component.paramString()`.

SAVE

PURPOSE The file dialog mode that specifies a save file dialog.

SYNTAX `public static final int SAVE`

DESCRIPTION This integer constant is used to specify a save file dialog when a file dialog is created.

EXAMPLE See the class example.

setDirectory()

PURPOSE Sets the file dialog's directory property.

SYNTAX `public void setDirectory(String dir)`

DESCRIPTION If `dir` is `null` or specifies an invalid directory, no exception is raised. The behavior of the file dialog in this case depends on the platform, but typically some default directory is displayed.

This method should be called *before* the file dialog is made visible. It should not be called when the file dialog is visible.

PARAMETERS

`dir` The string specifying the directory to display in the file dialog. May be `null`.

EXAMPLE See the class example.

setFile()

PURPOSE Sets the file dialog's file property.

SYNTAX `public void setFile(String file)`

DESCRIPTION When the file dialog is displayed, its filename text field contains the string `file`. If the file dialog's current directory has a file with the name `file`, that file will be selected. If `file` is `null`, it defaults to "".

This method should be called *before* the file dialog is made visible. It should not be called when the file dialog is visible.

PARAMETERS

`file` The string specifying the initial value of the filename text field in the file dialog. May be `null`.

EXAMPLE See the class example.

setFilenameFilter()

PURPOSE Sets the file dialog's filename filter.

SYNTAX `public void setFilenameFilter(FilenameFilter filter)`

DESCRIPTION This method installs `filter` as the file dialog's filename filter. The file dialog will display only files whose names are accepted by the filename filter. If `filter` is `null`, the file dialog displays all files.

PARAMETERS

`filter` The possibly `null` filename filter for the file dialog.

SEE ALSO `FilenameFilter`.

EXAMPLE See the class example.

FileDialogPeer

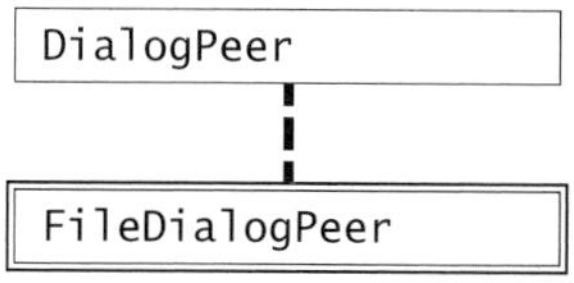

Syntax

```
public interface FileDialogPeer extends DialogPeer
```

Description

The file dialog component (see the `FileDialog` class) in the Abstract Windowing Toolkit (AWT) uses the platform's native implementation of a file dialog box. So that the AWT file dialog box behaves the same on all platforms, the file dialog box is assigned a peer, whose task is to translate the behavior of the platform's native file dialog box to the behavior of the AWT file dialog box.

AWT programmers normally do not directly use peer classes and interfaces. Instead they deal with AWT components in the `java.awt` package. These in turn automatically manage their peers. Only someone who is porting the AWT to another platform should be concerned with the peer classes and interfaces. Consequently, most peer documentation refers to `java.awt` counterparts.

See `Component` and `Toolkit` for additional information about component peers.

MEMBER SUMMARY	
Peer Methods	
`setDirectory()`	Sets the file dialog's directory property.
`setFile()`	Sets the file dialog's file property.
`setFilenameFilter()`	Sets the file dialog's filename filter.

See Also

`Component`, `FileDialog`, `Toolkit`.

B C D E F G H I J K L M N O P Q R S T U V W X Y Z

setDirectory()

PURPOSE Sets the file dialog's directory property.

SYNTAX `void setDirectory(String dir)`

PARAMETERS

`dir` The string specifying the directory to display in the file dialog.

SEE ALSO `FileDialog.setDirectory()`.

setFile()

PURPOSE Sets the file dialog's file property.

SYNTAX `void setFile(String file)`

PARAMETERS

`file` The string specifying the initial value of the filename text field in the file dialog.

SEE ALSO `FileDialog.setFile()`.

setFilenameFilter()

PURPOSE Sets the file dialog's filename filter.

SYNTAX `void setFilenameFilter(FilenameFilter filter)`

PARAMETERS

`filter` The possibly `null` filename filter for the file dialog.

SEE ALSO `FileDialog.setFilenameFilter()`.

FileInputStream

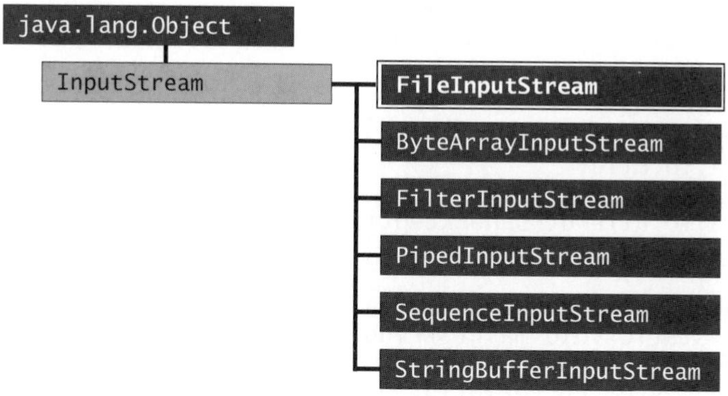

Syntax

```
public class FileInputStream extends InputStream
```

Description

The `FileInputStream` class provides methods for reading input from a file (Figure 91).

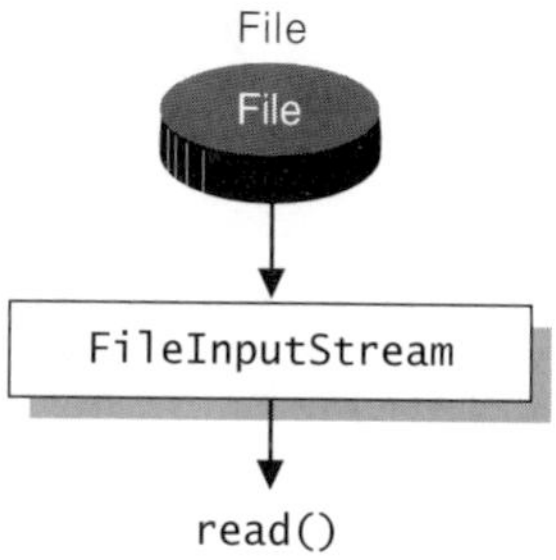

FIGURE 91 **`FileInputStream`**

MEMBER SUMMARY	
Constructor	
`FileInputStream()`	Constructs a new file input stream.
Input Methods	
`available()`	Determines the number of bytes that can be read without blocking.
`read()`	Reads bytes from this file input stream.
`skip()`	Skips bytes from this file input stream.
Methods for Closing the Stream	
`close()`	Closes this file input stream.
`finalize()`	Closes this file input stream when it is garbage collected.
File Descriptor Method	
`getFD()`	Retrieves the file descriptor used by this file input stream.

available()

See Also

File, FileDescriptor, FileOutputStream, InputStream.

Example

This example shows the use of a file input stream to read in a file and print out its contents, with any whitespace characters removed.

```
import java.io.FileInputStream;
import java.io.File;
import java.io.IOException;
import java.io.FileNotFoundException;

class Main {
    // read a file and print out all the non-spaces
    public static void main(String[] args) {
        if (args.length != 1) {
            System.err.println("Usage: java Main <input_file>");
            System.exit(-1);
        }
        File file = new File(args[0]);
        try {
            FileInputStream in = new FileInputStream(file);
            int c;

            while ((c=in.read()) > -1) {
                if (!Character.isSpace((char)c))
                    System.out.print((char)c);
            }
            in.close();
            System.out.flush();
        } catch (FileNotFoundException e) {
            System.err.println(file + " is not found");
        } catch (IOException e) {
            e.printStackTrace();
        }
    }
}
```

available()

PURPOSE Determines the number of bytes that can be read without blocking.

SYNTAX `public native int available() throws IOException`

DESCRIPTION This method returns the number of bytes that can be read from this file input stream without blocking. When this file input stream is first opened, this num-

A B C D E F G H I J K L M N O P Q R S T U V W X Y Z

ber equals the number of bytes in the file. As bytes are read from this stream, this number is decremented accordingly.

RETURNS The number of bytes that can be read without blocking.

EXCEPTIONS

`IOException` If an IO error occurred.

OVERRIDES `InputStream.available()`.

EXAMPLE This example demonstrates the use of `available()` and `skip()`. It opens a file and uses `available()` to determine the number of bytes in the file and then skips to the end of the file.

```
import java.io.FileInputStream;
import java.io.IOException;
import java.io.FileNotFoundException;

class Skip {
    public static void main(String[] args) {
        if (args.length != 1) {
            System.err.println("Usage: java Skip <input_file>");
            System.exit(-1);
        }
        try {
            FileInputStream in = new FileInputStream(args[0]);
            // create reference to same file
            FileInputStream in2 = new FileInputStream(in.getFD());
            int avail = in2.available();        // size of file

            System.out.print(args[0] + ": " + avail + " bytes");

            // skip to end of file
            System.out.println("; skipped " + in2.skip(avail) +
                " bytes");

            // should have nothing left in file for reading
            int c;
            while ((c=in.read()) > -1)
                System.out.print((char)c);

            in2.close();        // closes both in2 and in
            System.out.flush();
        } catch (FileNotFoundException e) {
            System.err.println(args[0] + " is not found");
        } catch (IOException e) {
            e.printStackTrace();
        }
    }
}
```

A B C D E F G H I J K L M N O P Q R S T U V W X Y Z

close()

PURPOSE Closes this file input stream.

SYNTAX

```
public native void close() throws IOException
```

DESCRIPTION This method closes this file input stream. It releases any resources, such as file descriptors, used by this file input stream. If the file has already been closed, this method does not do anything.

EXCEPTIONS

`IOException` If an IO error occurred.

OVERRIDES `InputStream.close()`.

EXAMPLE See `available()`.

FileInputStream()

PURPOSE Constructs a new file input stream.

SYNTAX

```
public FileInputStream(String filename) throws
    FileNotFoundException

public FileInputStream(File file) throws FileNotFoundException
public FileInputStream(FileDescriptor fd)
```

DESCRIPTION There are three forms of this constructor for `FileInputStream`. The first creates a file input stream for the file with name `filename`. `filename` is a platform-dependent name of the file. It can be an absolute or a relative pathname of the file. If absolute, it is resolved relative to the root of the file system. If relative, it is resolved relative to the current directory in which the Java program was started. The second form creates a file input stream for the file identified by the `File` object `file`. The third form creates a file input stream using the opened file descriptor `fd`.

The file input stream can be created only if the current execution context is allowed, by the security manager and the underlying file system, to read the specified file.

PARAMETERS

`fd` The opened file descriptor of the file.
`file` The `File` object of the file.
`filename` The string name of the file.

EXCEPTIONS

`FileNotFoundException`
If the file is not found.

`SecurityException`
If the file cannot be read due to security reasons.

SEE ALSO `File`, `FileDescriptor`, `SecurityManager.checkRead()`.

EXAMPLE See the class example, `available()`.

finalize()

PURPOSE Closes this file input stream when it is garbage collected.

SYNTAX `protected void finalize() throws IOException`

DESCRIPTION This method ensures that this file input stream is closed when it is garbage collected.

OVERRIDES `Object.finalize()`.

SEE ALSO `close()`, `System.gc()`, `System.runFinalization()`.

EXAMPLE This example shows the implementation of `FileInputStream.finalize()`.

```
protected void finalize() throws IOException {
    if (fd != null) close();
}
```

getFD()

PURPOSE Retrieves the file descriptor used by this file input stream.

SYNTAX `public final FileDescriptor getFD() throws IOException`

RETURNS The (non-`null`) file descriptor used by this file input stream.

EXCEPTIONS

`IOException` If the file has already been closed and consequently no longer has a file descriptor.

SEE ALSO `FileDescriptor`.

EXAMPLE See `available()`.

read()

PURPOSE Reads bytes from this file input stream.

SYNTAX
```
public native int read() throws IOException
public int read(byte[] buffer) throws IOException
public int read(byte[] buffer, int offset, int count) throws
    IOException
```

DESCRIPTION The three forms of this method read bytes from this file input stream. The first reads a single byte (8 bits) from this file input stream and returns it as a 32-bit `int`. The first three bytes of the `int` are not used. `read()` blocks until a byte is available for reading from this input stream. If end-of-file is reached on this stream, `read()` returns `-1`.

The second and third forms read bytes from this file input stream and store the bytes read into the byte array `buffer`. If `count` is specified, it reads at most `count` number of bytes from this stream; otherwise it reads at most `buffer.length` number of bytes. If `offset` is specified, `read()` stores the bytes read in `buffer` starting at `offset`; otherwise, the bytes are stored starting at index `0`. `read()` returns the number of bytes actually read from this stream. If end-of-file is reached on this stream before any bytes are read, `read()` returns `-1`.

PARAMETERS

`buffer`	The byte array into which the data read is stored.
`count`	The maximum number of bytes to read.
`offset`	The index in `buffer` at which to start placing the data.

RETURNS The first form returns the byte read; The second and third forms return the actual number of bytes read. All forms return `-1` if end-of-file has been reached before any bytes have been read.

EXCEPTIONS

`IOException` If an IO error occurred while attempting to read.

OVERRIDES `InputStream.read()`.

SEE ALSO `skip()`.

EXAMPLE See the class example.

A B C D E F G H I J K L M N O P Q R S T U V W X Y Z

skip()

PURPOSE Skips bytes from this file input stream.

SYNTAX `public native long skip(long count) throws IOException`

DESCRIPTION This method skips `count` number of bytes from this file input stream. Bytes that are skipped will not be returned in subsequent `read()` calls. `skip()` returns the actual number of bytes skipped.

PARAMETERS

`count` The number of bytes to be skipped.

RETURNS The actual number of bytes skipped.

EXCEPTIONS

`IOException` If an IO error occurred while attempting to read.

OVERRIDES `InputStream.skip()`.

EXAMPLE See `available()`.

A B C D E F G H I J K L M N O P Q R S T U V W X Y Z

java.io

FilenameFilter

```
FilenameFilter
```

Syntax

`public interface FilenameFilter`

Description

Given a list of filenames, you can use a *filename filter* to obtain a subset of those filenames. The filename filter defines the properties that a filename must have in order to pass the filter. For example, a filename filter might be one that only accepts filenames with a `.DOC` extension. The `FilenameFilter` interface is used for creating filename filters.

MEMBER SUMMARY	
Filter Method	
`accept()`	Determines whether a filename passes this filename filter.

See Also

`File`.

Example

This example defines a filename filter that accepts only files with the `.java` file extension.

```
import java.io.FilenameFilter;
import java.io.File;

class JavaSrcFilter implements FilenameFilter {
    public boolean accept(File dir, String name) {
        return (name.endsWith(".java"));
    }
}

class Main {
    public static void main (String[] args) {
        String dir = ".";
        if (args.length == 1)
            dir = args[0];
```

```
        File f1 = new File(dir);
        int i;
        String[] ls;
        FilenameFilter filter = new JavaSrcFilter();
        System.out.println("Java Source Files: " );
        for (ls = f1.list(filter), i = 0;
             ls != null && i < ls.length;
             System.out.println("\t" + ls[i++]));
    }
}
```

accept()

PURPOSE Determines whether a filename passes this filename filter.

SYNTAX `boolean accept(File dir, String name)`

DESCRIPTION This method determines whether a file from the directory `dir` with filename `name` has the properties required to pass this filename filter. It returns `true` if the filename passes the filter; `false` otherwise.

PARAMETERS

`dir` The directory in which the file is found.

`name` The name of the file.

RETURNS `true` if the specified file passes this filename filter; `false` otherwise.

SEE ALSO `File.list()`.

EXAMPLE See the class example.

java.io

FileNotFoundException

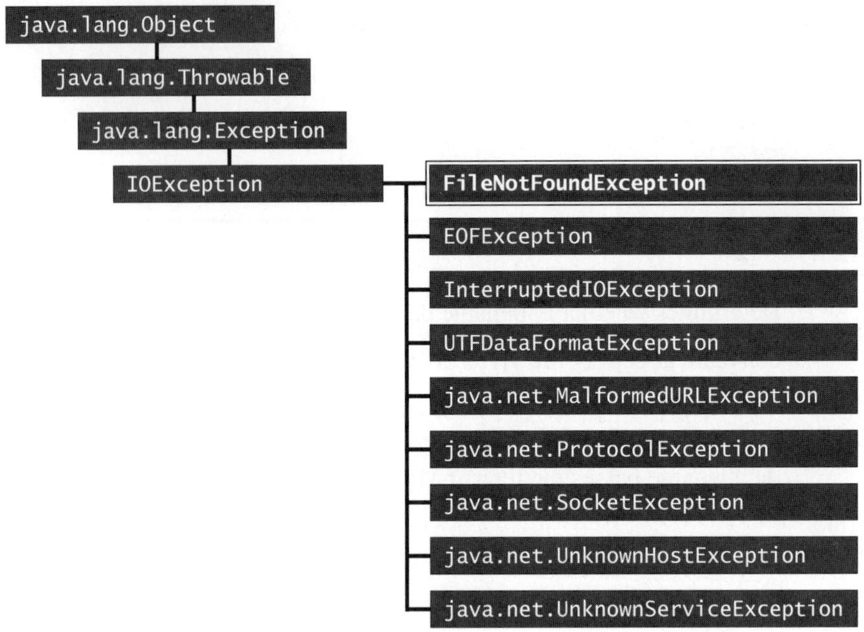

Syntax

```
public class FileNotFoundException extends IOException
```

Description

`FileNotFoundException` is an IO exception that is thrown when a program attempts to read from a nonexistent file or to write to a file in a nonexistent directory.

A method that throws `FileNotFoundException` must declare it or any of its superclasses in its `throws` clause.

MEMBER SUMMARY	
Constructor	
`FileNotFoundException()`	Constructs a `FileNotFoundException` instance.

See Also

`FileInputStream`, `FileOutputStream`, `IOException`.

Example

This example echoes a file's contents, throwing `FileNotFoundException` if the file does not exist.

```
import java.io.FileInputStream;
import java.io.FileNotFoundException;
import java.io.IOException;

class Main {
    public static void main(String[] args) {
        if (args.length == 0) {
            System.err.println("java Main <inputfile>");
            System.exit(-1);
        }
        try {
            FileInputStream in = new FileInputStream(args[0]);
            int ch;
            while ((ch = in.read()) > -1)
                System.out.print((char)ch);
        } catch (FileNotFoundException e) {
            System.err.println("File " + args[0] + " not found");
        } catch (IOException e) {
            e.printStackTrace();
        }
    }
}
```

FileNotFoundException()

PURPOSE Constructs a `FileNotFoundException` instance.

SYNTAX

```
public FileNotFoundException()
public FileNotFoundException(String msg)
```

DESCRIPTION These constructors create a new instance of `FileNotFoundException`. An optional string `msg` can be supplied that describes this particular instance of the exception.

PARAMETERS

`msg` A string that gives details about this exception.

java.io
FileOutputStream

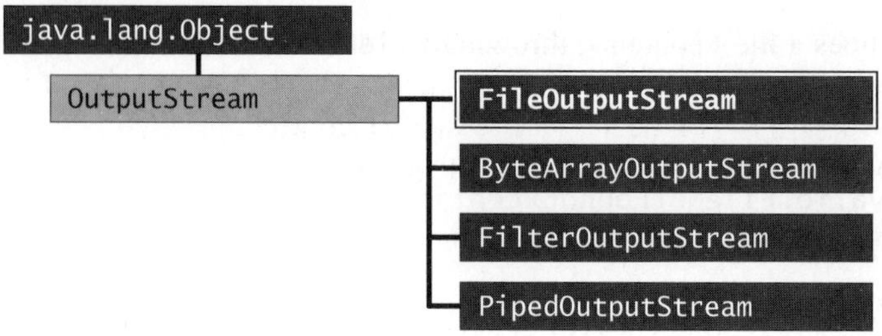

Syntax

```
public class FileOutputStream extends OutputStream
```

Description

The `FileOutputStream` class provides methods for writing data to a file (Figure 92).

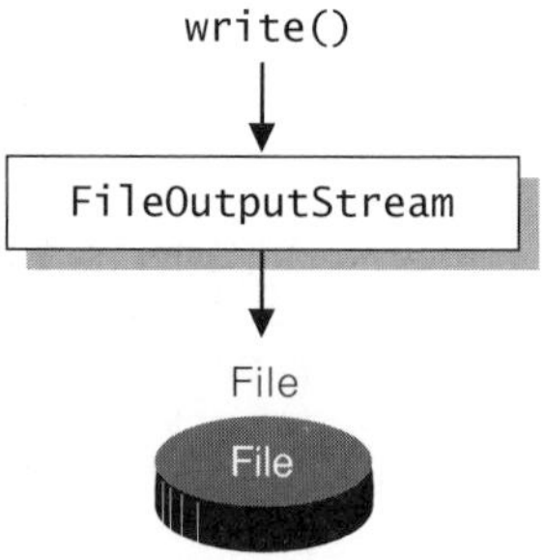

FIGURE 92 `FileOutputStream`

MEMBER SUMMARY

Constructor	
`FileOutputStream()`	Constructs a new file output stream.
Output Method	
`write()`	Writes bytes to this file output stream.
Methods for Closing Stream	
`close()`	Closes this file output stream.
`finalize()`	Closes this file output stream when it is garbage-collected.
File Descriptor Method	
`getFD()`	Retrieves the file descriptor used by this file output stream.

See Also

`File`, `FileDescriptor`, `FileInputStream`, `OutputStream`.

Example

This example creates a `FileOutputStream` using the filename supplied in the command line. It then creates a second `FileOutputStream` using the file descriptor of the first `FileOutputStream`. Both of these point to the same file. A “`Hello World`” string is then written to each of these streams. The result is two lines of “`Hello World`” in the output file.

```
import java.io.FileOutputStream;
import java.io.IOException;

class Main {
    public static void main (String[] args) {
        if (args.length != 1) {
            System.err.println(“Usage: java Main <output_file>”);
            System.exit(-1);
        }
        try {
            FileOutputStream out = new FileOutputStream(args[0]);
            FileOutputStream out2 = new FileOutputStream(out.getFD());

            String str = “Hello World\n”;
            byte[] buf = new byte[str.length()];
            str.getBytes(0, str.length(), buf, 0);

            out.write(buf);
            out2.write(buf);

            out2.close();  // will close ‘out’ too
        } catch (IOException e) {
            e.printStackTrace();
        }
    }
}
```

close()

PURPOSE Closes this file output stream.

SYNTAX `public native void close() throws IOException`

DESCRIPTION This method closes this file output stream. It releases any resources, such as file descriptors, used by this file output stream. If the file has already been closed, this method does not do anything.

EXCEPTIONS

`IOException` If an IO error occurred.

OVERRIDES `OutputStream.close()`.

EXAMPLE See the class example.

FileOutputStream()

PURPOSE Constructs a new file output stream.

SYNTAX
```
public FileOutputStream(String filename) throws IOException
public FileOutputStream(File file) throws IOException
public FileOutputStream(FileDescriptor fd)
```

DESCRIPTION There are three forms of this constructor for `FileOutputStream`. The first creates a file output stream for the file with name `filename`. `filename` is a platform-dependent name of the file. It can be an absolute or a relative path-name of the file. If absolute, it is resolved relative to the root of the file system. If relative, it is resolved relative to the current directory in which the Java program was started.

The second form creates a file output stream for the file identified by the `File` object `file`. The third form creates a file output stream using the opened file descriptor `fd`.

The file output stream can be created only if the current execution context is allowed, by the security manager and the underlying file system, to write to the specified file.

PARAMETERS

`fd` The opened file descriptor of the file.
`file` The `File` object of the file.
`filename` The string name of the file.

EXCEPTIONS

`IOException` If the file is not found or some other IO error occurred while attempting to open the file for writing.

`SecurityException`
The file cannot be opened for writing due to security reasons.

SEE ALSO `File`, `FileDescriptor`, `SecurityManager.checkWrite()`.

EXAMPLE See the class example.

A B C D E F G H I J K L M N O P Q R S T U V W X Y Z

finalize()

PURPOSE Closes this file output stream when it is garbage collected.

SYNTAX `protected void finalize() throws IOException`

DESCRIPTION This method ensures that this file output stream is closed when it is garbage collected.

OVERRIDES `Object.finalize()`.

SEE ALSO `close()`, `System.gc()`, `System.runFinalization()`.

EXAMPLE This example shows the implementation of `FileOutputStream.finalize()`.

```
protected void finalize() throws IOException {
    if (fd != null) close();
}
```

getFD()

PURPOSE Retrieves the file descriptor used by this file output stream.

SYNTAX `public final FileDescriptor getFD() throws IOException`

RETURNS The (non-`null`) file descriptor used by this file output stream.

EXCEPTIONS

`IOException` If the file has already been closed and consequently no longer has a file descriptor.

SEE ALSO `FileDescriptor`.

EXAMPLE See the class example.

write()

PURPOSE Writes bytes to this file output stream.

SYNTAX
```
public void write(int oneByte) throws IOException
public void write(byte[] buffer) throws IOException
public void write(byte[] buffer, int offset, int count) throws
    IOException
```

DESCRIPTION The three forms of this method write bytes to this file output stream. The first writes a single byte (8 bits) to this file output stream. The lowest-order byte from `oneByte` is written to the stream. The second and third forms of this method write bytes from the byte array `buffer` to this file output stream. If `offset` and `count` are specified, `count` number of bytes starting at index `offset` in `buffer` are written to this stream; otherwise all the bytes from `buffer` are written. All three forms of `write()` block until all the bytes have been written to this stream.

PARAMETERS

`buffer`	The byte array containing the bytes to be written.
`count`	The number of bytes to be written.
`offset`	The index in `buffer` from which to start getting the bytes to be written.
`oneByte`	The byte to be written.

EXCEPTIONS

`IOException`	If an IO error occurred while attempting to write the bytes.

OVERRIDES `OutputStream.write()`.

EXAMPLE See the class example.

java.awt.image
FilteredImageSource

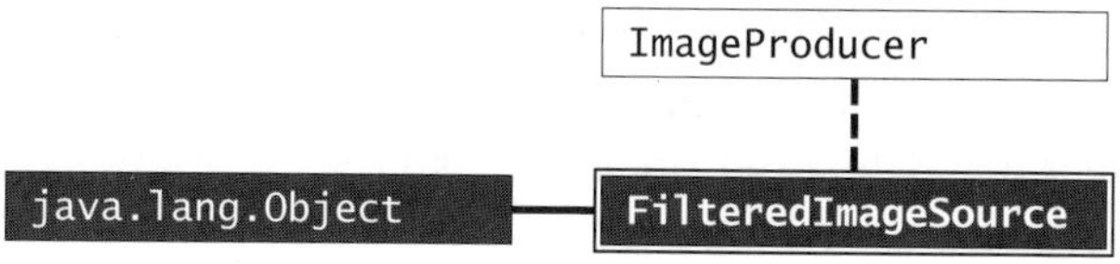

Syntax

`public class FilteredImageSource implements ImageProducer`

Description

This class is used to build a stream of image filters. This class takes an image producer and an image filter (see `ImageFilter`) and creates a new image producer. This new image producer can be combined with yet another image filter to create yet another image producer. Image consumers that get pixels from the new image producer will get pixels that have been modified by the associated image filter.

MEMBER SUMMARY	
Constructor	
`FilteredImageSource()`	Constructs a new `FilteredImageSource` object.
Image Producer Methods	
`addConsumer()`	Registers an image consumer with this image producer.
`isConsumer()`	Determines if an image consumer is registered with this image producer.
`removeConsumer()`	Removes a registered image consumer from this image producer.
`requestTopDownLeftRightResend()`	Request by an image consumer to retransmit pixels in top-down, left-right order.
`startProduction()`	Adds an image consumer to the list of consumers interested in pixels.

See Also

`ImageConsumer`, `ImageFilter`, `ImageProducer`.

A B C D E F G H I J K L M N O P Q R S T U V W X Y Z

Example

This example creates a filter stream with two image filters. See Figure 93. The first image filter closest to the source image is a crop filter that extracts a portion of the source image. In this example, the bottom quarter of the image is removed. The next filter down the pixel stream is an RGB filter that swaps the red and blue components of all the colors in the image.

FIGURE 93 `FilteredImageSource`

```
import java.awt.*;
import java.awt.image.*;
import java.net.*;
import java.util.*;
class Main extends Frame {
    Main(String filename) {
        super("FilteredImageSource Example");
        try {
            Image image = getToolkit().getImage(filename);

            // Use a media tracker object to wait until all the pixels
            // have been retrieved.
            MediaTracker tracker = new MediaTracker(this);
            tracker.addImage(image, 0);
            tracker.waitForID(0);

            add("Center", new ImageCanvas(image));
        } catch (Exception e) {
            e.printStackTrace();
        }
        resize(50, 100);
        show();
    }

    static public void main(String[] args) {
        if (args.length == 1) {
            new Main(args[0]);
        } else {
            System.err.println("usage: java Main <image file>");
        }
    }
}

class ImageCanvas extends Canvas {
    Image newImage;

    ImageCanvas(Image image) {
        ImageProducer ip = image.getSource();

        ip = new FilteredImageSource(ip, new CropImageFilter(0, 0,
                                     image.getWidth(this),
                                     image.getHeight(this)*3/4));
```

```
        ip = new FilteredImageSource(ip, new RedBlueSwapFilter());
        newImage = getToolkit().createImage(ip);
        //repaint();
    }

    public void paint(Graphics g) {
        g.drawImage(newImage, 0, 0, this);
    }
}

class RedBlueSwapFilter extends RGBImageFilter {
    public RedBlueSwapFilter() {
        canFilterIndexColorModel = true;
    }

    public int filterRGB(int x, int y, int rgb) {
        return ((rgb & 0xff00ff00)
                | ((rgb & 0xff0000) >> 16)
                | ((rgb & 0xff) << 16));
    }
}
```

addConsumer()

PURPOSE Registers an image consumer with this image producer.

SYNTAX `public synchronized void addConsumer(ImageConsumer ic)`

DESCRIPTION See `ImageProducer.addConsumer()` for details on how an image consumer should use this method.

PARAMETERS

`ic` The non-`null` image consumer to register.

SEE ALSO `ImageConsumer`.

EXAMPLE See `ImageProducer.addConsumer()`.

FilteredImageSource()

PURPOSE Constructs a new `FilteredImageSource` object.

SYNTAX `public FilteredImageSource(ImageProducer ip, ImageFilter filter)`

DESCRIPTION This constructor constructs a new filtered image source that combines an image producer with an image filter. The new filtered image source becomes a new image producer, which takes pixels from `ip`, converts them using `filter`, and then passes them onto its registered image consumers.

PARAMETERS

`filter` The non-`null` image filter.

`ip` The non-`null` image producer.

SEE ALSO `ImageFilter`, `ImageProducer`.

EXAMPLE See the class example.

isConsumer()

PURPOSE Determines if an image consumer is registered with this image producer.

SYNTAX `public synchronized boolean isConsumer(ImageConsumer ic)`

DESCRIPTION See `ImageProducer.isConsumer()` for details on how an image consumer should use this method.

PARAMETERS

`ic` The possibly `null` image consumer to check if registered.

RETURNS `true` if `ic` has been registered; `false` otherwise.

SEE ALSO `ImageConsumer`.

EXAMPLE See `ImageProducer.isConsumer()`.

removeConsumer()

PURPOSE Removes a registered image consumer from this image producer.

SYNTAX `public synchronized void removeConsumer(ImageConsumer ic)`

DESCRIPTION See `ImageProducer.removeConsumer()` for details on how an image consumer should use this method.

PARAMETERS

`ic` The non-`null` image consumer to be removed.

EXAMPLE See `ImageProducer.removeConsumer()`.

requestTopDownLeftRightResend()

PURPOSE Request by an image consumer to retransmit pixels in top-down, left-right order.

SYNTAX `public void requestTopDownLeftRightResend(ImageConsumer ic)`

DESCRIPTION See `ImageProducer.requestTopDownLeftRightResend()` for details on how an image consumer should use this method.

PARAMETERS

`ic` The non-`null` image consumer requesting the retransmission.

SEE ALSO `ImageConsumer`.

EXAMPLE See `ImageProducer.requestTopDownLeftRightResend()`.

startProduction()

PURPOSE Adds an image consumer to the list of consumers interested in pixels.

SYNTAX `public void startProduction(ImageConsumer ic)`

DESCRIPTION See `ImageProducer.startProduction()` for details on how an image consumer should use this method.

PARAMETERS

`ic` The non-`null` image consumer ready to receive pixels.

SEE ALSO `ImageConsumer`.

EXAMPLE See `ImageProducer.startProduction()`.

java.io
FilterInputStream

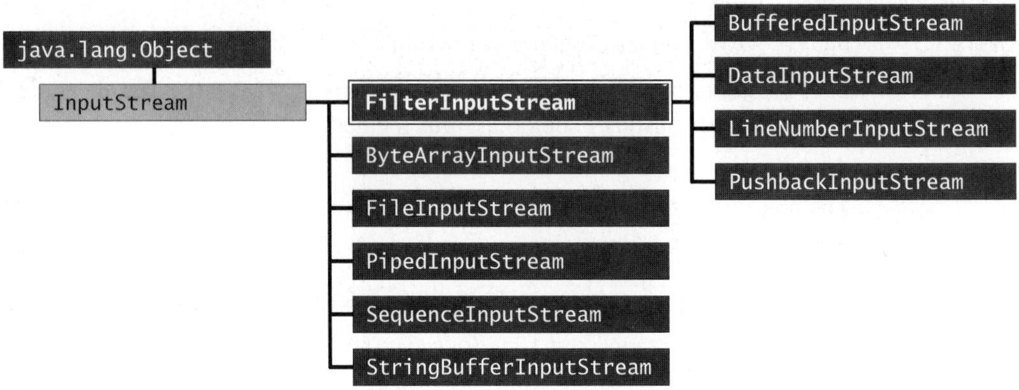

Syntax

```
public class FilterInputStream extends InputStream
```

Description

A *filter input stream* takes input from a stream and “filters” it so that when you read from this filter input stream, you get a filtered view of the input (see Figure 94). A stream that reads input and buffers it is an example of a filter input stream. Another example is a stream that reads Unicode characters from a stream and turns it into localized characters. In both cases, the filter input stream is adding functionality to the original stream. In the buffered stream case, the filter is providing buffering. In the localized stream case, the filter is serving a translation function.

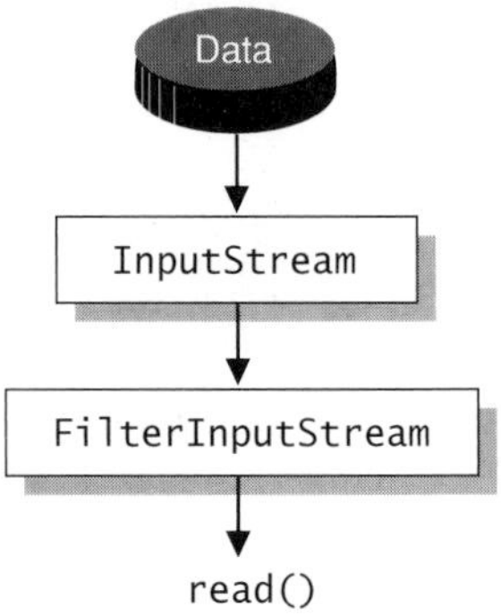

FIGURE 94 **FilterInputStream**

Filter input streams can be composed with other filter input streams. For example, you can have a buffered stream that translates Unicode characters to localized characters.

Note the different stages at which filtering occurs for filter input streams and filter output streams. A filter output stream performs processing on the stream *before* sending it to its eventual destination, while a filter input stream does processing *after* reading data from its original source.

The `FilterInputStream` class represents a filter input stream. A class extends `FilterInputStream` and overrides its input methods in order to add functionality to the stream that it is filtering.

MEMBER SUMMARY	
Constructor	
`FilterInputStream()`	Constructs a new filter input stream for an input stream.
Input Methods	
`available()`	Determines the number of bytes that can be read without blocking.
`read()`	Reads bytes from this filter input stream.
`skip()`	Skips bytes from this filter input stream.
Mark/Reset Methods	
`mark()`	Marks the current position in the filter input stream
`markSupported()`	Determines whether this filter input stream supports mark/reset.
`reset()`	Resets the current read position to the last marked position.
Method for Closing Stream	
`close()`	Closes this filter input stream.
Protected Field	
`in`	The input stream that is being filtered.

See Also

`BufferedInputStream`, `DataInputStream`, `FilterOutputStream`, `InputStream`, `LineNumberInputStream`, `PushbackInputStream`.

Example

This example defines a `FilterInputStream` that skips every other byte read from the input stream.

```
import java.io.*;

// a filter input stream that skips every other byte in the stream

class SkipFilterInputStream extends FilterInputStream {
    public SkipFilterInputStream (InputStream in) {
        super(in);
    }
    public synchronized int read() throws IOException {
        int c = in.read();
        in.skip(1);
        return (c);
    }
    public synchronized int read(byte[] b, int off, int len)
        throws IOException {
```

A B C D E F G H I J K L M N O P Q R S T U V W X Y Z

```
            byte[] tmp = new byte[len+len];

            int howmany = in.read(tmp);
            int real_count = off;
            for (int i = 0; i < howmany; i += 2) {
                b[real_count++] = tmp[i];
            }
            return (real_count);
        }
        public synchronized int read(byte[] b) throws IOException {
            return (this.read(b, 0, b.length));
        }
        public synchronized long skip(long n) throws IOException {
            byte[] b = new byte[(int)n];
            return (this.read(b));
        }
        public synchronized int available() throws IOException {
            return (in.available() / 2);
        }
        public boolean markSupported() {
            return in.markSupported();
        }
        public synchronized void mark(int readlimit) {
            in.mark(readlimit + readlimit);
        }
        public synchronized void reset() throws IOException {
            in.reset();
        }
        public synchronized void close() throws IOException {
            in.close();
        }
    }

    class Main {
        public static void main(String[] args) {
            if (args.length != 1) {
                System.err.println("Usage: java Main <input_file>");
                System.exit(-1);
            }
            try {
                FileInputStream f1 = new FileInputStream(args[0]);
                SkipFilterInputStream s1 = new SkipFilterInputStream(f1);

                // read of single char
                for(int c = s1.read(); c > -1; c = s1.read()) {
                    System.out.print((char)c);
                }
                s1.close();

                // read of buffer again, this time check mark/reset/skip
                f1 = new FileInputStream(args[0]);
                s1 = new SkipFilterInputStream(f1);
                byte[] buf = new byte[32];
```

```
            int howmany;
            while ((howmany = s1.read(buf)) > 0) {
                for (int i = 0; i < howmany; i++)
                    System.out.print((char)buf[i]);
                if (s1.skip(32) != 32)
                    break;
                if (s1.markSupported()) {
                    s1.mark(50);
                    if (s1.skip(32) != 32)
                        break;
                    s1.reset();
                }
            }
            s1.close();
        } catch (IOException e) {
            System.out.println(e);
        }
    }
}
```

available()

PURPOSE Determines the number of bytes that can be read without blocking.

SYNTAX `public int available() throws IOException`

DESCRIPTION This method returns the number of bytes that can be read from this filter input stream without blocking. In the default implementation of `FilterInputStream`, this number is determined by the number of bytes available from the stream that is being filtered (`in`).

RETURNS The number of bytes that can be read without blocking.

EXCEPTIONS
`IOException` If an IO error occurred.

OVERRIDES `InputStream.available()`.

SEE ALSO `in`.

EXAMPLE See the class example.

close()

PURPOSE Closes this filter input stream.

SYNTAX `public void close() throws IOException`

A B C D E F G H I J K L M N O P Q R S T U V W X Y Z

DESCRIPTION This method closes this filter input stream. By default, it closes the stream that is being filtered (`in`). Other resources related to the filter might also need to be released, depending on the nature of the filter.

EXCEPTIONS
`IOException` If an IO error has occurred.

OVERRIDES `InputStream.close()`.

SEE ALSO `in`.

EXAMPLE See the class example.

FilterInputStream()

PURPOSE Constructs a new filter input stream for an input stream.

SYNTAX `protected FilterInputStream(InputStream in)`

DESCRIPTION This method creates a new filter input stream for the input stream `in`. Data read from `in` is filtered by this new filter input stream before being returned by the `read()` method.

PARAMETERS
`in` The input stream to filter.

SEE ALSO `in`.

EXAMPLE See the class example.

in

PURPOSE The input stream being filtered.

SYNTAX `protected InputStream in`

DESCRIPTION This is the input stream with which this filter input stream has been created. It is the stream that this filter input stream reads from in order to satisfy the read/skip requests.

SEE ALSO `FilterInputStream()`.

EXAMPLE See the class example.

mark()

PURPOSE Marks the current position in the filter input stream.

SYNTAX `public synchronized void mark(int readlimit)`

DESCRIPTION This method marks the current position in the input stream so that a subsequent call to `reset()` will reposition the stream to this marked position. This allows subsequent `read()` calls to reread the same bytes that have already been read. `readlimit` is the number of bytes that can be read before the mark position becomes invalid. The default implementation uses the `mark()` method of the stream that is being filtered (`in`).

PARAMETERS

`readlimit` The number of bytes that can be read before the mark becomes invalid.

OVERRIDES `InputStream.mark()`.

SEE ALSO `in`, `markSupported()`, `reset()`.

EXAMPLE See the class example.

markSupported()

PURPOSE Determines whether this filter input stream supports mark/reset.

SYNTAX `public boolean markSupported()`

DESCRIPTION This method determines whether this filter input stream supports mark/reset. It returns `true` if mark/reset is supported and `false` otherwise. By default, whether mark/reset is supported is determined by the stream that is being filtered (`in`).

RETURNS `true` if mark/reset is supported; `false` otherwise.

OVERRIDES `InputStream.markSupported()`.

SEE ALSO `in`, `mark()`, `reset()`.

EXAMPLE See the class example.

read()

PURPOSE Reads bytes from this filter input stream.

SYNTAX

```
public int read() throws IOException
public int read(byte[] buffer) throws IOException
public int read(byte[] buffer, int offset, int count) throws
    IOException
```

DESCRIPTION The three forms of this method read bytes from this filter input stream. They are usually overridden because a filter input stream typically performs some postprocessing after reading the bytes from the stream that it is filtering (`in`).

The first form reads a single byte (8 bits) from this filter input stream and returns it as a 32-bit `int`. The first three bytes of the `int` are not used. `read()` blocks until a byte is available for reading from this input stream. If end-of-file is reached on this stream, `read()` returns `-1`.

The second and third forms read bytes from this filter input stream and store the bytes read into the byte array `buffer`. If `offset` and `count` are specified, `read()` reads at most `count` number of bytes from this stream and stores them in `buffer` starting at index `offset`. Otherwise `read()` reads at most `buffer.length` number of bytes and stores them in `buffer` starting at index `0`. `read()` returns the number of bytes actually read from this stream. If end-of-file is reached on this stream before any bytes are read, `read()` returns `-1`.

PARAMETERS

`buffer`	The byte array in which to store the bytes read.
`count`	The number of bytes to read.
`offset`	The index in `buffer` at which to start storing the bytes read.

RETURNS The first form returns the byte read. The second and third forms return the actual number of bytes read. All forms return `-1` if end-of-file is reached before any bytes are read.

EXCEPTIONS

`IOException` If an IO error occurred while attempting to read.

OVERRIDES `InputStream.read()`.

SEE ALSO `in`, `skip()`.

EXAMPLE See the class example.

reset()

PURPOSE Resets the current read position to the last marked position.

SYNTAX

```
public synchronized void reset() throws IOException
```

DESCRIPTION This method resets the current read position of this filter input stream to be the last marked position (the read position when `mark()` was last called). The default implementation invokes the `reset()` method of the stream being filtered (`in`).

EXCEPTIONS

`IOException` If no mark has been set or if the mark is invalid.

OVERRIDES `InputStream.reset()`.

SEE ALSO `in`, `mark()`, `markSupported()`.

EXAMPLE See the class example.

skip()

PURPOSE Skips bytes from this filter input stream.

SYNTAX `public long skip(long count) throws IOException`

DESCRIPTION This method skips `count` number of bytes from this filter input stream. Bytes that are skipped will not be returned by subsequent `read()` calls (except if mark/reset is used). The default implementation skips `count` number of bytes from the stream being filtered (`in`). This method returns the number of bytes actually skipped.

PARAMETERS

`count` The number of bytes to skip.

RETURNS The actual number of bytes skipped.

EXCEPTIONS

`IOException` If an IO error occurred.

OVERRIDES `InputStream.skip()`.

SEE ALSO `in`, `read()`.

EXAMPLE See the class example.

java.io
FilterOutputStream

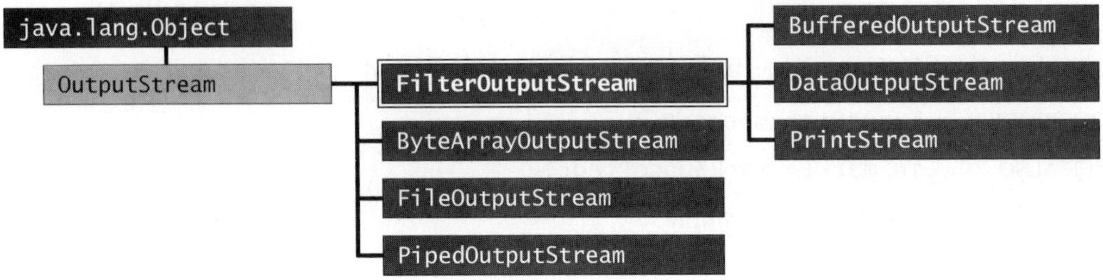

Syntax

```
public class FilterOutputStream extends OutputStream
```

Description

A *filter output stream* takes output to be written to a stream and "filters" it so that when you write to this filter output stream, the resulting output is "filtered" (see Figure 95). A stream that buffers output is an example of a filter output stream. Another example is a stream that accepts Unicode characters written to it and translates them into localized characters. In each case, the filter output stream is adding functionality to the original stream. In the buffered stream case, the filter is providing buffering. In the localized output stream case, the filter is serving a translation function.

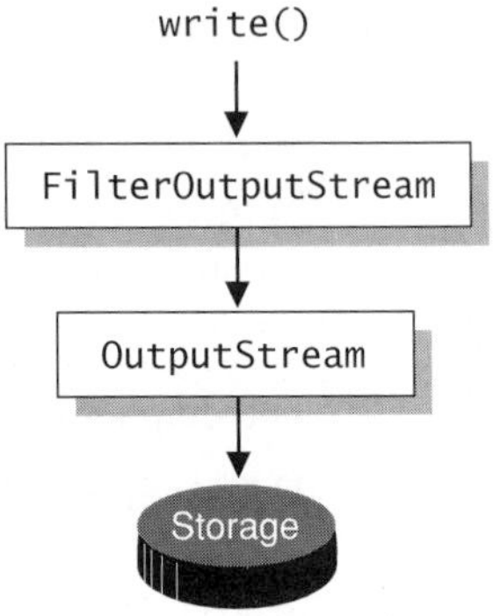

FIGURE 95 **`FilterOutputStream`**

Filter output streams can be composed with other filter output streams. For example, you can have a buffered stream that translates Unicode characters to localized characters.

Note the different stages at which filtering occurs for filter input streams and filter output streams. A filter output stream performs processing on the stream *before* sending it out to its eventual destination. A filter input stream does processing *after* reading data from its original source.

The `FilterOutputStream` class represents a filter output stream. A class extends `FilterOutputStream` and overrides its output methods in order to add functionality to the stream that it is filtering.

MEMBER SUMMARY

Constructor	
`FilterOutputStream()`	Constructs a new filter output stream for an output stream.
Output Methods	
`flush()`	Flushes this filter output stream.
`write()`	Writes bytes to this filter output stream.
Method for Closing Stream	
`close()`	Closes this filter output stream.
Protected Field	
`out`	The output stream that is being filtered.

See Also

`BufferedOutputStream`, `DataOutputStream`, `FilterInputStream`, `OutputStream`, `PrintStream`.

Example

This example defines a `FilterOutputStream` for producing line-numbered output.

```
import java.io.IOException;
import java.io.FilterOutputStream;
import java.io.FileInputStream;
import java.io.OutputStream;

class LineNumberOutputStream extends FilterOutputStream {
    private int linenumber = 0;
    private boolean neednewline = true;
    public LineNumberOutputStream (OutputStream out) {
        super(out);
    }

    protected void newline() {
        String prefix = ++linenumber + "\t";
        byte[] p = new byte[prefix.length()];
        prefix.getBytes(0, prefix.length(), p, 0);
        try {
            out.write(p);
        } catch (IOException e) {
            System.err.println(e);
        }
    }

    public void write(int b) throws IOException {
        if (neednewline) {
```

```
                newline();
                neednewline = false;
            }
            out.write(b);
            if (b == '\n') {
                neednewline = true;
            }
        }
    }
    class Main {
        public static void main(String[] args) {
            if (args.length == 0) {
                System.err.println("java Main <input file>");
                System.exit(-1);
            }
            try {
                FileInputStream in = new FileInputStream(args[0]);
                LineNumberOutputStream out =
                    new LineNumberOutputStream(System.out);

                for (int c = in.read(); c > -1; c = in.read())
                    out.write((char)c);
                out.flush();
                out.close();
            } catch (IOException e) {
                System.out.println(e);
            }
        }
    }
```

close()

PURPOSE Closes this filter output stream.

SYNTAX `public void close() throws IOException`

DESCRIPTION This method closes this filter output stream. By default, it closes the stream that is being filtered (`out`). Other resources related to the filter might also need to be released, depending on the nature of the filter.

EXCEPTIONS

`IOException` If an IO error occurred.

OVERRIDES `OutputStream.close()`.

SEE ALSO `out`.

EXAMPLE See the class example.

FilterOutputStream()

PURPOSE Constructs a new filter output stream for an output stream.

SYNTAX `public FilterOutputStream(OutputStream out)`

DESCRIPTION This method creates a new filter output stream for the output stream `out`. Data written to this new stream is processed by this filter before being sent to `out`.

PARAMETERS

`out` The output stream being filtered.

SEE ALSO `out`.

EXAMPLE See the class example.

flush()

PURPOSE Flushes this filter output stream.

SYNTAX `public void flush() throws IOException`

DESCRIPTION This method flushes any buffered bytes in this filter output stream. The default implementation simply flushes any bytes buffered by the stream being filtered (`out`). If this filter output stream does any buffering, `flush()` should be overridden to flush the buffered bytes as well.

EXCEPTIONS

`IOException` If an IO error occurred.

OVERRIDES `OutputStream.flush()`.

SEE ALSO `BufferedOutputStream.flush()`, `out`.

EXAMPLE See the class example.

out

PURPOSE The output stream being filtered.

SYNTAX `protected OutputStream out`

DESCRIPTION This is the output stream with which this filter output stream has been created. Data written to this filter output stream is processed by this filter output stream and then written to `out`.

SEE ALSO `FilterOutputStream()`.

EXAMPLE See the class example.

write()

PURPOSE Writes bytes to this filter output stream.

SYNTAX
```
public void write(int oneByte) throws IOException
public void write(byte[] buffer) throws IOException
public void write(byte[] buffer, int offset, int count) throws
   IOException
```

DESCRIPTION The three forms of this method write bytes to this filter input stream. These methods are usually overridden because a filter output stream typically performs some preprocessing before writing the bytes to the stream that it is filtering (`out`).

The first form of `write()` writes a single byte to this filter output stream. It writes the lowest-order byte from `oneByte`. The second form writes the bytes from the byte array `buffer` to this filter output stream. The third form writes `count` number of bytes starting at index `offset` from the byte array `buffer` to this filter output stream.

PARAMETERS

`buffer`	The byte array containing the bytes to be written.
`count`	The number of bytes to write.
`offset`	The index in `buffer` from which to start getting the bytes to be written.
`oneByte`	The byte to be written.

EXCEPTIONS

`IOException` If an IO error occurred.

OVERRIDES `OutputStream.write()`.

EXAMPLE See the class example.

A B C D E F G H I J K L M N O P Q R S T U V W X Y Z

java.lang
Float

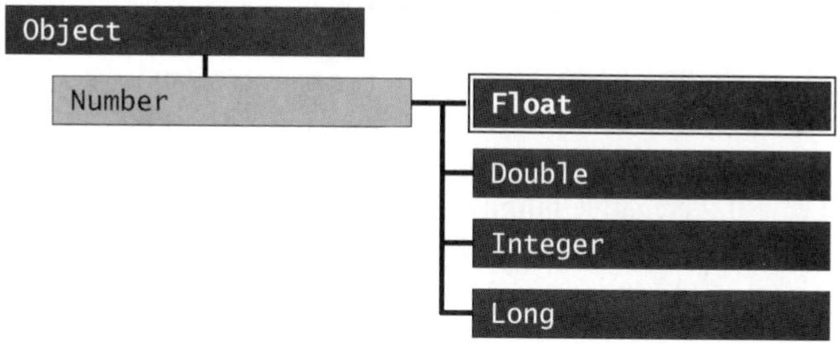

Syntax

```
public final class Float extends Number
```

Description

A `float` in Java is a 32-bit floating-point number. The `Float` class provides an object wrapper for `float` data value. This wrapper allows floating-point numbers to be passed to methods in Java class libraries that accept Java objects as parameters. In addition, the `Float` class provides methods that convert to and from floats and performs other operations on floats.

`Float` instances cannot be used in arithmetic expressions in place of `float`. For example, the following are not allowed.

```
Float f1 = new Float(243.34);
Float f2 = new Float(5);
Float f3 = f1 * f2;      // Illegal
```

To perform an arithmetic operation using a `Float` instance, you first must use access methods defined in the `Float` class to obtain its numeric value, as follows:

```
float f3 = f1.floatValue() * f2.floatValue();
double d1 = f1.floatValue() + f2.doubleValue();
```


A B C D E F G H I J K L M N O P Q R S T U V W X Y Z

MEMBER SUMMARY

Constructor

`Float()`	Constructs a `Float` object using a number or a string.

Constant Fields

`MAX_VALUE`	The maximum value a `float` value can have.
`MIN_VALUE`	The smallest positive value a `float` value can have.
`NaN`	The special Not-a-Number value.
`NEGATIVE_INFINITY`	Negative infinity for a float.
`POSITIVE_INFINITY`	Positive infinity for a float.

Number Methods

`doubleValue()`	Retrieves the value of this object as a `double`.
`floatValue()`	Retrieves the value of this object as a `float`.
`intValue()`	Retrieves the value of this object as an `int`.
`longValue()`	Retrieves the value of this object as a `long`.

Methods for Converting to/from Other Representations

`floatToIntBits()`	Retrieves the bit representation of a `float` value .
`intBitsToFloat()`	Retrieves the `float` value corresponding to a given bit representation.
`toString()`	Generates the string representation of a `float` or a `Float` object.
`valueOf()`	Creates a new `Float` object using its string representation.

Comparison Methods

`equals()`	Compares this object with another object for equality.
`isInfinite()`	Determines whether a `float` is infinitely large in magnitude.
`isNaN()`	Determines whether a `float` is Not-a-Number (`NaN`).

Hash Code Method

`hashCode()`	Computes the hash code for this object.

See Also

`Double`, `Int`, `Number`, `Long`.

doubleValue()

PURPOSE Retrieves the value of this object as a `double`.

SYNTAX `public double doubleValue()`

DESCRIPTION This method returns the value of this object as a `double` by casting its `float` value to a `double` value.

RETURNS The value of this object as a `double`.

EXAMPLE

```
Float fobj = new Float(0.47712f);

double dval = fobj.doubleValue(); // get double value
float fval = fobj.floatValue();   // get float value
int ival = fobj.intValue();       // round to 0
long lval = fobj.longValue();     // round to 0
```

equals()

PURPOSE Compares this object with another object for equality.

SYNTAX `public boolean equals(Object obj)`

DESCRIPTION This method compares the `float` value of this object against that of the object `obj`. It returns `true` if the two values are equal. It returns `false` if the two values are not equal or if `obj` is `null` or not a `Float` object. This method considers two `NaN` `float` values to be equal in order to be useful in hashtables. This is contrary to the IEEE specification.

PARAMETERS

`obj` The object against which this object will be compared.

RETURNS `true` if `obj` has the same `float` value as this object; `false` otherwise.

OVERRIDES `Object.equals()`.

EXAMPLE

```
Float f1 = new Float(4.8123f);
Float f2 = new Float(4.8123f);

// Check whether the value of two Floats are equal
if (f1.equals(f2))
    System.out.println("equal");
```

Float()

PURPOSE Constructs a `Float` object using a number or a string.

A B C D E F G H I J K L M N O P Q R S T U V W X Y Z

SYNTAX
```
public Float(float fval)
public Float(double dval)
public Float(String sval) throws NumberFormatException
```

DESCRIPTION The three forms of this constructor create new instances of `Float` using either a floating-point number (`fval` or `dval`) or the string representation `sval` of a floating-point number.

PARAMETERS

`fval` The `float` value used to construct this object.

`dval` The `double` value used to construct this object.

`sval` The string representation of a `float` value.

EXCEPTIONS

`NumberFormatException`
If `sval` cannot be parsed into a `float`.

SEE ALSO `valueOf()`.

EXAMPLE

```
Float pi = new Float(3.14159f);         // using float
Float num = new Float(8.23e13);         // using double
if (num.equals(pi))
  ...
try {
    Float f = new Float("1.23");        // using string
        ...
} catch (NumberFormatException e) {
  ...
}
```

floatToIntBits()

PURPOSE Retrieves the bit representation of a `float` value .

SYNTAX `public static native int floatToIntBits(float value)`

DESCRIPTION A `float` is a 32-bit floating-point number. This method returns in an `int` the bit representation of the `float` value `value`. The bit representation is the IEEE standard format for 32-bit floating-point numbers. This method is the inverse of `intBitsToFloat()`.

PARAMETERS

`value` The `float` value.

RETURNS An `int` containing the bit representation of `value`.

SEE ALSO intBitsToFloat().

EXAMPLE

```
float fnum = 22.45915f;
int bitrepr = Float.floatToIntBits(fnum);      // get bit repr
float reconst = Float.intBitsToFloat(bitrepr); // reconstruct fnum

if (reconst == fnum) // should be true
    System.out.println("correct");
```

floatValue()

PURPOSE Retrieves the value of this object as a `float`.

SYNTAX `public float floatValue()`

RETURNS The value of this object as a `float`.

EXAMPLE See `doubleValue()`.

hashCode()

PURPOSE Computes the hash code for this object.

SYNTAX `public int hashCode()`

DESCRIPTION This method returns the hash code for this `Float` object. The hash code for a `Float` object is calculated using the object's `float` value. Two `Float`s that have the same `float` value will have the same hash code. However, two `Float`s with the same hash code may not necessarily have the same `float` value.

RETURNS An `int` representing the hash code.

OVERRIDES `Object.hashCode()`.

EXAMPLE

```
int[] hits = new int[1023];
Float fnum = new Float(1.61803f);
int hashval = fnum.hashCode();          // generate hash code
++hits[Math.abs(hashval%hits.length)]; // count hits
```

intBitsToFloat()

PURPOSE Retrieves the `float` value corresponding to a given bit representation.

SYNTAX `public static native float intBitsToFloat(int bits)`

DESCRIPTION This method returns the `float` value corresponding to the bit representation `bits`. It is the inverse of the method `floatToIntBits()`.

PARAMETERS

`bits` The bits used to generate the `float` value.

RETURNS The `float` value represented by `bits`.

SEE ALSO `floatToIntBits()`.

EXAMPLE See `floatToIntBits()`.

intValue()

PURPOSE Retrieves the value of this object as an `int`.

SYNTAX `public int intValue()`

DESCRIPTION This method returns the value of this object as an `int` by casting its `float` value to an `int`. The `float` is rounded to a whole number.

RETURNS The value of this object as an `int`.

EXAMPLE See `doubleValue()`.

isInfinite()

PURPOSE Determines whether a `float` is infinitely large in magnitude.

SYNTAX

```
public boolean isInfinite()
public static boolean isInfinite(float value)
```

DESCRIPTION The first form of this method returns `true` if the `float` value of this `Float` object is infinitely large in magnitude. It returns `false` otherwise. The second form returns `true` if the `float` value `value` is infinitely large in magnitude. It returns `false` otherwise.

PARAMETERS

`value` The `float` value to check for infinity.

A B C D E F G H I J K L M N O P Q R S T U V W X Y Z

RETURNS `true` if the `float` value is infinitely large in magnitude; `false` otherwise.

EXAMPLE

```
Float fnum = new Float(1.6878f);
 ...
if (fnum.isInfinite())          // instance version
    throw new ArithmeticException();
if (Float.isInfinite(85.1f))    // class version
    break;
```

isNaN()

PURPOSE Determines whether a `float` is the special Not-a-Number (`NaN`) value.

SYNTAX
```
public boolean isNaN()
public static boolean isNan(float value)
```

DESCRIPTION The first form of this method returns `true` if the `float` value of this `Float` object is the special `NaN` value. It returns `false` otherwise. The second form returns `true` if the `float` value `value` is the special `NaN`. It returns `false` otherwise.

PARAMETERS

`value` The `float` value to check whether it is a `NaN` value.

RETURNS `true` if the `float` value is the `NaN` value; `false` otherwise.

EXAMPLE

```
Float fnum = new Float(1.523E24f);
if (fnum.isNaN())                   // instance version
    throw new ArithmeticException();
if (Float.isNaN(fnum.floatValue())) // class version
 ...
```

longValue()

PURPOSE Retrieves the value of this object as a `long`.

SYNTAX
```
public long longValue()
```

DESCRIPTION This method returns the value of this object as a `long` by casting its `float` value to a `long` value. The `float` value is rounded to a whole number.

RETURNS The value of this object as a `long`.

EXAMPLE See `doubleValue()`.

MAX_VALUE

PURPOSE The maximum value a `float` can have.

SYNTAX `public static final float MAX_VALUE`

DESCRIPTION This constant represents the maximum value a `float` can have, which is 3.40282346638528860e+38.

EXAMPLE

```
// test if number is less than MAX_VALUE
float fnum = 3.1415927f;
if (fnum < Float.MAX_VALUE)
    fnum *= 100;
```

MIN_VALUE

PURPOSE The minimum value a `float` can have.

SYNTAX `public static final float MIN_VALUE`

DESCRIPTION This constant represents the smallest positive value a `float` can have, which is 1.40129846432481707e-45.

EXAMPLE

```
// test if number is greater than MIN_VALUE
float fnum = 2.71828f;
if (fnum > Float.MIN_VALUE)
    fnum = 1/fnum;
```

NaN

PURPOSE The special Not-a-Number (`NaN`) value.

SYNTAX `public static final float NaN`

DESCRIPTION This constant represents the special Not-a-Number (NaN). The value of NaN is not equal to anything, including NaN itself. However, in order to be useful in hash tables, the Float.equals() method considers two NaNs equal, which is contrary to the IEEE specification. However, the equals operator ('==') considers two float NaNs to be not equal. This is consistent with the IEEE specification.

EXAMPLE

```
float fnum = Float.NaN;
// test if number is Not-A-Number
if (Float.isNaN(fnum))                  // succeeds
    System.out.println("correct");
if (Float.isNaN(Float.NaN))             // succeeds
    System.out.println("correct");

// A NaN is not equal to itself except when using equals()
if (fnum == Float.NaN)                  // fails
    System.out.println("incorrect");
Float f1 = new Float(Float.NaN);
Float f2 = new Float(Float.NaN);
if (f1.equals(f2))                      // succeeds
    System.out.println("correct");
```

NEGATIVE_INFINITY

PURPOSE Negative infinity for a float value.

SYNTAX `public static final float NEGATIVE_INFINITY`

EXAMPLE

```
float fnum;
 ...
// reset to 0 if number reached neg infinity
if (fnum == Float.NEGATIVE_INFINITY)
    fnum = 0;
```

POSITIVE_INFINITY

PURPOSE Positive infinity for a float value.

toString()

SYNTAX `public static final float POSITIVE_INFINITY`

EXAMPLE

```
float fnum;
 ...
// reset to 0 if number reached pos infinity
if (fnum == Float.POSITIVE_INFINITY)
    fnum = 0;
```

toString()

PURPOSE Generates the string representation for this object.

SYNTAX
```
public String toString()
public static String toString(float value)
```

DESCRIPTION The two forms of this method return the string representation of a `float` value. This first form returns the string representation of this `Float` object (basically the string form of its `float` value). This method is the inverse of `valueOf()`.

The second form returns the string representation of the `float` value `value`.

PARAMETERS

`value` The `float` for which to generate the string representation.

RETURNS The string representation of `value` or the `float` value of this `Float` object.

OVERRIDES `Object.toString()`.

SEE ALSO `Hashtable`, `valueOf()`.

EXAMPLE

```
Float fnum = new Float(0.843f);
String str = fnum.toString();        // get string form of number
String str2 = Float.toString(1.523E24f);
String pstr = "The two floats are " + str + " and " + str2;
```

valueOf()

PURPOSE Creates a new `Float` object using its string representation.

SYNTAX
```
public static native Float valueOf(String str) throws
    NumberFormatException
```

DESCRIPTION This method creates a new `Float` object by parsing the string `str` into a `float` value. This method is the inverse of `toString()`.

PARAMETERS

`str` The string to be parsed.

RETURNS A new `Float` object with the `float` value of the number parsed from `str`.

SEE ALSO `toString()`.

EXCEPTIONS

`NumberFormatException`

If `str` cannot be parsed into a `float` value.

EXAMPLE

```
String str = "1.0871E3f";
try {
    Float r = Float.valueOf(str);
     ...
} catch (NumberFormatException e) {
    System.err.println("Could not convert string to number " + str);
}
```

java.awt
FlowLayout

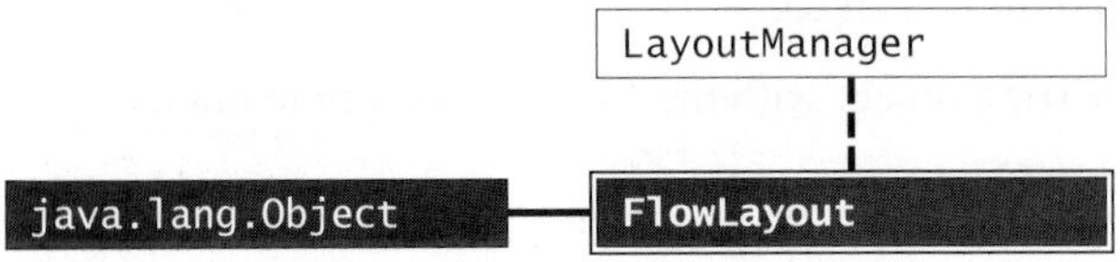

Syntax

```
public class FlowLayout implements LayoutManager
```

Description

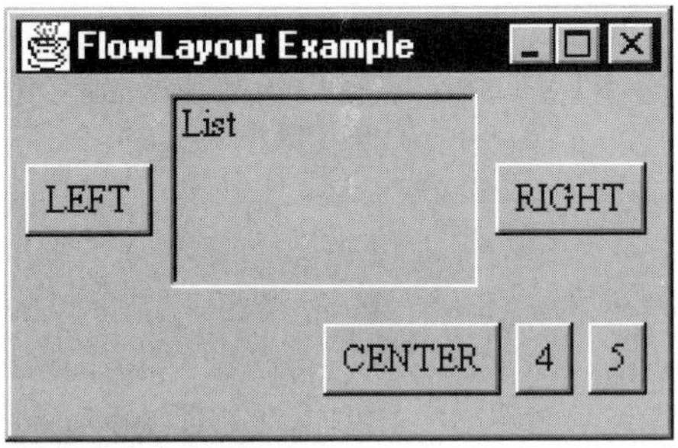

FIGURE 96 `FlowLayout`

The flow layout manager places components in rows in left-to-right, top-to-bottom order. When a component cannot be placed on a row without being clipped, a new row is created. The components are centered vertically on each row.

A flow layout has an alignment property that determines how each row distributes empty space. The alignment can be one of three values: `LEFT`, `CENTER`, or `RIGHT`. A flow layout with left alignment moves the empty space to the right of the row, thereby moving all the components left. A flow layout with right alignment moves the empty space to the left. A flow layout with center alignment divides the empty space and distributes it at the left and right ends of the rows, thereby centering all the components.

Gaps

The flow layout manager allows you to separate the components with gaps. The vertical gap specifies the space between rows, while the horizontal gap specifies the space between components.

The vertical and horizontal gaps are also applied around the edges of the container. If you do not want this space, you can eliminate it only by subclassing the container and overriding its `insets()` method. The override should retrieve the peer's required insets (if a peer exists), subtract the `vgap` and `hgap` from the peer's insets, and return the result. Doing this might make the insets negative, but it will eliminate the gaps around the edges.

MEMBER SUMMARY

Constructor	
`FlowLayout()`	Creates new `FlowLayout` instance.
Alignment Constant Fields	
`CENTER`	Alignment constant specifying center alignment.
`LEFT`	Alignment constant specifying left alignment.
`RIGHT`	Alignment constant specifying right alignment.
Layout Manager Methods	
`addLayoutComponent()`	This method is a no-op.
`layoutContainer()`	Lays out the container's components according to the settings of the layout manager.
`minimumLayoutSize()`	Calculates the minimum dimensions needed to lay out the components.
`preferredLayoutSize()`	Calculates the preferred dimensions needed to lay out the components.
`removeLayoutComponent()`	This method is a no-op.
Debugging Method	
`toString()`	Generates a string representation of the layout manager's state.

Example

This example creates a frame with a flow layout manager (see Figure 96). Three buttons labeled LEFT, CENTER, and RIGHT control the alignment of the flow layout . A list component is added to the container to introduce a different height in the row to demonstrate that the components in a row are centered vertically.

```
import java.awt.*;

class Main extends Frame {
    Main() {
        super("FlowLayout Example");
        List list = new List();

        setLayout(new FlowLayout(FlowLayout.RIGHT));
        add(new Button("LEFT"));
        list.addItem("List");
        add(list);
        add(new Button("RIGHT"));
        add(new Button("CENTER"));
        add(new Button("4"));
        add(new Button("5"));
```

```
            resize(100, 200);
            show();
        }
        public boolean action(Event evt, Object what) {
            FlowLayout l = null;
            if ("LEFT".equals(what)) {
                l = new FlowLayout(FlowLayout.LEFT);
            } else if ("CENTER".equals(what)) {
                l = new FlowLayout(FlowLayout.CENTER);
            } else if ("RIGHT".equals(what)) {
                l = new FlowLayout(FlowLayout.RIGHT);
            }
            if (l != null) {
                setLayout(l);
                invalidate();
                validate();
                return true;
            }
            return false;
        }
        public static void main(String[] args) {
            new Main();
        }
    }
```

addLayoutComponent()

PURPOSE This method is a no-op.

SYNTAX `public void addLayoutComponent(String name, Component comp)`

DESCRIPTION This method is called by the container when a component is added with a name. However, component names are ignored by the flow layout manager, so this method does not do anything. This method needs to be defined in order to satisfy the `LayoutManager` interface.

PARAMETERS

`comp` The non-`null` named component that has just been added to the container. Ignored.

`name` The name of the component. Ignored.

CENTER

PURPOSE Alignment constant specifying center alignment.

SYNTAX `public static final int CENTER`

DESCRIPTION The center alignment causes all the components in a row to be packed together and centered.

EXAMPLE See the class example.

FlowLayout()

PURPOSE Constructs a new `FlowLayout` instance.

SYNTAX

```
public FlowLayout()
public FlowLayout(int align)
public FlowLayout(int align, int hgap, int vgap)
```

DESCRIPTION The three forms of this constructor construct a new flow layout manager instance with the alignment `align` and the gaps `hgap` and `vgap`. If the alignment is not specified, it defaults to `CENTER`. If the gaps are not defined, they both default to `5`.

An instance of the flow layout manager can be shared by more than one container. Also, the flow layout manager can be set on a container at any time, regardless of the number of the components already in the container.

PARAMETERS

`align`	The alignment, which must be one of `LEFT`, `CENTER`, or `RIGHT`.
`hgap`	A non-negative integer specifying the horizontal gap in pixels.
`vgap`	A non-negative integer specifying the vertical gap in pixels.

SEE ALSO `BorderLayout()`, `CardLayout()`, `GridLayout()`, `GridBagLayout()`.

EXAMPLE See the class example.

layoutContainer()

PURPOSE Lays out the container's components according to the settings of the layout manager.

SYNTAX

```
public void layoutContainer(Container cont)
```

DESCRIPTION This method is called by the container `cont` when the layout is invalidated and needs to be redone. In placing the components, the flow layout manager sets the width of the rows to be the current width of the container and resizes the components based on their preferred sizes.

A B C D E F G H I J K L M N O P Q R S T U V W X Y Z

PARAMETERS

`cont`	The non-`null` container using this layout instance.
SEE ALSO	`Container`.
EXAMPLE	See `LayoutManager.layoutContainer()`.

LEFT

PURPOSE	Alignment constant specifying left alignment.
SYNTAX	`public static final int LEFT`
DESCRIPTION	The left alignment causes all the components in a row to be packed together and moved against the left edge of the container.
EXAMPLE	See the class example.

minimumLayoutSize()

PURPOSE	Calculates the minimum dimensions needed to lay out the components.
SYNTAX	`public Dimension minimumLayoutSize(Container cont)`
DESCRIPTION	This method calculates the minimum dimensions needed to lay out the components in the container `cont`. The minimum dimension of a flow layout is based on a layout of a single row. More precisely, the minimum dimension is calculated by determining each visible component's minimum size. The height of the result is determined by the maximum height of these minimum sizes plus 2 * the vertical gap plus any insets required by the container. The width of the result is the combined width of all the minimum widths + (number-of-components+1) * the horizontal gap plus any insets required by the container.

PARAMETERS

`cont`	The non-`null` container using this layout instance.
RETURNS	A non-`null` `Dimension` object containing the minimum size of the flow layout.
SEE ALSO	`Component.minimumSize()`, `preferredLayoutSize()`.

preferredLayoutSize()

PURPOSE Calculates the preferred dimensions needed to lay out the components.

SYNTAX `public Dimension preferredLayoutSize(Container cont)`

DESCRIPTION This method calculates the preferred dimensions needed to lay out the components in the container `cont`. The preferred dimension of a flow layout is based on a layout of a single row. More precisely, the preferred dimension is calculated by determining each visible component's preferred size. The height of the result is determined by the maximum height of these preferred sizes plus 2 * the vertical gap plus any insets required by the container. The width of the result is the combined width of all the preferred widths + (number-of-components+1) * the horizontal gap + any insets required by the container.

PARAMETERS

`cont` The non-`null` container using this layout instance.

RETURNS A non-`null` `Dimension` object containing the preferred size of the flow layout.

SEE ALSO `Component.preferredSize()`, `minimumLayoutSize()`.

removeLayoutComponent()

PURPOSE This method is a no-op.

SYNTAX `public void removeLayoutComponent(Component comp)`

DESCRIPTION This method is called by the container `comp` whenever a component is removed from `comp`. Since the flow layout manager ignores component names, this method does not do anything. This method needs to be defined in order to satisfy the `LayoutManager` interface.

PARAMETERS

`comp` The component about to be removed from the container. Ignored.

RIGHT

PURPOSE Alignment constant specifying right alignment.

SYNTAX `public static final int RIGHT`

DESCRIPTION The right alignment causes all the components in a row to be packed together and moved against the right edge of the container.

EXAMPLE See the class example.

toString()

PURPOSE Generates a string representation of the layout manager's state.

SYNTAX `public String toString()`

DESCRIPTION This method generates the string representation of this layout manager's state. The string contains the layout manager's class name, the size of the two gaps, and the alignment.

This method is typically used for debugging.

RETURNS A non-`null` string representing the layout manager's state.

OVERRIDES `Object.toString()`.

EXAMPLE See `Object.toString()`.

java.awt
Font

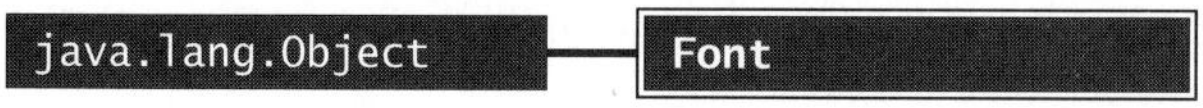

Syntax

```
public class Font
```

Description

A *font* determines how text looks when it is painted. In particular, a font is used when painting text on a `Graphics` context and as a property of AWT components. A font has three properties that contribute to the appearance of the text: the *logical name*, the *style*, and the *point size*. The properties of a font are specified at the time the font is created; they cannot be changed later.

FIGURE 97 Font

The Default Font

The font of an AWT component can be changed at any time. If an AWT component has a font whose value is `null`, the component will inherit its font from the closest ancestor whose font is not `null`.

Logical Font Name

The logical name determines the shape of the font characters. For example, the logical name `Helvetica` specifies a font with variable-width characters, while `Courier` specifies a font with fixed-width characters. The method `Toolkit.getFontList()` returns a list of valid logical font names. Currently, the supported logical font names are `Helvetica`, `TimesRoman`, `Courier`, `Dialog`, `DialogInput`, `Symbol`. Figure 97 shows a window that displays text in each of these logical font names. The `Font` class provides methods and variables to retrieve the properties of a font.

Description

Font Style

A font's style determines the weight (thickness) and slant of the font. The font style is really a combination of *style bits*. The plain style bit specifies a normal weight font with no slant. The bold style bit specifies heavy-weight font. The italic style bit specifies a font with slanted characters. The bold style bit can be combined with the italic style bit. Figure 97 shows text in various font styles.

Font Point Size

A font's point size determines the size of the font. One point is equal to approximately 1/72 of an inch. Although the AWT system tries to map the logical font names to scalable fonts, the process isn't guaranteed. So some requested point sizes may end up being mapped to a different point size. To ensure your painting code will work on all platforms, you should always retrieve and use a font's metrics when painting text in the font (see `FontMetrics`).

Font Family

The font family is a platform-specific font name. The platform-independent logical name is automatically translated to the font family at the time the `Font` object is created. The font name-to-font family translation map is specified via system properties; it cannot be specified when the `Font` object is created.

Font System Resources

The `Font` object is only a specification for a font. The actual font system resource that the platform uses to render text in a specified font is created only when needed. These system resources are automatically managed and in fact cannot be accessed via any AWT methods. You should not worry too much about trying to minimize the creation of these `Font` objects.

MEMBER SUMMARY

Constructor	
`Font()`	Constructs a new `Font` instance.
Property Methods and Fields	
`getName()`	Retrieves the logical name of the font.
`getSize()`	Retrieves the point size of the font.
`getStyle()`	Retrieves the style of the font.
`isBold()`	Determines if the font is bold.
`isItalic()`	Determines if the font is italic.
`isPlain()`	Determines if the font is plain.
`name`	Contains the font's logical name.
`size`	Contains the font's point size.
`style`	Contains the font's style.

MEMBER SUMMARY	
Style Bits	
`BOLD`	This style bit is used in creating a bold style font.
`ITALIC`	This style bit is used in creating an italic style font.
`PLAIN`	This style bit is used in creating a plain style font.
Font Methods	
`getFamily()`	Retrieves the platform-specific family name of the font.
`getFont()`	Creates a font based on the value of a system property.
General Methods	
`equals()`	Compares this object with another object for equality.
`hashCode()`	Computes the hashcode for the font.
`toString()`	Generates the string representation of the font.

See Also

`FontMetrics`.

Example

This example creates a frame and displays in it all available fonts in all four possible font styles (see Figure 97).

```
import java.awt.*;
class Main extends Frame {
    int[] styles = {
        Font.PLAIN, Font.ITALIC, Font.BOLD, Font.BOLD|Font.ITALIC};
    String[] styleNames = {
        "plain", "italic", "bold", "bold-italic",
        "plain-bold-italic"};

    Main() {
        super("Font Example");

        resize(300, 400);
        show();
    }

    public void paint(Graphics g) {
        int y = 5;

        String[] fontNames =
            Toolkit.getDefaultToolkit().getFontList();
        for (int i=0; i<fontNames.length; i++) {
```

```
                for (int j=0; j<styles.length; j++) {
                    Font f = new Font(fontNames[i], styles[j], 13);
                    FontMetrics fm = g.getFontMetrics(f);

                    y += fm.getAscent();
                    g.setFont(f);
                    g.drawString(fontNames[i]+" "+styleNames[j]
                        +" ("+f.getFamily()+")", 5, y);
                    y += fm.getLeading();
                }
                y += 13;
            }
        }

        static public void main(String[] args) {
            new Main();
        }
    }
```

BOLD

PURPOSE This style bit is used in creating a bold style font.

SYNTAX `public static final int BOLD`

DESCRIPTION This style bit can be or'ed with the `ITALIC` style bit to specify a bold-italic style font.

SEE ALSO `ITALIC`, `PLAIN`, `getStyle()`, `isBold()`.

EXAMPLE These statements create a bold and bold-italic style font.

```
    Font f1 = new Font("Dialog", Font.BOLD, 12);
    Font f2 = new Font("Dialog", Font.BOLD|Font.ITALIC, 12);
```

equals()

PURPOSE Compares this object with another object for equality.

SYNTAX `public boolean equals(Object object)`

DESCRIPTION Two font objects are equal only if their logical names, styles, and point sizes are equal. This method returns `true` if the two fonts are equal. If they are not equal or if `object` is `null` or is not of class `Font`, this method returns `false`.

PARAMETERS

`object` The object with which to compare.

RETURNS `true` if the objects are equal; `false` otherwise.

OVERRIDES `Object.equals()`.

EXAMPLE This method displays a string. The specified font is selected into the graphics context only if it differs from the currently selected font.

```
Font curFont;
void paintString(Graphics g, Font f, String s) {
   if (!curFont.equals(f)) {
      g.setFont(f);
      curFont = f;
   }
   g.drawString(s, x ,y);
}
```

Font()

PURPOSE Constructs a new `Font` instance.

SYNTAX `public Font(String name, int style, int size)`

DESCRIPTION This method constructs a new font with the specified logical name, style, and point size. The logical name of the font must be one of `Courier`, `Dialog`, `DialogInput`, `Helvetica`, `TimesRoman`, or `Symbol`. If `name` is not one of these, a default font is chosen. The actual font chosen is platform-dependent. The new `Font` instance can be used in more than one AWT object. For example, you could set the font in a number of button instances.

PARAMETERS

`name` The font's logical name.

`size` The font's point size.

`style` The font's style.

SEE ALSO `Toolkit.getFontList()`.

EXAMPLE This code fragment creates a 36-point bold Times Roman font and sets it to two buttons.

```
Font f = new Font("TimesRoman", Font.BOLD, 36);
Button b1 = new Button("OK");
Button b2 = new Button("Cancel");

b1.setFont(f);
b2.setFont(f);
```

getFamily()

PURPOSE Retrieves the font's family name.

SYNTAX `public String getFamily()`

DESCRIPTION The font family is the platform-specific font name that's assigned to the font's logical name. The font family name is determined at the time the font is created and cannot be changed.

RETURNS The font's family name as a non-`null` string.

EXAMPLE This example prints out the family name for each available logical font name.

```
import java.awt.*;
class Main extends Frame {
    static public void main(String[] args) {
        String[] fontNames =
            Toolkit.getDefaultToolkit().getFontList();

        for (int i=0; i<fontNames.length; i++) {
            Font f = new Font(fontNames[i], Font.PLAIN, 12);
            System.out.println(fontNames[i] + " -> " + f.getFamily());
        }
    }
}
```

OUTPUT

```
Dialog -> Dialog
Helvetica -> Helvetica
TimesRoman -> TimesRoman
Courier -> Courier
Symbol -> Symbol
```

getFont()

PURPOSE Creates a font based on the value of a system property.

SYNTAX

```
public static Font getFont(String propName)
public static Font getFont(String propName, Font defaultFont)
```

DESCRIPTION The two forms of this method create and return a `Font` object associated with the system property name `propName`. The font specification in the system property value has the following form:

```
<logical font name>-<style>-<point size>
```

Each of the three font properties are separated by a dash (-). The logical font name must be one of the valid logical font names. The style can be one of `plain`, `italic`, `bold`, or `bolditalic`. The point size can be any positive integer. Table 10 shows some examples of font specifications and their equivalent constructor statements:

TABLE 10 Examples of Font Properties

`Courier-bold-14`	`new Font("Courier", Font.BOLD, 14)`
`Courier-plain`	`new Font("Courier", Font.PLAIN, 12)`
`TimesRoman--18`	`new Font("TimesRoman", Font.PLAIN, 18)`
`Helvetica`	`new Font("Helvetica", Font.PLAIN, 12)`
`Dialog-bolditalic-16`	`new Font("Dialog", Font.BOLD|Font.ITALIC, 16)`

The logical font name is required, but the style and point size are optional. If the style is not specified or is blank or invalid, `plain` is assumed. If the point size is not specified, 12 is assumed.

If the system property `propName` is not defined and `defaultFont` is specified, `defaultFont` is returned. Also, if there is some error in the font specification, `defaultFont` is returned. However, if both the system property and `defaultFont` are not specified, `null` is returned.

PARAMETERS

`defaultFont` The font that is returned if the system property `propName` is not defined.

`propName` A non-`null` string specifying the system property name.

RETURNS A `Font` object or `null`.

EXCEPTIONS

`NullPointerException`

If `propName` is `null`.

SEE ALSO `System.getProperty()`.

EXAMPLE This example searches for a system property called "`myapp.button.font`" and creates a font based on the value of this property.

```
Font f = Font.getFont("myapp.button.font",
   new Font("Courier", Font.PLAIN, 12));
```

getName()

PURPOSE Retrieves the font's logical name.

SYNTAX `public String getName()`

DESCRIPTION The font's logical name is specified during the creation of the `Font` object and cannot be changed.

RETURNS The font's logical name as a non-`null` string.

SEE ALSO `Font`, `name`.

EXAMPLE This example method returns `true` if the logical names for `f1` and `f2` are the same.

```
boolean compareFontNames(Font f1, Font f2) {
    return f1.getName().equals(f2.getName());
}
```

getSize()

PURPOSE Retrieves the font's point size.

SYNTAX `public int getSize()`

DESCRIPTION The font's point size is specified during the creation of the `Font` object and cannot be changed.

RETURNS The font's point size.

SEE ALSO `Font`.

EXAMPLE This example increases the point size of a font by 1.

```
Font increasePointSize(Font f) {
    return new Font(f.getName(), f.getStyle(), f.getSize()+1);
}
```

getStyle()

PURPOSE Retrieves the font's style.

SYNTAX `public int getStyle()`

DESCRIPTION The font style is a collection of font style bits. To test whether a style bit is included in the font style, use the bitwise "and" operator (see the example).

The plain style differs from the other style bits in that it is really the absence of all style bits; hence it has the value `0`. So to test if the font style is plain, test it against the value `0` (see the example).

This method is typically used when saving the font style or using it to create another font with the same style. When determining which style bits are included in the font style, it is better to use the methods `isBold()`, `isItalic()`, and `isPlain()`.

RETURNS The font's style.

SEE ALSO `isBold()`, `isItalic()`, `isPlain()`.

EXAMPLE This example retrieves the default font of a frame and prints its styles.

```
import java.awt.*;
class Main {
    static public void main(String[] args) {
        Frame f = new Frame();
        f.pack();  // otherwise the default font is null.
        int s = f.getFont().getStyle();

        System.out.println("plain: " + (s == 0));
        System.out.println("bold: " + ((s&Font.BOLD) != 0));
        System.out.println("italic: " + ((s&Font.ITALIC) != 0));
    }
}
```

OUTPUT

```
plain: true
bold: false
italic: false
```

hashCode()

PURPOSE Computes the hash code for the font.

SYNTAX `public int hashCode()`

DESCRIPTION The font's hash code is an integer that's calculated from the font's properties. Two `Font` objects with the same properties will have the same hash code. However, two `Font` objects that do not have the same properties might also have the same hash code, although the hash code algorithm minimizes this possibility. The hash code is typically used as the key in a hash table.

Note, it's not really necessary to cache `Font` objects, since they are reasonably small. The actual system font resources contain all the necessary information for the system to paint text and so can be much larger. These are automatically maintained by the AWT system and cannot be accessed.

RETURNS The font's hash code.

OVERRIDES `Object.hashCode()`.

SEE ALSO `Hashtable`.

EXAMPLE

```
Hashtable ht = new Hashtable();
Font f = new Font("Dialog", Font.PLAIN, 12);
ht.put(f.hashCode(), f);
```

isBold()

PURPOSE Determines if the font's style includes the bold style bit.

SYNTAX `public boolean isBold()`

RETURNS `true` if the font's style includes the `BOLD` style bit.

SEE ALSO `BOLD`, `Font()`.

EXAMPLE These statements remove a font's bold style, if present.

```
if (f.isBold()) {
    f = new Font(f.getName(), f.getStyle()&~Font.BOLD, f.getSize());
}
```

isItalic()

PURPOSE Determines if the font's style includes the italic style bit.

SYNTAX `public boolean isItalic()`

RETURNS `true` if the font's style includes the `ITALIC` style bit.

SEE ALSO `ITALIC`, `Font()`.

EXAMPLE These statements remove a font's italic style, if present.

```
if (f.isItalic()) {
    f = new Font(f.getName(), f.getStyle()&~Font.ITALIC, f.getSize());
}
```

A B C D E F G H I J K L M N O P Q R S T U V W X Y Z

isPlain()

PURPOSE Determines if the font's style is plain.

SYNTAX `public boolean isPlain()`

RETURNS `true` if the font's style does not include any style bits besides `PLAIN`.

SEE ALSO `BOLD`, `Font()`, `ITALIC`, `PLAIN`.

EXAMPLE These statements force a font to a plain style.

```
if (!f.isPlain()) {
    f = new Font(f.getName(), Font.PLAIN, f.getSize());
}
```

ITALIC

PURPOSE Used in creating an italic style font.

SYNTAX `public static final int ITALIC`

DESCRIPTION This constant can be or'ed with the `BOLD` style bit to specify a bold-italic style font.

SEE ALSO `BOLD`, `getStyle()`, `isBold()`, `PLAIN`.

EXAMPLE These statements create an italic and a bold-italic font.

```
Font f1 = new Font("Courier", Font.ITALIC, 12);
Font f2 = new Font("courier", Font.BOLD|Font.ITALIC, 12);
```

name

PURPOSE Contains the font's logical name.

SYNTAX `protected String name`

DESCRIPTION This field is accessible only by subclasses of `Font`. It is meant to be read only and should not be changed.

SEE ALSO `getName()`.

PLAIN

PURPOSE This style bit is used in creating a plain font.

SYNTAX `public static final int PLAIN`

DESCRIPTION The `PLAIN` style bit isn't really a style bit. It's actually the absence of all other style bits, which means it has the value `0`. However, it's convenient to use when creating a plain style font.

SEE ALSO `BOLD`, `getStyle()`, `isPlain()`, `ITALIC`.

EXAMPLE This statement creates a plain font.

```
Font f = new Font("Courier", Font.PLAIN, 12);
```

size

PURPOSE Contains the font's point size.

SYNTAX `protected int size`

DESCRIPTION The value in this field is identical to the one returned via `getSize()`. This field is accessible only by subclasses of `Font`. It is meant to be read-only and should not be changed.

SEE ALSO `getSize()`.

style

PURPOSE Contains the font's style.

SYNTAX `protected int style`

DESCRIPTION The value in this field is identical to the one returned via `getStyle()`. This field is accessible only by subclasses of `Font`. It is meant to be read-only and should not be changed.

SEE ALSO `getStyle()`.

A B C D E F G H I J K L M N O P Q R S T U V W X Y Z

toString()

PURPOSE Generates the string representation of the font.

SYNTAX `public String toString()`

RETURNS A non-`null` string representing the properties of the font. This method is used for debugging output.

OVERRIDES `Object.toString()`.

EXAMPLE These statements print a string representation of a font.

```
Font f = new Font("Courier", Font.BOLD|Font.ITALIC, 12);
System.out.println(f.toString());
System.out.println(f);
```

java.awt
FontMetrics

`java.lang.Object` — `FontMetrics`

Syntax

```
public abstract class FontMetrics
```

Description

A `FontMetrics` instance for a particular font contains information about the visual attributes of the font, such as its height and character widths.

Figure 98 shows the attributes of a font. The values of these attributes are available through its font metrics.

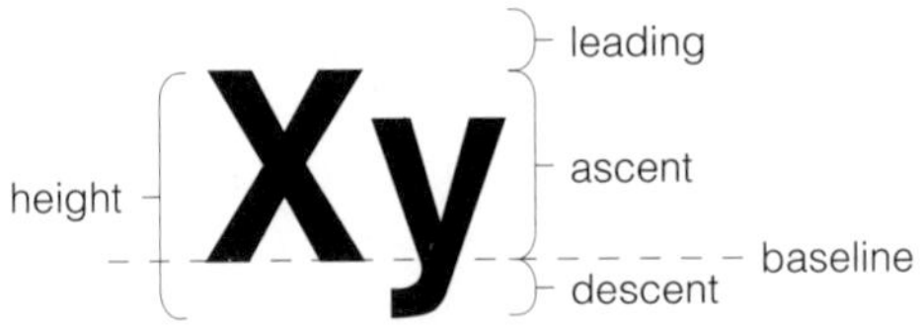

FIGURE 98 **`FontMetrics` Attributes**

Baseline

The baseline is an imaginary horizontal line that cuts through the characters in the font. The bottom of the character 'X', for example, is aligned on the font's baseline. Characters with descenders, such as the letter 'y', are aligned such that only the descender extends below the baseline. When you are painting text of different font sizes, the text should be painted such that their baselines connect.

Ascent

The ascent of a font is the distance from the top of the font to the baseline. The ascent is typically used to determine the location of the font's baseline. The font's ascent is not the same as the maximum ascent of all the characters in the font. Some characters may extend beyond the font's ascent. The maximum ascent of all characters is called the font's maximum ascent and is available in a font metrics.

Descent

The descent of a font is the distance from the bottom of the font to the baseline. The font's descent is not the same as the maximum descent of all the characters in the font. Some characters may extend below the descent depth. The maximum descent of all characters is called the font's maximum descent and is available in a font metrics.

Leading

The leading is the spacing between rows of painted text. If the text were painted without the leading, the rows would touch each other. In the case of when the ascent does not match the maximum ascent or the descent does not match the maximum descent, parts of the character may appear in the leading space.

Height

The height of a font is the sum of the font's ascent, descent, and leading. When painting rows of text, the distance between baselines should be the font's height. The font's maximum height is the sum of its maximum ascent, maximum descent, and leading.

MEMBER SUMMARY	
Constructor	
`FontMetrics`	Constructs a new `FontMetrics` instance.
Size Methods	
`bytesWidth()`	Determines the width of an array of bytes.
`charsWidth()`	Determines the width of an array of characters.
`charWidth()`	Retrieves the width of a character in the font.
`getWidths()`	Retrieves the width of the first 256 characters in the font.
`stringWidth()`	Determines the pixel width of a string.
Font Metric Attribute Methods	
`getAscent()`	Retrieves the font's ascent.
`getDescent()`	Retrieves the font's descent.
`getHeight()`	Retrieves the font's height.
`getLeading()`	Retrieves the font's leading.
`getMaxAdvance()`	Retrieves the width of the widest character in the font.
`getMaxAscent()`	Retrieves the font's maximum ascent.
`getMaxDescent()`	Retrieves the font's maximum descent.
Font Fields and Methods	
`font`	The font from which the font metrics were created.
`getFont()`	Retrieves the font used to create the font metrics.
Debugging Method	
`toString()`	Generates a string representation of the font metrics.

Example

This somewhat elaborate example demonstrates how to display text in multiple font styles and sizes. The text is input from a file and formatting codes are embedded in the text. The text is painted in a default font, and the formatting codes can change one attribute of the font at a time—its name, style, or size. Figure 99 shows a screen shot of the example. Figure 100 shows the input file used to generate the screen shot.

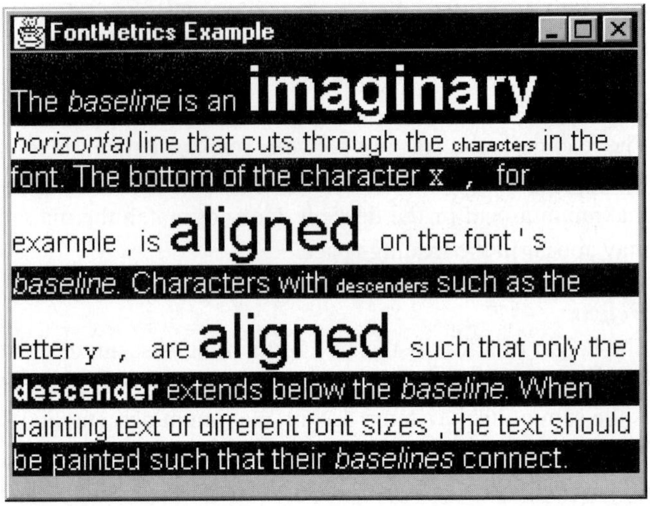

FIGURE 99 `FontMetrics`

```
<15 <Helvetica The <i baseline <p <15 is an <32 <b
imaginary <15 <i horizontal <p line that cuts through
the <9 characters <15 in the font.
The bottom of the character <Courier X,
<Helvetica for example, is <32 aligned <15 on the font''s
<i baseline. <p <15  Characters with <9 descenders <15 such as
the letter <Courier y, <Helvetica are <32 aligned
<15 such that only the <b descender <p extends below
the <i baseline. <p <15  When painting text of different
font sizes, the text should be painted such that their
<i baselines <p <15 connect.
```

FIGURE 100 `FontMetrics` **Example Input File**

Input Format

A formatting code begins with the left angle character ‘<’. If the text that follows the ‘<’ is a number, the current font size is changed to that number. If the code is ‘<b’, the font style is changed to bold. If the code is ‘<i’, the font style is changed to italics. If the code is ‘<p’, the font style is changed to plain. Otherwise, the font’s name becomes the text following the ‘<’ character.

To make it clearer to see the rectangles in which each line of text is painted, the background of each line alternates between black and white.

Implementation Notes: The leading for text is displayed above that line, except for the first line, which does not have any leading. The leading used is the maximum leading for all the fonts that appear on that line. For simplicity's sake, the text is parsed into words and formatting codes; all the words and formatting codes are kept in a `Vector` object.

```
import java.awt.*;
import java.io.*;
import java.util.*;

class Main extends Frame {
    Vector tokens = new Vector();
    Font defaultFont = new Font("TimesRoman", Font.PLAIN, 12);

    Main(String filename) throws IOException {
        super("FontMetrics Example");
        StreamTokenizer st =
            new StreamTokenizer(new FileInputStream(filename));
        Font f = defaultFont;;

        int t = st.nextToken();
        do {
            switch (t) {
            case '<':
                t = st.nextToken();
                switch (t) {
                case StreamTokenizer.TT_NUMBER:
                    f = new Font(f.getName(), f.getStyle(),
                        (int)st.nval);
                    break;
                case StreamTokenizer.TT_WORD:
                    switch (st.sval.charAt(0)) {
                    case 'b':
                        f = new Font(f.getName(), Font.BOLD,
                            f.getSize());
                        break;
                    case 'i':
                        f = new Font(f.getName(), Font.ITALIC,
                            f.getSize());
                        break;
                    case 'p':
                        f = new Font(f.getName(), Font.PLAIN,
                            f.getSize());
                        break;
                    default:
                        f = new Font(st.sval, f.getStyle(),
                            f.getSize());
                        break;
                    }
                }
                tokens.addElement(f);
                break;
            case StreamTokenizer.TT_WORD:
                tokens.addElement(st.sval);
```

Example

```
                break;
            case StreamTokenizer.TT_NUMBER:
                tokens.addElement(String.valueOf((int)st.nval));
                break;
            case StreamTokenizer.TT_EOL:
                break;
            default:
                tokens.addElement(String.valueOf((char)t));
                break;
            }
            t = st.nextToken();
        } while (t != StreamTokenizer.TT_EOF);
        resize(300, 300);
        show();
    }

    int line = 0;
    void paintLine(Graphics g, Font f, int start, int end,
                   int y, int ht, int ac) {
        int x = 0;
        FontMetrics fm = g.getFontMetrics(f);

        if (line++ % 2 == 0) {
            g.setColor(Color.black);
            g.fillRect(0, y, size().width, ht);
            g.setColor(Color.white);
        } else {
            g.setColor(Color.white);
            g.fillRect(0, y, size().width, ht);
            g.setColor(Color.black);
        }
        g.setFont(f);
        for (int i=start; i<end; i++) {
            Object tk = tokens.elementAt(i);
            if (tk instanceof Font) {
                g.setFont(f = (Font)tk);
                fm = g.getFontMetrics();
            } else {
                g.drawString((String)tk, x, y + ac);
                x += fm.stringWidth((String)tk) + fm.charWidth(' ');
            }
        }
    }

    public void paint(Graphics g) {
        Insets insets = insets();
        int w = size().width-insets.left-insets.right;
        Font f = defaultFont;
        Font startFont = f;
        FontMetrics fm = g.getFontMetrics(f);

        g.clearRect(0, 0, w, size().height);
        g.setFont(f);
```

```
        int start = 0, x = 0, y = 0;
        int ht = fm.getMaxAscent() + fm.getLeading();
        int base = fm.getMaxAscent();
        line = 0;
        for (int i=0; i<tokens.size(); i++) {
            Object token = tokens.elementAt(i);
            if (token instanceof Font) {
                f = (Font)token;
                g.setFont(f);
                fm = g.getFontMetrics(f);
            } else {
                x += fm.stringWidth((String)token);
                if (x > w) {
                    paintLine(g, startFont, start, i, y, ht, base);
                    startFont = f;
                    start = i--;
                    y += ht;
                    x = ht = base = 0;
                } else {
                    if (y == 0) {
                        ht = Math.max(ht, fm.getMaxAscent() +
                             fm.getDescent());
                        base = Math.max(base, fm.getMaxAscent());
                    } else {
                        ht = Math.max(ht, fm.getHeight());
                        base = Math.max(base, fm.getAscent()+
                             fm.getLeading());
                    }
                    x += fm.charWidth(' ');
                }
            }
        }
        paintLine(g, startFont, start, tokens.size(), y, ht, base);
    }

    static public void main(String[] args) {
        try {
            new Main(args[0]);
        } catch (IOException e) {
            e.printStackTrace();
        }
    }
}
```

bytesWidth()

PURPOSE Determines the width of an array of bytes.

SYNTAX `public int bytesWidth(byte[] data, int offset, int count)` charsWidth()

B C D E F G H I J K L M N O P Q R S T U V W X Y Z

DESCRIPTION This method determines the width of `count` number of bytes in the byte array `data` starting at the index `offset` when displayed using this font metrics. The bytes represent 8-bit characters. The bytes are converted to 16-bit `chars` and then supplied to `charsWidth()`.

PARAMETERS

`count` The number of bytes to consider. `count + offset` must be less than the length of `data`.

`data` The non-`null` array of bytes.

`offset` The index of the first byte to consider in `data`. `offset` must be less than the length of `data`.

RETURNS The pixel width of the bytes in `data` that are displayed.

SEE ALSO `charsWidth()`, `stringWidth()`.

EXAMPLE See `getMaxAdvance()`.

charsWidth()

PURPOSE Determines the width of an array of characters.

SYNTAX `public int charsWidth(char[] data, int offset, int count)`

DESCRIPTION This method determines the width of `count` number of characters in the character array `data` starting at the index `offset`.

PARAMETERS

`count` The number of characters to consider. `count + offset` must be less than the length of `data`.

`data` The non-`null` array of characters.

`offset` The index of the first byte to consider in `data`. `offset` must be less than the length of `data`.

RETURNS The pixel width of the characters in `data` when displayed.

SEE ALSO `bytesWidth()`, `stringWidth()`.

EXAMPLE See `getMaxAdvance()`.

charWidth()

PURPOSE Retrieves the width of a character in the font.

SYNTAX
```
public int charWidth(char ch)
public int charWidth(int i)
```

DESCRIPTION This method retrieves the width of the character `ch` in the font of this font metric. If an integer `i` is specified, it is equivalent to `charWidth((char)i)`.

PARAMETERS

`ch` The character whose width is to be retrieved.

`i` The character whose width is to be retrieved. `i` is first converted to a `char`.

RETURNS The pixel width of the character when displayed.

SEE ALSO `stringWidth()`.

EXAMPLE See the class example.

font

PURPOSE The font from which the font metrics were created.

SYNTAX `protected Font font`

SEE ALSO `getFont()`.

FontMetrics()

PURPOSE Constructs a new `FontMetrics` instance.

SYNTAX `protected FontMetrics(Font font)`

DESCRIPTION This constructor creates a new `FontMetrics` instance using the font `font`.

PARAMETERS

`font` The non-`null` font.

EXAMPLE This example demonstrates the most common use of the `FontMetrics` class—painting lines of text. The example prints two lines of output. Notice that when using `Graphics.drawString`, you need to add the font's ascent to the *y*-coordinate. See Figure 101.

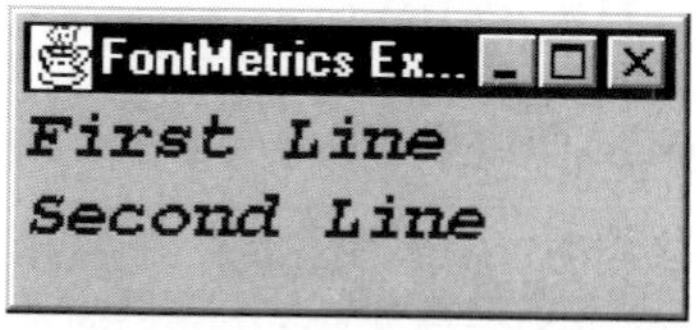

FIGURE 101 `FontMetrics()`

```
import java.awt.*;
class Main extends Frame {
```

```
        Main() {
            super("FontMetrics Example");
            resize(150, 75);
            show();
        }

        public void paint(Graphics g) {
            Font f = new Font("Courier", Font.ITALIC+Font.BOLD, 18);
            FontMetrics fm = g.getFontMetrics(f);
            int y = 0;

            g.setColor(Color.blue);
            g.setFont(f);
            g.drawString("First Line", 0, y + fm.getAscent());
            y += fm.getHeight();
            g.drawString("Second Line", 0, y + fm.getAscent());
        }

        public static void main(String[] args) {
            new Main();
        }
    }
```

getAscent()

PURPOSE	Retrieves the font's ascent.
SYNTAX	`public int getAscent()`
RETURNS	The font's ascent in pixels.
SEE ALSO	`getMaxAscent()`.
EXAMPLE	See the class example.

getDescent()

PURPOSE	Retrieves the font's descent.
SYNTAX	`public int getDescent()`
RETURNS	The font's descent in pixels.
SEE ALSO	`getMaxDescent()`.
EXAMPLE	See the class example.

getFont()

PURPOSE Retrieves the font used to create the font metrics.

SYNTAX `public Font getFont()`

RETURNS The non-`null` font used to create the font metrics.

EXAMPLE See the `getMaxAdvance()`.

getHeight()

PURPOSE Retrieves the font's height.

SYNTAX `public int getHeight()`

DESCRIPTION This method retrieves the font's height, which is the sum of the values `getLeading() + getAscent() + getDescent()`.

The font's height is used to determine the pixel distance between the baselines of adjacent lines of text.

RETURNS The font's height in pixels.

EXAMPLE See the class example.

getLeading()

PURPOSE Retrieves the font's leading.

SYNTAX `public int getLeading()`

DESCRIPTION This method returns the font's leading, which is the line spacing between adjacent lines of text.

RETURNS The font's leading in pixels.

EXAMPLE See the class example.

getMaxAdvance()

PURPOSE Retrieves the width of the widest character in the font.

SYNTAX `public int getMaxAdvance()`

RETURNS The maximum width of the widest character in the font in pixels; -1 if the value is not available.

EXAMPLE This example takes an array of characters and displays each character in a box. See Figure 102. All the boxes are of equal size. The maximum ascent, descent, and advance values are used to ensure that the characters do not extend outside the boxes. The font's leading size is used to separate the boxes and pad the interior of the boxes. Pressing the '+' key increases the size of the font; pressing the '-' key decreases the size of the font.

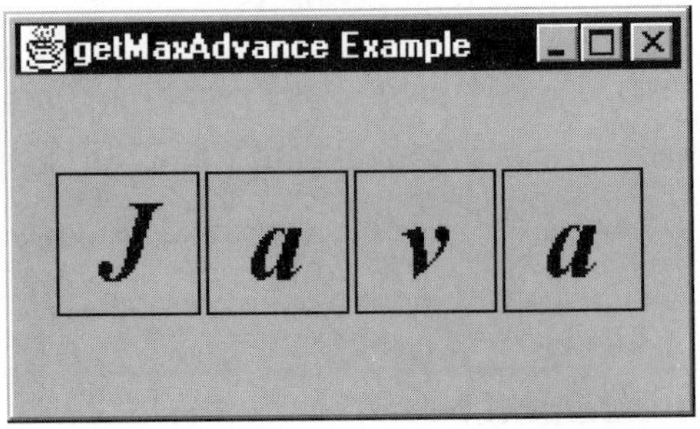

FIGURE 102 `FontMetrics.getMaxAdvance()`

```
import java.awt.*;
class Main extends Frame {
    int fontPointSize = 40;
    char[] message = {'J', 'a', 'v', 'a'};

    Main() {
        super("getMaxAdvance Example");
        resize(300, 150);
        show();
    }

    public void paint(Graphics g) {
        Insets insets = this.insets();
        int w = size().width-insets.left-insets.right;
        int h = size().height-insets.top-insets.bottom;
        FontMetrics fm = g.getFontMetrics(
            new Font("TimesRoman", Font.BOLD+Font.ITALIC,
                fontPointSize));

        // Determine size of one box.  Add some padding
        //     (use the leading
        // value) around the inside of each box.
        Dimension dim = new Dimension(fm.getMaxAdvance()+
            2*fm.getLeading(),
            fm.getMaxAscent() + fm.getMaxDescent() +
            2*fm.getLeading());

        // Determine bounding rectangle for all boxes; include
        //     some spacing
        // between the boxes.
        Rectangle r = new Rectangle(0, 0,
            message.length * dim.width + (message.length-1) *
                fm.getLeading(), dim.height);
```

```
        //Now center the rectangle.
        r.move((w-r.width)/2, (h-r.height)/2);

        g.clearRect(0, 0, w, h);
        g.setFont(fm.getFont());
        for (int i=0; i<message.length; i++) {
            int cW = fm.charsWidth(message, i, 1);
            int cH = fm.getMaxAscent() + fm.getMaxDescent() +
                fm.getLeading();

            g.drawChars(message, i, 1, r.x + (dim.width-cW)/2,
                r.y + (dim.height-cH)/2 + fm.getMaxAscent());
            g.drawRect(r.x, r.y, dim.width-1, r.height-1);
            r.x += dim.width + fm.getLeading();
        }
    }

    public boolean keyDown(Event evt, int key) {
        if (key == '+') {
            fontPointSize++;
        } else if (key == '-') {
            fontPointSize--;
        }
        repaint();
        return true;
    }

    static public void main(String[] args) {
        new Main();
    }
}
```

getMaxAscent()

PURPOSE Retrieves the font's maximum ascent.

SYNTAX `public int getMaxAscent()`

RETURNS The font's maximum ascent in pixels.

SEE ALSO `getAscent()`.

EXAMPLE See `getMaxAdvance()`.

getMaxDecent()

PURPOSE For backward compatibility only.

SYNTAX	`public int getMaxDecent()`
DESCRIPTION	This method is for backward compatibility only. It should no longer be used.
SEE ALSO	`getMaxDescent()`.
EXAMPLE	See `getMaxAdvance()`.

getMaxDescent()

PURPOSE	Retrieves the font's maximum descent.
SYNTAX	`public int getMaxDescent()`
RETURNS	The font's maximum descent.
SEE ALSO	`getDescent()`.
EXAMPLE	See `getMaxAdvance()`.

getWidths()

PURPOSE	Retrieves the width of the first 256 characters in the font.
SYNTAX	`public int[] getWidths()`
RETURNS	A 256-element array containing the widths of the first 256 characters in the font.

EXAMPLE This example displays text in columns, in top-to-bottom and left-to-right order. See Figure 103. The string can contain the new-line character, which starts a new column. The descent of the font is used to determine the spacing between columns.

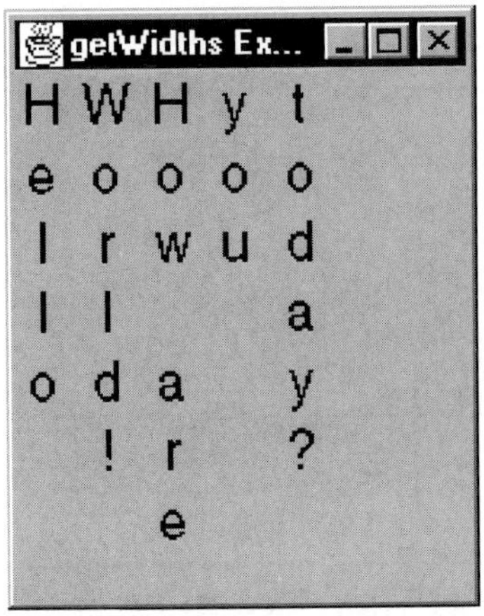

FIGURE 103 `FontMetrics.getWidths()`

```
import java.awt.*;
import java.io.*;
import java.util.*;

class Main extends Frame {
    StringBufferInputStream is =
```

```
        new StringBufferInputStream
            ("Hello\nWorld!\nHow are\nyou\ntoday?");
    int[] charWidths;


    Main() {
        super("getWidths Example");
        setFont(new Font("Helvetica", Font.PLAIN, 20));
        resize(300, 200);
        show();
    }

    public void paint(Graphics g) {
        int x = 0, y = 0;
        int ch;
        char[] chs = new char[1];
        FontMetrics fm = g.getFontMetrics();

        if (charWidths == null) {
            charWidths = fm.getWidths();
        }
        is.reset();
        while ((ch = is.read()) != -1) {
            if (ch == '\n') {
                x += fm.getMaxAdvance() + fm.getDescent();
                y = 0;
                continue;
            }
            chs[0] = (char)ch;
            g.drawChars(chs, 0, 1,
                x + (fm.getMaxAdvance()-charWidths[ch])/2,
                y + fm.getAscent());
            y += fm.getHeight();
        }
    }

    static public void main(String[] args) {
    new Main();
    }
}
```

stringWidth()

PURPOSE Determines the pixel width of a string.

SYNTAX `public int stringWidth(String string)`

DESCRIPTION This method determines the pixel width of a string. The result is equivalent to using `charWidth()` to add together the widths of the individual characters.

RETURNS The width of the string in pixels.

PARAMETERS	
`string`	The non-`null` string whose width is to be determined.
SEE ALSO	`bytesWidth()`, `charsWidth()`.
EXAMPLE	See the class example.

toString()

PURPOSE	Generates a string representation of this font metrics.
SYNTAX	`public String toString()`
DESCRIPTION	This method returns the string representation of this font metric. The result string contains the values for all the font metrics's attributes. This method is typically used for debugging.
RETURNS	A non-`null` string representing the font metrics's state.
OVERRIDES	`Object.toString()`.

java.awt

Frame

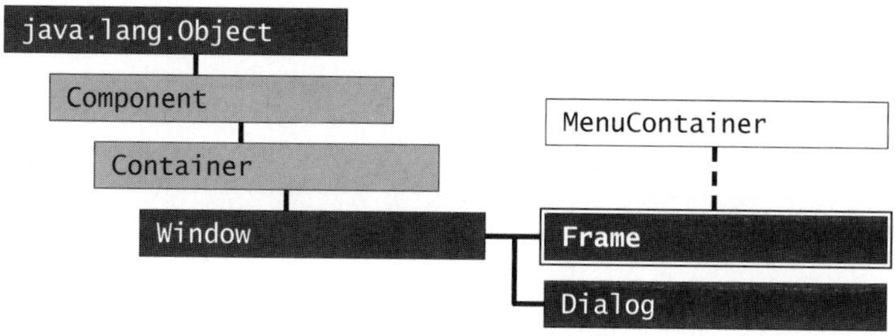

Syntax

```
public class Frame extends Window implements MenuContainer
```

Description

A *frame* is a window with additional properties: a title bar, a menu bar, a border, a cursor, and an icon image.

The Title Property

The *title bar* is a strip across the top of the frame that displays a short description of the frame, called the title. The title can be changed at any time.

The Resizable Property

A *resizable* frame can be resized by the user. The resizable property can be changed at any time. The precise steps to resize the frame are platform-dependent.

The Cursor Property

The frame normally displays the *default cursor*—typically an arrow—when the cursor is moved anywhere in the frame. This cursor shape can be changed at any time. The exact cursor shapes available are platform-dependent.

The IconImage Property

A frame can be assigned an *icon image*. The icon image is a way to graphically represent the frame. It is up to the platform windowing system as to how the icon image is used. For example, most platforms will display the frame's icon when the frame is iconified.

Coordinates and Sizes

A frame has a nonempty inset because of the title bar, menu bar, and border. The frame has an interior area in which you can paint and place components. The insets of a frame can change because of the menu bar. For example, if the window is made small enough so that the menu bar requires additional lines in order to display the menu labels, `insets().top` will increase.

The origin of the frame is at the top-left corner of the frame. The *x*- and *y*-coordinates in the frame's bounds indicate the location of the frame on the screen.

Events

The frame generates the same events as a window. See the `Window` class for more details.

MEMBER SUMMARY	
Constructor	
`Frame()`	Constructs a new `Frame` instance.
Cursor Types	
`CROSSHAIR_CURSOR`	The cursor type specifying a crosshair cursor.
`DEFAULT_CURSOR`	The cursor type specifying the default cursor.
`E_RESIZE_CURSOR`	The cursor type specifying a type of resizing cursor.
`HAND_CURSOR`	The cursor type specifying a hand cursor.
`MOVE_CURSOR`	The cursor type specifying a moving cursor.
`N_RESIZE_CURSOR`	The cursor type specifying a type of resizing cursor.
`NE_RESIZE_CURSOR`	The cursor type specifying a type of resizing cursor.
`NW_RESIZE_CURSOR`	The cursor type specifying a type of resizing cursor.
`S_RESIZE_CURSOR`	The cursor type specifying a type of resizing cursor.
`SE_RESIZE_CURSOR`	The cursor type specifying a type of resizing cursor.
`SW_RESIZE_CURSOR`	The cursor type specifying a type of resizing cursor.
`TEXT_CURSOR`	The cursor type specifying a caret cursor.
`W_RESIZE_CURSOR`	The cursor type specifying a resizing cursor.
`WAIT_CURSOR`	The cursor type specifying an hourglass cursor.
The Property Methods	
`getCursorType()`	Retrieves the frame's cursor type.
`getIconImage()`	Retrieves the frame's icon image.
`getTitle()`	Retrieves the frame's title.
`isResizable()`	Retrieves the frame's resizable state.
`setCursor()`	Sets the frame's cursor.
`setIconImage()`	Sets the image to display when this frame is iconified.
`setResizable()`	Sets the resizable property.
`setTitle()`	Sets the frame's title.
Menu Bar Methods	
`getMenuBar()`	Retrieves the frame's menu bar.
`remove()`	Removes the frame's menu bar.
`setMenuBar()`	Sets the frame's menu bar.

MEMBER SUMMARY	
Peer Methods	
`addNotify()`	Creates the frame's peer hierarchy.
`dispose()`	Destroys the frame's peer hierarchy.
Debugging Method	
`paramString()`	Generates a string representing the frame's state.

Example

This example creates a frame whose interior is exactly 150 pixels high and 150 pixels wide. If you click anywhere in the interior, a new frame will appear. Its northwest corner will be at the exact position you clicked (see Figure 104).

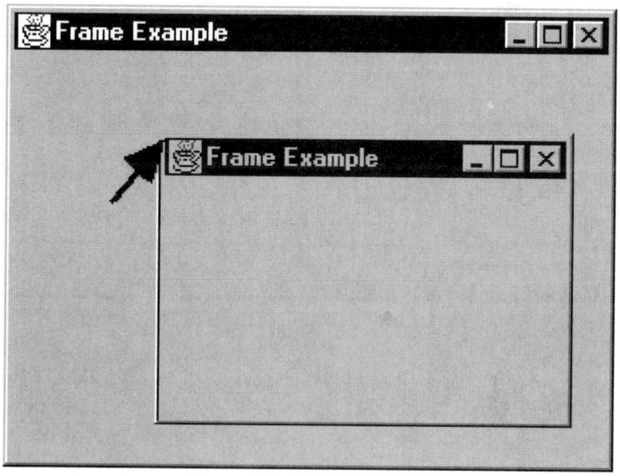

FIGURE 104 Frame

```
import java.awt.*;
class Main extends Frame {
    // The contructor creates a frame with a window size that gives
    // the desired interior size.
    Main() {
        super("Frame example");
        // Calling addNotify() creates the peers; otherwise insets()
        // does not return the right values.
        addNotify();

        Insets insets = insets();
        resize(insets.left + insets.right + 150,
               insets.top + insets.bottom + 150);
    }
    public boolean mouseDown(Event evt, int x, int y) {
        // x, y are in interior coordinates and must be translated
        // first to window coordinates and then to screen coordinates.
        Insets insets = insets();
        Rectangle bounds = bounds();
        Main m = new Main();
```

```
            x += insets.left + bounds.x;
            y += insets.top + bounds.y;
            m.move(x, y);
            m.show();
            return true;
        }
        static public void main(String[] args) {
            (new Main()).show();
        }
    }
```

addNotify()

PURPOSE Creates the frame's peer hierarchy.

SYNTAX `public synchronized void addNotify()`

DESCRIPTION This method creates the frame's peer hierarchy, if necessary. The frame's peer is created by calling the `Toolkit.createFrame()` method. This method should be called before the frame's minimum or preferred size is calculated. The methods `pack()` and `show()` automatically call `addNotify()`.

OVERRIDES `Window.addNotify()`.

SEE ALSO `Component`, `Component.minimumSize()`, `Component.preferredSize()`, `Toolkit`, `Window.pack()`, `Window.show()`.

EXAMPLE See the class example.

CROSSHAIR_CURSOR

PURPOSE The cursor type specifying a crosshair cursor.

SYNTAX `public static final int CROSSHAIR_CURSOR`

DESCRIPTION This cursor type is typically displayed when drawing graphics.

EXAMPLE See `setCursor()`.

DEFAULT_CURSOR

PURPOSE The cursor type specifying the default pointer cursor.

SYNTAX `public static final int DEFAULT_CURSOR`

A B C D E F G H I J K L M N O P Q R S T U V W X Y Z

DESCRIPTION This cursor type should be displayed when the cursor is not over a special kind of window or if the application is not in any mode.

EXAMPLE See `setCursor()`.

dispose()

PURPOSE Destroys the frame's peer hierarchy.

SYNTAX `public synchronized void dispose()`

DESCRIPTION This method destroys the frame's peer hierarchy, if it exists, thereby freeing any resources used by the peers. The state of the frame hierarchy is left intact and can be reused. The peer hierarchy can be restored by calling `addNotify()`.

OVERRIDES `Window.dispose()`.

EXAMPLE This example creates two buttons: One creates a frame and the other disposes it. See Figure 105. Upon initialization, the dispose button is disabled. When a frame is created, the create button is disabled and the dispose button is enabled. The original frame also handles the `Event.WINDOW_DESTROY` event and disposes itself.

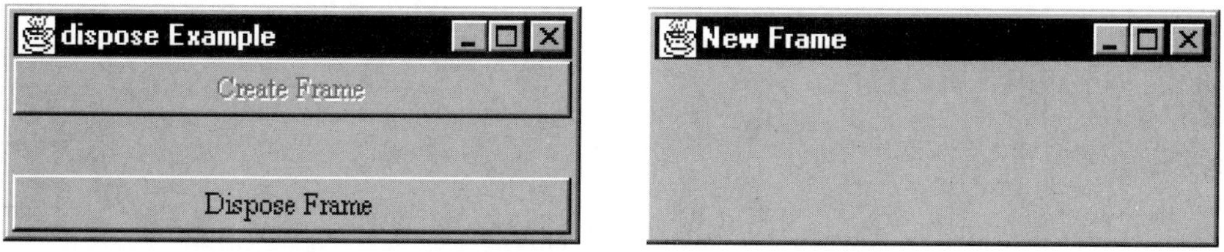

FIGURE 105 `Frame.dispose()`: Initial Frame and Newly Created Frame

```
import java.awt.*;
class Main extends Frame {
    Button btnCreate = new Button("Create Frame");
    Button btnDispose = new Button("Dispose Frame");
    Frame f;

    Main() {
        super("dispose Example");

        btnDispose.disable();
        add("North", btnCreate);
```

```
        add("South", btnDispose);
        resize(100, 100);
        show();
    }

    public boolean action(Event evt, Object arg) {
        if (evt.target == btnCreate) {
            btnCreate.disable();
            btnDispose.enable();
            f = new Frame("New Frame");
            f.reshape(100, 100, 100, 100);
            f.show();
            return true;
        } else if (evt.target == btnDispose) {
            btnCreate.enable();
            btnDispose.disable();
            f.dispose();
            return true;
        }
        return false;
    }

    public boolean handleEvent(Event evt) {
        if (evt.id == Event.WINDOW_DESTROY) {
            dispose();
            return true;
        }
        return super.handleEvent(evt);
    }

    static public void main(String[] args) {
        new Main();
    }
}
```

E_RESIZE_CURSOR

PURPOSE The cursor type specifying a type of resizing cursor.

SYNTAX `public static final int E_RESIZE_CURSOR`

DESCRIPTION This cursor type is typically displayed while the user is resizing the eastern border of an object.

EXAMPLE See `setCursor()`.

Frame()

PURPOSE Constructs a new `Frame` instance.

SYNTAX
```
public Frame()
public Frame(String title)
```

DESCRIPTION The two forms of this constructor create a new invisible `Frame` instance with the title `title`. If `title` is not specified, it defaults to "Untitled". The icon image property is initially `null`. The cursor is initially `DEFAULT_CURSOR`. The frame is initially resizable. The new frame has a border layout manager (see `BorderLayout`).

PARAMETERS

`title` The string specifying the frame's title.

EXAMPLE This example creates two frames: one with a title and one without. The second frame is created at a different location.

```
import java.awt.*;
class Main {
    static public void main(String[] args) {
        Frame f1 = new Frame("Frame Example");
        Frame f2 = new Frame();

        f1.resize(100, 100);
        f1.show();
        f2.reshape(100, 100, 100, 100);
        f2.show();
    }
}
```

getCursorType()

PURPOSE Retrieves the frame's cursor type.

SYNTAX `public int getCursorType()`

DESCRIPTION The frame's cursor type. The return value is one of the valid cursor types.

RETURNS The frame's cursor type.

EXAMPLE See `setCursor()`.

getIconImage()

PURPOSE Retrieves the frame's icon image.

SYNTAX `public Image getIconImage()`

RETURNS The frame's icon image. The return value can be `null`, which means the icon image has not yet been changed.

getMenuBar()

PURPOSE Retrieves the frame's menu bar.

SYNTAX `public MenuBar getMenuBar()`

RETURNS The frame's menu bar. The return value is `null` if the frame does not have a menu bar.

EXAMPLE See `MenuBar.add()`.

getTitle()

PURPOSE Retrieves the frame's title.

SYNTAX `public String getTitle()`

RETURNS A string containing the frame's title. The result value may be `null`.

SEE ALSO `setTitle()`.

EXAMPLE See `setTitle()`.

HAND_CURSOR

PURPOSE The cursor type specifying a hand cursor.

SYNTAX `public static final int HAND_CURSOR`

DESCRIPTION This cursor type is typically displayed if the cursor is over an object that can be dragged.

EXAMPLE See `setCursor()`.

isResizable()

PURPOSE Retrieves the frame's resizable state.

SYNTAX `public boolean isResizable()`

RETURNS `true` if the frame is currently resizable; `false` otherwise.

EXAMPLE See `setResizable()`.

MOVE_CURSOR

PURPOSE The cursor type specifying a moving cursor.

SYNTAX `public static final int MOVE_CURSOR`

DESCRIPTION This cursor type is typically displayed while the user is moving an object.

EXAMPLE See `setCursor()`.

N_RESIZE_CURSOR

PURPOSE The cursor type specifying a type of resizing cursor.

SYNTAX `public static final int N_RESIZE_CURSOR`

DESCRIPTION This cursor type is typically displayed while the user is resizing the north border of an object.

EXAMPLE See `setCursor()`.

NE_RESIZE_CURSOR

PURPOSE The cursor type specifying a type of resizing cursor.

SYNTAX `public static final int NE_RESIZE_CURSOR`

DESCRIPTION This cursor type is typically displayed while the user is resizing the northeastern border of an object.

EXAMPLE See `setCursor()`.

NW_RESIZE_CURSOR

PURPOSE The cursor type specifying a type of resizing cursor.

SYNTAX `public static final int NW_RESIZE_CURSOR`

DESCRIPTION This cursor type is typically displayed while the user is resizing the northwestern border of an object.

EXAMPLE See `setCursor()`.

paramString()

PURPOSE Generates a string representing the frame's state.

SYNTAX `protected String paramString()`

DESCRIPTION A subclass of this class should override this method and return a concatenation of its state with the results of `super.paramString()`. This method is called by the `toString()` method and is typically used for debugging.

RETURNS A non-`null` string representing the frame's state.

OVERRIDES `Container.paramString()`.

SEE ALSO `Object.toString()`.

EXAMPLE This example shows how to override the `paramString()` method. The subclass appends an extra piece of state (`myData`) to the result.

```
import java.awt.*;
class Main extends Frame {
    String myData = "Testing";

    Main() {
        super("paramString Example");
    }

    protected String paramString() {
        String str = super.paramString();
        if (myData != null) {
            str += ",myData=" + myData;
        }
        return str;
    }
```

```
    static public void main(String[] args) {
        Main m = new Main();
        System.out.println(m);
    }
}
```

remove()

PURPOSE Removes the frame's menu bar.

SYNTAX `public synchronized void remove(MenuComponent menubar)`

DESCRIPTION This method removes the menu bar `menubar` from the frame. If the `menubar` is not installed in the frame, this method call is ignored.

FIGURE 106 `Frame.remove()`

PARAMETERS

`menubar` The non-`null` menu bar to remove from the frame.

EXAMPLE This example creates a frame with a menu bar and a checkbox component. If the checkbox state is `true`, then the menu bar is visible; otherwise the menu bar is removed. See Figure 106.

```
import java.awt.*;
class Main extends Frame {
    MenuBar mb = new MenuBar();
    Checkbox cb = new Checkbox("Display Menu Bar");

    Main() {
        super("remove Example");
        Menu m = new Menu("Menu");

        m.add("MenuItem");
        mb.add(m);

        add("South", cb);
        pack();
        show();
    }

    public boolean action(Event evt, Object what) {
        if (evt.target == cb) {
            if (cb.getState()) {
                setMenuBar(mb);
```

```
                } else {
                    remove(mb);
                }
                return true;
            }
            return false;
        }

        static public void main(String[] args) {
            new Main();
        }
    }
```

S_RESIZE_CURSOR

PURPOSE The cursor type specifying a type of resizing cursor.

SYNTAX `public static final int S_RESIZE_CURSOR`

DESCRIPTION This cursor type is typically displayed while the user is resizing the southern border of an object.

EXAMPLE See `setCursor()`.

SE_RESIZE_CURSOR

PURPOSE The cursor type specifying a type of resizing cursor.

SYNTAX `public static final int SE_RESIZE_CURSOR`

DESCRIPTION This cursor type is typically displayed while the user is resizing the southeastern border of an object.

EXAMPLE See `setCursor()`.

SW_RESIZE_CURSOR

PURPOSE The cursor type specifying a type of resizing cursor.

SYNTAX `public static final int SW_RESIZE_CURSOR`

DESCRIPTION This cursor type is typically displayed while the user is resizing the southwestern border of an object.

EXAMPLE See `setCursor()`.

setCursor()

PURPOSE Sets the frame's cursor.

SYNTAX `public void setCursor(int cursorType)`

DESCRIPTION This method sets this frame's cursor to be `cursorType`.

PARAMETERS

`cursorType` An integer specifying one of the valid cursor types.

EXCEPTIONS

`IllegalArgumentException`

If `cursorType` is not a valid cursor type.

EXAMPLE This example creates a list containing the names of all available cursor types. Selecting a cursor name from the list sets that cursor. The program also creates a background thread that simply waits 10 seconds, sets the cursor to the `WAIT_CURSOR`, waits 2 seconds and then restores the cursor. See Figure 107.

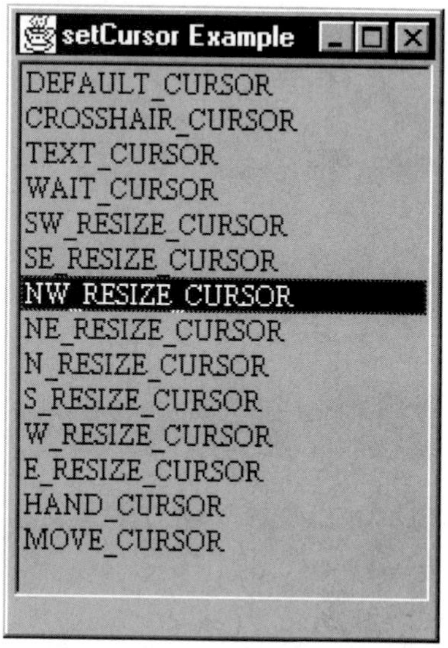

FIGURE 107 `Frame.setCursor()`

```
import java.awt.*;
class Main extends Frame implements Runnable {
    List l = new List();
    String[] cursors = {
        "DEFAULT_CURSOR",
        "CROSSHAIR_CURSOR",
        "TEXT_CURSOR",
        "WAIT_CURSOR",
        "SW_RESIZE_CURSOR",
        "SE_RESIZE_CURSOR",
        "NW_RESIZE_CURSOR",
        "NE_RESIZE_CURSOR",
        "N_RESIZE_CURSOR",
        "S_RESIZE_CURSOR",
        "W_RESIZE_CURSOR",
        "E_RESIZE_CURSOR",
        "HAND_CURSOR",
        "MOVE_CURSOR",};

    Main() {
        super("setCursor Example");
        for (int i=0; i<cursors.length; i++) {
            l.addItem(cursors[i]);
```

```
        }
        add("Center", l);
        (new Thread(this)).start();
        pack();
        show();
    }

    public boolean action(Event evt, Object what) {
        if (evt.target == l) {
            setCursor(l.getSelectedIndex());
            return true;
        }
        return false;
    }

    public void run() {

        while (true) {
            try {
                int cursor = getCursorType();

                setCursor(WAIT_CURSOR);
                Thread.sleep(2000);
                setCursor(cursor);
                Thread.sleep(10000);
            } catch (Exception e) {
            }
        }
    }

    static public void main(String[] args) {
        new Main();
    }
}
```

setIconImage()

PURPOSE Sets the image to display when this frame is iconified.

SYNTAX `public void setIconImage(Image image)`

DESCRIPTION This method sets `image` to be the image displayed when this frame is iconified. Note that not all platforms support the concept of iconifying a window.

PARAMETERS

`image` The non-`null` icon image.

setMenuBar()

PURPOSE Sets the frame's menu bar.

SYNTAX `public synchronized void setMenuBar(MenuBar menubar)`

DESCRIPTION This method sets the frame's menu bar to be `menubar`. If the frame already has a menu bar, the current menu bar is first removed. The frame becomes the menu bar's parent.

PARAMETERS

`menubar` The non-`null` menu bar to set.

EXAMPLE This example creates two menu bars and two buttons. Clicking one button installs one of the menu bars; clicking the other installs the other menu bar. See Figure 108.

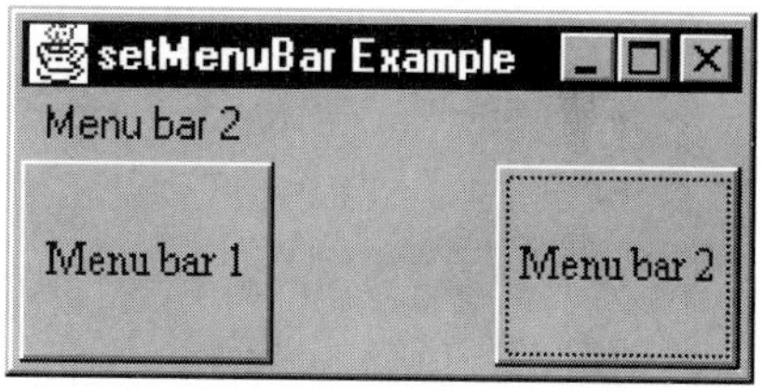

FIGURE 108 `Frame.setMenuBar()`

```
import java.awt.*;
class Main extends Frame {
    MenuBar mb1 = new MenuBar();
    MenuBar mb2 = new MenuBar();

    Main(String title) {
        super(title);
        Menu menu;

        menu = new Menu("Menu bar 1");
        menu.add("One");
        mb1.add(menu);
        setMenuBar(mb1);

        menu = new Menu("Menu bar 2");
        menu.add("Two");
        mb2.add(menu);

        add("West", new Button("Menu bar 1"));
        add("East", new Button("Menu bar 2"));
        pack();
        show();
    }

    public boolean action(Event evt, Object what) {
        if ("Menu bar 1".equals(what)) {
            setMenuBar(mb1);
            return true;
        } else if("Menu bar 2".equals(what)) {
```

```
                setMenuBar(mb2);
                return true;
            }
            return false;
        }

        static public void main(String[] args) {
            Main m = new Main("setMenuBar Example");
        }
    }
```

setResizable()

PURPOSE Sets the resizable property.

SYNTAX `public void setResizable(boolean resizable)`

DESCRIPTION This method sets this frame to be resizable or non-resizable. If `resizable` is `true`, the frame becomes resizable; otherwise it becomes non-resizable.

PARAMETERS

`resizable` If `true`, the frame becomes resizable; otherwise the frame becomes non-resizable.

EXAMPLE This example creates a frame with a checkbox indicating whether the frame should be resizable. Clicking the checkbox changes the resizable property of the frame. See Figure 109.

FIGURE 109 `Frame.setResizable()`

```
    import java.awt.*;
    class Main extends Frame {
        Checkbox cb = new Checkbox("Resizable", null, true);
        Main() {
            super("setResizable Example");
            add("North", cb);
            pack();
            show();
        }

        public boolean action(Event evt, Object what) {
            if (evt.target == cb) {
                setResizable(cb.getState());
                return true;
            }
            return false;
        }
```

```
    static public void main(String[] args) {
        new Main();
    }
}
```

setTitle()

PURPOSE Sets the frame's title.

SYNTAX `public void setTitle(String title)`

DESCRIPTION This method sets this frame's title to be the string `title`.

PARAMETERS

`title` The string specifying the frame's new title. A value of `null` clears the title.

SEE ALSO `getTitle()`.

EXAMPLE This example creates a text field in a frame, initialized with the frame's current title. Pressing Return in the text field sets the frame's title to the text in the text field. See Figure 110.

FIGURE 110 **`Frame.setTitle()`**

```
import java.awt.*;
class Main extends Frame {
    TextField t = new TextField(50);

    Main() {
        super("setTitle Example");
        t.setText(getTitle());    // Initialize with current title.
        add("North", t);
        pack();
        show();
    }

    public boolean action(Event evt, Object what) {
        if (evt.target == t) {
            setTitle((String)what);
            return true;
        }
        return false;
    }
```

```
        static public void main(String[] args) {
            new Main();
        }
    }
```

TEXT_CURSOR

PURPOSE The cursor type specifying a caret cursor.

SYNTAX `public static final int TEXT_CURSOR`

DESCRIPTION This cursor type is typically displayed while the cursor is over an object and text on the object can be selected.

EXAMPLE See `setCursor()`.

W_RESIZE_CURSOR

PURPOSE The cursor type specifying a type of resizing cursor.

SYNTAX `public static final int W_RESIZE_CURSOR`

DESCRIPTION This cursor type is typically displayed while the user is resizing the western border of an object.

EXAMPLE See `setCursor()`.

WAIT_CURSOR

PURPOSE The cursor type specifying an hourglass cursor.

SYNTAX `public static final int WAIT_CURSOR`

DESCRIPTION This cursor type is typically displayed while the application is busy and cannot respond to user input.

EXAMPLE See `setCursor()`.

java.awt.peer

FramePeer

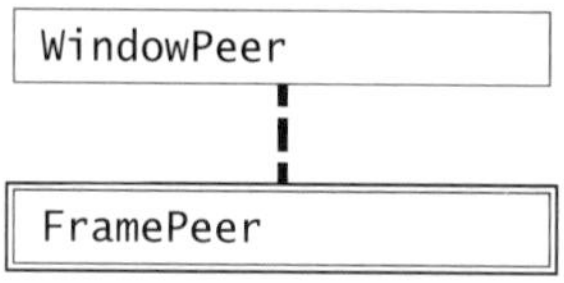

Syntax

```
public interface FramePeer extends WindowPeer
```

Description

The frame component (see the `Frame` class) in the Abstract Windowing Toolkit (AWT) uses the platform's native implementation of a frame. So that the AWT frame behaves the same on all platforms, the frame is assigned a peer, whose task is to translate the behavior of the platform's native frame to the behavior of the AWT frame.

AWT programmers normally do not directly use peer classes and interfaces. Instead they deal with AWT components in the `java.awt` package. These in turn automatically manage their peers. Only someone who is porting the AWT to another platform should be concerned with the peer classes and interfaces. Consequently, most peer documentation refers to `java.awt` counterparts.

See `Component` and `Toolkit` for additional information about component peers.

MEMBER SUMMARY

Peer Methods	
`setCursor()`	Sets this frame's cursor.
`setIconImage()`	Sets the image to display when this frame is iconified.
`setMenuBar()`	Sets this frame's menu bar.
`setResizable()`	Sets this frame's resizable property.
`setTitle()`	Sets this frame's title.

See Also

`Component`, `Frame`, `Toolkit`.

A B C D E F G H I J K L M N O P Q R S T U V W X Y Z

setCursor()

PURPOSE Sets this frame's cursor.

SYNTAX `void setCursor(int cursorType)`

PARAMETERS
`cursorType` An integer specifying one of the valid cursor types.

SEE ALSO `Frame.setCursor()`.

setIconImage()

PURPOSE Sets the image to display when this frame is iconified.

SYNTAX `void setIconImage(Image image)`

PARAMETERS
`image` The icon image to be displayed.

SEE ALSO `Frame.setIconImage()`.

setMenuBar()

PURPOSE Sets this frame's menu bar.

SYNTAX `void setMenuBar(MenuBar menubar)`

PARAMETERS
`menubar` The non-`null` menu bar to set.

SEE ALSO `Frame.setMenuBar()`.

setResizable()

PURPOSE Sets this frame's resizable property.

SYNTAX `void setResizable(boolean resizable)`

PARAMETERS
`resizable` If `true`, the frame becomes resizable; otherwise the frame becomes non-resizable.

SEE ALSO `Frame.setResizable()`.

setTitle()

PURPOSE Sets this frame's title.

SYNTAX `void setTitle(String title)`

PARAMETERS

`title` The string specifying the frame's new title. A value of `null` clears the title.

SEE ALSO `Frame.setTitle()`.

A B C D E F G H I J K L M N O P Q R S T U V W X Y Z

A B C D E F G H I J K L M N O P Q R S T U V W X Y Z

java.awt
Graphics

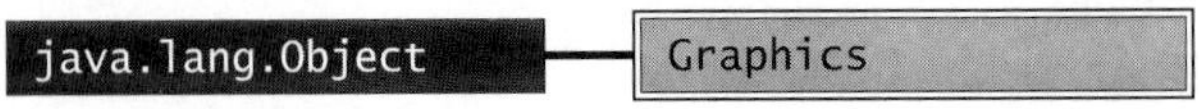

Syntax

```
public abstract class Graphics
```

Description

The *graphics context* is an object used to paint on a *drawing surface*. The drawing surface is a rendering device such as a screen or a printer. The drawing surface can also be an off-screen image (see Figure 111). A drawing surface has three properties that affect a graphics context: a background color, a foreground color, and a font. These three properties are used to initialize any new graphics contexts created on a drawing surface.

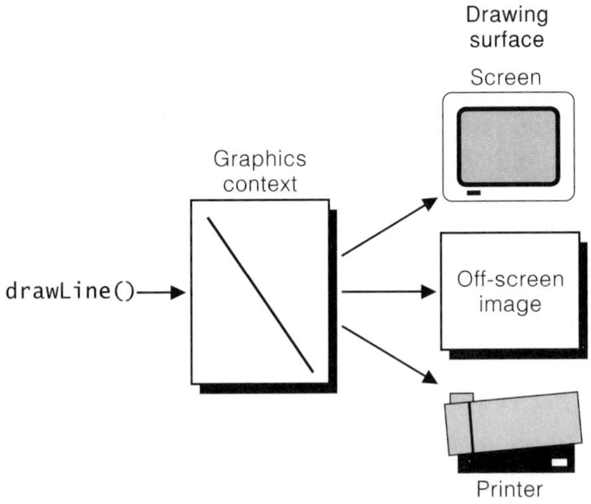

FIGURE 111 Graphics Context Drawing Surfaces

When you are painting to the screen or a printer, the AWT system supplies you with a graphics context via the `Component.paint()` and `Component.update()` methods. See the `Component` class for details. When painting to an off-screen image, you create a graphics context on the image that you can paint to any time you wish. However, if you want to paint any part of the off-screen image to the screen, you need to do it indirectly through the `Component.repaint()` method. See the `Component` class for details.

There can be more than one graphics context for a drawing surface, and they can be used simultaneously. Graphics contexts also can be cloned, and each graphics context can have a different property set. Having more than one graphics context, each with different properties, can be useful in some situations when you need to constantly switch properties while painting a complex image.

In general, graphics contexts should be disposed of as soon as they are no longer needed. This is because a graphics context is usually associated with a system resource, and such system resources are typically large and limited.

The Origin and Coordinates

The *x*-coordinates of a graphics context moves from left to right; the left edge has coordinate 0. The *y*-coordinates of a graphics context moves from top to bottom; the top edge has coordinate 0.

The graphics context has an origin, which is initially at the coordinates (0, 0) (see Figure 112). The coordinates supplied by the graphics operations are relative to the origin. The origin can be moved at any time. For example, if the origin is at (10, 10) and a circle is painted at (5, 5), the circle will appear on the drawing surface at (15, 15).

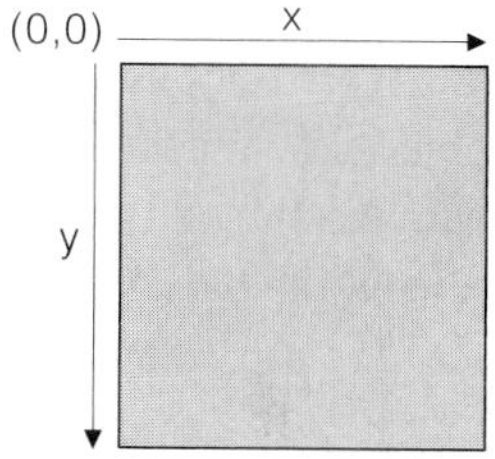

FIGURE 112 **Graphics Coordinates**

It is important to note that coordinates from mouse events usually need to be translated to graphics context coordinates before they can be used. For example, suppose you want a pixel at the cursor position *p* colored when the user clicks the mouse. You need to subtract the origin from *p*; the pixel location at the resulting point will be directly under the cursor. Graphics context coordinates can be determined from event coordinates by subtracting the origin from the event coordinates.

Background and Foreground Colors

A graphics context has both a *background* and *foreground* color. The background color is inherited from the drawing surface. The graphics context is created using the drawing surface's background at the time the graphics context is created. It cannot be changed, even if the background color on the drawing surface is changed. The only method that uses the background color is `clearRect()`.

The foreground color is used by all the other painting operations and can be changed at any time. The foreground color also is inherited from the drawing surface.

Font

The graphics context has a font that is used when you are painting text. The initial font of the graphics context is copied from the current font of the drawing surface. Changes to the drawing surface's current font do not affect the font in the graphics context. The graphics context's font can be changed at any time. See `setFont()` for an example that uses fonts.

Paint Modes

A graphics context can be in one of two paint modes: *normal* or *xor*. In normal paint mode, the background colors have no effect on the paint operation. That is, if you paint a black circle, it will appear as a black circle no matter on what color background it was painted.

Xor paint mode is more complicated. In the simplest terms, if you paint the same object twice while you are in xor mode, the object disappears. Also, when you paint the object for the first time, it won't appear in the correct colors. The color that appears is based on both the foreground and background colors; the exact color chosen is platform-dependent.

In xor paint mode, one special color called the xor color will not affect the foreground color. That is, if you paint on an xor color colored background the foreground color will come out as expected. However, the previous rule of painting the same object twice still applies.

One final effect of xor paint mode: If the foreground color is the same as the xor color, the painting operation is ignored.

Xor mode is typically used in dragging operations. During the drag, the outline of the object is painted in xor mode. After the object is moved, the old outline is erased simply by painting the outline in the same place. This optimization is much more efficient than having to repaint the background to erase the old outline of the object.

See `setXORMode()` for an example that uses xor paint mode.

The Clipping Rectangle

The *clipping rectangle* is used to constrain the results of the painting operations so that they affect only a specific area. The graphics context's clipping rectangle can only shrink; it can never enlarge. If you need two separate clipped areas on one drawing surface, you should first copy the graphics context and then adjust the clipping rectangle on each of them. See `create()` for an example of how to do this.

MEMBER SUMMARY

Constructors and Destructors	
`create()`	Constructs a new `Graphics` object that has the same properties as the graphics context.
`dispose()`	Releases the graphics context's system resources.
`finalize()`	Releases the graphics context's system resources.
`Graphics()`	Constructs a new `Graphics` object.
Color Methods	
`getColor()`	Retrieves the graphics context's foreground color.
`setColor()`	Sets the graphics context's foreground color.
Paint Mode Methods	
`setPaintMode()`	Sets the graphics context to normal paint mode.
`setXORMode()`	Sets the graphics context to xor paint mode.
Clipping Methods	
`clipRect()`	Shrinks the graphics context's clipping rectangle.
`getClipRect()`	Retrieves the graphics context's current clipping rectangle.
Painting Methods	
`clearRect()`	Paints a rectangle with the background color on the graphics context.

MEMBER SUMMARY

`copyArea()`	Copies an area of the drawing surface to another area of the drawing surface.
`draw3DRect()`	Paints a 3D outline around a rectangle on the graphics context.
`drawArc()`	Paints an elliptical arc inside a rectangle on the graphics context.
`drawLine()`	Paints a line on the graphics context.
`drawOval()`	Paints an oval outline inside a rectangle.
`drawPolygon()`	Paints a nonclosed polygon outline.
`drawRect()`	Paints an outline around a rectangle.
`drawRoundRect()`	Paints an outline of a rectangle with rounded corners.
`fill3DRect()`	Paints a rectangle that has a 3D outline.
`fillArc()`	Paints a filled elliptical arc inside a rectangle.
`fillOval()`	Paints an oval area.
`fillPolygon()`	Paints a closed polygon.
`fillRect()`	Paints a rectangular area.
`fillRoundRect()`	Paints a rectangle with rounded corners on the graphics context.
Font and String Methods	
`drawBytes()`	Paints an array of bytes as characters on the graphics context.
`drawChars()`	Paints an array of characters on the graphics context.
`drawString()`	Paints a string.
`getFont()`	Retrieves the graphics context's font.
`getFontMetrics()`	Retrieves the font metrics for a font.
`setFont()`	Sets the graphics context's font.
Image Methods	
`drawImage()`	Paints an image on the graphics context.
Translate Method	
`translate()`	Moves the graphics context's origin.
Debugging Method	
`toString()`	Generates a string representation of the graphics context's state.

Example

This example paints three colored figures. It demonstrates the simplest example of painting on the screen. See Figure 113.

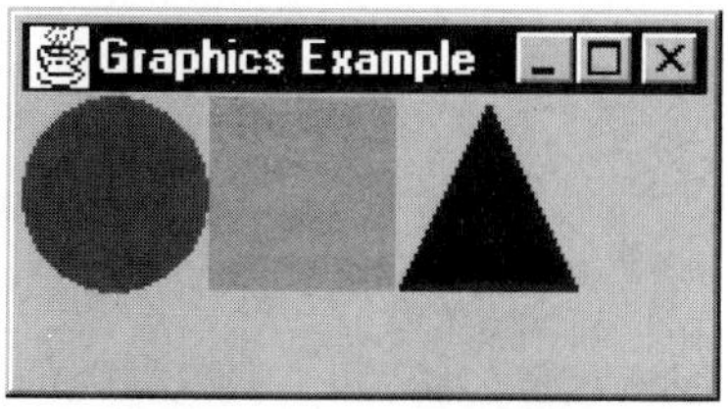

FIGURE 113 Simple Graphics

```
import java.awt.*;
class Main extends Frame {
```

```
        Main() {
            super("Graphics Example");
            resize(200, 100);
            show();
        }

        public void paint(Graphics g) {
            Polygon polygon = new Polygon();
            polygon.addPoint(125, 0);
            polygon.addPoint(100, 50);
            polygon.addPoint(150, 50);

            g.setColor(Color.red);
            g.fillOval(0, 0, 50, 50);
            g.setColor(Color.green);
            g.fillRect(50, 0, 50, 50);
            g.setColor(Color.blue);
            g.fillPolygon(polygon);
        }

        static public void main(String[] args) {
            new Main();
        }
    }
```

clearRect()

PURPOSE Paints a rectangle with the background color on the graphics context.

SYNTAX `public abstract void clearRect(int x, int y, int width, int height)`

DESCRIPTION This method paints the area defined by `x`, `y`, `width`, and `height` with the graphics context's background color. If either `width` or `height` is less than or equal to `0`, the method call is ignored.

PARAMETERS

`height`	The height of the rectangular area in pixels.
`width`	The width of the rectangular area in pixels.
`x`	The *x*-coordinate in pixels.
`y`	The *y*-coordinate in pixels.

SEE ALSO `drawRect()`, `fillRect()`.

EXAMPLE This example paints successively smaller and smaller rectangles, alternating between the background and foreground colors. See Figure 114.

FIGURE 114
`Graphics.clearRect()`

```
import java.awt.*;
class Main extends Frame {
    Main() {
        super("clearRect Example");
        setBackground(Color.black);
        resize(200, 200);
        show();
    }

    public void paint(Graphics g) {
        Insets insets = this.insets();
        int x = 0, y = 0;
        int w = size().width-insets.left-insets.right;
        int h = size().height-insets.top-insets.bottom;

        g.setColor(Color.red);
        while (w > 0 && h > 0) {
            g.clearRect(x++, y++, w, h);
            g.fillRect(x++, y++, w-2, h-2);
            w -= 4;
            h -= 4;
        }
    }

    static public void main(String[] args) {
        new Main();
    }
}
```

clipRect()

PURPOSE Shrinks the clipping rectangle.

SYNTAX `public abstract void clipRect(int x, int y, int width, int height)`

DESCRIPTION This method makes the new clipping rectangle at the intersection of the current clipping rectangle and the rectangle defined by `x`, `y`, `width`, and `height`.

PARAMETERS

`height` The height of the rectangle in pixels.
`width` The width of the rectangle in pixels.

A B C D E F G H I J K L M N O P Q R S T U V W X Y Z

x	The *x*-coordinate in pixels.
y	The *y*-coordinate in pixels.

SEE ALSO `getClipRect()`.

EXAMPLE See `create()`.

copyArea()

PURPOSE Copies an area of the drawing surface to another area of the drawing surface.

SYNTAX

```
public abstract void copyArea(int x, int y, int width, int
   height, int deltax, int deltay)
```

DESCRIPTION This method copies the pixels on the screen in the rectangular area defined by `x`, `y`, `width`, and `height` to the area defined by `x+deltax`, `y+deltay`, `width`, and `height`.

If some window is partially occluding the scrolled area, the `paint()` method will be called to repaint the damaged area. Optimally, the clipping rectangle of the graphics context supplied by the `paint()` method will be exactly as large as needed. However, on some platforms this may not be the case.

PARAMETERS

`deltax`	The horizontal distance from the source in pixels.
`deltay`	The vertical distance from the source in pixels.
`height`	The height of the source in pixels.
`width`	The width of the source in pixels.
`x`	The *x*-coordinate of the source in pixels.
`y`	The *y*-coordinate of the source in pixels.

EXAMPLE This example creates a canvas that paints a scrolling histogram. See Figure 115. The histogram is scrolled 1 pixel to the right, and a new line of data is added on the left. The `copyArea()` method is straightforward, unless some window is partially occluding the area being scrolled. In this case, the `paint()` method is called to paint the "damaged" areas. A blue rectangle is painted to indicate a complete paint, while a red rectangle is painted to indicate a partial paint. A paint call is partial if the dimensions of `getClipRect()` are smaller than `size()`.

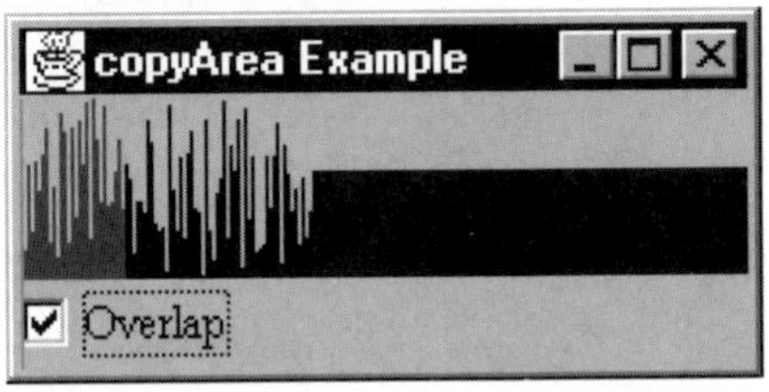

FIGURE 115 `Graphics.copyArea()`

A checkbox component allows you to show or hide a 1-pixel-wide window that will overlap the scrolling histogram to invoke a partial paint.

The scrolling histogram is embedded in another panel to guarantee that the overlapping window will overlap the scrolling histogram. If the overlapping window is a sibling of the scrolling histogram, there is no way to control whether the overlapping window will appear above or below the scrolling histogram.

```
import java.awt.*;
class Main extends Frame {
    Panel panel = new Panel();

    MainCanvas cv = new MainCanvas();
    Canvas overlap = new Canvas();
    Checkbox cb = new Checkbox("Overlap", null, false);

    Main() {
        super("copyArea Example");
        panel.setLayout(new BorderLayout());
        panel.add("Center", cv);

        add(overlap);
        add(panel);
        add(cb);
        overlap.setBackground(Color.green);
        overlap.hide();
        resize(400, 100);
        show();
    }

    // In order to get the overlapping window to overlap another,
    // we need to implement our own specific layout.
    public synchronized void layout() {
        Insets insets = this.insets();
        Dimension d = cb.preferredSize();
        int w = size().width - insets.left-insets.right;
        int h = size().height - insets.top-insets.bottom;

        panel.reshape(insets.left, insets.top, w, h-d.height);
        cb.reshape(insets.left, size().height-insets.bottom-d.height,
                   w, d.height);
        overlap.reshape(insets.left, insets.top, 1, h);
    }

    public boolean action(Event evt, Object what) {
        if (evt.target == cb) {
            overlap.show(cb.getState());
            return true;
        }
        return false;
    }
```

```
    static public void main(String[] args) {
        new Main();
    }
}

class MainCanvas extends Canvas implements Runnable {
    MainCanvas() {
        (new Thread(this)).start();
    }

    //  Returns an integer in the range [0..r-1].
    int random(int r) {
        return (int)(Math.floor(Math.random()*r));
    }

    public void update(Graphics g) {
        int w = size().width;
        int h = size().height;

        // shift right by 1 pixel.
        g.copyArea(0, 0, w-1, h, 1, 0);
        g.clearRect(0, 0, 1, h);
        g.drawLine(0, random(h), 0, h);
    }

    public void paint(Graphics g) {
        int w = size().width;
        int h = size().height;
        Rectangle r = g.getClipRect();

        if (r == null || (r.width == w && r.height == h)) {
            g.setColor(Color.blue); // full repaint
        } else {
            g.setColor(Color.red); // partial repaint
        }
        g.fillRect(0, random(h), w, h);
    }

    public void run() {
        while (true) {
            try {Thread.sleep(100);} catch (Exception e) {};
            repaint();
        }
    }
}
```

create()

PURPOSE Constructs a new `Graphics` object that has the same properties as the graphics context.

SYNTAX

```
public Graphics create()
public Graphics create(int x, int y, int width, int height)
```

DESCRIPTION If `x`, `y`, `width`, and `height` are specified, the new graphics context will be translated by `x` and `y` and a clipping rectangle assigned. More precisely, the second overload is equivalent to

```
Graphics g2 = g.create();
g2.translate(x, y);
g2.clipRect(0, 0, width, height);
```

PARAMETERS

`height`	The height of the area.
`width`	The width of the area.
`x`	The *x*-coordinate.
`y`	The *y*-coordinate.

FIGURE 116 `Graphics.create()`

RETURNS A non-`null` graphics context.

SEE ALSO `translate()`.

EXAMPLE This example requires three different non-overlapping clipping rectangles on the drawing surface. See Figure 116. Two copies of the supplied graphics context are created and a clipping rectangle is set on the copies. Finally, the original graphics context is clipped, since no more clipping rectangles need to be set.

```
import java.awt.*;
class Main extends Frame {
    Main() {
        super("create Example");
        resize(200, 200);
        show();
    }

    void paintFigure(Graphics g, int w, int h) {
        g.clipRect(5, 5, w-10, h-10);
        g.fillOval(0, 0, w, h);
    }
    public void paint(Graphics g) {
        Insets insets = this.insets();
        int x = 0, y = 0;
        int w = size().width-insets.left-insets.right;
        int h = size().height-insets.top-insets.bottom;

        Graphics g2 = g.create(0, 0, w/3, h);
        g2.setColor(Color.red);
        paintFigure(g2, w/3, h);
        g2.dispose();

        g2 = g.create(w/3, 0, w/3, h);
        g2.setColor(Color.green);
```

A B C D E F G H I J K L M N O P Q R S T U V W X Y Z

```
            paintFigure(g2, w/3, h);
            g2.dispose();

            // Safe to use original one.
            g.translate(w*2/3, 0);
            g.clipRect(0, 0, w/3, h);
            g.setColor(Color.blue);
            paintFigure(g, w/3, h);
        }

        static public void main(String[] args) {
            new Main();
        }
    }
```

dispose()

PURPOSE Releases the graphics context's system resources.

SYNTAX `public abstract void dispose()`

DESCRIPTION This method releases any system resources that the graphics context has been using. Any further method calls on this object after it has been disposed of are ignored.

Calling this method is not strictly necessary because the garbage collector will eventually call the graphics context's finalize method, which in turn will call `dispose()`. However, in situations when graphics contexts are created at a fast rate the overall system performance may be helped by explicitly disposing of the graphics context.

SEE ALSO `finalize()`.

EXAMPLE See `create()`.

draw3DRect()

PURPOSE Paints a 3D outline around a rectangle on the graphics context.

SYNTAX `public void draw3DRect(int x, int y, int width, int height, boolean raised)`

DESCRIPTION This method paints a 1-pixel-thick outline *around* the rectangle defined by `x`, `y`, `width`, and `height`. The left and top edges of the outline are within the specified rectangle, but the right and bottom edges are just outside the defined rectangle. Hence this method actually draws `width+1` horizontal lines and `height+1` vertical lines. Note that this method will paint a single pixel if width and height are both 0. Use draw3DRect(x, y, width-1, height-1) to paint the 3D outline inside the specified rectangle. If either width or height is less than 0, the method call is ignored.

If raised is true, the 3D effect is done by lightening the left and top edges and darkening the right and bottom edges. If raised is false, the left and top edges are darker and the right and bottom edges are lighter. The lighter and darker color shades are generated by the Color.brighter() and Color.darker() methods, respectively.

This method uses the foreground color to calculate the lighter and darker colors for the 3D rectangle. A common mistake is to forget to set the foreground color before calling this method. Generally, the foreground color should be set to the background color so that the 3D colors are based on the background. However, depending on the background color, the calculated 3D colors are not always very good. So you may have to experiment with different colors to achieve a better 3D effect.

PARAMETERS

height	The height of the rectangular area in pixels.
raised	Specifies whether the area should be raised or lowered.
width	The width of the rectangular area in pixels.
x	The *x*-coordinate in pixels.
y	The *y*-coordinate in pixels.

FIGURE 117 Graphics.draw3DRect(): Raised Border

SEE ALSO Color.brighter(), Color.darker(), fill3DRect().

EXAMPLE This example paints a 3D border just within the frame's paintable area. The 3D border is thicker than 1 pixel. Clicking toggles the 3D border between a raised border and a lowered border. Figure 117 shows a raised border. Figure 118 shows a lowered border.

FIGURE 118 Graphics.draw3DRect(): Lowered Border

```
import java.awt.*;
class Main extends Frame {
    int borderWidth = 5;
    boolean raised = true;

    Main() {
        super("draw3DRect Example");
        resize(200, 200);
        show();
    }
```

```
    public void paint(Graphics g) {
        Insets insets = this.insets();
        int x = 0, y = 0;
        int w = size().width-insets.left-insets.right;
        int h = size().height-insets.top-insets.bottom;

        w -= 1;        // draw inside the rectangle.
        h -= 1;        // draw inside the rectangle.
        g.setColor(getBackground());
        for (int i=0; i<borderWidth; i++) {
            g.draw3DRect(x++, y++, w, h, raised);
            w -= 2;
            h -= 2;
        }
        g.fillRect(x, y, w+1, h+1);
    }

    public boolean mouseDown(Event evt, int x, int y) {
        raised = !raised;
        repaint();
        return true;
    }

    static public void main(String[] args) {
        new Main();
    }
}
```

drawArc()

PURPOSE Paints an elliptical arc inside a rectangle on the graphics context.

SYNTAX
```
public abstract void drawArc(int x, int y, int width, int height,
    int startAngle, int arcAngle)
```

DESCRIPTION This method paints a 1-pixel-thick elliptical arc in the foreground color within the rectangle defined by `x`, `y`, `width`, and `height`. If either `width` or `height` is less than `0`, the method call is ignored.

Logically, you form the arc first by using the `drawOval()` method to paint an oval inside the rectangle. Next, define a horizontal line that originates from the oval's center and extends to the containing rectangle's right edge. Then anchor the line at the oval's center and rotate the line `startAngle` degrees from its starting position. If `startAngle` is positive, rotate counterclockwise; if `startAngle` is negative, rotate clockwise. The intersection of this line and the oval's outline is the starting point for the arc. Finally, continue rotating the line `arcAngle` degrees. Again, if `arcAngle` is positive, rotate counterclockwise;

otherwise rotate clockwise. All the points that intersect this line and the oval's outline during the rotation are included in the arc.

PARAMETERS

`arcAngle`	The angle in degrees (360 degrees in a circle) that specifies the end of the arc. `arcAngle` is relative to `startAngle`.
`height`	The height of the rectangular area in pixels.
`startAngle`	The angle in degrees (360 degrees in a circle) that specifies the start of the arc; a value of `0` is at the 3 o'clock position.
`width`	The width of the rectangular area in pixels.
`x`	The *x*-coordinate in pixels.
`y`	The *y*-coordinate in pixels.

SEE ALSO `fillArc()`.

EXAMPLE This example draws a 270-degree arc starting at 0 degrees. Four labels are used to show the start angle positions. See Figure 119.

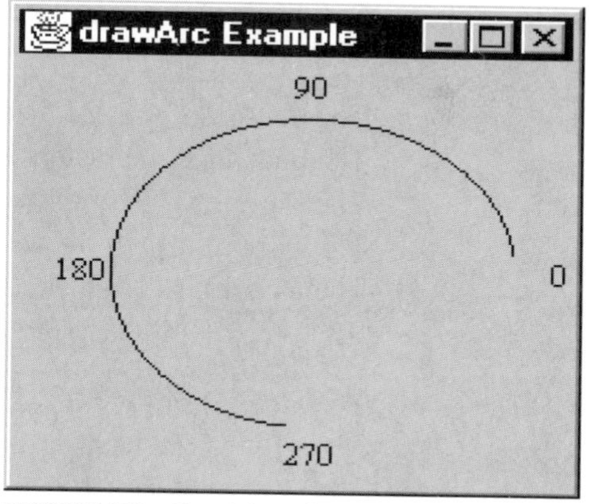

FIGURE 119 `Graphics.drawArc()`

```
import java.awt.*;
class Main extends Frame {
    Main() {
        super("drawArc Example");
        add("Center", new MainCanvas());
        add("North", new Label("90", Label.CENTER));
        add("South", new Label("270", Label.CENTER));
        add("East", new Label("0"));
        add("West", new Label("180"));
        resize(200, 200);
        show();
    }

    static public void main(String[] args) {
        new Main();
    }
}

class MainCanvas extends Canvas {
    public void paint(Graphics g) {
        g.drawArc(0, 0, size().width, size().height, 0, 270);
    }

}
```

drawBytes()

PURPOSE Paints an array of bytes as characters on the graphics context.

SYNTAX
```
public void drawBytes(byte[] buf, int offset, int count, int x,
    int y)
```

DESCRIPTION This method is equivalent to `drawString(new String(buf, 0, offset, count));`.

See the `drawString()` method for details.

PARAMETERS

`buf`	The non-`null` array of bytes to paint.
`count`	The number of characters in `buf` to paint.
`offset`	The starting index of the first character in `buf` to paint.
`x`	The *x*-coordinate of the baseline in pixels.
`y`	The *y*-coordinate of the baseline in pixels.

SEE ALSO `drawChars()`, `drawString()`, `FontMetrics`.

EXAMPLE See `drawString()`.

drawChars()

PURPOSE Paints an array of characters on the graphics context.

SYNTAX
```
public void drawChars(char[] buf, int offset, int count, int x,
    int y)
```

DESCRIPTION This method is equivalent to `drawString(new String(buf, offset, count));`.

See the `drawString()` method for details.

PARAMETERS

`buf`	The non-`null` array of characters to paint.
`count`	The number of characters in `buf` to paint.
`offset`	The index of the first character in `buf` to paint.
`x`	The *x*-coordinate of the baseline in pixels.
`y`	The *y*-coordinate of the baseline in pixels.

SEE ALSO `drawBytes()`, `drawString()`, `FontMetrics`.

EXAMPLE See `drawString()`.

drawImage()

PURPOSE Paints an image on the graphics context.

SYNTAX

```
public abstract boolean drawImage(Image image, int x, int y,
   ImageObserver observer)
public abstract boolean drawImage(Image image, int x, int y, Color
   bgColor, ImageObserver observer)
public abstract boolean drawImage(Image image, int x, int y, int
   width, int height, ImageObserver observer)
public abstract boolean drawImage (Image image, int x, int y, int
   width, int height, Color bgColor, ImageObserver observer)
```

DESCRIPTION The four forms of this method paint the image `image` such that its northwest corner is at pixel location (`x`, `y`). If `width` and `height` are specified, the image is scaled so that its width is `width` and its height is `height`. If `observer` is non-`null`, `observer` will receive updates as the image is loaded. See the `ImageObserver` class for more information.

PARAMETERS

`bgColor`	The color to use for transparent pixels in the image. If `null`, no color is used.
`height`	The height of the scaled image in pixels.
`image`	The image to paint.
`observer`	The image update observer. This value may be `null`.
`width`	The width of the scaled image in pixels.
`x`	The *x*-coordinate in pixels.
`y`	The *y*-coordinate in pixels.

RETURNS `true` if the image is completely loaded and was painted successfully; `false` otherwise.

SEE ALSO `Image`, `ImageObserver`.

EXAMPLE This example paints three colored figures on the screen. See Figure 120. The same colored figures are also painted on an off-screen image. The image is then scaled down and painted at the northwest corner. The instance fields `tinyIm` and `tinyImG` could have been local variables in the `paint()` method. However, the usage in this example is more typical, since it avoids the overhead of constantly creating an off-screen image and graphics context. This overhead would be much more significant if the program involved some animation.

FIGURE 120 `Graphics.drawImage()`

A B C D E F G H I J K L M N O P Q R S T U V W X Y Z

```
import java.awt.*;
class Main extends Frame {
    Image tinyIm;
    Graphics tinyImG;

    Main() {
        super("drawImage Example");
        resize(200, 100);
        show();
    }

    public void paint(Graphics g) {
        Insets insets = this.insets();
        int x = 0, y = 0;
        int w = size().width-insets.left-insets.right;
        int h = size().height-insets.top-insets.bottom;

        g.setColor(Color.black);
        paintFigure(g, w, h);
        if (tinyIm == null || tinyIm.getWidth(null) != w
                || tinyIm.getHeight(null) != h) {
            if (tinyImG != null) tinyImG.dispose();
            tinyIm = createImage(w, h);
            tinyImG = tinyIm.getGraphics();
            paintFigure(tinyImG, w, h);
        }
        g.drawRect(0, 0, w/4+1, h/4+1);
        g.drawImage(tinyIm, 1, 1, w/4, h/4, null);
    }

    public void paintFigure(Graphics g, int w, int h) {
        Color c = g.getColor();
        Polygon polygon = new Polygon();
        polygon.addPoint(w/6, 0);
        polygon.addPoint(0, h);
        polygon.addPoint(w/3, h);

        g.setColor(Color.red);
        g.fillPolygon(polygon);
        g.setColor(Color.green);
        g.fillOval(w/3, 0, w/3, h);
        g.setColor(Color.blue);
        g.fillRect(w*2/3, 0, w/3, h);
        g.setColor(c);
    }

    static public void main(String[] args) {
        new Main();
    }
}
```

drawLine()

PURPOSE Paints a line on the graphics context.

SYNTAX `public abstract void drawLine(int x1, int y1, int x2, int y2)`

DESCRIPTION This method paints a 1-pixel-thick line between the coordinates (`x1`, `y1`) and (`x2`, `y2`) in the foreground color. The pixel at (`x2`, `y2`) is included in the line. The `drawLine()` object always draws at least 1 pixel.

PARAMETERS

`x1` The first point's *x*-coordinate in pixels.

`y1` The first point's *y*-coordinate in pixels.

`x2` The second point's *x*-coordinate in pixels.

`y2` The second point's *y*-coordinate in pixels.

EXAMPLE This example paints a series of connected lines. See Figure 121. Each time the mouse is clicked or dragged, a new line is added to the line list. This example also demonstrates how to use the `update()` method to avoid redrawing all the lines and thus avoid flicker.

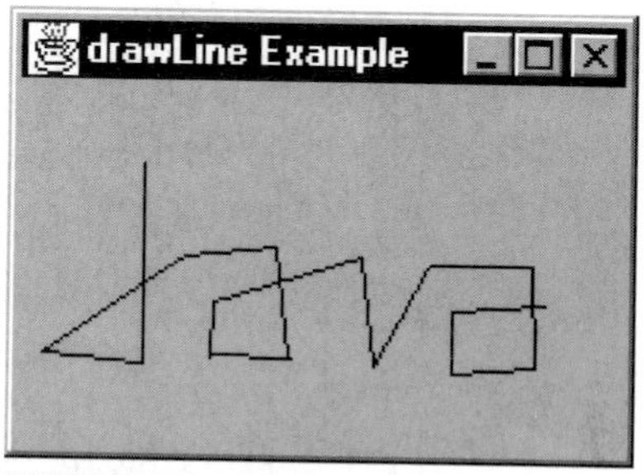

FIGURE 121 `Graphics.drawLine()`

```
import java.awt.*;
import java.util.*;
class Main extends Frame {
    Vector points = new Vector();
    int lastDrawnPoint = 0;

    Main() {
        super("drawLine Example");
        resize(200, 200);
        show();
    }

    public void paint(Graphics g) {
        Point curPt = null;
        for (int i=0; i<points.size(); i++) {
            Point pt = (Point)points.elementAt(i);

            if (curPt != null) {
                g.drawLine(curPt.x, curPt.y, pt.x, pt.y);
            }
            curPt = pt;
        }
        lastDrawnPoint = points.size();
    }
```

```
    public void update(Graphics g) {
        Point curPt = null;
        lastDrawnPoint = Math.max(0, lastDrawnPoint-1);
        for (int i=lastDrawnPoint; i<points.size(); i++) {
            Point pt = (Point)points.elementAt(i);

            if (curPt != null) {
                g.drawLine(curPt.x, curPt.y, pt.x, pt.y);
            }
            curPt = pt;
        }
        lastDrawnPoint = points.size();
    }

    public boolean mouseDown(Event evt, int x, int y) {
        Point pt = new Point(x, y);
        points.addElement(pt);
        repaint();
        return true;
    }

    public boolean mouseDrag(Event evt, int x, int y) {
        Point pt = new Point(x, y);
        points.addElement(pt);
        repaint();
        return true;
    }

    static public void main(String[] args) {
        new Main();
    }
}
```

drawOval()

PURPOSE Paints an oval outline inside a rectangle.

SYNTAX `public abstract void drawOval(int x, int y, int width, int height)`

DESCRIPTION This method paints a 1-pixel-thick oval outline in the foreground color within the rectangle defined by `x`, `y`, `width`, and `height`. If either `width` or `height` is less than `0`, the method call is ignored.

PARAMETERS

`height`	The height of the rectangular area in pixels.
`width`	The width of the rectangular area in pixels.
`x`	The *x*-coordinate in pixels.
`y`	The *y*-coordinate in pixels.

A B C D E F G H I J K L M N O P Q R S T U V W X Y Z

SEE ALSO `fillOval()`.

EXAMPLE This example creates a frame and reads numbers from standard input. See Figure 122. Each line from standard input contains a coordinate. When two coordinates are retrieved, they form a point and a circle is painted around the point.

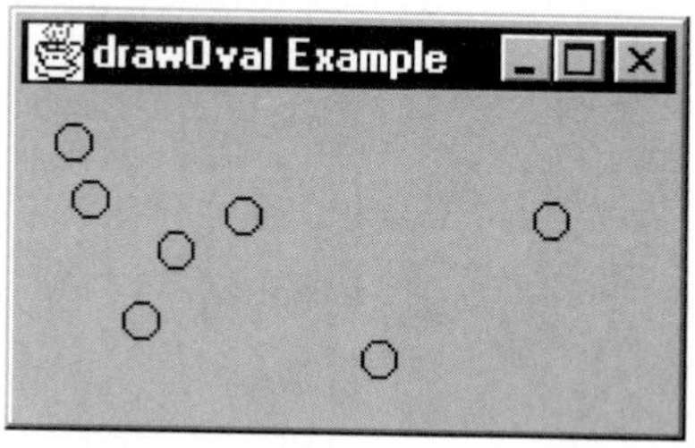

FIGURE 122 `Graphics.drawOval()`

```
import java.awt.*;
import java.util.*;
import java.io.*;
class Main extends Frame {
    Vector points = new Vector();

    Main() {
        super("drawOval Example");
        resize(200, 200);
        show();
    }

    void addPoint(Point p) {
        points.addElement(p);
        repaint();
    }

    public void paint(Graphics g) {
        for (int i=0; i<points.size(); i++) {
            Point p = (Point)points.elementAt(i);
            g.drawOval(p.x-5, p.y-5, 10, 10);
        }
    }

    static public void main(String[] args) {
        Main m = new Main();
        DataInputStream dis = new DataInputStream(System.in);

        while (true) {
            try {
                m.addPoint(new Point(
                    Integer.parseInt(dis.readLine()),
                    Integer.parseInt(dis.readLine())));
            } catch (Exception e) {
                e.printStackTrace();
                System.exit(1);
            }
        }
    }
}
```

A B C D E F G H I J K L M N O P Q R S T U V W X Y Z

drawPolygon()

PURPOSE Paints a non-closed polygon outline.

SYNTAX
```
public void drawPolygon(Polygon polygon)
public abstract void drawPolygon(int[] xPoints, int[] yPoints, int
   nPoints)
```

DESCRIPTION A *polygon* is a collection of lines connecting a series of points. The polygon is not closed, which means a line is not automatically drawn between the first and last points. This method paints a 1-pixel-thick polygon in the foreground color using the specified set of points.

The points are either specified by the polygon `polygon` or by two arrays `xPoints` and `yPoints`. In the latter form, `xPoints[i]` and `yPoints[i]` together specify a point in the polygon. The series of points from index `0` to `nPoints-1` specifies the ordered list of points in the polygon.

PARAMETERS

`nPoints`	The number of points in `xPoints` and `yPoints`.
`polygon`	The non-`null` polygon to paint.
`xPoints`	The non-`null` array of *x*-coordinates (in pixels) in the polygon.
`yPoints`	The non-`null` array of *y*-coordinates (in pixels) in the polygon.

SEE ALSO `fillPolygon()`, `Polygon`.

EXAMPLE This example paints a polygon. When the mouse is clicked or dragged, a new point is added to the polygon. See Figure 123.

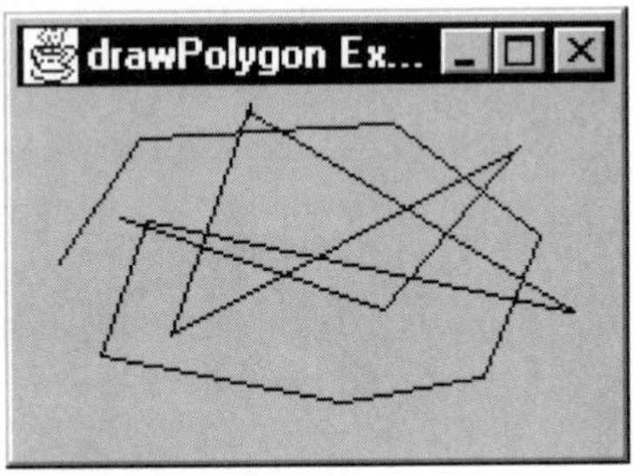

FIGURE 123
`Graphics.drawPolygon()`

```
import java.awt.*;
class Main extends Frame {
    Polygon polygon = new Polygon();

    Main() {
        super("drawPolygon Example");
        resize(200, 200);
        show();
    }

    public void paint(Graphics g) {
        g.drawPolygon(polygon);
    }

    // The default update method clears the screen which causes
    // flicker.  This override avoids this.
    public void update(Graphics g) {
        paint(g);
    }
```

```
    public boolean mouseDown(Event evt, int x, int y) {
        polygon.addPoint(x, y);
        repaint();
        return true;
    }

    public boolean mouseDrag(Event evt, int x, int y) {
        polygon.addPoint(x, y);
        repaint();
        return true;
    }

    static public void main(String[] args) {
        new Main();
    }
}
```

drawRect()

PURPOSE Paints an outline around a rectangle.

SYNTAX `public void drawRect(int x, int y, int width, int height)`

DESCRIPTION This method paints a 1-pixel-thick outline *around* the rectangle defined by `x`, `y`, `width`, and `height`. The left and top edges of the outline are within the specified rectangle, but the right and bottom edges are just outside the defined rectangle. Hence this method actually draws `width+1` horizontal lines and `height+1` vertical lines. Note that this method will paint a single pixel if `width` and `height` are both `0`. Use `drawRect(x, y, width-1, height-1)` to paint the outline inside the specified rectangle. If either `width` or `height` is less than `0`, the method call is ignored.

PARAMETERS

`height` The height of the rectangular area in pixels.

`width` The width of the rectangular area in pixels.

`x` The *x*-coordinate in pixels.

`y` The y-coordinate in pixels.

SEE ALSO `clearRect()`, `fillRect()`.

EXAMPLE This example demonstrates how to implement an "outline rectangle," which is typically used for selecting objects in a user interface or for defining the size and location of new objects. See Figure 124.

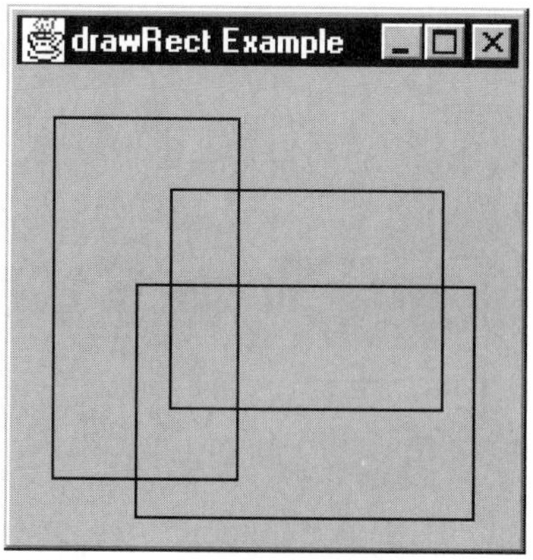

FIGURE 124 `Graphics.drawRect()`

B C D E F G H I J K L M N O P Q R S T U V W X Y Z

In this example, you can create a rectangle by clicking and dragging an outline of a rectangle until you are satisfied with the size of the rectangle. When you release the mouse, a permanent rectangle is drawn on the display. The outline rectangle is painted using xor paint mode, so it is not necessary to repaint the entire background each time the outline rectangle changes size. See `setXORMode()` for more details.

```
import java.awt.*;
import java.util.*;
class Main extends Frame {
    Main() {
        super("drawRect Example");
        add("Center", new MainCanvas());
        resize(200, 200);
        show();
    }
    static public void main(String[] args) {
        new Main();
    }
}

class MainCanvas extends Canvas {
    Vector rects = new Vector();
    int startX, startY;
    Rectangle oldRect, newRect;

    public void paint(Graphics g) {
        update(g);
    }

    public void update(Graphics g) {
        // First erase old rect.
        if (oldRect != null) {
            g.setXORMode(Color.white);
            g.drawRect(oldRect.x, oldRect.y, oldRect.width,
                  oldRect.height);
            g.setPaintMode();
        }
        // Now paint rectangles.
        for (int i=0; i<rects.size(); i++) {
            Rectangle r = (Rectangle)rects.elementAt(i);
            g.drawRect(r.x, r.y, r.width, r.height);
        }
        if (newRect != null) {
            g.setXORMode(Color.white);
            g.drawRect(newRect.x, newRect.y, newRect.width,
                  newRect.height);
            g.setPaintMode();
        }
        oldRect = newRect;
        newRect = null;
    }
```

```
    public boolean mouseDown(Event evt, int x, int y) {
        startX = x;
        startY = y;
        newRect = new Rectangle(x, y, 1, 1);
        repaint();
        return true;
    }

    public boolean mouseDrag(Event evt, int x, int y) {
        newRect = new Rectangle(startX, startY, x-startX, y-startY);
        repaint();
        return true;
    }

    public boolean mouseUp(Event evt, int x, int y) {
        rects.addElement(new Rectangle(startX, startY, x-startX,
             y-startY));
        newRect = null;
        repaint();
        return true;
    }
}
```

drawRoundRect()

PURPOSE Paints an outline of a rectangle with rounded corners.

SYNTAX `public abstract void drawRoundRect(int x, int y, int width, int height, int arcWidth, int arcHeight)`

DESCRIPTION This method paints a 1-pixel-thick rounded-rectangular outline in the foreground color within the rectangle defined by `x`, `y`, `width`, and `height`. If either `width` or `height` is less than `0`, the method call is ignored.

`arcWidth` and `arcHeight` specify the shape and size of the arc to use for each corner. Logically, the arcs are formed by defining a rectangle of width `arcWidth` and height `arcHeight` and calling `drawOval()` using this rectangle. The rectangle is then sliced into four equal-sized quadrants. Each quadrant yields an arc for one of the rectangle's corners. If either `arcWidth` or `arcHeight` is `0`, the painted rectangle will not have rounded corners. If either `arcWidth` or `arcHeight` is less than `0`, both `arcWidth` and `arcHeight` are set to `0`.

PARAMETERS

`arcHeight` The height, in pixels, of the ellipse used to generate the rounded corners.

`arcWidth` The width, in pixels, of the ellipse used to generate the rounded corners.

`height` The height of the rectangular area in pixels.

`width`	The width of the rectangular area in pixels.
`x`	The *x*-coordinate in pixels.
`y`	The *y*-coordinate in pixels.
SEE ALSO	`fillRoundRect()`.
EXAMPLE	This example implements a button with rounded corners. If the button is clicked, the outline and text changes color. See Figure 125.

FIGURE 125
`Graphics.drawRoundRect()`

```
import java.awt.*;
class Main extends Frame {
    Main() {
        super("drawRoundRect Example");
        add("Center", new MainCanvas());
        resize(150, 80);
        show();
    }

    static public void main(String[] args) {
        new Main();
    }
}

class MainCanvas extends Canvas {
    String label = "Round Button";
    boolean down;

    public boolean mouseDown(Event evt, int x, int y) {
        down = true;
        repaint();
        return true;
    }

    public boolean mouseUp(Event evt, int x, int y) {
        down = false;
        repaint();
        return true;
    }

    public void paint(Graphics g) {
        int w = size().width;
        int h = size().height;
        FontMetrics fm = g.getFontMetrics();

        if (down) {
            g.setColor(Color.red);
        } else {
            g.setColor(Color.black);
        }
        g.drawRoundRect(0, 0, w-1, h-1, 20, 20);
        g.drawString(label, (w-fm.stringWidth(label))/2,
```

```
            (h-fm.getHeight())/2+fm.getAscent());
        }
    }
```

drawString()

PURPOSE Paints a string.

SYNTAX `public abstract void drawString(String string, int x, int y)`

DESCRIPTION This method paints the string at position `x, y` using the current font and foreground color. Only the characters of the string are painted, not the background of the characters. The color of the characters is determined by the graphics context's foreground color.

The position `x, y` specifies the baseline of the string (not the northwest corner of the string as do most other methods). To paint the string such that the northwest corner of the string is at a point `p`, add the font ascent to `p.y`. For example:

```
Font fm = getFontMetrics();
          // get metrics of current font
drawString(string, p.x, p.y+fm.getAscent();
```

PARAMETERS

`string`	The non-`null` string to be painted.
`x`	The *x*-coordinate of the baseline in pixels.
`y`	The *y*-coordinate of the baseline in pixels.

SEE ALSO `Font.getAscent()`, `drawBytes()`, `drawChars()`.

EXAMPLE This example defines a canvas that paints a line of text on top of a colored background. It also creates a choice component to let you adjust the size of the font. See Figure 126.

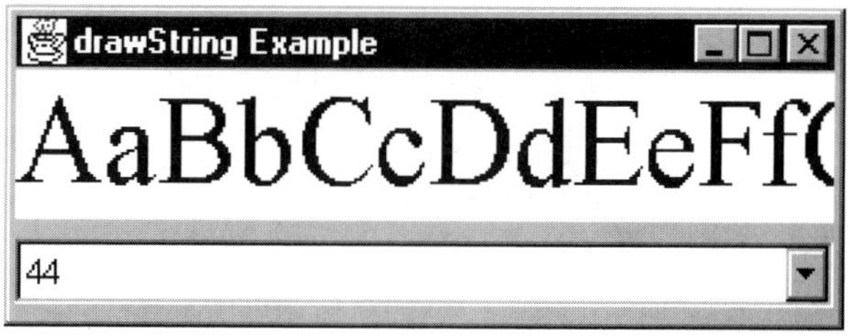

FIGURE 126 **`Graphics.drawString()`**

```
import java.awt.*;
class Main extends Frame {
    MainCanvas cv = new MainCanvas();
    Choice choice = new Choice();
```

A B C D E F G H I J K L M N O P Q R S T U V W X Y Z

```
    Main() {
        super("drawString Example");

        for (int i=4; i<60; i += 4) {
            choice.addItem(""+i);
        }
        choice.select(0);
        cv.setFontSize(4);
        cv.resize(300, 100);
        add("Center", cv);
        add("South", choice);
        pack();
        show();
    }

    public boolean action(Event evt, Object what) {
        if (evt.target ==  choice) {
            cv.setFontSize(Integer.parseInt((String)what));
            return true;
        }
        return false;
    }

    static public void main(String[] args) {
        new Main();
    }
}

class MainCanvas extends Canvas {
    void setFontSize(int size) {
        Font f = getFont();

        if (f == null) {
            f = new Font("TimesRoman", Font.PLAIN, size);
        } else {
            f = new Font(getFont().getName(), getFont().getStyle(),
                   size);
        }
        setFont(f);
        repaint();
    }

    public void paint(Graphics g) {
        String s =
              "AaBbCcDdEeFfGgHhIiJjKkLlMmNnOoPpQqRrSsTtUuVvWwXxYyZz";
        FontMetrics fontM = g.getFontMetrics();

        g.setColor(Color.white);
        g.fillRect(0, 0, fontM.stringWidth(s), fontM.getHeight());
        g.setColor(Color.black);
        g.drawString(s, 0, fontM.getAscent());
    }
}
```

fill3DRect()

PURPOSE Paints a rectangle that has a 3D outline.

SYNTAX

```
public void fill3DRect(int x, int y, int width, int height,
   boolean raised)
```

DESCRIPTION This method paints a rectangle defined by `x`, `y`, `width`, and `height` and a 3D outline *around* this rectangle. The left and top edges of the outline are within the specified rectangle, but the right and bottom edges are just outside the defined rectangle. Hence this method actually draws `width+1` horizontal lines and `height+1` vertical lines. Note that this method will paint a single pixel if `width` and `height` are both `0`. Use `fill3DRect(x, y, width-1, height-1)` to paint the 3D outline inside the specified rectangle. If either `width` or `height` is less than `0`, the method call is ignored.

If `raised` is `true`, the 3D effect is done by lightening the left and top edges and darkening the right and bottom edges. If `raised` is `false`, the left and top edges are darker and the right and bottom edges are lighter. The lighter and darker color shades are generated by the `Color.brigher()` and `Color.darker()` methods, respectively.

PARAMETERS

`height`	The height of the rectangular area in pixels.
`raised`	Specifies whether the 3D effect should appear raised or lowered.
`width`	The width of the rectangular area in pixels.
`x`	The *x*-coordinate in pixels.
`y`	The *y*-coordinate in pixels.

SEE ALSO `Color.brighter()`, `Color.darker()`, `draw3DRect()`.

EXAMPLE This example paints a 3D border just within the frame's paintable area. See Figure 127. The 3D border is thicker than 1 pixel. Clicking toggles the 3D border between a raised border and a lowered border.

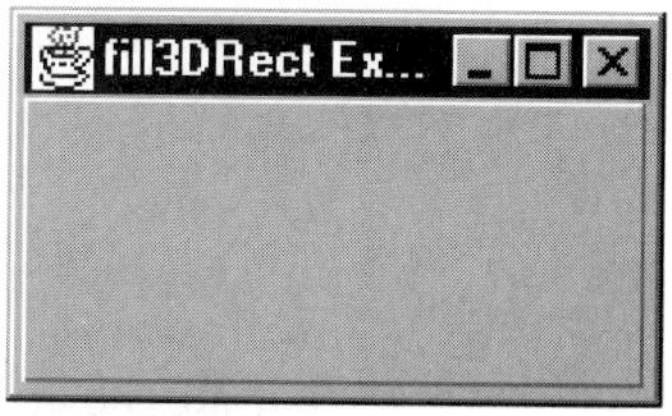

FIGURE 127
`Graphics.fill3DRect()`

```
import java.awt.*;
class Main extends Frame {
    boolean raised = true;

    Main() {
        super("fill3DRect Example");
        resize(200, 200);
        show();
    }
```

```
        public void paint(Graphics g) {
            Insets insets = this.insets();
            int x = 0, y = 0;
            int w = size().width-insets.left-insets.right;
            int h = size().height-insets.top-insets.bottom;

            w -= 1;    // draw inside the rectangle.
            h -= 1;    // draw inside the rectangle.
            g.setColor(getBackground());
            g.fill3DRect(x++, y++, w, h, raised);
        }

        public boolean mouseDown(Event evt, int x, int y) {
            raised = !raised;
            repaint();
            return true;
        }

        static public void main(String[] args) {
            new Main();
        }
    }
```

fillArc()

PURPOSE Paints a filled elliptical arc inside a rectangle.

SYNTAX

```
public abstract void fillArc(int x, int y, int width, int height,
    int startAngle, int arcAngle)
```

DESCRIPTION This method paints a filled elliptical arc in the foreground color within the rectangle defined by `x`, `y`, `width`, and `height`. If either `width` or `height` is less than `0`, the method call is ignored.

Logically, you form the arc first by using the `drawOval()` method to paint an oval inside the rectangle. Next, define a horizontal line that originates from the oval's center and extends to the containing rectangle's right edge. Then anchor the line at the oval's center and rotate the line `startAngle` degrees from its starting position. If `startAngle` is positive, rotate counterclockwise; if `startAngle` is negative, rotate clockwise. The intersection of this line and the oval's outline is the starting point for the arc.

Next, continue rotating the line `arcAngle` degrees. Again, if `arcAngle` is positive, rotate counterclockwise; otherwise rotate clockwise. All the points that intersect this line and the oval's outline during the rotation are included in the arc.

PARAMETERS

arcAngle — The angle in degrees (360 degrees in a circle) that specifies the end of the arc. arcAngle is relative to startAngle.

height — The height of the rectangular area in pixels.

startAngle — The angle in degrees (360 degrees in a circle) that specifies the start of the arc.

width — The width of the rectangular area in pixels.

x — The *x*-coordinate in pixels.

y — The *y*-coordinate in pixels.

SEE ALSO — drawArc().

EXAMPLE — This example draws a 270-degree arc starting at 0 degrees. Four labels are used to show the startAngle positions. See Figure 128.

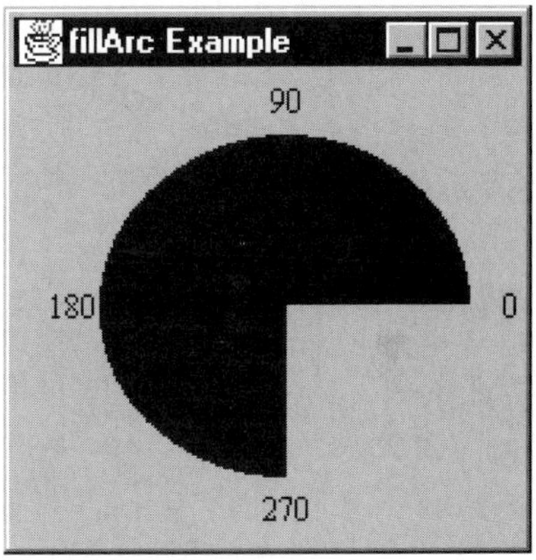

FIGURE 128 Graphics.fillArc()

```
import java.awt.*;
class Main extends Frame {
    Main() {
        super("fillArc Example");
        add("Center", new MainCanvas());
        add("North", new Label("90", Label.CENTER));
        add("South", new Label("270", Label.CENTER));
        add("East", new Label("0"));
        add("West", new Label("180"));
        resize(200, 200);
        show();
    }

    static public void main(String[] args) {
        new Main();
    }
}

class MainCanvas extends Canvas {
    public void paint(Graphics g) {
        g.fillArc(0, 0, size().width, size().height, 0, 270);
    }
}
```

fillOval()

PURPOSE — Paints an oval area.

A B C D E F G H I J K L M N O P Q R S T U V W X Y Z

SYNTAX `public abstract void fillOval(int x, int y, int width, int height)`

DESCRIPTION This method paints an oval area, which is defined to be the largest oval that fits into the rectangle defined by `x`, `y`, `width`, and `height`. The oval area is filled with the foreground color. If either `width` or `height` is less than or equal to `0`, the method call is ignored.

PARAMETERS

`height` The height of the rectangular area in pixels.
`width` The width of the rectangular area in pixels.
`x` The *x*-coordinate in pixels.
`y` The *y*-coordinate in pixels.

SEE ALSO `drawOval()`.

EXAMPLE This example creates and initializes an off-screen image with a circle-shaped pattern. See Figure 129. The image is then used to "texture" the frame's paintable area. For demonstration purposes, the image is scaled to half its size when painted.

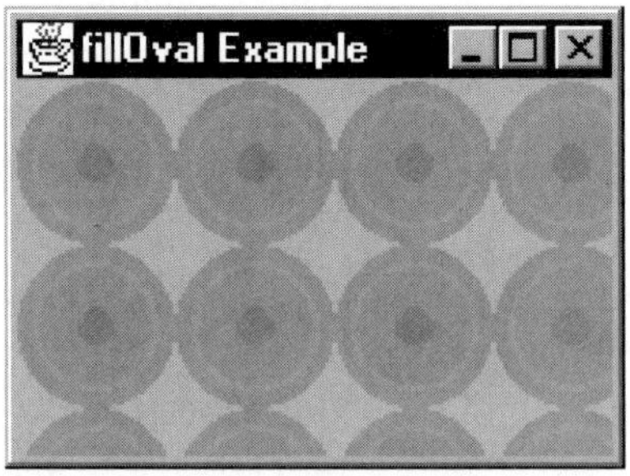

FIGURE 129 `Graphics.fillOval()`

```
import java.awt.*;
class Main extends Frame {
    Main() {
        super("fillOval Example");
        resize(400, 200);
        show();
    }

    public void paint(Graphics g) {
        int iSize = 50;
        Insets insets = this.insets();
        int w = size().width-insets.left-insets.right;
        int h = size().height-insets.top-insets.bottom;
        Image image = createImage(iSize);

        for (int y=0; y<h; y += iSize) {
            for (int x=0; x<w; x += iSize) {
                g.drawImage(image, x, y, iSize, iSize, null);
            }
        }
    }

    Image createImage(int size) {
        Image im = createImage(size, size);
        Graphics g = im.getGraphics();
        Rectangle r = new Rectangle(size, size);
```

```
        g.setColor(getBackground());
        g.fillRect(0, 0, size, size);
        while (!r.isEmpty()) {
            int c = r.x * 2 * 63 / size;
            g.setColor(new Color(255-c, 150, c+150));
            g.fillOval(r.x, r.y, r.width, r.height);
            r.grow(-1, -1);
        }
        return im;
    }

    static public void main(String[] args) {
        new Main();
    }
}
```

fillPolygon()

PURPOSE Paints a closed polygon.

SYNTAX
```
public void fillPolygon(Polygon p)
public abstract void fillPolygon(int[] xPoints, int[] yPoints, int
   nPoints)
```

DESCRIPTION A *polygon* is a collection of lines connecting a series of points. The polygon is closed, which means a line is automatically drawn between the first and last points. This method paints a polygon in the foreground color using the specified set of points. The points are either specified by the polygon `polygon` or by two arrays `xPoints` and `yPoints`. In the latter form, `xPoint[i]` and `yPoints[i]` together specify a point in the polygon. The series of points from index `0` to `nPoints-1` specify the ordered list of points in the polygon.

If the number of points is fewer than 3, the method call is ignored. If parts of the polygon overlap, the even-odd fill rule (otherwise known as an alternating rule) is applied.

PARAMETERS

`nPoints`	The number of points in `xPoints` and `yPoints`.
`polygon`	The non-`null` polygon to paint.
`xPoints`	The non-`null` array of *x*-coordinates (in pixels) in the polygon.
`yPoints`	The non-`null` array of *y*-coordinates (in pixels) in the polygon.

SEE ALSO `drawPolygon()`, `Polygon`.

EXAMPLE This example paints a filled polygon. See Figure 130. When the mouse is clicked or dragged, a new point is added to the polygon. Double-clicking clears the polygon.

FIGURE 130:
`Graphics.fillPolygon()`

```
import java.awt.*;
class Main extends Frame {
    Polygon polygon = new Polygon();

    Main() {
        super("fillPolygon Example");
        resize(200, 200);
        show();
    }

    public void paint(Graphics g) {
        g.fillPolygon(polygon);
    }

    public boolean mouseDown(Event evt, int x, int y) {
        if (evt.clickCount > 1) {    // double-click
            polygon = new Polygon();
        }
        polygon.addPoint(x, y);
        repaint();
        return true;
    }

    static public void main(String[] args) {
        new Main();
    }
}
```

fillRect()

PURPOSE Paints a rectangular area.

SYNTAX `public abstract void fillRect(int x, int y, int width, int height)`

DESCRIPTION This method paints the area defined by `x`, `y`, `width`, and `height` with the foreground color. If either `width` or `height` is less than or equal to `0`, the method call is ignored.

PARAMETERS

`height` The height of the rectangular area in pixels.

`width`	The width of the rectangular area in pixels.
`x`	The *x*-coordinate in pixels.
`y`	The *y*-coordinate in pixels.

SEE ALSO `clearRect()`, `drawRect()`.

EXAMPLE This example creates a frame with two choices and a drawing area. See Figure 131. The choices specify the color and shape of a figure. Clicking anywhere in the drawing area draws the specified figure at the mouse coordinates. `fillRect()` is used to draw the rectangle and squares.

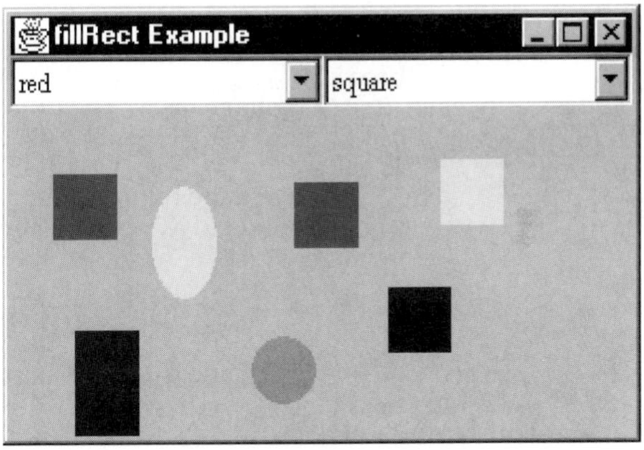

FIGURE 131 **`Graphics.fillRect()`**

```
import java.awt.*;
class Main extends Frame {
    String[] figureNames = {“circle”, “oval”, “square”, “rectangle”};
    String[] colorNames = {“red”, “green”, “blue”, “yellow”};
    Color[] colorValues = {Color.red, Color.green,
                           Color.blue, Color.yellow};
    Choice chFigure = new Choice();
    Choice chColor = new Choice();
    int curX, curY;

    Main() {
        super(“fillRect Example”);
        Panel p = new Panel();

        for (int i=0; i<figureNames.length; i++) {
            chFigure.addItem(figureNames[i]);
        }
        for (int i=0; i<colorNames.length; i++) {
            chColor.addItem(colorNames[i]);
        }
        p.setLayout(new GridLayout(1, 0));
        p.add(chColor);
        p.add(chFigure);
        add(“North”, p);
        resize(300, 300);
        show();
    }
```

```
    public void update(Graphics g) {
        g.setColor(colorValues[chColor.getSelectedIndex()]);
        switch (chFigure.getSelectedIndex()) {
        case 0: // circle
            g.fillOval(curX, curY, 30, 30);
            break;
        case 1: // oval
            g.fillOval(curX, curY, 30, 50);
            break;
        case 2: // square
            g.fillRect(curX, curY, 30, 30);
            break;
        case 3: // rectangle
            g.fillRect(curX, curY, 30, 50);
            break;
        }
    }

    public boolean mouseDown(Event evt, int x, int y) {
        curX = x;
        curY = y;
        repaint();
        return true;
    }

    static public void main(String[] args) {
        new Main();
    }
}
```

fillRoundRect()

PURPOSE Paints a rectangle with rounded corners on the graphics context.

SYNTAX `public abstract void fillRoundRect(int x, int y, int width, int height, int arcWidth, int arcHeight)`

DESCRIPTION This method paints a rounded rectangle in the foreground color within the rectangle defined by `x`, `y`, `width`, and `height`. If either `width` or `height` is less than `0`, the method call is ignored.

`arcWidth` and `arcHeight` specify the shape and size of the arc to use for each corner. Logically, you form the arcs by defining a rectangle of width `arcWidth` and height `arcHeight` and calling `drawOval()` using this rectangle. Then slice the rectangle into four equal-sized quadrants. Each quadrant yields an arc for one of the rectangle's corners. If either `arcWidth` or `arcHeight` are `0`, the painted rectangle will not have rounded corners. If either `arcWidth` or `arcHeight` is less than `0`, both `arcWidth` and `arcHeight` are set to `0`.

PARAMETERS

`arcHeight`	The height, in pixels, of the ellipse used to generate the rounded corners.
`arcWidth`	The width, in pixels, of the ellipse used to generate the rounded corners.
`height`	The height of the rectangular area in pixels.
`width`	The width of the rectangular area in pixels.
`x`	The *x*-coordinate in pixels.
`y`	The *y*-coordinate in pixels.

SEE ALSO `drawRoundRect()`.

EXAMPLE This example implements a simple framework for measuring the cost of operations in the `Graphics` class. See Figure 132. You select the graphics operation to time using the choice component at the bottom of the window. Clicking the canvas starts a timer thread and calls the `repaint()` method. This method causes the `paint()` method to be called. `paint()` enters a tight loop executing the selected operation. The timer thread waits for 5 seconds and then signals the `paint()` method to exit its tight loop. The results are then printed to standard output.

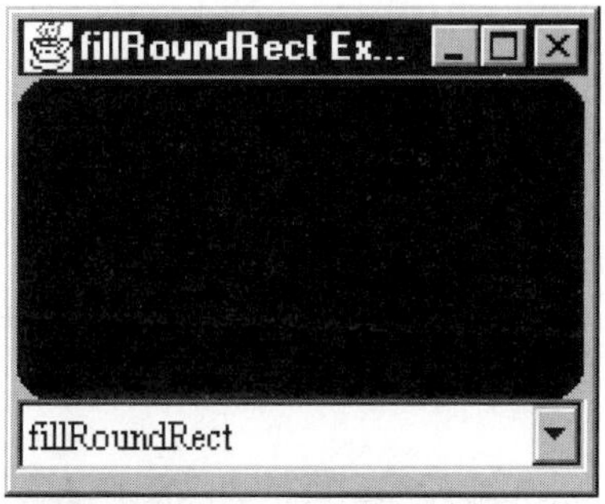

FIGURE 132
`Graphics.fillRoundRect()`

```
import java.awt.*;
class Main extends Frame {
    MainCanvas cv = new MainCanvas();
    Choice c = new Choice();
    Main() {
        super("fillRoundRect Example");
        add("Center", cv);

        c.addItem("create/dispose");
        c.addItem("drawRect");
        c.addItem("drawRoundRect");
        c.addItem("fillRect");
        c.addItem("fillRoundRect");
        add("South", c);
        resize(200, 200);
        show();
    }

    public boolean action(Event evt, Object arg) {
        if (evt.target == c) {
            cv.operation = c.getSelectedIndex();
            return true;
        }
```

```
        return false;
    }

    static public void main(String[] args) {
        new Main();
    }
}
class MainCanvas extends Canvas implements Runnable {
    int operation;
    Thread timerThread;

    public void paint(Graphics g) {
        int w = size().width-1;
        int h = size().height-1;
        if (timerThread != null) {
            int count = 0;
            long startTime = System.currentTimeMillis();

            switch (operation) {
              case 0:
                while (timerThread != null) {
                    Graphics g2 = g.create();
                     g2.dispose();
                     count++;
                }
              case 1:
                while (timerThread != null) {
                    g.drawRect(0, 0, w, h);
                     count++;
                }
              case 2:
                while (timerThread != null) {
                    g.drawRoundRect(0, 0, w, h, 20, 20);
                     count++;
                }
              case 3:
                while (timerThread != null) {
                    g.fillRect(0, 0, w, h);
                     count++;
                }
              case 4:
                while (timerThread != null) {
                    g.fillRoundRect(0, 0, w, h, 20, 20);
                     count++;
                }
            }
            System.out.print((double)count*1000.0
                / (double)(System.currentTimeMillis()-startTime));
            System.out.println(" paints/second");
        }
    }

    public void run() {
        try {
```

```
            Thread.sleep(5000);
        } catch (InterruptedException e) {
        }
        timerThread = null;
    }

    public boolean mouseDown(Event evt, int x, int y) {
        if (timerThread == null) {
            timerThread = new Thread(this);
            timerThread.start();
            repaint();
        }
        return true;
    }
}
```

A B C D E F G H I J K L M N O P Q R S T U V W X Y Z

finalize()

PURPOSE Releases the graphics context's system resources.

SYNTAX `public void finalize()`

DESCRIPTION This method simply calls the `dispose()` method. The graphics context can no longer be used after this call. This method is normally called by the garbage collector after the graphics context has been reclaimed.

OVERRIDES `Object.finalize()`.

SEE ALSO `dispose()`.

EXAMPLE See `Object.finalize()`.

getClipRect()

PURPOSE Retrieves the graphics context's current clipping rectangle.

SYNTAX `public abstract Rectangle getClipRect()`

DESCRIPTION If the return value is `null`, the clipping rectangle is the visible area of the surface.

RETURNS A new `Rectangle` object containing the current clipping area. The return value may be `null`.

SEE ALSO `clipRect()`.

A B C D E F G H I J K L M N O P Q R S T U V W X Y Z

EXAMPLE

This example shows that the area supplied to the `repaint()` method actually sets the graphics context clipping rectangle that you get in the `paint()` method callback. See Figure 133. Two threads are created that simply generate repaint requests at random intervals to update a particular area of the display. The area is then repainted using xor paint mode so that it is easy to see the affected area. What you see is the affected area flashing between red and the background color.

FIGURE 133
Graphics.getClipRect()

This example also demonstrates that the areas supplied to `repaint()` can sometimes be combined into a single area. When this happens, you will notice a larger area changing between red and the background color.

```
import java.awt.*;
class Main extends Frame implements Runnable {
    Main() {
        super("getClipRect Example");
        resize(200, 200);
        show();
        (new Thread(this)).start();
        (new Thread(this)).start();
    }

    public void update(Graphics g) {
        paint(g);
    }

    public void paint(Graphics g) {
        Insets insets = this.insets();
        int w = size().width-insets.left-insets.right;
        int h = size().height-insets.top-insets.bottom;

        g.setXORMode(Color.red);
        g.setColor(getBackground());
        g.fillOval(0, 0, w, h);
    }


    public void run() {
        while (true) {
            try {
                Thread.sleep((int)(Math.random()*400));
                if (Math.random() > .5) {
                    repaint(0, 0, 40, 40);
```

```
                } else {
                    repaint(80, 80, 40, 40);
                }
            } catch (Exception e) {}
        }
    }

    static public void main(String[] args) {
        new Main();
    }
}
```

getColor()

PURPOSE Retrieves the graphics context's foreground color.

SYNTAX `public abstract Color getColor()`

RETURNS The non-`null` foreground color.

SEE ALSO `setColor()`.

EXAMPLE See `drawImage()`.

getFont()

PURPOSE Retrieves the graphics context's font.

SYNTAX `public abstract Font getFont()`

RETURNS The current non-`null` font.

SEE ALSO `Font`, `setFont()`.

EXAMPLE This example displays the attributes of the frame's default font. See Figure 134.

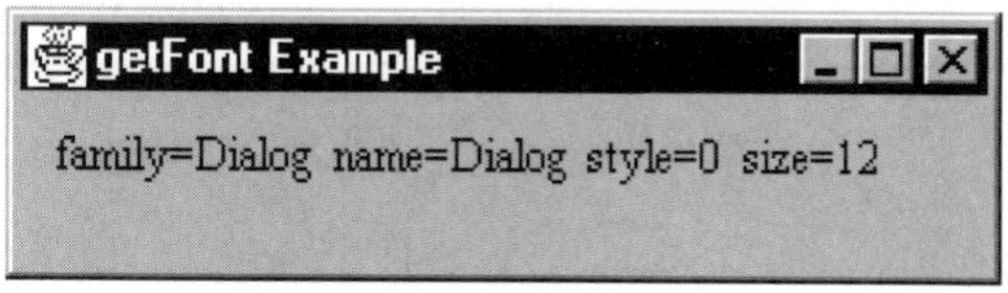

FIGURE 134 `Graphics.getFont()`

```
import java.awt.*;
class Main extends Frame {
    Main() {
        super("getFont Example");
        resize(100, 100);
        show();
    }
```

```
        public void paint(Graphics g) {
            Font f = g.getFont();
            FontMetrics fm = g.getFontMetrics(f);

            g.drawString("family="+f.getFamily()+"  name="+f.getName()
                +"  style="+f.getStyle()+"  size="+f.getSize(),
                10, 20);
        }

        public static void main(String[] args) {
            new Main();
        }
    }
```

getFontMetrics()

PURPOSE Retrieves the font metrics for a font.

SYNTAX
```
public FontMetrics getFontMetrics()
public abstract FontMetrics getFontMetrics(Font font)
```

DESCRIPTION The two forms of this method retrieve the font metrics for the font `font`. If `font` is not specified, it defaults to the graphics context's current font.

PARAMETERS

`font` The non-`null` font.

RETURNS The non-`null` font metrics for `font`.

SEE ALSO `Font`, `FontMetrics`, `getFont()`.

EXAMPLE See the `FontMetrics` class example.

Graphics()

PURPOSE Constructs a new graphics context.

SYNTAX
```
protected Graphics()
```

DESCRIPTION The background and foreground color and font are inherited from the drawing surface. The initial paint mode is normal.

A graphics context cannot be directly created from this constructor (note that the constructor is protected). It is supplied by classes that provide a drawing surface; for example, `Component.getGraphics()` and `Image.getGraphics()`.

SEE ALSO create().

EXAMPLE See Component.getGraphics(), Image.getGraphics().

setColor()

PURPOSE Sets the graphics context's foreground color.

SYNTAX `public abstract void setColor(Color color)`

DESCRIPTION This method sets the graphics context's foreground color to color.

PARAMETERS

color The non-null new foreground color.

SEE ALSO Color, getColor().

EXAMPLE This example is a set of random colored dots. A thread is created to continually change the colors of the dots. See Figure 135.

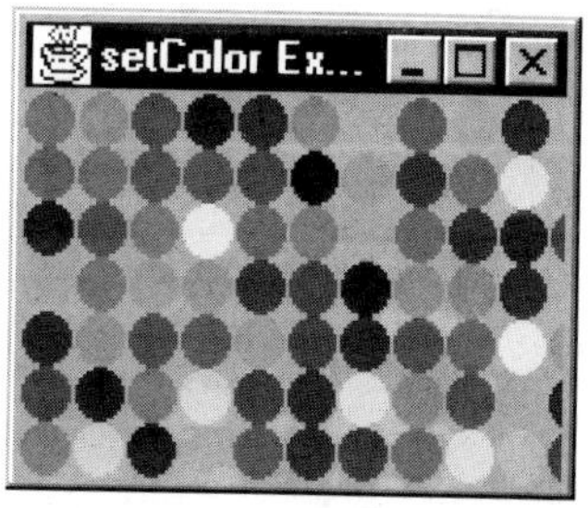

FIGURE 135
Graphics.setColor()

```
import java.awt.*;
class Main extends Frame implements Runnable
{
    int dotSize = 15;

    Main() {
        super("setColor Example");
        resize(150, 150);
        show();
        (new Thread(this)).start();
    }

    // Returns an integer in the range [0..r-1].
    int random(int r) {
        return (int)(Math.floor(Math.random()*r));
    }

    public void update(Graphics g) {
        Insets insets = this.insets();
        int w = size().width-insets.left-insets.right;
        int h = size().height-insets.top-insets.bottom;

        for (int i=0; i<10; i++) {
            int x = random(w), y = random(h);
            g.setColor(new Color(random(256), random(256),
                random(256)));
            g.fillOval(x-x%dotSize, y-y%dotSize, dotSize, dotSize);
        }
    }
```

```
        public void run() {
            while (true) {
                try {Thread.sleep(100);} catch (Exception e) {}
                repaint();
            }
        }

        static public void main(String[] args) {
            new Main();
        }
    }
```

setFont()

PURPOSE Sets the graphics context's font.

SYNTAX `public abstract void setFont(Font font)`

DESCRIPTION Sets the graphics context's font to `font`. The font affects only the string drawing operations.

PARAMETERS

`font` The non-`null` font.

SEE ALSO `drawBytes()`, `drawChars()`, `drawString()`, `Font`, `getFont()`.

EXAMPLE This example paints some text at different point sizes. The text is white painted on a black background. See Figure 136.

FIGURE 136 `Graphics.setFont()`

```
    import java.awt.*;
    class Main extends Frame {
        Main() {
            super("setFont Example");
            setBackground(Color.black);
            setForeground(Color.white);
            resize(200, 200);
            show();
        }

        public void paint(Graphics g) {
            int y = 0;
            for (int i=8; i<8*10; i+= 8) {
                Font f = new Font("TimesRoman", Font.PLAIN, i);
                FontMetrics fm = g.getFontMetrics(f);
```

```
            g.setFont(f);
            g.drawString(f.getName()+" at "+i+" points.",
                0, y+fm.getAscent());
            y += fm.getHeight();
        }
    }

    static public void main(String[] args) {
        new Main();
    }
}
```

setPaintMode()

PURPOSE Sets the graphics context to normal paint mode.

SYNTAX `public abstract void setPaintMode()`

DESCRIPTION This method sets the graphics context to normal paint mode. See the class description for details about paint modes.

SEE ALSO `setXORMode()`.

EXAMPLE See `setXORMode()`.

setXORMode()

PURPOSE Sets the graphics context to xor paint mode.

SYNTAX `public abstract void setXORMode(Color xorColor)`

DESCRIPTION This method sets the graphics context to xor paint mode using the xor color `xorColor`. See the class description for details of how xor paint mode uses the current foreground color and `xorColor`. Pixels of colors other than those two colors will be changed in an unpredictable, but reversible, manner. If you draw the same figure twice, all pixels will be restored to their original values.

PARAMETERS

`xorColor` The non-`null` xor color.

SEE ALSO `setPaintMode()`.

EXAMPLE This example creates a four-band colored background and paints a black circle on the background in xor paint mode. See Figure 137. The circle can be moved around the background so that you can see the xor mode paint effect. Black is xor'ed with green so that when the circle is on green, it appears as black and when it is on black, it appears green. When the black circle is on some other color, it simply appears in some color other than black. Four lines in different colors are also painted to see the xor mode paint effect. Notice that the green line does not show up at all.

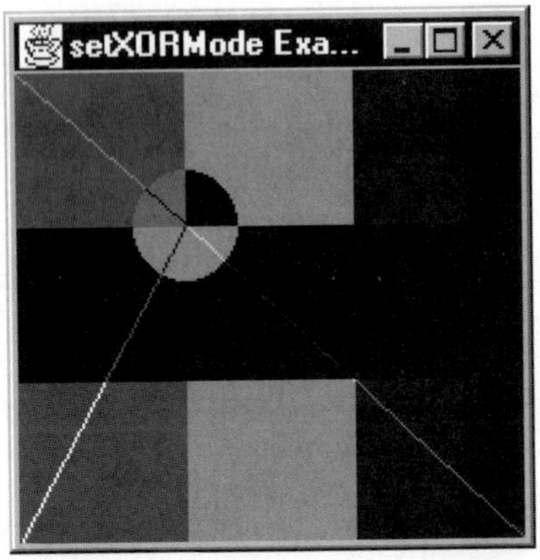

FIGURE 137 `Graphics.setXORMode()`

```
import java.awt.*;
class Main extends Frame {
    int curX, curY, newX, newY;

    Main() {
        super("setXORMode Example");
        resize(200, 200);
        show();
    }

    public boolean mouseMove(Event evt, int x, int y) {
        newX = x;
        newY = y;
        repaint();
        return true;
    }

    void drawLines(Graphics g, int x, int y, int w, int h) {
        g.setXORMode(Color.green);
        g.setColor(Color.red);
        g.drawLine(0, 0, x, y);
        g.setColor(Color.green);
        g.drawLine(w, 0, x, y);
        g.setColor(Color.blue);
        g.drawLine(0, h, x, y);
        g.setColor(Color.yellow);
        g.drawLine(w, h, x, y);
        g.setColor(Color.black);
        g.fillOval(x-20, y-20, 40, 40);
    }

    public void update(Graphics g) {
        Insets insets = this.insets();
```

```
        int w = size().width-insets.left-insets.right;
        int h = size().height-insets.top-insets.bottom;

        // Erase old image.
        drawLines(g, curX, curY, w, h);
        // Paint new one.
        drawLines(g, newX, newY, w, h);
        curX = newX;
        curY = newY;
    }

    public void paint(Graphics g) {
        Insets insets = this.insets();
        int w = size().width-insets.left-insets.right;
        int h = size().height-insets.top-insets.bottom;

        g.setPaintMode();
        g.setColor(Color.red);
        g.fillRect(0, 0, w/3, h);
        g.setColor(Color.green);
        g.fillRect(w/3, 0, w/3, h);
        g.setColor(Color.blue);
        g.fillRect(w*2/3, 0, w/3, h);
        g.setColor(Color.black);
        g.fillRect(0, h/3, w, h/3);
        drawLines(g, newX=curX=w/2, newY=curY=h/2, w, h);
    }

    static public void main(String[] args) {
        new Main();
    }
}
```

toString()

PURPOSE Generates the string representation of the graphics context's state.

SYNTAX `public String toString()`

DESCRIPTION This method generates the string representation of this graphics context. The string contains the graphics context's class name and the results of calling `paramString()`.

This method is typically used for debugging.

RETURNS A non-`null` string representing the graphics context's state.

OVERRIDES `Object.toString()`.

SEE ALSO `Component.paramString()`.

EXAMPLE See `Object.toString()`.

A B C D E F G H I J K L M N O P Q R S T U V W X Y Z

translate()

PURPOSE Moves the graphics context's origin.

SYNTAX `public abstract void translate(int x, int y)`

DESCRIPTION This method moves the graphics context's origin to `x, y` relative to the current origin. The coordinates of all subsequent graphics operations are interpreted relative to the new origin.

Note that the new origin is located relative to the current one. So if you call `translate(5, 5)`, `translate(0, 0)` will not restore the origin to its original location. To do that, you need to call `translate(-5, -5)`.

PARAMETERS

`x` The *x*-coordinate in pixels.

`y` The *y*-coordinate in pixels.

EXAMPLE This example creates a canvas that paints a histogram and a scrollbar to scroll the histogram. See Figure 138. The histogram is always twice as high as the available display area. The histogram is always painted in its entirety, and the scrollbar shifts the origin using the `translate()` method. You can select one of the histogram bars by clicking it. The example also demonstrates how to translate a position in mouse coordinates into graphics context coordinates.

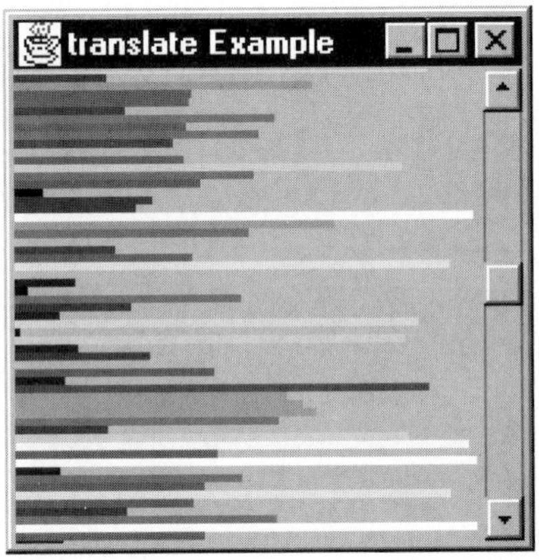

FIGURE 138 `Graphics.translate()`

```
import java.awt.*;
class Main extends Frame {
    MainCanvas cv = new MainCanvas();
    Scrollbar sb = new Scrollbar(Scrollbar.VERTICAL, 0, 50, 0, 100);

    Main() {
        super("translate Example");
        add("Center", cv);
        add("East", sb);
        resize(200, 200);
        show();
    }

    public boolean handleEvent(Event evt) {
        if (evt.target == sb) {
            cv.setOrigin(0, -cv.size().height * sb.getValue() / 100);
```

```
            return true;
        }
        return super.handleEvent(evt);
    }

    static public void main(String[] args) {
        new Main();
    }
}

class MainCanvas extends Canvas {
    int thick;
    double[] values = new double[100];
    int curX, curY;
    int originX, originY;

    MainCanvas() {
        for (int i=0; i<values.length; i++) {
            values[i] = Math.random();
        }
    }

    void setOrigin(int x, int y) {
        originX = x;
        originY = y;
        repaint();
    }

    public void paint(Graphics g) {
        int w = size().width;
        thick = size().height*2/values.length;

        g.translate(originX, originY);
        for (int i=0; i<values.length; i++) {
            int c = (int)(Math.floor(255 * values[i]));
            if (curY >= i * thick && curY < (i+1) * thick) {
                g.setColor(Color.red);
            } else {
                g.setColor(new Color(c, c, c));
            }
            g.fillRect(0, i * thick, (int)(w * values[i]), thick);
        }
    }

    public boolean mouseDown(Event evt, int x, int y) {
        curX = x - originX;
        curY = y - originY;
        repaint();
        return true;
    }
}
```

A B C D E F G H I J K L M N O P Q R S T U V W X Y Z

java.awt

GridBagConstraints

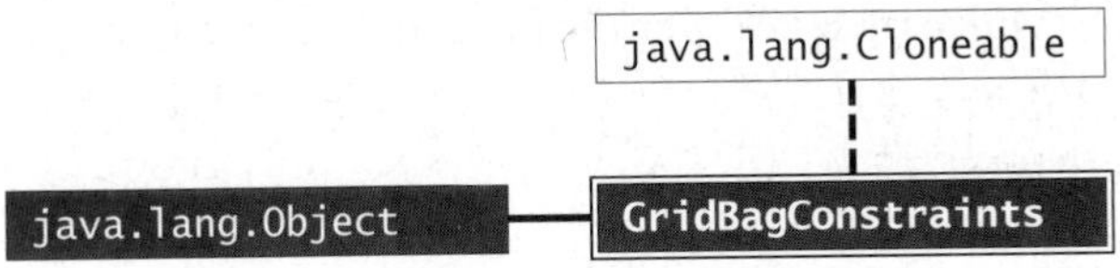

Syntax

`public class GridBagConstraints implements Cloneable`

Description

A *gridbag* is a collection of components laid out using the gridbag layout manager (see `GridBagLayout`). Each component in the gridbag has a set of constraints that determine its size and position in the gridbag. These constraints are defined with a `GridBagConstraints` instance and are associated with a component. There are seven gridbag constraints.

Fill

The *fill* constraint determines whether to stretch a component to fill the component's display area. There are four fill types. See `fill` later in this section for an example that uses these fill types.

Anchor

If a component is not stretched to completely fill its display area, the *anchor* constraint specifies the component's position in its display area. There are nine anchor types. See `anchor` later in this section for an example that uses these anchor types.

Size

A component can span more than one column or row. The *size* constraint specifies the number of columns or rows that the component occupies.

Internal Padding

The *internal padding* constraint is used to adjust the width and height of a component after `Component.minimumSize()` or `Component.preferredSize()` is called. Separate values control the width and height. See `ipadx` later in this section for an example that uses internal padding.

Insets

The *insets* constraint for a component is applied to a component's display area. An inset has four values to control the inset at the four edges. A positive inset at an edge reduces the display area at that edge. See `insets` later in this section for an example that uses insets.

A B C D E F G H I J K L M N O P Q R S T U V W X Y Z

Position

A component can be positioned at a particular cell location in the gridbag. Cells in the gridbag are addressed by *x*- and *y*-coordinates.

Weights

Each component in the gridbag has a non-negative gridbag weight constraint. Together the component weights define a weight for each column and row in the gridbag. This calculation for doing this is discussed below.

The column and row weights determine how columns and rows stretch and shrink when the container is made larger or smaller and how extra space is distributed among the columns and rows. The extra space is determined by subtracting the container size from the preferred size for the gridbag. The preferred size of the gridbag is calculated by laying out all the components in the gridbag using their preferred sizes. Here is how the extra space is distributed. First, no space is given to any row or column with zero weight. The amount that a column (or row) gets depends on its weight in relation to the total weight for all the columns (or rows) of the gridbag. For example, if the weight of a column *c* is 1 and the total weight is 10 (including *c*'s weight), column *c* gets one tenth of the total extra space.

If the total weight for all the columns (or rows) is 0, then the extra space is distributed around the gridbag. For example, if the total weight of all the columns is 0, the gridbag will be horizontally centered in its container.

It is important to note that if two components *C* and *D* both have weight 1, they will not necessarily be the same size. Only if *C*'s and *D*'s preferred sizes are identical will they be the same size. This is because only the extra space (after *C*'s and *D*'s preferred sizes are subtracted from the total available space) is distributed to *C* and *D*. For example, if *C*'s preferred size is 10, *D*'s preferred size is 20, and the extra space is 40 pixels, *C* will be 30 pixels wide while *D* will be 40 pixels wide.

The following steps describe how column and row weights are derived from component weights:

1. Consider all the components in a column whose grid widths are 1. The weight for that column is the maximal weight for those components.
2. Now consider all the components whose grid widths are greater than 1. Consider them in the order that they were inserted into the container. Suppose component *C* spans columns *ci..cj* and that the combined weight of these columns is *w*. If *C*'s weight is less than *w*, nothing happens. If *C*'s weight is greater than *w*, the extra weight is distributed among the columns. The distribution is based on the relative weight of the columns, so if one column has a weight of 1 while another has a weight of 5, the first column gets one sixth of the extra weight. After the extra weight has been distributed any remaining weight is given to the last column of the span. A zero weight column never gets any extra weight unless the column is the last column of the span and all the columns in the span have zero weights. The above rules also apply to each row.

If the container's dimensions are smaller than the gridbag's preferred size, the gridbag layout manager either attempts to shrink some rows or columns smaller than their preferred sizes or simply clips the components so that they appear off the container's visible area. You cannot control how the gridbag layout manager decides to fit a gridbag layout into an area smaller than the preferred size.

MEMBER SUMMARY

Constructor	
`GridBagConstraints()`	Constructs a new `GridBagConstraints` instance.
Size Type Constant Fields	
`RELATIVE`	Size type that specifies that subsequent cells in the row or column be occupied except for the last cell.
`REMAINDER`	Size type that specifies that subsequent cells in the row or column be occupied.
Fill Type Constant Fields	
`BOTH`	Fill type that specifies a fill in both directions
`NONE`	Fill type that specifies no fill (the default).
`HORIZONTAL`	Fill type that specifies a horizontal-only fill.
`VERTICAL`	Fill type that specifies a vertical-only fill.
Anchor Type Constant Fields	
`CENTER`	Anchor type that specifies center positioning.
`EAST`	Anchor type that specifies east positioning.
`NORTH`	Anchor type that specifies north positioning.
`NORTHEAST`	Anchor type that specifies northeast positioning.
`NORTHWEST`	Anchor type that specifies northwest positioning.
`SOUTH`	Anchor type that specifies south positioning.
`SOUTHEAST`	Anchor type that specifies southeast positioning.
`SOUTHWEST`	Anchor type that specifies southwest positioning.
`WEST`	Anchor type that specifies west positioning.
Fields	
`anchor`	This field holds the component's anchor constraint.
`fill`	This field holds the component's fill constraint.
`gridheight`	This field holds the component's height in cells.
`gridwidth`	This field holds the component's width in cells.
`gridx`	This field holds the *x*-coordinate cell location for the component.
`gridy`	This field holds the *y*-coordinate cell location for the component.
`insets`	This field holds the insets constraints for the component.

MEMBER SUMMARY	
`ipadx`	This field holds the internal padding for the component's width.
`ipady`	This field holds the internal padding for the component's height.
`weightx`	This field holds the component's column weight.
`weighty`	This field holds the component's row weight.
Copy Method	
`clone()`	Creates a copy of the gridbag constraints.

Example

See `GridBagLayout`.

anchor

PURPOSE This field holds the component's anchor constraint.

SYNTAX `public int anchor`

DESCRIPTION There are nine anchor types, one for each edge and each corner of a display area and one for the center of the display area: `CENTER`, `EAST`, `NORTH`, `NORTHEAST`, `NORTHWEST`, `SOUTH`, `SOUTHEAST`, `SOUTHWEST`, `WEST`.

EXAMPLE This example creates a 3-×-3 gridbag with nine buttons. See Figure 139. Each button represents an anchor type. All but the center button have a fill constraint of `BOTH`. Clicking a button modifies the center button's anchor constraint.

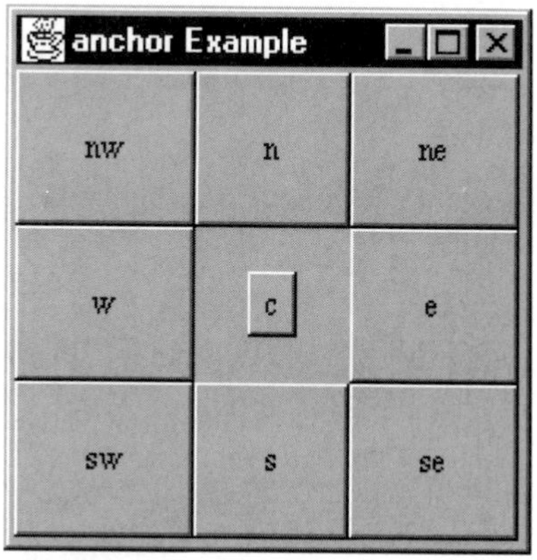

FIGURE 139
`GridBagConstraints.anchor`

```
import java.awt.*;
public class Main extends Frame {
    Component centerButton;
    GridBagLayout gbl = new
        GridBagLayout();
```

```
Main() {
super("anchor Example");
    GridBagConstraints c = new GridBagConstraints();

    setLayout(gbl);
    c.fill = GridBagConstraints.BOTH;
    c.weightx = 1;
    c.weighty = 1;

    makeButton(this, "nw", c, 0, 0);
    makeButton(this, "n", c, 1, 0);
    makeButton(this, "ne", c, 2, 0);
    makeButton(this, "w", c, 0, 1);
    makeButton(this, "e", c, 2, 1);
    makeButton(this, "sw", c, 0, 2);
    makeButton(this, "s", c, 1, 2);
    makeButton(this, "se", c, 2, 2);

       Make center button.
    c.fill = GridBagConstraints.NONE;
    centerButton = makeButton(this, "c", c, 1, 1);

    resize(200, 200);
    show();
}

    // Returns the new button.
Component makeButton(Container cont, String label,
        GridBagConstraints c, int x, int y) {
    GridBagLayout gbl = (GridBagLayout)cont.getLayout();
    Button b = new Button(label);

    cont.add(b);
    c.gridx = x;
    c.gridy = y;
    gbl.setConstraints(b, c);
    return b;
}

public boolean action(Event evt, Object arg) {
    GridBagConstraints c = gbl.getConstraints(centerButton);

    if ("n".equals(arg)) {
        c.anchor = GridBagConstraints.NORTH;
    } else if ("s".equals(arg)) {
        c.anchor = GridBagConstraints.SOUTH;
    } else if ("e".equals(arg)) {
        c.anchor = GridBagConstraints.EAST;
    } else if ("w".equals(arg)) {
        c.anchor = GridBagConstraints.WEST;
    } else if ("nw".equals(arg)) {
        c.anchor = GridBagConstraints.NORTHWEST;
    } else if ("ne".equals(arg)) {
        c.anchor = GridBagConstraints.NORTHEAST;
```

```
            } else if ("sw".equals(arg)) {
                c.anchor = GridBagConstraints.SOUTHWEST;
            } else if ("se".equals(arg)) {
                c.anchor = GridBagConstraints.SOUTHEAST;
            } else if ("c".equals(arg)) {
                c.anchor = GridBagConstraints.CENTER;
            }
            gbl.setConstraints(centerButton, c);
            invalidate();
            validate();
            return true;
        }

        static public void main(String[] args) {
            new Main();
        }
    }
```

BOTH

PURPOSE Fill type that specifies a fill in both directions.

SYNTAX `public static final int BOTH`

DESCRIPTION This constant field specifies that the component is to be stretched both horizontally and vertically to fill its display area. This constant is used in the `fill` field.

SEE ALSO `fill`.

EXAMPLE See `fill`.

CENTER

PURPOSE Anchor type that specifies center positioning.

SYNTAX `public static final int CENTER`

DESCRIPTION This constant field specifies that the center of the component is to be anchored to the center of its display area. This constant is used in the `anchor` field.

SEE ALSO `anchor`.

EXAMPLE See `anchor`.

clone()

PURPOSE Creates a copy of the gridbag constraints.

SYNTAX `public Object clone()`

DESCRIPTION This method makes a copy of the gridbag constraints. The new gridbag constraints have a complete copy of all the values, including a new copy of the insets object. Changing any value in the new gridbag constraints will not affect this instance.

RETURNS A copy of this gridbag constraints.

OVERRIDES `Object.clone()`.

EXAMPLE

```
GridBagConstraints c = new GridBagConstraints();
GridBagConstraints cCopy = (GridBagConstraints)c.clone();
```

EAST

PURPOSE Anchor type that specifies east positioning.

SYNTAX `public static final int EAST`

DESCRIPTION This constant field specifies that the east corner of the component is to be anchored to the east corner of the component's display area and centered vertically. This constant is used in the `anchor` field.

SEE ALSO `anchor`.

EXAMPLE See `anchor`.

fill

PURPOSE This field holds the fill constraint for a component.

SYNTAX `public int fill`

DESCRIPTION The fill type specifies how the component is stretched within its display area.

SEE ALSO `NONE`, `VERTICAL`, `HORIZONTAL`, `BOTH`.

EXAMPLE This example creates a 2-×-2 gridbag with four buttons. Each button has a different fill constraint. See Figure 140.

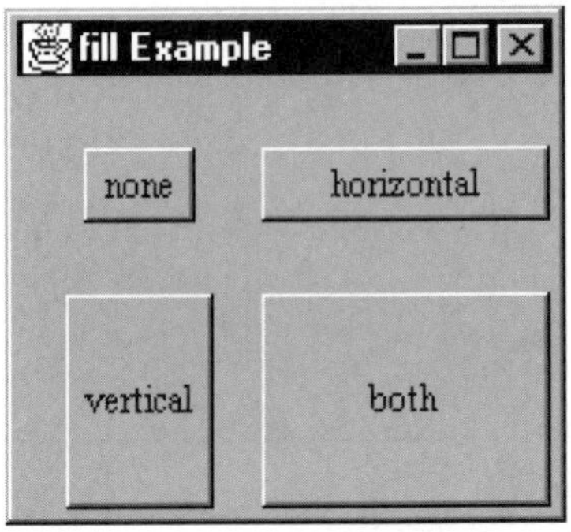

FIGURE 140 `GridBagConstraints.fill`

```
import java.awt.*;
public class Main {
    static void makeButton(Container cont, String label,
            GridBagConstraints c, int fill) {
        GridBagLayout gbl = (GridBagLayout)cont.getLayout();
        Button b = new Button(label);

        cont.add(b);
        c.fill = fill;
        gbl.setConstraints(b, c);
    }

    static public void main(String[] args) {
        GridBagLayout gbl = new GridBagLayout();
        GridBagConstraints c = new GridBagConstraints();
        Frame f = new Frame("fill Example");

        f.setLayout(gbl);
        c.weightx = 1;
        c.weighty = 1;
        makeButton(f, "none", c, GridBagConstraints.NONE);
        c.gridwidth = GridBagConstraints.REMAINDER;
        makeButton(f, "horizontal", c, GridBagConstraints.HORIZONTAL);
        c.gridwidth = 1;    // Restore default value.
        makeButton(f, "vertical", c, GridBagConstraints.VERTICAL);
        makeButton(f, "both", c, GridBagConstraints.BOTH);
        f.resize(200, 200);
        f.show();
    }
}
```

GridBagConstraints()

PURPOSE Constructs a new `GridBagConstraints` instance.

SYNTAX `public GridBagConstraints ()`

DESCRIPTION This constructor creates a new `GridBagConstraints` instance with the defaults given in Table 11.

TABLE 11 `GridBagConstraints` Defaults

`anchor`	`CENTER`
`fill`	`NONE`
`gridx`	`RELATIVE`
`gridy`	`RELATIVE`
`gridwidth`	`1`

Continued

TABLE 11 `GridBagConstraints` Defaults

`gridheight`	`1`
`ipadx`	`0`
`ipady`	`0`
`insets`	`new Insets(0, 0, 0, 0)`
`weightx`	`0`
`weighty`	`0`

EXAMPLE See the class example.

gridheight

PURPOSE This field holds the component's height in cells.

SYNTAX `public int gridheight`

DESCRIPTION The component's height is measured in cells and must be non-negative. For example, a grid height of 2 means the component will be 2 cells high. If the grid height is `REMAINDER`, the component will occupy all the cells below it. A grid height of 0 is the same as `REMAINDER`. If the grid height is `RELATIVE`, the component will occupy all the cells below it except for the last cell. Also, the grid height of the component that follows must be `REMAINDER`.

SEE ALSO `gridwidth`, `RELATIVE`, `REMAINDER`.

EXAMPLE See `gridwidth`.

gridwidth

PURPOSE This field holds the component's width in cells.

SYNTAX `public int gridwidth`

DESCRIPTION The component's width is measured in cells and must be non-negative. For example, a grid width of 2 means the component will be 2 cells wide.

If the grid width is `REMAINDER`, the component will occupy all the cells below it. A grid width of 0 is the same as `REMAINDER`.

If the grid width is `RELATIVE`, the component will occupy all the cells below it except for the last cell. Also, the grid width of the component that follows must be `REMAINDER`.

SEE ALSO `RELATIVE`, `REMAINDER`.

EXAMPLE This example creates a 6-×-3 gridbag with 18 buttons. See Figure 141. The button at the end of each row has the grid width constraint of `REMAINDER`. This means it will consume all remaining cells in that row. Each of the non-`REMAINDER` buttons will increase its grid width by 1 (up to 4) when pushed. Using this program, you can experiment with the effects of nonuniform grid widths in a gridbag.

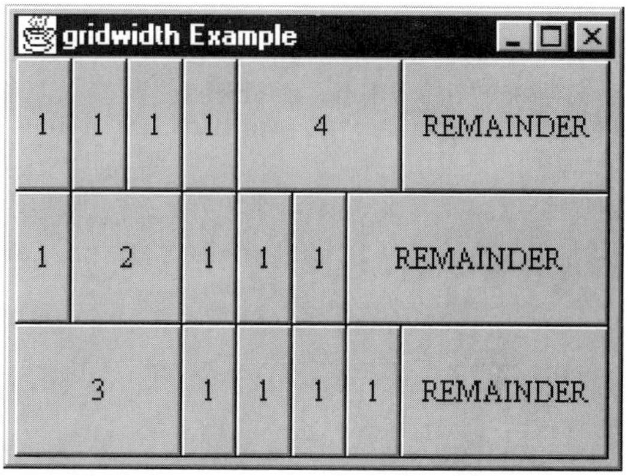

FIGURE 141 `GridBagConstraints.gridwidth` and `GridBagConstraints.gridheight`

```
import java.awt.*;
public class Main extends Frame {
    GridBagLayout gbl = new GridBagLayout();

    Main() {
        super("gridwidth Example");
        setLayout(gbl);
        for (int i=0; i<18; i++) {
            if (i % 6 == 5) {
                makeButton("REMAINDER", GridBagConstraints.REMAINDER);
            } else {
                makeButton("1", 1);
            }
        }
        resize(300, 300);
        show();
    }

    void makeButton(String label, int w) {
        GridBagConstraints c = new GridBagConstraints();
        Button b = new Button(label);

        c.gridwidth = w;
        c.gridheight = 1;
        c.fill = GridBagConstraints.BOTH;
        c.weightx = 1;
        c.weighty = 1;
        gbl.setConstraints(b, c);
        add(b);
    }
```

```
        public boolean action(Event evt, Object arg) {
            Button b = (Button)evt.target;
            GridBagConstraints gbc = gbl.getConstraints(b);

            if (gbc.gridwidth != GridBagConstraints.REMAINDER) {
                if (++gbc.gridwidth > 4) {
                    gbc.gridwidth = 1;
                }
                gbl.setConstraints(b, gbc);
                b.setLabel("" + gbc.gridwidth);
                invalidate();
                validate();
            }
            return true;
        }

        static public void main(String[] args) {
            new Main();
        }
    }
```

gridx

PURPOSE This field holds the *x*-coordinate cell location for a component.

SYNTAX `public int gridx`

DESCRIPTION The cell locations are 0-based. This means the location of the cell at the gridbag's northwest corner is (0, 0).

SEE ALSO `gridy`

EXAMPLE This example creates a 3-×-3 gridbag with eight buttons and one empty cell. See Figure 142. Pressing a button adjacent to the empty cell moves that button into the empty cell.

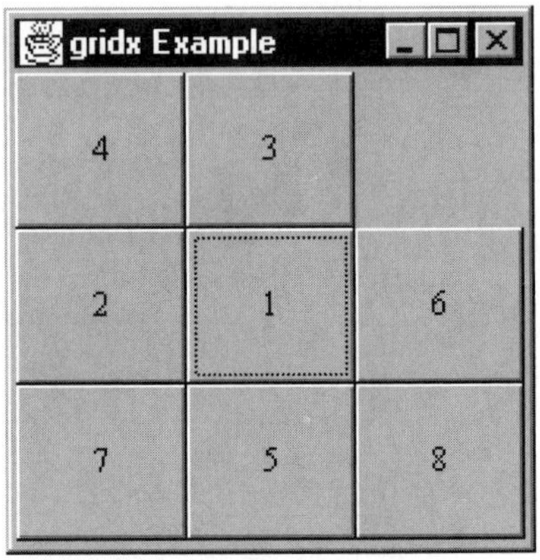

FIGURE 142 `GridBagConstraints.gridx` and `GridBagConstraints.gridy`

```
    import java.awt.*;
    public class Main extends Frame {
        GridBagLayout gbl = new GridBagLayout();
        Point free = new Point(2, 2);

        Main() {
            super("gridx Example");
            Component c = null;
```

```
        setLayout(gbl);
        for (int i=0; i<3; i++) {
            for (int j=0; j<3; j++) {
                c = makeButton(String.valueOf((char)('1'+i+3*j)),
                                    i, j);
            }
        }
        remove(c);        // remove the last button
        resize(200, 200);
        show();
    }

    // Returns the new button.
    Component makeButton(String label, int x, int y) {
        GridBagConstraints c = new GridBagConstraints();
        Button b = new Button(label);

        c.gridx = x;
        c.gridy = y;
        c.fill = GridBagConstraints.BOTH;
        c.weightx = 1;
        c.weighty = 1;
        gbl.setConstraints(b, c);
        add(b);
        return b;
    }

    public boolean action(Event evt, Object arg) {
        GridBagConstraints gbc = gbl.getConstraints
             ((Component)evt.target);
        Point p = new Point(gbc.gridx, gbc.gridy);

        if ((p.x == free.x && Math.abs(p.y-free.y) == 1)
               || (p.y == free.y && Math.abs(p.x-free.x) == 1)) {
            gbc.gridx = free.x;
            gbc.gridy = free.y;
            gbl.setConstraints((Component)evt.target, gbc);
            free = p;
            invalidate();
            validate();
        }
        return true;
    }

    static public void main(String[] args) {
        new Main();
    }
}
```

gridy

PURPOSE This field holds the *y*-coordinate cell location for a component.

SYNTAX `public int gridy`

DESCRIPTION The cell locations are 0-based. This means the location of the cell at the gridbag's northwest corner is (0, 0).

SEE ALSO `gridx`.

EXAMPLE See `gridx`.

HORIZONTAL

PURPOSE Fill type that specifies a horizontal-only fill.

SYNTAX `public static final int HORIZONTAL`

DESCRIPTION This constant field specifies that the component is to be stretched horizontally to fill its display area. The component's height is not changed. This constant is used in the `fill` field.

SEE ALSO `fill`.

EXAMPLE See `fill`.

insets

PURPOSE This field holds the insets constraints for the component.

SYNTAX `public Insets insets`

DESCRIPTION The insets constraint affects the dimensions of the component's display area. Although rare, an inset can be negative. This allows a component to extend outside its display area.

SEE ALSO `Insets`.

EXAMPLE This example creates a 4-×-4 gridbag with nine buttons. See Figure 143. There are two buttons along each edge of the gridbag that when pressed modify the center button's inset for that edge. The label of the center button shows the current values of the insets.

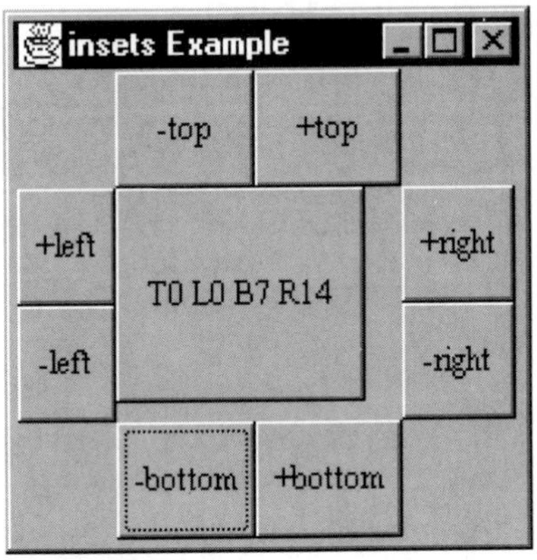

FIGURE 143
`GridBagConstraints.insets`

```
import java.awt.*;
public class Main extends Frame {
    Button centerButton;
    GridBagLayout gbl = new GridBagLayout();

    Main() {
        super("insets Example");
        GridBagConstraints c = new GridBagConstraints();

        setLayout(gbl);
        c.fill = GridBagConstraints.BOTH;
        c.weightx = 1;
        c.weighty = 1;

        makeButton(this, "-top", c, 1, 0);
        makeButton(this, "+top", c, 2, 0);
        makeButton(this, "+left", c, 0, 1);
        makeButton(this, "-left", c, 0, 2);
        makeButton(this, "-bottom", c, 1, 3);
        makeButton(this, "+bottom", c, 2, 3);
        makeButton(this, "+right", c, 3, 1);
        makeButton(this, "-right", c, 3, 2);

        // Make center button.
        c.gridwidth = c.gridheight = 2;
        c.fill = GridBagConstraints.BOTH;
        centerButton = makeButton(this, "T0 L0 B0 R0", c, 1, 1);

        resize(200, 200);
        show();
    }

    // Returns the new button.
    Button makeButton(Container cont, String label,
            GridBagConstraints c, int x, int y) {
        GridBagLayout gbl = (GridBagLayout)cont.getLayout();
        Button b = new Button(label);

        cont.add(b);
        c.gridx = x;
        c.gridy = y;
        gbl.setConstraints(b, c);
        return b;
    }

    public boolean action(Event evt, Object arg) {
        if (evt.target instanceof Button) {
            GridBagConstraints c = gbl.getConstraints(centerButton);
            String s = (String)arg;
            int sign = s.charAt(0) == '+' ? 1 : -1;

            s = s.substring(1);
            if ("top".equals(s)) {
                c.insets.top += sign;
```

```
                } else if ("left".equals(s)) {
                    c.insets.left += sign;
                } else if ("bottom".equals(s)) {
                    c.insets.bottom += sign;
                } else if ("right".equals(s)) {
                    c.insets.right += sign;
                }
                gbl.setConstraints(centerButton, c);
                centerButton.setLabel("T"+c.insets.top+" L"+c.insets.left
                    +" B"+c.insets.bottom+" R"+c.insets.right);
                invalidate();
                validate();
            }
            return true;
        }

        static public void main(String[] args) {
            new Main();
        }
    }
```

ipadx

PURPOSE This field holds the internal padding for the component's width.

SYNTAX `public int ipadx`

DESCRIPTION This field increases the minimum or preferred width of a component by `ipadx` pixels.

SEE ALSO `ipady`.

FIGURE 144 **GridBagConstraints.ipadx andGridBagConstraints.ip**

EXAMPLE This example creates a three-cell gridbag with three buttons. See Figure 144. One button has negative padding, one has no padding, and the last has positive padding.

```
import java.awt.*;
public class Main {
    static public void main(String[] args) {
        GridBagConstraints c = new GridBagConstraints();
        Frame f = new Frame("ipadx Example");

        f.setLayout(new GridBagLayout());
        c.gridwidth = GridBagConstraints.REMAINDER;
        c.ipadx = -6;
        makeButton(f, "- pad", c);
        c.ipadx = 0;
        makeButton(f, "0 pad", c);
```

```
        c.ipadx = 6;
        makeButton(f, "+ pad", c);
        f.resize(200, 200);
        f.show();
    }

    static void makeButton(Container cont, String label,
                           GridBagConstraints c) {
        GridBagLayout gbl = (GridBagLayout)cont.getLayout();
        Button b = new Button(label);

        cont.add(b);
        gbl.setConstraints(b, c);
    }
}
```

ipady

PURPOSE This field holds the internal padding for a component's height.

SYNTAX `public int ipady`

DESCRIPTION This field increases the minimum or preferred height of a component by `ipady` pixels.

SEE ALSO `ipadx`.

EXAMPLE See `ipadx`.

NONE

PURPOSE Fill type that specifies no fill (the default).

SYNTAX `public static final int NONE`

DESCRIPTION This constant field specifies that the component cannot be stretched in any direction. This constant is used in the `fill` field.

SEE ALSO `fill`.

EXAMPLE See `fill`.

NORTH

PURPOSE Anchor type that specifies north positioning.

A B C D E F G H I J K L M N O P Q R S T U V W X Y Z

SYNTAX `public static final int NORTH`

DESCRIPTION This constant field specifies that the north corner of the component is to be anchored to the north corner of the component's display area and centered horizontally. This constant is used in the `anchor` field.

SEE ALSO `anchor`.

EXAMPLE See `anchor`.

NORTHEAST

PURPOSE Anchor type that specifies northeast positioning.

SYNTAX `public static final int NORTHEAST`

DESCRIPTION This constant field specifies that the northeast corner of the component is to be anchored to the northeast corner of the component's display area. This constant is used in the `anchor` field.

SEE ALSO `anchor`.

EXAMPLE See `anchor`.

NORTHWEST

PURPOSE Anchor type that specifies northwest positioning.

SYNTAX `public static final int NORTHWEST`

DESCRIPTION This constant field specifies that the northwest corner of the component is to be anchored to the northwest corner of the component's display area. This constant is used in the `anchor` field.

SEE ALSO `anchor`.

EXAMPLE See `anchor`.

RELATIVE

PURPOSE Size type that specifies that subsequent cells in the row or column are to be occupied except for the last cell.

SYNTAX `public static final int RELATIVE`

DESCRIPTION If a component's grid width (or grid height) is RELATIVE, the component will occupy all the cells to the right of (or below) it except for the last cell. Also, the grid width (or grid height) of the component that follows must be REMAINDER.

SEE ALSO `gridheight`, `gridwidth`, REMAINDER.

EXAMPLE See REMAINDER.

REMAINDER

PURPOSE Size type that specifies that subsequent cells in the row or column are to be occupied.

SYNTAX `public static final int REMAINDER`

DESCRIPTION If a component's grid width (or grid height) is REMAINDER, the component will occupy all the cells to the right of (or below) it. A grid height of 0 is the same as REMAINDER. The component that follows will start a new row (or column).

SEE ALSO `gridheight`, `gridwidth`, RELATIVE.

EXAMPLE This example creates a gridbag with three rows. See Figure 145. All the cells in the first row are occupied by a component. In the second row, the button labeled REMAINDER consumes all but the first cell. In the third row, the button labeled RELATIVE consumes all but the first and last cells.

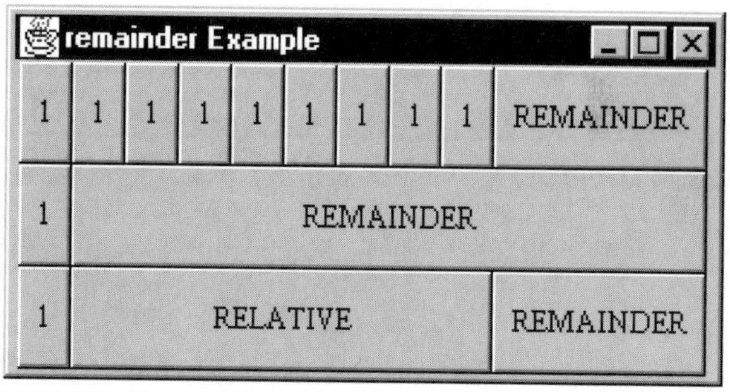

FIGURE 145 GridBagConstraints.REMAINDER

```
import java.awt.*;
public class Main extends Frame {
    GridBagLayout gbl = new GridBagLayout();

    Main() {
        super("remainder Example");
        setLayout(gbl);
        for (int i=0; i<9; i++) makeButton("1", 1);
        makeButton("REMAINDER", GridBagConstraints.REMAINDER);

        makeButton("1", 1);
        makeButton("REMAINDER", GridBagConstraints.REMAINDER);
```

```
            makeButton("1", 1);
            makeButton("RELATIVE", GridBagConstraints.RELATIVE);
            makeButton("REMAINDER", GridBagConstraints.REMAINDER);

            resize(300, 150);
            show();
        }

        void makeButton(String label, int w) {
            GridBagConstraints c = new GridBagConstraints();
            Button b = new Button(label);

            c.gridwidth = w;
            c.gridheight = 1;
            c.fill = GridBagConstraints.BOTH;
            c.weightx = 1;
            c.weighty = 1;
            gbl.setConstraints(b, c);
            add(b);
        }

        static public void main(String[] args) {
            new Main();
        }
    }
```

SOUTH

PURPOSE Anchor type that specifies south positioning.

SYNTAX `public static final int SOUTH`

DESCRIPTION This constant field specifies that the south corner of the component is to be anchored to the south corner of the component's display area and centered horizontally. This constant is used in the `anchor` field.

SEE ALSO `anchor`.

EXAMPLE See `anchor`.

SOUTHEAST

PURPOSE Anchor type that specifies southeast positioning.

SYNTAX `public static final int SOUTHEAST`

DESCRIPTION This constant field specifies that the southeast corner of the component is to be anchored to the southeast corner of the component's display area. This constant is used in the `anchor` field.

SEE ALSO `anchor`.

EXAMPLE See `anchor`.

SOUTHWEST

PURPOSE Anchor type that specifies southwest positioning.

SYNTAX `public static final int SOUTHWEST`

DESCRIPTION This constant field specifies that the southwest corner of the component is to be anchored to the southwest corner of the component's display area. This constant is used in the `anchor` field.

SEE ALSO `anchor`.

EXAMPLE See `anchor`.

VERTICAL

PURPOSE Fill type that specifies a vertical-only fill.

SYNTAX `public static final int VERTICAL`

DESCRIPTION This constant field specifies that the component is to be stretched vertically to fill its display area. The component's width is not changed. This constant is used in the `fill` field.

SEE ALSO `fill`.

DESCRIPTION See `fill`.

weightx

PURPOSE This field holds the component's column weight.

SYNTAX `public double weightx`

A B C D E F G H I J K L M N O P Q R S T U V W X Y Z

DESCRIPTION See the class description for details on gridbag weights. This value must be non-negative.

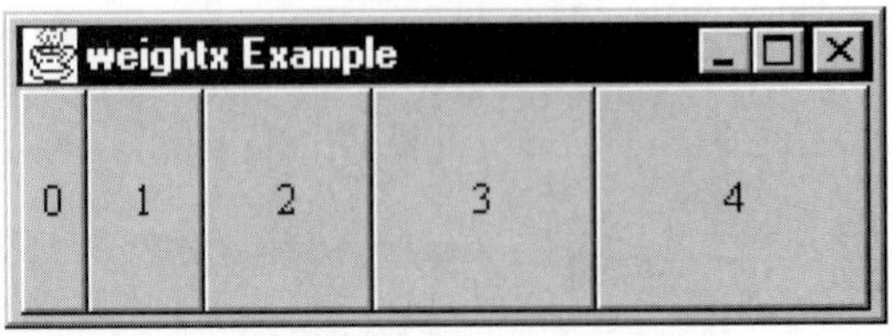

FIGURE 146 `GridBagConstraints.weightx` and `GridBagConstraints.weighty`

EXAMPLE This example creates a row of five buttons, each with a different weight. See Figure 146. Pressing a button increases its weight by 1. When the weight reaches 4, it is set back to 0.

```
import java.awt.*;
public class Main extends Frame {
    GridBagLayout gbl = new GridBagLayout();

    Main() {
        super("weightx Example");
        setLayout(gbl);
        for (int i=0; i<5; i++) {
            makeButton(i);
        }
        resize(300, 150);
        show();
    }

    void makeButton(int w) {
        GridBagConstraints c = new GridBagConstraints();
        Button b = new Button("" + w);

        c.weightx = w;
        c.weighty = 1;
        c.fill = GridBagConstraints.BOTH;
        gbl.setConstraints(b, c);
        add(b);
    }

    public boolean action(Event evt, Object arg) {
        Button b = (Button)evt.target;
        GridBagConstraints gbc = gbl.getConstraints(b);

        if (++gbc.weightx > 4) {
            gbc.weightx = 0;
        }
        gbl.setConstraints(b, gbc);
        b.setLabel("" + gbc.weightx);
        invalidate();
        validate();
        return true;
    }
```

```
    static public void main(String[] args) {
        new Main();
    }
}
```

weighty

PURPOSE This field holds the component's row weight.

SYNTAX `public double weighty`

DESCRIPTION See the class description for details on gridbag weights. This value must be non-negative.

EXAMPLE See `weightx`.

WEST

PURPOSE Anchor type that specifies west positioning.

SYNTAX `public static final int WEST`

DESCRIPTION This constant field specifies that the west edge of the component is to be anchored to the west edge of the component's display area and centered vertically. This constant is used in the `anchor` field.

SEE ALSO `anchor`.

EXAMPLE See `anchor`.

A B C D E F G H I J K L M N O P Q R S T U V W X Y Z

java.awt

GridBagLayout

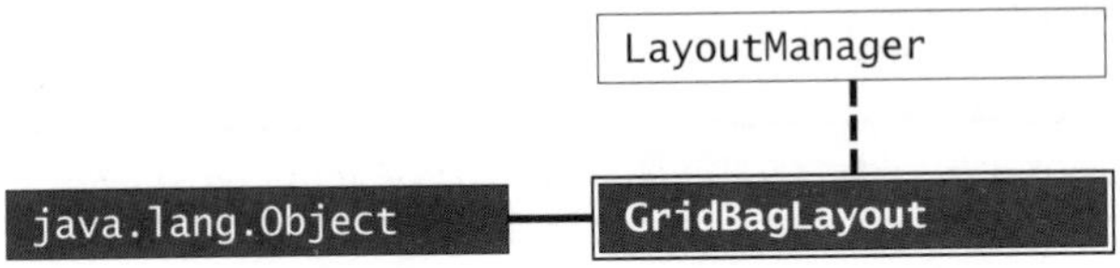

Syntax

```
public class GridBagLayout implements LayoutManager
```

Description

A *gridbag* is a container with a gridbag layout manager. The gridbag layout manager implements a 2D grid of cells where all cells in a column have the same width and all cells in a row have the same height. Multiplying the number of columns by the number of rows in the gridbag yields the total number of cells in the gridbag. Unlike with the grid layout manager (see `GridLayout`), the columns in a gridbag can have different widths; similarly for rows.

A cell in a gridbag is addressed by the *x*- and *y*-coordinates. The coordinates are 0-based, so the first cell is at location (0, 0). A gridbag is initially created with no cells. Cells are automatically created as components are added. For example, if the first component were added to location (10, 10), the grid would automatically create 11-×-11 cells. See `getLayoutDimensions()` on how to obtain the gridbag's current dimensions.

A component can be located anywhere within the grid of cells (see Figure 147). A component can occupy one or more contiguous cells which themselves must form a smaller but rectangular grid of cells. Not all cells must be occupied. (The gridbag allows more than one component to overlap a cell. However, this is considered a programming error.) The cell or cells that a component occupies is called the *component's display area.*

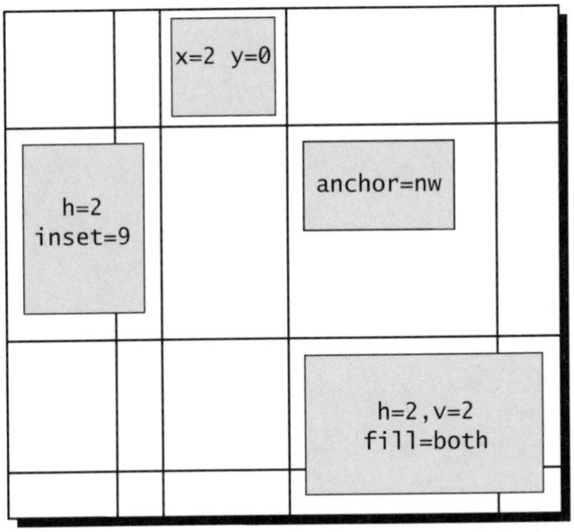

FIGURE 147 Cells in a `GridbagLayout`

A component's location in the gridbag is specified with what are called gridbag constraints. Every component in the gridbag has associated with it gridbag constraints. The gridbag layout manager uses all the component gridbag constraints to do the layout. See the `GridBagConstraints` class for details about available gridbag constraints and their effect on the component.

MEMBER SUMMARY

Constructor	
`GridBagLayout()`	Constructs a new `GridBagLayout` instance.
Constant Fields	
`MAXGRIDSIZE`	Specifies the maximum number of cells in the gridbag.
`MINSIZE`	Layout constant specifying that calculations should use a component's minimum size.
`PREFERREDSIZE`	Layout constant specifying that calculations should use a component's preferred size.
Layout Fields	
`columnWeights`	This field holds the overrides to the column weights.
`columnWidths`	This field holds the overrides to the column minimum widths.
`comptable`	This hash table maintains the association between a component and its gridbag constraints.
`layoutInfo`	This field holds the gridbag's layout information.
`rowHeights`	This field holds the overrides to the row minimum heights.
`rowWeights`	This field holds the overrides to the row weights.
Constraints Methods and Field	
`defaultConstraints`	This field holds a gridbag constraints instance containing the default values.
`getConstraints()`	Retrieves the gridbag constraints for a component.
`lookupConstraints()`	Retrieves the constraints for a component.
`setConstraints()`	Sets the gridbag constraints for a component.
Layout Methods	
`AdjustForGravity()`	Adjusts the position of a component within its display area.
`ArrangeGrid()`	Lays out the container's components using the components' constraints.
`getLayoutDimensions()`	Retrieves the dimensions of each row and column in the gridbag.
`GetLayoutInfo()`	Calculates the layout for a gridbag container.
`getLayoutOrigin()`	Retrieves the gridbag's location within its container.
`getLayoutWeights()`	Retrieves the gridbag's row and column weights.
`GetMinSize()`	Retrieves the minimum dimension of the gridbag.
`location()`	Retrieves the cell location using a pixel location.

Continued

A B C D E F G H I J K L M N O P Q R S T U V W X Y Z

MEMBER SUMMARY	
Layout Manager Interface Methods	
`addLayoutComponent()`	This method is a no-op.
`layoutContainer()`	Lays out the container's components using the components' constraints.
`minimumLayoutSize()`	Calculates the minimum dimensions needed to lay out the components.
`preferredLayoutSize()`	Calculates the preferred dimensions needed to lay out the components.
`removeLayoutComponent()`	This method is a no-op.
Debugging Method	
`toString()`	Generates a string representation of the gridbag.

Example

This example creates three sample layouts. The first is a simulation of the `BorderLayout` layout manager (Figure 148). The second is a popular use of the gridbag layout: implementing a form-like layout (Figure 149). The third simply demonstrates the kinds of layouts that are possible (Figure 150).

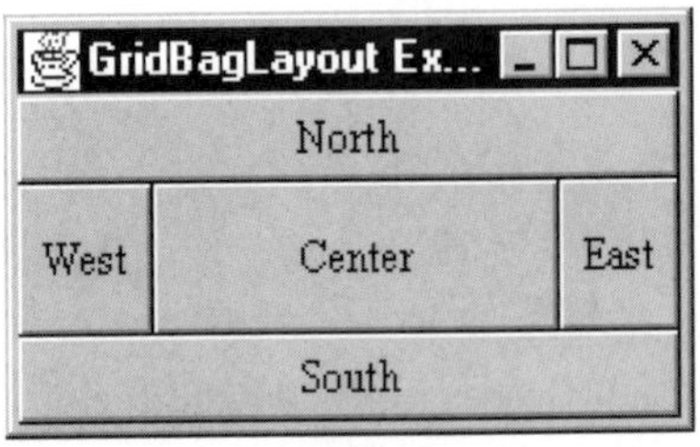

FIGURE 148 **`GridBagLayout` Simulating `BorderLayout`**

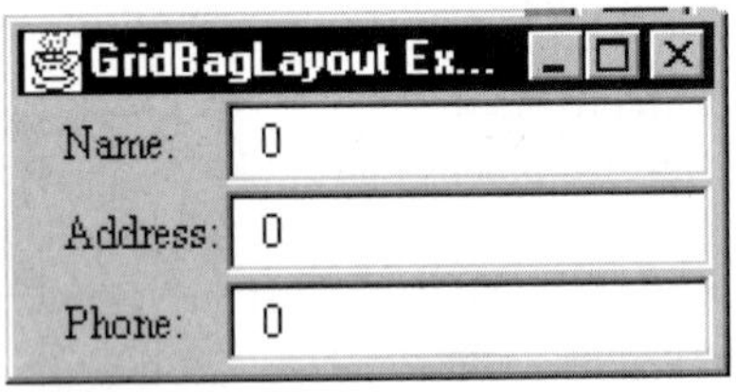

FIGURE 149 **`GridBagLayout` Implementing a Form**

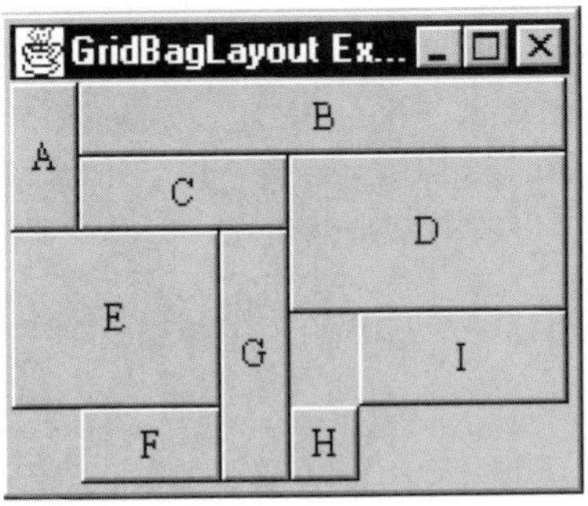

FIGURE 150 **`GridBagLayout`**

```
import java.awt.*;
public class Main {
    static void makeCrazyLayout() {
        Frame f = new Frame("GridBagLayout Example 1");

        f.setLayout(new GridBagLayout());
        makeButton(f, "A", 0, 0, 1, 2, 0.0, 0.0);
        makeButton(f, "B", 1, 0, 4, 1, 2.0, 0.0);
        makeButton(f, "C", 1, 1, 2, 1, 0.0, 0.0);
        makeButton(f, "D", 3, 1, 2, 2, 0.0, 2.0);
        makeButton(f, "E", 0, 2, 2, 2, 0.0, 0.0);
        makeButton(f, "F", 1, 4, 1, 1, 0.5, 0.0);
        makeButton(f, "G", 2, 2, 1, 3, 0.0, 0.0);
        makeButton(f, "H", 3, 4, 1, 1, 0.0, 0.0);
        makeButton(f, "I", 4, 3, 1, 1, 1.0, 0.5);
        f.pack();
        f.show();
    }

    static void makeBorderLayout() {
        Frame f = new Frame("GridBagLayout Example 2");

        f.setLayout(new GridBagLayout());
        makeButton(f, "North", 0, 0, 3, 1, 0.0, 0.0);
        makeButton(f, "South", 0, 2, 3, 1, 0.0, 0.0);
        makeButton(f, "West", 0, 1, 1, 1, 0.0, 1.0);
        makeButton(f, "East", 2, 1, 1, 1, 0.0, 1.0);
        makeButton(f, "Center", 1, 1, 1, 1, 1.0, 1.0);
        f.pack();
        f.show();
    }

    static void makeTableLayout() {
        Frame f = new Frame("GridBagLayout Example 3");

        f.setLayout(new GridBagLayout());
        makeButton(f, new Label("Name:"), 0, 0, 1, 1, 0.0, 0.0);
        makeButton(f, new Label("Address:"), 0, 1, 1, 1, 0.0, 0.0);
        makeButton(f, new Label("Phone:"), 0, 2, 1, 1, 0.0, 0.0);
        makeButton(f, new TextField("0", 5), 1, 0, 1, 1, 1.0, 0.0);
        makeButton(f, new TextField("0", 5), 1, 1, 1, 1, 1.0, 0.0);
        makeButton(f, new TextField("0", 5), 1, 2, 1, 1, 1.0, 0.0);
        f.pack();
        f.show();
    }

    static void makeButton(Container cont, Object arg,
            int x, int y, int w, int h, double weightx, double weighty)
```

```
        {
            GridBagLayout gbl = (GridBagLayout)cont.getLayout();
            GridBagConstraints c = new GridBagConstraints();
            Component comp;

            c.fill = GridBagConstraints.BOTH;
            c.gridx = x;
            c.gridy = y;
            c.gridwidth = w;
            c.gridheight = h;
            c.weightx = weightx;
            c.weighty = weighty;
            if (arg instanceof String) {
                comp = new Button((String)arg);
            } else {
                comp = (Component)arg;
            }
            cont.add(comp);
            gbl.setConstraints(comp, c);
        }

        static public void main(String[] args) {
            makeCrazyLayout();
            makeBorderLayout();
            makeTableLayout();
        }
    }
```

addLayoutComponent()

PURPOSE This method is a no-op.

SYNTAX `public void addLayoutComponent(String name, Component comp)`

DESCRIPTION This method is called by the container when a component is added with a name. However, component names are ignored by the gridbag layout manager, so this method does not do anything. This method needs to be defined in order to satisfy the `LayoutManager` interface.

PARAMETERS

`comp` The non-`null` named component that has just been added to the container. Ignored.

`name` The name of the component. Ignored.

EXAMPLE See `LayoutManager`.

AdjustForGravity()

PURPOSE Adjusts the position of a component within its display area.

SYNTAX
```
protected void AdjustForGravity(GridBagConstraints constraints,
    Rectangle displayArea)
```

DESCRIPTION The gridbag constraints `constraints` are used to adjust the component's bounds within its display area, which is represented by `displayArea`. In particular, the insets, fill, size, and anchor gridbag constraints are used to determine the component's bounds. After this method call, `displayArea` will contain the component's new bounds.

PARAMETERS

`constraints` The non-`null` component gridbag constraints.

`displayArea` A non-`null` rectangle representing a component's display area.

ArrangeGrid()

PURPOSE Lays out the container's components using the components' constraints.

SYNTAX
```
protected void ArrangeGrid(Container container)
```

DESCRIPTION This method is equivalent to `layoutContainer()`.

PARAMETERS

`container` The non-`null` container using this layout instance.

EXAMPLE See `layoutContainer()`.

columnWeights

PURPOSE This field holds the overrides to the column weights.

SYNTAX
```
public double[] columnWeights
```

DESCRIPTION If this field is non-`null`, the values in the field are applied to the gridbag after all the column weights have been calculated. If `columnWeights[i]` is greater than the weight for column `i`, then column `i` is assigned the weight in `columnWeights[i]`. If `columnWeights` has more elements than the number of columns, the excess elements in `columnWeights` are ignored. In particular, they do not cause more columns to be created.

EXAMPLE This example creates a 3-×-3 gridbag with nine buttons. The gridbag is set with some row/column weight and size overrides. See Figure 151.

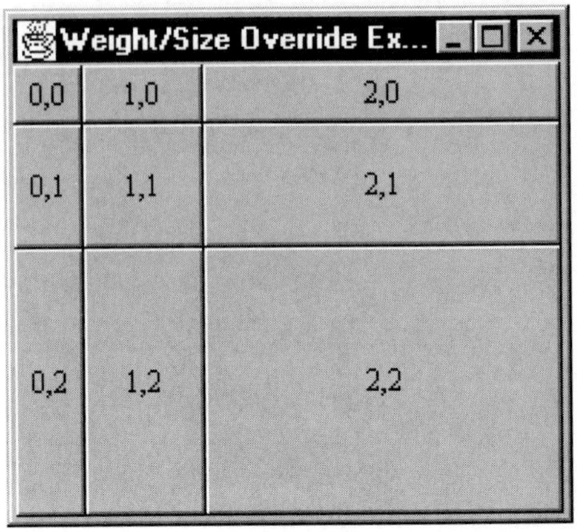

FIGURE 151 `GridBagLayout` Weights/Sizes

```
import java.awt.*;
public class Main extends Frame {
    GridBagLayout gbl = new
        GridBagLayout();

    Main() {
        super("Weight/Size Override Example");
        GridBagConstraints c = new GridBagConstraints();
        double rowWeights[] = {0, 0, 1.0};
        double colWeights[] = {0, 0, 1.0};
        int rowHeights[] = {20, 50};
        int colWidths[] = {20, 50};

        gbl.rowWeights = rowWeights;
        gbl.columnWeights = colWeights;
        gbl.rowHeights = rowHeights;
        gbl.columnWidths = colWidths;
        setLayout(gbl);

        c.fill = GridBagConstraints.BOTH;
        for (int i=0; i<3; i++) {
            for (int j=0; j<3; j++) {
                Button b = new Button(""+i+","+j);
                c.gridx = i;
                c.gridy = j;
                add(b);
                gbl.setConstraints(b, c);
            }
        }
        resize(250, 150);
        show();
    }

    static public void main(String[] args) {
        new Main();
    }
}
```

columnWidths

PURPOSE This field holds the overrides to the column minimum widths.

SYNTAX `public int[] columnWidths`

DESCRIPTION If this field is non-`null`, the values in the field are applied to the gridbag after all the minimum column widths have been calculated. If `columnWidths` has more elements than the number of columns, columns are added to the gridbag to match the number of elements in `columnWidths`.

EXAMPLE See `columnWeights`.

comptable

PURPOSE This hashtable maintains the association between a component and its gridbag constraints.

SYNTAX `protected Hashtable comptable`

DESCRIPTION The keys in `comptable` are the components and the values are the instances of `GridBagConstraints`.

defaultConstraints

PURPOSE This field holds a gridbag constraints instance containing the default values.

SYNTAX `protected GridBagConstraints defaultConstraints`

DESCRIPTION If a component is found not to have a gridbag constraints instance associated with it, the component is assigned a copy of `defaultConstraints`.

getConstraints()

PURPOSE Retrieves the gridbag constraints for a component.

SYNTAX `public GridBagConstraints getConstraints(Component comp)`

DESCRIPTION This method retrieves a clone of gridbag constraints for the component `comp`.

PARAMETERS

`comp`	The non-`null` component to be queried.

RETURNS A non-`null` copy of the component's gridbag constraints.

EXAMPLE See `getLayoutWeights()`.

getLayoutDimensions()

PURPOSE Retrieves the dimensions of each row and column in the gridbag.

SYNTAX

```
public int[][] getLayoutDimensions ()
```

DESCRIPTION If `w = getLayoutDimensions()`, then `w[0].length` contains the number of columns and `w[0][0]...w[0][w[0].length-1]` are the column widths. `w[1].length` contains the number of rows and `w[1][0]...w[1][w[1].length-1]` are the row heights. The resulting information is based on the most recent validation. So if the container is invalid or a constraint has been modified, the gridbag should be validated before this method is called.

RETURNS A non-`null` 2D array containing the row and column weights.

EXAMPLE See `getLayoutWeights()`.

GetLayoutInfo()

PURPOSE Calculates the layout for a gridbag container.

SYNTAX

```
protected GridBagLayoutInfo GetLayoutInfo(Container container,
    int sizeflag)
```

DESCRIPTION If `sizeflag` is `MINSIZE`, then the layout is based on the component's minimum size. If `sizeflag` is `PREFERREDSIZE`, then the layout is based on the component's preferred size.

PARAMETERS

`container`	The non-`null` container to query.
`sizeflag`	Can be either `MINSIZE` or `PREFERREDSIZE`.

RETURNS A non-`null` `GridBagLayoutInfo` instance containing the layout information.

getLayoutOrigin()

PURPOSE Retrieves the gridbag's location within its container.

SYNTAX `public Point getLayoutOrigin()`

DESCRIPTION The gridbag's origin is the position of the gridbag's northwest corner in relation to its container. The resulting information is based on the most recent validation. So if the container is invalid or a constraint has been modified, the gridbag should be validated before this method is called.

RETURNS A new non-`null` `Point` instance containing the gridbag's origin.

EXAMPLE This example creates a gridbag with two checkboxes whose default weights are 0. This means that the extra space is distributed around the gridbag rather than to some gridbag column or row. See Figure 152. A red dot is painted centered at the gridbag's origin within the container. Clicking a checkbox, thereby changing its weight, changes the gridbag size as well as its origin.

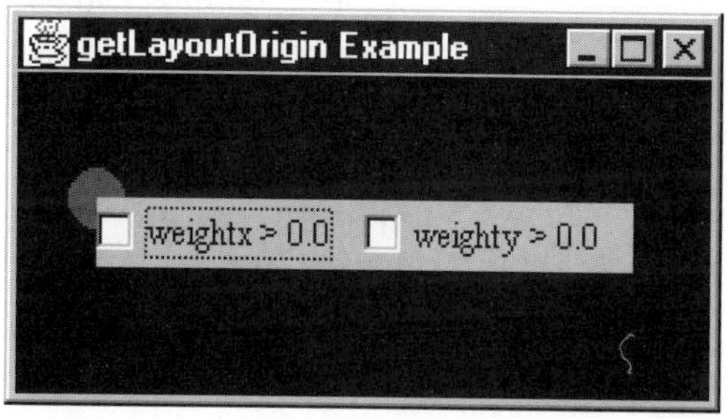

FIGURE 152 `GridBagLayout.getLayoutOrigin()`

```
import java.awt.*;
public class Main extends Frame {
    GridBagLayout gbl = new GridBagLayout();
    Main() {
        super("getLayoutOrigin Example");
        GridBagConstraints c = new GridBagConstraints();
        Checkbox cb;

        c.fill = GridBagConstraints.BOTH;
        setLayout(gbl);
        add(cb = new Checkbox("weightx > 0.0"));
        gbl.setConstraints(cb, c);
        add(cb = new Checkbox("weighty > 0.0"));
        gbl.setConstraints(cb, c);
        resize(300, 100);
        show();
    }

    public void paint(Graphics g) {
        Insets insets = this.insets();
        int dotSize = 20;
        Point p = gbl.getLayoutOrigin();
```

```
            g.setColor(Color.black);
            g.fillRect(0, 0, size().width, size().height);
            g.setColor(Color.red);
            g.fillOval(p.x-dotSize/2-insets.left,
                p.y-dotSize/2-insets.top,
                dotSize, dotSize);
        }

        public boolean action(Event evt, Object arg) {
            if (evt.target instanceof Checkbox) {
                Checkbox cb = (Checkbox)evt.target;
                GridBagConstraints c = gbl.getConstraints(cb);

                if ("weightx > 0.0".equals(cb.getLabel())) {
                    c.weightx = cb.getState() ? 1 : 0;
                } else {
                    c.weighty = cb.getState() ? 1 : 0;
                }
                gbl.setConstraints(cb, c);
                invalidate();
                validate();
                repaint();
                return true;
            }
            return false;
        }
        static public void main(String[] args) {
            new Main();
        }
    }
```

getLayoutWeights()

PURPOSE Retrieves the gridbag's row and column weights.

SYNTAX `public double[][] getLayoutWeights()`

DESCRIPTION If `w = getLayoutWeights()`, then `w[0].length` contains the number of columns and `w[0][0]...w[0][w[0].length-1]` are the column weights. `w[1].length` contains the number of rows and `w[1][0]...w[1][w[1].length-1]` are the row weights. The resulting information is based on the most recent validation. So if the container is invalid or a constraint has been modified, the gridbag should be validated before this method is called.

RETURNS A non-`null` two-dimensional array containing the row and column weights.

EXAMPLE

This example creates a gridbag with four buttons. See Figure 153. Pressing a button changes either its `weightx` or `weighty` gridbag constraints. The gridbag is then relaid out. After the constraints are changed, all the new row and column weights and dimensions are printed to `System.out`.

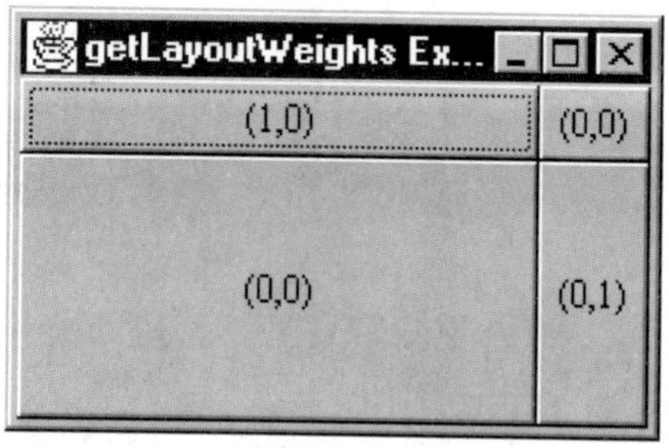

FIGURE 153
`GridBagLayout.getLayoutWeights()`

```
import java.awt.*;
public class Main extends Frame {
    GridBagLayout gbl = new GridBagLayout();

    Main() {
        super("getLayoutWeights Example");
        setLayout(gbl);
        printLayoutData(gbl);

        makeButton(0, 0);
        makeButton(0, 1);
        makeButton(1, 0);
        makeButton(1, 1);
        resize(200, 200);
        show();
    }

    void printLayoutData(GridBagLayout gbl) {
        System.out.println("===================================");
        // print layout weights
        System.out.println("Layout Weights");
        System.out.println("--------------");
        double[][]weights = gbl.getLayoutWeights();
        System.out.print("    "+weights[0].length+" columns: ");
        for (int i=0; i<weights[0].length; i++)  {
            System.out.print(weights[0][i]+" ");
        }
        System.out.println();
        System.out.print("    "+weights[1].length+" rows: ");
        for (int i=0; i<weights[1].length; i++) {
            System.out.print(weights[1][i]+" ");
        }

        // print layout dimensions
        System.out.println();
        System.out.println("Layout Dimensions");
        System.out.println("-----------------");
        int[][]dims = gbl.getLayoutDimensions();
        System.out.print("    "+dims[0].length+" columns: ");
        for (int i=0; i<dims[0].length; i++) {
```

A B C D E F G H I J K L M N O P Q R S T U V W X Y Z

```
            System.out.print(dims[0][i]+" ");
        }
        System.out.println();
        System.out.print("    "+dims[1].length+" rows: ");
        for (int i=0; i<dims[1].length; i++) {
            System.out.print(dims[1][i]+" ");
        }
        System.out.println();
    }

    void makeButton(int x, int y) {
        GridBagConstraints c = new GridBagConstraints();
        Button b = new Button("(0,0)");

        add(b);
        c.fill = GridBagConstraints.BOTH;
        c.gridx = x;
        c.gridy = y;
        gbl.setConstraints(b, c);
    }

    public boolean action(Event evt, Object arg) {
        if (evt.target instanceof Button) {
            Button b = (Button)evt.target;
            GridBagConstraints c = gbl.getConstraints(b);

            if (c.weightx == 0 && c.weighty == 0) {
                c.weighty = 1;
            } else if (c.weightx == 0 && c.weighty == 1) {
                c.weightx = 1;
            } else if (c.weightx == 1 && c.weighty == 1) {
                c.weighty = 0;
            } else {
                c.weightx = 0;
            }
            b.setLabel("("+c.weightx+","+c.weighty+")");
            gbl.setConstraints(b, c);
            invalidate();
            validate();
            printLayoutData(gbl);
        }
        return true;
    }

    static public void main(String[] args) {
        new Main();
    }
}
```

GetMinSize()

PURPOSE Retrieves the minimum dimension of the gridbag.

SYNTAX
```
protected Dimension GetMinSize(Container container,
    GridBagLayoutInfo info)
```

DESCRIPTION The minimum dimension of the gridbag is based on the layout information in `info`. Also, the insets of the container `container` are included in the result.

PARAMETERS

`container` The non-`null` gridbag's container.

`info` The non-`null` layout information.

RETURNS A new non-`null` `Dimension` instance containing the minimum dimensions of the gridbag.

GridBagLayout()

PURPOSE Constructs a new `GridBagLayout` instance.

SYNTAX
```
public GridBagLayout()
```

DESCRIPTION By default, the gridbag has no cells.

EXAMPLE See the class example.

layoutContainer()

PURPOSE Lays out the container's components using the components' constraints.

SYNTAX
```
public void layoutContainer(Container container)
```

DESCRIPTION This method is called by `container` when the layout is invalidated and needs to be redone. The gridbag layout manager uses the component's preferred size when calculating the layout.

PARAMETERS

`container` The non-`null` container using this layout instance.

EXAMPLE See `LayoutManager`.

A B C D E F G H I J K L M N O P Q R S T U V W X Y Z

layoutInfo

PURPOSE: This field holds the gridbag's layout information.

SYNTAX:
```
protected GridBagLayoutInfo layoutInfo
```

DESCRIPTION: The data in this field is based on the most recent validation of the gridbag. A value of `null` means either there are no components in the gridbag or the gridbag has not yet been validated.

EXAMPLE: See `GetLayoutInfo()`.

location()

PURPOSE: Retrieves the cell location using a pixel location.

SYNTAX:
```
public Point location(int x, int y)
```

DESCRIPTION: This method retrieves the cell location at pixel location (`x`, `y`). The cell locations are 0-based, so the top-left cell is at (0, 0). The cell at the bottom-right corner is at (number of column-1, number of rows-1). If `x` is to the left of the gridbag, it is set to 0; similarly for `y`. If `x` is to the right of the gridbag, it is set to the number of columns; similarly for `y`.

This calculation uses the data from the gridbag's most recent validation. Therefore, if the container is invalid or a constraint has been modified, the gridbag should be validated before calling this method.

PARAMETERS

`x` The *x*-coordinate relative to the gridbag container's inset area.

`y` The *y*-coordinate relative to the gridbag container's inset area.

RETURNS: A new non-`null` `Point` instance containing the coordinates of the cell.

EXAMPLE: This example creates a frame with four custom canvases. See Figure 154. The canvas displays its cell position and forwards mouse motion events to its parent which is the frame. The frame receives those events and uses them to locate a cell in the gridbag. The cell location is displayed at the bottom of the frame.

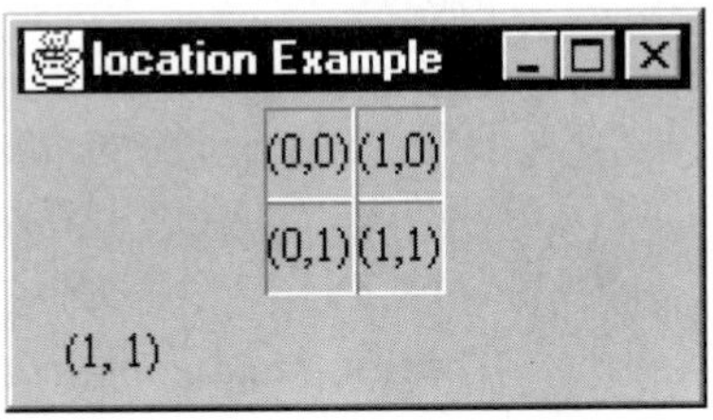

FIGURE 154 `GridBagLayout.location()`

```
import java.awt.*;
public class Main extends Frame {
    GridBagLayout gbl = new GridBagLayout();
    Label l = new Label();

    Main() {
        super("location Example");
        Panel p = new Panel();
        p.setLayout(gbl);
        for (int i=0; i<2; i++) {
            for (int j=0; j<2; j++) {
                makeCanvas(p, "("+i+","+j+")", i, j);
            }
        }
        add("Center", p);
        add("South", l);
        pack();
        show();
    }

    public boolean mouseMove(Event evt, int x, int y) {
        Insets insets = this.insets();
        Point p = gbl.location(x-insets.left, y-insets.top);

        l.setText("("+p.x+", "+p.y+")");
        return true;
    }

    void makeCanvas(Container cont, String label, int x, int y) {
        GridBagConstraints c = new GridBagConstraints();
        MainCanvas cv = new MainCanvas(label);

        cont.add(cv);
        cv.resize(25, 25);
        c.gridx = x;
        c.gridy = y;
        gbl.setConstraints(cv, c);
    }

    static public void main(String[] args) {
        new Main();
    }
}

class MainCanvas extends Canvas {
    String label;

    MainCanvas(String label) {
        this.label = label;
    }

    public void paint(Graphics g) {
        int w = size().width;
        int h = size().height;
```

```
            FontMetrics fm = g.getFontMetrics();

            g.drawString(label, (w-fm.stringWidth(label))/2,
                (h-fm.getHeight())/2+fm.getAscent());
            g.setColor(getBackground());
            g.draw3DRect(0, 0, w-1, h-1, false);
        }
    }
```

lookupConstraints()

PURPOSE Retrieves the constraints for a component.

SYNTAX `protected GridBagConstraints lookupConstraints(Component comp)`

DESCRIPTION This method retrieves the constraints for the component `comp`. The return value is not a copy; it is the actual constraints instance used by the layout mechanism.

PARAMETERS

`comp` The non-`null` component to be queried.

RETURNS The non-`null` constraints for the component.

SEE ALSO `getConstraints()`.

MAXGRIDSIZE

PURPOSE This constant specifies the maximum number of cells in the gridbag.

SYNTAX `protected static final int MAXGRIDSIZE`

minimumLayoutSize()

PURPOSE Calculates the minimum dimensions needed to lay out the components.

SYNTAX `public Dimension minimumLayoutSize(Container container)`

DESCRIPTION This method lays out the gridbag using the components' minimum sizes and returns the dimensions of the resulting gridbag.

PARAMETERS

`container` The non-`null` container using this layout instance.

RETURNS — A new non-null `Dimension` instance containing the minimum size of the gridbag.

SEE ALSO — `Component.minimumSize()`.

EXAMPLE — See `LayoutManager`.

MINSIZE

PURPOSE — Layout constant specifying that calculations should use a component's minimum size.

SYNTAX — `protected static final int MINSIZE`

DESCRIPTION — This constant is used in various layout methods. When a component's dimensions are needed, this constant specifies that the dimensions should be retrieved using `Component.minimumSize()` rather than `Component.preferredSize()`.

SEE ALSO — `PREFERREDSIZE`.

EXAMPLE — See `GetLayoutInfo()`.

preferredLayoutSize()

PURPOSE — Calculates the preferred dimensions needed to lay out the components.

SYNTAX — `public Dimension preferredLayoutSize(Container container)`

DESCRIPTION — This method lays out the gridbag using the components' preferred sizes and returns the dimensions of the resulting gridbag.

PARAMETERS

`container` — The non-null container using this layout instance.

RETURNS — A new non-null `Dimension` instance containing the preferred size of the gridbag.

SEE ALSO — `Component.preferredSize()`.

EXAMPLE — See `LayoutManager`.

A B C D E F G H I J K L M N O P Q R S T U V W X Y Z

PREFERREDSIZE

PURPOSE Layout constant specifying that calculations should use a component's preferred size.

SYNTAX `protected static final int PREFERREDSIZE`

DESCRIPTION This constant is used in various layout methods. When a component's dimensions are needed, this constant specifies that the dimensions should be retrieved using `Component.preferredSize()` rather than `Component.minimumSize()`.

SEE ALSO `MINSIZE`.

EXAMPLE See `GetLayoutInfo()`.

removeLayoutComponent()

PURPOSE This method is a no-op.

SYNTAX `public void removeLayoutComponent(Component comp)`

DESCRIPTION This method is called by the layout manager's container whenever a component is removed from the container.

This method does not do anything. This method needs to be defined in order to satisfy the `LayoutManager` interface.

PARAMETERS

`comp` The non-`null` component about to be removed from the container. Ignored.

EXAMPLE See `LayoutManager`.

rowHeights

PURPOSE This field holds the overrides to the row minimum heights.

SYNTAX `public int rowHeights[]`

DESCRIPTION If this field is non-`null`, the values in the field are applied to the gridbag after all the minimum row heights have been calculated. If `rowHeights` has more elements than the number of rows, rows are added to the gridbag to match the number elements in `rowHeights`.

EXAMPLE See `rowWeights`.

rowWeights

PURPOSE This field holds the overrides to the row weights.

SYNTAX `public double[] rowWeights`

DESCRIPTION If this field is non-`null`, the values in the field are applied to the gridbag after all the row weights have been calculated. If `rowWeights[i]` is greater than the weight for row `i`, then row `i` is assigned the weight in `rowWeights[i]`. If `rowWeights` has more elements than the number of rows, the excess elements in `rowWeights` are ignored. In particular, they do not cause more rows to be created.

EXAMPLE See `columnWeights`.

setConstraints()

PURPOSE Sets the gridbag constraints for a component.

SYNTAX
```
public void setConstraints(Component comp, GridBagConstraints
   constraints)
```

DESCRIPTION This method associates the gridbag constraints `constraints` to the component `comp`. The caller is free to modify `constraints`, since this method creates and uses a clone of `constraints`.

PARAMETERS

`comp` The non-`null` component to associate with `constraints`.

`constraints` The non-`null` gridbag constraints to associate with `comp`. The values in `constraints` are copied.

SEE ALSO `GridBagConstraints.clone()`.

EXAMPLE See the class example.

toString()

PURPOSE Generates the string representation of the gridbag.

SYNTAX `public String toString()`

DESCRIPTION This method generates the string representation of this gridbag. The result string contains the gridbag's class name.

This method is typically used for debugging.

RETURNS A non-`null` string containing the gridbag's class name.

OVERRIDES `Object.toString()`.

EXAMPLE See `Object.toString()`.

A B C D E F G H I J K L M N O P Q R S T U V W X Y Z

java.awt

GridLayout

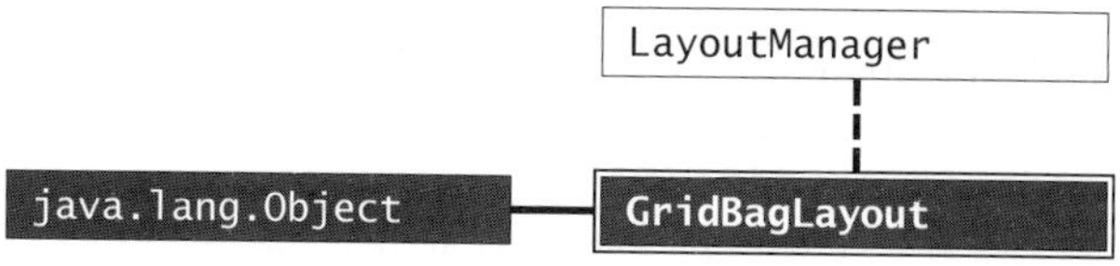

Syntax

```
public class GridLayout implements LayoutManager
```

Description

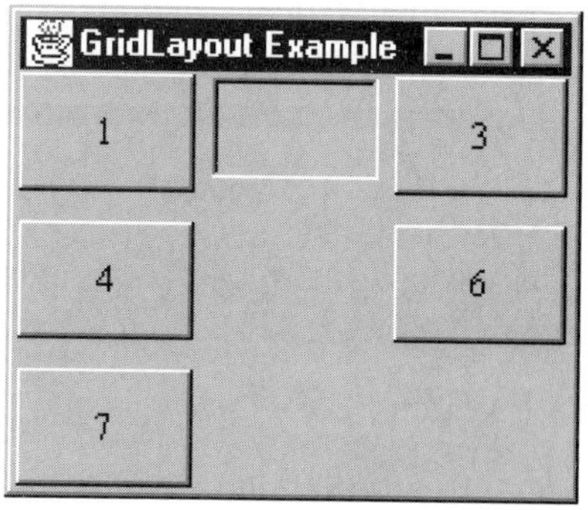

FIGURE 155 **`GridLayout`**

The grid layout manager places components in a grid of rows and columns. The components are laid out in left-to-right, top-to-bottom order. Figure 155 shows a container with a grid layout manager set to display a grid of three rows and three columns. The cells in the grid are exactly the same size and are as large as possible such that all cells are completely visible. Any remaining space is distributed to the right and bottom of the container. Every component is allocated a cell, regardless of whether the component is visible. Invisible components simply show up as an empty cell.

When creating a grid layout manager, you specify the number of rows and columns of the grid. Either of the dimensions can be set to "any," meaning the number of rows (or columns) in that dimension depends on the other dimension. For example, if the number of rows is "any" and the number of columns is 2, then the number of rows will be (number-of-components+1)/2. An exception is thrown if both dimensions are set to "any." If the number of rows is not "any," then the number of specified columns is ignored.

The grid layout manager does not use the names of the components, so any name that is supplied with the `addLayoutComponent()` method call is ignored.

Gaps

The grid layout manager allows you to separate the cells by gaps. The vertical gap specifies the space between rows, while the horizontal gap specifies the space between columns.

MEMBER SUMMARY

Constructor	
`GridLayout()`	Constructs a grid layout with the specified rows, columns.
Layout Manager Interface Methods	
`addLayoutComponent()`	Adds a component to the layout.
`layoutContainer()`	Lays out the container's components according to the settings of the layout manager.
`minimumLayoutSize()`	Calculates the minimum dimensions needed to layout the components.
`preferredLayoutSize()`	Calculates the preferred dimensions needed to layout the components.
`removeLayoutComponent()`	Removes a component from the layout.
Debugging Method	
`toString()`	Generates a string representation of the grid layout's values.

Example

This example creates a 3-×-3 grid layout with 5 pixels between columns and 10 pixels between rows (See Figure 155). Notice that button "5" is not visible, but it still occupies a cell.

```
import java.awt.*;
class Main {
    static public void main(String[] args) {
        Frame f = new Frame("GridLayout Example");
        Button b;
        f.setLayout(new GridLayout(3, 4, 5, 10));
        f.add(new Button("1"));
        f.add(new List());
        f.add(new Button("3"));
        f.add(new Button("4"));
        f.add(b = new Button("5"));
        f.add(new Button("6"));
        f.add(new Button("7"));
        f.pack();
        f.show();
        b.hide();
    }
}
```

addLayoutComponent()

PURPOSE Adds a component to the layout.

SYNTAX `public void addLayoutComponent(String name, Component comp)`

DESCRIPTION This method is called by the container when a component is added with a name. However, component names are ignored by the grid layout manager, so this method does not do anything. This method needs to be defined in order to satisfy the `LayoutManager` interface.

PARAMETERS

`comp` The named component that has just been added to the container. Ignored.

`name` The name of the component. Ignored.

EXAMPLE See `LayoutManager`.

GridLayout()

PURPOSE Constructs a new `GridLayout` instance.

SYNTAX

```
public GridLayout(int rows, int cols)
public GridLayout(int rows, int cols, int hgap, int vgap)
```

DESCRIPTION The two forms of this constructor create a new grid layout manager instance with the specified rows, columns, vertical gap, and horizontal gap. If `rows` is greater than `0`, the value of `cols` is ignored and is treated like `0`, that is, any number of columns (see the class description for more details). If `hgap` and `vgap` are not specified, they default to `0`.

An instance of the grid layout manager can be shared by more than one container. Also, the grid layout manager can be set on a container at any time, regardless of the number of the components already in the container.

PARAMETERS

`cols` A non-negative integer specifying the number of columns in the grid; `0` means "any number" of columns.

`hgap` A non-negative integer specifying the space between columns in pixels.

`rows` A non-negative integer specifying the number of rows in the grid; `0` means "any number."

`vgap` A non-negative integer specifying the space between rows in pixels.

EXCEPTIONS

`IllegalArgumentException`

If the `rows` and `cols` are both `0`.

EXAMPLE See the class example.

layoutContainer()

PURPOSE Lays out the container's components according to the settings of the layout manager.

SYNTAX `public void layoutContainer(Container cont)`

DESCRIPTION This method is called by the container when the layout is invalidated and needs to be redone.

The number of cells is determined by the number of specified rows and columns and the number of components in the container. The cell height is the largest integer such that rows * cellHeight + (rows-1) * (the vertical gap) does not exceed the current height of the container; likewise for the cell width. Neither the minimum nor preferred sizes of the components are used in the calculations. All the components are resized to the cell size and then placed in order from left-to-right and top-to-bottom. Any remaining space is distributed to the right and bottom of the container.

PARAMETERS

`cont` The non-`null` container using this layout instance.

SEE ALSO `Container`.

EXAMPLE See `LayoutManager`.

minimumLayoutSize()

PURPOSE Calculates the minimum dimensions needed to lay out the components.

SYNTAX `public Dimension minimumLayoutSize(Container cont)`

DESCRIPTION The minimum dimension is calculated by determining each component's minimum size. The maximum of these minimum dimensions determines the size of a cell. The minimum dimensions of the entire layout is based on this cell size and all the gaps between them.

PARAMETERS

`cont` The non-`null` container using this layout instance.

RETURNS A non-`null` `Dimension` object containing the minimum size of the grid layout.

SEE ALSO `Component.minimumSize()`.

EXAMPLE See `LayoutManager`.

preferredLayoutSize()

PURPOSE Calculates the preferred dimensions needed to lay out the components.

SYNTAX `public Dimension preferredLayoutSize(Container cont)`

DESCRIPTION The preferred dimension is calculated by determining each component's preferred size. The maximum of these preferred dimensions determines the size of a cell. The preferred dimensions of the entire layout is based on this cell size and all the gaps between them.

PARAMETERS

`cont` The non-`null` container using this layout instance.

RETURNS A non-`null` `Dimension` object containing the preferred size of the grid layout.

SEE ALSO `Component.preferredSize()`.

EXAMPLE See `LayoutManager`.

removeLayoutComponent()

PURPOSE Removes a component from the layout.

SYNTAX `public void removeLayoutComponent(Component comp)`

DESCRIPTION This method is called by the layout manager's container whenever a component is removed from the container. Since the grid layout does not use named components, this method does not do anything. It needs to be defined in order to satisfy the `LayoutManager` interface.

PARAMETERS

`comp` The component about to be removed from the container. Ignored.

EXAMPLE See `LayoutManager`.

toString()

PURPOSE Generates a string representation of the layout manager's state.

SYNTAX `public String toString()`

toString()

DESCRIPTION This method generates the string that contains the layout manager's class name, the size of the two gaps, and the number of rows and columns.

This method is typically used for debugging.

RETURNS A non-`null` string representing the layout manager's state.

OVERRIDES `Object.toString()`.

EXAMPLE See `Object.toString()`.

java.util

Hashtable

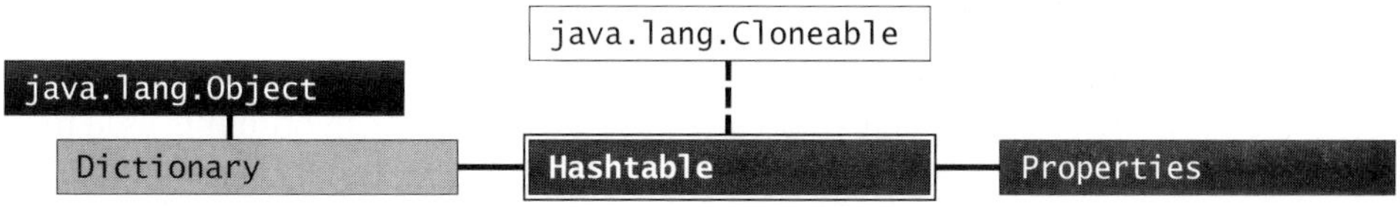

Syntax

```
public class Hashtable extends Dictionary implements Cloneable
```

Description

The `Hashtable` class represents a *hash table*. A hash table consists of an array of *hash buckets*. Each hash bucket contains zero or more *hash table entries*. Each hash table entry consists of a *key/element* pair; neither the key nor the element can be `null`. When an entry is added to the hash table, its key is used to *hash* to one of the buckets in the hash table. The hash table entry is stored in the bucket. More than one key can hash to a single bucket, but a key always hashes to the same bucket (in a hash table of the same size). Keys that hash to the same bucket are said to *collide*.

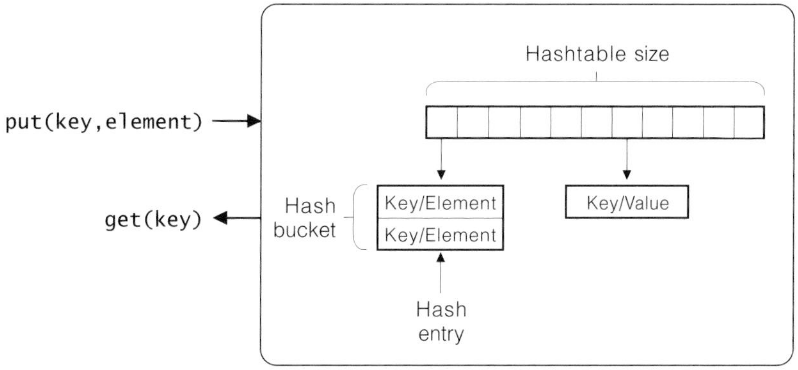

FIGURE 156 `Hashtable`

During the process of finding an entry in the hash table, the key is used to hash to the bucket in which its entry is located. If that bucket has more than one entry, the key is compared with the key of each entry (using `equals()`) to locate the right entry.

Hash Algorithm

The hash value of an object is obtained using its `hashCode()` method. The `Object` class defines a default implementation for `hashCode()` that uses the object's reference. Many classes override this default implementation to generate hash codes that are suited towards themselves. For example, the `Number` subclasses (`Double`, `Long`, `Int`, `Float`) define `hashCode()` to be a function of the object's numeric value. The hash value of a key is used in combination with the hash table's size to determine in which bucket the entry is placed. Using a prime number as the hash table's size helps distribute the entries among the different buckets (this is an artifact of the distribution algorithm used).

Hash Buckets

More than one key can hash to the same bucket. When that happens, these keys (and their elements) share the same bucket. When you search for a key, the hash algorithm is used to locate the bucket. Then a linear search is performed in the bucket to locate the entry with the target key. (`equals()` is used when comparing keys for equality.) As the bucket grows larger, searching for a key in that bucket takes longer. A desirable characteristic of a hash table is that entries in it are distributed evenly among all of its buckets.

Extensibility and Load Factor

This hash table implementation is an *extensible hash table*. This means that as the hash table becomes full, it will grow automatically to accommodate all the hash table entries. When a table grows to a larger size, all existing hash table entries must be rehashed using the new table size. Growing a table can be quite a costly operation, depending on the size of the table.

When you create a hash table, you can control when you want the table to grow by specifying a *load factor*. The load factor is the fraction of the number of entries in the hash table over the size of the hash table. When the hash table's load factor exceeds the load factor specified in its constructor, the table is grown. For example, a load factor of 0.5 means that when the table reaches half full (50%), it will be grown to its next size. A low load factor means the table will be grown when it is sparse, thereby leading to the probability of fewer collisions. A high load factor means the table will be grown when it is fairly full, thereby decreasing the number of times that the table is grown and saving the overhead of growing the table that many times. However, a higher load factor means a higher probability of hash collisions. This leads to larger hash buckets.

A larger hash table size also means more memory is required. A small load factor means few of the buckets in the hash table are being used, and consequently, the hash table is not making efficient use of memory.

MEMBER SUMMARY	
Constructor	
`Hashtable()`	Constructs a new, empty hash table.
Dictionary Methods	
`elements()`	Retrieves a list of all the elements in this hash table.
`isEmpty()`	Determines whether this hash table has any elements.
`get()`	Retrieves the element associated with a key from this hash table.
`keys()`	Retrieves a list of all keys from this hash table.

MEMBER SUMMARY

`put()`	Adds a key/element pair to this hash table.
`remove()`	Removes a key/element pair from this hash table.
`size()`	Retrieves the number of elements in this hash table.
Hash Table Methods	
`clear()`	Removes all keys and elements from this hash table.
`contains()`	Determines whether an element is in this hash table.
`containsKey()`	Determines whether a key is in this hash table.
Object Override Methods	
`clone()`	Creates a clone of this hash table.
`toString()`	Generates the string representation of this hash table.
Protected Method	
`rehash()`	Rehashes the content of this hash table into a larger hash table.

See Also

`Dictionary`, `Enumeration`, `Object.equals()`, `Object.hashCode()`.

Example

This example implements a juke box using `Hashtable`, with each element in `Hashtable` being a `Disc`. A disc consists of the title and singer of the song on the disc. The example creates the juke box, adds a few elements to it, displays its contents, searches by name and content for a disc, and finally clears it. The `print()` method uses many of the `Dictionary` methods, including the enumeration ones, to print the contents of the juke box.

```
import java.util.Hashtable;
import java.util.Enumeration;

class Disc {
    public String title;
    public String singer;

    Disc(String t, String s) {
        title = t;
        singer = s;
    }
    public String toString() {
        return ("‘" + title + "‘ by " + singer);
    }
}
class Main {
```

A B C D E F G H I J K L M N O P Q R S T U V W X Y Z

```
        // print the contents of the jukebox
        public static void print(String msg, Hashtable box, boolean all) {
            if (msg != null)
                System.out.print(msg + ": ");
            if (box.isEmpty())
                System.out.println("The juke box is empty");
            else {
                System.out.println("There are " + box.size()
                                   + " discs in the juke box:");
                for(Enumeration e = (all ? box.elements() : box.keys());
                    e.hasMoreElements();
                    System.out.println("\t" + e.nextElement()));
            }
        }
        public static void main (String[] args) {
            // create a jukebox with initial capacity of 13 and 0.5 load
            // factor
            Hashtable jukebox = new Hashtable(13, 0.5f);
            Disc houndDog;

            jukebox.put("Hound Dog", houndDog = new Disc("Hound Dog",
                        "Elvis"));
            jukebox.put("Yesterday", new Disc("Yesterday", "Beatles"));
            jukebox.put("On Top of the World",
                        new Disc("On Top of the World", "Carpenters"));
            jukebox.put("Only You", new Disc("Only You", "Platters"));

            print("jukebox after adding 4 titles", jukebox, true);

            // search by title
            System.out.println("Yesterday is " +
                (jukebox.containsKey("Yesterday") ? "" : "not ") +
                " in the jukebox");
            // search by content
            System.out.println(houndDog + " is " +
                (jukebox.contains(houndDog) ? "" : "not ") +
                " in the jukebox");

            // empty jukebox
            jukebox.clear();
            print("jukebox after clearing it", jukebox, true);
        }
    }
```

clear()

PURPOSE Removes all keys and elements from this hash table.

SYNTAX `public synchronized void clear()`

EXAMPLE See the class example.

clone()

PURPOSE Creates a clone of this hash table.

SYNTAX `public synchronized Object clone()`

DESCRIPTION This method creates a clone of this hash table by making a copy of the entire table and copies of all the hash table entries. Each hash table entry contains references to the key and element of that entry; the key and element objects are *not* cloned. If you make changes to this hash table (add a new entry or delete an old one), such changes will not affect the new copy of the hash table. Conversely, if you make changes to the new copy of the hash table, such changes will not affect this original hash table. However, if you subsequently change the key or element object themselves, such changes are reflected in both the new and old hash tables (because the references would point to the modified objects).

RETURNS A copy of this hash table.

OVERRIDES `Object.clone()`.

EXAMPLE See `get()`.

contains()

PURPOSE Determines whether an element is in this hash table.

SYNTAX `public synchronized boolean contains(Object obj)`

DESCRIPTION This method searches this hash table for an entry whose element is equal to `obj`. Equality is determined by using the `equals()` method. If such an entry is found, this method returns `true`; otherwise it returns `false`. Searching for an element is an expensive operation. Its cost increases linearly with the number of entries in this hash table.

PARAMETERS

`obj` The non-`null` element for which to search.

RETURNS `true` if `obj` is an element in this hash table; `false` otherwise.

SEE ALSO `containsKey()`, `Object.equals()`.

EXAMPLE See the class example.

containsKey()

PURPOSE Determines whether a key is in this hash table.

SYNTAX `public synchronized boolean containsKey(Object obj)`

DESCRIPTION This method searches this hash table for an entry whose key is equal to `obj`. Equality is determined using the `equals()` method. If such an entry is found, this method returns `true`; otherwise it returns `false`.

PARAMETERS

`obj` The non-`null` key for which to search.

SEE ALSO `contains()`, `Object.equals()`.

EXAMPLE See the class example.

elements()

PURPOSE Retrieves a list of all the elements in this hash table.

SYNTAX `public synchronized Enumeration elements()`

DESCRIPTION This method returns a list of all the elements in this hash table in the form of an `Enumeration`. Methods in the `Enumeration` class can then be used to retrieve the elements from this list one at a time.

Whether modifications to this hash table during enumeration affect the results of the enumeration depends on where the modifications occurred. For example, if a new key/element pair was added to the front of the hash table and the enumeration is nearing the end of the table, the newly added element would not be returned by this enumeration.

SEE ALSO `keys()`, `Enumeration`.

EXAMPLE See the class example.

get()

PURPOSE Retrieves the element associated with a key from this hash table.

SYNTAX `public synchronized Object get(Object key)`

DESCRIPTION This method retrieves the element associated with the key `key` in this hash table. If this hash table has no such key, `null` is returned.

PARAMETERS

key — The non-`null` key for which to search.

RETURNS — The element associated with `key`; `null` if `key` is not in this hash table.

SEE ALSO — `put()`.

EXAMPLE — This example uses the `Disc` declaration in the class example. It creates a few entries in the juke box and then clones it (`oldies`). After making changes to the original juke box, it checks that these changes have not affected the clone.

```
import java.util.Hashtable;
import java.util.Enumeration;

class Main {
    public static void main(String[] args) {
        Hashtable jukebox = new Hashtable(13, 0.5f);

        jukebox.put("Hound Dog", new Disc("Hound Dog", "Elvis"));
        jukebox.put("Yesterday", new Disc("Yesterday", "Beatles"));

        // Make a copy of it
        Hashtable oldies = (Hashtable)jukebox.clone();

        // find houndDog in jukebox
        System.out.println("looking for hounddog: " +
                           jukebox.get("Hound Dog"));
        System.out.println("removing it: " +
                           jukebox.remove("Hound Dog"));
        System.out.println("looking for it again: " +
                           jukebox.get("Hound Dog"));

        // find houndDog in oldies (should still be there)
        System.out.println("looking for hounddog in oldies: " +
                           oldies.get("Hound Dog"));
    }
}
```

Hashtable()

PURPOSE — Constructs a new hash table.

SYNTAX

```
public Hashtable()
public Hashtable(int initialSize)
public Hashtable(int initialSize, float loadFactor)
```

DESCRIPTION — There are three forms of the constructor for `Hashtable`. The first creates a new hash table with the initial size of `101` buckets and a load factor of `0.75`. The second creates a new hash table with initial size `initialSize` and a

A B C D E F G H I J K L M N O P Q R S T U V W X Y Z

load factor of `0.75`. The third form creates a new hash table with initial size `initialSize` and a load factor of `loadFactor`. When the hash table reaches the load specified by its load factor, it will automatically grow.

PARAMETERS

`initialCapacity`
The initial size of the hash table. It must be a positive value. The default capacity is 101. It is a good idea to use a prime number as the size because prime numbers help make the keys more evenly distributed in the hash table.

`loadFactor` A number in the range `0.0` (exclusive) and `1.0` (inclusive) stating how full the hash table should be before it is increased in size and rehashed. `1.0` means 100% full; `0.5` means 50% full. The smaller the load factor, the sooner the table will be increased. A small load factor also means that because the table is likely to be sparse, collisions (hashing a key to the same bucket) are less likely. Smaller buckets mean fewer comparisons are required before finding a key. However, increasing the hash table size is a costly operation because it involves rehashing all existing entries in the hash table for the new table size. A larger load factor means the table should be fuller before it is increased and rehashed. `1.0` means that the table should be completely full before it is increased.

SEE ALSO `rehash()`.

EXAMPLE See the class example and `get()`.

isEmpty()

PURPOSE Determines whether this hash table has any elements.

SYNTAX `public boolean isEmpty()`

RETURNS `true` if this hash table has no elements; `false` otherwise.

EXAMPLE See the class example.

keys()

PURPOSE Retrieves the element associated with a key from this hash table.

SYNTAX `public synchronized Enumeration keys()`

DESCRIPTION This method returns a list of all the keys in this hash table in the form of an `Enumeration`. Methods in the `Enumeration` class can then be used to retrieve the keys from this list one at a time.

Whether modifications to this hash table during enumeration affect the results of the enumeration depends on where the modifications occurred. For example, if a new key/element pair is added to the front of the hash table and the enumeration is nearing the end of the table, the newly added key will not be returned by this enumeration.

SEE ALSO `elements()`, `Enumeration`.

EXAMPLE See the class example.

put()

PURPOSE Adds a key/element pair to this hash table.

SYNTAX `public synchronized Object put(Object key, Object elem)`

DESCRIPTION This method adds the entry consisting of the key `key` and element `elem` into this hash table. `key` is hashed to determine in which bucket of this hash table this entry will be placed. If `key` already is in this hash table, the old element associated with `key` is returned by this method. If `key` is not in this hash table, `null` is returned.

PARAMETERS

`elem` The non-`null` element of the entry to add.

`key` The non-`null` key of the entry to add.

RETURNS The old element associated with `key`; `null` if `key` was not in this hash table.

SEE ALSO `get()`.

EXAMPLE See the class example and `get()`.

rehash()

PURPOSE Rehashes the content of the table into a larger table.

SYNTAX `protected void rehash()`

DESCRIPTION When adding a new entry to the hash table (using `put()`), if the load factor (the number of entries in the table as a fraction of the total table size) exceeds that specified by the load factor argument in this hash table's constructor, the table is automatically increased in size by using `rehash()`. The new size is at least double the old size. After the table has been grown, all existing entries in the table are rehashed using this new table size and then placed into their new buckets.

A subclass of `Hashtable` can override this method if it does not want to use this rehash policy.

SEE ALSO `Hashtable()`, `put()`.

remove()

PURPOSE Removes a key/element pair from this hash table.

SYNTAX `public synchronized Object remove(Object key)`

DESCRIPTION This method removes the key/element pair with key `key` from this hash table. It returns the element associated with `key`; if `key` is not present in this hash table, it returns `null`.

PARAMETERS

`key` The non-`null` key associated with the entry to remove.

RETURNS The element associated with `key`; `null` if `key` is not present.

SEE ALSO `put()`.

EXAMPLE See `put()`.

size()

PURPOSE Retrieves the number of elements in this hash table.

SYNTAX `public int size()`

RETURNS The number of elements in this hash table.

EXAMPLE See the class example.

toString()

PURPOSE Generates the string representation of this hash table.

SYNTAX `public synchronized String toString()`

DESCRIPTION The string representation of a hash table is a comma-separated list of all key/element pairs, with each key and element separated by an equals character ('=')).

RETURNS The string representation of this hash table.

OVERRIDES `Object.toString()`.

SEE ALSO `elements()`, `keys()`.

EXAMPLE

```
Hashtable tab = new Hashtable(13);

tab.put("Foo", new Integer(1245));
tab.put("Bar", new Float(5.4f));

System.out.println(tab.toString()); // "{Bar=5.4,Foo=1245}"
```

java.lang

IllegalAccessError

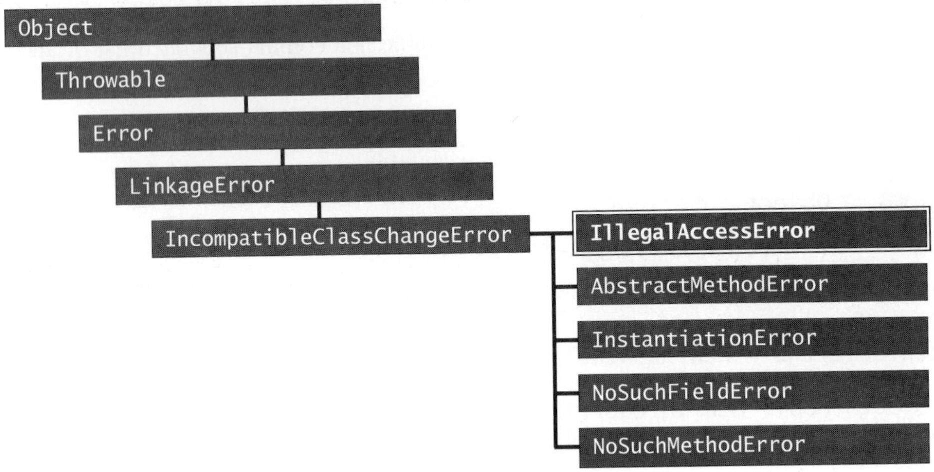

Syntax

```
public class IllegalAccessError extends IncompatibleClassChangeError
```

Description

`IllegalAccessError` is a runtime linkage error that is thrown when the program attempts to access a member of a class (field, member, or constructor) to which it does not have access. For example, this error will be thrown when the program tries to access a private or protected class or a private or protected method of a class. Normally, when you compiled these classes, you would get a compilation error pinpointing the problem so that a linkage error at runtime would not occur. However, the access problem could be introduced when classes of a program become inconsistent, for example, if you were to make an incompatible change and then recompile only some of its classes.

`IllegalAccessError` and `IllegalAccessException` both report the same error; namely, the requested access cannot be made due to access restrictions declared by the class. `IllegalAccessError`, however, is thrown by the Java virtual machine when it tries to perform the requested access. In contrast, `IllegalAccessException` is thrown when access is made explicitly via the program (for example, via the `Object.newInstance()` call).

`IllegalAccessError` should not be caught or declared in the `throws` clause of a method.

MEMBER SUMMARY

Constructor	
`IllegalAccessError()`	Constructs an `IllegalAccessError` instance.

See Also

`Error`, `IllegalAccessException`, `IncompatibleClassChangeError`, `LinkageError`.

Example

In this example, an `IllegalAccessError` is thrown when `main()` attempts to call `A`'s constructor after `A` has been made private within `pkg2`.

In `Main.java`:

```
import pkg2.A;

class Main {
    public static void main(String[] args) {
        System.out.println("IllegalAccessError example");
        A a = new A(10);
    }
}
```

In original `pkg2/A.java`:

```
package pkg2;

public class A {
    public A(int i) {
        System.out.println("A created");
    }
}
```

In modified `pkg2/A.java`:

```
package pkg2;

class A {
    public A(int i) {
        System.out.println("A created");
    }
}
```

IllegalAccessError()

PURPOSE Constructs an `IllegalAccessError` instance.

SYNTAX

```
public IllegalAccessError()
public IllegalAccessError(String msg)
```

DESCRIPTION The two forms of this constructor create a new instance of `IllegalAccessError`. An optional string `msg` can be supplied that describes this particular instance of the error.

PARAMETERS

`msg` A string that gives details about this error.

IllegalAccessException

Syntax

```
public class IllegalAccessException extends Exception
```

Description

`IllegalAccessException` is an exception that is thrown when the program attempts to access a member of a class (field, member, or constructor) to which it does not have access. For example, this exception will be thrown when the program tries to access a private or protected method of a class.

Normally, when you compile a program's classes, you would get a compilation error pinpointing the problem. However, in addition to using classes that a program has been compiled with, a program can also use other classes and invoke methods on them through the use of class loaders and the methods in the `Class` class. Access to these classes and their methods are checked by the Java runtime just like any other classes. Hence an `IllegalAccessException` can arise if an attempt is made to access the protected or private methods of these classes.

A method that throws `IllegalAccessException` must declare it or any of its superclasses in its `throws` clause.

MEMBER SUMMARY	
`IllegalAccessException()`	Constructs an `IllegalAccessException` instance.

See Also

`Exception`, `IllegalAccessError`, `Class.newInstance()`.

Example

In the following example, an `IllegalAccessException` is thrown when `main()` attempts to do a `newInstance()` on class `A` because `A`'s constructor is private.

In `Main.java`:

```
class Main {
    public static void main(String[] args) {
        System.out.println("IllegalAccessException example");
        try {
            Class c = Class.forName("A");
            Object a = c.newInstance();
        } catch (InstantiationException e) {
            e.printStackTrace();
        } catch (IllegalAccessException e) {
            e.printStackTrace();
        } catch (ClassNotFoundException e) {
            e.printStackTrace();
        }
    }
}
```

In `A.java`:

```
class A {
    private A() {
        System.out.println("A created");
    }
}
```

IllegalAccessException()

PURPOSE Constructs an `IllegalAccessException` instance.

SYNTAX

```
public IllegalAccessException()
public IllegalAccessException(String msg)
```

A B C D E F G H I J K L M N O P Q R S T U V W X Y Z

DESCRIPTION The two forms of this constructor create a new instance of `IllegalAccessException`. An optional string `msg` can be supplied that describes this particular instance of the exception.

PARAMETERS

`msg` A string that gives details about this exception.

java.lang
IllegalArgumentException

Syntax

```
public class IllegalArgumentException extends RuntimeException
```

Description

`IllegalArgumentException` is thrown by methods in the Java class libraries as well as by user-defined methods when they detect that any one of the arguments being supplied to the method is not a valid argument. For example, a method that expects a positive number as an argument will throw an `IllegalArgumentException` if it receives a negative number.

`IllegalArgumentException` should not be caught or declared in the `throws` clause of a method.

MEMBER SUMMARY	
Constructor	
`IllegalArgumentException()`	Constructs an `IllegalArgumentException` instance.

See Also

`IllegalThreadStateException`, `NumberFormatException`, `RuntimeException`.

Example

This example defines a square root function that checks that its argument is non-negative before taking its square root. It will throw an `IllegalArgumentException` when `sqrt(-4)` is called.

```
class Main {
    static double sqrt(double i)
        if (i < 0)
            throw new IllegalArgumentException(
                "Cannot take square root of a negative number");

        return (Math.sqrt(i));
    }
    public static void main(String[] args) {
        System.out.println("IllegalArgumentException example");

        System.out.println(sqrt(-4));
    }
}
```

IllegalArgumentException()

PURPOSE Constructs an `IllegalArgumentException` instance.

SYNTAX
```
public IllegalArgumentException()
public IllegalArgumentException(String msg)
```

DESCRIPTION The two forms of this constructor create a new instance of `IllegalAccessException`. An optional string `msg` can be supplied that describes this particular instance of the exception.

PARAMETERS

`msg` A string that gives details about this exception.

java.lang

IllegalMonitorStateException

Syntax

`class IllegalMonitorStateException extends RuntimeException`

Description

`IllegalMonitorStateException` is thrown when the program attempts to use a synchronization method (`wait()` or `notify()`) on an object for which it does not have the monitor. For example, the following code will throw an `IllegalMonitorStateException` when it executes `a.wait()` because `wait()` is not being executed inside of a synchronized method or block.

```
class Main {
    public static void main(String[] args) {
        Integer a = new Integer(10);
```

```
            try {
                a.wait();
            } catch (InterruptedException e) {
                e.printStackTrace();
            }
        }
    }
```

`IllegalMonitorStateException` should not be caught or declared in the `throws` clause of a method.

MEMBER SUMMARY	
Constructor	
`IllegalMonitorStateException()`	Constructs an `IllegalMonitorStateException` instance.

See Also

`Object.notify()`, `Object.notifyAll()`, `Object.wait()`, `RuntimeException`, `Thread`.

IllegalMonitorStateException()

PURPOSE Constructs an `IllegalMonitorStateException` instance.

SYNTAX
```
public IllegalMonitorStateException()
public IllegalMonitorStateException(String msg)
```

DESCRIPTION The two forms of this constructor create a new instance of `IllegalMonitorStateException`. An optional string `msg` can be supplied that describes this particular instance of the exception.

PARAMETERS

`msg` A string that gives details about this exception.

java.lang

IllegalThreadStateException

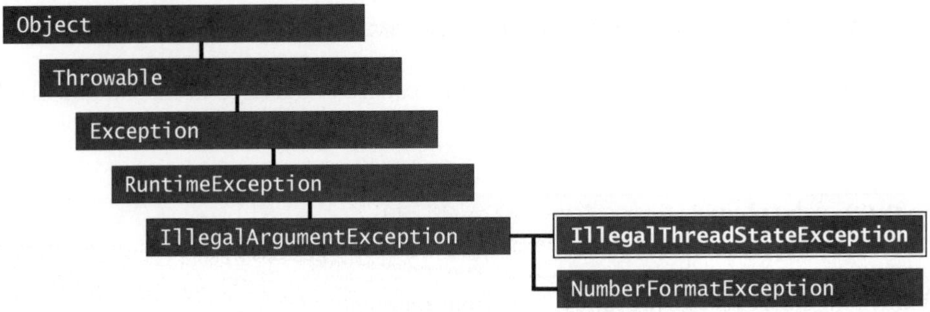

Syntax

```
public class IllegalThreadStateException extends IllegalArgumentException
```

Description

`IllegalThreadStateException` is an exception thrown by the runtime system when it detects that the program is attempting to perform an operation on a thread while the thread is in a state unsuitable for that operation. Table 12 contains a list of the methods that can throw `IllegalThreadStateException` and the corresponding condition under which each will be thrown.

TABLE 12 Methods That Throw an `IllegalThreadStateException`

`Thread.countStackFrames()`	Thread is not suspended.
`Thread.setDaemon()`	Thread is already active.
`Thread.start()`	Thread has already started.

`IllegalThreadStateException` should not be caught or declared in the `throws` clause of a method.

MEMBER SUMMARY	
Constructor	
`IllegalThreadStateException()`	Constructs an `IllegalThreadStateException` instance.

See Also

`IllegalArgumentException`, `RuntimeException`, `Thread.start()`, `Thread.countStackFrames()`, `Thread.setDaemon()`.

Example

This example will throw `IllegalThreadStateException` when it attempts to call `start()` on the thread the second time.

```
import java.util.Date;

class T extends Thread {
    public void run() {
        System.out.println(new Date());
    }
}
class Main {
    public static void main(String[] args) {
        T th = new T();
        th.start();
        th.start(); // will raise IllegalThreadStateException
    }
}
```

IllegalThreadStateException()

PURPOSE Constructs an `IllegalThreadStateException` instance.

SYNTAX
```
public IllegalThreadStateException()
public IllegalThreadStateException(String msg)
```

DESCRIPTION The two forms of this constructor create a new instance of `IllegalThreadStateException`. An optional string `msg` can be supplied that describes this particular instance of the exception.

PARAMETERS

`msg` A string that gives details about this exception.

java.awt

Image

java.lang.Object — Image

Syntax

```
public abstract class Image
```

Description

Image Producers and Consumers

An *image* is a repository of pixel values. Images are typically created by way of an image stream that involves an image producer—the object that supplies pixel values—and an image consumer—the object that takes the pixel values and places them in an image object. In this architecture, an image can be created without having all the pixels in it. Typically methods that return images actually return an image object immediately and then deliver the pixels later. The image object can then be used regardless of whether all the pixels are available. An object can register for updates as the image data becomes available (see "Image Observer" later in this section).

If an error does occur during the delivery of the pixels, none of the methods that operate on the image (e.g., `Graphics.drawImage()`) will fail, although the image will not appear correctly on the screen. The program must explicitly check for errors to determine if an error occurred (see `Component.checkImage()`).

One or more image filters can be inserted between an image producer and the image consumer to modify the pixel values as they pass through the filters. See the `ImageFilter` class for more details.

It is not possible to directly retrieve the pixels in an image. It must be done indirectly by retrieving the image's producer (using `getSource()`) and then reading the pixels as the producer delivers them. The `PixelGrabber` class makes this process more convenient. See the `PixelGrabber` class for more details.

Image Observer

An image observer is an object that is interested in some information about an image that is not yet available. Two methods in this interface take an image observer as a parameter—`getWidth()` and `getHeight()`. If an image's dimensions are not yet available, these methods return `-1`. If an image observer is registered (that is, the image observer is not `null`), the image observer will immediately be notified via the `ImageObserver.imageUpdate()` method as soon as the dimension information is available. See `ImageObserver` class for more details.

Off-screen and Produced Images

There are two kinds of images: *produced* and *off-screen*. Produced images are generated via an image producer. Off-screen images are created with the method `Component.createImage()`. The main difference between the two is that graphics contexts can be created only for an off-screen image. If it is necessary to paint on a produced image, you must first copy the produced image to an off-screen image.

Image Properties

An *image property* is an arbitrary value that an image producer associates with an image. For example, an image producer that decodes GIF images might make the comments embedded in the image available as a property. Another example is image filters that set the "filters" property so that the final image consumer can determine how the image has been filtered. There is no predefined set of image properties that an image might have. So you need to consult the image producer's documentation to discover what image properties it might set. Note that any image filters used in creating an image may also add their own image properties to the image as the image flows through the filter.

By convention, the property name "comment" is used to store an optional comment that can be presented to the user as a description of the image, its source, or its author.

MEMBER SUMMARY

Property Field and Methods	
`getProperty()`	Retrieves an image property.
`UndefinedProperty`	This object is returned by `getProperty()` if the property is not defined.
Dimensions Methods	
`getHeight()`	Retrieves the height of the image.
`getWidth()`	Retrieves the width of the image.
Painting Method	
`getGraphics()`	Retrieves a graphics context for this image.
Image Producer Method	
`getSource()`	Retrieves the image's producer.
Clean Up Method	
`flush()`	Destroys all resources used by this image.

Description

Example

This example reads in an image and then displays the image along with a scaled-up version of the image. See Figure 157. To scale the image, the pixels of the image are retrieved using the `PixelGrabber` class. Each of the image's pixels are duplicated in a separate buffer. The new pixels are then converted back into an image using the `MemorySourceImage` class.

FIGURE 157 **Image**

```
import java.awt.*;
import java.awt.image.*;
import java.net.*;
class Main extends Frame {
    Main(String filename) {
        super("Image Example");
        try {
            // Retrieve the image.
            URL url = new URL("file:///" +
                System.getProperty("user.dir")
              + "/" + filename);

            add("Center",
                new ImageCanvas(getToolkit().getImage(url)));
        } catch (Exception e) {
            e.printStackTrace();
        }
        resize(300, 300);
        show();
    }

    static public void main(String[] args) {
        if (args.length == 1) {
            new Main(args[0]);
        } else {
            System.err.println("usage: java Main <image file>");
        }
    }
}

class ImageCanvas extends Canvas {
    int scale = 3;
    Image image;
    Image scaledImage;

    ImageCanvas(Image image) {
        this.image = image;
        prepareImage(image, this);
    }
```

```
    public void paint(Graphics g) {
        update(g);
    }

    public void update(Graphics g) {
        int w = image.getWidth(this);
        int h = image.getHeight(this);

        if (w >= 0 || h >= 0) {
            if (g.drawImage(image, 0, 0, this) && scaledImage == null)
                {
                // The image has been completely loaded.

                // Display any comments.
                if (image.getProperty("comment", this) !=
                    Image.UndefinedProperty) {
                        System.out.println(
                           image.getProperty("comment", this));
                }

        // Create a pixel grabber and retrieve the pixels.
        int[] pixels = new int[w * h];
        try {
            PixelGrabber pg = new PixelGrabber(
                image, 0, 0, w, h, pixels, 0, w);
            pg.grabPixels();

            // Check for errors.
            if ((pg.status() & ImageObserver.ABORT) != 0) {
                System.err.println("Error while fetching image");
                System.exit(1);
            }
        } catch (Exception e) {
            e.printStackTrace();
            System.exit(1);
        }

        // Now replicate the pixels.
        int d = 0, s = 0;
        int[] newpixels = new int[w * h * scale * scale];
        for (int i=0; i<h; i++)
            for (int j=0; j<scale; j++)
                for (int k=0; k<w; k++)
                   for (int l=0; l<scale; l++)
                       newpixels[d++] = pixels[i*w + k];

        scaledImage = getToolkit().createImage(
            new MemoryImageSource(w*scale, h*scale,
            ColorModel.getRGBdefault(), newpixels, 0, w*scale));
         }
    }
    if (scaledImage != null) {
        g.drawImage(scaledImage, w, 0, this);
    }
     }
}
```

flush()

PURPOSE Destroys all resources used by this image.

SYNTAX `public abstract void flush()`

DESCRIPTION This method is used to explicitly free any resources that may be used by the image. This includes any cached information and any system resources used to store the image. All the image data is automatically regenerated if the image is used again.

Explicitly calling `flush()` is not necessary, since the `Object.finalize()` method calls this method when the `Image` object is reclaimed. However, in some cases it may be desirable to free up some memory quickly if it is certain the image will not be used again or is unlikely to be used for a while.

EXAMPLE See the class example.

getGraphics()

PURPOSE Retrieves a graphics context for this image.

SYNTAX `public abstract Graphics getGraphics()`

DESCRIPTION This method succeeds only for off-screen images (see `Component.createImage()`). Attempting to call `getGraphics()` for an image that is not an off-screen image results in a `ClassCastException` being thrown.

RETURNS A non-`null` `Graphics` object that can be used to paint on the image.

SEE ALSO `Component.createImage()`, `Graphics`.

EXAMPLE This example allows you to draw over an image read from the file system. See Figure 158. Since you cannot draw on a produced image, the program first copies the produced image to an off-screen image and then makes all drawing operations to the off-screen image.

FIGURE 158
`Image.getGraphics()`

```
import java.awt.*;
import java.awt.image.*;
import java.net.*;
class Main extends Frame {
    Main(String filename) {
        super("getGraphics Example");
        try {
```

A B C D E F G H I J K L M N O P Q R S T U V W X Y Z

```
            // Retrieve the image.
            URL url = new URL("file:///" +
                System.getProperty("user.dir")
              + "/" + filename);

            add("Center", new ImageCanvas(getToolkit().getImage(url)));
        } catch (Exception e) {
            e.printStackTrace();
        }
        resize(200, 200);
        show();
    }

    static public void main(String[] args) {
        if (args.length == 1) {
            new Main(args[0]);
        } else {
            System.err.println("usage: java Main <image file>");
        }
    }
}

class ImageCanvas extends Canvas {
    Image image;
    Image backBuffer;
    Graphics backBufferG;

    ImageCanvas(Image image) {
        this.image = image;
        prepareImage(image, this);
    }

    public void paint(Graphics g) {
        update(g);
    }

    public void update(Graphics g) {
        if (backBuffer == null) {
            if (g.drawImage(image, 0, 0, this) && backBuffer == null) {
                int w = image.getWidth(this);
                int h = image.getHeight(this);

                backBuffer = createImage(w, h);
                backBufferG = backBuffer.getGraphics();
                backBufferG.setColor(getBackground());
                backBufferG.fillRect(0, 0, w, h);
                backBufferG.drawImage(image, 0, 0, this);
            }
            return;
        }
        g.drawImage(backBuffer, 0, 0, this);
    }

    public boolean mouseDrag(Event evt, int x, int y) {
        backBufferG.setColor(Color.red);
```

```
            backBufferG.fillOval(x, y, 5, 5);
            repaint();
            return true;
        }
    }
```

getHeight()

PURPOSE Retrieves the height of the image.

SYNTAX `public abstract int getHeight(ImageObserver observer)`

DESCRIPTION The height of the image may not yet be available. In this case, `-1` is returned and if `observer` is non-`null`, `observer` will be notified when the height becomes available.

PARAMETERS

`observer` The image observer to register for image updates; if `null`, no updates are desired.

RETURNS The height of the image or `-1` if not yet available.

SEE ALSO `getWidth()`, `ImageObserver`.

EXAMPLE See the example.

getProperty()

PURPOSE Retrieves an image property.

SYNTAX `public abstract Object getProperty(String name, ImageObserver observer)`

DESCRIPTION This method retrieves the image property called `name`. The image properties that are available depend on the image producer. If `name` refers to an image property that is not defined by an image producer, the `UndefinedProperty` object is returned. If `name` refers to an image property whose value is not yet available, `null` is returned.

If the `name` image property is not yet available and `observer` is not `null`, `observer` will be notified when the property does become available.

PARAMETERS

`name` The non-`null` image property name.

`observer` The possibly `null` image observer.

RETURNS The value of the property called `name`. `UndefinedProperty` is returned if the property is not defined. `null` is returned if the value of the property is not yet available.

SEE ALSO `ImageObserver.imageUpdate()`, `UndefinedProperty`.

EXAMPLE See the class example.

getSource()

PURPOSE Retrieves the image's producer.

SYNTAX `public abstract ImageProducer getSource()`

DESCRIPTION The image producer is used to regenerate the image's pixels and is typically used in conjunction with image filters.

SEE ALSO `ImageFilter`, `ImageProducer`.

EXAMPLE This example reads in an image and scrambles it by swapping the left and right sides of the image. See Figure 159. A subimage of the original image is created with the help of the `CropImageFilter` class. The image producer of the original image is retrieved and used to create an image stream that passes through the crop image filter. An off-screen image holds the new scrambled image.

FIGURE 159 `Image.getSource()`

```
import java.awt.*;
import java.awt.image.*;
import java.net.*;
class Main extends Frame {
    Main(String filename) {
        super("getSource Example");
        try {
            // Retrieve the image.
            URL url = new URL("file:///" +
                System.getProperty("user.dir")
              + "/" + filename);

           add("Center", new ImageCanvas(getToolkit().getImage(url)));
        } catch (Exception e) {
            e.printStackTrace();
        }
        resize(100, 100);
        show();
```

```
        }

        static public void main(String[] args) {
            if (args.length == 1) {
                new Main(args[0]);
            } else {
                System.err.println("usage: java Main <image file>");
            }
        }
    }

    class ImageCanvas extends Canvas {
        Image oldImage;
        Image image;

        ImageCanvas(Image image) {
            oldImage = image;
            waitForImage(image);
        }

        void waitForImage(Image image) {
            try {
                // Use a media tracker object to wait until all the pixels
                // have been retrieved.
                MediaTracker tracker = new MediaTracker(this);
                tracker.addImage(image, 0);
                tracker.waitForID(0);
            } catch (Exception e) {
                e.printStackTrace();
            }
        }

        Image getSubImage(Image image, Rectangle r) {
            // Create crop image using a CropImageFilter.
            CropImageFilter imgf = new CropImageFilter(
                r.x, r.y, r.width, r.height);
            ImageProducer ip = image.getSource();

            ip = new FilteredImageSource(ip, imgf);
            Image result = getToolkit().createImage(ip);
            waitForImage(result);
            return result;
        }

        public void paint(Graphics g) {
            int w = oldImage.getWidth(this);
            int h = oldImage.getHeight(this);
            if (image == null) {

                image = createImage(w, h);
                Graphics g2 = image.getGraphics();
                g2.drawImage(getSubImage(oldImage,
                    new Rectangle(0, 0, w/2, h)),
                    w/2, 0, this);
```

```
            g2.drawImage(getSubImage(oldImage,
                new Rectangle(w/2, 0, w/2, h)),
                0, 0, this);
            g2.dispose();
        }
        g.drawImage(image, (size().width-w)/2,
            (size().height-h)/2, this);
    }
}
```

getWidth()

PURPOSE
Retrieves the width of the image.

SYNTAX
`public abstract int getWidth(ImageObserver observer)`

DESCRIPTION
This method retrieves the width of the image. If the width is not available, `-1` is returned. If `observer` is non-`null`, `observer` will be notified when the width becomes available.

PARAMETERS

`observer`
The image observer to register for image updates; if `null`, no updates are desired.

RETURNS
The width of the image; `-1` if not yet available.

SEE ALSO
`getHeight()`, `ImageObserver`.

EXAMPLE
See the class example.

UndefinedProperty

PURPOSE
This object is returned by `getProperty()` if the property is not defined.

SYNTAX
`public static final Object UndefinedProperty`

SEE ALSO
`getProperty()`.

EXAMPLE
See the class example.

A B C D E F G H I J K L M N O P Q R S T U V W X Y Z

java.awt.image
ImageConsumer

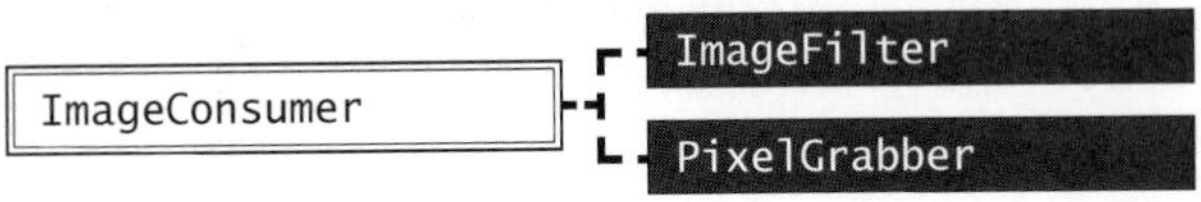

Syntax

```
public interface ImageConsumer
```

Description

Images are painted on a surface using a streaming architecture that involves an *image producer*, which is responsible for supplying a stream of pixel data, and an *image consumer*, which is responsible for displaying that stream. This architecture allows progressive rendering of images as the pixels are delivered from a remote source.

The `ImageConsumer` interface defines all the methods necessary for a class to receive pixels from an image producer. See the `ImageProducer` interface for details on how to register an image consumer to receive pixels from an image producer.

Hints

A *hint* is a bit of information about pixel delivery that the image producer gives to the image consumer prior to delivering the pixels. Using these hints, the image consumer might be able to implement some optimizations that would speed up the processing time.

Multiframe Images

The image can contain multiple frames, as in the case of a video source. This is the default, in the absence of the `SINGLEFRAME` hint from the image producer.

MEMBER SUMMARY

Image Completion Status Constants	
`IMAGEABORTED`	Status bit specifying that the image production was aborted.
`IMAGEERROR`	Status bit specifying an error occurred.
`SINGLEFRAMEDONE`	Status bit specifying that one frame of a multiframe image is complete.
`STATICIMAGEDONE`	Status bit specifying that the image is complete.
Pixel Delivery Hints	
`COMPLETESCANLINES`	Hint specifying that pixels will be delivered in complete scanlines.

MEMBER SUMMARY

Subclass Overrides	
`imageComplete()`	Called by the image producer to deliver completion status to the image consumer.
`setColorModel()`	Called by the image producer to set the color model for the source image.
`setDimensions()`	Called by the image producer to set the dimension of the source image.
`setHints()`	Called by the image producer to specify how the pixels will be delivered.
`setPixels()`	Called by the image producer to deliver pixels.
`setProperties()`	Called by the image producer to set the properties for the source image.
Pixel Retransmit Method	
`resendTopDownLeftRight()`	Retransmits the pixels in top-down, left-right order.
Consumer Field	
`consumer`	Contains the image consumer of the pixel data.

Example

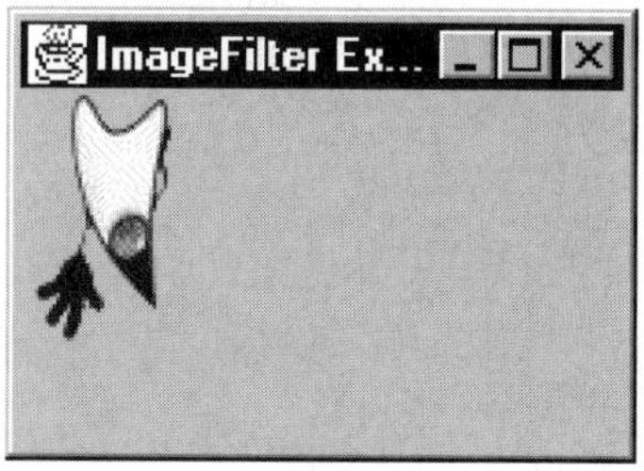

FIGURE 160 `ImageFilter`

This example implements a type of image filter that flips the image horizontally or vertically. See Figure 160. The image is displayed in the `ImageCanvas` class. If you click the canvas, it flips the image either horizontally or vertically. The overridden `setDimensions()` method records the width and height of the image. These are used in moving the pixels to the new location as they pass through the filter. The `setHints()` override sets the `ImageConsumer.RANDOMPIXELORDER` bit and clears the `ImageConsumer.TOPDOWNLEFTRIGHT` because as the pixels pass through the image filter, they are translated in an order different from what the filter's producer intended.

In the `setPixels()` override, notice that a temporary buffer must be allocated to store the displaced pixels. In other words, the image filter subclass cannot modify the pixel array supplied by `setPixels()`.

In the `setProperties()` override, the flip filter adds the `flipH` and `flipV` properties using the current flip values. If there is more than one flip filter in the pixel stream, the final values of the `flipH` and `flipV` properties will reflect the resulting transformation. That is, if there are two filters that flip the image vertically, they will cancel out each other and the resulting `flipV` property value will be false.

A B C D E F G H I J K L M N O P Q R S T U V W X Y Z

Example

```
import java.awt.*;
import java.awt.image.*;
import java.util.*;
class Main extends Frame {
    Main(String filename) {
        super("ImageFilter Example");
        add("Center", new ImageCanvas(
            getToolkit().getImage(filename)));
        resize(50, 100);
        show();
    }

    static public void main(String[] args) {
        if (args.length == 1) {
            new Main(args[0]);
        } else {
            System.err.println("usage: java Main <image file>");
        }
    }
}

class ImageCanvas extends Canvas {
    Image flipImage;
    Image image;
    boolean flipH = true, flipV = true;
    FlipFilter imgf = new FlipFilter();

    ImageCanvas(Image image) {
        this.image = image;
        processImage();
    }

    public void paint(Graphics g) {
        g.drawImage(flipImage, 0, 0, this);
    }

    void processImage() {
        ImageProducer ip = image.getSource();

        imgf.setFlip(flipH, flipV);
        ip = new FilteredImageSource(ip, imgf);
        flipImage = getToolkit().createImage(ip);
        repaint();
    }

    public boolean mouseDown(Event evt, int x, int y) {
        if (flipH & flipV) {
            flipH = flipV = false;
        } else if (flipV) {
            flipH = true;
            flipV = false;
        } else {
            flipV = true;
        }
```

```
        processImage();
        return true;
    }
}

class FlipFilter extends ImageFilter {
    int width, height;
    boolean flipH, flipV;

    public void setFlip(boolean flipH, boolean flipV) {
        this.flipH = flipH;
        this.flipV = flipV;
    }

    public void setDimensions(int w, int h) {
        super.setDimensions(width = w, height = h);
    }

    public void setProperties(Hashtable props) {
        boolean h = false;
        boolean v = false;
        Object bh = props.get("flipH");
        Object bv = props.get("flipV");

        if (bh != null) {
            h = ((Boolean)bh).booleanValue();
        }
        if (bv != null) {
            v = ((Boolean)bv).booleanValue();
        }
        h ^= flipH;
        v ^= flipV;
        props.put("flipH", new Boolean(h));
        props.put("flipV", new Boolean(v));
        consumer.setProperties(props);
    }

    public void setHints(int h) {
        h |= ImageConsumer.RANDOMPIXELORDER;
        h &= ~ImageConsumer.TOPDOWNLEFTRIGHT;
        super.setHints(h);
    }

    public void setColorModel(ColorModel model) {
        super.setColorModel(model);
    }

    public void setPixels(int srcX, int srcY, int srcW, int srcH,
          ColorModel model, byte pixels[], int srcOff, int srcScan) {
        int s = srcOff;
        byte[] tempBuff = new byte[srcW * srcH];

        for (int y=0; y<srcH; y++) {
            for (int x=0; x<srcW; x++) {
```

```
                int d = 0;
                if (flipV) {
                    d += (srcH-y-1)*srcW;
                } else {
                    d += y*srcW;
                }
                if (flipH) {
                    d += (srcW-x-1);
                } else {
                    d += x;
                }
                tempBuff[d] = pixels[s];
                s++;
            }
        }

        if (flipH) {
            srcX = width - (srcX+srcW);
        }
        if (flipV) {
            srcY = height - (srcY+srcH);
        }
        super.setPixels(srcX, srcY, srcW, srcH, model, tempBuff, 0,
            srcScan);
    }

    public void setPixels(int srcX, int srcY, int srcW, int srcH,
          ColorModel model, int pixels[], int srcOff, int srcScan) {
        int s = srcOff;
        int[] tempBuff = new int[srcW * srcH];

        for (int y=0; y<srcH; y++) {
            for (int x=0; x<srcW; x++) {
                int d = 0;
                if (flipV) {
                    d += (srcH-y-1)*srcW;
                } else {
                    d += y*srcW;
                }
                if (flipH) {
                    d += (srcW-x-1);
                } else {
                    d += x;
                }
                tempBuff[d] = pixels[s];
                s++;
            }
        }
        if (flipH) {
            srcX = width - (srcX+srcW);
        }
        if (flipV) {
            srcY = height - (srcY+srcH);
        }
```

```
        super.setPixels(srcX, srcY, srcW, srcH, model, tempBuff, 0,
            srcScan);
    }

    public synchronized void imageComplete(int status) {
        super.imageComplete(status);
    }
}
```

clone()

PURPOSE Constructs a clone of this image filter.

SYNTAX `public Object clone()`

DESCRIPTION The default implementation calls `Object.clone()`, which creates a new instance of this image filter that has a shallow copy of the variables. If the image filter refers to other objects or arrays that are modified during the filtering, this method must be overridden in order to clone these objects or arrays.

RETURNS A copy of this image filter.

OVERRIDES `Object.clone()`.

EXAMPLE See `Object.clone()`.

consumer

PURPOSE Contains the image consumer of the pixel data.

SYNTAX `protected ImageConsumer consumer`

DESCRIPTION The image filter delivers pixel data to the image consumer referred to by this field. This field is initialized by a `getFilterInstance()` method call, typically by the `FilteredImageSource` class during the construction of a pixel stream.

SEE ALSO `getFilterInstance()`, `ImageConsumer`.

getFilterInstance()

PURPOSE Creates an instance of this filter.

SYNTAX `public ImageFilter getFilterInstance(ImageConsumer ic)`

DESCRIPTION This method returns a unique instance of this image filter that will deliver pixels to the image consumer `ic`. This method is typically used by `FilteredImageSource` during the construction of an image stream. By default, this method calls `clone()` and returns the result.

PARAMETERS

`ic` The non-`null` image consumer of the new image filter instance.

RETURNS A non-`null` instance of this image filter.

imageComplete()

PURPOSE Called by the image producer to deliver completion status to the image consumer.

SYNTAX `public void imageComplete(int status)`

DESCRIPTION By default, this method calls the consumer's `imageComplete()` method by using `status`. See `ImageConsumer.imageComplete()` for details on how to override this method and how to interpret `status`. An image filter need not remove itself from the image producer's registered list of consumers, since the image consumer at the end of the stream will do that.

PARAMETERS

`status` A combination of the status bits as defined in the `ImageConsumer` class.

SEE ALSO `ImageConsumer`, `imageComplete()`.

resendTopDownLeftRight()

PURPOSE Retransmits the pixels in top-down, left-right order.

SYNTAX `public void resendTopDownLeftRight(ImageProducer ip)`

DESCRIPTION This method is called by the image consumer of this filter if the image consumer wants the pixels to be retransmitted in top-down, left-right order. `ip` should be the image producer that is sending pixels to this filter.

The image filter can respond to this request in one of three ways:

1. If the filter does not move around the pixels, it can forward the request to the image producer by calling `requestTopDownLeftRightResend()`, using itself as the image consumer. This is the default behavior.
2. If the filter has the pixels and can retransmit them in the right order, it

should override this method and do so. See the `ImageProducer.requestTopDownLeftRightResend()` method for details on how it should deliver the pixels to the image consumer.

3. The filter can ignore this call, and no retransmission will occur.

PARAMETERS

`ip` The non-`null` image producer that supplies this image filter with pixels.

SEE ALSO `ImageProducer.requestTopDownLeftRightResend()`.

setColorModel()

PURPOSE Called by the image producer to set the color model for the source image.

SYNTAX `public void setColorModel(ColorModel model)`

DESCRIPTION This method should be overridden to process `setColorModel()` calls from the image producer. The default implementation simply passes `model` to the image consumer.

PARAMETERS

`model` The non-`null` color model of the source image.

SEE ALSO `ImageConsumer.setColorModel()`.

EXAMPLE See the class example.

setDimensions()

PURPOSE Called by the image producer to set the dimension of the source image.

SYNTAX `public void setDimensions(int width, int height)`

DESCRIPTION This method should be overridden to intercept `setDimensions()` calls from the image producer. The default implementation simply passes the dimensions `width` and `height` to the image consumer.

PARAMETERS

`height` The height of the source image in pixels.

`width` The width of the source image in pixels.

SEE ALSO `ImageConsumer.setDimensions()`.

EXAMPLE See the class example.

A B C D E F G H I J K L M N O P Q R S T U V W X Y Z

setHints()

PURPOSE Called by image producer to specify how the pixels will be delivered.

SYNTAX
```
public void setHints(int hintFlags)
```

DESCRIPTION By default, the image filter simply passes the hints `hintFlags` to the image consumer. However, if the image filter moves pixels around, it must override this method and adjust the hints appropriately before sending them to the image consumer. See the `ImageConsumer` interface for the possible set of hints and what they mean.

PARAMETERS

`hintFlags` A set of bits that specify how pixels will be delivered.

SEE ALSO `ImageConsumer.setHints()`.

EXAMPLE See the class example.

setPixels()

PURPOSE Called by the image producer to deliver pixels.

SYNTAX
```
public void setPixels(int x, int y, int w, int h, ColorModel
   model, byte[] pixels, int offset, int scansize)
public void setPixels(int x, int y, int w, int h, ColorModel
   model, int[] pixels, int offset, int scansize)
```

DESCRIPTION By default, the image filter simply passes off the pixels, unchanged, to the image consumer. If the image filter needs to modify the pixels, it must override both `setPixels()` methods. See `ImageConsumer.setPixels()` for details on how the parameters are used.

PARAMETERS

`h` The height of the rectangle in which the pixels are destined.
`model` The non-`null` color model used to translate the pixel values.
`offset` The index of the first pixel in the pixel array `pixels`.
`pixels` The non-`null` array of pixel values.
`scansize` The width to use when extracting pixels from the pixel array `pixels`.
`w` The width of the rectangle in which the pixels are destined.
`x` The *x*-coordinate of the rectangle in which the pixels are destined.
`y` The *y*-coordinate of the rectangle in which the pixels are destined.

SEE ALSO `ImageConsumer.setPixels()`.

EXAMPLE See the class example.

setProperties()

PURPOSE Called by the image producer to set the properties for the source image.

SYNTAX `public void setProperties(Hashtable props)`

DESCRIPTION By default, the image filter passes along the properties after adding its name to the "filters" property. The filter should override this method if it wants to add or query a property.

PARAMETERS

`props` The non-`null` properties of the source image.

SEE ALSO `ImageConsumer.setProperties()`.

EXAMPLE See the class example.

java.awt.image

ImageObserver

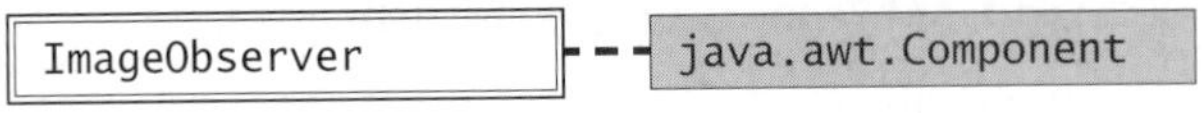

Syntax

```
public interface ImageObserver
```

Description

An object that implements the `ImageObserver` interface can register itself for progress information as an image is loaded. For example, an AWT canvas might want to progressively display the image as it is being loaded. Methods such as `Image.drawImage()` and `Image.getWidth()` accept image observers and automatically register them with the image producer.

When an image observer is registered, it receives all progress information via the `imageUpdate()` method call. However, only progress information that the image observer asks for is delivered to the `imageUpdate()` method. For example, if the image observer were to call `Image.getWidth()` and the `Image.getWidth()` width information was not yet available (that is, returned `-1`), `imageUpdate()` would be called as soon as the width became available. Otherwise if `Image.getWidth()` were not called or if `Image.getWidth()` returned the width, the `imageUpdate()` method would not be called.

MEMBER SUMMARY	
Image Update Method	
`imageUpdate()`	Called by an image consumer to deliver status information about the loading of an image.
Image Update Status Bits	
`ABORT`	Indicates that the image loading process was aborted.
`ALLBITS`	Indicates that the entire image has been successfully loaded.
`ERROR`	Indicates that an error was encountered while the image was being loaded.
`FRAMEBITS`	Indicates that a frame of a multiframe image has been successfully loaded.
`HEIGHT`	Indicates that the height of the image is now available.
`PROPERTIES`	Indicates that the image properties are now available.
`SOMEBITS`	Indicates that additional pixels are now available.
`WIDTH`	Indicates that the width of the image is now available.

Example

This example creates an image observer that can be wrapped around another image observer in order to "spy" on the calls to the `imageUpdate()` method. The information is printed on standard output. See Figure 161.

FIGURE 161 `ImageObserver`

```
import java.awt.*;
import java.awt.image.*;
import java.net.*;
import java.util.*;
class Main extends Frame {
    Main(String filename) {
        super("ImageObserver Example");
        try {
            // Retrieve the image.
            Image image = getToolkit().getImage(filename);

            add("Center", new ImageCanvas(image));
        } catch (Exception e) {
            e.printStackTrace();
        }
        resize(50, 100);
        show();
    }

    static public void main(String[] args) {
        if (args.length == 1) {
            new Main(args[0]);
        } else {
            System.err.println("usage: java Main <image file>");
        }
    }
}

class ImageCanvas extends Canvas {
    Image image;
    ImageObserverSpy spy = new ImageObserverSpy(this);

    ImageCanvas(Image image) {
        this.image = image;
        image.getWidth(spy);
        image.getHeight(spy);
        image.getProperty("test", spy);
    }

    public void paint(Graphics g) {
        g.drawImage(image, 0, 0, spy);
    }
}

class ImageObserverSpy implements ImageObserver {
```

Example

```
        ImageObserver obs;

        ImageObserverSpy(ImageObserver obs) {
            this.obs = obs;
        }

        public boolean imageUpdate(Image img, int infoflags,
            int x, int y, int width, int height) {
            System.out.print("x="+x+" ");
            System.out.print("y="+y+" ");
            System.out.print("width="+width+" ");
            System.out.print("height="+height+" ");
            System.out.print("  infoflags=");
            if ((infoflags & ABORT) != 0) System.out.print("ABORT ");
            if ((infoflags & ALLBITS) != 0) System.out.print("ALLBITS ");
            if ((infoflags & ERROR) != 0) System.out.print("ERROR ");
            if ((infoflags & FRAMEBITS) != 0)
                System.out.print("FRAMEBITS ");
            if ((infoflags & HEIGHT) != 0) System.out.print("HEIGHT ");
            if ((infoflags & PROPERTIES) != 0)
                System.out.print("PROPERTIES ");
           if ((infoflags & SOMEBITS) != 0) System.out.print("SOMEBITS ");
            if ((infoflags & WIDTH)!= 0) System.out.print("WIDTH ");
            System.out.println();
            return obs.imageUpdate(img, infoflags, x, y, width, height);
        }
    }
```

OUTPUT

```
    x=0 y=0 width=55 height=68   infoflags=WIDTH HEIGHT
    x=0 y=0 width=55 height=1   infoflags=SOMEBITS
    x=0 y=1 width=55 height=1   infoflags=SOMEBITS
    x=0 y=2 width=55 height=1   infoflags=SOMEBITS
    x=0 y=3 width=55 height=1   infoflags=SOMEBITS
    x=0 y=4 width=55 height=1   infoflags=SOMEBITS

        <many similar lines deleted>

    x=0 y=59 width=55 height=1   infoflags=SOMEBITS
    x=0 y=60 width=55 height=1   infoflags=SOMEBITS
    x=0 y=61 width=55 height=1   infoflags=SOMEBITS
    x=0 y=62 width=55 height=1   infoflags=SOMEBITS
    x=0 y=63 width=55 height=1   infoflags=SOMEBITS
    x=0 y=64 width=55 height=1   infoflags=SOMEBITS
    x=0 y=65 width=55 height=1   infoflags=SOMEBITS
    x=0 y=66 width=55 height=1   infoflags=SOMEBITS
    x=0 y=67 width=55 height=1   infoflags=SOMEBITS
    x=0 y=0 width=55 height=68   infoflags=ALLBITS
```

ABORT

PURPOSE Indicates that the image loading process was aborted.

SYNTAX `public static final int ABORT`

DESCRIPTION If the `ABORT` status bit is present in the status flags passed to the `imageUpdate()` method, no further status will be delivered via the `imageUpdate()` method. Unless the `ERROR` status bit is also present, the loading of the image can be restarted.

In the absence of any other status bits, the `x`, `y`, `width`, and `height` parameters passed to the `imageUpdate()` method should be ignored.

SEE ALSO `ERROR`, `imageUpdate()`.

EXAMPLE See the class example.

ALLBITS

PURPOSE Indicates that the entire image has been successfully loaded.

SYNTAX `public static final int ALLBITS`

DESCRIPTION If the `ALLBITS` status bit is present in the status flags passed to the `imageUpdate()` method, no further status will be delivered via the `imageUpdate()` method. If the image has only one frame the `ALLBITS` status bit is used (see the `ImageConsumer` interface for more information about multiframe images). If the image is multiframe, the `FRAMEBITS` status bit is used instead.

This status bit is delivered only if `Image.drawImage()` was called and returned `false`. In the absence of any other status bits, the `x`, `y`, `width`, and `height` parameters passed to the `imageUpdate()` method should be ignored.

SEE ALSO `Image.drawImage()`, `imageUpdate()`.

EXAMPLE See the class example.

ERROR

PURPOSE Indicates that an error was encountered while the image was being loaded.

SYNTAX `public static final int ERROR`

DESCRIPTION If the `ERROR` status bit is present in the status flags passed to the `imageUpdate()` method, no further status will be delivered via the `imageUpdate()` method. As a convenience, the `ABORT` flag is also set in the status flags whenever the `ERROR` flag is set. So if there is no need to distinguish between `ABORT` and `ERROR`, it is safe to test only for the `ABORT` flag.

SEE ALSO `imageUpdate()`.

EXAMPLE See the class example.

FRAMEBITS

PURPOSE Indicates that a frame of a multiframe image has been successfully loaded.

SYNTAX `public static final int FRAMEBITS`

DESCRIPTION If the image consists of only one frame, then the `ALLBITS` status bit is used instead to indicate that the image is complete.

DESCRIPTION This status bit is delivered only if `Image.drawImage()` was called and returned `false`. In the absence of any other status bits, the `x`, `y`, `width`, and `height` parameters passed to the `imageUpdate()` method should be ignored.

SEE ALSO `Image.drawImage()`, `imageUpdate()`.

EXAMPLE See the class example.

HEIGHT

PURPOSE Indicates that the height of the image is now available.

SYNTAX `public static final int HEIGHT`

DESCRIPTION If the `HEIGHT` status bit is present in the status flags passed to the `imageUpdate()` method, the height parameter contains the height of the image. This height can be retrieved also by using the `Image.getHeight()` method.

This status bit is delivered only if `Image.getHeight()` was called and returned `-1`.

SEE ALSO `Image.getHeight()`, `imageUpdate()`.

EXAMPLE See the class example.

imageUpdate()

PURPOSE Called by an image consumer to deliver status information about the loading of an image.

SYNTAX
```
public boolean imageUpdate(Image img, int infoflags, int x, int
   y, int width, int height)
```

DESCRIPTION This method is called when the image observer asks for a particular piece of information and the information is not yet available. For example, if the image observer called `Image.getWidth()` and the width information was not yet available (that is, `Image.getWidth()` returned `-1`), the `imageUpdate()` method would be called as soon as the width became available.

`infoflags` contains a combination of status bits that indicate the type of status information being provided. For example, the `WIDTH` status bit indicates that the width of the image is now available. `infoflags` may contain more than one status bit. To test for the presence of a bit, use the bitwise 'and' operator; for example:

```
if ((infoflags & WIDTH) != 0) {
   System.out.println("width information is now
    available");
}
```

The values that are supplied in `x`, `y`, `width`, and `height` depend on status bits present in `infoflags`. For example, if `infoflags` contains `WIDTH`, only the `width` parameter contains any information. See the other status bits in this interface for details on how the parameters should be interpreted.

PARAMETERS

`height`	This value depends on the status bits enabled in `infoflags`.
`img`	The non-`null` image being updated.
`infoflags`	A set of status bits.
`width`	This value depends on the status bits enabled in `infoflags`.
`x`	This value depends on the status bits enabled in `infoflags`.
`y`	This value depends on the status bits enabled in `infoflags`.

RETURNS `true` if no further calls to the `imageUpdate()` are needed.

EXAMPLE See the class example.

PROPERTIES

PURPOSE Indicates that the image properties are now available.

SYNTAX `public static final int PROPERTIES`

DESCRIPTION This status bit indicates that the properties of the image are now available. In the absence of any other status bits, the `x`, `y`, `width`, and `height` parameters passed to the `imageUpdate()` method should be ignored.

SEE ALSO `Image.getProperty()`, `imageUpdate()`.

EXAMPLE See the class example.

SOMEBITS

PURPOSE Indicates that additional pixels are now available.

SYNTAX `public static final int SOMEBITS`

DESCRIPTION The `x`, `y`, `width`, `height` parameters to the `imageUpdate()` method indicate which pixels of the image are available.

SEE ALSO `imageUpdate()`.

EXAMPLE See the class example.

WIDTH

PURPOSE Indicates that the width of the image is now available.

SYNTAX `public static final int WIDTH`

DESCRIPTION If the `WIDTH` status bit is present in the status flags passed to the `imageUpdate()` method, the `width` parameter contains the width of the image. This width can be retrieved also by using the `Image.getWidth()` method.

This status bit is delivered only if `Image.getWidth()` was called and returned `-1`.

SEE ALSO `Image.getWidth()`, `imageUpdate()`.

EXAMPLE See the class example.

ImageProducer

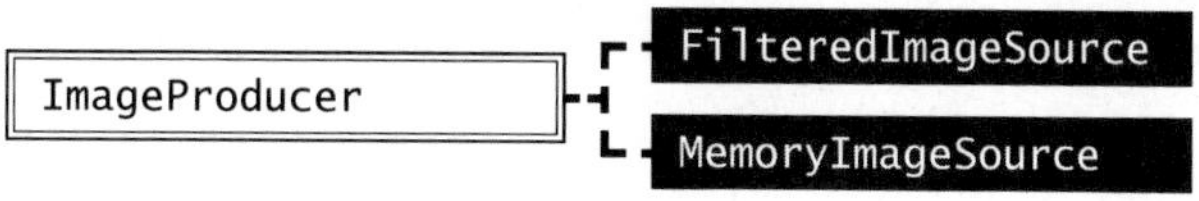

Syntax

`public interface ImageProducer`

Description

Images are painted on a surface using a streaming architecture that involves an *image producer*, which is responsible for supplying a stream of pixel data, and an *image consumer*, which is responsible for displaying that stream. The reason for this architecture is to allow progressive rendering of images as the pixels are delivered from a remote source.

This interface defines all the methods that are necessary for a class to generate pixels as an image producer. See the `ImageConsumer` interface for details on what an image consumer expects from an image producer.

MEMBER SUMMARY	
Image Consumer Registration Methods	
`addConsumer()`	Registers an image consumer with this image producer.
`isConsumer()`	Determines if an image consumer is registered with this image producer.
`removeConsumer()`	Removes a registered image consumer from this image producer.
Pixel Delivery Methods	
`requestTopDownLeftRightResend()`	Requests that pixel data be retransmitted in left-right, top-down order.
`startProduction()`	Triggers the delivery of image data.

See Also

`ImageConsumer`.

Example

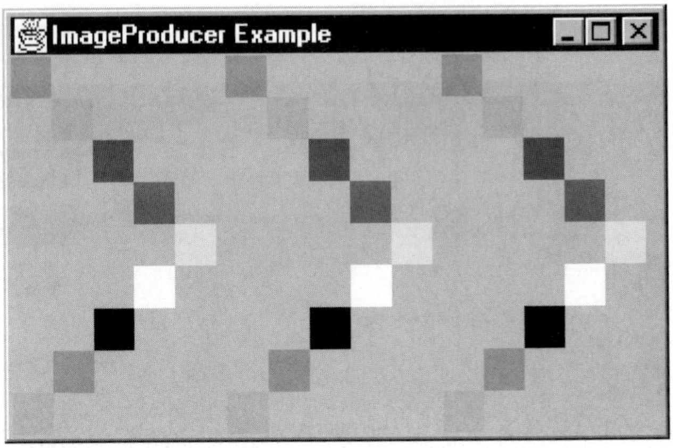

FIGURE 162 ImageProducer

This example demonstrates how one might build a new kind of image decoder. See Figure 162. The image producer reads information from a file and then interprets the data to build an image. The format and sample image file follow the example code. The image producer decodes the image file at the first request for the pixel data. Once the image is decoded, the image producer delivers the pixel data in an incremental fashion so that the image can be rendered incrementally. After all the pixels are delivered to an image consumer, that consumer is automatically removed from the list of consumers.

An image consumer that makes a request for pixels while the image producer is producing pixels is added to the list of consumers and is given the pixel data as soon as possible. The example creates three images using the image producer to test the code that supports multiple consumers.

In response to the `requestTopDownLeftRightResend()` method, all the pixel data is sent in a single call to `setPixels()`.

```
import java.awt.*;
import java.awt.image.*;
import java.io.*;
import java.util.*;
class Main extends Frame {
    BlockImageDecoder ip;

    Main(String filename) {
        super("ImageProducer Example");
        Panel p = new Panel();

        try {
            ip = new BlockImageDecoder(new FileInputStream(filename));
        } catch (IOException e) {
            e.printStackTrace();
            System.exit(1);
        }
        p.setLayout(new GridLayout(1, 0));
        p.add(new ImageCanvas(ip));
        p.add(new ImageCanvas(ip));
        p.add(new ImageCanvas(ip));
        add("Center", p);
```

```
        resize(325, 220);
        show();
    }

    public static void main(String[] args) {
        if (args.length == 1) {
            new Main(args[0]);
        } else {
            System.err.println("usage: java Main <image file>");
        }
    }
}

class ImageCanvas extends Canvas {
    ImageProducer ip;
    Image image;

    ImageCanvas(ImageProducer ip) {
        this.ip = ip;
        image = createImage(ip);
    }

    public void paint(Graphics g) {
        g.drawImage(image, 0, 0, this);
    }

    public boolean mouseDown(Event evt, int x, int y) {
        image = createImage(ip);
        repaint();
        return true;
    }
}

class BlockImageDecoder implements ImageProducer {
    StreamTokenizer st;
    ColorModel model;
    Vector consumers = new Vector();
    Hashtable properties = new Hashtable();
    byte[] pixels;
    int width = -1, height = -1;
    Rectangle[] rects;
    byte[] rectColors;


    BlockImageDecoder(InputStream is) {
        st = new StreamTokenizer(is);
    }

    public synchronized void addConsumer(ImageConsumer ic) {
        if (rects != null) {
            produce(ic);
        } else if (!consumers.contains(ic)) {
            consumers.addElement(ic);
```

Example

```
        }
    }

    public synchronized boolean isConsumer(ImageConsumer ic) {
        return consumers.contains(ic);
    }

    public synchronized void removeConsumer(ImageConsumer ic) {
        consumers.removeElement(ic);
    }

    private int getInt() throws IOException {
        if (st.nextToken() != StreamTokenizer.TT_NUMBER) {
            throw (new IOException("format error"));
        }
        return (int)st.nval;
    }

    // Convert the contents of the input file to image data.
    private synchronized void processImage() {
        try {
            // Read width and height
            width = getInt();
            height = getInt();

            // Read colors
            int numColors = getInt();
            byte cmap[] = new byte[numColors * 3];
            for (int i=0; i<cmap.length; i++) {
                cmap[i] = (byte)getInt();
            }

            // Create color model.
            int n = numColors-1;
            int nbits = 0;
            while (n > 0) {
                n >>>= 1;
                nbits++;
            }
            model = new IndexColorModel(nbits, numColors, cmap, 0,
               false, 0);

            // Read rectangles and their colors
            rects = new Rectangle[getInt()];
            rectColors = new byte[rects.length];

            for (int i=0; i<rects.length; i++) {
               rects[i] = new Rectangle(getInt(), getInt(), getInt(),
                    getInt());
                rectColors[i] = (byte)getInt();
            }
        } catch (Exception e) {
            e.printStackTrace();
        }
    }
```

A B C D E F G H I J K L M N O P Q R S T U V W X Y Z

```
    public void startProduction(ImageConsumer ic) {
        if (ic != null) {
            addConsumer(ic);
            if (rects == null) {
                processImage();
            }
            for (int i=consumers.size()-1; i>=0; i--) {
                ic = (ImageConsumer)consumers.elementAt(i);
                produce(ic);
                consumers.removeElement(ic);
            }
        }
    }

    private void produce(ImageConsumer ic) {
        if (width < 0) {
            ic.imageComplete(ImageConsumer.IMAGEERROR);
            return;
        }
        ic.setDimensions(width, height);
        ic.setProperties(properties);
        ic.setColorModel(model);
        ic.setHints(ImageConsumer.SINGLEPASS |
                    ImageConsumer.SINGLEFRAME);
        pixels = new byte[width * height];
        ic.setPixels(0, 0, width, height, model, pixels, 0, width);
        for (int i=0; i<rects.length; i++) {
            Rectangle r = rects[i];

            for (int y=r.y; y<r.y+r.height; y++) {
                for (int x=r.x; x<r.x+r.width; x++) {
                    pixels[y*width+x] = rectColors[i];
                }
            }
            ic.setPixels(r.x, r.y, r.width, r.height, model,
                         pixels, r.x+r.y*width, width);
        }
        ic.imageComplete(ImageConsumer.STATICIMAGEDONE);
    }

    public void requestTopDownLeftRightResend(ImageConsumer ic) {
        if (pixels != null) {
            ic.setDimensions(width, height);
            ic.setProperties(properties);
            ic.setColorModel(model);
            ic.setHints(ImageConsumer.SINGLEPASS |
                        ImageConsumer.TOPDOWNLEFTRIGHT |
                        ImageConsumer.SINGLEFRAME);
           ic.setPixels(0, 0, width, height, model, pixels, 0, width);
        }
    }
}
```

Input File

```
100 180             // image size
8                   // number of colors
0 0 255             // color 0 transparent
0 255 0             // color 1
0 255 255           // color 2
255 0 0             // color 3
255 0 255           // color 4
255 255 0           // color 5
255 255 255         // color 6
0 0 0               // color 7
9                   // number of rectangles
0 0 20 20 1         // rectangle 0
20 20 20 20 2       // rectangle 1
40 40 20 20 3       // rectangle 2
60 60 20 20 4       // rectangle 3
80 80 20 20 5       // rectangle 4
60 100 20 20 6      // rectangle 5
40 120 20 20 7      // rectangle 6
20 140 20 20 1      // rectangle 7
0 160 20 20 2       // rectangle 0
```

addConsumer()

PURPOSE Registers an image consumer with this image producer.

SYNTAX `public void addConsumer(ImageConsumer ic)`

DESCRIPTION This method registers the image consumer `ic` with this image producer. The image producer may or may not start delivering the image data to the image consumer immediately. The delivery of the image data can be triggered by a call to the `startProduction()` method.

PARAMETERS

`ic` The non-`null` image consumer to register.

SEE ALSO `startProduction()`.

EXAMPLE See the class example.

isConsumer()

PURPOSE Determines if an image consumer is registered with this image producer.

SYNTAX `public boolean isConsumer(ImageConsumer ic)`

PARAMETERS

`ic` The possibly `null` image consumer to check if registered.

RETURNS `true` if `ic` has been registered; `false` otherwise.

EXAMPLE See the class example.

removeConsumer()

PURPOSE Removes a registered image consumer from this image producer.

SYNTAX `public void removeConsumer(ImageConsumer ic)`

DESCRIPTION This method removes the given `ImageConsumer` object from the image producer's registered list of image consumers. The image producer will stop sending pixel data to `ic` as soon as it is feasible. This method call is ignored if `ic` has not been registered with this image producer.

PARAMETERS

`ic` The non-`null` image consumer to be removed.

EXAMPLE See the class example.

requestTopDownLeftRightResend()

PURPOSE Requests that pixel data be retransmitted in left-right, top-down order.

SYNTAX `public void requestTopDownLeftRightResend(ImageConsumer ic)`

DESCRIPTION This method is used by an image consumer to request that the pixels be retransmitted in top-down, left-right order. Some algorithms can produce higher-quality output more efficiently if the pixels are received in this order.

In response to this request, if the image producer can retransmit the data in the requested order, it should call `setHints()` again but this time including the `TOPDOWNLEFTRIGHT` hint.

The image producer can ignore this call if it cannot retransmit the data in the requested order.

PARAMETERS

`ic` The non-`null` image consumer requesting the retransmission.

SEE ALSO `ImageConsumer.imageComplete()`, `ImageConsumer.setHints()`, `ImageConsumer.setPixels()`.

EXAMPLE See the class example.

startProduction()

PURPOSE Triggers the delivery of image data.

SYNTAX `public void startProduction(ImageConsumer ic)`

DESCRIPTION This method registers the image consumer `ic`, if not already registered, and starts the delivery of image data to the list of registered consumers.

PARAMETERS

`ic` The non-`null` image consumer awaiting image data.

SEE ALSO `addConsumer()`.

EXAMPLE See the class example.

java.lang
IncompatibleClassChangeError

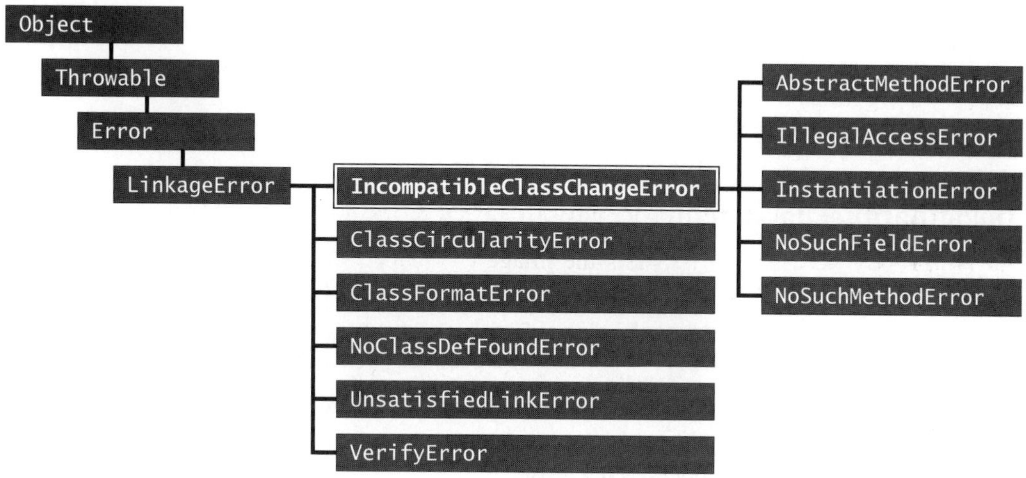

Syntax

`public class IncompatibleClassChangeError extends LinkageError`

Description

`IncompatibleClassChangeError` is the superclass of errors that occur when the Java virtual machine detects that the program is attempting to load or access a member of a class in a way that violates Java language rules. Normally, such errors are caught by the compiler when the program is compiled. However, problems could be introduced when classes used by a program become inconsistent, for example, if you were to make an incompatible change and then recompile only some of the classes.

`IncompatibleClassChangeError` should not be caught or declared in the `throws` clause of a method.

MEMBER SUMMARY	
Constructor	
`IncompatibleClassChangeError()`	Constructs an `IncompatibleClassChangeError` instance.

See Also

AbstractMethodError, Error, IllegalAccessError, InstantiationError, LinkageError, NoSuchFieldError, NoSuchMethodError.

Example

See examples of subclasses.

IncompatibleClassChangeError()

PURPOSE Constructs an IncompatibleClassChangeError instance.

SYNTAX
```
public IncompatibleClassChangeError()
public IncompatibleClassChangeError(String msg)
```

DESCRIPTION The two forms of this constructor create a new instance of IncompatibleClassChangeError. An optional string msg can be supplied that describes this particular instance of the error.

PARAMETERS

msg A string that gives details about this error.

IndexColorModel

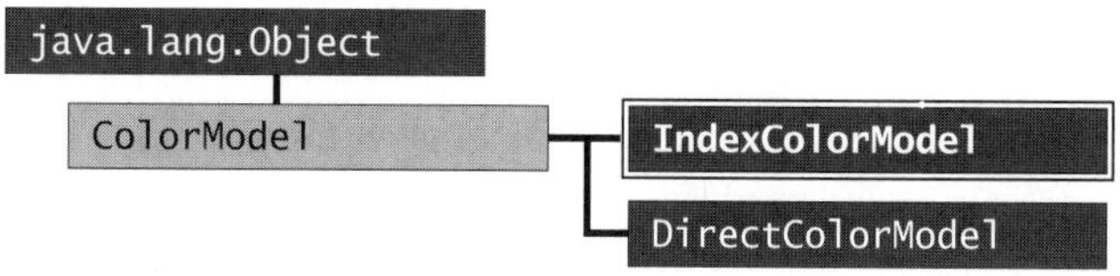

Syntax

```
public class IndexColorModel extends ColorModel
```

Description

An *index color model* maintains a particular palette of colors. Pixel values using the index color model are simply indexes into the palette of colors (see Figure 163). The number of colors in the palette is called the *color map size*. For more information about color models, see the `ColorModel` class.

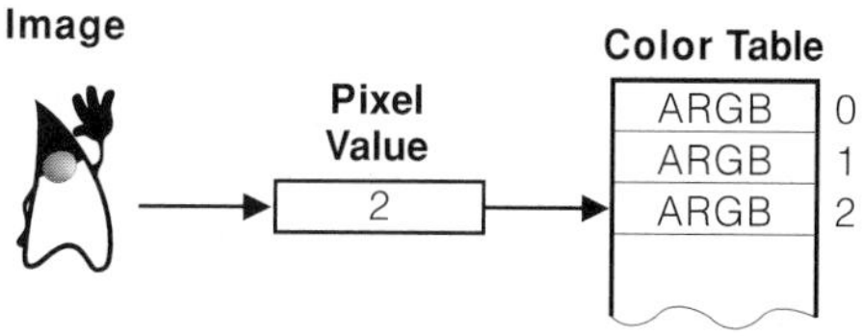

FIGURE 163 Index Color Model Pixel Values

MEMBER SUMMARY

Constructor	
`IndexColorModel()`	Constructs an `IndexColorModel` instance.
Color Map Size Method	
`getMapSize()`	Retrieves the color map size of this index color model.
Component Access Methods	
`getAlpha()`	Retrieves the alpha component of a pixel value.
`getAlphas()`	Retrieves the alpha component of all the colors in this index color model.
`getBlue()`	Retrieves the blue component of a pixel value.
`getBlues()`	Retrieves the blue component of all the colors in this index color model.
`getGreen()`	Retrieves the green component of a pixel value.
`getGreens()`	Retrieves the green component of all the colors in this index color model.
`getRed()`	Retrieves the red component of a pixel value.

Continued

A B C D E F G H I J K L M N O P Q R S T U V W X Y Z

MEMBER SUMMARY	
`getReds()`	Retrieves the red component of all the colors in this index color model.
`getRGB()`	Converts a pixel value to a pixel value in the default color model.
`getTransparentPixel()`	Retrieves the index of the transparent pixel in this index color model.

Example

This example implements an image filter that can adjust the alpha component of the colors in an index color model. See Figure 164. The program creates a frame with an image canvas and a text field. The image canvas displays the image after it passes through the image filter. In the text field, you can type in a number in the range `0.0` to `1.0`. The alpha components in an index color model are multiplied by this value, thereby increasing the transparency of the colors. A value of `0.0` forces all the colors to be transparent.

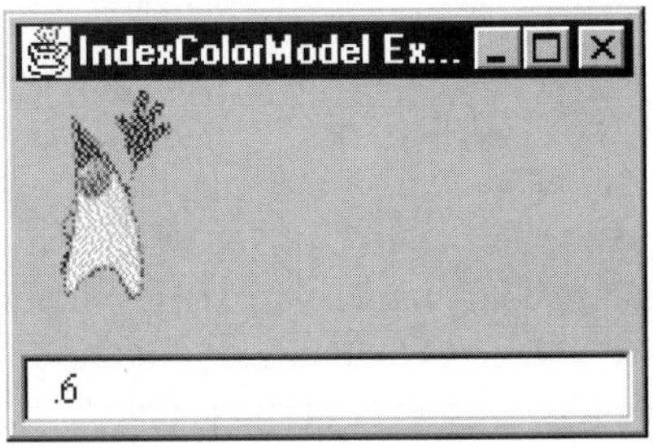

FIGURE 164 `IndexColorModel`

The `setColorModel()` method checks to see if the color model is an index color model. If it is, a copy of the color model is made combining the old colors with the new alpha value. The new color model is forwarded to the image consumer. The `setPixels()` method substitutes the new color model and then forwards the pixels to the image consumer. (For brevity's sake, the `setPixels()` method does not properly handle the case whereby the color model is not the same as the one supplied to `setColorModel()`.)

```
import java.awt.*;
import java.awt.image.*;
import java.net.*;
import java.util.*;
class Main extends Frame {
    TextField textField = new TextField();
    ImageCanvas icv;

    Main(String filename) {
        super("IndexColorModel Example");
        try {
            // Retrieve the image.
            URL url = new URL("file:///"
               + System.getProperty("user.dir")
               + "/" + filename);
```

```
            Image urlImage = getToolkit().getImage(url);

            add("Center", icv = new ImageCanvas(urlImage));
            add("South", textField);
        } catch (Exception e) {
            e.printStackTrace();
        }
        resize(50, 100);
        show();
    }

    public boolean action(Event evt, Object arg) {
        if (evt.target == textField) {
            icv.setAlphaFactor(Double.valueOf(
                textField.getText()).doubleValue());
            return true;
        }
        return false;
    }

    static public void main(String[] args) {
        if (args.length == 1) {
            new Main(args[0]);
        } else {
            System.err.println("usage: java Main <image file>");
        }
    }
}

class ImageCanvas extends Canvas {
    Image newImage;
    Image image;
    AlphaFilter imgf = new AlphaFilter();

    ImageCanvas(Image image) {
        this.image = image;
        processImage();
    }

    void setAlphaFactor(double afactor) {
        imgf.setAlphaFactor(afactor);
        processImage();
    }

    public void paint(Graphics g) {
        g.drawImage(newImage, 0, 0, this);
    }

    void processImage() {
        ImageProducer ip = image.getSource();

        ip = new FilteredImageSource(ip, imgf);
```

```
            newImage = getToolkit().createImage(ip);
            repaint();
        }
    }

    class AlphaFilter extends ImageFilter {
        double afactor;
        ColorModel transColorModel;

        void setAlphaFactor(double afactor) {
            this.afactor = afactor;
        }

        public void setColorModel(ColorModel model) {
            if (model instanceof IndexColorModel) {
                IndexColorModel icm = (IndexColorModel)model;
                byte[] reds = new byte[icm.getMapSize()];
                byte[] greens = new byte[icm.getMapSize()];
                byte[] blues = new byte[icm.getMapSize()];
                byte[] alphas = new byte[icm.getMapSize()];
                byte[] cmap = new byte[icm.getMapSize() * 4];

                icm.getReds(reds);
                icm.getGreens(greens);
                icm.getBlues(blues);
                icm.getAlphas(alphas);

                int j = 0;
                for (int i=0; i<icm.getMapSize(); i++) {
                    cmap[j++] = reds[i];
                    cmap[j++] = greens[i];
                    cmap[j++] = blues[i];
                    cmap[j++] = (byte)((alphas[i]&0xff)*afactor);
                }
                transColorModel = new IndexColorModel(icm.getPixelSize(),
                    icm.getMapSize(), cmap, 0, true,
                        icm.getTransparentPixel());
            } else {
                transColorModel = model;
            }
            consumer.setColorModel(transColorModel);
        }

        public void setPixels(int x, int y, int w, int h,
              ColorModel model, byte pixels[], int off, int scansize) {
            consumer.setPixels(x, y, w, h, transColorModel,
                pixels, off, scansize);
        }

        public void setPixels(int x, int y, int w, int h,
              ColorModel model, int pixels[], int off, int scansize) {
            consumer.setPixels(x, y, w, h, transColorModel, pixels,
                off, scansize);
        }
    }
```

getAlpha()

PURPOSE	Retrieves the alpha component of a pixel value.
SYNTAX	`final public int getAlpha(int pixelValue)`
DESCRIPTION	This method retrieves the alpha component of the pixel value `pixelValue`. The return value must be in the range `0-255` where `0` means completely transparent and `255` means completely opaque.
PARAMETERS	
`pixelValue`	The pixel value specifying a color in the color model.
RETURNS	The alpha transparency component in the range `0-255`.
EXAMPLE	See the class example.

getAlphas()

PURPOSE	Retrieves the alpha component of all the colors in this index color model.
SYNTAX	`final public void getAlphas(byte[] a)`
DESCRIPTION	This method retrieves the alpha component of all the colors in this index color model and places the values in `a`. The number of values placed in `a` is determined by the color map size (see `getMapSize()`). `a` can be larger than the color map size; the unused array elements are not modified.
PARAMETERS	
`a`	A non-`null` array that is at least as large as the color map size.
SEE ALSO	`getMapSize()`.
EXAMPLE	See the class example.

getBlue()

PURPOSE	Retrieves the blue component of a pixel value.
SYNTAX	`final public int getBlue(int pixelValue)`
DESCRIPTION	This method retrieves the blue component of the pixel value `pixelValue`. The return value must be in the range `0-255`, where `0` means no blue and `255` means maximum blue.

A B C D E F G H I J K L M N O P Q R S T U V W X Y Z

PARAMETERS

`pixelValue` The pixel value specifying a color in the color model.

RETURNS The blue color component in the range `0-255`.

EXAMPLE See the class example.

getBlues()

PURPOSE Retrieves the blue component of all the colors in this index color model.

SYNTAX `final public void getBlues(byte[] b)`

DESCRIPTION This method retrieves the blue color component of all the colors in this index color model and places the values in `b`. The number of values placed in `b` is determined by the color map size (see `getMapSize()`). `b` can be larger than the color map size; the unused array elements are not modified.

PARAMETERS

`b` A non-`null` array that is at least as large as the color map size.

SEE ALSO `getMapSize()`.

EXAMPLE See the class example.

getGreen()

PURPOSE Retrieves the green component of a pixel value.

SYNTAX `final public int getGreen(int pixelValue)`

DESCRIPTION This method retrieves the green component of the pixel value `pixelValue`. The return value must be in the range `0-255`, where `0` means no green and `255` means maximum green.

PARAMETERS

`pixelValue` The pixel value specifying a color in the color model.

RETURNS The green color component in the range `0-255`.

EXAMPLE See the class example.

getGreens()

PURPOSE Retrieves the green component of all the colors in this index color model.

SYNTAX `final public void getGreens(byte[] g)`

DESCRIPTION This method retrieves the green color component of all the colors in this index color model and places the values in `g`. The number of values placed in `g` is determined by the color map size (see `getMapSize()`). `g` can be larger than the color map size; the unused array elements are not modified.

PARAMETERS

`g` A non-`null` array that is at least as large as the color map size.

SEE ALSO `getMapSize()`.

EXAMPLE See the class example.

getMapSize()

PURPOSE Retrieves the color map size of this index color model.

SYNTAX `final public int getMapSize()`

RETURNS The color map size.

EXAMPLE See the class example.

getRed()

PURPOSE Retrieves the red component of a pixel value.

SYNTAX `final public int getRed(int pixelValue)`

DESCRIPTION This method retrieves the red component of the pixel value `pixelValue`. The return value must be in the range `0-255`, where `0` means no red and `255` means maximum red.

PARAMETERS

`pixelValue` The pixel value specifying a color in the color model.

RETURNS The red color component in the range from `0-255`.

EXAMPLE See the class example.

getReds()

PURPOSE Retrieves the red component of all the colors in this index color model.

SYNTAX `final public void getReds(byte[] r)`

DESCRIPTION This method retrieves the red color component of all the colors in this index color model and places the values in `r`. The number of values placed in `r` is determined by the color map size (see `getMapSize()`). `r` can be larger than the color map size; the unused array elements are not modified.

PARAMETERS

`r` A non-`null` array that is at least as large as the color map size.

SEE ALSO `getMapSize()`.

EXAMPLE See the class example.

getRGB()

PURPOSE Converts a pixel value to a pixel value in the default color model.

SYNTAX `final public int getRGB(int pixelValue)`

DESCRIPTION The pixel value `pixelValue` is converted to an equivalent pixel value that must be interpreted using the default color model. The color of the new pixel value might not be identical to the color of `pixelValue`; there may be some loss of color information.

PARAMETERS

`pixelValue` The pixel value specifying a color in the index color model.

RETURNS A pixel value that specifies a color in the default color model.

OVERRIDES `ColorModel.getRGB()`.

SEE ALSO `ColorModel.getRGBdefault()`.

EXAMPLE See the `ColorModel` class example.

getTransparentPixel()

PURPOSE Retrieves the index of the transparent pixel in this index color model.

SYNTAX `final public int getTransparentPixel()`

RETURNS The index of the transparent pixel. A return value of -1 indicates that there is no transparent pixel in the color model.

EXAMPLE See the class example.

IndexColorModel()

PURPOSE Constructs an `IndexColorModel` instance.

SYNTAX

```
public IndexColorModel(int nbits, int size, byte[] reds, byte[]
   greens, byte[] blues)
public IndexColorModel(int nbits, int size, byte[] reds, byte[]
   greens, byte[] blues, int trans)
public IndexColorModel(int nbits, int size, byte[] reds, byte[]
   greens, byte[] blues, byte[] alphas)
public IndexColorModel(int nbits, int size, byte[] cmap, int
   start, boolean hasAlpha)
public IndexColorModel(int nbits, int size, byte[] cmap, int
   start, boolean hasAlpha, int trans)
```

DESCRIPTION The forms of this constructor construct an `IndexColorModel` from a list of `size` colors. `nbits` specifies the number of bits needed to represent `size` colors. The number of colors can be smaller than the maximum value that `nbits` bits can represent.

The list of colors can be specified in one of two ways: as four arrays or as a single array. In the case of four array, `reds` contains all the reds, `greens` contains all the greens, `blues` contains all the blues, and `alphas` contains all the alpha transparency values. The arrays must have at least `size` elements. `reds[i]`, `greens[i]`, `blues[i]`, and `alphas[i]` would hold the components for the `i`th color.

If `alphas` is not specified, then all the colors, except for the transparent color, are considered opaque (i.e., the value `255`).

If `trans` is specified, it specifies which color should be treated as transparent, regardless of its alpha value. If `trans` is not specified or is `-1`, none of the colors will be treated as transparent.

In the case of specifying the colors with a single array `cmap`, the colors are encoded so that `cmap[i*4+start]` contains the red component for color `i`, `cmap[i*4+1+start]` contains the green component for color `i`, `cmap[i*4+2+start]` contains the blue component for color `i`, and cmap[i*4+3+start] contains the alpha component for color i. However, if hasAlpha is false, cmap is packed as follows:

- cmap[i*3+start] contains the red component for color i.
- cmap[i*3+1+start] contains the green component for color i.
- cmap[i*3+2+start] contains the blue component for color i.

PARAMETERS

alphas	The non-null array containing the alpha component of all the colors.
blues	The non-null array containing the blue component of all the colors.
cmap	The non-null array of packed color components.
greens	The non-null array containing the green component of all the colors.
hasAlpha	If true, cmap contains alpha values; otherwise cmap does not contain alpha values.
nbits	The number of bits required to hold all the components of a color.
reds	The non-null array containing the red component of all the colors.
size	The color map size.
start	The starting offset of the first color component in cmap.
trans	The index of the fully transparent color.

EXAMPLE See the class example.

java.lang
IndexOutOfBoundsException

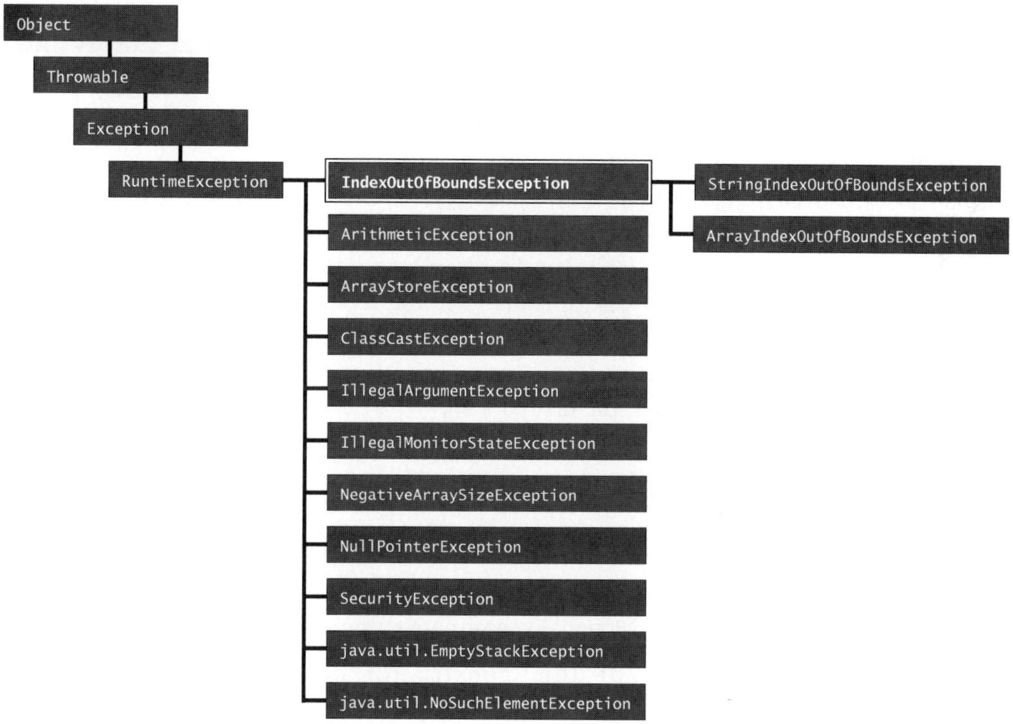

Syntax

`public class IndexOutOfBoundsException extends RuntimeException`

Description

`IndexOutOfBoundsException` is the superclass of exceptions thrown when the program attempts to use an index that is outside the bounds of the object that it is accessing. If the object is a `String`, a `StringIndexOutOfBoundsException` is thrown. If the object is an array, an `ArrayIndexOutOfBoundsException` is thrown.

`IndexOutOfBoundsException` should not be caught or declared in the `throws` clause of a method.

MEMBER SUMMARY	
Constructor	
`IndexOutOfBoundsException()`	Constructs a `IndexOutOfBoundsException` instance.

See Also

`ArrayIndexOutOfBoundsException`, `RuntimeException`, `StringIndexOutOfBoundsException`.

Example

See examples of subclasses.

IndexOutOfBoundsException()

PURPOSE Constructs an `IndexOutOfBoundsException` instance.

SYNTAX
```
public IndexOutOfBoundsException()
public IndexOutOfBoundsException(String msg)
```

DESCRIPTION The two forms of this constructor create a new instance of `IndexOutOfBoundsException`. An optional string `msg` can be supplied that describes this particular instance of the exception.

PARAMETERS

`msg` A string that gives details about this exception.

java.net
InetAddress

java.lang.Object — InetAddress

Syntax

```
public final class InetAddress
```

Description

The Internet is organized into smaller networks called *subnets*. There are different *classes* of subnets: A, B, and C. The Internet is made up of Class A and B subnets, which in turn contain hosts and Class C subnets. Machines and other objects in the Internet can belong to a subnet of any of these classes. Each subnet is allocated a range of addresses. Class A and B networks have a larger number of addresses to allocate than do Class C networks. The address is an *IP address*, a 32-bit number (actually four 8-bit numbers) used by the Internet Protocol (IP), the lower level protocol on which protocols like UDP and TCP are built. The four 8-bit numbers of an IP address provide a hierarchical space in which to allocate subnet and host addresses. IP addresses are often written in a dotted-string notation, with each 8-bit number separated by a dot. An example of an IP address in dotted-string notation is `129.143.15.32`.

The `InetAddress` class is used to represent an object on the Internet that has an address. An instance of an `InetAddress` consists of a host name and its corresponding IP address.

Host Name Resolution

Host name-to-Internet address resolution is accomplished through the use of a combination of local machine configuration information and network naming services such as the Internet Domain Name System (DNS) and Network Information Service (NIS). The particular naming service(s) being used is platform-dependent. The `InetAddress` class provides methods to resolve host names to their Internet addresses.

MEMBER SUMMARY

Host Name Resolution Methods

`getAllByName()`	Retrieves all of a host's addresses.
`getByName()`	Retrieves the address for a host.
`getLocalHost()`	Retrieves the address of the local host.

Continued

A B C D E F G H I J K L M N O P Q R S T U V W X Y Z

MEMBER SUMMARY	
Field Access Methods	
`getAddress()`	Retrieves the IP address in network byte order from this address.
`getHostAddress()`	Retrieves the dotted-string form of the IP address.
`getHostName()`	Retrieves the host name stored with this `InetAddress` object.
Object Override Methods	
`equals()`	Compares this object with another object for equality.
`hashCode()`	Computes the hash code for this object.
`toString()`	Generates the string representation of this object.

equals()

PURPOSE Compares this object with another for equality.

SYNTAX `public boolean equals(Object obj)`

DESCRIPTION This method compares this object with `obj` for equality. If `obj` is `null` or is not an object of class `InetAddress`, `equals()` returns `false`. If `obj` is of class `InetAddress` and has the same host name and IP address as this `InetAddress`, `equals()` returns `true`; otherwise it returns `false`. If a machine has multiple names, instances of `InetAddress` for different names of that same machine are not equal because they have different host names.

PARAMETERS

`obj` The object with which to compare. `obj` can be `null`.

RETURNS `true` if the objects are the same; `false` otherwise.

OVERRIDES `Object.equals()`.

SEE ALSO `hashCode()`, `Hashtable`.

EXAMPLE This example defines a method `localHostP()` that returns `true` if the specified hostname has the same `InetAddress` as the local host.

```
public static boolean localHostP(String hostname) {
    try {
        InetAddress target = InetAddress.getByName(hostname);
        return (target.equals(InetAddress.getLocalHost()));
    } catch (UnknownHostException e) {
        return (false);
    }
}
```

getAddress()

PURPOSE Retrieves the IP address in network byte order.

SYNTAX `public byte[] getAddress()`

DESCRIPTION This method returns the IP address associated with this `InetAddress` object. The IP address is returned in a byte array in network byte order (i.e., highest-order IP number first, lowest-order IP number last). A 32-bit IP address has an array with 4 bytes. For example, the address `129.144.50.23` would be returned in a 4-cell byte array with contents {`129, 144, 50, 23`}.

RETURNS A byte array with the IP address in network byte order.

EXAMPLE

```
try {
    byte[] addr = InetAddress.getLocalHost().getAddress();
    System.out.println("My address: " +
        (addr[0]&0xff) + "." + (addr[1]&0xff) + "." +
        (addr[2]&0xff) + "." + (addr[3]&0xff));
    System.out.println("Same thing, but easier: " +
        InetAddress.getLocalHost().getHostAddress());
} catch (UnknownHostException e) {
    e.printStackTrace();
}
```

getAllByName()

PURPOSE Retrieves all Internet addresses for a host.

SYNTAX `public static synchronized InetAddress[] getAllByName(String host) throws UnknownHostException`

DESCRIPTION This method retrieves all the Internet addresses for the machine with name `host`. The ordering of the addresses in the array returned is not significant. Host names that have been looked up previously are cached locally.

PARAMETERS

`host` The host name to resolve. If `host` is `null`, this means the local machine.

RETURNS An array of `InetAddress` objects.

EXCEPTIONS

`UnknownHostException`

If `host` could not be resolved.

getByName()

SEE ALSO getByName().

EXAMPLE

```
try {
    InetAddress[] alladdrs = InetAddress.getAllByName(target);
    for (int i = 0; i < alladdrs.length; i++)
        System.out.println(target + "[" + i + "] = " + alladdrs[i]);
} catch (UnknownHostException e) {
    System.err.println("Host not found: " + e);
}
```

getByName()

PURPOSE Retrieves the Internet address for a host.

SYNTAX `public static synchronized InetAddress getByName(String host) throws UnknownHostException`

DESCRIPTION This method retrieves the Internet address for the machine with name `host`. If the host has multiple addresses, only one is returned. Host names that have been looked up previously are cached. If `host` is `null`, the loopback address of this host is returned.

PARAMETERS

`host` The host name to resolve. If `host` is `null`, this means the local machine.

EXCEPTIONS

`UnknownHostException`
If `host` could not be resolved.

SEE ALSO `getAllByName()`.

EXAMPLE See `getHostName()`.

getHostAddress()

PURPOSE Retrieves the dotted-string form of the IP Address.

SYNTAX `public String getHostAddress()`

RETURNS The host name of this `InetAddress` object; `null` if this `InetAddress` is that of the local machine.

SEE ALSO `getByName()`, `getHostName()`.

EXAMPLE See `getAddress()`.

A B C D E F G H I J K L M N O P Q R S T U V W X Y Z

getHostName()

PURPOSE Retrieves the host name of this `InetAddress` object.

SYNTAX `public String getHostName()`

RETURNS The host name of this `InetAddress` object; `null` if this `InetAddress` is that of the local machine. If the host name cannot be determined, the dotted-string form of its IP address is returned.

SEE ALSO `getByName()`, `getHostAddress()`.

EXAMPLE

```
try {
    InetAddress somehost = InetAddress.getByName(target);
    String somehostName = somehost.getHostName();
    if (target.equals(somehostName))
        System.out.println("same name");
    else
        System.out.println("target is different from host name");
} catch (UnknownHostException e) {
    System.err.println("Host not found: " + e);
}
```

getLocalHost()

PURPOSE Retrieves the `InetAddress` object for the local host.

SYNTAX
```
public static InetAddress getLocalHost() throws
    UnknownHostException
```

DESCRIPTION If the security manager allows the current thread to connect to the local host using its host name, this method returns an `InetAddress` for the local host with that host name. If the security manager disallows this connection, an `InetAddress` for the loopback local host (i.e., with IP address `127.0.0.1`) is returned.

RETURNS The Internet address of the local host.

EXCEPTIONS

`UnknownHostException`
If cannot resolve the host name of this machine to an address.

SEE ALSO `getByName()`, `getAllByName()`, `SecurityManager.checkConnect()`.

EXAMPLE See `getAddress()`.

hashCode()

PURPOSE Generates the hash code for this object.

SYNTAX `public int hashCode()`

DESCRIPTION This method returns the hash code of this `InetAddress` object. The hash code of an `InetAddress` object is computed using its IP address. Two objects that have the same IP address will have the same hash code. However, two objects' having the same hash code does not necessarily mean they have the same IP address.

RETURNS An `int` representing the hash code for this object.

OVERRIDES `Object.hashCode()`.

SEE ALSO `Hashtable`.

EXAMPLE

```
try {
    int[] hits = new int[1023];
    InetAddress addr = InetAddress.getByName(target);
    int hashval = addr.hashCode();           // generate hash code
    ++hits[Math.abs(hashval%hits.length)];  // count hits
} catch (UnknownHostException e) {
    System.err.println("Host not found: " + e);
}
```

toString()

PURPOSE Generates the string representation of this object.

SYNTAX `public String toString()`

DESCRIPTION The string representation of an `InetAddress` object consists of its host name and its IP address in dotted-string notation (e.g., `129.144.50.23`). The `toString()` method returns the string representation for this `InetAddress` object.

RETURNS The string representation of this `InetAddress` object.

OVERRIDES `Object.toString()`.

SEE ALSO `getAddress()`, `getHostAddress()`, `getHostName()`.

EXAMPLE

```
try {
    InetAddress myAddr = InetAddress.getLocalHost();
    System.out.println(myAddr.toString()); // hostname/a.b.c.d
} catch (UnknownHostException e) {
    System.err.println("Host not found: " + e);
}
```

java.io

InputStream

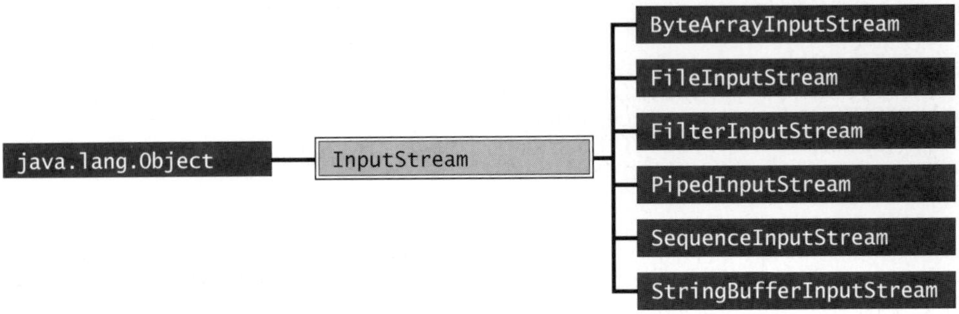

Syntax

```
public abstract class InputStream
```

Description

The `InputStream` class is the superclass of all input streams. It provides basic input methods for reading data from an input stream. Subclasses of `InputStream` override some or all of these basic methods for implementing their particular type of input stream. Figure 165 shows that you can either read directly from a subclass of `InputStream` or read from an input stream through filters.

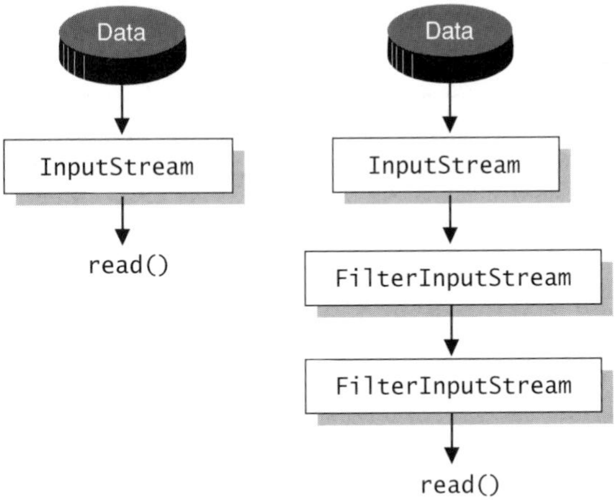

FIGURE 165 **`InputStream`**

Current Read Position and Mark/Reset

Each input stream has a current read position. As read operations occur, this current read position is incremented to reflect that the bytes have been read. In addition to conducting read operations, you also can skip bytes in the input stream. This is similar to reads except skipping a byte increments only the current read position; it does not return the byte skipped.

You can mark the current read position (using `mark()`) so that you can return to it (using `reset()`). This allows you to re-read previously read bytes. Mark/reset is useful for implementing parsers. You can mark the current read position and then read ahead in the stream to determine what action to take next. After making that determination, you then can reset the read position to that marked and pass the stream onto the appropriate processor.

MEMBER SUMMARY

Input Methods	
`available()`	Determines the number of bytes that can be read without blocking.
`read()`	Reads bytes from this input stream.
`skip()`	Skips bytes from this input stream.
Mark/Reset Methods	
`mark()`	Marks the current read position in the input stream.
`markSupported()`	Determines whether this input stream supports mark/reset.
`reset()`	Resets the current read position to be the last marked position.
Method for Closing Stream	
`close()`	Closes the input stream.

See Also

`OutputStream`, `BufferedInputStream`, `ByteArrayInputStream`, `DataInputStream`, `FileInputStream`, `FilterInputStream`, `IOException`, `LineNumberInputStream`, `PipedInputStream`, `PushbackInputStream`, `RandomAccessFile`, `SequenceInputStream`, `StringBufferInputStream`.

Example

This example counts the number bytes, words, and lines read from an input stream.

```
import java.io.InputStream;
import java.io.IOException;
import java.io.FileInputStream;

class Main {
    public static void wordCount(InputStream in) {
        int bytecount = 0;
        int wordcount = 0;
        int linecount = 0;
        try {
            int c;
            boolean newspace = true;
            while ((c = in.read()) > -1) {
                ++bytecount;
                if (c == '\n' || c == '\r')
                    ++linecount;
                if (Character.isSpace((char)c)) {
```

A B C D E F G H I J K L M N O P Q R S T U V W X Y Z

```
                    if (newspace) {
                        ++wordcount;
                        newspace = false;
                    }
                } else {
                    newspace = true;
                }
            }
            in.close();
        } catch (IOException e) {
            e.printStackTrace();
        }
        System.out.println(linecount + " " + wordcount + "
            " + bytecount);
    }
    public static void main(String[] args) {
        if (args.length == 1) {
            try {
                wordCount(new FileInputStream(args[0]));
            } catch (IOException e) {
                e.printStackTrace();
            }
        } else {
            System.err.println("Usage: java Main <file>");
            System.exit(-1);
        }
    }
}
```

available()

PURPOSE Determines the number of bytes that can be read without blocking.

SYNTAX `public int available() throws IOException`

DESCRIPTION This method returns the number of bytes that can be read without blocking. The default implementation of this method simply returns `0`.

RETURNS The number bytes that can be read without blocking.

EXCEPTIONS

`IOException` If an IO error occurred.

EXAMPLE See `mark()`.

close()

PURPOSE Closes this input stream.

SYNTAX `public void close() throws IOException`

DESCRIPTION This method closes this input stream. The default implementation does not do anything. Subclasses of `InputStream` should override this method to release any resources (especially system resources) used by this input stream, such as file descriptors and sockets.

EXCEPTIONS

`IOException` If an IO error occurred.

EXAMPLE See the class example.

mark()

PURPOSE Marks the current read position in the input stream.

SYNTAX `public synchronized void mark(int readlimit)`

DESCRIPTION This method marks the current position in the input stream so that a subsequent call to `reset()` will reposition the read position of the stream to this marked position. This marked position becomes invalid if you read more than `readlimit` number of bytes beyond this marked position. The default implementation of `mark()` does not do anything.

PARAMETERS

`readlimit` The number of bytes that can be read before this mark is invalidated.

SEE ALSO `markSupported()`, `reset()`.

EXAMPLE This is a slightly modified version of `URLConnect.guessContentTypeFromStream()`. It demonstrates the use of the `mark()/reset()` methods in probing the input stream to determine the content type and then resetting it so that the appropriate parser can complete the processing of the stream.

```
static protected String guessContentType(InputStream is)
    throws IOException {
    if (is.markSupported() && is.available() >= 6) {
        is.mark(6);
        int c1 = is.read();
        int c2 = is.read();
        int c3 = is.read();
        int c4 = is.read();
        int c5 = is.read();
        int c6 = is.read();
        is.reset();
        if (c1 == 'G' && c2 == 'I' && c3 == 'F' && c4 == '8')
            return "image/gif";
        if (c1 == '#' && c2 == 'd' && c3 == 'e' && c4 == 'f')
```

```
                return "image/x-bitmap";
            if (c1 == '!' && c2 == ' ' && c3 == 'X' &&
                c4 == 'P' && c5 == 'M' && c6 == '2')
                return "image/x-pixmap";
            if (c1 == '<')
                if (c2 == '!' || (c6 == '>'
                && (c2 == 'h' && (c3 == 't' && c4 == 'm' && c5 == 'l' ||
                                  c3 == 'e' && c4 == 'a' && c5 == 'd')
                    || c2 == 'b' && c3 == 'o' && c4 == 'd' && c5 == 'y')))
                return "text/html";
        }
        return null;
    }
```

markSupported()

PURPOSE Determines whether this input stream supports mark/reset.

SYNTAX `public boolean markSupported()`

DESCRIPTION This method returns `true` if this input stream supports mark/reset; `false` otherwise. The default implementation returns `false` (i.e., mark/reset is not supported).

RETURNS `true` if this input stream supports mark/reset; `false` otherwise.

SEE ALSO `mark()`, `reset()`.

EXAMPLE See `mark()`.

read()

PURPOSE Reads bytes from this input stream.

SYNTAX
```
abstract public int read() throws IOException
public int read(byte[] buffer) throws IOException
public int read(byte[] buffer, int offset, int count) throws
    IOException
```

DESCRIPTION The three forms of this method read bytes from this input stream. The first form is an abstract method whose implementation is supplied by the subclasses of `InputStream`. The other two forms are implemented using this first form and so usually should be overridden to be more efficient than performing reads a byte at a time. The second form reads `buffer.length` number of bytes from this input stream and stores those bytes into `buffer`. The third form reads `count` number of bytes from this input stream and stores those bytes into `buffer` starting at index `offset`.

PARAMETERS

`buffer`	The byte array in which the bytes read will be stored.
`count`	The number of bytes to read.
`offset`	The index in `buffer` at which to start storing the bytes read.

RETURNS The first form returns the byte read; the second and third forms return the actual number of bytes read. All forms return `-1` if end-of-file is reached before any bytes are read.

EXCEPTIONS

`IOException` If an IO error occurred.

SEE ALSO `mark()`, `reset()`, `skip()`.

EXAMPLE See the class example and `mark()`.

reset()

PURPOSE Resets the current read position to the last marked position.

SYNTAX `public synchronized void reset() throws IOException`

DESCRIPTION This method resets the current read position of this input stream to the last marked position. Subsequent invocations of `read()`/`skip()` will begin getting input from this marked position. The default implementation of `reset()` simply throws `IOException`.

EXCEPTIONS

`IOException` If the stream has not been marked or if the mark has been invalidated.

SEE ALSO `mark()`, `markSupported()`.

EXAMPLE See `mark()`.

skip()

PURPOSE Skips bytes from this input stream.

SYNTAX `public long skip(long count) throws IOException`

DESCRIPTION This method skips `count` number of bytes from this input stream. Skipped bytes will not be returned by subsequent `read()` calls (unless the read position has been changed using `reset()`). The default implementation of `skip()`

simply reads `count` number of bytes into a temporary buffer. This process is not efficient because a buffer must be allocated to store the bytes and the bytes need to be copied from this input stream to the buffer. This method should be overridden by subclasses of `InputStream`.

PARAMETERS

`count` The number of bytes to skip.

RETURNS The actual number of bytes skipped.

EXCEPTIONS

`IOException` If an IO error occurred.

EXAMPLE This example prints every other byte in the input stream.

```
static protected void skippy(InputStream in)
{
    try {
        int c;
        while ((c = in.read()) > -1) {
            System.out.print((char)c);
            if (in.skip(1) == 0)
                break;
        }
    } catch (IOException e) {
        e.printStackTrace();
    }
}
```

java.awt

Insets

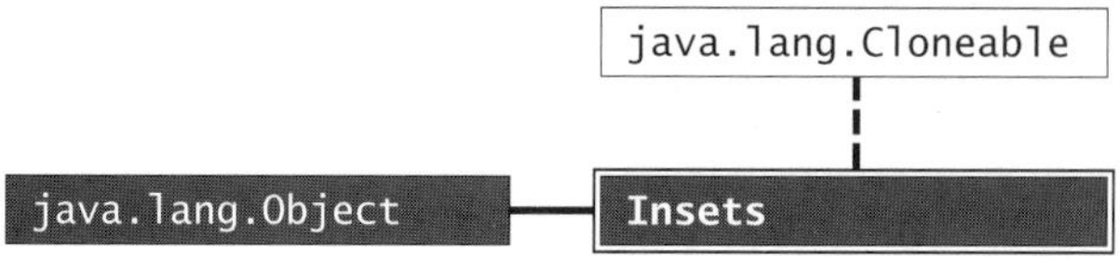

Syntax

`public class Insets implements Cloneable`

Description

An inset has four inset values, each defining the amount to adjust the sides of a rectangle. The four values are left, right, top, and bottom. The left value is added to the left edge of a rectangle to yield a new location for the edge. The other values and other edges are handled similarly.

Insets are typically used by layout managers in calculating the component positions. For example, a container returns an inset, which is applied to the container's bounds to yield its paintable area.

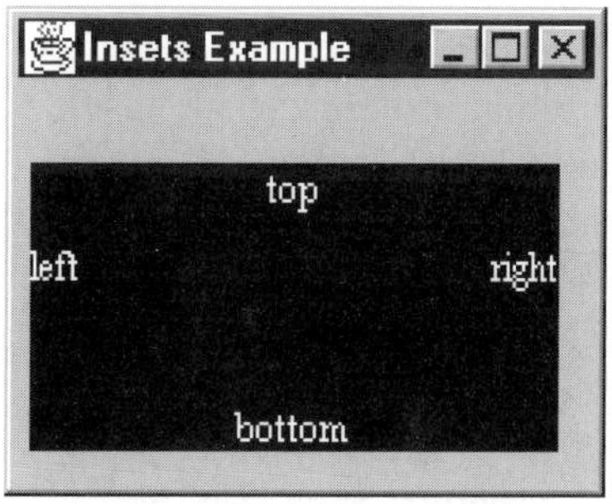

FIGURE 166 The Four Insets

In general, when returning an insets instance in a method call, either return a copy, if you need to retain the instance, or discard the instance after returning it. If you have an insets instance passed in a method call and wish to continue using the instance, note whether the method will retain the instance or copy the values.

MEMBER SUMMARY	
Constructor	
`Insets()`	Constructs a new `Insets` instance.
Fields	
`bottom`	Contains the inset's bottom value.
`left`	Contains the inset's left value.
`right`	Contains the inset's right value.
`top`	Contains the inset's top value.

Continued

Summary

MEMBER SUMMARY

General Methods

`clone()`	Creates a copy of the inset.
`toString()`	Generates the string representation of this inset.

Example

This example creates a frame that displays a black rectangle inside the frame's paintable area. See Figure 166. The size and position of the rectangle depends on the values of an insets object. The values of the object can be increased by pressing the l (left), r (right), t (top), and/or b (bottom) keys. If Shift is held down while pressing one of the keys, the affected inset is decreased. Each edge of the rectangle is labeled with a string that names the inset at that edge.

There are actually two insets involved in this example: `I` and `F`. `I` determines the size and position of the rectangle inside the container. However, since a frame is a container with an inset `F` (see `Container.insets()`), the frame's inset also needs to be taken into account. In this case, `F` is used to determine the size of the frame's paintable area. Once this is done, `I` is then applied to `F`, thereby yielding the area in which the rectangle is painted. This calculation would not be necessary if the rectangle were painted inside an "inset-less" container, such as a panel.

```
import java.awt.*;
class Main extends Frame {
    Insets insets = new Insets(0, 0, 0, 0);

    Main() {
        super("Insets Example");
        resize(150, 150);
        show();
    }

    public void paint(Graphics g) {
        int w = size().width - insets().right-insets().left;
        int h = size().height - insets().bottom-insets().top;
        FontMetrics fm = g.getFontMetrics();

        g.fillRect(insets.left, insets.top,
            w - insets.right - insets.left,
            h - insets.bottom - insets.top);
        g.setColor(Color.white);
        // top
        g.drawString("top", insets.left
              + (w-insets.left-insets.right-fm.stringWidth("top"))/2,
            insets.top+fm.getAscent());
        // left
```

```
    g.drawString("left", insets.left,
            insets.top
            + (h-insets.top-insets.bottom-fm.getHeight())/2);
    // bottom
    g.drawString("bottom", insets.left
            + (w-insets.left-insets.right-fm.stringWidth
                ("bottom"))/2,
        h-insets.bottom-fm.getDescent());
    // right
    g.drawString("right", w-insets.right-fm.stringWidth("right"),
            insets.top
            + (h-insets.top-insets.bottom-fm.getHeight())/2);
}

public boolean keyDown(Event evt, int key) {
    key = Character.toLowerCase((char)key);
    switch (key) {
        case 't':
            if (evt.shiftDown()) {
                if (insets.top > 0) {
                    insets.top--;
                }
            } else {
                insets.top++;
            }
            repaint();
            return true;
        case 'b':
            if (evt.shiftDown()) {
                if (insets.bottom > 0) {
                    insets.bottom--;
                }
            } else {
                insets.bottom++;
            }
            repaint();
            return true;
        case 'l':
            if (evt.shiftDown()) {
                if (insets.left > 0) {
                    insets.left--;
                }
            } else {
                insets.left++;
            }
            repaint();
            return true;
        case 'r':
            if (evt.shiftDown()) {
                if (insets.right > 0) {
                    insets.right--;
```

```
                    }
                } else {
                    insets.right++;
                }
                repaint();
                return true;
            }
            return false;
        }

        public static void main(String[] args) {
            new Main();
        }
    }
```

bottom

PURPOSE Contains the inset's bottom value.

SYNTAX `public int bottom`

EXAMPLE See the class example.

clone()

PURPOSE Creates a copy of the inset.

SYNTAX `public Object clone()`

DESCRIPTION Creates an insets instance with the same values as this inset.

RETURNS A non-`null` copy of the inset.

OVERRIDES `Object.clone()`.

EXAMPLE See `Object.clone()`.

Insets()

PURPOSE Constructs a new `Insets` instance.

SYNTAX `public Insets(int top, int left, int bottom, int right)`

DESCRIPTION This constructor creates a new `Insets` instance with the specified insets.

PARAMETERS

`bottom` The bottom inset.

`left` The left inset.

`right` The right inset.

`top` The top inset.

EXAMPLE See the class example.

left

PURPOSE Contains the inset's left value.

SYNTAX `public int left`

EXAMPLE See the class example.

right

PURPOSE Contains the inset's right value.

SYNTAX `public int right`

EXAMPLE See the class example.

top

PURPOSE Contains the inset's top value.

SYNTAX `public int top`

EXAMPLE See the class example.

toString()

PURPOSE Generates the string representation of this inset.

SYNTAX `public String toString()`

toString()

DESCRIPTION This method generates the string representation of this inset, which consists of the inset's values. This method is typically used for debugging.

RETURNS A non-`null` string representing the inset state.

OVERRIDES `Object.toString()`.

EXAMPLE See `Object.toString()`.

java.lang

InstantiationError

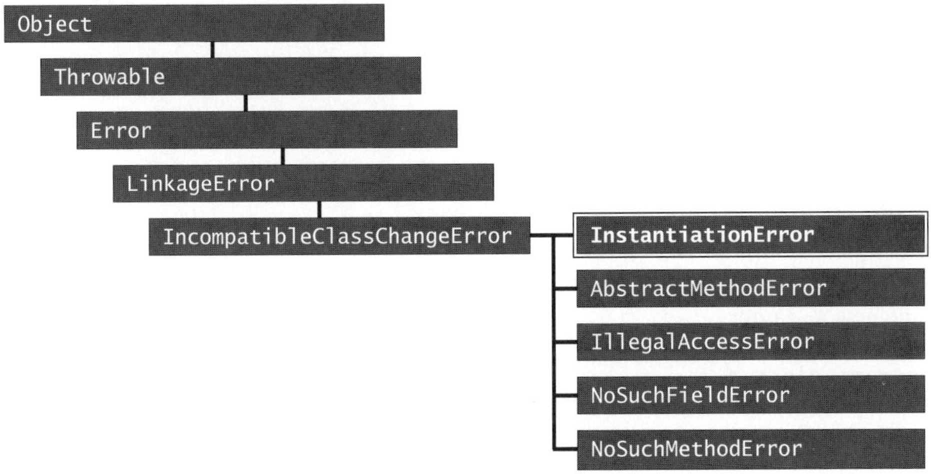

Syntax

```
public class InstantiationError extends IncompatibleClassChangeError
```

Description

`InstantiationError` is a runtime linkage error that is raised when the program attempts to instantiate an abstract class or an interface. Normally, when you compile a program that attempts to invoke an abstract method, you get a compilation error pinpointing the problem so that a linkage error at runtime will not occur. However, the problem could be introduced when classes used by the program become inconsistent, for example, if you were to make an incompatible change and then recompile only some of the classes.

`InstantiationError` and `InstantiationException` both report the same error, namely, that the class being instantiated is either an abstract class or an interface. They differ in that `InstantiationError` is thrown by the Java virtual machine when it detects this error when executing the program. In contrast `InstantiationException` is thrown when the program explicitly attempts to instantiate an object and fails (e.g., via `Class.newInstance()`). `InstantiationError` should not be caught or declared in the `throws` clause of a method.

MEMBER SUMMARY	
Constructor	
`InstantiationError()`	Constructs an `InstantiationError` instance.

B C D E F G H I J K L M N O P Q R S T U V W X Y Z

See Also

`IncompatibleClassChangeError`, `InstantiationException`, `LinkageError`.

Example

In this example, class `A` and `A.method1()` used to have the following definition:

```
class A {
    public void method1(int i) {
        System.out.println(i);
    }
}
```

Running `Main` after changing `A` as follows would throw `InstantiationError` because the Java runtime cannot instantiate an abstract method.

In the new `A.java`:

```
abstract class A {
    abstract public void method1(int i);
}
```

In `Main.java`:

```
class Main {
    public static void main(String[] args) {
        System.out.println("InstantiationError example");
        A a = new A();
        a.method1(0);
    }
}
```

InstantiationError()

PURPOSE	Constructs an `InstantiationError` instance.
SYNTAX	`public InstantiationError()` `public InstantiationError(String msg)`
DESCRIPTION	The two forms of this constructor create a new instance of `InstantiationError`. An optional string `msg` can be supplied that describes this particular instance of the error.
PARAMETERS	
`msg`	A string that gives details about this error.

InstantiationException

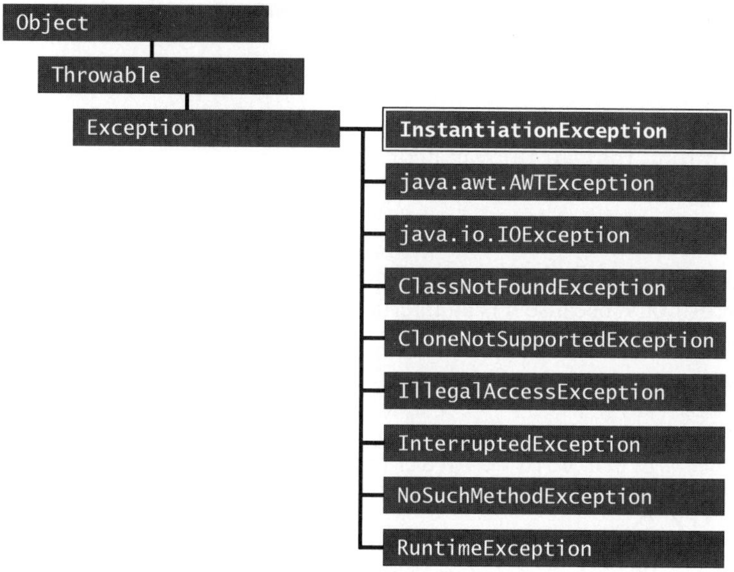

Syntax

```
public class InstantiationException extends Exception
```

Description

`InstantiationException` is an exception that is thrown when the program attempts to instantiate an abstract class or an interface.

Normally, when you compile a program's classes, you get a compilation error pinpointing the problem. However, in addition to a program's using classes that it has been compiled with, a program can also use other classes and invoke methods on them through the use of class loaders and the methods in the `Class` class. Access to these classes and their methods are checked by the Java runtime just like any other classes, and hence an `InstantiationException` can arise if one of these classes is an abstract class or an interface.

A method that throws `InstantionException` must declare it or any of its superclasses in its `throws` clause.

A B C D E F G H I J K L M N O P Q R S T U V W X Y Z

A B C D E F G H I J K L M N O P Q R S T U V W X Y Z

MEMBER SUMMARY

Constructor

`InstantiationException()`	Constructs an `InstantiationException` instance.

See Also

`Class`, `Exception`, `InstantiationError`.

Example

In the following example, `InstantiationException` is thrown when `main()` attempts to do a `newInstance()` on `A` because `A` is an interface.

In `Main.java`:

```
class Main {
    public static void main(String[] args) {
        System.out.println("InstantiationException example");
        try {
            Class c = Class.forName("A");
            Object a = c.newInstance();
        } catch (InstantiationException e) {
            e.printStackTrace();
        } catch (IllegalAccessException e) {
            e.printStackTrace();
        } catch (ClassNotFoundException e) {
            e.printStackTrace();
        }
    }
}
```

In `A.java`:

```
interface A {
    void methodX();
}
```

InstantiationException()

PURPOSE Constructs an `InstantiationException` instance.

SYNTAX

```
public InstantiationException()
public InstantiationException(String msg)
```

DESCRIPTION The two forms of this constructor create a new instance of `InstantiationException`. An optional string `msg` can be supplied that describes this particular instance of the exception.

PARAMETERS

`msg` A string that gives details about this exception.

java.lang

Integer

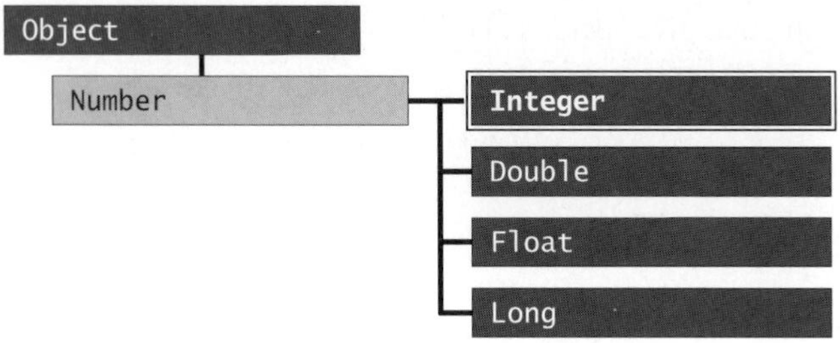

Syntax

```
public final class Integer extends Number
```

Description

An `int` in Java is a 32-bit signed integer. The `Integer` class provides an object wrapper for `int` data values. This allows integers to be passed to methods in Java class libraries that accept Java objects as parameters. In addition, the `Integer` class provides methods that convert to and from `int` values and performs other operations on `int` values.

`Integer` instances cannot be used in arithmetic expressions in place of `int`. For example, the following is not allowed:

```
Integer i1 = new Integer(50);
Integer i2 = new Integer(100);
Integer i3 = i1 * i2;        // Illegal
```

To perform arithmetic operations using an `Integer` instance, you first must use access methods defined in the `Integer` class to obtain its numeric value, as follows:

```
int i3 = i1.intValue() * i2.intValue();
long lnum = i1.longValue() + i2.intValue();
```

MEMBER SUMMARY	
Constructor	
`Integer()`	Constructs an `Integer` object using an `int` value or a string.
Constant Fields	
`MAX_VALUE`	The maximum value an `int` can have.

MEMBER SUMMARY	
`MIN_VALUE`	The minimum value an `int` can have.
Number Methods	
`doubleValue()`	Retrieves the value of this object as a `double`.
`floatValue()`	Retrieves the value of this object as a `float`.
`intValue()`	Retrieves the value of this object as an `int`.
`longValue()`	Retrieves the value of this object as a `long`.
Methods for Conversion from Strings	
`getInteger()`	Creates a new `Integer` object using the value of a system property.
`parseInt()`	Parses a string representation of an integer into an `int`.
`toBinaryString()`	Generates the string representation of an `int` as an unsigned binary number.
`toHexString()`	Generates the string representation of an `int` as an unsigned hexadecimal number.
`toOctalString()`	Generates the string representation of an `int` as an unsigned octal number.
`toString()`	Generates the string representation for an `int` or `Integer` object.
`valueOf()`	Creates a new `Integer` object using its string representation.
Comparison and Hash Code Methods	
`equals()`	Compares this object with another object for equality.
`hashCode()`	Computes the hash code for this object.

See Also

`Double`, `Float`, `Long`, `Number`.

doubleValue()

PURPOSE Retrieves the value of this object as a `double`.

SYNTAX `public double doubleValue()`

DESCRIPTION This method returns the value of this object as a `double` by casting its `int` value to a `double` value.

RETURNS The value of this object as a `double`.

EXAMPLE

```
Integer iobj = new Integer(855);

double dval = iobj.doubleValue(); // get double value
float fval = iobj.floatValue();   // get float value
int ival = iobj.intValue();       // get int value
long lval = iobj.longValue();     // get long value
```

equals()

PURPOSE Compares this object with another object for equality.

SYNTAX `public boolean equals(Object obj)`

DESCRIPTION This method compares the `int` value of this object with that of `obj`. It returns `true` if the two values are equal; it returns `false` otherwise. It also returns `false` if `obj` is `null` or is not an `Integer` object.

PARAMETERS

`obj` The object against which this object will be compared.

RETURNS `true` if `obj` has the same `int` value as this object; `false` otherwise.

OVERRIDES `Object.equals()`.

EXAMPLE

```
Integer i1 = new Integer(192);
Integer i2 = new Integer(192);

// Check whether the value of two Integers are equal
if (i1.equals(i2))
    System.out.println("equal");
```

floatValue()

PURPOSE Retrieves the value of this object as a `float`.

SYNTAX `public float floatValue()`

DESCRIPTION This method returns the value of this object as a `float` by casting its `int` value to a `float` value.

RETURNS The value of this object as a `float`.

EXAMPLE See `doubleValue()`.

getInteger()

PURPOSE
Creates an `Integer` object using the value of a system property.

SYNTAX

```
public static Integer getInteger(String prop)
public static Integer getInteger(String prop, int defval)
public static Integer getInteger(String prop, Integer defobj)
```

DESCRIPTION
The three forms of this method find the system property identified by `prop` and return the property's value as an `Integer` object. The property's value must be an integer (in radix 10), a hexadecimal number, or an octal number. A hexadecimal number is prefixed with either `0x` or `#`. An octal number has a leading zero (`0`). If `prop` does not exist or if `prop`'s value is not a number in the format described above, the first form of this method returns `null`. The second form returns an `Integer` object constructed using `defval` in the same situation, while the third form returns `defobj`.

PARAMETERS

`defobj` The default `Integer` object to return if `prop` does not exist.

`defval` The default `int` value to use for the resulting `Integer` object if `prop` does not exist.

`prop` The name of the property.

RETURNS
An `Integer` object containing the value of `prop` if it contains a valid integer. Otherwise it returns `null` if the first form of the method is used or a default `Integer` object as determined by `defval` or `defobj`.

SEE ALSO
`Properties`, `System.getProperty()`.

EXAMPLE

```
// set up properties
Properties props = System.getProperties();
props.put("os.maxusers", "250");        // radix 10 int property
props.put("os.maxfiles", "0xff");       // radix 16 int property
props.put("os.maxprinters", "#2a");     // radix 16 int property
props.put("os.maxfd", "065");           // radix 8 int property
props.put("os.version", "2.5.1");       // non-int property
System.setProperties(props);

// use the three forms of getInteger()
Integer maxusers = Integer.getInteger("os.maxusers");
Integer maxfiles = Integer.getInteger("os.maxfiles", 1024);
Integer maxprs = Integer.getInteger("os.maxprinters",
                                    new Integer(1));
Integer maxfd = Integer.getInteger("os.maxfd", 256);
Integer vers = Integer.getInteger("os.version", 1);
if (maxusers != null)
    System.out.println("max users: " + maxusers);
System.out.println("max files: " + maxfiles);
```

A B C D E F G H I J K L M N O P Q R S T U V W X Y Z

```
System.out.println("max printers: " + maxprs);
System.out.println("max fds: " + maxfd);
System.out.println("os version: " + vers);
```

hashCode()

PURPOSE Computes the hash code for this object.

SYNTAX `public int hashCode()`

DESCRIPTION This method returns the hash code for this `Integer` object. The hash code of an `Integer` object is calculated using its `int` value. Two `Integers` with the same `int` value will have the same hash code and vice versa.

RETURNS An `int` representing the hash code.

OVERRIDES `Object.hashCode()`.

SEE ALSO `Hashtable`.

EXAMPLE

```
int[] hits = new int[1023];
Integer inum = new Integer(3290);
int hashval = inum.hashCode();              // generate hash code
++hits[Math.abs(hashval%hits.length)];   // count hits
```

Integer()

PURPOSE Constructs an `Integer` object using an `int` value or a string.

SYNTAX
```
public Integer(int value)
public Integer(String str) throws NumberFormatException
```

DESCRIPTION The first form of this constructor constructs an `Integer` object using `value`. The second form parses `str`, the string representation of an integer in radix 10, and uses its numeric value to create the `Integer` object.

PARAMETERS

`str` The string representation of an integer in radix 10.
`value` The numeric value to use as the object's value.

EXCEPTIONS

`NumberFormatException`
If `str` cannot be parsed into an `int`.

SEE ALSO parseInt(), valueOf().

EXAMPLE

```
Integer width = new Integer(240);        // using integer
try {
    Integer height = new Integer("360"); // using string
    int area = width.intValue() * height.intValue();
} catch (NumberFormatException e) {
  ...
}
```

intValue()

PURPOSE Retrieves the value of this object as an `int`.

SYNTAX `public int intValue()`

RETURNS The value of this object as an `int`.

EXAMPLE See `doubleValue()`.

longValue()

PURPOSE Retrieves the value of this object as a `long`.

SYNTAX `public long longValue()`

DESCRIPTION This method returns the value of this object as a `long` by casting its `int` value into a `long`.

RETURNS The value of this object as a `long`.

EXAMPLE See `doubleValue()`.

MAX_VALUE

PURPOSE The maximum value an `int` can have.

SYNTAX `public static final int MAX_VALUE`

DESCRIPTION This constant represents the maximum value an `int` can have, which is `0x7fffffff`.

MIN_VALUE

EXAMPLE

```
// reset counter if maximum reached
int counter;
...
if (counter == Integer.MAX_VALUE)
    counter = 0;
else
    counter++;
```

MIN_VALUE

PURPOSE The minimum value an `int` can have.

SYNTAX `public static final int MIN_VALUE`

DESCRIPTION This constant represents the minimum value an `int` can have, which is `0x80000000`. This is a negative number.

EXAMPLE

```
// reset counter if minimum reached
int counter;
...
if (counter == Integer.MIN_VALUE)
    counter = 0;
else
    counter--;
```

parseInt()

PURPOSE Parses the string representation of an integer into an `int`.

SYNTAX

```
public static int parseInt(String str) throws
   NumberFormatException
public static int parseInt(String str, int radix) throws
   NumberFormatException
```

DESCRIPTION The two forms of this method parse the string `str` into an integer and return it as an `int`. If no radix is given, the radix used to parse `str` is 10. A negative integer has a leading minus (‘-’) character; a positive integer consists only of digits in the specified radix.

These methods are the inverse of `toString()`. `parseInt()` is similar to `valueOf()`, except `parseInt()` returns an `int`, while `valueOf()` returns an `Integer` object.

A B C D E F G H I J K L M N O P Q R S T U V W X Y Z

PARAMETERS

`radix` The radix to use when parsing `str`.

`str` The string containing the integer.

RETURNS An `int` containing the numeric value of the integer represented by `str`.

EXCEPTIONS

`NumberFormatException`

If `str` cannot be parsed into an integer of the specified radix.

SEE ALSO `Character.MAX_RADIX`, `Character.MIN_RADIX`, `toString()`, `valueOf()`.

EXAMPLE

```
try {
    int i = Integer.parseInt("25");
    int octnum = Integer.parseInt("065", 8);
} catch (NumberFormatException e) {
  ...
}
```

toBinaryString()

PURPOSE Generates the string representation of an `int` as an unsigned binary number.

SYNTAX `public static String toBinaryString(int inum)`

DESCRIPTION This method returns the string representation of `inum` as an unsigned binary number. This is not always equivalent to `toString(inum, 2)` because `toString()` always treats `inum` as a signed number.

PARAMETERS

`inum` The `int` for which to generate the string representation.

RETURNS The string representation of `inum` as an unsigned binary number.

SEE ALSO `parseInt()`, `toHexString()`, `toOctalString()`, `toString()`, `valueOf()`.

EXAMPLE This example shows the difference between using `toString()`, `toBinaryString()`, `toOctalString()` and `toHexString()` on a negative number. The output of this program is shown following the code.

```
class Main {
    public static void main(String[] args) {
        int inum = -279436;
        System.out.println(Integer.toString(inum, 10));
        System.out.println(Integer.toString(inum, 2));
        System.out.println(Integer.toString(inum, 8));
```

```
            System.out.println(Integer.toString(inum, 16));

            System.out.println(Integer.toString(inum));
            System.out.println(Integer.toBinaryString(inum));
            System.out.println(Integer.toOctalString(inum));
            System.out.println(Integer.toHexString(inum));
        }
    }
```

OUTPUT

```
    -279436
    -1000100001110001100
    -1041614
    -4438c
    -279436
    11111111111110111011110001110100
    37776736164
    fffbbc74
```

toHexString()

PURPOSE Generates the string representation of an `int` as an unsigned hexadecimal number.

SYNTAX `public static String toBinaryString(int inum)`

DESCRIPTION This method returns the string representation of `inum` as an unsigned hexadecimal number. The result is not always equivalent to `toString(inum, 16)` because `toString()` always treats `inum` as a signed number.

PARAMETERS

`inum` The `int` for which to generate the string representation.

RETURNS The string representation of `inum` as an unsigned hexadecimal number.

SEE ALSO `parseInt()`, `toBinaryString()`, `toOctalString()`, `toString()`, `valueOf()`.

EXAMPLE See `toBinaryString()`.

toOctalString()

PURPOSE Generates the string representation of an `int` as an unsigned octal number.

SYNTAX `public static String toHexString(int inum)`

DESCRIPTION This method returns the string representation of `inum` as an unsigned octal number. This is not always equivalent to `toString(inum, 8)` because `toString()` always treats `inum` as a signed number.

PARAMETERS

`inum` The `int` for which to generate the string representation.

RETURNS The string representation of `inum` as an unsigned octal number.

SEE ALSO `parseInt()`, `toBinaryString()`, `toHexString()`, `toString()`, `valueOf()`.

EXAMPLE See `toBinaryString()`.

toString()

PURPOSE Generates the string representation of an `int` or `Integer` object.

SYNTAX

```
public String toString()
public static String toString(int inum)
public static String toString(int inum, int radix)
```

DESCRIPTION The three forms of this method are used to generate a string representation of an `int`. The first form returns the string representation of the `int` value of this `Integer` object. The second form returns the string representation of `inum` in radix 10. The third form returns the string representation of `inum` in base `radix`.

PARAMETERS

`inum` The integer for which to generate the string representation.

`radix` The radix to use when generating the string representation. If `radix` is not in the inclusive range of `Character.MAX_RADIX` and `Character.MIN_RADIX`, it defaults to 10.

RETURNS The string representation of this `Integer` object, or `inum`.

OVERRIDES `Object.toString()`.

SEE ALSO `Character.MAX_RADIX`, `Character.MIN_RADIX`, `Integer.valueOf()`, `String.valueOf()`.

EXAMPLE Also see `toBinaryString()`.

```
Integer inum = new Integer(25);
String str = inum.toString();           // from Integer object
String str2 = Integer.toString(312);    // from radix 10 int
String str3 = Integer.toString(97, 8);  // from octal int
String pstr = “The three numbers are “ + str + “, “ + str2 + “ ,” +
        str3;
```

valueOf()

PURPOSE Creates an `Integer` object using its string representation.

SYNTAX
```
public static Integer valueOf(String str) throws
    NumberFormatException
public static Integer valueOf(String str, int radix) throws
    NumberFormatException
```

DESCRIPTION The two forms of this method parse the string `str` into an integer and return an `Integer` object constructed using the integer. If no radix is given, the radix used to parse `str` is 10. A negative integer has a leading minus (‘`-`’) character; a positive integer consists only of digits in the specified radix.

These methods are the inverse of `toString()`. `valueOf()` is similar to `parseInt()` except `valueOf()`, returns an `Integer` object, while `parseInt()` returns an `int`.

PARAMETERS

`radix` The radix to use when parsing `str`. `radix` must be inclusively between `Character.MAX_RADIX` and `Character.MIN_RADIX`.

`str` The string containing the integer.

EXCEPTIONS

`NumberFormatException`
If `str` cannot be parsed into an integer of the specified radix.

SEE ALSO `Character.MAX_RADIX`, `Character.MIN_RADIX`, `parseInt()`, `toString()`.

EXAMPLE
```
String str = "1243";
try {
    Integer i = Integer.valueOf(str);      // parse number in radix 10
    Integer i2 = Integer.valueOf(str, 16); // parse number in radix 16
     ...
} catch (NumberFormatException e) {
    System.err.println("Could not convert string to number " + str);
}
```

InternalError

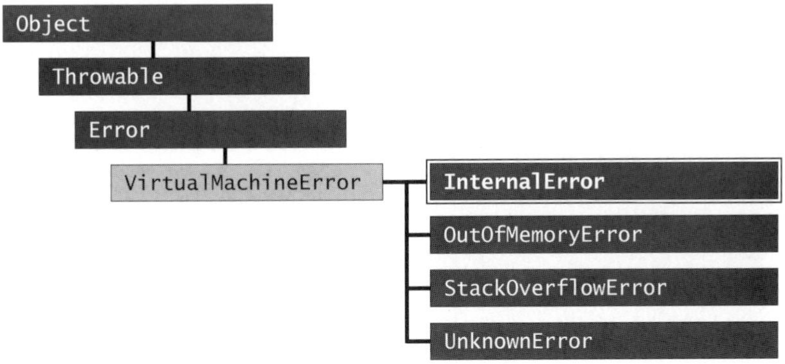

Syntax

```
public class InternalError extends VirtualMachineError
```

Description

`InternalError` is an error that is thrown when the Java virtual machine encounters an unrecoverable error that involves the virtual machine's internal logic (e.g. an unknown opcode).

`InternalError` should not be caught or declared in the `throws` clause of a method.

MEMBER SUMMARY	
Constructor	
`InternalError()`	Constructs an `InternalError` instance.

See Also

`Error`, `VirtualMachineError`.

InternalError()

PURPOSE Constructs an `InternalError` instance.

InternalError()

SYNTAX

```
public InternalError()
public InternalError(String msg)
```


DESCRIPTION The two forms of this constructor create a new instance of `InternalError`. An optional string `msg` can be supplied that describes this particular instance of the error.

PARAMETERS

`msg` A string that gives details about this error.

InterruptedException

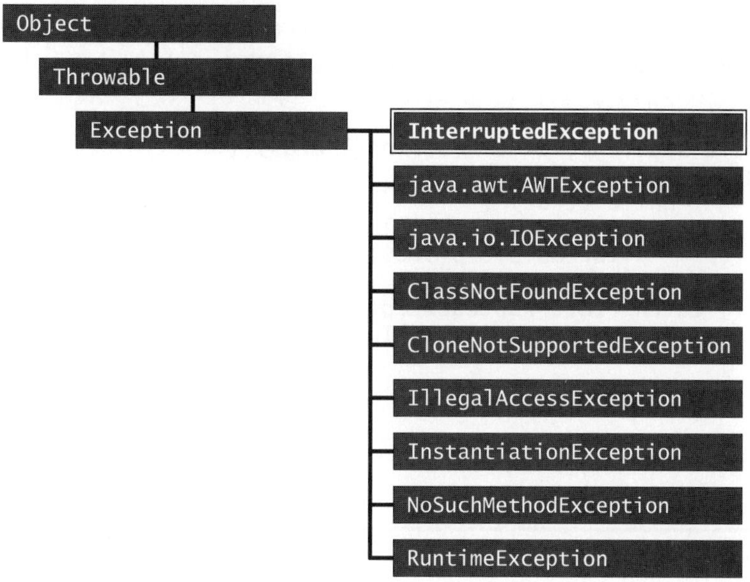

Syntax

```
public class InterruptedException extends Exception
```

Description

`InterruptedException` is thrown when a thread interrupts another thread. Methods that cause a thread to block (such as `Object.wait()` and `Thread.sleep()`) require the thread to have a `try/catch` clause for the `InterruptedException` so that it can deal with its being interrupted.

A method that throws `InterruptedException` must declare it or any of its superclasses in its `throws` clause.

MEMBER SUMMARY	
Constructor	
`InterruptedException()`	Constructs an `InterruptedException` instance.

A B C D E F G H I J K L M N O P Q R S T U V W X Y Z

See Also

`Exception`, `Object.notify()`, `Object.notifyAll()`, `Object.wait()`, `Thread`.

Example

This example loops, printing out the message "This is a test" every 5 seconds. It must use a `try/catch` clause to catch the `InterruptedException` that might be thrown by `sleep()`.

```
class Main {
    public static void main(String[] args) {
        try {
            while (true) {
                System.out.println("This is a test");
                Thread.sleep(5000);
            }
        } catch (InterruptedException e) {
            System.out.println("Interrupted!");
        }
    }
}
```

InterruptedException()

PURPOSE Constructs an `InterruptedException` instance.

SYNTAX
```
public InterruptedException()
public InterruptedException(String msg)
```

DESCRIPTION The two forms of this constructor create a new instance of `InterruptedException`. An optional string `msg` can be supplied that describes this particular instance of the exception.

PARAMETERS

`msg` A string that gives details about this exception.

java.io

InterruptedIOException

Syntax

```
public class InterruptedIOException extends IOException
```

Description

`InterruptedIOException` is an IO exception that is thrown when a program reading or writing to a stream receives an interrupt during its IO operation.

A method that throws `InterruptedIOException` must declare it or any of its superclasses in its `throws` clause.

MEMBER SUMMARY	
Constructor	
`InterruptedIOException()`	Constructs an `InterruptedIOException` instance.
Field	
`bytesTransferred`	The number of bytes transferred before interrupt.

A B C D E F G H I J K L M N O P Q R S T U V W X Y Z

A B C D E F G H I J K L M N O P Q R S T U V W X Y Z

See Also

IOException, InterruptedException, PipedInputStream, PrintStream.

Example

This is the implementation of PipedInputStream.receive() from the JDK. It throws an InterruptedIOException if it has been interrupted.

```
synchronized void receive(int b) throws IOException {
    writeSide = Thread.currentThread();
    while (in == out) {
        if ((readSide != null) && !readSide.isAlive()) {
            throw new IOException("Pipe broken");
        }
        /* full: kick any waiting readers */
        notifyAll();
        try {
            wait(1000);
        } catch (InterruptedException ex) {
            throw new java.io.InterruptedIOException();
        }
    }
    if (in < 0) {
        in = 0;
        out = 0;
    }
    buffer[in++] = (byte)(b & 0xFF);
    if (in >= buffer.length) {
        in = 0;
    }
}
```

bytesTransferred

PURPOSE	The number of bytes transferred before interrupt.
SYNTAX	`public int bytesTransferred`
DESCRIPTION	This field is typically set by the code that called the constructor. It is read by the code that catches InterruptedIOException. If not set, its default value is 0.

InterruptedIOException()

PURPOSE Constructs an `InterruptedIOException` instance.

SYNTAX
```
public InterruptedIOException()
public InterruptedIOException(String msg)
```

DESCRIPTION The two forms of this constructor create a new instance of `InterruptedIOException`. An optional string `msg` can be supplied that describes this particular instance of the exception.

PARAMETERS

`msg` A string that gives details about this exception.

java.io

IOException

Syntax

```
public class IOException extends Exception
```

Description

`IOException` and its subclasses are used to indicate that an exceptional condition has occurred with the input or output stream being operated on. A method that throws `IOException` must be declared it in its `throws` clause.

MEMBER SUMMARY	
Constructor	
`IOException()`	Constructs an `IOException` instance.

See Also

EOFException, FileNotFoundException, Exception, InputStream, OutputStream.

Example

See use of IOException in examples for EOFException and FileNotFoundException.

IOException()

PURPOSE Constructs an IOException instance.

SYNTAX
```
public IOException()
public IOException(String msg)
```

DESCRIPTION The two forms of this constructor create a new instance of IOException. An optional string msg can be supplied that describes this particular instance of the exception.

PARAMETERS

msg A string that gives details about this exception.

java.awt
Label

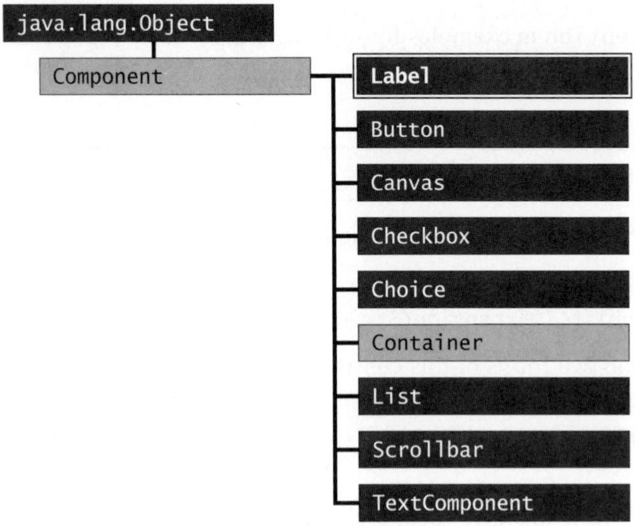

Syntax

```
public class Label extends Component
```

Description

A *label* is a component that displays a single line of text. The text can be modified by the program at any time but can never be modified by the user. A label is typically used in conjunction with other components that do not have labels, such as text fields and lists.

FIGURE 167 `Label`

Label Alignment

A label has an alignment mode that controls the placement of the label's text in relation to the label's bounds. The text is always vertically centered but can be horizontally aligned to the left, center, or right.

MEMBER SUMMARY	
Constructor	
`Label()`	Constructs a new `Label` instance.

MEMBER SUMMARY

Alignment Mode Constants

`CENTER`	The alignment mode specifying center alignment.
`LEFT`	The alignment mode specifying left alignment.
`RIGHT`	The alignment mode specifying right alignment.

Property Methods

`getAlignment()`	Retrieves the label's alignment.
`getText()`	Retrieves the label's text.
`setAlignment()`	Sets the label's alignment.
`setText()`	Sets the label's text

Peer Methods

`addNotify()`	Creates the label's peer.

Debugging Methods

`paramString()`	Generates a string representing the label's state.

Example

This example creates a label to serve as a status bar. The status bar displays mouse motion event information while the cursor is inside the frame's paintable area (see Figure 167).

```
import java.awt.*;
public class Main extends Frame {
    Label statusBar = new Label();

    Main() {
        super("Label Example");
        add("South", statusBar);
        resize(200, 200);
        show();
    }
    public boolean handleEvent(Event evt) {
        switch (evt.id) {
            case Event.MOUSE_MOVE:
            case Event.MOUSE_DRAG:
                String status = "("+evt.x+","+evt.y+") ";

                if (evt.controlDown()) status += "C";
                if (evt.shiftDown()) status += "S";
                if (evt.metaDown()) status += "M";
                statusBar.setText(status);
                return true;
        }
        return super.handleEvent(evt);
    }
```

B

C

D

```
        static public void main(String[] args) {
            new Main();
        }
    }
```

E

F

addNotify()

G

PURPOSE Creates the label's peer.

H

SYNTAX `public synchronized void addNotify()`

I

DESCRIPTION This method creates the label's peer if it does not yet exist. The peer is created by calling the `Toolkit.createLabel()` method. This method should never be called directly. It is normally called by the parent.

J

OVERRIDES `Component.addNotify()`.

K

SEE ALSO `Component`, `Toolkit`.

L

M

CENTER

N

PURPOSE The alignment mode specifying center alignment.

O

SYNTAX `public static final int CENTER`

P

DESCRIPTION In center-alignment mode, the text is displayed in the center of the label.

EXAMPLE See `setAlignment()`.

Q

R

getAlignment()

S

PURPOSE Retrieves the label's alignment.

T

SYNTAX `public int getAlignment()`

U

RETURNS The label's alignment. The return value is one of `LEFT`, `CENTER`, or `RIGHT`.

V

SEE ALSO `setAlignment()`.

EXAMPLE See `setAlignment()`.

W

X

Y

Z

A B C D E F G H I J K L M N O P Q R S T U V W X Y Z

getText()

PURPOSE Retrieves the label's text.

SYNTAX `public String getText()`

RETURNS A non-`null` string containing the label's text.

SEE ALSO `setText()`.

EXAMPLE See `setText()`.

Label()

PURPOSE Constructs a new `Label` instance.

SYNTAX
```
public Label()
public Label(String text)
public Label(String text, int alignment)
```

DESCRIPTION The three forms of this constructor create a new `Label` instance with the string text and `alignment` alignment. If `label` is `null` or not specified, it defaults to "". If `alignment` is not specified, it defaults to `LEFT`.

PARAMETERS

`alignment` The label's alignment. It must be one of `LEFT`, `CENTER`, or `RIGHT`.

`text` The string containing the label's text.

EXAMPLE See the class example.

LEFT

PURPOSE The alignment mode specifying left alignment.

SYNTAX `public static final int LEFT`

DESCRIPTION In left-alignment mode, the left edge of the text is pinned to the left edge of the label.

EXAMPLE See `setAlignment()`.

paramString()

PURPOSE Generates a string representing the label's state.

SYNTAX `protected String paramString()`

DESCRIPTION The returned string includes the label's alignment and text. A subclass of this class should override this method and return a concatenation of its state with the results of `super.paramString()`. This method is called by the `toString()` method and is typically used for debugging.

RETURNS A non-`null` string representing the label's state.

OVERRIDES `Component.paramString()`.

SEE ALSO `Object.toString()`.

EXAMPLE See `Component.paramString()`.

RIGHT

PURPOSE The alignment mode specifying right alignment.

SYNTAX `public static final int RIGHT`

DESCRIPTION In right-alignment mode, the right edge text is pinned to the right edge of the label.

EXAMPLE See `setAlignment()`.

setAlignment()

PURPOSE Sets the label's alignment.

SYNTAX `public void setAlignment(int alignment)`

DESCRIPTION This method sets the label's alignment to be `alignment`.

PARAMETERS

`alignment` The label's new alignment. It must be one of `LEFT`, `CENTER`, or `RIGHT`.

EXCEPTIONS

`IllegalArgumentException`

If alignment is not one of the values `LEFT`, `CENTER`, or `RIGHT`.

SEE ALSO `getAlignment()`.

EXAMPLE This example creates a label and a checkbox group. Use the checkbox group to change the label's alignment. See Figure 168.

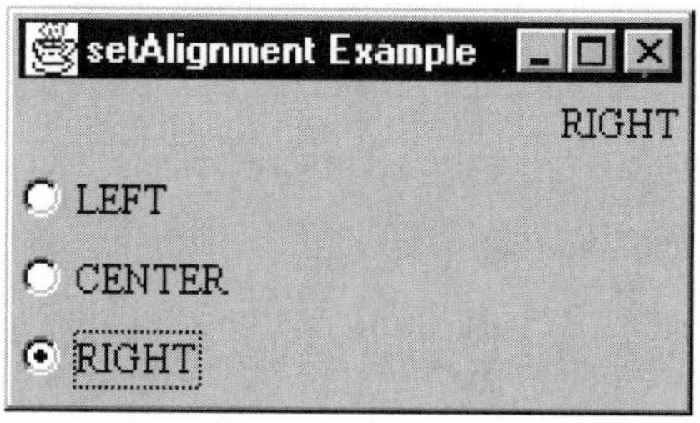

FIGURE 168 `Label.setAlignment()`

```
import java.awt.*;
class Main extends Frame {
    String[] alignLabels = {"LEFT", "CENTER", "RIGHT"};
    int[] alignValues = {Label.LEFT, Label.CENTER, Label.RIGHT};
    Label l = new Label("CENTER", Label.CENTER);

    Main() {
        super("setAlignment Example");
        CheckboxGroup cg = new CheckboxGroup();
        Panel p = new Panel();

        p.setLayout(new GridLayout(3, 0));
        for (int i=0; i<alignLabels.length; i++) {
            p.add(new Checkbox(alignLabels[i], cg,
                l.getAlignment() == alignValues[i]));
        }
        add("South", p);
        add("Center", l);
        pack();
        show();
    }

    public boolean action(Event evt, Object what) {
        if (evt.target instanceof Checkbox) {
            Checkbox cb = (Checkbox)evt.target;

            for (int i=0; i<alignLabels.length; i++) {
                if (alignLabels[i].equals(cb.getLabel())) {
                    l.setAlignment(alignValues[i]);
                    l.setText(alignLabels[i]);
                    return true;
                }
            }
        }
        return false;
    }

    static public void main(String[] args) {
        new Main();
    }
}
```

setText()

PURPOSE Sets the label's text.

SYNTAX `public void setText(String label)`

DESCRIPTION This method sets the label's text to be the string `label`. If `label` is `null`, it is treated like an empty string "".

Note that the minimum and preferred sizes of the label may change, so it may be necessary to resize the label. The example shows how to cause the label's parent to resize the label.

PARAMETERS

`label` The string specifying the label's new text. The value may be `null`.

SEE ALSO `getText()`.

EXAMPLE This example creates a label and a text field. Pressing Return in the text field causes the label's text to be set to the contents of the text field. When the text changes, so does its minimum size. This example also shows how to cause the label's parent to properly resize the label. See Figure 169.

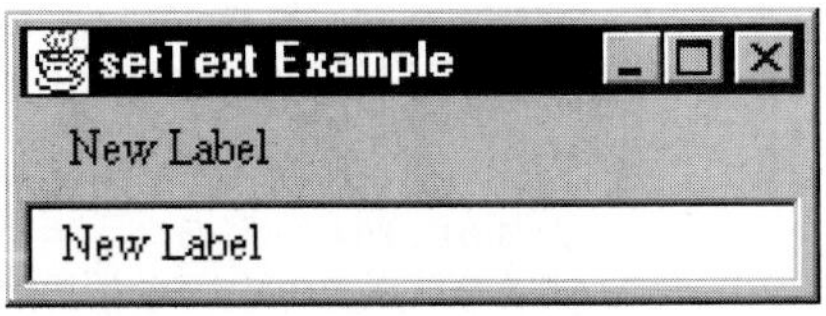

FIGURE 169 `Label.setText()`

```
import java.awt.*;
class Main extends Frame {
    Label l = new Label("Label", Label.LEFT);
    TextField tf = new TextField(40);

    Main() {
        super("setText Example");
        add("Center", new Canvas());
        add("West", l);
        add("South", tf);
        tf.setText(l.getText());     // init with current text
        pack();
        show();
    }

    public boolean action(Event evt, Object what) {
        if (evt.target == tf) {
            l.setText(tf.getText());

            // the size has changed so get parent to validate itself.
            invalidate();
            l.getParent().validate();
            return true;
        }
```

A B C D E F G H I J K L M N O P Q R S T U V W X Y Z

```
        return false;
    }

    static public void main(String[] args) {
        new Main();
    }
}
```

java.awt.peer
LabelPeer

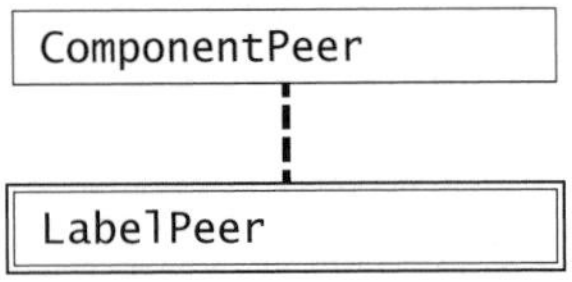

Syntax
`public interface LabelPeer extends ComponentPeer`

Description
The label component (see the `Label` class) in the Abstract Windowing Toolkit (AWT) uses the platform's native implementation of a label. So that the AWT label behaves the same on all platforms, the label is assigned a peer, whose task is to translate the behavior of the platform's native label to the behavior of the AWT label.

AWT programmers normally do not directly use peer classes and interfaces. Instead they deal with AWT components in the `java.awt` package. These in turn automatically manage their peers. Only someone who is porting the AWT to another platform should be concerned with the peer classes and interfaces. Consequently, most peer documentation refers to `java.awt` counterparts.

See `Component` and `Toolkit` for additional information about component peers.

MEMBER SUMMARY	
Peer Methods	
`setAlignment()`	Sets the label's alignment.
`setText()`	Sets the label's text.

See Also
`Component`, `Label`, `Toolkit`.

setAlignment()

PURPOSE Sets the label's alignment.

SYNTAX `void setAlignment(int alignment)`

PARAMETERS

`alignment` The label's new alignment.

SEE ALSO `Label.setAlignment()`.

setText()

PURPOSE Sets the label's text.

SYNTAX `void setText(String label)`

PARAMETERS

`label` The string specifying the label's new text. The value may be `null`.

SEE ALSO `Label.setText()`.

java.awt
LayoutManager

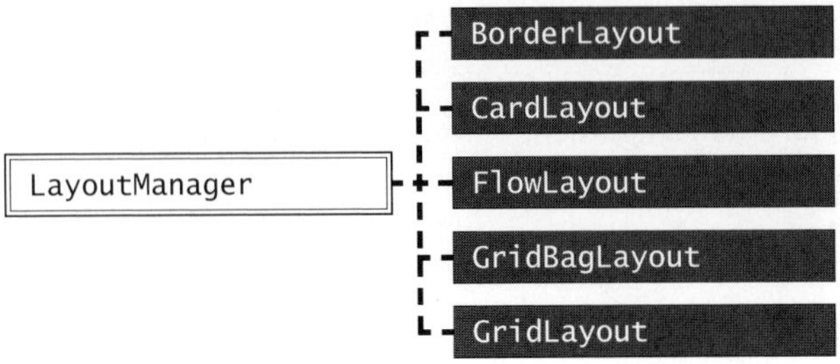

Syntax

`public interface LayoutManager`

Description

A layout manager is responsible for laying out components in a container. For example, the `FlowLayout` layout manager places the components in a left-to-right, top-down fashion. Figure 170 shows an example of a container with the `FlowLayout` layout manager.

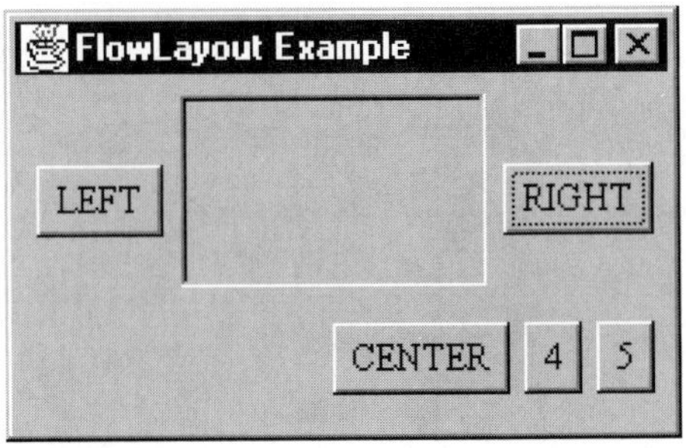

FIGURE 170 `FlowLayout`

Typically a newly created container has a default layout manager. For example, the default layout manager for the `Panel` container is `FlowLayout`. The layout manager for a container can be changed by calling `Container.setLayout()`, but deciding when it is safe to call this method is left to the layout manager. In general, any layout manager that maintains some state, such as the gridbag and border layout managers, can be safely set only when the container does not contain any components.

Container Validity

A container's layout manager is invoked only if the container is invalid. A container automatically becomes invalid if the container is resized or if a child component has been added, removed, or moved within the container. The system automatically calls the container's layout method if the user resizes the top-level window. However, if it is necessary to re-layout a container (perhaps because some layout parameter has changed), you must first call `Component.invalidate()` on the container, followed by `Component.validate()`.

Insets

When implementing the methods that return dimensions, you must always take into account the container's insets. That is, the components must be laid out within the area defined by the container's insets. See the `Container` class for a description of insets.

MEMBER SUMMARY	
Layout Manager Methods	
`addLayoutComponent()`	Adds a component to the layout.
`layoutContainer()`	Lays out the container in the specified panel.
`removeLayoutComponent()`	Removes the specified component from the layout.
Dimension Methods	
`minimumLayoutSize()`	Calculates the minimum size dimensions for the specified.
`preferredLayoutSize()`	Calculates the preferred size dimensions for the specified.

See Also

`BorderLayout`, `CardLayout`, `FlowLayout`, `GridBagLayout`, `GridLayout`.

Example

This example implements a layout manager that displays components in a horizontal or vertical list. See Figure 171. The name of the component specifies how the component should be stretched in the list. If the name is "*", the component will be stretched in both directions. If the name is "v", the component will be stretched only in the horizontal direction. If the name is "h", the component will be stretched only in the vertical direction. If the name is `null` or some other string, the component will not be stretched.

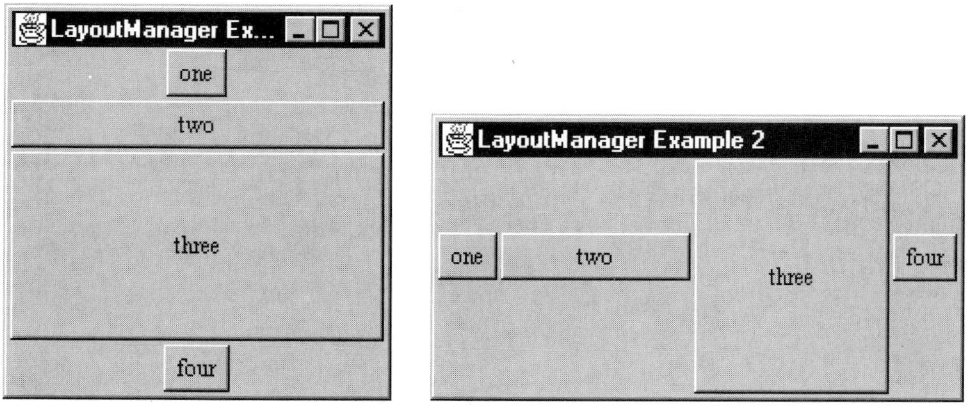

FIGURE 171 Horizontal and Vertical List Layouts

Example

```
import java.awt.*;
import java.util.*;
class Main extends Frame {
    Main(boolean vertical, String title) {
        super(title);
        setLayout(new FlexLayout(vertical, 2));
        add(new Button(“one”));
        add(“h”, new Button(“two”));
        add(“*”, new Button(“three”));
        add(new Button(“four”));
        resize(100, 200);
        show();
    }
    public static void main(String args[]) {
        new Main(true, “LayoutManager Example 1”);
        new Main(false, “LayoutManager Example 2”);
    }
}
class FlexLayout implements LayoutManager {
    int gap;
    boolean ver;
    Hashtable comps = new Hashtable();

    public FlexLayout(boolean v, int gap) {
        ver = v;
        this.gap = gap;
    }

    public void addLayoutComponent(String name, Component comp) {
        comps.put(comp, name);
    }

    public void removeLayoutComponent(Component comp) {
        comps.remove(comp);
    }

    public Dimension layoutSize(Container parent, boolean minimum) {
        Insets insets = parent.insets();
        int n = parent.countComponents();
        int w = 0, h = 0;

        for (int i=0; i<n; i++) {
            Component c = parent.getComponent(i);
            Dimension d = minimum ? c.minimumSize() :
                c.preferredSize();

            if (ver) {
                w = Math.max(w, d.width);
                h += d.height;
            } else {
                w += d.width;
                h = Math.max(h, d.height);
            }
        }
```

```
        if (n > 0) {
            if (ver) {
                h += (n-1)*gap;
            } else {
                w += (n-1)*gap;
            }
        }
        return new Dimension(insets.left + insets.right + w,
                             insets.top + insets.bottom + h);
    }

    public Dimension minimumLayoutSize(Container parent) {
        return layoutSize(parent, true);
    }

    public Dimension preferredLayoutSize(Container parent) {
        return layoutSize(parent, false);
    }

    public boolean isFlexible(Component c, boolean v) {
        String name = (String)comps.get(c);
        if (name == null) {
            return false;
        } else if (name.equals("*")) {
            return true;
        } else if (v) {
            return name.equals("v");
        }
        return name.equals("h");
    }

    public void layoutContainer(Container parent) {
        Insets insets = parent.insets();
        Dimension dim = layoutSize(parent, false);
        int n = parent.countComponents();
        int flexCnt = 0;
        int extra = 0;
        int add = 0;

        for (int i=0; i<n; i++) {
            if (isFlexible(parent.getComponent(i), ver)) {
                flexCnt++;
            }
        }
        if (flexCnt > 0) {
            if (ver) {
                extra = parent.size().height-dim.height;
            } else {
                extra = parent.size().width-dim.width;
            }
        }
        add = extra/flexCnt;

        if (ver) {
```

A
B
C
D
E
F
G
H
I
J
K
L
M
N
O
P
Q
R
S
T
U
V
W
X
Y
Z

B C D E F G H I J K L M N O P Q R S T U V W X Y Z

```
            int y = insets.top;
            for (int i=0; i<n; i++) {
                int x = insets.left;
                Component c = parent.getComponent(i);
                String name = (String)comps.get(c);
                Dimension d = c.preferredSize();

                if (isFlexible(c, ver)) {
                    d.height += add;
                    extra -= add;
                    if (extra < 0) {    // adjust for round off error
                        d.height += extra;
                    }
                }
                if (isFlexible(c, !ver)) {
                    d.width = parent.size().width - insets.left
                        - insets.right;
                } else {
                    x = (parent.size().width - d.width)/2;
                }
                c.reshape(x, y, d.width, d.height);
                y += d.height + gap;
            }
        } else {
            int x = insets.left;
            for (int i=0; i<n; i++) {
                int y = insets.top;
                Component c = parent.getComponent(i);
                String name = (String)comps.get(c);
                Dimension d = c.preferredSize();

                if (isFlexible(c, ver)) {
                    d.width += add;
                    extra -= add;
                    if (extra < 0) {    // adjust for round off error
                        d.width += extra;
                    }
                }
                if (isFlexible(c, !ver)) {
                    d.height = parent.size().height - insets.top
                        - insets.bottom;
                } else {
                    y = (parent.size().height - d.height)/2;
                }
                c.reshape(x, y, d.width, d.height);
                x += d.width + gap;
            }
        }
    }

    public String toString() {
        return getClass().getName() + "[ver=" + ver + ",gap=" + gap
            + "]";
    }
}
```

addLayoutComponent()

PURPOSE — Adds a component to the layout manager's list of components.

SYNTAX

```
void addLayoutComponent(String name, Component comp)
```

DESCRIPTION — When a component is added to a container along with an accompanying name (i.e., the `Container.add(String, Component)` method is called), the container not only adds the component to its list of components but also calls this method with the component and its name. The container does not call this method if the component is added without a name (`null` is a valid name). The container does not use the component name at all, nor does it remember the name, so this method must maintain the name-component association if necessary.

The name is, more accurately, layout information that the layout manager uses to place the component. The name does not have to be unique. Nor does it have to be non-`null` — it's up to the layout manager to decide what is a valid name. For example, in the `BorderLayout` layout manager, the name determines at which edge the component should be placed. Using the name "North" causes the component to be placed against the top edge of the container. `BorderLayout` expects the names of the components to be chosen from a fixed set of names and to be unique; the results are undefined if this rule is violated.

By the time this method is called, `comp` is already added to the container and a peer created if necessary.

Note that the `Container` class does not include an `add()` method in which both the name and a position can be specified. To work around this deficiency, you can first insert the component without an accompanying name and then call `addLayoutComponent()` directly to assign a name to the component.

PARAMETERS

`comp` — The non-`null` named component that has just been added to the container.

`name` — A possibly `null` string specifying the name of the component.

SEE ALSO — `Container.add()`.

EXAMPLE — See the class example.

layoutContainer()

PURPOSE — Lays out the components in a container.

SYNTAX

```
void layoutContainer(Container cont)
```

DESCRIPTION This method is called by the container's parent to lay out the components in `cont`. The size of `cont` can be retrieved by calling `cont.size()`, which will include the container's insets. The components should be laid out using `Component.reshape()` and placed inside the area defined by the insets. When retrieving the dimensions of a component, the component's preferred size should be used.

PARAMETERS

`cont` The non-`null` container using this layout instance.

EXAMPLE See the class example.

minimumLayoutSize()

PURPOSE Calculates the layout's minimum size dimensions.

SYNTAX `Dimension minimumLayoutSize(Container cont)`

DESCRIPTION This method calculates the minimum size dimensions for the container `cont`. The minimum sizes of the components are used in the calculations. The result includes the container's insets.

PARAMETERS

`cont` The non-`null` container using this layout instance.

RETURNS The non-`null` dimension containing the container's preferred size.

SEE ALSO `preferredLayoutSize()`.

EXAMPLE See the class example.

preferredLayoutSize()

PURPOSE Calculates the layout's preferred size dimensions.

SYNTAX `Dimension preferredLayoutSize(Container cont)`

DESCRIPTION This method calculates the preferred size dimensions for the container `cont`. The preferred sizes of the components are used in the calculations. The result includes the container's insets.

PARAMETERS

`cont` The non-`null` container using this layout instance.

RETURNS The non-`null` dimension containing the container's preferred size.

SEE ALSO `minimumLayoutSize()`.

EXAMPLE See the class example.

removeLayoutComponent()

PURPOSE Removes a component from the layout manager's list of components.

SYNTAX `void removeLayoutComponent(Component comp)`

DESCRIPTION This method is called by a container whenever a component is removed from the container, regardless of whether the component was named. At the time this method is called, `comp` is not yet removed from the container.

PARAMETERS

`comp` The non-`null` component about to be removed from the container.

EXAMPLE See the class example.

java.io
LineNumberInputStream

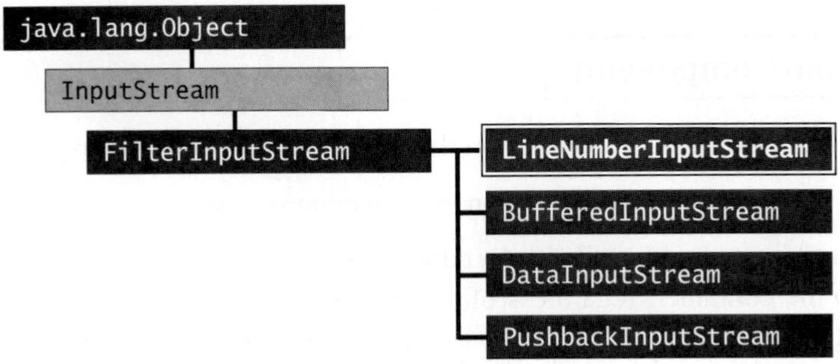

Syntax

`public class LineNumberInputStream extends FilterInputStream`

Description

A *line number input stream* is a filter input stream that counts the number of line terminators as data is read from the input stream that it is filtering. See Figure 172. A line terminator is one of

- a newline character (`'\n'`),
- a carriage return character (`'\r'`), or
- a carriage return character followed by a newline character (`'\r\n'`).

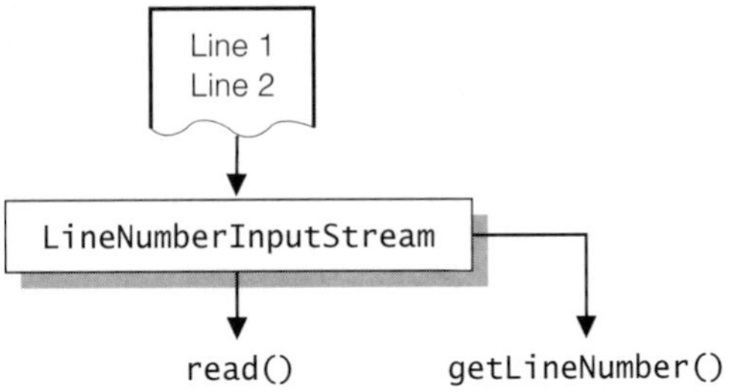

FIGURE 172 **`LineNumberInputStream`**

The line number of the stream starts at 1 and is incremented as each line terminator is encountered.

The `LineNumberInputStream` class is used to represent a line number input stream.

MEMBER SUMMARY

Constructor	
`LineNumberInputStream()`	Constructs a new line number input stream for an input stream.
Input Methods	
`available()`	Determines the number of bytes that can be read without blocking.

A B C D E F G H I J K L M N O P Q R S T U V W X Y Z

MEMBER SUMMARY	
`read()`	Reads bytes from this line number input stream.
`skip()`	Skips bytes from this line number input stream.
Mark/Reset Methods	
`mark()`	Marks the current read position in this line number input stream.
`reset()`	Repositions the read position to the last marked position.
Line Number Methods	
`getLineNumber()`	Retrieves the current line number.
`setLineNumber()`	Sets the current line number.

See Also

`FilterInputStream`, `InputStream`.

Example

This example echoes the input supplied to it and labels each line with its corresponding line number.

```
import java.io.*;

class Main {
    // reads input from 'in' and writes the bytes out to 'out'
    // with line numbers on the left
    public static void echo(InputStream i, OutputStream o) {
        try {
            LineNumberInputStream in = new LineNumberInputStream(i);
            PrintStream out = new PrintStream(o);
            int c, oldLineNumber = 0, newLineNumber = 0;
            boolean writePrefix = true;

            while((c = in.read()) > -1) {
                if (writePrefix) {
                    out.print(newLineNumber+1);
                    out.write('\t');
                }
                out.write(c);
                if (writePrefix =
                    ((newLineNumber = in.getLineNumber()) !=
                        oldLineNumber))
                    oldLineNumber = newLineNumber;
            }
            in.close();                    // close streams
            out.close();
        } catch (IOException e) {
            e.printStackTrace();
```

A B C D E F G H I J K L M N O P Q R S T U V W X Y Z

```
            }
        }
        public static void main(String[] args) {
            try {
                InputStream in;
                if (args.length == 0)
                    in = System.in;
                else
                    in = new FileInputStream(args[0]);
                echo(in, System.out);
            } catch (IOException e) {
                e.printStackTrace();
            }
        }
    }
```

available()

PURPOSE Determines the number of bytes that can be read without blocking.

SYNTAX `public int available() throws IOException`

DESCRIPTION The number of bytes that can be read without blocking is determined by counting the number of bytes that can be read from the underlying stream that this stream filters.

RETURNS The number of bytes that can be read without blocking.

EXCEPTIONS
`IOException` If an IO error occurred.

OVERRIDES `FilterInputStream.available()`.

EXAMPLE This example counts the number of bytes and the number of lines in a file and prints the first 100 bytes of that file. It uses `available()` and `skip()` to determine the counts and uses `mark()`/`reset()` to return to the beginning of the file to print the first 100 bytes. `BufferedInputStream` is used to enable `reset()` to work (`FileInputStream` does not support `reset()` directly).

```
import java.io.LineNumberInputStream;
import java.io.FileInputStream;
import java.io.BufferedInputStream;
import java.io.IOException;

class LCount {
    // prints the number of lines and bytes in a file
    // and prints the first 100 bytes of that file
    public static void main(String[] args) {
        if (args.length != 1) {
            System.err.println("Usage: java LCount <file>");
```

```
            System.exit(-1);
        }
        try {
            LineNumberInputStream in =
                new LineNumberInputStream(
               new BufferedInputStream(new FileInputStream(args[0])));

            int bytecount = in.available();
            in.mark(bytecount); // mark at beginning of stream
            in.skip(bytecount); // skip to end of buffer
            int linecount = in.getLineNumber();

            System.out.println("\t" + linecount + "\t" + bytecount +
                                  "\t" + args[0]);
            in.reset();
            int i, c;
            for (i = 0; i < 100 && ((c = in.read()) > -1); i++)
                System.out.write(c);
            if (i >= 100)
                System.out.println("\n...");
            System.out.flush();                   // flush output

            in.close();

        } catch (IOException e) {
            e.printStackTrace();
        }
    }
}
```

getLineNumber()

PURPOSE Retrieves the current line number.

SYNTAX `public int getLineNumber()`

RETURNS The current line number.

SEE ALSO `setLineNumber()`.

EXAMPLE See the class examples and the examples for `available()`and `setLineNumber()`.

LineNumberInputStream()

PURPOSE Constructs a new line number input stream for an input stream.

SYNTAX `public LineNumberInputStream(InputStream in)`

A B C D E F G H I J K L M N O P Q R S T U V W X Y Z

DESCRIPTION This constructor creates a new line number input stream for the input stream `in`. This line number input stream will count the line terminating characters (`'\n'`, `'\r'`, and `'\n\r'`) as input is read from `in`.

PARAMETERS

`in` The input stream for which to create the line number input stream.

SEE ALSO `FilterInputStream()`, `getLineNumber()`.

EXAMPLE See the class example and `available()` and `setLineNumber()`.

mark()

PURPOSE Marks the current read position in this line number input stream.

SYNTAX `public void mark(int readlimit)`

DESCRIPTION This method marks the current read position and line number of this line number input stream so that a subsequent call to `reset()` will reset the read position to this marked position and line number. `readlimit` number of bytes can be read after this mark has been set. If you read more than `readlimit` number of bytes, the mark becomes invalid.

`mark()` on this stream is supported only if it is supported by the stream being filtered.

PARAMETERS

`readlimit` The number of bytes that can be read before this mark becomes invalidated.

OVERRIDES `FilterInputStream.mark()`.

SEE ALSO `InputStream.markSupported()`, `reset()`.

EXAMPLE See `available()`.

read()

PURPOSE Reads bytes from this line number input stream.

SYNTAX
```
public int read() throws IOException
public int read(byte[] buffer, int offset, int count) throws
    IOException
```

DESCRIPTION The two forms of this method read bytes from the input stream. The first form reads and returns a single byte from the line number input stream, incrementing the line number if a line terminator has been encountered. If a line terminator has been encountered, the byte returned is the newline character ('\n'). The second form reads `count` number of bytes from this line number input stream and stores them into the byte array `buffer` starting at index `offset`. It returns the actual number of bytes read. This second form also increments the line number as line terminators are encountered. It does this in the same way that the first form does. A multicharacter line terminator (`'\r\n'`) is treated as a single byte.

PARAMETERS

`buffer`	The byte array in which to store the bytes read.
`count`	The number of bytes to read.
`offset`	The index in `buffer` at which to start storing the bytes read.

RETURNS The first form returns the byte read; the second form returns the actual number of bytes read. All forms return `-1` if end-of-file has been reached in the stream before any bytes have been read.

EXCEPTIONS

`IOException` If an IO error occurred while attempting to read the bytes.

OVERRIDES `FilterInputStream.read()`.

SEE ALSO `getLineNumber()`, `skip()`.

EXAMPLE See the class example, `setLineNumber()`.

reset()

PURPOSE Resets the read position to be the last marked position.

SYNTAX `public void reset() throws IOException`

DESCRIPTION This method resets the current read position to be the last marked position. It also resets the line number to be the line number of the last marked position. Subsequent invocations of the `read()`/`skip()` methods will begin getting input from this marked position. Subsequent invocations of `getLineNumber()` will return this reset line number.

`reset()` on this stream is supported only if it is supported by the stream being filtered.

EXCEPTIONS

`IOException` If no mark has been previously set or if the mark has been invalidated.

OVERRIDES `FilterInputStream.reset()`.

SEE ALSO `InputStream.markSupported()`, `getLineNumber()`, `mark()`.

EXAMPLE See `available()`.

setLineNumber()

PURPOSE Sets the current line number.

SYNTAX `public void setLineNumber(int lineNumber)`

DESCRIPTION This method sets the current line number to be `lineNumber`.

PARAMETERS

`lineNumber` The line number to which to set.

SEE ALSO `getLineNumber()`.

EXAMPLE This example is a variation of the class example. It prints the line number with each line but resets the line number for each new page.

```
import java.io.*;

class Page {
    // reads input from 'in' and writes the bytes out to 'out'
    // with line numbers on the left, resetting after each page
    public static void echo(InputStream i, OutputStream o,
        int pagesize) {
        try {
            LineNumberInputStream in = new LineNumberInputStream(i);
            PrintStream out = new PrintStream(o);
            int c, oldLineNumber = 0, newLineNumber = 0;
            boolean writePrefix = true;

            while((c = in.read()) > -1) {
                if (writePrefix) {
                    out.print(newLineNumber+1);
                    out.write('\t');
                }
                out.write(c);
                if (writePrefix =
                    ((newLineNumber = in.getLineNumber()) !=
                        oldLineNumber)) {
                    oldLineNumber = newLineNumber;
                    if (newLineNumber >= pagesize)
                        in.setLineNumber(newLineNumber=0);
                }
            }
            in.close();                 // close streams
            out.close();
        } catch (IOException e) {
            e.printStackTrace();
        }
    }
    public static void main(String[] args) {
        try {
            InputStream in;
            if (args.length == 0)
```

```
            in = System.in;
        else
            in = new FileInputStream(args[0]);
        echo(in, System.out, 10);
    } catch (IOException e) {
        e.printStackTrace();
    }
  }
}
```

skip()

PURPOSE Skips bytes from this line number input stream.

SYNTAX `public long skip(long count) throws IOException`

DESCRIPTION This method skips `count` number of bytes from this line number input stream. The line number is incremented as line terminators are encountered in the `count` number of bytes skipped. A multicharacter line terminator (`'\r\n'`) counts as a single byte.

PARAMETERS

`count` The number of bytes to skip.

RETURNS The actual number of bytes skipped.

EXCEPTIONS

`IOException` If an IO error occurred.

OVERRIDES `FilterInputStream.skip()`.

EXAMPLE See `available()`.

A B C D E F G H I J K L M N O P Q R S T U V W X Y Z

java.lang

LinkageError

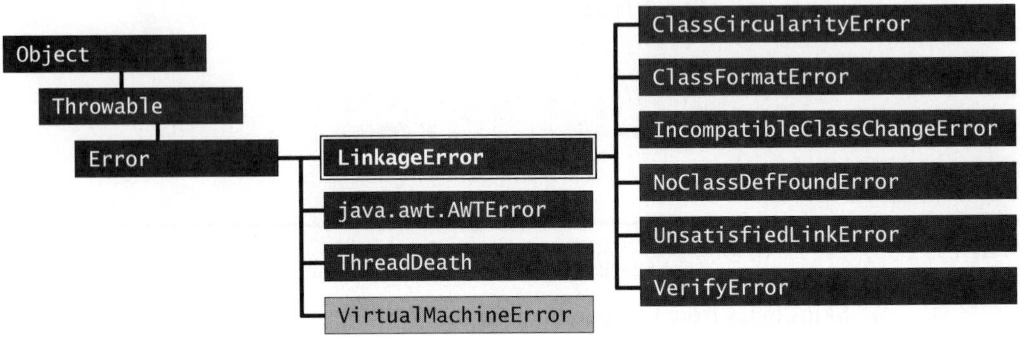

Syntax

`public class LinkageError extends Error`

Description

`LinkageError` and its subclasses of errors indicate that the classes that a class depends on have been changed in an incompatible way. This can happen if some of the classes were changed and compiled independently (without recompiling all the classes).

`LinkageError` and its subclasses should not be caught or declared in the `throws` clause of a method.

MEMBER SUMMARY	
Constructor	
`LinkageError()`	Constructs a `LinkageError` instance.

See Also

`ClassCircularityError`, `ClassFormatError`, `Error`, `IncompatibleClassChangeError`, `NoClassDefFoundError`, `UnsatisfiedLinkError`, `VerifyError`.

Examples

See examples of subclasses.

LinkageError()

PURPOSE Constructs a `LinkageError` instance.

SYNTAX
```
public LinkageError()
public LinkageError(String msg)
```

DESCRIPTION The two forms of this constructor create a new instance of `LinkageError`. An optional string `msg` can be supplied that describes this particular instance of the error.

PARAMETERS

`msg` A string that gives details about this error.

java.awt
List

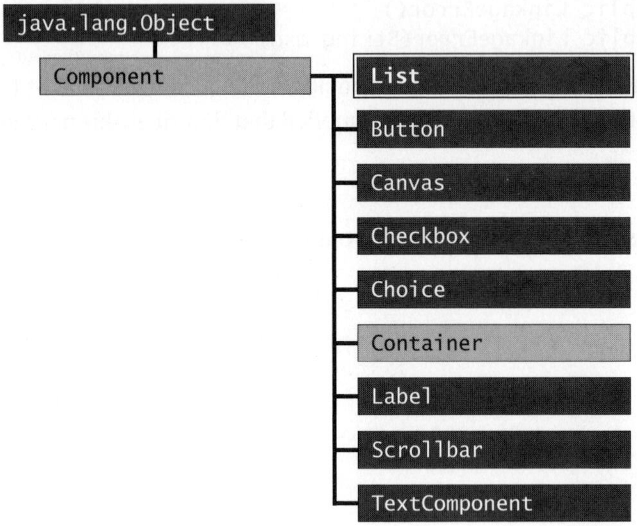

Syntax

```
public class List extends Component
```

Description

The list component is a scrollable vertical list of string items. The user can select an item from the list.

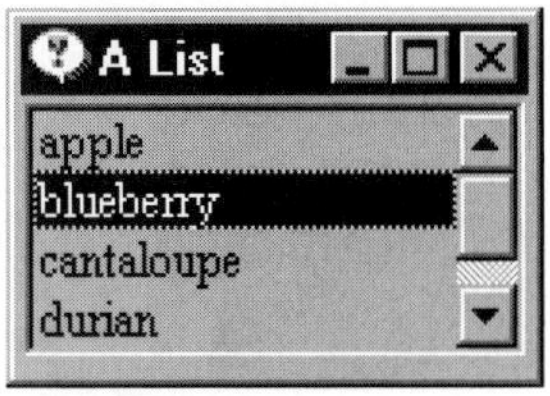

FIGURE 173 `List`

Selection Methods

The list component can be in either single- or multiple-selection mode. When it is in single-selection mode, only one item can be selected at a time. When it is in multiple-selection mode, more than one item can be selected. The gesture by which a selected item is deselected depends on the platform. For example, on Windows 95 a selected item is deselected by a click on the selected item.

The `List` class provides methods to modify and retrieve the set of selected items.

MEMBER SUMMARY

Constructor	
`List()`	Constructs a new `List` instance.
Visibility Methods	
`getVisibleIndex()`	Retrieves the index of the item that was last made visible.
`makeVisible()`	Scrolls the list so that an item is visible.
Item Methods	
`addItem()`	Adds an item to the list.
`clear()`	Removes all items from the list.
`countItems`	Retrieves the number of items in the list.
`delItem()`	Deletes an item from the list.
`delItems()`	Deletes a range of items from the list.
`getItem()`	Retrieves an item from the list.
`getRows()`	Retrieves the number of rows in the list.
`replaceItem()`	Replaces an item in the list.
Selection Methods	
`allowsMultipleSelections()`	Retrieves the list's selection mode.
`deselect()`	Deselects an item in the list.
`getSelectedIndex()`	Retrieves the index of the selected item.
`getSelectedIndexes()`	Retrieves the indices of the selected item.
`getSelectedItem()`	Retrieves the list's selected item.
`getSelectedItems()`	Retrieves the list's selected items.
`isSelected()`	Determines whether an item is selected.
`select()`	Selects an item in the list.
`setMultipleSelections()`	Sets the list's selection mode.
Layout Methods	
`minimumSize()`	Calculates the minimum dimensions of the list.
`preferredSize()`	Calculates the preferred dimensions needed for the list.
Peer Methods	
`addNotify()`	Creates the list's peer.
`removeNotify()`	Destroys the list's peer.
Debugging Method	
`paramString()`	Generates a string representing the list's state.

Example

For a simple example using the list component, see the example for the `List()` constructor. The more elaborate example presented here creates two lists and several buttons for moving items from one list to the other. See Figure 174. One or more items on either list can be selected and then moved to the other list. Making a selection on one list automatically clears all the selections on the other list. Double-clicking an item adds an asterisk to the item's name (this was done just to demonstrate the use of `replaceItem()`).

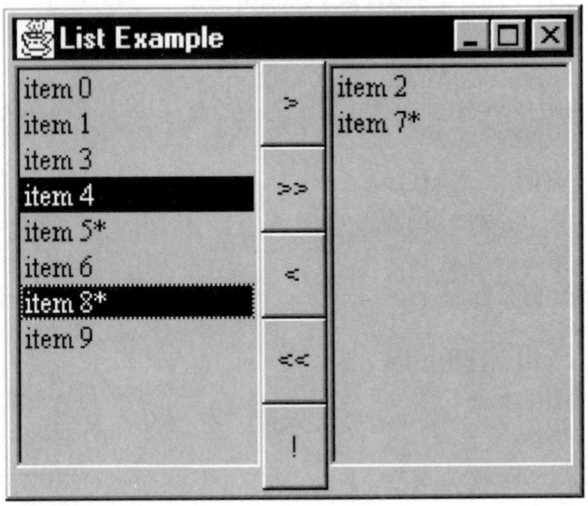

FIGURE 174 `List`

The > button moves the selected items in the left list to the right list; the < button does exactly the opposite. The >> button moves all the items in the left list to the right list; the << button does exactly the opposite. The ! button deselects the selected items and selects unselected items. This operation is applied to the list that has at least one selection. If neither list has any selections, this operation is ignored.

The example uses a grid bag layout manager (see `GridBagLayout`) to lay out the lists and buttons. The center column is not given any weight, so the first and last columns stretch with the window.

```
import java.awt.*;
class Main extends Frame {
    final static int ITEMS = 10;
    List ltList = new List(ITEMS, true);
    List rtList = new List(0, true);

    Main() {
        super("List Example");
        GridBagLayout gbl = new GridBagLayout();

        setLayout(gbl);
        add(ltList, 0, 0, 1, 5, 1.0, 1.0);
        add(rtList, 2, 0, 1, 5, 1.0, 1.0);
        add(new Button(">"), 1, 0, 1, 1, 0, 1.0);
        add(new Button(">>"), 1, 1, 1, 1, 0, 1.0);
        add(new Button("<"), 1, 2, 1, 1, 0, 1.0);
        add(new Button("<<"), 1, 3, 1, 1, 0, 1.0);
        add(new Button("!"), 1, 4, 1, 1, 0, 1.0);

        for (int i=0; i<ITEMS; i++) {
           ltList.addItem("item "+i);
        }
        pack();
        show();
        }
```

```
void add(Component comp,
        int x, int y, int w, int h, double weightx, double weighty)
{
    GridBagLayout gbl = (GridBagLayout)getLayout();
    GridBagConstraints c = new GridBagConstraints();

    c.fill = GridBagConstraints.BOTH;
    c.gridx = x;
    c.gridy = y;
    c.gridwidth = w;
    c.gridheight = h;
    c.weightx = weightx;
    c.weighty = weighty;
    add(comp);
    gbl.setConstraints(comp, c);
}

void reverseSelections(List l) {
    for (int i=0; i<l.countItems(); i++) {
        if (l.isSelected(i)) {
            l.deselect(i);
        } else {
            l.select(i);
        }
    }
}

void deselectAll(List l) {
    for (int i=0; i<l.countItems(); i++) {
        l.deselect(i);
    }
}

void replaceItem(List l, String item) {
    for (int i=0; i<l.countItems(); i++) {
        if (l.getItem(i).equals(item)) {
            l.replaceItem(item + "*", i);
        }
    }
}

void move(List l1, List l2, boolean all) {
    if (all) {
        for (int i=0; i<l1.countItems(); i++) {
            l2.addItem(l1.getItem(i));
        }
        l1.delItems(0, l1.countItems()-1);    // or l1.clear();
    } else {
        String[] items = l1.getSelectedItems();
        int[] itemIndexes = l1.getSelectedIndexes();

        deselectAll(l2);
        for (int i=0; i<items.length; i++) {
            l2.addItem(items[i]);        // add it
```

Example

```
                l2.select(l2.countItems()-1);// and select it
                if (i == 0) {
                    l2.makeVisible(l2.countItems()-1);
                }
            }
            for (int i=itemIndexes.length-1; i>=0; i--) {
                l1.delItem(itemIndexes[i]);
            }
        }
    }

    public boolean action(Event evt, Object arg) {
        if (">".equals(arg)) {
            move(ltList, rtList, false);
        } else if (">>".equals(arg)) {
            move(ltList, rtList, true);
        } else if ("<".equals(arg)) {
            move(rtList, ltList, false);
        } else if ("<<".equals(arg)) {
            move(rtList, ltList, true);
        } else if ("!".equals(arg)) {
            if (ltList.getSelectedItems().length > 0) {
                reverseSelections(ltList);
            } else if (rtList.getSelectedItems().length > 0) {
                reverseSelections(rtList);
            }
        } else if (evt.target == rtList || evt.target == ltList) {
            replaceItem((List)evt.target, (String)arg);
        } else {
            return false;
        }
        return true;
    }

    public boolean handleEvent(Event evt) {
        if (evt.id == Event.LIST_SELECT
                || evt.id == Event.LIST_DESELECT) {
            if (evt.target == ltList) {
                deselectAll(rtList);
            } else if (evt.target == rtList) {
                deselectAll(ltList);
            }
            return true;
        }
        return super.handleEvent(evt);
    }

    public static void main(String[] args) {
        new Main();
    }
}
```

A B C D E F G H I J K L M N O P Q R S T U V W X Y Z

addItem()

PURPOSE
Adds an item to the list.

SYNTAX
```
public synchronized void addItem(String item)
public synchronized void addItem(String item, int posn)
```

DESCRIPTION
The two forms of this method add the item `item` to the list. `posn` specifies the position in the list at which to add `item`. If `posn` is not specified, `item` is added to the end of the list. If `posn` is `0`, the item becomes the first item in the list.

The set of selected items does not change.

PARAMETERS

`item` A non-`null` string to be added to the list.

`posn` The position at which to add the item.

EXAMPLE
See the class example.

addNotify()

PURPOSE
Creates the list's peer.

SYNTAX
```
public synchronized void addNotify()
```

DESCRIPTION
This method calls the `Toolkit.createList()` method to create the list's peer. This method should never be called directly. It is normally called by the component's container.

OVERRIDES
`Component.addNotify()`.

SEE ALSO
`Container`, `Toolkit`.

EXAMPLE
See `Component.addNotify()`.

allowsMultipleSelections()

PURPOSE
Retrieves the selection mode of the list.

SYNTAX
```
public boolean allowsMultipleSelections()
```

RETURNS
`true` if the list is in multiple-selection mode; `false` otherwise.

SEE ALSO
`setMultipleSelections()`.

EXAMPLE
See `setMultipleSelections()`.

A B C D E F G H I J K L M N O P Q R S T U V W X Y Z

clear()

PURPOSE Removes all items from the list.

SYNTAX `public synchronized void clear()`

DESCRIPTION The effect of calling `clear()` is the same as calling `delItem()` for every item in the list.

SEE ALSO `delItem()`.

EXAMPLE See the class example.

countItems()

PURPOSE Retrieves the number of items in the list.

SYNTAX `public int countItems()`

RETURNS The number of items in the list. The result is always >= `0`.

SEE ALSO `getItem()`.

EXAMPLE See the class example.

delItem()

PURPOSE Deletes an item from the list.

SYNTAX `public synchronized void delItem(int posn)`

DESCRIPTION This method deletes the item at index `posn` from the list. This method does not affect the selected state of the other items in the list.

PARAMETERS

`posn` The 0-based index of the item in the list.

EXCEPTIONS

`ArrayIndexOutOfBoundsException`

If `posn` is less than `0` or greater than `countItems()-1`.

SEE ALSO `clear()`, `delItems()`.

EXAMPLE See the class example.

A B C D E F G H I J K L M N O P Q R S T U V W X Y Z

delItems()

PURPOSE Deletes a range of items from the list.

SYNTAX `public synchronized void delItems(int start, int end)`

DESCRIPTION This method deletes the items at index `start` and at index `end` and all items in between. Only one item is deleted if `start` equals `end`. No items are deleted if `end` is less than `start`.

PARAMETERS

`end` The 0-based index of the last item in the range.

`start` The 0-based index of the first item in the range.

EXCEPTIONS

`ArrayIndexOutOfBoundsException`

If `end >= start` and either `start` or `end` is an invalid item index.

SEE ALSO `clear()`, `delItem()`.

EXAMPLE See the class example.

deselect()

PURPOSE Deselects an item in the list.

SYNTAX `public synchronized void deselect(int posn)`

DESCRIPTION This method deselects the item specified at index `posn`. The call is ignored if the item is not selected. The other selections are not affected.

PARAMETERS

`posn` The 0-based index of the item in the list.

SEE ALSO `select()`, `getSelectedItem()`, `isSelected()`.

EXAMPLE See the class example.

getItem()

PURPOSE Retrieves an item from the list.

SYNTAX `public String getItem(int posn)`

DESCRIPTION This method retrieves the item at index `posn`.

B C D E F G H I J K L M N O P Q R S T U V W X Y Z

PARAMETERS

posn — The 0-based index of the item in the list.

RETURNS — The item. The return string is never `null`.

EXCEPTIONS

`ArrayIndexOutOfBoundsException`
If `posn` is less than `0` or greater than `countItems()-1`.

SEE ALSO — `countItems()`.

EXAMPLE — See the class example.

getRows()

PURPOSE — Retrieves the number of rows in the list.

SYNTAX — `public int getRows()`

DESCRIPTION — The number of rows is specified when the list is created, and it never changes, even if the dimensions of the list change. See the `List()` constructor for more details about rows.

RETURNS — The number of rows.

SEE ALSO — `List()`.

EXAMPLE — See the class example.

getSelectedIndex()

PURPOSE — Retrieves the index of the selected item.

SYNTAX — `public synchronized int getSelectedIndex()`

RETURNS — The 0-based index of the selected item or `-1` if no item is selected. If the list is in multiple-selection mode, `-1` is always returned.

SEE ALSO — `getSelectedItem()`.

EXAMPLE — See the class example.

getSelectedIndexes()

PURPOSE — Retrieves the indices of the selected items.

SYNTAX `public synchronized int[] getSelectedIndexes()`

RETURNS A non-`null` array containing the list of indices. The return array is never `null` but may have length 0, which indicates that no items were selected.

SEE ALSO `getSelectedIndex()`, `getSelectedItem()`.

EXAMPLE See the class example.

getSelectedItem()

PURPOSE Retrieves the selected item.

SYNTAX `public synchronized String getSelectedItem()`

RETURNS The selected item; `null` if no items are selected. If the list is in multiple-selection mode, `null` is always returned.

SEE ALSO `getSelectedIndex()`, `getSelectedIndexes()`.

EXAMPLE This example creates a frame containing a list. As you click any item in the list, the currently selected item is printed. See Figure 175.

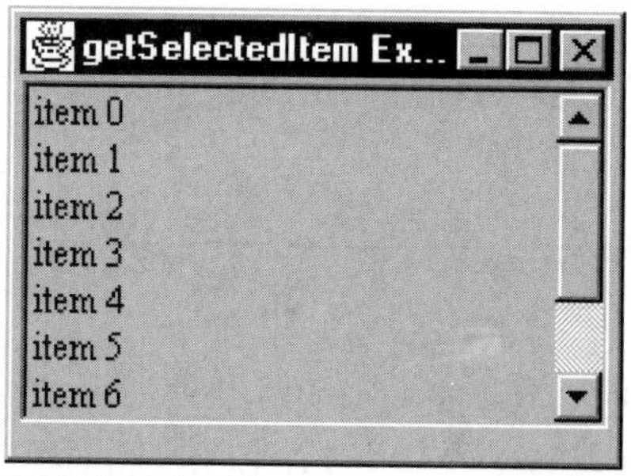

FIGURE 175 `List.getSelectedItem()`

```
import java.awt.*;
class Main extends Frame {
    static final int ITEMS = 10;
    static List l = new List(ITEMS, false);

    Main() {
        super("getSelectedItem Example");

        for (int i = 0; i < ITEMS; i++) {
           l.addItem("item "+i);
        }
        add("Center", l);
        pack();
        show();
    }

    public boolean handleEvent(Event evt) {
        if (evt.target == l) {
            System.out.println(l.getSelectedItem());
            return true;
        }
        return false;
    }
```

```
        static public void main(String[] args) {
            new Main();
        }
    }
```

getSelectedItems()

PURPOSE Retrieves the selected items in the list.

SYNTAX `public synchronized String[] getSelectedItems()`

RETURNS A non-`null` array containing the names of the selected items on the list.

SEE ALSO `getSelectedIndexes()`, `getSelectedItem()`.

EXAMPLE See the class example.

getVisibleIndex()

PURPOSE Retrieves the index of the item that was last made visible.

SYNTAX `public int getVisibleIndex()`

DESCRIPTION The item that was last made visible is the item passed to the most recent call to `makeVisible()`.

RETURNS The 0-based index of the item that was last made visible with the `makeVisible()` method. If `makeVisible()` has not yet been called, `0` is returned.

SEE ALSO `makeVisible()`.

isSelected()

PURPOSE Determines whether an item in the list is selected.

SYNTAX `public synchronized boolean isSelected(int posn)`

DESCRIPTION This method determines whether the item at index `posn` on the list is selected.

RETURNS `true` if the item at index `posn` is selected; `false` otherwise.

PARAMETERS

`posn` The 0-based index of the item.

SEE ALSO `select()`.

EXAMPLE See the class example.

List()

PURPOSE Constructs a new list component.

SYNTAX

```
public List()
public List(int nrows, boolean multipleSelections)
```

DESCRIPTION The two forms of this constructor create a new list component tall enough to display `nrows` visible rows. If `nrows` is not specified, it defaults to a platform-independent value. The number of rows can be retrieved at any time with `getRows()`. However, this value never changes, even if the dimensions of the list change. If `multipleSelections` is true, the list is set in multiple-selection mode; otherwise the list is set in single-selection mode. If `multipleSelections` is not specified, it defaults to `false`. The width of the list component is set to a platform-dependent value.

PARAMETERS

`nrows` The number of rows in the list is defined to be the number of items that can be visible at one time, where the first visible item is completely visible and the last visible item is at least partially visible. (Note that in implementations that allow both the first and last visible items to be partially visible, it's possible for more than `nrows` items to be visible.) In implementations in which a horizontal scrollbar automatically appears if needed, the number of visible items may be fewer than `nrows` when the scrollbar is present.

`multipleSelections`
Specifies the selection mode of the list.

EXAMPLE This example creates a list component with two items. See Figure 176. The program prints out the current item whenever an item in the list is double-clicked.

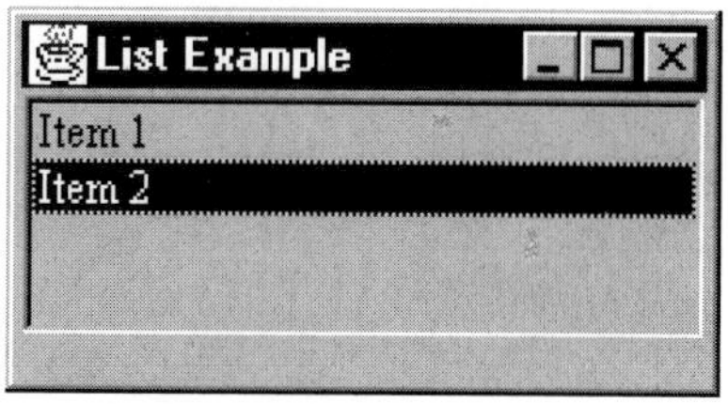

FIGURE 176 `List()`

```
import java.awt.*;
class Main extends Frame {
    Main() {
        super("List Example");
        List list = new List();
```

```
            list.addItem("Item 1");
            list.addItem("Item 2");
            add("Center", list);
            resize(200, 200);
            show();
        }

        public boolean action(Event evt, Object arg) {
            if (evt.target instanceof List) {
                System.out.println(arg);
                return true;
            }
            return false;
        }

        static public void main(String[] args) {
            new Main();
        }
    }
```

makeVisible()

PURPOSE Scrolls the list so that an item is visible.

SYNTAX `public void makeVisible(int posn)`

DESCRIPTION This method scrolls the list so that the item at index `posn` is visible.

PARAMETERS

`posn` The 0-based index of the item.

SEE ALSO `getVisibleIndex()`.

EXAMPLE See the class example.

minimumSize()

PURPOSE Calculates the minimum dimensions of the list.

SYNTAX
```
public Dimension minimumSize()
public Dimension minimumSize(int rows)
```

DESCRIPTION This method calculates the minimum dimensions needed for the list given that the specified number of rows must be visible. If `rows` is not specified, the value of `getRows()` is used.

If the list's peer does not exist, the result of `Component.size()` is returned.

On most platforms, the preferred and minimum dimensions for the list are the same.

PARAMETERS

`rows` The number of rows.

RETURNS The non-`null` minimum dimensions of the list.

OVERRIDES `Component.minimumSize()`.

SEE ALSO `preferredSize()`.

EXAMPLE See `LayoutManager.minimumSize()`.

paramString()

PURPOSE Generates a string representing the list's state.

SYNTAX `protected String paramString()`

DESCRIPTION A subclass of this class should override this method and return a concatenation of its state with the results of `super.paramString()`. This method is called by the `toString()` method and is typically used for debugging.

RETURNS A non-`null` string representing the list's state.

OVERRIDES `Component.paramString()`.

SEE ALSO `Object.toString()`.

EXAMPLE See `Component.paramString()`.

preferredSize()

PURPOSE Calculates the preferred dimensions needed for the list.

SYNTAX

```
public Dimension preferredSize()
public Dimension preferredSize(int rows)
```

DESCRIPTION This method calculates the preferred dimensions needed for the list given that the specified number of rows must be visible. If `rows` is not specified, the value of `getRows()` is used.

If the list's peer does not exist, the result of `Component.size()` is returned. On most platforms, the preferred and minimum dimensions for the list are the same.

A B C D E F G H I J K L M N O P Q R S T U V W X Y Z

PARAMETERS

`rows`	The number of rows.
RETURNS	The non-`null` preferred dimensions of the list.
OVERRIDES	`Component.preferredSize()`.
EXAMPLE	See `LayoutManager.preferredSize()`.

replaceItem()

PURPOSE	Replaces an item in the list.
SYNTAX	`public synchronized void replaceItem(String newItem, int posn)`
DESCRIPTION	This method replaces the item at the index `posn` with `newItem`.
PARAMETERS	
`newItem`	The non-`null` new item.
`posn`	The 0-based index of the item.
SEE ALSO	`addItem()`.
EXAMPLE	See the class example.

removeNotify()

PURPOSE	Destroys the list's peer.
SYNTAX	`public synchronized void removeNotify()`
DESCRIPTION	This method should never be called directly. It is normally called by the component's container.
OVERRIDES	`Component.removeNotify()`.
SEE ALSO	`Component`.
EXAMPLE	See `Component.show()`.

select()

PURPOSE	Selects an item in the list.
SYNTAX	`public synchronized void select(int posn)`

DESCRIPTION This method selects the item at the index `posn`. The call is ignored if the item is already selected.

PARAMETERS

`posn` The 0-based index of the item.

EXCEPTIONS

`ArrayIndexOutOfBoundsException`

If `posn` is less than `0` or greater than `countItems()-1`.

SEE ALSO `deselect()`, `getSelectedItem()`, `isSelected()`.

EXAMPLE See the class example.

setMultipleSelections()

PURPOSE Sets the list's selection mode.

SYNTAX `public void setMultipleSelections(boolean on)`

DESCRIPTION If `on` is `true`, this method sets the list control in multi-selection mode; otherwise it sets the list control in single-selection mode.

PARAMETERS

`on` Specifies the new selection mode of the list.

SEE ALSO `allowsMultipleSelections()`.

EXAMPLE This example creates a frame containing a list and a checkbox control. The checkbox control is used to toggle the multiple-selection model of the list control. See Figure 177.

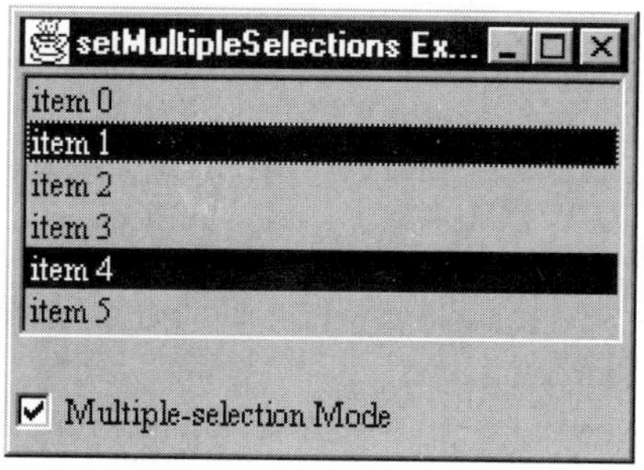

FIGURE 177
`List.setMultipleSelections()`

```
import java.awt.*;
class Main extends Frame {
    static final int ITEMS = 10;
    static List l = new List(ITEMS, false);
    static Checkbox b = new Checkbox("Multipleselection Mode",
        null, false);

    Main() {
        super("setMultipleSelections Example");

        for (int i = 0; i < ITEMS; i++) {
           l.addItem("item "+i);
```

```
        }
        add("Center", l);
        add("South", b);
        pack();
        show();
    }

    public boolean action(Event evt, Object what) {
        if (evt.target == b) {
            l.setMultipleSelections(!l.allowsMultipleSelections());
        }
        return true;
    }

    static public void main(String[] args) {
        new Main();
    }
}
```

ListPeer

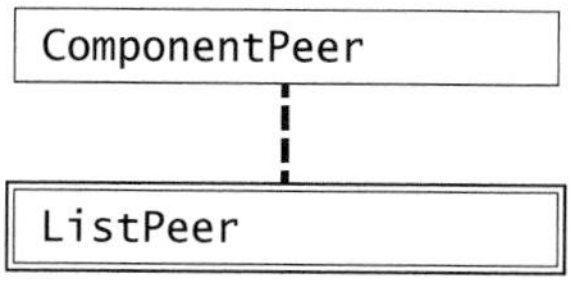

Syntax

```
public interface ListPeer extends ComponentPeer
```

Description

The list component (see the `List` class) in the Abstract Windowing Toolkit (AWT) uses the platform's native implementation of a list. So that the AWT list behaves the same on all platforms, the list is assigned a peer, whose task is to translate the behavior of the platform's native list to the behavior of the AWT list.

AWT programmers normally do not directly use peer classes and interfaces. Instead they deal with AWT components in the `java.awt` package. These in turn automatically manage their peers. Only someone who is porting the AWT to another platform should be concerned with the peer classes and interfaces. Consequently, most peer documentation refers to `java.awt` counterparts.

See `Component` and `Toolkit` for additional information about component peers.

MEMBER SUMMARY

Peer Methods

`addItem()`	Adds an item to the list.
`clear()`	Removes all items from the list.
`delItems()`	Deletes a range of items from the list.
`deselect()`	Deselects an item in the list.
`getSelectedIndexes()`	Retrieves the indices of the selected items.
`makeVisible()`	Scrolls the list so that an item is visible.
`minimumSize()`	Calculates the minimum dimensions of the list.
`preferredSize()`	Calculates the preferred dimensions of the list.
`select()`	Selects an item in the list.
`setMultipleSelections()`	Sets the selection mode of the list.

A B C D E F G H I J K L M N O P Q R S T U V W X Y Z

See Also

`Component`, `List`, `Toolkit`.

addItem()

PURPOSE	Adds an item to the list.
SYNTAX	`void addItem(String item, int index)`
PARAMETERS	
`item`	The item to be added.
`index`	The position in the list to which to add the item.
SEE ALSO	`List.addItem()`.

clear()

PURPOSE	Removes all items from the list.
SYNTAX	`void clear()`.
SEE ALSO	`List.clear()`.

delItems()

PURPOSE	Deletes a range of items from the list.
SYNTAX	`void delItems(int start, int end)`
PARAMETERS	
`end`	The 0-based index of the last item in the range.
`start`	The 0-based index of the first item in the range.
SEE ALSO	`List.delItems()`.

deselect()

PURPOSE	Deselects an item in the list.

SYNTAX `void deselect(int index)`

PARAMETERS

`index` The 0-based index of the item to deselect.

SEE ALSO `List.deselect()`.

getSelectedIndexes()

PURPOSE Retrieves the indices of the selected items.

SYNTAX `int[] getSelectedIndexes()`

RETURNS An array containing the list of indices.

SEE ALSO `List.getSelectedIndexes()`.

makeVisible()

PURPOSE Scrolls the list so that an item is visible.

SYNTAX `void makeVisible(int index)`

PARAMETERS

`index` The 0-based index of the item to make visible.

SEE ALSO `List.makeVisible()`.

minimumSize()

PURPOSE Calculates the minimum dimensions of the list.

SYNTAX `Dimension minimumSize(int rows)`

PARAMETERS

`rows` The number of rows the list must accommodate.

RETURNS The minimum dimensions of the list.

SEE ALSO `List.minimumSize()`.

preferredSize()

PURPOSE Calculates the preferred dimensions of the list.

SYNTAX `Dimension preferredSize(int rows)`

PARAMETERS

`rows` The number of rows the list must accommodate.

RETURNS The preferred dimensions of the list.

SEE ALSO `List.preferredSize()`.

select()

PURPOSE Selects an item in the list.

SYNTAX `void select(int index)`

PARAMETERS

`index` The index of the item to select.

SEE ALSO `List.select()`.

setMultipleSelections()

PURPOSE Sets the selection mode of the list.

SYNTAX `void setMultipleSelections(boolean on)`

PARAMETERS

`on` `true` means set the list control in multiple-selection mode; `false` means single-selection mode.

SEE ALSO `List.setMultipleSelections()`.

Long

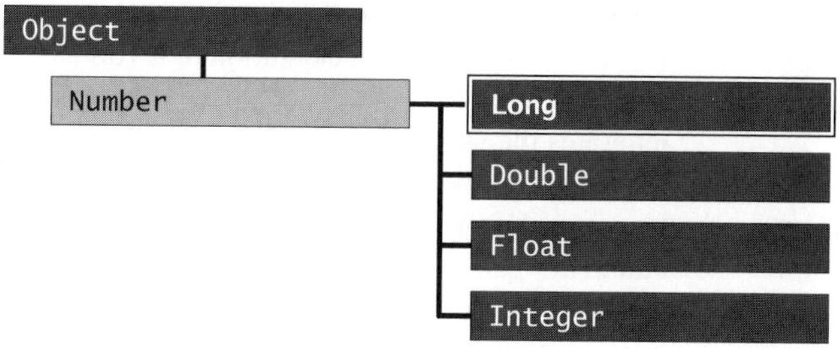

Syntax

```
public final class Long extends Number
```

Description

A `long` in Java is a 64-bit signed integer. The `Long` class provides an object wrapper for `long` data values. This allows `long` integers to be passed to methods in Java class libraries that accept Java objects as parameters. In addition, the `Long` class provides methods that convert to and from `long` values and performs other operations on `long` values.

`Long` instances cannot be used in arithmetic expressions in place of `long`. For example, the following is not allowed:

```
Long l1 = new Long(193);
Long l2 = new Long(5);
Long l3 = l1 * l2;       // Illegal
```

To perform arithmetic operations using a `Long` instance, you first must use access methods defined in the `Long` class to obtain its numeric value, as follows:

```
long l3 = l1.longValue() * l2.longValue();
double d1 = l1.intValue() + l2.doubleValue();
```

MEMBER SUMMARY

Constructor	
`Long()`	Constructs a `Long` object using a `long` or a string.
Constant Fields	
`MAX_VALUE`	The maximum value a `long` can have.
`MIN_VALUE`	The minimum value a `long` can have.

Continued

MEMBER SUMMARY	
Methods for Converting to/from Strings	
`getLong()`	Creates a `Long` object using the value of a system property.
`parseLong()`	Parses the string representation of an integer into a `long`.
`toBinaryString()`	Generates the string representation of a `long` as an unsigned binary number.
`toHexString()`	Generates the string representation of a `long` as an unsigned hexadecimal number.
`toOctalString()`	Generates the string representation of a `long` as an unsigned octal number.
`toString()`	Generates the string representation of a `long` or a `Long` object.
`valueOf()`	Creates a `Long` object using its string representation.
Comparison and Hash Code Methods	
`equals()`	Compares this object with the given object for equality.
`hashCode()`	Computes the hash code for this object.
Number Methods	
`doubleValue()`	Retrieves the value of this object as a `double`.
`floatValue()`	Retrieves the value of this object as a `float`.
`intValue()`	Retrieves the value of this object as an `int`.
`longValue()`	Retrieves the value of this object as a `long`.

See Also

`Double`, `Float`, `Integer`, `Number`.

doubleValue()

PURPOSE Retrieves the value of this object as a `double`.

SYNTAX `public double doubleValue()`

DESCRIPTION This method returns the value of this object as a `double` by casting its `long` value to a `double`.

RETURNS The value of this object as a `double`.

EXAMPLE

```
Long longobj = new Long(69521);
```

```
double dval = longobj.doubleValue(); // get double value
float fval = longobj.floatValue();   // get float value
int ival = longobj.intValue();       // get int value
long lval = longobj.longValue();     // get long value
```

equals()

PURPOSE Compares this object with the specified object for equality.

SYNTAX `public boolean equals(Object obj)`

DESCRIPTION This method compares the `long` value of this object with that of `obj`. It returns `true` if the two values are equal; it returns `false` otherwise. It also returns `false` if `obj` is `null` or is not a `Long` object.

PARAMETERS

`obj` The object against which this object will be compared.

RETURNS `true` if the objects are the same; `false` otherwise.

OVERRIDES `Object.equals()`.

EXAMPLE

```
Long l1 = new Long(35661);
Long l2 = new Long(2341);

// Check whether the value of two Longs are equal
if (l1.equals(l2))
    System.out.println("equal");
```

floatValue()

PURPOSE Retrieves the value of this object as a `float`.

SYNTAX `public float floatValue()`

DESCRIPTION This method returns the value of this object as a `float` by casting its `long` value into a `float`.

RETURNS The value of this object as a `float`.

EXAMPLE See `doubleValue()`.

A B C D E F G H I J K L M N O P Q R S T U V W X Y Z

getLong()

PURPOSE Creates a Long object using the value of a system property.

SYNTAX

```
public static Long getLong(String prop)
public static Long getLong(String prop, long defval)
public static Long getLong(String prop, Long defobj)
```

DESCRIPTION The three forms of this method find the system property identified by prop and return the property's value as a Long object. The property's value must be an integer (in radix 10), a hexadecimal number, or an octal number. A hexadecimal number is prefixed with either "0x" or "#". An octal number has a leading zero. If prop does not exist or if prop's value is not a number in the format described above, the first form of this method returns null. The second form returns a Long object constructed using defval in the same situation, while the third form returns defobj.

PARAMETERS

defobj The default Long object to return if prop does not exist.

defval The default long value to use for the resulting Long object if prop does not exist.

prop The name of the property.

RETURNS A Long object containing the value of prop if it contains a valid integer; otherwise null if the first form of the method is used or a default Long object as determined by defval or defobj.

SEE ALSO Properties, System.getProperty().

EXAMPLE

```
// set up properties
Properties props = System.getProperties();
props.put("test.bignum", "1048576");        // radix 10 int property
props.put("test.bighex", "0xeffffffffff"); // radix 16 int property
props.put("test.hex2", "#2");               // radix 16 int property
props.put("test.octal", "065");             // radix 8 int property
props.put("test.nonnum", "2.5.1");          // non-int property
System.setProperties(props);

// use the three forms of getLong()
Long p1 = Long.getLong("test.bignum");
Long p2 = Long.getLong("test.bighex", 1024);
Long p3 = Long.getLong("test.hex2", new Long(0));
Long p4 = Long.getLong("test.octal", 256);
Long p5 = Long.getLong("test.nonnum", 1);
```

```
System.out.println("bignum: " + p1);
System.out.println("bighex: " + p2);
System.out.println("hex2: " + p3);
System.out.println("octal: " + p4);
System.out.println("nonnum: " + p5);
```

hashCode()

PURPOSE Computes the hash code for this object.

SYNTAX `public int hashCode()`

DESCRIPTION This method returns the hash code for this `Long` object. The hash code of a `Long` object is calculated using its `long` value. Two `Longs` with the same `long` value will have the same hash code, but two `Longs` with the same hash code may not necessarily have the same `long` value.

RETURNS An `int` representing the object's hash code.

OVERRIDES `Object.hashCode()`.

SEE ALSO `Hashtable`.

EXAMPLE

```
int[] hits = new int[1023];
Long lnum = new Long(3290);
int hashval = lnum.hashCode();          // generate hash code
++hits[Math.abs(hashval%hits.length)]; // count hits
```

intValue()

PURPOSE Retrieves the value of this object as an `int`.

SYNTAX `public int intValue()`

DESCRIPTION This method returns the value of this object as an `int` by casting its `long` value to an `int`.

RETURNS The value of this object as an `int`.

EXAMPLE See `doubleValue()`.

A B C D E F G H I J K L M N O P Q R S T U V W X Y Z

Long()

PURPOSE Constructs a Long object using a long or a string.

SYNTAX
```
public Long(long value)
public Long(String str) throws NumberFormatException
```

DESCRIPTION The first form of this constructor constructs a Long object using value. The second form parses str, the string representation of a radix 10 integer, and uses its numeric value to create the Long object.

PARAMETERS

str The string to be parsed into a long.

value The numeric value to use as the object's value.

EXCEPTIONS

NumberFormatException

If str cannot be parsed into an integer.

SEE ALSO parseLong(), valueOf().

EXAMPLE

```
Long lobj = new Long(1024);           // using long
try {
    Long lobj2 = new Long("1048576"); // using string
    long div = lobj2.longValue() / lobj.longValue();
} catch (NumberFormatException e) {
  ...
}
```

longValue()

PURPOSE Retrieves the value of this object as a long.

SYNTAX
```
public long longValue()
```

RETURNS The value of this object as a long.

EXAMPLE See doubleValue().

MAX_VALUE

PURPOSE The maximum value a long can have.

SYNTAX `public static final long MAX_VALUE`

DESCRIPTION This constant represents the maximum value a `long` can have, which is `0x7fffffffffffffff`.

EXAMPLE

```
// reset counter if maximum reached
long counter;
...
if (counter == Long.MAX_VALUE)
    counter = 0;
else
    counter++;
```

MIN_VALUE

PURPOSE The minimum value a `long` can have.

SYNTAX `public static final long MIN_VALUE`

DESCRIPTION This constant represents the minimum value a `long` can have, which is `0x8000000000000000`. This is a negative number.

EXAMPLE

```
// reset counter if minimum reached
long counter;
...
if (counter == Long.MIN_VALUE)
    counter = 0;
else
    counter--;
```

parseLong()

PURPOSE Parses the string representation of an integer into a `long`.

SYNTAX
```
public static long parseLong(String str) throws
   NumberFormatException
public static long parseLong(String str, int radix) throws
   NumberFormatException
```

DESCRIPTION The two forms of this method parse the string `str` into an integer and return it as a `long` value. If no radix is given, the radix used to parse `str` is 10. A negative

B C D E F G H I J K L M N O P Q R S T U V W X Y Z

integer has a leading minus ('-') character; a positive integer consists only of digits of the specified radix.

These methods are the inverse of `toString()`. `parseLong()` is similar to `valueOf()`, except `parseLong()` returns a `long`, while `valueOf()` returns a `Long` object.

PARAMETERS

`radix` The radix to use when parsing `str`. `radix` must be inclusively between `Character.MAX_RADIX` and `Character.MIN_RADIX`.

`str` The string to be parsed.

RETURNS A `long` containing the numeric value of the integer represented by `str`.

EXCEPTIONS

`NumberFormatException`
If `str` cannot be parsed into an integer of the specified radix.

SEE ALSO `Character.MAX_RADIX`, `Character.MIN_RADIX`, `toString()`, `valueOf()`.

EXAMPLE

```
try {
    long lnum = Long.parseLong("8861212097");
    long hexnum = Long.parseLong("8a24fe3", 16);
} catch (NumberFormatException e) {
  ...
}
```

toBinaryString()

PURPOSE Generates the string representation of a `long` as an unsigned binary number.

SYNTAX `public static String toBinaryString(long lnum)`

DESCRIPTION This method returns the string representation of `lnum` as an unsigned binary number. This is not always equivalent to `toString(lnum, 2)` because `toString()` always treats `lnum` as a signed number.

PARAMETERS

`lnum` The `long` for which to generate the string representation.

RETURNS The string representation of `lnum` as an unsigned binary number.

SEE ALSO `parseLong()`, `toHexString()`, `toOctalString()`, `toString()`, `valueOf()`.

EXAMPLE This example shows the difference between using `toString()`, `toBinaryString()`, `toOctalString()` and `toHexString()` on a negative number. The output of this program is shown after the code.

```
class Main {
    public static void main(String[] args) {
        long lnum = -1234567890123l;
        System.out.println(Long.toString(lnum, 10));
        System.out.println(Long.toString(lnum, 2));
        System.out.println(Long.toString(lnum, 8));
        System.out.println(Long.toString(lnum, 16));

        System.out.println(Long.toString(lnum));
        System.out.println(Long.toBinaryString(lnum));
        System.out.println(Long.toOctalString(lnum));
        System.out.println(Long.toHexString(lnum));
    }
}
```

OUTPUT

```
-1234567890123
-10001111101110001111110110000010011001011
-21756176602313
-11f71fb04cb
-1234567890123
1111111111111111111111101110000010001110000001001111101100110101
1777777756021601175465
fffffee08e04fb35
```

toHexString()

PURPOSE Generates the string representation of a `long` as an unsigned hexadecimal number.

SYNTAX `public static String toBinaryString(long lnum)`

DESCRIPTION This method returns the string representation of `lnum` as an unsigned hexadecimal number. This is not always equivalent to `toString(lnum, 16)` because `toString()` always treats `lnum` as a signed number.

PARAMETERS

`lnum` The `long` for which to generate the string representation.

RETURNS The string representation of `lnum` as an unsigned hexadecimal number.

SEE ALSO `parseLong()`, `toBinaryString()`, `toOctalString()`, `toString()`, `valueOf()`.

EXAMPLE See `toBinaryString()`.

A B C D E F G H I J K L M N O P Q R S T U V W X Y Z

A B C D E F G H I J K L M N O P Q R S T U V W X Y Z

toOctalString()

PURPOSE — Generates the string representation of a `long` as an unsigned octal number.

SYNTAX

```
public static String toHexString(long lnum)
```

DESCRIPTION — This method returns the string representation of `lnum` as an unsigned octal number. This is not always equivalent to `toString(lnum, 8)` because `toString()` always treats `lnum` as a signed number.

PARAMETERS

`lnum` — The `long` for which to generate the string representation.

RETURNS — The string representation of `lnum` as an unsigned octal number.

SEE ALSO — `parseLong()`, `toBinaryString()`, `toHexString()`, `toString()`, `valueOf()`.

EXAMPLE — See `toBinaryString()`.

toString()

PURPOSE — Generates the string representation of a `long` or a `Long` object

SYNTAX

```
public String toString()
public static String toString(long lnum)
public static String toString(long lnum, int radix)
```

DESCRIPTION — The three forms of this method are used to generate the string representation of a `long`. The first form returns the string representation of the `long` value of this `Long` object. The second form returns the string representation of `lnum` in base 10. The third form returns the string representation of `lnum` in base `radix`.

These methods are the inverse of `parseLong()` and `valueOf()`.

PARAMETERS

`lnum` — The number for which to generate the string representation.

`radix` — The radix to use when generating the string representation. If `radix` is not in the inclusive range of `Character.MAX_RADIX` and `Character.MIN_RADIX`, it defaults to 10.

RETURNS — The string representation of this `Long` object, or `lnum`.

OVERRIDES — `Object.toString()`.

SEE ALSO — `Character.MAX_RADIX`, `Character.MIN_RADIX`, `parseLong()`, `String.valueOf()`, `valueOf()`.

EXAMPLE

```
Long lnum = new Long(7981828);
String str = lnum.toString();                    // string of Long object
String str2 = Long.toString(312123412);          // string of long
String str3 = Long.toString(123318811, 16); // string of hex long
String pstr = "The three numbers are " + str + ", " + str2 + " ," +
    str3;
```

valueOf()

PURPOSE Creates a `Long` object using its string representation.

SYNTAX
```
public static Long valueOf(String str) throws
    NumberFormatException
public static Long valueOf(String str, int radix) throws
    NumberFormatException
```

DESCRIPTION These methods parse the string `str` into an integer and return a `Long` object constructed using the integer. If no radix is given, the radix used to parse `str` is 10. A negative integer has a leading minus ('`-`') character. A positive integer consists only of digits in the specified radix.

These methods are the inverse of `toString()`. `valueOf()` is similar to `parseLong()`, except `valueOf()` returns a `Long` object, while `parseLong()` returns a `long`.

PARAMETERS

`radix` The radix to use when parsing `str`. `radix` must be inclusively between `Character.MAX_RADIX` and `Character.MIN_RADIX`.

`str` The string to be parsed.

EXCEPTIONS

`NumberFormatException`
If `str` cannot be parsed into an integer of the specified radix.

SEE ALSO `Character.MAX_RADIX`, `Character.MIN_RADIX`, `parseLong()`, `toString()`.

EXAMPLE

```
String str = "89618291243";
try {
    Long l1 = Long.valueOf(str);      // parse number in radix 10
    Long l2 = Long.valueOf(str, 16); // parse number in radix 16
     ...
} catch (NumberFormatException e) {
    System.err.println("Could not convert string to number " + str);
}
```

java.net
MalformedURLException

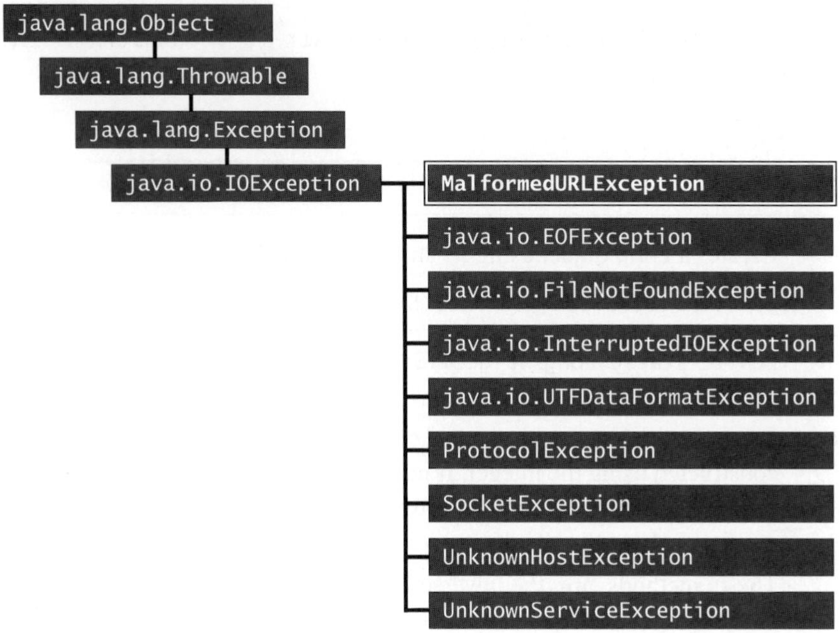

Syntax

```
public class MalformedURLException extends IOException
```

Description

URL stands for *Uniform Resource Locator*. It identifies the location of a resource on the World Wide Web. The `URL` class has constructors that allow you to create `URL` instances. If the arguments supplied to these constructors cannot be used to form a valid `URL`, `MalformedURLException` is thrown.

A method that throws `MalformedURLException` must declare it (or any of its superclasses) in its `throws` clause.

MEMBER SUMMARY	
Constructor	
`MalformedURLException()`	Constructs a `MalformedURLException` instance.

See Also

IOException, URL.

Example

This example throws MalformedURLException when it attempts to create a URL with an unknown protocol "funnyprot".

```
import java.net.URL;
import java.net.MalformedURLException;

class Main {
    public static void main(String[] args) {
        System.out.println("MalformedURLException example");
        try {
            URL url = new URL("funnyProt://www.test.com");
        } catch (MalformedURLException e) {
            e.printStackTrace();
        }
    }
}
```

MalformedURLException()

PURPOSE Constructs a MalformedURLException instance.

SYNTAX

```
public MalformedURLException()
public MalformedURLException(String msg)
```

DESCRIPTION The two forms of this constructor create a new instance of MalformedURLException. An optional string msg can be supplied that describes this particular instance of the exception.

PARAMETERS

msg A string that gives details about this exception.

java.lang
Math

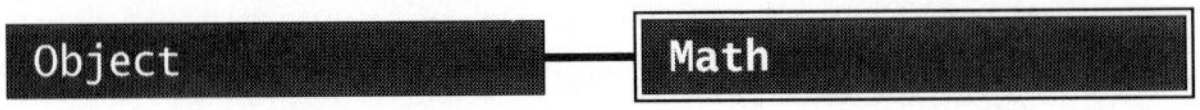

Syntax

```
public final class Math
```

Description

The `Math` class defines methods in the standard Math library. The library includes methods for calculating trigonometric functions, for rounding floating-point numbers into whole numbers, and for performing calculations using numbers. All methods and variables that this class defines are static.

This class cannot be subclassed or instantiated.

The ways by which these methods handle out-of-range or invalid results are platform-dependent.

MEMBER SUMMARY

Constant Fields	
`E`	The value of *e*.
`PI`	The value of π.
Methods for Rounding	
`ceil()`	Rounds a number to the smallest whole number greater than or equal to it.
`floor()`	Rounds a number to the largest whole number less than or equal to it.
`rint()`	Rounds a floating-point number to its closest whole number.
`round()`	Rounds a floating-point number to a whole number and casts it to an `int` or `long`.
Methods for Trigonometry	
`acos()`	Calculates the arc cosine of a number.
`asin()`	Calculates the arc sine of a number.
`atan()`	Calculates the arc tangent of a number.
`atan2()`	Converts rectangular coordinates to polar coordinates.
`cos()`	Calculates the trigonometric cosine of an angle.
`sin()`	Calculates the trigonometric sine of an angle.
`tan()`	Calculates the trigonometric tangent of an angle.

A B C D E F G H I J K L M N O P Q R S T U V W X Y Z

MEMBER SUMMARY

Other Methods

`abs()`	Calculates the absolute value of a number.
`exp()`	Calculates the result of *e* raised to a specified power.
`IEEEremainder()`	Calculates the remainder of the division between two floating-point numbers.
`log()`	Calculates the natural logarithm of a number.
`max()`	Determines the greater of two numbers.
`min()`	Determines the smaller of two numbers.
`pow()`	Calculates the result of raising a number to a specified power.
`random()`	Generates a random number between 0.0 and 1.0.
`sqrt()`	Calculates the square root of a number.

abs()

PURPOSE Calculates the absolute value of a number.

SYNTAX

```
public static int abs(int num)
public static long abs(long num)
public static float abs(float num)
public static double abs(double num)
```

DESCRIPTION The forms of this method return the absolute value of `num` in the same data type as `num`.

PARAMETERS

`num` The number of which to take the absolute value.

RETURNS The absolute value of `num` in the same type as `num`.

EXAMPLE

```
int inum = 10;
long lnum = -2934;
float fnum = -0.1243f;
double dnum = 21341390.8;

// take the total of the absolute values
double sum = Math.abs(inum) + Math.abs(lnum) +
    Math.abs(fnum) + Math.abs(dnum);
```

acos()

PURPOSE Calculates the arc cosine of a number.

SYNTAX `public static native double acos(double x)`

DESCRIPTION This method returns the arc cosine of a number, x, where $-1 \le x \le 1$. The result is between $0 \le \text{acos}\, x \le \pi$. If x is not in the range of -1 and 1, then the result is NaN.

PARAMETERS

x The cosine of an angle, where $-1 \le x \le 1$.

RETURNS The arc cosine of x, where $-1 \le x \le 1$; Double.NaN otherwise.

EXAMPLE

```
double x;
double alpha;
  ...
alpha = Math.acos(x);
```

asin()

PURPOSE Calculates the arc sine of a number.

SYNTAX `public static native double asin(double x)`

DESCRIPTION This method returns the arc sine of a number x, where $-1 \le x \le 1$. The result is between $-\pi/2 \le \text{asin}\, x \le \pi/2$.

PARAMETERS

x The sine of an angle, where $-1 \le x \le 1$.

RETURNS The arc sine of x, where $-1 \le x \le 1$; Double.NaN otherwise.

EXAMPLE

```
double x;
double alpha;
  ...
alpha = Math.asin(x);
```

atan()

PURPOSE Calculates the arc tangent of a number.

SYNTAX `public static native double atan(double x)`

DESCRIPTION This method returns the arc tangent of a number x, where $-\infty < x < \infty$. The result is between $-\pi/2 < \mathrm{atan}\, x < \pi/2$.

PARAMETERS

x The tangent of an angle, where $-\infty < x < \infty$.

RETURNS The arc tangent of x.

EXAMPLE

```
double x;
double alpha; // place holder for atan(x)
 ...
if (x >= 0)
    alpha = (Math.PI / 2) - Math.atan(1 / x);
```

atan2()

PURPOSE Converts rectangular coordinates to polar coordinates.

SYNTAX `public static native double atan2(double y, double x)`

DESCRIPTION This method converts rectangular coordinates (x,y) to polar coordinates (r, θ). r is called the radius vector and θ is called the vectorial angle. This method computes and returns the vectorial angle θ in the range –π to π. The radius vector can be computed using the formula $\sqrt{x^2 + y^2}$.

PARAMETERS

x The *x* part of the rectangular coordinates.

y The *y* part of the rectangular coordinates.

RETURNS The vectorial angle θ in radians.

EXAMPLE

```
double x, y;
x = -2.33;
y = 0;
double alpha = Math.atan2(y, x); // == pi;
```

ceil()

PURPOSE Rounds a number to the smallest whole number greater than or equal to it.

SYNTAX `public static native double ceil(double x)`

DESCRIPTION This method returns the ceiling of x. This is the smallest whole number greater than or equal to x.

PARAMETERS

x The floating-point number being rounded.

RETURNS The ceiling of x as a double.

SEE ALSO floor(), rint(), round().

EXAMPLE

```
double x = 879.327;
double ceilx = Math.ceil(x); // == 880
```

cos()

PURPOSE Calculates the trigonometric cosine of an angle.

SYNTAX `public static native double cos(double x)`

DESCRIPTION This method returns the cosine of the angle x.

PARAMETERS

x An angle measured in radians.

RETURNS The cosine of x.

EXAMPLE

```
// Calculate the cosine of a 60 degree angle
double angle = Math.PI / 3;
double cos = Math.cos(angle);
```

E

PURPOSE The value of *e*.

SYNTAX `public static final double E`

DESCRIPTION The floating-point representation (double) of the value of *e*, which is 2.718281828459045 2354.

EXAMPLE

```
// Calculate e**2
double e2 = Math.E * Math.E;
```

exp()

PURPOSE Calculates the result of e raised to a specified power.

SYNTAX `public static native double exp(double x)`

DESCRIPTION This method returns e^x.

PARAMETERS

x The power to raise e.

RETURNS e^x.

EXAMPLE

```
// Calculate e**pi
double ep = Math.exp(Math.PI);
```

floor()

PURPOSE Rounds a number to the largest whole number less than or equal to it.

SYNTAX `public static native double floor(double x)`

DESCRIPTION This method returns the floor of `x`. This is the largest whole number less than or equal to `x`.

PARAMETERS

x The floating-point number of which to take the floor.

RETURNS The floor of `x`.

SEE ALSO `ceil()`, `rint()`, `round()`.

EXAMPLE

```
double x = 879.327;
double floorx = Math.floor(x); // == 879
```

IEEEremainder()

PURPOSE Calculates the remainder of the division between two floating-point numbers.

SYNTAX `public static native double IEEEremainder(double f1, double f2)`

DESCRIPTION This method returns the remainder of dividing `f1` by `f2` as defined by IEEE754.

PARAMETERS

`f1`	The dividend.
`f2`	The divisor.

RETURNS The remainder.

EXAMPLE

```
double x = 8.892e20;
double y = 4.3109e3;
double rem = Math.IEEEremainder(x, y);
```

log()

PURPOSE Calculates the natural logarithm of a number.

SYNTAX `public static native double log(double x)`

DESCRIPTION This method returns $\log_e x$.

PARAMETERS

`x` The number to take the natural log of. $x \geq 0$.

EXCEPTIONS

`ArithmeticException`
If $x < 0$.

EXAMPLE

```
double x = 1.383e2;
double natural_log = Math.log(x);
```

max()

PURPOSE Determines the greater of two numbers.

SYNTAX
```
public static int max(int x, int y)
public static long max(long x, long y)
public static float max(float x, float y)
public static double max(double x, double y)
```

DESCRIPTION The four forms of this method return the greater of the numbers `x` and `y`. There is a method for each of the numeric types `int`, `long`, `float`, and `double`.

PARAMETERS

`x`	A number to be compared.
`y`	A number to be compared.

RETURNS The greater of x and y.

SEE ALSO `min()`.

EXAMPLE

```
int i1 = 28, i2 = 3, imax, imin;
long l1 = 960876, l2 = 78768, lmax, lmin;
float f1 = 1.384f, f2 = -2.83e2f, fmax, fmin;
double d1 = -2.3498e18, d2 = 8.792e8, dmax, dmin;

imax = Math.max(i1, i2);
lmax = Math.max(l1, l2);
fmax = Math.max(f1, f2);
dmax = Math.max(d1, d2);

imin = Math.min(i1, i2);
lmin = Math.min(l1, l2);
fmin = Math.min(f1, f2);
dmin = Math.min(d1, d2);
```

min()

PURPOSE Determines the smaller of two numbers.

SYNTAX

```
public static int min(int x, int y)
public static long min(long x, long y)
public static float min(float x, float y)
public static double min(double x, double y)
```

DESCRIPTION The four forms of the method return the smaller of the numbers x and y. There is a method for each of the numeric types `int`, `long`, `float`, and `double`.

PARAMETERS

x A number to be compared.

y A number to be compared.

RETURNS The smaller of x and y.

SEE ALSO `max()`.

EXAMPLE See `max()`.

PI

PURPOSE The value of π.

SYNTAX `public static final double PI`

DESCRIPTION The floating-point representation (`double`) of the value π, which is `3.14159265358979323846`.

EXAMPLE

```
public static double circleArea(double radius) {
    // area of a circle is pi*r**2
    return (Math.PI * Math.pow(radius, 2));
}
```

pow()

PURPOSE Calculates the result of raising a number to the specified power.

SYNTAX `public static native double pow(double x, double y)`

DESCRIPTION This method returns x^y. If x is 0, then y must be greater than 0. If x is 0 or negative, then y must be a whole number.

PARAMETERS

`x` The number to raise.

`y` The power by which to raise `x`. Must be a whole number unless `x` is a non-zero, positive number.

RETURNS x^y.

EXCEPTIONS

`ArithmeticException`
If x = 0 and y ≤ 0.

`ArithmeticException`
If x ≤ 0 and y is not a whole number.

EXAMPLE

```
double pow1 = Math.pow(21.2, 2.5);
double pow2 = Math.pow(-12, 2); // == 144
double pow3 = Math.pow(2, -1);  // == 0.5
```

random()

PURPOSE Generates a random number between 0.0 and 1.0.

SYNTAX `public static synchronized double random()`

DESCRIPTION This method returns a number between 0.0 and 1.0 using a *pseudorandom* number generator. Random number generators are often referred to as pseudorandom number generators because the numbers produced tend to repeat themselves after some number of calls.

RETURNS A pseudorandom number between 0.0 (inclusive) and 1.0 (exclusive).

SEE ALSO `Random`.

EXAMPLE

```
// Returns a number between 1 and 5 (inclusive)
public static short dice() {
    return (short)(Math.floor(Math.random() * 5) + 1);
}
```

rint()

PURPOSE Rounds a floating-point number to its closest whole number.

SYNTAX `public static native double rint(double x)`

DESCRIPTION This method rounds `x` into a whole number according to the IEEE754 rounding direction and returns it as a floating-point number (`double`). The rounding is to the closest whole number (same algorithm as `round()`, discussed next).

This method is similar to `round()`, except `rint()` returns the result as a `double`, while `round()` returns the result as an `int` or a `long`.

PARAMETERS

`x` The floating-point number to round.

RETURNS The value of `x` rounded and returned as a `double`.

SEE ALSO `ceil()`, `floor()`, `round()`.

EXAMPLE

```
double round1 = Math.rint(21.345); // == 21
double round2 = Math.rint(21.534); // == 22
```

round()

PURPOSE Rounds a floating-point number to its closest whole number.

SYNTAX
```
public static int round(float x)
public static long round(double x)
```

B

C DESCRIPTION The two forms of this method round `x` to its closest whole number by first adding 0.5 to `x` and then returning the largest integer that is less than or equal to this new value. A `float` is rounded to an `int`; a `double` is rounded to a `long`. When the resulting number does not fit into an `int` or a `long`, the result is that of `Integer.MAX_VALUE` or `Integer.MIN_VALUE`, or of `Long.MAX_VALUE` or `Long.MIN_VALUE`, respectively.

`round()` is similar to `rint()`, except `round()` returns the result as an `int` or a `long`, while `rint()` returns the result as a `double`.

PARAMETERS

`x` The number to round.

RETURNS The rounded off whole number. If `x` is a `float`, the return type is an `int`. If `x` is a `double`, the return type is a `long`.

SEE ALSO `ceil()`, `floor()`, `round()`.

EXAMPLE

```
int round = Math.round(5.62e2f);      // == 562
long lround = Math.round(1243.45);    // == 1243
```

sin()

PURPOSE Calculates the trigonometric sine of an angle.

SYNTAX `public static native double sin(double x)`

DESCRIPTION This method returns the sine of the angle `x`.

PARAMETERS

`x` An angle measured in radians.

RETURNS The sine of `x`.

EXAMPLE

```
// Calculate the sine of a 30 degree angle
double angle = Math.PI / 6;
double sin = Math.sin(angle);
```

sqrt()

PURPOSE Calculates the square root of a number.

SYNTAX `public static native double sqrt(double x)`

DESCRIPTION This method returns the square root of the positive number `x`.

PARAMETERS

`x` The number of which to take the square root. `x` must be a positive number.

RETURNS The square root of `x`.

EXCEPTIONS

`ArithmeticException`

If `x` is negative.

EXAMPLE

```
double sqrt1 = Math.sqrt(2);
```

tan()

PURPOSE Calculates the trigonometric tangent of an angle.

SYNTAX `public static native double tan(double x)`

DESCRIPTION This method returns the trigonometric tangent of the angle `x`.

PARAMETERS

`x` An angle measured in radians.

RETURNS The tangent of `x`.

EXAMPLE

```
double angle = 3 * Math.PI / 4;
double tan = Math.tan(angle);
```

A B C D E F G H I J K L M N O P Q R S T U V W X Y Z

java.awt
MediaTracker

java.lang.Object — **MediaTracker**

Syntax

```
public class MediaTracker
```

Description

The imaging routines in the AWT are designed to allow images to be used before they're completely loaded or generated. However, in some cases, you may want or need to wait until all the pixels of an image are available before rendering the image. For example, an application may wish to display an image for the user to view, while in the background it loads another image. Once the other image is loaded, the application replaces the currently displayed image.

The media tracker is used to manage the loading of images. It makes it convenient to determine when all the pixels have been received or if an error occurred.

The media tracker also makes it convenient to track the loading status of a set of images. It does this by allowing you to choose an arbitrary integer called the *id* and then associating all the images in the set with the id. By using the id, you can treat the entire set of images as one image. For example, you can start the loading of all the images in the set, or you can check if any image in the set has encountered an error, or you can wait until all the images have been loaded and then determine if every image loaded successfully.

Media tracker ids are often used with an animation frame, which consists of many images that need to be loaded or generated. Typically, all the images must be complete, otherwise none of the images can be used. That is, if any one of the images in the set encounters an error during its construction, then the whole set should be considered invalid.

MEMBER SUMMARY

Constructor	
`MediaTracker()`	Constructs a `MediaTracker` object.
Status Flag Constants	
`ABORTED`	Specifies that the image loading process was aborted.
`COMPLETE`	Specifies that the image loading process was completed successfully.
`ERRORED`	Specifies that the image loading process encountered an error.
`LOADING`	Specifies that the image loading process is in progress.

MEMBER SUMMARY

Status Methods	
`checkAll()`	Determines if all images have been loaded.
`checkID()`	Determines if all images tagged with an id have been loaded.
`getErrorsAny()`	Retrieves a list of all images that have encountered an error.
`getErrorsID()`	Retrieves a list of all images tagged with an id that have encountered an error.
`isErrorAny()`	Determines if any image encountered an error during loading.
`isErrorID()`	Determines if any image tagged with an id encountered an error during loading.
`statusAll()`	Determines the combined status of all images.
`statusID()`	Determines the combined status of all images tagged with ids.
Image Methods	
`addImage()`	Adds a scaled image to the list of images being tracked.
`imageUpdate()`	Should not be used.
`waitForAll()`	Waits for all images to be loaded.
`waitForID()`	Waits for all images tagged with lan id to be loaded.

Example

FIGURE 178 `MediaTracker`

This example implements a slide show program. See Figure 178. The program is invoked with a list of files that contain images. The images are displayed in the order in which they appear in the list. They also are loaded in the same order; that is, an image does not begin loading until the previous image has been completely loaded.

The program provides two buttons—Next and Previous—for moving through the slides. The Next button displays the next image in the list. However, it is enabled only if the next image has been completely loaded.

A thread is used to successively load each image in order. So while the user views an image, the program is busily loading the next image. If an error occurs in the loading of an image, the image appears as a red rectangle. After all the images have been loaded, the program prints status information about each image.

To implement the enabling and disabling of the two buttons, the program uses `statusID()` instead of `checkID()`. This is because `checkID()` returns `true` if an id has not been used (i.e., no image has been added using it), whereas `statusID()` returns `0` if the id has not been used.

Using statusID() makes it easy to disable the buttons for the id preceding the first image and following the last image. It might have been clearer simply to test for (curImage-1 < 0) or (curImage+1 > images.length), but we wanted to demonstrate the difference between statusID() and checkID().

```
import java.awt.*;
import java.awt.image.*;
class Main extends Frame implements Runnable {
    MediaTracker tracker;
    Image[] images;
    ImageCanvas icv = new ImageCanvas();
    Button btnNext = new Button("Next");
    Button btnPrevious = new Button("Previous");

    Main(String[] files) {
        super("MediaTracker Example");

        tracker = new MediaTracker(icv);
        images = new Image[files.length];
        for (int i=0; i<images.length; i++) {
            images[i] = getToolkit().getImage(files[i]);
            tracker.addImage(images[i], i);
        }

        // First image is progressively rendered.
        if (images.length > 0) {
            icv.setImage(images[0]);
        }

        add("Center", icv);
        add("North", btnPrevious);
        add("South", btnNext);
        resize(460, 250);
        show();
        (new Thread(this)).start();

        // Print overall status information.
        try {
            // We don't use waitForAll() because it forces
            // all images to start loading; we want to load
            // images one at a time.
            // tracker.waitForAll();
            while (!tracker.checkAll()) {
                Thread.sleep(1000);
            }
        } catch (Exception e) {
            e.printStackTrace();
            System.exit(1);
        }
        if (tracker.isErrorAny()) {
            System.out.println
                ("Not all images have been successfully loaded.");
            Object[] list = tracker.getErrorsAny();
```

```
            for (int i=0; i<list.length; i++) {
                System.out.println(list[i]);
            }
        } else {
            System.out.println
                ("All images have been successfully loaded");
        }
        for (int i=0; i<images.length; i++) {
            int s = tracker.statusID(i, false);

            System.out.print(files[i] + ": ");
            if ((s & MediaTracker.ABORTED) != 0)
                    System.out.print("ABORTED ");
            if ((s & MediaTracker.COMPLETE) != 0)
                    System.out.print("COMPLETE ");
            if ((s & MediaTracker.ERRORED) != 0)
                    System.out.print("ERRORED ");
            if ((s & MediaTracker.LOADING) != 0)
                    System.out.print("LOADING ");
            System.out.println();
        }
    }

    int curImage;
    final int DONE = (MediaTracker.ABORTED | MediaTracker.ERRORED
                      | MediaTracker.COMPLETE);
    public void paint(Graphics g) {
        if (tracker.isErrorID(curImage)) {
            icv.setImage(null);
        } else {
            icv.setImage(images[curImage]);
        }
        btnNext.enable((tracker.statusID(curImage+1, false)&DONE)
              != 0);
        btnPrevious.enable((tracker.statusID(curImage-1, false)&DONE)
              != 0);

        /* See example description for explanation:
        btnNext.enable(tracker.checkID(curImage+1));
        btnPrevious.enable(tracker.checkID(curImage-1));
        */
    }

    public boolean action(Event evt, Object arg) {
        if ("Next".equals(arg)) {
            if (curImage < images.length-1) {
                ++curImage;
                repaint();
            }
            return true;
        } else if ("Previous".equals(arg)) {
            if (curImage > 0) {
                --curImage;
                repaint();
```

```
                }
                return true;
            }
            return false;
        }

        public void run() {
            for (int i=0; i<images.length; i++) {
                try {
                    tracker.waitForID(i);
                } catch (Exception e) {
                    e.printStackTrace();
                }
                repaint();
            }
        }

        static public void main(String[] args) {
            new Main(args);
        }
    }

    class ImageCanvas extends Canvas {
        Image image;
        boolean clear;

        public void setImage(Image image) {
            this.image = image;
            clear = true;
            repaint();
        }

        public void update(Graphics g) {
            paint(g);
        }

        public void paint(Graphics g) {
            if (image == null) {
                g.setColor(Color.red);
                g.fillRect(0, 0, size().width, size().height);
            } else {
                if (clear) {
                    g.clearRect(0, 0, size().width, size().height);
                    clear = false;
                }
                int w = image.getWidth(this);
                int h = image.getHeight(this);
                if (w >= 0 && h >= 0) {
                    g.drawImage(image, (size().width-w)/2,
                        (size().height-h)/2, this);
                }
            }
        }
    }
```

ABORTED

PURPOSE Specifies that the image loading process was aborted.

SYNTAX `public static final int ABORTED`

DESCRIPTION This field is a status flag that specifies that the image loading process was aborted.

SEE ALSO `statusAll()`, `statusID()`.

EXAMPLE See the class example.

addImage()

PURPOSE Adds a scaled image to the list of images being tracked.

SYNTAX
```
public void addImage(Image image, int id)
public synchronized void addImage(Image image, int id, int w,
   int h)
```

DESCRIPTION The two forms of this method associates an image with the media tracker id `id`. Several images can be associated with `id`. The image will eventually be rendered at the indicated size.

PARAMETERS

`h` The height in pixels at which the image will be rendered.
`id` The identifier used to later track this image.
`image` The non-`null` image to be tracked.
`w` The width in pixels at which the image will be rendered.

EXAMPLE See the class example.

checkAll()

PURPOSE Determines if all images have been loaded.

SYNTAX
```
public boolean checkAll()
public synchronized boolean checkAll(boolean load)
```

DESCRIPTION The two forms of this method return `true` if all the images have been loaded. An image is defined to be loaded if either the image successfully loaded or it encountered an error. In other words, this method returns `true` if none of the images will receive more pixels. The method `isErrorAny()` can be used to determine if an error occurred during the loading of at least one image in the media tracker.

If `load` is `true` and not all the images have started loading, the loading process is started for all images. If `load` is not specified, it defaults to `false`.

PARAMETERS

`load` If `true`, the loading process is started for all images.

RETURNS `true` if all images are loaded.

SEE ALSO `checkID()`, `isErrorAny()`, `statusAll()`.

EXAMPLE See the class example.

checkID()

PURPOSE Determines if all images tagged with an id have been loaded.

SYNTAX

```
public boolean checkID(int id)
public synchronized boolean checkID(int id, boolean load)
```

DESCRIPTION This method returns `true` if all the images tagged with `id` have been loaded. An image is defined to be loaded if either it successfully loaded or it encountered an error. In other words, this method returns `true` if no image tagged with `id` will receive more pixels. The method `isErrorID()` can be used to determine if an error occurred during the loading of at least one of the images tagged with `id`.

If load is `true` and the images tagged with `id` have not started loading, the loading process is started for these images. If `load` is not specified, it defaults to `false`.

If no images are associated with `id`, this method returns `true`.

PARAMETERS

`id` The media tracker id.

`load` If `true`, the loading process is started for all images tagged with `id`.

RETURNS `true` if all images tagged with `id` are loaded.

SEE ALSO `checkID()`, `isErrorID()`, `statusID()`.

COMPLETE

PURPOSE Specifies that the image loading process was completed successfully.

SYNTAX

```
public static final int COMPLETE
```

DESCRIPTION	This field is a status flag that specifies that the image loading process was completed successfully.
SEE ALSO	`statusAll()`, `statusID()`.
EXAMPLE	See the class example.

ERRORED

PURPOSE	Specifies that the image loading process encountered an error.
SYNTAX	`public static final int ERRORED`
DESCRIPTION	This field is a status flag that specifies that the image loading process encountered an error.
SEE ALSO	`statusAll()`, `statusID()`.
EXAMPLE	See the class example.

getErrorsAny()

PURPOSE	Retrieves a list of all images that have encountered an error.
SYNTAX	`public synchronized Object[] getErrorsAny()`
DESCRIPTION	This method returns a list of all images that have encountered errors so far.
RETURNS	`null` if there are no errors or an array of all images that have encountered errors.
SEE ALSO	`getErrorsID()`, `isErrorAny()`.
EXAMPLE	See the class example.

getErrorsID()

PURPOSE	Retrieves a list of all images tagged with an id that have encountered an error.
SYNTAX	`public synchronized Object[] getErrorsID(int id)`
DESCRIPTION	This method returns a list of images tagged with `id` that have encountered errors so far.

A B C D E F G H I J K L M N O P Q R S T U V W X Y Z

PARAMETERS

`id`	The media tracker id.

RETURNS `null` if there are no errors or an array of all images that have encountered errors.

SEE ALSO `isErrorID()`, `isErrorAny()`.

EXAMPLE See the class example.

imageUpdate()

PURPOSE This method should not be used.

SYNTAX
```
public boolean imageUpdate(Image img, int infoflags, int x,
    int y, int w, int h)
```

DESCRIPTION The `MediaTracker` class implements this method as part of the `ImageConsumer` interface. It should not be used.

PARAMETERS

`h`	This value depends on the status bits enabled in `infoflags`.
`img`	The non-`null` image being updated.
`infoflags`	A set of status bits.
`w`	This value depends on the status bits enabled in `infoflags`.
`x`	This value depends on the status bits enabled in `infoflags`.
`y`	This value depends on the status bits enabled in `infoflags`.

RETURNS `true` if no further calls to the `imageUpdate()` are needed.

isErrorAny()

PURPOSE Determines if any images encountered an error during loading.

SYNTAX `public synchronized boolean isErrorAny()`

RETURNS `true` if any images encountered an error during loading; `false` otherwise.

SEE ALSO `getErrorsAny()`, `isErrorID()`.

EXAMPLE See the class example.

isErrorID()

PURPOSE Determines if any images tagged with an id encountered an error during loading.

SYNTAX `public synchronized boolean isErrorID(int id)`

PARAMETERS

`id` The media tracker id.

RETURNS `true` if any of the images tagged with `id` encountered an error during loading; `false` otherwise.

SEE ALSO `getErrorsID()`, `isErrorAny()`.

EXAMPLE See the class example.

LOADING

PURPOSE Specifies that the image loading process is in progress.

SYNTAX `public static final int LOADING`

DESCRIPTION This field is a status flag that specifies that the image loading process is in progress.

SEE ALSO `statusAll()`, `statusID()`.

EXAMPLE See the class example.

MediaTracker()

PURPOSE Constructs a `MediaTracker` object.

SYNTAX `public MediaTracker(Component comp)`

DESCRIPTION Constructs a new `MediaTracker` object for the component `comp`. The media tracker will register `comp` with the image producers of the images it maintains (see `ImageProducer`) and will process the `imageUpdate()` notifications from the image producers; these notifications are not passed onto `comp`. However, even if the media tracker has registered `comp`, `comp` is free to register itself with the same image producer if it also desires update notifications.

The `comp` object is used only in a call to `comp.prepareImage()` to start the loading of the image pixels.

B

C PARAMETERS

comp The non-null component on which the images will eventually be drawn.

D EXAMPLE See the class example.

E

F

statusAll()

G PURPOSE Determines the combined status of all images.

H SYNTAX `public int statusAll(boolean load)`

I DESCRIPTION This method determines the status of all images in the media tracker and combines them together as one status. For example, if some image is still in the process of being loaded, this method returns a status with the `LOADING` flag set. The status for an image that has not started loading is 0.

J

K If `load` is `true` and the images have not started loading, the loading process is started for these images.

L PARAMETERS

M `load` If `true`, the loading process is started for all images.

RETURNS The bitwise "or" of the status of all images.

N SEE ALSO `ABORTED`, `COMPLETE`, `ERRORED`, `LOADING`, `statusID()`.

O EXAMPLE See the class example.

P

Q

statusID()

R PURPOSE Determines the combined status of all images tagged with an id.

S SYNTAX `public int statusID(int id, boolean load)`

T DESCRIPTION This method determines the status of all images tagged with `id` and combines them together as one status. For example, if one of the images tagged with `id` is still in the process of being loaded, this method returns a status with the `LOADING` flag set. The status for an image that has not started loading is 0.

U

V If `load` is `true` and the images tagged with `id` have not started loading, the loading process is started for these images.

W PARAMETERS

X `id` The media tracker id.

`load` If `true`, the loading process is started for all images tagged with `id`.

Y

Z

RETURNS The bitwise "or" of the status of all images tagged with `id`.

SEE ALSO `ABORTED`, `COMPLETE`, `ERRORED`, `LOADING`, `statusAll()`.

EXAMPLE See the class example.

waitForAll()

PURPOSE Waits for all images to be loaded.

SYNTAX
```
public void waitForAll() throws InterruptedException
public synchronized boolean waitForAll(long ms) throws
   InterruptedException
```

DESCRIPTION The two forms of this method return only when all the images have been loaded or when `ms` milliseconds have expired. An image is defined to be loaded if either it successfully loaded or it encountered an error. In other words, this method returns `true` if no image will receive more pixels. The method `isErrorAny()` can be used to determine if an error occurred during the loading of at least one image in the media tracker.

This method starts the loading process for any images that have not been loaded. If `ms` is not specified, this method does not return until all images have been loaded.

PARAMETERS

`ms` The length of time in milliseconds to wait for the loading to complete.

RETURNS `true` if all images were successfully loaded.

EXCEPTIONS

`InterruptedException`

If another thread interrupted this thread.

SEE ALSO `isErrorAny()`, `waitForID()`.

EXAMPLE See the class example.

waitForID()

PURPOSE Waits for all images tagged with an id to be loaded.

SYNTAX
```
public void waitForID(int id) throws InterruptedException
public synchronized boolean waitForID(int id, long ms) throws
   InterruptedException
```

DESCRIPTION The two forms of this method return only when all the images tagged with `id` have been loaded or when `ms` milliseconds have expired. An image is defined to be loaded if either it successfully loaded or it encountered an error. In other words, this method returns `true` if no image will receive more pixels. The method `isErrorID()` can be used to determine if an error occurred during the loading of at least one image in the media tracker.

This method starts the loading process for any images tagged with `id` that have not been loaded. If `ms` is not specified, this method does not return until all images have been loaded.

PARAMETERS

`id` The media tracker id.

`ms` The length of time in milliseconds to wait for the loading to complete.

RETURNS `true` if all images tagged with `id` were successfully loaded.

EXCEPTIONS

`InterruptedException`

If another thread interrupted this thread.

SEE ALSO `isErrorID()`, `waitForAll()`.

EXAMPLE See the class example.

java.awt.image
MemoryImageSource

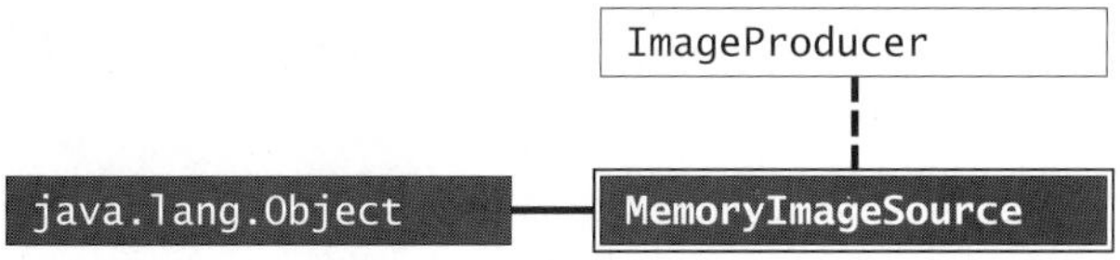

Syntax

```
public class MemoryImageSource implements ImageProducer
```

Description

The `MemoryImageSource` class is used to create an image producer that delivers pixels from a buffer in memory. This class is most often used when an image is generated in memory using an algorithm and then needs to be converted into an image.

For a description of the image consumer and image producer framework, see the `ImageConsumer` interface.

MEMBER SUMMARY

Constructor	
`MemoryImageSource()`	Constructs a new `MemoryImageSource` instance.
Image Producer Methods	
`addConsumer()`	Registers an image consumer with this image producer.
`isConsumer()`	Determines if an image consumer is registered with this image producer.
`removeConsumer()`	Removes a registered image consumer from this image producer.
`requestTopDownLeftRightResend()`	Request by an image consumer to retransmit pixels in top-down, left-right order.
`startProduction()`	Triggers the delivery of image data.

A B C D E F G H I J K L M N O P Q R S T U V W X Y Z

Example

This example generates the Mandelbrot set in a pixel buffer and uses the `MemoryImageSource` image producer to create an image pixel buffer. A 16-color index color model is used to represent the pixel values. See Figure 179.

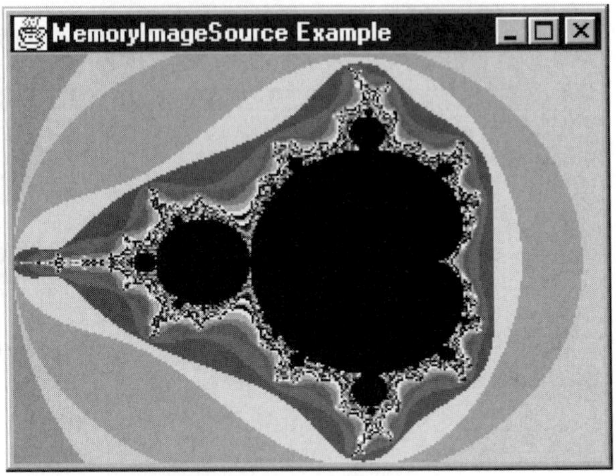

FIGURE 179 `MemoryImageSource`

```
import java.awt.*;
import java.awt.image.*;
import java.net.*;
import java.util.*;
class Main extends Frame {
    Main() {
        super("MemoryImageSource Example");
        try {
            add("Center", new MandelbrotCanvas());
        } catch (Exception e) {
            e.printStackTrace();
        }
        resize(300, 200);
        show();
    }

    static public void main(String[] args) {
        new Main();
    }
}

class MandelbrotCanvas extends Canvas {
    Image image;

    public void paint(Graphics g) {
        if (image == null ) {
            image = getToolkit().createImage(
                new MemoryImageSource(300, 200,
                generateColorModel(), generatePixels(300, 200), 0,
                    300));
        }
        g.drawImage(image, 0, 0, this);
    }

    IndexColorModel generateColorModel() {
        byte[] r = new byte[16];
        byte[] g = new byte[16];
        byte[] b = new byte[16];
```

```
        r[0] = 0; g[0] = 0; b[0] = 0;
        r[1] = 0; g[1] = 0; b[1] = (byte)192;
        r[2] = 0; g[2] = 0; b[2] = (byte)255;
        r[3] = 0; g[3] = (byte)192; b[3] = 0;
        r[4] = 0; g[4] = (byte)255; b[4] = 0;
        r[5] = 0; g[5] = (byte)192; b[5] = (byte)192;
        r[6] = 0; g[6] = (byte)255; b[6] = (byte)255;
        r[7] = (byte)192; g[7] = 0; b[7] = 0;
        r[8] = (byte)255; g[8] = 0; b[8] = 0;
        r[9] = (byte)192; g[9] = 0; b[9] = (byte)192;
        r[10] = (byte)255; g[10] = 0; b[10] = (byte)255;
        r[11] = (byte)192; g[11] = (byte)192; b[11] = 0;
        r[12] = (byte)255; g[12] = (byte)255; b[12] = 0;
        r[13] = (byte)80; g[13] = (byte)80; b[13] = (byte)80;
        r[14] = (byte)192; g[14] = (byte)192; b[14] = (byte)192;
        r[15] = (byte)255; g[15] = (byte)255; b[15] = (byte)255;

        return new IndexColorModel(4, 16, r, g, b);
    }

    final float xmin = -2.0f;
    final float xmax = 1.2f;
    final float ymin = -1.2f;
    final float ymax = 1.2f;
    byte[] generatePixels(int w, int h) {
        byte[] pixels = new byte[w * h];
        int pIx = 0;
        float[] p = new float[w];
        float q = ymin;
        float dp = (xmax-xmin)/w;
        float dq = (ymax-ymin)/h;

        p[0] = xmin;
        for (int i=1; i<w; i++) {
            p[i] = p[i-1] + dp;
        }

        for (int r=0; r<h; r++) {
            for (int c=0; c<w; c++) {
                int color = 1;
                float x = 0.0f;
                float y = 0.0f;
                float xsqr = 0.0f;
                float ysqr = 0.0f;
                do {
                    xsqr = x*x;
                    ysqr = y*y;
                    y = 2*x*y + q;
                    x = xsqr - ysqr + p[c];
                    color++;
                } while (color < 512 && xsqr + ysqr < 4);
                pixels[pIx++] = (byte)(color % 16);
            }
            q += dq;
```

```
            }
            return pixels;
        }
    }
```

addConsumer()

PURPOSE Registers an image consumer with this image producer.

SYNTAX `public synchronized void addConsumer(ImageConsumer ic)`

DESCRIPTION See `ImageProducer.addConsumer()` for details on how an image consumer should use this method.

PARAMETERS

`ic` The non-`null` image consumer to register.

SEE ALSO `ImageConsumer`.

EXAMPLE See `ImageProducer.addConsumer()`.

isConsumer()

PURPOSE Determines if an image consumer is registered with this image producer.

SYNTAX `public synchronized boolean isConsumer(ImageConsumer ic)`

DESCRIPTION See `ImageProducer.isConsumer()` for details on how an image consumer should use this method.

PARAMETERS

`ic` The possibly `null` image consumer to check if registered.

RETURNS `true` if `ic` has been registered; `false` otherwise.

SEE ALSO `ImageConsumer`.

EXAMPLE See `ImageProducer.isConsumer()`.

MemoryImageSource()

PURPOSE Constructs a new `MemoryImageSource` instance.

SYNTAX

```
public MemoryImageSource(int w, int h, int[] pix, int off, int
   scansize)
public MemoryImageSource(int w, int h, int[] pix, int off, int
   scansize, Hashtable props)
public MemoryImageSource(int w, int h, ColorModel cm, byte[] pix,
   int off, int scansize)
public MemoryImageSource(int w, int h, ColorModel cm, int[] pix,
   int off, int scansize)
public MemoryImageSource(int w, int h, ColorModel cm, byte[] pix,
   int off, int scansize, Hashtable props)
public MemoryImageSource(int w, int h, ColorModel cm, int[] pix,
   int off, int scansize, Hashtable props)
```

DESCRIPTION The six forms of this constructor construct an image producer that delivers pixels from a memory buffer.

`w` and `h` specify the width and height of the image.

`pix` contains the pixel values of the image. The first pixel value is located at `pix[off]` and each row of pixel values in `pix` occupies `scansize` elements. In summary, the pixel `(x, y)` (the top-left corner pixel of the image) is stored in the pix array at `[x + y * scansize + off]`.

`cm` specifies the color model in which the pixel values in `pix` are encoded. If `cm` is not specified, the default color model is used (see the `ColorModel` class).

`props` is a hash table of image properties (see `ImageConsumer`) that the new image producer should deliver to the image consumer. If `props` is not specified or is `null`, an empty hash table is delivered to the image consumer.

PARAMETERS

`cm`	The non-`null` color model.
`h`	The height of the image in pixels.
`off`	The index of the first pixel value in `pix`.
`pix`	The buffer of pixel values.
`props`	The possibly `null` hash table of image properties.
`scansize`	The width to use when extracting pixels from the `pix` array.
`w`	The width of the image in pixels.

SEE ALSO `ColorModel.getRGBdefault()`.

EXAMPLE See the class example.

removeConsumer()

PURPOSE Removes a registered image consumer from this image producer.

SYNTAX `public synchronized void removeConsumer(ImageConsumer ic)`

DESCRIPTION See `ImageProducer.removeConsumer()` for details on how an image consumer should use this method.

PARAMETERS

`ic` The non-`null` image consumer to be removed.

EXAMPLE See `ImageProducer.removeConsumer()`.

requestTopDownLeftRightResend()

PURPOSE Requests by an image consumer to retransmit pixels in top-down, left-right order.

SYNTAX `public void requestTopDownLeftRightResend(ImageConsumer ic)`

DESCRIPTION See `ImageProducer.requestTopDownLeftRightResend()` for details on how an image consumer should use this method.

PARAMETERS

`ic` The non-`null` image consumer requesting the retransmission.

SEE ALSO `ImageConsumer`.

EXAMPLE See `ImageProducer.requestTopDownLeftRightResend()`.

startProduction()

PURPOSE Triggers the delivery of image data.

SYNTAX `public void startProduction(ImageConsumer ic)`

DESCRIPTION See `ImageProducer.startProduction()` for details on how an image consumer should use this method.

PARAMETERS

`ic` The non-`null` image consumer ready to receive pixels.

SEE ALSO `ImageConsumer`.

EXAMPLE See `ImageProducer.startProduction()`.

Menu

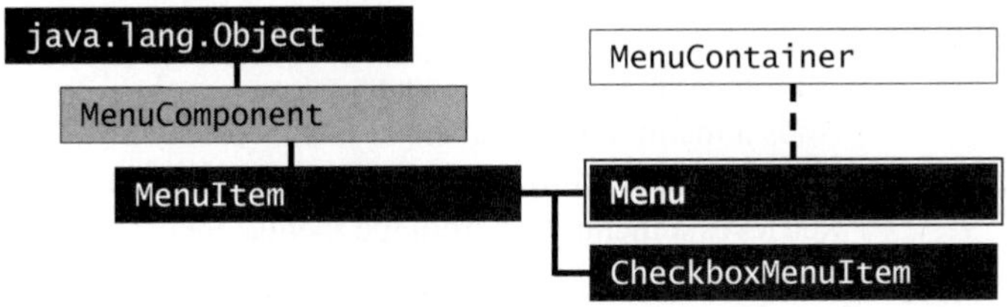

Syntax

```
public class Menu extends MenuItem implements MenuContainer
```

Description

A *menu* is an object that is inserted into a menu bar. Menus in turn contain menu items. Figure 180 shows a menu bar with two menus. The File menu is active; it contains two menu items.

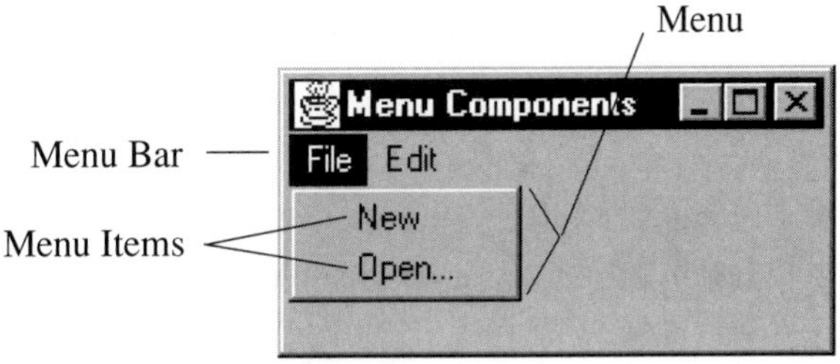

FIGURE 180 The Three Kinds of Menu Components

The Label Property

A menu has a *label*, which is used when inserted into a menu bar. The menu bar normally displays only the menu's label. When the user clicks the menu's label, the menu appears.

The Tear-off Property

Some platforms support the menu *tear-off* property. If this property is supported and enabled, the user can make a user interface gesture to clone the menu as a top-level window. When a menu is torn off, both the original menu on the menu bar and the torn-off menu can be used to select menu items. The torn-off menu can be deleted by the user when it is no longer needed.

A B C D E F G H I J K L M N O P Q R S T U V W X Y Z

MEMBER SUMMARY

Constructor	
`Menu()`	Constructs a new `Menu` instance.
Menu Item Methods	
`add()`	Adds a menu item to the menu.
`addSeparator()`	Adds a menu item separator to the menu.
`countItems()`	Retrieves the number of menu items in the menu.
`getItem()`	Retrieves a menu item from the menu.
`remove()`	Removes a menu item from the menu.
Property Method	
`isTearOff()`	Determines if the menu is a tear-off menu.
Peer Methods	
`addNotify()`	Creates the menu's peer hierarchy.
`removeNotify()`	Destroys the menu's peer hierarchy.

Example

This example uses a menu. (For a simpler example using a menu, see the `Menu` constructor example.) See Figure 181. It creates a Command menu that maintains a fixed list of commands. Each time a command is executed, it gets added to the top of the menu. If a command already appears in the menu, it is moved to the top of the menu. The menu can hold only 10 commands, so if the menu is full, the menu item at the bottom of the list is first removed before a new command is added.

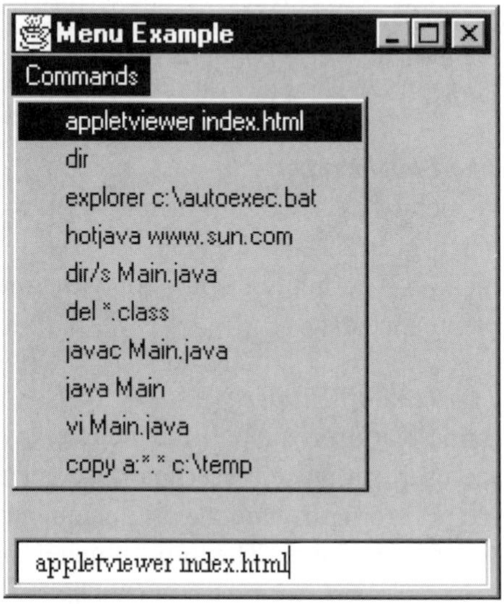

FIGURE 181 `Menu`

```
import java.awt.*;
import java.util.*;
class Main extends Frame {
    Vector commands = new Vector();
    Menu m = new Menu("Commands");

    Main() {
        super("Menu Example");
        MenuBar mb = new MenuBar();

        // Add menu to menu bar.
        mb.add(m);
```

```
        // Set the menu bar on the frame.
        setMenuBar(mb);
        add("South", new TextField());
        resize(100, 50);
        show();
    }

    void updateMenu(Menu m) {
        // First remove all the menu items.
        while (m.countItems() > 0) {
            m.remove(0);
        }
        // Then add them back in.
        for (int i=0; i<commands.size(); i++) {
            m.add((String)commands.elementAt(i));
        }
    }

    public void addCommand(String cmd) {
        for (int i=0; i<m.countItems(); i++) {
            MenuItem mi = (MenuItem)m.getItem(i);
            if (mi.getLabel().equals(cmd)) {
                // Move command to top of list.
                commands.removeElementAt(i);
                commands.insertElementAt(cmd, 0);
                updateMenu(m);
                return;
            }
        }
        if (m.countItems() >= 10) {
            // Remove last command from list.
            commands.removeElementAt(commands.size()-1);
        }
        commands.insertElementAt(cmd, 0);
        updateMenu(m);
    }

    public boolean action(Event evt, Object what) {
        if (evt.target instanceof TextField) {
            addCommand((String)what);
            return true;
        }
        return false;
    }

    static public void main(String[] args) {
        new Main();
    }
}
```

add()

PURPOSE Adds a menu item to the menu.

SYNTAX
```
public void add(MenuItem menuItem)
public void add(String label)
```

DESCRIPTION The two forms of this method add the menu item `menuItem` to the end of the menu. If the string `label` is specified instead of a menu item, a menu item with the label `label` is automatically created and added to the menu. If `label` is "-," a separator is added to the menu. If the menu item already has a parent, it is first removed from its parent before being added to the menu.

PARAMETERS

`label` The non-`null` string specifying the label of the menu item.

`menuItem` The non-`null` menu item.

EXAMPLE See the class example.

addNotify()

PURPOSE Creates the menu's peer hierarchy.

SYNTAX
```
public synchronized void addNotify()
```

DESCRIPTION This method creates the menu's peer hierarchy if it does not yet exist. The menu's peer is created by calling the `Toolkit.createMenu()` method. This method should never be called directly. It is normally called by the menu component's container.

OVERRIDES `MenuItem.addNotify()`,

SEE ALSO `Toolkit`.

EXAMPLE See `Component.show()`.

addSeparator()

PURPOSE Adds a menu item separator to the menu.

SYNTAX
```
public void addSeparator()
```

DESCRIPTION This method creates a menu item with the label "-" and adds it to the end of the menu.

EXAMPLE See the class example.

A B C D E F G H I J K L M N O P Q R S T U V W X Y Z

countItems()

PURPOSE Retrieves the number of menu items in the menu.

SYNTAX `public int countItems()`

DESCRIPTION This method retrieves the number of menu items in this menu, including any menu item separators.

RETURNS The number of menu items in the menu.

EXAMPLE See the class example.

getItem()

PURPOSE Retrieves a menu item from the menu.

SYNTAX `public MenuItem getItem(int pos)`

DESCRIPTION This method retrieves the menu item at index `pos` in this menu.

RETURNS The menu item at the index `pos`.

PARAMETERS

`pos` The 0-based index of the menu item in the menu.

EXAMPLE See the class example.

isTearOff()

PURPOSE Determines if the menu is a tear-off menu.

SYNTAX `public boolean isTearOff()`

DESCRIPTION See the class description for more information about tear-off menus.

RETURNS `true` if the menu is a tear-off menu; `false` otherwise.

Menu()

PURPOSE Constructs a new `Menu` instance.

SYNTAX

```
public Menu(String label)
public Menu(String label, boolean tearOff)
```

DESCRIPTION The two forms of this constructor create a new `menu` with the label `label`. If `tearOff` is `true`, then the menu can be torn off. If `tearOff` is not specified, it defaults to `false`.

PARAMETERS

`label` The non-`null` string specifying the menu's label.

`tearOff` Specifies whether the menu can be torn off.

EXAMPLE See the class example.

remove()

PURPOSE Removes a menu item from the menu.

SYNTAX
```
public synchronized void remove(int pos)
public synchronized void remove(MenuComponent menuItem)
```

DESCRIPTION The two forms of this method remove the menu item `menuitem` from this menu. If `menuItem` is not in the menu, this method call is ignored. If `pos` is specified instead of `menuItem`, then the menu item at index `pos` is removed.

PARAMETERS

`menuItem` The non-`null` menu item in the menu.

`pos` The 0-based index of the menu item in the menu.

EXAMPLE See the class example.

removeNotify()

PURPOSE Destroys the menu's peer hierarchy.

SYNTAX
```
public void removeNotify()
```

DESCRIPTION This method should never be called directly. It is normally called by the component's container.

OVERRIDES `MenuComponent.removeNotify()`.

EXAMPLE See `Component.show()`.

java.awt
MenuBar

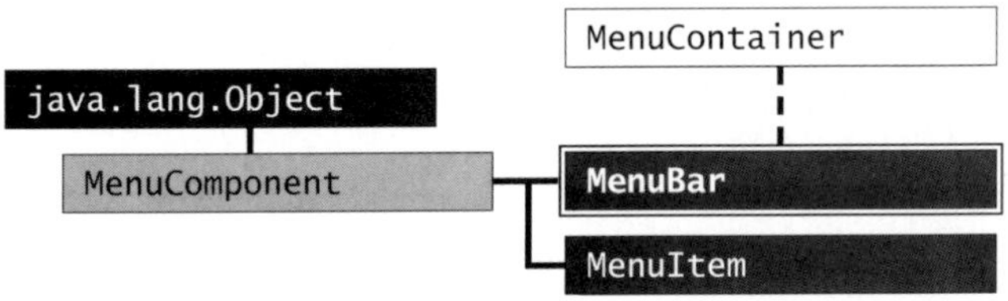

Syntax

```
public class MenuBar extends MenuComponent implements MenuContainer
```

Description

The *menu bar* is a strip across the top of a frame. If the frame has a title bar, the menu bar is located directly under the title bar. On some platforms, the menu bar appears at the top of the screen. The menu bar contains menus. Normally, only the menu labels are displayed. If the user clicks a menu label, the menu associated with the label appears.

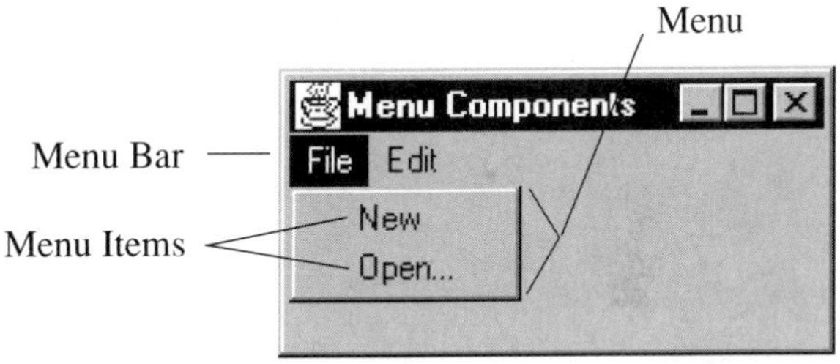

FIGURE 182 The Three Kinds of Menu Components

Figure 182 shows a frame with both a title bar and a menu bar. The menu bar contains two menus: File and Edit. The File menu is being displayed; it contains two menu items: New and Open....

The list of menus in a menu bar can be modified at any time, regardless of whether the menu bar is installed. However, a menu can be inserted in only one menu bar at a time.

The only valid parent for a menu bar is a `Frame` instance.

The Help Menu

There is a special menu designated the Help menu. The only thing special about the Help menu is that on some platforms, the Help menu appears at the right edge of the menu bar.

Events

Among menu components, only the menu item generates events. In particular, a menu item generates only action events. These events are passed onto the frame that contains the menu bar. You can handle these events by overriding the frame's `handleEvent()` method. To handle

A B C D E F G H I J K L M N O P Q R S T U V W X Y Z

menu item events in a menu or menu bar, you need to override the menu or menu bar's `postEvent()` method.

Since `MenuBar` does not subclass `Component`, you cannot handle events generated by a menu item in the normal way, that is, by overriding the `Component.handleEvent()` and related event methods. Instead, you must override the `postEvent()` method to filter events. However, events generated by a menu bar are automatically passed onto the frame, so the events can be handled in the frame.

MEMBER SUMMARY

Constructor	
`MenuBar()`	Constructs a new `MenuBar` instance.
Menu Methods	
`add()`	Adds a menu to the menu bar.
`countMenus()`	Retrieves the number of menus on the menu bar.
`getMenu()`	Retrieves a menu on the menu bar.
`remove()`	Removes a menu from the menu bar.
Help Menu Methods	
`getHelpMenu()`	Retrieves the Help menu.
`setHelpMenu()`	Replaces the Help menu.
Peer Methods	
`addNotify()`	Creates the menu bar's peer.
`removeNotify()`	Destroys the menu bar's peer.

Example

This example creates a menu bar with three menus. See Figure 183. To keep it short, only the File menu contains two menu items. This example also shows how to catch action events generated by menu items. For details on these events, see the `MenuItem` class.

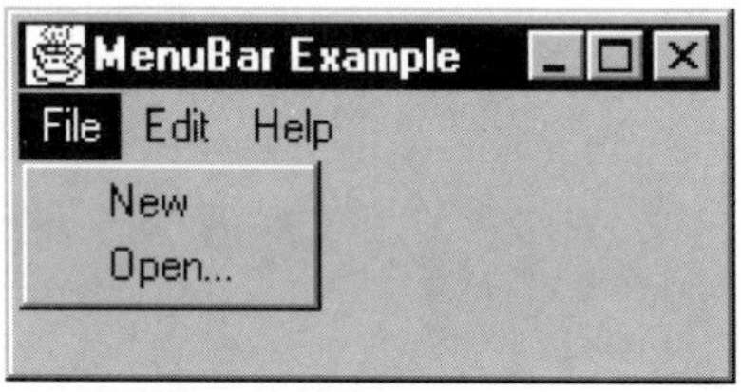

FIGURE 183 MenuBar

```
import java.awt.*;
class Main extends Frame {
    Main() {
        super("MenuBar Example");
        MenuBar mb = new MenuBar();
        Menu m = new Menu("File");
```

```
        m.add("New");
        m.add("Open...");
        mb.add(m);

        // To keep it short, these menus don't have menu items.
        mb.add(new Menu("Edit"));
        mb.setHelpMenu(new Menu("Help"));

        // Set the menu bar on the frame.
        setMenuBar(mb);
        resize(200, 100);
        show();
    }

    public boolean action(Event evt, Object what) {
        if ("New".equals(what)) {
            // do new
            return true;
        } else if ("Open...".equals(what)) {
            // do open
            return true;
        }
        return false;
    }

    static public void main(String[] args) {
        new Main();
    }
}
```

add()

PURPOSE Adds a menu to the menu bar.

SYNTAX `public synchronized Menu add(Menu menu)`

DESCRIPTION This method adds a menu to the end of the menu bar. If the menu already has a parent, it is first removed from its parent before being added to the menu bar. This means that the same menu cannot be inserted into more than one menu bar.

There is currently no way to insert a menu in the middle of a menu bar. To work around this, you need to remove all the menus and reinsert them, placing the new menu in the desired spot.

PARAMETERS

menu — The non-null menu to be added to the menu bar.

SEE ALSO — Menu.

EXAMPLE — This example creates a frame with a checkbox. Only when the checkbox is checked does the Edit menu appear on the menu bar. Figure 184 shows the Edit menu absent, and Figure 185 shows the Edit menu present.

FIGURE 184 Before MenuBar.add()

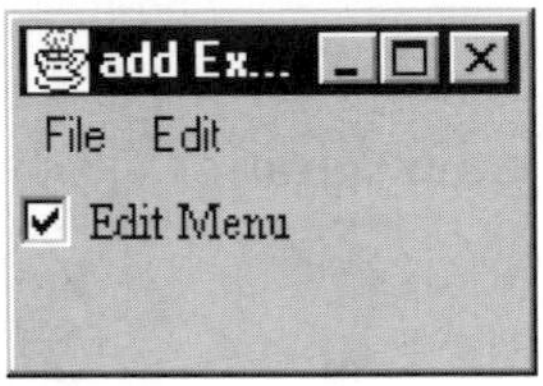

FIGURE 185 After MenuBar.add()

```
import java.awt.*;
class Main extends Frame {
    Menu editMenu = new Menu("Edit");
    Checkbox editMenuCheckbox = new
        Checkbox("Edit Menu");

    Main() {
        super("add Example");
        MenuBar mb = new MenuBar();

        mb.add(new Menu("File"));
        add("North", editMenuCheckbox);
        setMenuBar(mb);
        pack();
        show();
    }

    static public void main(String[] args) {
        Main m = new Main();
    }

    public boolean action(Event evt, Object what) {
        if (evt.target == editMenuCheckbox) {
            if (editMenuCheckbox.getState()) {
                getMenuBar().add(editMenu);
            } else {
                getMenuBar().remove(editMenu);
            }
            return true;
        }
        return false;
    }
}
```

addNotify()

PURPOSE — Creates the menu bar's peer hierarchy.

SYNTAX `public synchronized void addNotify()`

DESCRIPTION This method creates the menu bar's peer hierarchy, if it does not exist. The menu bar's peer is created by calling the `Toolkit.createMenuBar()` method. This method should never be called directly. It is normally called by the menu component's parent.

SEE ALSO `Component`, `Toolkit`.

countMenus()

PURPOSE Retrieves the number of menus on the menu bar.

SYNTAX `public int countMenus()`

DESCRIPTION This method retrieves the number of menus on the menu bar, including the Help menu.

RETURNS The number of menus on the menu bar.

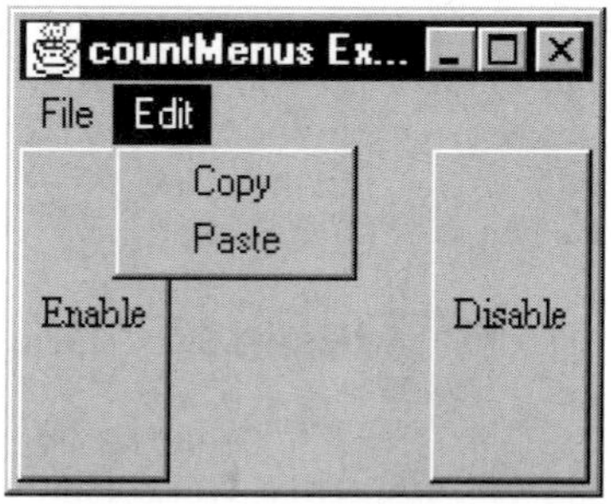

FIGURE 186 Enabled Menu Items

EXAMPLE This example enables or disables all menu items in all the menus in the menu bar. See Figure 186 and 187.

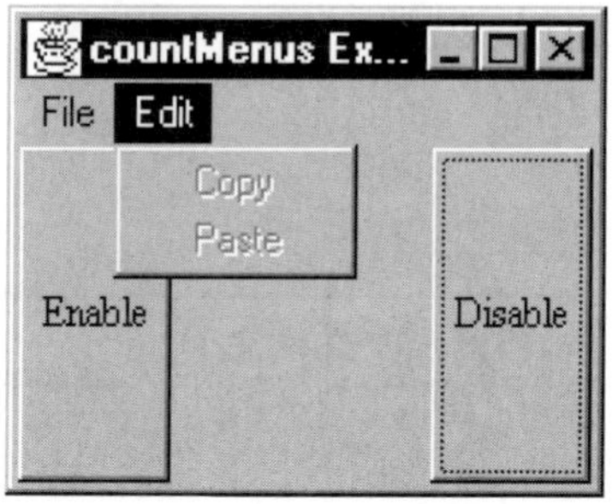

FIGURE 187 Disabled Menu Items

```
import java.awt.*;
class Main extends Frame {

    Main(String title) {
        super(title);
        MenuBar mb = new MenuBar();
        Menu menu = new Menu("File");

        menu.add("New");
        menu.add("Open...");
        mb.add(menu);

        menu = new Menu("Edit");
        menu.add("Copy");
        menu.add("Paste");
        mb.add(menu);

        setMenuBar(mb);
```

```
            add("West", new Button("Enable"));
            add("East", new Button("Disable"));

            pack();
            show();
        }

        static public void main(String[] args) {
            Main m = new Main("countMenus Example");
        }

        void enableMenuItems(boolean enable) {
            for (int i=0; i<getMenuBar().countMenus(); i++) {
                Menu menu = getMenuBar().getMenu(i);
                for (int j=0; j<menu.countItems(); j++) {
                    MenuItem menuitem = menu.getItem(j);
                    menuitem.enable(enable);
                }
            }
        }

        public boolean action(Event evt, Object what) {
            boolean enable = "Enable".equals(what);

            if (enable || "Disable".equals(what)) {
                enableMenuItems(enable);
                return true;
            }
            return false;
        }
    }
```

getHelpMenu()

PURPOSE Retrieves the Help menu on the menu bar.

SYNTAX `public Menu getHelpMenu()`

RETURNS The menu bar's Help menu. A return value of `null` means a Help menu has not been set.

SEE ALSO `setHelpMenu()`.

EXAMPLE This method removes the Help menu from the menu bar.

```
    void removeHelpMenu(MenuBar menubar) {
        Menu hm = menubar.getHelpMenu();
        if (hm != null) {
            menubar.remove(hm);
        }
    }
```

getMenu()

PURPOSE Retrieves a menu on the menu bar.

SYNTAX `public Menu getMenu(int pos)`

DESCRIPTION This method retrieves a menu on the menu bar.

PARAMETERS

`pos` The 0-based index of the menu on the menu bar.

RETURNS The non-`null` menu at the 0-based index `pos`.

SEE ALSO `addMenu()`, `getHelpMenu()`.

EXAMPLE This method prints the labels of all the menus on a menu bar.

```
void printMenuLabels(MenuBar menubar) {
    for (int i=0; i<menubar.countMenus(); i++) {
        System.out.println(menubar.getMenu(i).getLabel());
    }
}
```

MenuBar()

PURPOSE Constructs a new `MenuBar` instance.

SYNTAX `public MenuBar()`

DESCRIPTION This constructor creates a new `MenuBar` instance, which must be installed in a frame before it can be used by the user. A frame is the only valid parent that a `MenuBar` can have. The `MenuBar` instance can be assigned to only one frame.

SEE ALSO `Frame.setMenuBar()`.

EXAMPLE This example creates a frame that has a menu bar, which displays the menu labels in a large font.

```
import java.awt.*;
class Main {
    static public void main(String[] args) {
        Frame f = new Frame();
        MenuBar menubar = new MenuBar();

        f.setMenuBar(menubar);
        menubar.setFont(new Font("Courier", Font.PLAIN, 18));
        menubar.add(new Menu("File"));
        f.resize(100, 100);
        f.show();
    }

}
```

remove()

PURPOSE Removes a menu from the menu bar.

SYNTAX
```
public synchronized void remove(int pos)
public synchronized void remove(MenuComponent menu)
```

DESCRIPTION The two forms of this method remove the menu `menu` from the menu bar.

PARAMETERS

`menu` The non-`null` menu to be removed.

`pos` The 0-based index of the menu in the menu bar.

SEE ALSO `add()`.

EXAMPLE See `add()`.

removeNotify()

PURPOSE Destroys the menu bar's peer.

SYNTAX
```
public void removeNotify()
```

DESCRIPTION This method should never be called directly. It is normally called by the component's container.

OVERRIDES `MenuComponent.removeNotify()`.

SEE ALSO `MenuComponent`.

EXAMPLE See `Component.show()`.

setHelpMenu()

PURPOSE Replaces the Help menu.

SYNTAX
```
public synchronized void setHelpMenu(Menu menu)
```

DESCRIPTION This method sets the menu `menu` to be the Help menu. If a help menu already exists, the current Help menu is removed from the menu bar and `menu` becomes the new Help menu.

PARAMETERS

`menu` The non-`null` menu to be set.

EXAMPLE This example creates a frame with a Help menu that contains three menu items. See Figure 188.

FIGURE 188
MenuBar.setHelpMenu()

```
import java.awt.*;
class Main extends Frame {
    Main(String title) {
        super(title);
        MenuBar mb = new MenuBar();
        Menu menu = new Menu("Help");

        menu.add("Help Topics...");
        menu.add("Search...");
        menu.addSeparator();
        menu.add("About...");
        mb.setHelpMenu(menu);

        // Set the menu bar on the frame.
        setMenuBar(mb);
        resize(200, 200);
        show();
    }

    static public void main(String[] args) {
        Main m = new Main("setHelpMenu Example");
    }
}
```

java.awt.peer

MenuBarPeer

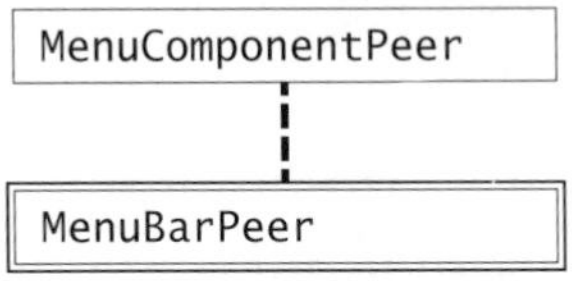

Syntax

`public interface MenuBarPeer extends MenuComponentPeer`

Description

The menu bar component (see the `MenuBar` class) in the Abstract Windowing Toolkit (AWT) uses the platform's native implementation of a menu bar. So that the AWT menu bar behaves the same on all platforms, the menu bar is assigned a peer, whose task is to translate the behavior of the platform's native menu bar to the behavior of the AWT menu bar.

AWT programmers normally do not directly use peer classes and interfaces. Instead they deal with AWT components in the `java.awt` package. These in turn automatically manage their peers. Only someone who is porting the AWT to another platform should be concerned with the peer classes and interfaces. Consequently, most peer documentation refers to `java.awt` counterparts.

See `Component` and `Toolkit` for additional information about component peers.

MEMBER SUMMARY

Peer Methods

`addHelpMenu()`	Replaces the Help menu.
`addMenu()`	Adds a menu to the menu bar.
`delMenu()`	Removes a menu from the menu bar.

See Also

`Component`, `MenuBar`, `Toolkit`.

addHelpMenu()

PURPOSE Replaces the Help menu.

SYNTAX `void addHelpMenu(Menu menu)`

PARAMETERS

`menu` The non-`null` menu to be set.

SEE ALSO `MenuBar.setHelpMenu()`.

addMenu()

PURPOSE Adds a menu to the menu bar.

SYNTAX `void addMenu(Menu menu)`

PARAMETERS

`menu` The non-`null` menu to be added to the menu bar.

SEE ALSO `MenuBar.add()`.

delMenu()

PURPOSE Removes a menu from the menu bar.

SYNTAX `void delMenu(int pos)`

PARAMETERS

`pos` The 0-based index of the menu in the menu bar.

SEE ALSO `MenuBar.remove()`.

java.awt
MenuComponent

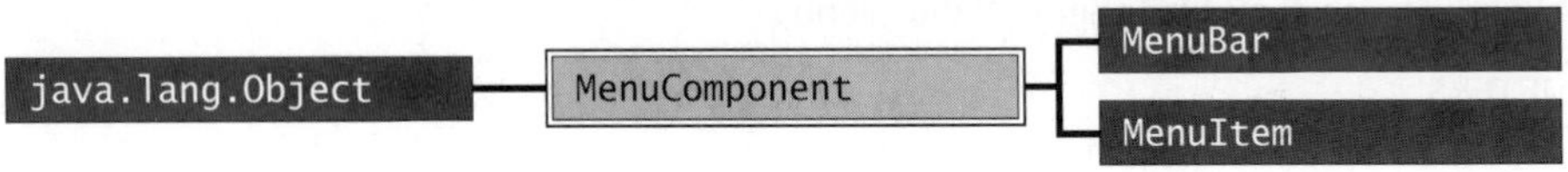

Syntax

`public abstract class MenuComponent`

Description

This class serves as the superclass of all menu-related components. There are presently three kinds of menu components in the AWT package, as shown in Figure 189.

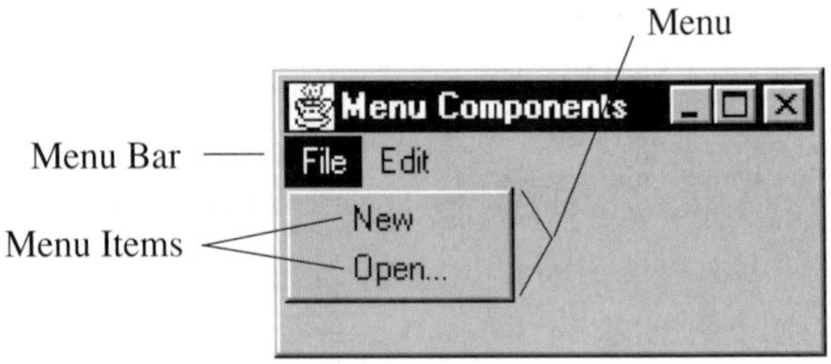

FIGURE 189 The Three Kinds of Menu Components

The `MenuComponent` class is similar to the `Component` class in that it is the superclass of all other AWT components. The reason why menu-related components are not `Component` is because menu components do not have most of the capabilities available to components. For example, you can't paint on menu components, you can't control their layout (only their ordering), you can't make them invisible, and you can't change their colors. Moreover, no other events are generated by menu components, other than the action event generated by a menu item when it is selected.

Events

Menu components participate in the AWT event flow in the same way that `Component` objects do. That is, events are passed through the ancestor chain until some component handles it. However, menu components do not handle events like `Component` objects, where you override the `action()` and `handleEvent()` methods. A menu component that needs to filter or handle events can do so by subclassing the `postEvent()` method. Events that are not handled should be passed on by calling the `postEvent()` method of the menu component's superclass.

MEMBER SUMMARY

Font Methods

`getFont()`	Retrieves the menu component's font.
`setFont()`	Sets the menu component's font.

A B C D E F G H I J K L M N O P Q R S T U V W X Y Z

MEMBER SUMMARY

Parent Method	
`getParent()`	Retrieves the menu component's parent.
Event Method	
`postEvent()`	Posts an event to the menu component's parent.
Peer Method	
`getPeer()`	Retrieves the menu component's peer.
`removeNotify()`	Destroys the menu component's peer hierarchy.
Debugging Methods	
`paramString()`	Generates a string representation of the menu component's state.
`toString()`	Generates a string representation of the menu component's state.

getFont()

PURPOSE Retrieves the menu component's font.

SYNTAX `public Font getFont()`

DESCRIPTION The menu component's font. The return value may be `null`. This means that neither the menu component nor any of its ancestors have been assigned a font.

RETURNS The menu component's current font, which may be `null`.

getParent()

PURPOSE Retrieves the menu component's parent.

SYNTAX `public MenuContainer getParent()`

RETURNS The menu component's parent. The return value may be `null`. This means that the menu component does not yet have a parent.

getPeer()

PURPOSE Retrieves the menu component's peer.

SYNTAX `public MenuComponentPeer getPeer()`

RETURNS The menu component's peer. The return value may be `null`. This means that the menu component does not yet have a peer.

paramString()

PURPOSE Generates a string representation of the menu component's state.

SYNTAX `protected String paramString()`

DESCRIPTION A subclass of this class should override this method and return a concatenation of its state with the results of `super.paramString()`. This method is called by the `toString()` method and is typically used for debugging.

RETURNS A non-`null` string representing the menu component's state.

SEE ALSO `toString()`.

EXAMPLE `Component.paramString()`.

postEvent()

PURPOSE Posts an event to the menu component's parent.

SYNTAX `public boolean postEvent(Event evt)`

DESCRIPTION If the menu component's parent is not `null`, this method calls the parent's `postEvent()` method with `evt`. A menu component does not typically handle events. Events are simply allowed to pass through the menu component hierarchy and end up at the frame, where they are finally handled.

If your menu component subclass handles events, you need to override this method in order to see the event. If your subclass does not handle the event, you should pass the event to the parent by calling `super.postEvent()`.

PARAMETERS

`evt` The non-`null` event to be posted.

RETURNS `true` if the event was handled by some component; `false` otherwise.

removeNotify()

PURPOSE Destroys the menu component's peer hierarchy.

SYNTAX `public void removeNotify()`

DESCRIPTION This method destroys the menu component's peer hierarchy, if it exists. This method should never be called directly. It is normally called by the component's container.

SEE ALSO `Component`.

EXAMPLE See `Component.show()`.

setFont()

PURPOSE Sets the menu component's font.

SYNTAX `public void setFont(Font font)`

DESCRIPTION This method sets the menu component's font to `font`. The value may be `null`. In this case, the default font is to be used.

PARAMETERS

`font` The font to be set.

toString()

PURPOSE Generates the string representation of the menu component's state.

SYNTAX `public String toString()`

DESCRIPTION The result string contains the menu component's class name and the results of calling `paramString()`.

This method is typically used for debugging.

RETURNS A non-`null` string representing the menu component's state.

OVERRIDES `Object.toString()`.

SEE ALSO `paramString()`.

EXAMPLE See `Object.toString()`.

java.awt.peer

MenuComponentPeer

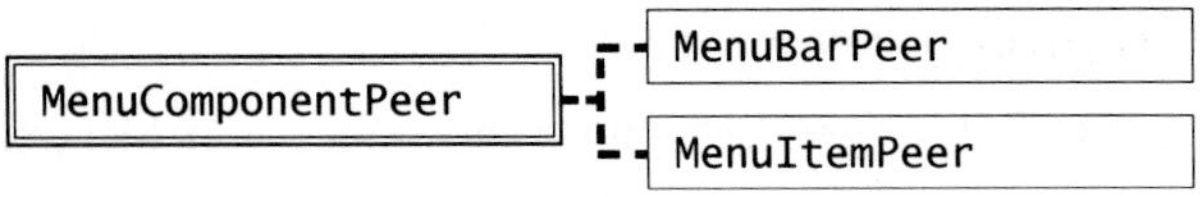

Syntax

```
public interface MenuComponentPeer
```

Description

The menu component (see the `MenuComponent` class) in the Abstract Windowing Toolkit (AWT) uses the platform's native implementation of a menu component. So that the AWT menu component behaves the same on all platforms, the menu component is assigned a peer, whose task is to translate the behavior of the platform's native menu component to the behavior of the AWT menu component.

AWT programmers normally do not directly use peer classes and interfaces. Instead they deal with AWT components in the `java.awt` package. These in turn automatically manage their peers. Only someone who is porting the AWT to another platform should be concerned with the peer classes and interfaces. Consequently, most peer documentation refers to `java.awt` counterparts.

See `Component` and `Toolkit` for additional information about component peers.

MEMBER SUMMARY	
Peer Method	
`dispose()`	Destroys the peer.

See Also

`Component`, `MenuComponent`, `Toolkit`.

dispose()

PURPOSE Destroys the peer.

SYNTAX `void dispose()`

SEE ALSO `MenuComponent.removeNotify()`.

java.awt

MenuContainer

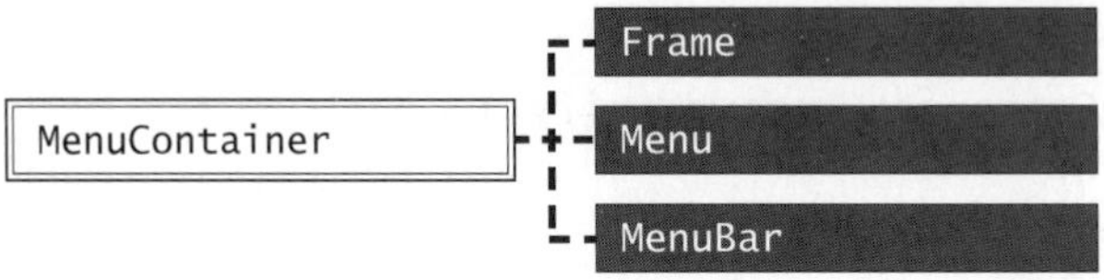

Syntax

```
public interface MenuContainer
```

Description

This interface is implemented by classes that contain menu components. The AWT package has three menu component containers: `Menu`, `MenuBar`, and `Frame`.

MEMBER SUMMARY	
Menu Container Methods	
`getFont()`	Retrieves the menu container's font.
`postEvent()`	Posts an event to the menu container.
`remove()`	Removes a menu component from the menu Container.

Example

This example implements a new type of menu container. It takes a list of menus and displays them all in one frame. See Figure 190. Each menu label and menu item label is displayed one per line. When the user clicks a menu item, an event is generated for that menu item.

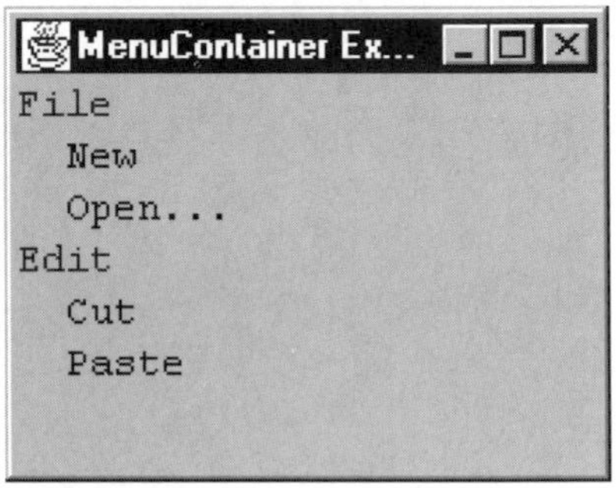

FIGURE 190 `MenuContainer`

```
import java.awt.*;
import java.util.*;
public class Main extends Frame implements MenuContainer {
    Font font = new Font("Courier", Font.PLAIN, 14);
    FontMetrics fontM;
```

```
// Contains all the menu in this container.
Vector menus = new Vector();

// Contains all the menu items in this container.
Vector menuItems = new Vector();

Main(Vector menus) {
    super("MenuContainer Example");
    this.menus = menus;
    Vector labels = getLabels();
    int width = 0;

    // Determine how large the frame should be to show all the
    // labels.
    fontM = getFontMetrics(font);
    for (int i=0; i<labels.size(); i++) {
        width = Math.max(width,
            fontM.stringWidth((String)labels.elementAt(i)));
    }
    resize(width, labels.size() * fontM.getHeight());
    show();
}

public Font getFont() {
    return font;
}

// Generates a vector of labels.  The menu item labels are
        indented.
Vector getLabels() {
    Vector result = new Vector();
    int width = 0;
    int i;

    for (i=0; i<menus.size(); i++) {
        Menu menu = (Menu)menus.elementAt(i);
        result.addElement(menu.getLabel());
        menuItems.addElement(null);
        for (int j=0; j<menu.countItems(); j++) {
            result.addElement("  "+menu.getItem(j).getLabel());
            menuItems.addElement(menu.getItem(j));
        }
    }
    return result;
}

// Paints the labels.
public void paint(Graphics g) {
    Vector labels = getLabels();
    int y = fontM.getAscent();

    g.setFont(font);
    for (int i=0; i<labels.size(); i++) {
        String label = (String)labels.elementAt(i);
```

Example

```
                // Paint menu label blue
                if (label.charAt(0) != ' ') {
                    g.setColor(Color.blue);
                }
                g.drawString(label, 0, y);
                y += fontM.getHeight();
                g.setColor(Color.black);
            }
        }

        // Determines which item was clicked on and generates an event for
        // that item.
        public boolean mouseDown(Event evt, int x, int y) {
            Vector labels = getLabels();
            int item = y / fontM.getHeight();

            // Don't generate events when the click is not on a label.
            if (item < labels.size()) {
                String label = ((String)labels.elementAt(item));

                //Don't generate event for menu labels.
                if (label.charAt(0) == ' ') {
                    evt = new Event(menuItems.elementAt(item),
                                    Event.ACTION_EVENT, label.trim());
                    postEvent(evt);
                    System.out.println(evt);
                    return true;
                }
            }
            return false;
        }

        public void remove(MenuComponent mcomp) {
            menus.removeElement(mcomp);
        }

        static public void main(String[] args) {
            // Now create a few menus.
            Vector menus = new Vector();
            Menu menu = new Menu("File");

            menu.add("New");
            menu.add("Open...");
            menus.addElement(menu);
            menu = new Menu("Edit");
            menu.add("Cut");
            menu.add("Paste");
            menus.addElement(menu);
            new Main(menus);
        }
    }
```

getFont()

PURPOSE Retrieves the menu container's font.

SYNTAX `Font getFont()`

RETURNS The menu container's font. A result value of `null` means neither the menu container nor any of its ancestors have been assigned a font.

EXAMPLE See the class example.

postEvent()

PURPOSE Posts an event to the menu container.

SYNTAX `public boolean postEvent(Event evt)`

DESCRIPTION This method posts the event `evt` to this menu container.

PARAMETERS

`evt` The non-`null` event to post.

RETURNS `true` if the event was handled by some menu component or `Component` object; `false` otherwise.

SEE ALSO `Component.postEvent()`.

EXAMPLE See the class example.

remove()

PURPOSE Removes a menu component from the menu container.

SYNTAX `void remove(MenuComponent mcomp)`

DESCRIPTION This method removes the menu component `mcomp` from this menu container.

PARAMETERS

`mcomp` The non-`null` menu component to remove from the menu container.

EXAMPLE See the class example.

java.awt
MenuItem

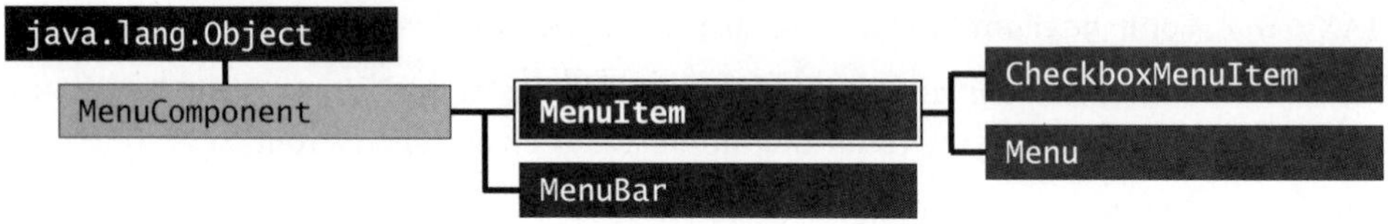

Syntax

`public class MenuItem extends MenuComponent`

Description

A *menu item* is a menu component that must exist in a menu. A menu item is typically used to invoke commands in the applications. Menu items are similar to buttons in function and use, except they take up less screen space. The trade off is that they are not as convenient to activate as buttons.

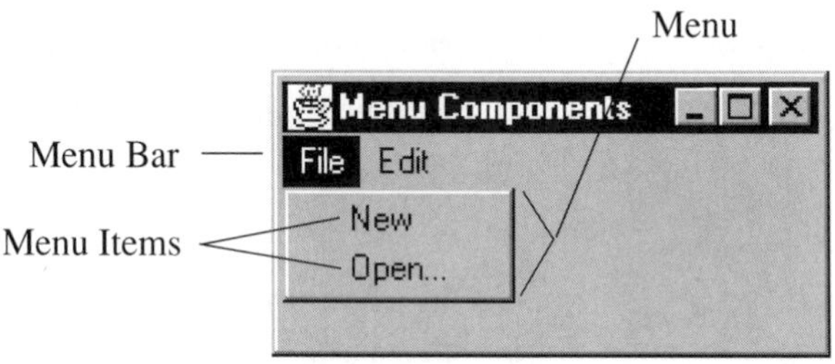

FIGURE 191 The Three Kinds of Menu Components

Figure 191 shows the three menu components in the AWT package. The displayed File menu contains two menu items: New and Open.….

The Enabled Property

A menu item can be either enabled or disabled. When enabled, it can be selected by the user, and when selected, it will generate an event. A disabled menu item cannot be selected nor will it generate events. Enabled menu items look different from disabled menu items so that both can be visually distinguished.

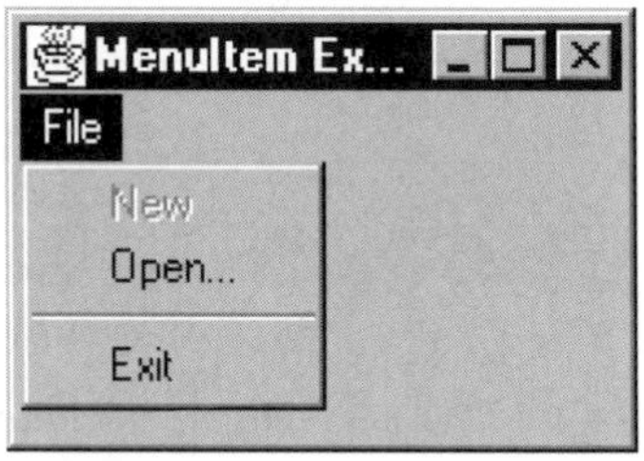

FIGURE 192 `MenuItem`

Figure 192 shows a menu with two enabled menu items (Open… and Exit) and one disabled menu item (New).

The Label Property and the Separator

The label of a menu item can be any string. There is one particular label, "-", which is treated specially. This label causes the menu item to become a separator. Separators are used to visually separate groups of menu items. This is useful if the menu has many menu items.

A B C D E F G H I J K L M N O P Q R S T U V W X Y Z

Separators are always disabled and never generate events. Figure 192 shows a menu with a separator between the Open... and Exit menu items.

Events

A menu item generates an action event when selected. See the `Event` class for details on how to filter or handle events. Table 13 describes how a menu item fills the fields in the event.

TABLE 13 `MenuItem` Action Event

`arg`	The label of the menu item.
`clickCount`	Not used.
`id`	`Event.ACTION`
`key`	Not used.
`modifiers`	The state of the modifier keys when the component was selected.
`target`	Handle to the component that generated this event.
`when`	The time, in milliseconds, that the event was generated.
`x`	Not used.
`y`	Not used.

MEMBER SUMMARY

Constructor	
`MenuItem()`	Constructs a new `MenuItem` instance.
Enable Methods	
`disable()`	Disables the menu item.
`enable()`	Enables or disables the menu item.
`isEnabled()`	Determines the menu item's enabled state.
Label Methods	
`getLabel()`	Retrieves the menu item's label.
`setLabel()`	Sets the label to be the specified label.
Peer Method	
`addNotify()`	Creates the menu item's peer.
Debugging Method	
`paramString()`	Generates a string representing the state of the menu item.

A B C D E F G H I J K L M N O P Q R S T U V W X Y Z

Example

This example creates a menu with two menu items, one enabled and one disabled. The menu is installed in a menu bar, which in turn is installed in a frame. This example also shows you how to handle events generated by menu items. See Figure 192.

```
import java.awt.*;
class Main extends Frame {
    Main() {
        super("MenuItem Example");
        MenuBar mb = new MenuBar();
        Menu m = new Menu("File");
        MenuItem mi;

        mi = new MenuItem("New");
        mi.disable();
        m.add(mi);
        m.add("Open...");
        m.add("-");
        m.add("Exit");
        mb.add(m);

        // Set the menu bar on the frame.
        setMenuBar(mb);
        resize(100, 50);
        show();
    }

    public boolean action(Event evt, Object what) {
        if ("New".equals(what)) {
            // do new
            return true;
        } else if ("Open...".equals(what)) {
            // do open
            return true;
        }
        return false;
    }

    static public void main(String[] args) {
        new Main();
    }
}
```

A B C D E F G H I J K L M N O P Q R S T U V W X Y Z

addNotify()

PURPOSE Creates the menu item's peer.

SYNTAX `public synchronized void addNotify()`

DESCRIPTION This method creates the menu item's peer if it does not yet exist. The peer is created by calling the `Toolkit.createMenuItem()` method. This method should never be called directly. It is normally called by the menu component's parent.

SEE ALSO `Component`.

EXAMPLE See `Component.show()`.

disable()

PURPOSE Disables the menu item.

SYNTAX `public void disable()`

DESCRIPTION This method disables this menu item. It is ignored if the menu item is already disabled.

EXAMPLE See `enable()`.

enable()

PURPOSE Enables or disables the menu item.

SYNTAX
```
public void enable()
public void enable(boolean on)
```

DESCRIPTION The two forms of this method enable or disable this menu item. If `on` is not specified, the menu item is enabled. The method call is ignored if the enabled property of the menu item is not changed.

PARAMETERS

`on` If `true`, the menu item is enabled; otherwise the menu item is disabled.

SEE ALSO `disable()`.

EXAMPLE This example creates a frame with two buttons. One button disables all menu items in the menu bar, and the other enables them. See Figure 193.

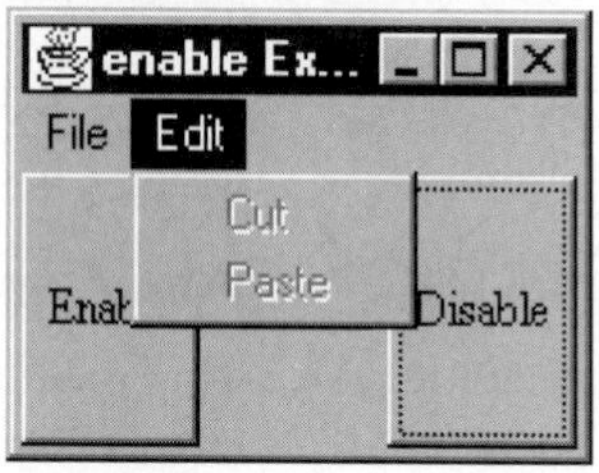

FIGURE 193
`MenuItem.enable()`

```
import java.awt.*;
class Main extends Frame {
    Main() {
        super("enable Example");
        MenuBar mb = new MenuBar();
        Menu m = new Menu("File");

        m.add("New");
        m.add("Open...");
        mb.add(m);
        m = new Menu("Edit");
        m.add("Cut");
        m.add("Paste");
        mb.add(m);

        // Add the two enable/disable buttons.
        add("West", new Button("Enable"));
        add("East", new Button("Disable"));

        // Set the menu bar on the frame.
        setMenuBar(mb);
        pack();
        show();
    }

    public boolean action(Event evt, Object what) {
        boolean enable = "Enable".equals(what);

        if (enable || "Disable".equals(what)) {
            for (int i=0; i<getMenuBar().countMenus(); i++) {
                Menu m = getMenuBar().getMenu(i);

                for (int j=0; j<getMenuBar().getMenu(i).countItems();
                     j++) {
                    m.getItem(j).enable(enable);
                    // The following would also work
                    // if (enable) {
                    //      m.getItem(j).enable();
                    // } else {
                    //     m.getItem(j).disable();
                    // }
                }
            }
            return true;
        }
        return false;
    }
```

```
    static public void main(String[] args) {
        new Main();
    }
}
```

getLabel()

PURPOSE Retrieves the menu item's label.

SYNTAX `public String getLabel()`

RETURNS The menu item's label. The return value may be `null`.

EXAMPLE This example prints all menu item labels in a menu.

```
void printLabels(Menu m) {
    for (int i=0; i<m.countItems(); i++) {
        System.out.println(m.getItem(i).getLabel());
    }
}
```

isEnabled()

PURPOSE Determines the menu item's enabled state.

SYNTAX `public boolean isEnabled()`

RETURNS `true` if the menu item is enabled; `false` otherwise.

EXAMPLE This example prints all enabled states of all menu items in a menu.

```
void printLabels(Menu m) {
    for (int i=0; i<m.countItems(); i++) {
        System.out.println(m.getItem(i).getLabel() + ": "
            + (m.getItem(i).isEnabled() ? "enabled" : "disabled"));
    }
}
```

MenuItem()

PURPOSE Creates a new `MenuItem` instance.

SYNTAX `public MenuItem(String label)`

DESCRIPTION This constructor creates a new `MenuItem` instance that has the label `label`. If `label` is "-", the menu item becomes a separator. The menu item is enabled by default.

PARAMETERS

`label` The non-`null` string specifying the menu item's label.

EXAMPLE See the class example.

paramString()

PURPOSE Generates a string representation of the menu item's state.

SYNTAX `public String paramString()`

DESCRIPTION The string includes the menu item's label and enabled state. This method is called by the `toString()` method and is typically used for debugging.

RETURNS A non-`null` string representing the menu item's state.

SEE ALSO `toString()`.

EXAMPLE See `Component.paramString()`.

setLabel()

PURPOSE Sets the menu item's label.

SYNTAX `public void setLabel(String label)`

DESCRIPTION This method sets the label of this menu item to be the string `label`.

PARAMETERS

`label` The non-`null` string specifying the menu item's new label.

EXAMPLE This example creates a menu with a single menu item and two buttons, One and Two. Clicking a button sets the label of the menu item to the label of the button. See Figure 194.

FIGURE 194
`MenuItem.setLabel()`

```
import java.awt.*;
class Main extends Frame {
    MenuItem mi = new MenuItem("One");

    Main() {
        super("setLabel Example");
```

```
        MenuBar mb = new MenuBar();
        Menu m = new Menu("Menu");

        // Add menu item.
        m.add(mi);

        // Add the two buttons.
        add("West", new Button("One"));
        add("East", new Button("Two"));

        // Set the menu bar on the frame.
        mb.add(m);
        setMenuBar(mb);
        pack();
        show();
    }

    public boolean action(Event evt, Object what) {
        if (evt.target instanceof Button) {
            mi.setLabel((String)what);
            return true;
        }
        return false;
    }

    static public void main(String[] args) {
        new Main();
    }
}
```

java.awt.peer

MenuItemPeer

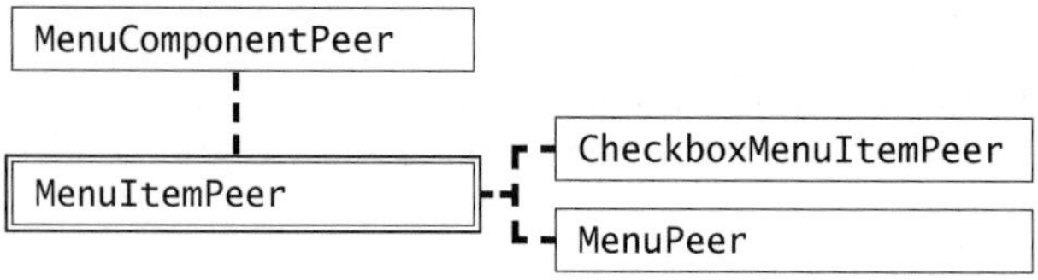

Syntax

```
public interface MenuItemPeer extends MenuComponentPeer
```

Description

The menu item (see the `MenuItem` class) in the Abstract Windowing Toolkit (AWT) uses the platform's native implementation of a menu item. So that the AWT menu item behaves the same on all platforms, the menu item is assigned a peer, whose task is to translate the behavior of the platform's native menu item to the behavior of the AWT menu item.

AWT programmers normally do not directly use peer classes and interfaces. Instead they deal with AWT components in the `java.awt` package which in turn automatically manage their peers. Only someone who is porting the AWT to another platform should be concerned with the peer classes and interfaces. Consequently, most peer documentation refers to `java.awt` counterparts.

See `Component` and `Toolkit` for additional information about component peers.

MEMBER SUMMARY

Peer Methods

`disable()`	Disables the menu item.
`enable()`	Enables the menu item.
`setLabel()`	Sets the menu item's label.

See Also

`Component`, `MenuItem`, `Toolkit`.

disable()

PURPOSE Disables the menu item.

SYNTAX `void disable()`

SEE ALSO `MenuItem.disable()`.

enable()

PURPOSE Enables the menu item.

SYNTAX `void enable()`

SEE ALSO `MenuItem.enable()`.

setLabel()

PURPOSE Sets the menu item's label.

SYNTAX `void setLabel(String label)`

PARAMETERS

`label` The string specifying the menu item's label.

SEE ALSO `MenuItem.setLabel()`.

java.awt.peer
MenuPeer

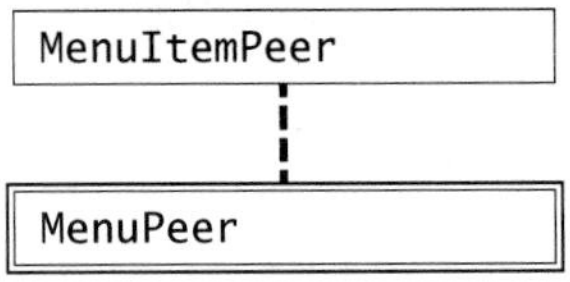

Syntax

```
public interface MenuPeer extends MenuItemPeer
```

Description

The menu (see the `Menu` class) in the Abstract Windowing Toolkit (AWT) uses the platform's native implementation of a menu. So that the AWT menu behaves the same on all platforms, the menu is assigned a peer, whose task is to translate the behavior of the platform's native menu to the behavior of the AWT menu.

AWT programmers normally do not directly use peer classes and interfaces. Instead they deal with AWT components in the `java.awt` package. These in turn automatically manage their peers. Only someone who is porting the AWT to another platform should be concerned with the peer classes and interfaces. Consequently, most peer documentation refers to `java.awt` counterparts.

See `Component` and `Toolkit` for additional information about component peers.

MEMBER SUMMARY

Peer Methods

`addItem()`	Adds a menu item to the menu.
`addSeparator()`	Adds a menu item separator to the menu.
`delItem()`	Removes a menu item from the menu.

See Also

`Component`, `Menu`, `Toolkit`.

addItem()

PURPOSE Adds a menu item to the menu.

SYNTAX `void addItem(MenuItem menuItem)`

PARAMETERS

`menuItem` The non-`null` menu item.

SEE ALSO `Menu.add()`.

addSeparator()

PURPOSE Adds a menu item separator to the menu.

SYNTAX `void addSeparator()`

SEE ALSO `Menu.addSeparator()`.

delItem()

PURPOSE Removes a menu item from the menu.

SYNTAX `void delItem(int pos)`

PARAMETERS

`pos` The 0-based index of the menu item in the menu.

SEE ALSO `Menu.remove()`.

java.lang

NegativeArraySizeException

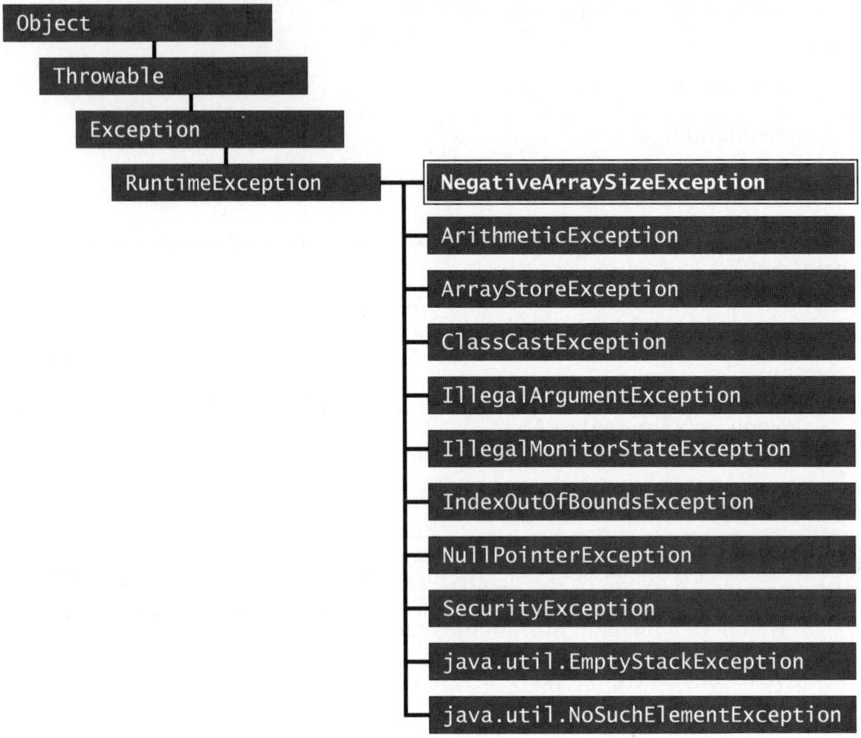

Syntax

```
public class NegativeArraySizeException extends RuntimeException
```

Description

`NegativeArraySizeException` is thrown when the program attempts to create an array with a negative size. It should not be caught or declared in the `throws` clause of a method.

MEMBER SUMMARY	
Constructor	
`NegativeArraySizeException()`	Constructs a `NegativeArraySizeException` instance.

See Also

RuntimeException.

Example

This example throws NegativeArraySizeException.

```
class Main {
    public static void main(String[] args) {
        System.out.println("NegativeArraySizeException example");
        int[] intArray = new int[-5];
        intArray[3] = 10;
    }
}
```

NegativeArraySizeException()

PURPOSE Constructs a NegativeArraySizeException instance.

SYNTAX
```
public NegativeArraySizeException()
public NegativeArraySizeException(String msg)
```

DESCRIPTION The two forms of this constructor create a new instance of NegativeArraySizeException. An optional string msg can be supplied that describes this particular instance of the exception.

PARAMETERS

msg A string that gives details about this exception.

java.lang
NoClassDefFoundError

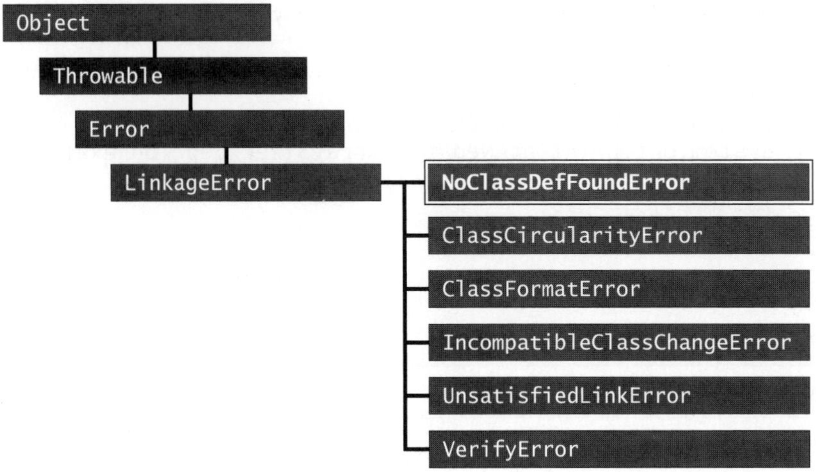

Syntax

```
public class NoClassDefFoundError extends LinkageError
```

Description

`NoClassDefFoundError` is a runtime linkage error that is thrown when the system's default class loader cannot find the class to load. Normally, when you compile a program's classes, you get a compilation error saying that the class is missing. However, if the class file was removed subsequent to compilation, then the runtime will not be able to find it, and so `NoClassDefFoundError` will be thrown.

`ClassNotFoundException` and `NoClassDefFoundError` both report the same error; namely, that the requested class cannot be found. They differ in that `ClassNotFoundException` is an exception thrown by a program-defined class loader or the user's invocation of a method to find a class (such as the use of `Class.for Name()` and `ClassLoader.findSystemClass()`). On the other hand, `NoClassDefFoundError` is a runtime linkage error thrown by the Java virtual machine when it is attempting to load and resolve class references.

`NoClassDefFoundError` should not be caught or declared in the `throws` clause of a method.

MEMBER SUMMARY	
Constructor	
`NoClassDefFoundError()`	Constructs a `NoClassDefFoundError` instance.

See Also

`ClassNotFoundException`, `ClassLoader.findSystemClass()`, `Error`, `LinkageError`.

Example

This example throws a `NoClassDefFoundError` if after compilation of `Main.java`, the class file for `A` is deleted.
In `A.java`:

```
class A {
}
```

In `Main.java`:

```
class Main {
        public static void main(String[] args) {
            System.out.println("NoClassDefFoundError Example");
            A a = new A();
        }
    }
```

NoClassDefFoundError()

PURPOSE Constructs a `NoClassDefFoundError` instance.

SYNTAX

```
public NoClassDefFoundError()
public NoClassDefFoundError(String msg)
```

DESCRIPTION The two forms of this constructor create a new instance of `NoClassDefFoundError`. An optional string `msg` can be supplied that describes this particular instance of the error.

PARAMETERS

`msg` A string that gives details about this error.

java.util

NoSuchElementException

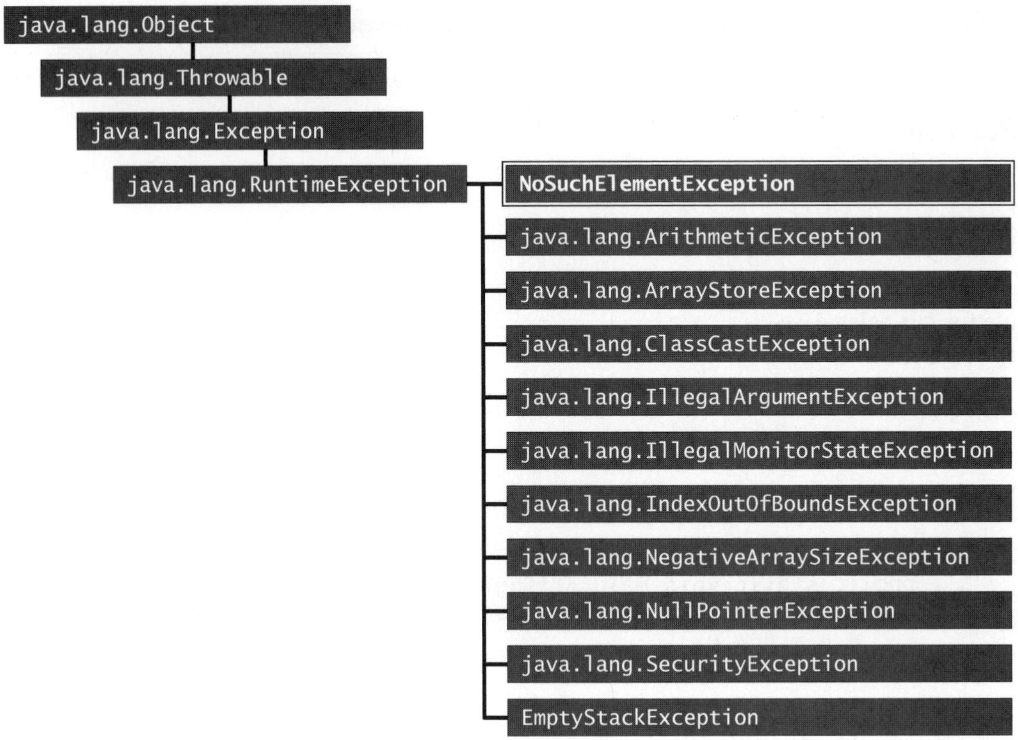

Syntax

```
public class NoSuchElementException extends RuntimeException
```

Description

`NoSuchElementException` is a runtime exception that is thrown when the program attempts to access an element in an enumeration after the enumeration has finished.

`NoSuchElementException` should not be caught or declared in the `throws` clause of a method.

MEMBER SUMMARY	
Constructor	
`NoSuchElementException()`	Constructs a `NoSuchElementException` instance.

See Also

Enumeration, RuntimeException.

Example

This example incorrectly avoids using Enumeration.hasMoreElements() and instead just loops, calling Enumeration.nextElement() until the enumeration has completed. After the enumeration has completed, a call to Enumeration.nextElement() throws a NoSuchElementException.

```
import java.util.Hashtable;
import java.util.Enumeration;

class Main {
    public static void main(String[] args) {
        Hashtable tab = new Hashtable(13);

        tab.put("Jones", "station wagon");
        tab.put("Smith", "race car");
        tab.put("Graham", "sedan");

        Enumeration e = tab.keys();
        Object elem;
        while ((elem = e.nextElement()) != null)
            System.out.println(elem);
    }
}
```

NoSuchElementException()

PURPOSE Constructs a NoSuchElementException instance.

SYNTAX
```
public NoSuchElementException()
public NoSuchElementException(String msg)
```

DESCRIPTION The two forms of this constructor create a new instance of NoSuchElementException. An optional string msg can be supplied that describes this particular instance of the exception.

PARAMETERS

msg A string that gives details about this exception.

java.lang

NoSuchFieldError

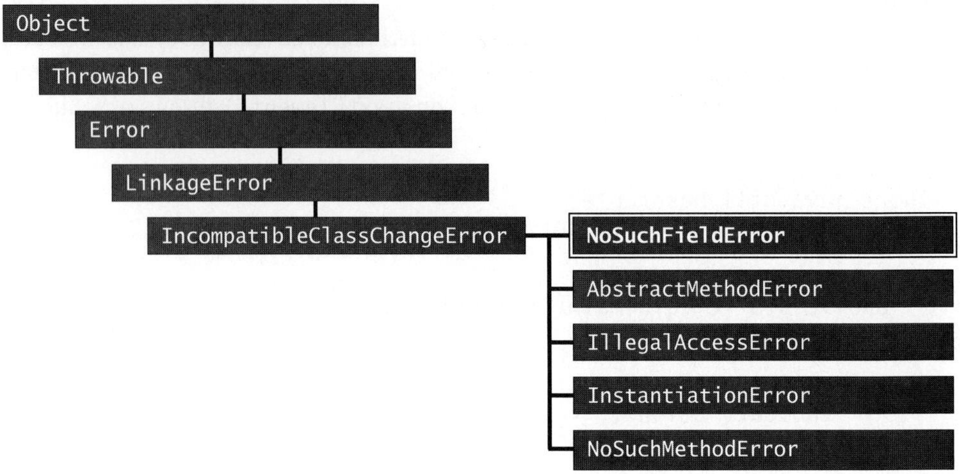

Syntax

`public class NoSuchFieldError extends IncompatibleClassChangeError`

Description

`NoSuchFieldError` is a runtime linkage error that is thrown when the program attempts to access a nonexistent field of a class. Normally, when you compile a program's classes, you get a compilation error pinpointing the problem so that a linkage error at runtime does not occur. However, this problem could be introduced when classes of a program become inconsistent, for example, if you were to make an incompatible change and then recompile only some of its classes.

`NoSuchFieldError` should not be caught or declared in the `throws` clause of a method.

MEMBER SUMMARY	
Constructor	
`NoSuchFieldError()`	Constructs a `NoSuchFieldError` instance.

See Also

`IncompatibleClassChangeError`, `LinkageError`, `NoSuchMethodError`.

A B C D E F G H I J K L M N O P Q R S T U V W X Y Z

Example

In this example, when `fieldA` is deleted from class A and recompiled, the main program raises a `NoSuchFieldError`.
In the original `A.java`:

```
class A {
public int fieldA = 100;
public int fieldB = 200;
}
```

In the modified `A.java`:

```
class A {
//    public int fieldA = 100;
        public int fieldB = 200;
}
```

In `Main.java`:

```
    class Main {
        public static void main(String[] args) {
            System.out.println("NoSuchFieldError example");
            A a = new A();

            System.out.println(a.fieldA);
            System.out.println(a.fieldB);
        }
    }
```

NoSuchFieldError()

PURPOSE Constructs a `NoSuchFieldError` instance.

SYNTAX
```
public NoSuchFieldError()
public NoSuchFieldError(String msg)
```

DESCRIPTION The two forms of this constructor create a new instance of `NoSuchFieldError`. An optional string `msg` can be supplied that describes this particular instance of the error.

PARAMETERS

`msg` A string that gives details about this error.

java.lang
NoSuchMethodError

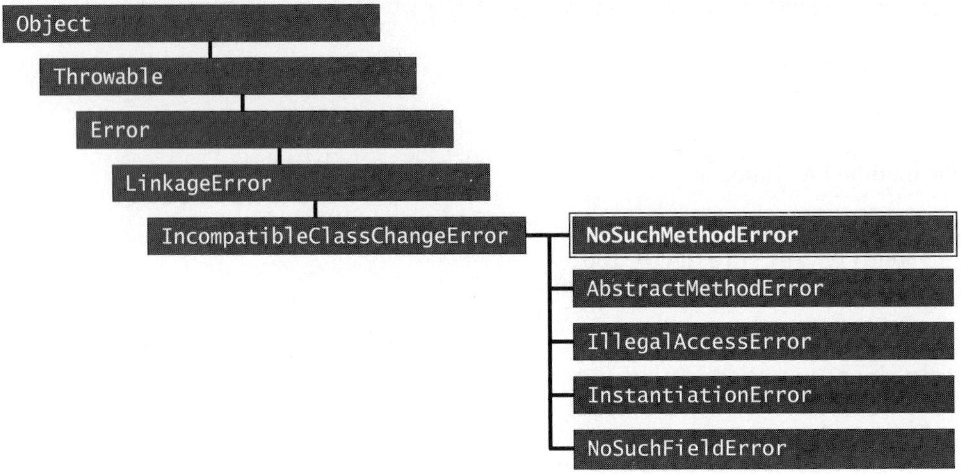

Syntax

```
public class NoSuchMethodError extends IncompatibleClassChangeError
```

Description

`NoSuchMethodError` is a runtime linkage error that is thrown when the program attempts to access a nonexistent method of a class. Normally, when you compile a program's classes, you get a compilation error pinpointing the problem so that a linkage error at runtime does not occur. However, this problem could be introduced when classes of a program become inconsistent, for example, if you were to make an incompatible change and then recompile only some of its classes.

`NoSuchMethodError` and `NoSuchMethodException` both report the same error, namely, that the requested method cannot be found. They differ in that `NoSuchMethodException` is an exception thrown by a program-defined class loader or the user's invocation of a method to find a class (such as the use of `Class.forName()` or `ClassLoader.findSystemClass()`). On the other hand, `NoSuchMethodError` is a runtime linkage error thrown by the Java virtual machine when it is attempting to invoke a nonexistent method.

`NoSuchMethodError` should not be caught or declared in the `throws` clause of a method.

MEMBER SUMMARY

Constructor	
`NoSuchMethodError()`	Constructs a `NoSuchMethodError` instance.

See Also

`IncompatibleClassChangeError`, `LinkageError`, `NoSuchFieldError`, `NoSuchMethodException`.

Example

In this example, when the `methodA` line is commented out in class `A` and the program recompiled, the main program raises a `NoSuchMethodError`.

In the original `A.java`:

```
class A {
    public int methodA() { return 100; }
    public int methodB() { return 200; }
}
```

In the modified `A.java`:

```
class A {
//    public int methodA() { return 100; }
    public int methodB() { return 200; }
}
```

In `Main.java`:

```
class Main {
    public static void main(String[] args) {
        System.out.println("NoSuchMethodError example");
        A a = new A();

        System.out.println(a.methodA());
        System.out.println(a.methodB());
    }
}
```

A
B
C
D
E
F
G
H
I
J
K
L
M
N
O
P
Q
R
S
T
U
V
W
X
Y
Z

NoSuchMethodError()

PURPOSE Constructs a `NoSuchMethodError` instance.

SYNTAX
```
public NoSuchMethodError()
public NoSuchMethodError(String msg)
```

DESCRIPTION The two forms of this constructor create a new instance of `NoSuchMethodError`. An optional string `msg` can be supplied that describes this particular instance of the error.

PARAMETERS

`msg` A string that gives details about this error.

NoSuchMethodException

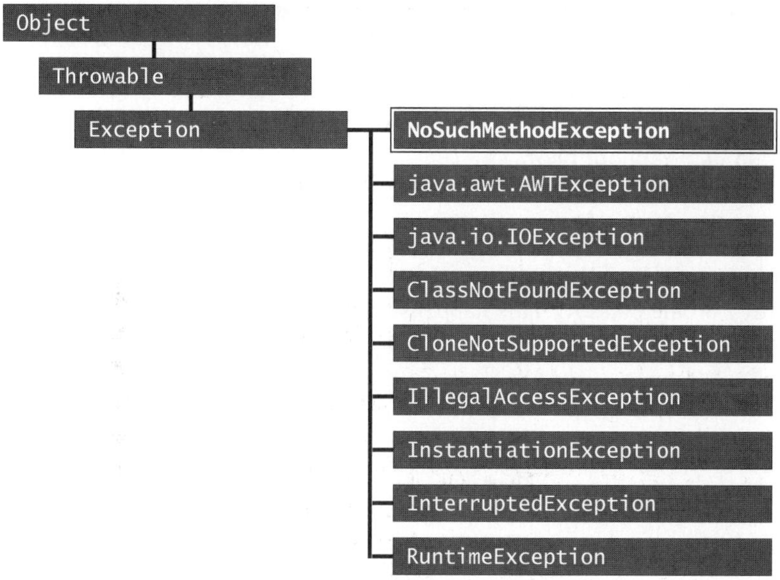

Syntax

```
public class NoSuchMethodException extends Exception
```

Description

`NoSuchMethodException` is an exception that is thrown when the program attempts to access a nonexistent method of a class. Normally, when you compile a program's classes, you get a compilation error pinpointing the problem so that a linkage error at runtime does not occur. But in addition to the classes that the program is compiled with, you can also dynamically link in classes and invoke methods on them through the use of class loaders and the methods in the `Class` class. When the program attempts to invoke a nonexistent method in one of these classes, a `NoSuchMethodException` is thrown.

`NoSuchMethodError` and `NoSuchMethodException` both report the same error, namely, that the requested method cannot be found. The difference is that `NoSuchMethodException` is an exception thrown by a program-defined class loader or the user's invocation of a method to find a class (such as the use of `Class.forName()` or `ClassLoader.findSystemClass()`). On the other hand, `NoSuchMethodError` is a runtime linkage error thrown by the Java virtual machine when it is attempting to invoke a nonexistent method.

MEMBER SUMMARY	
Constructor	
`NoSuchMethodException()`	Constructs a `NoSuchMethodException` instance.

See Also

`Exception`, `NoSuchMethodError`.

Example

In this example, a `NoSuchMethodException` is thrown when `main()` attempts to do a `newInstance()` on the class `A`. This happens because `A` does not have an empty constructor (one that accepts no arguments).

In `A.java`:

```
class A {
    public A(int i, int j) {
        System.out.println(i + j);
    }
}
```

In `Main.java`:

```
class Main {
    public static void main(String[] args) {
        System.out.println("NoSuchMethodException example");
        try {
            Class c = Class.forName("A");
            Object a = c.newInstance();
        } catch (InstantiationException e) {
            e.printStackTrace();
        } catch (IllegalAccessException e) {
            e.printStackTrace();
        } catch (ClassNotFoundException e) {
            e.printStackTrace();
        }
    }
}
```

NoSuchMethodException()

PURPOSE Constructs a `NoSuchMethodException` instance.

SYNTAX
```
public NoSuchMethodException()
public NoSuchMethodException(String msg)
```

DESCRIPTION The two forms of this constructor create a new instance of `NoSuchMethodException`. An optional string `msg` can be supplied that describes this particular instance of the exception.

PARAMETERS

`msg` A string that gives details about this exception.

java.lang
NullPointerException

Syntax

```
public class NullPointerException extends RuntimeException
```

Description

`NullPointerException` is thrown when the program attempts to dereference a `null` object reference. A typical example of this is a method that expects an object reference as an argument but instead gets a `null`.

```
class Main {
    public static void test(Object obj) {
        System.out.println(obj.toString());
    }
    public static void main(String[] args) {
```

```
        System.out.println("NullPointerException example");
        test(null);
    }
}
```

NullPointerException should not be caught or declared in the throws clause of a method.

MEMBER SUMMARY	
Constructor	
NullPointerException()	Constructs a NullPointerException instance.

See Also

RuntimeException.

NullPointerException()

PURPOSE Constructs a NullPointerException instance.

SYNTAX
```
public NullPointerException()
public NullPointerException(String msg)
```

DESCRIPTION The two forms of this constructor create a new instance of NullPointerException. An optional string msg can be supplied that describes this particular instance of the exception.

PARAMETERS

msg A string that gives details about this exception.

java.lang

Number

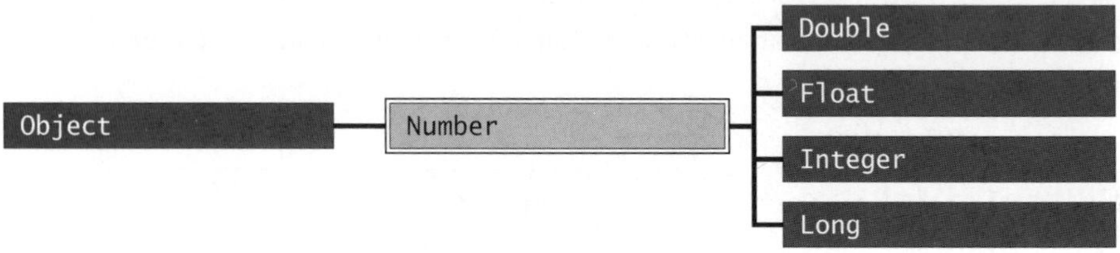

Syntax

```
public abstract class Number
```

Description

`Number` is an abstract superclass for numeric scalar types. `Integer`, `Long`, `Float`, and `Double` are subclasses of `Number` that implement the abstract methods in the `Number` class for the basic numeric types in Java.

MEMBER SUMMARY

Number Methods

`doubleValue()`	Retrieves the value of this object as a `double`.
`floatValue()`	Retrieves the value of this object as a `float`.
`intValue()`	Retrieves the value of this object as an `int`.
`longValue()`	Retrieves the value of this object as a `long`.

See Also

`Double`, `Float`, `Integer`, `Long`.

Example

```
import java.util.Vector;
import java.util.Enumeration;

class Main {
    // Calculate the double sum of a vector of Number objects
    public static double doubleSum(Vector v) {
        double sum = 0;
```

```
        for (Enumeration e = v.elements();
             e.hasMoreElements();
             sum += ((Number)e.nextElement()).doubleValue());
        return (sum);
    }
    public static void main(String[] args) {
        Vector numvec = new Vector(6);

        // Prepare contents of vector
        numvec.addElement(new Integer(1995));
        numvec.addElement(new Double(6.4e3));
        numvec.addElement(new Integer(32));
        numvec.addElement(new Float(7.821e3f));
        numvec.addElement(new Double(22.32e2));
        numvec.addElement(new Long(7927928));
        numvec.addElement(new Long(10424300));

        System.out.println("double total: " + doubleSum(numvec));
    }
}
```

doubleValue()

PURPOSE Retrieves the value of this object as a `double`.

SYNTAX `public abstract double doubleValue()`

DESCRIPTION This method returns the value of this object as a `double`. This may involve casting if the value of this object is not already a `double`.

RETURNS The value of this object as a `double`.

EXAMPLE

```
// Calculate the double sum of a vector of Number objects
public static double doubleSum(Vector v) {
    double sum = 0;
    for (Enumeration e = v.elements();
         e.hasMoreElements();
         sum += ((Number)e.nextElement()).doubleValue());
    return (sum);
}
```

floatValue()

PURPOSE Retrieves the value of this object as a `float`.

SYNTAX `public abstract float floatValue()`

DESCRIPTION This method returns the value of this object as a `float`. This may involve casting (and possibly loss of precision) if the value of this object is not already a `float`.

RETURNS The value of this object as a `float`.

EXAMPLE

```
// Calculate the float sum of a vector of Number objects
public static float floatSum(Vector v) {
    float sum = 0;
    for (Enumeration e = v.elements();
         e.hasMoreElements();
         sum += ((Number)e.nextElement()).floatValue());
    return (sum);
}
```

intValue()

PURPOSE Retrieves the value of this object as an `int`.

SYNTAX `public abstract int intValue()`

DESCRIPTION This method returns the value of this object as an `int`. This may involve casting and rounding (and possibly loss of precision) if the value of this object is not already an `int`. Casting a number that does not fit into an `int` results in an `int` with the value of `-1`.

RETURNS The value of this object as an `int`.

EXAMPLE

```
// Calculate the int sum of a vector of Number objects
public static int intSum(Vector v) {
    int sum = 0;
    for (Enumeration e = v.elements();
         e.hasMoreElements();
         sum += ((Number)e.nextElement()).intValue());
    return (sum);
}
```

longValue()

PURPOSE Retrieves the value of this object as a `long`.

SYNTAX `public abstract long longValue()`

DESCRIPTION This method returns the value of this object as a `long`. This may involve rounding if the value of this object is not already a whole number.

RETURNS The value of this object as a `long`.

EXAMPLE

```
// Calculate the long sum of a vector of Number objects
public static long longSum(Vector v) {
    long sum = 0;
    for (Enumeration e = v.elements();
         e.hasMoreElements();
         sum += ((Number)e.nextElement()).longValue());
    return (sum);
}
```

java.lang

NumberFormatException

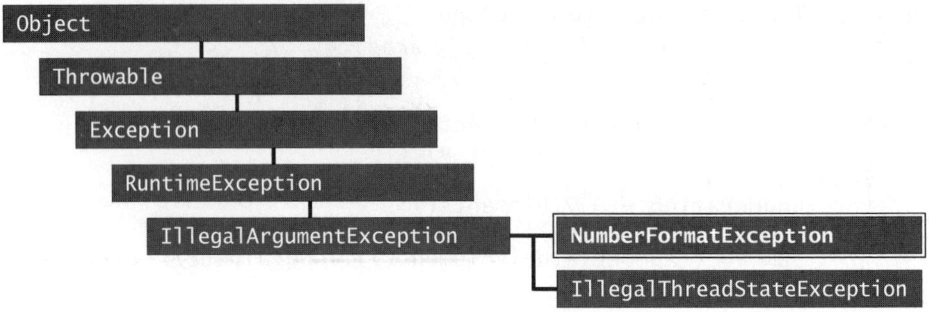

Syntax

`public class NumberFormatException extends IllegalArgumentException`

Description

`NumberFormatException` is an exception that is thrown when a method detects that the string it is parsing is an invalid format. It is thrown by methods in the runtime classes `Double`, `Float`, `Integer`, and `Long` when parsing a string in their respective formats. It could also be thrown by methods in user-supplied classes.

A method that throws `NumberFormatException` must declare it or any of its superclasses in its `throws` clause.

MEMBER SUMMARY	
Constructor	
`NumberFormatException()`	Constructs a `NumberFormatException` instance.

See Also

`Double`, `Float`, `IllegalArgumentException`, `Integer`, `Long`.

Example

In this example, a `NumberFormatException` is thrown because the string representation of an integer cannot contain a dot character ('.').

```
class Main {
    public static void main(String[] args) {
        System.out.println("NumberFormatException example");
        Integer inum = new Integer("36.5"); // format problem
    }
}
```

NumberFormatException()

PURPOSE Constructs a `NumberFormatException` instance.

SYNTAX
```
public NumberFormatException ()
public NumberFormatException (String msg)
```

DESCRIPTION The two forms of this constructor create a new instance of `NumberFormatException`. An optional string `msg` can be supplied that describes this particular instance of the exception.

PARAMETERS

`msg` A string that gives details about this exception.

java.lang

Object

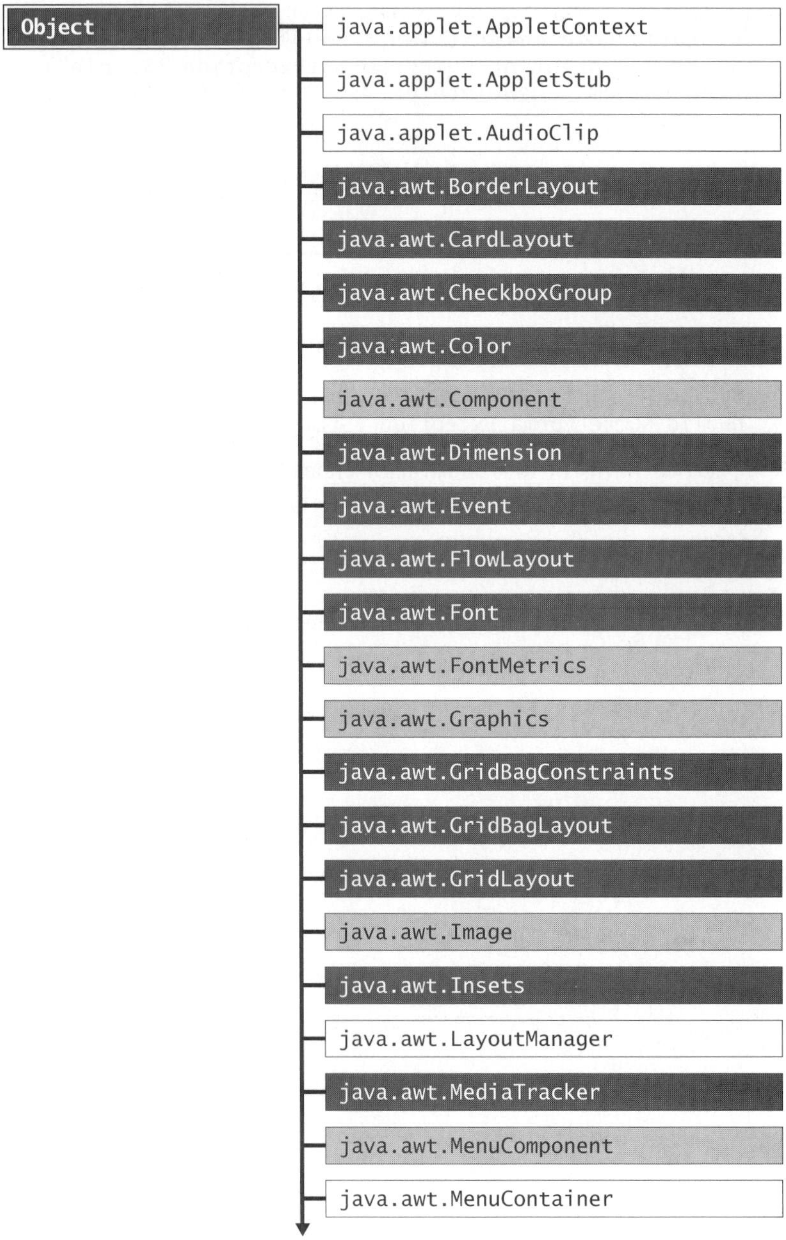
Object
java.applet.AppletContext
java.applet.AppletStub
java.applet.AudioClip
java.awt.BorderLayout
java.awt.CardLayout
java.awt.CheckboxGroup
java.awt.Color
java.awt.Component
java.awt.Dimension
java.awt.Event
java.awt.FlowLayout
java.awt.Font
java.awt.FontMetrics
java.awt.Graphics
java.awt.GridBagConstraints
java.awt.GridBagLayout
java.awt.GridLayout
java.awt.Image
java.awt.Insets
java.awt.LayoutManager
java.awt.MediaTracker
java.awt.MenuComponent
java.awt.MenuContainer

- java.awt.Point
- java.awt.Polygon
- java.awt.Rectangle
- java.awt.Toolkit
- java.awt.image.ColorModel
- java.awt.image.FilteredImageSource
- java.awt.image.ImageConsumer
- java.awt.image.ImageFilter
- java.awt.image.ImageObserver
- java.awt.image.ImageProducer
- java.awt.image.MemoryImageSource
- java.awt.image.PixelGrabber
- java.awt.peer.ButtonPeer
- java.awt.peer.CanvasPeer
- java.awt.peer.CheckboxMenuItemPeer
- java.awt.peer.CheckboxPeer
- java.awt.peer.ChoicePeer
- java.awt.peer.ComponentPeer
- java.awt.peer.ContainerPeer
- java.awt.peer.DialogPeer
- java.awt.peer.FileDialogPeer
- java.awt.peer.FramePeer
- java.awt.peer.LabelPeer
- java.awt.peer.ListPeer
- java.awt.peer.MenuBarPeer
- java.awt.peer.MenuComponentPeer
- java.awt.peer.MenuItemPeer
- java.awt.peer.MenuPeer

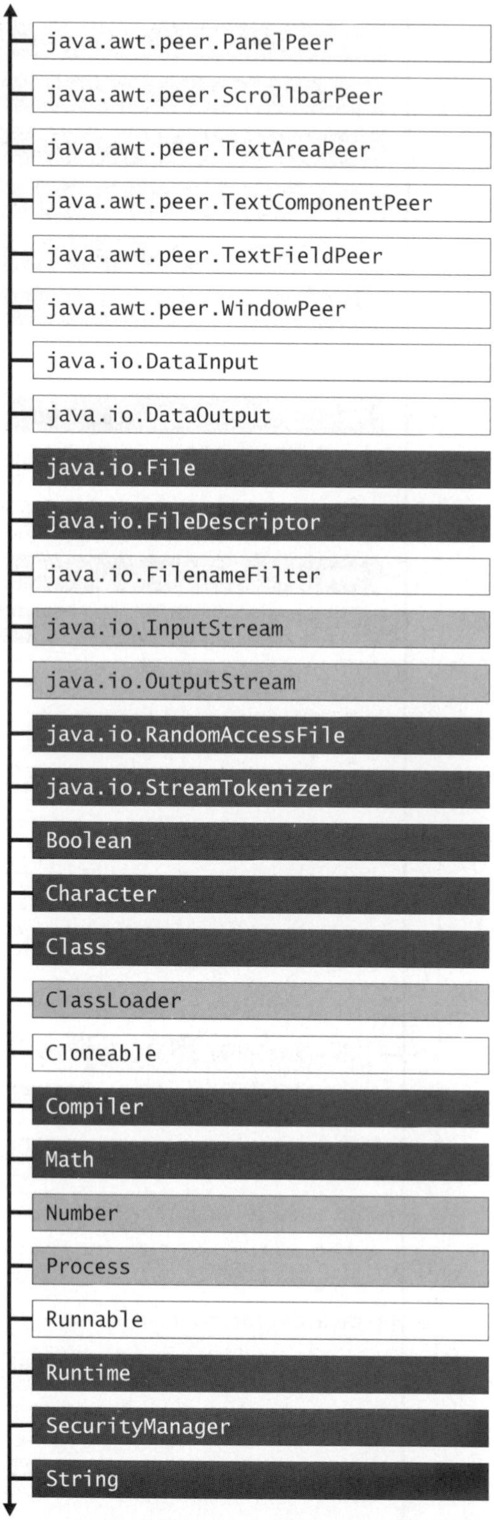
java.awt.peer.PanelPeer
java.awt.peer.ScrollbarPeer
java.awt.peer.TextAreaPeer
java.awt.peer.TextComponentPeer
java.awt.peer.TextFieldPeer
java.awt.peer.WindowPeer
java.io.DataInput
java.io.DataOutput
java.io.File
java.io.FileDescriptor
java.io.FilenameFilter
java.io.InputStream
java.io.OutputStream
java.io.RandomAccessFile
java.io.StreamTokenizer
Boolean
Character
Class
ClassLoader
Cloneable
Compiler
Math
Number
Process
Runnable
Runtime
SecurityManager
String

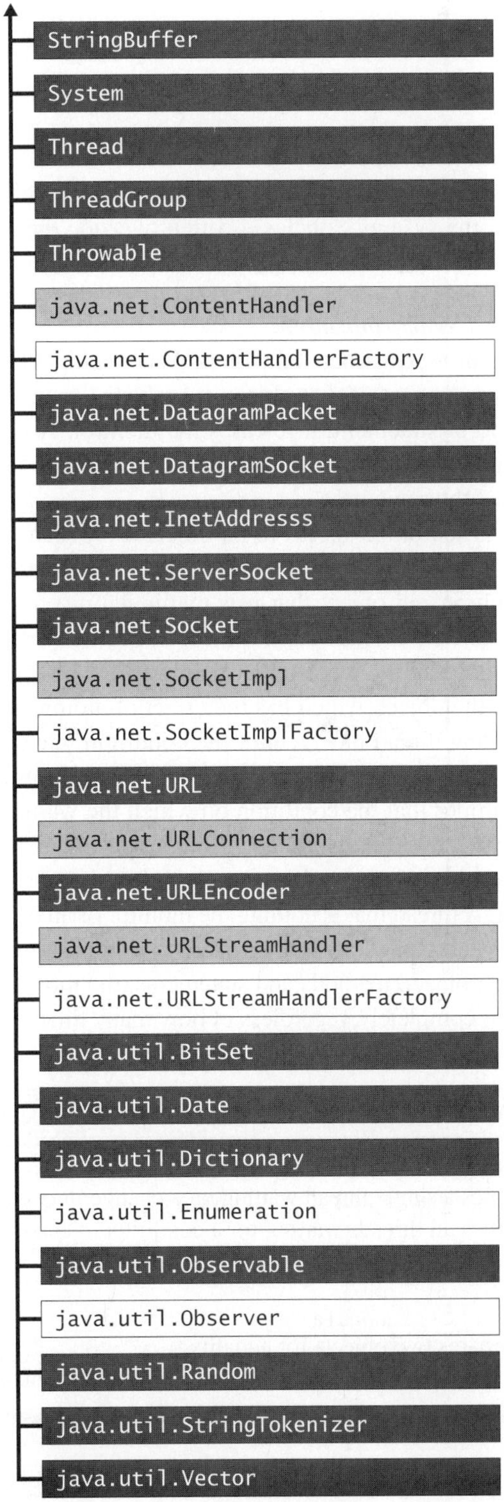
StringBuffer
System
Thread
ThreadGroup
Throwable
java.net.ContentHandler
java.net.ContentHandlerFactory
java.net.DatagramPacket
java.net.DatagramSocket
java.net.InetAddresss
java.net.ServerSocket
java.net.Socket
java.net.SocketImpl
java.net.SocketImplFactory
java.net.URL
java.net.URLConnection
java.net.URLEncoder
java.net.URLStreamHandler
java.net.URLStreamHandlerFactory
java.util.BitSet
java.util.Date
java.util.Dictionary
java.util.Enumeration
java.util.Observable
java.util.Observer
java.util.Random
java.util.StringTokenizer
java.util.Vector

A
B
C
D
E
F
G
H
I
J
K
L
M
N
O
P
Q
R
S
T
U
V
W
X
Y
Z

Syntax

```
public class Object
```

Description

The `Object` class is the ultimate superclass of all classes in Java; it is at the root of the Java class hierarchy. Every method defined in the `Object` class is available in all of its subclasses and hence in all objects in the system. Subclasses often override the implementation of some of these methods (such as `clone()`, `hashCode()`, and `equals()`).

Object Locking and Thread Synchronization

Each object has a *monitor* (or *lock*) associated with it. When a thread executes a synchronized method or a synchronized statement of that object, it grabs the monitor for that object. When the thread exits the method or statement, it releases the monitor. No two threads can grab an object's monitor at the same time. Hence no two threads can enter synchronized methods or statements for that object at the same time.

Multiple threads can synchronize access to an object with each other through the use of `wait()/notify()` calls. During the course of execution, a thread may need to wait for a condition (related to the synchronized object that it is manipulating) to occur before continuing execution. As mentioned earlier, when a thread is executing a synchronized method or synchronized statement, it is holding the monitor for that object. The thread waits for the condition by calling `wait()` on the object, which has the effect of atomically releasing the monitor that it is holding. The waiting thread blocks until the condition that it is waiting for has been satisfied. Effectively, the waiting thread is waiting for the monitor of the object to be returned to it. When a thread determines that the condition on which the waiting thread is awaiting has been satisfied, it invokes `notify()` on the object. This unblocks the waiting thread and allows the unblocked thread to grab the object's monitor when it has a chance to run.

Monitors are reentrant. A thread that is holding the monitor of an object can grab the monitor again by calling another synchronized method or synchronized statement of that object. When the thread exits all its synchronized methods and statements, the monitor is released. A `wait()` call will release the monitor completely, regardless of how many times the thread grabbed it.

MEMBER SUMMARY

Synchronization Methods	
`notify()`	Notifies a single thread waiting on a change in condition.
`notifyAll()`	Notifies all threads waiting for a condition to change.
`wait()`	Causes a thread to wait until it is notified.
General Methods	
`equals()`	Compares two objects for equality.
`getClass()`	Retrieves the name of the class associated with this object.

MEMBER SUMMARY	
`hashCode()`	Computes the hash code for this object.
`toString()`	Generates the string representation of this object.
Protected Methods	
`clone()`	Creates a clone of this object.
`finalize()`	Cleans up this object's state when it is being garbage-collected.

See Also

`Class`, `Cloneable`, `Hashtable`, `System.gc()`, `Thread`.

clone()

PURPOSE Creates a clone of this object.

SYNTAX `protected native Object clone()`

DESCRIPTION In general, a *clone* of an object should be a complete copy of the object. For example, a clone of a tree of objects is a complete copy of the tree, with copies of all the objects in the original tree.

`clone()` creates a clone of this object. The default implementation of `clone()` is defined by the `Object` class. In this default implementation, a new instance of this object's class is allocated and the contents of this object is bitwise-copied into the new instance. For example, if you are cloning a tree object that has not overridden its `clone()` method, invoking `clone()` on the tree object will simply copy the root object of the tree. The objects contained in the original tree will not be copied, but this newly cloned tree will point to those objects in the original tree. If any object in the original tree subsequently changes, those changes will be visible to the newly cloned tree.

A class whose `clone()` method should do more than just bitwise-copy (for example, making clones of objects to which it refers) must override the `clone()` method *and* implement the `Cloneable` interface.

RETURNS A copy of this object.

EXCEPTIONS

`CloneNotSupportedException`
If this object does not support the `Cloneable` interface.

`OutOfMemoryError`
If there is not enough memory to create the clone.

SEE ALSO Cloneable.

EXAMPLE See the Cloneable class example.

equals()

PURPOSE Compares this object with another for equality.

SYNTAX `public boolean equals(Object obj)`

DESCRIPTION This method compares this object with obj for equality. It returns true if the objects are equal; it returns false otherwise. The implementation of equals() in the Object class defines equality between two objects as that of *object reference equivalence*. That is, two objects are equal if they refer to the same object (they have the same object reference).

Subclasses of Object often override equals() with their own definitions of equality. For example, the Number classes (Integer, Long, Double, and Float) define equality in terms of equality of the object's numeric value and its Class.

The runtime system uses equals() when storing an Object in a hash table.

PARAMETERS

obj The object against which to compare.

RETURNS true if this object is equal to obj; false otherwise.

SEE ALSO hashCode(), Hashtable.

EXAMPLE The Hashtable class uses hashCode() and equals() to locate an object in a hash table.

```
public class Hashtable extends Dictionary implements Cloneable {
    ...
    public synchronized Object get(Object key) {
        HashtableEntry tab[] = table;
        int hash = key.hashCode();
        int index = (hash & 0x7FFFFFFF) % tab.length;
        for (HashtableEntry e = tab[index] ; e != null ; e = e.next) {
            if ((e.hash == hash) && e.key.equals(key)) {
                return e.value;
            }
        }
        return null;
    }
}
```

A B C D E F G H I J K L M N O P Q R S T U V W X Y Z

finalize()

PURPOSE Cleans up this object's state when it is garbage-collected.

SYNTAX `protected void finalize() throws Throwable`

DESCRIPTION This method is called by the system's garbage collector. By default, this method does not do anything. Subclasses of `Object` should override this method if there are resources held by instances of the subclass that need to be freed. In such cases, the class should override this method to include code that releases the resources held by an instance.

SEE ALSO `System.gc()`, `System.runFinalization()`.

EXAMPLE This example shows the `finalize()` method of the `DatagramSocket` class. This method ensures that the socket used by this instance of `DatagramSocket` is always closed before the object is garbage-collected.

```
public class DatagramSocket {
    ...
    protected synchronized void finalize() {
        datagramSocketClose();
    }
}
```

getClass()

PURPOSE Retrieves the class associated with this object.

SYNTAX `public final native Class getClass()`

DESCRIPTION Every object in Java is an instance of a class. For each class, Java maintains an immutable `Class` object containing information about the class. The `getClass()` method returns the `Class` object associated with this object.

RETURNS This object's `Class` object.

SEE ALSO `Class`.

EXAMPLE

```
public static void printClassName(Object obj) {
    System.out.println("The class of " + obj + " is " +
                       obj.getClass().getName());
}
```

hashCode()

PURPOSE
Computes the hash code for this object.

SYNTAX
`public native int hashCode()`

DESCRIPTION
Each `Object` in the Java system has a *hash code*, which is a *signed* number (`int`) that is usually different for different objects (i.e., hash codes can be negative). The hash code of an object is used when storing the object in hash tables.

An object's hash code is computed by calling its `hashCode()` method. The algorithm used to compute a hash code can differ for different classes of objects; most algorithms are based on the values in the object. In general, if `equals()` is `true` for two objects, they have the same hash code. However, the converse is not always true; two objects having the same hash code are not necessarily equal. Subclasses of `Object` override the default implementation of `hashCode()` if it wants to change the way hash codes are generated for its class of objects.

RETURNS
An `int` representing the hash code of the object.

SEE ALSO
`equals()`, `Hashtable`.

EXAMPLE
See `equals()`.

notify()

PURPOSE
Notifies a waiting thread of a change in condition.

SYNTAX
`public final native void notify()`

DESCRIPTION
A thread notifies another thread of a change in condition related to this object by calling `notify()`. This method unblocks one of the waiting threads and allows the unblocked thread to grab the object's monitor when it has a chance to run. If there are multiple waiting threads, the choice of which thread is unblocked is implementation-dependent. Other threads waiting for the condition to change remain blocked until other `notify()` or `notifyAll()` calls are invoked or until their specified time-out periods (if any) expire. If no thread is waiting for that condition, `notify()` does nothing. No state is kept that a `notify()` was done on the object.

The `notify()` method of an object can be called only by the thread holding the monitor for that object.

EXCEPTIONS

`IllegalMonitorStateException`

If the current thread is not holding the object's monitor.

SEE ALSO `wait()`, `notifyAll()`, `Thread`.

EXAMPLE This example illustrates the use of `wait()/notify()` in synchronizing access to a shared stack, defined by the class `Stack`. If the stack is full, `push()` waits until there is room in the stack before pushing another item onto the stack. If the stack is empty, `pop()` waits until there is an item on the stack to pop. If the stack was previously empty, `push()` notifies any thread that was waiting for an item to pop. If the stack was previously full, `pop()` notifies any thread that was waiting for space on the stack. The `Retriever` and `Stacker` classes are threads that, respectively, pop and push items onto the shared stack.

```
// A stack that has a 3 item limit
class Stack {
    static final int STACK_SIZE = 3;
    private int[] stack_store = new int[STACK_SIZE];
    private int stack_ptr = 0;

    // push item onto stack
    // If stack is full, wait until it has room
    synchronized public void push(int item) {
        while (stack_ptr >= STACK_SIZE) {
            try {
                wait();
            } catch (InterruptedException e) {
                // ignore
            }
        }
        if (stack_ptr == 0)
            notify();   // pop was awaiting stack to fill
        stack_store[stack_ptr++] = item;
    }

    // pop item off top of stack
    // If stack is empty, wait until it has item
    synchronized public int pop() {
        while (stack_ptr == 0) {
            try {
                wait();
            } catch (InterruptedException e) {
                // ignore
            }
        }
        if (stack_ptr >= STACK_SIZE)
            notify();  // push was awaiting stack to drain
        return(stack_store[--stack_ptr]);
    }
}
```

```
// Thread that loops, pushing items onto the stack, and then
// sleeping a random period of time
class Stacker extends Thread {
    Stack s;
    Stacker(Stack s) {
        super();
        this.s = s;
    }
    public void run() {
        while (true) {
            int rand = Math.round((float)((Math.random()* 6)));
            s.push(rand);
            System.out.println("push: " + rand);
            try {
                Thread.sleep(Math.round(Math.random()*100));
            } catch (InterruptedException e) {
            }
        }
    }
}

// Thread that loops, popping an item off the stack, and then
// sleeping a random period of time
class Retriever extends Thread {
    Stack s;
    Retriever(Stack s) {
        super();
        this.s = s;
    }
    public void run() {
        while (true) {
            int top = s.pop();
            System.out.println("pop: " + top);
            try {
                Thread.sleep(Math.round(Math.random()*100));
            } catch (InterruptedException e) {
            }
        }
    }
}

class Main {
    public static void main(String[] args) {
        Stack s = new Stack();  // create stack

        // create threads
        Thread rthread = new Retriever(s);
        Thread sthread = new Stacker(s);

        // start threads
        sthread.start();
        rthread.start();
    }
}
```

notifyAll()

PURPOSE Notifies all threads waiting for a condition to change.

SYNTAX `public final native void notifyAll()`

DESCRIPTION `notifyAll()` unblocks all threads waiting for a condition to change. If no thread is waiting for that condition, `notifyAll()` does nothing. The current thread must be holding the object's monitor.

EXCEPTIONS

`IllegalMonitorStateException`
If the current thread is not holding the object's monitor.

SEE ALSO `wait()`, `notify()`, `Thread`.

EXAMPLE

```
// wait until all workers are idle
while (workers_active > 0) {
    try {
        wait();
    } catch (InterruptedException e) {
        // ignore
    }
}
fillTaskList();
notifyAll();
```

toString()

PURPOSE Generates the string representation of this object.

SYNTAX `public String toString()`

DESCRIPTION This method returns the string representation of this object. By convention, all Java objects have a `toString()` method that returns the string representation of the object. When an object appears in a location where a `String` is expected, the compiler automatically invokes the `toString()` method of that object to get its string representation. All subclasses should override this method so that their string representation displays information relevant for that class.

RETURNS The string representation of this object.

A B C D E F G H I J K L M N O P Q R S T U V W X Y Z

EXAMPLE

```
Object obj = new Hashtable();

// the toString() invoked
// will be the overridden toString() defined by Hashtable
System.out.println(obj.toString());
```

wait()

PURPOSE Causes a thread to wait until it is notified.

SYNTAX
```
public final void wait() throws InterruptedException
public final void wait(long timeout) throws InterruptedException
public final void wait(long timeout, int nanos) throws
   InterruptedException
```

DESCRIPTION During the course of execution, a thread may need to wait for a condition related to this object to occur before continuing execution. It does this by calling `wait()`, which causes it to block until another thread invokes `notify()` on the object to indicate that the condition has been satisfied. The `wait()` method of an object can be called only by the thread holding the monitor for that object.

There are three forms of the `wait()` method; they vary in the time-out period to use for the wait. For all three forms, the wait can be interrupted by another thread (that invokes `interrupt()` on the thread). The first form of `wait()` blocks indefinitely until it has been notified. The second form blocks either until it has been notified or until `timeout` milliseconds has passed. A `timeout` of 0 means to wait indefinitely. The third form is like the second form, except it allows more precision in the time-out period by allowing nanoseconds to be specified as part of the time-out period. A `timeout` and `nanos` of 0 mean to wait indefinitely.

`wait()` is usually called in a loop. This is because there is no guarantee that the reason the thread was unblocked was because of a change in the condition that the thread has been waiting on. The thread could have been unblocked due to an interrupt or an expired time-out period. `wait()` is typically used by including the `wait()` statement in the body of a while loop. The condition at the top of the while loop checks that the condition that the thread is waiting on has not changed. If the condition has changed, the while loop is exited. Otherwise, the thread continues with the `wait()` call inside the while loop. An example of this is shown in the `notify()` example.

PARAMETERS

`timeout`	The maximum number of milliseconds to wait.
`nanos`	In addition to `timeout` milliseconds, wait `nanos` nanoseconds. `nanos` is a number between 0–999999 inclusive.[1]

EXCEPTIONS

`IllegalMonitorStateException`
If the current thread is not the owner of the object's monitor.

`InterruptedException`
If another thread has interrupted this thread.

SEE ALSO `notify()`, `notifyAll()`, `Thread`.

EXAMPLE See `notify()`.

1. In JDK 1.0.2, `nanos` is rounded to the nearest millisecond.

java.util
Observable

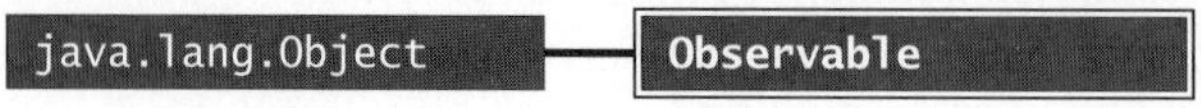

Syntax

```
public class Observable
```

Description

An *observable* is an object that holds some data. An *observer* is an object that monitors changes to the data in an observable object. You can associate a set of observers with an observable object (see Figure 195(a)). When a change is made to this observable object (see Figure 195(b)), the set of observers are notified of the change (see Figure 195(c)). Typically, a change in this observable object will result in some state changes in, or action by, the observers. Each observer must implement the `Observer` interface, but it otherwise is unrestricted as to its implementation. You can have observers of different subclasses observing the same observable object.

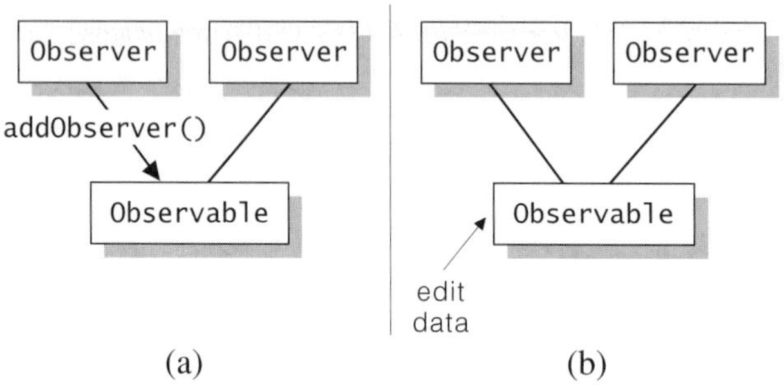

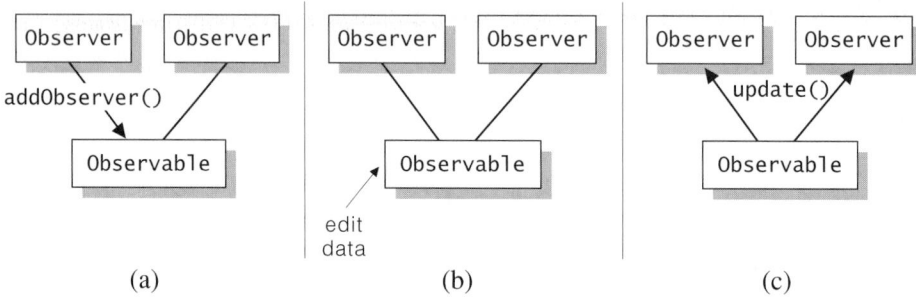

FIGURE 195 Observable and Observer Objects

The observable object must be a subclass of the `Observable` class. An example of an observable object could be the balance of a bank account. Observers of that observable could be an overdraft monitor, a financial advising tool, and the account owner's beeper. Whenever the balance was updated, you would notify these three objects of the change (perhaps including the account's delta as part of the arguments passed to notify these observers).

An Observable's Changed State

Each observable object has a state that records whether this object has changed. This state is either "changed" or "unchanged", and is set using `setChanged()` or `clearChanged()`, respectively. The typical sequence of steps are as follows:

1. Make changes to the data of an observable object.
2. Call `setChanged()` on the object to indicate that it has changed.
3. Notify observers of the change (using `notifyObservers()`), thereby automatically calling `clearChanged()`.

MEMBER SUMMARY

Observer Management Methods	
`addObserver()`	Adds an observer for this observable.
`countObservers()`	Determines the number of observers observing this observable.
`deleteObserver()`	Deletes an observer for this observable.
`deleteObservers()`	Deletes all observers for this observable.
Observable Status Change Methods	
`clearChanged()`	Records that this observable has not changed.
`hasChanged()`	Determines whether this observable has changed.
`notifyObservers()`	Notifies observers that this observable has changed.
`setChanged()`	Records that this observable has changed.

See Also

`Observer`.

Example

This example is an observable that tracks changes of an item from one color to another. It is used with the class examples in `Observer`.

```
import java.util.Observable;

class ColorObservable extends Observable {
    public static String colorName(int i) {
        switch (i) {
        case 1: return ("Red");
        case 0: return ("White");
        case 2: return ("Blue");
        default: return (null);
            }
    }
    public void changeColor(int i) {
        setChanged();
```

```
            notifyObservers(new Integer(i));
            clearChanged(); // not necessary;
                            // notifyObservers() already clears it
        }
    }
```

addObserver()

PURPOSE Adds an observer for this observable.

SYNTAX `public synchronized void addObserver(Observer obs)`

DESCRIPTION This method adds the observer `obs` as an observer for this observable. If there are already observers for this observable, `obs` is added to the list of observers. `obs` is notified of changes in this observable.

PARAMETERS

`obs` The non-`null` observer to add.

SEE ALSO `deleteObserver()`, `notifyObservers()`.

EXAMPLE This example uses the classes in the `Observable` and `Observer` class examples. It first creates the observable (`colors`) and then creates and adds the observers (`Statistician` and `Echoer`) for it. After performing some changes to the observable item, it prints a summary and then removes first one, and then all, of the observers.

```
import java.util.Observable;
import java.util.Observer;

class Main {
    final static int white = 0;
    final static int red = 1;
    final static int blue = 2;

    public static void main(String[] args) {
        colorObservable colors = new colorObservable();
        Statistician counter = new Statistician(3);

        // Assign Observers
        colors.addObserver(counter);
        colors.addObserver(new Echoer());
        System.out.println("Number of observers: "
            + colors.countObservers());

        // Make changes to Observable
        colors.changeColor(blue);
        colors.changeColor(white);
```

A B C D E F G H I J K L M N O P Q R S T U V W X Y Z

```
        colors.changeColor(red);
        colors.changeColor(blue);

        counter.report();

        // Remove one Observer
        colors.deleteObserver(counter);
        System.out.println("Number of observers: "
            + colors.countObservers());
        // Remove all Observers
        colors.deleteObservers();
        System.out.println("Number of observers: "
            + colors.countObservers());
    }
}
```

clearChanged()

PURPOSE Records that this observable has not changed.

SYNTAX `protected synchronized void clearChanged()`

DESCRIPTION This method clears the changed state recorded for this observable. If this observable was recorded earlier as having been changed, this method resets that state to "unchanged."

This method is the inverse of `setChanged()`.

SEE ALSO `hasChanged()`, `setChanged()`.

EXAMPLE See the class example.

countObservers()

PURPOSE Determines the number of observers for this observable.

SYNTAX `public synchronized int countObservers()`

RETURNS The number of observers observing this observable.

SEE ALSO `addObserver()`, `deleteObserver()`.

EXAMPLE See `addObserver()`.

deleteObserver()

PURPOSE Deletes an observer for this observable.

SYNTAX `public synchronized void deleteObserver(Observer obs)`

DESCRIPTION This method deletes the observer `obs` from the observers observing this observable. This method does not do anything if `obs` is not one of the observers for this observable.

This method is the inverse of `addObserver()`.

PARAMETERS

`obs` The (non-`null`) observer to delete.

SEE ALSO `addObserver()`, `deleteObservers()`.

EXAMPLE See `addObserver()`.

deleteObservers()

PURPOSE Deletes all observers for this observable.

SYNTAX `public synchronized void deleteObservers()`

SEE ALSO `deleteObserver()`.

EXAMPLE See `addObserver()`.

hasChanged()

PURPOSE Determines whether this observable has changed.

SYNTAX `public synchronized boolean hasChanged()`

DESCRIPTION An observable's changed state is set and cleared using `setChanged()` and `clearChanged()`, respectively. `hasChanged()` returns this observable's change state. It returns `true` if the observable has changed and `false` if the observable has not changed.

RETURNS `true` if this observable has changed; `false` if it has not changed.

SEE ALSO `clearChanged()`, `setChanged()`.

EXAMPLE See the class example.

notifyObservers()

PURPOSE Notifies observers that this observable has changed.

SYNTAX

```
public void notifyObservers()
public synchronized void notifyObservers(Object arg)
```

DESCRIPTION If this observable has changed, this method notifies its observers of the change and the changed state of this observable is cleared. The object `arg` is passed to each observer as part of the notification process. If `arg` is not specified, it defaults to `null`.

If this observable has not changed, this method does nothing.

PARAMETERS

`arg` The argument to be passed to the observers when notifying them.

SEE ALSO `clearChanged()`, `hasChanged()`, `Observer.update()`, `setChanged()`.

EXAMPLE See the class example.

setChanged()

PURPOSE Records that this observable has changed.

SYNTAX

```
protected synchronized void setChanged()
```

DESCRIPTION This method is the inverse of `clearChanged()`.

SEE ALSO `clearChanged()`, `hasChanged()`, `notifyObservers()`.

EXAMPLE See the class example.

A B C D E F G H I J K L M N O P Q R S T U V W X Y Z

java.util
Observer

```
Observer
```

Syntax

`public interface Observer`

Description

An *observable* is an object that holds some data. An *observer* is an object that monitors changes to the data in an observable object. You can associate a set of observers with an observable object. When a change is made to this observable object, the set of observers are notified of the change. Typically, a change in this observable object will result in some state changes in, or action by, the observers. Each observer must implement the `Observer` interface, but otherwise it is unrestricted as to its implementation. You can have observers of different subclasses observing the same observable object.

An example of an observable object could be the balance of a bank account. Observers of that observable could be an overdraft monitor, a financial advising tool, and the account owner's beeper. Whenever the balance was updated, you would notify these three objects of the change (perhaps including the account's delta as part of the arguments passed to notify these observers). Doing this would cause the `update()` method of each observer to be invoked to react to the change. The overdraft monitor object (which is an observer) would check whether the change in the account caused the new balance to fall below zero, and if so, it would take action to automatically transfer funds to cover the overdraft.

MEMBER SUMMARY

Observer Method

`update()`	Updates this observer using the supplied information.

See Also

`Observable`.

Example

The following contains two examples of observers: `Statistician` and `Echoer`. These use the `ColorObservable` class defined in the class example of `Observable`. The example in `Observable.addObserver()` shows how these observers are added. `Statistician` maintains an array that counts the number of times an object has been accessed. `Echoer` prints out information about the change that has been made.

```
import java.util.Observer;
import java.util.Observable;

// Observer that counts number of times the Integer 'arg' has been
// accessed
class Statistician implements Observer {
    private int[] counts;
    Statistician(int array_size) {
        counts = new int[array_size];
    }
    public void update(Observable o, Object arg) {
        Integer int_obj = (Integer)arg;
        if (int_obj.intValue() < counts.length)
            ++counts[int_obj.intValue()];
    }
    public void report() {
        System.out.println("Record of changes: ");
        for (int i = 0; i < counts.length; i++)
            System.out.println(ColorObservable.colorName(i) + ": " +
                counts[i]);
    }
}

// Observer that prints out arg each time that it is accessed
class Echoer implements Observer {
    int current_color;
    public void update(Observable o, Object arg) {
        int new_color = ((Integer)arg).intValue();
        System.out.println("Changing from " +
                               ColorObservable.colorName(current_color) +
                               " to " +
                               ColorObservable.colorName(new_color));
        current_color = new_color;
    }
}
```

update()

PURPOSE Updates this observer using the supplied information.

SYNTAX `void update(Observable observed, Object arg)`

update()

DESCRIPTION This method updates this observer, which is observing the object `observed`. This observer is notified that `observed` has changed and that `arg` is the argument that accompanies this notification. Each class that implements the `Observer` interface must supply an implementation for this method.

PARAMETERS

`arg`	The argument to supply to this observer when updating it.
`observed`	The observed object that has changed.

SEE ALSO `Observable.notifyObservers()`, `Observable.setChanged()`.

EXAMPLE See the class example.

java.lang

OutOfMemoryError

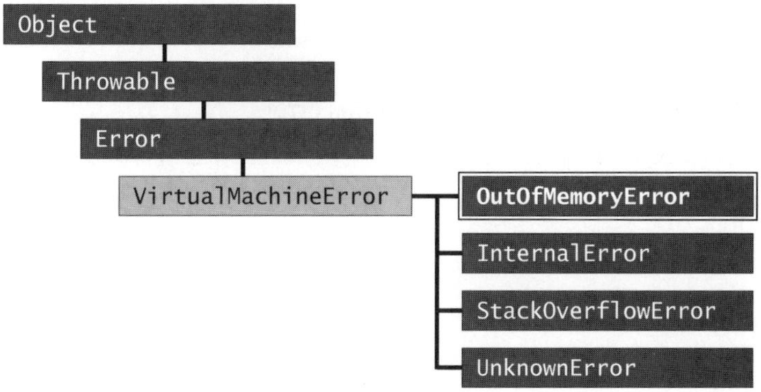

Syntax

```
public class OutOfMemoryError extends VirtualMachineError
```

Description

`OutOfMemoryError` is an unrecoverable error raised by the Java virtual machine when no more memory is available for continuing the execution of the program. It should not be caught or declared in the `throws` clause of a method.

MEMBER SUMMARY	
Constructor	
`OutOfMemoryError()`	Constructs an `OutOfMemoryError` instance.

See Also

`Error`, `VirtualMachineError`.

OutOfMemoryError()

PURPOSE Constructs an `OutOfMemoryError` instance.

A B C D E F G H I J K L M N O P Q R S T U V W X Y Z

OutOfMemoryError()

SYNTAX

```
public OutOfMemoryError()
public OutOfMemoryError(String msg)
```

DESCRIPTION The two forms of this constructor create a new instance of `OutOfMemoryError`. An optional string `msg` can be supplied that describes this particular instance of the error.

PARAMETERS

`msg` A string that gives details about this error.

java.io
OutputStream

Syntax
`public abstract class OutputStream`

Description
The `OutputStream` class is the superclass of all output streams. It provides basic output methods for writing data to an output stream. Subclasses of `OutputStream` override some or all of these basic methods for implementing their particular type of output stream. Figure 196 shows that you can either write directly to a subclass of `OutputStream` or write to an output stream through filters.

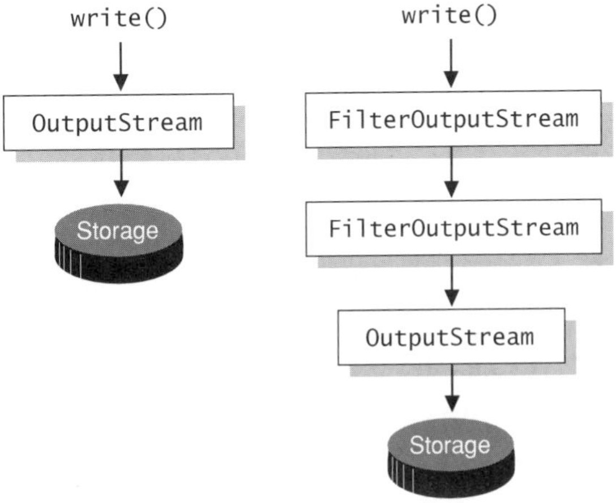

FIGURE 196 `OutputStream` and `FilterOutputStream`

MEMBER SUMMARY	
Output Methods	
`flush()`	Flushes any buffered bytes from this output stream.
`write()`	Writes bytes to this output stream.
Method for Closing Stream	
`close()`	Closes this output stream.

A B C D E F G H I J K L M N O P Q R S T U V W X Y Z

See Also

BufferedOutputStream, ByteArrayOutputStream, DataOutputStream, FileOutputStream, FilterOutputStream, InputStream, PipedOutputStream, PrintStream.

Example

This example shows an echo() method that takes input from an input stream and writes the bytes read directly to an output stream.

```
import java.io.*;

class Main {
    // reads input from 'in' and writes the bytes out to 'out'
    public static void echo(InputStream in, OutputStream out) {
        try {
            int c;
            while((c = in.read()) > -1)
                out.write(c);
            out.flush();                    // flush output

            in.close();                     // close streams
            out.close();
        } catch (IOException e) {
            e.printStackTrace();
        }
    }
    public static void main(String[] args) {
        try {
            InputStream in;
            if (args.length == 0)
                in = System.in;
            else
                in = new FileInputStream(args[0]);
            echo(in, System.out);
        } catch (IOException e) {
            e.printStackTrace();
        }
    }
}
```

close()

PURPOSE Closes this output stream.

SYNTAX `public void close() throws IOException`

DESCRIPTION This method closes this output stream. The default implementation does nothing. Subclasses of `OutputStream` should override this method to release any resources (especially system resources) used by this output stream, such as file descriptors and sockets.

EXCEPTIONS

`IOException` If an IO error occurred.

EXAMPLE See the class example.

flush()

PURPOSE Flushes any buffered bytes from this output stream.

SYNTAX

```
public void flush() throws IOException
```

DESCRIPTION Some output streams buffer the bytes written to them. `flush()` writes out any buffered bytes. The default implementation of `flush()` does nothing.

EXCEPTIONS

`IOException` If an IO error occurred.

EXAMPLE See the class example.

write()

PURPOSE Writes bytes to this output stream.

SYNTAX

```
public void write(int oneByte) throws IOException
public void write(byte[] buffer) throws IOException
public void write(byte[] buffer, int offset, int count) throws
   IOException
```

DESCRIPTION The three forms of this method write bytes to this output stream. The first form is an abstract method whose implementation is supplied by the subclasses of `OutputStream`. It writes the lowest-order byte from `oneByte` to this output stream. The other two forms are implemented using this first form and consequently should usually be overridden to be more efficient than performing writes a byte at a time. The second form writes `buffer.length` number of bytes from the byte array `buffer` to this output stream. The third form writes `count` number of bytes from the byte array `buffer`, starting at index `offset`, to this output stream.

write()

PARAMETERS

`buffer`	The byte array containing the bytes to be written.
`count`	The number of bytes to write.
`offset`	The index in `buffer` at which to start getting bytes to be written.
`oneByte`	The byte to be written.

EXCEPTIONS

`IOException`	If an IO error occurred while attempting to write.

EXAMPLE This example reimplements the `echo()` method in the class example. It writes the bytes out into a buffer and then when the buffer becomes full, writes the buffer out to the output stream.

```
public static void echo(InputStream in, OutputStream out) {
    try {
        int c, i = 0;
        byte[] buffer = new byte[1024];        // buffer for bytes
        while((c = in.read()) > -1) {
            if (i < buffer.length)
                buffer[i++] = (byte)c;         // get lowest order byte
            else {
                out.write(buffer);
                out.flush();                   // flush output
                i = 0;                         // reset
            }
        }
        if (i > 0) {
            out.write(buffer, 0, i);           // write remaining bytes
        }
        in.close();                            // close streams
        out.close();
    } catch (IOException e) {
        e.printStackTrace();
    }
}
```

A B C D E F G H I J K L M N O P Q R S T U V W X Y Z

Panel

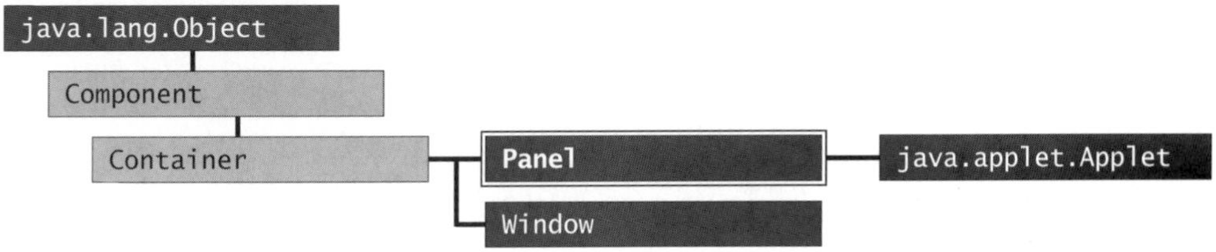

Syntax

```
public class Panel extends Container
```

Description

A *panel* is a component and a component container. Since a panel is itself a component, panels can be freely nested. Panels are typically used in the layout of components in a user interface. For example, suppose a user interface has two columns of buttons, one on the left and one on the right. In between the two columns is a display area that expands as the user expands the window. This layout would be implemented with three panels: a border layout panel (see `BorderLayout`) with two nested grid layout panels (see `GridLayout`).

A panel has no border or title, hence its insets are always (0, 0, 0, 0).

See the `Container` class for more information about insets and layout managers.

Events

The panel generates the same events as a component. See the `Component` class for details.

MEMBER SUMMARY	
Constructor	
`Panel()`	Constructs a new `Panel` instance.
Peer Method	
`addNotify()`	Creates the panel's peer hierarchy.

A B C D E F G H I J K L M N O P Q R S T U V W X Y Z

A B C D E F G H I J K L M N O P Q R S T U V W X Y Z

Example

This example creates four panels named "one", "two", "three", and "four". These four panels are in turn embedded in another panel with a card layout manager. Each panel contains from one to four buttons. Four buttons are provided on the left side of the frame to control which of the four panels are displayed. See Figure 197.

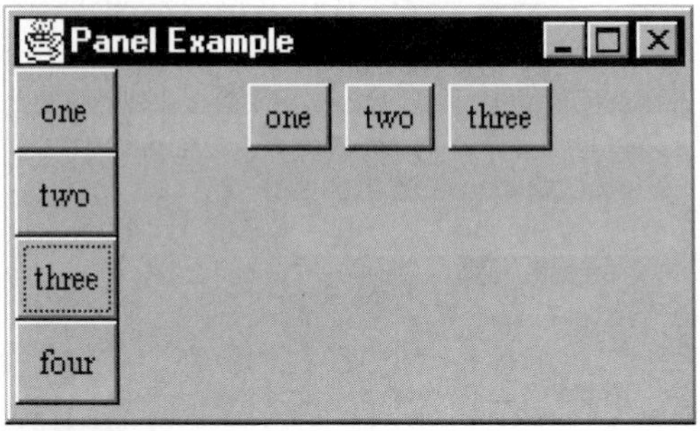

FIGURE 197 Panel

```
import java.awt.*;
class Main extends Frame {
    CardLayout cardLayout = new CardLayout();
    Panel cardPanel = new Panel();
    String[] names = {"one", "two", "three", "four"};

    Main() {
        super("Panel Example");
        Panel p = new Panel();

        p.setLayout(new GridLayout(0, 1));
        for (int i=0; i<names.length; i++) {
            p.add(new Button(names[i]));
        }
        add("West", p);

        cardPanel.setLayout(cardLayout);
        for (int i=0; i<names.length; i++) {
            addPanel(cardPanel, i+1);
        }
        add("Center", cardPanel);
        resize(300, 150);
        show();
    }

    // Creates a panel with 'count' buttons.
    void addPanel(Panel parent, int count) {
        Panel p = new Panel();
        for (int i=0; i<count; i++) {
            p.add(new Button(names[i]));
        }
        parent.add(names[count-1], p);
    }

    public boolean action(Event evt, Object what) {
        cardLayout.show(cardPanel, (String)what);
        return true;
    }
```

```
    static public void main(String[] args) {
        new Main();
    }
}
```

addNotify()

PURPOSE Creates the panel's peer hierarchy.

SYNTAX `public synchronized void addNotify()`

DESCRIPTION This method creates the panel's peer hierarchy, if necessary. The panel's peer is created by calling the `Toolkit.createPanel()` method. This method should never be called directly. It is normally called by the panel's parent.

OVERRIDES `Container.addNotify()`.

SEE ALSO `Component`, `Toolkit`.

Panel()

PURPOSE Constructs a new `Panel` instance.

SYNTAX `public Panel()`

DESCRIPTION This constructor creates a new visible `Panel` instance. The default layout manager for a panel is `FlowLayout`.

EXAMPLE See the class example.

java.awt.peer

PanelPeer

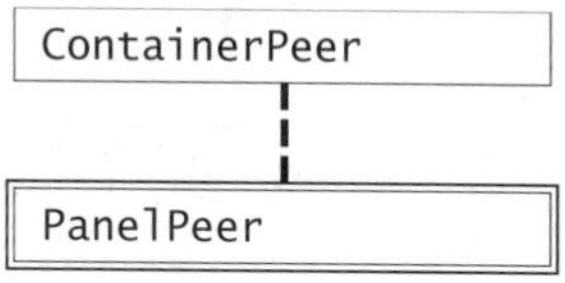

Syntax

```
public interface PanelPeer extends ContainerPeer
```

Description

The panel component (see the `Panel` class) in the Abstract Windowing Toolkit (AWT), uses the platform's native implementation of a panel. So that the AWT panel behaves the same on all platforms, the panel is assigned a peer, whose task is to translate the behavior of the platform's native panel to the behavior of the AWT panel.

AWT programmers normally do not directly use peer classes and interfaces. Instead they deal with AWT components in the `java.awt` package. These in turn automatically manage their peers. Only someone who is porting the AWT to another platform should be concerned with the peer classes and interfaces. Consequently, most peer documentation refers to `java.awt` counterparts.

See `Component` and `Toolkit` for additional information about component peers.

See Also

`Component`, `Panel`, `Toolkit`.

PipedInputStream

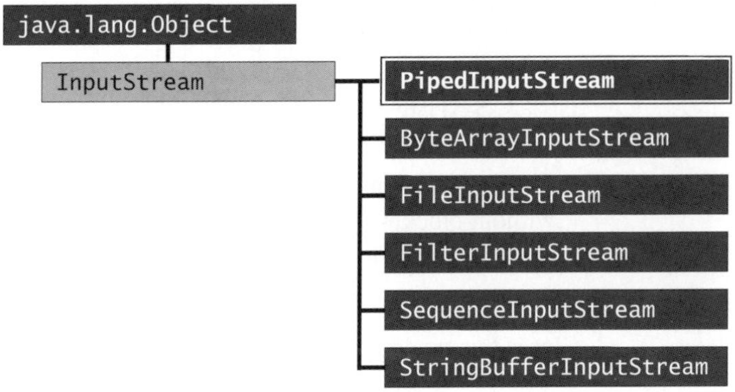

Syntax

```
public class PipedInputStream extends InputStream
```

Description

When writing a program, you may sometimes find it useful to be able to use a *pipe* as a communications stream between two threads. One thread communicates with another thread by sending output to the pipe. The other thread receives data from its counterpart by reading data from the pipe. Such a paradigm is useful when the threads have a producer/consumer relationship and the best way to transfer data between the two threads is via a pipe. For example, in a process monitoring program one thread could be collecting raw data from various monitoring devices and sending the data through a pipe to another thread. The other thread would then read data from the pipe and process the raw data in order to update status indicators.

The `PipedInputStream` class is used to provide an input stream to a pipe. A `PipedInputStream` is connected with a `PipedOutputStream` to create a pipe, whereby one thread can send data to the pipe while another thread reads the data from the pipe (see Figure 198). The pipe buffers any unread bytes. When the pipe becomes full, the writing thread

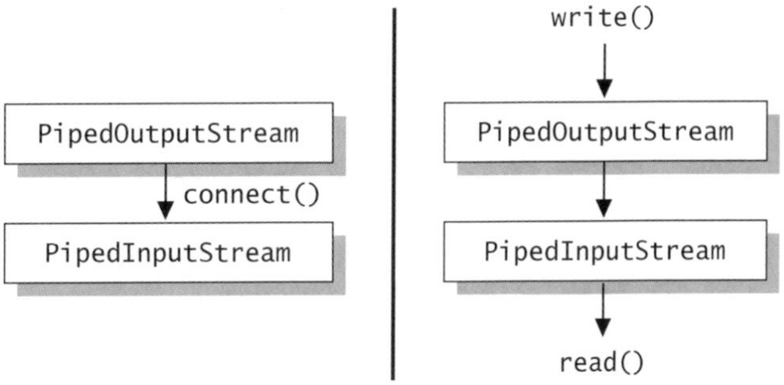

FIGURE 198 **`PipedInputStream` and `PipedOutputStream`**

A B C D E F G H I J K L M N O P Q R S T U V W X Y Z

blocks until there is room in the pipe to write more bytes. If the pipe is empty, the reading thread blocks until there are bytes in the pipe to be read.

MEMBER SUMMARY	
Constructor	
`PipedInputStream()`	Constructs a new piped input stream instance.
Input Method	
`available()`	Determines the number of bytes that can be read from the pipe without blocking.
`read()`	Reads bytes from this piped input stream.
Pipe Methods	
`close()`	Closes this piped input stream.
`connect()`	Connects this piped input stream to a piped output stream.

See Also

`InputStream`, `PipedOutputStream`.

Example

This example illustrates the use of piped input and output streams for two threads to communicate with each other. The `RunningAverage` thread is a thread that reads from the input stream a sequence of numbers and computes its running average. The `NumberGenerator` is a thread that generates a sequence of numbers and writes it out to an output stream. This particular implementation uses `Random()` to generate the numbers, but one could imagine other data generators like speedometers and temperature sensors.

```
import java.io.*;
import java.util.Random;

// reads numbers from input stream and compute running average
class RunningAverage extends Thread {
    private DataInputStream in;
    double total = 0;
    long count = 0;

    public RunningAverage(InputStream i) {
        in = new DataInputStream(i);
    }
    public void run() {
        while (true) {
```

```
            try {
                double num = in.readDouble();
                total += num;
                count++;
                System.out.println(count + ": " + num + " avg = "
                                   + total/count);
            } catch (IOException e) {
                e.printStackTrace();
            }
        }
    }
}
class NumberGenerator extends Thread {
    private DataOutputStream out;
    private Random gen = new Random();
    private final long RANGE = 10000;

    public NumberGenerator(OutputStream o) {
        out = new DataOutputStream(o);
    }
    public void run() {
        while (true) {
            try {
                double num = gen.nextFloat() * RANGE;
                out.writeDouble(num);
                out.flush();
                sleep(500);  // sleep for 500 milliseconds
            } catch (IOException e) {
                e.printStackTrace();
            } catch (InterruptedException e) {
                e.printStackTrace();
            }
        }
    }
}
class Main {
    public static void main(String[] args) {
        try {
            PipedOutputStream producer = new PipedOutputStream();
            PipedInputStream consumer = new PipedInputStream(producer);

            RunningAverage avg = new RunningAverage(consumer);
            NumberGenerator gen = new NumberGenerator(producer);

            gen.start();
            avg.start();
        } catch (IOException e) {
            e.printStackTrace();
        }
    }
}
```

available()

PURPOSE Determines the number of bytes that can be read from this pipe without blocking.

SYNTAX `public synchronized int available() throws IOException`

DESCRIPTION This method determines the number of bytes that have been written to the pipe but not yet read.

RETURNS The number of bytes that can be read from this pipe without blocking.

EXCEPTIONS
`IOException` If an IO error occurred.

OVERRIDES `InputStream.available()`.

EXAMPLE See `InputStream.mark()`.

close()

PURPOSE Closes this piped input stream.

SYNTAX `public void close() throws IOException`

DESCRIPTION This method closes this piped input stream. Once the stream has been closed, you can no longer read from it.

EXCEPTIONS
`IOException` If an IO error occurred.

OVERRIDES `InputStream.close()`.

SEE ALSO `read()`.

EXAMPLE See `connect()`.

connect()

PURPOSE Connects this piped input stream to a piped output stream.

SYNTAX `public void connect(PipedOutputStream src) throws IOException`

DESCRIPTION This method connects this piped input stream to the piped output stream `src`. Once these are connected, output written to `src` can be read from this piped input stream by using `read()`.

PARAMETERS

`src` The output stream to which to connect.

EXCEPTIONS

`IOException` If an IO error occurred while attempting to connect this stream to `src`.

SEE ALSO `PipedInputStream()`, `PipedOutputStream.connect()`.

EXAMPLE This example is a modification of the class example. It connects the pipe explicitly using `connect()` and runs for only 5 seconds before terminating the threads and closing the streams.

```
import java.io.*;

class Main2 {
    public static void main(String[] args) {
        try {
            PipedOutputStream producer = new PipedOutputStream();
            PipedInputStream consumer = new PipedInputStream();

            consumer.connect(producer);        // connect pipes

            RunningAverage avg = new RunningAverage(consumer);
            NumberGenerator gen = new NumberGenerator(producer);

            gen.start();                // start threads
            avg.start();

            try {
                Thread.sleep(5000);  // sleep for 5 seconds
            } catch (InterruptedException e) {
            }

            gen.stop();                 // stop threads
            avg.stop();

            producer.close();           // close streams
            consumer.close();
        } catch (IOException e) {
            e.printStackTrace();
        }
    }
}
```

PipedInputStream()

PURPOSE Constructs a new piped input stream instance.

SYNTAX

```
public PipedInputStream ()
public PipedInputStream (PipedOutputStream src) throws IOException
```

DESCRIPTION There are two forms of this constructor for `PipedInputStream`. The first form creates a piped input stream that is not connected to any piped output stream. Before this piped input stream can be used, it must be subsequently connected to a piped output stream using `connect()`. The second form creates a piped input stream that is connected to the piped output stream `src`. Output from `src` can be read from this newly created piped input stream.

PARAMETERS

`src` The output stream to which to connect.

EXCEPTIONS

`IOException` If an IO error occurred while attempting to connect this new stream to `src`.

SEE ALSO `connect()`, `PipedOutputStream`.

EXAMPLE See class example and `connect()`.

read()

PURPOSE Reads bytes from this piped input stream.

SYNTAX

```
public synchronized int read() throws IOException
public synchronized int read(byte[] buffer, int offset, int count)
   throws IOException
```

DESCRIPTION The two forms of this method read bytes from this piped input stream. The first form reads a single byte from this piped input stream and returns it as an `int` (the lowest-order byte of the `int`). The second form reads `count` number of bytes from this piped input stream and stores it into the byte array `buffer` starting at index `offset`.

The bytes read are obtained from the piped output stream to which this piped input stream is connected. If no output is available yet, `read()` waits until some output is available.

PARAMETERS

`buffer` The byte array in which to store the bytes read.
`count` The number of bytes to read.
`offset` The index in `buffer` at which to start storing the bytes read.

RETURNS The first form returns the byte read; the second form returns the actual number of bytes read. Both forms return `-1` when the end of the stream is reached before any bytes are read.

A B C D E F G H I J K L M N O P Q R S T U V W X Y Z

EXCEPTIONS

`IOException`	If an IO error occurred.
OVERRIDES	`InputStream.read()`.
SEE ALSO	`PipedOutputStream.write()`.
EXAMPLE	See the class example.

A B C D E F G H I J K L M N O P Q R S T U V W X Y Z

java.io
PipedOutputStream

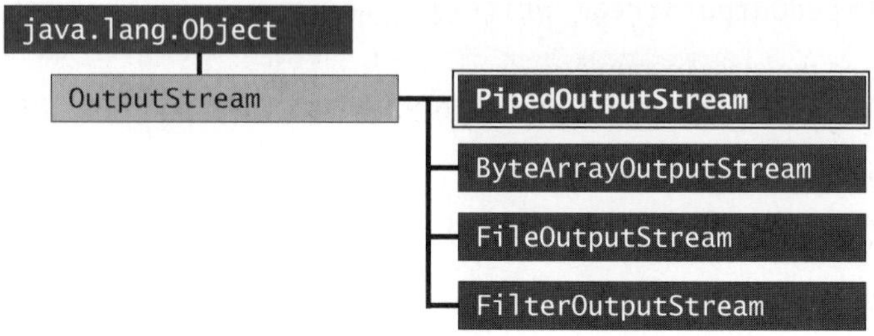

Syntax

```
public class PipedOutputStream extends OutputStream
```

Description

When writing a program, you may sometimes find it useful to be able to use a *pipe* as a communications stream between two threads. One thread communicates with another thread by sending output to the pipe. The other thread receives data from its counterpart by reading data from the pipe. Such a paradigm is useful when the threads have a producer/consumer relationship and the best way to transfer data between the two threads is via a pipe. For example, in a process monitoring program one thread could be collecting raw data from various monitoring devices and sending the data through a pipe to another thread. The other thread would then read data from the pipe and process the raw data in order to update status indicators.

The `PipedOutputStream` class is used to provide an output stream to a pipe. A `PipedInputStream` is connected with a `PipedOutputStream` to create a pipe, whereby one thread could send data to the pipe while another thread reads the data from the pipe. The pipe buffers any unread bytes. When the pipe becomes full, the writing thread blocks until there is room in the pipe to write more bytes. If the pipe is empty, the reading thread blocks until there are bytes in the pipe to be read.

MEMBER SUMMARY	
Constructor	
`PipedOutputStream()`	Constructs a new piped output stream.
Output Methods	
`flush()`	Notifies the piped input stream readers that bytes can be read from this pipe.

MEMBER SUMMARY

`write()`	Writes bytes to this piped output stream.
Pipe Methods	
`close()`	Closes this piped output stream.
`connect()`	Connects this piped output stream to a piped input stream.

See Also

`OutputStream`, `PipedInputStream`.

Example

See the class example of `PipedInputStream`.

close()

PURPOSE Closes this piped output stream.

SYNTAX `public void close() throws IOException`

DESCRIPTION This method closes this piped output stream. Once the stream has been closed, you can no longer send data to it.

EXCEPTIONS

`IOException` If an IO error occurred.

OVERRIDES `OutputStream.close()`.

SEE ALSO `write()`.

EXAMPLE See `PipedInputStream.connect()`.

connect()

PURPOSE Connects this piped output stream to a piped input stream.

SYNTAX `public void connect(PipedInputStream dest) throws IOException`

DESCRIPTION This method connects this piped output stream to the piped input stream `dest`. Data written to this piped output stream can be read from `dest`.

PARAMETERS

`dest`	The piped input stream to which to connect.

EXCEPTIONS

`IOException`	If an IO error occurred.

SEE ALSO `PipedInputStream.connect()`, `PipedOutputStream`.

EXAMPLE This example is a modification of the one in `PipedInputStream.connect()`. Instead of invoking `connect()` on the `PipedInputStream`, call `connect()` on the `PipedOutputStream`. Both ways produce the same effect.

```
import java.io.*;
class Main {
    public static void main(String[] args) {
        try {
            PipedOutputStream producer = new PipedOutputStream();
            PipedInputStream consumer = new PipedInputStream();

            producer.connect(consumer);        // connect pipe
              ...
```

flush()

PURPOSE Notifies the piped input stream readers that bytes can be read from this pipe.

SYNTAX `public synchronized void flush() throws IOException`

OVERRIDES `OutputStream.flush()`.

EXAMPLE See the `PipedInputStream` class example.

PipedOutputStream()

PURPOSE Constructs a new piped output stream.

SYNTAX
```
public PipedOutputStream()
public PipedOutputStream(PipedInputStream dest) throws
   IOException
```

DESCRIPTION There are two forms of the constructor for `PipedOutputStream`. The first form creates a piped output stream that is not connected to any piped input streams. Before this piped output stream can be used, it must be subsequently connected to a piped input stream using `connect()`. The second form creates a piped output stream that is connected to the piped input stream `dest`. Output from this newly created piped output stream can be read from `dest`.

PARAMETERS

`dest` The input stream to which to connect.

EXCEPTIONS

`IOException` If an IO error occurred while attempting to connect `dest` to this new piped output stream.

SEE ALSO `connect()`, `PipedInputStream`.

EXAMPLE See the class example of `PipedInputStream` and `PipedInputStream.connect()`.

write()

PURPOSE Writes bytes to this piped output stream.

SYNTAX

```
public void write(int oneByte) throws IOException
public void write(byte[] buffer, int offset, int count) throws
   IOException
```

DESCRIPTION The two forms of this method write bytes to this piped output stream. The first form writes a single byte to this piped output stream. The byte written is the lowest-order byte of `oneByte`. The second form writes `count` number of bytes from the byte array `buffer`, starting at index `count`.

The bytes written to this piped output stream can be read by the piped input stream to which this output stream is connected. Bytes that are not yet read are buffered by the pipe. If the pipe becomes full, `write()` blocks until there is room in the pipe to write more bytes.

PARAMETERS

`buffer` The byte array containing the bytes to be written.
`count` The number of bytes to write.
`offset` The index in `buffer` at which to start getting the bytes for writing.
`oneByte` The byte to write.

EXCEPTIONS

`IOException` If an IO error occurred.

OVERRIDES `OutputStream.write()`.

SEE ALSO `PipedInputStream.read()`.

EXAMPLE See the class example of `PipedInputStream`.

A B C D E F G H I J K L M N O P Q R S T U V W X Y Z

java.awt.image
PixelGrabber

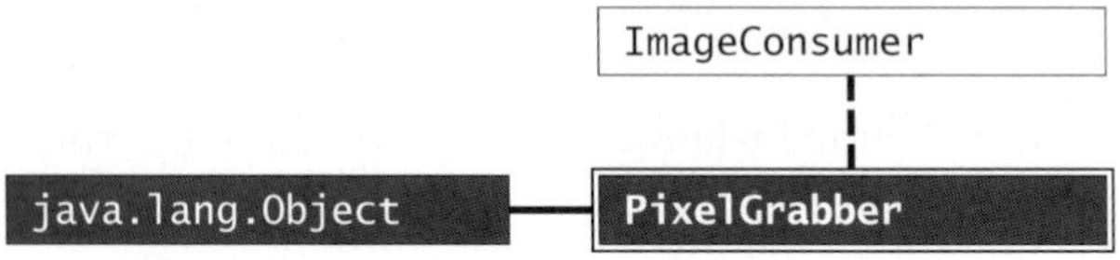

Syntax

```
public class PixelGrabber implements ImageConsumer
```

Description

The `PixelGrabber` class is used to retrieve the pixels in an image or from an image producer. The retrieved pixel values are colors in the default color model (see `ColorModel.getRGBdefault()`).

MEMBER SUMMARY

Constructor Method	
`PixelGrabber()`	Constructs a new `PixelGrabber` instance.
Pixel Method	
`grabPixels()`	Starts the action of retrieving the pixels.
Status Method	
`status()`	Determines the current state of the pixels.
Image Consumer Methods	
`imageComplete()`	Called by the image producer to deliver completion status.
`setColorModel()`	Called by the image producer to deliver the color model for the source image.
`setDimensions()`	Called by the image producer to deliver the dimensions of the source image.
`setHints()`	Called by the image producer to specify how the pixels will be delivered.
`setPixels()`	Called by the image producer to deliver pixels.
`setProperties()`	Called by the image producer to deliver the properties for the source image.

Example

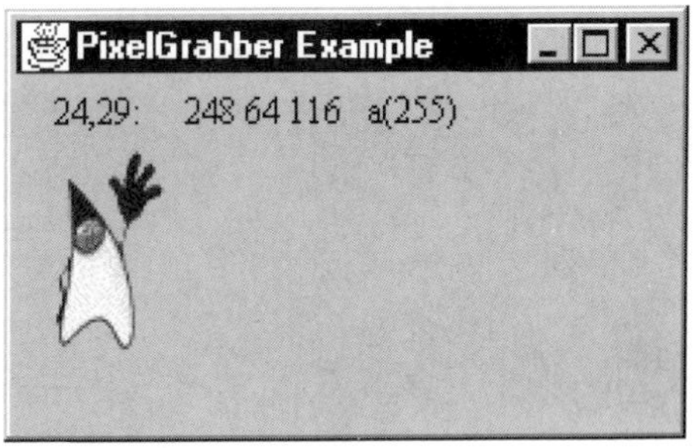

FIGURE 199 PixelGrabber

This example displays an image and retrieves the pixel values of the image. See Figure 199. The program displays the color components of the pixel directly under the cursor. If you click the pixel, the program colors all identical pixels in the image red. The program also displays the number of times that pixel value appears in the image.

The frame creates a label on the top and an `ImageCanvas` object in the center. The `ImageCanvas` object is created with an image and a label. It displays the image and watches the cursor. Using the supplied label, the `ImageCanvas` object displays the color components of the pixel directly under the cursor.

```
import java.awt.*;
import java.awt.image.*;
class Main extends Frame {
    Main(String filename) {
        super("PixelGrabber Example");
        Label label = new Label();

        add("North", label);
        add("Center", new
            ImageCanvas(getToolkit().getImage(filename), label));
        resize(300, 300);
        show();
    }

    static public void main(String[] args) {
        if (args.length == 1) {
            new Main(args[0]);
        } else {
            System.err.println("usage: java Main <image file>");
        }
    }
}

class ImageCanvas extends Canvas {
    Image image;
    Label label;
    int[] pixels;
    boolean paintTargetPixels;
    int targetPixelValue;

    ImageCanvas(Image image, Label label) {
        this.image = image;
        this.label = label;
    }

    void paintPixels(Graphics g, int w, int h) {
```

```
        int count = 0;
        g.setColor(Color.red);
        for (int x=0; x<w; x++) {
            for (int y=0; y<h; y++) {
                int p = pixels[y * w + x];
                if (p == targetPixelValue) {
                    g.fillRect(x, y, 1, 1);
                    count++;
                }
            }
        }
        label.setText("count: " + count);
    }

    public void update(Graphics g) {
        paint(g);
    }
    public void paint(Graphics g) {
        if (image != null) {
            g.drawImage(image, 0, 0, this);

            int w = image.getWidth(this);
            int h = image.getHeight(this);
            if (w < 0 || h < 0) return;
            if (paintTargetPixels) {
                paintPixels(g, w, h);
            }

            if (pixels == null) {
                // Create a pixel grabber and retrieve the pixels.
                pixels = new int[w * h];
                try {
                    PixelGrabber pg = new PixelGrabber(
                        image, 0, 0, w, h, pixels, 0, w);
                    pg.grabPixels();

                    // Check for errors.
                    if ((pg.status() & ImageObserver.ABORT) != 0) {
                        System.err.println("Error while fetching
                            image");
                        System.exit(1);
                    }
                } catch (Exception e) {
                    e.printStackTrace();
                    System.exit(1);
                }
            }
        }
    }

    public boolean mouseMove(Event evt, int x, int y) {
        if (pixels == null
              || x >= image.getWidth(this) || y >=
                 image.getHeight(this)) {
```

A B C D E F G H I J K L M N O P Q R S T U V W X Y Z

```
            label.setText("");
            return false;
        }
        ColorModel cm = ColorModel.getRGBdefault();
        int p = pixels[y * image.getWidth(this) + x];

        // The pixel value is translated into a color using
        // the default color model.
        label.setText(x + "," + y + ":     " + cm.getRed(p) + " "
            + cm.getGreen(p) + " " + cm.getBlue(p)
            + "   a("+cm.getAlpha(p) + ")");
        return true;
    }

    public boolean mouseDown(Event evt, int x, int y) {
        if (pixels == null
             || x >= image.getWidth(this) || y >=
                 image.getHeight(this)) {
            return false;
        }
        targetPixelValue = pixels[y * image.getWidth(this) + x];
        paintTargetPixels = true;
        repaint();
        return true;
    }
    public boolean mouseUp(Event evt, int x, int y) {
        paintTargetPixels = false;
        repaint();
        return true;
    }
}
```

grabPixels()

PURPOSE Starts the action of retrieving the pixels.

SYNTAX

```
public synchronized boolean grabPixels() throws
   InterruptedException
public synchronized boolean grabPixels(long ms) throws
   InterruptedException
```

DESCRIPTION The two forms of this method cause the image or image producer to start delivering pixels to the pixel grabber. This method returns when all the images in the desired rectangle (as specified in the constructor) are retrieved. If `ms` is specified and is greater than `0`, this method returns either when all the pixels are retrieved or when `ms` milliseconds have elapsed.

If this method returns `false`, the pixels were not successfully retrieved and the cause can be determined using the `status()` method.

This method can be called more than once and will return immediately if either all the pixels have been retrieved or if there has been an error. Typically, this method is called more than once if a time-out has been specified.

PARAMETERS

`ms` The number of milliseconds to wait for the image pixels. This value must be greater than `0`.

RETURNS `true` if the pixels were successfully retrieved; `false` otherwise.

EXCEPTIONS

`InterruptedException`
If another thread interrupted this thread.

SEE ALSO `status()`.

EXAMPLE See the class example.

imageComplete()

PURPOSE Called by the image producer to deliver completion status to the pixel grabber.

SYNTAX `public synchronized void imageComplete(int status)`

DESCRIPTION The `PixelGrabber` class implements this method as part of the `ImageConsumer` interface. It should not be used.

PARAMETERS

`status` A combination of the status bits as defined in the `ImageConsumer` class.

SEE ALSO `ImageConsumer.imageComplete()`.

EXAMPLE See `ImageConsumer`.

PixelGrabber()

PURPOSE Constructs a new `PixelGrabber` instance.

SYNTAX
```
public PixelGrabber(Image img, int x, int y, int w, int h, int[]
   pix, int off, int scansize)
public PixelGrabber(ImageProducer ip, int x, int y, int w, int h,
   int[] pix, int off, int scansize)
```

DESCRIPTION The two forms of this constructor construct a new `PixelGrabber` instance to retrieve the pixels in the rectangle defined by `(x, y, w, h)`. If the image `img` is specified, the pixels are retrieved from `img`. If the image producer `ip` is specified, the pixels are retrieved from `ip`.

The pixel values are stored in the `pix` integer array in the default color model. The pixel value for pixel `(i, j)`, where `(i, j)` is inside the rectangle `(x, y, w, h)`, is stored in the array at `pix[(j - y) * scansize + (i - x) + off]`.

The action of retrieving the pixels is not started until the `grabPixels()` method is called.

PARAMETERS

`h`	The height of the rectangle of pixels to retrieve.
`img`	The non-`null` image.
`ip`	The non-`null` image producer.
`off`	The offset into the array of where to store the first retrieved pixel.
`scansize`	The width of one row of pixels in `pix` (not necessarily the same as `w`).
`w`	The width of the rectangle of pixels to retrieve.
`x`	The *x*-coordinate of the upper-left corner of the rectangle.
`y`	The *y*-coordinate of the upper-left corner of the rectangle.
`pix`	The non-`null` array of integers to hold the retrieved pixels.

SEE ALSO `ColorModel.getRGBdefault()`.

EXAMPLE See the class example.

setColorModel()

PURPOSE Called by the image producer to deliver the color model for the source image.

SYNTAX `public void setColorModel(ColorModel model)`

DESCRIPTION The `PixelGrabber` class implements this method as part of the `ImageConsumer` interface. It should not be used.

PARAMETERS

`model` A non-`null` color model.

SEE ALSO `ImageConsumer.setColorModel()`.

EXAMPLE See `ImageConsumer`.

setDimensions()

PURPOSE Called by the image producer to deliver the dimensions of the source image.

SYNTAX `public void setDimensions(int width, int height)`

DESCRIPTION The `PixelGrabber` class implements this method as part of the `ImageConsumer` interface. It should not be used.

PARAMETERS

`height` The height of the image in pixels.

`width` The width of the image in pixels.

SEE ALSO `ImageConsumer.setDimensions()`.

EXAMPLE See `ImageConsumer`.

setHints()

PURPOSE Called by the image producer to specify how the pixels will be delivered.

SYNTAX `public void setHints(int hints)`

DESCRIPTION The `PixelGrabber` class implements this method as part of the `ImageConsumer` interface. It should not be used.

PARAMETERS

`hints` A set of bits that specify how pixels will be delivered.

SEE ALSO `ImageConsumer.setHints()`.

EXAMPLE See `ImageConsumer`.

setPixels()

PURPOSE Called by the image producer to deliver pixels to the image consumer.

SYNTAX

```
public void setPixels(int x, int y, int w, int h, ColorModel
   model, byte pixels[], int offset, int scansize)
public void setPixels(int x, int y, int w, int h, ColorModel
   model, int pixels[], int offset, int scansize)
```

DESCRIPTION The `PixelGrabber` class implements this method as part of the `ImageConsumer` interface. It should not be used.

PARAMETERS

`h` The height of the rectangle in which the pixels are destined.

`model` The non-`null` color model used to translate the pixel values.

`offset` The index of the first pixel in the pixel array.

`pixels` The non-`null` array of pixel values.

`scansize`	The width to use when extracting pixels from `pixels`.
`w`	The width of the rectangle in which the pixels are destined.
`x`	The *x*-coordinate of the rectangle in which the pixels are destined.
`y`	The *y*-coordinate of the rectangle in which the pixels are destined.

SEE ALSO `ImageConsumer.setPixels()`.

EXAMPLE See `ImageConsumer`.

setProperties()

PURPOSE Called by the image producer to deliver the properties for the source image.

SYNTAX `public void setProperties(Hashtable props)`

DESCRIPTION The `PixelGrabber` class implements this method as part of the `ImageConsumer` interface. It should not be used.

PARAMETERS

`props` A non-`null` hashtable of properties.

SEE ALSO `ImageConsumer.setProperties()`.

EXAMPLE See `ImageConsumer`.

status()

PURPOSE Determines the current state of the pixels.

SYNTAX `public synchronized int status()`

DESCRIPTION The result value indicates the current state of the pixels. The result value is a bitwise "or" of flags in the `ImageObserver` interface. See the `ImageObserver` class for details on available status bits.

SEE ALSO `ImageObserver`.

EXAMPLE See the class example

java.awt
Point

`java.lang.Object` — **`Point`**

Syntax

```
public class Point
```

Description

A *point* represents a location on a 2D plane. The coordinates of the point are integers, so only integral locations can be represented. A point is typically used in conjunction with AWT painting operations and with layout managers. In the AWT coordinate system, the *y*-coordinates increase downward rather than upward, as in classical analytical geometry.

In general when returning a point instance in a method call, either return a copy if you need to retain the instance or discard the instance after returning it. If you pass a point instance in a method call and wish to continue using the instance, note whether the method will retain the instance or will copy the values.

MEMBER SUMMARY	
Constructor	
`Point()`	Constructs a new `Point` instance.
Point Methods	
`move()`	Moves the point to a new location.
`translate()`	Adds an offset to the point.
Fields	
`x`	Contains the *x*-coordinate.
`y`	Contains the *y*-coordinate.
General Methods	
`equals()`	Determines the equality of two points.
`hashCode()`	Calculates the hash code for the point.
`toString()`	Generates a string representation of the point.

Example

This example creates a "mine field" of hidden random points. If you move the cursor over a point, it turns red. See Figure 200.

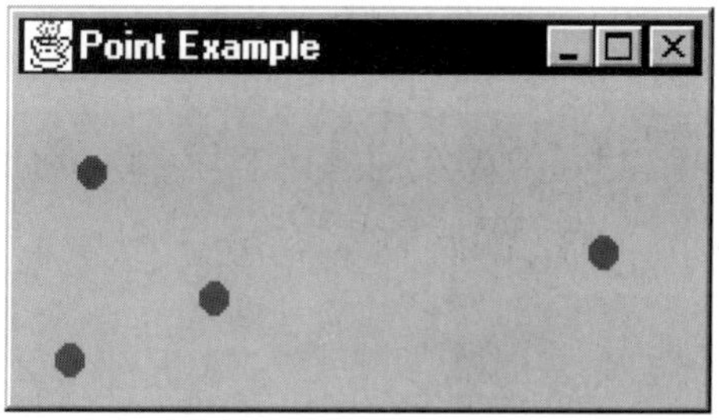

FIGURE 200 `Point`

```
import java.awt.*;
class Main extends Frame {
    int dotSize = 10;
    Point[] pts = new Point[100];

    Main() {
        super("Point Example");
        for (int i=0; i<pts.length; i++) {
            pts[i] = new Point(0, 0);
        }
        setForeground(Color.red);
        resize(100, 100);
        show();
    }

    // Returns a random integer in the range [0..r-1].
    int random(int r) {
        r = Math.max(r, 0);
        return (int)(Math.floor(Math.random()*r));
    }

    public void paint(Graphics g) {
        Insets insets = insets();
        int w = size().width-insets.left-insets.right;
        int h = size().height-insets.top-insets.bottom;

        for (int i=0; i<pts.length; i++) {
            pts[i].move(random(w-dotSize), random(h-dotSize));
        }
    }

    public void update(Graphics g) {
        for (int i=0; i<pts.length; i++) {
            if (pts[i].x < 0) {
                g.fillOval(-pts[i].x, -pts[i].y, dotSize, dotSize);
            }
        }
    }

    public boolean mouseMove(Event evt, int x, int y) {
        Point p = new Point(x-dotSize/2, y-dotSize/2);

        for (int i=0; i<pts.length; i++) {
            if (p.equals(pts[i])) {
                pts[i].x = -pts[i].x;
```

```
                    pts[i].y = -pts[i].y;
                    repaint();
                    break;
                }
            }
            return true;
        }

        static public void main(String[] args) {
            new Main();
        }
    }
```

equals()

PURPOSE Determines the equality of two points.

SYNTAX `public boolean equals(Object object)`

DESCRIPTION Two points are equal if both their *x*- and *y*-coordinates are equal.

PARAMETERS

`object` The point to which to compare.

RETURNS `true` if `object` is a `Point` object (or a subclass) and is equal to this point; `false` otherwise.

OVERRIDES `Object.equals()`.

EXAMPLE See the class example.

hashCode()

PURPOSE Calculates the hash code for the point.

SYNTAX `public int hashCode()`

DESCRIPTION The point's hash code is an integer that is calculated from the point's *x*- and *y*-coordinates. If `equals(p1, p2)` is true, then `p1` and `p2` will have the same hash code. Otherwise `p1` and `p2` will very likely have different hash codes.

RETURNS The point's hash code.

OVERRIDES `Object.hashCode()`.

SEE ALSO `equals()`.

EXAMPLE This method uses a hashtable to associate a point with an integer count.

```
Hashtable ht = new Hashtable();
void inc(Point p) {
    int i = 0;
    Integer integer = (Integer)ht.get(p);
    if (integer != null) {
        i = integer.intValue();
    }
    ht.put(p, new Integer(i+1));
}
```

move()

PURPOSE Moves the point to a new location.

SYNTAX `public void move(int x, int y)`

DESCRIPTION This method changes the *x*- and *y*-coordinates of the point to be `x` and `y`.

PARAMETERS

`x` The new *x*-coordinate.

`y` The new *y*-coordinate.

EXAMPLE See the class example.

Point()

PURPOSE Constructs a new `Point` instance.

SYNTAX `public Point(int x, int y)`

DESCRIPTION This constructor creates a new `Point` object and initializes it with the coordinates `x` and `y`.

PARAMETERS

`x` The *x*-coordinate.

`y` The *y*-coordinate.

EXAMPLE See the class example.

toString()

PURPOSE Generates the string representation of the point.

SYNTAX `public String toString()`

DESCRIPTION This method generates this point's string representation, which consists of the point's coordinates. This method is typically used for debugging output.

RETURNS A non-`null` string containing the coordinates of the point.

OVERRIDES `Object.toString()`.

EXAMPLE These statements print identical string representations of the point.

```
Point p = new Point(10, 20);
System.out.println("p = " + p.toString());
System.out.println("p = " + p);
```

translate()

PURPOSE Adds an offset to the point.

SYNTAX `public void translate(int x, int y)`

DESCRIPTION This method adds `x` to the point's *x*-coordinate and adds `y` to the point's *y*-coordinate.

PARAMETERS

`x` The offset to add to the point's *x*-coordinate.

`y` The offset to add to the point's *y*-coordinate.

EXAMPLE This method paints a red square with a shadow at point `p`.

```
public void paintShadowRect(Graphics g, Point p) {
    p.translate(5, 5);
    g.setColor(Color.gray);
    g.fillRect(p.x, p.y, 100, 100);
    p.translate(-5, -5);
    g.setColor(Color.red);
    g.fillRect(p.x, p.y, 100, 100);
}
```

x

PURPOSE Contains the *x*-coordinate of the point.

SYNTAX `public int x`

EXAMPLE See the class example.

y

PURPOSE Contains the *y*-coordinate of the point.

SYNTAX `public int y`

EXAMPLE See the class example.

java.awt

Polygon

java.lang.Object — **Polygon**

Syntax

```
public class Polygon
```

Description

A polygon is a data structure that maintains a list of points. This class is primarily used in conjunction with `Graphics.drawPolygon()` and `Graphics.fillPolygon()`. The polygon maintains a *bounding box*, which is the smallest rectangle that includes all the points in the polygon. See `getBoundingBox()` for more details.

MEMBER SUMMARY	
Constructor	
`Polygon()`	Constructs a new `Polygon` instance.
Fields	
`npoints`	Contains the number of points in the polygon.
`xpoints`	Array containing the x-coordinates of the polygon's points.
`ypoints`	Array containing the *y*-coordinates of the polygon's points.
Point Methods	
`addPoint()`	Adds a point to the polygon.
`inside()`	Determines if a point is inside the polygon.
Bounding Box Method	
`getBoundingBox()`	Calculates the polygon's bounding box.

Example

This example generates a random polygon and allows you to flip it. See Figure 201. There are three buttons that modify the polygon. The New button creates a new random polygon based on the current size of the canvas. The Flip Ver button flips the polygon around the *x*-axis. The Flip Hor button flips the polygon around the *y*-axis.

Also, a label at the top indicates whether the position pointed to by the cursor is considered to be inside or outside the polygon.

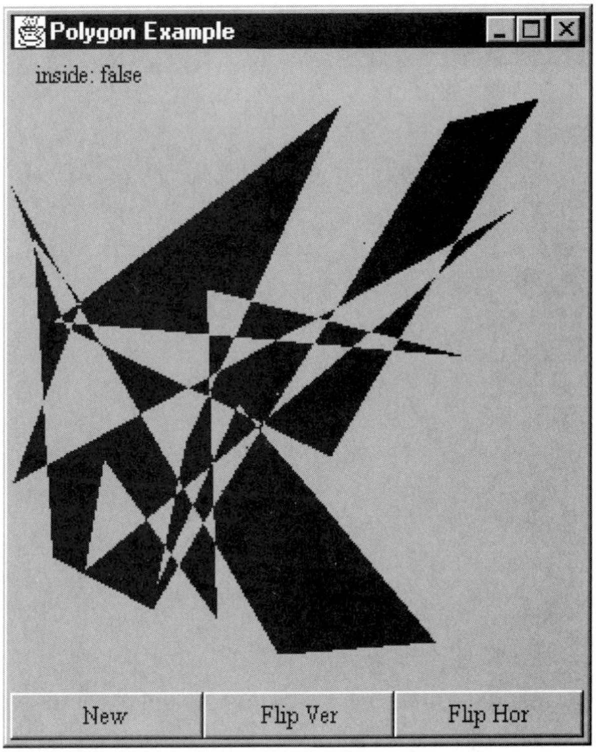

FIGURE 201 Polygon

```
import java.awt.*;
public class Main extends
    Frame {
    Label l = new
        Label();
    MainCanvas cv = new MainCanvas(l);

    Main() {
        super("Polygon Example");
        Panel p = new Panel();

        p.setLayout(new GridLayout(1, 0));
        p.add(new Button("New"));
        p.add(new Button("Flip Ver"));
        p.add(new Button("Flip Hor"));
        add("South", p);

        cv.resize(300, 300);
        add("Center", cv);
        add("North", l);
        pack();
        show();
    }

    public boolean action(Event evt, Object what) {
        if (evt.target instanceof Button) {
            if ("New".equals(what)) {
                cv.polygon = null;
```

```
            } else if (cv.polygon != null) {
                boolean ver =  "Flip Ver".equals(what);
                Rectangle r = cv.polygon.getBoundingBox();

                r.add(0, 0);
                for (int i=0; i<cv.polygon.npoints; i++) {
                    if (ver) {
                        cv.polygon.ypoints[i] = r.height -
                            cv.polygon.ypoints[i];
                    } else {
                        cv.polygon.xpoints[i] = r.width -
                            cv.polygon.xpoints[i];
                    }
                }
            }
            cv.repaint();
            return true;
        }
        return false;
    }

    static public void main(String[] args) {
        new Main();
    }
}

class MainCanvas extends Canvas {
    Label label;
    Polygon polygon;

    MainCanvas(Label label) {
        this.label = label;
    }
    // Returns a random number in the range [0..r-1].
    int random(int r) {
        return (int)(Math.floor(Math.random()*r));
    }

    public void paint(Graphics g) {
        int w = size().width;
        int h = size().height;

        if (polygon == null) {
            polygon = new Polygon();
            for (int i=0; i<25; i++) {
                // Points need to be one pixel from the
                // right and bottom edges otherwise the polygon
                // will extend outside the canvas bounds.
                polygon.addPoint(random(w-1), random(h-1));
            }
        }
        g.fillPolygon(polygon);
    }
```

```
    public boolean mouseMove(Event evt, int x, int y) {
        if (polygon != null) {
            label.setText("inside: " + polygon.inside(x, y));
        }
        return true;
    }

}
```

addPoint()

PURPOSE Adds a point to the polygon.

SYNTAX `public void addPoint(int x, int y)`

DESCRIPTION This method adds the point `(x, y)` to the polygon. After this method, the point will be included in the polygon's bounding box.

If you call `getBoundingBox()` and retain a handle to the rectangle instance, the values in the rectangle instance will be automatically updated after calling `addPoint()`.

PARAMETERS

`x` The *x*-coordinate of the new point.

`y` The *y*-coordinate of the new point.

SEE ALSO `getBoundingBox()`.

EXAMPLE See the class example.

getBoundingBox()

PURPOSE Calculates the polygon's bounding box.

SYNTAX `public Rectangle getBoundingBox()`

DESCRIPTION The bounding box is defined to be the smallest rectangle that includes all the points in the polygon. The values in the returned rectangle are updated automatically as points are added to the polygon.

If either `getBoundingBox()` or `inside()` has been called, you should not directly modify any of the fields `npoints`, `xpoints`, or `ypoints`. Modifying these fields after the bounding box has been calculated once will invalidate the bounding box. However, there's no way to recalculate the bounding box, except to create a new polygon instance.

A B C D E F G H I J K L M N O P Q R S T U V W X Y Z

RETURNS	A non-`null` rectangle defining the bounds of the polygon. Do not modify the rectangle.
EXAMPLE	See the class example.

inside()

PURPOSE	Determines if a point is inside the polygon.
SYNTAX	`public boolean inside(int x, int y)`
DESCRIPTION	This method determines if point (`x`, `y`) is inside the polygon. It uses an even-odd insideness rule (otherwise known as an alternating rule).
PARAMETERS	
`x`	The *x*-coordinate of the point to be tested.
`y`	The *y*-coordinate of the point to be tested.
RETURNS	`true` if the point is inside the polygon; `false` otherwise.
EXAMPLE	See the class example.

npoints

PURPOSE	Contains the number of points in the polygon.
SYNTAX	`public int npoints`
DESCRIPTION	Do not modify this field if either `getBoundingBox()` or `inside()` has been called. See `getBoundingBox()` for details.
SEE ALSO	`getBoundingBox()`.
EXAMPLE	See the class example.

Polygon()

PURPOSE	Constructs a new `Polygon` instance.
SYNTAX	`public Polygon()` `public Polygon(int[] xpoint, int[] ypoints, int npoints)`

DESCRIPTION The two forms of this constructor create a new `Polygon` instance with `npoints` points. The point coordinates are specified in the arrays `xpoints` and `ypoints`. The *x*- and *y*-coordinates of point `i` are, respectively, `xpoints[i]` and `ypoints[i]`. If no parameters are specified, the polygon is created with no points.

PARAMETERS

`npoints` The number of supplied points in `xpoints` and `ypoints`.

`xpoints` The non-`null` array of *x*-coordinates.

`ypoints` The non-`null` array of *y*-coordinates.

EXAMPLE See the class example.

xpoints

PURPOSE Array containing the *x*-coordinates of the polygon's points.

SYNTAX `public int[] xpoints`

DESCRIPTION Do not modify this field if either `getBoundingBox()` or `inside()` has been called. See `getBoundingBox()` for details.

SEE ALSO `getBoundingBox()`.

EXAMPLE See the class example.

ypoints

PURPOSE Array containing the *y*-coordinates of the polygon's points.

SYNTAX `public int[] ypoints`

DESCRIPTION Do not modify this field if either `getBoundingBox()` or `inside()` has been called. See `getBoundingBox()` for details.

SEE ALSO `getBoundingBox()`.

EXAMPLE See the class example.

java.io
PrintStream

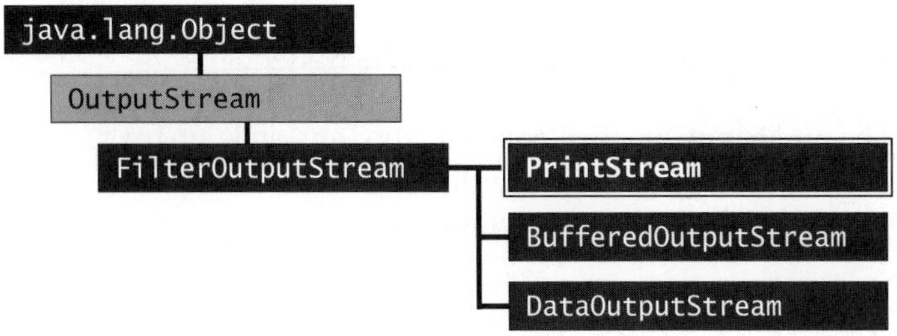

Syntax

```
public class PrintStream extends FilterOutputStream
```

Description

A *print stream* is a filter stream that accepts Java data values and writes out their string representations. Figure 202 shows a print stream accepting an `int`, a `char`, and a string. Typically, you use a print stream to generate output to be displayed to users. `System.out` and `System.err` are examples of print streams.

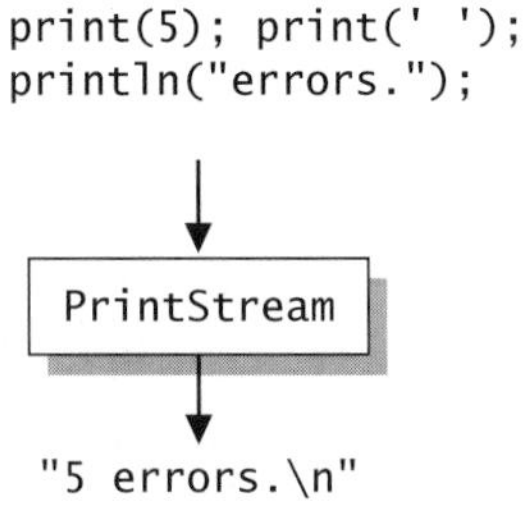

FIGURE 202 `PrintStream`

MEMBER SUMMARY	
Constructor	
`PrintStream()`	Constructs a new print stream.
Output Methods	
`flush()`	Flushes any buffered output from this print stream.
`print()`	Prints a data value.
`println()`	Prints a data value followed by a newline.
`write()`	Writes bytes to this print stream.
Error Checking Method	
`checkError()`	Determines whether this stream has had any exceptions.
Method for Closing Stream	
`close()`	Closes this print stream.

See Also

OutputStream, System.err, System.out.

Example

This example shows how different data types can be passed as an argument to print() and println().

```
import java.io.PrintStream;
import java.util.Date;

class Main {
    public static void main(String[] args) {
        String str = "abc";
        char[] chs = new char[str.length()];
        str.getChars(0, str.length(), chs, 0);

        System.out.print(new Date());          // Printing objects
        System.out.println(new Date());        // date
        System.out.flush();

        System.out.print(str);                 // String
        System.out.println(str);
        System.out.print(chs);                 // char[]
        System.out.println(chs);
        System.out.print(' ');                 // char
        System.out.println(' ');
        System.out.print(5);                   // int
        System.out.println(5);
        System.out.print(5L);                  // long
        System.out.println(5L);
        System.out.print(1.23f);               // float
        System.out.println(1.23f);
        System.out.print(1.23);                // double
        System.out.println(1.23);
        System.out.print(true);                // boolean
        System.out.println(true);

        // flush stream and check if we got any errors from those
        // print() and println() calls
        if (System.out.checkError()) {
            System.err.println("Got errors printing");
            System.exit(-1);
        }

        // can also 'write' to a print stream
        System.out.write('A');
        byte[] b = new byte[str.length()];
        str.getBytes(0, str.length(), b, 0);
        System.out.write(b, 0, b.length);
        System.out.close();
    }
}
```

checkError()

PURPOSE Determines whether this stream has had any exceptions.

SYNTAX `public boolean checkError()`

DESCRIPTION This method flushes any buffered output from this print stream. It then returns a `boolean` value indicating whether an exception has occurred earlier on this print stream. None of the output methods raise exceptions. When these output methods encounter an `IOException`, they record that the exception has occurred, but they do not raise the exception to the caller. The caller can subsequently check whether the output method succeeded by invoking `checkError()`. Once an exception has occurred, any subsequent call to `checkError()` on this print stream will always return `true`, regardless of which output method recorded the exception.

RETURNS `true` if this print stream has encountered an exception; `false` otherwise.

SEE ALSO `close()`, `flush()`, `write()`.

EXAMPLE See the class example.

close()

PURPOSE Closes this print stream.

SYNTAX `public void close()`

DESCRIPTION This method closes this print stream by closing the output stream that it filters. If an `IOException` occurs while attempting to close the stream, this fact is recorded and can be checked later using `checkError()`.

OVERRIDES `FilterOutputStream.close()`.

SEE ALSO `checkError()`, `FilterOutputStream`, `PrintStream()`.

EXAMPLE See the class example.

flush()

PURPOSE Flushes any buffered output from this print stream.

SYNTAX `public void flush()`

DESCRIPTION This method flushes any buffered output from this print stream. If an `IOException` occurs while attempting to flush the stream, this fact is recorded and can be checked later using `checkError()`.

OVERRIDES `FilterOutputStream.flush()`.

SEE ALSO `checkError()`, `PrintStream()`.

EXAMPLE See the class example.

print()

PURPOSE Prints a data value to this print stream.

SYNTAX

```
public void print(boolean bool)
public void print(int inum)
public void print(long lnum)
public void print(float fnum)
public void print(double dnum)
public void print(Object obj)
synchronized public void print(String str)
public void print(char ch)
synchronized public void print(char[] charArray)
```

DESCRIPTION The nine forms of this method print a data value to this print stream. The output generated is the string representation of the data value to be printed. `String.valueOf()` is used on the data value to obtain its string representation.

The actual sending of data to the stream is done using `write()`. If this print stream is an autoflush stream and the string representation of the data value being written contains a newline, the stream is automatically flushed.

PARAMETERS

`bool`	The `boolean` value (`true` or `false`) to print.
`ch`	The `char` value to print.
`charArray`	The `char` array to print.
`dnum`	The `double` value to print.
`fnum`	The `float` value to print.
`inum`	The `int` value to print.
`lnum`	The `long` value to print.
`obj`	The `object` to print (`null` is accepted).
`str`	The string to print (`null` is accepted).

SEE ALSO `flush()`, `String.valueOf()`, `write()`.

EXAMPLE See the class example.

println()

PURPOSE Prints a data value followed by a newline to this print stream.

SYNTAX

```
synchronized public void println(boolean bool)
synchronized public void println(int inum)
synchronized public void println(long lnum)
synchronized public void println(float fnum)
synchronized public void println(double dnum)
synchronized public void println(Object obj)
synchronized public void println(String str)
synchronized public void println(char ch)
synchronized public void println(char[] charArray)
```

DESCRIPTION The nine forms of this method print a data value followed by a newline to this print stream. The output generated is the string representation of the data value to be printed. `String.valueOf()` is used on the data value to obtain its string representation.

The actual sending of data to the stream is done using `write()`. If this print stream is an autoflush stream, the output is flushed after it has been written.

PARAMETERS

`bool`	The `boolean` value (`true` or `false`) to print.
`ch`	The `char` value to print.
`charArray`	The `char` array to print.
`dnum`	The `double` value to print.
`fnum`	The `float` value to print.
`inum`	The `int` value to print.
`lnum`	The `long` value to print.
`obj`	The `object` to print (`null` is accepted).
`str`	The string to print (`null` is accepted).

SEE ALSO `flush()`, `String.valueOf()`, `write()`.

EXAMPLE See the class example and `PrintStream()`.

PrintStream()

PURPOSE Constructs a new print stream.

SYNTAX

```
public PrintStream(OutputStream out)
public PrintStream(OutputStream out, boolean autoflush)
```

DESCRIPTION There are two forms of this constructor for `PrintStream`. The first form creates a new print stream for the output stream `out`. Output sent to this print stream is not automatically flushed. The second form creates a new print stream for the output stream. If `autoflush` is `true`, the stream will be flushed automatically after each newline has been written to the stream. If `autoflush` is `false`, no automatic flushing is done.

PARAMETERS

`autoflush` `true` means this print stream will automatically flush output after each newline is written. `false` means no automatic flushing will be performed.

`out` The output stream for which to create the print stream filter.

SEE ALSO `FilterOutputStream`, `flush()`, `OutputStream`.

EXAMPLE This example shows how to create a print stream for another output stream. It prints the HTTP server response header to that stream. For simplicity's sake, the output stream is `System.out`. But it would work equally well if the output stream is a socket's output stream.

```
import java.io.PrintStream;
import java.io.OutputStream;
import java.util.Date;

class Main2 {
    private static final String myServerVersion = "RLPCBrowse/1.0";
    private static final String mimeVersion = "1.0";
    private static final int goodStatus = 200;

    // writes HTTP server response header for text/html type
    public static void writeHTTPHeader(Date modDate,
        OutputStream orig) {
        PrintStream out = new PrintStream(orig, false);
        // no autoflush

        out.println("HTTP/1.0 " + goodStatus + " OK");
        out.println("Date: " + (new Date()).toGMTString());
        out.println("Server: " + myServerVersion);
        out.println("MIME-version: " + mimeVersion);
        out.println("Content-type: text/html");
        out.println("Last-modified: " + modDate.toGMTString());
        out.println();

        out.flush();
    }
    public static void main(String[] args) {
        writeHTTPHeader(new Date(), System.out);
    }
}
```

B C D E F G H I J K L M N O P Q R S T U V W X Y Z

write()

PURPOSE Writes bytes to this print stream.

SYNTAX
```
public void write(int oneByte)
public void write(byte[] buffer, int offset, int count)
```

DESCRIPTION The two forms of this method write bytes to this print stream. The first form writes a single byte (the lowest-order byte in `oneByte`) to this print stream. If this print stream is an autoflush stream and `oneByte` is the newline character (`'\n'`), the stream is flushed. The second form writes to this print stream `count` number of bytes from the byte array `buffer`, starting at index `offset`, and if it is an autoflush stream, flushes the stream. The bytes are written to the output stream that this print stream is filtering. If an `IOException` occurs during the write, this fact is recorded and can be checked subsequently using `checkError()`.

PARAMETERS

`buffer` The byte array containing the bytes to write.
`count` The number of bytes to write.
`offset` The index in `buffer` at which to start getting the bytes to write.
`oneByte` The byte to write.

OVERRIDES `FilterOutputStream.write()`.

SEE ALSO `checkError()`.

EXAMPLE See the class example.

java.lang
Process

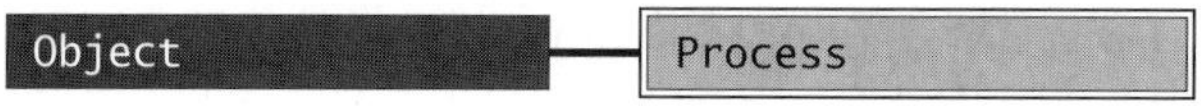

Syntax

```
public abstract class Process
```

Description

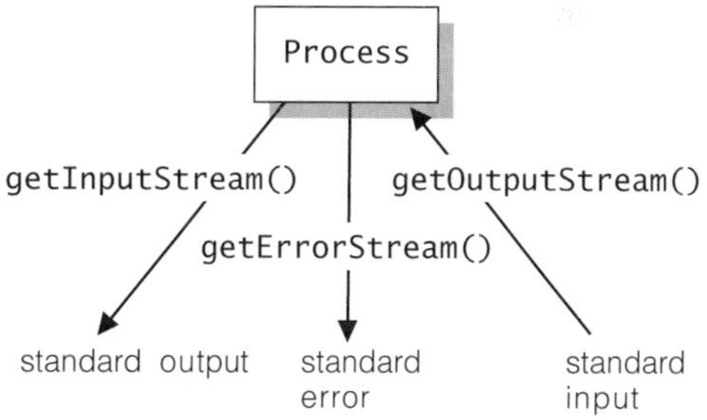

FIGURE 203 Communicating with a Process Through Standard IO

Java allows a program to spawn processes to execute *system programs* (*commands*). System programs are programs found in the native operating system on which Java is running. The `Runtime` class contains various `exec()` methods for executing system programs. An `exec()` method spawns a process to execute the specified program and returns to the caller a `Process` object containing information about the process just created. This information includes how to communicate with the process through its standard IO streams (see Figure 203), stop the process, and retrieve the exit status of the process. For example, the following code lists the output of the UNIX command `ls`.

```
    // some code that captures output from ‘ls’
try {
    Process child = Runtime.getRuntime().exec(“/bin/ls”);
    InputStream in = child.getInputStream();
    int c;
    // echo output of ‘ls’
    while ((c = in.read()) != -1) {
        System.out.print((char)c);
    }
    in.close();
    // Wait for subprocess to exit
    try {
        child.waitFor();
    } catch (InterruptedException e) {
        e.printStackTrace();
    }
    // Display exit status of subprocess
    System.out.println(“child exited with “ + child.exitValue());
} catch (IOException e) {
    System.err.println(e);
}
```

destroy()

The Process class is an abstract class that defines methods that all subclasses of Process must support. Subclasses of Process (such as implementations for Windows95 or UNIX) define specific implementations for these methods.

A process is destroyed when all references to its associated Process object have been dropped. There is no requirement that the process execute asynchronously with the existing Java process.

MEMBER SUMMARY

Methods for Communicating with the Process

getErrorStream()	Retrieves an input stream for reading error output from the process.
getInputStream()	Retrieves an input stream for reading output from the process.
getOutputStream()	Retrieves an output stream for sending data to the process.

Process Management Methods

destroy()	Destroys the process.
exitValue()	Retrieves the exit value of the process.
waitFor()	Waits for the process to terminate.

See Also

InputStream, OutputStream, Runtime.exec(), System.

destroy()

PURPOSE Destroys the process.

SYNTAX `abstract public void destroy()`

DESCRIPTION A process can be destroyed at any time before it is completed by invoking a destroy() method on the Process object associated with the process. Any streams obtained from the process are invalidated when the process is destroyed.

EXAMPLE This example executes the ls program, reads five lines from its output, and then destroys the process.

```
try {
    // read first 5 lines from 'ls' and then destroy process
    Process child = rt.exec("/bin/ls");
```

```
        InputStream in = child.getInputStream();
        int c, newline = 0;
        // read first 5 lines and then stop
        while ((c = in.read()) != -1 && newline < 5) {
            char ch = (char)c;
            System.out.print(ch);
            if (ch == '\n')
                ++newline;
        }
        in.close();
        child.destroy(); // destroy process
    } catch (IOException e) {
        System.err.println(e);
    }
```

exitValue()

PURPOSE Retrieves the exit value of the process.

SYNTAX `abstract public int exitValue()`

DESCRIPTION When a process terminates, it records the status of the system program just completed. This status is referred to as the *exit value* of the process. An exit status of `0` indicates success; all other exit values indicate failure. The meaning of nonzero exit values is program- and platform-dependent. This method returns the exit value of a process. If `exitvalue()` is called before the process has terminated, an `IllegalThreadStateException` is thrown.

RETURNS The exit value of the process. `0` means the program executed successfully; otherwise the program failed.

EXCEPTIONS

`IllegalThreadStateException`

If the process has not yet terminated.

EXAMPLE This example executes the `ls` command, waits for the command to terminate, and reports the execution status of the command by examining the command's exit value.

```
    try {
        Process child = rt.exec("/bin/ls");
     ...
        // Wait for child to finish
        try {
            child.waitFor();
        } catch (InterruptedException e) {
        }
        // Display exit status of subprocess
```

```
        int status = child.exitValue();
        if (status == 0)
            System.out.println("process successfully completed.");
        else
            System.out.println("process exited with " + status);
    } catch (IOException e) {
        System.err.println(e);
    }
```

getErrorStream()

PURPOSE Retrieves an input stream for reading error output from the process.

SYNTAX `abstract public InputStream getErrorStream()`

DESCRIPTION The standard IO of a process consists of an input stream, an output stream, and an error stream. The error stream is an output stream generated by the process to display information about erroneous conditions. `getErrorStream()` allows the caller to obtain an input stream connected to this error stream so that the caller can then use methods like `InputStream.read()` to obtain the output sent by the process to the error steam.

There is only one error stream per process. Hence multiple calls to `getErrorStream()` return the same `InputStream` object.

This stream is typically unbuffered.

RETURNS An input stream for reading error output from the process.

EXAMPLE This example executes the `ls` command on a nonexistent directory and hence forces a failure. It reads from the error output stream of the command the error reported by the command.

```
    try {
        Process child = rt.exec("/bin/ls /notthere");
        // get error output from child process
        InputStream child_err = child.getErrorStream();
        int c;
        while ((c = child_err.read()) != -1) {
            System.out.print((char)c);
        }
        child_err.close();
    } catch (IOException e) {
        System.err.println(e);
    }
```

getInputStream()

PURPOSE Retrieves an input stream for reading output from the process.

SYNTAX `abstract public InputStream getInputStream()`

DESCRIPTION The standard IO of a process consists of an input stream, an output stream, and an error stream. The output stream is where the process sends output intended for display to the user. `getInputStream()` allows the caller to obtain an input stream that is connected to this output stream so that the caller can then use methods like `InputStream.read()` on the input stream to obtain the output of the process.

There is only one standard output stream per process. Hence multiple calls to `getInputStream()` return the same `InputStream` object.

This stream is typically buffered, which means output generated by the process is stored until it is read (from this stream).

RETURNS An input stream for reading output from the process.

EXAMPLE This example executes the `ls` command and echoes the command's output.

```
try {
    Process child = rt.exec("/bin/ls");
    // get output from child process
    InputStream child_in = child.getInputStream();
    int c;
    while ((c = child_in.read()) != -1) {
        System.out.print((char)c);
    }
    child_in.close();
} catch (IOException e) {
    System.err.println(e);
}
```

getOutputStream()

PURPOSE Retrieves an output stream for sending data to the process.

SYNTAX `abstract public OutputStream getOutputStream()`

DESCRIPTION The standard IO of a process consists of an input stream, an output stream, and an error stream. The input stream is where the process reads its input from the user. getOutputStream() allows the caller to obtain an output stream that is connected to this input stream so that the caller can then use methods like OutputStream. write() to send data to the process.

There is only one standard input stream per process. Hence multiple calls to getOutputStream() return the same OutputStream object.

This stream is typically buffered, which means data sent to this stream is stored until the process reads it.

RETURNS An output stream for feeding input to the process.

EXAMPLE This example executes the cat command and sends "hello world!" to cat by opening an output stream to it.

```
try {
    Process child = rt.exec("/bin/cat");
    // stream for feeding input to child process
    OutputStream child_out = child.getOutputStream();
    PrintStream out = new PrintStream(child_out);
    out.println("hello world!");
    out.close();
} catch (IOException e) {
    System.err.println(e);
}
```

waitFor()

PURPOSE Waits for the process to terminate.

SYNTAX `abstract public int waitFor() throws InterruptedException`

DESCRIPTION A program can wait for its process to terminate using waitFor(). If the process has already terminated, the exit value of the process is returned. If the process has not terminated, this call blocks until the process terminates and returns the process's exit value.

RETURNS The exit value of the process. An exit value of 0 indicates the process executed successfully; all other values indicate failure.

EXCEPTIONS

InterruptedException

If another thread has interrupted this thread while it is waiting.

SEE ALSO exitValue().

EXAMPLE This example executes the `ls` command, waits for the command to terminate, and reports the execution status of the command by examining the command's exit value returned by `waitFor()`.

```
try {
    Process child = rt.exec("/bin/ls");
  ...
    // Wait for child to finish
    int status;
    try {
        status = child.waitFor();
    } catch (InterruptedException e) {
        status = -1;
    }
    // Display exit status of subprocess
    if (status == 0)
        System.out.println("process successfully completed.");
    else
        System.out.println("process exited with " + status);
} catch (IOException e) {
    System.err.println(e);
}
```

java.util

Properties

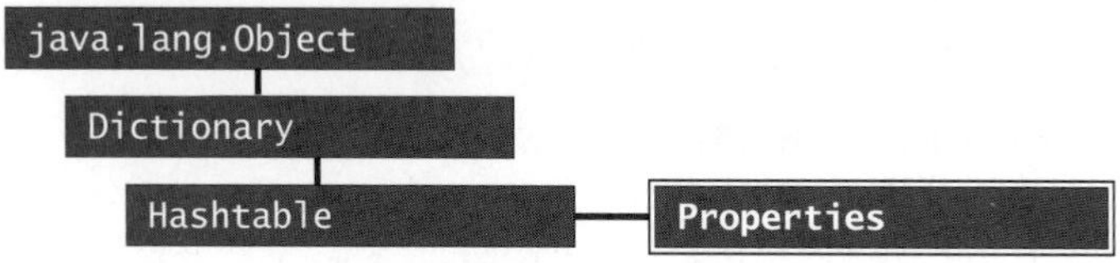

Syntax

```
public class Properties extends Hashtable
```

Description

The `Properties` class is used to represent a *properties list*. Each item on the list is called a *property* and consists of a *property name* and a *property value*. Each property name and property value is a Unicode string. If the properties list is to be used only internally within the Java program, there are no restrictions on the format of these strings. If the properties list is to be loaded or stored from IO streams, then syntactic rules apply that the property names and values must follow. These rules are described in the following section, "Formats of Properties." Also, some programs may have conventions for naming properties and their values.

Defaults

Each instance of the `Properties` class actually contains two properties lists: a *main* properties list and a *default* properties list. When you create a new `Properties` instance, you can supply a default properties list. This list is consulted when a requested property is not found in the main properties list. It also is a `Properties` instance, so it therefore can contain its own list of defaults. You can use this support of default properties lists to chain properties lists together.

Properties can be loaded from and saved into input/output streams. Properties loaded from a stream are added to the main properties list. Since `Properties` is a subclass of `Hashtable`, you can also use methods from the `Hashtable` class to add and remove items from a `Properties` instance. Such changes affect the main properties list, not the default properties list. To make changes to the default properties list, perform the `Properties` methods directly on the reference of the default properties list.

System Properties

The `System` class uses `Properties` to represent *system properties*, which are information about the system and environment in which the Java program is running. Examples of system properties are the name of the user running the Java program, the version of the Java interpreter being used, and the name of the operating system on which the Java program is running. A complete list of the system properties is given in Table 17 under the `System` class.

The Java system properties have a hierarchical naming convention for its property names, for example, "`user.name`", "`user.home`", "`java.vendor`".

The class libraries contain methods that will parse the strings of system property values into Java data types (`Boolean.getBoolean()`, `Integer.getInteger()`, `Long.getLong()`).

Formats of Properties

A property consists of a property name and a property value. A property name can contain any Unicode character except for the following: equals ('='), colon ('`:`'), space (' '), newline ('`\n`'), tab ('`\t`'), and return ('`\r`'). The property value is a Unicode string. A backslash, newline, return, or tab that appears in the string is encoded by writing the character as *two* characters. For example, newline (`'\n'`) is represented by two characters: a backslash (`'\'`) followed by the letter `'n'`. A property value cannot be `null`. If a property name does not have a corresponding value, it is as if the property does not exist.

A properties list can be read from an input stream. The input stream can use localized character sets, but when they are read in, they are translated into Unicode. Conversely, a properties list can be written out to an output stream. Java will attempt to write out the list using the localized character set, if it is appropriate. If the properties are not being written out to a localized stream, a character that is not in the printable range is encoded using its Unicode value; such a value has the format \u*dddd*, where *d* is a hexadecimal character (one of `0–9`, `a–e`, `A–E`) (see `Character`). If the properties are written out to a localized stream, the Unicode characters will be translated to their localized representation by the localized stream.

When a properties list is written out, the property name is separated by an equals character ('='). Each property name /property value pair is written on a single line terminated by a newline character.

When a properties list is read in, lines beginning with the hash character ('#') or the exclamation character ('!') are treated as comment lines and are ignored (no property name/value are derived from them). Empty lines (those containing only whitespace characters, newlines, or returns) are also ignored. If a property name appears on a line with no property value, the property value is `null`.

The following is an example of an output file containing a properties list. It was generated using `Properties.save()` (see the example in `load()`).

```
#/* testing */
#Sun Feb 18 23:53:45 PST 1996
java.home=/export/home/java/1.0.2/bin/..
java.version=1.0.2
file.separator=/
line.separator=\n
java.vendor=Sun Microsystems Inc.
user.name=rosanna
os.arch=sparc
os.name=Solaris
java.vendor.url=http://www.sun.com/
user.dir=/export/home/users/rosanna/java-docs/egs/util/Properties
```

```
java.class.path=.:/export/home/java/1.0.2/bin/../classes:/export/
home/java/1.0.2/bin/../lib/classes.zip
java.class.version=45.3
os.version=2.x
path.separator=:
user.home=/home/rosanna
```

MEMBER SUMMARY

Constructor	
`Properties()`	Constructs a new properties list.
Property Methods	
`getProperty()`	Retrieves the value of a property in this properties list.
`list()`	Writes this properties list to a print output stream.
`load()`	Reads properties from an input stream and adds them to this properties list.
`propertyNames()`	Retrieves the list of property names from this properties list.
`save()`	Writes this properties list to an output stream.
Protected Field	
`defaults`	The default properties.

See Also

`Hashtable`, `System.getProperties()`.

defaults

PURPOSE The default properties.

SYNTAX `protected Properties defaults`

DESCRIPTION This field contains the default properties for this properties list. It is an optional argument supplied to the `Properties()` constructor. If the constructor was called with no defaults, `defaults` is `null`.

`getProperty()` will search `defaults` when the requested property is not found in the main properties list.

SEE ALSO `getProperty()`, `Properties()`.

EXAMPLE This example shows the use of defaults in the implementation of getProperty().

```
public String getProperty(String key) {
    String val = (String)super.get(key);
        return ((val == null) && (defaults != null)) ?
                defaults.getProperty(key) : val;
    }
```

getProperty()

PURPOSE Retrieves the value of a property in this properties list.

SYNTAX
```
public String getProperty(String propName)
public String getProperty(String propName, String defVal)
```

DESCRIPTION The two forms of this method find the property with name propName from this properties list and return the property's value as a string. If propName is not in the main properties list, the default properties list, if any, associated with this properties list is searched. If propName is still not found and no defVal is specified, null is returned. If propName is not found and defVal is specified, defVal is returned.

PARAMETERS

defVal The default value to return if propName is not found.

propName The name of the property to retrieve.

RETURNS The value associated with propName if propName is found; otherwise, defVal. If defVal is not specified, null.

SEE ALSO Boolean.getBoolean(), Color.getColor()defaults, Integer.getInteger(), Long.getLong(), System.getProperty().

EXAMPLE

```
// Look for property
System.out.println("java.version: " +
                    props.getProperty("java.version"));

// Look for property with default
System.out.println("notthere: " +
                    props.getProperty("notthere", "default"));
```

A B C D E F G H I J K L M N O P Q R S T U V W X Y Z

list()

PURPOSE Writes this list of properties to a print output stream.

SYNTAX `public void list(PrintStream out)`

DESCRIPTION This method writes this list of properties to the print output stream `out`. Unlike `save()`, *both* the default properties list and the main properties list are printed. If a property appears in both lists, only the one in the main list is printed.

Each property is printed, one per line, in the format

`propertyName=propertyValue`

If the property value is too long (over 40 characters), only a prefix of it is printed. No special provisions are made for special characters (like newlines and returns). The format of the output generated by this method is not the same as that generated by `save()` and cannot be read in using `load()`.

PARAMETERS

`out` The print output stream to print the properties.

SEE ALSO `PrintStream`, `save()`.

EXAMPLE See the `load()` example.

```
Properties props_copy = new Properties(props); // Make copy
props.list(System.out);                        // print out
```

load()

PURPOSE Reads properties from an input stream and adds them to this properties list.

SYNTAX `public synchronized void load(InputStream in) throws IOException`

DESCRIPTION This method reads properties from the input stream `in` and adds them to this properties list's main properties list (i.e., not to the default list). If a property being added already exists in the main properties list, the newly added property's value overrides the existing value. These properties override any corresponding properties in the default properties list (but does not change the properties in the default properties list). The format of the data in the input stream is expected to be in the format described in the `Properties` class description. If the data contains two properties with the same name, the last one to be loaded overrides the previously loaded one.

A B C D E F G H I J K L M N O P Q R S T U V W X Y Z

Because `Properties` is a subclass of `Hashtable`, `Hashtable.put()` can also be used to add to the properties list.

PARAMETERS

`in` The input stream from which to read.

EXCEPTIONS

`IOException` If an IO error occurred when reading from `in`.

SEE ALSO `Hashtable.put()`, `save()`.

EXAMPLE

```
Properties props = new Properties();  // empty list
Properties sysprops = System.getProperties();
try {
    FileOutputStream out = new FileOutputStream("/tmp/props");
    sysprops.save(out, "/* testing */");
    FileInputStream in = new FileInputStream("/tmp/props");

    props.load(in);

    System.out.println("Got properties from /tmp/props");
    props.list(System.out);
} catch (IOException e) {
    System.out.println(e);
}
```

Properties()

PURPOSE Constructs a new properties list.

SYNTAX `public Properties()`
SYNTAX `public Properties(Properties defs)`

DESCRIPTION There are two forms of the constructor for the `Properties` class. The first form creates an empty properties list with no default properties list. The second form creates an empty main properties list with default `defs`. If a requested property is not found in the main properties list, the properties list in `defs` is searched. Modifications to the contents of `defs` subsequent to calling this constructor will be visible to this `Properties` instance.

PARAMETERS

`defs` The default properties list.

SEE ALSO `defaults`, `getProperty()`, `load()`.

EXAMPLE See `list()` and `load()`.

propertyNames()

PURPOSE Retrieves the list of property names from this properties list.

SYNTAX `public Enumeration propertyNames()`

DESCRIPTION This method returns the property names of all the properties in the main properties list and default properties list in this properties list. If there are duplicates in the main and default lists, the properties in the default list are overridden. Modifications made to either list during enumeration do not affect the enumeration.

If you are interested only in the properties in the main properties list, you can use `Hashtable.keys()`.

RETURNS An enumeration of all the property names in this properties list.

SEE ALSO `Hashtable.keys()`.

EXAMPLE

```
// Enumeration properties
for (Enumeration e = props.propertyNames();
     e.hasMoreElements();
     System.out.println("\t" + (String)e.nextElement()));
```

save()

PURPOSE Writes this properties list to an output stream.

SYNTAX `public synchronized void save(OutputStream out, String comment)`

DESCRIPTION This method writes this properties list to the output stream `out`. Only the main properties list is written. If the string `comment` is not `null`, it is written out as the first line in the stream as a comment preceded by a hash character ('#'). Before the properties are written, a comment with the current time of day is written out to the stream. The properties are then written out in the format described in the `Properties` class description.

PARAMETERS

`comment`	The possibly `null` comment to write to the stream.
`out`	The output stream to which to write.

SEE ALSO `list()`, `load()`.

EXAMPLE See `load()`.

java.net

ProtocolException

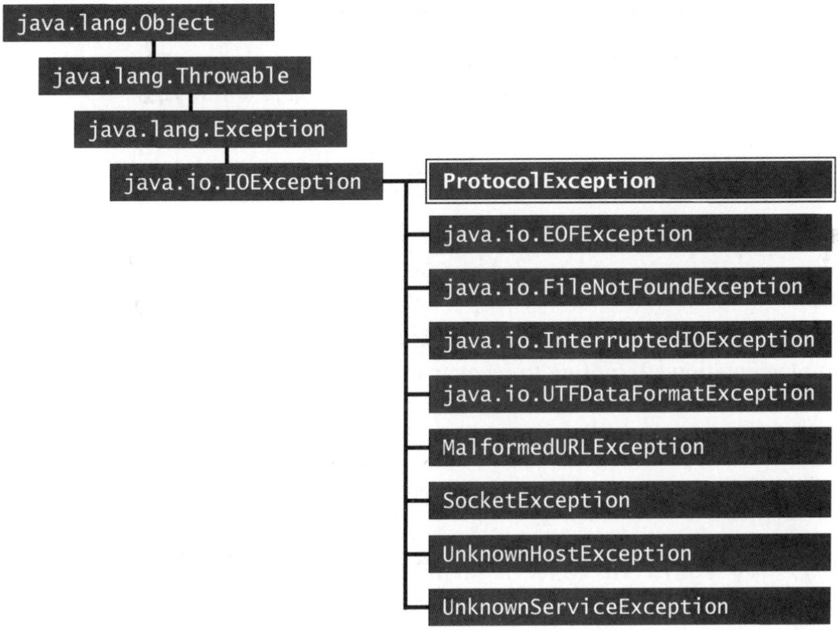

Syntax

```
public class ProtocolException extends IOException
```

Description

`ProtocolException` is an IO exception that is thrown when an attempt is made to connect a socket of the wrong type (stream versus nonstream). For example, an attempt to connect a datagram socket to a protocol that accepts only streams would raise `ProtocolException`. `ProtocolException` is typically caught within the socket implementation classes. It handles the exception by attempting a connection using a stream; hence, usually it is not seen by the user program. If an attempt is made to connect a stream socket for a protocol that supports only datagrams, a `SocketException` is thrown.

A method that throws `ProtocolException` must declare it or any of its superclasses in its `throws` clause.

A
B
C
D
E
F
G
H
I
J
K
L
M
N
O
P
Q
R
S
T
U
V
W
X
Y
Z

MEMBER SUMMARY	
Constructor	
`ProtocolException()`	Constructs a new `ProtocolException` instance.

See Also

`IOException`, `SocketImpl.connect()`, `SocketException`.

Example

This example is taken from `PlainSocketImpl.connect()` from the JDK. It shows the socket implementation attempting to recover from a `ProtocolException`.

```
IOException pending = null;
try {
    socketConnect(address, port);
    return;
} catch (ProtocolException e) {
    // Try again in case of a protocol exception
    socketClose();
    fd = new FileDescriptor();
    socketCreate(true); // use 'stream' this time
    pending = e;
} catch (IOException e) {
    // Let someone else deal with this exception
    socketClose();
    throw e;
}
```

ProtocolException()

PURPOSE Constructs a new `ProtocolException` instance.

SYNTAX
```
public ProtocolException()
public ProtocolException(String host)
```

DESCRIPTION The two forms of this constructor create a new instance of `ProtocolException`. An optional string `host` can be supplied that describes this particular instance of the exception. Typically, `host` is the name of the remote machine to which the socket is attempting to connect, but `host` can be any arbitrary message.

PARAMETERS

`host` The machine for which this exception was thrown.

java.io
PushbackInputStream

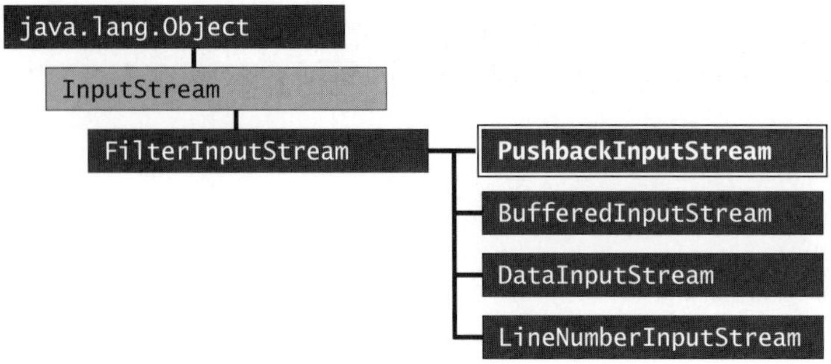

Syntax

```
public class PushbackInputStream extends FilterInputStream
```

Description

A *pushback input stream* is a filter stream that allows bytes to be "pushed back" (or unread) from the stream. For example, you can read a byte and subsequently push it back onto the stream so that the next read operation will return the byte that was pushed back. In Figure 204, the character 'a' is read once, and then pushed back, and then read again.

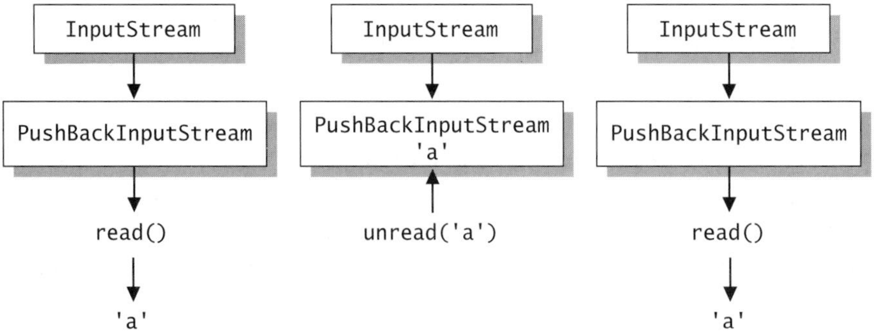

FIGURE 204 **`PushbackInputStream`**

This capability is useful when building parsers that need to read ahead in the stream in order to decide how to process the stream. This is a restricted form of the more general mark/reset capability available in some types of input streams (such as `BufferedInputStream`).

The PushbackInputStream implements a pushback input stream that has a single byte buffer. This means the stream can have at most one pushed-back byte in its stream. Once you have read the pushed-back byte, you can push another byte back onto the stream.

MEMBER SUMMARY	
Constructor	
PushbackInputStream()	Constructs a new pushback input stream for an input stream.
Pushback Method	
unread()	Pushes back a byte that has already been read.
Bytes Available Method	
available()	Determines the number of bytes that can be read without blocking.
Mark/Reset Methods	
markSupported()	Determines whether this stream supports mark/reset.
read()	Reads bytes from this pushback input stream.
Protected Field	
pushBack	The byte that has been pushed back.

See Also

BufferedInputStream, FilterInputStream, InputStream.

Example

This example shows how the pushback input stream is used to parse a sequence of numeric or string tokens. There are two parsing routines: readNumber() and readString(). Each of these keeps reading from the input stream until it encounters a character that does not belong to its token. At this point, it will push back the character onto the stream for the other parser to read.

```
import java.io.PushbackInputStream;
import java.io.IOException;
import java.util.Vector;

class Main {
    // read a stream and parse it into a sequence of numeric or string
    // tokens
    public static void main(String[] args) {
        Vector vec = new Vector();
```

Example

```
            PushbackInputStream pushin = new PushbackInputStream
                (System.in);
            boolean eof;
            while (true) {
                if (eof = readNumber(pushin, vec))
                    break;
                if (eof = readString(pushin, vec))
                    break;
            }
            System.out.println(vec);
        }
        private static boolean readNumber(PushbackInputStream in, Vector
             vec) {
            StringBuffer sb = new StringBuffer();
            int c = -1;
            // read number
            try {
                for (c = in.read(); c >= 0; c = in.read()) {
                    if (Character.isDigit((char)c)) {
                        sb.append((char)c);
                    } else {
                        in.unread(c);
                        break;
                    }
                }
            } catch (IOException e) {
            }
            if (sb.length() > 0)
                vec.addElement(Integer.valueOf(sb.toString()));
            return (c == -1);
        }
        private static boolean readString(PushbackInputStream in, Vector
             vec) {
            StringBuffer sb = new StringBuffer();
            int c = -1;
            try {
                for (c = in.read(); c >= 0; c = in.read()) {
                    if (Character.isDigit((char)c)) {
                        in.unread(c);
                        break;
                    } else if (Character.isSpace((char)c))
                        break;
                    else
                        sb.append((char)c);
                }
            } catch (IOException e) {
            }
            vec.addElement(sb.toString());
            return (c == -1);
        }
    }
```

available()

PURPOSE Determines the number of bytes that can be read without blocking.

SYNTAX `public int available() throws IOException`

DESCRIPTION This method returns the number of bytes that can be read without blocking. This number includes the byte that has been pushed back (if any) plus the number of bytes available from the stream that this pushback input stream is filtering.

RETURNS The number of bytes that can be read without blocking.

EXCEPTIONS
`IOException` If an IO error occurred.

OVERRIDES `FilterInputStream.available()`.

EXAMPLE This example uses a pushback input stream to examine the header of a file. It uses the length of the file and this header information to determine which parser to use.

```
try {
    PushbackInputStream pushin =
        new PushbackInputStream(new FileInputStream(args[0]));
    if (pushin.available() > CLASSC_LIMIT) {
        // read header (first byte) to find out format
        int c = pushin.read();
        if (c >= 0)
            pushin.unread(c);  // let parsers deal with it
        switch (c) {
        case CLASSA:
            classAParser(pushin);
            break;
        case CLASSB:
            classBParser(pushin);
        }
    } else {
        classCParser(pushin);
    }
    pushin.close();
} catch (IOException e) {
    e.printStackTrace();
}
```

markSupported()

PURPOSE Determines whether this pushback input stream supports mark/reset.

SYNTAX `public boolean markSupported()`

DESCRIPTION Pushback input streams do not support mark/reset. This method always returns `false` for pushback input streams.

RETURNS `false`.

OVERRIDES `FilterInputStream.markSupported()`.

SEE ALSO `InputStream.mark()`, `InputStream.markSupported()`, `InputStream.reset()`.

EXAMPLE

```
PushbackInputStream pushin = new PushbackInputStream(System.in);
if (pushin.markSupported())
    System.out.println("Mark for pushback is supported");
else
    System.out.println("Mark for pushback is not supported");
```

pushBack

PURPOSE The byte that has been pushed back.

SYNTAX `protected int pushBack`

DESCRIPTION This field contains the byte that has been pushed back. Its value is `-1` if no byte has been pushed back.

SEE ALSO `unread()`, `read()`.

EXAMPLE This example is from the source of `PushbackInputStream.unread()`. It shows how the field `pushBack` is used.

```
public void unread(int ch) throws IOException {
    if (pushBack != -1) {
        throw new IOException
            ("Attempt to unread more than one character!");
    }
    pushBack = ch;
}
```

PushbackInputStream()

PURPOSE Constructs a new pushback input stream for an input stream.

SYNTAX `public PushbackInputStream(InputStream in)`

DESCRIPTION This constructor creates a new pushback input stream for the input stream `in`. When you read from this new pushback input stream, it reads from `in`, except when you have previously "pushed back" a byte to this pushback stream. In that case, the pushed-back byte is returned before new bytes are read from `in`.

PARAMETERS

`in` The input stream for which this pushback input stream is created.

SEE ALSO `FilterInputStream`, `unread()`.

EXAMPLE See the class example, `available()`, and `markSupported()`.

read()

PURPOSE Reads bytes from this pushback input stream.

SYNTAX

```
public int read() throws IOException
public int read(byte[] buffer, int offset, int count) throws
    IOException
```

DESCRIPTION The two forms of this method read bytes from this pushback input stream. If a byte has been previously pushed back (`unread()`), it is returned first before other bytes are read from the stream being filtered.

The first form of this method reads and returns the next byte from this pushback input stream. The second form of this method reads `count` number of bytes from this pushback input stream and stores the bytes in the byte array `buffer` starting at index `offset`. It returns the actual number of bytes read.

PARAMETERS

`buffer` The byte array in which to store the bytes read.

`count` The number of bytes to read.

`offset` The index in `buffer` at which to start storing the bytes read.

RETURNS The first form returns the byte read; the second form returns the number of bytes read. Both forms return `-1` if end-of-file has been reached before any bytes have been read.

EXCEPTIONS

`IOException` If an IO error occurred.

OVERRIDES `FilterInputStream.read()`.

SEE ALSO `unread()`.

EXAMPLE See the class example.

unread()

PURPOSE Pushes back a byte.

SYNTAX `public void unread(int oneByte) throws IOException`

DESCRIPTION This method pushes back the lowest-order byte in `oneByte` to this pushback input stream. The immediate next `read()` call on this pushback input stream will return `oneByte` first before returning other bytes read.

PARAMETERS
`oneByte` The byte to push back.

EXCEPTIONS
`IOException` If an attempt is made to push back a byte when another byte has already been pushed back and has not yet been read.

SEE ALSO `pushBack`, `read()`.

EXAMPLE See the class example and `available()`.

java.util
Random

java.lang.Object — Random

Syntax

```
public class Random
```

Description

A *random-number generator* produces a sequence of numbers that are picked randomly from among a set or range of numbers. The appearance of a number at a particular position in this sequence is purely random. A *pseudorandom-number generator* produces a sequence of *pseudorandom numbers*. A pseudorandom-number generator is created with a *seed*. Two pseudorandom-number generators that have been created with the same seed value will produce two identical sequences of pseudorandom-numbers. Consequently, pseudorandom numbers are not really random numbers in the true sense. Rather, they exhibit randomness within any *single* sequence of pseudorandom numbers of a given seed.

The `Random` class is used to represent a pseudorandom-number generator for generating a sequence of pseudorandom numbers. You create a pseudorandom-number generator by giving it a seed. The generator uses the seed in the algorithm for generating the pseudorandom numbers.

Distribution of Pseudorandom Numbers

The numbers returned by the pseudorandom-number generator are of two distributions. One is *uniform distribution*. This means the numbers are uniformly distributed between the target range of numbers. For example, if the range is between 0.0 (inclusive) and 1.0 (exclusive), the numbers returned will be uniformly distributed between 0.0 and 1.0. The probability of returning any number in this range is equal. This is the distribution used for `nextDouble()`, `nextFloat()`, `nextInt()`, and `nextLong()`.

The second distribution is the *Gaussian distribution*. This is a bell-curved distribution with a mean of 0.0 and a standard deviation of 1.0.

MEMBER SUMMARY	
Constructor	
`Random()`	Constructs a new pseudorandom-number generator.
Seed Method	
`setSeed()`	Sets the seed of this pseudorandom-number generator.

Continued

MEMBER SUMMARY	
Generation Methods	
`nextDouble()`	Generates a pseudorandom uniformly distributed `double` value.
`nextFloat()`	Generates a pseudorandom uniformly distributed `float` value.
`nextGaussian()`	Generates a pseudorandom Gaussian distributed `double` value.
`nextInt()`	Generates a pseudorandom uniformly distributed `int` value.
`nextLong()`	Generates a pseudorandom uniformly distributed `long` value.

See Also

`Math.random()`.

Example

This example uses the pseudorandom-number generator to simulate a sequence of roulette spins. The pseudorandom-number generator is first created with the current time of day. When the dealer is changed, the generator is given a new seed (based on the new current time of day). The test program makes 20 spins and then changes the dealer and does 20 more spins.

```
import java.util.Random;
class Roulette {
    Random generator = new Random();
    // Spin the wheel and return a string (00, 0, 1-36)
    String spin() {
        int rand = generator.nextInt();
        int num = Math.abs(rand % 38);

        switch (num) {
        case 37: return ("00");
        case 36: return ("0");
       default: return (Integer.toString(num + 1)); // 1- 36 inclusive
        }
    }
    // Use a new seed when we change dealer
    void changeDealer() {
        generator.setSeed(System.currentTimeMillis());
    }
}
class Main {
    public static void main(String[] args) {
        Roulette r = new Roulette();

        // Spin 20 times
        for (int i = 0; i < 20; i++)
            System.out.println(i + ": " + r.spin());
```

```
        // change dealer
        r.changeDealer();

            // Spin 20 times again
        for (int i = 0; i < 20; i++)
            System.out.println(i + ": " + r.spin());
    }
}
```

nextDouble()

PURPOSE Generates a pseudorandom uniformly distributed `double` value.

SYNTAX `public double nextDouble()`

RETURNS A `double` between 0.0 (inclusive) and 1.0 (exclusive).

SEE ALSO `nextFloat()`.

EXAMPLE This example generates a sequence of random `double` values.

```
for(int i = 0; i < n; i++)
    System.out.println(rand.nextDouble());
```

nextFloat()

PURPOSE Generates a pseudorandom uniformly distributed `float` value.

SYNTAX `public float nextFloat()`

DESCRIPTION Generates a pseudorandom uniformly distributed `float` value between 0.0 and 1.0.

RETURNS A `float` between 0.0 (inclusive) and 1.0 (exclusive).

SEE ALSO `nextDouble()`.

```
if (rand.nextFloat() < 0.5)
        System.out.print("heads");
else
        System.out.print("tails");
```

nextGaussian()

PURPOSE Generates a pseudorandom Gaussian distributed `double` value.

SYNTAX `synchronized public double nextGaussian()`

DESCRIPTION This method generates a pseudorandom Gaussian distributed `double` value with mean 0.0 and standard deviation 1.0.

RETURNS A pseudorandom Gaussian distributed `double` value.

SEE ALSO `nextDouble()`.

EXAMPLE This example prints out a sequence of `n` pseudorandom Gaussian values.

```
for(int i = 0; i < n; i++)
    System.out.println(rand.nextGaussian());
```

nextInt()

PURPOSE Generates a pseudorandom uniformly distributed `int` value.

SYNTAX `public int nextInt()`

RETURNS An `int` value that ranges over all possible `int` values (positive and negative).

SEE ALSO `Integer.MAX_VALUE`, `Integer.MIN_VALUE`, `nextLong()`.

EXAMPLE See the class example.

nextLong()

PURPOSE Generates a pseudorandom uniformly distributed `long` value.

SYNTAX `public long nextLong()`

RETURNS A `long` in the range of all positive and negative `long` values.

SEE ALSO `Long.MAX_VALUE`, `Long.MIN_VALUE`, `nextInt()`.

EXAMPLE This example prints out a sequence of `n` pseudorandom `long` values.

```
for(int i = 0; i < n; i++)
    System.out.println(rand.nextLong());
```

Random()

PURPOSE Creates a new pseudorandom-number generator.

SYNTAX
```
public Random()
public Random(long seed)
```

DESCRIPTION There are two constructors for `Random()`. The first constructor creates a new pseudorandom-number generator using the current time of day as the seed. The second constructor creates a new pseudorandom-number generator using the number `seed`. In both cases, the seed can be replaced subsequently by using `setSeed()` to reset the generator and to start a new sequence using the new seed.

PARAMETERS

`seed` The seed to use for generating a sequence of pseudorandom numbers.

SEE ALSO `setSeed()`.

EXAMPLE See the class example.

```
Random time_based = new Random();
Random seed_based = new Random(41991);
```

setSeed()

PURPOSE Sets the seed of this pseudorandom-number generator.

SYNTAX
```
synchronized public void setSeed(long seed)
```

DESCRIPTION This method resets this pseudorandom-number generator and sets its seed to be `seed`. This seed is used to generate a new sequence of pseudorandom numbers for satisfying subsequent "next" calls. Doing this is effectively the same as creating a new pseudorandom-number generator.

PARAMETERS

`seed` The seed to use for generating a new sequence of pseudorandom numbers.

SEE ALSO `Random()`.

EXAMPLE See the class example.

java.io

RandomAccessFile

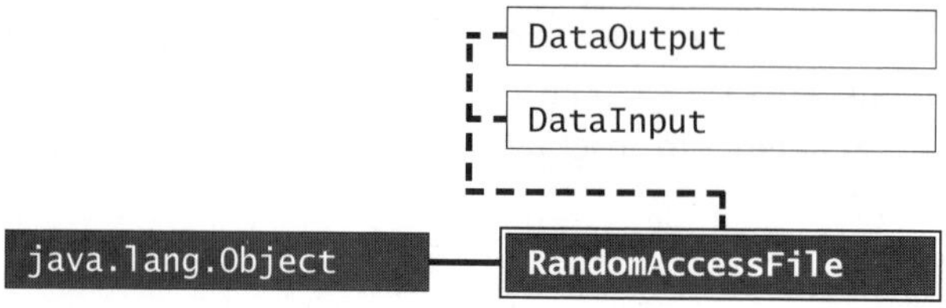

Syntax

```
public class RandomAccessFile implements DataOutput, DataInput
```

Description

A random-access file is a file in which you can point anywhere in the file and perform input/output operations on the file at that point. The `RandomAccessFile` class represents a random-access file. It provides methods for setting the *current file pointer* (the position in the file where the input/output will be effected). It also provides methods defined in the `DataInput` and `DataOutput` interfaces to allow primitive data values to be read from and written to the file.

MEMBER SUMMARY	
Constructor	
`RandomAccessFile()`	Constructs a new `RandomAccessFile` object.
Random Access Methods	
`getFilePointer()`	Retrieves the current file pointer of this file.
`seek()`	Sets the file pointer of this file.
Input Methods	
`read()`	Reads bytes from this file.
`readBoolean()`	Reads a `boolean` from this file.
`readByte()`	Reads an 8-bit `byte` from this file.
`readChar`	Reads a 16-bit `char` from this file.
`readDouble()`	Reads a 64-bit `double` from this file.
`readFloat()`	Reads a 32-bit `float` from this file.
`readFully()`	Reads bytes from this file, blocking until all bytes are read.
`readInt()`	Reads a 32-bit `int` from this file.
`readLine()`	Reads a line from this file.
`readLong()`	Reads a 64-bit `long` from this file.

MEMBER SUMMARY

`readShort()`	Reads a 16-bit `short` from this file.
`readUnsignedByte()`	Reads an unsigned 8-bit `byte` from this file.
`readUnsignedShort()`	Reads an unsigned 16-bit `short` from this file.
`readUTF()`	Reads a Unicode string in UTF from this file.
`skipBytes()`	Skips bytes from this file.
Output Methods	
`write()`	Writes bytes to this file.
`writeBoolean()`	Writes a `boolean` to this file.
`writeByte()`	Writes an 8-bit `byte` to this file.
`writeBytes()`	Writes a string to this file as a sequence of `byte`s.
`writeChar()`	Writes a 16-bit `char` to this file.
`writeChars()`	Writes a string to this file as a sequence of `char`s.
`writeDouble()`	Writes a 64-bit `double` to this file.
`writeFloat()`	Writes a 32-bit `float` to this file.
`writeInt()`	Writes a 32-bit `int` to this file.
`writeLong()`	Writes a 64-bit `long` to this file.
`writeShort()`	Writes a 16-bit `short` to this file.
`writeUTF()`	Writes a string in UTF to this file.
Information Methods	
`length()`	Determines the number of bytes in this file.
`getFD()`	Retrieves the file descriptor of this file.
Method for Closing File	
`close()`	Closes the file.

See Also

`DataInput`, `DataInputStream`, `DataOutput`, `DataOutputStream`, `File`, `FileDescriptor`.

Example

This example opens a random-access file for writing, writes using the different write methods, and then reads the data back using the read methods.

```
import java.io.*;

class Main {
    public static void main(String[] args) {
        if (args.length != 1) {
            System.err.println(
                "Usage: java Main <output file>");
            System.exit(-1);
```

Example

```
        }
        try {
           RandomAccessFile raf = new RandomAccessFile(args[0], "rw");

            char a = 'a';
            byte b = 2;
            String c = "abc";
            short d = 4;
            byte[] b2 = {'a', 'b', 'c'};

            // write some stuff out
            long file_start = raf.getFilePointer();
            raf.write(b);
            raf.write(b2, 0, b2.length);
            raf.writeBoolean(true);
            raf.writeChar(a);
            raf.writeBytes(c);
            raf.writeChars(c);
            raf.writeDouble(123.456);
            raf.writeFloat(123.456f);
            raf.writeInt(678);
            raf.writeLong(678l);
            raf.writeShort(d);
            raf.writeUTF(c);
            raf.writeUTF("abc\n");
            raf.write(b);
            raf.writeShort(d);

            System.out.println("Length of file: " + raf.length());

            // read the stuff back
            raf.seek(file_start);

            b2 = new byte[1];
            b = raf.readByte();
            System.out.println("Byte: " + b);
            raf.read(b2);
            System.out.println("Byte[0]: " + (char)b2[0]);
            raf.read(b2, 0, b2.length);
            System.out.println("Byte[0]: " + (char)b2[0]);
            int ub = raf.readUnsignedByte();
            System.out.println("Unsigned Byte: " + b);
            System.out.println("Boolean: " + raf.readBoolean());
            a = raf.readChar();
            System.out.println("Char: " + a);

            byte[] b3 = new byte[3];
            raf.readFully(b3);
            System.out.println("readFully: " + (char)b3[0] +
              (char)b3[1] +
                                  (char)b3[2]);
            raf.skipBytes(6); // skip string 'abc'
            double d1 = raf.readDouble();
            float f1 = raf.readFloat();
```

```
            int i = raf.readInt();
            long l = raf.readLong();
            short s = raf.readShort();
            String str = raf.readUTF();
            ub = raf.readUnsignedByte();
            int us = raf.readUnsignedShort();
            System.out.println("UTF String" + str);

            raf.close();
        } catch (IOException e) {
            System.err.println(e);
        }
    }
}
```

close()

PURPOSE Closes the file.

SYNTAX `public native void close() throws IOException`

DESCRIPTION This method closes this random-access file. It releases any resources, such as file descriptors, used by this file.

EXCEPTIONS

`IOException` If an IO error occurred while attempting to close this file.

EXAMPLE See the class example.

getFD()

PURPOSE Retrieves the file descriptor used by this file.

SYNTAX `public final FileDescriptor getFD() throws IOException`

DESCRIPTION When this `RandomAccessFile` is constructed, it is opened and assigned a file descriptor to use for accessing the file (from the underlying file system). This method returns this file descriptor.

RETURNS The file descriptor used by this file.

EXCEPTIONS

`IOException` If this file has already been closed.

SEE ALSO `FileDescriptor`.

A B C D E F G H I J K L M N O P Q R S T U V W X Y Z

getFilePointer()

PURPOSE Retrieves the current file pointer of this file.

SYNTAX `public native long getFilePointer() throws IOException`

DESCRIPTION The current file pointer is the position in the file at which the next read/write method will operate. For example, if the file is opened for read, the current file pointer is the position at which the next byte from the file will be read. If the file is opened for write, the current file pointer is the position at which the bytes will be written. The current file pointer is incremented after each read/write/skip and is set using `seek()`.

RETURNS The current file pointer of this file.

EXCEPTIONS
`IOException` If an IO error occurred while retrieving the current file pointer.

SEE ALSO `seek()`, `skipBytes()`, `read*()`, `write*()`.

EXAMPLE See the class example.

length()

PURPOSE Determines the number of bytes in this file.

SYNTAX `public native long length() throws IOException`

DESCRIPTION This method returns the number of bytes between the beginning of the file and the end of the file.

EXCEPTIONS
`IOException` If an IO error occurred.

EXAMPLE See the class example.

RandomAccessFile()

PURPOSE Constructs a new `RandomAccessFile` instance.

SYNTAX
```
public RandomAccessFile(String fileName, String mode) throws
   IOException
public RandomAccessFile(File file, String mode) throws IOException
```

DESCRIPTION There are two forms of the constructor for `RandomAccessFile`. The first form creates a new instance of `RandomAccessFile` for the file with the file pathname `fileName`. The second form creates a new instance of `RandomAccessFile` for the file as described by the `File` instance `file`. When the `RandomAccessFile` instance is created, it opens the file specified in the mode as specified by the string `mode`. `mode` can be "r", which means to open the file in read-only mode, or "rw", which means to open the file in read-write mode. Any other values of `mode` will raise an `IllegalArgumentException`.

The file can be opened only if allowed by the security manager.

PARAMETERS

`file` The `File` of the file to open.

`fileName` The string name of the file to open.

`mode` The access mode ("r" or "rw").

EXCEPTIONS

`IOException` If an IO error occurred while attempting to open the specified file.

`IllegalArgumentException`
If `mode` is neither "r" nor "rw".

`SecurityException`
If the file could not be opened in the mode specified due to security reasons.

SEE ALSO `FileDescriptor`, `SecurityManager.checkRead()`, `SecurityManager.checkWrite()`.

EXAMPLE See the class example.

read()

PURPOSE Reads bytes from this file.

SYNTAX

```
public int read() throws IOException
public int read(byte[] buffer) throws IOException
public int read(byte[] buffer, int offset, int count) throws
    IOException
```

DESCRIPTION The three forms of this method read bytes from this file. The first form reads a single byte and returns it in the lowest-order byte of an `int`. The other two forms read bytes and store them in `buffer`. If `offset` and `count` are specified, `count` bytes are read and placed into `buffer` starting at index `offset`. If these are not specified, `buffer.length` bytes are read and placed into `buffer` starting at index `0`. These methods might block if no bytes are available to be read. The requested number of bytes to be read (either `count` or `buffer.length`) might not all be read if there are not that many bytes available. If you want to block waiting for all the number of bytes requested, use `readFully()`.

PARAMETERS

`buffer`	The byte array to store the bytes read.
`count`	The number of bytes to read.
`offset`	The index in `buffer` at which to start storing the bytes read.

RETURNS The first form of `read()` returns the byte read; the other two forms return the actual number of bytes read. All forms return `-1` when end-of-file has been reached before any bytes have been read.

EXCEPTIONS

`IOException`	If an IO error has occurred.

SEE ALSO `readByte()`, `readBytes()`, `readFully()`, `readLine()`, `readUnsignedByte()`.

EXAMPLE See the class example.

readBoolean()

PURPOSE Reads a `boolean` from this file.

SYNTAX `public final boolean readBoolean() throws IOException`

DESCRIPTION This method reads a `boolean` value from this random-access file. A `boolean` is represented as a single byte. If the byte is nonzero, the `boolean` value is `true`. If the byte is zero, the `boolean` value is `false`.

RETURNS The `boolean` value read (`true` or `false`).

EXCEPTIONS

`EOFException`	If end-of-file was reached while attempting to read from this file.
`IOException`	If an IO error occurred while attempting to read from this file.

SEE ALSO `writeBoolean()`.

EXAMPLE See the class example.

readByte()

PURPOSE Reads a `byte` from this file.

SYNTAX `public final byte readByte() throws IOException`

RETURNS The 8-bit `byte` read.

EXCEPTIONS

`EOFException` If end-of-file was reached while attempting to read from this file.

`IOException` If an IO error occurred while attempting to read from this file.

SEE ALSO `writeByte()`, `writeBytes()`, `readUnsignedByte()`.

EXAMPLE See the class example.

readChar()

PURPOSE Reads a 16-bit `char` from this file.

SYNTAX `public final char readChar() throws IOException`

DESCRIPTION A Unicode `char` is represented by a 16-bit unsigned integer. This method reads a `char` by reading two consecutive bytes from this random-access file and interpreting them as a 16-bit unsigned integer (first byte read is the high-order byte) to be used as the value of the `char`.

RETURNS The `char` read.

EXCEPTIONS

`EOFException` If end-of-file was reached while attempting to read from this file.

`IOException` If an IO error occurred while attempting to read from this file.

SEE ALSO `writeChar()`, `writeChars()`.

EXAMPLE See the class example.

readDouble()

PURPOSE Reads a 64-bit `double` from this file.

SYNTAX `public final double readDouble() throws IOException`

DESCRIPTION This method reads 8 bytes from this random-access file and returns the `double` value represented by the bits of those 8 bytes.

RETURNS The `double` value read.

EXCEPTIONS

`EOFException` If end-of-file was reached while attempting to read from this file.

`IOException` If an IO error occurred while attempting to read from this file.

SEE ALSO `writeDouble()`, `Double.longBitsToDouble()`.

EXAMPLE See the class example.

A B C D E F G H I J K L M N O P Q R S T U V W X Y Z

readFloat()

PURPOSE Reads a 32-bit `float` from this file.

SYNTAX `public final float readFloat() throws IOException`

DESCRIPTION This method reads 4 bytes from the random-access file and returns the `float` value represented by the bits of those 4 bytes.

RETURNS The `float` value read.

EXCEPTIONS

`EOFException` If end-of-file was reached while attempting to read from this file.

`IOException` If an IO error occurred while attempting to read from this file.

SEE ALSO `writeFloat()`, `Float.intBitsToFloat()`.

EXAMPLE See the class example.

readFully()

PURPOSE Reads the requested number of bytes from this file.

SYNTAX

```
public final void readFully(byte[] buffer) throws IOException
public final void readFully(byte[] buffer, int offset, int count)
   throws IOException
```

DESCRIPTION The two forms of this method read bytes from this random-access file and copy them into the byte array `buffer`. If `offset` and `count` are specified, `count` bytes are read and placed into `buffer` starting at index `offset`. If these are not specified, `buffer.length` bytes are read and placed into `buffer` starting at index `0`. These methods will block waiting for all the requested number of bytes to be read (either `count` or `buffer.length`) .

PARAMETERS

`buffer` The byte array into which the data is read.

`count` The maximum number of bytes to read.

`offset` The index in `buffer` at which to start putting the bytes read.

EXCEPTIONS

`EOFException` If end-of-file was reached while attempting to read from this file.

`IOException` If an IO error occurred while attempting to read from this file.

EXAMPLE See the class example.

readInt()

PURPOSE Reads a 32-bit `int` from this file.

SYNTAX `public final int readInt() throws IOException`

DESCRIPTION This method reads 4 bytes from this random-access file and returns the `int` value represented by the bits of those 4 bytes. The higher-order bytes are read in order from the file.

RETURNS The `int` value read.

EXCEPTIONS

`EOFException` If end-of-file was reached while attempting to read from this file.

`IOException` If an IO error occurred while attempting to read from this file.

SEE ALSO `writeInt()`.

EXAMPLE See the class example.

readLine()

PURPOSE Reads a line from this file.

SYNTAX `public final String readLine() throws IOException`

DESCRIPTION This method reads a line from this random-access file and returns it as a string. A line is defined as a sequence of bytes terminated by an `'\n'` or end-of-file. The string does not include the line terminator character.

RETURNS A string copy of a line read from this file; `null` if no character is read before end-of-file is reached.

EXCEPTIONS

`IOException` If an IO error occurred while attempting to read from this stream.

SEE ALSO `writeBytes()`.

EXAMPLE See the class example.

readLong()

PURPOSE Reads a 64-bit `long` from this file.

SYNTAX `public final long readLong() throws IOException`

DESCRIPTION This method reads 8 bytes from this random-access file and returns the `long` value represented by the bits of those 8 bytes. The higher-order bytes are read in order from the file.

RETURNS The `long` value read.

EXCEPTIONS

`EOFException` If end-of-file was reached while attempting to read from this file.

`IOException` If an IO error occurred while attempting to read from this file.

SEE ALSO `writeLong()`.

EXAMPLE See the class example.

readShort()

PURPOSE Reads a 16-bit `short` from this file.

SYNTAX `public final short readShort() throws IOException`

DESCRIPTION This method reads 2 bytes from this random-access file and returns the `short` value represented by the bits of those 2 bytes. The higher-order byte is read first from the file.

RETURNS The `short` value read.

EXCEPTIONS

`EOFException` If end-of-file was reached while attempting to read from this stream.

`IOException` If an IO error occurred while attempting to read from this stream.

SEE ALSO `readUnsignedShort()`, `writeShort()`.

EXAMPLE See the class example.

readUnsignedByte()

PURPOSE Reads an unsigned 8-bit byte from this file.

SYNTAX `public final int readUnsignedByte() throws IOException`

DESCRIPTION This method reads a byte from this random-access file and returns it as the lowest byte in an `int`. The only difference between this method and `readByte()` is that this method returns the byte in an `int`, while `readByte()` returns the byte in a `byte`. Because `byte` is a signed type, the highest-order bit will determine the sign of the value. When a byte is returned in an `int`, the higher-order 3 bytes are unused (0). Consequently, the `int` value returned is always unsigned.

RETURNS An `int` containing the byte read.

EXCEPTIONS

`EOFException` If end-of-file was reached while attempting to read from this stream.

`IOException` If an IO error occurred while attempting to read from this stream.

SEE ALSO `readByte()`, `writeByte()`.

EXAMPLE See the class example.

readUnsignedShort()

PURPOSE Reads a 16-bit `short` from this file.

SYNTAX `public final int readUnsignedShort() throws IOException`

DESCRIPTION This method reads 2 bytes from this random-access file and returns the unsigned integer value represented by the bits of those 2 bytes. The higher-order byte is read first from the input stream. The only difference between this method and `readShort()` is that this method returns the result as an `int`, while `readShort()` returns the result as a `short`. Because `short` is a signed type, the highest-order bit will determine the sign of the value. When a `short` is returned in an `int`, it occupies the lower-order 2 bytes of the `int`; the higher-order 2 bytes are unused (0). Consequently, the `int` value returned is always unsigned.

RETURNS An `int` containing the 16-bit `short` value read.

EXCEPTIONS

`EOFException` If end-of-file was reached while attempting to read from this stream.

`IOException` If an IO error occurred while attempting to read from this stream.

SEE ALSO `readShort()`, `writeShort()`.

EXAMPLE See the class example.

readUTF()

PURPOSE Reads a Unicode string from this file.

SYNTAX `public final String readUTF() throws IOException`

DESCRIPTION This method reads a Unicode string and returns it as a `String`. UTF stands for *Unicode Transfer Format*, an encoding scheme for Unicode characters. Write a string to a file using `writeUTF()`. Read it back using `readUTF()`.

RETURNS The Unicode string read as a `String`.

EXCEPTIONS

`EOFException` If end-of-file was reached while attempting to read the string.

`IOException` If an IO error occurred while attempting to read the string.

`UTFDataFormatException`
If the string being read is not in UTF.

SEE ALSO `writeUTF()`.

EXAMPLE See the class example.

seek()

PURPOSE Sets the file pointer of this file.

SYNTAX `public native void seek(long pos) throws IOException`

DESCRIPTION This method sets the current file pointer of this random-access file to be `pos`. Subsequent read/write/skip operations will operate on the file starting at this new file pointer.

PARAMETERS

`pos` The absolute position to which to set the file pointer.

EXCEPTIONS

`IOException` If an IO error occurred.

SEE ALSO `getFilePointer()`.

EXAMPLE See the class example.

skipBytes()

PURPOSE Skips bytes from this file.

SYNTAX `public int skipBytes(int count) throws IOException`

DESCRIPTION This method skips `count` number of bytes from this random-access file. It updates the current file pointer to reflect the number of bytes skipped. This method returns the actual number of bytes skipped.

PARAMETERS

`count` The number of bytes to skip.

RETURNS The actual number of bytes skipped.

EXCEPTIONS

IOException If an IO error occurred.

SEE ALSO seek().

EXAMPLE See the class example.

write()

PURPOSE Writes bytes to this file.

SYNTAX

```
public void write(int oneByte) throws IOException
public void write(byte[] buffer) throws IOException
public void write(byte[] buffer, int offset, int count) throws
   IOException
```

DESCRIPTION The three forms of the `write()` method write the specified byte or bytes to this file. The first form writes a single byte `oneByte` to this file. The second form writes all the bytes from `buffer` to this file. The third form of `write()` writes `count` bytes from the byte array `buffer` starting at index `offset` to this stream.

PARAMETERS

`buffer` The byte array containing bytes to be written.

`count` The number of bytes from `buffer` to write.

`offset` The index in `buffer` of the bytes to be written.

`oneByte` The byte to be written.

EXCEPTIONS

IOException If an IO error occurred while attempting to write.

SEE ALSO readByte(), readLine(), readFully(), readUnsignedByte(), writeByte(), writeBytes().

EXAMPLE See the class example.

writeBoolean()

PURPOSE Writes a `boolean` to this file.

SYNTAX

```
public final void writeBoolean(boolean val) throws IOException
```

DESCRIPTION This method writes the `boolean` value `val` to this file. The output consists of a single byte whose value is `1` if `val` is `true` and `0` if `val` is `false`.

A B C D E F G H I J K L M N O P Q R S T U V W X Y Z

PARAMETERS

`val` The `boolean` to be written.

EXCEPTIONS

`IOException` If an IO error occurred while attempting to write.

SEE ALSO `readBoolean()`.

EXAMPLE See the class example.

writeByte()

PURPOSE Writes an 8-bit byte to this file.

SYNTAX `public final void writeByte(int val) throws IOException`

DESCRIPTION This method writes the 8-bit byte (in the lowest-order byte of `val`) to this file. The output consists of a single byte whose value is the lowest-order byte of `val`.

PARAMETERS

`val` The byte value to be written.

EXCEPTIONS

`IOException` If an IO error occurred while attempting to write.

SEE ALSO `read()`, `readByte()`, `readFully()`, `readLine()`, `readUnsignedByte()`, `write()`.

EXAMPLE See the class example.

writeBytes()

PURPOSE Writes a string as a sequence of bytes.

SYNTAX `public final void writeBytes(String str) throws IOException`

DESCRIPTION This method writes the string `str` to this file as a sequence of bytes (8 bits). Because a string consists of 16-bit Unicode `char` values and the output is only 8-bit bytes, the high-order bytes of the `char` values are lost (and not written). Use `writeChar()` and `writeChars()` to write all 16 bits of a Unicode `char` or `char` string.

PARAMETERS

`str` The string to be written.

EXCEPTIONS

IOException If an IO error occurred while attempting to write.

SEE ALSO `read()`, `readByte()`, `readFully()`, `readLine()`, `readUnsignedByte()`, `writeChar()`, `writeChars()`.

EXAMPLE See the class example.

writeChar()

PURPOSE Writes a 16-bit `char` to this file.

SYNTAX `public final void writeChar(int val) throws IOException`

DESCRIPTION This method writes a 16-bit Unicode `char val` to this file. Only the lower-order 2 bytes of `val` are written. The output consists of two bytes (higher-order written first), which represent the Unicode value of `val`.

PARAMETERS

`val` The `char` value to be written.

EXCEPTIONS

`IOException` If an IO error occurred while attempting to write.

SEE ALSO `readChar()`, `writeByte()`, `writeChars()`.

EXAMPLE See the class example.

writeChars()

PURPOSE Writes a string as a sequence of 16-bit `chars` to this file.

SYNTAX `public final void writeChars(String str) throws IOException`

DESCRIPTION This method writes the string `str` to the output stream as a sequence of `chars` (16 bits). Each `char` written consists of 2 bytes (higher-order written first), which represent its Unicode value.

PARAMETERS

`str` The string to be written.

EXCEPTIONS

`IOException` If an IO error occurred while attempting to write.

SEE ALSO `readChar()`, `writeBytes()`, `writeChar()`, `writeUTF()`.

EXAMPLE See the class example.

A B C D E F G H I J K L M N O P Q R S T U V W X Y Z

writeDouble()

PURPOSE Writes a `double` to this file.

SYNTAX `public final void writeDouble(double val) throws IOException`

DESCRIPTION This method writes the `double` value `val` to this file. The output generated consists of 8 bytes, which make up the bit representation of `val`.

PARAMETERS

`val` The `double` value to be written.

EXCEPTIONS

`IOException` If an IO error occurred while attempting to write.

SEE ALSO `readDouble()`, `Double.doubleToLongBits()`.

EXAMPLE See the class example.

writeFloat()

PURPOSE Writes a `float` to this file.

SYNTAX `public final void writeFloat(float val) throws IOException`

DESCRIPTION This method writes the `float` value `val` to this file. The output generated consists of 4 bytes, which make up the bit representation of `val`.

PARAMETERS

`val` The `float` value to be written.

EXCEPTIONS

`IOException` If an IO error occurred while attempting to write.

SEE ALSO `readFloat()`, `Float.floatToIntBits()`.

EXAMPLE See the class example.

writeInt()

PURPOSE Writes a 32-bit `int` to this file.

SYNTAX `public final void writeInt(int val) throws IOException`

DESCRIPTION This method writes the `int` value `val` to this file. The output generated consists of 4 bytes, in highest-to-lowest byte order, that represent the value of `val`.

PARAMETERS

`val` The `int` value to be written.

EXCEPTIONS

`IOException` If an IO error occurred while attempting to write.

SEE ALSO `readInt()`.

EXAMPLE See the class example.

writeLong()

PURPOSE Writes a 64-bit `long` to this file.

SYNTAX `public final void writeLong(long val) throws IOException`

DESCRIPTION This method writes the `long` value `val` to this file. The output generated consists of 8 bytes, in highest-to-lowest byte order, that represent the value of `val`.

PARAMETERS

`val` The `long` value to be written.

EXCEPTIONS

`IOException` If an IO error occurred while attempting to write.

SEE ALSO `readLong()`.

EXAMPLE See the class example.

writeShort()

PURPOSE Writes a 16-bit `short` to this file.

SYNTAX `public final void writeShort(int val) throws IOException`

DESCRIPTION This method writes the `short` value `val` to this file (the lower-order 2 bytes of `val` are used). The output generates 2 bytes, with the higher-order byte written first.

PARAMETERS

`val` The value to be written. The two lower-order bytes of `val` are used as the value of the `short` to be written.

EXCEPTIONS

`IOException` If an IO error occurred while attempting to write.

SEE ALSO `readShort()`, `readUnsignedShort()`.

EXAMPLE See the class example.

writeUTF()

PURPOSE Writes a Unicode string in UTF.

SYNTAX `public final void writeUTF(String str) throws IOException`

DESCRIPTION This method writes a string `str` to this file in UTF. UTF stands for *Unicode Transfer Format*, an encoding scheme for Unicode characters. Write a string to a file using the `writeUTF()` method. Read it back using `readUTF()`.

PARAMETERS

`str` The string to be written.

EXCEPTIONS

`IOException` If an IO error occurred while attempting to write.

SEE ALSO `readUTF()`, `writeBytes()`, `writeChars()`.

EXAMPLE See the class example.

java.awt
Rectangle

java.lang.Object — **Rectangle**

Syntax

```
public class Rectangle
```

Description

A rectangle represents a rectangular area on a 2D plane. A rectangle is defined by four values: *x*, *y*, *width*, and *height*. *x* and *y* define the northwest corner of the rectangle; *width* and *height* define the size of the rectangle. Rectangles are typically used in the layout of components and in graphics operations.

When using the methods in this class, note whether a new rectangle is returned. Some methods modify the current instance, while others return a new instance. In general, when having a rectangle instance returned in a method call, either have a copy returned, if you need to retain the instance or—have the instance discarded after it is returned. If you have passed a rectangle instance in a method call and wish to continue using the instance, note whether the method will either retain the instance or copy the values.

MEMBER SUMMARY

Constructor	
`Rectangle()`	Creates a new `Rectangle` instance.
Rectangle Tests	
`equals()`	Determines if two rectangles are equal.
`inside()`	Determines if a point lies inside the rectangle.
`intersects()`	Determines if two rectangles intersect.
`isEmpty()`	Determines if the rectangle is empty.
Rectangle Operations	
`add()`	Enlarges the rectangle.
`grow()`	Shifts all four edges of the rectangle.
`intersection()`	Calculates the intersection of two rectangles.
`move()`	Moves the rectangle to a new location.
`reshape()`	Modifies the rectangle's bounds.

Continued

MEMBER SUMMARY

`resize()`	Modifies the rectangle's size.
`translate()`	Moves the rectangle by a relative distance.
`union()`	Calculates the union of two rectangles.
Fields	
`height`	This field holds the rectangle's height.
`width`	This field holds the rectangle's width.
`x`	This field holds the rectangle's *x*-coordinate.
`y`	This field holds the rectangle's *y*-coordinate.
Hash Code Method	
`hashCode()`	Calculates the hash code for the rectangle.
Debugging Method	
`toString()`	Generates a string representation of the rectangle.

Example

This example demonstrates how to implement drag and drop. The program creates three coins and three slots in the three primary colors. The coins can be dragged over a slot and dropped on it. A coin changes color only if it's over the same-colored slot. If the coin is dropped on the proper slot, the coin disappears. See Figure 205.

The double-buffering technique is used to eliminate flicker during the dragging of the coins.

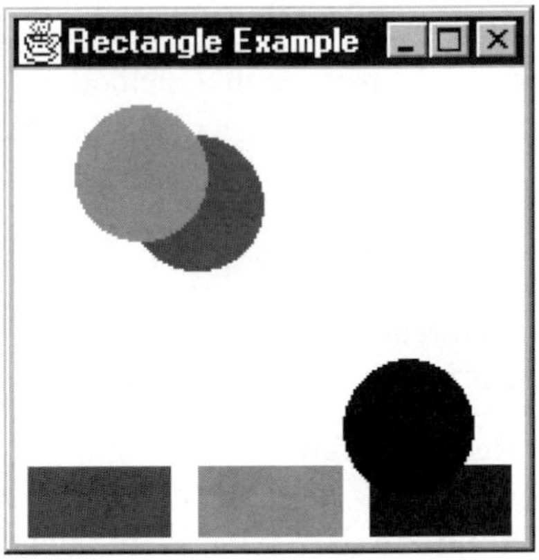

FIGURE 205 **Rectangle**

```
import java.awt.*;
class Main extends Frame {
    Main() {
        super("Rectangle Example");
        add("Center", new ImageCanvas());
        resize(200, 200);
        show();
    }

    public static void main(String[] args) {
        new Main();
    }
}

class ImageCanvas extends Canvas {
    int numCoins = 3;
```

A B C D E F G H I J K L M N O P Q R S T U V W X Y Z

```
Rectangle[] coins = new Rectangle[numCoins];
Rectangle[] slots = new Rectangle[numCoins];
Color[] colors = {Color.red, Color.green, Color.blue};
Image bbuf;
Graphics bbufG;

ImageCanvas() {
    for (int i=0; i<numCoins; i++) {
        coins[i] = new Rectangle(rand(50), rand(50), 50, 50);
        slots[i] = new Rectangle();
    }
}

int rand(int r) {
    return (int)Math.floor(Math.random()*r);
}

public void paint(Graphics g) {
    update(g);
}

public void update(Graphics g) {
    int w = size().width;
    int h = size().height;

    if (bbuf == null
        || w > bbuf.getWidth(null)
        || h > bbuf.getHeight(null)) {
        bbuf = createImage(w, h);
        bbufG = bbuf.getGraphics();
    }

    bbufG.setColor(Color.white);
    bbufG.fillRect(0, 0, size().width, size().height);

    // paint slots
    for (int i=0; i<numCoins; i++) {
        slots[i].reshape(i*w/3, h-30, w/3, 30);
        slots[i].grow(-5, -2);
        bbufG.setColor(colors[i]);
        bbufG.fillRect(slots[i].x, slots[i].y,
            slots[i].width, slots[i].height);
    }

    // paint coins
    for (int i=0; i<numCoins; i++) {
        if (!coins[i].isEmpty()) {
            if (dragging == i && coins[i].intersects(slots[i])) {
                bbufG.setColor(Color.black);
            } else {
                bbufG.setColor(colors[i]);
            }
            bbufG.fillOval(coins[i].x, coins[i].y,
                coins[i].width, coins[i].height);
```

```
                }
            }
            g.drawImage(bbuf, 0, 0, this);
        }

        int dragging = -1;
        Point offset;
        public synchronized boolean mouseDown(Event evt, int x, int y) {
       for (int i=coins.length-1; i>=0; i--) {
           if (!coins[i].isEmpty() && coins[i].inside(x, y)) {
                   dragging = i;
                   offset = new Point(coins[i].x-x, coins[i].y-y);
                   return true;
           }
       }
            return false;
        }

        public synchronized boolean mouseDrag(Event evt, int x, int y) {
            if (dragging >= 0) {
                coins[dragging].move(x, y);
                coins[dragging].translate(offset.x, offset.y);
                repaint();
                return true;
            }
            return false;
        }

        public synchronized boolean mouseUp(Event evt, int x, int y) {
            if (dragging >= 0) {
                if (coins[dragging].intersects(slots[dragging])) {
                    coins[dragging].width = 0;    // make it empty
                    dragging = -1;
                }
                repaint();
                return true;
            }
            return false;
        }
    }
```

add()

PURPOSE Enlarges the rectangle.

SYNTAX
```
public void add(int x, int y)
public void add(Point point)
public void add(Rectangle rectangle)
```

DESCRIPTION The three forms of this method enlarge the rectangle, if necessary, to include another point or rectangle. If `x` and `y` are specified, they define a point; the rectangle's bounds are modified to be just large enough to include the point. If `point` is specified, the rectangle's bounds are modified to be just large enough to include the point. If `rectangle` is specified, the rectangle's bounds are modified to be just large enough to include all the points in the rectangle.

The following invariants for `add()` hold:

After `r.add(x, y)`, `r.inside(x, y)` is `true`.

After `r.add(point)`, `r.inside(point.x, point.y)` is `true`.

After `r.add(rectangle)`, `r.equals(r.union(rectangle))` is `true`.

PARAMETERS

`point`	The non-`null` point to include.
`rectangle`	The non-`null` rectangle to include.
`x`	The *x*-coordinate of the point to include.
`y`	The *y*-coordinate of the point to include.

EXAMPLE This example takes points defined by clicking the mouse and adding them to a rectangle.

```
Rectangle rect = new Rectangle();

public boolean mouseDown(Event evt, int x, int y) {
   rect.add(x, y);
   downX = x;
   downY = y;
   return true;
}
```

equal()

PURPOSE Determines if two rectangles are equal.

SYNTAX `public boolean equals(Object object)`

DESCRIPTION Two rectangles are equal if their *x*- and *y*-coordinates, width, and height are identical.

PARAMETERS

`object`	The object to check for equality. This can be `null`.

RETURNS `true` if `object` is a rectangle and is equal to this rectangle; `false` otherwise.

OVERRIDES `Object.equals()`.

EXAMPLE This example defines a method that searches through an array of rectangles looking for one that exactly matches a particular rectangle. If a match exists, the method returns the index of the rectangle; otherwise it returns `-1`.

```
Rectangle[] rects = new Rectangle[100];

int findEqual(Rectangle r) {
   for (int i=0; i<rects.length; i++) {
      if (r.equals(rects[i]);
      return i;
   }
   return -1;
}
```

grow()

PURPOSE Shifts all four edges of the rectangle.

SYNTAX `public void grow(int hor, int ver)`

DESCRIPTION This method modifies the rectangle such that its left edge is shifted left by `hor` and its width is increased by 2 * `hor`. Also, its top edge is shifted up by `ver` and its height is increased by 2 * `ver`.

`hor` or `ver` can be negative. This causes the rectangle to shrink instead.

PARAMETERS

`hor` The amount to shift the rectangle's left and right edges.

`ver` The amount to shift the rectangle's top and bottom edges.

EXAMPLE This example defines a `keyDown()` method, whereby if 'g' is pressed, the rectangle increases in width and height by 2 pixels each and if 's' is pressed, the rectangle decreases in width and height by 2 pixels each.

```
public boolean keyDown(Event evt, int key) {
   if (key == 'g') {
      rect.grow(1, 1);
      return true;
   } else (key == 's') {
      rect.grow(-1, -1);
      return true;
   }
   return false;
}
```

hashCode()

PURPOSE Calculates the hash code for the rectangle.

SYNTAX `public int hashCode()`

DESCRIPTION The rectangle's hash code is an integer calculated from the rectangle's bounds. If `equals(r1, r2)` is `true`, then `r1` and `r2` will have the same hash codes; otherwise `r1` and `r2` will likely have different hash codes.

OVERRIDES `Object.hashCode()`.

RETURNS The rectangle's hash code.

EXAMPLE See `equals()` and `Object.hashCode()`.

height

PURPOSE This field holds the rectangle's height.

SYNTAX `public int height`

EXAMPLE This example paints a rectangle on the screen.

```
Rectangle rect = new Rectangle();

public void paint(Graphics g) {
    g.fillRect(rect.x, rect.y, rect.width, rect.height);
}
```

inside()

PURPOSE Determines if a point lies inside the rectangle.

SYNTAX `public boolean inside(int x, int y)`

DESCRIPTION A point is inside a rectangle if the following condition is true:

```
pt.x >= x && pt.y >= y && (pt.x-x) < width && (pt.y-y) < height
```

PARAMETERS

`x` The point's x-coordinate.

`y` The point's y-coordinate.

A B C D E F G H I J K L M N O P Q R S T U V W X Y Z

RETURNS `true` if the point is inside the rectangle; `false` otherwise.

EXAMPLE This example defines a `mouseDown()` method that responds only if the user clicks inside the rectangle `rect`.

```
Rectangle rect = new Rectangle();

public boolean mouseDown(Event evt, int x, int y) {
   if (rect.inside(x, y)) {
      // (x, y) are inside the rectangle
      return true;
   }
   return false;
}
```

intersection()

PURPOSE Calculates the intersection of two rectangles.

SYNTAX `public Rectangle intersection(Rectangle rectangle)`

DESCRIPTION The intersection of two rectangles is defined to be the set of all points that lie in both rectangles.

PARAMETERS

`rectangle` The non-`null` rectangle with which to intersect.

RETURNS A new non-`null` `Rectangle` instance that is the intersection of this rectangle and `rectangle`.

EXAMPLE This example paints two rectangles red and then paints their intersection red.

```
Rectangle r1 = new Rectangle();
Rectangle r2 = new Rectangle();

public void paint(Graphics g) {
   g.fillRect(r1.x, r1.y, r1.width, r1.height);
   g.fillRect(r2.x, r2.y, r2.width, r2.height);
   g.setColor(Color.red);
   Rectangle r = r1.intersection(r2);
   g.fillRect(r.x, r.y, r.width, r.height);
}
```

intersects()

PURPOSE Determines if two rectangles intersect.

SYNTAX `public boolean intersects(Rectangle rectangle)`

DESCRIPTION The intersection of two rectangles is defined to be the set of all points that lie in both rectangles. Two rectangles intersect if the intersection is not empty.

PARAMETERS

`rectangle` The non-`null` rectangle to intersect with this rectangle.

RETURNS `true` if this rectangle intersects `rectangle`; `false` otherwise.

EXAMPLE See the class example.

isEmpty()

PURPOSE Determines if the rectangle is empty.

SYNTAX `public boolean isEmpty()`

DESCRIPTION A rectangle is empty if either its width or height is less than or equal to `0`.

RETURNS `true` if the rectangle is empty; `false` otherwise.

EXAMPLE See the class example.

move()

PURPOSE Moves the rectangle to a new location.

SYNTAX `public void move(int x, int y)`

DESCRIPTION This method modifies the rectangle's northwest corner to be at `x` and `y`.

PARAMETERS

`x` The rectangle's new *x*-coordinate.

`y` The rectangle's new *y*-coordinate.

EXAMPLE This example defines a `mouseDrag()` method that drags around a rectangle.

```
Rectangle rect = new Rectangle();

public boolean mouseDrag(Event evt, int x, int y) {
    rect.move(x, y);
    repaint();
    return true;
}
```

A B C D E F G H I J K L M N O P Q R S T U V W X Y Z

Rectangle()

PURPOSE Constructs a new `Rectangle` instance.

SYNTAX
```
public Rectangle()
public Rectangle(int width, int height)
public Rectangle(int x, int y, int width, int height)
public Rectangle(Point point)
public Rectangle(Dimension dimension)
public Rectangle(Point point, Dimension dimension)
```

DESCRIPTION The six forms of this constructor create a new `Rectangle` instance with the specified bounds. Various ways are available to initialize the rectangle's bounds. If no parameters are specified, `x`, `y`, `width`, and `height` all default to `0`. If only `width` and `height` are specified, `x` and `y` default to `0`. If only a point is specified, the rectangle's northwest corner is at `point`, but `width` and `height` default to `0`. If only a dimension is specified, `x` and `y` default to `0` and `width` and `height` are taken from `dimension`. If both a point and a dimension are specified, the rectangle's northwest corner is at `point`, and `width` and `height` are taken from `dimension`.

PARAMETERS

`dimension`	The non-`null` dimension specifying the new rectangle's size.
`height`	The height of the rectangle.
`point`	The non-`null` point specifying the new rectangle's northwest corner.
`width`	The width of the rectangle.
`x`	The new rectangle's *x*-coordinate.
`y`	The new rectangle's *y*-coordinate.

EXAMPLE This example creates a hundred rectangles and lays them out in a 10-×-10 grid.

```
Rectangle[] rects = new Rectangle[100];

for (int x=0; x<10; x++) {
    for (int y=0; y<10; y++) {
        rects[i] = new Rectangle(x*10, y*10, 10, 10);
    }
}
```

reshape()

PURPOSE Modifies the rectangle's bounds.

SYNTAX
```
public void reshape(int x, int y, int width, int height)
```

DESCRIPTION This method modifies the rectangle's northwest corner to be at `x` and `y` and its size to be `width` and `height`.

PARAMETERS

`height`	The rectangle's new height.
`width`	The rectangle's new width.
`x`	The rectangle's new *x*-coordinate.
`y`	The rectangle's new *y*-coordinate.

EXAMPLE This example defines two mouse handlers that together allow the user to stretch a rectangle. The `mouseDown()` method sets the top-left corner of the rectangle, and the `mouseDrag()` method adjusts the dimensions of the rectangle.

```
Rectangle rect = new Rectangle();
int downX, downY;

public boolean mouseDown(Event evt, int x, int y) {
    downX = x;
    downY = y;
    return true;
}

public boolean mouseDrag(Event evt, int x, int y) {
    rect.reshape(downX, downY, x-downX, y-downY);
    return true;
}
```

resize()

PURPOSE Modifies the rectangle's size.

SYNTAX `public void resize(int width, int height)`

DESCRIPTION This method modifies the rectangle's size to be `width` and `height`.

PARAMETERS

`height`	The rectangle's new height.
`width`	The rectangle's new width.

EXAMPLE This example defines a `mouseDrag()` method that allows you to resize a rectangle.

```
Rectangle rect = new Rectangle();

public boolean mouseDrag(Event evt, int x, int y) {
    rect.resize(x-rect.x, y-rect.y);
    return true;
}
```

toString()

PURPOSE Generates a string representation of the rectangle.

SYNTAX `public String toString()`

DESCRIPTION This method generates this rectangle's string representation, which consists of the rectangle's bounds. This method is typically used for debugging.

RETURNS A non-`null` string representing the rectangle's state.

OVERRIDES `Object.toString()`.

EXAMPLE See `Object.toString()`.

translate()

PURPOSE Moves the rectangle by a relative distance.

SYNTAX `public void translate(int dx, int dy)`

DESCRIPTION This method modifies the rectangle so that its *x*-coordinate is shifted by `dx` and its *y*-coordinate is shifted by `dy`. In particular, the rectangle's new *x*-coordinate is `x+dx` and the rectangle's new *y*-coordinate is `y+dy`.

PARAMETERS

`dx` The amount to shift the rectangle's *x*-coordinate.

`dy` The amount to shift the rectangle's *y*-coordinate.

EXAMPLE This example creates a thread that moves a rectangle toward the southeast, one pixel at a time, every 30 milliseconds.

```
Rectangle rect = new Rectangle(;

public void run() {
    for (int i=0; i<100; i++) {
        rect.translate(1, 1);
        repaint();
        try {
            Thread.sleep(30);
        } catch (Exception e) {
            e.printStackTrace();
        }
    }
}
```

union()

PURPOSE Calculates the union of two rectangles.

SYNTAX `public Rectangle union(Rectangle rectangle)`

DESCRIPTION The union of two rectangles is defined to be the smallest rectangle that includes all points in both rectangles.

PARAMETERS

`rectangle` The non-`null` rectangle with which to perform the union.

RETURNS A new non-`null` rectangle instance that is the union of this rectangle and `rectangle`.

EXAMPLE This example paints two rectangles and then paints a box around them.

```
Rectangle r1 = new Rectangle();
Rectangle r2 = new Rectangle();

public void paint(Graphics g) {
    g.fillRect(r1.x, r1.y, r1.width, r1.height);
    g.fillRect(r2.x, r2.y, r2.width, r2.height);
    g.setColor(Color.red);
    Rectangle r = r1.union(r2);
    g.drawRect(r.x, r.y, r.width, r.height);
}
```

width

PURPOSE This field holds the rectangle's width.

SYNTAX `public int width`

EXAMPLE This example paints a rectangle on the screen.

```
Rectangle rect = new Rectangle();

public void paint(Graphics g) {
    g.fillRect(rect.x, rect.y, rect.width, rect.height);
}
```

x

PURPOSE This field holds the rectangle's *x*-coordinate.

SYNTAX `public int x`

EXAMPLE This example paints a rectangle on the screen.

```
Rectangle rect = new Rectangle();

public void paint(Graphics g) {
   g.fillRect(rect.x, rect.y, rect.width, rect.height);
}
```

y

PURPOSE This field holds the rectangle's *y*-coordinate.

SYNTAX `public int y`

EXAMPLE This example paints a rectangle on the screen.

```
Rectangle rect = new Rectangle();

public void paint(Graphics g) {
   g.fillRect(rect.x, rect.y, rect.width, rect.height);
}
```

RGBImageFilter

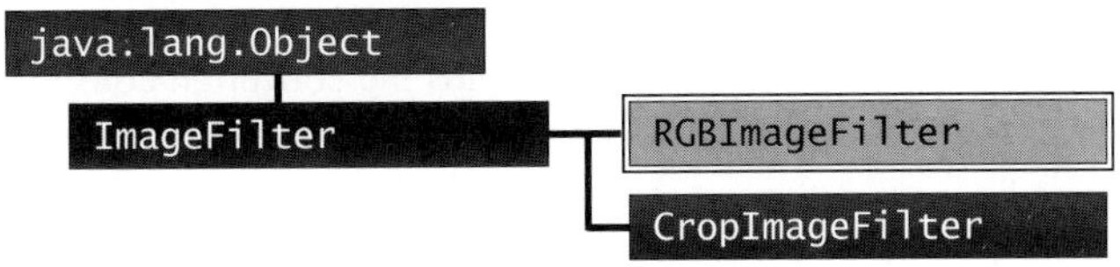

Syntax

```
public abstract class RGBImageFilter extends ImageFilter
```

Description

The `RGBImageFilter` class is used to modify the pixel values in an image. There are two ways to modify the pixel values in an image: either modify the colors in the color table of the image (if the image uses an index color model) or modify each pixel in the image. The former is much more efficient if color changes don't depend on the location of pixels. An example of this is a filter that simply brightens all color. The latter method is necessary if the color changes depend on the location of the pixels. An example of this is a filter that gradually darkens pixels toward one edge of the image.

This class is an abstract class and is meant to be subclassed. Only the `filterRGB()` method needs to be overridden. This method is responsible for converting pixel values. `filterRGB()` receives the coordinates of the pixel so that it can convert the color based on the location of the pixel. By default, all pixels in the image are filtered through `filterRGB()`. It is also possible to just filter the colors in the color table by setting the field `canFilterIndexColorModel` to `true`. When this happens, all the colors in the color table are passed through `filterRGB()` and a new color model is created. This new color model is then used for the pixels that flow through the filter.

MEMBER SUMMARY

Image Consumer Methods

`setColorModel()`	Called by the image producer to deliver the color model of the source image.
`setPixels()`	Called by the image producer to deliver pixels to the image filter.

Continued

MEMBER SUMMARY	
Fields	
`canFilterIndexColorModel`	Indicates whether color filtering is applied to the color table.
`newmodel`	This field holds the converted color model.
`origmodel`	This field holds the color model passed to the `setColorModel()` method.
Color Model Substitution	
`substituteColorModel()`	Replaces the color model of the source image.
Filter Methods	
`filterIndexColorModel()`	Filters the colors in the color table.
`filterRGB()`	Override to filter each pixel value.
`filterRGBPixels()`	Override to filter a batch of pixel values.

Example

This example implements a gradient filter using the `RGBImageFilter` class. See Figure 206. The example displays an image in a canvas, which in turn is embedded in a frame. The image is brightened at the top-left corner and is gradually darkened toward the bottom-right corner. Since the transformation of a pixel value depends on its location, `canFilterIndexColorModel` must be `false`.

FIGURE 206 `RGBImageFilter`

```
import java.awt.*;
import java.awt.image.*;
import java.util.*;
class Main extends Frame {
    Main(String filename) {
        super("RGBFilter Example");
        add("Center", new ImageCanvas(
            getToolkit().getImage(filename)));
        resize(50, 100);
        show();
    }

    static public void main(String[] args) {
        if (args.length == 1) {
            new Main(args[0]);
        } else {
            System.err.println("usage: java Main <image file>");
        }
    }
```

```
}

class ImageCanvas extends Canvas {
    Image gradientImage;

    ImageCanvas(Image image) {
        GradientFilter imgf = new GradientFilter();
        ImageProducer ip = image.getSource();
        ip = new FilteredImageSource(ip, imgf);
        gradientImage = getToolkit().createImage(ip);
        repaint();
    }

    public void paint(Graphics g) {
        g.drawImage(gradientImage, 0, 0, this);
    }
}

class GradientFilter extends RGBImageFilter {
    float[] hsb = new float[3];
    int width, height;

    public void setDimensions(int w, int h) {
        super.setDimensions(w, h);
        width = w;
        height = h;
    }

    public int filterRGB(int x, int y, int rgb) {
        Color c = new Color(rgb);
        Color.RGBtoHSB(c.getRed(), c.getGreen(), c.getBlue(), hsb);
        hsb[2] += .5f - (float)x / width;
        hsb[2] += .5f - (float)y / height;
        hsb[2] = Math.max(0.0f, Math.min(1.0f, hsb[2]));
        return Color.HSBtoRGB(hsb[0], hsb[1], hsb[2]);
    }
}
```

canFilterIndexColorModel

PURPOSE Indicates whether color filtering is applied to the color table.

SYNTAX `protected boolean canFilterIndexColorModel`

DESCRIPTION The subclass of this filter should set this `boolean` value to indicate whether to color filter just the color table or every pixel. If `canFilterIndexColorModel` is set to `true` and if the image's color model is indeed an index color model, then all the colors in the color model are transformed using the `filterRGB()` method and the pixel values flowing through the filter are not modified.

If the color filtering does not depend on the position of the pixel values in the image, then for the most efficient implementation, this field should be set to `true`.

SEE ALSO `filterRGB()`, `IndexColorModel`, `substituteColorModel()`.

EXAMPLE This example implements a brightness filter. An image is painted in a canvas, which is in turn embedded in a frame. See Figure 207. The image is passed through a brightness filter, which brightens or darkens all entries in the image's color map. Typing a '+' brightens the image by 10%, and typing a '-' darkens the image by 10%.

FIGURE 207
`canFilterIndexColorModel`

```
import java.awt.*;
import java.awt.image.*;
import java.util.*;
class Main extends Frame {
    Main(String filename) {
        super("canFilterIndexColorModel Example");
        add("Center", new ImageCanvas(
            getToolkit().getImage(filename)));
        resize(50, 100);
        show();
    }

    static public void main(String[] args) {
        if (args.length == 1) {
            new Main(args[0]);
        } else {
            System.err.println("usage: java Main <image file>");
        }
    }
}

class ImageCanvas extends Canvas {
    Image brightImage;
    Image image;
    BrightnessFilter imgf = new BrightnessFilter();

    ImageCanvas(Image image) {
        this.image = image;
        processImage();
    }

    public void paint(Graphics g) {
        g.drawImage(brightImage, 0, 0, this);
    }

    void processImage() {
```

```
        ImageProducer ip = image.getSource();

        ip = new FilteredImageSource(ip, imgf);
        brightImage = getToolkit().createImage(ip);
        repaint();
    }

    public boolean keyUp(Event evt, int key) {
        if (key == '+') {
            imgf.addBrightness(.1f);
        } else if (key == '-') {
            imgf.addBrightness(-.1f);
        }
        processImage();
        return true;
    }
}

class BrightnessFilter extends RGBImageFilter {
    float bDelta;
    float[] hsb = new float[3];
    int width, height;

    BrightnessFilter() {
        canFilterIndexColorModel = true;
    }

    public void setDimensions(int w, int h) {
        super.setDimensions(w, h);
        width = w;
        height = h;
    }

    public void addBrightness(float f) {
        bDelta += f;
    }

    public int filterRGB(int x, int y, int rgb) {
        // x and y are both -1
        Color c = new Color(rgb);
        Color.RGBtoHSB(c.getRed(), c.getGreen(), c.getBlue(), hsb);
        hsb[2] = Math.max(0.0f, Math.min(1.0f, hsb[2] + bDelta));
        return Color.HSBtoRGB(hsb[0], hsb[1], hsb[2]);
    }
}
```

filterIndexColorModel()

PURPOSE Filters the colors in the color table.

filterIndexColorModel()

SYNTAX `public IndexColorModel filterIndexColorModel(IndexColorModel icm)`

DESCRIPTION This method filters an index color model instance by running each entry in its color tables through the `filterRGB()` function that `RGBImageFilter` subclasses must implement. This method uses coordinates of -1 to indicate that a color table entry, rather than a pixel value taken from the image, is being filtered.

PARAMETERS

`icm` The index color model instance to be filtered.

RETURNS A new index color model representing the filtered colors.

EXAMPLE This example implements a filter that allows you to specify a color in the color table and highlight those pixels in an image that uses that color. The example changes the highlighted pixels to red. See Figure 208.

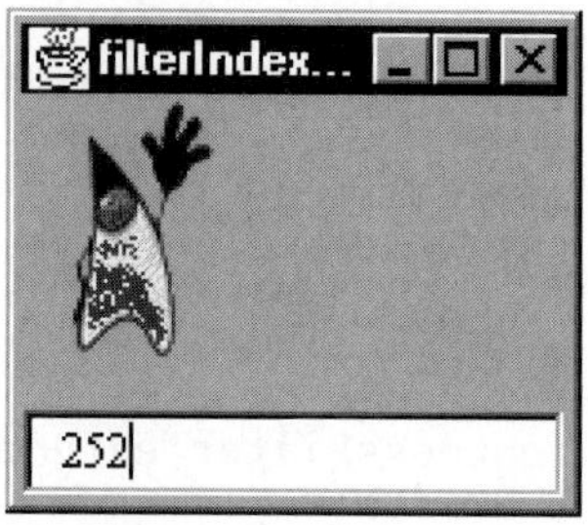

FIGURE 208
`RGBImageFilter.filterIndexColorModel()`

The frame contains a canvas, which displays the image. At the bottom of the frame is a text field in which you can type an index of a color in the color table.

```
import java.awt.*;
import java.awt.image.*;
import java.net.*;
import java.util.*;
class Main extends Frame {
    ImageCanvas icv;
    TextField textField = new TextField();

    Main(String filename) {
        super("filterIndexColorModel Example");
        try {
            add("Center", icv =
                new ImageCanvas(getToolkit().getImage(filename)));
            add("South", textField);
        } catch (Exception e) {
            e.printStackTrace();
        }
        resize(50, 100);
        show();
    }

    public boolean action(Event evt, Object arg) {
        if (evt.target == textField) {
            icv.seeColor(Integer.parseInt(textField.getText()));
            return true;
```

```
        }
        return false;
    }

    static public void main(String[] args) {
        if (args.length == 1) {
            new Main(args[0]);
        } else {
            System.err.println("usage: java Main <image file>");
        }
    }
}

class ImageCanvas extends Canvas {
    Image seeColorImage;
    Image image;
    SeeColorFilter imgf = new SeeColorFilter();

    ImageCanvas(Image image) {
        this.image = image;
        processImage();
    }

    void seeColor(int colorIndex) {
        imgf.seeColor(colorIndex);
        processImage();
    }

    public void paint(Graphics g) {
        g.drawImage(seeColorImage, 0, 0, this);
    }

    void processImage() {
        ImageProducer ip = image.getSource();

        ip = new FilteredImageSource(ip, imgf);
        seeColorImage = getToolkit().createImage(ip);
        repaint();
    }
}

class SeeColorFilter extends RGBImageFilter {
    int colorIndex = -1;

    SeeColorFilter() {
        canFilterIndexColorModel = true;
    }

    void seeColor(int colorIndex) {
        this.colorIndex = colorIndex;
    }

    public IndexColorModel filterIndexColorModel(IndexColorModel
         icm){
```

```
            int mapsize = icm.getMapSize();
            byte r[] = new byte[mapsize];
            byte g[] = new byte[mapsize];
            byte b[] = new byte[mapsize];

            icm.getReds(r);
            icm.getGreens(g);
            icm.getBlues(b);
            if (colorIndex >= 0) {
                r[colorIndex] = (byte)255;
                g[colorIndex] = 0;
                b[colorIndex] = 0;
            }
            return new IndexColorModel(icm.getPixelSize(), mapsize,
                                       r, g, b, icm.getTransparentPixel());
        }

        public int filterRGB(int x, int y, int rgb) {
            return rgb;
        }
    }
```

filterRGB()

PURPOSE Override to filter each pixel value.

SYNTAX `public abstract int filterRGB(int x, int y, int rgb)`

DESCRIPTION The `rgb` parameter is a pixel value encoded in the default color model (see `ColorModel.getRGBdefault ()`). `x` and `y` are the coordinates of the pixel value in the image.

Subclasses must specify a method to convert a single input pixel in the default RGB `ColorModel` to a single output pixel.

PARAMETERS

`rgb` The pixel value encoded in the default color model.

`x` The *x*-coordinate of the pixel value's location in the image; `-1` if the color table is being filtered.

`y` The *y*-coordinate of the pixel value's location in the image; `-1` if the color table is being filtered.

SEE ALSO `ColorModel.getRGBdefault()`, `filterRGBPixels()`.

EXAMPLE See the class example.

filterRGBPixels()

PURPOSE Override to filter a batch of pixel values.

SYNTAX

```
public void filterRGBPixels(int x, int y, int w, int h, int[]
    pixels, int offset, int scansize)
```

DESCRIPTION The pixel values in `pixels` are encoded in the default color model (see `ColorModel.getRGBdefault`). All pixels flowing through this filter pass through this method. By default, this method simply takes each pixel value in the `pixels` array and calls the `filterRGB()` method. It then stores the result back into the same location in the `pixels` array.

This method can be overridden to avoid calling `filterRGB()` for each pixel, thereby making for a more efficient implementation.

PARAMETERS

`h`	The height of the rectangle in which the pixels are destined.
`model`	The non-`null` color model used to translate the pixel values.
`offset`	The index of the first pixel in the pixel array `pixels`.
`pixels`	The non-`null` array of pixel values encoded in the default color model.
`scansize`	The width to use when extracting pixels from the pixel array `pixels`.
`w`	The width of the rectangle in which the pixels are destined.
`x`	The *x*-coordinate of the rectangle in which the pixels are destined.
`y`	The *y*-coordinate of the rectangle in which the pixels are destined.

SEE ALSO `ColorModel.getRGBdefault()`, `filterRGB()`.

EXAMPLE This example is identical to the class example, except that the `filterRGBPixels()` method, instead of the `filterRGB()` method, is overridden. Note that the `filterRGB()` method is defined even though it is not used; this is done to make the class nonabstract. See Figure 209.

FIGURE 209
`RGBImageFilter.filterRGBPixels()`

```
import java.awt.*;
import java.awt.image.*;
import java.net.*;
import java.util.*;
class Main extends Frame {
    Main(String filename) {
        super("filterRGBPixels Example");
        try {
            add("Center",
                new ImageCanvas(getToolkit().getImage(filename)));
        } catch (Exception e) {
            e.printStackTrace();
        }
        resize(50, 100);
        show();
    }
```

A B C D E F G H I J K L M N O P Q R S T U V W X Y Z

```
    static public void main(String[] args) {
        if (args.length == 1) {
            new Main(args[0]);
        } else {
            System.err.println("usage: java Main <image file>");
        }
    }
}

class ImageCanvas extends Canvas {
    Image gradientImage;

    ImageCanvas(Image image) {
        GradientFilter imgf = new GradientFilter();
        ImageProducer ip = image.getSource();
        ip = new FilteredImageSource(ip, imgf);
        gradientImage = getToolkit().createImage(ip);
        repaint();
    }

    public void paint(Graphics g) {
        g.drawImage(gradientImage, 0, 0, this);
    }
}

class GradientFilter extends RGBImageFilter {
    float[] hsb = new float[3];
    int width, height;

    public void setDimensions(int w, int h) {
        super.setDimensions(w, h);
        width = w;
        height = h;
    }

    public void filterRGBPixels(int x, int y, int w, int h,
                                int pixels[], int offset, int scansize) {
        int i = offset;
        for (int cy = 0; cy < h; cy++) {
            for (int cx = 0; cx < w; cx++) {
                Color c = new Color(pixels[i]);

                Color.RGBtoHSB(c.getRed(), c.getGreen(), c.getBlue(),
                        hsb);
                hsb[2] += .5f - (float)x / width;
                hsb[2] += .5f - (float)y / height;
                hsb[2] = Math.max(0.0f, Math.min(1.0f, hsb[2]));
                pixels[i] = Color.HSBtoRGB(hsb[0], hsb[1], hsb[2]);
                i++;
            }
            i += scansize - w;
```

```
        }
        consumer.setPixels(x, y, w, h, ColorModel.getRGBdefault(),
                               pixels, offset, scansize);
    }

    // Never called.
    public int filterRGB(int x, int y, int rgb) {
        return 0;
    }
}
```

newmodel

PURPOSE This field holds the converted color model.

SYNTAX `protected ColorModel newmodel`

DESCRIPTION If `canFilterIndexColorModel` is `true` and the color model of the source image is an index color model, this field holds the converted color model.

SEE ALSO `origmodel`.

origmodel

PURPOSE This field holds the color model passed to the `setColorModel()` method.

SYNTAX `protected ColorModel origmodel`

DESCRIPTION If `canFilterIndexColorModel` is `true` and the color model of the source image is an index color model, this field holds the original color model. If this field is not `null`, then the `setPixels()` method checks whether the color model it gets is the same as `origmodel`. If the field is `null`, then `newmodel` is substituted and the pixels are not modified.

SEE ALSO `newmodel`.

setColorModel()

PURPOSE Called by the image producer to deliver the color model of the source image.

SYNTAX `public void setColorModel(ColorModel model)`

DESCRIPTION This method is called by the image producer to deliver the color model of the source image to the image filter. Therefore it must not be called directly. Instead, it can be overridden if necessary to introduce behavior different from the default implementation. The default implementation checks the `canFilterIndexColorModel` field to see if it should set a new color model by calling `filterIndexColorModel()`. If `canFilterIndexColorModel` is `true` and `model` is an index color model, a new color model is created and enabled by calling `substituteColorModel()`. Otherwise the image filter passes the default color model to the image consumer.

PARAMETERS

`model` The non-`null` color model of the source image.

OVERRIDES `ImageFilter.setColorModel()`.

SEE ALSO `canFilterIndexColorModel`, `ColorModel.getRGBdefault()`, `filterIndexColorModel()`, `substituteColorModel()`.

EXAMPLE See `ImageConsumer.setColorModel()`.

setPixels()

PURPOSE Called by the image producer to deliver pixels to the image filter.

SYNTAX

```
public void setPixels(int x, int y, int w, int h, ColorModel model,
   byte[] pixels, int offset, int scansize)
public void setPixels(int x, int y, int w, int h, ColorModel model,
   int[] pixels, int offset, int scansize)
```

DESCRIPTION This method is called by the image producer to deliver pixels to the image filter. Therefore it must not be called directly. Instead, it can be overridden if necessary to introduce behavior different from the default `RGBImageFilter` implementation. The default implementation creates a temporary buffer, translates the pixel values in `pixels` to the default color model, saves the pixels in the temporary buffer, and then calls `filterRGBPixels()` with the temporary buffer of pixel values.

PARAMETERS

`h` The height of the rectangle in which the pixels are destined.
`model` The non-`null` color model used to translate the pixel values.
`offset` The index of the first pixel in the pixel array `pixels`.
`pixels` The non-`null` array of pixel values.

`scansize`	The width to use when extracting pixels from the pixel array `pixels`.
`w`	The width of the rectangle in which the pixels are destined.
`x`	The *x*-coordinate of the rectangle in which the pixels are destined.
`y`	The *y*-coordinate of the rectangle in which the pixels are destined.

OVERRIDES `ImageFilter.setPixels()`.

SEE ALSO `ColorModel.getRGBdefault()`, `filterRGBPixels()`, `ImageConsumer.setPixels()`.

EXAMPLE See `ImageConsumer.setPixels()`.

substituteColorModel()

PURPOSE Replaces the color model of the source image.

SYNTAX

```
public void substituteColorModel(ColorModel oldcm, ColorModel
    newcm)
```

DESCRIPTION As pixels flow through this filter via the `setPixels()` method, a check is made to see if the pixels have been encoded with the `oldcm` color model. If so, the pixels are not converted. They are simply forwarded to the image consumer with `newcm` as the color model.

PARAMETERS

`newcm`	The non-`null` color model to replace `oldcm` on the fly.
`oldcm`	The color model to be replaced by `newcm`. May be `null`.

SEE ALSO `setPixels()`.

java.lang

Runnable

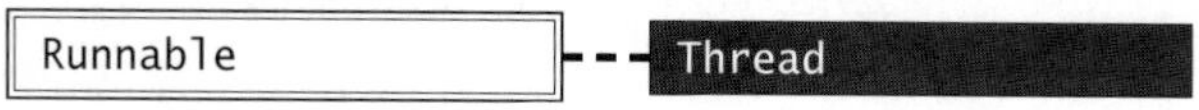

Syntax

`public interface Runnable`

Description

When defining a new thread, you typically define a class that subclasses `Thread`. When you create an instance of that class, a new thread is created. When you start that thread, it runs the code in the class's `run()` method. For example, the following code defines a class that prints a message every second:

```
// class that prints out "Lights On!" every second
class ThreadTest extends Thread {
    public void run() {
        while (true) {
            System.out.println("Lights On!");
            try {
                sleep(1000);
            } catch (InterruptedException e) {
                // ignore
            }
        }
    }
}
 ...
// create ThreadTest thread
ThreadTest tt = new ThreadTest();
tt.start();          // start thread
```

However, in some cases, you cannot or do not want a class to subclass `Thread`. Java is a language that supports single inheritance. Perhaps you want a class to inherit from something that is functionally similar to the class that you are defining. In that case, you declare the class to implement the `Runnable` interface and provide an implementation for the single `run()` method of the `Runnable` interface.

A class that implements `Runnable` provides a definition for `run()`, which contains the code that a thread will execute. To have a thread execute this code, you first create an instance of that class and then pass this instance as an argument to one of the `Thread` constructors. The `run()` method defined by this class will then be executed when the thread starts running. The following code is functionally equivalent to the `ThreadTest` example above, except it is implemented by declaring a class that is *not* a subclass of `Thread`. Instead, it implements the `Runnable` interface directly.

```
// class that prints out "Lights On!" every second
class RunTest implements Runnable {
    public void run() {
        while (true) {
            System.out.println("Lights On!");
            try {
                Thread.sleep(1000);
            } catch (InterruptedException e) {
                // ignore
            }
        }
    }
}
 ...
// create thread with 'RunTest' object
Thread tr = new Thread(new RunTest(), "runtest");
tr.start();          // start thread
```

MEMBER SUMMARY	
Abstract Method	
`run()`	Defines the code to be run.

See Also

`Thread`.

run()

PURPOSE Defines the code to be run.

SYNTAX `public abstract void run()`

DESCRIPTION This method is executed when a `Runnable` object is executed by a thread. A class that implements `Runnable` or a class that is a subclass of `Thread` must provide an implementation for `run()`.

SEE ALSO `Thread`, `Thread.run()`.

EXAMPLE See the class example.

java.lang

Runtime

Object — Runtime

Syntax

```
public class Runtime
```

Description

This class defines methods in the `Runtime` library. It contains methods that perform environment-related and system-related functions, such as loading libraries, executing system programs, turning on tracing, and performing garbage-collection. This class cannot be instantiated. You get a reference to an instance of `Runtime` by calling `getRuntime()`, as follows:

```
Runtime rt = Runtime.getRuntime();
```

You can then invoke methods on this `Runtime` object, as follows:

```
// display amount of free and total memory
System.out.println("free " + rt.freeMemory() +
                   " total " + rt.totalMemory());
```

MEMBER SUMMARY

Memory Management Methods	
`freeMemory()`	Retrieves the number of free bytes in the Java system memory.
`gc()`	Runs the garbage collector.
`runFinalization()`	Runs the finalization method of objects that are pending finalization.
`totalMemory()`	Retrieves the total number of bytes in the Java system memory.
Methods for Debugging	
`traceInstructions()`	Enables/disables the tracing of instructions.
`traceMethodCalls()`	Enables/disables the tracing of method calls.
General Methods	
`exec()`	Executes a system program.
`exit()`	Exits the virtual machine.

MEMBER SUMMARY

`getLocalizedInputStream()`	Creates a localized input stream.
`getLocalizedOutputStream()`	Creates a localized output stream.
`getRuntime()`	Retrieves the reference to the `Runtime` object.
`load()`	Loads a dynamic library when given its full pathname.
`loadLibrary()`	Loads a dynamic library when given its library name.

exec()

PURPOSE Executes a system program.

SYNTAX

```
public Process exec(String prog) throws IOException
public Process exec(String prog, String[] envp) throws IOException
public Process exec(String[] progarray) throws IOException
public Process exec(String[] progarray, String[] envp) throws
    IOException
```

DESCRIPTION The four forms of this method execute the system program specified by `prog` or `progarray[0]`. The absolute pathname of the program must be used when specifying the `prog` or `progarray[0]`. Path variables (such as $PATH) that specify the search path when executing system programs in the native environment are not consulted. `exec()` returns a `Process` object, which has methods for obtaining the standard input, standard output, and standard error of the newly created process.

These methods can be executed only if permitted by the security manager.

PARAMETERS

`progarray` `progarray[0]` contains the pathname of the system program to be executed; arguments to the program are supplied in the rest of `progarray`.

`prog` The pathname of the system program to execute.

`envp` Environment variable settings to use when executing the system program. Each string in this array has the format *variable_name=value*.

RETURNS A (non-`null`) `Process` object representing the process created for the execution of the system program.

EXCEPTIONS

`IOException` `program` or `progarray[0]` does not name a valid system program.

SEE ALSO `Process`, `SecurityManager.checkExec()`.

exit()

EXAMPLE

```
try {
    // set up command, arguments, and environment variables
    String[] progarray = new String[2];
    String[] envp = new String[1];
    String prog = "/bin/ls";
    progarray[0] = prog;
    progarray[1] = "/";
    envp[0] = "TERM=vt100";

    Process p1 = rt.exec(prog);                  // '/bin/ls'
    Process p2 = rt.exec(prog, envp);            // '(TERM=vt100; ls)'
    Process p3 = rt.exec(progarray);             // '/bin/ls /'
    Process p4 = rt.exec(progarray, envp);       // '(TERM=vt100; ls /)'
  ...
} catch (IOException e) {
    System.err.println("exec error:" + e);
}
```

exit()

PURPOSE Exits the virtual machine.

SYNTAX `public void exit(int status)`

DESCRIPTION This method causes the virtual machine to terminate with exit code `status`. All running threads are terminated. All resources associated with the process, such as threads and file descriptors, are released. This method does not return.

This method can be executed only if permitted by the security manager.

PARAMETERS

`status` The exit status. A value of `0` indicates success; all other values indicate failure.

SEE ALSO `SecurityManager.checkExit()`.

EXAMPLE

```
Runtime rt = Runtime.getRuntime();
  ...
rt.exit(0); // exit with status code 0
```

freeMemory()

PURPOSE Retrieves the number of free bytes in the Java system memory.

SYNTAX `public native long freeMemory()`

DESCRIPTION This method returns an estimate of the free memory available in the Java run-time system. Additional free memory might be obtained by calling `runFinalization()` or `gc()`, depending on whether there are any objects that need to be finalized or garbage-collected.

RETURNS The number of free bytes in system memory.

SEE ALSO `gc()`, `Object.finalize()`, `runFinalization()`, `totalMemory()`.

EXAMPLE

```
// display amount of free and total memory
System.out.println("free " + rt.freeMemory() +
                   " total " + rt.totalMemory());
```

gc()

PURPOSE Runs the garbage collector.

SYNTAX `public native void gc()`

DESCRIPTION The system's garbage collector is run asynchronously by the garbage collector thread to free memory tied up in objects no longer referenced. Those objects determined by the system to be no longer referenced are garbage-collected. The particular algorithm used to make this determination is implementation-dependent. However, all `gc()` implementations ensure that circular references are freed. For example, if two objects reference each other but they themselves are not referenced by any other object in the system, both objects will be garbage-collected. After determining the objects to be garbage-collected, the garbage-collector uses a finalization thread to execute the `finalize()` methods defined for each object to be collected before reclaiming the memory occupied by the objects.

The garbage collector is run automatically (and asynchronously) by the run-time system. However, you can give an indication to the system that you want the garbage collector to run by invoking the `gc()` method. Doing this, however, does not guarantee that the garbage collector will run immediately; a call to `gc()` acts only as a hint to the system.

SEE ALSO `Object.finalize()`, `runFinalization()`.

EXAMPLE

```
Runtime rt = Runtime.getRuntime();
 ...
rt.gc();         // indicate that Garbage Collector should run
```

getLocalizedInputStream()

PURPOSE Creates a localized input stream.

SYNTAX `public InputStream getLocalizedInputStream(InputStream in)`

DESCRIPTION This method creates a *localized* input stream using the given input stream `in`. A localized input stream will automatically translate the input from the format of the current locale into Unicode. This means the input source can be in a locale-specific format, but readers of the localized stream can always expect the data to be Unicode.

PARAMETERS

`in` The input stream for which to create the localized stream.

RETURNS A localized input stream that emits Unicode characters.

SEE ALSO `getLocalizedOutputStream()`, `InputStream`.

REMARKS In JDK1.0.2, this method does not do any localization; it just returns `in`.

EXAMPLE

```
// Turn standard input into localized input
InputStream in = rt.getLocalizedInputStream(System.in);
try {
    int c;
    while ((c = in.read()) != -1) {
        char ch = (char)c;
    ...
    }
    in.close();
} catch (IOException e) {
    System.err.println(e);
}
```

getLocalizedOutputStream()

PURPOSE Creates a localized output stream.

SYNTAX `public OutputStream getLocalizedOutputStream(OutputStream out)`

DESCRIPTION This method creates a localized output stream using the given output stream `out`. A localized output stream will automatically translate the output from Unicode into the format of the current locale. This means that the program sending output to the localized output stream can send the data in Unicode, but the eventual output of the stream will be in a format specific to the current locale.

PARAMETERS

out — The output stream for which to create a localized stream.

RETURNS — A localized output stream.

SEE ALSO — getLocalizedInputStream(), OutputStream.

REMARKS — In JDK1.0.2, this method does not do any localization; it just returns out.

EXAMPLE

```
// Turn standard output into localized output
OutputStream out = rt.getLocalizedOutputStream(System.out);
try {
    String str = "Hello World\n";
    byte[] buf = new byte[str.length()];
    str.getBytes(0, buf.length, buf, 0);
    for (int i = 0; i < buf.length; i++) {
        out.write((char)buf[i]);
    }
} catch (IOException e) {
    System.err.println(e);
}
```

getRuntime()

PURPOSE — Retrieves a reference to the Runtime object.

SYNTAX — public static Runtime getRuntime()

DESCRIPTION — A reference to the Runtime object is required to invoke the runtime library methods. This method returns the reference to Runtime object.

RETURNS — A reference to the Runtime object.

SEE ALSO — System.getRuntime().

EXAMPLE

```
Runtime rt = Runtime.getRuntime();
```

load()

PURPOSE — Loads a dynamic library when given its full pathname.

SYNTAX — public synchronized void load(String pathname)

DESCRIPTION This method loads in the dynamic library named by `pathname`. The syntax of `pathname` is platform-dependent. Loading a library makes the symbols and functions exported by that library available to the program. You can call `load()` on a library as many times as you want, but only the first call does anything.

If you use `load()` from `java_g`, it will automatically insert "_g" before the "`.so`". For example, if `pathname` is `/usr/lib/libc.so`, `java_g` will look for `/usr/lib/libc_g.so`; `/usr/lib/libc.so` will not be consulted.

A library can be loaded only if permitted by the security manager.

PARAMETERS

`pathname` The pathname of the library.

EXCEPTIONS

`UnsatisfiedLinkError`

If `pathname` does not name a library or the library could not be linked successfully (for example because of unresolved references).

SEE ALSO `loadLibrary()`, `SecurityManager.checkLink()`.

EXAMPLE

```
rt.load("/usr/lib/libc.so");          // load library as named by
                                      // pathname
```

loadLibrary()

PURPOSE Loads a dynamic library when given its library name.

SYNTAX `public synchronized void loadLibrary(String libname)`

DESCRIPTION This method loads in the dynamic library, `libname`, that it finds in the directory or directories specified by the platform-dependent library search path. On Solaris and Windows95, the library search path is specified by the environment variable `LD_LIBRARY_PATH`.

Loading a library makes the symbols and functions exported by that library available to the program. You can call `loadLibrary()` on a library as many times as you want, but only the first call does anything.

If you use `loadLibrary()` from `java_g`, it will automatically add "_g" to the library name. In other words, "_g" is inserted before the "`.so`" or "`.dll`". For example, if `libname` is `libc.so`, `java_g` will look for `libc_g.so`; `libc.so` will not be consulted.

A library can be loaded only if permitted by the security manager.

PARAMETERS

`libname` The name of the library.

EXCEPTIONS

`UnsatisfiedLinkError`
If the library does not exist or the library could not be linked successfully (for example, as a result of unresolved references).

SEE ALSO `load()`, `SecurityManager.checkLink()`.

EXAMPLE

```
rt.loadLibrary("net");        // use library search path to find
library
```

runFinalization()

PURPOSE Runs the finalization method of any objects that are pending finalization.

SYNTAX `public native void runFinalization()`

DESCRIPTION Each object has a `finalize()` method that must be run before the object can be garbage-collected. The `Object` class declares a default `finalize()` method, but subclasses override this method when special clean-ups must be done to release resources held by objects in those classes. For example, a `finalize()` method is typically defined to free system resources used by an object.

The garbage collector uses an asynchronous finalization thread to run the `finalize()` methods of objects that are to be garbage-collected. You can force the `finalize()` method of these objects to be executed by calling the `runFinalization()` method.

SEE ALSO `gc()`, `Object.finalize()`.

EXAMPLE

```
rt.runFinalization();        // run finalize() methods
```

totalMemory()

PURPOSE Retrieves the total number of bytes in the Java system memory.

SYNTAX `public native long totalMemory()`

RETURNS The number of bytes of total memory available in the Java system.

SEE ALSO `freeMemory()`.

EXAMPLE See `freeMemory()`.

traceInstructions()

PURPOSE Enables/disables the tracing of instructions.

SYNTAX `public native void traceInstructions(boolean on)`

DESCRIPTION This method turns the tracing of byte code instructions on and off. When tracing is set to *on*, each byte code instruction that is executed, as well as all entries and exits from method calls, is displayed to standard error output. A voluminous amount of output is generated when tracing is set to *on*. For a less-detailed trace of your program, use `traceMethodCalls()`.

`traceInstructions()` can be used for debugging your Java program when using `java_g`; it does not do anything when using the normal `java` interpreter.

PARAMETERS

`on` If `true`, turns tracing on; otherwise turns tracing off.

SEE ALSO `traceMethodCalls()`.

EXAMPLE

```
// trace all instructions executed for creating Date instance
rt.traceInstructions(true);        // trace on
Date d = new Date();
rt.traceInstructions(false);       // trace off
```

traceMethodCalls()

PURPOSE Enables/disables the tracing of method calls.

SYNTAX `public native void traceMethodCalls(boolean on)`

DESCRIPTION This method turns the tracing of method calls on and off. When tracing is set to *on*, output is displayed to standard error output each time a method is entered or exited, showing the name of the method involved. For more-detailed information about the execution of your program, use `traceInstructions()`.

traceMethodCalls() can be used for debugging your Java program when using java_g; it does not do anything when using the normal java interpreter.

PARAMETERS

on — if true, turns tracing on; otherwise turns tracing off.

SEE ALSO — traceInstructions().

EXAMPLE

```
// trace all methods executed for creating Date instance
rt.traceMethodCalls(true);          // trace on
Date d = new Date();
rt.traceMethodCalls(false);         // trace off
```

java.lang

RuntimeException

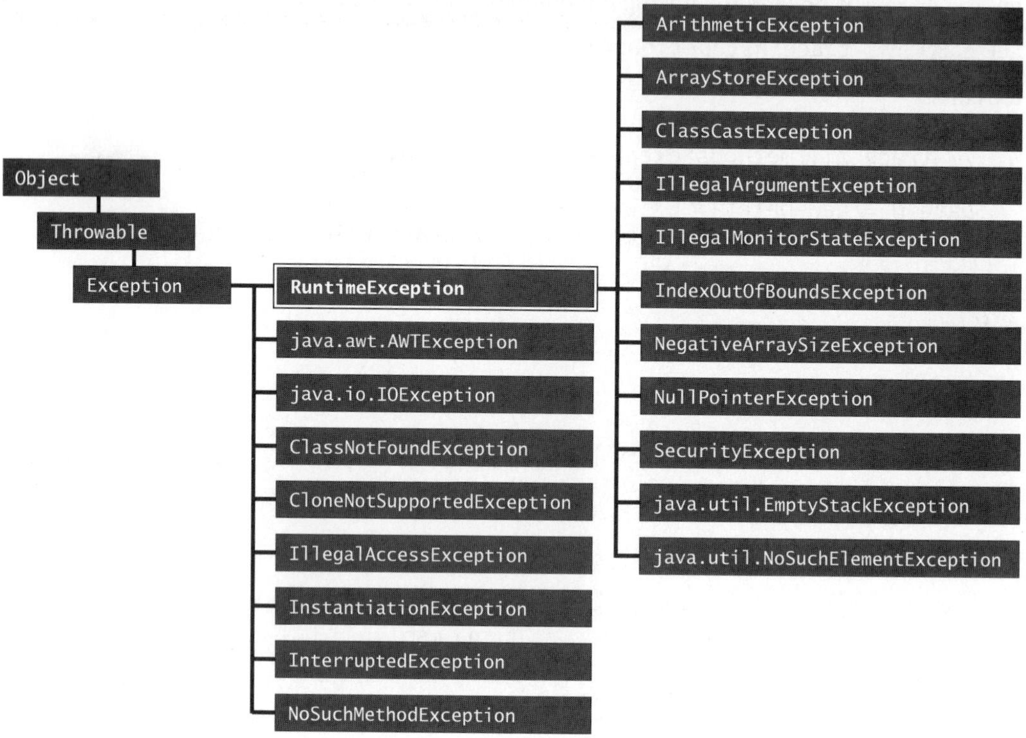

Syntax

```
public class RuntimeException extends Exception
```

Description

`RuntimeException` and its subclasses are exceptions thrown by the Java runtime. They indicate unrecoverable conditions indicative of programming errors. Consequently, they should not be declared in the `throws` clause of a method. Nor should they be caught using `try/catch` statements. These exceptions should be allowed to percolate to the top level of the user's program, where they will be dealt with by the Java runtime system. The Java runtime system displays to the user executing the faulty program a stack trace of where the `RuntimeException` occurred. User programs should not subclass `RuntimeException` or its subclasses; these are reserved for the Java runtime system.

MEMBER SUMMARY

Constructor	
`RuntimeException()`	Constructs a `RuntimeException` instance.

See Also

`ArithmeticException`, `ArrayStoreException`, `ClassCastException`, `Exception`, `IllegalArgumentException`, `IndexOutOfBoundsException`, `NegativeArraySizeException`, `NullPointerException`, `SecurityException`.

Example

See examples of subclasses.

RuntimeException()

PURPOSE Constructs a `RuntimeException` instance.

SYNTAX

```
public RuntimeException()
public RuntimeException(String msg)
```

DESCRIPTION The two forms of this constructor create a new instance of `RuntimeException`. An optional string `msg` can be supplied that describes this particular instance of the exception.

PARAMETERS

`msg` A string that gives details about this exception.

java.awt

Scrollbar

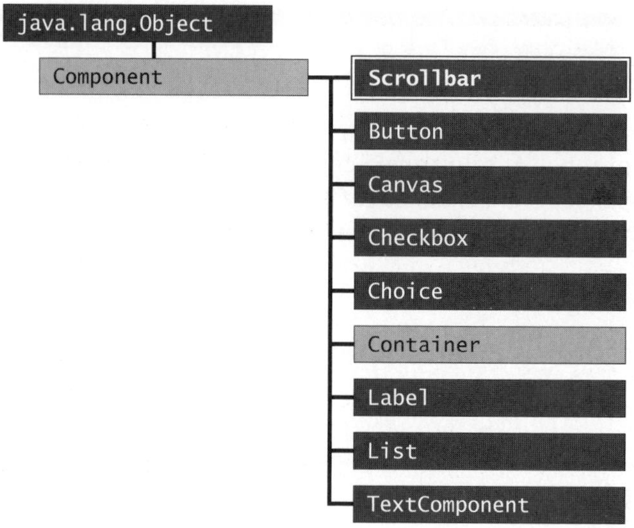

Syntax

```
public class Scrollbar extends Component
```

Description

The `Scrollbar` component is used to specify a particular integer value in a range of values. A scrollbar has an orientation that can be either vertical or horizontal. The orientation is specified as the scrollbar is created and cannot be changed. Figure 210 shows a horizontal scrollbar with labels on all its parts.

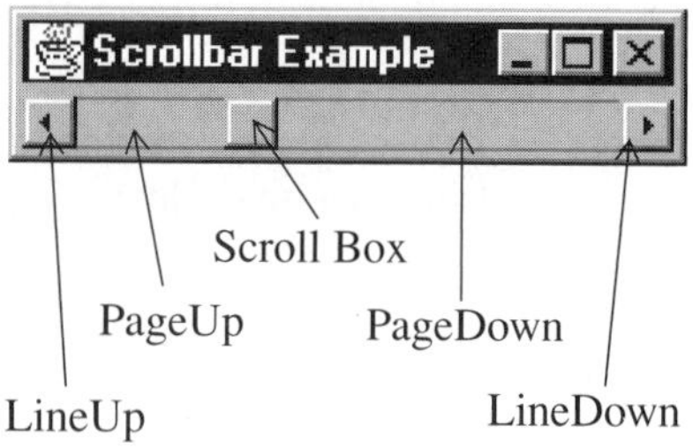

FIGURE 210 Parts of a Horizontal Scrollbar

The Scrollbar Range and Value

A scrollbar has a scrollbar range, which is defined by two integer values: the *minimum* and the *maximum*. The range can be any integer value, positive or negative. However, the maximum value must be greater than or equal to the minimum value. The range can be modified at any time.

The scrollbar maintains a scrollbar value, which controls the location of the scrollbar's scroll box. The scrollbar value must be within the scrollbar range. The actual location of the

A B C D E F G H I J K L M N O P Q R S T U V W X Y Z

scroll box within the scrollbar matches the relative position of the scrollbar value within the scrollbar range. The scrollbar value can be changed at any time, and the scroll box will move accordingly. When the user moves the scroll box, the scrollbar value is automatically updated and an event is generated.

The Scrollbar Visible Size

If the scrollbar is used to pan around a large image, it is useful to have an indication of what fraction of the entire image is visible. The size of the scroll box in relation to the size of the entire scrollbar is typically used to indicate the size of the visible area in proportion to the entire image. For example, if the scroll box is about half the size of the scrollbar, then about half of the image is visible. The scrollbar's "visible size" property controls the size of the scroll box (note that not all platforms support variable-sized scroll boxes).

The Scrollbar Increments

The scrollbar line and page increments control how much the line up/line down and page up/ page down buttons update the scrollbar value when pressed. If applying the increment modifies the scrollbar value outside the scrollbar range, the scrollbar value is adjusted to either the maximum or minimum value. The scrollbar line and page increments can be changed at any time.

Events

Table 14 shows the events that the scrollbar can generate when some part of the scrollbar is pressed.

TABLE 14 `ScrollBar` Events

`Event.SCROLL_LINE_UP`	When the line up button is pressed.
`Event.SCROLL_LINE_DOWN`	When the line down button is pressed
`Event.SCROLL_PAGE_UP`	When the page up button is pressed.
`Event.SCROLL_PAGE_DOWN`	When the page down button is pressed.
`Event.SCROLL_ABSOLUTE`	When the scroll box is dragged.

Except for the `SCROLL_ABSOLUTE` event, the scrollbar does not generate an event if the scrollbar value does not change. So if the scroll box is at the bottom of the scrollbar, pressing the line down/page down buttons does not generate an event.

See the `Event` class for details on how to filter or handle events. Table 15 describes how a scrollbar fills the fields in the event.

Summary

TABLE 15 Action Event from a `Scrollbar`

`arg`	The new scrollbar value.
`clickCount`	Not used.
`id`	One of the scrollbar events given in Table 14.
`key`	Not used.
`modifiers`	The state of the modifier keys when the component was clicked.
`target`	A reference to the component that generated this event.
`when`	The time, in milliseconds, when the event was generated.
`x`	*x*-coordinate of the component in pixels.
`y`	*y*-coordinate of the component in pixels.

MEMBER SUMMARY

Constructor	
`Scrollbar()`	Constructs a new `Scrollbar` instance.
Orientation Constant Fields	
`HORIZONTAL`	The orientation constant specifying a horizontal scrollbar.
`VERTICAL`	The orientation constant specifying a vertical scrollbar.
Property Methods	
`getLineIncrement()`	Retrieves the scrollbar's line increment value.
`getMaximum()`	Retrieves the scrollbar's maximum value.
`getMinimum()`	Retrieves the scrollbar's minimum value.
`getOrientation()`	Retrieves the scrollbar's orientation.
`getPageIncrement()`	Retrieves the scrollbar's page increment value.
`getValue()`	Retrieves the scrollbar's value.
`getVisible()`	Retrieves the scrollbar's visible value.
`setLineIncrement()`	Sets the scrollbar's line increment.
`setPageIncrement()`	Sets the scrollbar's page increment.
`setValue()`	Sets the scrollbar's value.
`setValues()`	Sets various scrollbar values.
Peer Method	
`addNotify()`	Create the scrollbar's peer.
Debugging Method	
`paramString()`	Generates a string representing the scrollbar's state.

Example

This example creates a canvas that paints a very large grid and two scrollbars to pan around the grid. See Figure 211. The maximum values of the scrollbars are set to the pixel size of the grid so that the value of the scrollbar can be used to determine the location of the visible area. For simplicity, the `paint()` method always paints the entire grid such that the top-left corner is at (0, 0), and the `Graphics.translate()` method is used to adjust the graphics context's origin so that the correct part of the grid will be visible. A more efficient implementation would paint only the visible portion of the grid.

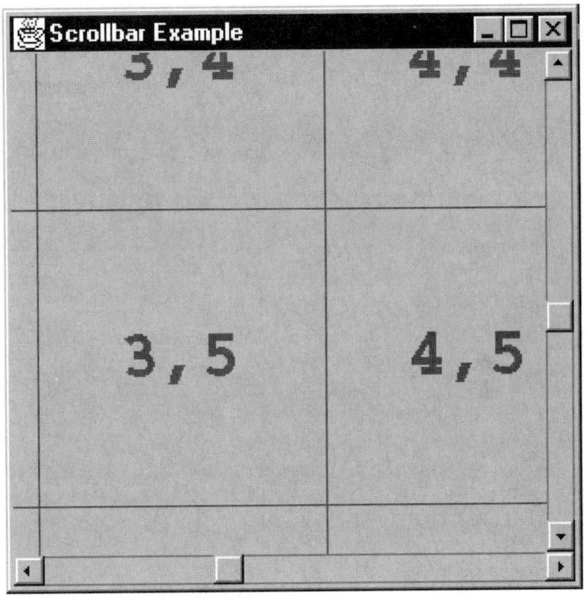

FIGURE 211 `Scrollbar`

```
import java.awt.*;
class Main extends Frame {
    Scrollbar sbVer = new Scrollbar(Scrollbar.VERTICAL);
    Scrollbar sbHor = new Scrollbar(Scrollbar.HORIZONTAL);
    MainCanvas cv = new MainCanvas(sbVer, sbHor);

    Main() {
        super("Scrollbar Example");
        add("Center", cv);
        add("East", sbVer);
        add("South", sbHor);
        resize(200, 200);
        show();
    }

    public boolean handleEvent(Event evt) {
        if (evt.target == sbVer || evt.target == sbHor) {
            Scrollbar sb = (Scrollbar)evt.target;

            System.out.println(
                ((sb.getOrientation() == Scrollbar.VERTICAL) ?
                    "ver" : "hor")
                + " li=" + sb.getLineIncrement()
                + " pi=" + sb.getPageIncrement()
                + " max=" + sb.getMaximum()
```

```
                + " vis=" + sb.getVisible());
            cv.sbChanged();
            return true;
        }
        return super.handleEvent(evt);
    }

    static public void main(String[] args) {
        new Main();
    }
}

// Creates a very large square grid.
// Each grid cell is labelled to help with navigation.
class MainCanvas extends Canvas {
    int gridSize = 1500;
    int gridCells = 10;
    int cellSize = gridSize/gridCells;
    int originX, originY;
    Scrollbar sbVer;
    Scrollbar sbHor;

    MainCanvas(Scrollbar sbVer, Scrollbar sbHor) {
        this.sbVer = sbVer;
        this.sbHor = sbHor;
        setFont(new Font("Courier", Font.BOLD, 36));
    }

    public void sbChanged() {
        originY = -sbVer.getValue();
        originX = -sbHor.getValue();
        repaint();
    }

    // If the size of the canvas changes, we need to update
    // the scrollbar values.
    public void layout() {
        super.layout();
        int w = size().width;
        int h = size().height;

        sbVer.setValues(sbVer.getValue(), h, sbVer.getMinimum(),
            gridSize);
        sbVer.setPageIncrement(Math.min(cellSize, h));
        sbVer.setLineIncrement(Math.min(cellSize, h/5));
        sbHor.setValues(sbHor.getValue(), w, sbHor.getMinimum(),
            gridSize);
        sbHor.setPageIncrement(Math.min(cellSize, w));
        sbHor.setLineIncrement(Math.min(cellSize, w/5));

        // This ensures that if the grid is larger than the viewable
        // area, you will never see space around the grid.
        originX = -Math.max(0, Math.min
            (gridSize-w, sbHor.getValue()));
```

```
            originY = -Math.max(0, Math.min
                (gridSize-h, sbVer.getValue()));
        }

        public void paint(Graphics g) {
            FontMetrics fm = g.getFontMetrics();

            // Using translate() simplifies the painting code
            // since it doesn't have to worry about origin changes.
            g.translate(originX, originY);
            g.setColor(Color.red);
            for (int i=0; i<gridCells; i++) {
                int c = i * cellSize;
                g.drawLine(c, 0, c, gridSize);
                g.drawLine(0, c, gridSize, c);
            }
            g.drawRect(0, 0, gridSize-1, gridSize-1);
            for (int i=0; i<gridCells; i++) {
                for (int j=0; j<gridCells; j++) {
                    String str = "" + i + "," + j;
                    int x = i * cellSize;
                    int y = j * cellSize;

                    g.drawString(str, x+(cellSize-fm.stringWidth(str))/2,
                        y+(cellSize-fm.getHeight())/2+fm.getAscent());
                }
            }
        }
    }
```

addNotify()

PURPOSE Creates the scrollbar's peer.

SYNTAX `public synchronized void addNotify()`

DESCRIPTION This method creates the peer if it does not yet exist. The peer is created by calling the `Toolkit.createScrollbar()` method. This method should never be called directly. It is normally called by the parent.

OVERRIDES `Component.addNotify()`.

SEE ALSO `Component`, `Toolkit`.

getLineIncrement()

PURPOSE Retrieves the scrollbar's line increment value.

SYNTAX `public int getLineIncrement()`

DESCRIPTION The scrollbar line increment controls how much the line up/line down buttons update the scrollbar value when pressed. If applying the increment modifies the scrollbar value outside the scrollbar range, the scrollbar value is adjusted to either the maximum or minimum value. The scrollbar line increments can be changed at any time by using the `setLineIncrement()` method.

RETURNS The scrollbar's line increment value.

SEE ALSO `setLineIncrement()`.

EXAMPLE See the class example.

getMaximum()

PURPOSE Retrieves the scrollbar's maximum value.

SYNTAX `public int getMaximum()`

DESCRIPTION See the class description for more information about the scrollbar's maximum value.

RETURNS The scrollbar's maximum value.

SEE ALSO `getMinimum()`, `getValue()`.

EXAMPLE See the class example.

getMinimum()

PURPOSE Retrieves the scrollbar's minimum value.

SYNTAX `public int getMinimum()`

DESCRIPTION See the class description for more information about the scrollbar's minimum value.

RETURNS The scrollbar's minimum value.

SEE ALSO `getMaximum()`, `getValue()`.

EXAMPLE See the class example.

getOrientation()

PURPOSE Retrieves the scrollbar's orientation.

SYNTAX `public int getOrientation()`

DESCRIPTION See the class description for more information about the scrollbar's orientation.

RETURNS The scrollbar's orientation. This value can be either `VERTICAL` or `HORIZONTAL`.

EXAMPLE See the class example.

getPageIncrement()

PURPOSE Retrieves the scrollbar's page increment value.

SYNTAX `public int getPageIncrement()`

DESCRIPTION The scrollbar page increments control how much the page up/page down buttons update the scrollbar value when pressed. If applying the increment modifies the scrollbar value outside the scrollbar range, the scrollbar value is adjusted to either the maximum or minimum value. The scrollbar page increments can be changed at any time using the `setPageIncrement()` method.

RETURNS The scrollbar's page increment value.

EXAMPLE See the class example.

getValue()

PURPOSE Retrieves the scrollbar's value.

SYNTAX `public int getValue()`

DESCRIPTION See the class description for more information about the scrollbar's value.

RETURNS The scrollbar's value.

SEE ALSO `getMaximum()`, `getMinimum()`.

EXAMPLE See the class example.

getVisible()

PURPOSE	Retrieves the scrollbar's visible value.
SYNTAX	`public int getVisible()`
DESCRIPTION	The scrollbar's visible value controls the size of the scroll box. It is typically used to indicate how much of the document is visible. For example, if only one third of the document is visible, the scrollbar's visible value should be set to `(getMaximum()-getMinimum())/3` so that the size of the scroll box will be one third the size of the whole scrollbar.
RETURNS	The scrollbar's visible value.
EXAMPLE	See the class example.

HORIZONTAL

PURPOSE	The orientation constant specifying a horizontal scrollbar.
SYNTAX	`public static final int HORIZONTAL`
EXAMPLE	See the class example.

paramString()

PURPOSE	Generates a string representing the scrollbar's state.
SYNTAX	`protected String paramString()`
DESCRIPTION	A subclass of this class should override this method and return a concatenation of its state with the results of `super.paramString()`. This method is called by the `toString()` method and is typically used for debugging.
RETURNS	A non-`null` string representing the scrollbar's state.
OVERRIDES	`Component.paramString()`.
SEE ALSO	`Object.toString()`.
EXAMPLE	See `Component.paramString()`.

Scrollbar()

PURPOSE Constructs a new `Scrollbar` instance.

SYNTAX

```
public Scrollbar()
public Scrollbar(int orientation)
public Scrollbar(int orientation, int value, int visible, int
   minimum, int maximum)
```

DESCRIPTION The three forms of this constructor create a new `Scrollbar` instance with the orientation `orientation` and initial values and range. If `orientation` is not specified, it defaults to `VERTICAL`. If `value`, `visible`, `minimum`, and `maximum` are not specified, they default to `0`. The line increment defaults to `1` and the page increment defaults to `10`. The supplied values are adjusted if necessary to satisfy the following constraint:

```
minimum <= value <= maximum
```

The constraint is achieved with the following rules. If `maximum < minimum`, `maximum` is set to `minimum`. If `value > maximum`, `value` is set to `maximum`; if `value < minimum`, `value` is set to `minimum`. The visible size can be larger than the `maximum`. In this case, the scroll box is as large as the scrollbar and prevents the scrollbar from generating any events.

PARAMETERS

`maximum`	The scrollbar's maximum value.
`minimum`	The scrollbar's minimum value.
`orientation`	Specifies the orientation of the scrollbar.
`value`	The scrollbar's initial value.
`visible`	The scrollbar's visible size.

EXCEPTIONS

`IllegalArgumentException`
If `orientation` is not valid.

EXAMPLE This example creates a horizontal scrollbar and prints out all events generated by the scrollbar. See Figure 212.

FIGURE 212 `Scrollbar()`

```
import java.awt.*;
public class Main extends Frame {
    Scrollbar sb = new Scrollbar(Scrollbar.HORIZONTAL,
        50, 50, 0, 100);
```

```
        Main() {
            super("Scrollbar Example");
            add("South", sb);
            pack();
            show();
        }

        public boolean handleEvent(Event evt) {
            if (evt.target == sb) {
                System.out.println(evt);
                return true;
            }
            return false;
        }

        static public void main(String[] args) {
            new Main();
        }
    }
```

setLineIncrement()

PURPOSE Sets the scrollbar's line increment.

SYNTAX `public void setLineIncrement(int increment)`

DESCRIPTION This method sets the scrollbar's line increment to `increment`. The scrollbar line increment controls how much the line up/line down buttons update the scrollbar value when pressed. If applying the increment modifies the scrollbar value outside the scrollbar range, the scrollbar value is adjusted to either the maximum or minimum value.

PARAMETERS

`increment` The non-negative line increment.

EXAMPLE See the class example.

setPageIncrement()

PURPOSE Sets the scrollbar's page increment.

SYNTAX `public void setPageIncrement(int increment)`

DESCRIPTION This method sets the scrollbar's page increment to be `increment`. The scroll-bar page increment controls how much the page up/page down buttons update the scrollbar value when pressed. If applying the increment modifies the scrollbar value outside the scrollbar range, the scrollbar value is adjusted to either the maximum or minimum value.

PARAMETERS

`increment` The non-negative page increment.

EXAMPLE See the class example.

setValue()

PURPOSE Sets the scrollbar's value.

SYNTAX `public void setValue(int value)`

DESCRIPTION This method updates the position of the scrollbar's scroll box to be `value`. `value` is adjusted if necessary to be greater than or equal to the scrollbar's minimum value and less than or equal to the scrollbar's maximum value.

PARAMETERS

`value` The scrollbar's new value.

SEE ALSO `getValue()`.

EXAMPLE See the class example.

setValues()

PURPOSE Sets various scrollbar values.

SYNTAX

```
public void setValues(int value, int visible, int minimum, int
   maximum)
```

DESCRIPTION The supplied values are adjusted if necessary to satisfy the following constraint:

```
minimum <= value <= maximum.
```

The constraint is achieved with the following rules. If `maximum < minimum`, `maximum` is set to `minimum`. If `value > maximum`, `value` is set to `maximum`; if `value < minimum`, `value` is set to `minimum`. The visible size can be larger than the maximum. In this case, the scroll box is as large as the scrollbar and prevents the scrollbar from generating any events.

PARAMETERS

`maximum` The scrollbar's maximum value.

`minimum` The scrollbar's minimum value.

`value`	The scrollbar's value.
`visible`	The scrollbar's visible size.

EXAMPLE See the class example.

VERTICAL()

PURPOSE The orientation constant specifying a vertical scrollbar.

SYNTAX `public static final int VERTICAL`

EXAMPLE See the class example.

java.awt.peer
ScrollbarPeer

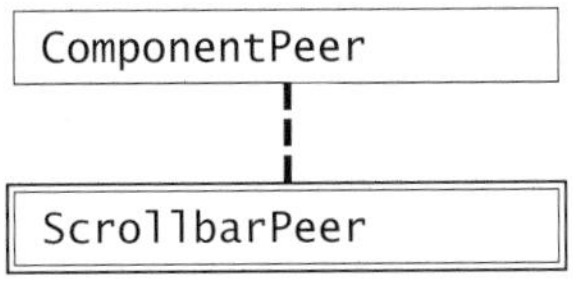

Syntax

```
public interface ScrollbarPeer extends ComponentPeer
```

Description

The scrollbar (see `Scrollbar` class) in the Abstract Windowing Toolkit (AWT) uses the platform's native implementation of a scrollbar. So that the AWT scrollbar behaves the same on all platforms, the scrollbar is assigned a peer, whose task is to translate the behavior of the platform's native scrollbar to the behavior of the AWT scrollbar.

AWT programmers normally do not directly use peer classes and interfaces. Instead they deal with AWT components in the `java.awt` package. These in turn automatically manage their peers. Only someone who is porting the AWT to another platform should be concerned with the peer classes and interfaces. Consequently, most peer documentation refers to `java.awt` counterparts.

See `Component` and `Toolkit` for additional information about component peers.

MEMBER SUMMARY	
Peer Methods	
`setLineIncrement()`	Sets the scrollbar's line increment.
`setPageIncrement()`	Sets the scrollbar's page increment.
`setValue()`	Sets the scrollbar's value.
`setValues()`	Sets various scrollbar values.

See Also

`Component`, `Scrollbar`, `Toolkit`.

A B C D E F G H I J K L M N O P Q R S T U V W X Y Z

setLineIncrement()

PURPOSE Sets the scrollbar's line increment.

SYNTAX `void setLineIncrement(int increment)`

PARAMETERS

`increment` The non-negative line increment.

SEE ALSO `Scrollbar.setLineIncrement()`.

setPageIncrement()

PURPOSE Sets the scrollbar's page increment.

SYNTAX `void setPageIncrement(int increment)`

PARAMETERS

`increment` The non-negative page increment.

SEE ALSO `Scrollbar.setPageIncrement()`.

setValue()

PURPOSE Sets the scrollbar's value.

SYNTAX `void setValue(int value)`

PARAMETERS

`value` The scrollbar's new value.

SEE ALSO `Scrollbar.setValue()`.

setValues()

PURPOSE Sets various scrollbar values.

SYNTAX `void setValues(int value, int visible, int minimum, int maximum)`

PARAMETERS

`maximum`	The scrollbar's maximum value.
`minimum`	The scrollbar's minimum value.
`value`	The scrollbar's value.
`visible`	The scrollbar's visible size.

SEE ALSO `Scrollbar.setValues()`.

java.lang

SecurityException

Syntax

```
public class SecurityException extends RuntimeException
```

Description

`SecurityException` is a runtime exception that is thrown by the Java runtime library when a method cannot be executed for security reasons. When `SecurityException` is thrown, it indicates that the program has violated security constraints on the system.

`SecurityException` is a runtime exception and should not be caught or declared in the `throws` clause of a method.

MEMBER SUMMARY	
Constructor	
`SecurityException()`	Constructs a `SecurityException` instance.

See Also

`SecurityManager`.

Example

Here are some examples of methods that throw `SecurityException`.

```
protected SecurityManager() {
    if (System.getSecurityManager() != null) {
        throw new SecurityException("can't create SecurityManager");
    }
}
public void checkConnect(String host, int port) {
    if (port > 1024)
        throw new SecurityException();
}
```

SecurityException()

PURPOSE
Constructs a `SecurityException` instance.

SYNTAX

```
public SecurityException()
public SecurityException(String msg)
```

DESCRIPTION
The two forms of this constructor create a new instance of `SecurityException`. An optional string `msg` can be supplied that describes this particular instance of the exception.

PARAMETERS

`msg` A string that gives details about this exception.

java.lang

SecurityManager

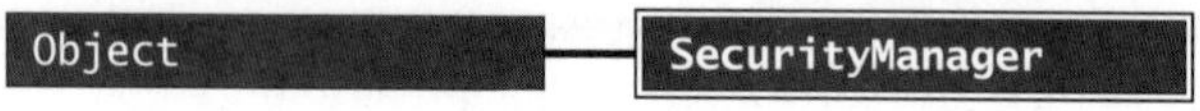

Syntax

```
public abstract class SecurityManager
```

Description

A security manager enforces security policies related to what a program is allowed to do. Some of these policies include inspection of the execution stack, access to local files, access to system properties, and permission to execute system commands.

The Java runtime system by default does not use a security manager. This means there are no security checks on any operation and all operations are allowed. However, applications like Web browsers typically define a security manager and use `System.setSecurityManager()` to install it. Only one security manager can be installed. Once installed, it cannot be replaced.

Permission Checking

When you define a security manager, you must override some or all of the permission checking methods, depending on the policies the security manager enforces. With the exception of `checkTopLevelWindow()`, all of these methods by default simply throw `SecurityException`, meaning the operation is not allowed for security reasons. For example, if your security manager wants to allow the program to be able to read any file (allowed by the underlying operating system), then it must supply its own implementation for `checkRead()` as follows:

```
public void checkRead(String filename) {
}
public void checkRead(FileDescriptor fd) {
}
```

These two methods override the existing implementations of `checkRead()` and permit any file to be read. If all other policies are to remain unchanged, then these are the only method definitions your security manager must supply.

Current Execution Context

When permission checks are made, they are always done with respect to the *current execution context*, sometimes called the current *security context*. The current execution context is a platform-dependent collection of information that the system has about the currently executing thread (including the thread group to which it belongs, the identity of the user executing the

Java program, and the machine on which the Java program is executing). The information in the current execution context can be used by the security manager to do permission checks.

Execution Stack Information

The *execution stack* is a record of the method calls that were made from the main program to the current method. It indicates all the methods that are in progress and pending termination of the current method call. For example, if `main()` calls `foo()`, which in turn calls `bar()`, the execution stack when executing inside `bar()` would be `bar() -> foo() -> main()`. For some methods to perform some of the permission checking, they may need to inspect the execution stack to find out information about the current execution context. The `SecurityManager` class provides protected methods that can be used by subclasses of `SecurityManager` for this purpose.

MEMBER SUMMARY

Constructor	
`SecurityManager()`	Constructs a new `SecurityManager` instance.
Permission Checking Methods	
`checkAccept()`	Determines if allowed to accept a socket connection.
`checkAccess()`	Determines if allowed to modify a thread or thread group.
`checkConnect()`	Determines if allowed to establish a socket connection.
`checkCreateClassLoader()`	Determines if allowed to create a class loader.
`checkDelete()`	Determines if allowed to delete a file.
`checkExec()`	Determines if allowed to execute a system program.
`checkExit()`	Determines if allowed to exit the virtual machine.
`checkLink()`	Determines if allowed to load and link in a library.
`checkListen()`	Determines if allowed to bind to a local port.
`checkPackageAccess()`	Determines if allowed to access a package.
`checkPackageDefinition()`	Determines if allowed to add class definitions to a package.
`checkPropertiesAccess()`	Determines if allowed to read and update the system properties.
`checkPropertyAccess()`	Determines if allowed to access a system property.
`checkRead()`	Determines if allowed to read a file.
`checkSetFactory()`	Determines if allowed to set the networking-related object factories.
`checkTopLevelWindow()`	Determines if allowed to create a top-level window.
`checkWrite()`	Determines if allowed to write to a file.
Methods for Checking Security Manager's State	
`getInCheck()`	Determines whether there is a security check in progress.
`getSecurityContext()`	Retrieves a security context for performing security checks.

Continued

A B C D E F G H I J K L M N O P Q R S T U V W X Y Z

MEMBER SUMMARY

Methods and Field for Examining the Execution Stack

`classDepth()`	Finds the first occurrence of a class on the execution stack.
`classLoaderDepth()`	Finds the first occurrence of a class created by a class loader on the execution stack.
`currentClassLoader()`	Finds the class loader on the execution stack.
`getClassContext()`	Retrieves the context of the execution stack.
`inCheck`	Field for recording whether there is a security check in progress.
`inClass()`	Determines whether a class is on the execution stack.
`inClassLoader()`	Determines whether there is a class loader on the execution stack.

See Also

`System.getSecurityManager()`, `System.setSecurityManager()`.

checkAccept()

PURPOSE Determines if allowed to accept a socket connection.

SYNTAX `public void checkAccept(String host, int port)`

DESCRIPTION This method determines whether the current execution context is allowed to accept a socket connection from the machine `host` on the remote port `port`.

PARAMETERS

`host` The machine name to check. The syntax of the name is platform-dependent. For example, if the machine has an Internet host name, `host` could be a domain-qualified name like `foobar.widget.com` or a nonqualified name like `foobar`.

`port` The remote port number to check.

EXCEPTIONS

`SecurityException`

If the connection cannot be accepted due to security reasons.

SEE ALSO `checkListen()`, `checkRead()`, `checkWrite()`, `ServerSocket.accept()`.

checkAccess()

PURPOSE Determines if allowed to modify a thread or thread group.

SYNTAX
```
public void checkAccess(Thread thrd)
public void checkAccess(ThreadGroup thrdGroup)
```

DESCRIPTION The first form of this method determines whether the current execution context is allowed to modify the thread `thrd`. Modifications include stopping, suspending, and resuming the thread and changing its priority, name, and daemon status.

The second form of this method determines whether the current thread is allowed to modify the thread group `thrdGroup`. Modifications include stopping, suspending, resuming, and destroying threads in the thread group, joining the thread group, and changing the thread group's daemon status and maximum priority.

PARAMETERS

`thrd` The thread to be checked.

`thrdGroup` The thread group to be checked.

EXCEPTIONS

`SecurityException`
If the current thread is not allowed to modify `thrd` or `thrdGroup` for security reasons.

SEE ALSO `Thread.checkAccess()`, `Thread.resume()`, `Thread.setDaemon()`, `Thread.setName()`, `Thread.setPriority()`, `Thread.stop()`, `Thread.suspend()`, `Thread.Thread()`, `ThreadGroup.checkAccess()`, `ThreadGroup.destroy()`, `ThreadGroup.setDaemon()`, `ThreadGroup.setPriority()`, `ThreadGroup.resume()`, `ThreadGroup.stop()`, `ThreadGroup.suspend()`, `ThreadGroup.ThreadGroup()`.

checkConnect()

PURPOSE Determines if allowed to establish a socket connection.

SYNTAX
```
public void checkConnect(String host, int prt)
public void checkConnect(String host, int prt, Object ctx)
```

DESCRIPTION The two forms of this method check whether the current execution context is allowed to establish a connection to the port `prt` on the machine `host`. If `prt` is `-1`, the methods check whether any connection to *any* port on `host` is allowed. If a context `ctx` is specified, the security manager determines whether *both* the current execution context and `ctx` are allowed to establish the connection.

PARAMETERS

`ctx`	The additional context to check.
`host`	The machine name to check.
`prt`	The port to check. If `prt` is `-1`, checks whether any ports are allowed.

EXCEPTIONS

`SecurityException`
If the connection cannot be established for security reasons.

SEE ALSO `DatagramSocket.send()`, `DatagramSocket.receive()`, `InetAddress.InetAddress()`, `Socket.Socket()`.

checkCreateClassLoader()

PURPOSE Determines if allowed to create a class loader.

SYNTAX `public void checkCreateClassLoader()`

DESCRIPTION This method determines whether the current execution context is allowed to create a class loader.

EXCEPTIONS

`SecurityException`
If a class loader cannot be created due to security reasons.

SEE ALSO `ClassLoader.ClassLoader()`.

checkDelete()

PURPOSE Determines if allowed to delete a file.

SYNTAX `public void checkDelete(String fileName)`

DESCRIPTION This method determines whether the current execution context is allowed to delete the file `fileName`.

PARAMETERS

`fileName` The system-dependent filename to check.

EXCEPTIONS

`SecurityException`
If `fileName` cannot be deleted for security reasons.

SEE ALSO `File.delete()`.

A B C D E F G H I J K L M N O P Q R S T U V W X Y Z

checkExec()

PURPOSE Determines if allowed to execute a system program.

SYNTAX `public void checkExec(String prog)`

DESCRIPTION This method determines whether the current execution context is allowed to execute the system program `prog`. Executing system programs has security implications because certain programs can make unexpected and sometimes undesirable updates to the system environment.

PARAMETERS

`prog` The system-dependent name of the program to check.

EXCEPTIONS

`SecurityException`

If `prog` cannot be executed for security reasons.

SEE ALSO `Runtime.exec()`.

checkExit()

PURPOSE Determines if allowed to exit the virtual machine.

SYNTAX `public void checkExit(int stat)`

PURPOSE This method determines whether the current execution context is allowed to exit the virtual machine with status `stat`. Exiting the virtual machine has security implications because it effectively stops the entire Java program. The exit status is significant because it is sometimes used by other programs to check whether a program executed correctly.

PARAMETERS

`stat` The exit status to check.

EXCEPTIONS

`SecurityException`

If the virtual machine cannot be exited with `stat` for security reasons.

SEE ALSO `Runtime.exit()`.

checkLink()

PURPOSE Determines if allowed to load and link a library.

SYNTAX	`public void checkLink(String lib)`
DESCRIPTION	This method determines whether the current execution context is allowed to load and link the library `lib` into the system. Loading libraries has security implications because it makes the symbols being exported by the libraries visible to the program. This could possibly override the definition of symbols (to be loaded in the future) of functions that have security importance, such as functions for getting passwords, resolving host names, and getting machine licenses.

PARAMETERS

`lib`	Either the filename or library name of the library to load.

EXCEPTIONS

`SecurityException`
If `lib` cannot be loaded for security reasons.

SEE ALSO `Runtime.load()`, `Runtime.loadLibrary()`.

checkListen()

PURPOSE	Determines if allowed to bind to a local port.
SYNTAX	`public void checkListen(int lport)`
DESCRIPTION	This method determines whether the current execution context is allowed to bind to the local port `lport`.

PARAMETERS

`lport`	The local port to check.

EXCEPTIONS

`SecurityException`
If `lport` cannot be bound due to security reasons.

SEE ALSO `DatagramSocket.DatagramSocket()`, `ServerSocket.ServerSocket()`.

checkPackageAccess()

PURPOSE	Determines if allowed to access a package.
SYNTAX	`public void checkPackageAccess(String pkg)`
DESCRIPTION	This method determines whether the current execution context is allowed to access the package `pkg`.

PARAMETERS

`pkg` The name of the package to check (e.g., "java.io").

EXCEPTIONS

`SecurityException`
If `pkg` cannot be accessed due to security reasons.

checkPackageDefinition()

PURPOSE Determines if allowed to add class definitions to a package.

SYNTAX `public void checkPackageDefinition(String pkg)`

DESCRIPTION This method determines whether the current execution context is allowed to add class definitions to the package `pkg`.

PARAMETERS

`pkg` The name of the package to check (e.g., "java.io").

EXCEPTIONS

`SecurityException`
If class definitions cannot be added to `pkg` due to security reasons.

checkPropertiesAccess()

PURPOSE Determines if allowed to access the system properties.

SYNTAX `public void checkPropertiesAccess()`

DESCRIPTION This method determines whether the current execution context is allowed to access the system properties. This method controls both the reading and updating of system properties.

EXCEPTIONS

`SecurityException`
If the system properties cannot be accessed due to security reasons.

SEE ALSO `Properties`, `System.getProperties()`, `System.setProperties()`.

checkPropertyAccess()

PURPOSE Determines if allowed to access a system property .

SYNTAX
```
public void checkPropertyAccess(String prop)
public void checkPropertyAccess(String prop, String defval)
```

DESCRIPTION The two forms of this method determine whether the current execution context is allowed to access the system property `prop`. If `defval` is supplied, a check is made to see whether `defval` is allowed to be returned as the default value for `prop` if `prop` does not exist.

PARAMETERS

`defval` The default value for `prop` to check.

`prop` The system property to check.

EXCEPTIONS

`SecurityException`
If `prop` cannot be accessed due to security reasons.

SEE ALSO `System.getProperty()`.

checkRead()

PURPOSE Determines if allowed to read a file.

SYNTAX
```
public void checkRead(FileDescriptor fd)
public void checkRead(String fileName)
public void checkRead(String fileName, Object ctx)
```

DESCRIPTION The three forms of this method check whether the current execution context is allowed to read the specified file. The first form of this method determines whether the security manager allows reading from the open file descriptor, `fd`. This is useful for checking objects such as sockets that more commonly have file descriptors rather than filenames.

The other two forms of this method check whether the current execution context is allowed to read the file named `fileName`. If `ctx` is supplied, both the current execution context and `ctx` must be allowed to read `fileName`.

PARAMETERS

`ctx` The additional execution context to be checked.

`fd` The file descriptor of the file to check.

`fileName` The system-dependent file name to check.

EXCEPTIONS

`SecurityException`
If `fileName` or `fd` cannot be read due to security reasons.

SEE ALSO `File.canRead()`, `File.exists()`, `File.isDirectory()`, `File.isFile()`, `File.lastModified()`, `File.length()`, `File.list()`,

`FileInputStream.FileInputStream()`,
`RandomAccessFile.RandomAccessFile()`.

checkSetFactory()

PURPOSE Determines if allowed to set networking-related object factories.

SYNTAX `public void checkSetFactory()`

DESCRIPTION The networking classes use the concept of a *factory* to allow different underlying implementations to be used at the discretion of the Java program. A `Foo` factory is an object that generates instances of class `Foo`. There are factories for sockets, URL protocol handlers, and URL content handlers. The program can set a particular factory *once* during the life of the program. This factory defines for the rest of the program the implementation for that class.

`checkSetFactory()` determines whether the current execution context is allowed to set networking-related object factories.

EXCEPTIONS

`SecurityException`

If not allowed to set any networking-related object factory due to security reasons.

SEE ALSO `ServerSocket.setSocketFactory()`,
`Socket.setSocketImplFactory()`,
`URL.setURLStreamHandlerFactory()`,
`URLConnection.setContentHandlerFactory()`.

checkTopLevelWindow()

PURPOSE Determines if top-level windows can be created.

SYNTAX `public boolean checkTopLevelWindow(Object window)`

DESCRIPTION This method determines whether the current execution context is allowed to create the top-level window `window`. Creating top-level windows has security implications because a program may impersonate security-related applications (e.g., login windows) and mislead the user to supply security-sensitive information (e.g., passwords).

`checkTopLevelWindow()` returns `false` if the window creation is allowed, but the window must have visual warnings that it is a window generated by the Java program. The method returns `true` if creation is allowed without restrictions. To disallow the creation entirely, `checkTopLevelWindow()` should throw a `SecurityException`. The default implementation of this method simply returns `false`.

PARAMETERS

`window` The new window being created.

RETURNS `true` if top-level windows can be created without restrictions; `false` if top-level windows should be created with an accompanying visual warning.

EXCEPTIONS

`SecurityException`

If `window` cannot be created due to security reasons.

SEE ALSO `Window.Window()`.

checkWrite()

PURPOSE Determines if allowed to write to a file.

SYNTAX
```
public void checkWrite(FileDescriptor fd)
public void checkWrite(String fileName)
```

DESCRIPTION The two forms of this methods determine whether the current execution context is allowed to write to the file named `fileName` or to the open file descriptor `fd`. `fd` is useful for checking objects such as sockets that more commonly have file descriptors rather than filenames.

PARAMETERS

`fd` The file descriptor to check.

`fileName` The system-dependent filename to check.

EXCEPTIONS

`SecurityException`

If `fd` or `fileName` cannot be written to for security reasons.

SEE ALSO `File.canWrite()`, `File.mkdir()`, `File.renameTo()`, `FileOutputStream.FileOutputStream()`, `RandomAccessFile.RandomAccessFile()`.

classDepth()

PURPOSE Finds the first occurrence of a class on the execution stack.

SYNTAX
```
protected native int classDepth(String className)
```

DESCRIPTION By convention, the current stack frame is on "top" of the execution stack; it has position `0`. The oldest stack frame is on the "bottom" of the execution stack. This is a utility method for security managers. It searches the current execution stack starting from the top looking for a stack frame executing a method of the class `className`. If such a stack frame is found, its position is returned; otherwise, `-1` is returned.

EXAMPLE This example creates two different execution stacks and shows the class depth values of classes on those stacks. Since the `classDepth()` method is protected, it cannot be called directly. Hence, this example creates a subclass of `SecurityManager` with a public method that provides access to the `classDepth()` method.

```
public class Main {
    public static void main(String[] args) {
        MySecurityManager sm = new MySecurityManager();

        System.setSecurityManager(sm);
        sm.printClassDepth("C");                          // -1
        sm.printClassDepth("MySecurityManager");          // 0
        sm.printClassDepth("Main");                       // 1

        C.printClassDepth("C");                           // 1
        C.printClassDepth("MySecurityManager");           // 0
        C.printClassDepth("Main");                        // 2
    }
}

class MySecurityManager extends SecurityManager {
    public void printClassDepth(String name) {
        System.out.println(classDepth(name));
    }
}

class C {
    static void printClassDepth(String name) {
        ((MySecurityManager)
         System.getSecurityManager()).printClassDepth(name);
    }
}
```

PARAMETERS

`className` The fully qualified name of the class for which to look.

RETURNS The position of the stack frame found; `-1` if not found.

classLoaderDepth()

PURPOSE Finds the first occurrence of a class created by a class loader on the execution stack.

SYNTAX `protected native int classLoaderDepth()`

DESCRIPTION By convention, the current stack frame is on "top" of the execution stack; it has position `0`. The oldest stack frame is on the "bottom" of the execution stack. This is a utility method for security managers. It searches the current execution stack starting from the top looking for a stack frame executing a method of a class that was created with a class loader other than the defaults system class loader. If such a stack frame is found, its position is returned; otherwise, `-1` is returned.

RETURNS The top-most stack frame executing a method whose class was created with a class loader.

SEE ALSO `ClassLoader`, `currentClassLoader()`, `inClassLoader()`.

currentClassLoader()

PURPOSE Finds the class loader on the execution stack.

SYNTAX `protected native ClassLoader currentClassLoader()`

DESCRIPTION This method searches the current execution stack of the current thread for a stack frame executing a method of a class created by a class loader other than the defaults system class loader. If such a stack frame is found, the class loader for the class is returned.

RETURNS The class loader for the most recent stack frame executing a method of a class created by a class loader. `null` is returned if such a stack frame does not exist.

SEE ALSO `ClassLoader`, `classLoaderDepth()`, `inClassLoader()`.

getClassContext()

PURPOSE Retrieves the context of the execution stack.

SYNTAX `protected native Class[] getClassContext()`

DESCRIPTION This is a utility method for security managers. It scans the current execution stack and determines the class of the method being invoked in each stack frame. For each class, its `Class` object is returned.

RETURNS An array containing the `Class` objects of the methods on the execution stack. Index `0` holds the `Class` object of the method in the most recent stack frame.

EXAMPLE This example prints out the context for an execution stack. Since the `getClassContext()` method is protected, it can not be called directly. Hence, this example creates a subclass of `SecurityManager` with a public method that provides access to the `getClassContext()` method.

```
public class Main {
    public static void main (String[] args) {
        System.setSecurityManager(new MySecurityManager());

        C.printContext();
    }
}

class MySecurityManager extends SecurityManager {
    public void printContext() {
        Class[] c = getClassContext();

        for (int i=0; i<c.length; i++) {
            System.out.println(c[i]);
        }
    }
}

class C {
    static void printContext() {
        ((MySecurityManager)
            System.getSecurityManager()).printContext();
    }
}
```

OUTPUT

```
class MySecurityManager
class C
class Main
```

getInCheck()

PURPOSE Determines whether there is a security check in progress.

SYNTAX `public boolean getInCheck()`

RETURNS `true` if a security check is in progress; `false` otherwise.

SEE ALSO `inCheck`.

getSecurityContext()

PURPOSE Retrieves a security context for performing security checks.

SYNTAX `public Object getSecurityContext()`

DESCRIPTION This method returns the current execution context. This is an implementation-dependent `Object` that encapsulates enough information about the current execution environment to perform subsequent security checks.

RETURNS The current execution context.

inCheck()

PURPOSE Field for recording whether there is a security check in progress.

SYNTAX `protected boolean inCheck`

SEE ALSO `getInCheck()`.

inClass()

PURPOSE Determines whether a class is on the execution stack.

SYNTAX `protected boolean inClass(String className)`

DESCRIPTION This method determines whether the class `className` is on the current execution stack.

PARAMETERS

`className` The name of the class for which to look.

RETURNS `true` if `className` is on the execution stack; `false` otherwise.

SEE ALSO `classDepth()`.

inClassLoader()

PURPOSE Determines whether a class loader is on the execution stack.

SYNTAX `protected boolean inClassLoader()`

DESCRIPTION This method searches the current execution stack of the current thread for a stack frame executing a method of a class created by a class loader other than the defaults system class loader.

RETURNS `true` if some class on the execution stack has been created by a class loader; `false` otherwise.

SEE ALSO `ClassLoader`, `currentClassLoader()`.

SecurityManager()

PURPOSE Constructs a new `SecurityManager` object.

SYNTAX `protected SecurityManager()`

DESCRIPTION This method creates a new `SecurityManager` object. If no security manager has been previously set, this newly created object can be installed as the security manager by calling `System.setSecurityManager()`. If a security manager has already been set, a `SecurityException` is thrown. That is, a new security manager cannot be created if one is already installed.

EXCEPTIONS

`SecurityException`

If a security manager has already been set or a security manager cannot be created.

SEE ALSO `System.getSecurityManager()`, `System.setSecurityManager()`.

java.io

SequenceInputStream

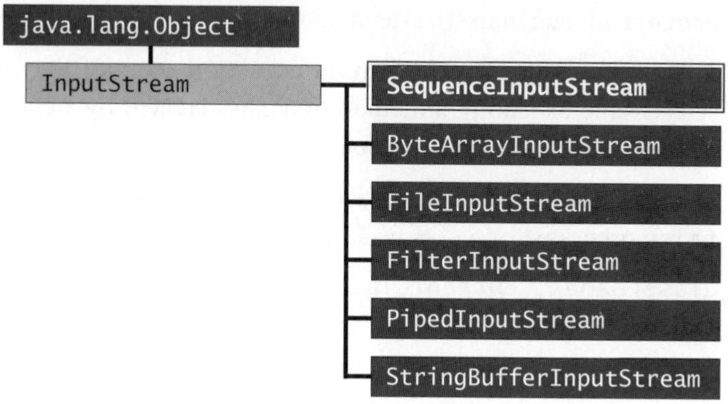

Syntax

```
public class SequenceInputStream extends InputStream
```

Description

The `SequenceInputStream` class is used to represent a *sequence input stream.* A sequence input stream is a stream in which the contents of the input stream is composed of the contents of an ordered list of input streams. You create a sequence input stream by giving it a list of input streams, as show in Figure 213.

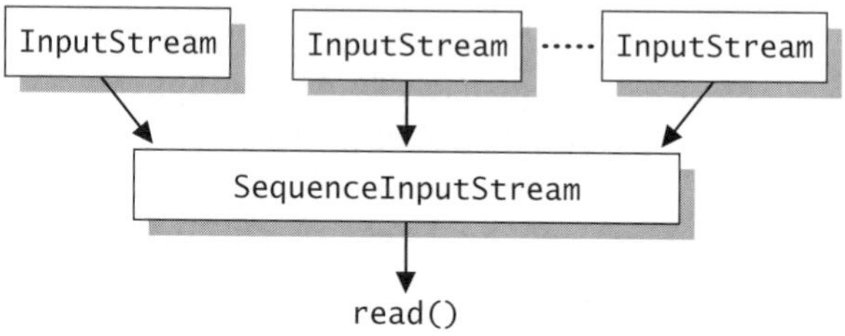

FIGURE 213 **`SequenceInputStream`**

When reading from the sequence input stream, you start reading from the first input stream. Then when data is exhausted from that stream, you go on to the next input stream in the sequence, and so on, until the entire list of input streams have been exhausted. To the reader reading from the sequence input stream, there is no visible boundary as the sequence input stream moves from one input stream to the next. It is as if the sequence input stream is one whole stream.

For example, you can use a sequence input stream to process data spread over multiple files by creating a sequence input stream that consists of `FileInputStream`s for those files (see the class example).

MEMBER SUMMARY	
Constructor	
`SequenceInputStream()`	Constructs a new sequence input stream using multiple streams.
Input Method	
`read()`	Reads bytes from this sequence input stream.
Method for Closing Stream	
`close()`	Closes this sequence input stream.

See Also

`InputStream`.

Example

This example shows how `SequenceInputStream` can be used to implement a program that takes a list of file names and prints their contents to standard output (similar to the Unix `cat` command).

```
import java.io.SequenceInputStream;
import java.io.FileInputStream;
import java.io.IOException;
import java.util.Vector;

class Main {
    // This implements a form of 'cat' that echoes all files named
    // on command line to standard output
    public static void main(String[] args) {
        try {
            Vector streams = new Vector(args.length);
            for (int i = 0; i < args.length; i++)
                streams.addElement(new FileInputStream(args[i]));

            SequenceInputStream in =
                new SequenceInputStream(streams.elements());

            byte[] b = new byte[256];
            int howmany;
            while ((howmany = in.read(b, 1, b.length - 1)) > 0)
                for(int i = 0; i < howmany; i++)
                    System.out.print((char)b[i]);
```

```
                System.out.flush();
                in.close();
            } catch (IOException e) {
                e.printStackTrace();
            }
        }
    }
```

close()

PURPOSE	Closes this sequence input stream.
SYNTAX	`public void close() throws IOException`
DESCRIPTION	This method closes this sequence input stream by closing all the input streams in its sequence that have not yet been closed.
EXCEPTIONS	
`IOException`	If an IO error occurred in attempting to close the input streams in its sequence.
OVERRIDES	`InputStream.close()`.
EXAMPLE	See the class example.

read()

PURPOSE Reads bytes from this sequence input stream.

SYNTAX

```
public int read() throws IOException
public int read(byte[] buffer, int offset, int count) throws
    IOException
```

DESCRIPTION The two forms of this method read bytes from this sequence input stream. The first form reads a single byte from this sequence input stream and returns it. The second form reads `count` number of bytes from this sequence input stream and stores the bytes read into the byte array `buffer`, starting at index `offset`. It returns the number of bytes actually read.

Bytes read from this sequence input stream are read from the current input stream of this sequence. When end-of-file is reached on the current input stream, the input stream is closed. The next stream in the sequence becomes current and bytes are then read from it. When end-of-file has been reached on all input streams of this sequence input stream, both forms of `read()` return `-1`.

PARAMETERS

`buffer`	The byte array in which to store the bytes read.
`count`	The number of bytes to read.
`offset`	The index in `buffer` at which to start storing the bytes read.

EXCEPTIONS

`IOException`	If an IO error occurred.

OVERRIDES `InputStream.read()`.

EXAMPLE See the class example.

SequenceInputStream()

PURPOSE Constructs a new sequence input stream using multiple streams.

SYNTAX

```
public SequenceInputStream(InputStream s1, InputStream s2)
public SequenceInputStream(Enumeration streams)
```

DESCRIPTION The first form of this constructor creates a sequence using the input streams `s1` and `s2`. Bytes read from this new sequence input stream are first read from `s1` until end-of-file is reached on the stream. Then bytes are read from `s2`. The second form creates a sequence using the list of input streams in the enumeration `streams`. When bytes are read from this new sequence input stream, the streams are read in the same order in which they appear in the enumeration.

PARAMETERS

`s1`	The first input stream to use for this sequence input stream.
`s2`	The second input stream to use for this sequence input stream.
`streams`	The list of streams to use for this sequence input stream.

SEE ALSO `Enumeration`, `InputStream`.

EXAMPLE See the class example.

A B C D E F G H I J K L M N O P Q R S T U V W X Y Z

java.net

ServerSocket

java.lang.Object — **ServerSocket**

Syntax

`public final class ServerSocket`

Description

A *socket* is a communications endpoint. A *server socket* is an endpoint (used by the server) in a connection-oriented protocol.

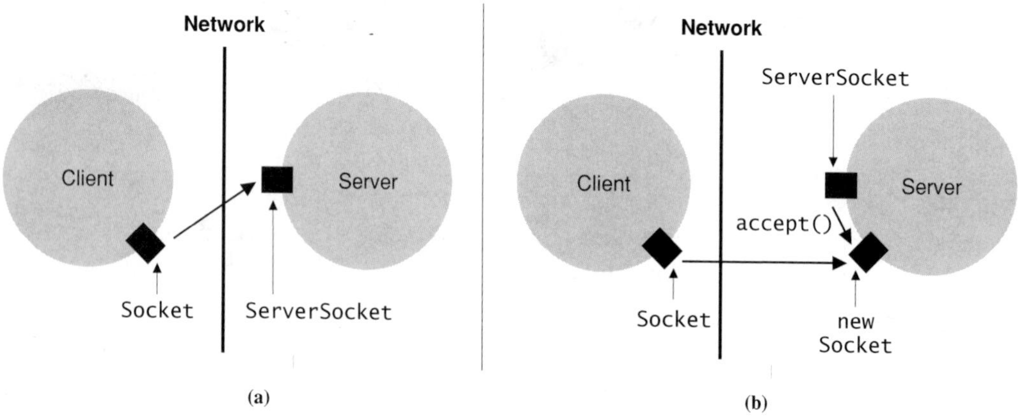

FIGURE 214 Socket and ServerSocket

In a client/server application, the server typically creates a server socket and binds it to a well-known port. Clients learn of this well-known port either by convention or through a naming service that maps service names to port numbers. This server then listens on this well-known port for connection. Any connections made to this server are then queued. The client sends a connection request to the server (see Figure 214(a)).The server accepts a connection from a client by creating a new socket. This establishes a connection between the client's socket and this new socket through which the client and server can communicate with each other (see Figure 214(b)). The original well-known port is still open for accepting new connections. New connections that arrive while the server is interacting with clients are queued until the server is ready to accept them. The following class example illustrates the use of these methods.

The `ServerSocket` class is used to represent a server socket. The actual implementation of server sockets is supplied by a subclass of `SocketImpl` and is configurable by the application.

This allows the application to choose its socket implementation depending on the security properties of the network, such as its firewall implementation.

MEMBER SUMMARY	
Constructor	
`ServerSocket()`	Constructs a server socket and binds it to the specified local port.
Communications Methods	
`accept()`	Accepts a connection on this server socket.
`close()`	Closes this server socket.
Socket Information Methods	
`getInetAddress()`	Retrieves the address to which this server socket is connected.
`getLocalPort()`	Retrieves this server socket's local port.
`toString()`	Generates the string representation of this object.
Socket Factory Method	
`setSocketFactory()`	Sets the system's server socket implementation factory.

See Also

`DatagramPacket`, `DatagramSocket`, `Socket`, `SocketImpl`, `SocketImplFactory`.

Example

The following example illustrates a server that uses multiple threads to accept connections, thereby allowing concurrent handling of requests. The example consists of two classes: the main server `ClockServer` and `ClockWorker`. A request to the server returns the worker id (a single-digit character) followed by the current time of day.

```
import java.net.*;
import java.io.*;
import java.util.Date;

class ClockWorker extends Thread {
    private Socket sock;
    char id;
    public ClockWorker(Socket ss, int i) {
        super();
        sock = ss;
        id = Character.forDigit(i, 10);        // id of worker thread
    }
    public void run() {
        try {
            OutputStream out = sock.getOutputStream();
```

Example

```
                String answer = (new Date()).toString();
                byte[] b = new byte[answer.length()];
                answer.getBytes(0, answer.length(), b, 0);
                out.write(id); // first byte indicates worker id
                out.write(b, 0, b.length);
                out.write('\n');
                out.flush();
                sock.close();
            } catch (IOException e) {
                e.printStackTrace();
            }
        }
    }

    class ClockServer extends Thread {
        private ServerSocket srvSock = null;
        public ClockServer(int port, int backlog) {
            super();
            try {
                srvSock = new ServerSocket(port, backlog);
               System.err.println("Server Socket: " + srvSock.toString());
                System.err.println("Socket is connected to: " +
                                        srvSock.getInetAddress());
                System.err.println("Local port: " +
                    srvSock.getLocalPort());
            } catch (IOException e) {
                e.printStackTrace();
            }
        }
        public void run() {
            if (srvSock == null)
                return;
            Socket sock;
            ClockWorker worker;
            int id = 0;
            while (true) {
                try {
                    sock = srvSock.accept();
                    worker = new ClockWorker(sock, id++);
                    worker.start();
                } catch (IOException e) {
                    e.printStackTrace();
                }
            }
        }
        protected void finalize() {
            if (srvSock != null) {
                try {
                    srvSock.close();
                } catch (IOException e) {
                    e.printStackTrace();
                }
                srvSock = null;
            }
```

```
    }
}

class Main {
    static int date_port = 1258;

    public static void getDate(InetAddress dst, int port) {
        try {
            Socket client = new Socket(dst, port);
            InputStream in = client.getInputStream();

            for (int ch = in.read(); ch > 0; ch = in.read()) {
                System.out.print((char)ch);
            }
            client.close();
        } catch (IOException e) {
            e.printStackTrace();
        }
    }

    public static void main(String[] args) {
        // start server
        ClockServer srv = new ClockServer(date_port, 5);
        srv.setDaemon(true);
        srv.start();

        try {
            String msg = "\n";
            InetAddress dst = InetAddress.getLocalHost();

            for (int i = 0; i < 5; i++)
                getDate(dst, date_port);
        } catch (UnknownHostException e) {
                System.err.println("Host not found: " + e);
        }
    }
}
```

accept()

PURPOSE Accepts a connection on this server socket.

SYNTAX `public Socket accept() throws IOException`

DESCRIPTION `accept()` retrieves the first connection on the queue of pending connections and creates a new socket to handle that connection. If there are no pending connections, `accept()` blocks until a connection is present. The new socket is used to read and write data to and from the socket at the other end of the connection. The new socket is closed when the connection is terminated and is not used to accept more connections. This server socket remains open for accepting further connections and queues them for future processing.

RETURNS A new socket for communicating with the socket at the other end of the connection.

EXCEPTIONS

`IOException` If an IO error occurs while waiting for the connection.

`SecurityException`
If it cannot accept a connection from the sending socket due to security reasons.

SEE ALSO `SecurityManager.checkAccept()`, `SocketImpl.accept()`.

EXAMPLE See the class example.

close()

PURPOSE Closes this server socket.

SYNTAX `public void close() throws IOException`

DESCRIPTION A server socket should be closed when it is no longer needed. Closing the server socket frees up resources associated with the socket (e.g., file descriptors, socket descriptors) and allows the port that was bound to the socket to be reused. After a server socket has been closed, the server cannot accept connections from it. Any attempts to connect to it by a client will fail. `close()` closes this server socket.

EXCEPTIONS

`IOException` If an IO error occurred when closing the socket.

SEE ALSO `SocketImpl.close()`.

EXAMPLE See the class example.

getInetAddress()

PURPOSE Retrieves the address to which this server socket is bound.

SYNTAX `public InetAddress getInetAddress()`

DESCRIPTION When you create a server socket, it is bound to a local port on the local machine. `getInetAddress()` returns the address of the machine on which this server socket was created.

RETURNS The Internet address to which this server socket is bound.

SEE ALSO `InetAddress`, `ServerSocket()`, `SocketImpl.getInetAddress()`.

EXAMPLE See the class example.

getLocalPort()

PURPOSE Retrieves this server socket's local port.

SYNTAX `public int getLocalPort()`

DESCRIPTION When a server socket is created, you can specify the local port to use or leave it to the system to select any available ports. `getLocalPort()` returns this port number (whether specified by you or selected by the system).

RETURNS This server socket's port number.

SEE ALSO `ServerSocket()`, `SocketImpl.getLocalPort()`.

EXAMPLE See the class example.

ServerSocket()

PURPOSE Constructs a server socket and binds it to the specified local port.

SYNTAX
```
public ServerSocket(int port) throws IOException
public ServerSocket(int port, int backlog) throws IOException
```

DESCRIPTION The two forms of this constructor create a server socket, bind it to the specified local port `port`, and listen to it for connections. If `port` is `0`, the socket is bound to any locally available port. Use of certain ports is restricted (for example, those well-known ports for Internet protocols such as FTP, Telnet, and SMTP) and use of *any* port is permitted only if allowed by the security manager.

`backlog` specifies the maximum number of pending connections that this socket can have. If `backlog` is not specified, the default is `50` pending connections. When `backlog` number of connections are pending, clients making further requests for connections will fail with `IOException`.

PARAMETERS

`backlog` The maximum number of pending connections this socket can have.

`port` The local port to use. If `port` is `0`, use any available port.

EXCEPTIONS

`IOException` If an IO error occurred while creating the socket.

`SecurityException`
If `port` cannot be used due to security reasons.

SEE ALSO `accept()`, `SecurityManager.checkListen()`, `setSocketFactory()`, `SocketImpl.create()`, `SocketImpl.bind()`, `SocketImpl.listen()`.

EXAMPLE See the class example.

setSocketFactory()

PURPOSE Sets the system's server socket implementation factory.

SYNTAX
```
public static synchronized void
   setSocketFactory(SocketImplFactory factory) throws
   IOException
```

DESCRIPTION The actual implementation of server sockets is supplied by a subclass of `SocketImpl` and is configurable by the application. This allows the application to choose its socket implementation depending on the security properties of the network, such as its firewall implementation.

`setSocketFactory()` sets `factory` to be the server socket implementation factory. `factory` is responsible for creating an instance of (subclasses of) `SocketImpl` whenever a new server socket is created.

`setSocketFactory()` can be executed only if permitted to do so by the security manager. If permitted it can be executed only once during the lifetime of the application.

PARAMETERS

`factory` The server socket implementation factory to use.

EXCEPTIONS

`IOException` If an IO error occurred while setting the factory.

`SecurityException`
If not allowed to set the socket implementation factory due to security reasons.

`SocketException`
If a socket implementation factory has already been set.

SEE ALSO `SecurityManager.checkSetFactory()`, `SocketImpl`, `SocketImplFactory`.

EXAMPLE

```
try {
    ServerSocket.setSocketFactory(new DebugSocketImplFactory());
} catch (IOException e) {
    e.prinStackTrace();
}
```

toString()

PURPOSE Generates the string representation of this object.

SYNTAX `public String toString()`

DESCRIPTION The string representation of a server socket consists of its local address and local port number. `toString()` returns the string representation for this server socket.

RETURNS The string representation of this server socket.

OVERRIDES `Object.toString()`.

SEE ALSO `getInetAddress()`, `getLocalPort()`.

EXAMPLE See the class example.

A B C D E F G H I J K L M N O P Q R S T U V W X Y Z

java.net
Socket

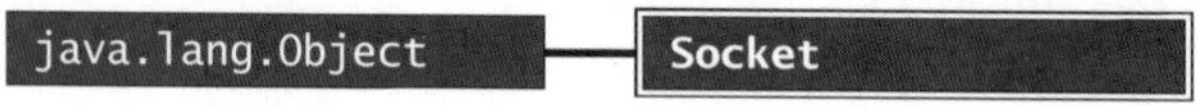

Syntax

```
public final class Socket
```

Description

A *socket* is a communications endpoint. It can be used by both the client and the server in a client/server application or by peers in a peer-to-peer application. It can be used for connection-oriented or connectionless protocols.

In a client/server application, once the server has created on a server socket, it can accept the next pending connection from the socket. This connnection returns to the server a new socket that it can use to communicate with the client. The client communicates with the server by creating a socket with the server's address and port number. The client can then create input and/or output streams with the socket in order to receive from and/or send data to the server, respectively.

The `Socket` class is used to represent a socket. The actual implementation of sockets is supplied by a subclass of `SocketImpl` and is configurable by the application. This allows the application to choose its socket implementation depending on the security properties of the network, such as its firewall implementation.

MEMBER SUMMARY	
Constructor	
`Socket()`	Constructs a socket to the specified destination.
Communications Methods	
`close()`	Closes the socket.
`getInputStream()`	Creates an input stream for this socket.
`getOutputStream()`	Creates an output stream to this socket.
Socket Information Methods	
`getInetAddress()`	Retrieves the address to which the socket is connected.
`getLocalPort()`	Retrieves this socket's local port.
`getPort()`	Retrieves this socket's remote port.
`toString()`	Generates the string representation for this object.
Socket Factory Method	
`setSocketImplFactory()`	Sets the system's socket implementation factory.

See Also

DatagramSocket, ServerSocket, SocketImpl, SocketImplFactory.

Example

This following example is a client-side routine that creates a connection to a destination and reads and echoes the data from the input stream.

```
public static void echoer(InetAddress dst, int port) {
    try {
        Socket client = new Socket(dst, port);
        InputStream in = client.getInputStream();

        for (int ch = in.read(); ch > 0; ch = in.read()) {
            System.out.print((char)ch);
        }
        client.close();
    } catch (IOException e) {
        e.printStackTrace();
    }
}
```

close()

PURPOSE Closes this socket.

SYNTAX `public synchronized void close() throws IOException`

DESCRIPTION A socket should be closed when it is no longer needed because sockets are a limited system resource. Closing a socket frees up resources associated with the socket (e.g., streams, file descriptors, socket descriptors) and allows the ports that were bound to the socket to be reused. You cannot send or receive data from a socket once it has been closed.

`close()` closes this socket.

EXCEPTIONS

`IOException` If an IO error occurred when closing the socket.

SEE ALSO `SocketImpl.close()`.

EXAMPLE See the class example.

getInetAddress()

PURPOSE Retrieves the Internet address to which this socket is connected.

SYNTAX `public InetAddress getInetAddress()`

DESCRIPTION This method returns the Internet address of the remote host to which this socket is connected.

RETURNS The address of this socket's remote host.

SEE ALSO `SocketImpl.getInetAddress()`.

EXAMPLE

```
public static void socketDetails(Socket s) {
    System.out.println("Socket is " + s.toString());
    System.out.println("Socket is to " + s.getInetAddress() +
                       "(" + s.getPort() + ")" +
                       " from local port" + s.getLocalPort());
}
```

getInputStream()

PURPOSE Creates an input stream for this socket.

SYNTAX `public InputStream getInputStream() throws IOException`

DESCRIPTION This method creates an input stream for this socket so that you can read data from this socket. You can compose this stream with input streams that have other properties by using filter streams. For example, filtering could be used to obtain the data in the expected format or to improve performance of the stream by buffering so that not all reads require direct interaction with the socket. Data sent by the remote host to this socket can be read from this input stream. Input streams and output streams can coexist on a socket.

Once a socket has been closed, any input streams created from it are also closed. Attempting to read from an input stream of a closed socket raises an IO exception.

RETURNS An input stream that allows reading data from the socket.

SEE ALSO `BufferedInputStream`, `FilterInputStream`, `InputStream`, `getOutputStream()`, `SocketImpl.getInputStream()`.

EXAMPLE See the class example.

getLocalPort()

PURPOSE Retrieves this socket's local port.

SYNTAX `public int getLocalPort()`

DESCRIPTION A socket has two endpoints: the sending end and the receiving end. Each end of the socket is identified by the Internet address of the machine that it is connected to and the port on the machine being used. `getLocalPort()` returns the port number that is being used by this socket on the local machine to send and receive data.

RETURNS The port number being used for the socket on the local machine.

SEE ALSO `DatagramPacket.getPort()`, `getInetAddress()`, `getPort()`, `SocketImpl.getLocalPort()`.

EXAMPLE See `getInetAddress()`.

getOutputStream()

PURPOSE Creates an output stream to this socket.

SYNTAX `public OutputStream getOutputStream() throws IOException`

DESCRIPTION This method creates an output stream to this socket so that you can send data to the remote host connected to this socket. You can compose this stream with output streams that have other properties by using filter streams. For example, filtering could be used to send the data in the desired format or to improve the performance of the stream by buffering the data so that not all output operations interact directly with the socket. Data to this stream can be read from the other endpoint of the socket (using `getInputStream()`). Input streams and output streams can coexist on a socket.

Once a socket has been closed, any output streams created from it are also closed. Attempting to send data to an output stream of a closed socket raises an IO exception.

RETURNS An output stream for sending data to the remote host.

SEE ALSO `BufferedOutputStream`, `FilterOutputStream`, `getInputStream()`, `OutputStream`, `SocketImpl.getOutputStream()`.

EXAMPLE

```
// write string to socket
public static void writeToSocket(Socket s, String msg) {
```

```
        try {
            OutputStream out = s.getOutputStream();
            if (out != null) {
                byte[] ob = new byte[msg.length()];
                msg.getBytes(0, ob.length, ob, 0);
                out.write(ob, 0, ob.length);
                out.flush();
                // close() will happen when socket gets closed
            }
        } catch (IOException e) {
            System.err.println("Had problems with writing to socket: " +
                e);
        }
    }
```

getPort()

PURPOSE Retrieves this socket's remote port.

SYNTAX `public int getPort()`

DESCRIPTION A socket has two endpoints: the sending end and the receiving end. Each end of the socket is identified by the Internet address of the machine that it is connected to and the port on the machine being used. `getPort()` returns the port number that is being used by this socket on the remote machine to send and receive data.

RETURNS The port number being used for the socket on the remote machine.

SEE ALSO `getInetAddress()`, `getLocalPort()`, `SocketImpl.getPort()`.

EXAMPLE See `getInetAddress()`.

setSocketImplFactory()

PURPOSE Sets the system's client socket implementation factory.

SYNTAX
```
public static synchronized void
   setSocketImplFactory(SocketImplFactory factory) throws
   IOException
```

DESCRIPTION The actual implementation of sockets is supplied by a subclass of `SocketImpl` and is configurable by the application. This allows the application to choose its socket implementation depending on the security properties of the network, such as its firewall implementation.

`setSocketImplFactory()` sets `factory` to be the socket implementation factory. `factory` is responsible for creating an instance of (subclasses of) `SocketImpl` whenever a new socket is created.

`setSocketImplFactory()` can be executed only if permitted to do so by the security manager. If it is permitted, it can be executed only once during the lifetime of the application.

PARAMETERS

`factory` The socket implementation factory to use.

EXCEPTIONS

`IOException` If an IO exception occurred while setting the socket implementation factory.

`SecurityException`
If not allowed to set the socket implementation factory due to security reasons.

`SocketException`
If a socket implementation factory has already been defined.

SEE ALSO `SecurityManager.checkSetFactory()`, `Socket()`, `SocketImpl`, `SocketImplFactory`.

EXAMPLE

```
try {
    Socket.setSocketImplFactory(new DebugSocketImplFactory());
} catch (IOException e) {
    System.out.println("Cannot set Socket factory: " + e);
}
```

Socket()

PURPOSE Constructs a socket to the specified destination.

SYNTAX
```
public Socket(String hostName, int port) throws
   UnknownHostException, IOException
public Socket(String hostName, int port, boolean stream) throws
   UnknownHostException, IOException
public Socket(InetAddress dst, int port) throws IOException
public Socket(InetAddress dst, int port, boolean stream) throws
   IOException
```

DESCRIPTION The four forms of this constructor create a socket for communicating with the specified destination. The destination can be specified using either the host name `hostName` of the remote machine or the address `dst` of the remote machine. In either case, you must specify the port number `port` on the remote machine to use. In addition, you can specify whether you want a datagram socket or a stream (connection-oriented) socket. If `stream` is not supplied or if `stream` is `true`, a stream socket is created; otherwise a datagram socket is created. After creating a socket, you can then create input and/or output streams for it so that you can communicate with the destination. When you no longer need the socket, be sure to close it to free up resources associated with it.

You can create a socket to the destination specified (the target machine's address and port number) only if allowed to do so by the security manager.

PARAMETERS

`dst`	The destination's Internet address.
`hostName`	The destination's host name.
`port`	The destination's port number.
`stream`	`true` means to create a stream socket; `false` means to create a datagram socket.

RETURNS A new socket for communicating with the remote host.

EXCEPTIONS

`IOException` If an IO error occurred while creating the socket.

`SecurityException`
If the connection to the destination cannot be made due to security reasons.

`UnknownHostException`
If `hostName` cannot be resolved (cannot find its Internet address).

SEE ALSO `DatagramSocket`, `SecurityManager.checkConnect()`, `SocketImpl.create()`, `SocketImpl.connect()`.

EXAMPLE See the class example.

```
try {
    //  9 == 'discard' port, false == not a stream socket
    Socket sock = new Socket("localhost", 9, false);

    socketDetails(sock);
    writeToSocket(sock, "this is a test");
    sock.close();
} catch (IOException e) {
    e.printStackTrace();
}
```

toString()

PURPOSE Generates the string representation of this object.

SYNTAX `public String toString()`

DESCRIPTION The string representation of a socket consists of its remote address and port and its local port. `toString()` returns the representation of this socket.

RETURNS The string representation of this socket.

OVERRIDES `Object.toString()`.

SEE ALSO `getInetAddress()`, `getLocalPort()`, `getPort()`.

EXAMPLE See `getInetAddress()`.

java.net

SocketException

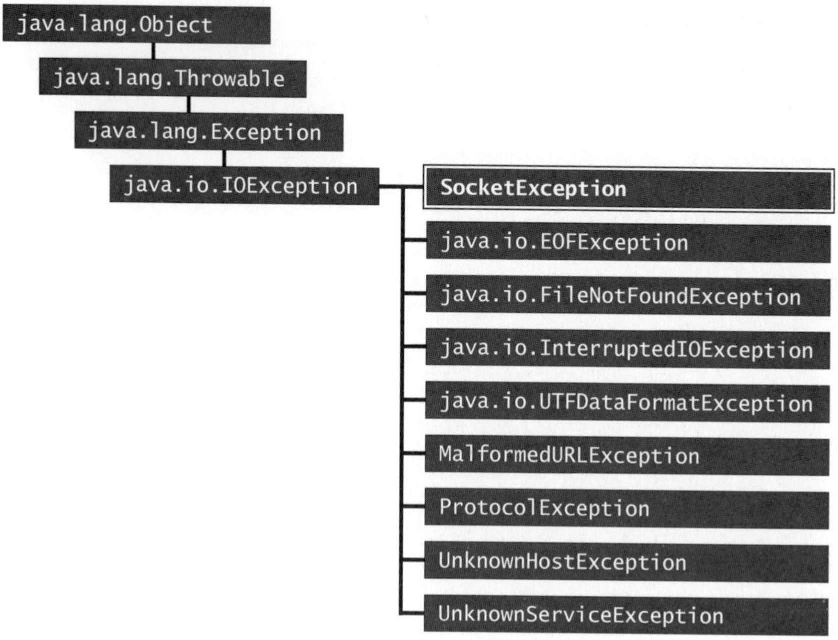

Syntax

```
public class SocketException extends IOException
```

Description

`SocketException` is an exception that is raised when attempting to create a socket or when attempting to set a program's socket factory when one has already been set.

A method that throws `SocketException` must declare it or any of its superclasses in its `throws` clause.

MEMBER SUMMARY

Constructor	
`SocketException()`	Constructs a new `SocketException` instance.

See Also

`DatagramSocket`, `IOException`, `ProtocolException`, `ServerSocket`, `Socket`, `SocketImpl`.

Example

This example raises a `SocketException` when it attempts to connect using a stream socket to a service that supports only datagrams (UDP).

```
import java.net.Socket;
import java.net.SocketException;
import java.io.IOException;

class Main {
    public static void main(String[] args) {
        try {
            // 69 == TFTP
            // ask for stream when only udp is available
            Socket sock = new Socket("localhost", 69, true);
            sock.close();
        } catch (SocketException e) {
            e.printStackTrace();
        } catch (IOException e) {
            e.printStackTrace();
        }
    }
}
```

SocketException()

PURPOSE Constructs a new `SocketException` instance.

SYNTAX

```
public SocketException()
public SocketException(String msg)
```

DESCRIPTION The two forms of this constructor create a new instance of `SocketException`. An optional string `msg` can be supplied that describes this particular instance of the exception.

PARAMETERS

`msg` A string that gives details about this exception.

java.net
SocketImpl

java.lang.Object → SocketImpl

Syntax

```
public abstract class SocketImpl
```

Description

In socket programming, Java programs use the methods in the `Socket` and `ServerSocket` classes. To allow a program (such as a Web browser) to choose its socket implementation depending on the security properties of the network, such as its firewall implementation, Java defines a socket implementation class, `SocketImpl`, which is used by the `Socket` and `ServerSocket` classes. It is a subclass (provided by the program) of `SocketImpl` that provides the actual implementation for sockets. A program configures the socket implementation to use by invoking `Socket.setSocketImplFactory()` and `ServerSocket.setSocketFactory()`.

To define a socket implementation, you define a subclass of `SocketImpl` that provides implementations for its abstract methods. You can use `SocketImpl` to implement both stream sockets and datagram sockets.

A *stream* socket is a socket in which a connection is established between the two endpoints of the socket. Data sent via a stream socket has reliable, ordered delivery. A *datagram* socket is a socket in which each packet sent is self-contained and has no relationship to other packets sent through the socket. Data sent via a datagram socket has unreliable delivery with no ordering guarantees. Also, data sent via a datagram socket is limited to the size of the packet, whereas data sent via a stream socket has no such limits.

Changing Socket State

The first step in using a socket is to create an unconnected socket. A socket must be connected before it is used. Once it is connected, you can get input and/or output streams on it in order to send and/or receive data. When you no longer need the socket, you must close it in order to free this limited resource. These are the steps taken by the peers of a datagram socket and the client of a stream socket.

A server that accepts stream socket connections must first create an unconnected stream socket and bind its own address to it. It then listens on the socket for connections and queues them as they arrive. It accepts a connection by creating a new socket to communicate with the client, while keeping the original stream socket open for listening for and queueing more connections. The server must close each new socket created for accepting a connection as the connection is terminated.

MEMBER SUMMARY

Methods for Changing Socket State (Abstract)	
`accept()`	Accepts a connection for this socket.
`bind()`	Binds this socket to the local port.
`close()`	Closes this socket.
`connect()`	Connects this socket to a destination.
`create()`	Creates a new unconnected socket.
`listen()`	Listens for connections on this stream socket.
Methods for Communicating via Sockets (Abstract)	
`available()`	Determines the number of bytes that can be read without blocking.
`getInputStream()`	Creates an input stream for this socket.
`getOutputStream()`	Creates an output stream for this socket.
Socket Information Fields and Methods	
`address`	The Internet address to which this socket is connected.
`fd`	This socket's file descriptor.
`getFileDescriptor()`	Retrieves the file descriptor used by this socket.
`getInetAddress()`	Retrieves the Internet address to which this socket is connected.
`getLocalPort()`	Retrieves this socket's local port number.
`getPort()`	Retrieves this socket's remote port number.
`localport`	This socket's local port number.
`port`	This socket's remote port number.
`toString()`	Generates the string representation for this object.

See Also

`DatagramSocket`, `ServerSocket`, `Socket`, `SocketImplFactory`.

Example

The JDK contains a package private class `PlainSocketImpl` that implements sockets using native methods that have no security checks. This is the implementation that is used when no socket implementation factory has been set. Typically, the application (e.g., a Web browser) installs its own socket implementation factory for security reasons, and this default implementation is not used. `PlainSocketImpl` gives you a good idea of how to build socket implementations. The following example extends `PlainSocketImpl` to give some debugging output. Because this new class is being added to the `java.net` package, the class file for the following must be installed in `$JAVAHOME/classes/java/net`.

Example

```
package java.net;

import java.io.*;
import java.net.PlainSocketImpl;

/**
 * Wrapper around default socket implementation that
 * provides debugging information.
 */

public class DebugSocketImpl extends PlainSocketImpl
{
    protected synchronized void create(boolean stream) throws
        IOException {
        System.err.println("Creating " +
                           (stream ? "virtual circuit" : "datagram") +
                           " socket.");
        super.create(stream);
    }

    protected void connect(String host, int port)
        throws UnknownHostException, IOException
    {
        System.err.println("Connecting to " + host + " at port "
            + port);
        super.connect(host, port);
    }

    protected void connect(InetAddress address, int port) throws
        IOException {
        System.err.println("Connect to " + address + " at port "
            + port);
        super.connect(address, port);
    }

    protected synchronized void bind(InetAddress address, int lport)
        throws IOException
    {
        System.err.println("Binding " + address + " at local port "
            + lport);
        super.bind(address, lport);
    }

    protected synchronized void listen(int count) throws IOException {
        System.err.println("Listening for " + count + " msec");
        super.listen(count);
    }

    protected synchronized void accept(SocketImpl s) throws
        IOException {
        System.err.println("Accepting connection for " + s.toString());
        super.accept(s);
    }
```

```
    protected synchronized InputStream getInputStream() throws
        IOException {
        System.err.println("Returning input stream for this socket");
        return super.getInputStream();
    }

    protected synchronized OutputStream getOutputStream() throws
        IOException {
        System.err.println("Returning output stream for this socket");
        return super.getOutputStream();
    }

    protected synchronized void close() throws IOException {
        System.err.println("Closing socket");
        super.close();
    }

    protected synchronized void finalize() throws IOException {
        System.err.println("Finalizing socket");
        super.finalize();
    }
}
```

accept()

PURPOSE Accepts a connection for this socket.

SYNTAX

```
protected abstract void accept(SocketImpl newSocket) throws
    IOException
```

DESCRIPTION This method creates a new socket for accepting the next pending connection on this socket using `newSocket`. If there are no pending connections, `accept()` blocks until one arrives.

`newSocket` is created before being passed to `accept()`. The Internet address, port numbers, and file descriptor fields of `newSocket` will be filled in by `accept()` when the connection is made. After `accept()` returns, `newSocket` can be used to send and receive data to and from the remote host of the accepted connection. When the connection is terminated, `newSocket` must be closed. This socket remains available for listening and queueing pending connections.

PARAMETERS

`newSocket` The new socket created for establishing the accepted connection.

EXCEPTIONS

`IOException` If an IO error occurred while accepting the next connection.

EXAMPLE This example shows how an existing socket implementation creates a new socket implementation for accepting a new connection.

```
SocketImpl impl = factory.createSocketImpl();
impl.create(true);                          // create stream socket
impl.address = new InetAddress();           // use package private constructor
impl.fd = new FileDescriptor();
this.accept(impl);   // accept connection and fill in address, ports, fd
```

address

PURPOSE The Internet address to which this socket is connected.

SYNTAX `protected InetAddress address`

DESCRIPTION For a datagram socket or a client stream socket, `address` is the Internet address of this socket's remote host. For a server stream socket (the one on which the server is listening), `address` is the local machine's Internet address to which the socket is bound.

SEE ALSO `getAddress()`.

EXAMPLE See `accept()`.

available()

PURPOSE Determines the number of bytes that can be read from this socket without blocking.

SYNTAX `protected abstract int available() throws IOException`

RETURNS The number of bytes that can be read without blocking.

SEE ALSO `getInputStream()`.

EXAMPLE

```
SocketImpl impl = factory.createSocketImpl();
    ...
System.out.println("Bytes available from socket: " +
    impl.available());
```

A B C D E F G H I J K L M N O P Q R S T U V W X Y Z

bind()

PURPOSE Binds the socket to the local port.

SYNTAX `protected abstract void bind(InetAddress src, int lport) throws IOException`

DESCRIPTION After a stream socket has been created, it must be bound to a local address and port before it can listen for connections. This method binds this socket to the specified local port `lport` on the local machine. Use of certain ports is restricted (e.g., those well-known ports for Internet protocols such as FTP, Telnet, and SMTP). `src` specifies the Internet address of the local machine to use for the binding.

PARAMETERS

`lport` The local port number to use for this socket. If `port` is `0`, any available port is used.

`src` The Internet address of this machine to use.

EXCEPTIONS

`IOException` If an IO error occurred while attempting to bind this socket to the local address and port.

SEE ALSO `listen()`, `ServerSocket.ServerSocket()`.

EXAMPLE This code fragment shows the typical steps involved in setting up a server socket.

```
SocketImpl impl = factory.createSocketImpl();
impl.create(true);
impl.bind(InetAddress.anyLocalAddress, port);
impl.listen(queueSize);
```

close()

PURPOSE Closes this socket.

SYNTAX `protected abstract void close() throws IOException`

DESCRIPTION This method closes this socket. A `close()` method typically frees up the resources used for this socket, such as its file descriptor, streams, and port numbers.

EXCEPTIONS

`IOException`

If an IO error occurred when closing the socket.

SEE ALSO ServerSocket.close(), Socket.close().

EXAMPLE See connect().

connect()

PURPOSE Connects this socket to a destination.

SYNTAX
```
protected abstract void connect(String hostName, int port) throws
    IOException
protected abstract void connect(InetAddress dst, int port) throws
    IOException
```

DESCRIPTION After a socket has been created, it must be connected to a destination before it can be used. connect() connects this socket to the port port on the machine named by hostName or on the machine with Internet address dst. After a socket has been connected, the socket can then send and receive data.

For a datagram socket, connect() associates the destination information with this socket and usually takes no other actions (e.g., it does not attempt to contact the destination). You can change the destination of a datagram socket at different times during the lifetime of the socket by calling connect() multiple times. In this way, you can reuse the same socket to talk to different destinations.

For a stream socket, connect() typically attempts to contact the destination as part of the operation. Typically, connect() is called only once on a stream socket to establish a connection with the destination. It is not called thereafter to change the destination.

PARAMETERS

dst	The Internet address of the remote host.
hostName	The name of the remote host.
port	The port number on the remote host.

EXCEPTIONS

IOException	If an IO error occurred while attempting to connect to the destination.

SEE ALSO create(), getInputStream(), getOutputStream(), Socket.Socket().

EXAMPLE This code fragment shows how a client creates a socket to a destination (destHost, destPort).

```
SocketImpl impl = factory.createSocketImpl();
impl.create(true); // create stream
impl.connect(destHost, destPort);
```

A B C D E F G H I J K L M N O P Q R S T U V W X Y Z

```
...
impl.close();
```

create()

PURPOSE Creates a new unconnected socket.

SYNTAX `protected abstract void create(boolean stream) throws IOException`

DESCRIPTION This method creates a stream socket if `stream` is true; otherwise it creates a datagram socket. Creation of a socket typically involves allocating a file descriptor to be used for the socket.

A socket must be connected before any data may be sent or received on it.

PARAMETERS

`stream` `true` means create a stream socket; `false` means create a datagram socket.

EXCEPTIONS

`IOException` If an IO error occurred during the creation of the stream.

SEE ALSO `bind()`, `connect()`, `DatagramSocket.DatagramSocket()`, `ServerSocket.ServerSocket()`, `Socket.Socket()`.

EXAMPLE See `accept()`.

fd

PURPOSE This socket's file descriptor.

SYNTAX `protected FileDescriptor fd`

SEE ALSO `getFileDescriptor()`.

EXAMPLE See `accept()`.

getFileDescriptor()

PURPOSE Retrieves this socket's file descriptor.

SYNTAX `protected FileDescriptor getFileDescriptor()`

DESCRIPTION A socket typically has a file descriptor that is used for doing input and/or output. `getFileDescriptor()` returns the file descriptor associated with this socket.

RETURNS This socket's file descriptor.

SEE ALSO fd, FileDescriptor, getInputStream(), getOutputStream().

EXAMPLE This code fragment prints information about a socket.

```
System.out.println("fd: " + impl.getFileDescriptor());
System.out.println("inetAddr: " + impl.getInetAddress());
System.out.println("port: " + impl.getPort());
System.out.println("local port: " + impl.getLocalPort());
```

getInetAddress()

PURPOSE Retrieves the Internet address to which this socket is connected.

SYNTAX `protected InetAddress getInetAddress()`

DESCRIPTION For a datagram socket or a client stream socket, `getInetAddress()` returns the Internet address of this socket's remote host. For a server stream socket (the one on which the server is listening), `getInetAddress()` returns the local machine's Internet address used for binding this socket.

RETURNS The Internet address to which this socket is connected.

SEE ALSO address, InetAddress, Socket.getInetAddress(), ServerSocket.getInetAddress().

EXAMPLE See getFileDescriptor().

getInputStream()

PURPOSE Creates an input stream for this socket.

SYNTAX
```
protected abstract InputStream getInputStream() throws
    IOException
```

DESCRIPTION After a socket has been connected, you can receive data from it by first creating an input stream for it and then reading data from this input stream. A typical implementation would use the file descriptor of this socket for creating its input stream.

RETURNS An input stream for receiving data from this socket.

EXCEPTIONS

IOException If an IO error occurred while creating the input stream.

SEE ALSO `getOutputStream()`, `InputStream`, `Socket.getInputStream()`.

EXAMPLE See the class example.

getLocalPort()

PURPOSE Retrieves this socket's local port number.

SYNTAX `protected int getLocalPort()`

RETURNS This socket's local port number.

SEE ALSO `localport`, `ServerSocket.getLocalPort()`.

EXAMPLE See `getFileDescriptor()`.

getOutputStream()

PURPOSE Creates an output stream for this socket.

SYNTAX
```
protected abstract OutputStream getOutputStream() throws
    IOException
```

DESCRIPTION After a socket has been connected, you can send data to the socket by first creating an output stream to it and then sending data to this output stream. `getOutputStream()` creates an output stream for this socket. A typical implementation would use the file descriptor of this socket for creating its output stream.

RETURNS An output stream for sending data to the remote host.

EXCEPTIONS

`IOException` If an IO error occurred while creating the output stream.

SEE ALSO `getInputStream()`, `OutputStream`, `Socket.getOutputStream()`.

EXAMPLE See the class example.

getPort()

PURPOSE Retrieves this socket's remote port number.

SYNTAX `protected int getPort()`

RETURNS This socket's remote port number.

SEE ALSO `port`, `Socket.getPort()`.

EXAMPLE See `getFileDescriptor()`.

listen()

PURPOSE Listens for connections on this stream socket.

SYNTAX `protected abstract void listen(int backlog) throws IOException`

DESCRIPTION After a stream socket has been created and bound, the `listen()` call is used to set the socket into "listening" mode. In this mode, connection set-up requests sent to this socket are queued until the server is ready to accept them. `backlog` specifies the maximum number of pending connections this socket can have. When this socket has `backlog` number of pending connections, clients attempting to make further connections to this socket will fail with an `IOException`.

`listen()` can be invoked only on stream sockets; they do not apply to datagram sockets.

PARAMETERS

`backlog` The maximum number of pending connections this socket can have.

EXCEPTIONS

`IOException` If an IO error occurred while listening for connections.

SEE ALSO `accept()`, `ServerSocket.ServerSocket()`.

EXAMPLE See `bind()`.

localport

PURPOSE This socket's local port number.

SYNTAX `protected int localport`

SEE ALSO `getLocalPort()`.

EXAMPLE

```
SocketImpl impl = factory.createSocketImpl();
    ...
System.out.println("Local port:" + impl.localport);
System.out.println("Remote port: " + impl.port);
```

port

PURPOSE This socket's remote port number.

SYNTAX `protected int port`

SEE ALSO `getPort()`.

EXAMPLE See `localport`.

toString()

PURPOSE Generates the string representation of this object.

SYNTAX `public String toString()`

DESCRIPTION The string representation of a socket consists of its destination address (Internet address plus remote port number) and the local port number being used for the socket. `toString()` returns the string representation of this socket.

RETURNS The string representation of this socket.

OVERRIDES `Object.toString()`.

SEE ALSO `getInetAddress()`, `getLocalPort()`, `getPort()`.

EXAMPLE

```
SocketImpl impl = factory.createSocketImpl();
System.out.println("This is what a newly created SocketImpl looks like: "
    + impl.toString());
```

java.net

SocketImplFactory

`java.lang.Object` — `SocketImpl`

Syntax

```
public interface SocketImplFactory
```

Description

This interface defines a factory for `SocketImpl` instances. It is used by the socket classes to create socket implementations that implement various policies.

In socket programming, Java programs use the methods in the `Socket` and `ServerSocket` classes. To allow a program (such as a Web browser) to choose its socket implementation depending on the security properties of the network, such as its firewall implementation, Java defines a socket implementation class, `SocketImpl`, which is used by the `Socket` and `ServerSocket` classes. It is a subclass (provided by the program) of `SocketImpl` that provides the actual implementation for sockets.

Different instances of `SocketImpl` are created by the `SocketImplFactory` object used by the program (usually a Web browser). A program configures the socket implementation to use by first selecting (and creating) its socket implementation factory object. It then uses `Socket.setSocketImplFactory()` and `ServerSocket.setSocketFactory()` to install this object as the factory for the entire program. These methods can be invoked only once. Once installed, the socket implementation factory cannot be replaced.

MEMBER SUMMARY	
Implementation Creation Method	
`createSocketImpl()`	Creates a new socket implementation.

See Also

`ServerSocket.setSocketFactory()`, `Socket.setSocketImplFactory()`, `SocketImpl`.

A B C D E F G H I J K L M N O P Q R S T U V W X Y Z

Example

This example defines a socket implementation factory `DebugSocketImplFactory` that creates and returns a new instance of `DebugSocketImpl` (see `SocketImpl`) for each request to create a new socket implementation.

```
import java.net.*;

public class DebugSocketImplFactory implements SocketImplFactory {
    public SocketImpl createSocketImpl() {
        return new DebugSocketImpl();
    }
}
```

createSocketImpl()

PURPOSE Creates a new socket implementation.

SYNTAX `SocketImpl createSocketImpl()`

DESCRIPTION This method creates a new instance of `SocketImpl`. It is used by the constructors in `ServerSocket` and `Socket` when instances of `ServerSocket` and `Socket` classes, respectively, are created.

SEE ALSO `ServerSocket.ServerSocket()`, `Socket.Socket()`.

EXAMPLE See the class example.

java.util
Stack

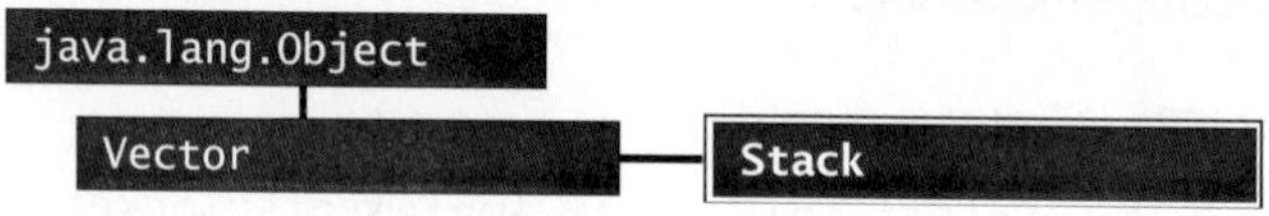

Syntax

`public class Stack extends Vector`

Description

The `Stack` class represents a last-in/first-out (LIFO) stack of objects. It provides methods for popping and pushing possibly `null` objects onto the stack. There is no limit to the size of the stack. If you try to pop objects from an empty stack, an `EmptyStackException` will be raised.

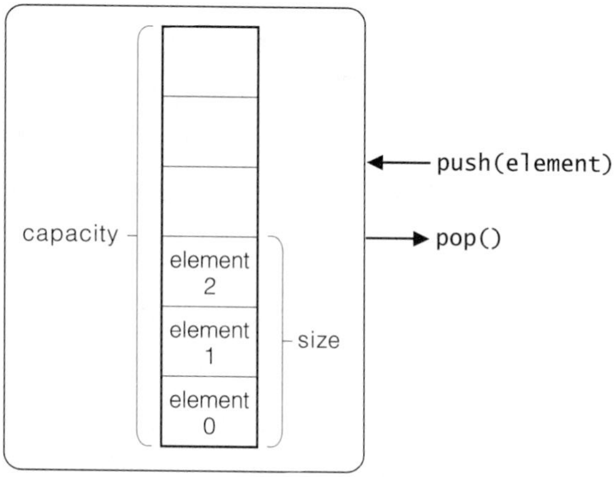

FIGURE 215 `Stack`

MEMBER SUMMARY	
Stack Methods	
`empty()`	Determines whether this stack is empty.
`peek()`	Retrieves the top object of this stack without removing it.
`pop()`	Removes the top object from this stack.
`push()`	Pushes an object onto the top of this stack.
`search()`	Searches for an object on this stack.

See Also

`Vector`.

Example

This example uses a stack to maintain a stack of newspapers. A newspaper that is pushed on top of another newspaper must first be removed (popped) before the newspaper beneath it can be removed. This example shows the use of the various methods in the Stack class.

```
import java.util.Stack;
import java.util.Date;
import java.util.EmptyStackException;

class Newspaper {
    Date date;
    String publisher;
    Newspaper(String pub, Date d) {
        date = d;
        publisher = pub;
    }
    Newspaper(String pub) {
        this(pub, new Date()); // use today's date
    }
    public String toString() {
        return (publisher + " " + date);
    }
}
class Main {
    public static void main(String[] args) {
        Stack newspapers = new Stack();

        Newspaper NYT = new Newspaper("New York Times");
        Newspaper SJM = new Newspaper("San Jose Mercury News");
        Newspaper SFC = new Newspaper("San Francisco Chronicle");
        Newspaper WSJ = new Newspaper("Wall Street Journal");

        // push onto stack
        newspapers.push(NYT);
        newspapers.push(SJM);
        newspapers.push(SFC);

        int where = newspapers.search(SJM);
        System.out.println(SJM + " is at the " + where + " position");

        where = newspapers.search(WSJ);
        if (where > 0)
            System.out.println(WSJ + " is at the " + where +
                " position");
        else
            System.out.println(WSJ + " is not on the stack");

        try {
            Newspaper top = (Newspaper) newspapers.peek();
            System.out.println("Top contains " + top);

            do {
                top = (Newspaper) newspapers.pop();
```

```
                System.out.println("Popped off " + top);
            } while (!newspapers.empty());

        } catch (EmptyStackException e) {
            System.out.println("Trying to go beyond bottom of stack");
        }
    }
}
```

empty()

PURPOSE Determines whether this stack is empty.

SYNTAX `public boolean empty()`

RETURNS `true` if this stack is empty; `false` otherwise.

EXAMPLE See the class example.

peek()

PURPOSE Retrieves the top object from this stack without removing it.

SYNTAX `public Object peek()`

RETURNS The top object from this stack; `null` if the top object is `null`.

EXCEPTIONS

`EmptyStackException`
If this stack is empty.

SEE ALSO `pop()`.

EXAMPLE See the class example.

pop()

PURPOSE Removes the top object of this stack.

SYNTAX `public Object pop()`

DESCRIPTION This method removes the top object from this stack and returns it.

RETURNS The top object from this stack; `null` if the top object is `null`.

EXCEPTIONS

`EmptyStackException`
If this stack is empty.

SEE ALSO `peek()`, `push()`.

EXAMPLE See the class example.

push()

PURPOSE Pushes an object onto the top of this stack.

SYNTAX `public Object push(Object obj)`

DESCRIPTION This method pushes the object `obj` onto the top of this stack and returns `obj`.

PARAMETERS

`obj` The object to push can be `null`.

RETURNS `obj`.

SEE ALSO `peek()`, `pop()`.

EXAMPLE See the class example.

search()

PURPOSE Searches for an object on this stack.

SYNTAX `public int search(Object obj)`

DESCRIPTION This method searches for the object `obj` on this stack. If `obj` is on this stack, this method returns its position on the stack as measured from the top of the stack. For example, if `obj` is at the top of the stack, its position is 0; if `obj` is next to the top on the stack, its position is 1, and so on. If `obj` is not on this stack, `-1` is returned. If more than one instance of `obj` is on the stack, the position of the one closest to the top of the stack is returned.

PARAMETERS

`obj` The object for which to search. `obj` cannot be `null`.

RETURNS The position of `obj` on the stack (0 is top of stack); `-1` if `obj` is not found.

EXAMPLE See the class example.

java.lang
StackOverflowError

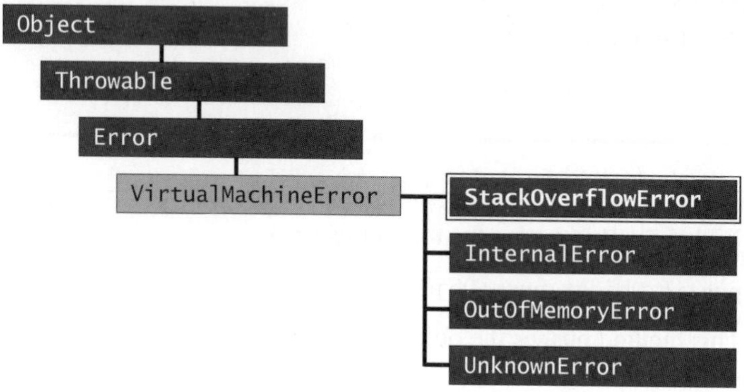

Synta x

```
public class StackOverflowError extends VirtualMachineError
```

Description

When the Java virtual machine executes a program, the execution environment (parameters, variables) of each method that it calls is placed on an execution stack. For example, if method `A` were to call method `B`, which in turn called method `C`, the execution stack would contain `{C, B, A}`. `StackOverflowError` is an unrecoverable error raised by the Java virtual machine when the execution stack overflows as it is attempting to execute a method. Usually, this indicates a problem with the calling sequence of methods, rather than a problem with the limit of the execution stack. For example, a nonterminating, tail-recursive program would overflow the stack because the execution stack cannot be infinitely large.

`StackOverflowError` should not be caught or declared in the `throws` clause of a method.

MEMBER SUMMARY	
Constructor	
`StackOverflowError()`	Constructs a `StackOverflowError` instance.

See Also

`Error`, `VirtualMachineError`.

Example

This example throws a `StackOverflowError` because the calling sequence never terminates.

```
class Main {
    public static void method1() {
        method2();
    }
    public static void method2() {
        method1();
    }
    public static void main(String[] args) {
        System.out.println("StackOverflowError example");
        method1();
    }
}
```

StackOverflowError()

PURPOSE Constructs a `StackOverflowError` instance.

SYNTAX
```
public StackOverflowError()
public StackOverflowError(String msg)
```

DESCRIPTION The two forms of this constructor create a new instance of `StackOverflowError`. An optional string `msg` can be supplied that describes this particular instance of the error.

PARAMETERS

`msg` A string that gives details about this error.

A B C D E F G H I J K L M N O P Q R S T U V W X Y Z

java.io

StreamTokenizer

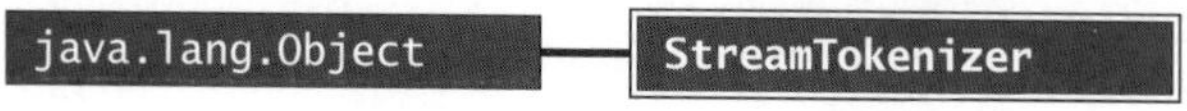

Syntax

```
public class StreamTokenizer
```

Description

The `StreamTokenizer` class reads from an input stream to produce a stream of tokens (see Figure 216). The input stream is parsed according to the syntax defined by the stream tokenizer. The stream tokenizer is defined using the elements defined in Table 16.

By default, the stream tokenizer defines various settings for which characters are word characters, which characters are whitespace characters, and so on. You can customize your stream tokenizer by changing these settings using the methods provided by the `StreamTokenizer` class.

You use the stream tokenizer first by calling its constructor to create it. Then you call various syntax specifying methods to customize the stream tokenizer. Finally, you call `nextToken()` in a loop to parse the stream into tokens.

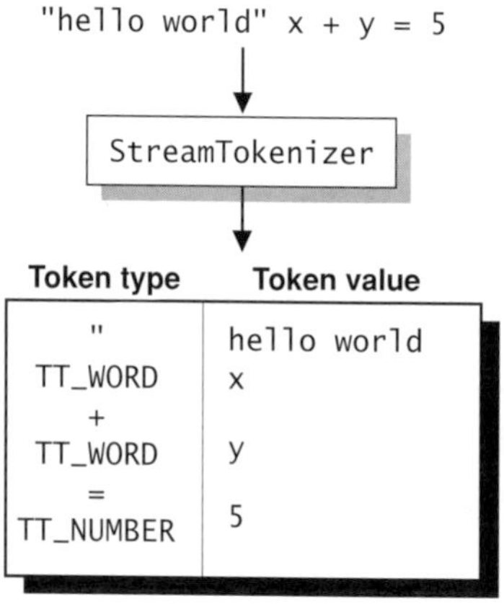

FIGURE 216 `StreamTokenizer`

TABLE 16 Elements of a Stream Tokenizer

`number`	A sequence of digits characters of a double-precision floating-point number.
`word`	A sequence of consecutive word characters delimited by whitespace characters.
`string`	A sequence of characters delimited by matching quote characters.
`comment`	Characters that are for comments only and not parsed as tokens.
`EOF`	An end-of-file has been reached on the stream.
`EOL`	An end-of-line has been encountered in the stream.
`white space`	Whitespace characters are used to separate word tokens from word tokens and number tokens from number tokens.

MEMBER SUMMARY

Constructor	
`StreamTokenizer()`	Constructs a stream tokenizer for an input stream.
Syntax Specification Methods	
`commentChar()`	Specifies a character as the start of a single-line comment.
`eolIsSignificant()`	Specifies whether an end-of-line is recognized as a token.
`lowerCaseMode()`	Specifies whether word tokens are automatically lowercased.
`ordinaryChar()`	Specifies a character as being ordinary.
`ordinaryChars()`	Specifies characters in a range as ordinary.
`parseNumbers()`	Specifies that digit characters are used for numbers.
`quoteChar()`	Specifies a character as a quote character.
`resetSyntax()`	Resets the syntax table so that all characters are ordinary.
`slashSlashComments()`	Specifies whether to recognize C++-style comments.
`slashStarComments()`	Specifies whether to recognize C-style comments.
`whitespaceChars()`	Specifies that characters in this range are whitespace characters.
`wordChars()`	Specifies that characters in this range are word characters.
Parsing Methods	
`lineno()`	Retrieves the current input line number.
`pushBack()`	Pushes back a token onto the input stream.
`nextToken()`	Parses a token from the input stream.
Token Fields	
`nval`	The numeric value of the number token.
`sval`	The string value of the word or string token.
`ttype`	The type of the token returned.
Token Type Fields (static final)	
`TT_EOF`	The end-of-file token.
`TT_EOL`	The end-of-line token.
`TT_NUMBER`	The number token type.
`TT_WORD`	The word token type.
Description Method	
`toString()`	Generates the string representation of the token.

See Also

`StringTokenizer`.

Summary

Example

This example uses the stream tokenizer to parse a list of key/value pairs and places them into a hash table. The key is separated from the value using either whitespace characters or an equals character ('=').

```
import java.io.StreamTokenizer;
import java.io.InputStream;
import java.util.Hashtable;
import java.io.IOException;

class KeyValue {
    public static void parser(InputStream in, Hashtable h) {
        StreamTokenizer p = new StreamTokenizer(in);

        // key values are separated by white spaces or '='
        p.whitespaceChars('=', '=');
        int c;
        String key = null;
        boolean errFlag = false;
        boolean expecting_value = false;
        try {
        out:
            while (true) {
                c = p.nextToken();
                switch (c) {
                case StreamTokenizer.TT_EOF:
                    break out;
                case StreamTokenizer.TT_EOL:
                    // should not see this because we didn't make
                    // EOL significant
                    System.err.println(
                        "warning: unexpected EOL token"); break;
                case StreamTokenizer.TT_NUMBER:
                    if (expecting_value) {
                        h.put(key, new Double(p.nval));
                        expecting_value = false;
                    } else {
                        // cannot have numeric keys
                        errFlag = true;
                        break out;
                    }
                    break;
                case StreamTokenizer.TT_WORD:
                    if (expecting_value) {
                        h.put(key, p.sval);
                        expecting_value = false;
                    } else {
                        expecting_value = true;
                        key = p.sval;
                    }
                    break;
                default:
                    errFlag = true;
```

A B C D E F G H I J K L M N O P Q R S T U V W X Y Z

```
                    break out;
                }
            }
            if (errFlag)
                System.err.println(
                    "Error encountered around '" + key +"'");
        } catch (IOException e) {
            e.printStackTrace();
        }
    }
    public static void main(String[] args) {
        Hashtable h = new Hashtable();
        parser(System.in, h);
        System.out.println(h.toString());
    }
}
```

commentChar()

PURPOSE Specifies a character as the start of a single-line comment.

SYNTAX `public void commentChar(int ch)`

DESCRIPTION This method specifies that the character `ch` is used to denote the start of a single-line comment. When `ch` is encountered in the input stream, all characters between `ch` and the end of the line are treated as a single-line comment. Comments are not returned by the parser (`nextToken()`).

There can be many such comment characters. By default, the forward slash character ('/') is a comment character.

PARAMETERS

`ch` The character to be used as the start of a single-line comment.

SEE ALSO `nextToken()`, `slashSlashComments()`, `slashStarComments()`.

EXAMPLE This example shows the different ways that comments can be specified to the stream tokenizer. This example turns on both // and /* comments. It also uses # to begin single-line comments. The default / comment character must be turned off in order for /* comments to be recognized.

```
import java.io.StreamTokenizer;
import java.io.IOException;

class Comments {
    public static void main(String[] args) {
        try {
            StreamTokenizer tokens = new StreamTokenizer(System.in);
            // turn off single slash as comment char, this is required
            // for slashStar comments to work properly
```

A B C D E F G H I J K L M N O P Q R S T U V W X Y Z

```
                tokens.ordinaryChar('/');
                tokens.slashStarComments(true);
                tokens.slashSlashComments(true);

                tokens.commentChar('#');
                int c;
            out:
                while (true) {
                    switch (c=tokens.nextToken()) {
                    case StreamTokenizer.TT_EOF:
                        break out;
                    case StreamTokenizer.TT_EOL:
                        System.out.print("\n" + tokens.lineno() + "\t");
                        break;
                    case StreamTokenizer.TT_NUMBER:
                        System.out.println("Number: " + tokens.nval);
                        break;
                    case StreamTokenizer.TT_WORD:
                        System.out.println("Identifier: " + tokens.sval);
                        break;
                    }
                }
            } catch (IOException e) {
                e.printStackTrace();
            }
        }
    }
```

eolIsSignificant()

PURPOSE Specifies whether an end-of-line is recognized as a token.

SYNTAX `public void eolIsSignificant(boolean eolSign)`

DESCRIPTION This method specifies whether end-of-line characters are significant. If they are, then when an end-of-line (one of `\n`, `\r`, or `\r\n`) is encountered, the token type `TT_EOL` is returned in `ttype`. If they are not significant, end-of-line characters are treated as whitespace characters. If `eolSign` is `true`, end-of-line characters are significant; if `eolSign` is `false`, end-of-line characters are not significant. By default, they are not significant.

PARAMETERS

`eolSign` `true` means end-of-lines are significant; `false` means end-of-lines are treated as white spaces.

SEE ALSO `TT_EOL`, `ttype`.

EXAMPLE See `nextToken()`.

lineno()

PURPOSE Retrieves the current input line number.

SYNTAX `public int lineno()`

RETURNS The current input line number.

EXAMPLE See `nextToken()`.

lowerCaseMode()

PURPOSE Specifies whether word tokens are automatically lowercased.

SYNTAX `public void lowerCaseMode(boolean lower)`

DESCRIPTION This method specifies whether word tokens parsed from this stream will be automatically lowercased before being returned. If `lower` is `true`, word tokens (`sval`) are lowercased before returned in `sval`. If `lower` is `false`, the case of characters in word tokens are left unchanged. By default, word tokens are left unchanged.

PARAMETERS

`lower` `true` means to automatically lowercase word tokens; `false` means to leave word tokens as is.

SEE ALSO `sval`, `TT_WORD`.

EXAMPLE See `nextToken()`.

nextToken()

PURPOSE Parses a token from the input stream.

SYNTAX `public int nextToken() throws IOException`

DESCRIPTION This method parses the next token in the input stream. It uses the syntax as specified by the program to determine what defines a token. `nextToken()` returns the token type of the token or the character read from the stream (this is, the same as the value of `ttype`). If the token type is `TT_NUMBER`, the value of the token is returned in `nval`. If the token type is `TT_WORD` or one of the quote characters, the value of the token is returned in `sval`. `TT_EOL` indicates an end-of-line has been encountered; `TT_EOF` indicates the end-of-file has been encountered in the stream. If the return value is none of TT_NUMBER, TT_WORD, TT_EOL, or TT_EOF, it is the character read from the input stream.

RETURNS The token type of the next token (one of TT_NUMBER, TT_WORD, TT_EOL, or TT_EOF), or the next character in the input stream.

EXCEPTIONS

`IOException` If an IO error occurred while attempting to read the next token.

SEE ALSO `nval`, `sval`, TT_EOF, TT_EOL, TT_NUMBER, TT_WORD, `ttype`.

EXAMPLE See also the class example, `commentChar()`, and `parseNumbers()`. This example demonstrates the use of `nextToken()` and various syntax specifiers. To have digit characters be treated as word characters, you must first reset the syntax and then add back the word characters and whitespace characters.

```
import java.io.StreamTokenizer;
import java.io.IOException;

class Parser {
    public static void main(String[] args) {
        try {
            StreamTokenizer tokens = new StreamTokenizer(System.in);

            tokens.resetSyntax();
            tokens.wordChars('0', '9');          // make digit
                chars word chars
            tokens.wordChars('a', 'z');
            tokens.wordChars('A', 'Z');
            tokens.eolIsSignificant(true);
            tokens.quoteChar('"');               // " is quoted
                string delimiter
            tokens.whitespaceChars(0, ' ');
            tokens.whitespaceChars('$', '$');   // treat $ as
                white space
            tokens.lowerCaseMode(true);          // turn tokens to
                lowercase
            int c;
        out:
            while (true) {
                switch (c=tokens.nextToken()) {
                case StreamTokenizer.TT_EOF:
                    break out;
                case StreamTokenizer.TT_EOL:
                    System.out.print("\n" + tokens.lineno() + "\t");
                    break;
                case StreamTokenizer.TT_NUMBER:
                    // unexpected because we made digit chars words
                    System.err.println(
                        "warning: unexpected number: " + tokens.nval);
                    break;
                case StreamTokenizer.TT_WORD:
                    System.out.println("Identifier: " + tokens.sval);
```

```
                        break;
                    case '"':
                        System.out.println("Quoted String: " +
                                           tokens.sval); break;
                    default:
                        System.out.println("Default: " + (char)c);
                    }
                }
            } catch (IOException e) {
                e.printStackTrace();
            }
        }
    }
```

nval

PURPOSE The numeric value of the number token.

SYNTAX `public double nval`

DESCRIPTION This field stores the numeric value of the token being returned by `nextToken()`. Numeric tokens are returned only if the syntax specifies that digit characters should be treated as numbers. Otherwise digit characters are treated as ordinary characters.

SEE ALSO `nextToken()`, `parseNumbers()`, `TT_NUMBER`.

EXAMPLE See the class example, `commentChar()`, and `nextToken()`.

ordinaryChar()

PURPOSE Specifies a character as being ordinary.

SYNTAX `public void ordinaryChar(int ch)`

DESCRIPTION This method specifies that the character `ch` is ordinary. When `ch` is encountered in the input stream, it will not be treated as a word character, comment, string, whitespace character, or number character. It is simply returned as is by `nextToken()`.

All other characters not set by the `StreamTokenizer` constructor are by default ordinary characters. You can call `ordinaryChar()` or `ordinaryChars()` several times to set different ranges of characters to be ordinary characters. You can set a character that is an ordinary character to be some other type of character by calling `wordChars()` or other syntax-specifying methods.

A B C D E F G H I J K L M N O P Q R S T U V W X Y Z

PARAMETERS

`ch` The character to be classified as ordinary.

SEE ALSO `ordinaryChars()`, `StreamTokenizer()`.

EXAMPLE See `commentChar()`.

ordinaryChars()

PURPOSE Specifies characters in a range as ordinary.

SYNTAX `public void ordinaryChars(int low, int hi)`

DESCRIPTION This method specifies that the characters in the range of Unicode characters `low` to `hi`, inclusive, are ordinary. Any of these characters encountered in the input stream will not be treated as a word character, comment, string, whitespace character, or number character. They are simply returned as is by `nextToken()`.

All other characters not set by the `StreamTokenizer` constructor are by default ordinary characters. You can call `ordinaryChar()` or `ordinaryChars()` several times to set different ranges of characters to be ordinary characters. You can set a character that is an ordinary character to be some other type of character by calling `wordChars()` or other syntax-specifying methods.

PARAMETERS

`hi` The last Unicode character in the range of ordinary characters.
`low` The first Unicode character in the range of ordinary characters.

SEE ALSO `ordinaryChar()`, `StreamTokenizer()`.

EXAMPLE See use of `ordinaryChar()` in the `commentChar()` example for an example of similar usage.

parseNumbers()

PURPOSE Specifies that digit characters are used for number tokens.

SYNTAX `public void parseNumbers()`

DESCRIPTION This method specifies that the digit characters (0–9, period (.), and minus (-)) are to be used in constructing number tokens. Digit characters also can appear as part of a word if they occur in the second or higher position of the word. When a number token (any double-precision floating-point number) is encountered in the input stream, `nextToken()` returns `TT_NUMBER` and sets the field `nval` to be the numeric value of the token. Once `parseNumbers()` has been invoked, the only way to undo its effects (i.e., specify that digit characters are not to be used for number tokens) is to call `ordinaryChar()` or `wordChars()` explicitly on those characters.

The default `StreamTokenizer` constructor calls `parseNumbers()`.

SEE ALSO `nextToken()`, `nval`, `TT_NUMBER`.

EXAMPLE This example recognizes only numbers as tokens; all other nonwhitespace characters are not returned as tokens but treated as individual characters.

```
import java.io.StreamTokenizer;
import java.io.IOException;

class ParseNum {
    public static void main(String[] args) {
        try {
            StreamTokenizer tokens = new StreamTokenizer(System.in);

            tokens.resetSyntax();                 // turn off
                everything else
            tokens.parseNumbers();
            tokens.whitespaceChars(0, ' ');     // must put spaces back

            int c;
          out:
            while (true) {
                c = tokens.nextToken();
                switch (tokens.ttype) {           // same as value of 'c'
                case StreamTokenizer.TT_EOF:
                    break out;
                case StreamTokenizer.TT_NUMBER:
                    System.out.println(tokens.toString());
                    break;
                case StreamTokenizer.TT_WORD:
                    System.err.println(
                        "warning: unexpected identifier: "
                            + tokens.sval);
                    break;
                default:
                    System.out.println("Default: " + (char)c);
                }
            }
        } catch (IOException e) {
            e.printStackTrace();
        }
    }
}
```

A B C D E F G H I J K L M N O P Q R S T U V W X Y Z

pushBack()

PURPOSE Pushes back a token onto the input stream.

SYNTAX `public void pushBack()`

DESCRIPTION This method pushes back the last token obtained via `nextToken()` onto the input stream. The next call to `nextToken()` will return this same token. Calling `pushBack()` consecutive times has the same effect as calling it once.

SEE ALSO `nextToken()`.

EXAMPLE This example shows part of an expression parser that uses `pushBack()`.

```
public static Node parseExpr(StreamTokenizer tokens)
    throws IOException {
    Node left, op, right;
    int c = tokens.nextToken();
    switch (c) {
    case '(':
           left = parseToken(tokens);
           op = parseToken(tokens);
           right = parseToken(tokens);
           if (tokens.nextToken() != (int)')')  {
               System.err.print("Unbalanced parenthesis");
               return (null);
           }
           return new Node(op, left, right);
    default:
           tokens.pushBack();
           return (parseToken(tokens));
    }
}
public static Node parseToken(StreamTokenizer tokens)
    throws IOException {
        switch (tokens.nextToken()) {
        case StreamTokenizer.TT_EOF:
            return (null);
        case StreamTokenizer.TT_NUMBER:
            return (new Node(tokens.ttype, tokens.nval));
        case StreamTokenizer.TT_WORD:
            return (new Node(tokens.ttype, tokens.sval));
        case '+':
        case '-':
        case '*':
        case '/':
            return (new Node(Node.TT_OPERATOR,
                (char)tokens.ttype));
        case '(':
            tokens.pushBack();
            return (parseExpr(tokens));
        }
        return (null);
}
```

quoteChar()

PURPOSE Specifies a character as a quote character.

SYNTAX `public void quoteChar(int ch)`

DESCRIPTION This method specifies that the character `ch` is a quote character. `ch` will delimit the start and end of a string token. When `nextToken()` encounters `ch`, all characters appearing between the starting and ending `ch` are returned as a string token in `sval`. `nextToken()` itself returns `ch` (`ttype` is also set to `ch`). There can be multiple quote characters in the syntax, but the same quote character must be used to delimit a single string token. Other quote characters that appear within a string token are not treated as quote characters for that string token.

PARAMETERS

`ch` The character to be used as a quote character.

SEE ALSO `nextToken()`, `sval`.

EXAMPLE See `nextToken()`.

resetSyntax()

PURPOSE Resets the syntax so that all characters are ordinary.

SYNTAX `public void resetSyntax()`

SEE ALSO `ordinaryChar()`, `ordinaryChars()`.

EXAMPLE See `nextToken()`, `parseNumbers()`.

slashSlashComments()

PURPOSE Specifies whether to recognize C++-style comments.

SYNTAX `public void slashSlashComments(boolean cpp)`

DESCRIPTION A C++-style comment is delimited by two consecutive forward slash characters ('/') and the end of the line. `slashSlashComments()` is used to specify whether the parser should recognize C++-style comments. If `cpp` is `true`, double slashes are recognized as the start of comments; otherwise they are not treated as the start of comments.

Note that by default, the single forward slash ('/') is a comment character. This mean that turning on C++-style comments does not do anything because the first slash would be recognized as a comment character and the rest of the line would be treated as a comment. `slashSlashComments()` is useful only if the slash character has been explicitly turned into a word character or an ordinary character.

PARAMETERS

`cpp` `true` means recognize C++-style comments; `false` means do not recognize C++-style comments.

SEE ALSO `commentChar()`, `nextToken()`, `slashStarComments()`.

EXAMPLE See `commentChar()`.

slashStarComments()

PURPOSE Specifies whether to recognize C-style comments.

SYNTAX `public void slashStarComments(boolean cp)`

DESCRIPTION A C-style comment is delimited by the string "/*" and the string ("*/"). Any characters that occur between "/*" and "*/" are treated as comments. `slashStarComments()` is used to specify whether the parser should recognize C-style comments. If `cp` is `true`, C-style comments are recognized; otherwise "/*" strings are not treated specially.

Note that by default, the single forward slash ('/') is a comment character. This means that turning C-style comments on does not work by default because the first slash would be recognized as a comment character and the rest of the line would be treated as a comment. `slashStarComments()` works only if the slash character has been explicitly turned into a word character or an ordinary character.

PARAMETERS

`cp` `true` means recognize C-style comments; `false` means do not recognize C-style comments.

SEE ALSO `commentChar()`, `nextToken()`, `slashStarComments()`.

EXAMPLE See `commentChar()`.

StreamTokenizer()

PURPOSE Constructs a new stream tokenizer for an input stream.

SYNTAX `public StreamTokenizer (InputStream in)`

DESCRIPTION The constructor for `StreamTokenizer` creates a stream tokenizer for the input stream `in`. The default settings are as follows:

- a–z, A–Z, and characters with Unicode values 160–255 are word characters.
- Forward slash (/) is a comment character.
- Characters with Unicode values 0–32 are whitespace characters (this includes, among others, space, escape, newline (`\n`), carriage return (`\r`), backspace, and delete).
- Single quote (`'`) and double quote (") are quote characters.
- 0–9, period (`.`), and minus (`-`) are digit characters.

To override these defaults, call the appropriate syntax specifier methods after the stream tokenizer has been created.

PARAMETERS

`in` The input stream for which to create the stream tokenizer.

SEE ALSO `commentChar()`, `eolIsSignificant()`, `parseNumbers()`, `ordinaryChar()`, `quoteChar()`, `resetSyntax()`, `slashSlashComments()`, `slashStarComments()`, `whiteSpaceChars()`, `wordChars()`.

EXAMPLE See the class example, `commentChar()`, `nextToken()`, and `parseNumbers()`.

sval

PURPOSE The string value of the word or string token.

SYNTAX `public String sval`

DESCRIPTION When `nextToken()` encounters a word token or a quoted string, it sets `sval` to be the word token or quoted string. For the quoted string, the beginning and ending quote characters are not included in `sval`.

SEE ALSO `nextToken()`, `quoteChar()`, `TT_WORD`, `wordChars()`.

EXAMPLE See the class example, `commentChar()`, and `nextToken()`.

A B C D E F G H I J K L M N O P Q R S T U V W X Y Z

toString()

PURPOSE Generates the string representation of the token.

SYNTAX `public String toString()`

DESCRIPTION This method returns the string representation of the token that `nextToken()` just returned (i.e., the token most recently parsed). It consists of a string description of the token and the line number at which the token occurred in the input stream.

RETURNS The string representation of the token.

OVERRIDES `Object.toString()`.

EXAMPLE See `parseNumbers()`.

TT_EOF

PURPOSE The end-of-file token.

SYNTAX `public static final int TT_EOF`

DESCRIPTION This constant field represents the end-of-file token. It is returned by `nextToken()` when the end-of-file has been reached on the input stream.

SEE ALSO `nextToken()`, `ttype`.

EXAMPLE See the class example, `commentChar()`, `nextToken()`, and `parseNumbers()`.

TT_EOL

PURPOSE The end-of-line token.

SYNTAX `public static final int TT_EOL`

DESCRIPTION This constant field represents the end-of-line token. It is returned by `nextToken()` when an end-of-line has been encountered in the input stream *and* if end-of-line has been made significant via `eolIsSignificant()`.

SEE ALSO `eolIsSignificant()`, `nextToken()`, `ttype`.

EXAMPLE See the class example, `commentChar()`, and `nextToken()`.

TT_NUMBER

PURPOSE The number token type.

SYNTAX `public static final int TT_NUMBER`

DESCRIPTION This constant field represents the number token type. It is returned by `nextToken()` when a number token has been encountered in the input stream. When `nextToken()` returns `TT_NUMBER`, it sets `nval` to be the numeric value of the token. `nextToken()` recognizes number tokens only if `parseNumbers()` has been called (it is called by default in the `StreamTokenizer` constructor).

SEE ALSO `nextToken()`, `nval`, `parseNumbers()`, `StreamTokenizer()`, `ttype`.

EXAMPLE See the class example, `commentChar()`, `nextToken()`, and `parseNumbers()`.

TT_WORD

PURPOSE The word token type.

SYNTAX `public static final int TT_WORD`

DESCRIPTION This constant field represents the word token type. It is returned by `nextToken()` when a word token has been encountered in the input stream. When `nextToken()` returns `TT_WORD`, it sets `sval` to be the value of the word token. `nextToken()` recognizes word tokens by the setting of word characters via calls to `wordChars()`. Some default word characters are set by default in the `StreamTokenizer` constructor.

SEE ALSO `nextToken()`, `sval`, `StreamTokenizer()`, `wordChars()`, `ttype`.

EXAMPLE See the class example, `commentChar()`, `nextToken()`, and `parseNumbers()`.

ttype

PURPOSE The type of the token returned.

SYNTAX `public int ttype`

DESCRIPTION This field holds the type of the token parsed by `nextToken()`. It is identical to the value returned by `nextToken()`. Its value is one of `TT_EOF`, `TT_EOL`, `TT_NUMBER`, or `TT_WORD` or the character just read from the input stream token if it is none of the special characters recognized by the tokenizer.

A B C D E F G H I J K L M N O P Q R S T U V W X Y Z

SEE ALSO `nextToken()`, `quoteChar()`, `TT_EOF`, `TT_EOL`, `TT_NUMBER`, `TT_WORD`.

EXAMPLE See `parseNumbers()`.

whitespaceChars()

PURPOSE Specifies characters as whitespace characters.

SYNTAX `public void whitespaceChars(int low, int hi)`

DESCRIPTION This method specifies that the characters with Unicode value `low` to Unicode value `hi` should be treated as whitespace characters. Whitespace characters are used to separate word tokens and number tokens.

By default, the `StreamTokenizer` constructor sets the characters with Unicode values 0–32 to be whitespace characters (this includes, among other characters, space, escape, newline (\n), carriage return (\r), backspace, and delete). You can call `whiteSpaceChars()` several times to set different ranges of characters to be whitespace characters. You can reset a character that is a whitespace character to be some other type of character by calling `ordinaryChar()` or other syntax-specifying methods.

PARAMETERS

`hi` The last Unicode character in the range of whitespace characters.

`low` The first Unicode character in the range of whitespace characters.

SEE ALSO `eolIsSignificant()`, `nextToken()`, `StreamTokenizer()`.

EXAMPLE See the class example, `nextToken()`, and `parseNumbers()`.

wordChars()

PURPOSE Specifies characters as word characters.

SYNTAX `public void wordChars(int low, int hi)`

DESCRIPTION This method specifies that the characters with Unicode value `low` to Unicode value `hi` should be treated as word characters. A word consists of a word character, followed by consecutive word or digit characters. Words are separated by whitespaces, end-of-lines, or an end-of-file. When `nextToken()` encounters a word, it returns `TT_WORD` and sets `sval` to be the word just parsed.

By default, the `StreamTokenizer` constructor sets the characters a–z, A–Z, and characters with Unicode values 160–255 to be word characters. Calls to wordChars() are cumulative. You can call wordChars() several times to set different ranges of characters to be word characters. You can reset a character that is a word character to be some other type of character by calling ordinaryChar() or other syntax-specifying methods.

PARAMETERS

hi	The last Unicode character in the range of word characters.
low	The first Unicode character in the range of word characters.

SEE ALSO nextToken(), sval, TT_WORD, whiteSpaceChars().

EXAMPLE See nextToken().

java.lang
String

Object — String

Syntax

```
public final class String
```

Description

The `String` class is used to represent a sequence of characters. Once created, the contents of a `String` cannot be modified. The `String` class contains methods for examining and searching the contents of a `String` and methods for creating new `Strings` using existing `String` objects and other data types.

Creating New Strings

The `String` class provides methods for creating new `String` objects by using other `String` objects or other data types. There are also methods that take an existing `String` and create a variation of that `String`, for example, the `toLowerCase()` method takes an existing `String` and creates a new version of it in which all the characters are converted to lowercase.

The Java language supports not only these methods but also the creation of `String` objects using `String` constants and the concatenation operator ('+'). For example, in the following `str1` and `str2` are equivalent and `str3` and `str4` are equivalent:

```
String str1 = “abc”;
char data[] = {‘a’, ‘b’, ‘c’};
String str2 = new String(data);

String str3 = str1.concat(str2);
String str4 = str1 + str2;
```

Note that these methods all create a *new, immutable* `String` object.

Character and Substring Searches

The `String` class provides methods that do character and substring searches. Character positions (or *indices*) within a `String` range from 0 to $n - 1$, where n is the number of characters in the string. An index of `0` is the position of the first character; an index of $n - 1$ is the position of the last character in the `String`.

Strings to Other Representations

The `String` class provides methods for converting strings to and from other types, such as integers and byte arrays.

MEMBER SUMMARY

Constructor	
`String()`	Constructs a new `String` object using characters from a character array, byte array, or `String`.
Methods for Creating New Strings	
`concat()`	Creates a string that is the concatenation of two strings.
`copyValueOf()`	Creates a string using characters from a character array.
`replace()`	Creates a string by replacing all occurrences of a character with another character.
`substring()`	Creates a string that is a substring of this string.
`toLowerCase()`	Creates a string by turning all characters of this string into lowercase.
`toUpperCase()`	Creates a string by turning all characters of this string into uppercase.
`trim()`	Creates a string that removes leading and trailing whitespace from this string.
`valueOf()`	Creates the string representation of a data value.
Comparison Methods	
`compareTo()`	Compares this string to another string for equality and Unicode ordering.
`equals()`	Compares this string with another object for equality.
`equalsIgnoreCase()`	Performs a case-insensitive comparison of this string with another string.
Search Methods	
`endsWith()`	Determines whether this string ends with some suffix.
`indexOf()`	Finds the first occurrence of a character or substring within this string.
`lastIndexOf()`	Finds the last occurrence of a character or substring within this string.
`regionMatches()`	Determines whether a region of this string matches a region of another string.
`startsWith()`	Determines whether this string starts with some prefix.
Conversion Methods	
`charAt()`	Retrieves the character at an index.
`getBytes()`	Copies characters from this string into a byte array.
`getChars()`	Copies characters from this string into a character array.
`toCharArray()`	Creates a character array containing the characters from this string.
`toString()`	Generate the string representation of this object.

Continued

MEMBER SUMMARY	
General Methods	
`hashCode()`	Computes the hash code for this object.
`intern()`	Retrieves a string that has the same internal representation as this string.
`length()`	Retrieves the number of characters in this string.

See Also

`StringBuffer`.

charAt()

PURPOSE Retrieves the character at an index.

SYNTAX `public char charAt(int index)`

DESCRIPTION This method returns the character at the position, `index`, of this `String` object.

PARAMETERS

`index` The character position. `index` must be in the range `0` to `length()-1`, inclusive.

RETURNS The character at position `index`.

EXCEPTIONS

`StringIndexOutOfBoundsException`

If `index` is not in the range `0` to `length()-1`.

EXAMPLE

```
// method that returns true if 'str' contains a whitespace character
public static boolean hasWhiteSpace(String str) {
    for (int i = 0; i < str.length(); i++) {
        if (Character.isSpace(str.charAt(i)))
            return (true);
    }
    return (false);
}
```

compareTo()

PURPOSE Compares this string to another string for equality and Unicode ordering.

SYNTAX `public int compareTo(String str)`

DESCRIPTION This method compares this string with the string `str`, character-by-character, according to Unicode ordering. It returns an integer indicating whether the two strings are equal and, if they are not, the ordering of the two strings. If the two strings are identical (same length and same characters in same order), this method returns `0`. Otherwise it returns a negative value if the difference—i.e., the first different character—of this string precedes that of `str` in the Unicode code set. A negative value is also returned if this string is a prefix of `str`. `compareTo()` returns a positive value if the difference of `str` precedes that of this string in the Unicode code set. A positive value is also returned if `str` is a prefix of this string. For Roman character sets, the positive and negative return values could be used to order strings alphabetically.

PARAMETERS

`str` The string to be compared. `str` must not be `null`.

RETURNS `0` if the strings are identical; a negative value if the difference of this string is lower in the Unicode code set than that of `str`; a positive value if the difference of this string is higher in the Unicode code set.

SEE ALSO `equals()`, `equalsIgnoreCase()`.

EXAMPLE

```
String str = "this is a test";

int r1 = str.compareTo("this is a test and more");// negative
    (str shorter)
int r2 = str.compareTo("this is not a test");     // negative
    ('a' < 'n')
int r3 = str.compareTo("this is a test");         // 0
int r4 = str.compareTo("no, this is not a test"); // positive
    ('t' > 'n')
int r5 = str.compareTo("this");                   // positive
    (str longer)
```

concat()

PURPOSE Creates a string that is the concatenation of two strings.

SYNTAX `public String concat(String str)`

A B C D E F G H I J K L M N O P Q R S T U V W X Y Z

DESCRIPTION This method creates a new `String` object whose content is the string concatenation of this string and `str`. If `str` is an empty string (has a length of 0), this `String` object is simply returned. A new `String` object is not created because no concatenation is required.

PARAMETERS

`str` The string to be concatenated to the end of this string to make a new string. `str` must not be `null`.

RETURNS A new `String` object that is the concatenation of this string and `str`.

EXAMPLE

```
String str1 = "abc";

String str2 = str1.concat("cde");     // "abccde"
String str3 = str1 + "cde";           // "abccde"
```

copyValueOf()

PURPOSE Creates a `String` using characters from a character array.

SYNTAX
```
public static String copyValueOf(char[] data)
public static String copyValueOf(char[] data, int offset, int
   count)
```

DESCRIPTION The two forms of this method create a new `String` object using characters from the character array `data`. The first form of this method copies the characters from the entire array `data` for creating the new string. The second form of this method copies `count` characters starting at position `offset` within `data`. Changes to `data` after the creation of the string do not affect the contents of the new string.

`copyValueOf()` is equivalent to the `String()` constructor and `valueOf()` (the forms that take a `char` array as an argument).

PARAMETERS

`count` The number of characters from `data` to copy.

`data` The character array from which to copy the characters.

`offset` The position of the first character in `data` to copy. `offset` must be in the range `0` to `length()-1`.

RETURNS A new `String` object whose content is a copy of the characters from `data` (or a subset of it as specified by `offset` and `count`).

EXCEPTIONS

`ArrayIndexOutOfBoundsException`
If `offset` or `count` are outside the bounds of `data`.

SEE ALSO String(), valueOf().

EXAMPLE

```
char data[] = {'a', 'b', 'c'};
String abc = String.copyValueOf(data);
String bc = String.copyValueOf(data, 1, 2);
System.out.println("copy " + abc + " " + bc);
data[2] = 'e';         // updating 'data' doesn't affect abc or bc
System.out.println("copy after " + abc + " " + bc);
```

endsWith()

PURPOSE Determines whether this string ends with some suffix.

SYNTAX `public boolean endsWith(String suffix)`

DESCRIPTION This method determines whether this string ends with the string `suffix`. It returns `true` if this string ends with `suffix`; it returns `false` otherwise.

PARAMETERS

`suffix` The suffix to be compared. `suffix` must not be `null`.

RETURNS `true` if this string ends with `suffix`; `false` otherwise.

SEE ALSO `startsWith()`.

EXAMPLE

```
// method that checks whether 'file' has correct suffix
// to be Java source file
public static boolean validSrcFilename(String file) {
    return (file.endsWith(".java"));
}
```

equals()

PURPOSE Compares this string with another object for equality.

SYNTAX `public boolean equals(Object obj)`

DESCRIPTION This method compares this `String` object with `obj`. It returns `true` if `obj` is another `String` containing a string of the same length and with the same sequence of characters as this string; it returns `false` otherwise. It also returns `false` if `obj` is `null` or if `obj` is not a `String` object.

PARAMETERS

`obj` The object to be compared.

RETURNS `true` if `obj` is equal to this `String` object; `false` otherwise.

OVERRIDES `Object.equals()`.

SEE ALSO `compareTo()`, `equalsIgnoreCase()`, `regionMatches()`.

EXAMPLE

```
String abc = "abc";
String str = new String(abc);
if (str.equals(abc))
    System.out.println("correct");
```

equalsIgnoreCase()

PURPOSE Performs a case-insensitive comparison of this string with another string.

SYNTAX `public boolean equalsIgnoreCase(String str)`

DESCRIPTION This method performs a case-insensitive comparison of this string with another string `str`. It returns `true` if the two strings are equal when case is ignored; it returns `false` otherwise (including if `str` is `null`). The strings are considered equal if they have the same length and contain the same sequence of characters and they differ only in the case of the characters.

PARAMETERS

`str` The string to be compared.

RETURNS `true` if the strings are equal when ignoring case; `false` otherwise.

SEE ALSO `compareTo()`, `equals()`, `regionMatches()`.

EXAMPLE

```
String abc = "abc";
String str = new String("ABC");
if (str.equalsIgnoreCase(abc))
    System.out.println("correct");
```

getBytes()

PURPOSE Copies characters from this string into a byte array.

SYNTAX `public void getBytes(int srcOffset, int srcEnd, byte[] dst, int dstOffset)`

DESCRIPTION This method copies the characters of this string, from index `srcOffset` (inclusive) to index `srcEnd` (exclusive), to the byte array `dst` starting at `dstOffset` in `dst`. Since `dst` is a byte array, the 16-bit Unicode characters of this string are cast into 8-bit bytes when copied into `dst`. The top 8 bits of the Unicode character are ignored; the lower 8 bits are used for the byte.

PARAMETERS

`dst` The destination array.

`dstOffset` The start offset in `dst` into which to copy characters. `dstOffset` must be in the range `0` to `dst.length-1` inclusive.

`srcEnd` The index of the character in this string at which to stop copying. `srcEnd` must be in the range `0` to `length()` inclusive.

`srcOffset` The index of the character in this string at which to start copying. `srcOffset` must be in the range `0` to `length()-1` inclusive.

EXCEPTIONS

`ArrayIndexOutOfBoundsException`

If `srcOffset` or `srcEnd` are outside the bounds of this string or `dstOffset` is outside the bounds of `dst`.

SEE ALSO `getChars()`.

EXAMPLE

```
// method that writes out a String
public static void writeString(OutputStream out, String str) {
    byte[] buf = new byte[str.length()];
    str.getBytes(0, str.length(), buf, 0);
    try {
        out.write(buf);
    } catch (IOException e) {
        System.err.println(e);
    }
}
```

getChars()

PURPOSE Copies characters from this string into the specified character array.

SYNTAX

```
public void getChars(int srcOffset, int srcEnd, char[] dst, int
   dstOffset)
```

DESCRIPTION This method copies the characters of this string, from index `srcOffset` (inclusive) to index `srcEnd` (exclusive), to the character array `dst`, starting at `dstOffset` in `dst`. The character at `srcOffset` is copied, but the character at `srcEnd` is not.

A B C D E F G H I J K L M N O P Q R S T U V W X Y Z

PARAMETERS

`dst`	The (non-`null`) destination array.
`dstOffset`	The start offset in `dst` at which to copy characters. `dstOffset` must be between `0` and `dst.length-1` (inclusive).
`srcEnd`	The index of the character in this string at which to stop copying. `srcEnd` must be in the range `0` to `length()` (exclusive).
`srcOffset`	The index of the character in this string at which to start copying. `srcOffset` must be in the range `0` to `length()-1` (inclusive).

EXCEPTIONS

`ArrayIndexOutOfBoundsException`
If `srcOffset` or `srcEnd` are outside the bounds of this string or `dstOffset` is outside the bounds of `dst`.

SEE ALSO `getBytes()`, `toCharArray()`.

EXAMPLE

```
// method that splits a string into two and returns the head
public static String firstHalf(String str) {
    int half = str.length() / 2;
    char[] buf = new char[half];
    str.getChars(0, half, buf, 0);
    return (new String(buf));
}
```

hashCode()

PURPOSE Computes the hash code for this object.

SYNTAX `public int hashCode()`

DESCRIPTION This method generates the hash code for this `String` object. The hash code for a `String` object is calculated using its character values. Two strings with the same string value (characters) have the same hash code. However, two strings with the same hash code may not necessarily have the same string values.

RETURNS An `int` representing the hash code of this object.

OVERRIDES `Object.hashCode()`.

SEE ALSO `equals()`, `Hashtable`.

EXAMPLE

```
// Keep track of hits on hash code
int[] hits = new int[1023];
String str = "this is a test";
```

```
int hashval = str.hashCode();  // get hash code for str
++hits[Math.abs(hashval%hits.length)];  // count hits
```

indexOf()

PURPOSE Finds the first occurrence of a character or substring within this string.

SYNTAX

```
public int indexOf(int ch)
public int indexOf(int ch, int offset)
public int indexOf(String str, int offset)
```

DESCRIPTION The three forms of this method return the index within this string of the first occurrence of the given character `ch` or substring `str`. If `offset` is specified, the characters within this string that are considered during the search are those between `offset` and the end of this string (`length()-1`). If `offset` is not specified, this string is searched in its entirety. If `ch` or `str` does not occur in the specified portion of this string, this method returns `-1`.

PARAMETERS

`ch` The character for which to search.

`offset` The index in this string from which to start the search. The search is performed in the region between `offset` (inclusive) and the end of the string. `offset` must be in the range `0` to `length()-1` inclusive; if it is not, `-1` is returned.

`str` The substring for which to search. `str` must not be `null`.

RETURNS The index of the first occurrence of `ch` or `str`; `-1` if not found.

SEE ALSO `lastIndexOf()`.

EXAMPLE

```
// Method that counts number of tokens between separator char
public static int countTokens(String str, char separator) {
    int count, offset, where;

    for (count = 0, offset = 0;
         ((where = str.indexOf(separator, offset)) >= 0);
         offset = where + 1) {
        if (where > 0)
            ++count;
    }
    if (str.charAt(str.length()-1) != separator)
        ++count;
    return (count);
}

// Method that counts number of tokens between separator string
public static int countTokens(String str, String separator) {
```

```
        int count, offset, where;

        for (count = 0, offset = 0;
             ((where = str.indexOf(separator, offset)) >= 0);
             offset = where + separator.length()) {
            if (where > 0)
                ++count;
        }
        if (!str.endsWith(separator))
            ++count;
        return (count);
    }
```

intern()

PURPOSE Retrieves a string that has the same internal representation as this string.

SYNTAX `public String intern()`

DESCRIPTION This method retrieves a string that has the same internal representation as this `String` object. Two `String` objects with the same `intern()` result are guaranteed to be equal.

RETURNS A `String` object that is guaranteed to have the same internal representation as this `String` object.

EXAMPLE

```
// intern() values the same means strings are equal
if (s1.intern() == s2.intern())
    System.out.println("Strings are equal");
```

lastIndexOf()

PURPOSE Finds the last occurrence of a character or substring within this string.

SYNTAX
```
public int lastIndexOf(char ch)
public int lastIndexOf(char ch, int offset)
public int lastIndexOf(String str, int offset)
```

DESCRIPTION The three forms of this method return the index within this string of the last occurrence of the given character `ch` or substring `str`. If `offset` is specified, the characters within this string that are considered during the search are those between the start of the string and the index `offset`. If `offset` is not specified, this string is searched in its entirety. The search is performed backwards starting at offset (if specified) or the end of the string towards the front of the string. If the ch or str does not occur in the specified portion of this string, this method returns -1.

PARAMETERS

ch	The character for which to search.
offset	The index at which to start the reverse search. The search is performed in the region between 0 and offset (inclusive) of this string. offset must be in the range 0 to length()-1 (inclusive); if it is not, -1 is returned.
str	The substring for which to search. str must not be null.

RETURNS The index of the last occurrence of ch or str; -1 if not found.

SEE ALSO indexOf().

EXAMPLE

```
// Get file name without parent directories
public static String getAtomicFilename(String pathname, char
    separator) {
    int lastSep = pathname.lastIndexOf(separator);
    if (lastSep >= 0)
        return new String(pathname.substring(lastSep + 1,
            pathname.length()));
    else
        return new String(pathname); // atomic to begin with
}

// Find directory path of pathname
public static String getDirPath(String pathname, String separator) {
    // search pathname starting from index at end of pathname
    int lastSep = pathname.lastIndexOf(separator,
        pathname.length()-1);
    if (lastSep >= 0)
        return new String(pathname.substring(0, lastSep));
    else
        return null; // no directories in pathname
}
```

length()

PURPOSE Retrieves the length of the string.

SYNTAX `public int length()`

RETURNS The number of characters in this string.

EXAMPLE See charAt().

A B C D E F G H I J K L M N O P Q R S T U V W X Y Z

regionMatches()

PURPOSE Determines whether a region of this string matches a region of another string.

SYNTAX
```
public boolean regionMatches(int offset1, String str2, int
    offset2, int count)
public boolean regionMatches(boolean ignoreCase, int offset1,
    String str2, offset2, int count)
```

DESCRIPTION The two forms of this method determine whether a region of this string as specified by `offset1` and `count` matches the region of another string, `str2`, as specified by `offset2` and `count`. If `ignoreCase` is specified and is set to `true`, uppercase characters are considered equivalent to their corresponding lowercase characters. Otherwise the match is based on a character-by-character comparison.

PARAMETERS

`count` The number of characters in the region to match.

`ignoreCase` If `true`, case is ignored; otherwise case is considered.

`offset1` The start of the region in this string. `offset1` must be in the range `0` to `length()-1` (inclusive).

`offset2` The start of the region in `str2`. `offset2` must be in the range `0` to `str2.length()-1` (inclusive).

`str2` The string to be compared. `str2` must not be `null`.

RETURNS `true` if the regions match; `false` otherwise. `false` is also returned if the regions as specified by `offset1` and `count` or `offset2` and `count` are outside the bounds of their respective string object.

SEE ALSO `compareTo()`, `equals()`, `equalsIgnoreCase()`.

EXAMPLE

```
String s1 = “this is a test”;
String s2 = “testing”;
String s3 = “Testing”;
int testLoc = s1.indexOf(“test”, 0);
if (testLoc >= 0) {
    if (s1.regionMatches(testLoc, s2, 0, 4))
        System.out.println(“regions match”);
    // try again using case-insensitive match
    if (s1.regionMatches(true, testLoc, s3, 0, 4))
        System.out.println(“regions match when case ignored”);
}
```

replace()

PURPOSE
Creates a string by replacing all occurrences of a character with another character.

SYNTAX
`public String replace(char oldChar, char newChar)`

DESCRIPTION
This method creates a new `String` object that is a copy of this string, except all occurrences of `oldChar` are replaced with `newChar`.

PARAMETERS

`newChar` The character that replaces the old character.

`oldChar` The character to be replaced.

RETURNS
A new `String` object with `oldChar` replaced with `newChar`.

EXAMPLE

```
// method that replaces blanks with '#'
public static String blanksWithHash(String str) {
    return (str.replace(' ', '#'));
}
```

startsWith()

PURPOSE
Determines whether this string starts with some prefix.

SYNTAX
```
public boolean startsWith(String prefix)
public boolean startsWith(String prefix, int offset)
```

DESCRIPTION
The two forms of this method determine whether this string starts with the given string `prefix`. It returns `true` if this string starts with `prefix`; it returns `false` otherwise. If `offset` is specified, `prefix` is compared against this string starting at index `offset`. If `offset` is not specified, the comparison is done starting at index `0`.

PARAMETERS

`offset` The index of this string at which to start the comparison. `offset` must be in the range `0` to `length()-1` (inclusive).

`prefix` The prefix substring for which to search. `prefix` must not be `null`.

RETURNS
`true` if this string starts with `prefix`; `false` otherwise. `false` is also returned if `offset` is outside the bounds of this string.

SEE ALSO
`endsWith()`.

EXAMPLE

This example is a method that parses a string of octal, hexadecimal, or decimal numbers. Any string that starts with "0x" or "#" denotes a hexadecimal string, while any string that starts with "0" denotes an octal string. All other strings are considered to denote decimal numbers.

```
// Method that parses string of octal, hex, or decimal number
public static int parseNumber(String str) throws NumberFormatException
{
    if (str.startsWith("0x")) {
        return Integer.parseInt(str.substring(2), 16);
    }
    if (str.startsWith("#")) {
        return Integer.parseInt(str.substring(1), 16);
        }
    if (str.startsWith("0")) {
        return Integer.parseInt(str.substring(1), 8);
        }
    return Integer.parseInt(str, 10);
}
```

String()

PURPOSE

Constructs a new `String` object using characters from a character array, byte array, or `String`.

SYNTAX

```
public String()
public String(String src)
public String(char[] charArray)
public String(char[] charArray, int offset, int count)
public String(byte[] byteArray, int hibyte)
public String(byte[] byteArray, int hibyte, int offset, int count)
public String(StringBuffer buffer)
```

DESCRIPTION

The `String` class has seven constructors. Each creates an immutable `String` object by using characters from the arguments supplied. Any modifications to the arguments after the `String` object has been constructed do not affect the `String` object.

You can create an empty string using the first form of the constructor. It takes no arguments.

You also can create a new string from an existing string, `src`, using the second form. The result is a new `String` object that is a copy of `src`.

The third and fourth forms of the constructor allow you to create a string using characters from a character array, `charArray`. You can specify a region of charArray to copy characters from by using offset and count. Otherwise characters from the entire charArray are copied.

You can also create a string using characters from a byte array, byteArray (forms five and six). Because byteArray contains 8-bit bytes and chars are 16-bit Unicode characters, you must supply an argument, hibyte, that indicates how to pad the upper 8 bits of the char value. For example, if byteArray contains an array of ASCII characters, you set hibyte to 0. You can specify a region of byteArray to use by using offset and count. Otherwise bytes from the entire byteArray are used.

Finally, you can create a new string by supplying the constructor with a StringBuffer, buffer. The result is a new String object whose value is that of buffer. If buffer is subsequently modified, a new copy of buffer is created for the updates so that the modifications do not affect the string already created.

PARAMETERS

buffer	The StringBuffer from which to get characters. buffer must not be null.
byteArray	The byte array from which to copy the lower 8-bit bytes.
charArray	The character array from which to copy characters.
count	The number of elements from the array to use.
hibyte	The top 8 bits to pad each byte with when making a 16-bit Unicode char value.
offset	The offset into charArray or byteArray to start copying. offset must be in the range 0 to charArray.length-1 or byteArray.length-1 (inclusive).
src	The String object from which to copy. src must not be null.

EXCEPTIONS

StringIndexOutOfBoundsException

If offset or count is outside the bounds of byteArray or charArray.

SEE ALSO copyValueOf(), valueOf().

EXAMPLE

```
String s1 = new String();                  // empty string
String s2 = "abc";                         // use constant
String s3 = new String(s2);                // copy from String

s2 = "def";                                // won't affect s3


// copy from char array
char[] charArray = {'a', 'b', 'c'};
String s4 = new String(charArray);         // "abc"
```

```
charArray[1] = 'B'; // won't affect s4
String s5 = new String(charArray, 1, 1);    // "B"

// copy from byte array, using hi-byte of 0
byte[] byteArray = {'a', 'b', 'c'};
String s6 = new String(byteArray, 0);        // "abc"

byteArray[1] = 'x';                          // won't affect s6
String s7 = new String(byteArray, 0, 1, 1); // "x"

// copy from StringBuffer
StringBuffer buf = new StringBuffer("xyz");
String s8 = new String(buf);

buf.setLength(1);                            // won't affect s8
```

substring()

PURPOSE Creates a string object that is a substring of this string.

SYNTAX
```
public String substring(int offset)
public String substring(int offset, int endIndex)
```

DESCRIPTION The two forms of this method create a new string that is a substring of this string. The substring starts at the index `offset` and ends at the index `endIndex`. The character at `offset` is included in the substring, but the character at `endIndex` is not. The characters copied are those between `offset` and `endIndex-1` inclusive.

PARAMETERS

`endIndex` The ending index, exclusive. `endindex` must be in the range `0` and `length()`.

`offset` The beginning index, inclusive. `offset` must be in the range `0` to `length()-1`.

RETURNS A new string that is a substring of this string in the range (`offset, endIndex-1`) inclusive.

EXCEPTIONS

`StringIndexOutOfBoundsException`
If `offset` or `endIndex` is outside the bounds of this string.

EXAMPLE See `indexOf()`, `startsWith()`.

toCharArray()

PURPOSE Creates a character array using characters from this string.

SYNTAX `public char[] toCharArray()`

DESCRIPTION This method creates a new `char` array using the sequence of characters from this string.

RETURNS A `char` array containing the characters of this string.

SEE ALSO `getChars()`.

EXAMPLE

```
// return an upper case version of a string
public static String turnUpper(String str) {
    char[] contents = str.toCharArray();
    for(int i = 0; i < contents.length; i++) {
        contents[i] = Character.toUpperCase(contents[i]);
    }
    return (new String(contents));
}
```

toLowerCase()

PURPOSE Creates a new string by turning all characters in this string into lowercase.

SYNTAX `public String toLowerCase()`

DESCRIPTION This method creates a new string that has the same sequence of characters as this string, except all the characters are in their lowercase forms.

RETURNS A new string with all characters in lowercase.

SEE ALSO `Character.toLowerCase()`, `toUpperCase()`.

EXAMPLE

```
// creates new string with all lower case
System.out.println("This is a test".toLowerCase());
```

toString()

PURPOSE Generates the string representation of this object.

SYNTAX `public String toString()`

RETURNS A reference to this string.

OVERRIDES `Object.toString()`.

toUpperCase()

EXAMPLE

```
String s1 = "abc";
String s2 = s1.toString();
// s2 is just reference of s1
if (s1 == s2)
    System.out.println("same thing");
```

toUpperCase()

PURPOSE Creates a new string by turning all characters in this string into uppercase.

SYNTAX `public String toUpperCase()`

DESCRIPTION This method creates a new string that has the same sequence of characters as this string except all the characters are in their uppercase forms.

RETURNS A new string with all characters in uppercase.

SEE ALSO `Character.toUpperCase()`, `toLowerCase()`.

EXAMPLE

```
// creates new string with all upper case
System.out.println("This is a test".toUpperCase());
```

trim()

PURPOSE Creates a new string by trimming any leading and trailing whitespaces from this string.

SYNTAX `public String trim()`

DESCRIPTION This method creates a new string that has the same sequence of characters as this string, except any leading and trailing whitespace characters have been removed. See `Character.isSpace()` for the definition of a whitespace character.

RETURNS A new string with any leading and trailing whitespaces removed.

SEE ALSO `Character.isSpace()`.

EXAMPLE

```
String s1 = "  Start and end.  ";
String s2 = s1.trim(); // "Start and end."
```

valueOf()

PURPOSE Creates the string representation of a data value.

SYNTAX

```
public static String valueOf(boolean bool)
public static String valueOf(char ch)
public static String valueOf(int inum)
public static String valueOf(long lnum)
public static String valueOf(float fnum)
public static String valueOf(double dnum)
public static String valueOf(Object obj)
public static String valueOf(char[] data)
public static String valueOf(char[] data, int offset, count)
```

DESCRIPTION The nine forms of this method create the string representation of an object or a data value. After the string has been created, any modifications to the arguments do not affect the string already created.

PARAMETERS

`bool`	The `boolean` value (`true` or `false`) for which to create the string.
`ch`	The `char` value for which to create the string.
`count`	The number of characters to copy from `data`.
`data`	The `char` array for which to create the string.
`dnum`	The `double` value for which to create the string.
`fnum`	The `float` value for which to create the string.
`inum`	The `int` value for which to create the string.
`lnum`	The `long` value for which to create the string.
`obj`	The `object` for which to create the string. (`null` is accepted.)
`offset`	The index in `data` from which to start copying. `offset` must be in the range from `0` to `data.length-1` (inclusive).

RETURNS A new `String` object that represents the data value.

SEE ALSO `copyValueOf()`, `Boolean.toString()`, `Character.toString()`, `Double.toString()`, `Float.toString()`, `Integer.toString()`, `Long.toString()`, `Object.toString()`.

EXAMPLE

```
int inum = 512;
long lnum = Long.MAX_VALUE;
double dnum = 123.123e54;
float fnum = 3.1243f;
Object obj1 = null;
Object obj2 = new Vector();

String s1 = String.valueOf(true);      // "true"
String s2 = String.valueOf('A');       // "A"
String s3 = String.valueOf(inum);      // "512"
```

```
String s4 = String.valueOf(lnum);       // “9223372036854775807”
String s5 = String.valueOf(dnum);       // “1.23123e+56”
String s6 = String.valueOf(fnum);       // “3.1243”
String s7 = String.valueOf(obj1);       // “null”
String s8 = String.valueOf(obj2);       // “[]”

char[] charArray = {‘a’, ‘b’, ‘c’};
String s9 = String.valueOf(charArray); // “abc”
charArray[1] = ‘B’;                     // won’t affect s9
```

java.lang

StringBuffer

Object — **StringBuffer**

Syntax

```
public final class StringBuffer
```

Description

The `String` class is used to create immutable string objects. Each time you make an update to a string, a new `String` object is created. A more efficient way to deal with these updates is to store a string in a `StringBuffer`, make updates to it until a `String` form is needed, and then use the `StringBuffer` to create a `String` object.

The `StringBuffer` class implements a buffer for characters that allows updates in place and allows the buffer to grow and shrink as needed to accommodate the updates. The Java compiler uses `StringBuffer` to implement the "+" operator. For example,

```
"a" + 4 + "c"
```

is compiled to

```
new StringBuffer().append("a").append(4).append("c").toString()
```

Capacity

When you create a `StringBuffer`, you can create it with a *capacity*. A capacity is the amount of storage that has been allocated for the string buffer (see Figure 217). If you know approximately how big your string is going to be, you can supply that number as the capacity so that the string buffer does not have to expand each time more characters are added to it. After a `StringBuffer` has been created, you can set its capacity at any time by calling `ensureCapacity()`.

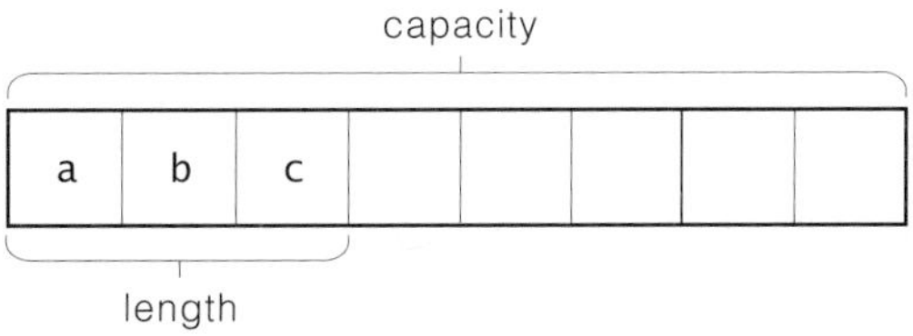

FIGURE 217 **`StringBuffer`**

MEMBER SUMMARY

Constructor	
`StringBuffer()`	Constructs a new `StringBuffer` instance.
Update Methods	
`append()`	Appends the string representation of an object or data value to this string buffer.
`insert()`	Inserts the string representation of an object or data value into this string buffer.
`reverse()`	Reverses the order of characters in this string buffer.
`setCharAt()`	Replaces a character in this string buffer.
`setLength()`	Truncates or expands this string buffer.
Access Methods	
`charAt()`	Retrieves a character from this string buffer.
`getChars()`	Copies a region of this string buffer to a character array.
Capacity and Length Methods	
`capacity()`	Retrieves the current capacity of this string buffer.
`ensureCapacity()`	Ensures that the capacity of this string buffer is at least a specified amount.
`length()`	Retrieves the number of characters in this string buffer.
String Method	
`toString()`	Generates the string representation of this object.

See Also

`ByteArrayOutputStream`, `String`.

append()

PURPOSE Appends the string representation of an object or data value to this string buffer.

SYNTAX

```
public StringBuffer append(boolean bool)
public synchronized StringBuffer append(char ch)
public StringBuffer append(int inum)
public StringBuffer append(long lnum)
public StringBuffer append(float fnum)
public StringBuffer append(double dnum)
public synchronized StringBuffer append(Object obj)
```

```
public synchronized StringBuffer append(String str)
public synchronized StringBuffer append(char[] data)
public synchronized StringBUffer append(char[] data, int offset,
   int count)
```

DESCRIPTION Each of the 10 forms of this method appends the string representation of its argument to this string buffer and returns the reference to the (updated) string buffer. The string buffer is automatically expanded as needed to accommodate additional characters. The data is copied into the string buffer, so any subsequent modifications to the arguments do not affect the string buffer. For example, subsequent changes to `data` will not affect the string buffer.

Although some forms of the method do not have the `synchronized` modifier, they eventually call a version of `append()` that does have the `synchronized` modifier, thus ensuring that all updates to the string buffer are done one at a time.

PARAMETERS

`bool`	The `boolean` whose string representation to append.
`ch`	The character to append.
`count`	The number of characters from `data` to use.
`data`	The `char` array for getting characters to append.
`dnum`	The `double` whose string representation to append.
`fnum`	The `float` whose string representation to append.
`inum`	The `int` whose string representation to append.
`lnum`	The `long` whose string representation to append.
`obj`	The object whose string representation to append. `obj` can be `null`.
`offset`	The index in `data` from which to start getting characters. `offset` must be in the range of `0` to `data.length-1` (inclusive).
`str`	The string to append.

RETURNS The updated `StringBuffer`, *not* a new one.

SEE ALSO `insert(), ensureCapacity()String.valueOf().`

EXAMPLE

```
// Return one string that represents the path constructed
// using the components, each separated by ‘sep’
// e.g. {{a}, {b}, {c}}, ‘/’ -> /a/b/c
public static String stringify(char[][]components, char sep) {
    StringBuffer str = new StringBuffer();
    for (int i = 0; i < components.length; i++) {
        str.append(sep).append(components[i]);
    }
    return (str.toString());
}

int inum = 512;
long lnum = Long.MAX_VALUE;
```

```
double dnum = 123.123e54;
float fnum = 3.1243f;
char sep = ' ';
Object obj1 = null;
Object obj2 = new Vector();
char[] charArray = {'a', 'b', 'c'};
StringBuffer buf = new StringBuffer(100);

// Keep appending all the data types above to buf
buf.append(inum).append(sep).append(lnum).append(sep);
buf.append(dnum).append(sep).append(dnum).append(sep);
buf.append(obj1).append(sep).append(obj2);
buf.append(sep).append(charArray);
buf.append(sep).append(charArray, 1, 2);
```

capacity()

PURPOSE Retrieves the current capacity of this string buffer.

SYNTAX `public int capacity()`

DESCRIPTION A *capacity* is the amount of storage that has been allocated for the string buffer. It differs from the *length* of the string buffer, which is the actual number of characters in the string buffer. If the number of characters to be added to the string buffer during an update exceeds the string buffer's capacity, the string buffer's capacity is increased to accommodate the additional characters. You can set the capacity when the string buffer is created or any time after creation by calling `ensureCapacity()`. `capacity()` returns the current capacity of this string buffer.

RETURNS The current capacity of this string buffer.

SEE ALSO `ensureCapacity()`, `length()`, `StringBuffer()`.

EXAMPLE

```
StringBuffer s0 = new StringBuffer();
StringBuffer s1 = new StringBuffer(20);
StringBuffer s2 = new StringBuffer("this is a test");

// capacity is different from length
// for s0 (cap 16, len 0)
// for s1 (cap 20, len 0),
// for s2 (cap 16+14, len 14)
System.out.println("s0: capacity " + s0.capacity() + " length " +
    s0.length());
System.out.println("s1: capacity " + s1.capacity() + " length " +
    s1.length());
System.out.println("s2: capacity " + s2.capacity() + " length " +
    s2.length());
```

charAt()

PURPOSE Retrieves a character from the string buffer.

SYNTAX `public synchronized char charAt(int index)`

DESCRIPTION This method returns the character at the index `index` of this string buffer.

PARAMETERS

`index` The index of the character to retrieve. `index` must be in the range of `0` to `length()-1` (inclusive).

RETURNS The character at `index`.

EXCEPTIONS

`StringIndexOutOfBoundsException`

If `index` is outside the range of (`0`, `length()-1`).

SEE ALSO `getChars()`, `setCharAt()`.

EXAMPLE

```
// Count null characters in buffer
public static int countNullChars(StringBuffer buf)
{
    int count = 0;
    for (int i = 0; i < buf.length(); i++) {
        if (buf.charAt(i) == '\0')
            ++count;
    }
    return (count);
}
```

ensureCapacity()

PURPOSE Ensures that the capacity of the string buffer is at least a specified amount.

SYNTAX `public synchronized void ensureCapacity(int minimumCapacity)`

DESCRIPTION A *capacity* is the amount of storage that has been allocated for the string buffer. It differs from the *length* of the string buffer, which is the actual number of characters in the string buffer. If the number of characters to be added to the string buffer during an update exceeds the string buffer's capacity, the string buffer's capacity is increased to accommodate the additional characters. If you know the approximate expected size of the final string, you should set the capacity of the string buffer to that number to avoid the number of times the capacity must be increased. You can set the capacity when the string buffer is created or any time after creation by calling `ensureCapacity()`. `ensureCapacity()` ensures that the capacity of the string buffer is at least `minimumCapacity`. If the capacity is less than `minimumCapacity`, it is increased to `minimumCapacity`. If the capacity is already at or greater than `minimumCapacity`, the capacity is left unchanged.

PARAMETERS

`minimumCapacity`
The minimum desired capacity.

SEE ALSO `capacity()`.

EXAMPLE

```
StringBuffer s1 = new StringBuffer("this is a test");
String filler = new String("simple yet powerful");

s1.ensureCapacity(10); // no op, already cap > 10
s1.ensureCapacity(100);

// buffer need not be expanded for following operations
s1.append(filler).append(filler).append(filler);
```

getChars()

PURPOSE Copies a region of the string buffer to a character array.

SYNTAX
```
public synchronized void getChars(int srcOffset, int srcEnd,
   char[] dst, int dstOffset)
```

DESCRIPTION This method copies the characters in the region specified by the starting index `srcOffset` (inclusive) and the ending index `srcEnd` (exclusive) of this string buffer into the character array `dst` starting at the array's `dstBegin` index.

PARAMETERS

`dst` The `char` array into which to copy the characters.

`dstOffset` The index in `dst` to which to start copying. `dstOffset` must be in the range of `0` to `dst.length-1` (inclusive).

`srcEnd` The index in this string buffer at which to stop copying (exclusive). `srcEnd` must be in the range of `0` to `length()` (inclusive).

`srcOffset` The index in this string buffer to start copying (inclusive). `srcOffset` must be in the range of `0` to `length()-1` (inclusive).

EXCEPTIONS

`StringIndexOutOfBoundsException`
: If `srcOffset` or `srcEnd` is outside the bounds of this string buffer.

`ArrayIndexOutOfBoundsException`
: If `dstOffset` is outside the bounds of `dst`.

SEE ALSO `charAt()`.

EXAMPLE

```
// Make a copy of StringBuffer
public static StringBuffer copyStringBuffer(StringBuffer buf) {
    char[] data = new char[buf.length()];
    buf.getChars(0, buf.length(), data, 0);
    StringBuffer answer = new StringBuffer(buf.length());
    answer.append(data);
    return (answer);
}
```

insert()

PURPOSE Inserts the string representation of an object or data value into this string buffer.

SYNTAX

```
public StringBuffer insert(int offset, boolean bool)
public synchronized StringBuffer insert(int offset, char ch)
public StringBuffer insert(int offset, int inum)
public StringBuffer insert(int offset, long lnum)
public StringBuffer insert(int offset, float fnum)
public StringBuffer insert(int offset, double dnum)
public synchronized StringBuffer insert(int offset, Object obj)
public synchronized StringBuffer insert(int offset, String str)
public synchronized StringBuffer insert(int offset, char[] data)
```

DESCRIPTION Each of the nine forms of this method inserts the string representation of its argument into this string buffer starting at index `offset`. Any characters occurring at or greater than `offset` are placed after the newly added characters. A call to `insert()` with an `offset` of `length()` is equivalent to a call to `append()`. This method returns the reference to the (updated) string buffer. The string buffer is automatically expanded as needed to accommodate additional characters. The data is copied into the string buffer, so any subsequent modifications to the arguments do not affect the string buffer. For example, subsequent changes to `data` will not affect the string buffer.

Although some forms of the method do not have the `synchronized` modifier, they eventually call a version of `insert()` that does have the `synchronized` modifier, thus ensuring that all updates to the string buffer are done one at a time.

PARAMETERS

`bool`	The `boolean` whose string representation to insert.
`ch`	The character to insert.
`data`	The `char` array for getting characters to insert.
`dnum`	The `double` whose string representation to insert.
`fnum`	The `float` whose string representation to insert.
`inum`	The `int` whose string representation to insert.
`lnum`	The `long` whose string representation to insert.
`obj`	The object whose string representation to insert. `obj` can be `null`.
`offset`	The index in this string buffer at which to start the insertion. `offset` must be in the range of `0` to `length()` (inclusive).
`str`	The string to insert.

RETURNS The updated `StringBuffer`, *not* a new one.

EXCEPTIONS

`StringIndexOutOfBoundsException`

If `offset` is not in the range of `0` to `length()`.

SEE ALSO `append()`, `ensureCapacity()String.valueOf()`.

EXAMPLE

```
int inum = 512;
long lnum = Long.MAX_VALUE;
double dnum = 123.123e54;
float fnum = 3.1243f;
char sep = ' ';
Object obj1 = null;
Object obj2 = new Vector();
char[] charArray = {'a', 'b', 'c'};
StringBuffer buf = new StringBuffer(100);

// Keep inserting at head of buffer all the data types above
buf.insert(0, inum).insert(0, sep).insert(0, lnum).insert(0, sep);
buf.insert(0, dnum).insert(0, sep).insert(0, dnum).insert(0, sep);
buf.insert(0, obj1).insert(0, sep).insert(0, obj2);
buf.insert(0, sep).insert(0, charArray);
```

length()

PURPOSE Retrieves the number of characters in this string buffer.

A B C D E F G H I J K L M N O P Q R S T U V W X Y Z

SYNTAX `public int length()`

RETURNS The number of characters in this string buffer.

SEE ALSO `capacity()`, `setLength()`.

EXAMPLE See `capacity()`.

reverse()

PURPOSE Reverses the order of characters in this string buffer.

SYNTAX `public synchronized StringBuffer reverse()`

RETURNS The updated `StringBuffer`, *not* a new one.

EXAMPLE

```
class Main {
    public static void main(String[] args) {
        StringBuffer sb = new StringBuffer("abcde");

        sb.reverse();
        System.out.println(sb);  // "edcba"
    }
}
```

setCharAt()

PURPOSE Replaces a character in this string buffer.

SYNTAX `public synchronized void setCharAt(int index, char ch)`

DESCRIPTION This method replaces the character at the index `index` of this string buffer with the character `ch`.

PARAMETERS

`index` The index of the character to update. `index` must be in the range of `0` to `length()-1`.

`ch` The character to use.

EXCEPTIONS

`StringIndexOutOfBoundsException`

If `index` is not in the range of `0` to `length()-1`.

SEE ALSO `charAt()`.

setLength()

EXAMPLE

```
// Set null characters in buffer to '#'
public static void markNullChars(StringBuffer buf)
{
    for (int i = 0; i < buf.length(); i++) {
        if (buf.charAt(i) == '\0')
            buf.setCharAt(i, '#');
    }
}
```

setLength()

PURPOSE Truncates or expands this string buffer.

SYNTAX `public synchronized void setLength(int newLength)`

DESCRIPTION This method sets the length of this string buffer to `newLength`. If `newLength` is less than the current length of the string buffer, the string buffer is truncated. Characters located at an index at or greater than `newLength` are lost. If `newLength` is greater than the current length of the string buffer, the newly added region is filled with null characters (`\0`).

PARAMETERS

`newLength` The new length of the string buffer. `newLength` must be non-negative.

EXCEPTIONS

`StringIndexOutOfBoundsException`
If `newLength` is negative.

EXAMPLE

```
StringBuffer s1 = new StringBuffer("this is a test");

// expand buffer
s1.setLength(20);
System.out.println(s1 + "(" + s1.length() + ")"); // added null chars

// truncate buffer
s1.setLength(4);
System.out.println(s1 + "(" + s1.length() + ")"); // "this"
```

StringBuffer()

PURPOSE Constructs a new `StringBuffer` instance.

SYNTAX
```
public StringBuffer()
public StringBuffer(int capacity)
public StringBuffer(String str)
```

DESCRIPTION The `StringBuffer` class has three constructors. The first form takes no arguments. It creates an empty `StringBuffer` with a default capacity of 16. The second form creates an empty `StringBuffer` that has the initial capacity of `capacity`. The third form takes a string, `str`, as the argument and creates a new `StringBuffer` by copying the characters from `str` into the new string buffer.

PARAMETERS

`capacity` The initial capacity of this string buffer.

`str` The initial value of the string buffer.

SEE ALSO `capacity()`, `ensureCapacity()`.

EXAMPLE See `capacity()`.

toString()

PURPOSE Generates the string representation of this object.

SYNTAX
```
public String toString()
```

DESCRIPTION This method returns a new `String` object that shares the internal string buffer of this `StringBuffer` object. The `StringBuffer` class enforces a copy-on-write policy on this shared buffer so that when this string buffer is updated in the future, a copy will be made to accommodate the new updates without affecting the `String` already returned.

RETURNS A new `String` object that shares the internal string buffer of this `StringBuffer` object.

OVERRIDES `Object.toString()`.

EXAMPLE See `append()`.

java.io

StringBufferInputStream

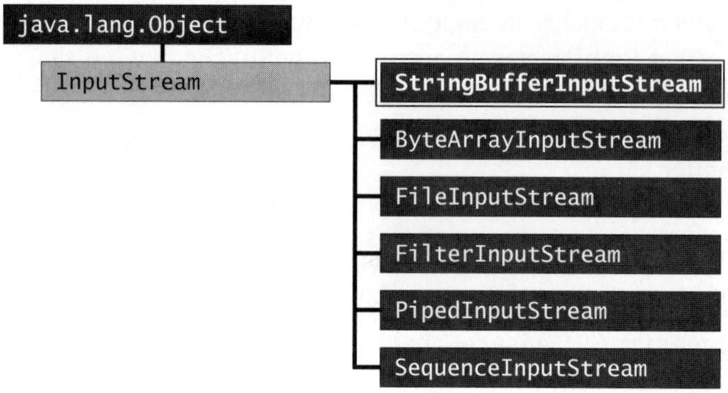

Syntax

```
public class StringBufferInputStream extends InputStream
```

Description

The `StringBufferInputStream` class allows a string buffer to be used as an input stream. For example, you can turn a string into a string buffer input stream so that you can perform input stream methods on that stream. Figure 218 shows an example of this. The string "This is a string" is turned into a `StringBufferInputStream`; a `read()` of the first four characters from this stream produces the string "This".

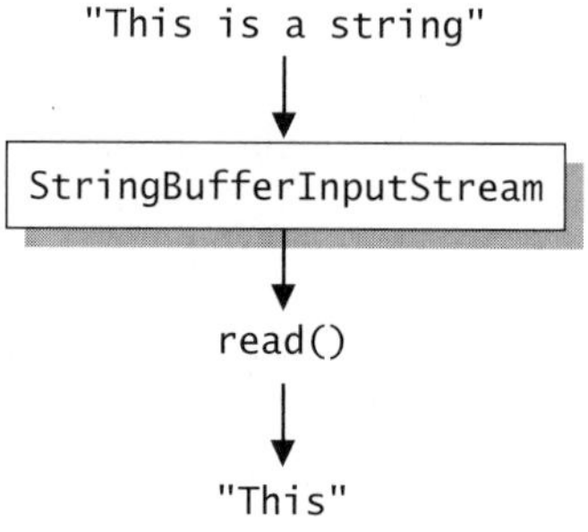

FIGURE 218 **`StringBufferInputStream`**

MEMBER SUMMARY	
Constructor	
`StringBufferInputStream()`	Constructs a new string buffer input stream using a string.
Input Methods	
`available()`	Determines the number of characters available in this stream.

MEMBER SUMMARY

`read()`	Reads bytes from this string buffer input stream.
`skip()`	Skips characters from this string buffer input stream.
Reset Method	
`reset()`	Resets the read position to the beginning of this string.
Protected Fields	
`buffer`	The string where data for this stream is stored.
`count`	The total number of characters in this string.
`pos`	The current read position of this stream.

See Also

`ByteArrayInputStream`, `InputStream`, `StringBuffer`.

Example

The following code uses a string buffer input stream to read its input from either the command line or standard input:

```
import java.io.StringBufferInputStream;
import java.io.InputStream;
import java.io.IOException;

class Main {
    private static long rand(InputStream in) {
        long sum = 0;
        try {
            int c;
            while ((c = in.read()) >= 0)
                sum += c;
        } catch (IOException e) {
        }
        return sum;
    }
    public static void main(String[] args) {
        InputStream in;
       // if no string specified in command line, read from standard in
        if (args.length != 1) {
            in = System.in;
        } else {
            in = new StringBufferInputStream(args[0]);
        }
```

```
            System.out.println(rand(in));
        }
    }
```

available()

PURPOSE Determines the number of characters available in this stream.

SYNTAX `public synchronized int available()`

DESCRIPTION The number of characters available in this string buffer input stream is the number of characters yet to be read from this stream. It is the number of characters that can be read before end-of-file on this stream is reached.

RETURNS The number of bytes available in this stream.

OVERRIDES `InputStream.available()`.

SEE ALSO `count`, `pos`.

EXAMPLE This example demonstrates the use of the various methods in `StringBufferInputStream`.

```
import java.io.StringBufferInputStream;

class Main2 {
    public static void main(String[] args) {
        StringBufferInputStream sb = new StringBufferInput-
            Stream("abcde\n");
        System.out.println("available: " + sb.available()); // 5
        sb.skip(2)                                            // skip 2
        for (int c = sb.read(); c > 0; c = sb.read())       // "cde"
            System.out.print((char)c);

        sb.reset();                                           // reset
        byte[] b = new byte[10];
        sb.read(b, 0, b.length);                              // read
        for (int i = 0; i < b.length; i++)                    // "abcde"
            System.out.print((char)b[i]);
    }
}
```

buffer

PURPOSE The string where data for this stream is stored.

SYNTAX `protected String buffer`

SEE ALSO count, pos.

EXAMPLE This example is taken from the source of StringBufferInputStream.read(). It demonstrates the use of the fields buffer, count, and pos.

```
public synchronized int read() {
    return (pos < count) ? buffer.charAt(pos++) : -1;
}
```

count

PURPOSE The total number of characters in this string.

SYNTAX `protected int count`

SEE ALSO buffer, pos.

EXAMPLE See buffer.

pos

PURPOSE The current read position of this stream.

SYNTAX `protected int pos`

DESCRIPTION This field keeps track of which character to read next from this string buffer input stream. It is incremented as each character is read/skipped from the stream, but it can be reset to 0 (the beginning of the string) using reset().

SEE ALSO buffer, count, read(), reset(), skip().

EXAMPLE See buffer.

read()

PURPOSE Reads bytes from this string buffer input stream.

SYNTAX
```
public synchronized int read()
public synchronized int read(byte[] buffer, int offset, int count)
```

DESCRIPTION The two forms of this method read bytes from this string buffer input stream. The first form reads the next character from this string buffer input stream and returns it as an int (the higher order 2 bytes are 0 and unused). The second form reads the next `count` number of characters from this string buffer input stream and stores the bytes in the byte array `buffer` starting at index `offset`. Only the lower-order byte of each character is stored in `buffer`; the higher-order byte of each character is ignored.

The next byte read is determined by the current read position, which is incremented as bytes are read from the stream. It can be reset to `0` using `reset()`.

PARAMETERS

`buffer`	The byte array in which to store the bytes read.
`count`	The number of bytes to read.
`offset`	The index in `buffer` at which to start storing the bytes read.

RETURNS The first form returns the character read; the second form returns the actual number of bytes read. Both forms return `-1` when the end of the string has been reached.

OVERRIDES `InputStream.read()`.

SEE ALSO `pos`, `reset()`, `skip()`.

EXAMPLE See the class example.

reset()

PURPOSE Resets the buffer to the beginning of the string.

SYNTAX `public synchronized void reset()`

DESCRIPTION This method resets the current read position to `0` so that subsequent `read()` and `skip()` calls will get characters from the beginning of the string.

OVERRIDES `InputStream.reset()`.

SEE ALSO `pos`.

EXAMPLE See `available()`.

skip()

PURPOSE Skips characters from this string buffer input stream.

SYNTAX `public synchronized long skip(long count)`

DESCRIPTION This method skips `count` number of characters from this string buffer input stream. It increments the current read position by `count` so that subsequent `read()/skip()` calls will not read those characters just skipped.

PARAMETERS

`count` The number of characters to skip.

RETURNS The actual number of characters skipped.

OVERRIDES `InputStream.skip()`.

SEE ALSO `pos, read()`.

EXAMPLE See `available()`.

StringBufferInputStream()

PURPOSE Constructs a new string buffer input stream using a string.

SYNTAX `public StringBufferInputStream(String str)`

DESCRIPTION This constructor creates a new string buffer input stream using the string `str` as data for the stream. The initial current read position (`pos`) of the stream is `0` (the beginning of `str`), and there are `str.length` (`count`) number of characters in this stream.

PARAMETERS

`str` The string to use for the new input stream. It is not copied.

SEE ALSO `pos, count`.

EXAMPLE See the class example and `available()`.

java.lang
StringIndexOutOfBoundsException

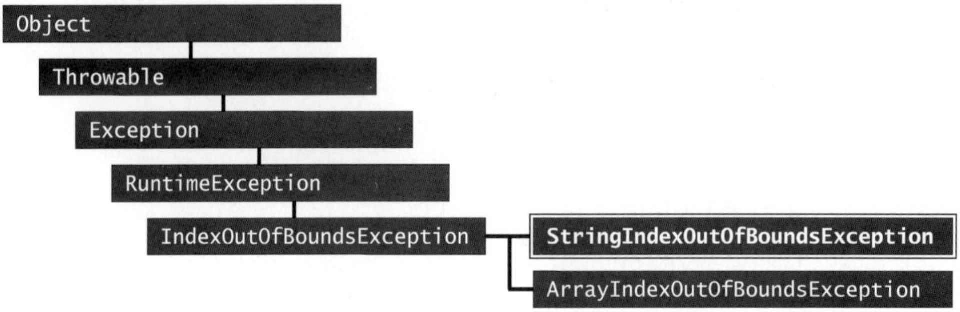

Syntax

```
public class StringIndexOutOfBoundsException extends IndexOutOfBoundsException
```

Description

`StringIndexOutOfBoundsException` is a runtime exception that is thrown when the program attempts to access a character within a `String` using an index that is not within the bounds of the `String`. Because `String` indices use a 0-based numbering scheme, the index is either negative or a number greater than or equal to the string's length.

`StringIndexOutOfBoundsException` is a runtime exception that should not be caught or declared in the `throws` clause of a method.

MEMBER SUMMARY	
Constructor	
`StringIndexOutOfBoundsException()`	Constructs a `StringIndexOutOfBoundsException` instance.

See Also

`IndexOutOfBoundsException`, `RuntimeException`.

Example

This example generates a StringIndexOutOfBoundsException.

```
class Main {
    public static void main(String[] args) {
        System.out.println("StringIndexOutOfBoundsException example");
        String str = "abc";
        System.out.println(str.charAt(3));
    }
}
```

StringIndexOutOfBoundsException()

PURPOSE Constructs a StringIndexOutOfBoundsException instance.

SYNTAX

```
public StringIndexOutOfBoundsException()
public StringIndexOutOfBoundsException(int idx)
public StringIndexOutOfBoundsException(String msg)
```

DESCRIPTION The three forms of this constructor create a new instance of StringIndexOutOfBoundsException. An optional string msg can be supplied that describes this particular instance of the exception. Alternatively, the index idx that caused the exception can be supplied to the constructor, which will use idx to construct a message for describing this exception.

PARAMETERS

idx The index that caused the exception.

msg A string that gives details about this exception.

java.util
StringTokenizer

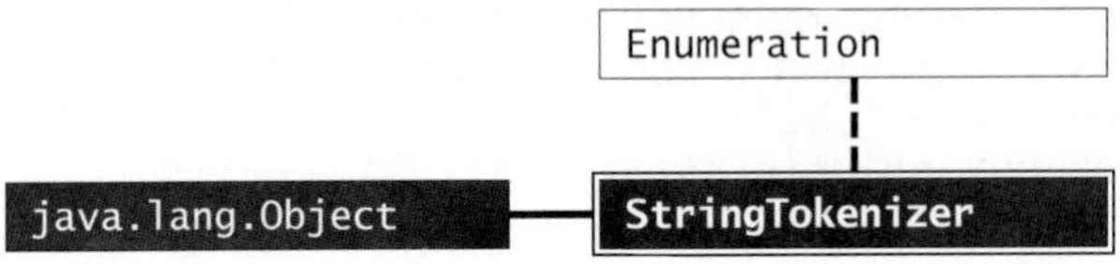

Syntax

```
public class StringTokenizer implements Enumeration
```

Description

The `StringTokenizer` class is for parsing a string into a sequence of *tokens*. A token is a string of characters separated by *delimiter characters* (or simply *delimiters*). An instance of a `StringTokenizer` is created with a string, a set of delimiters, and a flag indicating whether delimiters are to be returned as tokens. The delimiters can be replaced any time after the `StringTokenizer` has been created. The default delimiters are the whitespace characters (space, tab, newline, and return).

The following example shows a tokenizer that parses a string using the default delimiters (Figure 219):

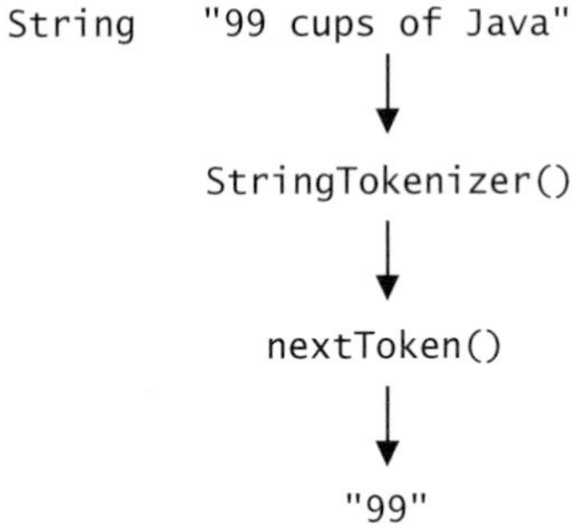

FIGURE 219 **`StringTokenizer`**

```
String s = "99 cups of Java";
StringTokenizer parser =
    new StringTokenizer(s);
try {
    while(parser.hasMoreTokens()) {
        System.out.println(
            parser.nextToken());
    }
} catch (NoSuchElementException e) {
    System.out.println(e);
}
```

This example produces the following output:

```
99
cups
of
Java
```

`StringTokenizer` implements the `Enumeration` interface. This means you can pass an instance of `StringTokenizer` to methods that accept enumerations. You can use the enumeration methods to enumerate the tokens in a `StringTokenizer`.

The following example shows a tokenizer that parses a string using the semicolon character (';') as the delimiter:

```
String s = "c:\\windows\\command;c:\\dos;c:\\bin;c:\\util";
StringTokenizer parser = new StringTokenizer(s, ";");
try
 {
    while(parser.hasMoreElements()) {
        System.out.println(parser.nextElement());
    }
} catch (NoSuchElementException e) {
    System.out.println(e);
}
```

It produces the following output.

```
c:\windows\command
c:\dos
c:\bin
c:\util
```

MEMBER SUMMARY

Constructor	
`StringTokenizer()`	Constructs a new string tokenizer.
Parsing Methods	
`countTokens()`	Determines the number of tokens remaining in this string tokenizer.
`hasMoreTokens()`	Determines whether this string tokenizer has any more tokens.
`nextToken()`	Retrieves the next token in this string tokenizer.
Enumeration Method	
`hasMoreElements()`	Determines whether this string tokenizer has any more tokens.
`nextElement()`	Retrieves the next token in this string tokenizer.

See Also

`Enumeration`, `StreamTokenizer`.

countTokens()

PURPOSE Determines the number of tokens remaining in this string tokenizer.

SYNTAX `public int countTokens()`

DESCRIPTION This method returns the number of tokens remaining in this string tokenizer. This is the number of times `nextToken()` can be called before it raises `NoSuchElementException`. `countToken()` does not affect the current position of the string tokenizer or the value returned by subsequent calls to `nextToken()`.

RETURNS The number of tokens remaining.

SEE ALSO `hasMoreTokens()`, `nextToken()`.

EXAMPLE This example shows a tokenizer that treats the delimiters as tokens. The output of this example follows its code.

```
String s = “a = b + c, d = e.”;
StringTokenizer parser = new StringTokenizer(s, “,.”, true);
System.out.println(“There are “ + parser.countTokens() + “ tokens”);
try {
    while (parser.hasMoreTokens()) {
        System.out.println(parser.nextToken());
    }
} catch (NoSuchElementException e) {
    e.printStackTrace();
}
```

OUTPUT

```
There are 4 tokens
a = b + c
,
 d = e
.
```

hasMoreElements()

PURPOSE Determines whether this string tokenizer has any more tokens.

SYNTAX `public boolean hasMoreElements()`

DESCRIPTION This method is the same as `hasMoreTokens()`. It is provided for the `Enumeration` interface implemented by `StringTokenizer`.

RETURNS `true` if there are more tokens; `false` otherwise.

SEE ALSO `Enumeration.hasMoreElements()`, `hasMoreTokens()`.

EXAMPLE See the class example.

A B C D E F G H I J K L M N O P Q R S T U V W X Y Z

hasMoreTokens()

PURPOSE Determines whether this string tokenizer has any more tokens.

SYNTAX `public boolean hasMoreTokens()`

DESCRIPTION This method checks this string tokenizer to see if it has any more unparsed tokens. It updates the current position of the string tokenizer to be at the starting position of the next token. If it is already at the start of the next token, the current position is not changed.

RETURNS `true` if there are more tokens; `false` otherwise.

SEE ALSO `countTokens()`, `hasMoreElements()`.

EXAMPLE See the class example.

nextElement()

PURPOSE Retrieves the next token from this string tokenizer.

SYNTAX `public Object nextElement()`

DESCRIPTION This method is the same as `nextToken()`. It is provided for the `Enumeration` interface implemented by `StringTokenizer`.

RETURNS The next token in this string tokenizer.

EXCEPTIONS
`NoSuchElementException`
If there are no more tokens in this string tokenizer.

SEE ALSO `Enumeration.nextElement()`, `nextToken()`.

EXAMPLE See the class example.

nextToken()

PURPOSE Retrieves the next token in this string tokenizer.

SYNTAX
```
public String nextToken()
public String nextToken(String delims)
```

DESCRIPTION The two forms of the method return the next token in this string tokenizer, delimited by any of the delimiters associated with this string tokenizer. If `delims` is specified, `nextToken()` first sets the delimiters of this string tokenizer to be delims and then returns the next token in its string delimited by any character in delims. delims will be used for subsequent nextToken() calls until it is replaced by another set of delimiters.

If this string tokenizer was created with retDelim set to true, any delimiter that is encountered in its string is also returned as a token, one character at a time. If it was created with retDelim set to false, delimiters are not returned as tokens.

PARAMETERS

delims — The delimiters to use for this string tokenizer. delims must not be null.

RETURNS — The next token in this string tokenizer.

EXCEPTIONS

NoSuchElementException — If there are no more tokens in this string tokenizer.

SEE ALSO — nextElement(), StringTokenizer().

EXAMPLE — This example shows the use of nextElement() to parse a quoted string. Initially, the tokenizer uses blanks and the single quote character as delimiters. When it encounters the quote character, it uses only the single quote character as the delimiter. This way, you can have embedded blanks within the quoted string. Once the quoted string has been parsed, the tokenizer switches back to accepting both blanks and single quote characters as delimiters. The output of this example follows its code.

```
String s = "frontstuff 'Welcome to our Home' endstuff";
StringTokenizer parser = new StringTokenizer(s, " '", true);
String token, new_delimiter = null;
boolean look_for_matching_quote = false;
try {
    while (parser.hasMoreTokens()) {
        if (new_delimiter != null) {
            token = parser.nextToken(new_delimiter);
            new_delimiter = null;
        } else {
            token = parser.nextToken();
        }
        if (token.equals(" "))
            continue;
        if (token.equals("'")) {
            if (look_for_matching_quote) {
                new_delimiter = " '";
                look_for_matching_quote = false;
            } else {
                new_delimiter = "'";  // can have embedded blanks
                look_for_matching_quote = true;
            }
        } else {
```

```
            System.out.println(token);
        }
    }
} catch (NoSuchElementException e) {
    e.printStackTrace();
}
```

OUTPUT

```
frontstuff
Welcome to our Home
endstuff
```

StringTokenizer()

PURPOSE Constructs a new string tokenizer.

SYNTAX

```
public StringTokenizer(String str)
public StringTokenizer(String str, String delims)
public StringTokenizer(String str, String delims, boolean
   retDelim)
```

DESCRIPTION There are three forms of the constructor for `StringTokenizer`. The first form creates a string tokenizer for the string `str` with delimiters " `\t\n\r`" (blank, tab, newline, and return). Delimiters that occur in `str` are not returned as tokens.

The second form creates a string tokenizer for the string `str`, with delimiters in the string `delims`. Delimiters that occur in `str` are not returned as tokens.

The third form creates a string tokenizer for the string `str`, with delimiters in the string `delims`. If `retDelim` is `true`, delimiters that occur in `str` are returned as tokens; if `retDelim` is `false`, delimiters are not returned.

PARAMETERS

`delims` Delimiters for this tokenizer. Each character in `delims` is used to delimit tokens that occur in `str`.

`retDelim` If `true`, the delimiters will be returned as a token a character at a time as they are encountered; if `false`, the delimiters will not be returned as tokens.

`str` The string to parse for this string tokenizer.

SEE ALSO `nextToken()`.

EXAMPLE See the class examples, `count()`, `nextToken()` for examples.

java.lang
System

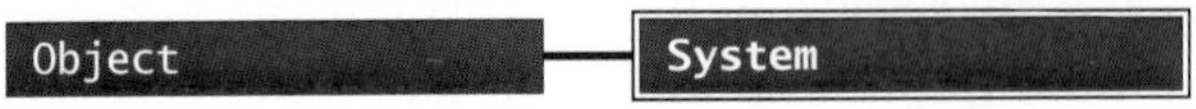

Syntax

```
public final class System
```

Description

The `System` class provides a collection of methods for examining and manipulating system-related information in a platform-independent manner. These methods include support for standard IO, memory management, and system properties.

This class cannot be instantiated or subclassed.

Standard IO

The `System` class provides support for user-level input/output. Three open streams are associated with the three standard open files: input, output, and error output. The standard input stream is used by the program to read character data from the user who is running the program. The standard output stream is used by the program to print text output for display to the user; for example:

```
System.out.println("Hello World!");
```

The standard error output stream is used by the program to print error messages to the user.

Security

A security manager enforces security policies related to what a program is allowed to do. Some of these policies deal with which class loaders to use, inspection of the execution stack, access to local files, access to system properties, and permission to execute system programs. The `System` class allows the program to set these policies by defining the security manager to use.

The Java runtime system by default does not use a security manager. However, applications such as Web browsers typically define a security manager and use `System.setSecurityManager()` to install it. Only one security manager can be installed. Once installed it cannot be replaced.

Runtime

The `System` class provides methods for performing runtime-related functions, such as loading libraries and memory management. These methods are also available directly from the

Runtime class; the System class methods are just short forms of the same methods. For example, calling

```
System.gc();
```

is equivalent to calling

```
Runtime.getRuntime().gc();
```

System Properties

A *system property* is a key-value pair that the Java runtime defines to describe the user, system environment, and Java system. Table 17 contains a list of the default system properties. Other properties also can be made available to a Java program by using the -D option to the Java interpreter. For example, running the interpreter as follows:

```
java -Dmyenviron=abc Main
```

will add the property myenviron with value "abc" to the list of properties visible to the program Main.

The System class provides methods that allow you to get all or selected properties, as well as a method to update the list of properties (if allowed by the security manager).

TABLE 17 Java System Properties

java.version	Java version number.
java.vendor	Java vendor-specific information.
java.vendor.url	Java vendor URL.
java.home	Directory name of where Java software has been installed.
java.class.version	Java class version number.
java.class.path	The setting of CLASSPATH.
os.name	Name of the operating system.
os.arch	Machine architecture.
os.version	Release version of the operating system.
file.separator	String used in file pathnames to separate directories.
path.separator	String used to separate components in a path variable.
line.separator	String used to separate lines.
user.name	User's account name.
user.home	Pathname of user's home directory.
user.dir	Pathname of user's current working directory.

MEMBER SUMMARY	
Standard IO	
`err`	Standard error output stream.
`in`	Standard input stream.
`out`	Standard output stream.
Security Methods	
`getSecurityManager()`	Retrieves the reference to the security manager.
`setSecurityManager()`	Sets the system's security manager.
Runtime Methods	
`exit()`	Exits the virtual machine.
`gc()`	Runs the garbage collector.
`load()`	Loads a dynamic library when given its full pathname.
`loadLibrary()`	Loads a dynamic library when given its library name.
`runFinalization()`	Runs the finalization method of objects that are pending finalization.
System Properties	
`getProperties()`	Retrieves the list of system properties.
`getProperty()`	Retrieves the named system property.
`setProperties()`	Updates the list of system properties.
Array Method	
`arraycopy()`	Copies a region of one array to another.
Time Method	
`currentTimeMillis()`	Retrieves the current time in milliseconds.

See Also

`Date`, `InputStream`, `OutputStream`, `PrintStream`, `Properties`, `Runtime`, `SecurityManager`.

arraycopy()

PURPOSE Copies a region of one array to another.

SYNTAX
```
public static native void arraycopy(Object src, int srcOffset,
    Object dst, int dstOffset, int count)
```

DESCRIPTION This method copies a region of one array, `src`, beginning at the array cell at `srcOffset`, to another array, `dst`, beginning at the array cell at `dstOffset`. `count` cells are copied. This method does not allocate memory for the destination array `dst`. The memory must already be allocated.

PARAMETERS

`count`	The number of cells to copy.
`dst`	The array into which to copy.
`dstOffset`	The first cell in `dst` into which to copy.
`src`	The array from which to copy.
`srcOffset`	The first cell in `src` from which to copy.

EXCEPTIONS

`ArrayIndexOutOfBoundsException`
: `count`, `dstOffset`, or `srcOffset`, are specified in such a way that the copy would cause access of data outside array bounds.

`ArrayStoreException`
: If an element in the `src` array could not be stored into the destination array due to a type mismatch.

EXAMPLE

```
// Implementation of String.getChars().
public void getChars(int srcBegin, int srcEnd,
    char dst[], int dstBegin) {
    System.arraycopy(value, offset + srcBegin, dst, dstBegin,
        srcEnd - srcBegin);
}
```

currentTimeMillis()

PURPOSE Retrieves the current time in milliseconds.

SYNTAX `public static native long currentTimeMillis()`

DESCRIPTION This method returns the current time in milliseconds GMT since the *epoch* (00:00:00 UTC, January 1, 1970). It is a signed 64-bit integer, so it will not overflow until the year 292280995.

RETURNS The current time in milliseconds.

SEE ALSO `Date`.

EXAMPLE

```
// Create a Date object using today's date
Date today = new Date(System.currentTimeMillis());
System.out.println("Today: " + today.toString());
```

err

PURPOSE Standard error output stream.

SYNTAX `public static PrintStream err`

DESCRIPTION The standard error output stream is used by the program to print messages to the user concerning errors about program execution. This is separate from the standard output stream, which is intended for normal, expected output to the user of the program.

`err` is a *print stream*. This means you can send data values like integers to it and those data values will automatically be converted into strings for printing. `err` is also a *buffered* stream, meaning output sent to it is stored and written out only when the buffer is either full or explicitly flushed.

SEE ALSO `BufferedOutputStream`, `out`, `PrintStream`.

EXAMPLE

```
public static void usage() {
    System.err.println("Usage: testprog <username> <age>");
    System.exit(-1);
}
```

exit()

PURPOSE Exits the virtual machine.

SYNTAX `public void exit(int status)`

DESCRIPTION This method is equivalent to `Runtime.exit()`. All threads are terminated and the executing program is halted.

PARAMETERS

`status` The exit status. A value of `0` indicates success; all other values indicate failure.

SEE ALSO `Runtime.exit()`, `SecurityManager.checkExit()`.

EXAMPLE See `err`.

gc()

PURPOSE Runs the garbage collector.

SYNTAX `public static void gc()`

A B C D E F G H I J K L M N O P Q R S T U V W X Y Z

DESCRIPTION This method is equivalent to `Runtime.gc()`.

SEE ALSO `Runtime.gc()`.

EXAMPLE

```
System.gc(); // indicate that garbage collector should run
```

getProperties()

PURPOSE Retrieves the list of system properties.

SYNTAX `public static Properties getProperties()`

DESCRIPTION This method returns the list of system properties currently defined. This includes the standard system properties listed in Table 17, as well as any environment variables set via the `-D` options to the Java interpreter (see the example given in the class description). If any changes, additions, or removals are made to the system properties via the `setProperties()` method, those will also be reflected in the list of properties returned.

The system properties can be accessed only if permitted by the security manager.

RETURNS The list of system properties currently defined.

SEE ALSO `getProperty()`, `SecurityManager.checkPropertiesAccess()`, `Properties`, `setProperties()`.

EXAMPLE

```
Properties props = System.getProperties(); // get list of properties
// Print properties using Enumeration
for (Enumeration enum = props.propertyNames();
    enum.hasMoreElements();) {
    String key = (String)enum.nextElement();
    System.out.println(key + " = " + (String)(props.get(key)));
}
```

getProperty()

PURPOSE Retrieves the named system property.

SYNTAX

```
public static String getProperty(String property)
public static String getProperty(String property, String defval)
```

DESCRIPTION The two forms of this method retrieve the system property identified by `property` and return the property's value as a string. If the property does not exist, the first form of this method returns `null`. The second form returns `defval` in the same situation.

The system property can be accessed only if permitted by the security manager.

PARAMETERS

`defval` The default value to return if `property` does not exist.

`property` The name of the property.

RETURNS The string value of `property` if `property` names a system property; otherwise, `defval`.

SEE ALSO `Boolean.getBoolean()`, `Color.getColor()`, `Integer.getInteger()`, `Long.getLong()`, `getProperties()`, `SecurityManager.checkPropertyAccess()`, `setProperties()`.

EXAMPLE

```
// get user's home directory
String homeDir = System.getProperty("user.home");
// If 'outDir' not found, use 'homeDir' as default
String dir = System.getProperty("outDir", homeDir);
```

getSecurityManager()

PURPOSE Retrieves the reference to the security manager.

SYNTAX `public static SecurityManager getSecurityManager()`

DESCRIPTION This method allows you to get a reference to the current security manager. If no security manager has been set, this method returns `null`. Otherwise, you can use the returned reference to perform various security-related checks (e.g., permission to do IO to files and permission to launch system programs).

RETURNS The reference to the security manager if it has been set; `null` otherwise.

SEE ALSO `SecurityManager`, `setSecurityManager()`.

EXAMPLE

```
// Implementation of Thread.checkAccess()
public final void checkAccess() {
    SecurityManager security = System.getSecurityManager();
    if (security != null) {
        security.checkAccess(this);
    }
}
```

A B C D E F G H I J K L M N O P Q R S T U V W X Y Z

in

PURPOSE Standard input stream.

SYNTAX `public static InputStream in`

DESCRIPTION The standard input stream is used by the program to read character data from the user. `in` is a *buffered* input stream, meaning input from the user is kept in a buffer until it is read by the program.

SEE ALSO `BufferedInputStream`, `err`, `InputStream`, `out`.

EXAMPLE

```
// reads a line from standard input
public static String getLine() {
    StringBuffer buf = new StringBuffer(80);
    int c;
    try {
        while ((c = System.in.read()) != -1) {
            char ch = (char) c;
            if (ch == '\n')
                break;
            buf.append(ch);
        }
    } catch (IOException e) {
        System.err.println(e);
    }
    return (buf.toString());
}
```

load()

PURPOSE Loads a dynamic library when given its full pathname.

SYNTAX `public static void load(String pathname)`

DESCRIPTION This method is equivalent to `Runtime.load()`.

PARAMETERS

`pathname` The pathname of the library to load.

EXCEPTIONS

`UnsatisfiedLinkError`
If `pathname` does not exist or does not name a library.

SEE ALSO `loadLibrary()`, `Runtime.load()`.

EXAMPLE

```
System.load("/usr/lib/libc.so");
```

A B C D E F G H I J K L M N O P Q R S T U V W X Y Z

loadLibrary()

PURPOSE Loads a dynamic library when given its library name.

SYNTAX `public static void loadLibrary(String libname)`

DESCRIPTION This method is equivalent to `Runtime.loadLibrary()`.

PARAMETERS
`libname` The name of the library.

EXCEPTIONS
`UnsatisfiedLinkError`
If `libname` does not exist.

SEE ALSO `load()`, `Runtime.loadLibrary()`.

EXAMPLE

```
System.loadLibrary("net");
```

out

PURPOSE Standard output stream.

SYNTAX `public static PrintStream out`

DESCRIPTION The standard output stream is used by the program to print text output for display to the user.

`out` is a *print stream*, meaning you can send data values like integers to it and those data values will automatically be converted into strings for printing. `out` is also a *buffered* stream, meaning output sent to it is stored and written out only when the buffer is either full or explicitly flushed.

SEE ALSO `BufferedOutputStream`, `err`, `in`, `PrintStream`.

EXAMPLE See `getProperties()`.

runFinalization()

PURPOSE Runs the finalization method of objects that are pending finalization.

SYNTAX `public static void runFinalization()`

DESCRIPTION This method is equivalent to `Runtime.runFinalization()`.

SEE ALSO `gc()`, `Runtime.runFinalization()`.

EXAMPLE

```
System.runFinalization();
```

setProperties()

PURPOSE Updates the list of system properties.

SYNTAX `public static void setProperties(Properties props)`

DESCRIPTION This method replaces the existing list of system properties with the new list, `props`. The list may contain deletions from and modifications and additions to the current list.

The system properties can be changed only if permitted by the security manager.

PARAMETERS

`props` The new list of system properties.

SEE ALSO `getProperties()`, `getProperty()`, `Properties`, `SecurityManager.checkPropertiesAccess()`.

EXAMPLE

```
Properties props = System.getProperties();
// Add 'outDir' property
props.put("outDir", "/tmp");
// overwrites System properties with new properties
System.setProperties(props);
```

setSecurityManager()

PURPOSE Sets the system's security manager.

SYNTAX `public static void setSecurityManager(SecurityManager s)`

DESCRIPTION This method sets the security manager of the current program to `s`. Once set, the security manager cannot be replaced.

PARAMETERS

`s` The security manager.

EXCEPTIONS

`SecurityException`
If the security manager has already been set.

SEE ALSO `getSecurityManager()`, `SecurityManager`.

EXAMPLE See `SecurityManager.classDepth()`.

TextArea

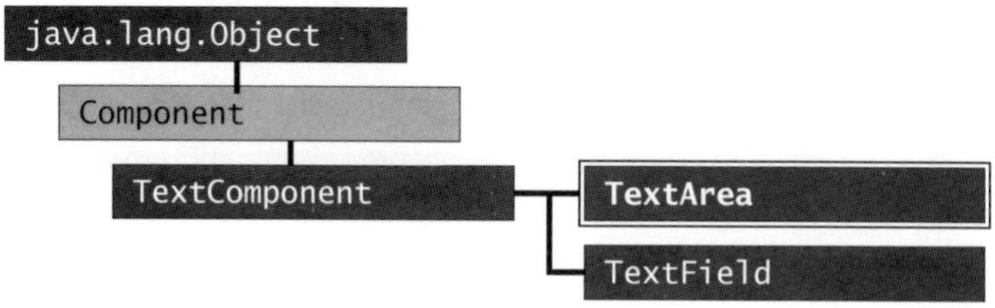

Syntax

```
public class TextArea extends TextComponent
```

Description

The *text area* is a text component that displays editable text. The text area is similar to the field component except that the text area can display multiple lines and has vertical and horizontal scrollbars.

The text area component is typically used for entering text messages or comments to a program and for displaying text output from a program.

Figure 220 shows an example of text area.

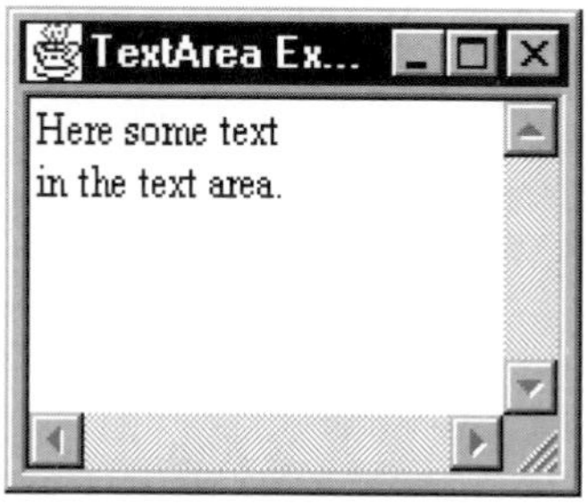

FIGURE 220 `TextArea`

MEMBER SUMMARY	
Constructor	
`TextArea()`	Constructs a new `TextArea` instance.
Layout Methods	
`getColumns()`	Retrieves the number of columns used to create the text area.
`getRows()`	Retrieves the number of rows used to create the text area.
`minimumSize()`	Calculates the minimum dimensions of the text area.
`preferredSize()`	Calculates the preferred dimensions of the text area.
Text Methods	
`appendText()`	Appends a string to the text area.
`insertText()`	Inserts a string in the text area.
`replaceText()`	Replaces a range of characters in the text area with another range of characters.

Continued

MEMBER SUMMARY	
Peer Method	
`addNotify()`	Creates the `TextArea`'s peer.
Debugging Method	
`paramString()`	Generates a string representing the text area's state.

Example

This example creates a text area and displays it in a frame. See Figure 220 for a screen shot of the example.

```
import java.awt.*;
class Main extends Frame {
    TextArea ta = new TextArea(1, 1);

    Main() {
        super("TextArea Example");
        add("Center", ta);
        pack();
        show();
    }

    static public void main(String[] args) {
        new Main();
    }
}
```

addNotify()

PURPOSE Creates the text area's peer.

SYNTAX `public synchronized void addNotify()`

DESCRIPTION This method creates the menu bar's peer if it does not yet exist. The text area's peer is created by calling the `Toolkit.createTextArea()` method. This method should never be called directly. It is normally called by the text area's parent.

OVERRIDES `Component.addNotify()`.

SEE ALSO Component, Toolkit.

EXAMPLE Component.show().

appendText()

PURPOSE Appends a string to the text area.

SYNTAX `public void appendText(String text)`

DESCRIPTION This method appends the string `text` to the end of the text area.

PARAMETERS

`text` The non-`null` string to be appended.

SEE ALSO `insertText()`, `replaceText()`.

EXAMPLE This example creates a frame containing a text area and a text field. The text typed in the text field is appended to the text area if you press Return. See Figure 221.

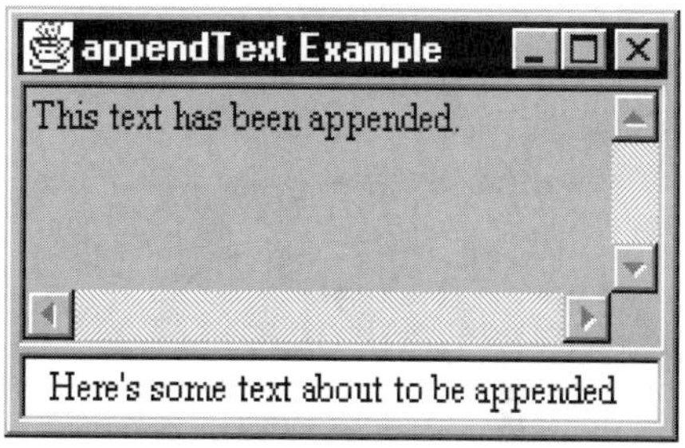

FIGURE 221 `TextArea.appendText()`

```
import java.awt.*;
class Main extends Frame {
    TextField tf = new TextField();
    TextArea ta = new TextArea();

    Main() {
        super("appendText Example");
        ta.setEditable(false);
        add("Center", ta);
        add("South", tf);
        pack();
        show();
    }

    public boolean action(Event evt, Object what) {
        if (evt.target == tf) {
            ta.appendText(tf.getText() + "\n");
            tf.setText("");
            return true;
        }
        return false;
    }
```

```
        static public void main(String[] args) {
            new Main();
        }
    }
```

getColumns()

PURPOSE Retrieves the number of columns used to create the text area.

SYNTAX `public int getColumns()`

DESCRIPTION This method retrieves the number of columns used to create the text area. The return value is identical to the one used to create the text area. This value does not change even if the text area is resized.

RETURNS The number of columns used to create the text area.

SEE ALSO `TextArea()`.

getRows()

PURPOSE Retrieves the number of rows used to create the text area.

SYNTAX `public int getRows()`

DESCRIPTION This method retrieves the number of rows used to create the text area. The return value is identical to the one used to create the text area. This value does not change even if the text area is resized.

RETURNS The number of rows used to create the text area.

SEE ALSO `TextArea()`.

insertText()

PURPOSE Inserts a string in the text area.

SYNTAX `public void insertText(String text, int pos)`

DESCRIPTION This method inserts the string `text` at index `pos` of this text area.

PARAMETERS

`pos` The 0-based index at which to insert the text.

`text` The non-null text to be inserted.

SEE ALSO `appendText()`, `replaceText()`.

EXAMPLE This example creates a frame containing a text area and a choice. The choice contains a number of words that can be inserted into the text area when selected. See Figure 222.

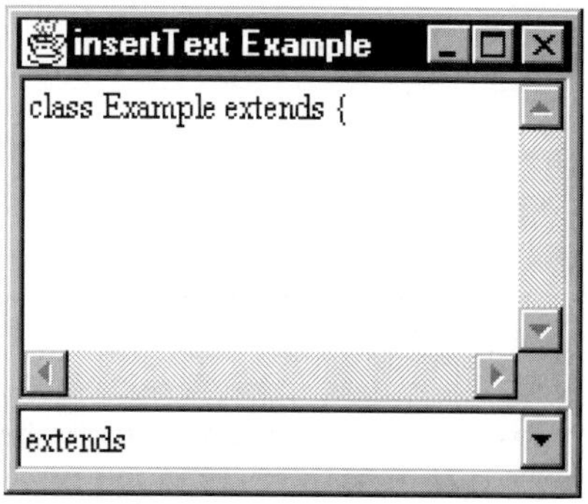

FIGURE 222 `TextArea.insertText()`

```
import java.awt.*;
class Main extends Frame {
    String[] keywords =
        {"class", "extends", "import", "interface", "synchronized"};
    TextArea ta = new TextArea();
    Choice c = new Choice();

    Main() {
        super("insertText Example");
        for (int i=0; i<keywords.length; i++) {
            c.addItem(keywords[i]);
        }
        add("Center", ta);
        add("South", c);
        pack();
        show();
    }

    public boolean action(Event evt, Object what) {
        if (evt.target == c) {
            ta.insertText((String)what,ta.getSelectionEnd());
            ta.requestFocus();
            return true;
        }
        return false;
    }

    static public void main(String[] args) {
        new Main();
    }
}
```

minimumSize()

PURPOSE Calculates the minimum dimensions of the text area.

SYNTAX
```
public Dimension minimumSize()
public Dimension minimumSize(int rows, int cols)
```

DESCRIPTION The minimum dimensions of a text area are based on the dimensions needed for displaying the specified number of rows and columns of characters. The size of a character depends on the text area's current font. If the text area's font has variable-width characters, then `cols` is based on the average size of a character and the result is an approximation. The average width of a character is a platform-dependent value. If `rows` and `cols` are not specified, they default to the same values that were used to create the text area.

If the text area's peer is not yet created, the resulting dimensions are (0, 0). On most platforms, the minimum and preferred dimensions are the same.

PARAMETERS

`cols` A non-negative integer specifying the width in characters.

`rows` A non-negative integer specifying the height in character lines.

RETURNS A new non-`null` `Dimension` instance containing the minimum dimensions of the text area.

OVERRIDES `Component.minimumSize()`.

paramString()

PURPOSE Generates the string representing the text area's state.

SYNTAX
```
protected String paramString()
```

DESCRIPTION A subclass of this class should override this method and return a concatenation of its state with the results of `super.paramString()`. This method is called by the `toString()` method and is typically used for debugging.

RETURNS A non-`null` string representing the text area's state.

OVERRIDES `TextComponent.paramString()`.

SEE ALSO `Object.toString()`.

EXAMPLE See `Component.paramString()`.

preferredSize()

PURPOSE Calculates the preferred dimensions of the text area.

SYNTAX

```
public Dimension preferredSize()
public Dimension preferredSize(int rows, int cols)
```

DESCRIPTION The preferred dimensions of a text area are based on the dimensions needed for displaying the specified number of rows and columns of characters. The size of a character depends on the text area's current font. If the text area's font has variable-width characters, then `cols` is based on the average size of a character and the result is an approximation. The average width of a character is a platform-dependent value. If `rows` and `cols` are not specified, they default to the same values that were used to create the text area.

If the text area's peer is not yet created, the resulting dimensions are (0, 0). On most platforms, the minimum and preferred dimensions are the same.

PARAMETERS

`cols` A non-negative integer specifying the width in characters.

`rows` A non-negative integer specifying the height in character lines.

RETURNS A new non-`null` `Dimension` instance containing the preferred dimensions of the text area.

OVERRIDES `Component.preferredSize()`.

replaceText()

PURPOSE Replaces a range of characters in the text area with another range of characters.

SYNTAX

```
public void replaceText(String str, int startPos, int endPos)
```

DESCRIPTION This method replaces the text between `startPos` and `endPos` with `str` in this text area. The length of the range is `endPosstartPos`.

PARAMETERS

`endPos` The end position of the range. The character at the 0-based index `end` is not included in the range.

`startPos` The 0-based index of the first character in the range.

`str` The non-`null` replacement string.

SEE ALSO `appendText()`, `insertText()`.

EXAMPLE This example creates a text area and two text fields. See Figure 223. In one text field, you specify a search string and in the other, you specify a replacement string. When you hit Return in either text field, an occurrence of the search string in the text area is replaced by the replacement string.

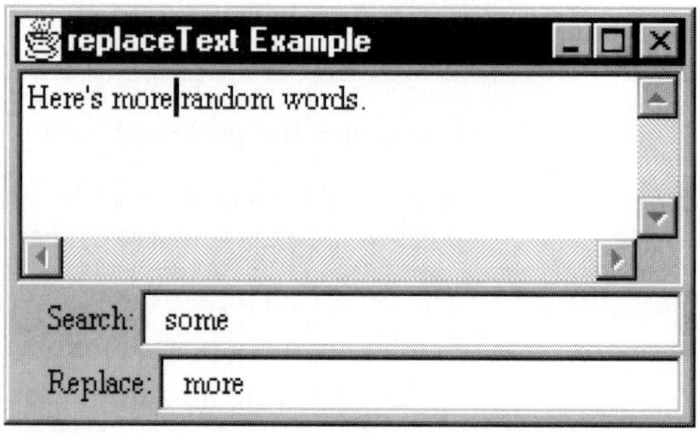

FIGURE 223 TextArea.replaceText()

```
import java.awt.*;
class Main extends Frame {
    TextField tfSearch = new TextField();
    TextField tfReplace = new TextField();
    TextArea ta = new TextArea(10, 40);

    Main() {
        super("replaceText Example");
        Panel southPanel = new Panel();
        Panel p;

        southPanel.setLayout(new GridLayout(2, 1));
        p = new Panel();
        p.setLayout(new BorderLayout());
        p.add("West", new Label("Search:"));
        p.add("Center", tfSearch);
        southPanel.add(p);

        p = new Panel();
        p.setLayout(new BorderLayout());
        p.add("West", new Label("Replace:"));
        p.add("Center", tfReplace);
        southPanel.add(p);

        add("Center", ta);
        add("South", southPanel);
        pack();
        show();
    }

    public boolean action(Event evt, Object what) {
        if (evt.target == tfSearch || evt.target == tfReplace) {
            String str = tfSearch.getText();
            int s = ta.getText().indexOf(str, ta.getSelectionStart());

            if (s < 0 && ta.getSelectionStart() > 0) {
                // Let's try from the beginning.
                s = ta.getText().indexOf(str, 0);
```

```
            }
            if (s >= 0) {
                String strRep = tfReplace.getText();
                ta.replaceText(strRep, s, s + str.length());
                ta.select(s + strRep.length(), s + strRep.length());
                ta.requestFocus();
            }
            return true;
        }
        return false;
    }

    static public void main(String[] args) {
        new Main();
    }
}
```

TextArea()

PURPOSE — Creates a new `TextArea` instance.

SYNTAX

```
public TextArea()
public TextArea(String text)
public TextArea(int rows, int cols)
public TextArea(String text, int rows, int cols)
```

DESCRIPTION — The four forms of this constructor create a new editable `TextArea` initialized using the string `text`. If `text` is not specified, it defaults to "".

`rows` and `cols` specify the initial size of the text area. It is based on the character size of the text area's font. If the font has variable-width characters, then `cols` is based on the average size of a character and the result is an approximation. The average width of a character is a platform-dependent value. If `rows` and `cols` are not specified, the defaults are chosen by the platform.

PARAMETERS

`cols` — A non-negative integer specifying the initial width in characters.

`rows` — A non-negative integer specifying the initial height in character lines.

`text` — The string specifying the initial text for the text component. May be `null`.

EXAMPLE — See the class example.

java.awt.peer

TextAreaPeer

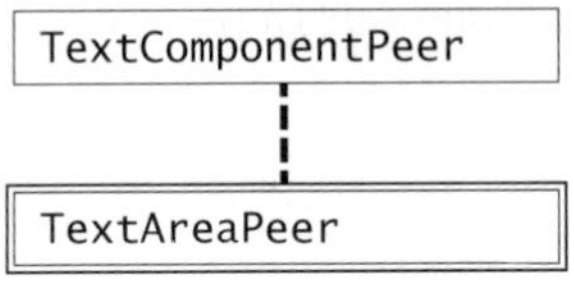

Syntax

```
public interface TextAreaPeer extends TextComponentPeer
```

Description

The text area component (see the `TextArea` class) in the Abstract Windowing Toolkit (AWT) uses the platform's native implementation of a text area. So that the AWT text area behaves the same on all platforms, the text area is assigned a peer, whose task is to translate the behavior of the platform's native text area to the behavior of the AWT text area.

AWT programmers normally do not directly use peer classes and interfaces. Instead they deal with AWT components in the `java.awt` package. These in turn automatically manage their peers. Only someone who is porting the AWT to another platform should be concerned with the peer classes and interfaces. Consequently, most peer documentation refers to `java.awt` counterparts.

See `Component` and `Toolkit` for additional information about component peers.

MEMBER SUMMARY

Peer Methods

`insertText()`	Inserts some text in the text area.
`minimumSize()`	Calculates the minimum dimensions of the text area.
`preferredSize()`	Calculates the preferred dimensions of the text area.
`replaceText()`	Replaces a range of characters in the text area with another range of characters.

See Also

`Component`, `TextArea`, `Toolkit`.

insertText()

PURPOSE Inserts some text in the text area.

SYNTAX `void insertText(String text, int pos)`

PARAMETERS

`pos` The 0-based position at which to insert the text.

`text` The non-`null` text to be inserted.

SEE ALSO `TextArea.insertText()`.

minimumSize()

PURPOSE Calculates the minimum dimensions of the text area.

SYNTAX `Dimension minimumSize(int rows, int cols)`

PARAMETERS

`cols` A non-negative integer specifying the width in characters.

`rows` A non-negative integer specifying the height in character lines.

RETURNS The non-`null` minimum dimensions for the text area.

SEE ALSO `TextArea.minimumSize()`.

preferredSize()

PURPOSE Calculates the preferred dimensions of the text area.

SYNTAX `Dimension preferredSize(int rows, int cols)`

PARAMETERS

`cols` A non-negative integer specifying the width in characters.

`rows` A non-negative integer specifying the height in character lines.

RETURNS The non-`null` minimum dimensions for the text area.

SEE ALSO `TextArea.minimumSize()`.

replaceText()

PURPOSE	Replaces a range of characters in the text area with another range of characters.
SYNTAX	`void replaceText(String str, int start, int end)`
PARAMETERS	
`end`	The end position.
`start`	The start position.
`str`	The non-`null` replacement string.
SEE ALSO	`TextArea.replaceText()`.

java.awt
TextComponent

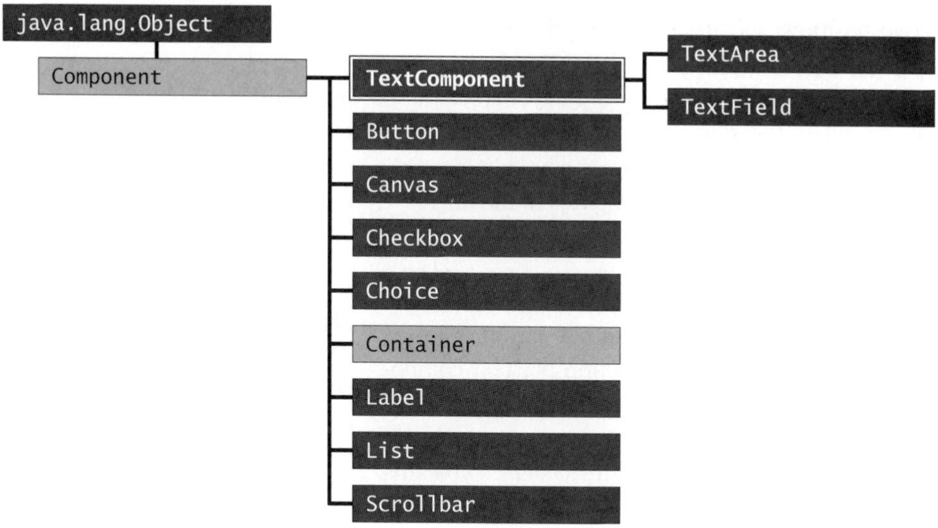

Syntax

```
public class TextComponent extends Component
```

Description

The text component is a component that displays editable text. The text can be modified by either the user or a program. There are two text components in the AWT package: the text field and text area. Both are subclasses of `TextComponent`. The `TextComponent` class itself is not instantiated. Its main purpose is to encapsulate the functionality that is common between the text field and text area components. Figure 224 shows a frame containing a text area and text field.

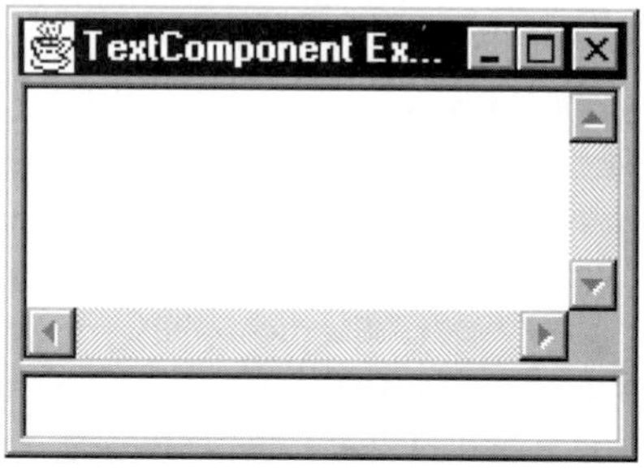

FIGURE 224 `TextArea` **and** `TextField`

The Editable Property

A text component has an editable property that controls whether the user can edit the text in the text component. The editable property affects only edits by the user; edits by a program are still allowed. On some platforms, the text component has some distinguishing visual feature to indicate its editable state.

Description

Text Component Positions

Text component positions refer to a character in the text. A position is 0-based, meaning the position of the first character in the text is 0 and the position of the last character is the length of the text minus 1. New line characters (`\n`) are treated as a single character.

Two positions specify a range of characters. The start position refers to the first character in the range. The end position also refers to a character in the text, but that character is not included in the range; the text before the character at the end position is included in the range. Therefore, when the start and end positions are the same, the range is empty. Moreover, to select the last characters in the text, you should set the end position to the length of the text. (end - start) is the number of characters in the range.

The Selection and Caret

A selection is a range of text in the text component. Both the user and a program can set and change the selection. There is only one selection per text component. The appearance and exact behavior of the selection is platform-dependent, but on most systems, only one selection is allowed in the entire system. Typically, the active selection is in the text component that is receiving keyboard input. Although the selections in other text components are not active, a program can still operate on the selection, modifying the range or the text in the range. Figure 225 shows the selection on the text "word" in the text area component as selected.

FIGURE 225 The Selection

A selection can become empty. It still has a position in the text component but does not contain any text. In fact, both the start and end positions are equal. When the active selection is empty, it becomes the "caret." The caret indicates where in the text component characters will appear as the user types. The caret moves forward with each character typed. As with the active selection, there is only one caret in the entire system.

Figure 226 shows the caret between the words "these words." On most platforms, when the user types a character at the active selection the text in the selection is first deleted, the active selection is then turned into a caret, and then the character is inserted.

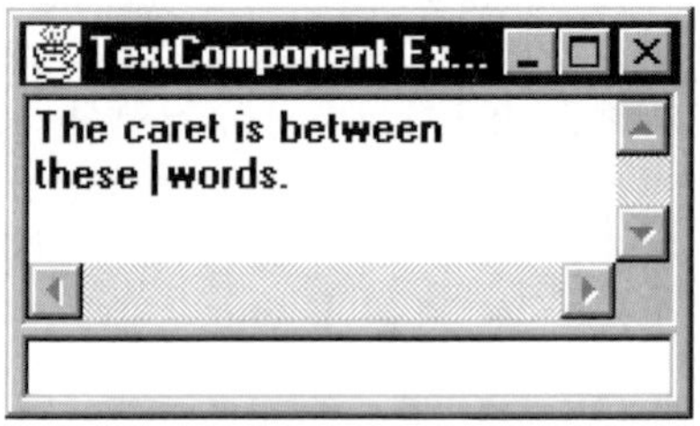

FIGURE 226 The Caret

Events

Text components generate the events defined in the `Event` class. See the `Event` class for details about available events and how to filter or handle events.

A text component can generate an action event. Table 18 describes how a text component fills the fields in an action event.

TABLE 18 Action Event from a `TextComponent`

`arg`	The contents of the text component.
`clickCount`	Not used.
`id`	`Event.ACTION`.
`key`	The key that caused the action event; usually a carriage return.
`modifiers`	The state of the modifier keys when the component was clicked.
`target`	A reference to the component that generated this event.
`when`	The time, in milliseconds, when the event was generated.
`x`	*x*-coordinate of the component in pixels.
`y`	*y*-coordinate of the component in pixels.

In the case of an `Event.KEY_ACTION` or `Event.KEY_PRESS` event, you can prevent the character from being inserted into the text component by returning `true` (see `Component.handleEvent()`). If the text component is not editable, key events are still generated, but they are not inserted into the text component.

MEMBER SUMMARY

Text Methods

`getText()`	Retrieves the text in the text component.
`setText()`	Sets the text of the text component.

Selection Methods

`getSelectedText()`	Retrieves the selected text in the text component.
`getSelectionEnd()`	Retrieves the selection's end position.
`getSelectionStart()`	Retrieves the selection's start position.
`select()`	Sets the selection in the text component.
`selectAll()`	Selects the text in the text component.

Editable Methods

`isEditable()`	Retrieves the text component's current editable state.
`setEditable()`	Sets the text component's editable state.

Peer Method

`removeNotify()`	Destroys the text component's peer.

Debugging Method

`paramString()`	Generates a string representation of the text component's state.

Example

This example creates a frame containing both kinds of text components: a text field and text area. See Figure 224 for a screen shot of the example.

```
import java.awt.*;
class Main {

    static public void main(String[] args) {
        Frame f = new Frame("TextComponent Example");
        f.add("South", new TextField());
        f.add("Center", new TextArea());
        f.pack();
        f.show();
    }
}
```

getSelectedText()

PURPOSE Retrieves the selected text in the text component.

SYNTAX `public String getSelectedText()`

DESCRIPTION This method retrieves the selected text in this text component. Each text component has a selection that may be empty.

RETURNS A non-`null` string containing the text in the selection. The length of the result value may be 0.

SEE ALSO `select()`.

EXAMPLE This example creates a frame containing both kinds of text components—the text field and the text area—and a print button. See Figure 227. Clicking the print button causes the current selection of both text components to be printed on standard output.

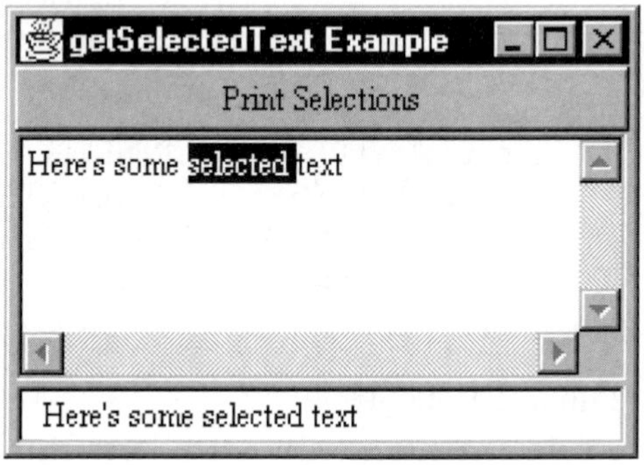

FIGURE 227
`TextComponent.getSelectedText()`

```
import java.awt.*;
class Main extends Frame {
    TextField tf = new TextField();
    TextArea ta = new TextArea();

    Main() {
        super("getSelectedText Example");
```

```
        add("North", new Button("Print Selections"));
        add("Center", ta);
        add("South", tf);
        pack();
        show();
    }

    public boolean action(Event evt, Object what) {
        System.out.println("------ text area -------");
        System.out.println(ta.getSelectedText());
        System.out.println("------ text field ------");
        System.out.println(tf.getSelectedText());
        return true;
    }

    static public void main(String[] args) {
        new Main();
    }
}
```

getSelectionEnd()

PURPOSE Retrieves the selection's end position.

SYNTAX `public int getSelectionEnd()`

DESCRIPTION The selection end position can be in the range 0 to the length of text in the text component. The selection's start position must be less than or equal to the selection's end position.

RETURNS The 0-based index of the selection's end position. Note that the character referred to by the index is not in the selection.

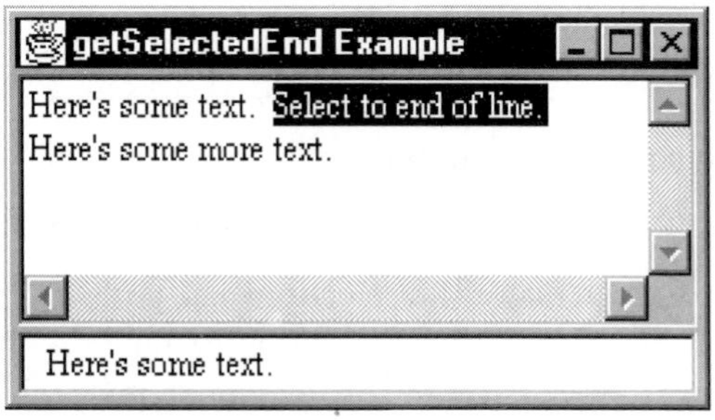

FIGURE 228
`TextComponent.getSelectedEnd()`

EXAMPLE This example creates a frame containing both kinds of text components—the text field and the text area. See Figure 228. Typing `ctl-e` in one of these components will extend the selection to the end-of-line, not including the newline character.

```
import java.awt.*;
class Main extends Frame {
    TextField tf = new TextField();
    TextArea ta = new TextArea();
```

```
        Main() {
            super("getSelectedEnd Example");
            add("Center", ta);
            add("South", tf);
            pack();
            show();
        }

        public boolean keyDown(Event evt, int key) {
            if (evt.target instanceof TextComponent && evt.key == 5
                  /*ctl-e*/) {
                TextComponent tc = (TextComponent)evt.target;
                String str = tc.getText();
                int e = str.indexOf('\n', tc.getSelectionEnd());

                tc.select(tc.getSelectionStart(), e < 0 ? str.length()
                          : e);
                return true;
            }
            return false;
        }

        static public void main(String[] args) {
            new Main();
        }
    }
```

getSelectionStart()

PURPOSE Retrieves the selection's start position.

SYNTAX `public int getSelectionStart()`

DESCRIPTION The selection start position can be in the range 0 to the length of text in the text component. The selection's end position must be greater than or equal to the selection's start position.

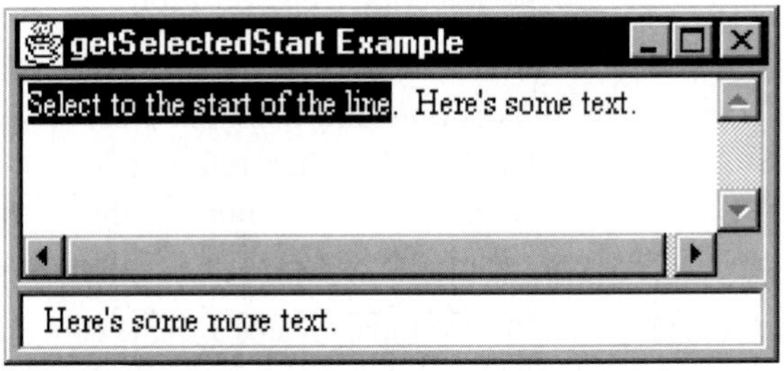

FIGURE 229 `TextComponent.getSelectedStart()`

RETURNS The 0-based index of the selection's start position.

EXAMPLE This example creates a frame containing both kinds of text components—the text field and the text area. See Figure 229. Typing `ctl-a` in one of these components will extend the selection to the start-of-line.

```
import java.awt.*;
class Main extends Frame {
    TextField tf = new TextField();
    TextArea ta = new TextArea();

    Main() {
        super("getSelectedStart Example");
        add("Center", ta);
        add("South", tf);
        pack();
        show();
    }

    public boolean keyDown(Event evt, int key) {
        if (evt.target instanceof TextComponent && evt.key == 1
              /*ctl-a*/) {
            TextComponent tc = (TextComponent)evt.target;
            String str = tc.getText();
            int s = str.lastIndexOf('\n', tc.getSelectionStart()-1)
                                        + 1;

            tc.select(s, tc.getSelectionEnd());
            return true;
        }
        return false;
    }

    static public void main(String[] args) {
        new Main();
    }
}
```

getText()

PURPOSE Retrieves the text in the text component.

SYNTAX `public String getText()`

RETURNS A non-`null` string containing the entire text in the text component.

SEE ALSO `setText()`.

EXAMPLE See `setText()`.

A B C D E F G H I J K L M N O P Q R S T U V W X Y Z

isEditable()

PURPOSE Retrieves the text component's current editable state.

SYNTAX `public boolean isEditable()`

RETURNS `true` if the text component is editable; `false` otherwise.

SEE ALSO `setEditable()`.

EXAMPLE This example creates a frame containing a text area and a text field. Typing `ctl-t` toggles the editable state of the text component. See Figure 230.

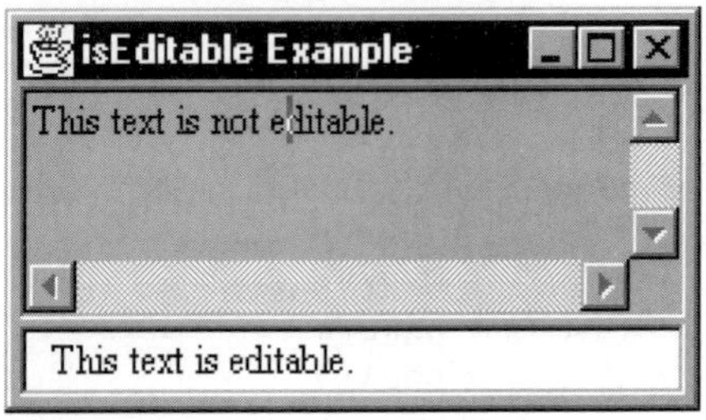

FIGURE 230
TextComponent.isEditable()

```
import java.awt.*;
class Main extends Frame {
    Main() {
        super("isEditable Example");
        add("Center", new TextArea());
        add("South", new TextField());
        pack();
        show();
    }

    public boolean keyDown(Event evt, int key) {
        if (evt.target instanceof TextComponent && key == 20
            /*ctl-t*/) {
            TextComponent tc = (TextComponent)evt.target;

            tc.setEditable(!tc.isEditable());
            return true;
        }
        return false;
    }

    static public void main(String[] args) {
        new Main();
    }
}
```

paramString()

PURPOSE Generates a string representation of the text component's state.

SYNTAX `protected String paramString()`

DESCRIPTION A subclass of this class should override this method and return a concatenation of its state with the results of `super.paramString()`. This method is called by the `toString()` method and is typically used for debugging.

RETURNS A non-`null` string representing the text component's state.

OVERRIDES `Component.paramString()`.

SEE ALSO `Object.toString()`.

EXAMPLE See `Component.paramString()`.

removeNotify()

PURPOSE Destroys the text component's peer.

SYNTAX `public void removeNotify()`

DESCRIPTION This method should never be called directly. It is normally called by the component's container.

OVERRIDES `Component.removeNotify()`.

SEE ALSO `Component`.

EXAMPLE See `Component.show()`.

select()

PURPOSE Sets the selection in the text component.

SYNTAX `public void select(int selStart, int selEnd)`

DESCRIPTION This method selects the text located between the positions `selStart` and `selEnd`, inclusive. If a position is negative, the position is set to `0`. If a position is greater than the length of text in the text component, the position is set to the length. If `selEnd` < `selStart`, `selEnd` is set to `selStart`.

PARAMETERS

`selEnd` The 0-based end position of the text range.

`selStart` The 0-based start position of the text range.

EXAMPLE This example creates a text area and a text field in a frame. See Figure 231. Pressing Return in the text field causes a search for the string in the text field.

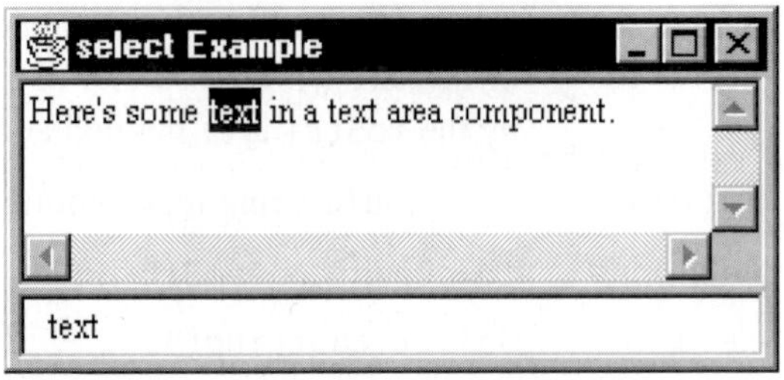

FIGURE 231 `TextComponent.select()`

```
import java.awt.*;
class Main extends Frame {
    TextField tf = new TextField();
    TextArea ta = new TextArea(10, 40);

    Main() {
        super("select Example");
        add("Center", ta);
        add("South", tf);
        pack();
        show();
    }

    public boolean action(Event evt, Object what) {
        if (evt.target == tf) {
            String str = tf.getText();
            int s = ta.getText().indexOf(str, ta.getSelectionStart());

            if (s < 0 && ta.getSelectionStart() > 0) {
                // Let's try from the beginning.
                s = ta.getText().indexOf(str, 0);
            }
            if (s >= 0) {
                ta.select(s, s + str.length());
                ta.requestFocus();
            }
            return true;
        }
        return false;
    }

    static public void main(String[] args) {
        new Main();
    }
}
```

selectAll()

PURPOSE Selects the text in the text component.

SYNTAX `public void selectAll()`

DESCRIPTION This method selects the entire text in the text component.

EXAMPLE This example creates a frame containing a menu bar and a text area. The menu bar contains an Edit menu with the item Select All, which causes the text area to request the focus and select all its text.

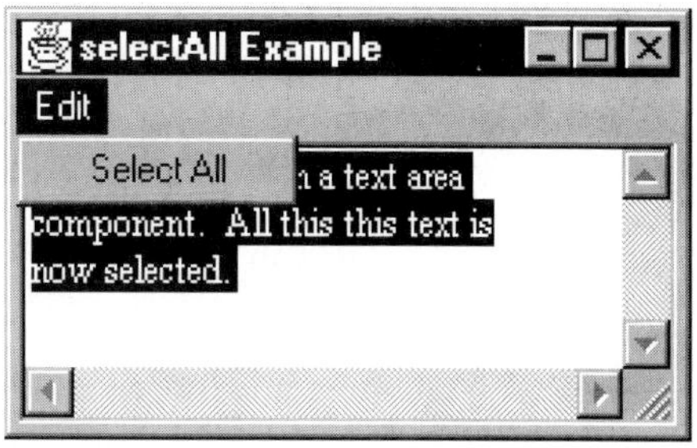

FIGURE 232
`TextComponent.selectAll()`

```
import java.awt.*;
class Main extends Frame {
    TextArea ta = new TextArea();

    Main() {
        super("selectAll Example");
        MenuBar mb = new MenuBar();
        Menu menu = new Menu("Edit");

        menu.add("Select All");
        mb.add(menu);
        setMenuBar(mb);
        add("Center", ta);
        pack();
        show();
    }

    public boolean action(Event evt, Object what) {
        if ("Select All".equals(what)) {
            ta.selectAll();
            ta.requestFocus();
            return true;
        }
        return false;
    }

    static public void main(String[] args) {
        new Main();
    }
}
```

setEditable()

PURPOSE Sets the text component's editable state.

SYNTAX `public void setEditable(boolean editable)`

PARAMETERS

`editable`	If `true`, the text component becomes editable; otherwise it becomes uneditable.
SEE ALSO	`isEditable()`.
EXAMPLE	This example creates a frame containing a text area and a checkbox. The checkbox sets the editable state of the text area. See Figure 233.

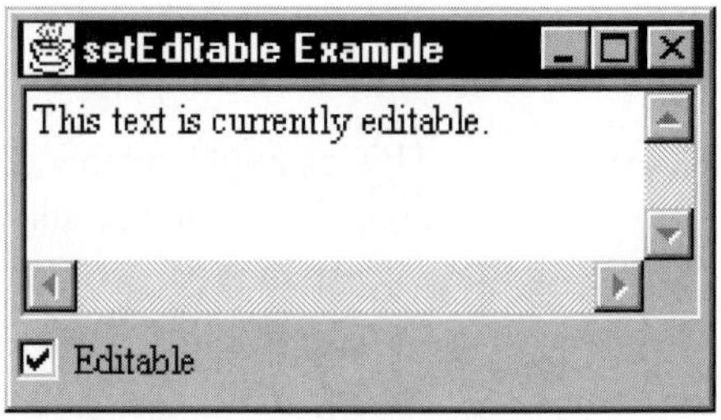

FIGURE 233
`TextComponent.setEditable()`

```
import java.awt.*;
class Main extends Frame {
    TextArea ta = new TextArea();
    Checkbox cb = new Checkbox("Editable", null, true);

    Main() {
        super("setEditable Example");
        add("Center", ta);
        add("South", cb);
        pack();
        show();
    }

    public boolean action(Event evt, Object what) {
        if (evt.target == cb) {
            ta.setEditable(cb.getState());
        }
        return true;
    }

    static public void main(String[] args) {
        new Main();
    }
}
```

setText()

PURPOSE	Sets the text of the text component.
SYNTAX	`public void setText(String text)`

DESCRIPTION This method replaces the entire text of the text component with the string `text`.

PARAMETERS

`text` A string containing the text. A value of `null` is the same as "".

SEE ALSO `getText()`.

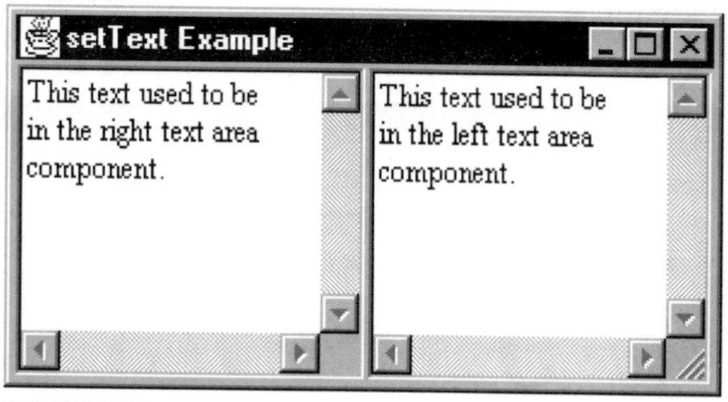

FIGURE 234 `TextComponent.setText()`

EXAMPLE This example creates a frame containing two text areas. Typing `ctl-t` swaps the text in the components. See Figure 234.

```
import java.awt.*;
class Main extends Frame {
    TextArea ta1 = new TextArea(null, 10, 40);
    TextArea ta2 = new TextArea(null, 10, 40);

    Main() {
        super("setText Example");
        setLayout(new GridLayout(1, 2));
        add(ta1);
        add(ta2);
        pack();
        show();
    }

    public boolean keyDown(Event evt, int key) {
        if (evt.target instanceof TextArea && key == 20 /*ctl-t*/) {
            String str = ta1.getText();

            ta1.setText(ta2.getText());
            ta2.setText(str);
            return true;
        }
        return false;
    }

    static public void main(String[] args) {
        new Main();
    }
}
```

java.awt.peer

TextComponentPeer

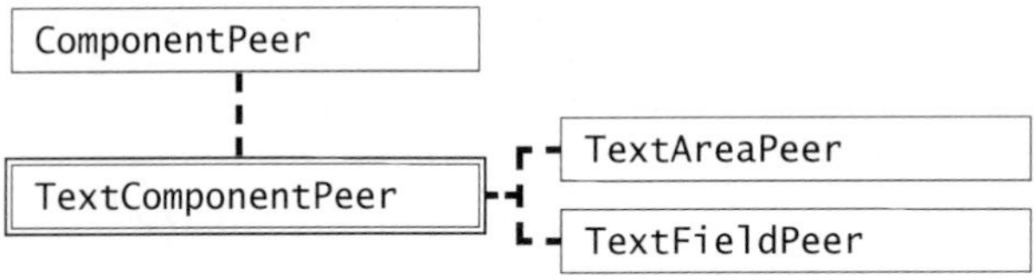

Syntax

```
public interface TextComponentPeer extends ComponentPeer
```

Description

The text component (see the `TextComponent` class) in the Abstract Windowing Toolkit (AWT) uses the platform's native implementation of a text component. So that the AWT text component behaves the same on all platforms, the text component is assigned a peer, whose task is to translate the behavior of the platform's native text component to the behavior of the AWT text component.

AWT programmers normally do not directly use peer classes and interfaces. Instead they deal with AWT components in the `java.awt` package. These in turn automatically manage their peers. Only someone who is porting the AWT to another platform should be concerned with the peer classes and interfaces. Consequently, most peer documentation refers to `java.awt` counterparts.

See `Component` and `Toolkit` for additional information about component peers.

MEMBER SUMMARY

Peer Methods

`getSelectionEnd()`	Retrieves the selection's end position.
`getSelectionStart()`	Retrieves the selection's start position.
`getText()`	Retrieves the text in the text component.
`select()`	Sets the selection in the text component.
`setEditable()`	Sets the text component's editable state.
`setText()`	Sets the text of the text component.

See Also

`Component`, `TextComponent`, `Toolkit`.

getSelectionEnd()

PURPOSE Retrieves the selection's end position.

SYNTAX `int getSelectionEnd()`

RETURNS The 0-based index of the selection's end position.

SEE ALSO `TextComponent.getSelectionEnd()`.

getSelectionStart()

PURPOSE Retrieves the selection's start position.

SYNTAX `int getSelectionStart()`

RETURNS The 0-based index of the selection's start position.

SEE ALSO `TextComponent.getSelectionStart()`.

getText()

PURPOSE Retrieves the text in the text component.

SYNTAX `String getText()`

RETURNS A non-`null` string containing the entire text in the text component.

SEE ALSO `TextComponent.getText()`.

select()

PURPOSE Sets the selection in the text component.

SYNTAX `void select(int selStart, int selEnd)`

PARAMETERS

`selEnd`	The 0-based end position of the text range.
`selStart`	The 0-based start position of the text range.

SEE ALSO `TextComponent.select()`.

setEditable()

PURPOSE Sets the text component's editable state.

SYNTAX `void setEditable(boolean editable)`

PARAMETERS

`editable` If `true`, the text component becomes editable; otherwise it becomes uneditable.

SEE ALSO `TextComponent.setEditable()`.

setText()

PURPOSE Sets the text of the text component.

SYNTAX `void setText(String text)`

PARAMETERS

`text` A string containing the text. A value of `null` is the same as "".

SEE ALSO `TextComponent.setText()`.

A B C D E F G H I J K L M N O P Q R S T U V W X Y Z

TextField

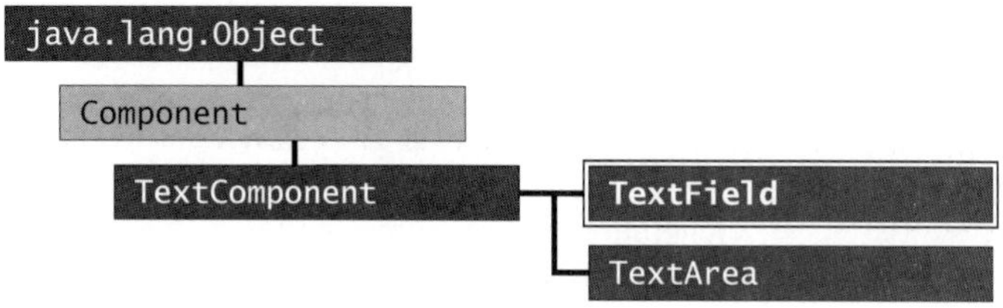

Syntax

```
public class TextField extends TextComponent
```

Description

A *text field* is a text component that displays editable text. The text field is similar to the text area component except that the text field holds only a single line of text.

A text field is typically used to obtain textual input from the user.

Figure 235 shows a text area and a text field.

FIGURE 235 `TextField`

The Echo Property

The text field can be set into a mode in which all characters typed into the text field are displayed as a different character called the *echo character*. The text field still maintains the original characters, but it disguises them as the echo character. The disguises can be removed by setting the echo character to 0.

MEMBER SUMMARY	
Constructor	
`TextField()`	Constructs a new `TextField` instance.
Echo Character Methods	
`echoCharIsSet()`	Determines if the text field's echo character has been set.
`getEchoChar()`	Retrieves the text field's echo character.
`setEchoCharacter()`	Sets the text field's echo character.
Layout Methods	
`getColumns()`	Retrieves the number of columns used to create the text field.

Continued

A B C D E F G H I J K L M N O P Q R S T U V W X Y Z

MEMBER SUMMARY	
`minimumSize()`	Calculates the minimum dimensions of the text field.
`preferredSize()`	Calculates the preferred dimensions of the text field.
Peer Method	
`addNotify()`	Creates the text field's peer.
Debugging Method	
`paramString()`	Generates a string representation of the text field's state.

Example

This simple example creates a frame with a text field. When you press Return in the text field, it prints the contents of the text field. See Figure 235 for a screen shot of the example.

```
import java.awt.*;
public class Main extends Frame {
    TextField tf = new TextField("TextField");

    Main() {
        super("TextField Example");
        add("Center", tf);
        pack();
        show();
    }

    public boolean action(Event evt, Object what) {
        if (evt.target == tf) {
            System.out.println(tf.getText());
            return true;
        }
        return false;
    }

    static public void main(String[] args) {
        new Main();
    }
}
```

addNotify()

PURPOSE Creates the text field's peer.

SYNTAX `public synchronized void addNotify()`

DESCRIPTION This method creates the text field peer if it does not yet exist. The text field's peer is created by calling the `Toolkit.createTextArea()` method. This method should never be called directly. It is normally called by the text field's parent.

OVERRIDES `Component.addNotify()`.

SEE ALSO `Component`, `Toolkit`.

EXAMPLE See `Component.show()`.

echoCharIsSet()

PURPOSE Determines if the text field's echo character has been set.

SYNTAX `public boolean echoCharIsSet()`

RETURNS `true` if the text field's echo character has been set; `false` otherwise.

SEE ALSO `getEchoChar()`, `setEchoCharacter()`.

EXAMPLE This example creates a text field. Typing `ctl-a` toggles whether or not an echo character is set for the text field. See Figure 236.

FIGURE 236
`TextField.echoCharIsSet()`

```
import java.awt.*;
class Main extends Frame {
    TextField tf = new TextField(40);

    Main() {
        super("echoCharIsSet Example");
        add("North", tf);
        pack();
        show();
    }

    public boolean keyDown(Event evt, int key) {
        if (evt.target == tf && key == 1 /*ctl-a*/) {
            if (tf.echoCharIsSet()) {
                key = 0;
            } else {
                key = '*';
            }
            tf.setEchoCharacter((char)key);
            return true;
        }
        return false;
    }
```

```
        static public void main(String[] args) {
            new Main();
        }
    }
```

getColumns()

PURPOSE Retrieves the number of columns used to create the text field.

SYNTAX `public int getColumns()`

DESCRIPTION This method retrieves the number of columns used to create the text field. This is identical to the value used to create the text field. This value does not change even if the text field is resized.

RETURNS The number of columns used to create the text field.

getEchoChar()

PURPOSE Retrieves the text field's echo character.

SYNTAX `public char getEchoChar()`

DESCRIPTION This method retrieves the text field's echo character. The result is not meaningful unless `echoCharIsSet()` returns `true`.

RETURNS The text field's echo character.

SEE ALSO `echoCharIsSet()`, `setEchoCharacter()`.

EXAMPLE See `setEchoCharacter()`.

minimumSize()

PURPOSE Calculates the minimum dimensions of the text field.

SYNTAX
```
public Dimension minimumSize()
public Dimension minimumSize(int cols)
```

DESCRIPTION The minimum dimensions of a text field are based on the dimensions needed for displaying one row of `cols` characters. The size of a character depends on the text field's current font. If the text field's font has variable-width characters, then `cols` is based on the average size of a character and the result is an approximation. The average width of a character is a platform-dependent value. If `cols` is not specified, it defaults to the same value used to create the text field.

If the text field's peer is not yet created, the resulting dimensions are (0, 0). On most platforms, the minimum and preferred dimensions are the same.

PARAMETERS

`cols` A non-negative integer specifying the width in characters.

RETURNS A new non-`null` `Dimension` instance containing the minimum dimensions of the text field.

OVERRIDES `Component.minimumSize()`.

paramString()

PURPOSE Generates a string representation of the text field's state.

SYNTAX `protected String paramString()`

DESCRIPTION A subclass of this class should override this method and return a concatenation of its state with the results of `super.paramString()`. This method is called by the `toString()` method and is typically used for debugging.

RETURNS A non-`null` string representing the text field's state.

OVERRIDES `Component.paramString()`.

SEE ALSO `Object.toString()`.

preferredSize()

PURPOSE Calculates the preferred dimensions of the text field.

SYNTAX
```
public Dimension preferredSize()
public Dimension preferredSize(int cols)
```

DESCRIPTION The preferred dimensions of a text field are based on the dimensions needed for displaying one row of `cols` characters. The size of a character depends on the text field's current font. If the text field's font has variable-width characters, then `cols` is based on the average size of a character and the result is an approximation. The average width of a character is a platform-dependent value. If `cols` is not specified, it defaults to the same value used to create the text field.

If the text field's peer is not yet created, the resulting dimensions are (0, 0). On most platforms, the minimum and preferred dimensions are the same.

PARAMETERS

`cols` A non-negative integer specifying the width in characters.

RETURNS A new non-`null` `Dimension` instance containing the preferred dimensions of the text field.

OVERRIDES `Component.preferredSize()`.

setEchoCharacter()

PURPOSE Sets the text field's echo character.

SYNTAX `public void setEchoCharacter(char ch)`

DESCRIPTION This method sets the echo character of this text field to be the character `ch`. `ch` can be any character and can be changed at any time. However, the value `0` is used to clear the echo character. After setting the echo character to `0`, the characters in the text field will be visible and `echoCharIsSet()` returns `true`.

PARAMETERS

`ch` The echo character. A value of `0` clears the echo character.

SEE ALSO `echoCharIsSet()`, `getEchoChar()`.

EXAMPLE This example creates two text fields. See Figure 237. In one text field, you specify an echo character. In the other text field, the echo character is used. If you type `ctl-a`, the echo character is cleared.

FIGURE 237
`TextArea.setEchoCharacter()`

```
import java.awt.*;
class Main extends Frame {
    TextField tf = new TextField();
    TextField tfEcho = new TextField();

    Main() {
        super("setEchoCharacter Example");
        Panel p = new Panel();

        p.setLayout(new BorderLayout());
        p.add("West", new Label("Echo Character:"));
        p.add("Center", tfEcho);
        add("South", p);
        add("North", tf);
```

A B C D E F G H I J K L M N O P Q R S T U V W X Y Z

```
            pack();
            show();
        }

        public boolean keyDown(Event evt, int key) {
            if (evt.target == tfEcho) {
                if (key == tf.getEchoChar()) {    // clear the echo char
                    key = 0;
                    tfEcho.setText("");
                } else {
                    tfEcho.setText(String.valueOf((char)key));
                }
                tf.setEchoCharacter((char)key);
                tf.requestFocus();
                return true;
            }
            return false;
        }

        static public void main(String[] args) {
            new Main();
        }
    }
```

TextField()

PURPOSE Creates a new `TextField` instance.

SYNTAX

```
public TextField()
public TextField(int cols)
public TextField(String text)
public TextField(String text, int cols)
```

DESCRIPTION The four forms of this constructor create a new `TextField` instance. If `text` is not specified or is `null`, it defaults to `""`. `cols` specifies the initial width of the text area. It is based on the character width of the text field's font. If the font has variable-width characters, then `cols` is based on the average size of a character and the result is an approximation. The average width of a character is a platform-dependent value. If `cols` is not specified, the default is chosen by the platform.

The echo character is initially not set.

PARAMETERS

`cols` A non-negative integer specifying the initial width in characters.

`text` The string specifying the initial text for the text component. May be `null`.

EXAMPLE See the class example.

java.awt.peer

TextFieldPeer

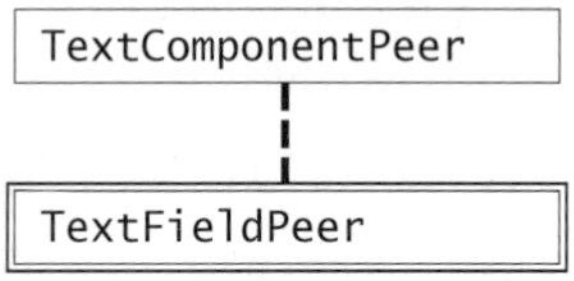

Syntax

```
public interface TextFieldPeer extends TextComponentPeer
```

Description

The text field component (see the `TextField` class) in the Abstract Windowing Toolkit (AWT) uses the platform's native implementation of a text field. So that the AWT text field behaves the same on all platforms, the text field is assigned a peer, whose task is to translate the behavior of the platform's native text field to the behavior of the AWT text field.

AWT programmers normally do not directly use peer classes and interfaces. Instead they deal with AWT components in the `java.awt` package. These in turn automatically manage their peers. Only someone who is porting the AWT to another platform should be concerned with the peer classes and interfaces. Consequently, most peer documentation refers to `java.awt` counterparts.

See `Component` and `Toolkit` for additional information about component peers.

MEMBER SUMMARY

Peer Methods

`minimumSize()`	Calculates the minimum dimensions of the text field.
`preferredSize()`	Calculates the preferred dimensions of the text field.
`setEchoCharacter()`	Sets the text field's echo character.

See Also

`Component`, `TextField`, `Toolkit`.

minimumSize()

PURPOSE Calculates the minimum dimensions of the text field.

SYNTAX `Dimension minimumSize(int cols)`

PARAMETERS

`cols` A non-negative integer specifying the width in characters.

RETURNS The non-`null` minimum dimensions for the text field.

SEE ALSO `TextField.minimumSize()`.

preferredSize()

PURPOSE Calculates the preferred dimensions of the text field.

SYNTAX `Dimension preferredSize(int cols)`

PARAMETERS

`cols` A non-negative integer specifying the width in characters.

RETURNS The non-`null` preferred dimensions for the text field.

SEE ALSO `TextField.preferredSize()`.

setEchoCharacter()

PURPOSE Sets the text field's echo character.

SYNTAX `void setEchoCharacter(char c)`

PARAMETERS

`c` The echo character. A value of `0` clears the echo character.

SEE ALSO `TextField.setEchoCharacter()`.

java.lang
Thread

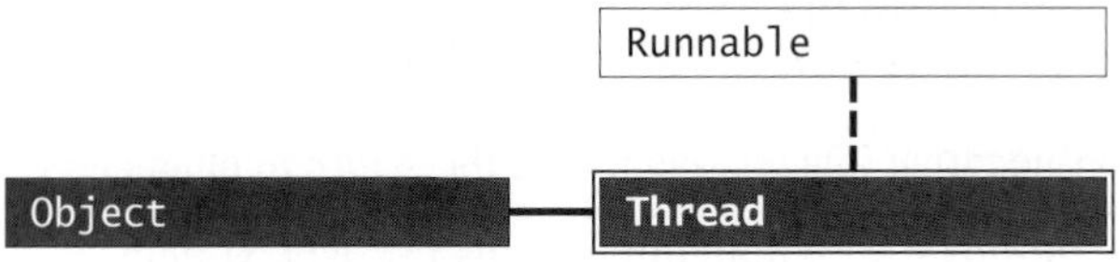

Syntax

```
public class Thread implements Runnable
```

Description

A *thread* is a single sequential flow of control within a process. A single process can have multiple concurrently executing threads.[1] For example, a process may have a thread reading input from the user, while at the same time another thread is updating a database containing the user's account balance, while at the same time a third thread is updating the display with the latest stock quotes. Such a process is called a *multithreaded process*; the program from which this process executes is called a *multithreaded program*.

The `Thread` class is used to represent a thread, with methods to control the execution state of a thread.

To create a new thread of execution, you first declare a new class that is a subclass of `Thread` and override the `run()` method with code that you want executed in this thread.

```
class PrimeThread extends Thread {
  public void run() {
       // compute primes...
  }
}
```

You then create an instance of this subclass, followed by a call to the `start()` method. That method will execute the `run()` method defined by this subclass.

```
PrimeThread pThread = new PrimeThread();
pThread.start();
...
```

You can achieve this same effect by having the class directly implement the `Runnable` interface.

1. JDK 1.0.2 on Solaris does not allow for true concurrency; it does not use native Solaris threads.

```
class Primes implements Runnable {
  public void run() {
       // compute primes...
  }
}
```

To create a thread to execute this `run()` method, do the following:

```
Primes p = new Primes();
Thread pThread = new Thread(p);
pThread.start();
...
```

Thread Priorities

Each thread has a priority that is used by the Java runtime in scheduling threads for execution. A thread that has a higher priority than another thread is typically scheduled ahead of the other thread. However, the way thread priorities precisely affect scheduling is platform-dependent. In some systems, priority-based scheduling is guaranteed, while in others, priorities act only as hints to the scheduler. Therefore you should not depend on priorities in designing your program.

A thread inherits its priority from the thread that created it. A thread's priority can be changed subsequent to the thread's creation at any time using the `setPriority()` method in the `Thread` class, if allowed by the security manager.

User Threads and Daemon Threads

Each thread has a *daemon* status that indicates whether the thread is a *user* thread or a *daemon* thread. User and daemon threads are the same in all respects, except a Java program will terminate only when all user threads have stopped running. The program will stop regardless of how many daemon threads are still running. Examples of daemon threads are the garbage collector thread and the finalization thread. An example of a user thread is the one that executes `main()` in a Java program.

A thread inherits its daemon status from the thread that created it. This status can be changed after creation, but before the thread has started. After a thread has been started, its daemon status cannot be changed.

Thread Groups

A *thread group* contains a set of threads and thread groups. It is the means by which you can organize threads into logical units for security and organizational reasons. When a thread is created, it is added to a thread group. The thread group is either specified as an argument to the thread's constructor or by default is the same thread group as that of the creating thread.

Thread State and Synchronization between Threads

When a thread is started, its state is *active*. Its state remains active until it has terminated execution or is stopped. An active thread can be executing or suspended. When a thread is first started, it starts executing its `run()` method. The `Thread` class provides methods for you to

A B C D E F G H I J K L M N O P Q R S T U V W X Y Z

suspend an executing thread, to resume execution of a suspended thread, and to stop a thread completely (it can no longer run unless restarted at the beginning of its `run()` method). These methods can be invoked only if allowed by the security manager.
In addition to these methods in the `Thread` class, you can also use synchronization methods available in the `Object` class (`wait()/notify()`) to control the execution of a thread.

Interrupts
A thread can send an *interrupt* to another thread. This sets a flag in the target thread to indicate that it has been interrupted. The target thread can then check for this flag at its discretion and react appropriately.

MEMBER SUMMARY

Constructor	
`Thread()`	Constructs a new `Thread` instance.
Thread Property Fields and Methods	
`getName()`	Retrieves this thread's name.
`getPriority()`	Retrieves this thread's priority.
`getThreadGroup()`	Retrieves this thread's thread group.
`isDaemon()`	Determines if this thread is a daemon thread.
`MAX_PRIORITY`	The maximum priority that a thread can have.
`MIN_PRIORITY`	The minimum priority that a thread can have.
`NORM_PRIORITY`	The default priority that is assigned to the first user thread.
`setDaemon()`	Changes this thread's daemon status.
`setName()`	Changes this thread's name.
`setPriority()`	Changes this thread's priority.
Thread State Methods	
`destroy()`	Destroys this thread without any cleanup.
`isAlive()`	Determines if this thread is active.
`join()`	Waits for this thread to terminate.
`resume()`	Resumes execution of this thread.
`run()`	The actual body of this thread.
`sleep()`	Causes the currently executing thread to sleep for a period of time.
`start()`	Starts execution of this thread.
`stop()`	Stops execution of this thread.
`suspend()`	Suspends execution of this thread.
`yield()`	Causes the currently executing thread object to yield to other threads.
Interrupt Methods	
`interrupt()`	Sends an interrupt to this thread.

MEMBER SUMMARY	
`interrupted()`	Determines if the currently executing thread has been interrupted.
`isInterrupted()`	Determines if this thread has been interrupted.
Stack Frame Methods	
`countStackFrames()`	Counts the number of stack frames in this thread.
`dumpStack()`	Prints a snapshot of the current execution stack trace.
Security Method	
`checkAccess()`	Determines if the currently executing thread is allowed to modify this thread.
Current Thread Methods	
`activeCount()`	Estimates the number of active threads in the current thread's threadgroup and its subgroup.
`currentThread()`	Retrieves the currently executing thread.
`enumerate()`	Enumerates the active threads in the currently executing thread's thread group.
Description Method	
`toString()`	Generates a string representation of the thread.

See Also

`Object`, `Runnable`, `ThreadGroup`, `SecurityManager`.

Example

This example implements a thread viewer that shows all the threads in the system at a certain point in time. See Figure 238. The thread viewer updates the list of threads every 5 seconds. The thread viewer can be paused and resumed by clicking the button at the top of the frame.

A thread can be stopped (via the `stop()` method) by clicking the thread name in the list. If the thread that is stopped is one of the `Main` class's thread, a message is printed on `System.out`.

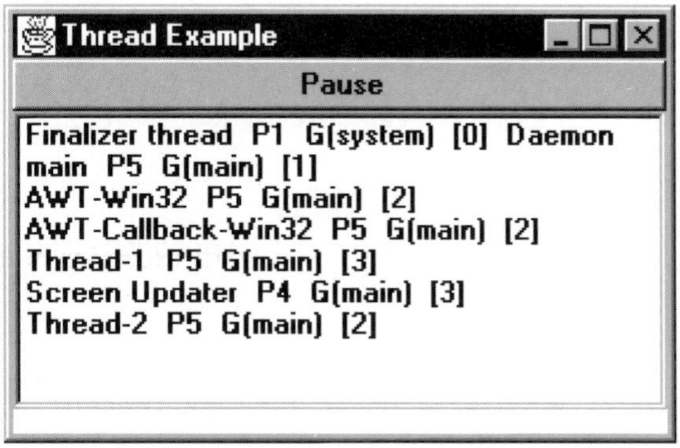

FIGURE 238 `Thread`

Example

In the ThreadViewer class, the handleEvent() and updateList() methods are synchronized because they share a number of fields. This prevents the two methods from seeing inconsistent values in the shared fields.

```
import java.awt.*;
class Main implements Runnable {
    public static void main(String args[] ) {
        try {
            new ThreadViewer();

            // periodically create a thread just to keep
            // things interesting
            while (true) {
                Thread.sleep((int)Math.floor(Math.random()*5000));
                (new Thread(new Main())).start();
            }
        } catch (Exception e) {
            e.printStackTrace();
        }
    }
    public void run() {
        try {
            Thread.sleep(5000);
        } catch (Exception e) {
            e.printStackTrace();
        } catch (ThreadDeath e) {
            System.out.println(Thread.currentThread().getName() +
                " has been stopped!");
        }
    }
}

class ThreadViewer extends Frame implements Runnable {
    Thread timerThread;

    // List of all threads in the system.
    Thread[] threads;

    // List component containing all the threads in the system.
    List threadList = new List();

    ThreadViewer() {
        super("Thread Example");
        add("Center", threadList);
        add("North", new Button("Pause"));

        resize(300, 300);
        show();
        timerThread = new Thread(this);
        timerThread.start();
    }

    public synchronized boolean handleEvent(Event evt) {
```

```
    if (evt.id == Event.WINDOW_DESTROY) {
        timerThread = null;
        dispose();
        return true;
    } else if (evt.target == threadList) {
        Thread t = threads[threadList.getSelectedIndex()];
        try {
            t.checkAccess();
            t.stop();
        } catch (SecurityException e) {
            System.out.println("No permission to stop thread " +
                t.getName());
        }
        return true;
    } else if ("Pause".equals(evt.arg)) {
        timerThread.suspend();
        ((Button)evt.target).setLabel("Resume");
        return true;
    } else if ("Resume".equals(evt.arg)) {
        timerThread.resume();
        ((Button)evt.target).setLabel("Pause");
        return true;
    }
    return false;
}

public void run() {
    try {
        while (timerThread == Thread.currentThread()) {
            updateList();
            Thread.sleep(5000);
        }
    } catch (Exception e) {
        e.printStackTrace();
    }
}

synchronized void updateList() {
    // Find the root thread group
    ThreadGroup rootGrp = Thread.currentThread().getThreadGroup();

    while (rootGrp.getParent() != null) {
        rootGrp = rootGrp.getParent();
    }

    threads = new Thread[rootGrp.activeCount()];
    int count = rootGrp.enumerate(threads, true);

    threadList.clear();
    for (int i=0; i<count; i++) {
        Thread t = threads[i];

        threadList.addItem(t.getName()
            + "  P" + t.getPriority()
            + "  G(" + t.getThreadGroup().getName() + ")"
```

```
                        + "   [" + t.countStackFrames() + "]"
                        + "   " + (t.isDaemon() ? "Daemon" : "")
                        + "   " + (t.isInterrupted() ? "" : "Interrupted")
                        + "   " + (t.isAlive() ? "" : "NotAlive"));
                }
            }
        }
```

activeCount()

PURPOSE Estimates the number of active threads in the current thread's thread group and its subgroups.

SYNTAX `public static int activeCount()`

DESCRIPTION This method estimates the number of active threads in the currently executing thread's thread group and its subgroups. This is an estimate because during this call, threads might be added to or removed from the thread group or its subgroups.

SEE ALSO `currentThread()`, `getThreadGroup()`, `isAlive()`, `ThreadGroup`.

EXAMPLE See the class example.

checkAccess()

PURPOSE Checks whether the currently executing thread is allowed to modify this thread.

SYNTAX `public void checkAccess()`

DESCRIPTION This method checks whether the security manager allows the currently executing thread to modify this thread. Modifications that require access checking include changing the state of the thread (e.g., suspend/resume) and changing the properties associated with a thread (its daemon status, priority).

EXCEPTIONS

`SecurityException`

If the currently executing thread is not allowed to modify this thread due to security reasons.

SEE ALSO `currentThread()`, `resume()`, `SecurityManager.checkAccess()`, `setDaemon()`, `setName()`, `setPriority()`, `stop()`, `suspend()`, `Thread()`,`ThreadGroup.checkAccess()`.

EXAMPLE See the class example.

countStackFrames()

PURPOSE Counts the number of stack frames in this thread.

SYNTAX `public native int countStackFrames()`

DESCRIPTION This method returns the number of stack frames in this thread. The thread must be suspended when this method is called.

RETURNS The number of stack frames in this thread.

EXCEPTIONS

`IllegalThreadStateException`
If this thread is not suspended.

SEE ALSO `suspend()`.

EXAMPLE See the class example.

currentThread()

PURPOSE Retrieves the currently executing thread.

SYNTAX `public static native Thread currentThread()`

RETURNS The reference to the currently executing thread.

EXAMPLE See the class example.

destroy()

PURPOSE Destroys this thread without any cleanup.

SYNTAX `public void destroy()`

DESCRIPTION This method destroys this thread without any cleanup. It removes the thread from its thread group. Any monitors the thread has locked remain locked.

SEE ALSO `isActive()`, `stop()`.

REMARKS This method has not been implemented in JDK 1.0.2.

A B C D E F G H I J K L M N O P Q R S T U V W X Y Z

dumpStack()

PURPOSE Prints a snapshot of the current execution stack trace.

SYNTAX `public static void dumpStack()`

DESCRIPTION A debugging procedure to print a stack trace for the current `Thread` to `System.err`.

SEE ALSO `currentThread()`, `System.err`, `Throwable.printStackTrace()`.

EXAMPLE This example simply calls a method recursively. On the tenth recursion, `dumpStack()` is called to print a stack trace. The output of this program is shown following the code.

```
class Main {
    static void method(int i) {
        if (i == 10) {
            Thread.currentThread().dumpStack();
        } else {
            method(++i);
        }
    }

    public static void main(String args[]) {
        method(0);
    }
}
```

OUTPUT

```
java.lang.Exception: Stack trace
        at java.lang.Thread.dumpStack(Thread.java:529)
        at Main.method(Main.java:4)
        at Main.method(Main.java:6)
        at Main.method(Main.java:6)
        at Main.method(Main.java:6)
        at Main.method(Main.java:6)
        at Main.method(Main.java:6)
        at Main.method(Main.java:6)
        at Main.method(Main.java:6)
        at Main.method(Main.java:6)
        at Main.method(Main.java:6)
        at Main.method(Main.java:6)
        at Main.main(Main.java:11)
```

enumerate()

PURPOSE Enumerates the active threads in the currently executing thread's thread group.

SYNTAX `public static int enumerate(Thread[] threads)`

DESCRIPTION This method recursively enumerates the active threads in the currently executing thread's thread group and its subgroups. It copies into the array `threads` the references to these active threads. You can use `activeCount()` to estimate the size of the array `threads` to allocate before calling `enumerate()`.

PARAMETERS

`threads` An existing array into which to copy the references.

RETURNS The number of active threads in the current thread's thread group and its subgroups.

SEE ALSO `activeCount()`, `currentThread()`, `getThreadGroup()`, `isAlive()`, `ThreadGroup`.

EXAMPLE See the class example.

getName()

PURPOSE Retrieves this thread's name.

SYNTAX `public final String getName()`

DESCRIPTION Each thread has a name when it is created. A thread's name can be changed subsequent to the thread's creation at any time using `setName()`. `getName()` returns the name of this thread.

DESCRIPTION This thread's name.

SEE ALSO `Thread()`, `setName()`.

EXAMPLE See the class example.

getPriority()

PURPOSE Retrieves the thread's priority.

SYNTAX `public final int getPriority()`

DESCRIPTION Each thread has a priority that is used by the Java runtime in scheduling threads for execution. A thread that has a higher priority than another thread is typically scheduled ahead of the other thread. However, the way thread priorities precisely affect scheduling is platform-dependent. In some systems, priority-based scheduling is guaranteed, while in others, priorities act only as hints to the scheduler.

A thread inherits its priority from the thread that created it. A thread's priority can be changed subsequent to the thread's creation at any time using `setPriority()`. `getPriority()` returns this thread's priority.

RETURNS This thread's priority.

SEE ALSO `MAX_PRIORITY`, `MIN_PRIORITY`, `NORM_PRIORITY`, `setPriority()`.

EXAMPLE See the class example.

getThreadGroup()

PURPOSE Retrieves this thread's thread group.

SYNTAX `public final ThreadGroup getThreadGroup()`

DESCRIPTION A *thread group* contains a set of threads and thread groups. It is the means by which you can organize threads into logical units for security and organizational reasons. When a thread is created, it is added to a thread group. The thread group is either specified as an argument to the thread's constructor or by default is the same thread group as that of the creating thread.

`getThreadGroup()` returns this thread's thread group.

RETURNS This thread's thread group.

SEE ALSO `Thread()`, `ThreadGroup`.

EXAMPLE See the class example.

interrupt()

PURPOSE Sends an interrupt to this thread.

SYNTAX `public void interrupt()`

DESCRIPTION A thread can send an interrupt to another thread by calling `interrupt()` on it. This sets a flag in the target thread to indicate that it has been interrupted. The target thread can then check for this flag at its discretion using `interrupted()` or `isInterrupted()`.

If a thread is sleeping, or waiting, calling `interrupt()` on it will send it an `InterruptedException`, which will wake it up.

SEE ALSO `InterruptedException`.

EXAMPLE See `ThreadGroup` class example.

interrupted()

PURPOSE Determines if the currently executing thread has been interrupted.

SYNTAX `public static boolean interrupted()`

DESCRIPTION A thread can send an interrupt to another thread by calling `interrupt()` on it. This sets a flag in the target thread to indicate that it has been interrupted. The target thread can then check for this flag at its discretion and react appropriately.

You can check whether the currently executing thread has been interrupted by using `interrupted()`. This method returns `true` if the currently executing thread has been interrupted; it returns `false` otherwise.

RETURNS `true` if the currently executing thread has been interrupted; `false` otherwise.

SEE ALSO `currentThread()`, `interrupt()`, `InterruptedException`, `isInterrupted()`.

EXAMPLE See `stop()`.

isAlive()

PURPOSE Determines if this thread is active.

SYNTAX `public final native boolean isAlive()`

DESCRIPTION A thread that has been started is active. It remains active until it has been stopped or destroyed. This method returns `true` if this thread is active.

RETURNS `true` if this thread is active; `false` otherwise.

SEE ALSO `activeCount()`, `destroy()`, `start()`, `stop()`.

EXAMPLE See the class example.

isDaemon()

PURPOSE Determines if this thread is a daemon thread.

SYNTAX `public final boolean isDaemon()`

DESCRIPTION Each thread has a daemon status that indicates whether the thread is a *user* thread or a *daemon* thread. User and daemon threads are the same in all respects, except a Java program will terminate only when all user threads have stopped running. The program will stop regardless of how many daemon threads are still running. Examples of daemon threads are the garbage collector thread and the finalization thread. An example of a user thread is the one that executes `main()` in a Java program.

A thread inherits its daemon status from the thread that created it. This status can be changed after creation, but before the thread has started, by using `setDaemon()`. You can determine the daemon status of a thread by calling `isDaemon()`. This method returns `true` if this thread is a daemon thread.

RETURNS `true` if this thread is a daemon thread; `false` if this thread is a user thread.

SEE ALSO `setDaemon()`, `Thread()`.

EXAMPLE See the class example.

isInterrupted()

PURPOSE Determines if this thread has been interrupted.

SYNTAX `public boolean isInterrupted()`

DESCRIPTION A thread can send an interrupt to another thread by calling `interrupt()` on it. This sets a flag in the target thread to indicate that it has been interrupted. The target thread can then check for this flag at its discretion and react appropriately.

You can check whether a thread has been interrupted by using `isInterrupted()`. This method returns `true` if this thread has been interrupted; it returns `false` otherwise.

RETURNS `true` if this thread has been interrupted; `false` otherwise.

SEE ALSO `interrupt()`, `interrupted()`, `InterruptedException`.

EXAMPLE See the class example.

A B C D E F G H I J K L M N O P Q R S T U V W X Y Z

join()

PURPOSE Waits for this thread to terminate.

SYNTAX
```
public final void join() throws InterruptedException
public final synchronized void join(long millis) throws
   InterruptedException
public final synchronized void join(long millis, int nanos) throws
   InterruptedException
```

DESCRIPTION The three forms of this method cause the currently executing thread to wait until this thread has terminated (stopped). The currently executing thread blocks until any one of the following events occur:

- The currently executing thread has been interrupted.
- This thread has terminated.
- The time specified has expired.

The time period to wait is specified in milliseconds `millis`. If finer granularity is desired, you can supply a nanosecond count `nanos`. If no time period has been specified, the currently executing thread waits indefinitely for the other two events to occur.

PARAMETERS

`millis` The time to wait in milliseconds.

`nanos` Additional nanoseconds to wait. `nanos` is in the range `0-999999`.[1]

EXCEPTIONS

`InterruptedException`

If the currently executing thread has been interrupted.

SEE ALSO `destroy()`, `Object.wait()`, `sleep()`, `stop()`.

EXAMPLE This example illustrates the use of worker threads and priorities. In this example, one worker is created for every priority level. Each worker does exactly the same amount of work; the only difference is their priority levels. The output of this program (shown following the code) shows that higher-priority threads (priority 9) are much more productive that lower-priority threads (priority 1).

```
class Main {
    public static void main(String args[] ) {
        // Create a slot for each priority level.
        Worker[] workers =
            new Worker[Thread.MAX_PRIORITY-Thread.MIN_PRIORITY];
```

1. In JDK 1.0.2, `nanos` is rounded to the nearest millisecond.

```
            // Create the workers.
            for (int i=0; i<workers.length; i++) {
                workers[i] = new Worker(Thread.MIN_PRIORITY+i);
                workers[i].start();
            }

            // Now wait for them to terminate.
            for (int i=workers.length-1; i >= 0; i--) {
                try {
                    workers[i].join();
                } catch (Exception e) {
                    e.printStackTrace();
                }
                System.out.println(workers[i].getName() + ": " +
                    workers[i].time + " ms");
            }
        }
    }

    class Worker extends Thread {
        // Record current time.
        long time = System.currentTimeMillis();

        Worker(int priority) {
            setPriority(priority);
            setName("Worker-"+priority);
        }

        public void run() {
            // Here is where the work gets done.
            String s = "";
            for (int i=0; i<1024; i++) {
                s += i;
            }

            // Record time.
            time = System.currentTimeMillis() - time;
        }
    }
```

OUTPUT

```
Worker-9: 1540 ms
Worker-8: 2700 ms
Worker-7: 4390 ms
Worker-6: 12190 ms
Worker-5: 12580 ms
Worker-4: 12470 ms
Worker-3: 14060 ms
Worker-2: 16200 ms
Worker-1: 16310 ms
```

MAX_PRIORITY

PURPOSE The maximum priority a thread can have.

SYNTAX `public final static int MAX_PRIORITY`

DESCRIPTION The maximal priority a thread can have is 10.

SEE ALSO `getPriority()`, `MIN_PRIORITY`, `NORM_PRIORITY`, `setPriority()`.

EXAMPLE See `join()`.

MIN_PRIORITY

PURPOSE The minimum priority that a thread can have.

SYNTAX `public final static int MIN_PRIORITY`

DESCRIPTION The minimum priority that a thread can have is 1.

SEE ALSO `getPriority()`, `MAX_PRIORITY`, `NORM_PRIORITY`, `setPriority()`.

EXAMPLE See `join()`.

NORM_PRIORITY

PURPOSE The default priority that is assigned to the first user thread.

SYNTAX `public final static int NORM_PRIORITY`

DESCRIPTION `NORM_PRIORITY` is the priority assigned to the first user thread created by the system. The value of `NORM_PRIORITY` is 5.

SEE ALSO `getPriority()`, `MAX_PRIORITY`, `MIN_PRIORITY`, `setPriority()`.

resume()

PURPOSE Resumes execution of this thread.

SYNTAX `public final void resume()`

DESCRIPTION This method causes this suspended thread to resume execution. It can be executed only if permitted by the security manager. If you resume a thread that has not been suspended, no action is taken.

run()

SEE ALSO `checkAccess()`, `suspend()`, `stop()`, `ThreadGroup.resume()`.

EXAMPLE See the class example.

run()

PURPOSE The actual body of this thread.

SYNTAX `public void run()`

DESCRIPTION This method defines the actual body of this thread. This is what the thread executes when it is started. You must either override this method by subclassing class `Thread` or create the thread with a `Runnable` target, which defines the `run()` method to execute.

SEE ALSO `Runnable`, `start()`, `stop()`.

EXAMPLE See the class example.

setDaemon()

PURPOSE Changes the daemon status of this thread.

SYNTAX `public final void setDaemon(boolean status)`

DESCRIPTION Each thread has a *daemon* status that indicates whether the thread is a *user* thread or a *daemon* thread. User and daemon threads are the same in all respects, except a Java program terminates only when all user threads have stopped running. The program will stop regardless of how many daemon threads are still running. Examples of daemon threads are the garbage collector thread and the finalization thread. An example of a user thread is the one that executes `main()` in a Java program.

A thread inherits its daemon status from the thread that created it. This status can be changed after creation, but before the thread has started, using `setDaemon()`. Once the thread has been started, you cannot change its daemon status. If `status` is `true`, the thread becomes a daemon thread. If `status` is `false`, the thread becomes a user thread.

`setDaemon()` can be executed only if permitted by the security manager.

PARAMETERS

`status` `true` means this thread becomes a daemon thread; `false` means this thread becomes a user thread.

EXCEPTIONS

`IllegalThreadStateException`

If this thread is active (i.e., has been started).

SEE ALSO `checkAccess()`, `isDaemon()`, `start()`, `Thread()`.

EXAMPLE This example creates a server thread (which does not do anything particularly useful) that continually waits for a socket connection. However, the server thread is made a daemon thread so that when the main program terminates, the server thread does not prevent the program from terminating.

```
import java.net.*;
class Main {
    public static void main(String[] args ) {
        (new Waiter()).start();

        try {
            Thread.sleep(5000);    // Wait 5 seconds.
        } catch (InterruptedException e) {
            e.printStackTrace();
        }
    }
}

class Waiter extends Thread {
    Waiter() {
        setDaemon(true);
    }

    public void run() {
        try {
            ServerSocket socket = new ServerSocket(2000);
            while (true) {
                Socket s = socket.accept();
                System.out.println("got a connection");
            }
        } catch (Exception e) {
            e.printStackTrace();
        }
    }
}
```

setName()

PURPOSE Changes this thread's name.

SYNTAX `public final void setName(String name)`

A B C D E F G H I J K L M N O P Q R S T U V W X Y Z

DESCRIPTION Each thread has a name when it is created. A thread's name can be changed subsequent to the thread's creation at any time using `setName()`. This method changes the name of this thread to `name`. It can be executed only if permitted by the security manager.

PARAMETERS

`name` The new name of this thread. `name` cannot be `null`.

SEE ALSO `checkAccess()`, `getName()`, `Thread()`, `toString()`.

EXAMPLE See `join()`.

setPriority()

PURPOSE Changes this thread's priority.

SYNTAX `public final void setPriority(int newPriority)`

DESCRIPTION Each thread has a priority that is used by the Java runtime in scheduling threads for execution. A thread that has a higher priority than another thread is typically scheduled ahead of the other thread. However, the way thread priorities precisely affect scheduling is platform-dependent. In some systems, priority-based scheduling is guaranteed, while in others, priorities act only as hints to the scheduler.

A thread inherits its priority from the thread that created it. A thread's priority can be changed subsequent to the thread's creation at any time using `setPriority()`. `setPriority()` sets this thread's priority to `newPriority`. If `newPriority` is greater than the thread group's maximum priority, the thread group's maximum is used as the new priority.

This method can be executed only if permitted by the security manager.

PARAMETERS

`newPriority` The new priority the thread is to have. `newPriority` must be in the range of `MIN_PRIORITY` and `MAX_PRIORITY`, inclusive.

EXCEPTIONS

`IllegalArgumentException`

If `newPriority` is not within the range of `MIN_PRIORITY` and `MAX_PRIORITY`.

SEE ALSO `checkAccess()`, `getPriority()`, `MAX_PRIORITY`, `MIN_PRIORITY`, `NORM_PRIORITY`, `ThreadGroup.getMaxPriority()`, `ThreadGroup.setMaxPriority()`.

EXAMPLE See `join()`.

sleep()

PURPOSE Causes the currently executing thread to sleep for a period of time.

SYNTAX

```
public static native void sleep(long millis) throws
    InterruptedException
public static void sleep(long millis, int nanos) throws
    InterruptedException
```

DESCRIPTION This method causes the currently executing thread to sleep for `millis` milliseconds. For finer granularity of the sleep period, you can supply a nanosecond count `nanos`.

The thread that is put to sleep remains in active state but is not scheduled to run until the sleep period has expired. It can be interrupted from its sleep by another thread.

PARAMETERS

`millis` The length of time to sleep, in milliseconds.

`nanos` Additional nanoseconds to sleep. `nanos` is in the range `0-999999`.[1]

EXCEPTIONS

`InterruptedException`

If another thread has interrupted the currently executing thread while the latter was sleeping.

SEE ALSO `currentThread()`, `interrupt()`, `suspend()`.

EXAMPLE See the class example, `setDaemon()`, and `stop()`.

start()

PURPOSE Starts execution of this thread.

SYNTAX

```
public synchronized native void start()
```

DESCRIPTION This method starts execution of this thread by calling the `run()` method associated with this thread. The state of this thread is set to *active*.

`start()` returns immediately.

EXCEPTIONS

`IllegalThreadStateException`

The thread was already started.

1. In JDK 1.0.2, `nanos` is rounded to the nearest millisecond.

stop()

SEE ALSO activeCount(), isActive(), run(), stop().

EXAMPLE See the class example.

stop()

PURPOSE Stops the execution of this thread.

SYNTAX
```
public final void stop()
public final synchronized void stop(Throwable e)
```

DESCRIPTION The two forms of this method stop the execution of this thread. A thread that has been stopped is no longer active and is removed from its thread group.

Normally, to stop a thread you call `stop()` with no arguments. Doing this causes the error `ThreadDeath` to be thrown. The Java runtime then catches this error and completes the termination. You can also call `stop()` with a `Throwable` object `e`, but this is rarely done unless you want to terminate the thread abnormally. If `e` is not an instance of `ThreadDeath` or its subclasses, it is not caught by the Java runtime and the uncaught exception is thrown to the top-level error handler, which prints out a stack trace of `e`.

When a thread is blocked doing a `wait()`, `join()`, or `sleep()`, it must come out of the wait before it can be stopped. The thread that is invoking the `stop()` method, however, is never blocked. `stop()` returns immediately regardless of when the waiting thread eventually stops.

This method can be executed only if permitted by the security manager.

PARAMETERS

`e` The object to be thrown when stopping this thread.

SEE ALSO checkAccess(), activeCount(), isActive(), start(), ThreadDeath, ThreadGroup.stop(), ThreadGroup.uncaughtException(), Throwable.

EXAMPLE This example implements a framework for measuring the performance of Java operations. A thread, called the *timer*, is created to perform a certain test. The timer thread executes the test by running an operation in a very tight loop. The timer thread doesn't check whether it should be terminated. Instead the creator of the timer thread calls `stop()` on the timer thread to terminate it. The text following the code shows the output of the example when run on a 90MHz Pentium laptop running Windows95.

```
class Main {
    public static void main(String args[]) {
        for (int i=0; i<Timer.NUM_TESTS; i++) {
            Timer timer = new Timer(i);
```

```
            long time = System.currentTimeMillis();
            double usPerOp;

            try {
                timer.start();
                Thread.sleep(5000);     // Wait 5 seconds.

                time = System.currentTimeMillis() - time;
                usPerOp = time * 1000.0 / timer.count;
                System.out.println(timer.label + ": " + usPerOp
                                  + " us/op");

                timer.stop();           // Stop the thread.

                Thread.sleep(1000);     // Wait a second.
            } catch (InterruptedException e) {
                e.printStackTrace();
            }
        }
    }
}

class Timer extends Thread {
    static int NUM_TESTS = 6;
    int count;
    int testType;
    String label;

    Timer(int testType) {
        this.testType = testType;
    }

    public void run() {
        switch (testType) {
          case 0:
            label = "i++";
            while (true) {
                count++;
            }
          case 1:
            label = "Non-synchronized method call";
            while (true) {
                nonSynchronizedMethod();
                count++;
            }
          case 2:
            label = "Synchronized method call";
            while (true) {
                synchronizedMethod();
                count++;
            }
          case 3:
            label = "Math.random()";
            while (true) {
```

```
                    Math.random();
                    count++;
                }
              case 4:
                label = "Thread.interrupted";
                while (true) {
                    interrupted();
                    count++;
                }
              case 5:
                label = "Thread.sleep(60)";
                while (true) {
                    try {
                        Thread.sleep(60);
                    } catch (InterruptedException e) {
                        e.printStackTrace();
                    }
                    count++;
                }
            }
        }

        synchronized void synchronizedMethod() {
        }

        void nonSynchronizedMethod() {
        }
    }
```

OUTPUT

```
i++: 2.22373 us/op
Non-synchronized method call: 4.39275 us/op
Synchronized method call: 22.3401 us/op
Math.random(): 101.539 us/op
Thread.interrupted: 6.31886 us/op
Thread.sleep(60): 68493.2 us/op
```

suspend()

PURPOSE Suspends the execution of this thread.

SYNTAX `public final void suspend()`

DESCRIPTION This method suspends the execution of this thread. When a thread has been suspended, it cannot run until it is resumed via a call to `resume()`. A thread that is suspended is still marked *active*.

This method can be executed only if permitted by the security manager.

SEE ALSO `checkAccess()`, `countStackFrames()`, `resume()`, `stop()`, `ThreadGroup.suspend()`.

EXAMPLE See the class example.

Thread()

PURPOSE Constructs a new `Thread` instance.

SYNTAX

```
public Thread()
public Thread(Runnable target)
public Thread(String threadName)
public Thread(ThreadGroup group, Runnable target)
public Thread(ThreadGroup group, String threadName)
public Thread(Runnable target, String threadName)
public Thread(ThreadGroup group, Runnable target, String
   threadName)
```

DESCRIPTION A `Thread` object is created with three arguments: its name, a `Runnable` object whose `run()` method will be the core of this thread, and the thread group `group` to which the new thread is to be added. All of these arguments are optional. The thread is created with the name `threadName`. If you do not supply a name for the thread, the thread will be created with an automatically generated name. If you supply `target`, the thread will run the `run()` method defined by `target` when it starts. If you do not supply a `Runnable` object, the `run()` method that will be used is that defined by the new thread itself. If you do not supply a thread group, the new thread will be added to the same thread group as the currently executing thread. If you supply a thread group `group` in which to add the new thread, the currently executing thread must be permitted by the security manager to access and update `group`.

When a thread is created, its status is *inactive*. It is remains that way until a `start()` method has been invoked on it, at which time its state is changed to *active* and the thread starts running. When a thread is created, its daemon status and priority are the same as those of the currently executing thread. These can be changed using `setDaemon()` and `setPriority()`, respectively, before the thread has been started.

PARAMETERS

`group` The thread group to which the new thread will be added. If `null`, the new thread is added to the same thread group as the currently executing thread.

`target` The object whose `run()` method will be called.

`threadName` The name of the new thread. `threadName` cannot be `null`.

B

C SEE ALSO checkAccess(), currentThread(), run(), Runnable, setDaemon(), setPriority(), start(), ThreadGroup.

D EXAMPLE See the class example.

E

F

toString()

G

PURPOSE	Generates the string representation of this thread.
SYNTAX	`public String toString()`
DESCRIPTION	The string representation of a thread includes the thread's name, priority, and thread group. `toString()` returns this string representation.
RETURNS	The string representation of a thread.
OVERRIDES	`Object.toString()`.
EXAMPLE	See `Object.toString()`.

H I J K L M

yield()

N O P Q R S T U V W

PURPOSE	Causes the currently executing thread to yield to other threads.
SYNTAX	`public static native void yield()`
DESCRIPTION	This method causes the currently executing thread to yield to other runnable threads for execution. This causes another runnable thread to execute. If no other runnable thread is found, the currently executing thread continues to execute. On some platforms, a thread that goes into a continuous loop takes control of the processor, thus starving other threads. So that this does not happen, such threads should call the `yield()` method to relinquish the processor to some other thread.
SEE ALSO	`currentThread()`, `resume()`, `stop()`, `suspend()`.
EXAMPLE	This example demonstrates the effect of the `yield()` method by creating several worker threads that perform intensive computation work. To show that a worker has just started running, the worker constantly checks a static field to see if it was the last running thread. If not, it prints its identification number to indicate that it is now running. Every worker thread does some amount of work and then prints an asterisk just before calling `yield()`.

X Y Z

The output of this program is shown below the code. Notice that just after an asterisk, a new thread starts to run. Also, notice that once in a while a thread can be preempted even without a call to `yield()`.

```
class Main {
    public static void main(String args[] ) {
        for (int i=0; i<10; i++) {
            (new Worker(i)).start();
        }
    }
}

class Worker extends Thread {
    int id;
    static int lastRunningWorker;

    Worker(int id) {
        this.id =  id;
    }

    public void run() {
        int i = 0;

        // Here is where the work gets done.
        while (true) {
            synchronized (this) {
                if (id != lastRunningWorker) {
                    System.out.print(id);
                    lastRunningWorker = id;
                }
            }
            if (i++ % 100 == 0) {
                System.out.print("*");
                Thread.yield();
            }
        }
    }
}
```

OUTPUT

```
*1*0*2*1*0*3*2*0*4*3*2*1*0*5*4*3*2*1*0*6*5
*4*3*2*1*0*7*6*5*4*3*2*1*08*7*6*5*4*3*2*1*0
*9*8*7*6*4*3*2*1*0*9*8*7*6*5*4*3*2*1*0*9*8
*7*6*5*4*
```

java.lang

ThreadDeath

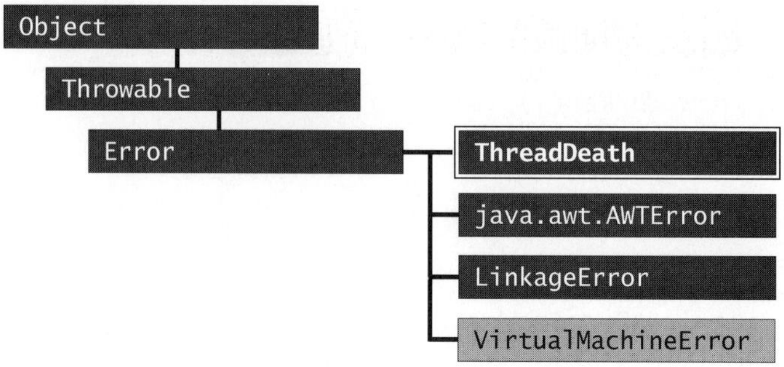

Syntax

```
public class ThreadDeath extends Error
```

Description

When a program invokes `thread.stop()` with no argument, the thread's execution is stopped and a `ThreadDeath` error is thrown. The Java virtual machine catches this error and completes the termination (e.g., it frees system resources such as monitors used by the thread). `ThreadDeath` is explicitly caught by the program only if the program needs to do some special clean- up for the thread. After `ThreadDeath` has been caught, it must be re-thrown so that it will be caught by the Java virtual machine to complete the thread termination.

You can declare subclasses of `ThreadDeath` for `Thread.stop()` to throw so as to indicate any special processing required for cleaning up a thread. Any error or exception thrown by `Thread.stop()` must be a subclass of `ThreadDeath`.

`ThreadDeath` is a special subclass of `Error`. Other subclasses of `Error` generated by the Java virtual machine indicate unrecoverable errors that cause the program to terminate. `ThreadDeath`, on the other hand, indicates only that a thread has been destroyed; the program continues to run with other existing threads.

See Also

`Error`, `Thread.stop()`, `ThreadGroup.uncaughtException()`.

Example

See `ThreadGroup.uncaughtException()`.

java.lang
ThreadGroup

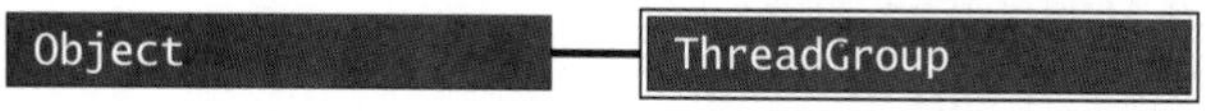

Syntax

```
public class ThreadGroup
```

Description

The `ThreadGroup` class represents a group of threads. A thread group can contain a set of threads and other thread groups (see Figure 239). A thread or thread group can be in at most one thread group. Thread groups allow you to organize groups so that you can manipulate the group of threads as a whole. For example, you can set the maximum priority of a thread group, suspend and resume all threads in a group, and so on.

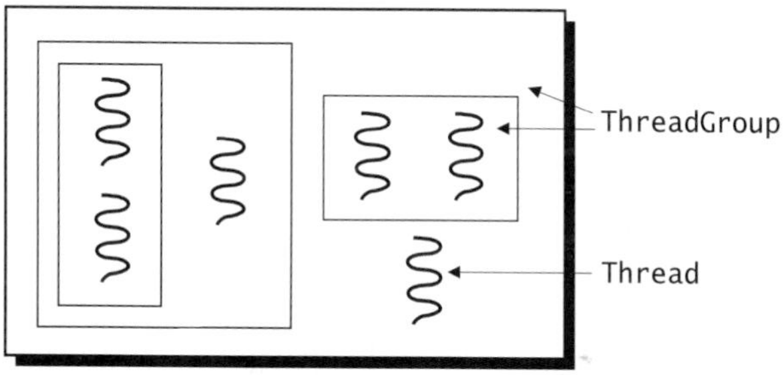

FIGURE 239 **ThreadGroup**

Security

You can also use thread groups to control manipulation of thread state between groups, if this is a policy enforced by the security manager. For example, the security manager's policy may allow a thread to access threads in its own thread group, but not in its parent's. The policies and restrictions of which thread group can manipulate which other thread group are dependent on the security manager in place.

Maximum Priority

A thread group's *maximum priority* places an upper bound on the priority to which threads and thread groups in this thread group can be set. When a thread group is created, its maximum priority is that of its parent thread group. This maximum can subsequently be lowered if permitted by the security manager.

Daemon Thread Groups

A *daemon* thread group is automatically destroyed when it becomes empty (contains no more threads or thread groups). A thread group that is not a daemon thread group must be destroyed explicitly. When a thread group is created, it inherits the daemon status of its parent thread group. You can change a thread group's daemon status subsequent to creation by using `setDaemon()`.

There is no relationship between daemon thread groups and daemon threads.

MEMBER SUMMARY

Constructor	
`ThreadGroup()`	Constructs a new `ThreadGroup` instance.
ThreadGroup Property Methods	
`getMaxPriority()`	Retrieves the maximum priority of this thread group.
`getName()`	Retrieves the name of this thread group.
`getParent()`	Retrieves the parent thread group of this thread group.
`isDaemon()`	Determines if this thread group is a daemon thread group.
`parentOf()`	Determines if this thread group is an ancestor of another group.
`setDaemon()`	Changes the daemon status of this thread group.
`setMaxPriority()`	Sets the maximum priority of this thread group and its subgroup.
ThreadGroup State Methods	
`activeCount()`	Estimates the number of active threads in this thread group.
`activeGroupCount()`	Estimates the number of active thread groups in this thread group.
`enumerate()`	Enumerates the threads or thread groups in this thread group.
`list()`	Prints the threads and thread groups in this thread group.
Thread State Methods	
`destroy()`	Destroys this thread group and its subgroups.
`resume()`	Resumes all the threads in this thread group and its subgroups.
`stop()`	Stops all the threads in this thread group and its subgroups.
`suspend()`	Suspends all the threads in this thread group and its subgroups.
Security Method	
`checkAccess()`	Checks to determine if allowed to modify this thread group.
Thread Exit Handling Method	
`uncaughtException()`	Handles a thread exit from this thread group due to an uncaught exception.
Description Method	
`toString()`	Generates the string representation of this thread group.

See Also

`Thread`, `SecurityManager`.

Example

This example implements a thread group viewer that shows all thread groups in the system at a certain point in time. The thread viewer updates the list of thread groups every 5 seconds. The thread group viewer can be paused and resumed by clicking the button at the top of the frame.

A thread group can be destroyed by clicking the thread group name in the list. In this example, the `handleEvent()` method first interrupts all the threads in the thread group and then waits for them to be stopped.

In the `ThreadViewer` class, the `handleEvent()` and `updateList()` methods are synchronized because they share a number of fields. Doing this prevents the two methods from seeing inconsistent values in the shared fields.

```
import java.awt.*;
class Main implements Runnable {
    public static void main(String args[] ) {
        try {
            new ThreadGViewer();          // Create the thread viewer

            // periodically create a thread group just to
            // keep things interesting
            for (int i=0; ; i++) {
                // Create a new thread group.
                ThreadGroup grp = new ThreadGroup("ThreadGroup-"+i);

                // And create a new thread in the thread group.
                (new Thread(grp, new Main())).start();

                Thread.sleep((int)Math.floor(Math.random()*5000));
            }
        } catch (Exception e) {
            e.printStackTrace();
        }
    }

    public void run() {
        try {
            while (true) {
                // Check if this thread has been interrupted.
                if (Thread.currentThread().isInterrupted()) {
                    break;
                }
               Thread.sleep(500);
            }
        } catch (Exception e) {
            e.printStackTrace();
        }
    }
}
```

Example

```
class ThreadGViewer extends Frame implements Runnable {
    Thread timerThread;

    // List of all thread groups in the system.
    ThreadGroup[] groups;

    // List component containing all the thread groups in the system.
    List threadList = new List();

    ThreadGViewer() {
        super("ThreadGroup Example");
        add("Center", threadList);
        add("North", new Button("Pause"));

        resize(300, 300);
        show();
        timerThread = new Thread(this);
        timerThread.start();
    }

    public synchronized boolean handleEvent(Event evt) {
        if (evt.id == Event.WINDOW_DESTROY) {
            timerThread = null;
            dispose();
            return true;
        } else if (evt.target == threadList) {
             ThreadGroup grp = groups[threadList.getSelectedIndex()];
            try {
                grp.checkAccess();

                // Interrupt and then wait until all threads
                // have stopped.
                Thread[] threads = new Thread[grp.activeCount()];
                int count = grp.enumerate(threads, false);
                for (int i=0; i<count; i++) {
                    threads[i].interrupt();
                    threads[i].join();
                }

                // Now destroy the group.
                grp.destroy();
            } catch (InterruptedException e) {
                e.printStackTrace();
            } catch (SecurityException e) {
                System.out.println("No permission to stop thread " +
                grp.getName());
            }
            return true;
        } else if ("Pause".equals(evt.arg)) {
            timerThread.suspend();
            ((Button)evt.target).setLabel("Resume");
            return true;
        } else if ("Resume".equals(evt.arg)) {
            timerThread.resume();
```

```
            ((Button)evt.target).setLabel("Pause");
            return true;
        }
        return false;
    }

    public void run() {
        try {
            while (timerThread == Thread.currentThread()) {
                updateList();
           Thread.sleep(5000);
            }
        } catch (Exception e) {
            e.printStackTrace();
        }
    }

    synchronized void updateList() {
        ThreadGroup curGrp = Thread.currentThread().getThreadGroup();
        ThreadGroup[] grps =
            new ThreadGroup[curGrp.activeGroupCount()];
        int count = curGrp.enumerate(grps, true);

        groups = new ThreadGroup[count];
        threadList.clear();
        int j = 0;
        for (int i=0; i<count; i++) {
            if (Thread.currentThread().getThreadGroup().parentOf(
                grps[i])) {
                ThreadGroup grp = grps[i];

                threadList.addItem(grp.getName()
                    + "  P" + grp.getMaxPriority()
                    + "  " + (grp.isDaemon() ? "Daemon" : ""));
                groups[j++] = grp;
            }
        }
    }
}
```

activeCount()

PURPOSE Estimates the number of active threads in this thread group.

SYNTAX `public synchronized int activeCount()`

DESCRIPTION This method returns an estimate of the number of active threads in this thread group and its subgroups. This includes (recursively) all descendents of this thread group. It is only an estimate because during this call, threads might have been added to or removed from this thread group or its subgroups.

RETURNS — An estimate of the total number of active threads in this thread group and its subgroups.

SEE ALSO — `activeGroupCount()`, `enumerate()`, `list()`.

EXAMPLE — See the class example.

activeGroupCount()

PURPOSE — Estimates the number of thread groups in this thread group.

SYNTAX

```
public synchronized int activeGroupCount()
```

DESCRIPTION — This method returns an estimate of the number of thread groups in this thread group and its subgroups. It is only an estimate because during this call, thread groups might have been added to or removed from this thread group or its subgroups.

RETURNS — An estimate of the total number of thread groups in this thread group and its subgroups.

SEE ALSO — `activeCount()`, `enumerate()`, `list()`.

EXAMPLE — See the class example.

checkAccess()

PURPOSE — Checks to determine if allowed to modify this thread group.

SYNTAX

```
public final void checkAccess()
```

DESCRIPTION — This method checks if the currently executing thread is allowed to modify this thread group. Modifications that require access checking include changing the state of the threads within the group (e.g. suspend/resume) and changing the properties of the thread group (its daemon status and maximum priority).

EXCEPTIONS

`SecurityException`
If the currently executing thread is not allowed to modify this thread group due to security reasons.

SEE ALSO — `destroy()`, `resume()`, `SecurityManager.checkAccess()`, `setDaemon()`, `setMaxPriority()`, `stop()`, `suspend()`, `ThreadGroup()`.

EXAMPLE — See the class example.

destroy()

PURPOSE Destroys this thread group and its subgroups.

SYNTAX `public final synchronized void destroy()`

DESCRIPTION This method destroys this thread group and its subgroups and removes this thread group from its parent's thread group. A thread group can be destroyed only if it and all its subgroups contain no more threads.

EXCEPTIONS
`IllegalThreadStateException`
If this thread group is not empty or if it has already been destroyed.

SEE ALSO `isDaemon()`, `setDaemon()`.

EXAMPLE See the class example.

enumerate()

PURPOSE Enumerates the threads or thread groups in this thread group.

SYNTAX
```
public int enumerate(Thread[] threads)
public int enumerate(Thread[] threads, boolean recurse)
public int enumerate(ThreadGroup[] groups)
public int enumerate(ThreadGroup[] groups, boolean recurse)
```

DESCRIPTION The four forms of this method enumerate the threads or thread groups in this thread group.

The first two forms enumerate the threads in this group. `enumerate()` copies to the array `threads` references of the `Thread` objects in this group. `recurse` specifies whether to recursively enumerate the threads in the subgroups of this thread group. If `recurse` is `true`, the subgroups are enumerated. If `recurse` is `false`, only this thread group is enumerated. If `recurse` is not specified, subgroups are enumerated. `threads` must have been allocated before calling `enumerate()`. If `threads` is too small to hold all the references, then when `threads` becomes full the enumeration terminates. You can use `activeCount()` to estimate the size of `threads`.

The last two forms enumerate the thread groups in this group. `enumerate()` copies to the array `groups` references of the `ThreadGroup` objects in this group. `recurse` specifies whether to recursively enumerate the thread groups in the subgroups of this thread group. If `recurse` is `true`, the subgroups are enumerated. If `recurse` is `false`, only this thread group is enumerated. If `recurse` is not specified, subgroups are enumerated. `groups` must have been allocated before calling `enumerate()`. If `groups` is too small to hold all the references, then when `groups` becomes full the enumeration terminates. You can use `activeGroupCount()` to estimate the size of `groups`.

PARAMETERS

`groups`	An existing array to hold the references to `ThreadGroup` objects.
`recurse`	Whether to enumerate recursively the subgroups of this thread group. `true` means to recursively enumerate subgroups; `false` means enumerate on this thread group, not its subgroups.
`threads`	An existing array to hold the references to `Thread` objects.

RETURNS The number of references filled in `groups` or `threads`.

SEE ALSO `activeCount()`, `activeGroupCount()`, `list()`.

EXAMPLE See the class example.

getMaxPriority()

PURPOSE Retrieves the maximum priority of this thread group.

SYNTAX `public final int getMaxPriority()`

DESCRIPTION A thread group's maximum priority places an upper bound on the priority to which threads and thread groups in this thread group can be set. When a thread is created, its priority is set to that of the thread that created it and is not limited by the thread group's maximum priority. The thread group's maximum priority is checked only when setting the thread's priority using `Thread.setPriority()`.

When a thread group is created, its maximum priority is that of its parent thread group. This maximum can subsequently be lowered using `setMaxPriority()` if permitted by the security manager.

`getMaxPriority()` returns the maximum priority of this thread group.

RETURNS The maximum priority of this thread group.

SEE ALSO `setMaxPriority()`, `Thread.setPriority()`, `ThreadGroup()`.

EXAMPLE See the class example.

getName()

PURPOSE Retrieves the name of this thread group.

A B C D E F G H I J K L M N O P Q R S T U V W X Y Z

SYNTAX `public final String getName()`

RETURNS The name of this thread group.

SEE ALSO `ThreadGroup()`.

EXAMPLE See the class example.

getParent()

PURPOSE Retrieves the parent thread group of this thread group.

SYNTAX `public final ThreadGroup getParent()`

RETURNS The parent of this thread group. `null` if this thread group is the first thread group created in the system.

SEE ALSO `parentOf()`, `ThreadGroup()`.

EXAMPLE See the `Thread` class example.

isDaemon()

PURPOSE Determines if this thread group is a daemon thread group.

SYNTAX `public final boolean isDaemon()`

DESCRIPTION A *daemon* thread group is automatically destroyed when it becomes empty (contains no more threads or thread groups). A thread group that is not a daemon thread group must be destroyed explicitly using `destroy()`. When a thread group is created, it inherits the daemon status of its parent thread group. You can change a thread group's daemon status using `setDaemon()`.

`isDaemon()` returns `true` if this thread group is a daemon thread group. It returns `false` if this thread group is not a daemon thread group.

There is no relationship between daemon thread groups and daemon threads.

RETURNS `true` if this thread group is daemon; `false` otherwise.

SEE ALSO `destroy()`, `setDaemon()`, `ThreadGroup()`.

EXAMPLE See the class example.

list()

PURPOSE Prints the threads and thread groups in this thread group.

SYNTAX `public synchronized void list()`

DESCRIPTION This method prints all the threads and thread groups in this thread group to `System.out`. This includes (recursively) all descendents of this thread group. This method is useful for debugging.

SEE ALSO `enumerate()`, `System.out`.

EXAMPLE This example simply creates a set of nested thread groups and then calls `list()`. The output of this program follows the following code.

```
import java.awt.*;
class Main {
    public static void main(String args[] ) {
        ThreadGroup grp = Thread.currentThread().getThreadGroup();

        for (int i=0; i<5; i++) {
            // Create a new thread group.
            ThreadGroup g = new ThreadGroup(grp, "group-"+i);

            grp = g;
        }
        Thread.currentThread().getThreadGroup().list();
    }
}
```

OUTPUT

```
java.lang.ThreadGroup[name=main,maxpri=10]
    Thread[main,5,main]
    java.lang.ThreadGroup[name=group-0,maxpri=10]
        java.lang.ThreadGroup[name=group-1,maxpri=10]
            java.lang.ThreadGroup[name=group-2,maxpri=10]
                java.lang.ThreadGroup[name=group-3,maxpri=10]
                    java.lang.ThreadGroup[name=group-4,maxpri=10]
```

parentOf()

PURPOSE Determines if this thread group is an ancestor of another group.

SYNTAX `public final boolean parentOf(ThreadGroup group)`

DESCRIPTION

This method determines whether this thread group is equal to `group` or is an *ancestor* of `group`. This thread group is an ancestor of `group` if this thread group is `group`'s parent, or `group`'s parent's parent, and so on.

PARAMETERS

`group` The thread group to check.

RETURNS

`true` if this thread group is equal to or is an ancestor of `group`; `false` otherwise.

SEE ALSO

`getParent()`, `ThreadGroup()`.

EXAMPLE

See the class example.

resume()

PURPOSE

Resumes all the threads in this thread group and its subgroups.

SYNTAX

```
public final synchronized void resume()
```

DESCRIPTION

This method can be executed only if permitted by the security manager.

SEE ALSO

`checkAccess()`, `stop()`, `suspend()`, `Thread.resume()`, `Thread.stop()`, `Thread.suspend()`.

EXAMPLE

See the class example.

setDaemon()

PURPOSE

Changes the daemon status of this thread group.

SYNTAX

```
public final void setDaemon(boolean daemon)
```

DESCRIPTION

A *daemon* thread group is automatically destroyed when it becomes empty (contains no more threads or thread groups). A thread group that is not a daemon thread group must be destroyed explicitly using `destroy()`. When a thread group is created, it inherits the daemon status of its parent thread group. You can change a thread group's daemon status using `setDaemon()`. If `daemon` is `true`, the thread group becomes a daemon thread group. If `daemon` is `false`, the thread group becomes a non-daemon thread group.

There is no relationship between daemon thread groups and daemon threads.

A B C D E F G H I J K L M N O P Q R S T U V W X Y Z

PARAMETERS

daemon — `true` changes the thread group to a daemon thread group; `false` changes the thread group to a non-daemon thread group.

SEE ALSO — `destroy()`, `isDaemon()`.

EXAMPLE — This example creates a daemon thread group containing a number of threads. When the threads in the thread group terminate, so does the thread group.

```
class Main {
    public static void main(String args[] ) {
        ThreadGroup grp = new ThreadGroup("Group");

        grp.setDaemon(true);
        // Create a few workers
        for (int i=0; i<5; i++) {
            (new Worker(grp)).start();
        }
    }
}

class Worker extends Thread {
    Worker(ThreadGroup grp) {
        super(grp, "Worker");
    }

    public void run() {
        try {
            Thread.sleep((int)Math.floor(Math.random()*5000));
            System.out.println("done");
        } catch (Exception e) {
            e.printStackTrace();
        }
    }
}
```

setMaxPriority()

PURPOSE — Sets the maximum priority of this thread group and its subgroups.

SYNTAX — `public final synchronized void setMaxPriority(int pri)`

DESCRIPTION — A thread group's maximum priority places an upper bound on the priority to which threads and thread groups this thread group can be set. When a thread is created, its priority is set to that of the thread that created it and is not limited by the thread group's maximum priority. The thread group's maximum priority is checked only when setting the thread's priority using `Thread.setPriority()`.

When a thread group is created, its maximum priority is that of its parent thread group.

`setMaxPriority()` lowers the maximum priority of this thread group and its subgroups to `pri`. `pri` is limited to the inclusive range `Thread.MIN_PRIORITY` and the current maximum. If `pri` is greater than the current maximum, the maximum remains unchanged.

`setMaxPriority()` does not change the priorities of threads that are already in this thread group and its subgroups, even if those priorities are higher than `pri`. However, if the priorities of these threads are subsequently changed (using `Thread.setPriority()`), the new thread group maximum priority will apply.

This method can be executed only if permitted by the security manager.

PARAMETERS

`pri`	The maximum priority of this group.

SEE ALSO `checkAccess()`, `getMaxPriority()`, `Thread.MAX_PRIORITY`, `Thread.MIN_PRIORITY`, `Thread.setPriority()`, `ThreadGroup()`.

EXAMPLE See `suspend()`.

stop()

PURPOSE Stops all the threads in this thread group and its subgroups.

SYNTAX `public final synchronized void stop()`

DESCRIPTION This method can be executed only if permitted by the security manager.

SEE ALSO `checkAccess()`, `resume()`, `suspend()`, `Thread.resume()`, `Thread.stop()`, `Thread.suspend()`.

EXAMPLE See `uncaughtException()`.

suspend()

PURPOSE Suspends all the threads in this thread group and its subgroups.

SYNTAX `public final synchronized void suspend()`

DESCRIPTION This method can be executed only if permitted by the security manager.

SEE ALSO `checkAccess()`, `resume()`, `stop()`, `Thread.resume()`, `Thread.stop()`, `Thread.suspend()`.

EXAMPLE

This example creates two thread groups: one whose maximum priority is normal (hiGroup) and one whose maximum priority is minimum (loGroup). See Figure 240. Two threads are created in each. The example also creates a frame with two labels, one for each group. The labels are used to show the progress of the threads.

FIGURE 240
ThreadGroup.suspend()

The threads in the hiGroup will get more work done than will the threads in the loGroup. Clicking the Suspend button in the frame will suspend the hiGroup, giving all the processor cycles to the threads in the loGroup.

```
import java.awt.*;
class Main extends Frame {
    Label loLabel = new Label();
    Label hiLabel = new Label();
    ThreadGroup hiGroup = new ThreadGroup(“High”);
    ThreadGroup loGroup = new ThreadGroup(“Low”);

    Main() {
        super(“suspend Example”);

        // Limit the priority in the low priority thread group.
        loGroup.setMaxPriority(Thread.MIN_PRIORITY);

        // Add a few threads.
        (new Worker(hiGroup, hiLabel)).start();
        (new Worker(hiGroup, hiLabel)).start();
        (new Worker(loGroup, loLabel)).start();
        (new Worker(loGroup, loLabel)).start();

        add(“North”, hiLabel);
        add(“South”, loLabel);
        add(“Center”, new Button(“suspend”));
        pack();
        show();
    }

    public synchronized boolean handleEvent(Event evt) {
        if (“suspend”.equals(evt.arg)) {
            hiGroup.suspend();
            ((Button)evt.target).setLabel(“resume”);
            return true;
        } else if (“resume”.equals(evt.arg)) {
            hiGroup.resume();
            ((Button)evt.target).setLabel(“suspend”);
            return true;
        }
        return false;
    }
```

```
    static public void main(String[] args) {
        new Main();
    }
}

class Worker extends Thread {
    Label label;

    Worker(ThreadGroup group, Label label) {
        super(group, "Worker");
        this.label = label;
    }

    public void run() {
        try {
            for (int i=0; ; i++) {
                if (i % 10 == 0) {
                    label.setText(""+i);
                }
                Thread.sleep(16);
            }
        } catch (Exception e) {
            e.printStackTrace();
        }
    }
}
```

ThreadGroup()

PURPOSE Constructs a new `ThreadGroup` object.

SYNTAX

```
public ThreadGroup()
public ThreadGroup(String name)
public ThreadGroup(ThreadGroup parent, String name)
```

DESCRIPTION `ThreadGroup` has three constructors. By default, the new thread group is created in the same thread group as the currently executing thread. You can specify that it be created in a different thread group by supplying a thread group `parent`. A thread group can be added to another thread group only if permitted by the security manager.

PARAMETERS

`name` The name of the new thread group being created. `name` can be `null`.

`parent` The thread group in which to create this new thread group. `parent` must not be `null`.

SEE ALSO `checkAccess()`, `Thread.currentThread()`, `Thread.getThreadGroup()`.

EXAMPLE See the class example.

toString()

PURPOSE Generates the string representation of this thread group.

SYNTAX `public String toString()`

DESCRIPTION The string representation of a thread group consists of the `ThreadGroup` class name, the thread group's name, and its maximum priority. `toString()` returns this string representation.

RETURNS The string representation of this thread group.

OVERRIDES `Object.toString()`.

SEE ALSO `getMaxPriority()`, `getName()`.

EXAMPLE See `Object.toString()`.

uncaughtException()

PURPOSE Handles a thread exit from this thread group due to an uncaught exception.

SYNTAX `public void uncaughtException(Thread thrd, Throwable e)`

DESCRIPTION When the thread `thrd` from this thread group throws an exception or error that has not been caught, `uncaughtException()` is called by the Java runtime to handle it. Normally, when a thread is destroyed, a `ThreadDeath` error is thrown. `uncaughtException()` checks that `e` is a subclass of `ThreadDeath`. If it is not, `uncaughtException()` prints a stack trace of `e`.

PARAMETERS

`e` The uncaught exception.
`thrd` The thread that threw `e`.

SEE ALSO `stop()`, `Thread.stop()`, `ThreadDeath`, `Throwable.printStackTrace()`.

EXAMPLE This example defines a thread group that overrides the `uncaughtException()` method. A thread is created in this group and then later stopped (via the `stop()` method. Since the thread does not catch `ThreadDeath` (which is thrown because of the `stop()`) the `uncaughtException()` method is invoked. The output generated by this program follows the following code:

```
class Main implements Runnable {
    public static void main(String args[]) {
        MainThreadGroup mtg = new MainThreadGroup("MainThreadGroup");
        Thread thread = new Thread(mtg, new Main());
```

```
        thread.start();

        // Wait 1 second ...
        try {
            Thread.sleep(1000);

            // And then stop the thread.
            thread.stop();
        } catch (InterruptedException e) {
            e.printStackTrace();
        }
    }

    public void run() {
        try {
            Thread.sleep(2000);
        } catch (Exception e) {
            e.printStackTrace();
        }
    }
}

class MainThreadGroup extends ThreadGroup {
    MainThreadGroup(String name) {
        super(name);
    }

    public void uncaughtException(Thread t, Throwable e) {
        System.out.println("UNCAUGHT EXCEPTION by " + t.getName());
        e.printStackTrace();
    }
}
```

OUTPUT

```
UNCAUGHT EXCEPTION by Thread-1
java.lang.ThreadDeath
   at Main.run(Main.java:21)
   at java.lang.Thread.run(Thread.java:294)
```

java.lang
Throwable

Syntax

```
public class Throwable
```

Description

The `Throwable` class is the superclass for `Error` and `Exception`, which in turn are the superclasses for all other system- and user-defined exceptions. Except for specially system-defined errors and runtime exceptions, the Java language requires that any method that throws an instance of `Throwable` or its subclasses to declare the throwable in its `throws` clause as part of the method's declaration. Any method that calls this method must either catch the throwable using `try/catch` statements or declare it in its own `throws` clause. The Java compiler will generate a compilation error for any code that does not follow these rules.

The following is an example of how to catch a throwable. In your programs, however, you should make use of the `Exception` class hierarchy when defining, throwing, or catching exceptions instead of using `Throwable` directly.

```
try {
    int a[] = new int[2];
    a[4]= 3;
} catch (Throwable e) {
    System.err.println("exception msg: " + e.getMessage());
    System.err.println("exception string: " + e.toString());
    e.printStackTrace();
}
```

When you create a throwable, it contain three pieces of information:

1. The class name of the throwable.
2. A snapshot of the current execution stack.
3. An optional string describing the details of this particular throwable.

The class name indicates the type of throwable. The stack trace is useful for pinpointing where the throwable was thrown. The optional string can be used to provide additional details about the throwable. For example, if the throwable is associated with a file, the filename could be supplied as this string.

MEMBER SUMMARY	
Constructor	
`Throwable()`	Constructs a new `Throwable` instance.
Stack Trace Methods	
`fillInStackTrace()`	Fills in the execution stack trace.
`printStackTrace()`	Prints the `Throwable` and its stack trace.
Field Access Method	
`getMessage()`	Retrieves the string with which the `Throwable` was created.
Description Method	
`toString()`	Generates the string representation of the `Throwable`.

See Also

`Error`, `Exception`.

fillInStackTrace()

PURPOSE Fills in the execution stack trace.

SYNTAX `public native Throwable fillInStackTrace()`

DESCRIPTION An instance of `Throwable` is created with a snapshot of the current stack trace. If the throwable is not thrown at the same point at which it was created or if the throwable is to be re-thrown, `fillInStackTrace()` can be called to update this snapshot to the current stack trace so that it reflects exactly where the throwable was thrown.

RETURNS The `Throwable` itself.

SEE ALSO `Throwable.printStackTrace()`.

EXAMPLE

```
int a = 0, b = 0, c = 0;
 ...
try {
    a = b / c;
} catch(Throwable e) {
    throw e.fillInStackTrace();
}
```

getMessage()

PURPOSE Retrieves the string with which the `Throwable` was created.

SYNTAX `public String getMessage()`

DESCRIPTION When you create an instance of `Throwable`, you can associate with it a string describing details of the throwable. This could be, for example, a file name or the string representation of a number. `getMessage()` returns this string. This string also is included in the throwable's string representation generated by `toString()`.

RETURNS The string that the throwable was created with; `null` if it was not created with a detail message.

SEE ALSO `Throwable()`, `toString()`.

EXAMPLE

```
try {
    FileInputStream out = new FileInputStream(args[0]);
...
} catch (IOException e) {
    System.err.println("cannot create stream: " + e.getMessage());
}
```

printStackTrace()

PURPOSE Prints the `Throwable` and its stack trace.

SYNTAX
```
public void printStackTrace()
public void printStackTrace(PrintStream s)
```

DESCRIPTION A `Throwable` has associated with it a stack trace. You can display this stack track using `printStackTrace()`. By default, the output is sent to `System.err`. If you supply a `PrintStream` argument `s`, the output will go to `s`.

PARAMETERS

`s` The print stream to send the output.

SEE ALSO `fillInStackTrace()`, `PrintStream`, `System.err`, `Throwable()`.

EXAMPLE

```
try {
    Long lobj2 = new Long("1048L576"); // using string
} catch (NumberFormatException e) {
```

```
    e.printStackTrace();             // output goes to System.err
    e.printStackTrace(System.out);   // send trace to stdout too
}
```

Throwable()

PURPOSE Constructs a new `Throwable` object.

SYNTAX

```
public Throwable()
public Throwable(String message)
```

DESCRIPTION This method creates a new `Throwable` object and records in it the current stack trace. If the string `message` is supplied to the constructor, it is recorded with the throwable. `message` is then included with the string representation of the throwable (the one generated by `toString()`). `message` can be retrieved from the throwable using `getMessage()`.

The snapshot of the stack trace recorded in the throwable can be displayed using `printStackTrace()`. It also can be updated after the throwable has been created using `fillInStackTrace()`.

PARAMETERS

`message` The string to associate with the throwable.

SEE ALSO `fillInStackTrace()`, `getMessage()`, `printStackTrace()`, `toString()`.

EXAMPLE

```
// Implementation of FileInputStream.getFD()
public final FileDescriptor getFD() throws IOException {
    if (fd != null) return fd;
    throw new IOException();
}
// Implementation of FileInputStream constructor
public FileInputStream(String name) throws FileNotFoundException {
    SecurityManager security = System.getSecurityManager();
    if (security != null) {
        security.checkRead(name);
    }
    try {
        fd = new FileDescriptor();
        open(name);
    } catch (IOException e) {
        throw new FileNotFoundException(name);
    }
}
```

toString()

PURPOSE Generates the string representation of the Throwable.

SYNTAX `public String toString()`

DESCRIPTION The string representation of a throwable includes its class name and the string that the throwable was created with (if any). `toString()` returns this string representation.

RETURNS The string representation of this object.

OVERRIDES `Object.toString()`.

SEE ALSO `getMessage()`, `printStackTrace()`.

EXAMPLE

```
try {
    FileInputStream out = new FileInputStream(args[0]);
...
} catch (IOException e) {
    System.err.println(e.toString());
}
```

Toolkit

java.lang.Object — Toolkit

Syntax

```
public abstract class Toolkit
```

Description

A component, such as a button, in the Abstract Windowing Toolkit (AWT) uses the platform's native implementation of a button. For example, on Solaris, the AWT button uses the Motif button widget, while on Windows95, the AWT button uses the button control. So that the AWT button component behaves the same on all platforms, the button is assigned a peer (see `Component`) that takes care of translating the behavior of the platform's native button to the behavior of the AWT button.

Each platform has its own complete set of peers to match each of the AWT components. The purpose of this abstract class `Toolkit` is to deliver the correct set of peers that are appropriate for the current platform. For example, when an AWT button object needs a button peer, it first calls `getDefaultToolkit()` to retrieve an instance of this class with which it can use to create a button peer.

There is only one instance of the `Toolkit` class in existence at any time. The instance is created with the first call to `getDefaultToolkit()`. There is an implementation of this class for each platform. To determine which instance to create, the `awt.toolkit` system property is used (see `Properties`). The `awt.toolkit` system property names the class (which must of course be a subclass of `Toolkit`) to create.

Most of the peer creation methods in this class are not typically used directly by AWT programmers, since they are indirectly available through other classes.

MEMBER SUMMARY	
Initialization Method	
`getDefaultToolkit()`	Retrieves the toolkit instance to use when creating component peers.
Peer Methods	
`createButton()`	Creates a button peer.
`createCanvas()`	Creates a canvas peer.
`createCheckbox()`	Creates a checkbox peer.

Continued

A B C D E F G H I J K L M N O P Q R S T U V W X Y Z

MEMBER SUMMARY	
`createCheckboxMenuItem()`	Creates a checkbox menu item peer.
`createChoice()`	Creates a choice peer.
`createDialog()`	Creates a dialog peer.
`createFileDialog()`	Creates a file dialog peer.
`createFrame()`	Creates a frame peer.
`createLabel()`	Creates a label peer.
`createList()`	Creates a list peer.
`createMenu()`	Creates a menu peer.
`createMenuBar()`	Creates a menu bar peer.
`createMenuItem()`	Creates a menu item peer.
`createPanel()`	Creates a panel peer.
`createScrollbar()`	Creates a scrollbar peer.
`createTextArea()`	Creates a text area peer.
`createTextField()`	Creates a text field peer.
`createWindow()`	Creates a window peer.
Color Method	
`getColorModel()`	Retrieves the color model for the screen.
Font Methods	
`getFontList()`	Retrieves a list of the names of all available AWT fonts.
`getFontMetrics()`	Retrieves the font metrics for a font.
Image Methods	
`checkImage()`	Retrieves the construction status of an image.
`createImage()`	Creates an image using image data supplied by an image producer.
`getImage()`	Retrieves an image from a file or URL.
`prepareImage()`	Triggers the loading of image data for an image.
Screen Methods	
`getScreenResolution()`	Retrieves the resolution of the screen.
`getScreenSize()`	Retrieves the size of the screen.
`sync()`	Flushes any pending operations on active graphics contexts.

Example

This example creates a frame and centers it on the screen. See Figure 241. The frame also displays the screen resolution and an estimate of the size of the screen based on the screen size and resolution.

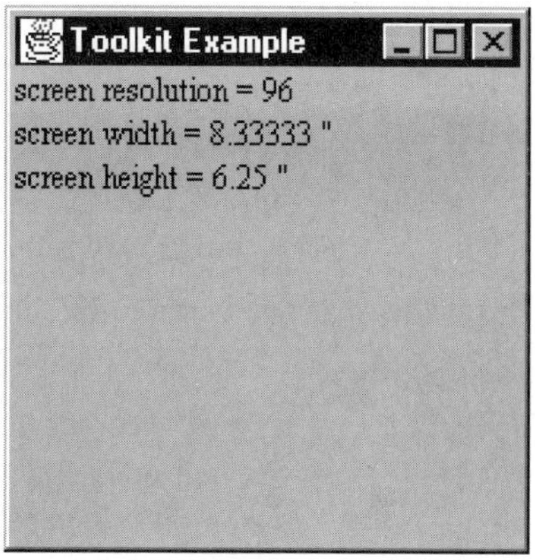

FIGURE 241 `Toolkit`

```
import java.awt.*;
class Main extends Frame {
    Main() {
        super("Toolkit Example");
        Dimension d = Toolkit.getDefaultToolkit().getScreenSize();

        resize(200, 200);
        move((d.width-bounds().width)/2,
            (d.height-bounds().height)/2);
        show();
    }

    public void paint(Graphics g) {
        FontMetrics fm = g.getFontMetrics();
        int resol = Toolkit.getDefaultToolkit().getScreenResolution();
        Dimension d = Toolkit.getDefaultToolkit().getScreenSize();
        int y = fm.getAscent();

        g.drawString("screen resolution = "+resol, 0, y);
        y += fm.getHeight();
        g.drawString("screen width = "
            + ((double)d.width/resol) + " \"", 0, y);
        y += fm.getHeight();
        g.drawString("screen height = "
            + ((double)d.height/resol) + " \"", 0, y);
    }

    public static void main(String[] args) {
        new Main();
    }
}
```

checkImage()

PURPOSE Retrieves the construction status of an image.

SYNTAX
```
public abstract int checkImage(Image image, int width, int
    height, ImageObserver obs)
```

DESCRIPTION See `Component.checkImage()` for a complete description of this method.

PARAMETERS

`height`	If >= `0`, specifies the height of the scaled version of the image to check.
`image`	The non-`null` image to check.
`obs`	If non-`null`, specifies the image observer to be notified whenever the status changes.
`width`	If >= `0`, specifies the width of the scaled version of the image to check.

RETURNS The combination of status bits as defined by the `ImageObserver` interface.

SEE ALSO `Component.checkImage()`.

EXAMPLE See `Component.checkImage()`.

createButton()

PURPOSE Creates a button peer.

SYNTAX
```
protected abstract ButtonPeer createButton(Button target)
```

DESCRIPTION This method is called by `Button.addNotify()` as the peers for a component hierarchy are created. For a complete description of the behavior of the peer, see the `Button` class.

PARAMETERS

`target`	The non-`null` AWT button requiring a peer.

RETURNS A button peer for the AWT button target.

SEE ALSO `Button`.

createCanvas()

PURPOSE Creates a canvas peer.

SYNTAX
```
protected abstract CanvasPeer createCanvas(Canvas target)
```

DESCRIPTION This method is called by `Canvas.addNotify()` as the peers for a component hierarchy are created. For a complete description of the behavior of the peer, see the `Canvas` class.

PARAMETERS

`target` The non-`null` AWT canvas requiring a peer.

RETURNS A canvas peer for the AWT canvas target.

SEE ALSO `Canvas`.

createCheckbox()

PURPOSE Creates a checkbox peer.

SYNTAX

```
protected abstract CheckboxPeer createCheckbox(Checkbox target)
```

DESCRIPTION This method is called by `Checkbox.addNotify()` as the peers for a component hierarchy are created. For a complete description of the behavior of the peer, see the `Checkbox` class.

PARAMETERS

`target` The non-`null` AWT checkbox requiring a peer.

RETURNS A checkbox peer for the AWT checkbox target.

SEE ALSO `Checkbox`.

createCheckboxMenuItem()

PURPOSE Creates a checkbox menu item peer.

SYNTAX

```
protected abstract CheckboxMenuItemPeer
   createCheckboxMenuItem(CheckboxMenuItem target)
```

DESCRIPTION This method is called by `CheckboxMenuItem.addNotify()` as the peers for a component hierarchy are created. For a complete description of the behavior of the peer, see the `CheckboxMenuItem` class.

PARAMETERS

`target` The non-`null` AWT checkbox menu item requiring a peer.

RETURNS A checkbox menu item peer for the AWT checkbox menu item target.

SEE ALSO `CheckboxMenuItem`.

createChoice()

PURPOSE Creates a choice peer.

SYNTAX `protected abstract ChoicePeer createChoice(Choice target)`

DESCRIPTION This method is called by `Choice.addNotify()` as the peers for a component hierarchy are created. For a complete description of the behavior of the peer, see the `Choice` class.

PARAMETERS

`target` The non-`null` AWT choice requiring a peer.

RETURNS A choice peer for the AWT choice target.

SEE ALSO `Choice`.

createDialog()

PURPOSE Creates a dialog peer.

SYNTAX `protected abstract DialogPeer createDialog(Dialog target)`

DESCRIPTION This method is called by `Dialog.addNotify()` as the peers for a component hierarchy are created. For a complete description of the behavior of the peer, see the `Dialog` class.

PARAMETERS

`target` The non-`null` AWT dialog requiring a peer.

RETURNS A dialog peer for the AWT dialog target.

SEE ALSO `Dialog`.

createFileDialog()

PURPOSE Creates a file dialog peer.

SYNTAX
```
protected abstract FileDialogPeer createFileDialog(FileDialog
    target)
```

DESCRIPTION This method is called by `FileDialog.addNotify()` as the peers for a component hierarchy are created. For a complete description of the behavior of the peer, see the `FileDialog` class.

PARAMETERS

`target` The non-`null` AWT file dialog requiring a peer.

RETURNS A file dialog peer for the AWT file dialog target.

SEE ALSO `FileDialog`.

createFrame()

PURPOSE Creates a frame peer.

SYNTAX `protected abstract FramePeer createFrame(Frame target)`

DESCRIPTION This method is called by `Frame.addNotify()` as the peers for a component hierarchy are created. For a complete description of the behavior of the peer, see the `Frame` class.

PARAMETERS

`target` The non-`null` AWT frame requiring a peer.

RETURNS A frame peer for the AWT frame target.

SEE ALSO `Frame`.

createImage()

PURPOSE Creates an image using image data supplied by an image producer.

SYNTAX `public abstract Image createImage(ImageProducer producer)`

DESCRIPTION This method creates an image based on the image data generated by the image producer `producer`. When this method returns, it does not contain any image information. The production of image information must be triggered by calling either `prepareImage()` or `Graphics.drawImage()`. Since the image is not loaded before this method returns, the image may become invalid later (when an error is eventually encountered). See the `Image` class description for more information about the asynchronous loading of image data.

PARAMETERS

`producer` The non-`null` image producer.

RETURNS A reference to a new image. `null` may be returned if the producer is not valid.

SEE ALSO `Image`, `ImageProducer`.

createLabel()

PURPOSE Creates a label peer.

SYNTAX `protected abstract LabelPeer createLabel(Label target)`

DESCRIPTION This method is called by `Label.addNotify()` as the peers for a component hierarchy are created. For a complete description of the behavior of the peer, see the `Label` class.

PARAMETERS
`target` The non-`null` AWT label requiring a peer.

RETURNS A label peer for the AWT label target.

SEE ALSO `Label`.

createList()

PURPOSE Creates a list peer.

SYNTAX `protected abstract ListPeer createList(List target)`

DESCRIPTION This method is called by `List.addNotify()` as the peers for a component hierarchy are created. For a complete description of the behavior of the peer, see the `List` class.

PARAMETERS
`target` The non-`null` AWT list requiring a peer.

RETURNS A list peer for the AWT list target.

SEE ALSO `List`.

createMenu()

PURPOSE Creates a menu peer.

SYNTAX `protected abstract MenuPeer createMenu(Menu target)`

DESCRIPTION This method is called by `Menu.addNotify()` as the peers for a component hierarchy are created. For a complete description of the behavior of the peer, see the `Menu` class.

PARAMETERS
`target` The non-`null` AWT menu requiring a peer.

RETURNS A menu peer for the AWT menu target.

SEE ALSO `Menu`.

createMenuBar()

PURPOSE Creates a menu bar peer.

SYNTAX `protected abstract MenuBarPeer createMenuBar(MenuBar target)`

DESCRIPTION This method is called by `MenuBar.addNotify()` as the peers for a component hierarchy are created. For a complete description of the behavior of the peer, see the `MenuBar` class.

PARAMETERS

`target` The non-`null` AWT menu bar requiring a peer.

RETURNS A menu bar peer for the AWT menu bar target.

SEE ALSO `MenuBar`.

createMenuItem()

PURPOSE Creates a menu item peer.

SYNTAX `protected abstract MenuItemPeer createMenuItem(MenuItem target)`

DESCRIPTION This method is called by `MenuItem.addNotify()` as the peers for a component hierarchy are created. For a complete description of the behavior of the peer, see the `MenuItem` class.

PARAMETERS

`target` The non-`null` AWT menu item requiring a peer.

RETURNS A menu item peer for the AWT menu item target.

SEE ALSO `MenuItem`.

createPanel()

PURPOSE Creates a panel peer.

SYNTAX `protected abstract PanelPeer createPanel(Panel target)`

A B C D E F G H I J K L M N O P Q R S T U V W X Y Z

DESCRIPTION This method is called by `Panel.addNotify()` as the peers for a component hierarchy are created. For a complete description of the behavior of the peer, see the `Panel` class.

PARAMETERS

`target` The non-`null` AWT panel requiring a peer.

RETURNS A panel peer for the AWT panel target.

SEE ALSO `Panel`.

createScrollbar()

PURPOSE Creates a scrollbar peer.

SYNTAX
```
protected abstract ScrollbarPeer createScrollbar(Scrollbar
    target)
```

DESCRIPTION This method is called by `Scrollbar.addNotify()` as the peers for a component hierarchy are created. For a complete description of the behavior of the peer, see the `Scrollbar` class.

PARAMETERS

`target` The non-`null` AWT scrollbar requiring a peer.

RETURNS A scrollbar peer for the AWT scrollbar target.

SEE ALSO `Scrollbar`.

createTextArea()

PURPOSE Creates a text area peer.

SYNTAX
```
protected abstract TextAreaPeer createTextArea(TextArea target)
```

DESCRIPTION This method is called by `TextArea.addNotify()` as the peers for a component hierarchy are created. For a complete description of the behavior of the peer, see the `TextArea` class.

PARAMETERS

`target` The non-`null` AWT text area requiring a peer.

RETURNS A text area peer for the AWT text area target.

SEE ALSO `TextArea`.

createTextField()

PURPOSE Creates a text field peer.

SYNTAX
```
protected abstract TextFieldPeer createTextField(TextField
    target)
```

DESCRIPTION This method is called by `TextField.addNotify()` as the peers for a component hierarchy are created. For a complete description of the behavior of the peer, see the `TextField` class.

PARAMETERS

`target` The non-`null` AWT text field requiring a peer.

RETURNS A text field peer for the AWT text field target.

SEE ALSO `TextField`.

createWindow()

PURPOSE Creates a window peer.

SYNTAX
```
protected abstract WindowPeer createWindow(Window target)
```

DESCRIPTION This is called by `Window.addNotify()` as the peers for a component hierarchy are created. For a complete description of the behavior of the peer, see the `Window` class.

PARAMETERS

`target` The non-`null` AWT window requiring a peer.

RETURNS A window peer for the AWT window target.

SEE ALSO `Window`.

getColorModel()

PURPOSE Retrieves the color model for the screen.

SYNTAX
```
public abstract ColorModel getColorModel()
```

RETURNS The non-`null` color model of the screen.

SEE ALSO `ColorModel`.

EXAMPLE See `ColorModel` for an example that displays the colors in the screen's color table.

getDefaultToolkit()

PURPOSE Retrieves the toolkit instance to use when creating component peers.

SYNTAX `public static synchronized Toolkit getDefaultToolkit()`

DESCRIPTION The first time this method is called, `getDefaultToolkit()` reads the `awt.toolkit` system property to determine which version of the `Toolkit` to create. The toolkit instance is created only once and cannot be replaced.

RETURNS The non-`null` toolkit instance.

EXCEPTIONS
`AWTError` If the toolkit could not be created.

EXAMPLE See the class example.

getFontList()

PURPOSE Retrieves a list of the names of all available AWT fonts.

SYNTAX `public abstract String[] getFontList()`

DESCRIPTION The returned list should not be modified.

RETURNS A non-`null` list of all available AWT font names.

EXAMPLE See the `Font` class.

getFontMetrics()

PURPOSE Retrieves the font metrics for a font.

SYNTAX `public abstract FontMetrics getFontMetrics(Font font)`

DESCRIPTION This method retrieves the font metrics for the font `font`.

PARAMETERS
`font` The non-`null` font.

RETURNS The non-`null` font metrics for `font`.

SEE ALSO `FontMetrics`, `Graphics.getFontMetrics()`.

getImage()

PURPOSE
Creates an image from a file or URL.

SYNTAX
```
public abstract Image getImage(String filename)
public abstract Image getImage(URL url)
```

DESCRIPTION
The two forms of this method return a reference to an `Image` object. The pixels contained in the file `filename` or at the URL `url` are not immediately loaded into the image. To start the loading of the pixel data, call `Component.prepareImage()` or `Graphics.drawImage()`. Since the image is not loaded before this method returns, the image may become invalid later (when an error is eventually encountered). See the `Image` class description for more information about the asynchronous loading of image data.

PARAMETERS
`filename` The non-`null` string specifying the file that contains the image.
`url` The non-`null` URL specifying the location of the image.

RETURNS
A reference to the image that will eventually contain the pixel data. `null` is returned if `filename` or `url` is invalid.

SEE ALSO
`URL`.

EXAMPLE
This example demonstrates how a URL can be derived from pathname. See Figure 242. The program creates a frame and a canvas in which to display the image. The image is scaled to the size of the canvas.

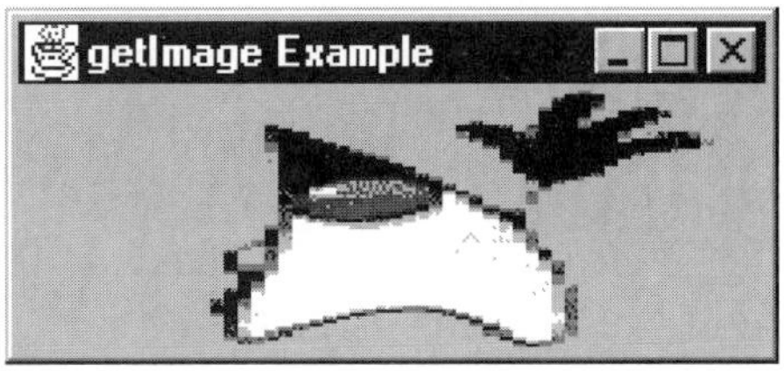

FIGURE 242 `Toolkit.getImage()`

```
import java.awt.*;
import java.net.*;
class Main extends Frame {
    Main(String filename) {
        super("getImage Example");
        try {
            // Retrieve the image.
            URL url = new URL("file:///" +
                              System.getProperty("user.dir")
                + "/" + filename);
            Image urlImage = getToolkit().getImage(url);

            add("Center", new ImageCanvas(urlImage));
        } catch (Exception e) {
            e.printStackTrace();
```

A B C D E F G H I J K L M N O P Q R S T U V W X Y Z

```
            }
            resize(50, 100);
            show();
        }

        static public void main(String[] args) {
            if (args.length == 1) {
                new Main(args[0]);
            } else {
                System.err.println("usage: java Main <image file>");
            }
        }
    }

    class ImageCanvas extends Canvas {
        Image image;

        ImageCanvas(Image image) {
            this.image = image;
        }

        public void paint(Graphics g) {
            update(g);
        }

        public void update(Graphics g) {
            g.drawImage(image, 0, 0, size().width, size().height, this);
        }
    }
```

getScreenResolution()

PURPOSE Retrieves the resolution of the screen.

SYNTAX `public abstract int getScreenResolution()`

DESCRIPTION Dividing the screen size by the screen resolution should yield the physical size of the screen.

RETURNS The resolution of the screen in dots-per-inch.

EXAMPLE See the class example.

getScreenSize()

PURPOSE Retrieves the size of the screen.

SYNTAX `public abstract Dimension getScreenSize()`

RETURNS The non-`null` dimensions of the screen in pixels.

EXAMPLE See the class example.

prepareImage()

PURPOSE Triggers the loading of image data for an image.

SYNTAX
```
public abstract boolean prepareImage(Image image, int width, int
    height, ImageObserver observer)
```

DESCRIPTION This method starts the loading or production of image data associated with image `image` or a scaled version of `image`. If `width` and `height` are `-1`, no scaling of `image` is done. If `width` and `height` are non-negative, they specify that `image` should not only be loaded but also scaled so that its width is `width` and its height is `height`.

This method is typically used to preload image data for an image or a scaled version of an image so that `Graphics.drawImage()` can operate as quickly as possible.

PARAMETERS

`height`	`-1` or the scaled height of the returned image.
`image`	The non-`null` image to load.
`observer`	The non-`null` image observer.
`width`	`-1` or the scaled width of the returned image.

RETURNS `true` if all the image data for image is available; `false` otherwise.

SEE ALSO `Component.checkImage()`.

EXAMPLE See `Component.checkImage()`.

sync()

PURPOSE Flushes any pending operations on active graphics contexts.

SYNTAX `public abstract void sync()`

DESCRIPTION This method is useful on platforms that batch painting calls to a graphics context. It currently is not used.

SEE ALSO `Graphics`.

A B C D E F G H I J K L M N O P Q R S T U V W X Y Z

java.lang
UnknownError

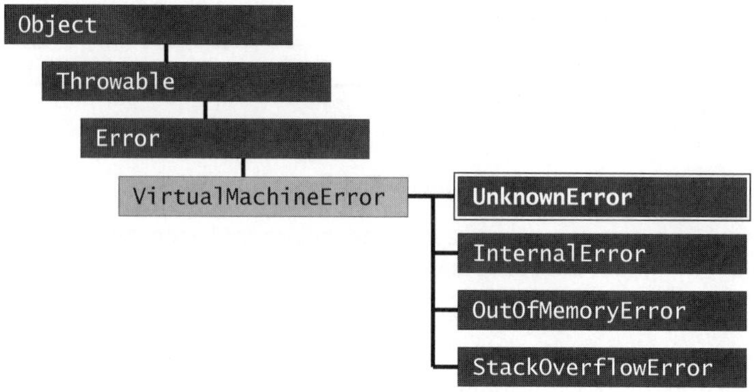

Syntax

```
public class UnknownError extends VirtualMachineError
```

Description

`UnknownError` is an error that is thrown when the Java virtual machine encounters an unrecoverable error that does not fit into any of the other error subclasses. It should not be caught or declared in the `throws` clause of a method.

MEMBER SUMMARY	
Constructor	
`UnknownError()`	Constructs an `UnknownError` instance.

See Also

`Error`, `VirtualMachineError`.

UnknownError()

PURPOSE Constructs an `UnknownError` instance.

SYNTAX `public UnknownError()`

DESCRIPTION This constructor creates a new instance of `UnknownError`. An optional string `msg` can be supplied that describes this particular instance of the error.

PARAMETERS

`msg` A string that gives details about this error.

java.net

UnknownHostException

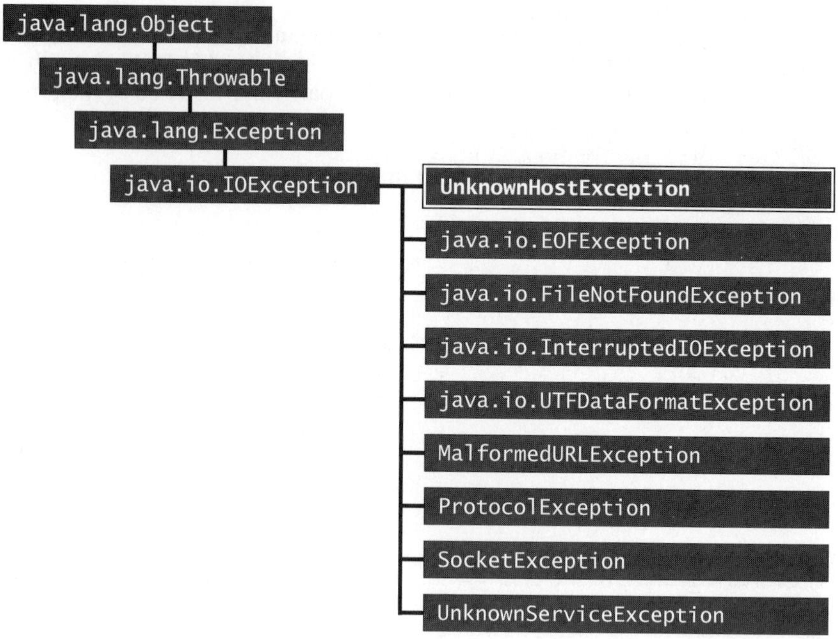

Syntax

```
public class UnknownHostException extends IOException
```

Description

`UnknownHostException` is an IO exception that is thrown when the name of a machine (*host*) cannot be resolved to an address. Such name resolution capability is required by the `InetAddress` and `URL` classes.

A method that throws `UnknownHostException` must declare it or any of its superclasses in its `throws` clause.

MEMBER SUMMARY	
Constructor	
`UnknownHostException()`	Constructs a new `UnknownHostException` instance.

See Also

IOException, InetAddress, URL.

Example

This example generates an UnknownHostException when trying to resolve the host name NeverFindThis.

```
import java.net.InetAddress;
import java.net.UnknownHostException;

class Main {
    public static void main(String[] args) {
        System.out.println("UnknownHostException example");
        try {
            InetAddress someAddr =
                InetAddress.getByName("NeverFindThis");
        } catch (UnknownHostException e) {
            System.err.println("Cannot resolve: " + e);
        }
    }
}
```

UnknownHostException()

PURPOSE Constructs a new UnknownHostException instance.

SYNTAX

```
public UnknownHostException()
public UnknownHostException(String host)
```

DESCRIPTION The two forms of this constructor create a new instance of UnknownHostException. An optional string host containing the name of the machine can be supplied.

PARAMETERS

host The machine for which this exception was thrown.

java.net
UnknownServiceException

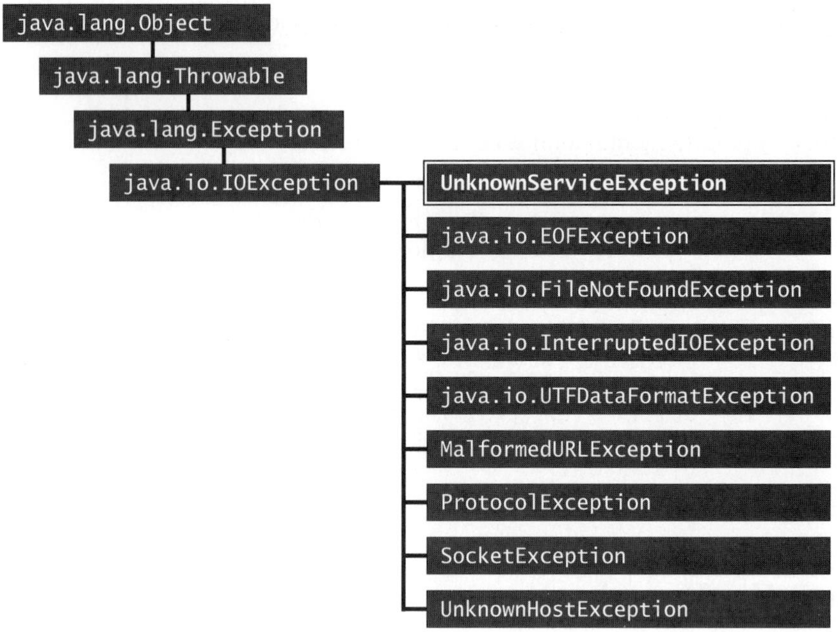

Syntax

```
public class UnknownServiceException extends IOException
```

Description

`UnknownServiceException` is an IO exception that is thrown when a URL connection does not support a particular service. Examples of services that a URL connection may support are reading from the connection as an input stream, writing to the connection as an output stream, and getting MIME-typed content from the connection.

A method that throws `UnknownServiceException` must declare it or any of its superclasses in its `throws` clause.

MEMBER SUMMARY	
Constructor	
`UnknownServiceException()`	Constructs a new `UnknownServiceException` instance.

See Also

IOException, URLConnection.

Example

This example throws an UnknownServiceException when it attempts to get an output stream for a file URL.

```
import java.net.*;
import java.io.IOException;
import java.io.OutputStream;

class Main {
    public static void main(String[] args) {
        try {
            URL u = new URL(
               "file://localhost/export/home/java/api/packages.html");
            URLConnection conn = u.openConnection();

            OutputStream out = conn.getOutputStream();
        } catch (UnknownServiceException e) {
            System.err.println("Cannot get output stream: "+ e);
        } catch (IOException e) {
            e.printStackTrace();
        }
    }
}
```

UnknownServiceException()

PURPOSE Constructs a new UnknownServiceException instance.

SYNTAX `public UnknownServiceException(String msg)`

DESCRIPTION This constructor creates a new instance of UnknownServiceException. An optional string msg can be supplied that describes this particular instance of the exception.

PARAMETERS

msg A string that gives details about this exception.

java.lang
UnsatisfiedLinkError

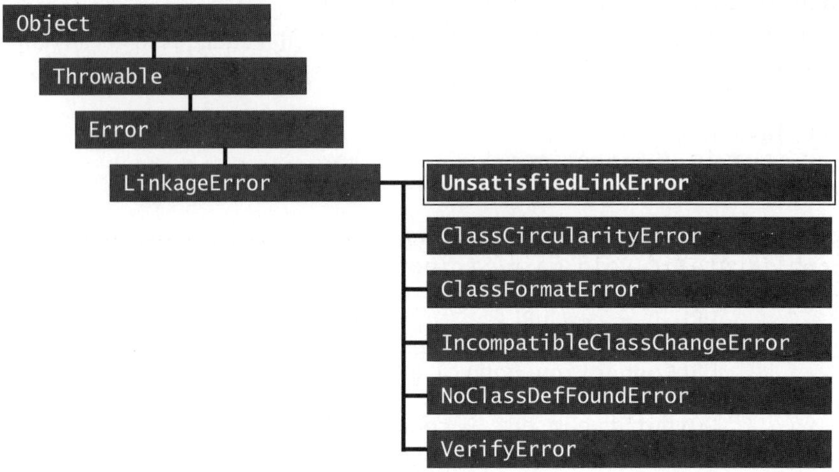

Syntax

```
public class UnsatisfiedLinkError extends LinkageError
```

Description

`UnsatisfiedLinkError` is a runtime linkage error that is thrown when a library cannot be loaded and linked successfully. This can occur, for example, if the requested library does not exist, or, if it does exist, it contains unresolved references that prevent it from being successfully loaded.

`UnsatisfiedLinkError` is an unrecoverable error that should not be caught or declared in the `throws` clause of a method.

MEMBER SUMMARY	
Constructor	
`UnsatisfiedLinkError()`	Constructs an `UnsatisfiedLinkError` instance.

See Also

`LinkageError`, `Runtime.load()`, `Runtime.loadLibrary()`, `System.load()`, `System.loadLibrary()`.

Example

This example generates an UnsatisfiedLinkError.

```
class Main {
    public static void main(String[] args) {
        System.out.println("UnsatisfiedLinkError example");

        System.load("NeverFindThisOne"); // link error
    }
}
```

UnsatisfiedLinkError()

PURPOSE
Constructs an UnsatisfiedLinkError instance.

SYNTAX
```
public UnsatisfiedLinkError()
public UnsatisfiedLinkError(String msg)
```

DESCRIPTION
The two forms of this constructor create a new instance of UnsatisfiedLinkError. An optional string msg can be supplied that describes this particular instance of the error.

PARAMETERS

msg
A string that gives details about this error.

java.net
URL

java.lang.Object — URL

Syntax

`public final class URL`

Description

A *Uniform Resource Locator* (URL) is a string that describes how to locate a resource on the Internet. The specification of a URL's syntax and semantics are described in the Internet RFC 1738.

In general, a URL consists of the following components (in order of their appearance in the URL):

protocol — This is an identifier that specifies which Internet protocol to use to access the resource. Examples of these are `http`, `ftp`, `gopher`, `news`, `telnet`, and `mailto`.

host name — The name of a host or domain to contact to access the resource. Examples of these are `ds.internic.net`, `localhost`, `jupiter`.

port number — The port number on the host to which to connect. It usually is optional. Most protocols have a default port number. For example, the default port number for HTTP is `80`; the default port number for Telnet is `23`.

file name — The filename identifies the file or directory on the file system exported by the host that contains the resource. Examples of these are `pub/beta/product.zip` and `apidocs/`. A trailing slash in the name indicates a directory.

reference — HTTP URLs also can contain fragment identifiers that name fragments of the document named by the filename of the URL. For example, suppose the document `notice.html` contains

```
<A name=READMEFIRST>
```

In the URL `http://jupiter/notice.html#READMEFIRST`, the reference is `READMEFIRST`. The URL would access the fragment of `notice.html` starting at the fragment marked with the label.

Here is an example of a complete URL:

```
http://ds.internic.net:80/rfc/rfc1738.txt
```

It uses the HTTP protocol and will contact the host `ds.internic.net` using port `80` to access the file `rfc/rfc1738.txt`. For more information on URLs, read the document named by this URL.

The `URL` class represents URLs and provides methods to construct and obtain components of the URL (its protocol, host name, port number, etc.). In addition, it provides methods that, after a URL has been created, uses the URL to retrieve the resource identified by the URL. It also supports lower-level methods such as opening a connection or input stream to the server that is managing the resource identified by the URL.

Protocol or Stream Handlers

URLs support many different protocols. Consequently, how the resource identified by the URL is retrieved and how connections or streams are opened to the server are very protocol-specific tasks. Java provides a flexible mechanism for supporting arbitrary protocols by using possibly program-defined implementations. The entity that supports a single protocol is called a *URL stream* (or *protocol*) *handler* and is implemented by a subclass of `URLStreamHandler`.

The Java runtime itself provides a handful of protocol handlers (e.g., HTTP, MailTo, and FTP) and allows new protocol handlers to be added dynamically. By using `setURLStreamHandlerFactory()`, the program can configure (if permitted to do so by the security manager) which implementations are selected for the protocol handlers, as well as which protocols are supported. This method sets the *stream handler factory* for the program. A stream handler factory defines the policy that dictates the list of protocols supported and their implementations.

If the program has not configured a stream handler factory, then by default the stream handler is defined to come from a package listed in the `java.protocol.handler.pkgs` property. This property contains a list of package prefixes, each separated by '`|`'; each package prefix in the property is tried in the order specified. The default package prefix is `sun.net.www.protocol`. Each stream handler is defined in a class named *protocol*.`Handler`. For example, the handler for HTTP would have the fully qualified name of

```
sun.net.www.protocol.http.Handler
```

MEMBER SUMMARY

Constructor

`URL()`	Constructs a new `URL` instance.

Field Access Methods

`getFile()`	Retrieves this URL's filename.
`getHost()`	Retrieves this URL's host name.
`getPort()`	Retrieves this URL's port number.
`getProtocol()`	Retrieves this URL's protocol name.
`getRef()`	Retrieves this URL's reference.
`set()`	Sets the fields of this URL.

Continued

A B C D E F G H I J K L M N O P Q R S T U V W X Y Z

MEMBER SUMMARY

Communications Methods	
`getContent()`	Retrieves the contents pointed to by this URL.
`openConnection()`	Opens this URL's connection.
`openStream()`	Opens an input stream on this URL's connection.
Comparison Methods	
`equals()`	Compares two URLs for equality.
`sameFile()`	Determines whether two URLs point to the same file.
Hash Code Methods	
`hashCode()`	Computes the hash code for this URL.
Description Methods	
`toExternalForm()`	Generates the string representation for this URL.
`toString()`	Generates the string representation for this URL.
Factory Method	
`setURLStreamHandlerFactory()`	Sets the `URLStreamHandler` factory.

See Also

`ContentHandler`, `ContentHandlerFactory`, `InputStream`, `URLConnection`, `URLStreamHandler`, `URLStreamHandlerFactory`.

equals()

PURPOSE Compares two URLs for equality.

SYNTAX `public boolean equals(Object obj)`

DESCRIPTION Two URLs are considered equal if they are both of class URL and they both have the same protocol, host name, port number, and filename. `equals()` returns `true` if `obj` is equal to this URL; it returns `false` otherwise.

This method is similar to `sameFile()` except `sameFile()` accepts only a `URL` as an argument, whereas `equals()` accepts an object of any class, including `null`.

PARAMETERS

`obj` The object against which to compare.

RETURNS `true` if `obj` is the same URL as this URL; `false` otherwise.

OVERRIDES `Object.equals()`.

SEE ALSO `sameFile()`.

EXAMPLE

```
try {
    URL u1 = new URL(“http://java.sun.com:80/new.html”);
    URL u2 = new URL(“http://java.sun.com/new.html”);
    URL u3 = new URL(“http://java.sun.com/new.html#_top_”);

    // u1 and u2 are not the same because of ‘port’
    System.out.println(u1 + (u1.equals(u2)? “ is “ : “ is not “) +
                       “the same as “ + u2);
    // u2 and u3 are the same because fragment is ignored
    System.out.println(u2 + (u2.equals(u3)? “ is “ : “ is not “) +
                       “the same as “ + u3);
} catch (MalformedURLException e) {
    e.printStackTrace();
}
```

getContent()

PURPOSE Retrieves the contents identified by this URL.

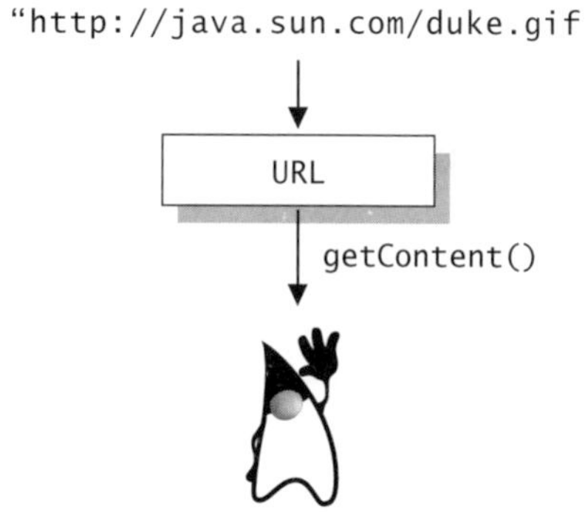

FIGURE 243 **URL.getContent()**

SYNTAX
```
public final Object
   getContent() throws
   IOException
```

DESCRIPTION This method retrieves the contents identified by this URL by first opening a connection to the destination named by the URL (if it has not been opened already) and then getting its contents. The mechanisms used for getting the contents are particular to the protocol and the content handler for that protocol. The use of various content handlers is configurable by the application through the use of the `ContentHandlerFactory`. Figure 243 shows the use of `getContent()` on an HTTP URL to retrieve a GIF image.

RETURNS The contents identified by this URL as an `Object`.

EXCEPTIONS

`IOException` If an IO error has occurred while attempting to get the contents of this URL.

SEE ALSO `ContentHandler`, `ContentHandlerFactory`, `URLConnection.getContent()`.

EXAMPLE See `URL()`, `URLStreamHandler`.

A B C D E F G H I J K L M N O P Q R S T U V W X Y Z

getFile()

PURPOSE Retrieves this URL's file name.

SYNTAX `public String getFile()`

DESCRIPTION The URLs for many protocols, such as FTP and HTTP, contain a file component that names a file or directory within the file system exported by the host of the URL. `getFile()` returns the file component of this URL.

RETURNS This URL's file/directory name.

SEE ALSO `URL()`.

EXAMPLE

```
try {
    URL u = new URL("http://java.sun.com/new.html#_top_");
    String protocol = u.getProtocol(); // "http"
    String host = u.getHost();         // "java.sun.com"
    int port = u.getPort();            // -1 (unspecified)
    String file = u.getFile();         // "new.html"
    String frag = u.getRef();          // "_top_"

    System.out.println(protocol + host + port + file + frag);
} catch (MalformedURLException e) {
    e.printStackTrace();
}
```

getHost()

PURPOSE Retrieves this URL's host name.

SYNTAX `public String getHost()`

DESCRIPTION A URL contains the name of a host to contact to access the resource. `getHost()` returns the name of this host.

RETURNS This URL's host name.

SEE ALSO `URL()`.

EXAMPLE See `getFile()`.

getPort()

PURPOSE Retrieves this URL's port number.

SYNTAX `public int getPort()`

DESCRIPTION A connection to the host of this URL is made to a particular port number. `getPort()` returns the port number that this URL's connection will use. `-1` means the default port number for this URL's protocol will be used.

RETURNS This URL's port number. If `-1`, uses the default port number for this protocol.

SEE ALSO `URL()`.

EXAMPLE See `getFile()`.

getProtocol()

PURPOSE Retrieves this URL's protocol.

SYNTAX `public String getProtocol()`

DESCRIPTION The first component of a URL is its protocol. The protocol component is a string identifier that names the Internet protocol to use to access the resource. Examples of identifiers of common protocols found in URLs are `http`, `gopher`, `ftp`, `news`, `telnet`, and `mailto`. `getProtocol()` returns this protocol identifier.

RETURNS This URL's protocol identifier.

SEE ALSO `URL()`.

EXAMPLE See `getFile()`.

getRef()

PURPOSE Retrieves this URL's reference.

SYNTAX `public String getRef()`

DESCRIPTION The reference field of a URL is the substring that appears after the '#' character. The '#' character may not necessarily be used in all protocols. For HTTP URLs, it is called a *fragment identifier* or *anchor identifier*; it refers to a named location within the document named by the filename component of the URL. `getRef()` returns this fragment identifier.

The reference field can be specified only when the URL constructor that takes a URL string (`spec`) is used. If the URL is constructed by passing the protocol, host name, and filename (and optionally the port number) as separate arguments, the reference is not parsed from the file component.

RETURNS This URL's reference.

SEE ALSO `URL()`.

EXAMPLE See `getFile()`.

hashCode()

PURPOSE Computes the hash code for this URL object.

SYNTAX `public int hashCode()`

DESCRIPTION This method returns the hash code for this URL object. The hash code of a URL is computed using the hash code of its protocol, the hash code of the Internet address of the host, and the hash code of its file. This means that two URLs with the same protocol, hostname, port number, and file fields, but with different reference fields, will have the same hash code.

RETURNS An `int` that represents the hash code of this URL object.

OVERRIDES `Object.hashCode()`.

SEE ALSO `equals()`, `sameFile()`.

EXAMPLE

```
try {
    int[] hits = new int[1023];
    URL u = new URL("http://java.sun.com/");
    int hashval = u.hashCode();
    ++hits[Math.abs(hashval%hits.length)];  // count hits
} catch (MalformedURLException e) {
    e.printStackTrace();
}
```

openConnection()

PURPOSE Opens a connection to the location identified by this URL.

SYNTAX `public URLConnection openConnection()throws IOException`

DESCRIPTION This method opens a connection to the location identified by this URL. Connections that have been opened previously are cached. If a connection to this URL is found in the cache, it is returned; a new one is not created. Creating a connection involves first creating the handler for the URL's protocol and then asking the handler to establish the connection.

RETURNS A connection to the location identified by this URL.

EXCEPTIONS

`IOException` If an IO exception occurred while attempting to open a connection to this URL.

SEE ALSO `URLConnection`, `URLStreamHandler`.

EXAMPLE

```
try {
    URL u = new URL(
        "file://localhost/export/home/java/api/packages.html");
    URLConnection uconn = u.openConnection();
    Object content = uconn.getContent();
    if (content != null) {
        System.out.println("class: " + content.getClass());
        System.out.println("obj: " + content);
    }
} catch (MalformedURLException e) {
    e.printStackTrace();
} catch (IOException e) {
    e.printStackTrace();
}
```

openStream()

PURPOSE Opens an input stream to this URL's connection.

SYNTAX `public final InputStream openStream() throws IOException`

DESCRIPTION This method returns an input stream for reading from the connection of this URL. If this URL's connection is not open, `openStream()` will open it before attempting to retrieve the stream. Closing this URL's connection also closes this input stream.

RETURNS The input stream of this URL's connection.

EXCEPTIONS

`IOException` If an IO exception occurred while attempting to open the input stream.

EXAMPLE See `URL()`.

sameFile()

PURPOSE Determines whether two URLs point to the same file.

SYNTAX `public boolean sameFile(URL other)`

DESCRIPTION This method determines whether two URLs point to the same file. All components of the URL (protocol, host name, port number, and filename) must be equal. The reference component of the URL (i.e., the one following the '#' character) is excluded from the comparison.

PARAMETERS

`other` The URL against which to compare. `other` cannot be `null`.

RETURNS `true` if `other` and this URL both point to the same file; `false` otherwise.

SEE ALSO `equals()`, `URL()`.

EXAMPLE

```
try {
    URL u1 = new URL("http://java.sun.com:80/new.html");
    URL u2 = new URL("http://java.sun.com/new.html");
    URL u3 = new URL("http://java.sun.com/new.html#_top_");
            // u1 and u2 are not the same because of 'port'
    System.out.println(u1 + (u1.sameFile(u2)? " is " : " is not ") +
                         "the same as " + u2);
    // u2 and u3 are the same because fragment is ignored
    System.out.println(u2 + (u2.sameFile(u3)? " is " : " is not ") +
                         "the same as " + u3);

} catch (MalformedURLException e) {
    e.printStackTrace();
}
```

set()

PURPOSE Sets the fields of the URL.

SYNTAX `protected void set(String protocol, String host, int port, String file, String ref)`

DESCRIPTION Subclasses of `URLStreamHandler` use this method to set the various fields of a URL. URL fields are otherwise constant after creation.

PARAMETERS

`protocol` The protocol to use.

`host` The name of the host to which to connect.

`port`	The port number to which to connect.
`file`	The filename on `host`.
`ref`	Additional arguments for operating on `file`.

SEE ALSO `URL()`, `URLStreamHandler`.

setURLStreamHandlerFactory()

PURPOSE Sets the `URLStreamHandler` factory.

SYNTAX
```
public static synchronized void
   setURLStreamHandlerFactory(URLStreamHandlerFactory factory)
```

DESCRIPTION The actual implementation of URL protocol handlers is supplied by a subclass of `URLStreamHandler` and is configurable by the application. `setURLStreamHandlerFactory()` sets `factory` to be the protocol handler factory. `factory` is responsible for creating an instance of (subclasses of) `URLStreamHandler` whenever a handler for a particular protocol is requested.

`setURLStreamHandlerFactory()` can be executed only if permitted by the security manager. If permitted, it can be executed only once during the lifetime of the application.

PARAMETERS

`factory` The URL protocol handler factory to use.

EXCEPTIONS

`Error` If the URL protocol handler factory has already been defined.

`SecurityException`
If not allowed to set the factory due to security reasons.

SEE ALSO `SecurityManager.checkSetFactory()`, `URLStreamHandler`, `URLStreamHandlerFactory`.

EXAMPLE See `URLConnection`, `URLStreamHandler`, and `URLStreamHandlerFactory` for related examples.

```
import java.io.IOException;
import java.net.*;

class Main {
    public static void main(String[] args) {
        URL.setURLStreamHandlerFactory(new TestFactory());
        String host = "localhost";
        if (args.length > 0)
            host = args[0];
        try {
            URL u = new URL("date://" + host);
```

```
                Object content = u.getContent();

                if (content != null) {
                    System.out.println("class: " + content.getClass());
                    System.out.println("obj: " + content);
                }
            } catch (MalformedURLException e) {
                e.printStackTrace();
            } catch (IOException e) {
                e.printStackTrace();
            }
        }
    }
```

toExternalForm()

PURPOSE Generates the string representation for this `URL`.

SYNTAX `public String toExternalForm()`

DESCRIPTION This method returns the string representation of this URL. Typically, this consists of the protocol, host name, port numbers, and filename fields of the URL. Except for the protocol, all other fields may be displayed in a protocol-dependent format. This method is identical to `toString()`.

RETURNS The string representation of this URL.

SEE ALSO `toString()`, `URL()`, `URLStreamHandler.toExternalForm()`.

EXAMPLE

```
try {
    URL u = new URL("http", "java.sun.com", 80, "new.html");
    if (u.toString().equals(u.toExternalForm()))
        System.out.println("external form is same as string form");
    else
        System.out.println("external form is different");
} catch (MalformedURLException e) {
    e.printStackTrace();
}
```

toString()

PURPOSE Generates the string representation for this URL.

SYNTAX `public String toString()`

DESCRIPTION The string representation of a URL consists of its protocol and a protocol-dependent string representation of the rest of the URL. `toString()` returns this string representation. It is identical to `toExternalForm()`.

RETURNS The string representation of this URL.

OVERRIDES `Object.toString()`.

SEE ALSO `toExternalForm()`, `URL()`.

EXAMPLE See `toExternalForm()`.

URL()

PURPOSE Constructs a new `URL` instance.

SYNTAX

```
public URL(String protocol, String host, int port, String file)
   throws MalformedURLException
public URL(String protocol, String host, String file) throws
   MalformedURLException
public URL(String spec) throws MalformedURLException
public URL(URL context, String spec) throws MalformedURLException
```

DESCRIPTION The four forms of the constructor of the `URL` class create a URL from the information supplied. The first two forms create a URL for the protocol `protocol` to host `host` at the port number `port`. If `port` is not supplied, the default port number for `protocol` is used. For example, for the HTTP protocol, the default port is `80`. `file` specifies the pathname and any arguments to use after reaching the host. `file` is parsed into a file pathname and arguments (if any) that occur after the hash character ('#') (these are recorded as the *reference* of the URL).

The last two forms construct a URL by parsing the URL string `spec`. An example of `spec` is `http://www.widget.com/cgi-bin/123.cgi#urllist`. This string gets parsed into a URL with host `www.widget.com`, default port `-1`, file `cgi-bin/123.cgi`, and reference `urllist`. If `context` is specified and non-`null`, it identifies the context in which to parse and construct the new URL if `spec` is a relative URL. If `spec` is an absolute URL (like in the previous example), `context` is ignored. If `context` is not specified or is `null`, `spec` must be an absolute URL. For example, if `context` is the URL `http://www.widget.com/cgi-bin/`, and `spec` is `formX`, the new URL would be `http://www.widget.com/cgi-bin/formX`.

Once a URL has been constructed, you can then open a connection to the location pointed to by the URL and read the data from that location.

URL()

PARAMETERS

`context`	The context to interpret `spec` if `spec` is a relative URL. If `null`, `spec` must be an absolute URL.
`host`	The name of the host to which to connect.
`file`	The file pathname (and any arguments) to use after reaching the host.
`port`	The port number to use.
`protocol`	The protocol to use.
`spec`	The URL string to parse.

EXCEPTIONS

`MalformedURLException`
If the protocol (either `protocol` or that determined from `spec`) is unspecified (`null`) or a protocol handler could not be found for it.

SEE ALSO `openConnection()`, `getContent()`, `URLStreamHandler.parseURL()`.

EXAMPLE

```
try {
    String protocol = "file";
    String host = "localhost";
    int port = 0;
    String file = "/export/home/java/api/packages.html";

    URL u1 = new URL(protocol, host, port, file);
    URL u2 = new URL(protocol, host, file);
    URL u3 = new URL(protocol + "://" + host + "/");
    URL u4 = new URL(u3, file + "#_top_");

    Object content = u4.getContent();
    if (content != null) {
        System.out.println("class: " + content.getClass());
        System.out.println("obj: " + content);
    }
    InputStream in = u4.openStream();
    if (in != null) {
        for(int c = in.read(); c > 0; c = in.read()) {
            System.out.print((char)c);
        }
    }
} catch (MalformedURLException e) {
    e.printStackTrace();
} catch (IOException e) {
    e.printStackTrace();
}
```

URLConnection

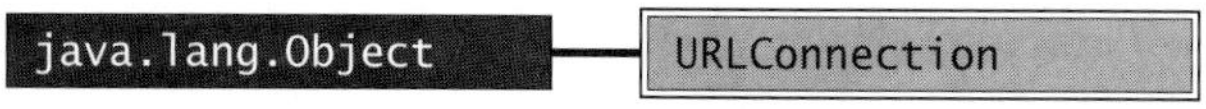

Syntax

```
abstract public class URLConnection
```

Description

The `URLConnection` class represents an active connection to the resource identified by a URL. It is an abstract class that must be subclassed to provide an implementation of `connect()`.

A `URLConnection` object goes through the following steps:

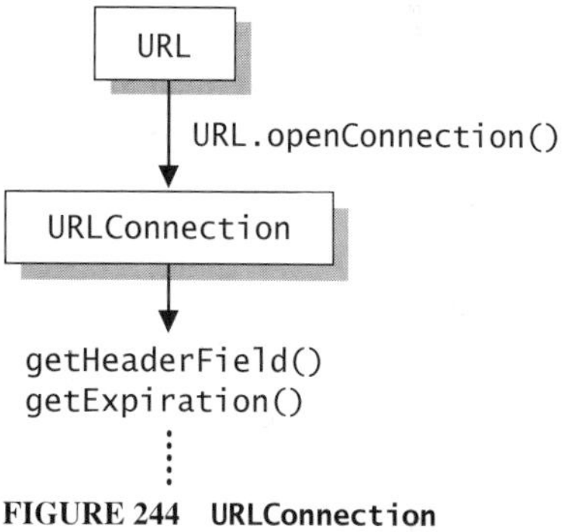

FIGURE 244 **`URLConnection`**

1. The `URLConnection` object is created for a particular URL.
2. (optional) Various options or characteristics about this connection are set.
3. A connection is established to the host destination named by the URL using the protocol specified.
4. A request is constructed using the information in the URL, the properties and characteristics of the connection, and information about the user and client environment making the request. The request is sent through the connection to the destination.
5. A response is received from the connection. Headers describing the response and its contents are decoded and returned to the caller.
6. The connection is closed.

Step 2 is accomplished through the use of the many get/set methods provided by the `URLConnection` class. These settings can be changed only prior to connection establishment. The implementation of `connect()` has responsibility for Steps 3–4. Step 5 is performed by the various methods for getting header fields and `getContent()`, whose particular implementation is determined by the type of content to be obtained.

Although this class could be used for other protocols, as is evident by the methods supported by `URLConnection`, it is designed to support HTTP in particular.

Protocol or Stream Handlers

`URLConnection` is an abstract class, so what provides the actual implementations for `URLConnection`? The answer is URL protocol handlers. Different protocols, by definition, specify different ways in which the client and server of a connection interact. Consequently, individual URL protocol handlers (`URLStreamHandler`) define their own implementations of `URLConnection` and create their own instances of a `URLConnection` in response to a request to open a connection to the resource specified by a given URL.

The selection of the particular implementation of protocol handlers used by a program is configurable by the program via the use of `URL.setURLStreamHandlerFactory()`.

useCaches

Some protocols support caching of documents. Occasionally, it is necessary to bypass the cache; for example, when reloading the document upon explicit directions from the user (e.g., support for the Reload button in a Web browser). When the `useCaches` flag is set on a connection, caches can be used by the protocol handler; otherwise caches are bypassed. An enabled `useCaches` does not mean the protocol handler *will* use caches. Some protocol handlers do not use caches at all. This flag indicates only that *if* the protocol handler does support caching, then it is allowed to use caches. The setting of this flag does not affect protocol handlers that have no caching support.

The `URLConnection` class provides methods for setting and getting the default value of this flag that all new URL connections will have. It also provides methods for getting and setting this flag for individual connections. Note that this flag can be set only before the connection has been established. Once the connection has been established, attempting to change the `useCaches` flag results in an error.

The `useCaches` setting is consulted when the protocol handler is constructing the request header (if caching is relevant for that protocol).

If-Modified-Since

For efficiency, some protocols allow reuse of documents even if the uncached copy (on the server) has been modified, within some specified grace period. The time when the document must be re-fetched is referred to as the `If-Modified-Since` time. Documents that have been modified before the `If-Modified-Since` time are not re-fetched. Documents that have been modified after the `If-Modified-Since` time must be re-fetched.

The `URLConnection` class provides methods for setting this modification time limit for a connection.

The `If-Modified-Since` setting is consulted when the protocol handler is constructing the request header (if the `If-Modified-Since` time is relevant for that protocol).

allowUserInteraction

Some connections require interaction with the user. For example, the user might need to fill in fields in a form or enter a password for a particular connection. The `URLConnection` class provides an `allowUserInteraction` flag and set/get methods for determining whether such interaction is allowed. This setting is consulted when processing the response.

HTTP Request Headers

An http request consists of the *method* to apply to the object (named by a URL), a *header* part, and a content part. The header contains *request header fields* that indicate to the server certain information about the client making the request, as well as information about the request itself. These fields are encoded in the RFC822 header style. A summary of the request header fields is given in Table 19.

TABLE 19 HTTP Request Header Fields

`Accept:` *`type/subtype`*	List of MIME content types acceptable to the client.
`Accept-Encoding:` *`type`*	List of data encoding types acceptable to the client.
`Accept-Language:` *`lang`*	List of languages preferred by the client.
`Authorization:` *`authinf`*	User authentication information and encryption scheme.
`Charge-To:` *`accountInf`*	Account information (format TBD).
`Content-Length:` *`length`*	Length of contents in bytes.
`Content-Type:` *`type/subtype`*	MIME content type of this message.
`From:` *`email_address`*	Email address of the user making the request.
`If-Modified-Since:` *`date`*	Directs that if the document requested hasn't changed since `date`, don't send it.
`Pragma:` *`server_directive`*	Special instructions to the server (e.g., `no-cache`).
`Referer:` *`URL`*	URL of the document from which this request originated.
`User-Agent:` *`product/vers`*	Product name and version number of the client software.

The `Accept`, `Accept-Encoding`, and `Accept-Language` fields are semicolon-separated lists and may appear more than once in the header. If the `Accept` field is absent, the client is assumed to be able to accept `text/plain` and `text/html`. All of these fields are optional.

The `useCaches` flag of the `URLConnection` class can be used to construct the no-cache `Pragma` field. The connection's `If-Modified-Since` time is used to construct the `If-Modified-Since` header field. Other header fields can be constructed using the get/set request property methods.

HTTP Response Header

Once an HTTP request has been sent through the URL connection, the server at the other end of the connection sends back an HTTP response. This response consists of the HTTP version number and a status code for the request. This is followed by (applicable) response header fields, which are given in Table 20, and then by the response data.

Description

TABLE 20 HTTP Response Header Fields[a]

`Allowed: methods*`	List of request methods the user is allowed to issue for this URL.
`Content-Encoding: type`	Encoding of this response message (`x-compress` or `x-gzip`).
`Content-Language: lang`	Language in which this response message is written.
`Content-Length: length`	Length of this response message.
`Content-Transfer-Encoding: type`	Encoding used for the MIME messages (default is 8-bit character encoding).
`Content-Type: type/subtype`	MIME content type of this document.
`Cost: TBS`	The cost of retrieving this document.
`Date: date`	Creation time (in GMT) of this document.
`Derived-From: verid`	The version of the document from which this document is derived.
`Expires: date`	Time (in GMT) at which this document expires and should be refetched.
`Last-Modified: date`	Last modified time (in GMT) of this document.
`Message-ID: URI`	Unique identifier for this message.
`Public: method*`	List of request methods anyone is allowed to issue for this URL.
`Title: string`	The title of this document.
`URI: url`	The URL of this document.
`Version: verid`	String identifying the version of this document.
`WWW-Authenticate: auth`	Encryption and authorization schemes the server wants to use.
`WWW-Link: href`	HTML link reference of this document.

a. This list is obtained from the HTTP/2.0 draft. There may be differences between this list and that of HTTP/1.0.

The `URLConnection` class provides methods that retrieve the common header fields (such as content types, length, and date) and generic methods for retrieving arbitrary header fields.

For a full discussion of the HTTP protocol, see

`http://www.w3.org/hypertext/WWW/Protocols/HTTP/HTTP2.html`

Content Handlers

Once a response header has been retrieved from a URL connection, its contents must be processed. The header information (more specifically, `Content-Type`) is used to determine which content handler to invoke to process the contents. If the `Content-Type` header field is missing from the response or if the field contains the wrong type, some heuristics are applied to "guess" the type of the response.

The `getContent()` method, whose implementation is provided by individual content handlers, processes the response data and generates an object of the appropriate type. For example, response data that is an image gets turned into an object of class `Image`. Typically, the program invokes `URL.getContent()`, which opens the URL connection and invokes `URLConnection.getContent()`.

The selection of the particular implementation of content handlers used by a program is configurable by the program via the use of `setContentHandlerFactory()`. If a program has not configured a content handler factory, then by default a content handler is defined to come from a package listed in the `java.content.handler.pkgs` property. This property contains a list of package prefixes, each separated by '|'; each package prefix in the property is tried in the order specified. The default package prefix is `sun.net.www.content.` Each content handler is defined in a class whose name is derived from its corresponding MIME type (i.e., the '/' is changed to '.'). For example, the handler for content with MIME type `text.html` will have the fully qualified name of

```
sun.net.www.content.text.html
```

MEMBER SUMMARY

Constructor	
`URLConnection()`	Constructs a URL connection.
Connection Establishment Fields and Methods	
`connect()`	Establishes this URL connection.
`connected`	Indicates whether connection has been established.
Content Processing Methods	
`getContent()`	Retrieves the contents of this URL as an object.
`getInputStream()`	Creates an input stream for reading from this connection.
`getOutputStream()`	Creates an output stream for writing to this connection.
`setContentHandlerFactory()`	Sets the content handler factory for this program.
`guessContentTypeFromName()`	Guesses the content type from its filename extension.
`guessContentTypeFromStream()`	Guesses the content type by inspecting the contents.

Continued

Description

MEMBER SUMMARY	
Response Header Methods	
getContentEncoding()	Retrieves the content encoding type of the response data.
getContentLength()	Retrieves the content length of the response data.
getContentType()	Retrieves the content type of the response data.
getDate()	Retrieves the creation date of the response data.
getExpiration()	Retrieves the expiration date of the response data.
getHeaderField()	Retrieves a header field from the response.
getHeaderFieldDate()	Retrieves a header field and parses its value as a GMT date.
getHeaderFieldInt()	Retrieves a header field and parses its value as an integer.
getHeaderFieldKey()	Retrieves the nth header field name.
getLastModified()	Retrieves the last modification date of the response data.
Request Header Methods	
getDefaultRequestProperty()	Retrieves the default value of a request header field for future connections.
getRequestProperty()	Retrieves the value of a request header field for this connection.
setDefaultRequestProperty()	Sets the default value for a request header field for future connections.
setRequestProperty()	Sets the value of a request header field for this connection.
Cache Field and Methods	
getDefaultUseCaches()	Determines if by default future connections can use caches.
getUseCaches()	Determines if this connection allows the use of caches.
setDefaultUseCaches()	Sets the default cache usage flag for future connections.
setUseCaches()	Sets the cache usage flag of this connection.
useCaches	Indicates whether this connection allows the use of caches.
If-Modified-Since Field and Methods	
getIfModifiedSince()	Retrieves the modification time that forces re-fetching of the document.
ifModifiedSince	Indicates that documents modified after this time must be re-fetched.
setIfModifiedSince()	Sets the modification time that forces re-fetching of the document.

MEMBER SUMMARY	
User Interaction Field and Methods	
`allowUserInteraction`	Indicates whether user interaction is allowed for this connection.
`getAllowUserInteraction()`	Determines if user interaction is allowed for this connection.
`getDefaultAllowUserInteraction()`	Determines if by default future connections will allow user interaction.
`setAllowUserInteraction()`	Sets the user interaction flag for this connection.
`setDefaultAllowUserInteraction()`	Sets the default user interaction flag for future connections.
User Input/Output Fields and Methods	
`doInput`	Indicates whether input is planned from this connection.
`doOutput`	Indicates whether output is planned to this connection.
`getDoInput()`	Determines whether input is planned from this connection.
`getDoOutput()`	Determines whether output is planned to this connection.
`setDoInput()`	Sets the indication of whether input from this connection is planned.
`setDoOutput()`	Sets the indication of whether output to this connection is planned.
URL Field and Method	
`url`	The URL associated with this connection.
`getURL()`	Retrieves the URL associated with this connection.
Description Method	
`toString()`	Generates the string representation of this object.

See Also

`URL`, `URL.getContent()`, `URL.setURLStreamHandlerFactory`, `URLContentHandler`, `URLContentHandlerFactory`, `URLStreamHandler`, `URLStreamHandlerFactory`.

Example

This example shows an implementation of a `URLConnection` for the Internet `daytime` protocol (port `13`), which uses UDP to return the time of day in a string in GMT format.

Example

DateURLConnection defines two methods: connect() and getContent(). connect() makes a connection to the host named in the URL, while getContent() reads the current date from the host and returns the answer in the form of a Date object. getContent() overrides the URLConnection.getContent() because it does not handle contents in the same style as HTTP does. Most methods in URLConnection, such as those related to content headers and input/output streams, are not relevant for this simple protocol.

See related examples in URLStreamHandler, URLStreamHandlerFactory, and URL.setURLStreamHandlerFactory() for how a program makes use of DateURLConnection.

```
import java.net.*;
import java.io.*;
import java.util.Date;

public class DateURLConnection extends URLConnection {
    DatagramSocket sock = null;
    public DateURLConnection(URL u) {
        super(u);
    }
    public void connect() throws IOException {
        InetAddress dst = InetAddress.getByName(getURL().getHost());
        byte[] outbuf = new byte[1];
        outbuf[0] = '\n';
        int port;
        if ((port = getURL().getPort()) == -1)
            port = 13;          // daytime

        DatagramPacket request =
            new DatagramPacket(outbuf, outbuf.length, dst, port);
        try {
            sock = new DatagramSocket();
            sock.send(request);
            connected = true;
        } catch (SocketException e) {
            sock = null;
            throw e;
        }
    }
    public Object getContent() throws IOException {
        if (!connected)
            connect();

        byte[] inbuf = new byte[256];  // default size
        DatagramPacket reply =
            new DatagramPacket(inbuf, inbuf.length);
        sock.receive(reply);
        sock.close();
        sock = null;
        connected = false;
        String dateStr = new String(reply.getData(), 0);
```

```
        if (dateStr != null)
            return (new Date(dateStr));

        return (null);
    }
}
```


allowUserInteraction

PURPOSE Indicates whether this URL connection allows user interaction.

SYNTAX `protected boolean allowUserInteraction`

DESCRIPTION This field records whether this URL connection allows interaction with the user. If `allowUserInteraction` is `true`, interaction is allowed; if `false`, interaction is not allowed. The default value for `allowUserInteraction` is `false` unless the default has been modified earlier in the program via `setDefaultAllowUserInteraction()`. `getDefaultAllowUserInteraction()` can be used to examine the default setting of `allowUserInteraction`.

This field should be accessed and manipulated through the `getAllowUserInteraction()` and `setAllowUserInteraction()` methods, respectively.

SEE ALSO `getDefaultAllowUserInteraction()`, `getAllowUserInteraction()`, `setDefaultAllowUserInteraction()`, `setAllowUserInteraction()`.

RETURNS `true` if this URL connection allows user interaction; `false` otherwise.

connect()

PURPOSE Establishes this URL connection.

SYNTAX `abstract public void connect() throws IOException`

DESCRIPTION After a `URLConnection` object has been created and (optionally) after various options (such as `useCaches` and `allowUserInteraction`) have been set, the connection can be established via a call to `connect()`. The implementation of this abstract method is provided by the `URLStreamHandler` for the protocol identified in the URL of this connection. The connection is established to the host and port number identified in the URL. A request is then sent to the connection. The request consists of information derived from the rest of the URL,

A B C D E F G H I J K L M N O P Q R S T U V W X Y Z

option settings on this connection, and user and client information. The particulars of the request depend on the protocol. A response is then returned from the connection. `connect()` is responsible for getting the connection to a state so that a subsequent call to `getContent()` will retrieve the contents of the response as an object. The steps required to achieve this are protocol-dependent.

Certain calls will call `connect()` automatically if their semantics are such that they make sense only after `connect()` has been called (e.g., `getContent()`, `getContentLength()`, `getInputStream()`).

The implementation of `connect()` should be idempotent, that is, if connection has already been established, `connect()` does not do anything. After a connection has been successfully established, it should set the field `connected` to `true`.

EXCEPTIONS

`IOException` If an IO error occurred while attempting to establish the connection.

SEE ALSO `connected`, `URLStreamHandler`.

EXAMPLE See the class example.

connected

PURPOSE The connected status of this URL connection.

SYNTAX `protected boolean connected`

DESCRIPTION A URL connection is first created and then connected. This field records whether this URL connection has been connected. If it has been, `connected` is `true`; otherwise it is `false`.

SEE ALSO `connect()`.

EXAMPLE See the class example.

doInput

PURPOSE Indicates whether this URL connection will be used for input.

SYNTAX `protected boolean doInput`

DESCRIPTION A URL connection can be used for input, output, or both. This field records whether this connection will be used for input. By default, it is `true` .

This field should be examined and manipulated through the use of the methods `getDoInput()` and `setDoInput()`, respectively.

SEE ALSO `getDoInput()`, `setDoInput()`.

doOutput

PURPOSE Indicates whether this URL connection will be used for output.

SYNTAX `protected boolean doOutput`

DESCRIPTION A URL connection can be used for input, output, or both. This field records whether this connection will be used for output. By default, it is `false`.

This field should be examined and manipulated through the use of the methods `getDoOutput()` and `setDoOutput()`, respectively.

SEE ALSO `getDoOutput()`, `setDoOutput()`.

getAllowUserInteraction()

PURPOSE Determines whether this URL connection allows user interaction.

SYNTAX `public boolean getAllowUserInteraction()`

DESCRIPTION This method returns a `boolean` flag indicating whether this connection allows user interaction. This flag can be changed prior to the connection's being established (before `connect()` is called) by using `setAllowUserInteraction()`.

RETURNS `true` if this connection allows user interaction; `false` otherwise.

SEE ALSO `getDefaultAllowUserInteraction()`, `setDefaultAllowUserInteraction()`, `setDefaultAllowUserInteraction()`, `allowUserInteraction`.

getContent()

PURPOSE Retrieves the contents of this connection's response as an object.

SYNTAX `public Object getContent() throws IOException`

DESCRIPTION	The particular implementation of this method is determined by the content handler selected for the content type of the response (obtained from the response header). The particular content handler implementation is determined by the content handler factory, which is set once by the program using the method `setContentHandlerFactory()`.
	`getContent()` returns an object whose class is determined by its content type. For example, a content with type `image` generates an object of subclass of `Image`; a content with type `text` generates an object of class `String`. The `instanceOf` operator should be used to determine the class of the object.
EXCEPTIONS	
`IOException`	If an IO error occurred while retrieving the contents.
SEE ALSO	`ContentHandler`, `ContentHandlerFactory`, `setContentHandlerFactory()`.
EXAMPLE	See the class example.

getContentEncoding()

PURPOSE	Retrieves the content encoding type of the response data.
SYNTAX	`public String getContentEncoding()`
DESCRIPTION	This method returns the content encoding type of the response data. The encoding type is obtained by examining the `Content-Encoding` header field in the response header. Currently, only two encodings are used in HTTP: `x-compress` and `x-gzip`. This method returns `null` if the `Content-Encoding` header field is not in the response.
RETURNS	An identifier specifying how the response data is encoded; `null` if this was not specified in the response.
SEE ALSO	`getContentType()`.

getContentLength()

PURPOSE	Retrieves the content length of the response data.
SYNTAX	`public int getContentLength()`
DESCRIPTION	This method returns the content length of the response data, in bytes. The length is obtained by examining the `Content-Length` header field in the

response header. If the header does not contain a `Content-Length` header field, this method returns `-1`. The end of the response data in HTTP is always indicated by a blank line (contains only one carriage return).

RETURNS The length of the response data, in bytes; `-1` if unknown.

SEE ALSO `getContentType()`.

getContentType()

PURPOSE Retrieves the content type of the response data.

SYNTAX `public String getContentType()`

DESCRIPTION This method returns the MIME type of the response data. The MIME type is specified in the `Content-Type` header field and has the form *type/subtype*. For example, `text/html` has type `text` and subtype `html`. If no `Content-Type` header field is found, this method returns `null`.

RETURNS The MIME content type of the response data; `null` if unknown.

SEE ALSO `guessContentTypeFromName()`, `guessContentTypeFromStream()`.

getDate()

PURPOSE Retrieves the creation date of the response data.

SYNTAX `public long getDate()`

DESCRIPTION This method returns the creation date of the response data by examining the `Date` header field in the response. If no `Date` header field is found, it returns `0`.

RETURNS The creation date in number of milliseconds since epoch; `0` if unknown.

SEE ALSO `Date`, `getExpiration()`, `getLastModified()`.

getDefaultAllowUserInteraction()

PURPOSE Determines whether new URL connections by default allow user interaction.

SYNTAX `public static boolean getDefaultAllowUserInteraction()`

DESCRIPTION This method returns a `boolean` flag indicating whether URL connections created in the future can by default allow user interaction. This may not

A B C D E F G H I J K L M N O P Q R S T U V W X Y Z

	necessarily be the same as what this URL connection allows. `getAllowUserInteraction()` can be used to find out whether this URL connection allows user interaction.
RETURNS	`true` if by default new connections allow user interaction; `false` if by default new connections do not allow user interaction.
SEE ALSO	`getAllowUserInteraction()`, `setDefaultAllowUserInteraction()`, `setAllowUserInteraction()`, `allowUserInteraction`.

getDefaultRequestProperty()

PURPOSE	Retrieves the default value of a request header field for future connections.
SYNTAX	`public static String getDefaultRequestProperty(String field)`
DESCRIPTION	This method returns the default value of the request header field `field` that will be used for future URL connections. When a new URL connection is created, it gets initialized with these default request header fields. Table 19 contains examples of request header fields. This method returns `null` if `field` does not have a default value.
PARAMETERS	
`field`	The name of the request header field.
RETURNS	The default value of `field`; `null` if it does not have a default value.
SEE ALSO	`setDefaultRequestProperty()`.

getDefaultUseCaches()

PURPOSE	Determines whether new URL connections can use caches by default.
SYNTAX	`public boolean getDefaultUseCaches()`
DESCRIPTION	This method returns a `boolean` flag indicating whether URL connections created in the future can use caches by default. This may not necessarily be the same as what this URL connection allows. `getUseCaches()` can be used to find out whether this URL connection can use caches.
RETURNS	`true` if by default new connections can use caches; `false` otherwise.
SEE ALSO	`getUseCaches()`, `setDefaultUseCaches()`, `setUseCaches()`, `useCaches`.

getDoInput()

PURPOSE Determines whether this connection intends to do any input.

SYNTAX `public boolean getDoInput()`

DESCRIPTION This method returns a `boolean` flag indicating whether this connection intends to do any input. This flag can be changed prior to the connection's being established (before `connect()` is called) by using `setDoInput()`.

RETURNS `true` if this connection intends to do input; `false` otherwise.

SEE ALSO `setDoInput()`, `doInput`.

getDoOutput()

PURPOSE Determines whether this connection intends to do any output.

SYNTAX `public boolean getDoOutput()`

DESCRIPTION This method returns a `boolean` flag indicating whether this connection intends to do any output. This flag can be changed prior to the connection's being established (before `connect()` is called) by using `setDoOutput()`.

RETURNS `true` if this connection intends to do output; `false` otherwise.

SEE ALSO `setDoOutput()`, `doOutput`.

getExpiration()

PURPOSE Retrieves the expiration date of the response data.

SYNTAX `public long getExpiration()`

DESCRIPTION This method returns the expiration date of the response data by examining the `Expires` header field in the response. If no `Expires` header field is found, it returns `0`. This date can be used by systems that implement caching to know when the data needs to be flushed from the cache.

RETURNS The expiration date in number of milliseconds since epoch; `0` if unknown.

SEE ALSO `Date. getDate()`, `getLastModified()`.

getHeaderField()

PURPOSE Retrieves a header field from the response header.

SYNTAX
```
public String getHeaderField(int posn)
public String getHeaderField(String field)
```

DESCRIPTION The two forms of this method retrieve the header field value identified from the response header. The first form returns the value of the header field at position `posn`. If there are fewer than `posn` fields, this method returns `null`. This method can be used in conjunction with `getHeaderFieldKey()` to iterate through all the response header fields in the message.

The second form returns the value of the header field named `field`. If no such field exists, it returns `null`.

PARAMETERS

`field` The name of the header field value to fetch.

`posn` The position of the header field value to fetch; the first field has position 0.

RETURNS The value of the header field specified; `null` if no such header field exists.

SEE ALSO `getHeaderFieldDate()`, `getHeaderFieldInt()`, `getHeaderFieldKey()`.

getHeaderFieldDate()

PURPOSE Retrieves a response header field and parses its value as a GMT date.

SYNTAX
```
public long getHeaderFieldDate(String field, long default)
```

DESCRIPTION This method retrieves the response header field from the response with name `field` and parses its value as a GMT date. It then returns this date value as the number of milliseconds since epoch. If `field` is not found, `default` is returned.

This method can be overridden by implementations that support preparsed headers and hence bypass the parsing altogether.

PARAMETERS

`default` The value to return if `field` is not in the response header.

`field` The name of the header field.

RETURNS The date value (in number of milliseconds since epoch) of the header field `field`; `default` if `field` is not found in the response header or if the value of `field` cannot be parsed into a date.

SEE ALSO `Date`, `getHeaderField()`, `getHeaderFieldInt()`.

getHeaderFieldInt()

PURPOSE Retrieves a response header field and parses its value as an integer.

SYNTAX
```
public int getHeaderFieldInt(String field, int default)
```

DESCRIPTION This method retrieves the response header field with name `field`, parses its value as an integer, and returns that value as an `int`. If `field` is not found, `default` is returned.

This method can be overridden by implementations that support preparsed headers and hence bypass the parsing altogether.

PARAMETERS

`default` The value to return if `field` is not in the response header.

`field` The name of the header field.

RETURNS The value of the header field `field` as an `int`; `default` if `field` is not found in the response header or if the value of `field` cannot be parsed into an `int`.

SEE ALSO `getHeaderField()`, `getHeaderFieldDate()`.

getHeaderFieldKey()

PURPOSE Retrieves the header field at the specified position in the response header.

SYNTAX
```
public String getHeaderFieldKey(int posn)
```

DESCRIPTION This method returns the name of the header field at position `posn` from the response header (e.g., "content-type"). If there are fewer than `posn` fields, this method returns `null`. This method can be used in conjunction with `getHeaderField()` to iterate through all the response header fields in the message.

PARAMETERS

`posn` The position of the header field to fetch; the first field has position 0.

RETURNS The name of the header field at position `posn`; `null` if there are fewer than `posn` fields.

SEE ALSO `getHeaderFieldDate()`, `getHeaderFieldInt()`, `getHeaderField()`.

getIfModifiedSince()

PURPOSE Retrieves the modification time that forces refetching of the document.

SYNTAX `public long getIfModifiedSince()`

DESCRIPTION This method returns the `if-modified-since` time of this connection (if the protocol associated with this connection makes use of `if-modified-since` times). This time is placed into the request header to indicate to the server that it should skip returning the document if the document has not been modified since the `if-modified-since` time. This value can be set and modified prior to the connection's being established (before `connect()` is called) by using `setIfModifiedSince()`.

RETURNS The `if-modified-since` time of this connection in milliseconds since epoch.

SEE ALSO `Date`, `if-modified-since`, `setIfModifiedSince()`.

getInputStream()

PURPOSE Creates an input stream for reading from this connection.

SYNTAX `public InputStream getInputStream() throws IOException`

DESCRIPTION This method creates an input stream from this URL connection. It must be overridden by protocol implementations that support reading input from the connection. This method should establish a connection with the server of the URL, if one has not been done yet.

RETURNS An input stream for reading from the connection.

EXCEPTIONS
`UnknownServiceException`
This protocol does not support input.

SEE ALSO `getContent()`, `getOutputStream()`.

getLastModified()

PURPOSE Retrieves the last modified date of the response data.

SYNTAX `public long getLastModified()`

DESCRIPTION This method returns the last modified date of the response data by examining the `Last-Modified` header field in the response. If no `Last-Modified` header field is found, it returns `0`.

RETURNS The last modified date in number of milliseconds since epoch; `0` if unknown.

SEE ALSO `Date`, `getDate()`, `getExpiration()`.

getOutputStream()

PURPOSE Creates an output stream for writing to this connection.

SYNTAX `public InputStream getInputStream() throws IOException`

DESCRIPTION This method creates an output stream for writing to this URL connection. It must be overridden by protocol implementations that support writing to the connection. This method should establish a connection to the server of the URL, if one has not been done yet.

RETURNS An output stream for writing to the connection.

EXCEPTIONS
`UnknownServiceException`
This protocol does not support output.

SEE ALSO `getContent()`, `getInputStream()`.

getRequestProperty()

PURPOSE Retrieves the value of a request header field for this connection.

SYNTAX `public String getRequestProperty(String field)`

DESCRIPTION This method returns the value of the request header field `field`. If there is no value for `field`, this method returns `null`. Table 19 contains examples of request header fields. The value of `field` can be changed prior to the connection's being established (before `connect()` is called) by using `setRequestProperty()`.

RETURNS The value of `field`; `null` if not found.

SEE ALSO `getDefaultRequestProperty()`, `setDefaultRequestProperty()`, `setRequestProperty()`.

A B C D E F G H I J K L M N O P Q R S T U V W X Y Z

getURL()

PURPOSE Retrieves the URL for this connection.

SYNTAX `public URL getURL()`

DESCRIPTION This method returns the URL of this connection. It is set initially by the `URLConnection` constructor and typically remains unchanged for the duration of the connection.

PARAMETERS

RETURNS The URL for this connection.

SEE ALSO `url`, `URLConnection()`.

getUseCaches()

PURPOSE Determines whether this connection allows caches to be used.

SYNTAX `public boolean getUseCaches()`

DESCRIPTION This method returns a `boolean` flag indicating whether this connection allows caches to be used. This flag can be changed prior to the connection's being established (before `connect()` is called) by using `setUseCaches()`.

RETURNS `true` if this connection can use caches; `false` otherwise.

SEE ALSO `getDefaultUseCaches()`, `setDefaultUseCaches()`, `setUseCaches()`, `useCaches`.

guessContentTypeFromName()

PURPOSE Guesses the content type by looking at the filename extension.

SYNTAX `protected static String guessContentTypeFromName(String url)`

DESCRIPTION This method extracts the file pathname component of the URL string `url` and examines the filename extension of that pathname to determine the content type of the document named by that URL. Any fragment identifier (follows the '#') is removed from the URL in order to find the filename extension. For example, a filename extension of 'html' or 'htm' results in the content-type of "text/html"; a filename extension of 'jpeg' or 'jpg' results in the content type of "image/jpeg".

`getContentType()` should be used to determine the content type of the response. However, sometimes the `Content-Type` field is not present. Hence this heuristic must be used to guess its type.

PARAMETERS

`url` The URL string to use for guessing.

RETURNS The MIME type deduced from the filename extension; `null` if the method cannot guess.

SEE ALSO `getContentType()`, `guessContentTypeFromStream()`.

guessContentTypeFromStream()

PURPOSE Guesses the content type by inspecting the contents of the document.

SYNTAX

```
static protected String
   guessContentTypeFromStream(InputStream stream)
   throws IOException
```

DESCRIPTION This method is used to guess the content type of a document by inspecting its contents. The bytes at the beginning of the document are examined loosely. The document is accessed via the input stream `stream`. `stream` must support `mark()` and `reset()` in order for this method to work. You can use `BufferedInputStream` as one of the filters to `stream` in order to enable `mark()/reset()` support.

This method is used in two cases. In the first, the document is lacking a `Content-Type` header field. In the second, the document contains an incorrect header field and `guessContentTypeFromName()` is not sufficient because of the use of nonstandard filename extensions. Use of this method allows the system to be able to recover from these problems.

PARAMETERS

`stream` The stream to read to inspect the contents.

RETURNS The MIME type deduced from the contents of the stream; `null` if the method cannot guess.

EXCEPTIONS

`IOException` If an IO error occurred while reading from `stream`.

SEE ALSO `BufferedInputStream`, `getContentType()`, `guessContentTypeFromName()`, `InputStream`.

setAllowUserInteraction()

PURPOSE Sets whether user interaction is allowed.

SYNTAX `public void setAllowUserInteraction(boolean allows)`

DESCRIPTION This method is used to indicate whether this connection allows user interaction. It can be invoked after the URL connection has been created but before the connection has been established (i.e., before `connect()` has been invoked on it).

PARAMETERS

`allows` A `boolean` flag indicating whether to allow user interaction. `true` means allow user interaction; `false` means do not allow user interaction.

EXCEPTIONS

`IllegalAccessError`

If this method is called after the connection has already been established.

SEE ALSO `allowUserInteraction`, `getDefaultAllowUserInteraction()`, `getAllowUserInteraction()`, `setDefaultAllowUserInteraction()`.

setContentHandlerFactory()

PURPOSE Sets the content handler factory.

SYNTAX

```
public static synchronized void
   setContentHandlerFactory(ContentHandlerFactory factory)
```

DESCRIPTION A content handler processes the content in the response data of a URL connection and generates an object representing that data. The actual implementation of content handlers is supplied by a subclass of `ContentHandler` and is configurable by the application. `setContentHandlerFactory()` sets `factory` to be the content handler factory. `factory` is responsible for creating an instance of (subclasses of) `ContentHandler` whenever a handler for a particular content type is requested.

`setContentHandlerFactory()` can be executed only if permitted by the security manager. If permitted, it can be executed only once during the lifetime of the application.

PARAMETERS

`factory` The content handler factory to use.

EXCEPTIONS

`Error` If the content handler factory has already been defined.

`SecurityException`
If not allowed to set the factory due to security reasons.

SEE ALSO `SecurityManager.checkSetFactory()`, `ContentHandler`, `ContentHandlerFactory`.

EXAMPLE This example sets the content handler factory to be `SampleFactory`. (See related examples in `ContentHandler` and `ContentHandlerFactory`.)

```
class Main {
    public static void main(String[] args) {

        if (args.length != 1) {
            System.err.println("Usage: java Main <URL>");
            System.exit(1);
        }

        // Configure system to use our own factory
        URLConnection.setContentHandlerFactory(new SampleFactory());
        try {
            URL url = new URL(args[0]);

            Object obj = url.getContent();
            if (obj != null) {
                System.out.println("class: " + obj.getClass());
                System.out.println("obj: " + obj);
            }
        } catch (MalformedURLException e) {
            e.printStackTrace();
        } catch (IOException e) {
            e.printStackTrace();
        }
    };
}
```

setDefaultAllowUserInteraction()

PURPOSE public static void setDefaultAllowUserInteraction(boolean allows)

DESCRIPTION This method sets the default flag for whether newly created URL connections allow user interaction. It applies to all new URL connections that will be created in the future. It does not apply to the current URL connection because this URL connection has already been created. The allow user interaction status of this URL connection can be modified only via `setAllowUserInteraction()`.

PARAMETERS

`allows` A `boolean` flag indicating whether to allow user interaction by default for all new URL connections. `true` means allow user interaction; `false` means do not allow user interaction.

SEE ALSO `allowUserInteraction`, `getDefaultAllowUserInteraction()`, `getAllowUserInteraction()`, `setAllowUserInteraction()`.

setDefaultRequestProperty()

PURPOSE Sets the default value of a request header field.

SYNTAX
```
public static void setDefaultRequestProperty(String field,
   String value)
```

DESCRIPTION This method sets the default value of the request header field `field` to be `value`. When a URL connection is created, it gets initialized with these request header fields. This call does not affect request header field settings already in place for the current URL connection. Table 19 contains examples of request header fields.

PARAMETERS

`field` The name of the request header field.

`value` The value of the request header field.

SEE ALSO `getDefaultRequestProperty()`, `getRequestProperty()`, `setRequestProperty()`.

setDefaultUseCaches()

PURPOSE public void setDefaultUseCaches(boolean useCaches)

DESCRIPTION This method sets the default flag for whether newly created URL connections can use caches. It applies to all new URL connections that will be created in the future. It does not apply to the current URL connection because this URL connection has already been created. This URL connection's cache usage can be modified only via `setUseCaches()`.

PARAMETERS

`useCaches` A `boolean` flag indicating whether to use caches by default for all URL connections. `true` means use caches; `false` means do not use caches.

SEE ALSO `getDefaultUseCaches()`, `getUseCaches()`, `setUseCaches()`, `useCaches`.

setDoInput()

PURPOSE Sets the indication of whether input from this connection is planned.

SYNTAX `public void setDoInput(boolean doinput)`

DESCRIPTION This method sets an indication of whether input from this URL connection is planned. It updates the field `doInput` with the value of the argument `doinput`. If `doinput` is `true`, input is expected; if `doinput` is `false`, input is not expected.

PARAMETERS

`doinput` Whether input from this connection is planned.

EXCEPTIONS

`IllegalAccessError`

If this connection has already been connected.

SEE ALSO `getDoInput()`.

setDoOutput()

PURPOSE Sets the indication of whether output to this connection is planned.

SYNTAX `public void setDoOutput(boolean dooutput)`

DESCRIPTION This method sets an indication of whether output to this URL connection is planned. It updates the field `doOutput` with the value of the argument `dooutput`. If `dooutput` is `true`, output is expected; if `dooutput` is `false`, output is not expected.

PARAMETERS

`dooutput` Whether output to this connection is planned.

EXCEPTIONS

`IllegalAccessError`

If this connection has already been connected.

SEE ALSO `getDoOutput()`.

setIfModifiedSince()

PURPOSE Sets the modification time that forces refetching of the document.

SYNTAX `public void setIfModifiedSince(long time)`

DESCRIPTION This method is used to set the `if-Modified-Since` time of this connection to `time`. This time is used to set the `If-Modified-Since` request header field to indicate to the server to not send the document unless it has been modified since `time`. It can be invoked after the URL connection has been created but before the connection has been established (i.e., before `connect()` has been invoked on it).

PARAMETERS

`time` The `if-Modified-Since` time for this connection in the number of milliseconds since epoch.

EXCEPTIONS

`IllegalAccessError`
If this method is called after the connection has already been established.

SEE ALSO `getIfModifiedSince()`, `ifModifiedSince`.

setRequestProperty()

PURPOSE Sets a request header field.

SYNTAX `public void setRequestProperty(String field, String value)`

DESCRIPTION This method sets the value of the request header field `field` to `value`. Table 19 contains examples of request header fields. The value of `field` can be changed prior to the connection's being established (before `connect()` is called). This method affects only this URL connection.

PARAMETERS

`field` The name of the request header field.
`value` The value of the request header field.

SEE ALSO `getDefaultRequestProperty()`, `setDefaultRequestProperty()`, `getRequestProperty()`.

setUseCaches()

PURPOSE Sets the cache usage flag of this connection.

SYNTAX `public void setUseCaches(boolean useCaches)`

DESCRIPTION This method is used to indicate whether this connection can use caches. It can be invoked after the URL connection has been created but before the connection has been established (i.e., before `connect()` has been invoked on it).

PARAMETERS

useCaches A `boolean` flag indicating whether to use caches. `true` means use caches; `false` means do not use caches.

EXCEPTIONS

`IllegalAccessError`
If this method is called after the connection has already been established.

SEE ALSO `getDefaultUseCaches()`, `getUseCaches()`, `setDefaultUseCaches()`, `useCaches`.

toString()

PURPOSE Generates the string representation for this object.

SYNTAX `public String toString()`

DESCRIPTION This method returns the string representation of this URL connection. The string representation of a URL connection consists of the name of the `URLConnection` class (usually a subclass specific for a particular protocol) and the URL of the connection.

RETURNS The string representation of this URL connection.

OVERRIDES `Object.toString()`.

url

PURPOSE The URL of this URL connection.

SYNTAX `protected URL url`

DESCRIPTION This field is used to hold the URL of this connection. It is set initially by the `URLConnection` constructor and typically remains unchanged for the duration of the connection.

SEE ALSO `getURL()`, `URLConnection()`.

URLConnection()

PURPOSE Constructs a URL connection for a URL.

SYNTAX `protected URLConnection (URL url)`

DESCRIPTION	This constructor creates a `URLConnection` object for the URL `url`. The constructor is protected and is typically called by the URL stream handler for a particular protocol (from its `openConnection()` method). After a `URLConnection` has been created, a connection can be made to the destination of `url` by invoking `connect()`.
PARAMETERS	
`url`	The URL for which to create the connection.
RETURNS	A URL connection.
SEE ALSO	`connect()`, `URLStreamHandler.openConnection()`.
EXAMPLE	See the class example for `URLStreamHandler`.

useCaches

PURPOSE	Indicates whether this connection allows the use of caches.
SYNTAX	`protected boolean useCaches`
DESCRIPTION	This field records whether this connection allows the use of caches. If `useCaches` is `true`, caching is allowed; if `false`, caches are bypassed. The default value for `useCaches` is `true` unless the default has been modified earlier in the program via `setDefaultUseCaches()`. `getDefaultUseCaches()` can be used to examine the default setting of `useCaches`. This field should be accessed and manipulated through the `getUseCaches()` and `setUseCaches()` methods, respectively.
SEE ALSO	`getDefaultUseCaches()`, `getUseCaches()`, `setDefaultUseCaches()`, `setUseCaches()`.

A B C D E F G H I J K L M N O P Q R S T U V W X Y Z

URLEncoder

java.lang.Object — **URLEncoder**

Syntax

```
public class URLEncoder
```

Description

URL Character Encoding

A URL consists of a sequence of (8-bit) characters that must meet certain requirements in terms of their "displayability" in different media (newspaper, electronic protocols, etc.). There is an encoding scheme defined for URLs to meet these requirements. Basically, all characters in a URL are drawn from a restricted subset of the printable US-ASCII character set. Nonprintable characters, plus those that are printable but considered unsafe or reserved, must be encoded by a triplet consisting of a percent character (%) followed by two hexadecimal digit characters representing the hexadecimal ISO-Latin-1 code of the character. For example, the hash character (#) is an unsafe character. Instead of the # character appearing as is in a URL, it must be encoded as the triplet `%35` (35 is the character code for #).

Here are the characters that may appear unencoded in a URL:

alphanumeric characters and `$ - _ . + ! , * ()'` (forward single quote)

These characters also can be encoded, in which case, they have the same meaning as when unencoded. `B` and `%66` both mean `B`.

The following are the unsafe characters. They must be encoded when they appear in a URL.

`{ } | \ ^ ~ [ ] ‘` (back single quote) space `< > " # %`

The following are the reserved characters.

`; / ? : @ = &`

A reserved character that appears unencoded in a URL has the special meaning for which it was reserved; when encoded, that character is "escaped" and does not hold the special meaning. The nonprintable characters have the character codes `80–ff,00–1f`, and `7f`. These must be encoded when they appear in a URL.

For example, a string

```
c=us/o=widget/ou=engineering
```

will appear encoded in a URL as

```
c%3dus%2fo%3dwidget%2fou%3dengineering
```

The application/x-www-form-urlencoded MIME Content Type

When the content type of a message is `application/x-www-form-urlencoded`, the content is a string of URL-encoded `FORM` name/value arguments used in the HTTP protocol. In this encoding, name/value pairs are listed in the string, with each pair separated by an ampersand (&) character. Each name/value pair has the format *name*=*value*. Names and values must follow the URL character encoding scheme described earlier in this section, except blank characters are replaced by the plus (+) character.

The following is an example of a string in `x-www-form-urlencoded` format:

```
country=Canada&province=Manitoba
```

This string consists of two name/value pairs: `country=Canada` and `province=Manitoba`.

The following is another example of a string in `x-www-form-urlencoded` format:

```
country=United+States&state=Ohio
```

This string consists of two name/value pairs: `country=United States` and `state=Ohio`. The blank character in "`United States`" has been replaced with a +.

URLEncoder Class

The `URLEncoder` class provides a method that encodes a string in `x-www-form-urlencoded` format. The string is expected to be the name or value in the name/value of a `FORM` argument. For example, `United States` gets encoded as `United+States`, but `a=b` gets encoded as `a%3db`. Each name and each value should be encoded separately. See Figure 245.

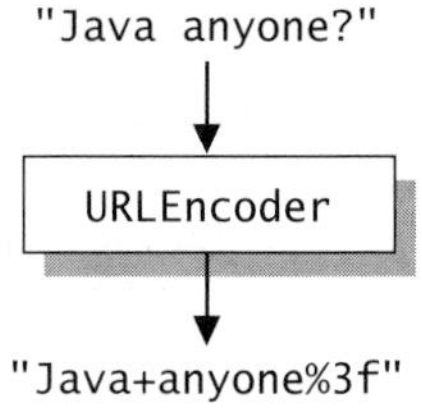

FIGURE 245 URLEncoder

The implementation of this method is conservative in that even some allowable characters are encoded with the % triplet.

MEMBER SUMMARY	
Encode Method	
`encode()`	Encodes a string in `x-www-form-urlencoded` format.

See Also

URL, URLConnection.

encode()

PURPOSE Encodes a string in x-www-form-urlencoded format.

SYNTAX `public static String encode(String str)`

DESCRIPTION This method encodes the string str as if it were a name or value expected by the x-www-form-urlencoded format. Alphanumeric characters and the underscore character (_) appear as is, but all other characters are encoded using the % hexadecimal code triplet.

PARAMETERS

str The string to be encoded.

RETURNS The string encoded in x-www-form-urlencoded format.

EXAMPLE

```
import java.net.URLEncoder;

class Main {
    public static void main(String[] args) {
        String x500name = new String("c=us/o=sun/ou=eng");
        String url = URLEncoder.encode(x500name);
            // "c%3dus%2fo%3dsun"

        String u2 = URLEncoder.encode("Open Sesame");// "Open+Sesame"

        System.out.println(url);
        System.out.println(u2);

    }
}
```

java.net

URLStreamHandler

`java.lang.Object` — `URLStreamHandler`

Syntax

```
public abstract class URLStreamHandler
```

Description

Different protocols can be used when specifying a URL for a resource. So that the resource can be obtained from its specified location (URL), support must be provided by, or accessible from, the Java runtime for the protocol specified. An object that provides this support is called a *URL protocol handler*, or *URL stream handler*. It is implemented by a subclass of the abstract class `URLStreamHandler`. A protocol handler implements a particular protocol and provides methods to open a connection to the service identified in the URL using that protocol. Each of the supported protocols has a protocol handler, as determined by the *URL stream handler factory*.

A URL stream handler factory creates instances of `URLStreamHandler` based on the protocol names of the instances (e.g., `telnet`, `ftp`, `http`). A default factory supports a handful of the popular protocols. It also supports dynamic addition of new protocol handlers. The program can configure its own factory to use, depending on factors such as network characteristics and security requirements. The selection of the particular implementation of protocol handlers used by a program is configurable by the program via the `URL.setURLStreamHandlerFactory()` method.

All subclasses of `URLStreamHandler` must provide an implementation for `openConnection()`, which returns a protocol-specific `URLConnection` object for communicating with the service identified in the URL.

MEMBER SUMMARY

Communications Method (Abstract)	
`openConnection()`	Creates a connection to the service identified in a URL.
URL Methods	
`parseURL()`	Parses a string URL into a URL object using the syntax of this protocol.
`setURL()`	Sets the components of a URL using the given arguments.
`toExternalForm()`	Generates the string representation of a URL in the syntax of this protocol.

See Also

URL, URLConnection, URLStreamHandlerFactory.

Example

This example shows an implementation of a URLStreamHandler that supports URL connections using dateURLConnection.

See related examples at URL.setURLStreamHandlerFactory(), URLConnection, and URLStreamHandlerFactory.

```
import java.net.*;
import java.io.IOException;

// given host name, communicates with host via the daytime port

public class TestdateHandler extends URLStreamHandler {
    protected URLConnection openConnection(URL u) throws IOException {
        return new DateURLConnection(u);
    }
}
```

openConnection()

PURPOSE Creates a connection to the service identified in a URL.

SYNTAX `abstract protected URLConnection openConnection(URL url) throws IOException`

DESCRIPTION This method creates a connection to the service identified in the URL url. The service is typically identified by the host name and port number specified in the URL. The implementation of this method is protocol-specific and must be provided by a subclass of URLStreamHandler. The connection created also is protocol-specific. Subsequent communication over this connection is achieved using the methods defined in the abstract class URLConnection.

PARAMETERS

url The URL for which to create a connection.

RETURNS A protocol-specific connection to the service identified by the URL.

EXCEPTIONS

IOException If an IO error occurred while attempting to create the connection.

SEE ALSO URL, URLConnection.

EXAMPLE See the class example.

A B C D E F G H I J K L M N O P Q R S T U V W X Y Z

parseURL()

PURPOSE Parses a URL string into a `URL` object using the syntax of this protocol.

SYNTAX
```
protected void parseURL(URL url, String spec, int offset, int
    endIndex)
```

DESCRIPTION This method parses the URL string `spec` into a `URL` object `url` using the syntax of this protocol. Any existing components in `url` not overridden by new components in `spec` remain unchanged. This allows a context to be specified in `url` prior to the calling of `parseURL()`. `offset` and `endIndex` specify the range of characters in `spec` that should be parsed. This substring should not include the protocol. For example, an acceptable string would be "`//java.sun.com/pub/JDK-beta2/`".

This method's default implementation uses the URL syntax for HTTP URLs. Most other URL protocol families also follow this syntax. If this protocol has a different syntax, then its protocol handler must override this method. This method is called by the `URL` constructor.

This method is the inverse of `toExternalForm()`.

PARAMETERS

`endIndex`	The ending index of `spec` at which to stop parsing, exclusive. `endindex` must be in the range of `0` to `spec.length()`.
`offset`	The beginning index of `spec` at which to start parsing, inclusive. `offset` must be in the range of 0 to `spec.length()-1`.
`spec`	The URL string to parse.
`url`	The `URL` object to update.

SEE ALSO `toExternalForm()`, `URL()`.

setURL()

PURPOSE Sets the components of a URL using the given arguments.

SYNTAX
```
protected void setURL(URL url, String protocol, String host, int
    port, String file, String ref)
```

DESCRIPTION This method sets the components of the URL `url` to the given arguments `protocol`, `host`, `port`, `file`, and `ref`.

PARAMETERS

`file`	The file pathname of the URL.
`host`	The host name of the URL.

`port`	The port number of the URL. `-1` means to use the protocol's default port number.
`protocol`	The name of the URL's protocol.
`ref`	The reference (fragment identifier) of the URL.
`url`	The URL to update.

SEE ALSO `URL()`, `URL.set()`.

toExternalForm()

PURPOSE Generates the string representation of a URL using the syntax of this protocol.

SYNTAX `protected String toExternalForm(URL url)`

DESCRIPTION This method generates the string representation of a URL using the syntax of this protocol. By default, the syntax used is that of HTTP URLs. This consists of the protocol name, host name, port number (if explicitly specified; used instead of the protocol's default port number), the file pathname, and, if present, the fragment identifier (reference). Appropriate separators ('//', '#', etc.) are used to separate these components according to the HTTP syntax.

If this protocol's syntax differs from the HTTP URL syntax, then the protocol handler should override this method. This method is called by `URL.toExternalForm()` (and consequently `URL.toString()`).

This method is the inverse of `parseURL()`.

PARAMETERS

`url` The URL for which to generate the string representation.

RETURNS The string representation of the (fully qualified) URL `url`.

SEE ALSO `URL.toExternalForm()`.

java.net

URLStreamHandlerFactory

`URLStreamHandlerFactory`

Syntax

`public interface URLStreamHandlerFactory`

Description

Different protocols can be used when specifying a URL for a resource. So that the resource can be obtained from its specified location (URL), support must be provided by, or accessible from, the Java runtime for the protocol specified. An object that provides this support is called a *URL protocol handler*, or *URL stream handler*. It is implemented by a subclass of the abstract class `URLStreamHandler`. A protocol handler implements a particular protocol and provides methods to open a connection to the service identified in the URL using that protocol. Each of the supported protocols has a protocol handler, as determined by the *URL stream handler factory*.

A URL stream handler factory creates instances of `URLStreamHandler` based on the protocol name of the instances (e.g., `telnet`, `ftp`, `http`). A default factory supports a handful of the popular protocols. It also supports dynamic addition of new protocol handlers. The program can configure its own factory to use, depending on factors such as network characteristics and security requirements. The selection of the particular implementation of protocol handlers used by a program is configurable by the program via the `URL.setURLStreamHandlerFactory()` method. Only one stream handler factory can be installed in a program at any one time. Once installed, the factory cannot be replaced.

Once a stream handler has been created, you use the `openConnection()` method implemented by the handler to create a connection for accessing the URL.

MEMBER SUMMARY	
Handler Creation Method	
`createURLStreamHandler()`	Creates a new URL stream handler for a protocol.

Example

This example shows a URLStreamHandlerFactory that uses its own algorithm for constructing the class name of the handler requested. Handlers that have been previously located are cached in a hash table.

See related examples at URL.setURLStreamHandlerFactory(), URLConnection, and URLStreamHandler.

```
import java.net.*;
import java.util.Hashtable;

public class TestFactory implements URLStreamHandlerFactory {
    static Hashtable handlers = new Hashtable();

    public URLStreamHandler createURLStreamHandler(String protocol) {
        // try cached handlers first
        URLStreamHandler handler =
            (URLStreamHandler)handlers.get(protocol);
        if (handler == null) {
            String className = "Test" + protocol + "Handler";
            try {
                handler = (URLStreamHandler)Class.
                    forName(className).newInstance();
            } catch (ClassNotFoundException e) {
                handler = null;                 // not found
            } catch (Exception e) {
                // all other exceptions, print out problem
                e.printStackTrace();
                handler = null;
            }

            if (handler != null)
                handlers.put(protocol, handler); // put into cache
        }
        return (handler);
    }
}
```

createURLStreamHandler()

PURPOSE Creates a new URL stream handler for a protocol.

SYNTAX `URLStreamHandler createURLStreamHandler(String protocol)`

DESCRIPTION This method creates a new URLStreamHandler instance for the protocol protocol.

PARAMETERS

`protocol`	The protocol for which to create the stream handler (e.g., `http`, `telnet`, `ftp`).
RETURNS	A new stream handler for `protocol`.
SEE ALSO	`URL`, `URLStreamHandler`.
EXAMPLE	See the class example.

UTFDataFormatException

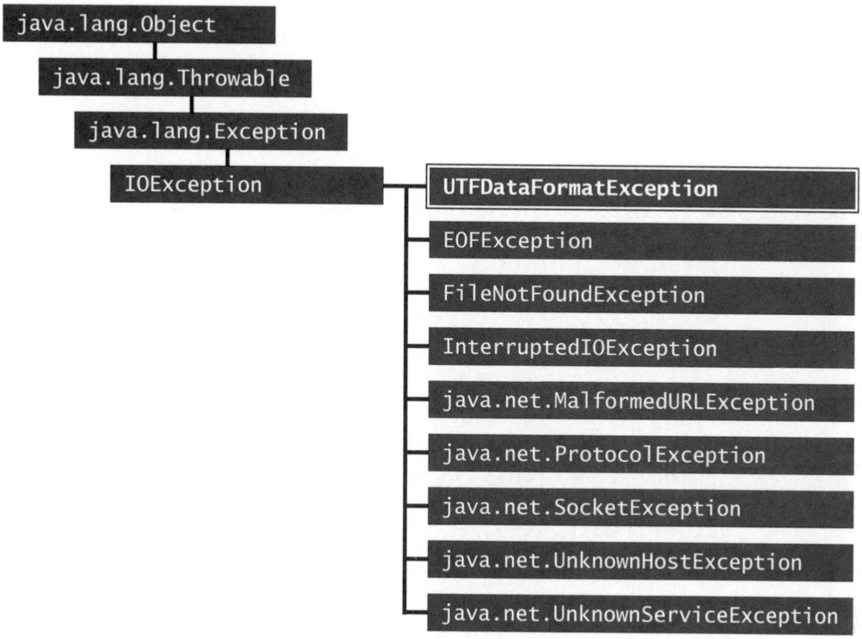

Syntax

`public class UTFDataFormatException extends IOException`

Description

UTF stands for *Unicode Transfer Format*. It is an encoding scheme for Unicode characters. When writing a string to a data stream, a program uses `DataOutputStream.writeUTF()`. It reads it back using `DataInputStream.readUTF()`. If `DataInputStream.readUTF()` encounters a malformed UTF string, it throws `UTFDataFormatException`.

A method that throws `UTFDataFormatException` must declare it or any of its superclasses in its `throws` clause.

MEMBER SUMMARY	
Constructor	
`UTFDataFormatException()`	Constructs a `UTFDataFormatException` instance.

A B C D E F G H I J K L M N O P Q R S T U V W X Y Z

A B C D E F G H I J K L M N O P Q R S T U V W X Y Z

See Also

`DataInputStream.readUTF()`, `DataOutputStream.writeUTF()`, `IOException`.

Example

This example throws a `UTFDataFormatException` when it attempts to read a UTF string (that has been purposely mangled).

```
import java.io.*;

class Main {
    public static void main(String[] args) {
        if (args.length != 1) {
            System.err.println(
                "Usage: java Main <temp output file>");
            System.exit(-1);
        }
        try {
            // write it out
            FileOutputStream fout = new FileOutputStream(args[0]);
            DataOutputStream out = new DataOutputStream(fout);
            String str = "This is a test\n";
            out.writeDouble(10.02); // introduce bogus value
            out.writeUTF(str);
            out.close();

            // read it back
            FileInputStream fin = new FileInputStream(args[0]);
            DataInputStream in = new DataInputStream(fin);

            System.out.println(in.readUTF());
        } catch (UTFDataFormatException e) {
            System.err.println("UTF error");
            e.printStackTrace();
        } catch (IOException e) {
            e.printStackTrace();
        }
    }
}
```

UTFDataFormatException()

PURPOSE Constructs a `UTFDataFormatException` instance.

SYNTAX

```
public UTFDataFormatException()
public UTFDataFormatException(String msg)
```

DESCRIPTION The two forms of this constructor create a new instance of `UTFDataFormatException`. An optional string `msg` can be supplied that describes this particular instance of the exception.

PARAMETERS

`msg` A string that gives details about this exception.

java.util

Vector

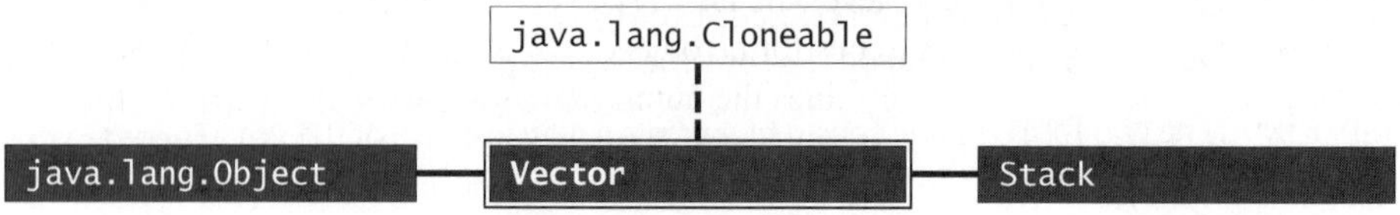

Syntax

```
public class Vector implements Cloneable
```

Description

The `Vector` class represents an expansible array consisting of an array of objects called *elements*. You manipulate a vector much like an array. They differ only in that you can add and remove objects from a vector and the vector will automatically grow or shrink. Elements can be `null`, but not all of the search methods supported by the `Vector` class accept `null` as an argument.

Vector Capacity

A *capacity* is the amount of storage that has been allocated for a vector. It differs from the *size* of a vector, which is the actual number of elements in the vector. If the number of elements added to a vector exceeds the vector's capacity, its capacity will be automatically increased to accommodate the additional elements. By default, the capacity is doubled when it needs to be increased. When you create the vector, you can set the initial capacity as well as the amount by which the capacity increases. The capacity can be changed anytime after creation by calling `ensureCapacity()`.

MEMBER SUMMARY

Constructor	
`Vector()`	Constructs an empty vector.
Access Methods	
`contains()`	Determines whether an object is in this vector.
`copyInto()`	Copies the references of the elements of this vector into an array.
`elementAt()`	Retrieves the element at the specified index in this vector.
`elements()`	Generates a list of the elements in this vector.
`firstElement()`	Retrieves the first element in this vector.

A B C D E F G H I J K L M N O P Q R S T U V W X Y Z

MEMBER SUMMARY

`indexOf()`	Searches for an object in this vector.
`isEmpty()`	Determines whether this vector is empty.
`lastElement()`	Retrieves the last element in this vector.
`lastIndexOf()`	Searches for an object starting from the end of this vector.
`size()`	Determines the number of elements in this vector.
Update Methods	
`addElement()`	Adds an element to the end of this vector.
`insertElementAt()`	Inserts an element in this vector.
`removeAllElements()`	Removes all elements from this vector.
`removeElement()`	Removes an element from this vector.
`removeElementAt()`	Removes the element at the specified index in this vector.
`setElementAt()`	Replaces the element at the specified index in this vector.
`setSize()`	Truncates or expands this vector.
Vector Capacity Methods	
`capacity()`	Determines the current capacity of this vector.
`ensureCapacity()`	Ensures that this vector has at least the specified capacity.
`trimToSize()`	Trims this vector's capacity to be the same as the vector's size.
Object Override Methods	
`clone()`	Clones this vector.
`toString()`	Generates the string representation for this vector.
Protected Fields	
`capacityIncrement`	The size of the increment to use when growing the capacity of this vector.
`elementCount`	The number of elements in `elementData`.
`elementData`	The buffer where elements of this vector are stored.

See Also

`StringBuffer`.

Example

`Vector` is useful when you do not know ahead of time the number of elements in an object. This example shows how `Vector` can be used to read a file of lines and write the lines out in reverse order.

```
import java.util.Vector;
import java.util.Enumeration;
import java.io.*;
```

```
class Main {
// reads in a file of lines and writes the lines out in reverse order
public static void main (String[] args) {
    if (args.length != 2) {
        System.err.println("Usage: inputfile outputfile");
        System.exit(1);
    }
    try {
        DataInputStream in =
            new DataInputStream(new FileInputStream(args[0]));
        DataOutputStream out =
            new DataOutputStream(new FileOutputStream(args[1]));
        Vector buf = new Vector(100);
        String str;

        while ((str = in.readLine()) != null)
            buf.addElement(str);
        in.close();

        for (int i = buf.size()-1; i >=0; i--) {
            out.writeBytes((String)buf.elementAt(i));
            out.writeByte('\n');
        }
        out.close();
    } catch (IOException e) {
        e.printStackTrace();
    }
}
}
```

addElement()

PURPOSE Adds an element to the end of this vector.

SYNTAX `public final synchronized void addElement(Object obj)`

DESCRIPTION This method adds the element `obj` to the end of this vector. The capacity of this vector is automatically increased if necessary to accommodate the new element.

PARAMETERS

`obj` The element to add.

SEE ALSO `ensureCapacity()`.

EXAMPLE See the class example, `copy()`, `toString()`.

A B C D E F G H I J K L M N O P Q R S T U V W X Y Z

capacity()

PURPOSE Determines the current capacity of this vector.

SYNTAX `public final int capacity()`

RETURNS The current capacity of this vector.

SEE ALSO `ensureCapacity()`, `size()`, `Vector()`.

EXAMPLE This example ensures that `capacity()` can hold `len` elements before they are added.

```
if (v.capacity() - v.size() < len )
    v.ensureCapacity(len+v.size());
for (int i = 0; i < len; i++)
   v.addElement(obj[i]);
```

capacityIncrement

PURPOSE The size of the increment to use when growing the capacity of this vector.

SYNTAX `protected int capacityIncrement`

DESCRIPTION The default value of this field is `0`, which means to double the capacity each time this vector is grown. This field is set when this vector is first created. It is an argument to its constructor.

SEE ALSO `capacity()`, `ensureCapacity()`, `Vector()`.

EXAMPLE The following is an excerpt from the JDK. It illustrates the use of the protected variables `capacityIncrement`, `elementCount`, and `elementData`.

```
public final synchronized void ensureCapacity(int minCapacity) {
    int oldCapacity = elementData.length;
    if (minCapacity > oldCapacity) {
        Object oldData[] = elementData;
        int newCapacity = (capacityIncrement > 0) ?
            (oldCapacity + capacityIncrement) : (oldCapacity * 2);
        if (newCapacity < minCapacity) {
            newCapacity = minCapacity;
        }
        elementData = new Object[newCapacity];
        System.arraycopy(oldData, 0, elementData, 0, elementCount);
    }
}
```

clone()

PURPOSE Clones this vector.

SYNTAX `public synchronized Object clone()`

DESCRIPTION This method makes a clone of this vector. The size, capacity, and capacity increment of the new vector are the same as those of this vector. The references to the objects in this vector are copied to the new vector, but the objects themselves are not cloned. Adding and deleting elements from this vector does not affect the new vector, and vice versa.

RETURNS A new copy of this vector.

OVERRIDES `Object.clone()`.

SEE ALSO `Cloneable`.

EXAMPLE See `setSize()`.

contains()

PURPOSE Determines whether an object is in this vector.

SYNTAX `public final boolean contains(Object obj)`

DESCRIPTION This method searches this vector for the object `obj`. It returns `true` if `obj` is an element in this vector; it returns `false` otherwise. `obj.equals()` is used when comparing `obj` with the elements for equality.

PARAMETERS

`obj` The non-`null` object for which to search.

RETURNS `true` if `obj` is in this vector; `false` otherwise.

SEE ALSO `indexOf()`, `lastIndexOf()`, `Object.equals()`.

EXAMPLE See `copyInto()`.

copyInto()

PURPOSE Copies the reference of the elements of this vector into an array.

SYNTAX `public final synchronized void copyInto(Object[] objArray)`

DESCRIPTION This method copies the reference of the elements of this vector into the array `objArray`. The elements themselves are not copied.

PARAMETERS

`objArray` The array into which to copy.

SEE ALSO `clone()`.

EXAMPLE This example takes an array of strings, adds and removes strings as requested, and returns an updated string array. It first creates a `Vector` of the original strings and then uses the `Vector` operations to add and remove items. After the modifications have been made, it uses `copyInto()` to get the data back into an array of string form.

```
public static String[] filter(String[] master,
                              String[] additions,
                              String[] deletions) {
    // make rough estimate of size needed
    Vector vec =
        new Vector(master.length+additions.length-deletions.length);
    for (int i = 0; i < master.length; i++)
        vec.addElement(master[i]);

    for (int i = 0; i < deletions.length; i ++)
        vec.removeElement(deletions[i]);

    for (int i = 0; i < additions.length; i++)
        if (!vec.contains(additions[i]))
        vec.addElement(additions[i]);

    String[] newmaster = new String[vec.size()];
    vec.copyInto((Object[])newmaster);
    return (newmaster);
}
```

elementAt()

PURPOSE Retrieves the element at the specified index in this vector.

SYNTAX `public final synchronized Object elementAt(int idx)`

DESCRIPTION This method returns the element at the index `idx` from this vector. If `idx` is not a valid index for this vector (it is either negative or larger than the index of the last element), an `ArrayIndexOutOfBoundsException` is thrown.

PARAMETERS

`idx` The index of the element to retrieve. `idx` must be in the range of `0` to `size()-1` (inclusive).

A B C D E F G H I J K L M N O P Q R S T U V W X Y Z

EXCEPTIONS

`ArrayIndexOutOfBoundsException`
If `idx` is negative or larger than `size()-1`.

SEE ALSO `element()`, `size()`.

EXAMPLE This example uses `elementAt()` to enumerate the objects in a vector for printing. Also see the class example and `insertElementAt()`.

```
public static void printVec(String msg, Vector vec) {
    if (msg != null)
        System.out.println(msg);
    if (vec.isEmpty())
        System.out.println("Empty vector");
    else
        for (int i=0; i < vec.size(); i++)
            System.out.println(vec.elementAt(i));
}
```

elementCount

PURPOSE The number of elements in `elementData`.

SYNTAX `protected int elementCount`

DESCRIPTION This field keeps track of the number of elements in `elementData`. It is decremented when an element is removed and incremented when an element is added. This is the value returned by `size()`.

SEE ALSO `addElement()`, `elementData`, `insertElementAt()`, `removeElement()`, `removeAllElements()`, `size()`.

EXAMPLE See `capacityIncrement`.

elementData

PURPOSE The buffer where elements of this vector are stored.

SYNTAX `protected Object[] elementData`

DESCRIPTION This field is the array that contains the elements of this vector. It is grown automatically when it becomes full or is grown manually using `ensureCapacity()`.

SEE ALSO `capacity()`, `capacityIncrement`, `ensureCapacity()`.

EXAMPLE See `capacityIncrement`.

elements()

PURPOSE Generates a list of all elements in this vector.

SYNTAX `public final synchronized Enumeration elements()`

DESCRIPTION This method generates a list of all elements in this vector and returns the list as an `Enumeration`. The methods in the `Enumeration` class can subsequently be used to retrieve objects from this list one at a time. Any changes to this vector may be visible in this enumeration, depending on where the changes were made and how far the enumeration has proceeded.

This is one way of enumerating the elements in a vector. The other way is to use `elementAt()` in a `for` loop.

RETURNS An enumeration of the elements in this vector.

SEE ALSO `elementAt()`, `Enumeration`.

EXAMPLE This example shows how to use `Enumeration` to print the elements of a vector. See the example for `elementAt()` for another way of doing the same thing.

```
public static void printVec2(String msg, Vector vec) {
    if (msg != null)
        System.out.println(msg);
    if (vec.isEmpty())
        System.out.println("Empty vector");
    else {
        Enumeration e = vec.elements();
        while (e.hasMoreElements())
             System.out.println("\t" + e.nextElement());
    }
}
```

ensureCapacity()

PURPOSE Ensures that this vector has at least the specified capacity.

SYNTAX `public final synchronized void ensureCapacity(int minCap)`

DESCRIPTION If you know approximately the expected size of the final vector, you should set the capacity of this vector to the expected size to minimize the number of times that the capacity must be increased. You can set the capacity at the time this vector is created or at any time after creation by calling `ensureCapacity()`. `ensureCapacity()` ensures that the capacity of this vector is at least `minCap`. If the current capacity is less than `minCap`, it is increased to `minCap`. If the current capacity is already at or greater than `minCap`, the capacity is left unchanged.

PARAMETERS

minCap The minimum capacity this vector should have.

SEE ALSO capacity().

EXAMPLE See capacity().

firstElement()

PURPOSE Retrieves the first element of this vector.

SYNTAX `public final synchronized Object firstElement()`

RETURNS The first element in this vector; `null` if the first element happens to be `null`.

EXCEPTIONS

`NoSuchElementException`
If this vector is empty.

SEE ALSO `elementAt()`, `isEmpty()`, `lastElement()`.

EXAMPLE This example swaps the first element of a vector with its last element.

```
public static void swapFirstLast(Vector vec) {
    try {
        Object fst = vec.firstElement();
        Object lst = vec.lastElement();
        vec.setElementAt(lst, 0);
        vec.setElementAt(fst, vec.size()-1);
    } catch (NoSuchElementException e) {
        System.out.println(e);
    }
}
```

indexOf()

PURPOSE Searches for an object in this vector.

SYNTAX
```
public final int indexOf(Object obj)
public final synchronized int indexOf(Object obj, int idx)
```

DESCRIPTION The two forms of this method search for the object `obj` in this vector. If `idx` is specified, the search begins at the index `idx` toward the end of this vector. If `idx` is not specified, the search begins at index `0`. Comparison of `obj` with the elements in this vector uses `Object.equals()` to test for equality.

PARAMETERS

`idx` The index in this vector at which to start the search; `idx` must be greater than or equal to `0`.

`obj` The non-`null` object for which to search.

RETURNS The index of `obj` in this vector; `-1` if `obj` is not in this vector in the range specified.

SEE ALSO `contains()`, `lastIndexOf()`, `Object.equals()`.

EXAMPLE This example replaces the first occurrence of an object `target` in a vector `vec` with another object `sub`.

```
public static boolean replaceFirst(Vector vec, Object target, Object
                                   sub) {
    int loc = vec.indexOf(target);
    if (loc >= 0) {
        vec.setElementAt(sub, loc);
        return (true);
    }
    return (false);
}
```

insertElementAt()

PURPOSE Inserts an element in this vector.

SYNTAX `public final synchronized void insertElementAt(Object obj, int idx)`

DESCRIPTION This method inserts object `obj` at index `idx` in this vector. The element that used to be at `idx` and all elements with an index greater than `idx` are shifted up one index position (toward the end of this vector). The size of this vector is increased by 1. When `idx` is equal to `size()`, this method is the same as `addElement()`.

PARAMETERS

`idx` The index in this vector to insert `obj`. `idx` must be in the range of `0` to `size()` (inclusive).

`obj` The possibly `null` object to insert.

EXCEPTIONS

`ArrayIndexOutOfBoundsException`
If `idx` is negative or is greater than `size()`.

SEE ALSO `addElement()`, `size()`.

EXAMPLE This example replaces the first occurrence of the object obj in the vector vec with all the elements from the vector replacement.

```
public static boolean replaceElementWithVec(Vector vec, Object obj,
                                            Vector replacement)
{
    int ind = vec.indexOf(obj);
    if (ind < 0)
        return (false);

    // Remove existing element and insert vector
    vec.removeElementAt(ind);
    for(int i = 0; i < replacement.size(); i++)
        vec.insertElementAt(replacement.elementAt(i), ind++);
    return (true);
}
```

isEmpty()

PURPOSE Determines whether this vector is empty.

SYNTAX `public final boolean isEmpty()`

RETURNS `true` if this vector is empty; `false` otherwise.

SEE ALSO `size()`.

EXAMPLE See `elementAt()` and `elements()`.

lastElement()

PURPOSE Retrieves the last element in this vector.

SYNTAX `public final synchronized Object lastElement()`

RETURNS The last element in this vector; `null` if the last element happens to be `null`.

EXCEPTIONS

`NoSuchElementException`
If this vector is empty.

SEE ALSO `elementAt()`, `firstElement()`, `size()`.

EXAMPLE See `firstElement()`.

lastIndexOf()

PURPOSE Searches for an object starting from the end of this vector.

SYNTAX
```
public final int lastIndexOf(Object obj)
public final synchronized int lastIndexOf(Object obj, int idx)
```

DESCRIPTION The two forms of this method search for the object `obj` in this vector. If `idx` is specified, the search begins at the index `idx` toward the start of this vector. If `idx` is not specified, the search begins at index `size()-1`. Comparison of `obj` with the elements in this vector uses `Object.equals()` to test for equality.

PARAMETERS

`idx` The index in this vector at which to start the backward search. `idx` must be less than `size()`.

`obj` The non-`null` object for which to search.

RETURNS The index of `obj` in this vector; `-1` if `obj` is not in this vector in the search range specified.

SEE ALSO `contains()`, `indexOf()`, `Object.equals()`.

EXAMPLE This method replaces the last occurrence of the object `target` in the vector `vec` with another object `sub`.

```
public static boolean replaceLast(Vector vec, Object target, Object
                                  sub) {
    int loc = vec.lastIndexOf(target);
    if (loc >= 0) {
        vec.setElementAt(sub, loc);
        return (true);
    }
    return (false);
}
```

removeAllElements()

PURPOSE Removes all elements from this vector.

SYNTAX
```
public final synchronized void removeAllElements()
```

DESCRIPTION This method removes all elements from this vector and leaves the vector empty. The size of the vector becomes zero, but the capacity of this vector remains unchanged.

SEE ALSO `capacity()`, `isEmpty()`, `size()`.

removeElement()

EXAMPLE

```
public static void clearVec(Vector vec) {
    vec.removeAllElements();          // remove all elements
    vec.trimToSize();                 // reclaim space
}
```

removeElement()

PURPOSE Removes an element from this vector.

SYNTAX `public final synchronized boolean removeElement(Object obj)`

DESCRIPTION This method removes the element `obj` from this vector. If `obj` is not found in this vector, this method returns `false`; otherwise it returns `true`. Comparison of `obj` with the elements in this vector uses `Object.equals()` to test for equality. If `obj` occurs more than once, only the first occurrence (from the beginning of the vector) is removed.

When `obj` is removed, all elements located at an index greater than where `obj` was are shifted down (toward the head of this vector). The size of this vector is decremented by one.

PARAMETERS

`obj` The non-`null` object to remove.

RETURNS `true` if `obj` is removed; `false` if `obj` is not in this vector.

SEE ALSO `Object.equals()`, `removeAllElements()`, `removeElementAt()`, `size()`.

EXAMPLE See `copyInto()`.

removeElementAt()

PURPOSE Removes the element at the specified index from this vector.

SYNTAX `public final synchronized void removeElementAt(int idx)`

DESCRIPTION This method removes the element at index `idx` from this vector. Elements at an index greater than `idx` are shifted down (toward the head of this vector). The size of this vector is decremented by 1.

PARAMETERS

`idx` The index of the element to remove. `idx` must be in the range of `0` to `size()-1` (inclusive).

EXCEPTIONS
`ArrayIndexOutOfBoundsException`
If `idx` is negative or greater than `size()-1`.

SEE ALSO `removeElement()`, `removeAllElements()`, `size()`.

EXAMPLE See `insertElementAt()`.

setElementAt()

PURPOSE Replaces the element at the specified index in this vector.

SYNTAX `public final synchronized void setElementAt(Object obj, int idx)`

DESCRIPTION This method replaces the element at index `idx` of this vector with the object `obj`.

PARAMETERS
`idx` The index of the element to replace; `idx` must be in the range of `0` to `size()-1` inclusive.
`obj` The object with which to replace the element.

EXCEPTIONS
`ArrayIndexOutOfBoundsException`
If `idx` is negative or greater than `size()-1`.

SEE ALSO `size()`.

EXAMPLE See `firstElement()`, `indexOf()`, `lastIndexOf()`.

setSize()

PURPOSE Truncates or expands this vector.

SYNTAX `public final synchronized void setSize(int newSize)`

DESCRIPTION This method sets the size of this vector to `newSize`. If `newSize` is less than the current size of this vector, the vector is truncated. Elements located at an index at or greater than `newSize` are lost. If `newSize` is greater than the current length of this vector, the newly added region is filled with `null`. `size()` becomes `newSize`.

PARAMETERS
`newSize` The new size of this vector. `newSize` must be non-negative.

size()

EXCEPTIONS

`ArrayIndexOutOfBoundsException`
If `newSize` is negative.

SEE ALSO `size()`.

EXAMPLE This method creates a vector that has the first `n` elements of a vector `orig`.

```
public static Vector vecNCopy(Vector orig, int n) {
    Vector vec = (Vector)orig.clone();
    vec.setSize(n);
    return (vec);
}
```

size()

PURPOSE Determines the number of elements in this vector.

SYNTAX `public final int size()`

DESCRIPTION This is the number of elements in this vector. Each time an element is added or removed, this number changes correspondingly.

SEE ALSO `capacity()`, `elementCount`, `lastElement()`, `setSize()`.

EXAMPLE See `copyInto()`, `elementAt()`, `firstElement()`, `insertElementAt()`.

toString()

PURPOSE Generates the string representation for this vector.

SYNTAX `public final synchronized String toString()`

DESCRIPTION The string representation of a vector is a comma-separated list of all the elements in the vector. The elements are listed from index `0` to index `size()-1`. `toString()` returns this string representation.

RETURNS The string representation of this vector.

OVERRIDES `Object.toString()`.

SEE ALSO `elements()`.

EXAMPLE

```
Vector v = new Vector(10);
v.addElement("a");
v.addElement("b");
```

```
v.addElement("c");
v.addElement("d");
v.addElement("e");
v.addElement("f");
System.out.println(v.toString());  // [a, b, c, d, e, f]
```

trimToSize()

PURPOSE Trims this vector's capacity to be the same as the vector's size.

SYNTAX `public final synchronized void trimToSize()`

DESCRIPTION This method trims the capacity of this vector down to its size. It removes the currently unused storage from this vector. If an object is subsequently added, the capacity will be increased.

SEE ALSO `capacity()`, `ensureCapacity()`, `size()`.

EXAMPLE See `removeAllElements()`.

Vector()

PURPOSE Constructs a new empty vector.

SYNTAX

```
public Vector()
public Vector(int initCap)
public Vector(int initCap, int capIncrement)
```

DESCRIPTION The `Vector` class has three forms of the constructor. The first form takes no arguments. It creates an empty vector with a default capacity of 10. The second form creates an empty vector with the initial capacity of `initCap`. Vectors created using these two forms increase their capacity as needed by doubling their existing capacity. The third form of the constructor creates a new empty vector with the initial capacity of `initCap` and capacity increment of `capIncrement`. When additional capacity is needed, the existing capacity is increased by `capIncrement`.

PARAMETERS

`capIncrement`
The amount to grow when additional capacity is needed.

`initCap` The initial capacity of this vector.

SEE ALSO `capacity()`, `capacityIncrement`, `ensureCapacity()`.

EXAMPLE See the class example, `copyInto()`, `toString()`.

java.lang
VerifyError

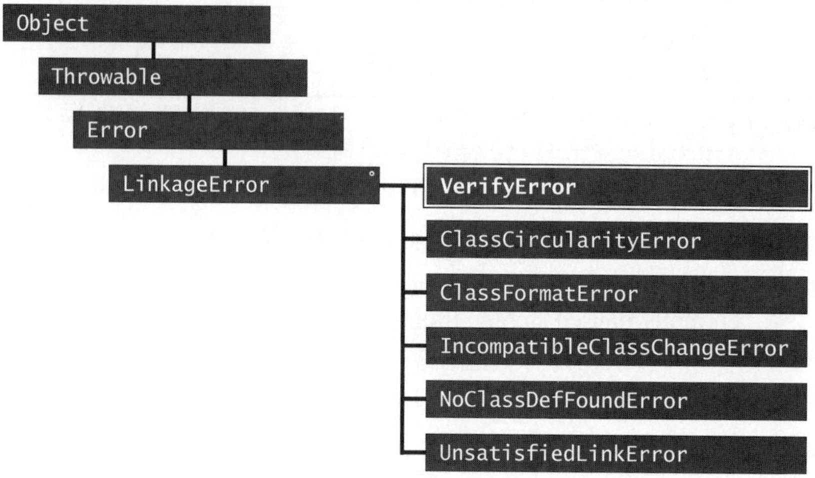

Syntax

```
public class VerifyError extends LinkageError
```

Description

When a class is to be loaded (by using either the system's default class loader or a user-defined class loader), its class definition must be verified before it is installed. This verification involves ensuring that all method names and signatures are valid, all field names and signatures are valid, and no final methods or classes are being overridden. If any of these verifications fail, the Java virtual machine throws a `VerifyError`.

`VerifyError` should not be caught or declared in the `throws` clause of a method.

MEMBER SUMMARY	
Constructor	
`VerifyError()`	Constructs a `VerifyError` instance.

See Also

`LinkageError`.

VerifyError()

PURPOSE Constructs a `VerifyError` instance.

SYNTAX
```
public VerifyError()
public VerifyError(String msg)
```

DESCRIPTION The two forms of the constructor create a new instance of `VerifyError`. An optional string `msg` can be supplied that describes this particular instance of the exception.

PARAMETERS

`msg` A string that gives details about this error.

java.lang
VirtualMachineError

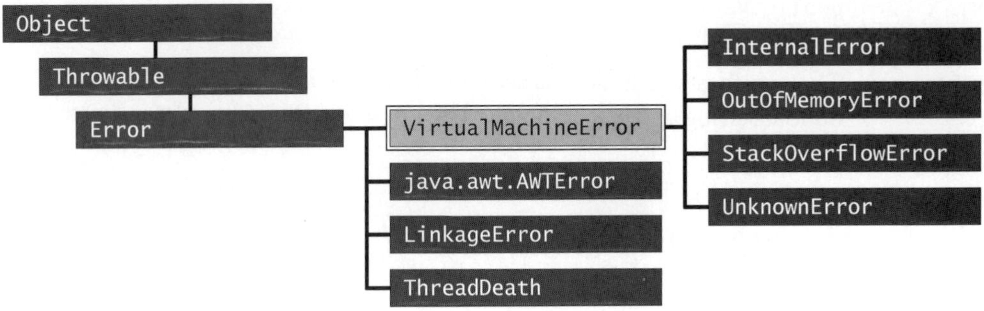

Syntax

```
abstract public class VirtualMachineError extends Error
```

Description

`VirtualMachineError` and its subclasses of errors indicate that the Java virtual machine has encountered an unrecoverable error or has ran out of system resources required to continue execution.

`VirtualMachineError` and its subclasses should not be caught or declared in the `throws` clause of a method.

MEMBER SUMMARY	
Constructor	
`VirtualMachineError()`	Constructs a `VirtualMachineError` instance.

See Also

`Error`, `InternalError`, `OutOfMemoryError`, `StackOverflowError`, `UnknownError`.

VirtualMachineError()

PURPOSE Constructs a `VirtualMachineError` instance.

SYNTAX

```
public VirtualMachineError()
public VirtualMachineError(String msg)
```

DESCRIPTION The two forms of this constructor create a new instance of `VirtualMachineError`. An optional string `msg` can be supplied that describes this particular instance of the error.

PARAMETERS

`msg` A string that gives details about this error.

java.awt
Window

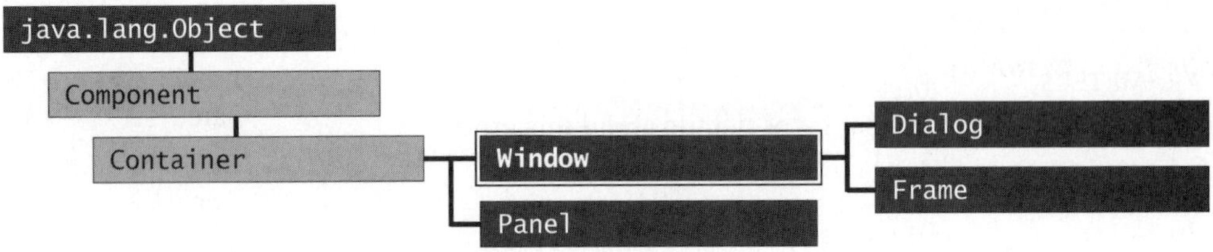

Syntax

```
public class Window extends Container
```

Description

A window is a top-level window with no title, menu bar, or border. It could be used to implement a pop-up menu.

The Modal Property

Windows can be modal or modeless. Modal windows, when visible, prevent all other AWT windows from responding. Modeless windows are completely independent of all other windows.

The Warning Message Property

The warning message is a string that is displayed in nonsecure windows. The warning message is not displayed for secure windows. A nonsecure window is a window that has a security manager is installed and calling `SecurityManager.checkTopLevelWinow()` on the window yields `false`. The warning message is displayed somewhere in the window and cannot be hidden or disguised by the application. The warning message prevents an application from disguising a window to look like a critical window, such as a login window, in order to steal information. Figure 246 shows a nonsecure window.

FIGURE 246 **A Nonsecure Window**

The default warning message string is retrieved from the `awt.appletWarning` system property. See the `Properties` class for more details about system properties.

Coordinates, Sizes, and Insets

The insets for a window are normally (0, 0, 0, 0) because a window has no title, menu bar, or border. However, if the window has a warning message that is displayed, the inset can be non-zero.

The Peer Hierarchy

The peers for most AWT components require that both the component's parent and peer exist. The window component (and its subclasses) is the exception. The window's peer can be created even if it does not have a parent. This means that the other components need to have a window at the root of their ancestor chain before their peers can be created.

The Toolkit Property

A toolkit is a factory that creates AWT components like buttons, scrollbars, and windows. The default toolkit that AWT uses supplies components that use the platform's native windowing toolkit. For example, when running an AWT application on Windows95, the default toolkit creates wrappers around Windows controls, while on Motif, the default toolkit creates wrappers around Motif widgets.

Events

A window generates all the events defined in the `Event` class. See the `Event` class for details.

MEMBER SUMMARY	
Constructor	
`Window()`	Constructs a new `Window` instance.
Property Methods	
`getToolkit()`	Retrieves the window's toolkit.
`getWarningString()`	Retrieves the window's warning message.
Visibility Methods	
`show()`	Makes the window visible.
`toBack()`	Moves the window behind all other windows.
`toFront()`	Moves the window in front of all other windows.
Peer Methods	
`addNotify()`	Creates the window's peer hierarchy.
`dispose()`	Destroys the window's peer hierarchy.
Layout Method	
`pack()`	Resizes the window to its preferred size.

Example

This example demonstrates how to create a pop-up menu. Clicking the frame creates a window at the point of the click. Releasing the mouse button disposes of the window. See Figure 247.

FIGURE 247 **Window**

```
import java.awt.*;
class Main extends Frame {
    PopupMenu pm;

    Main() {
        super("Window Example");
        resize(100, 100);
        show();
    }

    public boolean mouseDown(Event evt, int x, int y) {
        if (evt.target == this) {
            Rectangle r = bounds();

            pm = new PopupMenu(this);
            pm.reshape(r.x + x + insets().left,
                r.y + y + insets().top, 50, 100);
            pm.show();
            return true;
        }
        return false;
    }

    public boolean mouseUp(Event evt, int x, int y) {
        if (pm != null) {
            pm.dispose();
            pm = null;
            return true;
        }
        return false;
    }

    static public void main(String[] args) {
        new Main();
    }
}

class PopupMenu extends Window {
    PopupMenu(Frame f) {
        super(f);
    }

    public void paint(Graphics g) {
        FontMetrics fm = g.getFontMetrics();
        String s = "Popup Menu";
```

```
        g.drawString(s, (size().width-fm.stringWidth(s))/2,
            (size().height-fm.getHeight())/2 + fm.getAscent());
    }
}
```

addNotify()

PURPOSE Creates the window's peer hierarchy.

SYNTAX `public synchronized void addNotify()`

DESCRIPTION This method creates the window's peer hierarchy, if necessary. The window's peer is created by calling the `Toolkit.createWindow()` method. This method should be called before calculating the window's minimum or preferred size. The methods `pack()` and `show()` automatically call `addNotify()`.

OVERRIDES `Container.addNotify()`.

SEE ALSO `Component.addNotify()`.

dispose()

PURPOSE Destroys the window's peer hierarchy.

SYNTAX `public synchronized void dispose()`

DESCRIPTION The window's peer hierarchy is destroyed if it exists, thereby freeing any resources used by the peers. The state of the window hierarchy is left intact and can be reused. The peer hierarchy can be restored by calling `addNotify()`.

EXAMPLE See the class example.

getToolkit()

PURPOSE Retrieves the window's toolkit.

SYNTAX `public Toolkit getToolkit()`

DESCRIPTION This method calls `Toolkit.getDefaultToolkit()`and returns the result. If a window implements its own toolkit, it should override this method to return its own toolkit.

RETURNS The window's toolkit.

OVERRIDES `Component.getToolkit()`.

SEE ALSO `Toolkit.getDefaultToolkit()`.

EXAMPLE See `Toolkit`.

getWarningString()

PURPOSE Retrieves the window's warning message.

SYNTAX `public final String getWarningString()`

RETURNS The warning message. A return value of `null` means the window is a secure window.

EXAMPLE This example implements an applet that creates a window. Under most browsers, the security manager forces a warning message to be displayed on any external window an applet creates. In this example, the external window simply displays the warning message in its center. See Figure 248. Notice that the window's insets are used to calculate the center of the window's paintable area. The insets of a window are normally all zero, since a window does not have any window decorations such as a title or border. The only time this is not true is if the window displays a warning message.

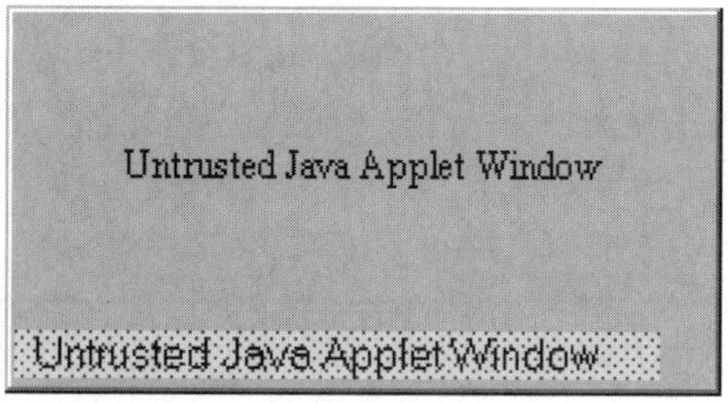

FIGURE 248 `Window.getWarningString()`

```
import java.awt.*;
import java.applet.*;
public class Main extends Applet {
    MyWindow w;

    public void init() {
        // Find the applet's frame.
        Component f = getParent();
        while (f != null && !(f instanceof Frame)) {
            f = f.getParent();
        }
```

```
        w = new MyWindow((Frame)f);
        w.reshape(0, 0, 150, 150);
        w.show();
    }

    public void start() {
        w.show();
    }

    public void stop() {
        w.hide();
    }

    public void destroy() {
        if (w != null) {
            w.dispose();
            w = null;
        }
    }
}

class MyWindow extends Window {
    MyWindow(Frame frame) {
        super(frame);
    }

    public void paint(Graphics g) {
        FontMetrics fm = g.getFontMetrics();
        String s = getWarningString();
        int w = size().width - insets().left - insets().right;
        int h = size().height - insets().top - insets().bottom;

        if (s != null) {
            g.drawString(s, (w-fm.stringWidth(s))/2,
                (h-fm.getHeight())/2 + fm.getAscent());
        }
    }

    public boolean mouseDown(Event evt, int x, int y) {
        hide();
        return true;
    }
}
```

INPUT Here is the HTML necessary to start the applet:

```
<applet code=Main width=100 height=100>
</applet>
```

pack()

PURPOSE Resizes the window to its preferred size.

SYNTAX `public synchronized void pack()`

DESCRIPTION This method resizes the window to its preferred size. It calls the `addNotify()` method before the window's preferred size is calculated. This is important to note because the preferred size of some components is valid only if its peer exists.

SEE ALSO `Container.preferredSize()`.

EXAMPLE See `show()`.

show()

PURPOSE Makes the window visible.

SYNTAX `public synchronized void show()`

DESCRIPTION This method calls the `addNotify()` method, validates the window's layout, and then makes the window visible. The window does not necessarily appear in front of all other windows; the exact behavior is platform-dependent. To force the window to be displayed in front of all other windows, call the `toFront()` method. If the window is already visible, the window is brought to the front.

OVERRIDES `Component.show()`.

EXAMPLE This example creates a window with a button that hides the window when pressed. The window reappears within 5 seconds. See Figure 249.

FIGURE 249 `Window.show()`

```
import java.awt.*;
class Main extends Window implements Runnable {
    Main() {
        super(null);
        add("Center", new Button("Hide"));
        pack();
        show();
        (new Thread(this)).start();
    }

    public boolean action(Event evt, Object what) {
        if ("Hide".equals(what)) {
```

```
            hide();
            return true;
        }
        return false;
    }

    public void run() {
        while (true) {
            try {
                show();
                Thread.sleep(5000);
            } catch (InterruptedException e) {};
        }
    }

    static public void main(String[] args) {
        new Main();
    }
}
```

toBack()

PURPOSE Moves the window behind all other windows.

SYNTAX `public void toBack()`

DESCRIPTION The window is moved behind all windows in the system, regardless of whether they are AWT windows. The position of the window with respect to other windows is not necessarily maintained; the exact behavior is platform-dependent. For example, if the window was behind some windows, hidden, and then shown again, it may not reappear behind the same windows.

SEE ALSO See `toFront()`.

toFront()

PURPOSE Moves the window in front of all other windows.

SYNTAX `public void toFront()`

DESCRIPTION The window is moved in front of all other windows in the system, regardless of whether they are AWT windows.

Window()

EXAMPLE This example creates a window with a button that sends the window to the back. The window returns to the front within 5 seconds. See Figure 250.

FIGURE 250 `Window.toFront()`

```
import java.awt.*;
class Main extends Window implements Runnable {
    Main() {
        super(null);
        add("Center", new Button("Back"));
        pack();
        show();
        (new Thread(this)).start();
    }

    public boolean action(Event evt, Object what) {
        if ("Back".equals(what)) {
            toBack();
            return true;
        }
        return false;
    }

    public void run() {
        while (true) {
            try {
                toFront();
                Thread.sleep(5000);
            } catch (InterruptedException e) {};
        }
    }

    static public void main(String[] args) {
        new Main();
    }
}
```

Window()

PURPOSE Constructs a new `Window` instance.

SYNTAX `public Window(Frame parent)`

DESCRIPTION This constructor creates a new invisible `Window` instance with the parent `parent`. If parent is `null`, the window is not modal; otherwise the window is modal and no other AWT window will respond to input until this window disappears. If `parent` is not `null`, events that are not handled by the window are forwarded to `parent`.

The new window has a border layout manager.

PARAMETERS

`parent` The owner of the window. May be `null`.

SEE ALSO `show()`.

EXAMPLE This example creates two buttons: one creates a modal window and the other creates a modeless window. The new window contains a Quit button that disposes of the new window. See Figure 251.

FIGURE 251 `Window()`

```
import java.awt.*;
import java.applet.*;
public class Main extends Applet {
    MyWindow w;

    public void init() {
        // Find the applet's frame.
        Component f = getParent();
        while (f != null && !(f instanceof Frame)) {
            f = f.getParent();
        }

        w = new MyWindow((Frame)f);
        w.reshape(0, 0, 150, 150);
        w.show();
    }

    public void start() {
        w.show();
    }

    public void stop() {
        w.hide();
    }

    public void destroy() {
        if (w != null) {
            w.dispose();
            w = null;
        }
    }
}

class MyWindow extends Window {
    MyWindow(Frame frame) {
        super(frame);
    }
```

```
        public void paint(Graphics g) {
            FontMetrics fm = g.getFontMetrics();
            String s = getWarningString();
            int w = size().width - insets().left - insets().right;
            int h = size().height - insets().top - insets().bottom;

            if (s != null) {
                g.drawString(s, (w-fm.stringWidth(s))/2,
                    (h-fm.getHeight())/2 + fm.getAscent());
            }
        }

        public boolean mouseDown(Event evt, int x, int y) {
            hide();
            return true;
        }
    }
```

java.awt.peer

WindowPeer

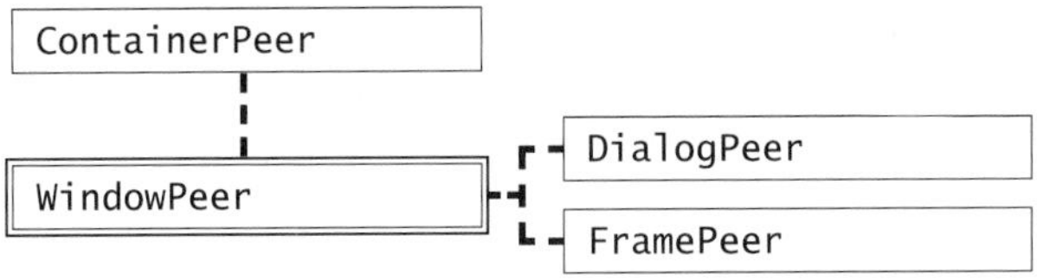

Syntax

`public interface WindowPeer extends ContainerPeer`

Description

The window component (see the `Window` class) in the Abstract Windowing Toolkit (AWT) uses the platform's native implementation of a window. So that the AWT window behaves the same on all platforms, the window is assigned a peer, whose task is to translate the behavior of the platform's native window to the behavior of the AWT window.

AWT programmers normally do not directly use peer classes and interfaces. Instead they deal with AWT components in the `java.awt` package. These in turn automatically manage their peers. Only someone who is porting the AWT to another platform should be concerned with the peer classes and interfaces. Consequently, most peer documentation refers to `java.awt` counterparts.

See `Component` and `Toolkit` for additional information about component peers.

MEMBER SUMMARY

Peer Methods	
`toBack()`	Moves the window behind all other windows.
`toFront()`	Moves the window in front of all other windows.

See Also

`Component`, `Toolkit`, `Window`.

A B C D E F G H I J K L M N O P Q R S T U V W X Y Z

toBack()

PURPOSE Moves the window behind all other windows.

SYNTAX `void toBack()`

SEE ALSO `Window.toBack()`.

toFront()

PURPOSE Moves the window in front of all other windows.

SYNTAX `void toFront()`

SEE ALSO `Window.toFront()`.

Index

B

D

E

F

H

I

L

M

O

P

Q

R

T

V

W

X

Y

Z